THE HUMAN FRONTAL LOBES

THE SCIENCE AND PRACTICE OF NEUROPSYCHOLOGY
A Guilford Series

Robert A. Bornstein, *Series Editor*

The Human Frontal Lobes: Functions and Disorders
Bruce L. Miller and Jeffrey L. Cummings, Editors

Forthcoming:

Pediatric Neuropsychology
Keith Owen Yeates, M. Douglas Ris, and H. Gerry Taylor, Editors

THE HUMAN FRONTAL LOBES

Functions and Disorders

BRUCE L. MILLER

JEFFREY L. CUMMINGS

Editors

THE GUILFORD PRESS
New York   London

The human frontal lobes

© 1999 The Guilford Press
A Division of Guilford Publications, Inc.
72 Spring Street, New York, NY 10012
http://www.guilford.com

Printed in the United States of America

This book is printed on acid-free paper.

Last digit is print number: 9 8 7 6 5 4 3 2 1

Library of Congress Cataloging-in-Publication Data

The human frontal lobes: functions and disorders / edited by Bruce L.
  Miller and Jeffrey L. Cummings.
    p. cm. — (The science and practice of neuropsychology
series)
    Includes bibliographical references and index.
    ISBN 1-57230-390-5 (hardcover)
    1. Frontal lobes—Physiology. 2. Frontal lobes—Pathophysiology.
I. Miller, Bruce L., 1949- . II. Cummings, Jeffrey L., 1948- . III. Series.
    [DNLM: 1. Frontal Lobe—physiology. 2. Brain Diseases. 3. Mental
Disorders. WL 307H918 1998]
QP382.F7H85 1999
612.8'25—dc21
DNLM/DLC
for Library of Congress   98-36944
                                                              CIP

Dedication

This volume is dedicated to the memory of D. F. "Frank" Benson, MD. Frank was mentor to the editors as well as to many of the contributors. Even those who didn't personally study with him were influenced by his reports and writings about the frontal lobes. Frank's interest in frontal lobe function spanned his entire career. During his years in Boston (1965–1979), he contributed to understanding Broca's aphasia, and he identified and characterized the "third alexia" occurring with left frontal dysfunction. In 1979, he and Dietrich Blumer edited *Psychiatric Aspects of Neurologic Disease,* which included a chapter they wrote on personality changes with frontal and temporal lobe lesions. This work represented a step forward in classifying the specific personality features associated with different focal brain lesions. They utilized the famous story of Phineas Gage—who manifested dramatic personality changes following a penetrating brain injury affecting the frontal lobes—as well as descriptions by Norman Geschwind of personality changes accompanying temporal lobe epilepsy. The book augmented these auspicious cases with descriptions of patients from their own rich clinical experience to introduce a nosology of brain-related personality alterations.

In the late 1970s, Frank and his colleagues in Boston initiated a series of studies of patients who had had frontal lobotomies. These investigations advanced understanding of how best to assess behavioral and cognitive changes in patients with frontal lobe lesions and revealed the residual deficits evident in these patients who had had their surgeries 30 or 40 years previously. These studies also illustrated Frank's great ability to take advantage of an available clinical population to advance understanding of brain–behavior relationships.

The collaboration that began between Donald Stuss, PhD, and Frank with the studies of lobotomy patients continued and eventually culminated in the publication of *The Frontal Lobes* in 1986. This book provided a comprehensive review of frontal lobe anatomy and function in humans as well as detailed descriptions of the behavioral changes associated with frontal lobe dysfunction. Like Frank's earlier book on psychiatric aspects of neurological disease, this volume was a benchmark in the evolving understanding of the role of the frontal lobes in humans.

After joining the faculty of the University of California at Los Angeles, Frank continued to pursue his interest in the frontal lobes. In this venue, his studies turned to patients with dementia syndromes. The availability of advanced neuroimaging techniques and of patients with a variety of dementia syndromes allowed him to pursue investigations of frontal lobe function in patients with Alzheimer's disease and other dementias. With his colleague Bruce Miller, MD, he assessed patients with frontotemporal dementias and brought his experience with frontal lobe disorders to bear on studies of this fascinating group of patients.

Throughout his career, Frank remained clinically active, examining patients and teaching in case conferences. He also built theories based on direct and personal case observation. His ideas speak most directly to the clinician because the clinic was the laboratory where his concepts originated. We have tried to preserve this tradition in the current volume, addressing topics of interest and relevance to understanding patients with frontal lobe disorders.

Frontal lobe dysfunction is common in neurological disease. In some cases it is subtle and contributes little to the clinical symptom complex; in others it is severe and determines the dominant features of the clinical syndrome. Understanding a patient with neurological disease nearly always requires at least a cursory assessment of frontal lobe function; sometimes a comprehensive evaluation is needed. Whenever clinicians examine a patient with a frontal lobe syndrome, they are participating in the legacy of Frank Benson.

About the Editors

Bruce L. Miller, MD, is a Professor of Neurology at the University of California, San Francisco, where he is the clinical director of the aging and dementia program and holds the A. W. and Mary Margaret Clausen Distinguished Chair. Dr. Miller is also Medical Director for the John Douglas French Foundation for Alzheimer's Disease Research where he has worked for the past decade. Dr. Miller's research has focused on the differential diagnosis of degenerative dementias, particularly frontotemporal dementia, which he has studied for the past decade. Frontotemporal dementia serves as a model for understanding the clinical consequences of frontal lobe injury, and Dr. Miller has outlined the behavioral and neuropsychological findings in this population. Dr. Miller has authored over 120 research publications, has edited books on the treatment of Alzheimer's disease, and is currently working on a nonfiction book entitled, *Social Brain Stories*. Recently, this work has appeared in the journals *Neurology, Archives of Neurology, Brain, Lancet, British Journal of Psychiatry,* and *Journal of the International Neuropsychological Society.*

Jeffrey L. Cummings, MD, is The Augustus S. Rose Professor of Neurology, Professor of Psychiatry and Biobehavioral Sciences, and Director of the University of California at Los Angeles Alzheimer's Disease Center at the UCLA School of Medicine. Dr. Cummings also serves as Fellowship Director of the Dementia and Neurobehavior Research Fellowship at UCLA. Dr. Cummings received his undergraduate degree with high honors from the University of Wyoming and went on to obtain his MD from the University of Washington School of Medicine. He completed fellowships in Behavioral Neurology at Boston University School of Medicine, and in Neuropathology and Neuropsychiatry at the National Hospital for Neurological Diseases in London. Dr. Cummings has authored and edited eight books on neuropsychiatry and dementia and has published over 250 scientific articles on Alzheimer's disease and related topics.

Contributors

Valerie Aubin-Brunet, MD, Memory Center, Department of Psychiatry, University of Nice Sophia Antipolis, Nice, France

Carol A. Banyas, MD, Neuropsychiatric Institute, Department of Geriatric Psychiatry, University of California, Los Angeles, Los Angeles, California

Kyle Brauer Boone, PhD, Department of Psychiatry, Harbor–UCLA Medical Center, Torrance, California

David L. Braff, MD, School of Medicine, University of California, San Diego, La Jolla, California

Arne Brun, MD, PhD, Department of Pathology, Lund University Hospital, Lund, Sweden

Tiffany W. Chow, MD, Department of Neurology, School of Medicine, University of California, Los Angeles, Los Angeles, California

Helena Chui, MD, Department of Neurology, University of Southern California, Los Angeles, Los Angeles, California; Geriatric Neurobehavior and Alzheimer Center, Rancho Los Amigos Medical Center, Downey, California

Guy Darcourt, MD, University Clinic of Psychiatry and Medical Psychology, Pasteur Hospital, Nice, France

Terri A. Edwards-Lee, MD, UCLA Medical Center, University of California, Los Angeles; West Los Angeles Veterans Affairs Medical Center, Los Angeles, California

Thierry Ettlin, MD, Rehaklinik Rheinfelden, Rheinfelden, Switzerland

David Feifel, MD, PhD, Department of Psychiatry, School of Medicine, University of California, San Diego, La Jolla, California

L. Jaime Fitten, MD, Department of Psychiatry and Biobehavioral Sciences, School of Medicine, University of California, Los Angeles, Los Angeles, California, VHA Southern California Systems of Clinics, Sepulveda, California

Joaquin M. Fuster, MD, PhD, Department of Psychiatry and Brain Research Institute, UCLA Neuropsychiatric Institute, University of California, Los Angeles, Los Angeles, California

Daniel H. Geschwind, MD, PhD, Program in Neurogenetics, Department of Neurology, School of Medicine, University of California, Los Angeles, Los Angeles, California

Michael Goldberg, MD, Autism Network, Los Angeles, California

Cheryl L. Grady, PhD, Rotman Research Institute, Baycrest Centre for Geriatric Care, University of Toronto, Toronto, Ontario, Canada

Jordan Grafman, PhD, Cognitive Neuroscience Section, National Institute of Neurological Disorders and Stroke, Bethesda, Maryland

Lars Gustafson, MD, PhD, Department of Psychogeriatrics, Lund University Hospital, Lund, Sweden

Klemens Gutbrod, PhD, Division of Neuropsychological Rehabilitation, Department of Neurology, University Hospital, Bern, Switzerland

Gordon J. Harris, PhD, Radiology Computer-Aided Diagnosis Laboratory, Massachusetts General Hospital, Boston, Massachusetts

Michael E. Hasselmo, MD, Department of Psychology, Boston University, Boston, Massachusetts

Craig Hou, MD, Department of Neurology, Washington University, St. Louis, Missouri

Marco Iacoboni, MD, PhD, Division of Brain Mapping, Department of Neurology and Psychiatry, School of Medicine, University of California, Los Angeles, Los Angeles, California,

William Jagust, MD, Department of Neurology, University of California, Davis, Davis, California

Daniel I. Kaufer, MD, Departments of Psychiatry and Neurology and the Center for the Neural Basis of Cognition, University of Pittsburgh School of Medicine, Pittsburgh, Pennsylvania

Andrew Kertesz, MD, FRCPC, Department of Clinical Neurological Sciences, St. Joseph's Health Centre, London, Ontario, Canada

Udo Kischka, MD, Rehaklinik Rheinfelden, Rheinfelden, Switzerland

David A. Lewis, MD, Departments of Psychiatry and Neuroscience and the Center for the Neural Basis of Cognition, University of Pittsburgh School of Medicine, Pittsburgh, Pennsylvania

Christiane Linster, MD, Department of Psychology, Boston University, Boston, Massachusetts

Irene Litvan, MD, Neuropharmacology Unit, Defense and Vietnam Head Injury Program, Henry M. Jackson Foundation and Medical Neurology Branch, National Institute of Neurological Disorders and Stroke, National Institutes of Health, Bethesda, Maryland

Jennifer E. McDowell, PhD, School of Medicine, University of California, San Diego, La Jolla, California

Ian G. McKeith, MD, Department of Old Age Psychiatry, Institute for the Health of the Elderly, Newcastle General Hospital, Newcastle-upon-Tyne, United Kingdom

Ismael Mena, MD, Catholic University, Santiago, Chile

Carol A. Miller, MD, Department of Pathology, School of Medicine, University of Southern California, Los Angeles, Los Angeles, California

Tomoko Y. Nakawatase, MD, Gallatin Medical Foundation, Downey, California; Department of Neurology, UCLA School of Medicine, University of California, Los Angeles, Los Angeles, California

Elaine K. Perry, PhD, MRC Neurochemical Pathology Unit, Newcastle General Hospital, Newcastle-upon-Tyne, United Kingdom

Robert H. Perry, MD, Department of Neuropathology, Newcastle General Hospital, Newcastle-upon-Tyne, United Kingdom

William Perry, PhD, School of Medicine, University of California, San Diego, La Jolla, California

Jonathan H. Pincus, MD, Department of Neurology, School of Medicine, Georgetown University, Washington, DC

Philippe H. Robert, MD, PhD, Memory Center, Department of Psychiatry, University of Nice Sophia Antipolis, Nice, France

Robert G. Robinson, MD, Department of Psychiatry, School of Medicine, University of Iowa, Iowa City, Iowa

Robert T. Rubin, MD, PhD, Center for Neurosciences Research, Allegheny General Hospital, Pittsburgh, Pennsylvania

Carole Samango-Sprouse, EdD, Department of Pediatrics, George Washington University and Children's National Medical Center, Washington, DC

Ronald E. Saul, MD, Department of Neurology, UCLA Medical Center, University of California, Los Angeles, Los Angeles, California

Douglas W. Scharre, MD, Division of Cognitive Neurology, Department of Neurology, Ohio State University, Columbus, Ohio

Armin Schnider, MD, Department of Rehabilitation, University Hospital, Geneva, Switzerland

Sergio E. Starkstein, MD, PhD, Department of Neuropsychiatry, Raul Carrea Institute of Neurological Research-FLENI, Buenos Aires, Argentina

J. Randolph Swartz, MD, Department of Psychiatry and Biobehavioral Sciences, University of California, Los Angeles, Los Angeles, California; Harbor–UCLA Medical Center, Torrance, California

Neal R. Swerdlow, MD, PhD, School of Medicine, University of California, San Diego, La Jolla, California

Seth M. Weingarten, MD, University of California, Los Angeles, Alzheimer Disease Center and Neurobehavior Program, Los Angeles, California

Lee Willis, PhD, Department of Neurology, University of Southern California, Los Angeles, Los Angeles, California; Geriatric Neurobehavior and Alzheimer Center, Rancho Los Amigos Medical Center, Downey, California

Gorsev G. Yener, MD, Department of Neurology, Medical Faculty, Dokuz Eylul University, Inciralti, Izmir, Turkey

Adam Zaffos, MD, Department of Physiology, School of Medicine, University of California, Los Angeles, Los Angeles, California

Series Editor Note

The publication of this volume, *The Human Frontal Lobes*, edited by Bruce L. Miller and Jeffrey L. Cummings, represents an auspicious beginning for the series, The Science and Practice of Neuropsychology. Given the current information explosion in the neurosciences, the role of the scientist–practitioner is vitally important. As such, the aim of the series is to integrate the scientific foundations of neuropsychology with the clinical applications of that knowledge.

In this series, neuropsychology is defined broadly as the study of brain–behavior relationships, incorporating the perspectives of a range of related disciplines. Although some of the volumes will undoubtedly be of greater interest to specific subsets of readers, it is intended that the series be of interest to scientists and practitioners in all the disciplines that address brain–behavior relationships. A wide range of topics will be covered and will include reviews of emerging technologies and their potential impact on the science and clinical understanding of neuropsychology.

This volume on the human frontal lobes is a timely reflection of the dramatic expansion of our understanding in the neurosciences. During the past decade, there has been a remarkable evolution in our knowledge about frontal subsystems, cortical–subcortical circuitry, and the role of the frontal lobes in a host of neurologic and psychiatric disorders. The contemporary insights into neuroanatomy, neurochemistry, neurophysiology, and neuropsychology of the frontal lobes have necessitated the abandonment of the so-called frontal lobe syndrome in favor of empirically refined conceptualizations of multiple frontal lobe syndromes. This volume presents an integration of a broad spectrum of current knowledge and demonstrates how the active exchange of information between the laboratory and clinic can contribute to mutual and complementary advances.

ROBERT A. BORNSTEIN, PhD

Preface

The frontal lobes have undergone a dramatic expansion during the evolution of the human species. They now comprise the largest lobe and account for almost one-third of the total human brain surface area. Despite their large size, their function remains enigmatic, and much remains to be learned about their roles in the cognitive and emotional aspects of human life. Dramatic behavioral changes are a hallmark of human frontal lobe dysfunction. An archetypal example is the case of Phineas Gage, who sustained a massive frontal lobe injury and underwent marked personality changes. Relinquishing the usual civil restraints on behavior, he became impulsive, disinhibited, and socially inappropriate. This case along with others focused attention on the potential importance of frontal lobes, and in 1928, Tilney prophesied that the 20th century would prove to be "the age of the frontal lobes." Tilney's proclamation was precocious, and during the first half of the 20th century little new was learned about the structure or function of the prefrontal cortex. With the advent of neuroimaging, behavioral neurology, neuropsychology, and neuroscience, however, there has been an impressive accumulation of basic and clinical information regarding the structure and function of the frontal lobes.

The explosion of data regarding the frontal lobes has made it nearly impossible for even the most diligent clinician or neuroscientist to keep track of the new discoveries. *The Human Frontal Lobes* provides an update and synthesizes evolving knowledge regarding this enigmatic brain region. This multiauthored text offers a contemporary perspective on frontal lobe neuroanatomy, neurochemistry, neurophysiology, and phylogeny, as well as on diseases of the prefrontal cortex. The accumulating knowledge of the frontal lobes is critically reviewed and summarized in a series of chapters organized into four main parts: Neuroanatomy; Neurochemistry and Neurophysiology; Neuropsychological Functions; and Diseases, divided into two subsections, Neurology and Psychiatry. The chapters offer a broad and comprehensive view of normal and abnormal frontal lobe function.

The gross morphology, structural and functional asymmetries, cortical anatomy and connectivity, pathology, evolution, and radiographic features of the frontal lobes are described in the section on Neuroanatomy, written by an international group of clinicians and scientists. In the section on Neurochemistry and Neurophysiology, the roles of serotonin, acetylcholine, dopamine, and neuropeptides in frontal lobe function are outlined by psychiatrists and cognitive psychobiologists. Implications for treatment are emphasized. Parallel chapters on primates and humans elucidate the anatomy and physiology of frontal lobe functions such as inhibition and working memory. The section on Neuropsychological Functions discusses the roles of the frontal lobe in language, attention, behavior, decision making, and memory. The effects of age and gender on frontal lobe function are presented as well. Both bedside and experimental paradigms for testing the frontal lobes are described, providing an opportunity for clinicians and cognitive scientists to learn about and adopt new procedures.

The part devoted to both Neurological Diseases and Psychiatric Diseases reviews the clinical conditions known to involve the frontal lobes. Neurological diseases described include the frontotemporal dementias, vascular dementia, dementia with Lewy bodies, psychosurgery, demyelinating and infectious disorders, traumatic brain injury, and frontal lobe tumors. An exciting area of research links frontal lobe dysfunction to a variety of psychiatric disorders. Clinical symptoms indicative of frontal dysfunction in schizophrenia, autism, obsessive–compulsive disorder, depression, crime and aggression, visual hallucinations, and childhood behavior are extensively reviewed by an international group of authors.

The Human Frontal Lobes presents a contemporary summary of recent advances in frontal lobe structure and function in health and disease. It offers a valuable perspective for both the novice and the experienced scientist.

BRUCE L. MILLER, MD
San Francisco

JEFFREY L. CUMMINGS, MD
Los Angeles

Acknowledgments

We could not have pursued the investigation of patients whose syndromes stimulated our interests in the frontal lobes without the support of the National Institute on Aging (Alzheimer's Disease Center Grant AG 10123) and the generous help of the Katherine Kagan and the Sidell-Kagan Foundation.

B.L.M and J.L.C.

I offer special thanks to my administrative assistant, Sunny Honsinger, who tirelessly helped with the organization and editing of this book.

B.L.M.

Contents

xix

Part III. Neuropsychological Functions of the Frontal Lobes

Part IV. Diseases of the Frontal Lobes

Section A. Neurology

Part I

NEUROANATOMY OF THE FRONTAL LOBES

1

Frontal–Subcortical Circuits

TIFFANY W. CHOW
JEFFREY L. CUMMINGS

Alexander, DeLong, and Strick (1986) introduced the concept of parallel but segregated frontal–subcortical circuits. Their description of five frontal–subcortical circuits provided a basis for subsequent elucidation of how those circuits influence both movement and behavior. This chapter describes the three frontal–subcortical circuits associated with neurobehavioral syndromes: circuits originating in dorsolateral, orbitofrontal, and anterior cingulate cortices. In addition, the chapter reviews the associated clinical syndromes, neuroanatomy, neurotransmitters, direct and indirect pathways, as well as closed and open connections of the circuits.

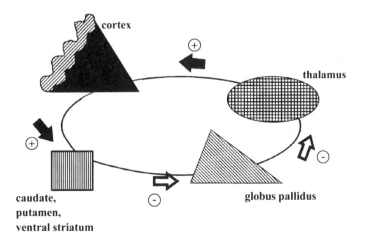

FIGURE 1.1. Basic organization of frontal–subcortical circuits.

As illustrated in Figure 1.1, each of the circuits circumnavigates the same member structures, including the frontal lobe, striatum, globus pallidus and substantia nigra, and thalamus. The indirect pathway of these circuits includes the subthalamic nucleus. In addition to sharing anatomical way stations, each circuit employs the same neurotransmitters. The relative anatomic positions of the circuits are preserved as they pass through striatum (caudate and putamen), globus pallidus, substantia nigra, and thalamus. Thus, the dorsolateral frontal cortex projects to the dorsolateral region of the caudate nucleus, the orbitofrontal region projects to the ventral caudate/ventral striatal areas, and the anterior cingulate cortex projects to the medical striatal/nucleus accumbens region (Kim, Nakano, Jayaraman, & Carpenter, 1976; Ilinsky, Jouandet, & Goldman-Rakic, 1985). The mediodorsal thalamus closes the circuit by projecting back to the circuit's origins in areas 9 and 10 of the dorsolateral frontal lobe (Giguere & Goldman-Rakic, 1988; Kievit & Kuypers, 1977). We describe indirect circuit connections later.

DORSOLATERAL CIRCUIT

The dorsolateral circuit subserves executive function (Cummings, 1993a), which includes the ability to organize a behavioral response to solve a complex problem (such as learning new information, copying complicated figures, and systematically searching memory), activation of remote memories, independence from environmental contingencies, shifting and maintaining behavioral sets appropriately, generating motor programs, and using verbal skills to guide behavior. Damage to the dorsolateral frontal lobe or any part of its circuit produces deficits in these abilities (see Tables 1.1 and 1.2). Successful performance of the Wisconsin Card Sorting Test (WCST) requires several of the functions mediated by this brain region, including set shifting and maintenance, strategy generation, and organization of information (Milner, 1963). Performance on verbal and design fluency (drawing novel designs) and alternating and reciprocal sequences also depends on executive function (Cummings, 1985; Jones-Gotman & Milner, 1977). Not all executive skills are reduced with all lesions. Patients with dorsolateral frontal cortical dysfunction evidence a spectrum of severity, as well as variation in the specific abilities that are compromised. A typical patient may present with inability to organize and plan an activity, such as cooking a meal, memory loss, and perseverative behaviors.

Executive dysfunction is a hallmark feature of subcortical dementia. The characteristic patient with subcortical dementia manifests a long response latency, apathy or depressed mood, retrieval memory deficits, and motor abnormalities, typically including dysarthria and gait disturbance (Albert, Feldman, & Willis, 1974; Cummings, 1990). The first contemporary descriptions of subcortical dementia (Albert et al., 1974) noted similarities between the characteristics of subcortical dementia and those of frontal lobe dysfunction. Lesions of the dorsolateral cortex and caudate nucleus result in poor recall with relative preservation of recognition abilities (Butters, Wolfe, Granholm, & Martone, 1986), whereas further along the circuit, thalamic lesions produce impairment of both recall and recognition (Stuss, Guberman, Nelson, & Larochelle, 1988). Lesions in the thalamus usually combine the amnesia of medial limbic dysfunction with features typical of subcortical dementia and frontal–subcortical circuit dysfunction (Deymeer, Smith, DeGirolami, & Drachman, 1989; Eslinger, Warner, Grattan, & Easton, 1991; Stuss et al., 1988) because the thalamus is poised at the intersection of the frontal–subcortical circuits and the circuit comprised of the hippocampus, fornix, and hypothalamus.

TABLE 1.1. Executive Cognitive Dysfunctions Associated with Disorders of the Dorsolateral Frontal–Subcortical Circuit

Classification	Impaired functions
Poor organizational strategies	Segmented drawing Impaired organization of material to be learned Poor word list generation Reduced design fluency Poor sorting behavior (WCST)
Poor memory search strategies	Reduced word list generation Poor recall of remote information Poor recall of recently learned information
Stimulus-bound behavior/ environmental dependency	Poor set shifting Concrete interpretation of abstract concepts and proverbs "Pull" toward high-stimulus objects Imitation behavior Utilization behavior Reduced design fluency Impaired reciprocal programs Poor go/no-go performance Poor response inhibition (Stroop Color Word Test)

Impaired set shifting and
maintenance
	Impaired card sorting (WCST)
	Poor alternation between concepts
	Perseveration on:
	  Multiple loops
	  Alternating programs
	  Reciprocal programs
	Go/no-go test
	Luria serial hand sequences

Verbal–manual dissociation	Impaired Luria serial hand sequences

Note. Items appear several times when they have multiple determinants.

ORBITOFRONTAL CIRCUIT

The orbitofrontal circuit is comprised of two parallel subcircuits originating in Brodmann areas 10 and 11 (see Figures 1.2 and 1.3). The lateral orbitofrontal circuit sends projections to the ventromedial caudate; the medial orbitofrontal circuit sends projections to the ventral striatum. Both orbitofrontal circuits then project to the most medial portion of the mediodorsal globus pallidus interna and to the rostromedial substantia nigra pars

TABLE 1.2. Etiologies of Dorsolateral Frontal–Subcortical Circuit Dysfunction or Associated Disease Processes

Corticobasal degeneration	Parkinson's disease
Dementia syndrome of depression	Progressive supranuclear palsy
Frontotemporal dementia	Schizophrenia
HIV dementia	Stroke
Huntington's disease	Subcortical dementia
Lacunar state/Binswanger's disease	Sydenham's chorea
Multiple systems atrophy	Tumor
Neuroacanthocytosis	Vascular dementia

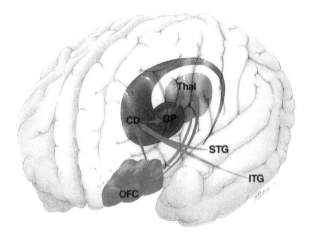

FIGURE 1.2. Neuroanatomy of the lateral orbitofrontal–subcortical circuit. From Zald and Kim (1996a). Copyright 1996 by American Psychiatric Press. Reprinted by permission.

reticulata (GPi/SNr) (Johnson & Rosvold, 1971). Axons extend from GPi/SNr to the medial section of the magnocellular division of the ventral anterior thalamus as well as the inferomedial sector of the magnocellular division of the mediodorsal thalamus (MDmc) (Selemon & Rakic, 1985). The circuit then closes with projections from this thalamic region back to lateral or medial orbitofrontal cortex (Ilinsky et al., 1985). The two subcircuits overlap greatly in anatomy and behavioral functions but differ at the cytological level. Table 1.3 enumerates their characteristics.

The orbitofrontal circuit mediates empathic, civil, and socially appropriate behavior; personality change is the hallmark of orbitofrontal dysfunction. Patients with lesions of this area may develop irritability, lability, tactlessness, and fatuous euphoria (Bogousslavsky & Regli, 1990; Hunter, Blackwood, & Bull, 1968; Logue, Durward, Pratt, Piercy, & Nixon, 1968). Patients do not respond appropriately to social cues, show undue familiarity, and cannot empathize with the feelings of others. Enslavement to environmental cues, exemplified by utilization behavior (inappropriate automatic use of tools

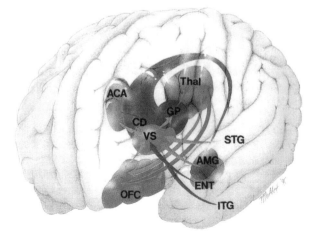

FIGURE 1.3. Neuroanatomy of the medial orbitofrontal–subcortical circuit. From Zald and Kim (1996a). Copyright 1996 by American Psychiatric Press. Reprinted by permission.

TABLE 1.3. Anatomy and Function of the Lateral and Medial Orbitofrontal–Subcortical Circuits

Lateral orbitofrontal cortex	Medial orbitofrontal cortex
Cytology 　Granular regions of orbitofrontal region	Agranular–dysgranular regions
Anatomy 　Cortex → caudate → globus pallidus 　　→ thalamus → cortex	Cortex Ä ventral striatum → caudate 　→ globus pallidus → thalamus → cortex
Personality change 　Emotional incontinence 　Tactlessness 　Impulsivity 　Irritability 　Undue familiarity	Emotional incontinence Impulsivity Antisocial behavior
Environmental dependency 　Utilization behavior 　Imitation behavior	Abnormal autonomic response to socially 　meaningful stimuli
Mood disorders 　Depression 　Lability 　Mania	
Obsessive–compulsive disorder 　Recognition of reinforcing stimuli 　Association of a visual representation of a 　　stimulus with its affective value 　Modulation of behavior in situations where 　　more than one choice is reinforced over time 　Difficulty with changing set, go/no-go tasks	Recognition of reinforcing stimuli Registration of the absence of an expected 　reinforcer (extinction) Poor direct stimulus–response learning

Note. Differentiation of personality changes due to lesions in either of the two divisions has not yet been clearly defined.

and utensils in the patient's environment) and automatic imitation of the gestures and actions of others, may occur with large lesions (Cummings, 1993b; Lhermitte, Pillon & Serdaru, 1986). Unlike individuals with dorsolateral lesions, patients with primarily orbitofrontal dysfunction perform card-sorting tasks normally (Laiacona et al., 1989). Similar behavioral changes are evident in patients with dysfunction of the subcortical structures of the orbitofrontal–subcortical circuit, including patients with Huntington's disease (caudate abnormalities) and manganese intoxication (globus pallidus lesions) (Folstein, 1989; Mena et al., 1967). Lesions in the orbitofrontal circuit may result in acquired obsessive–compulsive disorder (OCD) (Berthier, Kulisevsky, Gironell, & Heras, 1996), discussed later in the chapter (see Table 1.4).

TABLE 1.4. Etiologies of Orbitofrontal–Subcortical Circuit Dysfunction or Associated Disease Processes

Carbon monoxide toxicity	Multiple sclerosis
Creutzfeldt–Jakob disease	Neuroacanthocytosis
Frontotemporal dementia	Obsessive–compulsive disorder and
Gilles de la Tourette's syndrome	obsessive–compulsive spectrum disorders
Head trauma	Postencephalitic Parkinson's disease
Herpes simplex viral encephalitis	Ruptured anterior communicating artery aneurysm
Huntington's disease	Stroke
Manganese intoxication	Tumor

ANTERIOR CINGULATE CIRCUIT

Neurons of the anterior cingulate serve as the origin of the anterior cingulate–subcortical circuit. Input travels from Brodmann area 24 to the ventral striatum, which includes the ventromedial caudate, ventral putamen, nucleus accumbens, and olfactory tubercle (Selemon & Goldman-Rakic, 1985). Collectively, these structures comprise the limbic striatum. Projections from the ventral striatum then innervate the rostromedial GPi, rostrodorsal substantia nigra, and ventral pallidum (the region of the globus pallidus inferior to the anterior commissure). The anterior cingulate circuit continues to the dorsal portion of MDmc and closes with projections to the anterior cingulate (Goldman-Rakic & Porrino, 1985).

The anterior cingulate circuit mediates motivated behavior, and apathy betrays damage to the structures of this circuit, as shown in Table 1.5. Akinetic mutism occurs with bilateral lesions of the anterior cingulate (Barris & Schuman, 1953; Fesenmeier, Kuzniecky, & Garcia, 1990; Nielsen & Jacobs, 1951). With bilateral lesions, patients are profoundly apathetic; rarely moving, they are incontinent, eat and drink only when fed, and may have speech limited to monosyllabic responses to others' questions. Displaying no emotions, even when in pain, patients show complete indifference to their circumstances. Unilateral lesions produce less dramatic apathetic syndromes, including transient akinetic mutism (Damasio & Damasio, 1989). Failure of response inhibition on go/no-go tests is the major neuropsychological deficit (Drewe, 1975; Leimkuhler & Mesulam, 1985). Patients also experience a diminished ability to conceive new thoughts or participate in creative thought processes.

Apathy occurs in many disorders. Patients with Parkinson's disease, Huntington's disease, and thalamic lesions, which affect the subcortical links of the anterior cingulate circuit, commonly manifest apathy (Burns, Folstein, Brandt, & Folstein, 1990; Starkstein et al., 1992; Stuss et al., 1988). SPECT scans in Alzheimer's disease patients show significantly decreased cerebral blood flow in anterior cingulate, dorsolateral, orbitofrontal, and anterior temporal regions when apathy is a major behavioral characteristic (Craig et al., 1996). Table 1.6 lists etiologies of anterior cingulate circuit dysfunction.

DIRECT AND INDIRECT PATHWAYS

Each circuit introduced previously has an indirect, as well as a direct, connection within the subcortical portion of the circuitry. The indirect pathway projects from caudate to globus pallidus externa and then to the subthalamic nucleus. This connection with the subthalamic nucleus (STN) targets the GPi, which in turn affects the activity of the thalamus, specifically its excitatory thalamocortical connections. The direct loop of the circuit itself disinhibits the thalamus, whereas the indirect loop inhibits it. Both pathways

TABLE 1.5. Cognitive and Behavioral Abnormalities Associated with Disorders of the Anterior Cingulate Frontal–Subcortical Circuit

Impaired motivation	Reduced creative thought
Akinetic mutism	Poor response inhibition
Indifference to pain	Impaired go/no-go test performance
Marked apathy	
Poverty of spontaneous speech	
Psychic emptiness	

TABLE 1.6. Etiologies of Anterior Cingulate Frontal–Subcortical Circuit Dysfunction or Associated Disease Processes

Alzheimer's disease	Parkinson's disease/extrapyramidal syndromes
Creutzfeldt–Jakob disease	Postencephalitic Parkinson's disease
Epilepsy	Progressive supranuclear palsy
Frontotemporal dementia	Stroke
Huntington's disease	Trauma
Multiple sclerosis	Tumor

begin with excitatory, glutamatergic projections from the frontal cortex to specific areas within the striatum (caudate, putamen, and ventral striatum). Striatal output neurons then bifurcate to either internal or external globus pallidus to the direct loop or the indirect loop, respectively.

The direct pathway consists of inhibitory γ-aminobutyric acid (GABA) striatal fibers extending to the internal segment of the GPi/SNr. Cortical stimulation of the striatum inhibits GPi/SNr, reducing the effect of inhibitory GABAergic projections to the thalamus. The direct pathway inhibits GPi/SNr, which reduces tonic thalamic inhibition and thereby excites the thalamus through disinhibition and enhances thalamocortical excitation (see large arrow on Figure 1.4a).

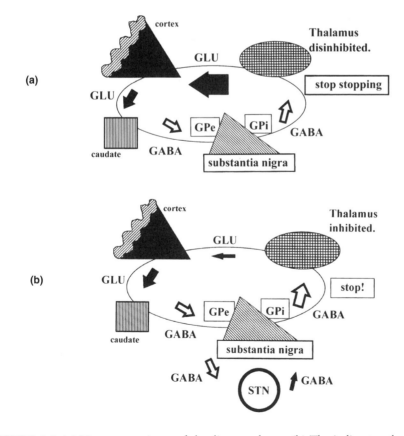

FIGURE 1.4. (a) Neurotransmitters of the direct pathway. (b) The indirect pathway: Inhibited by the globus pallidus externa (GPe), the subthalamic nucleus (STN) cannot keep the globus pallidus interna (GPi) from inhibiting the thalamus. GLU, glutamate; GABA, γ-amino-butyric acid.

The indirect pathway leads from striatum to external segment of the globus pallidus (GPe). The striatum inhibits GPe, which would otherwise exert a tonic inhibitory GABAergic influence on the STN. The STN glutamatergic efferent fibers to GPi/SNr then heighten inhibition of the thalamus, reducing thalamocortical excitation (see small arrow on Figure 1.4b).

In concert, the direct and indirect pathways modulate each frontal–subcortical circuit's activity and response to differential inputs. Dysfunction in the direct circuit results in abnormal thalamic inhibition, whereas indirect circuit abnormalities release the thalamus, leading to overactive thalamocortical excitation.

NEUROTRANSMITTERS

Several neurotransmitters play vital roles in the function of the circuits.

Glutamate

Glutamate (GLU) exerts its excitatory effects primarily via N-methyl-D-aspartate (NMDA) receptors, and drugs acting at these sites have profound behavioral consequences. Corticostriatal and thalamocortical projections are glutamatergic.

γ-Aminobutyric Acid

Within the basal ganglia, the predominant neurotransmitter is GABA. Striatal, pallidal, and substantia nigra interconnections and their projections to the thalamus are GABAergic. The serial arrangement of excitatory cortical tranmitters and inhibitory basal ganglia transmitters translates excitatory drive from the cortex into disinhibition of the thalamus and brainstem, as delineated in the previous section on direct and indirect pathways.

Dopamine

Dopamine (DA) acts on cholinergic interneurons within the striatum to regulate striatal output as well as directly influencing glutamatergic cortical and thalamic efferents (Masterman & Cummings, 1997). Dopaminergic projections from the substantia nigra pars compacta (SNpc) innervate the entire striatum, selectively making contact with the necks of striatal dendritic spines, whereas the heads of those spines receive synaptic inputs from cortex (Smith & Bolam, 1990).

The overall inhibitory or excitatory effects of DA are dependent to a large degree on the type of postsynaptic receptor with which it interacts. Five different DA receptor genes encode pharmacologically distinct receptor subtypes (D1–D5). They have been further grouped into receptor subfamilies based on their sequence homologies and pharmacological profiles, with D1 and D5 receptors sharing the same subfamily and D2, D3, and D4 subtypes another. Table 1.7 summarizes distinctions among receptor subtypes.

Dopaminergic modulation of all three frontal–subcortical circuits provides an anatomic basis for the multifaceted effects of dopaminergic agents, including improved motor function in Parkinson's disease, enhanced motivation in akinetic mutism, and

TABLE 1.7. Anatomical Distribution of Dopamine Receptor Subtypes

Subtype	Nucleus accumbens	Striatum–motor and limbic circuits	Limbic circuits	Effect on postsynaptic cyclic AMP
D1	×	×		Stimulates
D2	×	×		Inhibits
D3	×		×	(Not known)
D4	×		×	(Not known)
D5		×	×	(Not known)

Note. Limbic circuits include hippocampus, amygdala, olfactory tubercle, septal region, hypothalamus, and thalamus.

adverse effects such as hallucinations and delusions (Cummings, 1991; Ross & Stewart, 1981).

Acetylcholine

The striatum contains cholinergic interneurons which modulate thalamic activation of the cortex. Other cholinergic afferents to the thalamus originate in the pedunculopontine and laterodorsal tegmentum. Cortical regions involved in frontal–subcortical circuits receive cholinergic input from the nucleus basalis of Meynert, as part of an open-circuit communication (discussed later) and also due to the effects of the nucleus basalis of Meynert on other open-circuit contributors, the hippocampus and olfactory bulbs.

Acetylcholine–Dopamine Interaction

Acetylcholine (ACh) tonically facilitates striatal DA release via activation of both muscarinic and nicotinic receptors presumably located on presynaptic DA terminals (DiChiara & Morelli, 1993). Dopamine D2 receptors are located directly on cholinergic interneurons and tonically inhibit ACh release; D1 receptor agonists indirectly enhance ACh release (Stoof, Drukarch, DeBoer, Westerink & Groenewegen, 1992).

Glutamate–Dopamine–Acetylcholine Interactions

GLU stimulates striatal DA release through binding at both NMDA and non-NMDA types of receptors (Carlsson & Carlsson, 1990; DiChiara & Morelli, 1993). Blockade of NMDA receptors exerts reciprocal effects on D1 and D2 responses in experimental models of DA deficiency (Snyder-Keller, 1991). Dopaminergic nigrostriatal fibers may presynaptically inhibit striatal glutamate release via D2 receptors located on the terminals of corticostriatal neurons (Carlsson & Carlsson, 1990; Morelli, Fenu, Pinna, & DiChiara, 1992; Paul, Graybiel, David, & Robertson, 1992).

GLU also influences striatal cholinergic interneurons. Glutamatergic activation of NMDA receptors increases striatal ACh release, and cortical ablation or injection of glutamate antagonists reduces striatal ACh turnover (Scatton & Lehmann, 1982). In turn, ACh may presynaptically inhibit striatal GLU uptake (Nieoullon & Kerkerian-LeGoff, 1992). NMDA receptor blockade reduces basal ACh release and also prevents D1-dependent stimulation of ACh release in a complex interaction between GLU, DA, and Ach (Damsma, Robertson, Tham, & Fibiger, 1991). Carlsson (1988) sees this interaction as a corticostriatal–thalamocortical negative feedback loop, which guards the cortex against overstimulation.

Serotonin

Serotonin (5-hydroxytryptamine; 5-HT) receptors are differentially distributed in the frontal–subcortical circuits. The 5-HT1 receptor is the most abundant serotonin receptor in the basal ganglia with the exception of the ventral striatum, where 5-HT3 receptors dominate (Lavoie & Parent, 1990). 5-HT3 receptors appear also in hippocampus, septum, and amygdala (Mega & Cummings, 1994), contributing to modulation of mesocortial and mesolimbic dopaminergic pathways (Hagan, Kilpatrick, & Tyers, 1993). Serotonergic fibers modulate dopaminergic neurons, particularly when the dopaminergic neurons are activated (Palfreyman et al., 1993). A further interaction between 5-HT and DA has been suggested though a number of studies looking at schizophrenia and particularly the role of clozapine, a drug which antagonizes D2, D3, and D4 receptors as well as 5-HT2 receptors. Such an interaction between these two systems provides a possible basis for the modulating effects of 5-HT antagonists on states of presumed DA excess as in schizophrenia and substance abuse (Masterman & Cummings, 1997).

Neuropeptides

GABAergic efferents from striatum to GPe are rich in enkephalin and neurotensin; the parallel GABAergic neurons projecting from the striatum to GPi contain substance P and dynorphin. The levels of these neuropeptides appear to be regulated by differential DA input to the striatum. Levels of enkephalin and substance P increase with DA depletion or D2 blockade (Gerfen et al., 1990; Keefe & Gerfen, 1995). Compartmental shifts in peptide gene expression can be seen after treatments with dopaminergic agonists and antagonists (Ragsdale & Graybiel, 1990). Substance P-containing terminals synapse on the cell bodies of cholinergic interneurons, providing another level of regulation within the complex striatal circuitry (Emson et al., 1993). Neuropeptide Y (NPY) is discussed in the section "Striosome–Matrix Chemoarchitecture."

Two Different Transmitter Classes

As suggested by Graybiel (1990), neurotransmitters may act in the basal ganglia by (1) fast neurotransmission or (2) slow neurotransmission. Fast neurotransmitters include GLU and GABA; agents of slower transmission are DA and ACh acting at G-protein receptors and GLU acting at NMDA receptors. Modulatory transmitters use this slower action to produce tonic influences; the direct GLU and GABA connections are fast acting and exert phasic influences.

STRIOSOME–MATRIX CHEMOARCHITECTURE IN FRONTAL–SUBCORTICAL CIRCUITS

Direct and indirect connections create a dynamic balance within each of the frontal–subcortical circuits. This ability to modulate responses is further enhanced by cytochemical dichotomy in the dorsal striatum: striosomes and matrix.

Cytologically, the caudate and putamen appear identical. They are both composed of a large number of cells that exhibit no lamination. Approximately 90–95% of this striatal neuronal population is composed of GABAergic, efferent, medium spiny neurons (Kemp & Powell, 1971). When exposed to specific neurochemical markers for acetylcholinesterase (AChE) activity, though, the striatum reveals a mosaic structure consisting of (1) specialized striosomes and (2) an intervening matrix (Graybiel & Ragsdale, 1978) (see Table 1.8). Striosomes appear as 0.5-mm-wide ellipses and rings which stain poorly for AChE. They are especially evident in the head of the caudate nucleus and rostral putamen, whereas the posterior sensorimotor region of the putamen has few striosomes (Masterman & Cummings, 1997). The matrix component, by comparison, is rich in AChE, as well as D2 receptors and enkephalin. Further immunolabeling identifies somatostatin fibers and calbindin immunoreactive neurons in the matrix (Gerfen, Baimbridge, & Miller, 1985).

Neurochemical differences between striosomes and matrix may correspond to their separation of inputs and outputs. Inputs differ not only in their cortical region of origin but also by layer. Neurons in the substantia nigra and STN also project differentially to the striosome–matrix compartments.

The striatum, unlike the cortex, is unusual in that most of its neurons are efferent neurons rather than interneurons. Outputs of the striosome and matrix compartments are as distinct as their inputs. Striosomal GABAergic efferents target the dopaminergic SNpc and its neighbors; the matrix projects mainly to the SNr and globus pallidus.

Although interneurons constitute less than 5% of the striatal neuronal population, they play a disproportionately large role in the basal ganglia's complex circuitry because they provide an avenue of communication between the striosomes and matrix. Mainly incorporated into the matrix, several types of striatal interneurons differ in morphology and in the neuroactive substances they express, such as ACh, GABA, NPY, and

TABLE 1.8. Comparison of Striosomes and Matrix Characteristics

	Striosomes	Matrix
Neurotransmitters	+++D1 receptors +Muscarinic receptors +Opiate receptors Less serotonin, substance P, neurotensin, dynorphin, tyrosine hydroxylase, limbic-associated membrane protein	+++D2 receptors +++Muscarinic receptors, more cholinergic neurons
Limbic input	Prefrontal, orbitofrontal, insular, and temporal cortex Amygdala-centered input Cortical input from deep layers 5 and 6	
Neocortical input		Sensorimotor cortex, parietal–temporal–occipital association cortex, and the cingulate gyrus Cingulate and hippocampus-centered cortical input from superficial layer 5 and supragranular layers 2 and 3
Dopaminergic afferents	Ventral SNpc	Dorsal SNpc
Thalamic afferents	Midline nuclei of the thalamus	Centromedian–parafascicular complex (cell group A8 from the midbrain
GABAergic efferents	To medial SNpc	To GPe, GPi, and SNr

somatostatin. Cholinergic interneurons are large, aspiny cells with processes distributed throughout the striatum. They act directly upon striatal efferents and receive afferents from intrinsic GABAergic striatal medium spiny neurons, midbrain DA projections, glutamatergic thalamic neurons, and some direct corticostriate glutamatergic connections (Lapper & Bolam, 1992). The NPY interneurons show patterns of connectivity similar to the cholinergic interneurons and may play a similar integrative and modulatory role in the striatal circuitry. A differential distribution of these two interneuron subtypes places NPY fibers ventromedially and cholinergic fibers in the dorsolateral part of the striatum, suggesting that the cholinergic innervation serves the sensorimotor part of the striatum and that these two populations of interneurons may be involved in different cortico-striatal–thalamic circuits (Masterman & Cummings, 1997).

Organization of the striatum into both topographical regions corresponding to each frontal–subcortical circuit and a striosomal–matrix patchwork affords a luxurious versa-tility: Striatal regions closer together than a millimeter can support sharply different neurotransmitter repertoires based on where they lie on either side of a striosomal border. Although the neurochemical difference between striosomes and matrix is relative, the two systems are distinct enough to suggest that the same transmitter might have differential effects in each compartment (Graybiel, 1990).

Striosome–matrix compartmentalization accounts for cytoarchitectural organization of the dorsal striatum. The ventral striatum (e.g., nucleus accumbens) is divided into shell and core regions, where the core, organized into striosomes and matrix, rests within a shell that approximates the characteristics of the dorsal striatum's (Meredith, Blank, & Groenewegen, 1989; Voorn, Jorritsma-Byham, Van Dijk, & Buijs, 1986).

OPEN CONNECTIONS

As described thus far, each frontal–subcortical circuit comprises a closed loop. Dedicated neurons remain anatomically segregated from other parallel circuits in continuous loops, but afferent and efferent open elements also contribute to each circuit (Mega & Cummings, 1994).

An examination of the open aspects of each circuit facilitates understanding of how information processed in different brain regions can be integrated and synthesized in the processing cascade of the closed loops. Open elements of the circuits relate systematically to other brain regions that mediate related functions and have similar phylogenetic origins to the frontal–subcortical circuit involved. For example, the parvocellular and magnocel-lular regions of the dorsomedial thalamus project to the most differentiated and least differentiated prefrontal cortical areas, respectively.

Table 1.9 lists the principal afferents and efferents for the three frontal–subcortical circuits. Major cortical afferents to the dorsolateral frontal–subcortical circuit include Brodmann prefrontal area 46 (Selemon & Goldman-Rakic, 1985) and parietal area 7a (Yeterian & Pandya, 1993). These two areas are also richly interconnected to one another. Parietal area 7a participates in visual processing: attention to significant visual stimuli, visually guided reaching, and planning visuospatial strategies. Lesser afferents include limbic connections which contribute to the dorsolateral frontal–subcortical circuit via dopaminergic projections from SNpc to striatum.

The orbitofrontal–subcortical circuit takes open afferents from the superior temporal cortex and has many minor afferents in common with the dorsolateral frontal–subcortical circuit. Zald and Kim (1996a) point out that open afferents to the orbitofrontal cortex

TABLE 1.9. Open Afferent and Efferent Connections of Three Frontal–Subcortical Circuits

Category	Dorsolateral circuit	Orbitofrontal circuit	Anterior cingulate circuit
Major open afferents	Dorsofrontal area 46 Parietal area 7a	Superior temporal area 22 Orbitofrontal area 12	Hippocampus Entorhinal area 28 Perirhinal area 35
Major open efferents	Dorsofrontal area 46 Anterior frontal area 8	Orbitofrontal area 12 Mediofrontal area 25 Mediofrontal area 32	Pars compacta of substantia nigra Medial subthalamic nucleus Lateral hypothalamus
Minor open afferents	Dorsal parafascicular thalamus Medial pars compacta of sustantia nigra Dorsal raphe Central midbrain tegmentum Nucleus basalis of Meynert	Rostrimedial parafascicular thalamus Medial pars compacta of sustantia nigra Dorsal raphe Central midbrain tegmentum Nucleus basalis of Meynert Amygdala Entorhinal cortex Nucleus accumbens Olfactory tubercle	Subparafascicular thalamus Dorsal raphe Central midbrain tegmentum Nucleus basalis of Meynert Amygdala Orbitofrontal area 12
Minor open efferents	Anterior frontal area 6	Mediofrontal area 9 Anterior cingulate area 33 Anterior insula Temporal pole of area 38 Lateral hypothalamus Septal region	Midline thalamic nuclei Dorsal globus pallidus Lateral habenula Central gray matter Tegmenti pedunculopontine nucleus

Note. Connections specific to lateral or medial orbitofrontal–subcortical circuits have not been distinguished.

(OFC) consist of a heteromodal sensory division and a paralimbic division. The heteromodal sensory division enters the orbitofrontal–subcortical circuit at the same part of the caudate nucleus targeted by lateral OFC. Here, well-processed unimodal and polymodal, exteroceptive and interoceptive information from every sensory modality (olfactory, gustatory, visual, auditory, somatosensory) can be integrated with lateral OFC efferents. The polymodal afferents project from heteromodal areas of the temporal pole and insula (Chavis & Pandya, 1976; Jones & Powell, 1970; Mesulam & Mufson, 1982; Mufson & Mesulam, 1982). Afferents to the heteromodal sensory division tend to follow a general pattern of cytoarchitectural organization: More highly differentiated sensory association cortices project to the more differentiated regions of the OFC, whereas the more cytoarchitecturally primitive sensory association regions direct their projections to the agranular or dysgranular cortices in the relatively more posterior OFC region (Barbas, 1988; Morecraft, Geula, & Mesulam, 1992; Pandya & Yeterian, 1990). This pattern allows the OFC to receive multiple parallel sensory projections originating from association cortices of different phylogenetic age and with different functional relevance (Zald & Kim, 1996b).

The medial OFC loop is associated primarily with projections from limbic and paralimbic regions. Medial OFC merges with paralimbic input at the ventral striatum, which consists of the nucleus accumbens, part of the olfactory tubercle, and the extreme edge of the ventral caudate (Nauta, 1979; Zald & Kim, 1996a). The ventral striatum also receives projections from the basolateral nucleus of the amygdala, the anterior cingulate, entorhinal cortex, perirhinal cortex, and temporal lobe (Zald & Kim, 1996a).

These areas communicate directly with the OFC via numerous small cells, while the indirect connections travel through large neurons with long, radiating dendrites (Ray & Price, 1993; Russchen, Amaral, & Price, 1987). The paralimbic division of the orbitofrontal circuit distinguishes itself by providing the only major prefrontal projection to entorhinal cortex (Van Hoesen, Pandya, & Butters, 1975), which may influence medial temporal lobe mnemonic functions.

Of the frontal cortices involved in circuits, the OFC possesses the strongest association with the amygdala (Zald & Kim, 1996a). The medial OFC encounters afferents from the amygdala within rostral areas of the cingulate (Zald & Kim, 1996a). Because the amygdala is also the major source of efferents to brainstem and hypothalamus, the medial OFC appears to participate in modulating a spectrum of endocrine, autonomic, and involuntary behavioral responses (Amaral, Price, Pitkaenen, & Carmichel, 1992; Davis, 1992). The medial OFC sends prominent projections back to the basolateral and basal accessory nuclei of the amygdala, and the caudal OFC projects directly to the central nucleus of the amygdala (Laiacona et al., 1989; Van Hoesen, 1981). The amygdala also serves as a minor open afferent for the anterior cingulate circuit.

The OFC sends unreciprocated efferents to two important limbic structures: the lateral hypothalamus and the septal region (Parent, Bouchard, & Smith, 1984; Zald & Kim, 1996a). The MOFC plays an important role in regulating visceral responses to stimuli. A projection arising from a similar caudal section of the OFC appears to innervate the septal region (Nauta, 1971, 1973). These two open efferents contribute to the olfactory-centered paralimbic belt (Mesulam, 1985). The paralimbic belt is a transitional cortical zone from less differentiated paleocortex or archicortex to the more differentiated isocortex, and it has two functional centers: (1) the olfactory piriform paleocortex, which unites the orbitofrontal, insular, and temporopolar regions; and 2) the hippocampus, which provides the source of the archicortical system's spread into the cingulate and parahippocampal gyri.

The anterior cingulate frontal–subcortical circuit's open afferents originate in entorhinal cortex, the perirhinal area, and, most significantly, the hippocampus. While the orbitofrontal–subcortical circuit is phylogenetically older and involved with the internal state of the organism, the anterior cingulate center is the externally directed arm of the limbic system, enabling the intentional selection of environmental stimuli based on the internal relevance of those stimuli for the organism. The orbitofrontal circuit mediates information concerning the internal environment (Mega & Cummings, 1994).

The nucleus basalis of Meynert is a minor open afferent to all three frontal–subcortical circuits through its cholinergic projections to frontal cortex and the hippocampus. It has not been found to display any circuit specificity (Parent, Pare, Smith, & Steriade, 1988).

COMMENTS

Disruption of each of the three behaviorally related frontal–subcortical circuits leads to signature clinical syndromes. A lesion in the dorsalateral circuit causes frontal dysexecutive syndrome, a lesion in the orbitofrontal–subcortical circuit causes disinhibition, and a lesion of the anterior cingulate circuit causes apathy. Aside from these circuit-specific behavioral syndromes, there are circuit-related behavioral syndromes. Table 1.10 lists associations observed between circuit lesions and neuropsychiatric manifestations.

OCD has a basis in the orbitofrontal–subcortical circuit. OCD is a relatively frequent disorder characterized by the presence of intrusive and senseless ideas, thoughts, urges, and images (obsessions) as well as by repetitive cognitive and physical activities that are performed in a ritualistic way (compulsions) (American Psychiatric Association, 1994). The orbitofrontal cortex's participation in direct and indirect pathways has provided the basis for several biological models of OCD. Idiopathic and acquired OCD patients display similar behavioral disturbances and neuropsychological dysfunction. Etiologies for acquired OCD include pericallosal neoplasms compressing the posterior cingulate gyrus, left anterior cingulate contusion, epilepsy symptomatic of right anterior cingulate gyrus or unilateral temporal lobe anomalies, left anterior temporal or bitemporal arachnoid cysts, subcortical lesions (particularly involving the caudate nucleus), infarction of the right posterior putamen, and posttraumatic orbitofrontal contusions (Berthier et al., 1996). These observations provide clinicopathologic evidence of the significance of frontal–subcortical circuits in OCD, both at the cortical and at the subcortical level.

On the basis of the neurochemical properties of the basal ganglia loops, several authors have hypothesized that the core pathology of OCD arises from an excessive disinhibition of the mediodorsal thalamus, pars magnocellulare (Mdmc) (Baxter, 1990; Modell, Mountz, Curtis, & Greden, 1989; Rapoport & Wise, 1988). Three hypotheses might explain the pathogenesis: (1) disinhibition might allow information that would normally be inhibited in the thalamus to flow freely through the MDmc, leading to the adventitious release of information to the OFC (Baxter, 1990); (2) the reciprocal connections between the OFC and the MDmc both use the excitatory neurotransmitter glutamate as their primary neurotransmitter, and disinhibition of the thalamus could lead to the establishment of a positive feedback loop (Modell et al., 1989); or (3) disinhibition might also lead to a feedback loop involving the entire OFC–striatal–pallidal–MDmc loop (Penney & Young, 1983). These positive feedback loops would cause the MDmc–OFC axis to process information perseveratively (Zald & Kim, 1996b). Pre- and posttreatment positron emission tomograpy (PET) studies seem to confirm this hyperactivity model, in that responders to behavior therapy for OCD decrease morbid hypermetabolism in the caudate nucleus bilaterally. Schwartz and colleagues noted that PET studies on OCD patients show right-sided orbital gyri hyperactivity correlated with similar abnormalities in the ipsilateral caudate nucleus and thalamus (Schwartz, Stoessel, Baxter, Martin, & Phelps, 1996).

Obsessive–compulsive spectrum disorders include pathological gambling, kleptomania, risk-seeking behavior, and body dysmorphic disorder. Their relation to either the lateral or medial orbitofrontal–subcortical circuit is anticipated but yet to be determined.

TABLE 1.10. Neuropsychiatric Alterations Associated with Abnormalities of Specific Frontal–Subcortical Circuit Structures

Structure	Mood	Personality	OCD
Dorsolateral	Depression	UD	No
Orbitofrontal	Mania	Disinhibition, irritability	Yes
Anterior cingulate	No	Apathy	Yes
Caudate	Depression (L,B), mania (R,B)	Disinhibition, irritability	Yes
Nucleus accumbens	No	Apathy	No
Globus pallidus	UD	Apathy, irritability	Yes
Thalamus	Mania (R)	Apathy, irritability	No

Note. OCD, obsessive–compulsive disorder; UD, undetermined; L, left; R, right; B, bilateral. From Cummings (1993a). Copyright 1993 by American Medical Association. Reprinted by permission.

Depression has been linked to lesions in two structures of the frontal–subcortical circuits: the frontal lobes and the caudate nucleus. Studies of idiopathic depression reveal decreased metabolism in the dorsolateral prefrontal cortex and the caudate nucleus (Baxter et al., 1989); studies of depression in Parkinson's disease, Huntington's disease, and complex partial seizures demonstrate reduced metabolic activity in the OFC and caudate nucleus (Goldman-Rakic, 1994; Mayberg et al., 1990, 1992). Depression is also closely linked with lesions of the temporal lobes, however, and thus the disorder is not circuit specific (Cummings, 1993b; Irle, Peper, Wowra, & Kunze, 1994; Mayberg, 1994). Neuropsychiatric disturbances associated with dorsolateral circuit dysfunction include depression and anxiety. Caudate dysfunction from stroke and basal ganglia disorders can result in depression; stroke in the dorsolateral prefrontal area can manifest with depression and anxiety (Folstein, 1989; Robinson & Starkstein, 1990; Starkstein et al., 1990).

Mania is another circuit-related but not circuit-specific behavior. Secondary mania occurs with lesions or degenerative disorders affecting the OFC, caudate nucleus, and perithalamic areas (Bogousslavsky et al., 1988; Cummings & Mendez, 1984; Kulisevsky, Berthier, & Pujol, 1993; Starkstein, Pearlson, Boston, & Robinson, 1987; Trautner, Cummings, Read, & Benson, 1988). Lesions of the temporobasal regions including the amygdala and temporal stem, however, also produce mania, and these lesions are not obligatory members of the orbitofrontal–subcortical circuit (Berthier, Starkstein, Robinson, & Leiguarda, 1990; Lykestos et al., 1993; Starkstein et al., 1987). Subcortical lesions affecting the caudate nucleus and thalamus tend to produce a bipolar type of mood disorder with alternating periods of mania and depression, whereas lesions of the cortex that produce mania are not typically followed by a cyclic mood disorder (Starkstein, Fedoroff, Berthier, & Robinson, 1991). Nearly all focal lesions producing secondary mania have involved the right hemisphere (Cummings, 1995). The association of a dopaminergic second messenger system within the limbic striatum may provide insight into how lithium exerts its effects on mood and suggests that frontal–subcortical circuits may provide an anatomic basis for these effects (Mega & Cummings, 1994).

Psychosis is a circuit-related behavior. Psychosis may result from many disease entities, which affect frontal–subcortical circuits either structurally or neurochemically. Systemic lupus erythematosis and vascular dementia may cause psychosis due to infarction at the cortical or subcortical level. Human immunodeficiency virus dementia or acquired immunodeficiency syndrome dementia complex, metachromatic leukodystrophy, and neoplasms that manifest with psychosis may disrupt white matter tracts that constitute the subcortical component of the circuits (Hyde, Ziegler, & Weinberger, 1992). PET scans on Alzheimer's disease patients with psychosis show hypometabolism in temporal and frontal lobes (Sultzer et al., 1995). Late-life psychosis has been associated with infarctions of frontal lobe white matter, normal pressure hydrocephalus (Miller, Benson, Cummings, & Neshkes, 1986), and basal ganglia calcification (Cummings, Gosenfeld, Houlihan, & McCaffrey, 1983). PET studies using fluoro-L-dopa as a tracer demonstrate transient hypermetabolism in striatum of patients with psychosis, whether related to schizophrenia or to temporal lobe epilepsy. Reith et al. (1994) hypothesize that this hypermetabolism is an indication of dopamine receptor upregulation in response to frontal cortical insufficiency. L-Dopa-induced psychosis, as seen in treatment for Parkinson's disease, may have its pathogenesis in disturbing dopaminergic modulation of the limbic striatum. Caudate dysfunction in Huntington's disease is associated with psychosis

(Folstein, 1989; Cummings et al., 1983), but most lesions producing delusional syndromes involve the temporal lobe, particularly medial temporal–limbic structures (Gorman & Cummings, 1990). Studies on patients with temporal lobe epilepsy and psychosis describe onset of postictal psychosis after resection of either temporal lobe (Leinonen, Tuunainen, & Lepola, 1994).

Cortical–basal degeneration and Lewy body disorders violate the boundaries of the circuits but have clinical features overlapping the signature manifestations of frontal-subcortical circuit disruption.

Comments on laterality of the circuits have been based on a variety of disease entities, including epilepsy patients and frontotemporal dementia studies. Epileptics with electroencephalogram abnormalities in the left temporal lobe also showed hypoperfusion on SPECT (single photon emission computed tomography) in the same areas during psychotic episodes (Jibiki, Maeda, Kubota, & Yamaguchi, 1993). Right-sided atrophy in frontotemporal patients most commonly presents first with disinhibition. Aprosodia, mania, bizarre affect, and OCD are other features. In contrast, left-dominant frontotemporal dementia manifests first with anomia and may also feature depression. Bilaterally affected frontotemporal patients experienced decline in executive function as the most common initial change (R. Swartz & B. L. Miller, personal communication, October 1997).

Table 1.11 outlines the basis for common clinical disease entities and how frontal-subcortical circuits may relate to their manifestations.

SUMMARY

Five frontal–subcortical circuits provide a neuroanatomical basis for movement and behavior. Each of the circuits circumnavigates the same member structures, including the frontal lobe, striatum, globus pallidus, substantia nigra, and thalamus. The indirect pathway of these circuits includes the subthalamic nucleus. In addition to sharing anatomical way stations, each circuit employs the same neurotransmitters (glutamate, GABA, DA, ACh, serotonin, and various neuropeptides).

Frontal–subcortical circuits are named by either function or cortical site of origin. The dorsolateral circuit manages executive function. Executive dysfunction is a hallmark feature of subcortical dementia. The orbitofrontal circuit mediates empathic, civil, and socially appropriate behavior; personality change is a main characteristic of orbitofrontal dysfunction. The anterior cingulate circuit mediates motivated behavior, and apathy usually betrays damage to the structures of this circuit.

Each circuit is modulated by (1) *an indirect pathway*: the direct effect of the circuit itself is to disinhibit the thalamus, whereas an indirect pathway inhibits the thalamus; (2) *division of neurons into striosomes and matrix within each circuit*: striosomes and matrix differ with respect to neurotransmitter functions and afferent/efferent projections; and (3) *open afferent and efferent connections*: these allow posterior association cortices to affect frontally mediated behavior or to serve as communication points between the three circuits, as exemplified by the orbitofrontal–subcortical circuit's influence on the anterior cingulate circuit via the hippocampus-centered paralimbic belt.

OCD appears to be an orbitofrontal–subcortical mediated disorder of thalamocortical disinhibition. The exact lesion along the circuit which leads to this disinhibition is still unknown. Depression, mania, and psychosis are circuit-related behaviors but are not circuit specific.

TABLE 1.11. Summary of Common Neurological Disorders and Contributions of the Five Frontal–Subcortical Circuits

	Frontal–subcortical circuits				
Disorder	Dorsolateral	Orbitofrontal	Anterior cingulate	Motor	Oculomotor
Alzheimer's disease	Dysexective syndrome	Disinhibition	Apathy	Extrapyramidal signs	Decreased scanning
Obsessive–compulsive disorder	Dysexective syndrome	Obsessive–compulsive behaviors	Obsessive–compulsive behaviors	Tic	
Parkinson's disease	Dysexective syndrome, depression	Disinhibition, depression	Apathy, depression	Resting tremor, bradykinesia, postural instability, rigidity	Decreased extraocular movements
Progressive supranuclear palsy	Dysexective syndrome, depression	Disinhibition, depression	Apathy, depression	Resting tremor, bradykinesia, retropulsion, rigidity	Decreased vertical gaze
Huntington's disease	Dysexective syndrome, subcortical dementia, depression	Disinhibition, obsessive–compulsive behaviors, mania, bipolar affective disorder, antisocial behavior	Apathy, obsessive–compulsive behaviors, depression	Tremor, choreoathetosis, rigidity and bradykinesia in Westphal variant	Poor saccades and smooth pursuit
Frontotemporal dementia	Dysexective syndrome, subcortical, dementia, depression	Disinhibition, obsessive–compulsive behaviors, depression	Apathy, obsessive–compulsive behaviors, depression	May have upper motor neuronopathy or unilateral corticospinal tract signs	Poor saccades and smooth pursuit
Multiple sclerosis	Dysexective syndrome, subcortical, dementia, depression	Apathy, obsessive–compulsive behaviors, depression	Apathy, obsessive–compulsive behaviors, depression	May have upper motor neuronopathy or unilateral corticospinal tract signs	Poor saccades and smooth pursuit

ACKNOWLEDGMENTS

This project was supported by the Department of Veterans Affairs, a National Institute on Aging Alzheimer's Disease Center Grant (No. AG10123), and the Sidell–Kagan Research Fund.

REFERENCES

Albert, M. L., Feldman, R. G., & Willis, A. L. (1974). The "subcortical dementia" of progressive supranuclear palsy. *Journal of Neurology, Neurosurgery and Psychiatry, 37*(2), 121–130.

Alexander, G. E., DeLong, M. R., & Strick, P. L. (1986). Parallel organization of functionally segregated circuits linking basal ganglia and cortex. *Annual Review of Neuroscience, 9,* 357–381.

Amaral, D. G., Price, J. L., Pitkaenen A., & Carmichael, S. T. (1992). Anatomical organization of the primate amygdaloid complex. In J. P. Aggleton (Ed.), *The amygdala: Neurobiological aspects of emotion, memory, and mental dysfunction* (pp. 1–66). New York: Wiley.

American Psychiatric Association. (1994). *Diagnostic and statistical manual of mental disorders* (4th ed.). Washington, DC: Author.

Barbas, H. (1988). Anatomic organization of basoventral and mediodorsal visual recipient prefrontal regions in the rhesus monkey. *Journal of Comparative Neurology, 276*(3), 313–342.

Barris, R. W., & Schuman, H. R. (1953). Bilateral anterior cingulate gyrus lesions. *Neurology, 3*, 44–52.

Baxter, L. R. (1990). Brain imaging as a tool in establishing a theory of brain pathology in obsessive–compulsive disorder. *Journal of Clinical Psychiatry, 51*(Suppl.), 22–26.

Baxter, L. R., Schwartz, J. M., Phelps, M. E., Mazziotta, J. C., Guze, B. H., Selin, C. E., Gerner, R. H., & Sumida, R. M. (1989). Reduction of prefrontal cortex glucose metabolism common to three types of depression. *Archives of General Psychiatry, 46*(3), 243–250.

Berthier, M. L., Kulisevsky, J., Gironell, A., & Heras, J. A. (1996). Obsessive–compulsive disorder associated with brain lesions: Clinical phenomenology, cognitive function, and anatomic correlates. *Neurology, 47*(2), 353–361.

Berthier, M. L., Starkstein, S. E., Robinson, R. G., & Leiguarda, R. (1990). Limbic lesions in a patient with recurrent mania [letter]. *Journal of Neuropsychiatry and Clinical Neurosciences, 2*(2), 235–236.

Bogousslavsky, J., Ferrazzini, M., Regli, F., Assal, G., Tanabe, H., & Delaloye-Bischof, A. (1988). Manic delirium and frontal-like syndrome with paramedian infarction of the right thalamus. *Journal of Neurology, Neurosurgery and Psychiatry, 51*(1), 116–119.

Bogousslavsky, J., & Regli, F. (1990) Anterior cerebral artery territory infarction in the Lausanne stroke registry. *Archives of Neurology, 47*(2), 144–150.

Burns, A., Folstein, S., Brandt, J., & Folstein, M. (1990). Clinical assessment of irritability, aggression, and apathy in Huntington and Alzheimer disease. *Journal of Nervous and Mental Disease, 178*(1), 20–26.

Butters, N., Wolfe, J., Granholm, E., & Martone, M. (1986). An assessment of verbal recall, recognition and fluency abilities in patients with Huntington's disease. *Cortex, 22*(1), 11–32.

Carlsson, A. (1988). The current status of the dopamine hypothesis of schizophrenia. *Neuropsychopharmacology, 1*(3), 179–186.

Carlsson, M., & Carlsson, A. (1990). Interactions between glutamatergic and monoaminergic systems within the basal ganglia—implications for schizophrenia and Parkinson's disease. *Trends in Neurosciences, 13*(7), 272–276.

Chavis, D. A., & Pandya, D. N. (1976). Further observations on corticofrontal connections in the rhesus monkey. *Brain Research, 117*(3), 369–386.

Craig, A. H., Cummings, J. L., Fairbanks, L., Itti, L., Miller, B. L., Li, J., & Mena, I. (1996). Cerebral blood flow correlates of apathy in Alzheimer Disease. *Archives of Neurology, 53*(11), 1116–1120.

Cummings, J. L. (Ed.). (1985). *Clinical neuropsychiatry.* New York: Grune & Stratton.

Cummings, J. L. (1990). Introduction. In J. L. Cummings (Ed.), *Subcortical dementia* (pp. 3–16). New York: Oxford University Press.

Cummings, J. L. (1991). Behavioral complications of drug treatment of Parkinson's disease. *Journal of the American Geriatrics Society, 39*(7), 708–716.

Cummings, J. L. (1993a). Frontal–subcortical circuits and human behavior. *Archives of Neurology, 50*(8), 873–880.

Cummings, J. L. (1993b). The neuroanatomy of depression. *Journal of Clinical Psychiatry, 54*(Suppl.), 14–20.

Cummings, J. L. (1995). Anatomic and behavioral aspects of frontal–subcortical circuits. In J. Grafman, K. J. Holyoak, & F. Boller (Eds.), *Structure and functions of the human prefrontal cortex* (Vol. 769, pp. 1–13). New York: New York Academy of Sciences.

Cummings, J. L., Gosenfeld, L. F., Houlihan, J. P., & McCaffrey, T. (1983). Neuropsychiatric disturbances associated with idiopathic calcification of the basal ganglia. *Biological Psychiatry, 18*(5), 591–601.

Cummings, J. L., Mendez, M. F. (1984). Secondary mania with focal cerebrovascular lesions. *American Journal of Psychiatry, 141*(9), 1084–1087.

Damasio, H., & Damasio, A. R. (Eds.). (1989). Lesion analysis in neuropsychology. New York: Oxford University Press.

Damsma, G., Robertson, G. S., Tham, C. S., & Fibiger, H. C. (1991). Dopaminergic regulation of striatal acetylcholine release: Importance of D1 and D-methyl-*N*-aspartate receptors. *Journal of Pharmacology and Experimental Therapeutics, 259,* 1064–1072.

Davis, M. (1992). The role of the amygdala in fear and anxiety. *Annual Review of Neuroscience, 15*(3), 353–375.

Deymeer, F., Smith, T. W., DeGirolami, U., & Drachman, D. A. (1989). Thalamic dementia and motor neuron disease. *Neurology, 39*(1), 58–61.

DiChiara, G. & Morelli, M. (1993). Dopamine–acetylcholine–glutamate interactions in the striatum. *Advances in Neurology, 60,* 102–107.

Drewe, E. A. (1975). Go/no-go learning after frontal lobe lesions in humans. *Cortex, 11*(1), 8–16.

Emson, P. C., Augood, S. J., Senaris, R., Guerara Guzman, R., Kishimoto, J., Kadowaki, K., Norris, P. J., & Kendrick, K. M. (1993). Chemical signalling and striatal interneurones. *Progress in Brain Research, 99,* 155–165.

Eslinger, P. J., Warner, G. C., Grattan, L. M., & Easton, J. D. (1991). "Frontal lobe" utilization behavior associated with paramedian thalamic infarction. *Neurology, 41*(3), 450–452.

Fesenmeier, J. T., Kuzniecky, R., & Garcia, J. H. (1990). Akinetic mutism caused by bilateral anterior cerebral tuberculous obliterative arteritis. *Neurology 40*(6), 1005–1006.

Folstein, S. E. (Ed.). (1989). *Huntington's disease: A disorder of families.* Baltimore: Johns Hopkins University Press.

Gerfen, C. R., Baimbridge, K. G., & Miller, J. J. (1985). The neostriatal mosaic: Compartmental distribution of calcium binding protein and parvalbumin in the basal ganglia of the rat and monkey. *Proceedings of the National Academy of Sciences of the United States of America, 82*(24), 8780–8784.

Gerfen, C. R., Engber, T. M., Mahan, L. C., Susel, Z., Chase, T. N., Monsma, F. J. Jr., & Sibley, D. R. (1990). D1 and D2 dopamine receptor-regulated gene expression of striatonigral and striatopallidal neurons. *Science, 250*(4986), 1429–1432.

Giguere, M., & Goldman-Rakic, P. S. (1988). Mediodorsal nucleus: Areal, laminar, and tangential distribution of afferents and efferents in the frontal lobe of the rhesus monkey. *Journal of Comparative Neurology, 277*(2), 195–213.

Goldman-Rakic, P. S. (1994). Working memory dysfunction in schizophrenia. *Journal of Neuropsychiatry and Clinical Neuroscience, 6*(4), 348–357.

Goldman-Rakic, P. S., & Porrino, L. J. (1985). The primate mediodorsal (MD) nucleus and its projection to the frontal lobe. *Journal of Comparative Neurology, 242*(4), 535–560.

Gorman, D. G., & Cummings, J. L. (1990). Organic delusional syndrome. *Seminars in Neurology, 10*(3), 229–238.

Graybiel, A. M. (1990). Neurotransmitters and neuromodulators in the basal ganglia. *Trends in Neuroscience, 13*(7), 244–254.

Graybiel, A. M., & Ragsdale, C. W., Jr. (1978). Histochemically distinct compartments in the striatum of human, monkey and cat demonstrated by acetylcholinesterase staining. *Proceedings of the National Academy of Sciences of the United States of America, 75*(11), 5723–5726.

Hagan, R. M., Kilpatrick, G. H., & Tyers, M. B. (1993). Interactions between 5-HT3 receptors and cerebral dopamine function: Implications for the treatment of schizophrenia and psychoactive substance abuse. *Psychopharmacology, 112*(1 Suppl.), S68–S75.

Hunter, R., Blackwood, W., & Bull, J. (1968). Three cases of frontal meningiomas presenting psychiatrically. *British Medical Journal, 3*(609), 9–16.

Hyde, T. M., Ziegler, J. C., & Weinberger, D. R. (1992). Psychiatric disturbances in metachromatic leukodystrophy. Insights into the neurobiology of psychosis. *Archives of Neurology, 49*(4), 401–406.

Ilinsky, L. A., Jouandet, M. L., & Goldman-Rakic, P. S. (1985). Organization of the nigrothalamocortical system in the rhesus monkey. *Journal of Comparative Neurology, 236*(3), 315–330.

Irle, E., Peper, M., Wowra, B., & Kunze, S. (1994). Mood changes after surgery for tumors of the cerebral cortex. *Archives of Neurology, 51*(2), 164–174.

Jibiki, I., Maeda, T., Kubota, T., & Yamaguchi, N. (1993). 1231-IMP SPECT brain imaging in epileptic psychosis: A study of two cases of temporal lobe epilepsy with schizophrenia-like syndrome. *Neuropsychobiology, 28,* 207–211.

Johnson, T. N., & Rosvold, H. E. (1971). Topographic projections on the globus pallidus and substantia nigra of selectively placed lesions in the precommissural caudate nucleus and putamen in the monkey. *Experimental Neurology, 33,* 584–596.

Jones, E. G., & Powell, T. P. (1970). An anatomical study of converging sensory pathways within the cerebral cortex of the monkey. *Brain, 93,* 793–820.

Jones-Gotman, M., & Milner, B. (1977). Design fluency: The invention of nonsense drawings after focal cortical lesions. *Neuropsychologia, 15*(4–5), 653–674.

Keefe, K. A., & Gerfen, C. R. (1995). D1–D2 dopamine receptor synergy in striatum: Effects of intrastriatal infusions of dopamine agonists and antagonists on immediate early gene expression. *Neuroscience, 66*(4), 903–913.

Kemp, J. M., & Powell, T. P. S. (1971). The structure of the caudate nucleus of the cat: Light and electron microscopy. *Philosophical Transactions of the Royal Society of London. Series B. Biological Sciences, 262*(845), 383–401.

Kievit, J., & Kuypers, H. G. J. M. (1977). Organization of the thalamo-cortical connexions to the frontal lobe in the rhesus monkey. *Experimental Brain Research, 29*(3–4), 299–322.

Kim, R., Nakano, K., Jayaraman, A., & Carpenter, M. B. (1976). Projections of the globus pallidus and adjacent structures: An autoradiographic study in the monkey. *Journal of Comparative Neurology, 169*(3), 263–90.

Kulisevsky, J., Berthier, M. L., & Pujol, J. (1993). Hemiballismus and secondary mania following right thalamic infarction. *Neurology, 43*(7), 1422–1424.

Laiacona, M., De Santis, A., Barbarotto, R., Basso, A., Spagnoli, D., & Capitani, E. (1989). Neuropsychological follow-up of patients operated for aneurysms of anterior communicating artery. *Cortex, 25*(2), 261–273.

Lapper, S. R., & Bolam, J. P. (1992). Input from the frontal cortex and the parafasicular nucleus to cholinergic interneurons in the dorsal striatum of the rat. *Neuroscience, 51*(3), 533–545.

Lavoie, B., & Parent, A. (1990). Immunohistochemical study of the sertoninergic innervation of the basal ganglia in the squirrel monkey. *Journal of Comparative Neurology, 299*(1), 1–16.

Leimkuhler, M. E., & Mesulam, M.-M. (1985). Reversible go–no go deficits in a case of frontal lobe tumor. *Annals of Neurology, 18*(5), 617–619.

Leinonen, E., Tuunainen, A., & Lepola, U. (1994). Postoperative psychoses in epileptic patients after temporal lobectomy. *Acta Neurologica Scandinavica, 90*(6), 394–399.

Lhermitte, F., Pillon, B., & Serdaru, M. (1986). Human autonomy and the frontal lobes. I: Imitation and utilization behavior, a neuropsychological study of 75 patients. *Annals of Neurology, 19*(4), 326–334.

Logue, V., Durward, M., Pratt, R. T., Piercy, M., & Nixon, W. L. (1968). The quality of survival after an anterior cerebral aneurysm. *British Journal of Psychiatry, 114*(507), 137–160.

Lykestos, C., Stoline, A. M., Longstreet, P., Ranen, N. G., Lesser, R., Fisher, R., & Folstein, M. (1993). Mania in temporal lobe epilepsy. *Neuropsychiatry, Neuropsychology, and Behavioral Neurology, 6,* 19–25.

Masterman, D. M., & Cummings, J.L. (1997). Frontal–subcortical circuits: The anatomic basis of executive, social and motivated behaviors. *Journal of Psychopharmacology, 11*(2), 107–114.

Mayberg, H. S. (1994). Frontal lobe dysfunction in secondary depression. *Journal of Neuropsychiatry and Clinical Neurosciences, 6*(4), 428–442.

Mayberg, H. S., Starkstein, S. E., Peyser C. E., Brandt, J., Dannals, R. F., & Folstein, S. E. (1992). Paralimbic frontal lobe hypometabolism in depression associated with Huntington's disease. *Neurology, 42*(9), 1791–1797.

Mayberg, H. S., Starkstein, S. E., Sadzot, B., Preziosi, T., Andrezejewski, P. L., Dannals, R. F., Wagner, H. N., Jr., & Robinson, R. G. (1990). Selective hypometabolism in inferior frontal lobe in depressed patients with Parkinson's disease. *Annals of Neurology, 28*(1), 57–64.

Mega, M. S., & Cummings, J. L. (1994). Frontal–subcortical circuits and neuropsychiatric disorders. *Journal of Neuropsychiatry and Clinical Neurosciences, 6*(4), 358–370.

Mena, I., Marin, O., Fuenzalida, S., Horiuchi, K., Burke, K., & Cotzias, G. C. (1967). Chronic manganese poisoning. *Neurology, 17*(2), 128–136.

Meredith, G. E., Blank, B., & Groenewegen, H. J. (1989). The distribution and compartmental organization of the cholinergic neurons in nucleus accumbens of the rat. *Neuroscience, 31*(2), 327–345.

Mesulam, M.-M. (1985). Patterns in behavioral neuroanatomy: Association areas, the limbic system, and hemispheric specialization. In M.-M. Mesulam (Ed.), *Behavioral neurology* (pp. 1–70). Phildadelphia: F. A. Davis.

Mesulam, M.-M., & Mufson, E. J. (1982). Insula of the old world monkey: III. Efferent cortical output and comments on function. *Journal of Comparative Neurology, 212*(1), 38–52.

Miller, B. L., Benson, D. F., Cummings, J. L., & Neshkes, R. (1986). Late-life paraphrenia: An organic delusional syndrome. *Journal of Clinical Psychiatry, 47*(4), 204–207.

Milner, B. (1963). Effects of different brain lesions on card sorting. *Archives of Neurology, 9,* 90–100.

Modell, J. G., Mountz, J. M., Curtis, G. C., & Greden, J. F. (1989). Neurophysiologic dysfunction in basal ganglia/limbic striatal and thalamocortical circuits as a pathogenetic mechanism of obsessive–compulsive disorder. *Journal of Neuropsychiatry and Clinical Neurosciences, 1*(1), 27–36.

Morecraft, R. J., Geula, C., & Mesulam, M.-M. (1992). Cytoarchitecture and neural afferents of orbitofrontal cortex in the brain of the monkey. *Journal of Comparative Neurology, 323*(3), 341–358.

Morelli, M., Fenu, S., Pinna, A., & DiChiara, G. (1992). Opposite effects of NMDA receptor blockade on dopaminergic D1- and D2-mediated behavior in the 6-hydroxydopamine model of turning: Relationship to c-fos expression. *Journal of Pharmacology and Experimental Therapeutics, 260*(1), 402–408.

Mufson, E. J., & Mesulam, M.-M. (1982). Insula of the old world monkey: II. Afferent cortical input and comments on the claustrum. *Journal of Comparative Neurology, 212*(1), 23–37.

Nauta, W. J. H. (1971). The problem of the frontal lobe: A reinterpretation. *Journal of Psychiatric Research, 8*(3), 167–187.

Nauta, W. J. H. (1973). Connections of the frontal lobe with the limbic system. In L. V. Laitinen & K. E. Livingston (Eds.), *Surgical approaches in psychiatry* (pp. 303–314). Baltimore: University Park Press.

Nauta, W. J. H. (1979). A proposed conceptual reorganization of the basal ganglia and telenchephalon. *Neuroscience, 4*(12), 1875–1881.

Nielsen, J. M., & Jacobs, L. L. (1951). Bilateral lesions of the anterior cingulate gyri. *Bulletin of the Los Angeles Neurological Society, 16,* 231–234.

Nieoullon, A., & Kerkerian-LeGoff, L. (1992). Cellular interactions in the striatum involving neuronal systems using "classical" neurotransmitters: Possible functional implications. *Movement Disorders, 7*(4), 311–325.

Palfreyman, M. G., Schmidt, C. J., Sorensen, S. M., Dudley, M. W., Kehne, J. H., Moser, P., Gittos, M. W., & Carr, A. A. (1993). Electrophysiological, biochemical and behavioral evidence for 5-HT2 and 5-HT3 mediated control of dopaminergic function. *Psychopharmacology, 112*(1 Suppl.), S60–S67.

Pandya, D. N., & Yeterian, E. H. (1990). Prefrontal cortex in relation to other cortical areas in rhesus monkey: Architecture and connections. *Progress in Brain Research, 85,* 63–94.

Parent, A., Bouchard, C., & Smith, Y. (1984). The striatopallidal and striatonigral projections: Two distinct fiber systems in primate. *Brain Research, 303*(2), 385–390.

Parent, A., Pare, D., Smith, Y., & Steriade, M. (1988). Basal forebrain cholinergic and noncholinergic projections to the thalamus and brainstem in cats and monkeys. *Journal of Comparative Neurology, 277*(2), 281–301.

Paul, M. L., Graybiel, A. M., David, J. C., & Robertson, H. A. (1992). D1-like and D2-like dopamine receptors synergistically activate rotation and c-fos expression in the dopamine-depleted striatum in a rat model of Parkinson's disease. *Journal of Neuroscience, 12*(10), 3729–3742.

Penney, J. B., Jr., & Young, A. B. (1983). Speculations on the functional anatomy of basal ganglia disorders. *Annual Review of Neuroscience, 6,* 73–94.

Ragsdale, C. W., & Graybiel, A. M. (1990). A simple ordering of neocortical areas established by the compartmental organization of their striatal projections. *Proceedings of the National Academy of Sciences of the United States of America, 87*(16), 6196–6199.

Rapoport, J. L., & Wise, S. P. (1988). Obsessive–compulsive disorder: Evidence for basal ganglia dysfunction. *Psychopharmacology Bulletin, 24*(3), 380–384.

Ray, J. P., & Price J. L. (1993). The organization of projections from the mediodorsal nucleus of the thalamus to orbital and medial prefrontal cortex in macaque monkeys. *Journal of Comparative Neurology, 337*(1), 1–31.

Reith, J., Benkelfat, C., Sherwin, A., Yasuhara, Y., Kuwabara, H., Andermann, F., Bachneff, S., Cumming, P., Diksic, M., Dyve, S. E., Etienne, P., Evans, A. C., Lal, S., Shevell, M., Savard, G., Wong, D. F., Chouinard, G., & Gjedde, A. (1994). Elevated dopa decarboxylase activity in living brain of patients with psychosis. *Proceedings of the National Academy of Sciences of the United States of America, 91*(24), 11651–11654.

Robinson, R. G., & Starkstein, S. E. (1990). Current research in affective disorders following stroke. *Journal of Neuropsychiatry and Clinical Neurosciences, 2*(1), 1–14.

Ross, E. D., & Stewart, R. M. (1981). Akinetic mutism from hypothalamic damage: Successful treatment with dopamine agonists. *Neurology, 31*(11), 1435–1439.

Russchen, F. T., Amaral, D. G., & Price, J. L. (1987). The afferent input to the magnocellular division of the mediodorsal thalamic nucleus in the monkey, Macaca fascicularis. *Journal of Comparative Neurology, 256*(2), 175–210.

Scatton, B., & Lehmann, J. (1982). N-methyl-D-aspartate-type receptors mediate striatal 3H-acetylcholine release evoked by excitatory amino-acids. *Nature, 297*(5865), 422–424.

Schwartz, J. M., Stoessel, P. W., Baxter, L. R., Jr., Martin, K. M., & Phelps, M. E. (1996). Systematic changes in cerebral glucose metabolic rate after successful behavior modification treatment of obsessive–compulsive disorder. *Archives of General Psychiatry, 53*(2), 109–113.

Selemon, L. D., & Goldman-Rakic, P. S. (1985). Longitudinal topography and interdigitation of corticostriatal projections in the rhesus monkey. *Journal of Neuroscience, 5*(3), 776–794.

Smith, A. D., & Bolam, J. P. (1990). The neural network of the basal ganglia as revealed by the study of synaptic connections of identified neurones. *Trends in Neuroscience, 13*(7), 259–265.

Snyder-Keller, A. M. (1991). Striatal c-fos induction by drugs and stress in neonatally dopamine-depleted rats given nigral transplants: Importance of NMDA activation and relevance to sensitization phenomena. *Experimental Neurology, 113*(2), 155–65.

Starkstein, S. E., Cohen, B. S., Fedoroff, P., Parikh, R. M., Price, T. R., & Robinson, R. G. (1990). Relationship between anxiety disorders and depressive disorders in patients with cerebrovascular injury. *Archives of General Psychiatry, 47*(3), 246–251.

Starkstein, S. E., Fedoroff, P., Berthier, M. L., & Robinson, R. G. (1991). Manic–depressive and pure manic states after brain lesions. *Biological Psychiatry, 29*(2), 149–158.

Starkstein, S. E., Mayberg, H. S., Preziosi, T. J., Andrezejewski, P., Leiguarda, R., & Robinson, R. G. (1992). Reliability, validity, and clinical correlates of apathy in Parkinson's disease. *Journal of Neuropsychiatry and Clinical Neurosciences, 4*(2), 134–139.

Starkstein, S. E., Pearlson, G. D., Boston, J., & Robinson, R. G. (1987). Mania after brain injury. A controlled study of causative factors. *Archives of Neurology, 44*(10), 1069–1073.

Stoof, J. C., Drukarch, B., DeBoer, P., Westerink, B. H. C., & Groenewegen, H. J. (1992). Regulation of the activity of striatal cholinergic neurons by dopamine. *Neuroscience, 47*(4), 755–770.

Stuss, D. T., Guberman, A., Nelson, R., & Larochelle, S. (1988). The neuropsychology of paramedian thalamic infarction. *Brain and Cognition, 8*(3), 348–378.

Sultzer, D. L., Mahler, M. E., Mandelkern, M. A., Cummings, J. L., van Gorp, W. G., Hinkin, C. H., & Berisford, M. A. (1995). The relationship between psychiatric symptoms and regional cortical metabolism in Alzheimer's disease. *Journal of Neuropsychiatry and Clinical Neuroscience, 7*(4), 476–484.

Trautner, R. J., Cummings, J. L., Read, S. L., & Benson, D. F. (1988). Idiopathic basal ganglia calcification and organic mood disorder. *American Journal of Psychiatry, 145*(3), 350–353.

Van Hoesen, G. W. (1981). The differential distribution, diversity and sprouting of cortical projections to the amygdala in the rhesus monkey. In Y. Ben-Ari (Ed.), *The amygdaloid complex* (pp. 77–90). Amsterdam: Elsevier/North Holland.

Van Hoesen, G. W., Pandya, D. N., & Butters, N. (1975). Some connections of the entorhinal (area 28) and perirhinal (area 35) cortices of the rhesus monkey: II. Frontal lobe afferents. *Brain Research, 95*, 25–38.

Voorn, P., Jorritsma-Byham, B., Van Dijk, C., & Buijs, R. M. (1986). The dopaminergic innervation of the ventral striatum in the rat: A light- and electron-microscopical study with antibodies against dopamine. *Journal of Comparative Neurology, 251*(1), 84–99.

Yeterian, E. H., & Pandya, D. N. (1993). Striatal connections of the parietal association cortices in rhesus monkeys. *Journal of Comparative Neurology, 332*(2), 175–197.

Zald, D. H., & Kim, S. W. (1996a). Anatomy and function of the orbital frontal cortex: I. Anatomy, neurocircuitry, and obsessive-compulsive disorder. *Journal of Neuropsychiatry and Clinical Neuroscience, 8*(2), 125–138.

Zald, D. H. & Kim, S. W. (1996b). Anatomy and function of the orbital frontal cortex: II. Function and relevance to obsessive–compulsive disorder. *Journal of Neuropsychiatry and Clinical Neuroscience, 8*(3), 249–261.

2

Frontal Lobe Anatomy and Cortical Connectivity

DANIEL I. KAUFER
DAVID A. LEWIS

The human frontal lobes comprise the anterior half of the cerebral hemispheres. Within its boundaries, diverse functions ranging from fine motor control to working memory to complex social behaviors are subserved by a number of anatomically distinct regions. The identification and classification of frontal lobe regions, as with other areas of cerebral cortex, are based on morphological features of varying resolution, including the appearance of surface landmarks and the microscopic analysis of the constituent neurons. Aside from the central sulcus, which clearly separates frontal motor from parietal lobe sensory regions, few other gross surface landmarks within the frontal lobes can be used to reliably discriminate functionally related regions (Damasio, 1991). At the microscopic level, a number of different cytoarchitectonic maps of the cerebral cortex have been constructed, whereby regions are parcellated based on the laminar distribution and packing density of neurons (reviewed in Zilles, 1990). Although a modest degree of general agreement exists between areal maps prepared by different investigators, the boundaries and number of regions ascribed to the frontal lobes differ across investigators due to methodological differences, interindividual subject variation, and the absence of uniform morphological criteria. The human cytoarchitectonic map Brodmann (1909/1994), which delineates 43 cortical regions, is the most widely used and is emphasized in the following discussion.

Patterns of neuronal connectivity involving frontal regions critically determine the nature and diversity of frontal lobe-affiliated functions. Because technical and ethical considerations restrict the application of neural pathway tracing methods in humans, much of what we know about human cerebral connectivity has been inferred from work in nonhuman primates. However, compared to nonhuman primates, one of the most striking features of the human brain is the increased size and differentiation of the frontal lobes, including greater hemispheric asymmetries (see Chapters 3, 4, and 5, this volume). Although certain anatomical similarities are present between human and monkey frontal cortices, a comprehensive circuit-by-circuit comparison has yet to be achieved. Observations such as the cross-species similarities in the dopamine innervation of the prefrontal cortex (Lewis, Hayes, Lund, & Oeth, 1992) have important implications for current hypotheses of the neural circuitry underlying human frontal lobe functions, which are principally based on extrapolation from nonhuman primates (Goldman-Rakic, 1987; see also see Chapter 11, this volume).

For didactic purposes, the cortical classification scheme of Mesulam (1985, 1997) is used to review functional trends in frontal lobe anatomy. General features of frontal corticocortical connectivity are surveyed, emphasizing parallel and integrative aspects of functional circuitry. Two examples of altered frontal lobe cortical connectivity in disease states highlight gross morphometric relationships in degenerative dementias and local circuit interactions in schizophrenia.

FRONTAL LOBE ANATOMY

Functional Regions

The surface boundaries of the frontal lobes are demarcated by the central sulcus caudally and the lateral sulcus in each hemisphere (Figure 2.1). Within these gross borders, three primary functional regions on the lateral surface of the frontal lobes are recognized: motor, premotor, and prefrontal, essentially forming a caudal to rostral continuum (Nieuwenhuys, Voogd, & van Huijzen, 1988; Zilles, 1990). A fourth functional region, paralimbic or limbic, is located deep in the medial portion of the frontal lobes. As these zones are principally defined on the basis of cytoarchitectonic features, precision in specifying their boundaries relative to surface landmarks is lacking (Damasio, 1991; Damasio & Damasio, 1989; Mesulam, 1985).

Primary motor cortex (Brodmann's area 4) is the smallest and structurally most homogeneous of these regions, forming a narrow strip of tissue along the lateral surface of the frontal lobe and extending down around the medial bank of the cortical apex (see also Table 2.1). Rostrally, the premotor or motor association area (Brodmann's area 6) generally parallels the lateral and medial extent of primary motor cortex and may functionally overlap with it. The medial portion of this region is independently referred to as the suppplementary motor area. More rostrally located is Brodmann's area 8, which contains the frontal eye field, a region involved in oculomotor control. The most lateral and rostral extension of motor association cortex is Brodmann's area 44 (pars opercularis), which together with Brodmann's area 45 (pars triangularis) comprises Broca's area. Collectively, Brodmann's area 47 (pars orbitalis) and areas 44 and 45 form the frontal operculum.

Prefrontal regions occupy the largest portion of the frontal lobes and may be subdivided into the following three topographically segregated groups: dorsolateral prefrontal cortex, orbitofrontal cortex, and paralimbic regions. Rostromedial (areas 9, 10, and the rostral portion of area 32) and dorsolateral regions (area 46 and part of area 9) are generally referred to as prefrontal cortex, or when specifying regions located along the lateral convexity, dorsolateral prefrontal cortex (DLPFC). Brodmann's area 11 and the rostral portion of area 12 represent the main components of orbitofrontal cortex, which extends caudally into paralimbic zones (caudal area 12 and the subcallosal or paraolfactory region, area 25). The anterior cingulate (area 24) and the caudal portion of area 32 (mesial frontal cortex) constitute the largest paralimbic regions of the frontal lobes, forming a belt of tissue along the mesial hemisphere surface.

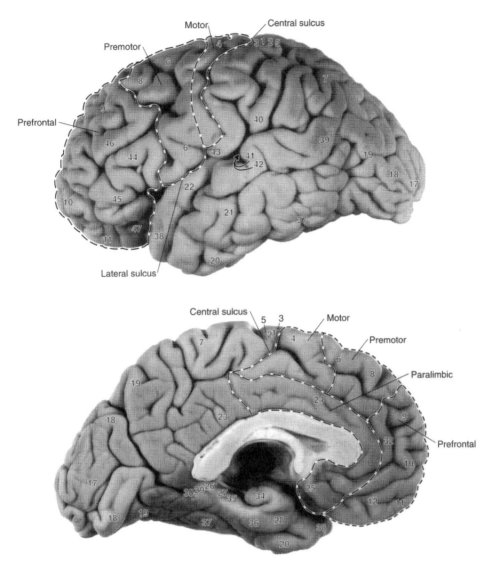

FIGURE 2.1. Lateral (top) and medial (bottom) views of the left cerebral hemishere of a human brain indicating the subdivisions of the frontal lobe. Numbers indicate the approximate location of Brodmann's areas.

Cortical Types

Following the nomenclature of Mesulam (1985, 1997), cerebral cortical areas are divided into three types: *idiotypic* (or koniocortex), *homotypic* (or isocortex), and *paralimbic* (or proisocortex and periallocortex) (Barbas & Pandya, 1989; Sanides, 1972). In general, idiotypic and homotypic cortices (neocortex) have six distinct cellular layers at some stage of development, whereas paralimbic regions may have fewer recognizable lamina, reflecting a transitional spectrum with more primitive limbic-associated cortical and nuclear regions. General trends in architectonic features spanning the range from

TABLE 2.1. Frontal Lobe Anatomy

Brodmann's area	Anatomic description	Cortical type	Functional region
4	Primary motor cortex	Primary motor	Motor
6	Premotor/supplementary motor area	Primary motor (caudal) Unimodal motor (rostral)	
44[a,b]	Pars opercularis	Unimodal motor	Premotor
8[c]	Motor association cortex	Unimodal motor (caudal) Heteromodal (?rostral)	
46	Dorsolateral prefrontal cortex	Heteromodal	
9	Superior prefrontal cortex	Heteromodal	
10	Inferior prefrontal cortex	Heteromodal	Prefrontal (dorsolateral)
45[a,b]	Pars triangularis	Heteromodal	
47[a]	Pars orbitalis	Heteromodal	
11[d]	Lateral orbitofrontal cortex	Heteromodal	
12[d]	Medial orbitofrontal cortex	Heteromodal (rostral) Paralimbic (caudal)	Prefrontal (orbitofrontal)
32	Medial frontal cortex	Heteromodal (rostral) Paralimbic (caudal)	
24	Anterior cingulate	Paralimbic	Paralimbic (medial frontal)
25	Paraolfactory region (subcallosal area)	Paralimbic	

Note. After Mesulam (1985) and Damasio and Damasio (1989).
[a] Frontal operculum; [b] Broca's area (left hemisphere); [c] frontal eye fields; [d] region numbers are reversed in nonhuman primates (Walker, 1940).

paralimbic to idiotypic cortex include a progressively more distinct laminar organization, an increase in myelin content, an emergent granular layer (layer IV), increased pyramidal cell size, and increased cellular density, particularly in the supragranular layers (Barbas & Pandya, 1989; Mesulam, 1985; Zilles, 1990).

Primary motor cortex (area 4) is the only idiotypical cortex in the frontal lobe. Giant pyramidal neurons (Betz cells) in layer V, which project to the spinal cord, are a prominent feature of primary motor cortex. A well-developed inner granular layer (IV) characteristic of primary sensory idiotypical (koniocortical) areas is absent in area 4, leading to its designation as "agranular" cortex. Brodmann's criterion for defining the borders between primary and nonprimary motor cortex on the basis of cell size alone has been vigorously contested and appears no longer tenable (see Zilles, 1990, for discussion).

The most abundant cortical type in the frontal lobe is homotypical cortex, carrying the functional connotation of association cortex. Two types of homotypical cortex are recognized: unimodal association, or modality-specific, and heteromodal association, representing multimodal or higher-order cortical regions. Although subtle cytoarchitectonic differences between unimodal and heteromodal association cortices may be present, functional properties are the primary basis for distinguishing these two types of association cortices. For example, an individual neuron in a given unimodal association area is typically responsive only to a single sensory (auditory, visual, somatosensory) or motor input; neurons in heteromodal association cortices, in contrast, respond to or influence the activity of neurons in multiple sensory modalities or are involved in integrated sensory and motor processing. Within the frontal lobes, Brodmann's area 6 and part of area 8 are unimodal motor association areas, whereas Brodmann's areas 9–11, 45–47, and portions of areas 8,

12, and 32 comprise integrative heteromodal association regions. Investigators (Benson, 1993) refer to rostral areas of prefrontal cortex suggested to mediate nonsensorimotor (cognitive) associative functions as supramodal association regions.

Paralimbic cortex is structurally heterogenous and exhibits gradations of features between more highly differentiated isocortex (idiotypical and homotypical) and less differentiated two-layered allocortex (hippocampus and olfactory cortex). A continuous belt of paralimbic cortex including portions of the frontal and temporal lobes (Broca's "limbic lobe") circumscribes the corpus callosum along the medial and basal hemispheric surface. From a phylogenetic perspective, paralimbic regions are viewed as being composed of two intersecting allocortical lines. One is the hippocampal trend, which includes the hippocampus, parahippocampal and cingulate regions, forming the caudal and superior portions of the "paralimbic belt"; the other is the olfactory-based line, emanating from olfactory piriform cortex, and extending into orbitofrontal, insular, and anterior temporal polar regions (Barbas & Pandya, 1989, 1991; Mesulam, 1985, 1997; Sanides, 1972).

CORTICOCORTICAL CONNECTIVITY

Laminar Distribution Patterns

Researchers have identified or suggested (Barbas & Pandya, 1989; Selemon & Goldman-Rakic, 1988; Zilles, 1990) several general trends in the laminar distribution of cortical projection systems. Short corticocortical association fibers most commonly arise from neurons in cortical layers II and superficial III; long corticocortical association tracts and commissural (interhemispheric) fibers are primarily associated with lamina III and, to a lesser extent, infragranular layers V and VI. In contrast, cortical–subcortical (i.e., striatum, thalamus, and brainstem) pathways traverse infragranular cortical lamina. A similar pattern of laminar distribution has also been suggested to occur among cortical areas based on their degree of differentiation (Barbas, 1986; Barbas & Pandya, 1989). That is, frontally directed cortical projections from less differentiated areas tend to have their cells of origin in infragranular layers V and VI, whereas projections from more differentiated cortical areas generally arise from supragranular layers. In the visual and auditory systems, functionality (i.e., the direction of information flow) is reflected by the laminar distribution of neural pathways (Galaburda & Pandya, 1983; Nieuwenhuys et al., 1988; Pandya & Yeterian, 1985; Rockland & Pandya, 1979; van Essen & Mausell, 1983). Feed-forward pathways, transferring information from primary sensory areas to secondary association areas, arise in supragranular areas and principally terminate in layer IV. Feedback projections in the reverse direction originate from both supra- and infragranular layers of association cortices and terminate outside layer IV. These two types of projections underscore the well-established findings that most connections between cortical association areas are reciprocal (Felleman & van Essen, 1991).

Functional Topography and Parallel Circuitry

Overview

The frontal lobes are reciprocally connected with temporal, parietal, and occipital cortices, where they receive higher-level auditory, somatosensory, and visual information. In addition, the frontal lobes have robust connections with limbic structures such as the hippocampus and amygdala, which mediate such processes as learning and memory, emotional and affective tone, autonomic regulation, drive, and motivation. The frontal lobes may thus be viewed as integrating information regarding the external world and internal states (Mesulam, 1985). Although portions of the frontal lobes are involved in processing sensory information about taste and smell, their primary role in this context is to mediate action. Frontal lobe motor output is directed to the brainstem and spinal cord, constituting the only direct cortical influence on these regions of the central nervous system. Motor and prefrontal areas of the frontal lobes are also connected in a series of parallel circuits involving portions of the striatum and thalamus, which have been implicated to subserve cognitive, motor, and behavioral regulatory processes (Alexander, DeLong, & Strick, 1986; Cummings, 1993). As a complement to discussion of frontal–subcortical circuitry (see Chapter 1, this volume), a survey of frontal corticocortical connectivity emphasizes functionally segregated, parallel circuitry involving motor/premotor, dorsolateral prefrontal, and medial/orbitofrontal regions of the frontal lobes. For the sake of clarity, discrepancies among investigators in observed patterns of connectivity and difficulties in mapping data obtained in monkeys to humans are largely ignored.

Motor/Premotor Circuits

Primary motor cortex is principally connected with neighboring premotor (Brodmann's area 6 and the supplementary motor area) and unimodal somatosensory cortices (mainly area 2). These connections are somatopically arranged, with the head and upper limb areas represented in ventral connections among these regions and more dorsally located interconnections representing the trunk and legs (Jones, Coulter, & Hendry, 1978; Nieuwenhuys et al., 1988). Premotor areas are principally connected with somatosensory association cortices in the superior parietal lobule (areas 5 and rostral 7; see Mesulam, 1985, for discussion of inconsistencies between Brodmann human and monkey maps of this region), as well as with more rostral prefrontal association areas across the lateral convexity (Barbas & Pandya, 1987; Petrides & Pandya, 1984). Prefrontal input to premotor areas is most concentrated in ventrolateral regions, corresponding to the somatotopic representations of the upper body (Lu, Preston, & Strick, 1994). In contrast to the predominantly somatosensory input to area 6, area 8 and the frontal eye fields receive sensory input from widespread unimodal (visual and auditory) and heteromodal association areas, including caudal portions of area 7, the inferior parietal lobule (supramarginal and angular gyri), the superior temporal sulcus, and posterior inferotemporal regions (Barbas & Mesulam, 1981; Barbas, 1992; Cavada & Goldman-Rakic, 1989; Petrides & Pandya, 1984; Seltzer & Pandya, 1989). Compared to prefrontal–premotor connections, prefrontal input to area 8 is more restricted to dorsal regions along the prefrontal lateral convexity (Barbas, 1992; Barbas & Pandya, 1989, 1991). The respective patterns of connections exhibited by areas 6 and 8 to other sensory and frontal cortices (including descending efferent outputs) have been suggested to represent two parallel systems for controlling movement: a somatomotor system governing movements of the limb and body in space and a visuomotor system for orienting the head and eyes to the environment (Passingham, 1993) (Figure 2.2).

Dorsolateral Prefrontal Circuits

Visual system projections to the frontal lobes originate from temporal, parietal, and occipital cortices. Two functionally and topographically segregated visual systems are recognized: a dorsal system, composed of visual association cortices in parieto-occipital

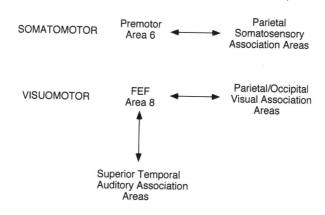

FIGURE 2.2. Schematic diagram of cortical connections for the somatic and visual motor systems. FEF, frontal eye fields. After Passingham (1993).

areas (caudal area 7 and dorsal portions 18 and 19), and a ventral system, composed of regions extending rostrally from the temporal–occipital border along the inferior and middle temporal gyri (ventral areas 18 and 19, and areas 37, 20, and 21) (Mishkin, Ungerleider, & Macko, 1983; van Essen & Maunsell, 1983) (Figure 2.3). Functionally, the dorsal system is primarily involved in processing motion and spatial dimensions of visual information ("where"); the ventral system is mainly associated with discriminative visual feature processing ("what"). In general, inferior temporal visual projections terminate in lateral orbital regions and the ventral part of area 46, whereas visual projections from the parietal cortex connections are primarily directed to more dorsal and lateral frontal cortices (e.g., areas 9 and dorsal 46), including robust connections

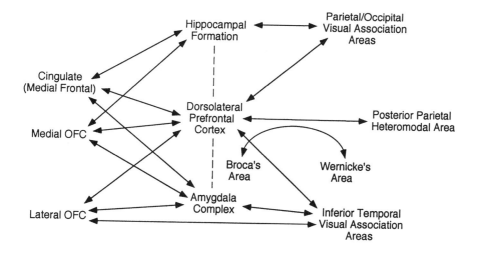

FIGURE 2.3. Schematic diagram of principal corticocortical connections within frontal lobe regions, including primary limbic connections, and between posterior sensory cortices and frontal lobe regions. Double-head arrows indicate that most connections are reciprocal. Relatively sparse direct connections between dorsolateral prefrontal cortex and limbic structures (hippocampal formation and amygdala nuclei) are depicted with a dashed line. OFC, orbitofrontal cortex.

with area 8 (Barbas, 1992; Cavada & Goldman-Rakic, 1989; Petrides & Pandya, 1984; Selemon & Goldman-Rakic, 1988). Single neuron recordings in monkeys have demonstrated that the parallel, segregated visual spatial and object processing streams remain functionally and anatomically distinct in these respective prefrontal cortical regions (Wilson, Scalaidhe, & Goldman-Rakic, 1993).

Functionally segregated processing streams akin to the "what" (ventral) and "where" (dorsal) visual systems have not been described for cortical auditory pathways. However, as information regarding sound intensity and spatial localization project bilaterally to primary auditory cortices from crossed brainstem central auditory pathways (Konishi, 1995), linguistic and nonlinguistic processing may represent the principal basis of functional segregation in cortical auditory pathways that are topographically distributed within the left and right hemispheres, respectively. Projections from auditory association cortex (area 22) in the superior temporal gyrus to dorsal area 8, lateral prefrontal areas 10 and 46, and medial frontal areas 32 and 25 are the main frontal–auditory cortical connections. Less robust auditory projections from superior temporal areas terminate in orbitofrontal regions (Barbas, 1992; Barbas & Pandya, 1991). Topographically, the latter projections and those to medial frontal paralimbic areas originate from anterior superior temporal regions; lateral frontal auditory pathways emanate from more posterior superior temporal areas. Wernicke's area includes a portion of auditory association cortex in the posterior one-third of the superior temporal gyrus and adjacent heteromodal regions in the left (dominant) hemisphere. Connections from Wernicke's to Broca's area in the frontal operculum (areas 44 and 45) accompany auditory association projections to ventral premotor areas (Nieuwenhuys et al., 1988).

Medial–Orbitofrontal Circuits

Prefrontal cortices are richly connected to paralimbic and allocortical areas (Amaral & Price, 1984; Carmichael & Price, 1995b; Rosene & van Hoesen, 1987). A general rostrocaudal gradient of limbic inervation has been described, whereby medial and orbital prefrontal areas have the highest proportion of limbic inputs, area 8 the lowest, and lateral prefrontal regions have an intermediate degree of limbic connections (Barbas, 1992; Barbas & Mesulam, 1981). Lateral prefrontal areas (DLPFC) are indirectly linked to limbic regions of the parahippocampal gyrus through connections with the anterior and posterior cingulate (areas 24 and 23) and medial frontal area 32 (Barbas, 1992). In addition, Goldman-Rakic, Selemon, & Schwartz, 1984) identified sparse connections between the DLPFC and entorhinal, presubicular, and (particularly) caudal parahippocampal regions (caudomedial lobule). Although the functional significance of these indirect and direct connections are not well defined, they represent parallel pathways between the DLPFC and hippocampus that have been implicated to play a role in maintaining contextual information on a moment-by-moment basis (i.e., working memory) (Goldman-Rakic, 1987).

The robust limbic and sensorimotor connections to medial–orbitofrontal cortices exhibit topographical selectivity (Carmichael & Price, 1995a, 1995b). Virtually all limbic areas project to posteriomedial orbitofrontal regions, including the hippocampus (via the subiculum), posterior parahippocampal areas, portions of the amygdala, entorhinal and perirhinal cortices, and the anterior temporal pole (via the uncinate fasiculus). Gustatory, olfactory, and somatosensory inputs also converge in posterior medial orbital regions. In contrast, lateral orbitofrontal areas receive limbic input only from the amygdala, temporopolar region, and entorhinal cortex but also are connected with somatosensory and inferior temporal visual association regions (Carmichael & Price, 1995a). Limbic input to medial prefrontal cortices arises primarily from the amygdala and entorhinal cortex, in addition to a small projection from the subiculum. Thus, medial orbital areas are predominantly affiliated with limbic structures, are involved in processing taste and smell information from neighboring posterior orbital areas, and include the primary hippocampal afferents (via the rostral subiculum) to orbitofrontal cortices. Lateral and posterior orbital regions, in contrast, receive more restricted limbic input, particularly from the amygdala, but are strongly connected to sensory and motor areas outside orbitofrontal regions. All three medial and orbital frontal regions are strongly connected to the amygdala (Amaral & Price, 1984). Posterior medial orbital area interconnections with gustatory, olfactory, visceral (limbic), somatosensory, and ventral premotor areas may form a network involved in feeding behavior (Carmichael & Price, 1995a). Similar functional networks involving visual and somatosensory projections to distinct lateral orbital areas, together with their associated limbic and premotor interconnections, may subserve the integration of affective and visceral influences with sensorimotor functions in guiding other aspects of behavior.

Interhemispheric Connectivity

It is estimated that 2–3% of all cortical neurons send projections to the contralateral hemisphere, the vast majority of which cross in the corpus callosum (Lamantia & Rakic, 1990). In general, patterns of interhemispheric cortical connectivity parallel intrahemispheric associational relationships (Innocenti, 1986; Pandya & Seltzer, 1986). Homotopical connections interconnect similar cortical areas in both hemispheres; heterotopical commissural fibers typically project to contralateral areas that correspond to the intrahemispheric distribution of fibers from that region but are usually less abundant than ipsilateral connections. Higher-order association areas tend to have the greatest density of commissural projections, whereas fewer interhemispheric connections are present between primary sensory and motor cortices. Among primary motor and sensory areas, axial and midline regions typically have robust interconnections; distal limb regions, in contrast, may have few, if any, interhemispheric connections. The differential density of sensorimotor commissural fibers between homologous body regions may account for the relative susceptibility of distal limb areas to lesion-induced autonomous activity (i.e., alien hand syndrome).

Most interhemispheric connections between the frontal lobes traverse the corpus callosum, although a small proportion of commissural fibers cross in the anterior commisssure. The general pattern of callosal connectivity between the frontal lobes, as with other cerebral cortices, broadly reflects cortical topography along the anterior–posterior hemispheric axis (Figure 2.4) (Barbas, 1992; Barbas & Pandya, 1984; Pandya & Seltzer, 1986). For example, premotor and motor fibers occupy the rostral body of the corpus callosum, exhibiting overlapping but generally respective rostral and caudal positions. Commissural fibers from the DLPFC generally cross in the genu of the corpus callosum, rostral to premotor and motor axons. Interhemispheric axons from dorsal regions of the DLPFC typically occupy more caudal regions of the genu relative to those from ventral DLPFC regions. The most rostral areas of the corpus callosum (lower genu and rostrum) contain commissural axons from rostral medial frontal (areas 25 and rostral area 32) and orbitofrontal areas. Some interhemispheric fibers from caudal orbitofrontal regions also cross in the anterior commissure. Commissural projections from the anterior cingulate are widely distributed throughout the rostral half of the corpus callosum,

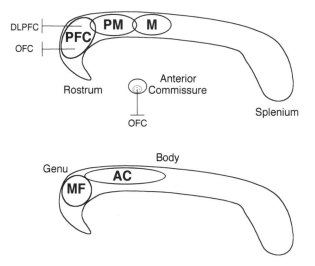

FIGURE 2.4. Schematic diagram indicating the approximate trajectories of lateral (top) and medial (bottom) hemispheric commissural fibers from frontal lobe regions in the corpus callosum and anterior commissure. As depicted, rostral–caudal hemispheric relationships are generally reflected in the regional distribution of commissural fibers in the corpus callosum. In contrast, commissural fibers from medial and lateral hemispheric regions exhibit significant overlap. M, primary motor area; PM, premotor areas (Brodmann's areas 6 and 8); PFC, prefrontal cortex; DLPFC, dorsolateral prefrontal cortex; OFC, orbitofrontal cortex; AC, anterior cingulate; MF, medial frontal. After Pandya and Seltzer (1986); Barbas (1992).

intermingling with fibers from premotor and motor areas in the superior portion of the callosum.

Modular Organization of Corticocortical Connections

The preceding discussion has reviewed general aspects of frontal lobe anatomy and cortical connectivity, focusing on architectonic features and topographically distributed functional circuitry. At a superordinate level of organization, contemporary models of brain function are based on multifocal patterns of synchronous activity in distributed networks consisting of neural nodes or modules (Damasio & Damasio, 1989; Mesulam, 1990). Although the physiological determinants of temporal coactivation within network circuitry remain speculative, insight into the anatomical substrates of spatially distributed network activity derives from axon terminal labeling experiments in rhesus monkeys (Selemon & Goldman-Rakic, 1988). In this work, axon terminals from labeled neurons in lateral prefrontal (Brodmann's areas 9 and 10) and posterior parietal (Brodmann's area 7) heteromodal regions were observed to converge in 15 different cortical regions. Among these common areas of intersection, research identified two general, but not all-inclusive, patterns of laminar terminal organization (Figure 2.5). The first pattern is characterized by the interdigitation of convergent prefrontal and posterior parietal inputs. As schematically illustrated (Figure 2.5, left), prefrontal and parietal fiber terminations were observed to span all cortical layers (being slightly more prominent in layer I) and typically formed adjacent, horizontally oriented columns. This pattern of fiber terminal segregation was observed throughout paralimbic cingulate regions. A different pattern of labeling was observed in heteromodal superior temporal cortex, as well as the frontoparietal opercu-

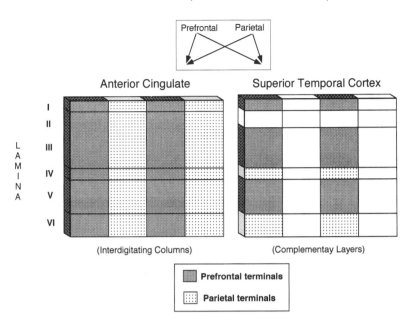

FIGURE 2.5. Schematic illustration of two general patterns of terminations observed for convergent prefrontal and posterior parietal labeled fibers in representative cortical areas of the rhesus monkey. See text for details. Adapted from Selemon and Goldman-Rakic (1988). Copyright 1988 by *The Journal of Neuroscience*. Adapted by permission.

lum (Figure 2.5, right). In these regions, alternating columns exhibited a vertically oriented pattern of laminar segregation; prefrontal terminals typically occupied layers I, III, and V, with alternating or "complementary" terminal labeling of layers IV and VI by fibers of parietal origin. In addition, convergent prefrontal and parietal fiber terminals were observed in the contralateral superior temporal cortex, which may account for the unlabeled intervening columnar spaces in the ipsilateral superior temporal cortex. Previous work by the same investigators (Schwartz & Goldman-Rakic, 1984) also observed columnar organization of contiguous, alternating ipsilateral parietal and contralateral prefrontal inputs to prefrontal cortex in rhesus monkeys. More recently, a similar type of cortical modular organization has been demonstrated for both intrinsic (i.e., local circuit) and long-distance associational connections within monkey prefrontal cortex (Pucak, Levitt, Lund, & Lewis, 1996). Together, these findings suggest that corticocortical connections may generally exhibit a modular functional architecture responsible for channeling patterns of activation in multifocal intra- and interhemispheric networks.

FRONTAL–CORTICAL CONNECTIVITY IN HUMAN DISEASE

Callosal Morphometry and Degenerative Dementias

Selective cortical neuronal loss in degenerative dementias such as Alzheimer's disease (AD) and frontotemporal dementia (FTD) involve differential pathological topographies. In AD, medial temporal limbic and temporoparietal association cortices are the sites of primary involvement, with relative sparing of primary sensory and motor areas (Arnold,

Hyman, Flory, Damasio, & van Hoesen, 1991). In contrast, pathological alterations in FTD predominantly affect frontal and anterior temporal lobe regions, typically most concentrated in prefrontal and paralimbic cortices (Lund and Manchester Groups, 1994). Relative differences in the anterior–posterior topographical distribution of pathological involvement may largely account for the distinctive yet overlapping clinical features of AD and FTD.

Although much is known about functional cerebral laterality, the fundamental mechanisms and clinical implications of impaired interhemispheric transmission between homotopical and heterotopical regions are poorly understood. Investigating regional callosal morphometry in degenerative and other neurological disorders may facilitate investigations of these interactions and provide insight into their functional significance. A recent study (Kaufer et al., 1997) comparing regional cross-sectional area of the corpus callosum in patients with AD and FTD observed marked focal atrophy of anterior (rostrum and genu) callosal areas in subjects with FTD (Figure 2.6). AD subjects, in contrast, exhibited more diffuse atrophy in the genu and body of the corpus callosum compared to the others, consistent with previous findings (Biegon et al., 1994; Janowsky, Kaye, & Carper, 1996). The observed patterns of regional callosal atrophy may reflect the functional nature (e.g., loss of commissural connections between association areas in AD) or topography (e.g., focal anterior hemispheric atrophy in FTD) of cortical involvement in these respective diseases. The overall degree of dementia severity showed no correlation with any callosal area measures in FTD but was directly correlated to the size of the anterior portion of the callosum in AD, presumably reflecting the loss of commissural projections between prefrontal association and paralimbic areas. Among all commissural fiber types, only the number of small commissural axons, which are concentrated in the genu of the corpus callosum and are thought to primarily interconnect association cortices, have been demonstrated to provide a reliable index of callosal

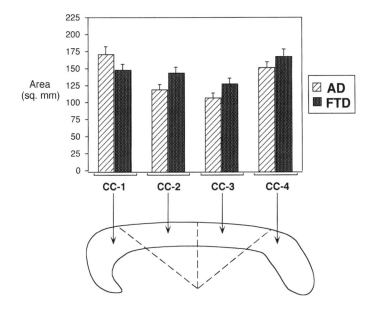

FIGURE 2.6. Comparison of mean regional areas (square millimeters) of the corpus callosum (lower inset) in Alzheimer's disease (AD; $n = 17$) and frontotemporal dementia (FTD; $n = 16$).

cross-sectional area (Aboitiz, Scheibel, Fisher, & Zaidel, 1992). The observed relationship between dementia severity and anterior callosal area in AD is consistent with other reports (Janowsky et al., 1996), including findings that the strongest correlate of cognitive impairment in AD identified to date is reduced synaptic density or loss of synaptic markers in frontal lobe regions (DeKosky & Scheff, 1990; Terry, Masliah, & Salmon, 1991).

Intrinsic Prefrontal Circuitry and Schizophrenia

Multiple lines of evidence implicate dysfunction of the DLPFC in the pathophysiology of schizophrenia. Deficits in spatial working memory are associated with DLPFC lesions (Goldman-Rakic, 1987), and these types of cognitive disturbances are a common feature of schizophrenia (Weinberger, Berman, & Illowsky, 1988). Developmental considerations suggest another link between the DLPFC and schizophrenia; schizophrenia typically has its onset in the postpubertal period, and performance on DLPFC-dependent tasks tends to reach adult levels around the time of puberty (Levin, Culhane, Hartmann, Evankovich, & Mattson, 1991). Within the DLPFC, excitatory pyramidal cells in layers II and III send intrinsic axon collaterals horizontally through the supragranular layers, and the terminal fields of these axons are organized as a series of stripes separated by similarly sized gaps (Levitt, Lewis, Yoshioka, & Lund, 1993) (Figure 2.7). The projections between interconnected stripes are reciprocal, and the majority of these axon terminals synapse on dendritic spines of other pyramidal cells (Pucak et al., 1996). Thus, the reciprocal monosynaptic connections between stripes may provide the anatomical substrate for reverberating excitatory circuits that maintain the activity of functionally related populations of DLPFC cells, a critical feature of working memory (Lewis & Anderson, 1995). During adolescence, the number of these pyramidal cell interconnections typically decreases (Woo, Pucak, Kye, Matus, & Lewis, 1996; Lewis, 1997), suggesting that the pruning of the intrinsic connections of layer III pyramidal neurons in the DLPFC may confer a selective vulnerability related to the clinical onset of schizophrenic symptoms after maturity. Consistent with this interpretation, layer III pyramidal cells have been reported to be decreased in size (Rajkowska, Selemon, & Goldman-Rakic, 1994) and to have fewer dendritic spines (Glantz & Lewis, 1995; Garey et al., 1995) in schizophrenic subjects. In addition, the activity of layer III pyramidal cells is modulated by inputs from certain inhibitory γ-aminobutyric acid–containing local circuit neurons, as well as by dopamine afferent fibers. Interestingly, these components of DLPFC circuitry also undergo substantial refinements during adolescence, and have been reported to be altered in schizophrenia (Lewis, 1997).

SUMMARY AND EMERGING PERSPECTIVES

This survey of frontal anatomy and related cortical circuitry emphasized general features of architectonic differentiation, functional topographical relationships, and associated patterns of connectivity. Separate visual and somatic motor systems (Passingham, 1993) and distinct spatial location and object recognition visual pathways are examples of parallel, functionally segregated circuits involved in sensory and motor processes. The more complex functional circuitry of prefrontal association and paralimbic areas reflects the generally more widespread connectivity (and functional diversity) of these areas to both cortical and subcortical areas, particularly to limbic-related cortices and nuclei

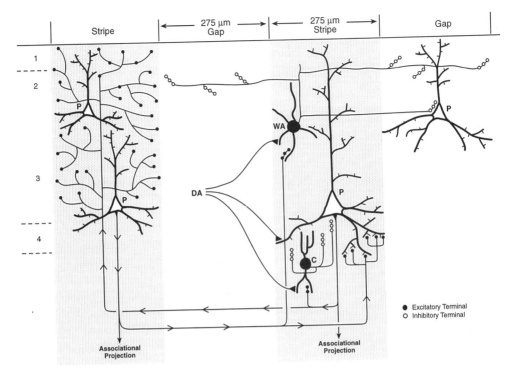

FIGURE 2.7. Schematic summary of intrinsic connectivity in monkey dorsolateral prefrontal cortex. Layer III pyramidal neurons (P) furnish horizontal axon collaterals (lower part of figure), which terminate in stripe-like arrays approximately 275 microns wide in the superficial cortical layers. Many of these excitatory axon terminals target dendritic spines of pyramidal neurons that provide reciprocal connections between stripes. A smaller proportion of these excitatory axon terminals also project to chandelier (C) and wide arbor (WA) neurons, which may, respectively, form inhibitory synapses within the same stripe and in adjacent gaps. Dopamine (DA) afferents project to the dendritic spines and shafts of excitatory pyramidal cells, as well as to local circuit inhibitory neurons. Adapted from Lewis (1997). Copyright 1997 by American College of Neuropsychopharmacology. Adapted by permission.

(Barbas & Pandya, 1989, 1991; Barbas, 1992; Mesulam, 1985). However, selectivity exists within the broad framework of limbic–prefrontal connections, as exemplified by the differential topography of hippocampal and amygdala projections to prefrontal cortices and the greater prominence of sensory and restricted limbic connections of lateral compared to medial–orbitofrontal regions. Two examples of altered frontal cortical connectivity in human disease, differential patterns of corpus callosum atrophy in AD and FTD, and aberrant DLPFC local circuit interactions in schizophrenia illustrate contrasting dimensions of frontal circuitry in terms of the level of analysis (gross vs. microscopic), the proximity of interaction (interhemispheric vs. local circuit), and age-related pathophysiological alterations (degenerative vs. developmental).

Although structure–function relationships have primarily been discussed from a frame of reference provided by Brodmann-defined areas, structural and functional heterogeneity within such regions suggests a modular functional organization of prefrontal association cortices (Goldman-Rakic, 1987; Pucak et al., 1996). Consistent with descriptions of posterior visual cortices in terms of functional modules (van Essen & Maunsell, 1983), detailed architectonic mapping of orbital and medial–prefrontal regions have identified at least 22 different areas which may constitute discrete functional zones or modules (Carmichael & Price, 1994, 1995a, 1995b). Concepts of modular cerebral cortical organization and functionally segregated, topographically distributed parallel pathways that have emerged from anatomical and electrophysiological studies in nonhuman primates have important implications for the study of functional connectivity in humans. Rapidly developing *in vivo* functional brain-mapping techniques provide a means for investigating task-specific patterns of human cerebral activation (see Chapter 12, this volume). In addition, neural network models based on the computational theory of parallel-distributed processing have been described, involving both large-scale, distributed functional networks (Mesulam, 1990) and individual neuronal interactions within local (prefrontal) circuits (Cohen & Servan-Schreiber, 1992). Together, these tools may offer complementary avenues for generating and testing hypotheses related to normal and pathological functioning of the human frontal lobes.

ACKNOWLEDGMENTS

This work was supported by U.S. Public Health Service Grant Nos. AG05133, MM00519, and MH45156, and by the Augustus Rose Fellowship of the John Douglas French Alzheimer's Foundation.

REFERENCES

Aboitiz, F., Scheibel, A. B., Fisher, R. S., & Zaidel, E. (1992). Fiber composition of the human corpus callosum. *Brain Research, 598,* 154–161.

Alexander, G. E., DeLong, M. R., & Strick, P. L. (1986). Parallel organization of functionally segregated circuits linking based ganglia and cortex. *Annual Review of Neuroscience, 9,* 357–381.

Amaral, D. G., & Price, J. L. (1984). Amygdalo-cortical projections in the monkey (*Macaca fascicularis*). *Journal of Comparative Neurology, 230,* 465–496.

Arnold, S. E., Hyman, B. T., Flory, J., Damasio, A. R., & van Hoesen, G. W. (1991). The topographical and neuroanatomical distribution of neurofibrillary tangles and neuriticplaques in the cerebral cortex of patients with Alzheimer's disease. *Cerebral Cortex, 1,* 103–116.

Barbas, H. (1986). Pattern in the laminar origin of corticocortical connections. *Journal of Comparative Neurology, 252,* 415–422.

Barbas, H. (1992). Architecture and cortical connections of the prefrontal cortex in the rhesus monkey. In P. Chauvel & H. V. Delgado-Escueta (Eds.), *Advances in neurology* (Vol. 57, pp. 91–115). New York: Raven Press.

Barbas, H., & Mesulam, M. M. (1981). Organization of afferent input to subdivisions of area 8 in the rhesus monkey. *Journal of Comparative Neurology, 200,* 407–431.

Barbas, H., & Pandya, D. N. (1984). Topography of commissural fibers of the prefrontal cortex in the rhesus monkey. *Experimental Brain Research, 55,* 187–191.

Barbas, H., & Pandya, D. (1987). Architecture and frontal cortical connections of the premotor cortex (area 6) in the rhesus monkey. *Journal of Comparative Neurology, 256,* 211–228.

Barbas, H., & Pandya, D. (1989). Architecture and intrinsic connections of the prefrontal cortex in rhesus monkeys. *Journal of Comparative Neurology, 286,* 353–375.

Barbas, H., & Pandya, D. (1991). Patterns of connections of the prefrontal cortex in the rhesus monkey associated with cortical architecture. In H. S. Levin, H. M. Eisenberg, & A. L. Benton (Eds.), *Frontal lobe function and dysfunction* (pp. 35–58). New York: Oxford University Press.

Benson, D. F. (1993). Progressive frontal dysfunction. *Dementia, 4,* 149–153.

Biegon, A., Eberling, J. L., Richardson, B. E., Roos, M. S., Wong, T. S., Reed, B. R., & Jagust, W. J. (1994). Human corpus callosum in aging and Alzheimer's disease: A magnetic resonance imaging study. *Neurobiology of Aging, 15,* 393–397.

Brodmann, K. (1994). *Localization in the cerebral cortex.* London: Smith-Gordon. (Original work published 1909)

Carmichael, S. T., & Price, J. L. (1994). Architectonic subdivision of the orbital and medial prefrontal cortex in the macaque monkey. *Journal of Comparative Neurology, 346,* 366–402.

Carmichael, S. T., & Price, J. L. (1995a). Limbic connections of the orbital and medial prefrontal cortex in macaque monkeys. *Journal of Comparative Neurology, 363,* 615–641.

Carmichael, S. T., & Price, J. L. (1995b). Sensory and premotor connections of the orbital and medial prefrontal cortex of macaque monkeys. *Journal of Comparative Neurology, 363,* 642–664.

Cavada, C., & Goldman-Rakic, P. S. (1989). Posterior parietal cortex in rhesus monkeys: II. Evidence for segregated corticocortical networks linking sensory and limbic areas with the frontal lobes. *Journal of Comparative Neurology, 287,* 422–445.

Cohen, J. D., & Servan-Schreiber, D. (1992). Context, cortex, and dopamine: A connectionist approach to behavior and biology in schizophrenia. *Psychology Review, 99,* 45–77.

Cummings, J. L. (1993). Frontal–subcortical circuits and human behavior. *Archives of Neurology, 50,* 873–880.

Damasio, H. C. (1991). Neuroanatomy of frontal lobe *in vivo:* A comment on methodology. In H. S. Levin, H. M. Eisenberg, & A. L. Benton (Eds.), *Frontal lobe function and dysfunction* (pp. 92–124). New York: Oxford University Press.

Damasio, H. C., & Damasio, A. R. (1989). *Lesion analysis in neuropsychology.* New York: Oxford University Press.

DeKosky, S. T., & Scheff, S. W. (1990). Synapse loss in frontal cortex biopsies in Alzheimer's disease: Correlation with cognitive severity. *Annals of Neurology, 27,* 457–464.

Felleman, D. J., & van Essen, D. C. (1991). Distributed hiearchical processing in the primate cerebral cortex. *Cerebral Cortex, 1,* 1–47.

Galaburda, A. M., & Pandya, D. N. (1983). The intrinsic architectonic and connectional organization of the superior temporal region of the rhesus monkey. *Journal of Comparative Neurology, 221,* 169–184.

Garey, L. J., Ong, W. Y., Patel, T. S., Kanani, M., Davis, C., Hornstein, C., & Bauer, M. (1995). reduction in dendritic spine number on cortical pyramidal neurons in schizophrenia. *Society of Neuroscience Abstracts, 21,* 237.

Glantz, L. A., & Lewis, D. A. (1995). Assessment of spine density on layer III pyramidal cells in the prefrontal cortex of schizophrenic subjects. *Society of Neuroscience Abstracts, 21,* 239.

Goldman-Rakic, P. S. (1987). Circuitry of primate prefrontal cortex and regulation of behavior by representational memory. In F. Plum (Ed.), *Handbook of physiology: The nervous system* (Vol. 5, pp. 373–417). Bethesda, MD: American Physiological Society.

Goldman-Rakic, P. S., Selemon, L. D., & Schwartz, M. S. (1984). Dual pathways connecting the dorsolateral prefrontal cortex with the hippocampal formation and parahippocampal cortex in the rhesus monkey. *Journal of Neuroscience, 12,* 719–743.

Innocenti, G. M. (1986). General organization of callosal connections in the cerebral cortex. In E. G. Jones & A. Peters (Eds.), *Cerebral cortex* (Vol. 5, pp. 291–353). New York: Plenum.

Janowsky, J. S., Kaye, J. A., & Carper, R. A. (1996). Atrophy of the corpus callosum in Alzheimer's disease versus healthy aging. *Journal of the American Geriatric Society, 44,* 798–803.

Jones, E. G., Coulter, J. D., & Hendry, S. H. C. (1978). Intracortical connectivity of architectonic fields in the somatic sensory, motor and parietal cortex of monkeys. *Journal of Comparative Neurology, 181,* 291–348.

Kaufer, D. I., Miller, B. L., Itti, L., Fairbanks, L., Li, J., Fishman, J., Kushi, J., & Cummings, J. L. (1997). Midline cerebral morphometry distinguishes frontotemporal dementia and Alzheimer's disease. *Neurology, 48,* 978–984.

Konishi, M. (1995). Neural mechanisms of auditory image formation. In M. S. Gazzaniga (Ed.), *The cognitive neurosciences* (pp. 269–278). Cambridge, MA: MIT Press.

Lamantia, A. S., & Rakic, P. (1990). Cytological and quantitative characteristics of four cerebral commissures in the rhesus monkey. *Journal of Comparative Neurology, 291,* 520–537.

Levin, H. S., Culhane, K. A., Hartmann, J., Evankovich, K., & Mattson, A. J. (1991). Developmental changes in performance on tests of purported frontal lobe functioning. *Developmental Neuropsychology, 7,* 377–395.

Levitt, J. B., Lewis, D. A., Yoshioka, T., & Lund, J. S. (1993). Topography of pyramidal neuron connections in macaque monkey prefrontal cortex (areas 9 & 46). *Journal of Comparative Neurology, 338, 360–376.*

Lewis, D. A. (1997). Development of the prefrontal cortex during adolescence: Insights into vulnerable schizophrenic circuits in schizophrenia. *Neuropsychopharmacology, 16,* 385–398.

Lewis, D. A., & Anderson, S. A. (1995). The functional architecture of the prefrontal cortex and schizophrenia. *Psychological Medicine, 25,* 887–894.

Lewis, D. A, Hayes, T. L., Lund, J. S., & Oeth, K. M. (1992). Dopamine and the neural circuitry of primate prefrontal cortex: Implications for schizophrenia research. *Neuropsychopharmacology, 6,* 127–134.

Lu, M. T., Preston, J. B., & Strick, P. L. (1994). Interconnections between the prefrontal cortex and the premotor areas in the frontal lobe. *Journal of Comparative Neurology, 341,* 375–392.

Lund and Manchester Groups. (1994). Clinical and neuropathological criteria for frontotemporal dementia: The Lund and Manchester Groups. *Journal of Neurology, Neurosurgery, and Psychiatry, 57,* 416–418.

Mesulam, M.-M. (1985). Patterns in behavioral neuroanatomy: association areas, the limbic system, and hemispheric specialization. In M.-M. Mesulam (Ed.), *Principles of behavioral neurology* (pp. 1–70). Philadelphia: F. A. Davis.

Mesulam, M.-M. (1990). Large-scale neurocognitve networks and distributed processing for attention, language, and memory. *Annals of Neurology, 28,* 597–613.

Mesulam, M.-M. (1997). Anatomic principles in behavioral neurology and neurospsychology. In T. E. Feinberg & M. J. Farah (Eds.), *Behavioral neurology and neuropsychology* (pp. 55–68). New York: McGraw-Hill.

Mishkin, M., Ungerleider, L. G., & Macko, K. A. (1983). Object vision and spatial vision: Two cortical pathways. *Trends in Neuroscience, 6,* 414–417.

Nieuwenhuys, R., Voogd, J., & van Huijzen, C. (1988). *The human central nervous system. A synopsis and atlas* (3rd ed. rev.). Berlin: Springer-Verlag.

Pandya, D. N., & Seltzer, B. (1986). The topography of commissural fibers. In F. Lepore, M. Ptito, & H. H. Jasper (Eds.), *Two hemispheres—One brain* (pp. 47–73). New York: Liss.

Pandya, D. N., & Yeterian, E. H. (1985). Architecture and connections of cortical association areas. In A. Peters & E. Jones (Eds.), *Cerebral cortex. Association and auditory cortices* (Vol. 4, pp. 3–61). New York: Plenum.

Passingham, R. (1993). *The frontal lobes and voluntary action.* Oxford: Oxford University Press.

Petrides, M., & Pandya, D. N. (1984). Projections to the frontal lobes from the posterior–parietal region in the rhesus monkey. *Journal of Comparative Neurology, 228,* 105–116.

Pucak, M. L., Levitt, J. B., Lund, J. S., & Lewis, D. A. (1996). Patterns of intrinsic and associational excitatory circuitry in monkey prefrontal cortex. *Journal of Comparative Neurology, 376,* 614–630.

Rajkowska, G., Selemon, L. D., & Goldman-Rakic, P. (1994). Reduction in neuronal sizes in prefrontal cortex of schizophrenics and Huntington patients. *Society of Neuroscience Abstracts, 20,* 620.

Rockland, K. S., & Pandya, D. S. (1979). Laminar origins and terminations of cortical connections of the occipital lobe in the rhesus monkey. *Brain Research, 179,* 3–20.

Rosene, D. L., & van Hoesen, G. W. (1987). The hippocampal formation of the primate brain. In E. G. Jones & A. G. Peters (Eds.), *Cerebral cortex* (pp. 345–456). New York: Plenum.

Sanides, F. (1972). Representation in the cerebral cortex and its areal lamination pattern. In G. H. Bourne (Ed.), *The structure and function of nervous tissue* (Vol. 5, pp. 329–453). New York: Academic Press.

Schwartz, M. S., & Goldman-Rakic, P. S. (1984). Callosal and intrahemispheric connectivity of the prefrontal association cortex in rhesus monkey: Relation between intraparietal and principal sulcal cortex. *Journal of Comparative Neurology, 226,* 403–420.

Selemon, L. D., & Goldman-Rakic, P. S. (1988). Common cortical and subcortical targets of the dorsolateral prefrontal and parietal cortices in the rhesus monkey: Evidence for a distributed neural network subserving spatially guided behavior. *Journal of Neuroscience, 8,* 4049–4068.

Seltzer, B., & Pandya, D. N. (1989). Frontal lobe connections of the superior temporal sulcus in the rhesus monkey. *Journal of Comparative Neurology, 281,* 97–113.

Terry, R. D., Masliah, E., & Salmon, D. P. (1991). Physical basis of cognitive alterations in Alzheimer's disease: Synapse loss is the major correlate of cognitive impairment. *Annals of Neurology, 30,* 572–580.

van Essen, D. C., & Maunsell, J. H. R. (1983). Hiearchical organization and functional streams in the visual cortex. *Trends in Neuroscience, 6,* 370–375.

Walker, A. E. (1940). A cytoarchitectural study of the prefrontal area of the macaque monkey. *Journal of Comparative Neurology, 73,* 59–86.

Weinberger, D. R., Berman, K. F., & Illowsky, B. P. (1988). Physiological dysfunction of dorsolateral prefrontal cortex in schizophrenia. III. A new cohort and evidence for a monoaminergic mechanism. *Archives of General Psychiatry, 45,* 609–615.

Wilson, F. A. W., Scalaidhe, S. P. O., & Goldman-Rakic, P. S. (1993). Dissociation of object and spatial processing domains in primate prefrontal cortex. *Science, 260,* 1955–1958.

Woo, T. U., Pucak, M. L., Kye, C. H., Matus, C. V., & Lewis, D. A. (1997). Peripubertal refinement of the intrinsic associational circuitry in monkey prefrontal cortex. *Journal of Neuroscience, 80,* 1149–1158.

Zilles, K. (1990). Cortex. In G. Paxinos (Ed.), *The human nervous system* (pp. 757–802). San Diego: Academic Press.

3

Structural and Functional Asymmetries of the Human Frontal Lobes

DANIEL H. GESCHWIND
MARCO IACOBONI

One of the most fundamental divisions of the human brain is that of the left and right cerebral hemispheres. Numerous studies reveal the consistent presence of both behavioral and anatomical asymmetries that reflect the specialized capacities of each hemisphere (Annett, 1985; Bogen, 1993; Galaburda, 1991; Gazzaniga, 1970; Geschwind & Galaburda, 1985). The significance of several of these asymmetries is controversial, and surprisingly little is known about asymmetries in the frontal lobe, arguably the area that contributes most to human cognitive and behavioral attributes. This chapter is not meant to solve all the mysteries of lateralized functions of the frontal lobes but merely to highlight anatomical and functional asymmetries as they relate to language, complex motor behaviors, and sensorimotor integration, areas where the most is currently known with regard to lateralized frontal lobe functions. In addition, we discuss the lateralization of prosody and emotion. The focus of our review is on patients with focal brain lesions and structural and functional brain imaging in healthy volunteers. Chronic progressive conditions such as progressive aphasia (Snowden, Neary, Mann, Goulding, & Testa, 1992) and the right frontal lobe variant of frontal–temporal dementia (Miller, Chang, Mena, Boone, & Lesser, 1993) present intriguing examples of lateralized behaviors but do not lend themselves as well to localization and therefore are not included in this brief review. Clinical lesion data is presented first when applicable, followed by functional imaging and morphological data relevant to each section.

It is often assumed that anatomical asymmetries invariably reflect functional asymmetries. However, physiological asymmetries, asymmetries in gene expression, or subtle differences in neuronal cytoskeletal architecture may play a more significant role in hemispheric specialization than do gross anatomical or cytoarchitectonic asymmetries. The identification of morphological asymmetries associated with language is important because of a wealth of evidence that these asymmetries are functionally relevant (Galaburda, LeMay, Kemper, & Geschwind, 1978; Geschwind & Galaburda, 1985; Geschwind & Levitsky, 1968; Witelson, 1977, 1992). Furthermore, a number of studies support the general notion that the amount of cerebral cortex dedicated to a particular function may reflect the brain capabilities in that area (Eccles, 1977; Garraghty & Kaas, 1992; Jerison, 1977).

However, the size of a brain region is not always positively correlated with its capabilities. Often, a larger cerebral hemisphere can be observed due to neuronal migration abnormalities or other cortical malformations. In the domain of language specifically, the brains of dyslexics appear to be more symmetric, with a larger than usual planum temporale on the right rather than a smaller planum temporale on the left (Galaburda, 1993; Kushch et al., 1993). Thus, anatomical asymmetries gross or fine cannot be viewed in isolation and must eventually be considered in the context of the physiology of the neuronal systems to which they contribute.

ASYMMETRIES IN LANGUAGE FUNCTION IN THE FRONTAL LOBES

Functional and anatomical asymmetries related to language functions have been the most widely studied asymmetries of the frontal lobes. Recently, functional imaging has provided a revealing view of areas involved in healthy and neurologically impaired subjects (Binder et al., 1995; Klein, Milner, Zatorre, Meyer, & Evans, 1995; Petersen, Fox, Posner, Mintun, & Raichle, 1988; Roland, 1984; Warburton et al., 1996). However, the study of hundreds of aphasic patients over the last century has provided the bulk of the fundamental observations related to language localization. Most observant clinicians have remarked on the variability and overlap of aphasic syndromes, especially in the immediate period following brain injury, as well as the individual differences in symptoms between patients with apparently similar lesions (Benson, 1986; Galaburda, Rosen, & Sherman, 1990). Individual variability in the gross morphology (see Figure 3.1) and detailed cytoarchitecture in humans (Adrianov, 1979; Rajkowska & Goldman-Rakic, 1995) and nonhuman primates (Lashley & Clark, 1946) has been well demonstrated and is likely to underlie the variability in clinical syndromes in humans. In light of this variability, the left-hemisphere superiority and proficiency for the majority of vocal, motor, and language functions is striking (Geschwind, 1970; Benson, 1986). The correspondence between this functional asymmetry for language and the anatomical asymmetries described later in this chapter provides the most compelling example of a structure–function relationship underlying cerebral hemispheric specializations. Even so, the extent to which these anatomical asymmetries contribute to functional asymmetry has not been totally clarified. The lateralization of any function including language is unlikely to be an all-or-none phenomenon, because language consists of many components. Thus, some language capacity exists in most right hemispheres (Iacoboni & Zaidel, 1996). Especially relevant to the discussion of the frontal lobes is the predominance of the right frontal lobe in the production of the melodic components that contribute to prosody, as well as the expression of the emotional content of language (discussed later).

As spoken and written language are human specializations, detailed animal models of the role of different frontal subregions serving language are not available. This is in contrast to the frontal lobe's participation in other cognitive functions, such as working memory and sensorimotor integration, in which studies in primates have vastly accelerated our knowledge of regional subspecializations and provided models that can be tested

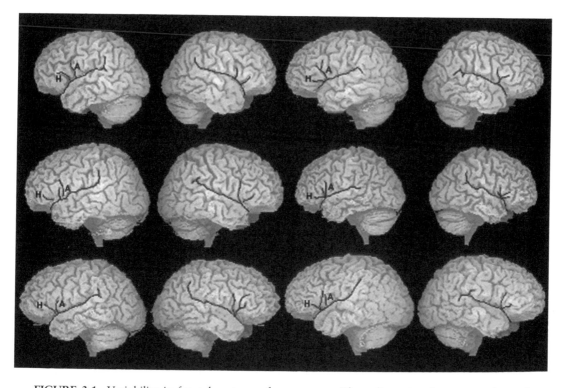

FIGURE 3.1. Variability in frontal cortex surface anatomy. Three-dimensional reconstructions of left and right magnetic resonance images from six different caucasian volunteers demonstrate the variability in surface morphology and emphasize the difficulty in defining Broca's region using surface landmarks alone. The sylvian fissure and the horizontal (H) and ascending (A) rami, which define the anterior and posterior boundary of the pars triangularis (Brodmann's area 45) are traced and labeled in the left side view of each pair. The pars opercularis (Brodmann's area 44) is directly posterior to the ascending ramus and extends posteriorly to border on the precentral gyrus in most individuals. The morphology of these fissures differs considerably between individuals, and in some cases, the landmarks that define Broca's area are difficult to identify. Given these ambiguities, cytoarchitectonic measurement of these areas may be necessary for a meaningful demonstration of morphological hemispheric asymmetries.

in humans (Funahashi, Bruce, & Goldman-Rakic, 1989; Fuster, 1995; Goldman-Rakic, 1987; Petrides, 1994; Wilson, Scalaidhe, & Goldman-Rakic, 1993). Thus, our discussion of structure–function relationships in frontal lobe language is relatively crude compared with the latter topics. Although the hope is that functional imaging studies will remedy this deficiency, the complexity of language tasks presents unique challenges in experimental design.

Clinical Lesion Studies in Aphasia

Broca's original belief that lesions confined to the posterior portion of the third left frontal gyrus (Figure 3.2) caused loss of articulatory language function ("aphemie") occurred on the background of the conviction, shared by his contemporaries, that the left and right frontal lobes were identical in size and anatomy (Berker, Berker, & Smith, 1986; Broca, 1865; Flourens, 1824). The recovery of language function occurred through the compen-

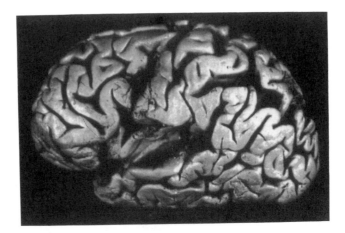

FIGURE 3.2. Lateral left view of Broca's second case. Broca's second case illustrates the gross extent of this patient's lesion. The area of damaged cortex extends beyond pars triangularis anteriorly and pars opercularis posteriorly, thus encompassing a region slightly larger than the posterior portion of the inferior frontal gyrus anterior to the motor strip (Brodmann's areas 44 and 45). The extent of surface damage supports the argument that lesions encompassing more than areas 44 and 45 are neccesary to produce the full syndrome of nonfluent aphasia. Furthermore, this brain was not sectioned or examined histologically to determine the extent of subcortical injury. From Finger (1993). Copyright 1993 by Oxford University Press. Reprinted by permission.

satory efforts of homologous, essentially equipotential regions in the right frontal lobe. Broca (1865) stated that the specialization of articulatory language and other functions occurred due to the earlier development of the left hemisphere (hence the preponderance of right-handers as well) and did not imply an underlying functional difference between the two hemispheres. Broca's conclusions were based on extensive lesions that encompassed regions beyond the pars triangularis and opercularis to include the primary motor cortex (see Figure 3.2). However, his fundamental observation of a cerebral asymmetry related to language provided the foundation for modern brain laterality research.

Following Broca, numerous cases supported the left-hemispheric localization of language in right-handers, while expanding the cerebral territory responsible for language functions (Broca, 1888; Jackson, 1880; Jackson, 1915; Wernicke, 1874). Jackson (1868) presented the first case of a left-handed man with aphasia and a right-sided lesion, further supporting a connection between hand dominance and language lateralization. More recent lesion studies confirmed the functional localization of language to the left hemisphere in 99% of right-handers (Annett, 1985; Benson, 1986; Hecaen, De, & Monzon, 1981). This relationship is less certain in left-handers, most demonstrating either left-hemisphere or bilateral language and, less frequently, right-hemisphere language (Geschwind, 1970; Geschwind & Galaburda, 1985; Hecaen et al., 1981).

However, the precise nature of the lesion necessary to produce nonfluent aphasia remains controversial (Hecean & Consoli, 1973; Marie, 1906; Mohr et al., 1978; Moutier, 1908; Nielsen, 1946; Zangwill, 1975). The majority of the frontal lobe anterior to Broca's area, the first frontal opercular gyrus, and all of the right hemisphere can be removed in patients with intractable epilepsy without producing lasting aphasia. In contrast, the removal of the first two to three gyri of the left frontal operculum pars opercularis (area 44) and triangularis (area 45) anterior to Brodmann's area 4 on the left in epilepsy surgery resulted in nonfluent aphasia in every case except one (Penfield & Roberts, 1959). Cortical stimulation studies by these same investigators demonstrated speech arrest from stimulation of the first two opercular gyri on the left but never on the right. Stimulation of the left supplementary motor area (SMA), and not right, produced speech arrest (Penfield & Roberts 1959). Lesions of the left SMA can produce transcortical motor aphasia, whereas similar lesions on the right do not, consistent with the proposed role of the SMA in speech initiation (Masdeu 1980; Freedman, Alexander, & Naeser, 1984). Further evidence from neuroimaging studies supports the contribution of the left SMA to language (see "Functional Imaging" section below), but no morphological asymmetries of the SMA have been documented.

Lesion studies support the presence of an anterior frontal lobe language area that encompasses Broca's area and additional perisylvian areas more posteriorly. In a series of patients with left-sided lesions of the posterior part of the inferior frontal gyrus, 17 out of 19 had difficulties in language fluency (Hecean & Consoli, 1973). The two patients without language difficulties suffered from congenital lesions, and it is likely that these anomalies displaced Broca's region. Patients with lesions largely confined to the cortical surface corresponding to Broca's region did not have significant agrammatism, or writing difficulties, whereas those with deeper lesions tended to have more profound language impairment. None of 15 patients with a homologous right-sided lesion demonstrated any language or articulatory deficits, confirming the relative specialization of the left inferior frontal gyrus for language output.

Numerous case studies have underscored the relationship between the extension of lesion into cortical regions adjacent to the third frontal gyrus and the severity of the Broca's aphasia (Tonkonogy & Goodglass, 1981). Articulatory disturbances (dysarthria and dysprosody) are typically associated with lesions that extend into the opercular precentral gyrus (Alexander, Naeser, & Palumbo, 1990). A combination of word-finding difficulties, paraphasias, and slowness in speech is observed with lesions of the pars triangularis and opercularis. Involvement of both regions typically leads to a more severe and lasting nonfluent aphasia. Mohr et al. (1978) also demonstrated that lesions localized to Broca's area lead to nonfluent aphasia or nonmotor articulatory disturbance, as well as to persistent apraxia and dysprosodia, but not to frank agrammatism as is paradigmatic in many current formulations of nonfluent (Broca's) aphasia. Those with typical Broca's aphasia have larger lesions that encompassed deeper white matter structures, the anterior insula and adjacent perisylvian regions (Mohr et al., 1978; Alexander et al., 1990). So, although the minimally sufficient lesion necessary to cause nonfluent aphasia in right-handers remains controversial, it is clear that even larger acute lesions on the right only rarely cause a similar disturbance in language function (Benson, 1986; Geschwind, 1970; Geschwind & Galaburda, 1985; Jackson, 1915; Moutier, 1908).

Functional Imaging

Many functional imaging studies done within the last decade employing positron emission tomography (PET) and functional magnetic resonance imaging (fMRI) have supported the functional specialization of the left frontal cortex in language and language-related tasks (Binder et al., 1995; Frith, Friston, Liddle, & Frackowiak, 1991; Just, Carpenter, Keller, Eddy, & Thulborn, 1996; Klein et al., 1995; McCarthy, Blamire, Rothman, Gruetter, & Shulman, 1993). Indeed, widespread areas of lateral frontal hypometabolism are even seen in aphasic patients with lesions in parietal and temporal cortex, further implicating the lateral left frontal cortex in language function and recovery (Metter,

1991). These imaging studies also confirmed that even simple language tasks, although highly lateralized, activate a network of widely distributed left-hemisphere cortical areas (Petersen et al., 1988; Binder et al., 1995; Just et al., 1996). The left-hemisphere activations are highly variable and extend beyond Broca's region, including the SMA and cingulate medially and the dorsolateral prefrontal cortex and premotor area laterally. In addition, in most careful PET or fMRI studies of language, homologous regions are often activated on the right side, although typically at far lower levels than those on the left (Habib, Demonet, & Frackowiak, 1996; Just et al., 1996; Warburton et al., 1996).

One of the factors confounding the interpretation of PET language data is the variability in activated areas across different studies. The overall variability in language PET studies is due to a variety of factors, including intersubject differences in cortical representation of language functions, differences in activation tasks, and differences in PET methodologies. However, in spite of this variability, left perisylvian regions in general, and Broca's area in particular, show consistent activation in language tasks. Thus, although language is a highly complex function that requires the activation of different cortical areas, the PET data support the wide body of information in patients with brain injury demonstrating that Broca's area is a critical cortical structure for language. However, the precise role of this famous section of frontal cortex in language remains controversial.

Indeed, it is unlikely that Broca's region should be considered as an area dedicated solely to language output. It is probable that because Broca's region comprises cytoarchitectonically and physiologically diverse areas, it may serve several language-related functions (Poppel, 1996). For instance, lesion studies, intraoperative electrical stimulation, and PET imaging studies confirm its role in phonological processing (Demonet, Price, Wise, & Frackowiak, 1994; Denny-Brown, 1975; Lecours & Lhermitte, 1970; Ojemann & Mateer, 1979; Zatorre, Meyer, Gjedde, & Evans, 1996). The phonemic paraphasias seen more typically with Broca's than with Wernicke's aphasia are consistent with these observations. Recent PET data indicate that Broca's region is activated in a wide variety of non-output-related language tasks, including listening tasks (Roland, 1984). Phonological discrimination tasks often engage verbal working-memory functions, which are typically associated with left frontal lobe predominance, as well (Milner & Petrides, 1984; Paulesu, Frith, & Frackowiak, 1993; Petrides, Alivisatos, Meyer, & Evans, 1993). Thus, it is conceivable that Broca's region is composed of contiguous areas that serve separate functions that can be simultaneously engaged in the same task. Later, in the section "Asymmetries in Sensorimotor Integration in the Frontal Lobe," we review some data pertaining to the activation of Broca's area in lip reading and grasping that are particularly relevant and raise important evolutionary considerations. Remarkable in this regard are the observations of Denny-Brown initiated over 30 years ago of the importance of visual input in language acquisition and visual influences on aphasia caused by lesions of Broca's area (Denny-Brown, 1965, 1975). Disruption of the integration of these visual inputs with other processing streams is likely a component of the literal alexia that can sometimes be observed in patients with Broca's area lesions (Benson, 1977; Boccardi, Bruzzone, & Vignolo, 1984).

Morphological Asymmetries

The recognition of the functional asymmetry for language observed over a century ago prompted investigators to search for morphological asymmetries underlying this left frontal lobe specialization. Investigators, prior to the latter half of this century, were limited to studying gross measures of asymmetry, due to methodological constraints.

Comparison of the weights of both hemispheres yielded variable and inconclusive results (Aresu, 1914; Broca, 1875; Thurnam, 1866; Von Bonin, 1962). Most morphometrical studies demonstrated a larger right frontal lobe and total right-hemisphere size overall. However, these studies do not consider the surface area accounted for by the vast amount of cortex contained in the folds of sulci. In this vein, the specific gravity of the left hemisphere is greater than the right, suggesting more cortical surface area overall on the left (Von Bonin, 1962).

Most gross morphological asymmetries of the frontal lobes described in humans are the result of indirect measurements taken of indentations in the skull, called petalias, that reflect outgrowth of the adjacent cerebral hemisphere. Although one of the most consistent findings is the presence of marked left occipitopetalia, the nature of frontal lobe asymmetries has been less obvious (Hadziselmovic & Cus, 1966; Tilney, 1927). However, most careful quantitative studies in adequate numbers of cases show a predominance of the right frontal petalia (Geschwind & Galaburda, 1985; Hadziselmovic & Cus, 1966).

LeMay and Kido (1978) made direct measurements of the frontal lobes and demonstrated that the width of the right frontal region was greater in 58% of right-handed patients and extended further forward in 31%, as opposed to only 14% that extended further forward on the left. Researchers observed a trend toward symmetry in left-handers. Several studies have consistently observed this gross structural asymmetry (Bear, Schiff, Saver, Greenberg, & Freeman, 1986; Geschwind & Galaburda, 1985; Glicksohn & Myslobodsky, 1993). However, the meaning of these observations is unclear. The petalias and even direct gross morphometry are imprecise measurements that do not reflect the total extent of cortical surface area in a given region, as much surface area is contained in the sulcal folds. This explanation is likely to hold for the studies of Wada, Clarke, and Hamm (1975), which demonstrated a right-sided size advantage when only the lateral cortical surface of areas 44 and 45 were measured. Nonhuman primates, including orangutans, chimpanzees, gorillas, and new and old world monkeys, also show a right frontal petalia, suggesting that these asymmetries are not related to strictly human cognitive abilities, such as language (Falk et al., 1990; Galaburda et al., 1978; Geschwind & Galaburda, 1985; Holloway & De La Coste-Lareymondie, 1982).

One of the first studies involving detailed measurements based on cytoarchitectonic divisions of the frontal lobes was carried out by Kononova (cited in Adrianov, 1979). This work on five right-handed subjects showed not only that the total area of the left frontal lobe was larger than the right by 16% but that Brodmann's areas 45 and 47 were larger on the left by a margin of 30% and 45%, respectively. Intriguingly, the results were reversed in the one left-handed patient studied. Kononova also observed a large amount of individual variation in these and other regions of the frontal lobe, highlighting the difficulty in drawing firm conclusions from this study of only six cases. Galaburda's detailed study of the magnocellular region of the pars opercularis, which largely coincides with area 44, demonstrated the left side to be larger than the right in the majority of 10 cases (Galaburda, 1980).

More recent investigations have demonstrated a population of magnopyramidal neurons that are 15% larger in left Brodmann's area 45 than on the right (Hayes & Lewis, 1993). No difference was seen between similar large pyramidal neurons in area 4 (Hayes & Lewis, 1995). However, in area 46 of the dorsolateral prefrontal cortex, the magnopyramidal neurons were about 10% smaller on the left. These differences are not large, and it is not known how these asymmetries relate to lateralization of frontal cortical functions. An additional problem in interpreting these findings is the small sample sizes studied, especially in light of current knowledge that highlights the striking individual variability in morphology (Figure 3.1) and cytoarchitectonics of the human frontal lobes (Adrianov, 1979; Rajkowska & Goldman-Rakic, 1995).

Other investigators have demonstrated consistent morphological asymmetries in more extensive regions of the third or inferior frontal gyrus using autopsy material and MRI in living patients (Albanese, Merlo, Albanese, & Gomez, 1989; Falzi, Perrone, & Vignolo, 1982; Foundas, Leonard, Gilmore, Fennell, & Heilman, 1996; Foundas, Leonard, & Heilman, 1995). Recently, Foundas et al. (1996) demonstrated a striking correlation between the direction of pars triangularis (area 45) asymmetry and hemispheric language lateralization, providing the most convincing evidence to date of the correspondence between language and anatomical asymmetries in the frontal lobe. Nine of 10 patients with Wada Test-proven lateralization of language to the left hemisphere displayed asymmetry in favor of the left pars triangularis. This is a striking finding, especially given the well-described individual differences in the surface landmarks that define this region and other frontal lobe areas (e.g., Figure 3.1).

Although it is most likely that an increased neuron number underlies the larger areas 44 and 45 of the left hemisphere (Galaburda, 1993), an increase in neuropil size could also account for the left-hemisphere predominance. Both pars triangularis and opercularis have been shown to have an increased complexity of higher-order dendritic branching on the left, relative to the primary motor cortex in both hemispheres and pars triangularis and opercularis on the right (Scheibel et al., 1985; Simonds & Scheibel, 1989). However, these dendritic specializations may develop independently of gross anatomical asymmetry, and their significance is uncertain. Because the majority of synapses occur on dendritic spines, it is possible that the shape and complexity of these dendritic arbors reflect the influence of experience on synapse elimination during the critical period of language acquisition.

ASYMMETRIES OF PROSODY AND EMOTION IN THE FRONTAL LOBE

Speech involves the communication of vocabulary and grammatical content as well as social and emotional content. The rhythmic, melodic intonation in speech that contributes these additional elements of meaning to language is termed "prosody." Several studies show that patients with right-hemisphere lesions can demonstrate deficiency in interpreting and expressing the emotional content of speech (Ross & Mesulam, 1979). The lesions described in loss of expressive prosody mostly involve large portions of the frontal lobe and often extend into the parietal lobe, hindering precise anatomical localization (Dordain, Degos, & Dordain, 1971; Ross & Mesulam, 1979). To what extent these lesions disrupt prosody by damaging frontal–subcortical circuits is an important, unresolved issue, given the involvement of the basal ganglia in prosody as demonstrated by lesion studies (Cancelliere & Kertesz, 1990; Starkstein, Federoff, Price, Leiguarda, & Robinson, 1994).

It is proposed that the prosodic deficit in cases of frontal lobe damage corresponds to the right-hemisphere homologue of Broca's region (Ross, 1981). The critical role of the right hemisphere in the melodic and musical aspects of speech and language output is also supported by the observation of preservation of simple singing ability in many patients with nonfluent aphasia (Yamadori, Osumi, Masuhara, & Okubo, 1977). In addition, a recent PET study supports the role of the right lateral prefrontal cortex in simple pitch discrimination, analogous to the role of Broca's area in phoneme perception

(Zatorre, Evans, & Meyer, 1994). A PET study of emotional prosody comprehension also suggests that right prefrontal cortex is preferentially active in tasks requiring perception and interpretation of emotional prosody and is not simply dedicated to prosodic expression (George et al., 1996).

The deficit in prosody observed after right frontal lesions is not entirely limited to the expression of emotional and melodic content, however, and can extend into nonemotional semantic aspects such as syllable stress (Weintraub, Mesulam, & Kramer, 1981). In addition, prosodic elements of speech comprehension and expression can also be impaired in anterior left-hemisphere lesions resulting in a Broca's aphasia (Benson, 1986; Danley & Shapiro, 1982). In the foreign accent syndrome, which can result from left frontal lesions involving Broca's area and neighboring cortical and subcortical regions, inappropriate syllable stress, phoneme misproduction, rhythm disturbances, and pauses occur, changing a patient's accent, often without chronically altering other aspects of language (Monrad-Krohn, 1947). However, other nonlinguistic elements of prosody, such as the ability to sing and produce melodic speech, are preserved, consistent with a right hemisphere role in these functions. Exaggerated prosody, sometimes observed in nonfluent aphasia, reflects the speaker's attempts to communicate using retained right frontal abilities in the face of minimal linguistic capabilities. Thus, although the evidence is not overwhelming, the left and right frontal lobes appear to have different relative contributions when it comes to prosody; the right specializes in melody and emotional valence whereas the left specializes in the linguistic elements.

Studies of patients with brain injury (Benson & Stuss, 1986) have established the role of the orbital frontal lobes in the regulation of emotion and mood. Asymmetries in frontal cortex in the mediation of emotional behavior were also described in several studies of patients with unilateral brain damage. Left frontal damage, especially damage to the anterior frontal lobes, is far more likely to cause depression than are similar lesions on the right (Gainotti, 1972; Iacoboni, Padovani, Di Piero, & Lenzi, 1995; Robinson, Kubos, Starr, Rao, & Price, 1984; Sackeim et al., 1982; Starkstein et al., 1991). Lesions on the right more frequently lead to mania (Jorge et al., 1993), especially regions of the orbitofrontal cortex (Starkstein, Pearlson, Boston, & Robinson, 1987; Starkstein et al., 1989). In healthy subjects, left prefrontal cortex cerebral blood flow increases when patients induce a state of dysphoria by thinking sad thoughts (Pardo, Fox, & Raichle, 1991; George et al., 1995). More recently, transcranial magnetic stimulation (causing transient hypofunctioning) of the left, but not right, prefrontal cortex resulted in decreased self-report of happiness and a significant increase in sadness ratings (Pascual-Leone, Catala, & Pascual-Leone, 1996).

Davidson (1992) developed a compelling model of human emotion in which frontal lobe asymmetries reflect affective reactivity and, hence, the potential for mania or depression given the appropriate stimulus. Electrophysiological evidence suggests that the left frontal lobe is more specialized for positive emotions related to approach and exploratory mechanisms, and the right for negative, avoidance-related reactions (Davidson, 1992; Davidson & Sutton, 1995). Similar frontal lobe asymmetries in electrical activity can predict a child's likelihood to engage in separation from his or her parents to explore novel elements in the environment, consistent with this model (Davidson, 1992). Because withdrawal and exploration are within the behavioral domain of nonhuman primates and lower animals, if this model were correct, similar asymmetries should exist in these lower species as well. Perhaps in the future, more precise physioanatomical models of lateralized frontal lobe contributions to emotional states and behavior can be developed in nonhuman primates.

ASYMMETRIES IN SENSORIMOTOR
INTEGRATION IN THE FRONTAL LOBE

The frontal lobe is undeniably one of the most critical cerebral structures involved in sensorimotor integration. Different regions of the frontal lobe receive segregated cortical inputs from a variety of cortical areas of sensory significance. In addition, the frontal lobe controls voluntary action through planning of movements in prefrontal areas, preparation of movements in premotor areas, and execution of movements in primary motor areas (Fuster, 1995). In this section, we review evidence from neurological patients and from functional neuroimaging studies that support the existence of functional asymmetries in the sensorimotor integration processes subserved by frontal lobe areas. Evidence concerning asymmetries in sensorimotor integration, first in the lateral wall and then in the medial wall of the frontal lobe, are reviewed. Unfortunately, few relevant data on structural asymmetries may relate to functional asymmetries in any of these processes.

The reader should be advised that we use sensorimotor integration in its broadest sense. Hence, in this section, we discuss known asymmetries in a number of cognitive functions that are necessary components of sensorimotor integration but that, in principle, are distinct cognitive functions (e.g., visuospatial working memory, complex motor functions, conditional motor learning, and attention).

Lateral Wall (Prefrontal, Premotor, and Primary Motor Cortex)

The lateral wall of the frontal lobe can be subdivided in three main sectors along the antero–posterior axis: prefrontal, premotor, and primary motor. Each of these sectors can further be subdivided in subsectors that are anatomically and functionally differentiated (Cavada & Goldman-Rakic, 1989; Fogassi et al., 1996; Fujii, Mushiake, & Tanji, 1996; Geyer et al., 1996; Matelli, Luppino, & Rizzolatti, 1985; Petrides, 1994; Rizzolatti, Fadiga, Gallese, & Fogassi, 1996; Stepniewska, Preuss, & Kaas, 1993). We review evidence for asymmetries in sensorimotor processes lateralized to the different sectors of the lateral wall of the frontal lobe starting from the prefrontal cortex, moving then to the premotor cortex, and finally concluding with the primary motor cortex.

Prefrontal Cortex: A Role in Working Memory

The prefrontal cortex in the lateral wall of the two cerebral hemispheres is known to be primarily involved in working memory processes (Goldman-Rakic, 1987). Neurophysiological studies in nonhuman primates and functional neuroimaging studies in humans have provided detailed models of the functional anatomy of the lateral prefrontal cortex and are reviewed later in this section. Lesion studies in neurological patients have not provided the same type of detailed information and thus are discussed only briefly here. However, these lesion studies in humans provided the foundations of laterality investigations in the prefrontal cortex, leading to models that were subsequently refined by neurophysiological and neuroimaging investigations.

Lesion Studies. In patients with brain injury, left frontal lobe damage typically leads to more profound verbal recall deficits than right-sided damage, whereas right frontal damage causes deficits in categorization (Incisa della Rocchetta, 1986; Incisa della

Rocchetta & Milner, 1993; Milner & Petrides, 1984). Although deficits in verbal fluency occur with either left or right frontal lesions, performance is worse with left frontal damage (Benson & Stuss, 1986). Deficits in the retrieval of verbal material in patients with left frontal damage may be specific to certain lexical categories in that injury to the left, but not the right, premotor areas produced a specific deficit in verb but not noun retrieval (Damasio & Tranel, 1993).

Consistent with the left-language, right-visuospatial specialization, patients with right frontal lesions are more likely to demonstrate poor use and representation of visuospatial data in a variety of tasks that require working memory, and left frontal lesions are more likely to result in disordered memory for episodic information (Kolb & Wishaw, 1985; Milner, 1975). Of patients with unilateral frontal damage, those with right frontal damage show the poorest performance in design fluency tasks (Benson & Stuss, 1986).

However, left-hemisphere deficits in short-term or working memory are not limited to the sphere of language and suggest the importance of the left prefrontal cortex in programming strategies, control of executive functions, and motor responses (Milner & Petrides, 1984). Left frontal lesions, but not those on the right, are more likely to cause impaired recall of words, especially when the task is based on a search strategy internally generated through the mental effort of the subject (Incisa della Rocchetta & Milner, 1993). In this regard, cuing or providing the patient with connected discourse ameliorates the retrieval difficulties experienced by patients with left frontal damage, emphasizing the importance of the dorsolateral left frontal lobe when a search strategy is not externally provided. Patients with frontal lesions that spare the dorsolateral prefrontal cortex do not exhibit these deficits (Goldman-Rakic, 1987). Thus, even though the known specialization of the left hemisphere for language and the right for visuospatial information is well supported in lesion studies of the frontal lobes, the use of internally and externally generated problem-solving strategies may be functionally lateralized as well.

Functional Imaging Studies. A specific framework of the neural substrates of human planning and executive functions comprising working memory suggests that the dorsolateral prefrontal cortex serves mechanisms of active manipulation and monitoring of sensorimotor information within working memory. In this model, the ventrolateral prefrontal cortex serves only working-memory mechanisms that support simple retrieval of information for sensory-guided sequential behavior (Petrides, 1994). Anatomical and physiological evidence presented here supports the functional distinction between these two systems.

The lateral prefrontal cortex receives strong input from extrastriate cortical areas of visual significance (Milner & Goodale, 1995). Hence, it is not surprising that some aspects of lateral prefrontal cortex organization replicate the pattern that has been described in occipitofugal corticocortical pathways. The occipitofugal corticocortical pathways consist of a dorsal occipito-parietal stream and a ventral occipitotemporal stream. Initially, the dorsal stream was conceived as concerned with the processing of spatial relationships, and the ventral stream as mainly concerned with the processing of object identity (Ungerleider & Mishkin, 1982). This view has been refined in that the dorsal stream is thought to be related primarily to pragmatic aspects of spatial behavior, whereas the ventral stream is related primarily to semantic aspects of spatial behavior (Goodale & Milner, 1992; Jeannerod, Arbib, Rizzolatti, & Sakata, 1995).

Single cell recordings in nonhuman primates have supported the differential role of dorsal and ventral aspects of the lateral prefrontal cortex in working memory. Working memory for spatial locations is served by the dorsolateral prefrontal, whereas working memory for object identity is served by the ventrolateral prefrontal cortex (Wilson et al., 1993). Research has not yet demonstrated a lateralization of working-memory functions in the nonhuman primate. Again, mirroring the organizational principles of the posterior occipitofugal streams, these two prefrontal areas can be regarded as the neural substrates of the pragmatic aspects of working-memory mechanisms (the dorsolateral prefrontal cortex) and of semantic aspects of working-memory mechanisms (the ventrolateral prefrontal cortex). Both dorsolateral and ventrolateral prefrontal cortex appear lateralized in the type of information that they process.

Indeed, PET studies have shown that listening to digits activates the left dorsolateral prefrontal cortex in normal subjects, when active monitoring and manipulation of external information held in memory are required only to make judgments about the same stimuli, and no active manipulation is required (Petrides et al., 1993). Similarly, visuospatial information activates the right dorsolateral prefrontal cortex in normal subjects when active manipulation and monitoring of information are required. The same visuospatial information activates only the right ventrolateral prefrontal cortex when only "reproduction" of information without active manipulation and monitoring is demanded by the task (Owen, Evans, & Petrides, 1996). Other PET studies on working memory, where the differentiation between active monitoring and passive reproduction of information was not specifically addressed, have confirmed the general pattern of lateralization of verbal working-memory functions to the left frontal lobe and of visuospatial working-memory functions to the right frontal lobe (Smith, Jonides, & Koeppe, 1996), consistent with the clinical lesion data.

The dorsolateral prefrontal cortex seems to be a critical structure in a number of delayed-response and conditional sensorimotor learning tasks in nonhuman primates (Goldman-Rakic, 1987). One functional aspect of the dorsolateral prefrontal cortex that makes this cerebral structure critical to delayed-response tasks and to conditional sensorimotor learning, seems to be related to the learning of association rules between stimuli and responses (Fuster, 1995). In conditional motor learning to visuospatial stimuli in normal volunteers, learning-related changes in regional cerebral blood flow (rCBF) in the dorsolateral prefrontal cortex of the left hemisphere recently were observed (see Figure 3.3; Iacoboni, Woods, & Mazziotta, 1996a). This would be consistent with neurophysiological evidence showing that the neuronal discharge in dorsolateral prefrontal neurons of monkeys performing conditional sensorimotor tasks is dependent on the learning component of the task (Fuster, 1995). Learning-related rCBF increases seem to be lateralized to the left dorsolateral prefrontal cortex even when learning effects in conditional motor tasks are largely parallel in both hands (Iacoboni et al., 1996a). This suggests that transfer of learning might occur through the anterior regions of the corpus callosum, interconnecting the prefrontal cortex of the two cerebral hemispheres (Iacoboni & Zaidel, 1995). In keeping with this, callosal lesions in primates interfere with transfer of visuomotor conditional learning (Eacott & Gaffan, 1990). The lateralization of conditional sensorimotor learning to the left prefrontal cortex may not be specific to the human brain. Indeed, a lateralized left prefrontal learning-dependent activity during sensorimotor learning has been recently reported in a nonhuman primate (Gemba, Miki, & Sasaki, 1995).

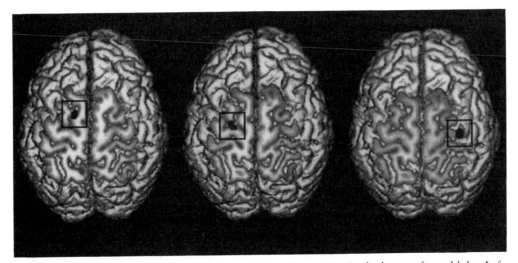

FIGURE 3.3. Functional asymmetries in sensorimotor integration in the human frontal lobe. Left: Rostral dorsal premotor activation in the left frontal lobe, subserving explicit stimulus–response associations. Center: Caudal dorsal premotor activation in the left frontal lobe, subserving implicit sensorimotor learning. Right: Primary motor activation in the right frontal lobe, subserving the merging of extrapersonal and personal space.

Premotor Cortex

There are four different cortical premotor fields in the lateral wall of the frontal lobe in the macaque brain. A variety of different nomenclatures have been used for these cortical fields. We follow here a nomenclature that seems the most intuitive. Independent anatomical and physiological evidence in nonhuman primates (Fogassi et al., 1996; Fujii et al., 1996; Matelli et al., 1985; Rizzolatti, Fadiga, Gallese, & Fogassi, 1996), and PET data in humans (Iacoboni, Woods, & Mazziotta, 1996b; Rizzolatti, Fadiga, & Matello, 1996) support the division of premotor cortex into four fields: a rostral (PMdr) and a caudal (PMdc) field in the dorsal premotor cortex and a rostral (PMvr) and a caudal (PMvc) field in the ventral premotor cortex. Neurophysiological evidence from studies of nonhuman primates suggests that PMdr is associated with saccade-, arm- and eye-, eye position-, and stimulus-related activity, whereas PMdc is associated with arm motor preparation- and arm movement-related activity (Fujii et al., 1996). The ventral premotor cortex seems to be associated with grasp representations and action recognition in PMvr (Rizzolatti, Fadiga, Gallese, & Fogassi, 1996) and with peripersonal space coding of somatosensory and visual stimuli in PMvc (Fogassi et al., 1996).

Lesion Studies. The dorsal premotor cortex is traditionally associated with neglect in extrapersonal space, with the selection and preparation of movements guided by external sensory stimuli, and with the retrieval of responses associated with specific sensory stimuli (Halsband & Freund, 1990; Passingham, 1993). The ventral premotor cortex is associated with neglect in peripersonal space (Rizzolatti, Matelli, & Pavcsi, 1983). There are no convincing data from studies of humans with focal premotor cortical damage that address the issue of functional or anatomical lateralization of premotor cortex.

Functional Imaging Studies. Recent PET evidence suggests a left-hemisphere lateralization in the human PMvr (inferior frontal gyrus, Brodmann's area 45) for the observation/execution matching system of grasping actions (Grafton, Arbib, Fadiga, & Rizzolatti, 1996; Rizzolatti, Fadiga, Matelli, et al., 1996). This functional lateralization is consistent with the hypothesis that primate communicative gestures would be the precursors of human language (MacNeilage, in press) and that the "grammar" of communicative gestures would be represented in nonhuman primate PMvr, considered as the anatomical homologue of human Broca's area (Rizzolatti, Fadiga, Gallese, & Fogassi, 1996). One of the interpretational limitations of these PET studies is that subjects were required to grasp objects, or to imagine grasping objects, or to observe others grasping objects, only with the dominant right hand. Thus, a left-hemisphere lateralization of brain activity might simply be caused by an asymmetry in the activation task. More convincingly, it has been shown with PET that the left PMvr (Brodmann's area 45) is activated in normal subjects while observing others making silent monosyllable mouth movements ("lip reading"), whereas no acoustic or language-receptive areas were activated (Grafton, Fadiga, Arbib, & Rizzolatti, 1996). This would be consistent with the hypothesis that visual information feeds forward to Broca's area in the left hemisphere, as emphasized by Denny-Brown (1975).

With regard to PET studies of the dorsal premotor cortex in humans, there seems to be a left PMdr superiority in establishing explicit stimulus–response associations and a left PMdc superiority in implicit sensorimotor learning (see Figure 3.3; Iacoboni et al., 1996b). This suggests a functional rostrocaudal fractionation of human dorsal premotor cortex similar to the one observed in nonhuman primates. The lateralization to the left dorsal premotor cortex also supports the notion, suggested by chronometric investigations, that the human left hemisphere is superior in tasks in which stimulus–response associations and response selection are required (Anzola, Bertoloni, Buchtel, & Rizzolatti, 1977). Finally, as in the dorsolateral prefrontal cortex, the sensorimotor learning is associated with blood flow increases only in PMdc. This suggests that in contrast with other types of learning that may be associated with blood flow decreases (Raichle et al., 1994), frontal lobe mechanisms of sensorimotor learning are generally associated with blood flow increases that correspond to an increase in neural activity.

Primary Motor Cortex

One of the most striking lateralized behaviors in humans is hand preference, which is typically, although not invariably, associated with manual skill (Annett, 1985). Fine manual coordination is lateralized to the left motor cortex in most right-handed individuals (Annett, 1985; Goldberg, 1985; Liepmann & Mass, 1907). Recent fMRI studies in humans demonstrate asymmetric activation of primary motor cortex during volitional fine movements of the hand (Kim et al., 1993; Kawashima et al., 1993). However, these activations involve a variety of prefrontal motor areas and are not restricted to primary motor cortex.

Some anatomical evidence suggests that the primary motor cortex in human and nonhuman primates is divided into a rostral sector and a caudal sector (Stepniewska et al., 1993; Geyer et al., 1996). Researchers proposed that this anatomical differentiation may correspond to a functional differentiation (Geyer et al., 1996). However, the functional asymmetries of the primary motor cortex that we discuss later do not differentiate between rostral and caudal sectors.

Lesion and Physiological Studies. Hemispatial neglect is typically associated with right temporal–parietal lesions but is observed with right frontal lobe lesions as well (Heilman & Valenstein, 1972; Heilman, Watson, & Valenstein, 1993). Patients with right prerolandic lesions, often encompassing primary motor areas, tend not to move the hand ipsilateral to the lesion in the contralateral hemispace (Bisiach, Geminiani, Berti, & Rusconi, 1990) and exhibit motor impersistence as well, which is thought to reflect an attentional deficit (Benson & Stuss, 1986). Under free vision, these patients typically fail to mark short lines lying on the left side of a paper sheet. Under mirror-reversed vision, in which only the left-right mirror image is possible, patients have to mark the lines on the left side of the paper sheet to mark the lines that they see on the right. Paradoxically, these patients tend to neglect lines seen on the left under free vision and lines seen on the right under mirror-reversed vision (Bisiach et al., 1995). Furthermore, a double dissociation in unilateral neglect patients is often seen: some patients have unilateral neglect only for near space and other patients have unilateral neglect only for far space (Halligan & Marshall, 1991). This double dissociation suggests that the representations of extrapersonal and personal space are differentiated and segregated in the human brain.

In the nonhuman primate, there is evidence for two parietofrontal circuits subserving extrapersonal and personal space. A dorsal parietofrontal circuit comprises area 7a, lateral intraparietal area, and dorsal premotor cortex, and codes extrapersonal space. A ventral parietofrontal circuit comprises area 7b, anterior intraparietal area, and ventral premotor cortex and codes personal space. These two circuits are anatomically largely independent, but both have input to primary motor cortex (Passingham, 1993). PET data, reviewed in the next section, suggest that the right motor cortex is involved in merging the information from these two parietofrontal circuits.

Functional Imaging Studies. A recent PET observation suggests that the right motor cortex is a critical structure in mapping extrapersonal onto personal space (Iacoboni, Woods, Lenzi, & Mazziotta, 1997). To test whether or not the merging of the two spaces occurred in primary motor cortex, rCBF was measured in normal volunteers while performing a task that required the coding of external stimuli in extrapersonal space and of motor responses in personal space. The critical manipulation was to ask subjects to respond half of the time with uncrossed arms (each arm in its homonymous hemispace) and half of the time with crossed arms (each hand in its heteronymous hemispace; i.e., left hand in right hemispace and right hand in left hemispace). The crossed-arms response position produced slower reaction times and increased rCBF in primary motor cortex in the right hemisphere (Figure 3.3). These increases in blood flow correlated with the lengthening of reaction times.

A number of functional neuroimaging studies suggest a major role for the primary motor cortex in motor learning (for a brief review, see Grafton, 1995). Most of these studies have also resulted in lateralized activation of the left primary motor cortex. However, these studies are inconclusive with regard to issues of functional asymmetries in motor learning, given that subjects were generally asked to use only the dominant right hand. The only studies in functional neuroimaging of which we are aware that have used an unbiased learning paradigm in which left-hand and right-hand motor activity was completely counterbalanced (Iacoboni et al., 1996a, 1996b, 1997) have resulted in blood flow increases consistently lateralized to the left frontal lobe. These blood flow increases occurred mainly in dorsal premotor cortex (Figure 3.3) and in dorsolateral prefrontal cortex and only sporadically in primary motor cortex (Iacoboni et al., 1996a).

Medial Wall (Supplementary Motor Area and Anterior Cingulate Cortex)

Two main regions of the medial wall of the frontal lobe have a critical role in sensorimotor integration mechanisms: the SMA and the anterior cingulate cortex. We review evidence from neurological literature and from neuroimaging techniques suggesting anatomical and functional parcellation and anatomical and functional asymmetries in these two areas.

SMA

According to recent anatomical and physiological evidence, two distinct areas can be differentiated in this region: a rostral area called pre-SMA and a caudal area called SMA proper. In macaques, pre-SMA is located mainly anteriorly to the genu of the arcuate sulcus, whereas SMA proper is located posteriorly to the genu of the arcuate sulcus. In the human brain, pre-SMA is located rostral to the level of the anterior commissure, and the SMA proper is located caudal to the level of the anterior commissure. Anatomical and neurophysiological evidence suggests that pre-SMA is related to selection and preparation of movements, whereas the SMA proper is more related to aspects of motor execution (Picard & Strick, 1996).

Lesion Studies. Evidence for asymmetrical functions of the SMA in general, without a precise distinction between pre-SMA and SMA proper, comes from observations in neurological patients. Patients with long-term unilateral medial frontal lobe lesions in the left hemisphere benefit from preparatory information regarding a motor response and can inhibit inappropriate responses. In contrast, patients with similar long-term lesions in the right hemisphere cannot benefit from preparatory information regarding a motor response and cannot inhibit an inappropriate motor response (Verfaellie & Heilman, 1987). In other words, there is a differential effect of contextual cues on motor performance in left and right SMA. We present evidence from PET studies of healthy subjects, later in this section, that is compatible with this hypothesis.

Another functional asymmetry that is observed in right-handed neurological patients with unilateral SMA lesions is related to the temporal control of movement sequences, a function generally subserved by the SMA (Tanji & Shima, 1994). Patients with left SMA lesions are much more impaired in reproducing rhythm patterns using the left hand, the right hand, or both hands in an alternating manner than are patients with right SMA lesions (Halsband, Ito, Tanji, & Freund, 1993). Furthermore, patients with left SMA lesions are more disturbed in the chronology of memory-guided saccade sequences than are patients with right SMA lesions (Gaymard, Rivaud, & Pierrot-Deseilligny, 1993).

The evidence for a differential role of the left and right SMA in sequential control of movements, at least in right-handers, might also explain why strategically placed callosal lesions producing motor disconnection tend to be associated with alien hand syndrome in the nondominant hand but not in the dominant hand in right-handers (Geschwind et al., 1995). If the motor areas of the right hemisphere that control the left hand do not receive inputs on sequential control of movements from the right SMA because of a callosal disconnection, then motor control disturbances in the left hand are likely to appear. We propose that this pathophysiological mechanism might be a unitary mechanism of praxis disturbances following callosal lesions (see brief review in Gonzalez-Rothi, Raade, & Heilman, 1994).

Functional Imaging Studies. A robust phenomenon in sensorimotor learning that may be associated with functional asymmetries in the medial wall of the frontal lobe in both the SMA and cingulate cortex is the contextual interference effect. When subjects perform sensorimotor tasks, practice in blocked fashion (where each task pattern is practiced separately from the others) produces a faster learning slope than does practice in random fashion (where each task pattern is practiced mixed with the others; Stelmach, 1996).

In a PET experiment on sensorimotor conditional learning, we have observed that contextual interference affects learning in the right hand more than in the left hand. This was associated with blood flow increases in the left SMA proper (Iacoboni, 1997, in press). In other words, the left SMA proper is more sensitive to contextual interference than is the right SMA proper, which might suggest that the differential contextual effect observed in patients with left and right SMA lesions occurs more specifically at the level of the SMA proper. An additional area of the medial wall of the frontal lobe that showed blood flow changes related to contextual interference effect is the cingulate cortex, discussed in the following section.

Anterior Cingulate Cortex

In the macaque, there are three areas, buried in the cingulate sulcus, that have significance in sensorimotor processes: the rostral cingulate motor area (CMAr), located anterior to the genu of the arcuate sulcus, and the dorsal (CMAd) and the ventral (CMAv) cingulate motor areas, located caudal to the genu of the arcuate sulcus (Picard & Strick, 1996). A recent review of PET findings in humans suggested at least two cortical fields in the human anterior cingulate cortex: a large rostral one, anterior to the anterior commissure, associated with complex sensorimotor tasks and with a somatotopic arrangement; and a small caudal one, posterior to the anterior commissure, associated with simple tasks and not showing a clear somatotopy (Picard & Strick, 1996).

Functional Imaging Studies. The anterior cingulate has been associated with attentional functions (Bench et al., 1993; Posner & Dehaene, 1994). However, asymmetries in the anterior cingulate in attentional mechanisms have not been systematically described (Pardo et al., 1991). Furthermore, widespread areas of right dorsolateral prefrontal cortex are preferentially activated during a variety of attentional tasks (Bench et al., 1993; Lewin et al., 1996; Vendrell et al., 1995). In terms of functional asymmetries, lateralized functional neuroimaging findings should be interpreted with caution in midline structures such as the cingulate region, given the spatial proximity of left and right cingulate cortex. If, in functional neuroimaging studies, the behavioral performance can be monitored on-line, then lateralized findings in the anterior cingulate are more likely to be reliable. For instance, in the contextual interference experiment cited in the previous section, we observed slower learning in the right hand in subjects practicing in a random fashion associated with blood flow increases in the left SMA-proper and in the left rostral anterior cingulate area, in a region overlapping with the arm representation in the human anterior cingulate cortex, according to Picard and Strick (1996). Taken together, behavioral data and rCBF findings suggest a greater sensitivity of the left rostral cingulate region to contextual cues. This is in line with a general role of the cingulate cortex in context-specific learning in other mammals (Freeman, Cuppernell, Flannery, & Gabriel, 1996).

Anatomical Studies. The most striking asymmetry in the anterior cingulate region is at the morphological level. In the left hemisphere there are often two cerebral sulci in the cingulate region, the cingulate sulcus and the paracingulate sulcus, whereas in the right hemisphere there is generally only one sulcus, the cingulate sulcus. It has been speculated that this asymmetry might be related to certain aspects of effortful versus automatic vocalization (Paus et al., 1996). Indeed, in a PET study that compared reversed speech (effortful) with overpracticed speech, foci of activation were largely observed overlapping the paracingulate sulcus in the left hemisphere (Paus, Petrides, Evans, & Meyer, 1993). It is not clear whether this asymmetry is related to the motor or linguistic components of speech.

CONCLUDING REMARKS: IS A COMPREHENSIVE MODEL OF FRONTAL LOBE LATERALIZATION REALISTIC?

A recent model of frontal lobe specialization proposes a dichotomy in which the right frontal lobe is specialized for novelty and the left frontal lobe for the routine (Goldberg & Podell, 1995). That the right frontal lobe is predominant in novelty processing fits with its role in attentional mechanisms (Heilman et al., 1993). PET studies in healthy volunteers demonstrate strikingly increased blood flow and metabolic activity in the right prefrontal cortex, including Brodmann's areas 8, 9, 44, and 46 during selective attention tasks in different sensory modalities (Roland, 1984; Pardo et al., 1991, Bench et al., 1993; Lewin et al., 1996). The lateralized role of the primary motor area in the merging of personal and extrapersonal space has been discussed previously. However, the role of the right hemisphere in attention or novelty processing does not neccesarily relegate the left hemisphere to the routine.

The dichotomization and polarization of the functions of the two cerebral hemispheres are recurrent themes in models of cerebral lateralization. In contrast, we believe that the specialization of one hemisphere for a given function does not require that the contralateral hemisphere is not involved in that function, or that it serves the polar opposite function. Recent PET and fMRI data demonstrate frequent bilateral (although still asymmetrical) activations in homologous regions in tasks previously considered completely lateralized. Furthermore, in this chapter, we saw that the frontal lobes consist of numerous functionally distinct areas on cytoarchitectonic and physiological grounds, and that these functionally distinct frontal areas demonstrate different laterality patterns. Thus, any attempt to unify lateralized frontal lobe functions under one model is simplistic and likely to be flawed.

In spite of the large number of frontal lobe functions that appear lateralized, the only functional asymmetry for which a corresponding structural asymmetry has been supported by a body of converging evidence is that of language and Broca's area. We anticipate that as physiological and anatomical studies in primates and fMRI studies in humans continue to aid in the segregation of functional units within the frontal lobe, the morphological, physiological, and molecular asymmetries that contribute to these functional asymmetries will be elucidated.

It is becoming clear that many of the functional asymmetries discussed in this chapter are in functions for which nonhuman primates are well adapted. Thus, a detailed study of the degree of lateralization in these nonlanguage functions and their anatomical correlates in primates should provide important insights into the evolutionary origins of frontal lobe asymmetries. In the same vein, how functional asymmetries in sensorimotor integration in humans correspond to language lateralization in individual subjects will be of great interest.

ACKNOWLEDGMENTS

We gratefully acknowledge support from the McDonnell–Pew Foundation in Cognitive Neuroscience (D.H.G), the International Human Frontier Science Program (M.I.), and National Institutes of Health Grant Nos. NS-01849-01 (D.H.G.), NS-20187 (M.I.), and RSA MH-00179 (M.I.).

REFERENCES

Adrianov, O. S. (1979). Structural basis for functional interhemispheric brain asymmetry. *Human Physiology, 5,* 359–363.

Albanese, E., Merlo, A., Albanese, A., & Gomez, E. (1989). Anterior speech region. Asymmetry and weight-surface correlation [see comments]. *Archives of Neurology, 46,* 307–310.

Alexander, M. P., Naeser, M. A., & Palumbo, C. (1990). Broca's area aphasias: Aphasia after lesions including the frontal operculum. *Neurology, 40,* 353–362.

Annett, M. (1985). *Left, right, hand and brain: The right shift theory.* London: Erlbaum.

Anzola, G. P., Bertoloni, G., Buchtel, H. A., & Rizzolatti, G. (1977). Spatial compatibility and anatomical factors in simple and choice reaction time. *Neuropsychologia, 15,* 295–302.

Aresu, M. (1914). La superficie cerebrale nell uomo. *Archives of Italian Anatomy Embriologio, 12,* 380–433.

Bear, D., Schiff, D., Saver, J., Greenberg, M., & Freeman, R. (1986). Quantitative analysis of cerebral asymmetries: Fronto-occipital correlation, sexual dimorphism and association with handedness. *Archives of Neurology, 43,* 598–603.

Bench, C. J., Frith, C. D., Grasby, P. M., Friston, K. J., Paulesu, E., Frackowiak, R. S., & Dolan, R. J. (1993). Investigations of the functional anatomy of attention using the Stroop Test. *Neuropsychologia, 31,* 907–922.

Benson, D. F. (1977). The third alexia. *Archives of Neurology, 34,* 327–331.

Benson, D. F. (1986). Aphasia and the lateralization of language. *Cortex, 22,* 71–86.

Benson, D. F., & Stuss, D. T. (1986). *The frontal lobes.* New York: Raven Press.

Berker, E. A., Berker, A. H., & Smith, A. (1986). Translation of Broca's 1865 report: Localization of speech in the third left frontal convolution. *Archives of Neurology, 43,* 1065–1072.

Binder, J. R., Rao, S. M., Hammeke, T. A., Frost, J. A., Bandettini, P. A., Jesmanowicz, A., & Hyde, J. S. (1995). Lateralized human brain language systems demonstrated by task subtraction functional magnetic resonance imaging. *Archives of Neurology, 52,* 593–601.

Bisiach, E., Geminiani, G., Berti, A., & Rusconi, M. L. (1990). Perceptual and premotor factors of unilateral neglect. *Neurology, 40,* 1278–1281.

Bisiach, E., Tegner, R., Ladavas, E., Rusconi, M. L., Mijovic, D., & Hjaltason, H. (1995). Dissociation of ophthalmokinetic and melokinetic attention in unilateral neglect. *Cerebral Cortex, 5,* 439–447.

Boccardi, E., Bruzzone, M. G., & Vignolo, L. A. (1984). Alexia in recent and late Broca's aphasia. *Neuropsychologia, 22,* 745–754.

Bogen, J. E. (1993). The callosal syndromes. In K. M. Heilman & E. Valenstein (Eds.), *Clinical neuropsychology* (pp. 337–407). New York: Oxford University Press.

Broca, P. (1865). Sur la faculté du langage articulé. *Bulletin de la Société Anatomique de Paris, 6*, 493–494.

Broca, P. (1875). Instructions craniologiques et craniometriques de la Société d'Anthropologie. *Bulletin de la Société d'Anthropologie (Paris), 6*, 534–536.

Broca, P. (1888). *Memoires sur le cerveau de l'homme*. Paris: Reinwald.

Cancelliere, A. E., & Kertesz, A. (1990). Lesion localization in acquired deficits of emotional expression and comprehension. *Brain and Cognition, 13*(2), 133–147.

Cavada, C., & Goldman-Rakic, P. S. (1989). Posterior parietal cortex in rhesus monkey: II. Evidence for segregated corticocortical networks linking sensory and limbic areas with the frontal lobe. *Journal of Comparative Neurology, 287*, 422–445.

Damasio, A. R., & Tranel, D. (1993). Nouns and verbs are retrieved with differently distributed neural systems. *Proceedings of the National Academy of Sciences, USA, 90*, 4957–4960.

Danly, M., & Shapiro, B. (1982). Speech prosody in Broca's aphasia. *Brain and Language, 16*(2), 171–190.

Davidson, R. J. (1992). Anterior cerebral asymmetry and the nature of emotion. *Brain and Cognition, 20*, 125–151.

Davidson, R. J., & Sutton, S. K. (1995). Affective neuroscience: The emergence of a discipline. *Current Opinion in Neurobiology, 5*, 217–224.

Demonet, J. F., Price, C., Wise, R., & Frackowiak, R. S. (1994). A PET study of cognitive strategies in normal subjects during language tasks: Influence of phonetic ambiguity and sequence processing on phoneme monitoring. *Brain, 117*(Pt. 4), 671–682.

Denny-Brown, D. (1965). Physiologic aspects of disturbances of speech. *Australian Journal of Experimental Biology and Medical Science, 43*, 455–474.

Denny-Brown, D. (1975). Cerebral dominance. In K. J. Zulch, O. Creutzfeldt, & G. C. Galbraith (Eds.), *Cerebral localization* (pp. 306–307). New York: Springer-Verlag.

Dordain, M., Degos, J. D., & Dordain, G. (1971). [Voice disorders in left hemiplegia]. *Revue de Laryngologie Otologie Rhinologie, 92*(3), 178–188.

Eacott, M. J., & Gaffan, D. (1990). Interhemispheric transfer of visuomotor conditional learning via the anterior corpus callosum of monkeys. *Behavioral Brain Research, 38*, 109–116.

Eccles, J. C. (1977). Evolution of the brain in relation to the development of the self-conscious mind. *Annals of the New York Academy of Sciences, 299*, 161–178.

Falk, D., Hildebolt, C., Cheverud, J., Vannier, M., Helmkamp, R. C., & Konigsberg, L. (1990). Cortical asymmetries in frontal lobes of rhesus monkeys (Macaca mulatta). *Brain Research, 512*(1), 40–45.

Falzi, G., Perrone, P., & Vignolo, L. A. (1982). Right–left asymmetry in anterior speech region. *Archives of Neurology, 39*, 239–240.

Finger, S. (1993). *The origins of neuroscience*. New York: Oxford University Press.

Flourens, P. (1824). *Recherches experimentales sur les propriétés et les fonctions du système nerveux dans les animaux vertébrés*. Paris: Crevot.

Fogassi, L., Gallese, V., Fadiga, L., Luppino, G., Matelli, M., & Rizzolatti, G. (1996). Coding of peripersonal space in inferior premotor cortex. *Journal of Neurophysiology, 76*, 140–157.

Foundas, A. L., Leonard, C. M., Gilmore, R. L., Fennell, E. B., & Heilman, K. M. (1996). Pars triangularis asymmetry and language dominance. *Proceedings of the National Academy of Sciences, USA, 93*, 719–722.

Foundas, A. L., Leonard, C. M., & Heilman, K. M. (1995). Morphologic cerebral asymmetries and handedness. The pars triangularis and planum temporale. *Archives of Neurology, 52*, 501–508.

Freedman, M., Alexander, M. P., & Naeser, M. A. (1984). Anatomic basis of transcortical motor aphasia. *Neurology, 34*(4), 409–417.

Freeman, J. H. Jr., Cuppernell, C., Flannery, K., & Gabriel, M. (1996). Context-specific multi-site cingulate cortical, limbic thalamic, and hippocampal neuronal activity during concurrent discriminative approach and avoidance training in rabbits. *Journal of Neuroscience, 16*, 1538–1549.

Frith, C. D., Friston, K. J., Liddle, P. F., & Frackowiak, R. S. (1991). A PET study of word finding. *Neuropsychologia, 29,* 1137–1148.

Fujii, N., Mushiake, H., & Tanji, J. (1996). Rostrocaudal differentiation of dorsal premotor cortex with physiological criteria [Abstract]. *Society for Neuroscience, 22,* 2024.

Funahashi, S., Bruce, C. J., & Goldman-Rakic, P. S. (1989). Mnemonic coding of visual space in the monkey's dorsolateral prefrontal cortex. *Journal of Neurophysiology, 61,* 331–349.

Fuster, J. M. (1995). *Memory in the cerebral cortex.* Cambridge, MA: MIT Press.

Gainotti, G. (1972). Emotional behavior and hemispheric side of the lesion. *Cortex, 8*(1), 41–55.

Galaburda, A. M. (1980). [Broca's region: Anatomic remarks made a century after the death of its discoverer]. *Revue Neurologique (Paris), 136,* 609–616.

Galaburda, A. M. (1991). Asymmetries of cerebral neuroanatomy. In J. Marsh & M. J. Bock (Eds.), *Biological asymmetry and handedness* (pp. 219–226). New York: Wiley.

Galaburda, A. M. (1993). Neurology of developmental dyslexia. *Optometry and Vision Science, 70,* 343–347.

Galaburda, A. M., LeMay, M., Kemper, T. L., & Geschwind, N. (1978). Right–left asymmetries in the brain. *Science, 199,* 852–856.

Galaburda, A. M., Rosen, G. D., & Sherman, G. F. (1990). Individual variability in cortical organization: Its relationship to brain laterality and implications to function. *Neuropsychologia, 28,* 529–546.

Garraghty, P. E., & Kaas, J. H. (1992). Dynamic features of sensory and motor maps. *Current Opinion in Neurobiology, 2,* 522–527.

Gaymard, B., Rivaud, S., & Pierrot-Deseilligny, C. (1993). Role of the left and right supplementary motor areas in memory-guided saccade sequences. *Annals of Neurology, 34*(3), 404–406.

Gazzaniga, M. S. (1970). *The bisected brain.* New York: Appleton Century Crofts.

Gemba, H., Miki, N., & Sasaki, K. (1995). Field potential change in the prefrontal cortex of the left hemisphere during learning processes of reaction time hand movement with complex tone in the monkey. *Neuroscience Letters, 190,* 93–6.

George, M. S., Ketter, T. A., Parekh, P. I., Horwitz, B., Herscovitch, P., & Post, R. M. (1995). Brain activity during transient sadness and happiness in healthy women. *American Journal of Psychiatry, 152*(3), 341–351.

George, M. S., Parekh, P. I., Rosinsky, N., Ketter, T. A., Kimbrell, T. A., Heilman, K. M., Herscovitch, P., & Post, R. M. (1996). Understanding emotional prosody activates right hemisphere regions. *Archives of Neurology, 53*(7), 665–670.

Geschwind, D. H., Iacoboni, M., Mega, M. S., Zaidel, D. W., Cloughesy, T., & Zaidel, E. (1995). The alien hand syndrome: Interhemispheric motor disconnection due to a lesion in the midbody of the corpus callosum. *Neurology, 45,* 802–808.

Geschwind, N. (1970). The organization of language and the brain. *Science, 170,* 940–944.

Geschwind, N., & Galaburda, A. (1985). Cerebral lateralization: Biological mechanisms, associations, and pathology. *Archives of Neurology, 42,* 428–458, 521–552.

Geschwind, N., & Levitsky, W. (1968). Human brain: Left–right asymmetries in temporal speech region. *Science, 161,* 186–187.

Geyer, S., Ledberg, A., Schleicher, A., Kinomura, S., Schorman, T., Burgelu, A., Klingberg, T., Larson, M., Zilles, K., & Roland, P. E. (1996). Two different areas within the primary motor cortex of man. *Nature, 382,* 805–807.

Glicksohn, J., & Myslobodsky, M. S. (1993). The representation of patterns of structural brain asymmetry in normal individuals. *Neuropsychologia, 31,* 145–159.

Goldberg, E., & Podell, K. (1995). Lateralization in the frontal lobes. In H. H. Jasper, S. Riggio, & P. Goldman-Rakic (Eds.), *Epilepsy and the functional anatomy of the frontal lobe* (pp. 85–96). New York: Raven Press.

Goldberg, G. (1985). Supplementary motor area structure and function: Review and hypotheses. *Behavioral and Brain Sciences, 8,* 567–616.

Goldman-Rakic, P. S. (1987). Circuitry of primate prefrontal cortex and regulation of behavior by representational memory. In V. B. Mountcastle (Ed.), *Handbook of physiology—The nervous system* (pp. 373–417). Bethesda, MD: American Physiological Society.

Gonzalez-Rothi, L. G., Raade, A. S., & Heilman, K. M. (1994). Localization of lesions in limb and buccofacial apraxia. In A. Kertesz (Ed.), *Localization and neuroimaging in neuropsychology* (pp. 407–428). San Diego, CA: Academic Press.

Goodale, M. A., & Milner, A. D. (1992). Separate visual pathways for perception and action. *Trends in Neurosciences, 15,* 20–25.

Grafton, S. T. (1995). Mapping memory systems in the human brain. *Seminars in Neuroscience, 7,* 157–163.

Grafton, S. T., Arbib, M. A., Fadiga, L., & Rizzolatti, G. (1996). Localization of grasp representations in humans by positron emission tomography. Observation compared with imagination. *Experimental Brain Research, 112,* 103–111.

Grafton, S. T., Fadiga, L., Arbib, M. A., & Rizzolatti, G. (1996). Activation of frontal motor areas during silent lip reading [Abstract]. *Society of Neuroscience, 22,* 1109.

Habib, M., Demonet, J. F., & Frackowiak, R. (1996). [Cognitive neuroanatomy of language: Contribution of functional cerebral imaging]. *Revue Neurologique (Paris), 152,* 249–260.

Hadziselmovic, H., & Cus, M. (1966). The appearance of internal structures of the brain in relation to configuration of the human skull. *Acta Anatomica, 63,* 289–299.

Halligan, P., & Marshall, J. (1991). Left neglect for near but not for far space in man. *Nature, 350,* 498–500.

Halsband, U., & Freund, H. J. (1990). Premotor cortex and conditional motor learning in man. *Brain, 113,* 207–222.

Halsband, U., Ito, N., Tanji, J., & Freund, H. J. (1993). The role of premotor cortex and the supplementary motor area in the temporal control of movement in man. *Brain, 116,* 243–266.

Hayes, T. L., & Lewis, D. A. (1993). Hemispheric differences in layer III pyramidal neurons of the anterior language area. *Archives of Neurology, 50,* 501–505.

Hayes, T. L., & Lewis, D. A. (1995). Anatomical specialization of the anterior motor speech area: Hemispheric differences in magnopyramidal neurons. *Brain and Language, 49,* 289–308.

Hecean, H., & Consoli, S. (1973). Analyse des troubles de langage au cours des lesions de l'aire de Broca. *Neuropsychologia, 11,* 377–388.

Hecaen, H., De, A. M., & Monzon, M. A. (1981). Cerebral organization in left-handers. *Brain and Language, 12,* 261–284.

Heilman, K. M., & Valenstein, E. (1972). Frontal lobe neglect in man. *Neurology, 22,* 660–664.

Heilman, K. M., Watson, R. T., & Valenstein, E. (1993). Neglect and related disorders. In K. M. Heilman & E. Valenstein (Eds.), *Clinical neuropsychology* (pp. 279–336). New York: Oxford University Press.

Holloway, R. L., & De La Coste-Lareymondie, M. (1982). Brain endocast asymmetry in pongids and hominids: Some preliminary findings on the paleontology of cerebral dominance. *American Journal of Physical Anthropology, 58,* 101–110.

Iacoboni, M. (1997). Word recognition in the split brain and PET studies of spatial stimulus–response compatibility support contextual integration. *Behavioral Brian Science, 20,* 690–691.

Iacoboni, M. (in press). Attention and sensorimotor integration: Mapping the embodied mind. In A. Toga & J. C. Mazziotta (Eds.), *Brain mapping: Applications.* San Diego, CA: Academic Press.

Iacoboni, M., Padovani, A., Di Pigro, V., & Lenzi, G. L. (1995). Post-stroke depression: Relationships with morphological damage and cognition over time. *Italian Journal of Neurological Sciences, 16,* 209–216.

Iacoboni, M., Woods, R. P., Lenzi, G. L., & Mazziotta, J. C. (1997). Merging of oculomotor and somatomotor space coding in the human right precentral gyrus. *Brain, 120(9),* 1635–1645.

Iacoboni, M., Woods, R. P., & Mazziotta, J. C. (1996a). Brain behavior relationships: Evidence from practice effects in spatial stimulus–response compatibility. *Journal of Neurophysiology, 76,* 321–331.

Iacoboni, M., Woods, R. P., & Mazziotta, J. C. (1996b). Blood flow increases in left dorsal premotor cortex during sensorimotor integration learning [Abstract]. *Society for Neuroscience, 22,* 720.

Iacoboni, M., & Zaidel, E. (1995). Channels of the corpus callosum: Evidence from simple reaction times to lateralized flashes in the normal and the split brain. *Brain, 118,* 779–788.

Iacoboni, M., & Zaidel, E. (1996). Hemispheric independence in word recognition: Evidence from unilateral and bilateral presentations. *Brain and Language, 53,* 121–140.

Incisa della Rocchetta, A. (1986). Classification and recall of pictures after unilateral frontal or temporal lobectomy. *Cortex, 22,* 189–211.

Incisa della Rocchetta, A., & Milner, B. (1993). Strategic search and retrieval inhibition: The role of the frontal lobes. *Neuropsychologia, 31,* 503–524.

Jackson, J. H. (1868). Deficit of intellectual expression (aphasia). with left hemiplegia. *Lancet, 1,* 457.

Jackson, J. H. (1880). On aphasia, with left hemiplegia. *Lancet, 1,* 637–638.

Jackson, J. H. (1915). Hughlings Jackson on aphasia and kindred affections of speech, together with a complete bibliography of his publications on speech and a reprint of some of the more important papers. *Brain, 38,* 1–190.

Jeannerod, M., Arbib, M. A., Rizzolatti, G., & Sakata, H. (1995). Grasping objects: The cortical mechanisms of visuomotor transformation. *Trends in Neurosciences, 18,* 314–320.

Jerison, H. J. (1977). The theory of encephalization. *Annals of the New York Academy of Sciences, 299,* 146–160.

Jorge, R. E., Robinson, R. G., Starkstein, S. E., Arndt, S. V., Forrester, A. W., & Geisler, F. H. (1993). Secondary mania following traumatic brain injury. *American Journal of Psychiatry, 150*(6), 916–921.

Just, M. A., Carpenter, P. A., Keller, T. A., Eddy, W. F., & Thulborn, K. R. (1996). Brain activation modulated by sentence comprehension. *Science, 274,* 114–116.

Kawashima, R., Yamada, K., Kinomura, S., Yamaguchi, T., Matsui, H., Yoshioka, S., & Fukuda, H. (1993). Regional cerebral blood flow changes of cortical motor areas and prefrontal areas in humans related to ipsilateral and contralateral hand movement. *Brain Research, 623*(1), 33–40.

Kim, S. G., Ashe, J., Hendrich, K., Ellerman, J. M., Merkle, H., Ugurbil, K., & Georgopoulos, A. P. (1993). Functional magnetic imaging of motor cortex. Hemispheric asymmetry and handedness. *Science, 261,* 615–616.

Klein, D., Milner, B., Zatorre, R. J., Meyer, E., & Evans, A. C. (1995). The neural substrates underlying word generation: A bilingual functional-imaging study. *Archives of Neurology, 92,* 2899–2903.

Kolb, D., & Wishaw, D. (1985). *Fundamentals of human neuropsychology.* San Francisco: W. H. Freeman.

Kushch, A., Gross, G. K., Jallad, B., Lubs, H., Rabin, M., & Feldman, E. (1993). Temporal lobe surface area measurements on MRI in normal and dyslexic readers. *Neuropsychologia, 31,* 811–821.

Lashley, K. S., & Clark, D. (1946). The cytoarchitecture of the cerebral cortex of ateles: A critical examination of architectonic studies. *Journal of Comparative Neurology, 85,* 223–305.

Lecours, A. R., & Lhermitte, F. (1970). *L'aphasie.* Paris: Flammarion.

LeMay, M., & Kido, D. K. (1978). Asymmetries of the cerebral hemispheres on computed tomograms. *Journal of Computer Assisted Tomography, 2,* 471–476.

Lewin, J. S., Friedman, L., Wu, D., Miller, D. A., Thompson, L. A., Klein, S. K., Wise, A. L., Hedera, P., Buckley, P., & Meltzer L. (1996). Cortical localization of human sustained attention: Detection with functional MR using a visual vigilance paradigm. *Journal of Computer Assisted Tomography, 20,* 695–701.

Liepmann, H., & Mass, O. (1907). Fall von linksseitiger agraphie und apraxie bei techtsseitiger lahmung. *Journal für Psychologie und Neurologie, 10,* 214–227.

MacNeilage, P. F. (in press). The frame/content theory of evolution of speech production. *Behavioral and Brain Sciences.*

Marie, P. (1906). La troisième circumconvolution frontale gauche ne joue aucun rôle special dans la fonction du langage. *Semaine Medicale, 26*, 241–247.

Masdeu, J. C. (1980). Aphasia after infarction of the left supplementary motor area. *Neurology, 30*, 359.

Matelli, M., Luppino, G., & Rizzolatti, G. (1985). Patterns of cytochrome oxidase activity in the frontal agranular cortex of macaque monkey. *Behavioral Brain Research, 18*, 125–137.

McCarthy, G., Blamire, A. M., Rothman, D. L., Gruetter, R., & Shulman, R. G. (1993). Echo-planar magnetic resonance imaging studies of frontal cortex activation during word generation in humans. *Proceedings of the National Academy of Sciences, USA, 90*, 4952–4956.

Metter, E. J. (1991). Brain–behavior relationships in aphasia studied by positron emission tomography. *Annals of the New York Academy of Science, 620*, 153–164.

Miller, B. L., Chang, L., Mena, I., Boone, K., & Lesser, I. M. (1993). Progressive right frontotemporal degeneration: Clinical, neuropsychological and SPECT characteristics. *Dementia, 4*, 204–213.

Milner, A. D., & Goodale, M. A. (1995). *The visual brain in action.* New York: Oxford University Press.

Milner, B. (1975). Psychological aspects of focal epilepsy and the neuropsychological management. *Advances in Neurology, 8*, 299–321.

Milner, B., & Petrides, M. (1984). Behavioral effects of frontal-lobe lesions in man. *Journal of Neuroscience, 7*(11), 403–407.

Mohr, J. P., Pessin, M. S., Finkelstein, S., Funkenstein, H. H., Duncan, G. W., & Davis, K. R. (1978). Broca aphasia: Pathologic and clinical. *Neurology, 28*, 311–324.

Monrad-Krohn, G. H. (1947). Dysprosody or alteration in "melody of language." *Brain, 70*, 405–415.

Moutier, F. (1908). *L'aphasie de Broca.* Paris: Steinheil.

Nielsen, J. M. (1946). *Agnosia, apraxia, aphasia: Their value in cerebral localization.* New York: Hoeber.

Ojemann, G., & Mateer, C. (1979). Human language cortex: Localization of memory, syntax, and sequential motor–phoneme identification systems. *Science, 205*(4413), 1401–1403.

Owen, A. M., Evans, A. C., & Petrides, M. (1996). Evidence for a two-stage model of spatial working memory processing within the lateral frontal cortex: A positron emission tomography study. *Cerebral Cortex, 6*, 31–38.

Pardo, J. V., Fox, P. T., & Raichle, M. E. (1991). Localization of a human system for sustained attention by positron emission tomography. *Nature, 349*, 61–64.

Pascual-Leone, A., Catala, M. D., & Pascual-Leone, A. (1996). Lateralized effect of rapid-rate transcranial magnetic stimulation of the prefrontal cortex on mood. *Neurology, 46*, 499–502.

Passingham, R. E. (1993). *The frontal lobes and voluntary action.* New York: Oxford University Press.

Paulesu, E., Frith, C. D., & Frackowiak, R. S. (1993). The neural correlates of the verbal component of working memory. *Nature, 362*, 342–345.

Paus, T., Petrides, M., Evans, A., & Meyer, E. (1993). Role of the human anterior cingulate cortex in the control of oculomotor, manual, and speech responses: A positron emission tomography study. *Neurophysiology, 70*, 453–469.

Paus, T., Tomaiuolo, F., Otaki, N., MacDonald, D., Petrides, M., Atlas, J., Morris, R., & Evans, A. C. (1996). Human cingulate and paracingulate sulci: Pattern, variability, asymmetry, and probabilistic map. *Cerebral Cortex, 6*(2), 207–214.

Penfield, W., & Roberts, L. (1959). *Speech and brain mechanisms.* Princeton, NJ: Princeton University Press.

Petersen, S. E., Fox, P. T., Posner, M. I., Mintun, M., & Raichle, M. E. (1988). Positron emission tomographic studies of the cortical anatomy of single-word processing. *Nature, 331*, 585–589.

Petrides, M. (1994). Frontal lobes and working memory: Evidence from investigations of the effects of cortical excisions in nonhuman primates. In F. Boller & J. Grafman (Eds.), *Handbook of neuropsychology* (Vol. 9, pp. 59–82). Amsterdam: Elsevier.

Petrides, M., Alivisatos, B., Meyer, E., & Evans, A. C. (1993). Functional activation of the human frontal cortex during the performance of verbal working memory tasks. *Proceedings of the National Academy of Sciences, USA, 90,* 878–882.

Picard, N., & Strick, P. L. (1996). Motor areas of the medial wall: A review of their location and functional activation. *Cerebral Cortex, 6,* 342–353.

Poppel, D. (1996). Some remaining questions about studying phonological processing with PET: Response to Demonet, Fiez, Paulesu, Petersen, and Zatorre. *Brain and Language, 55,* 380–385.

Posner, M. I., & Dehaene, S. (1994). Attentional networks. *Trends in Neurosciences, 2,* 75–79.

Raichle, M. E., Fiez, J. A., Videen, T. O., MacLeod, A. M., Pardo, J. V., Fox, P. T., & Petersen, S. E. (1994). Practice-related changes in human brain functional anatomy during nonmotor learning. *Cerebral Cortex, 4,* 8–26.

Rajkowska, G., & Goldman-Rakic, P. (1995). Cytoarchitectonic definition of prefrontal areas in the normal human cortex: II. Variability in locations of areas 9 and 46 and relationship to the Talaraich coordinate system. *Cerebral Cortex, 5,* 323–337.

Rizzolatti, G., Fadiga, L., Gallese, V., & Fogassi, L. (1996). Premotor cortex and the recognition of motor actions. *Cognitive Brain Research, 3,* 131–141.

Rizzolatti, G., Fadiga, L., Matelli, M., Bettinardi, V., Paulesu, E., Perani, D., & Fazio, F. (1996). Localization of grasp representations in humans by PET: 1. Observation versus execution. *Experimental Brain Research, 111,* 246–252.

Rizzolatti, G., Matelli, M., & Pavcsi, G. (1983). Deficits in attention and movement following the removal of postarcuate (area 6) and prearcuate (area 8) cortex in macaque monkeys. *Brain, 106,* 655–673.

Robinson, R. G., Kubos, K. L., Starr, L. B., Rao, K., & Price, T. R. (1984). Mood disorders in stroke patients: Importance of location of lesion. *Brain, 107*(Pt. 1), 81–93.

Roland, P. E. (1984). Metabolic measurements of the working frontal cortex in man. *Trends in Neurosciences, 7*(11), 430–435.

Ross, E. D. (1981). The aprosodias: Functional–anatomical organization of the affective components of language in the right hemisphere. *Archives of Neurology, 38,* 561–569.

Ross, E. D., & Mesulam, M. M. (1979). Dominant language functions of the right hemisphere: Prosody and emotional gesturing. *Archives of Neurology, 36,* 144–148.

Sackeim, H. A., Greenberg, M. S., Weiman, A. L., Gur, R. C., Hungerbuhler, J. P., & Geschwind, N. (1982). Hemispheric asymmetry in the expression of positive and negative emotions: Neurologic evidence. *Archives of Neurology, 39,* 210–218.

Scheibel, A. B., Paul, L. A., Fried, I., Forsythe, A. B., Tomiyasu, U., Wechsler, A., Kao, A., & Slotnick, J. (1985). Dendritic organization of the anterior speech area. *Experimental Neurology, 87,* 109–117.

Simonds, R. J., & Scheibel, A. B. (1989). The postnatal development of the motor speech area: A preliminary study. *Brain and Language, 37,* 42–58.

Smith, E. E., Jonides, J., & Koeppe, R. A. (1996). Dissociating verbal and spatial working memory using PET. *Cerebral Cortex, 6,* 11–20.

Snowden, J. S., Neary, D., Mann, D. M., Goulding, P. J. & Testa, H. J. (1992). Progressive language disorder due to lobar atrophy. *Annals of Neurology, 31,* 174–183.

Starkstein, S. E., Bryer, J. B., Berthier, M. L., Cohen, B., Price, T. R., & Robinson, R. G. (1991). Depression after stroke: The importance of cerebral hemisphere asymmetries. *Journal of Neuropsychiatry and Clinical Neurosciences, 3*(3), 276–85.

Starkstein, S. E., Federoff, J. P., Price, T. R., Leiguarda, R. C., & Robinson, R. G. (1994). Neuropsychological and neuroradiologic correlates of emotional prosody comprehension. *Neurology, 44*(Pt. 1), 515–522.

Starkstein, S. E., Pearlson, G. D., Boston, J., & Robinson, R. G. (1987). Mania after brain injury. A controlled study of causative factors. *Archives of Neurology, 44*(10), 1069–1073.

Starkstein, S. E., Robinson, R. G., Honig, M. A., Parikh, R. M., Joselyn, J., & Price, T. R. (1989). Mood changes after right-hemisphere lesions. *British Journal of Psychiatry, 155,* 79–85.

Stelmach, G. E. (1996). Motor learning: Toward understanding acquired representations. In J. R. Bloedel, T. J. Ebner, & S. P. Wise (Eds.), *The acquisition of motor behavior in vertebrates* (pp. 391–408). Cambridge, MA: MIT Press.

Stepniewska, I., Preuss, T. M., & Kaas, J. H. (1993). Architectonics, somatotopic organization, and ipsilateral cortical connections of the primary motor area (M1) of owl monkey. *Journal of Comparative Neurology, 330,* 238–271.

Tanji, J., & Shima, K. (1994). Role for supplementary motor area cells in planning several movements ahead. *Nature 371,* 413–416.

Thurnam, J. (1866, April). On the weight of the brain and the circumstances affecting it. *Journal of Mental Science.*

Tilney, F. (1927). The brain of prehistoric man. *Archives of Neurology and Psychiatry, 17,* 723–769.

Tonkonogy, J., & Goodglass, H. (1981). Language function, foot of the third frontal gyrus, and rolandic operculum. *Archives of Neurology, 38,* 486–490.

Ungerleider, L. G., & Mishkin, M. (1982). Two cortical visual systems. In D. J. Ingle, M. A. Goodale, R. J. W. Mansfield (Eds.), *Analysis of visual behavior* (pp. 549–586). Cambridge, MA: MIT Press.

Vendrell, P., Junque, C., Pujol, J., Jurado, M. A., Molet, J., & Grafman, J. (1995). The role of prefrontal regions in the Stroop task. *Neuropsychologia, 33,* 341–352.

Verfaellie, M., & Heilman, K. M. (1987). Response preparation and response inhibition after lesions of the medial frontal lobe. *Archives of Neurology, 44,* 1265–1271.

Von Bonin, G. (1962). Anatomical asymmetries of the cerebral hemispheres. In V. B. Mountcastle (Ed.), *Interhemispheric relations and cerebral dominance* (pp. 1–6). Baltimore: Johns Hopkins Press.

Wada, J. A., Clarke, R., & Hamm, A. (1975). Cerebral hemispheric asymmetry in humans. *Archives of Neurology, 32,* 239–246.

Warburton, E., Wise, R. J., Price, C. J., Weiller, C., Hadar, U., Ramsay, S., & Frackowiak, R. S. (1996). Noun and verb retrieval by normal subjects: Studies with PET. *Brain, 119,* 159–179.

Weintraub, S., Mesulam, M. M., & Kramer, L. (1981). Disturbances in prosody. A right-hemisphere contribution to language. *Archives of Neurology, 38*(12), 742–744.

Wernicke, C. (1874). *Der Aphasische Symptomenkomplex.* Breslau: Cohn & Weigert.

Wilson, F. A., Scalaidhe, S. P., & Goldman-Rakic, P. S. (1993). Dissociation of object and spatial processing domains in primate prefrontal cortex. *Science, 260,* 1955–1958.

Witelson, S. F. (1977). Anatomic asymmetry in the temporal lobes: Its documentation, phylogenesis and relationship to functional asymmetry. *Annals of the New York Academy of Sciences, 299,* 328–354.

Witelson, S. F. (1992). Cognitive neuroanatomy: A new era [editorial; comment]. *Neurology, 42,* 709–713.

Yamadori, A., Osumi, Y., Masuhara, S., & Okubo, M. (1977). Preservation of singing in Broca's aphasia. *Journal of Neurology, Neurosurgery and Psychiatry, 40*(3), 221–224.

Zangwill, O. (1975). Excision of Broca's area without persistent aphasia. In K. J. Zulch, O. Creutzfeldt, & G. C. Galbraith (Eds.), *Cerebral localization* (pp. 258–263). New York: Springer-Verlag.

Zatorre, R. J., Evans, A. C., & Meyer, E. (1994). Neural mechanisms underlying melodic perception and memory for pitch. *Journal of Neuroscience, 14,* 1908–1919.

Zatorre, R. J., Meyer, E., Gjedde, A., & Evans, A. C. (1996). PET studies of phonetic processing of speech: Review, replication, and reanalysis. *Cerebral Cortex, 6*(1), 21–30.

4

Gross Morphology and Architectonics of the Frontal Lobes

CAROL A. MILLER

The frontal lobes of the human cerebrum comprise, by far, the largest component of the cerebral cortex. They are also perhaps, functionally the least understood. Specific traumatic ablations such as that of Phineas Gage (Harlow, 1868) and the prefrontal lobotomies performed in the 1950s for behavioral modification of intractable schizophrenia provide some site-specific functional correlates. Congenital anomalies, including absence of the corpus callosum or split-brain surgical procedures have provided additional information (Gazzaniga, 1995; Gazzaniga, Bogen, & Sperry, 1962). More recently, the intensified investigations of certain neurodegenerative diseases such as Alzheimer's disease and the lobar dementias, including Pick's disease and frontotemporal dementia, have yielded additional insight at the regional and cellular level into behavioral correlates of frontal lobe function. This is especially exemplified by the selective vulnerability of certain neuronal subpopulations in these diseases (Lewis, Campbell, Terry, & Morrison, 1987; Miller, Rudnicka, Hinton, Blanks, & Kozlowski, 1987; Sinha, Hollen, & Miller, 1993).

Several levels of observations of the organization of the frontal lobes have emerged during the past century. Gross morphology, coupled with histochemical methods, including the silver impregnation methods of Bielschowsky and later, Golgi, initiated a detailed definition of the structure of the brain by Ramon y Cajal (1995). More recently, monoclonal antibodies (MAbs) have identified neuronal components including receptors specific to neurotransmitters and trophic factors, regulatory proteins, and cytoskeletal elements.

MAbs developed using immunogens of unknown specificities have also identified new neuronal specific markers, some of which define functionally related neuronal systems in the cerebral cortex of the cat (Hendry, Hockfield, Jones, & McKay, 1984). Some of the corresponding antigens are conserved phylogenetically (Miller & Benzer, 1983). In fact, it is now commonplace to search molecular databases for such information. Expression of neuron-specific genes, localized by *in situ* hybridization using cDNA probes, provides additional measures. This information demonstrates possible ontogenetically determined connectivities expressed architectonically, including within the frontal lobes.

In this chapter, I discuss the gross and microscopic architecture of the developing and mature frontal lobes defined by classic morphological techniques. These observations include molecular markers that define neuronal subpopulations.

DEVELOPMENT OF THE FRONTAL LOBES

Morphogenesis of the human brain is conveniently divided into two periods, with the end of the fifth month (20 weeks) of gestation as the demarcation point. The first half of fetal life includes the neural tube closure by day 28 (30–35 somites stage) (England, 1988), and the completion of the formation of the telencephalic vesicles by 10–12 weeks gestation (Figure 4.1A). Primitive neuroblasts are generated within the germinal matrix which lies adjacent to the cerebral ventricles (Figure 4.1B). A superficial cellular zone increases in width and later forms the white matter. Young neuroblasts migrate along radial glial fibers (Gadisseux & Evrard, 1985; Rakic, 1982). More recently, radial glia have been identified by the antibody to nestin, an intermediate filament protein in rodents thought to be neuronal in origin (Dahlstrand, Zimmerman, McKay, & Lendahl, 1992; McKay, 1989). The neuroblasts ultimately complete their migration to the cortical plate, with the oldest cells in the cortex located in layer I (Cajal–Retzius cells), and in the

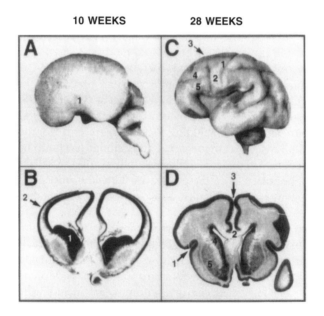

FIGURE 4.1. Development of the human frontal lobe. (A) At 10 weeks' gestation, the telencephalon, seen in lateral view, has a smooth external surface. A lateral fossa (1) inferiorally demarcates the anterior portion, which later develops into the frontal lobes. (B) A cross-section just anterior to this region reveals (1) the cellular germinal matrix just adjacent to the ventricles, and (2) a smooth cortical mantle (cresyl violet). (C) At 28 weeks, the frontal cortex has the primary and many secondary sulci in place, with well-defined motor, premotor, and prefrontal regions. Included are (1) central sulcus, (2) motor cortex (area 4), (3) superior, (4) middle, and (5) inferior frontal gyri. (D) Coronal section of the 28-week brain through the premotor area reveals a cellular cortical ribbon, broad white matter zone, depletion of the germinal matrix, and well-defined caudate nuclei and putamina: (1) Sylvian fissure; (2) corpus callosum; and (3) interhemispheric fissure. Adapted from Feess-Higgins and Larroche (1987). Copyright 1987 by Editions INSERM, Paris. Adapted by permission.

deepest layer, VI. These subpial (layer I) neurons originate from olfactory germinative epithelium and are stained with antibody to MAP-2 (Gadisseux, Goffinet, Lyon, & Evrard, 1992). These cells are transient, appearing around 16 weeks gestation and disappearing prior to birth (Duckett & Pearse, 1968). As migration proceeds, neurons occupy more superficial positions between the two primitive layers (Angevine & Sidman, 1961; Rakic, 1982). In the mature cortex at term, neurons forming layers V and VI are formed first and those in layer II last (Figure 4.2A).

This migratory pattern is the basis for the formation of the telencephalon into the two hemispheres and the development of the cortical mantle joined bilaterally by interhemispheric commissures, including the corpus callosum, by 10 weeks' gestation (Reed, Claireaux, & Bain, 1989). By the 12th week of gestation, the brain is externally smooth or lissencephalic (Figures 4.1A, 4.1B). Thereafter, the gyral pattern and concomitant sulcation is the result of this highly programmed migration. Sulcation begins with the callosal sulcus, Sylvian fissure and cingulate sulcus in place by 18 weeks' gestation. The frontal lobes are posteriorially demarcated from the parietal cortex by the Rolandic or central sulcus by 20 weeks' gestation, the time when neuronal migration is complete. By 24 weeks, differential growth including dendritic arborization, results in a six-layered isocortex or neocortex (Friede, 1989).

Subdivision of the frontal lobes occurs by 24 weeks with the appearance of the pre-Rolandic sulcus which segregates the primary motor from the premotor areas. The superior frontal and inferior frontal sulci appear by 25 and 28 weeks, respectively (Figure 4.1C). Thus, by the beginning of the third trimester, the division of the frontal lobes into three broad regions is complete. These include, the primary motor cortex (Brodmann's area 4, or MI), premotor (areas 6, 8, MII) and the prefrontal cortex. The lateral (areas, 9, 46, 10, 12), medial (areas 9, 25, 32, 14), and orbital (areas 13, 14, 11) components comprise the prefrontal cortex.

The morphogenesis of the cerebral cortices, especially the frontal lobes, is best understood by an unfortunate global failure of telencephalic migration beyond the lamina terminalis. This abnormality, termed "holoprosencephaly," is seen early, prior to 10 weeks gestation and results in partial or total absence of the frontal lobes and the corpus

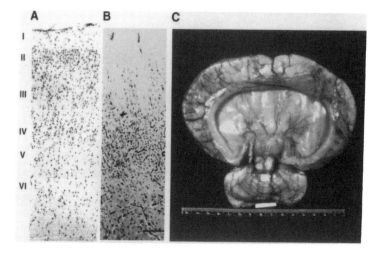

FIGURE 4.2. Developmental defects of the telencephalon. Nissl-stained sections of frontal cortex from (A) Normal full-term fetal brain. (B) Holoprosencephaly. In the latter, note failure of neuronal migration, especially of the superficial layers (bar = 140 μm). (C) Holoprosencephalic brain shows a single cerebral ventricle surrounded by a uniform cortex. Lobar formation is absent.

callosum (Figure 4.3C). In this instance, there is a single ventricle and, microscopically, a failure of formation of the normal six-layered cortex (Figure 4.2B). This defect, associated with chromosome 13 trisomy (Lyon & Beaugerie, 1988), is also coupled with the absence of limbic system development and a resultant arrhinencephaly.

Later in development, focal migration defects can occur with localized lissencephalic or smooth cortices, including the frontal lobe. Microscopically, there is abnormal, thickened cerebral lamination termed "pachygyria," yielding a four-layered cortex (not shown) rather than the normal six layers (Figure 4.2A).

GROSS MORPHOLOGY: ADULT

The gross morphology of the frontal lobes of the normal adult brain is demonstrated in Figure 4.3. The lateral convexity is posteriorly demarcated by the Rolandic or central sulcus, which separates the primary motor cortex (area 4) from the primary somatosensory cortex of the parietal lobe. Immediately anterior is the premotor region, which in

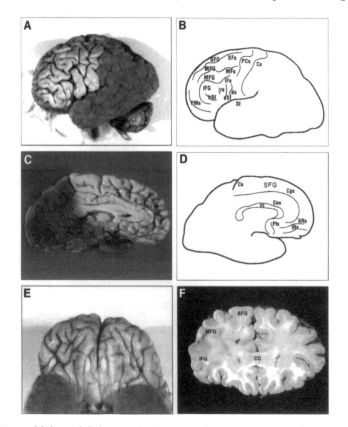

FIGURE 4.3. Frontal lobes adult human brain, external anatomy. (A) and (B) Lateral surface. (C) and (D) Medial surface. (E) Orbital view. (F) Coronal view. aSf, ascending ramus of Sylvian fissure; Cas, callosal sulcus; cc, corpus callosum; Cgs, cingulate sulcus; Cs, central sulcus; ds, diagonal sulcus; FMs, frontomarginal sulcus; FOs, fronto-orbital sulcus; hSf, horizontal ramus of the Sylvian fissure; IFG, inferior frontal gyrus; Ifs, inferior frontal sulcus; IRs, inferior rostral sulcus; MFG, middle frontal gyrus; MFs, middle frontal sulcus; PCs, precentral sulcus; Pfs, parolfactory sulcus; rs, radial sulcus; SFG, superior frontal gyrus; Sfs, superior frontal sulcus. Panels B and D from Rajkowska and Goldman-Rakic (1995). Copyright 1995 by Oxford University Press. Reprinted by permission.

turn, is segregated from the prefrontal region by the precentral sulcus. The premotor region serves as the primary association cortex of the primary motor region and is phylogenetically one of the regions specific to the human brain. The prefrontal region is divided into superior, middle and inferior gyri. The Sylvian fissure segregates these regions as well as the motor and premotor strips from the temporal and insular lobes. Broca's area, another unique human feature, resides along the Sylvian fissure and serves as a functional region for motor speech.

The medial face of the frontal lobes is bounded inferiorly by the corpus callosum. The cingulate sulcus separates the cingulate gyrus from the superior frontal gyrus and paracentral lobule (Figures 4.3C, 4.3D). The orbital surfaces shown in Figure 4.3E include the orbital gyri and, medially, the gyrus rectus upon which rests the olfactory nerve and bulb. A coronal section of the frontal lobes reveals the abundant white matter and the genu of the corpus callosum (Figure 4.3F).

ARCHITECTONICS

Classical morphological techniques have particularly used Nissl preparations, myelin stains or histochemical reactions for lipofuschin. The cortical ribbon of the frontal lobe consists entirely of the six-layered neocortex or the isocortex (Figure 4.4).

Based on studies in primates (Pandya & Yeterian, 1984), the isocortex with its six-layered organization evolved from archicortical (hippocampal) and paleocortical (olfactory or insular) cortices and gives rise to the proisocortex, which approximates six layers (Sanides, 1969, 1972). As Figure 4.4 illustrates, the isocortex is best visualized with the Nissl stain and consists of the molecular layer (I) the external granular layer (II), the external pyramidal layer (III), internal granule layer (IV), internal pyramidal layer (V), and multiform layer (VI). The width of the individual layers vary according to the relative numbers of pyramidal neurons in layers III and the granular neurons in layers II and IV (Figure 4.4).

Sanides (1972) proposed that the premotor and prefrontal cortices developed from two architectonic moieties: ventrally from the paleocortex of the olfactory region and insulae, which contributed to the granule cells of layers in areas 4 and 6, and dorsally, from the archicortex (hippocampus) of the paralimbic regions, giving rise to the dorsal regions of areas 4 and 6 and contributing to the pyramidal cell component. The same neuronal morphological subtypes are proposed for prefrontal regions, where granule cells predominate in layer IV (Figure 4.4C). Generally, the relative amounts of granule to pyramidal cells are based on the ratio of supragranule cells (layers II, III) to infragranule cells (layers V, VI) and are regionally determined, as shown in Figure 4.4A–4.4C. As Figure 4.4C demonstrates, association cortices (e.g., area 46) manifest more granule cell population than primary sensory or motor cortices (area 4) (Figure 4.4B). Primary association areas, such as the premotor cortex (area 6), (Figure 4.4A) have more laminar differentiation and supragranule component, whereas bimodal and multimodal association areas in the lateral prefrontal orbital and medial regions, respectively, show an increasing granular component.

HISTOLOGY OF CORTICAL NEURONS

Researchers have extensively studied the neuronal organization of the neocortex with the Golgi preparation, initially by Ramon y Cajal (1995). The value of this method is that

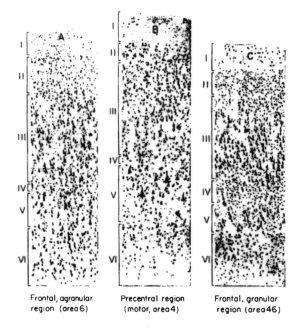

| Frontal, agranular region (area 6) | Precentral region (motor, area 4) | Frontal, granular region (area 46) |

FIGURE 4.4. Frontal cortex cytoarchitectonics: granular vs. agranular. Nissl-stained sections of representative areas of the frontal lobes: premotor (area 6)(A), motor (area 4)(B), and prefrontal (area 46)(C) cortices. In B, note the abundant, large pyramidal neurons in layers III and V; in C, the prominent granular layers II and IV, typical of the association cortical region. From Carpenter (1991). Copyright 1991 by Williams & Wilkins. Reprinted by permission.

within a plane of section, an entire neuron can be visualized, including its dendritic arbors, associated synaptic spines and axon.

Two main categories of neurons defined by this method are pyramidal and nonpyramidal cells (Jones, 1975). A third group, fusiform cells, is located in layer VI and lies vertical to the pial surface. Axons from all three neuronal types join in bundles oriented perpendicular to the pial surface and include both afferent and efferent processes. As Figure 4.5 illustrates, pyramidal neurons include a range of sizes and are found in layers II through VI, although most abundant in layers III and V. Axons of these projection neurons extend to adjacent ipsilateral areas to contralateral cortices and to various subcortical targets (Parnevelas, 1984). These cells are selectively vulnerable to degeneration in some cortical regions in Alzheimer's disease. Several functional regions of the frontal lobe mediate lateralized function. One example is Broca's area 45 in the left hemisphere. This region contains a subpopulation of magnocellular pyramidal neurons of layer III that are significantly larger than those in the homotopical region contralaterally (Hayes & Lewis, 1995). However, no such assymmetry is noted in layer III pyramidal neurons of primary motor cortex.

Nonpyramidal neurons or stellate cells are interneurons and show striking morphological variation, especially of their dendritic arbors (Figure 4.5). Many of these cells provide inhibitory input to the pyramidal neurons. They are classified according to their dendritic branching as multipolar, bitufted, and bipolar groups. They are further classified according to the abundance of their dendritic spines. For example, multipolar neurons are either smooth, sparsely spinous, or spinous. The majority of the multipolar or stellate neurons are basket cells which, in the superficial cortical layers, synapse with pyramidal cells and are inhibitory in function (Jones & Hendry, 1984).

Bitufted neurons are vertically oriented. They include a subgroup known as chandelier cells, which contact the initial segments of pyramidal neuron axons. The double bouquet cells are a second group of bitufted neurons which are in contact with pyramidal neuron dendrites. A third group, the horizontal cells of Cajal, lies in layer I, in contact

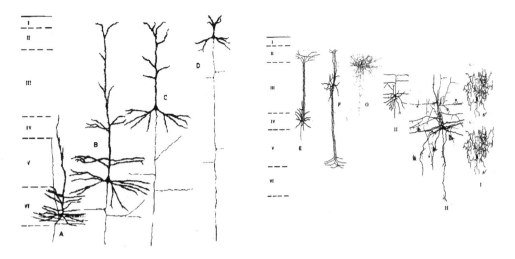

FIGURE 4.5. Neuronal subtypes in primates defined by Golgi stain. Camera lucida drawings of pyramidal neurons from the human cortex, show somas in layers II, III, V, and VI (A–D). Nonpyramidal neurons from several mammalian species are shown here in layers II–V and have striking variability in their dendritic arbors. *Left:* Pyramidal cells A–D. *Right:* Nonpyramidal cells. E, spiny stellate; F, double bouquet; G, small basket cell; H, large basket cells, I, chandelier cells. From Jones and Hendry (1984) and Jones and Peters (1984). Copyright 1984 by Plenum Press. Reprinted by permission.

with distal dendrites of pyramidal neurons. Bipolar or fusiform neurons, found predominantly in layer VI, have elongate perikarya and vertically oriented axons sending excitatory impulses across one or more cortical layers.

The sites of contacts of these various neurons are important distinguishing features that may have an impact on the specific functions of their target neurons. Clinical syndromes may specifically involve individual subgroups of interneurons, including within the frontal lobe. In Alzheimer's disease, pyramidal neurons are selectively vulnerable, specifically in the association cortices with increasing severity in multimodal cortices (Van Hoesen & Damasio, 1987). As Figure 4.6 shows, other neurons may be lost, for example, in Huntington's disease, and schizophrenia (Selemon, Rajkowska, & Goldman-Rakic, 1995).

MOLECULAR NEUROARCHITECTONICS

The identification, expression, and distribution of genes relevant to neuronal functions have come to the fore during the past two decades. The distribution of neuron-specific antigens of both known and yet unknown specificities has been defined with an array of monoclonal antibodies. These include pyramidal neuron-predominant antigens (Figures 4.7A, 4.7B), (Hinton, Blanks, Henderson, Rudnicka, & Miller, 1988) as well as proteoglycans specific to surfaces of interneurons (Figure 4.7C). Calcium-binding proteins, including parvalbumin and calbindin, have also been localized to γ-aminobutyric acidergic interneurons (Hendry et al., 1989; Hof & Morrison, 1991; Hof et al., 1991). Specifically, parvalbumin is localized to the chandelier and basket cells. Although the terminals of chandelier cells may be reduced in Alzheimer's disease (Fonseca, Soriano,

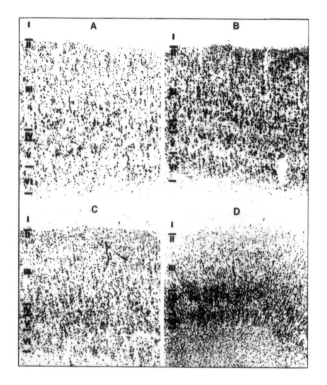

FIGURE 4.6. Abnormal layering of cortical neurons in disease. Selective loss of neurons is seen in Nissl-stained sections of area 9 in A, normal brain; B, schizophrenic brain; C, a schizoaffective cortex; D, a brain from a patient with Huntington's disease. Note that the schizophrenic and schizoaffective brains are slightly thinner than normal and layer IV is more prominent in the schizophrenic cortex relative to the normal control. In the Huntington's disease brain, there is a marked reduction of the infragranular (V, VI) layers (×44). From Selemon et al. (1995). Copyright 1995 by the American Medical Association. Reprinted by permission.

Ferrer, Martinez, & Tunon, 1993), these calcium-binding proteins may be neuroprotective and manifest resistence to hypoxia (Kalus & Senitz, 1996).

Another subset-specific and protective protein is nitric-oxide synthase (NOS), which is localized to nonpyramidal neurons of the cerebral cortex (Egberongbe et al., 1994), and Betz cells of the motorcortex (Wallace, Brown, Cox, & Harper, 1995). *In situ* hybridization also reveals decreased NOS in the subcortical white matter in the frontal cortex in Alzheimer's disease (Norris, Faull, & Emson, 1996).

A variety of receptors have been localized to certain neuronal subpopulations. Glutamate receptors (types 1 through 5) also are differentially distributed among pyramidal neurons and interneurons in humans and primates (Vickers et al., 1995; Vissavajjahala et al., 1996). Glycine receptors, identified by a specific MAb (4a) are found in frontal cortex, within apical dendrites of pyramidal neurons in layers III and V (Naas et al., 1991).

Signal transduction factors may be localized to neuronal subpopulations. The C-neu oncoprotein, a transmembrane tyrosine kinase, is expressed in pyramidal neurons in layer V (Kuhn & Miller, 1996).

Cytoskeletal proteins are specifically localized to certain neuronal subpopulations. SMI-32, an antibody against a nonphosphorylated neurofilament epitope, identifies a subpopulation of cortical neurons that preferentially degenerate in Alzheimer's and Huntington's disease (Gottron, Turetsky, & Choi, 1995). SMI-32 immunoreactive neurons fall into subgroups based on their perikaryal acetylcholinesterase activity (Mesulam & Geula, 1991). Similarly, large spindle neurons in the anterior cingulate cortex immunocytochemically have been shown to bear neurofilament triplet proteins but not calcium-binding proteins. These neurons are also lost in Alzheimer's disease (Nimchinsky, Vogt, Morrison, & Hof, 1995).

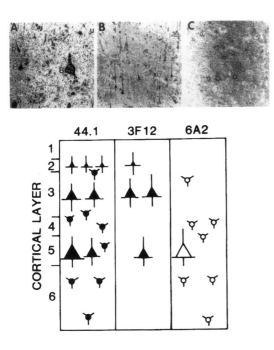

FIGURE 4.7. Neuronal subpopulations identified by monoclonal antibodies. Immunoperoxidase localization of neuronal antigens in motorcortex (area 4). In A, the pyramidal neurons (P) and the large pyramidal neurons or Betz cells (B) are identified by MAb 44.1 (×120). In B, a subpopulation of pyramidal neurons are seen with MAb 3F12 (×110). In C, there is surface labeling of nonpyramidal neurons (×100). Below, a schematic diagram of the motor cortex shows the distribution of the cell types identified by each of the three MAbs. MAb 44.1 reacts with a subpopulation of pyramidal cells and some nonpyramidal neurons, whereas MAb 3F12 reacts with a subpopulation of pyramidal neurons that overlaps with the MAb 44.1 population. MAb 6A2 reacts with rare pyramidal neurons and a subpopulation of nonpyramidal cells. From Hinton et al. (1988). Copyright 1988 by John Wiley & Sons. Reprinted by permission.

Neuropeptide- and neurotransmitter-related proteins are demonstrable in frontal cortex. Chromogranin A, found primarily in catecholaminergic neurons, is present in pyramidal and some nonpyramidal neurons (Adams, Ang, & Munoz, 1993). Biopsies of cerebral cortex reveal four neuropeptides (neuropeptide Y, somataglycan, substance P, and cholecystokinin) localized to interneurons. Cholecystokinin immunoreactivity is in neurons in supragranular layers, whereas the other three localize to the infragranular or deeper cortical layers. Cholecystokinin is the predominant peptide of the frontal lobe (Hornung, Detribolet, & Tork, 1992).

Neurotrophins are important in development and regeneration in the cerebral cortex. Although nerve growth factor (NGF) receptors are not identified by specific MAbs in young adults, expression of these receptors is seen in nonpyramidal neurons of laminae II–VI of temporal cortices in nondemented elderly as well as patients with Alzheimer's disease (Mufson & Kordower, 1992).

Large-surface macromolecules, primarily chondroitin sulfate proteoglycans, have been detected in regions of the frontal cortex by a variety of MAbs (Bertolotto, Rocca, Canavese, Migheli, & Schiffer, 1991; Hinton et al., 1988). Typically, these antigens are localized intersynaptically along somata of nonpyramidal neurons (Figure 4.7C). These proteoglycans enwrap presynaptic terminals and adjacent neuronal somas. Some of these are phosphacan molecules in other vertebrates (Rauch et al., 1991) or neurocan proteoglycans (Rauch, Karthikeyan, Maurel, Margolis, & Margolis, 1992). Chondroitin 4-sulfate proteoglycan are also found around some cortical neurons (Bertolotto et al., 1991). Other glycosylated molecules such as Gp135, a membrane glycoprotein, are enriched in the frontal cortex and are concentrated in neurons (Berglund, Thornell, & Stigbrand, 1991). This continually expanding panel of antibodies defines, both singly and combinatorially, a meshwork of neurons that may be functionally related and contribute to the unique and complex interactions within the frontal cortex. Some of these antibodies may be especially useful in the isolation of corresponding antigens, or cDNA species from expression libraries, and the identification of novel neuron-specific proteins which are expressed in the frontal lobes.

REFERENCES

Adams, L. A., Ang, L. C., & Munoz, D. G. (1993). Chromogranin-A, a soluble synaptic vesicle protein, is found in cortical neurons other than previously defined peptidergic neurons in the human neocortex. *Brain Research, 602*(2), 336–341.

Angevine, J. B., & Sidman, R. L. (1961). Autoradiographic study of cell migration during histogenesis of cerebral cortex of the mouse. *Nature, 192,* 766–768.

Berglund, E., Thornell, L. E., & Stigbrand, T. (1991). Intracerebral distribution of GP135: A new human brain glycoprotein. *Brain Research, 549*(2), 292–296.

Bertolotto, A., Rocca, G., Canavese, G., Migheli, A., & Schiffer, D. (1991). Chondroitin sulfate proteoglycan surrounds a subset of human and rat CNS neurons. *Journal of Neuroscience Research, 29*(2), 225–234.

Carpenter, M. B. (1991). *Core text of neuroanatomy.* Baltimore: Williams & Wilkins.

Dahlstrand, J., Zimmerman, L. B., McKay, R. D. G., & Lendahl, U. (1992). Characterization of the human nestin gene reveals a close evolutionary relationship to neurofilaments. *Journal of Cellular Science, 103,* 589–597.

Duckett, S., & Pearse, A. G. E. (1968). The cells of Cajal–Retzius in the developing human brain. *Journal of Anatomy, 102,* 183–188.

Egberongbe, Y. I., Gentleman, S. M., Falkai, P., Bogerts, B., Polak, J. M., & Roberts, G. W. (1994). The distribution of nitric-oxide synthase immunoreactivity in the human brain. *Neuroscience, 59*(3), 561–578.

England, M. A. (1988). Normal development of the central nervous system. In M. Levine, M. J. Bennett, & J. Punt (Eds.), *Fetal and neonatal neurology and neurosurgery* (Vol. 19, pp. 1–28). Edinburgh, NY: Churchill-Livingstone.

Feess-Higgins, A., & Larroche, J. C. (1987). *Development of the human fetal brain: An anatomical atlas.* Paris: Masson.

Fonseca, M., Soriano, E., Ferrer, I., Martinez, A., & Tunon, T. (1993). Chandelier cell axons identified by parvalbumin-immunoreactivity in the normal human temporal cortex and in Alzheimer's disease. *Neuroscience, 55*(4), 1107–1116.

Friede, R. L. (Ed.). (1989). *Developmental neuropathology.* New York: Springer-Verlag.

Gadisseux, J. F., & Evrard, P. (1985). Glial–neuronal relationship in the developing central nervous system. *Developmental Neurosurgery, 7,* 12–32.

Gadisseux, J. F., Goffinet, A. M., Lyon, G., & Evrard, P. (1992). The human transient subpial granular layer, immunohistochemical and ultrastructural analysis. *Journal of Comparative Neurology, 324,* 94–114.

Gazzaniga, M. (1995). Principles of human brain organization derived from split-brain studies. *Neuron, 14*(217), 228.

Gazzaniga, M. S. Bogen, J. E., & Sperry, R. W. (1962). Some functional effects of sectioning the cerebral commissure in man. *Proceedings of the National Academy of Sciences, USA, 48,* 1765–1769.

Gottron, F., Turetsky, D., & Choi, D. (1995). SM1-32 antibody against non-phosphorylated neurofilaments identifies a subpopulation of cultures cortical neurons hypersensitive to kainate toxicity. *Neuroscience Letters, 194,* 1–4.

Harlow, H. M. (1868). Recovery from the passage of an iron bar through the head. *Publication of the Massachusetts Medical Society, 2,* 327.

Hayes, T. L., & Lewis, D. A. (1995). Anatomical specialization of the anterior motor speech area—Hemispheric differences in magnopyramidal neurons. *Brain and Language, 49,* 289–308.

Hendry, S. H. C., Hockfield, S., Jones, E. G., & McKay, R. (1984). Monoclonal antibody that identifies subsets of neurons in the central visual system of monkey and cat. *Nature, 307,* 267–269.

Hendry, S. H. C., Jones, E. G., Emson, P. C., Lawson, D. E. M., Heizmann, C. W., & Strect, P. (1989). Two classes of cortical GABA neurons defined by differential calcium binding protein immunoreactivities. *Experimental Brain Research, 76,* 467–472.

Hinton, D. R., Blanks, J., Henderson, V., Rudnicka, M., & Miller, C. A. (1988). Monoclonal antibodies identify subpopulations in the human nervous system. *Journal of Comparative Neurology, 267,* 398–408.

Hof, P. R., Cox, K., Young, W. G., Celio, M. R., Rogers, J., & Morrison, J. H. (1991). Parvalbumin-immunoreactive neurons in the neocortex are resistant to degeneration in Alzheimer's disease. *Journal of Neuropathy and Experimental Neurology, 50,* 451–462.

Hof, P. R., & Morrison, J. H. (1991). Neocortical neuronal subpopulations labelled by a monoclonal antibody to calbindin exhibit differential vulnerability in Alzheimer's disease. *Experimental Neurology, 111,* 293–301.

Hornung, J. P., Detribolet, N., & Tork, I. (1992). Morphology and distribution of neuropeptide containing neurons in human cerebral cortex. *Journal of Neuroscience, 51(2),* 363–375.

Jones, E. G., (1975). Varieties and distribution of non-pyramidal cells in the somatic sensory cortex of the squirrel monkey. *Journal of Comparative Neurology, 160,* 205–267.

Jones, E. G., & Hendry, S. (1984). Basket cells. In E. G. Jones & A. Peters (Eds.), *Cerebral cortex* (Vol. 1, pp. 309–336). New York: Plenum Press.

Jones, E. G., & Peters, A. (Eds.). (1984). *Cerebral cortex,* (Vols. 1 and 2). New York: Plenum Press.

Kalus, P., & Senitz, D. (1996). Parvalbumin in the human anterior cingulate cortex—Morphological heterogeneity of inhibitory interneurons. *Brain Research, 729(1),* 45–54.

Kuhn, P. E., & Miller, M. W. (1996). C-neu oncoprotein in developing rostral cerebral cortex: Relationship to epidermal growth factor receptor. *Journal of Comparative Neurology, 372(2),* 189–203.

Lewis, D. A., Campbell, M. J., Terry, R. D., & Morrison, J. H. (1987). Laminar and regional distributions of neurofibrillary tangles and neuritic plaques in Alzheimer's disease: A quantitative study of visual and auditory cortices. *Journal of Neuroscience, 7,* 1799–1808.

Lyon, G., & Beaugerie, A. (1988). Congenital developmental malformations: In M. Levine, M. J. Bennett, & J. Punt (Eds.), *Fetal and neonatal neurology and neurosurgery* (Vol. 19, pp. 231–248). Edinburgh, NY: Churchill-Livingstone.

McKay, R. (1989). The origins of cellular diversity in the mammalian central nervous system. *Cell, 58,* 815–821.

Mesulam, M., & Geula, C. (1991). Differential distribution of a neurofilament protein epitope in acetylcholinesterase-rich neurons of human cerebral neocortex. *Brain Research, 544(1),* 169–173.

Miller, C. A., & Benzer, S. (1983). Monoclonal antibody cross-reaction between *Drosophila* and human brain. *Proceedings of the National Academy of Science, USA, 80,* 7641–7648.

Miller, C. A., Rudnicka, M., Hinton, D. R., Blanks, J. C., & Kozlowski, M. (1987). Monoclonal antibody identification of subpopulations of cerebral cortical neurons affected in Alzheimer's disease. *Proceedings of the National Academy of Science, USA, 84,* 8657–8661.

Mufson, E. J., & Kordower, J. H. (1992). Cortical neurons express nerve growth factor receptors in advanced age and Alzheimer's disease. *Proceedings of the National Academy of Science, USA, 89(2),* 569–573.

Naas, E., Zilles, K., Gnahn, H., Betz, H., Becker, C. M., & Schroder, H. (1991). Glycine receptor immunoreactivity in rat and human cerebral cortex. *Brain Research, 561(1),* 139–146.

Nimchinsky, E. A., Vogt, B. A., Morrison, J. H., & Hof, P. R. (1995). Spindle neurons of the human anterior cingulate cortex. *Journal of Comparative Neurology, 355(1),* 27–37.

Norris, P., Faull, R. L. M., Emson, P. C. (1996). Neuronal nitric oxide synthase (NNDS) messenger-RNA expression and NADPH-Diaphorase staining in the frontal-cortex, visual cortex and hippocampus of control and Alzheimer's disease brains. *Molecular Brain Research, 41,* 36–49.

Pandya, D. N., & Yeterian, E. H. (1984). Architecture and connections of cortical association area in cerebral cortex. In E. G. Jones & A. Peters (Eds.), *Cerebral cortex* (Vol. 4, pp. 3–55). New York: Plenum Press.

Parnevelas, J. G. (1984). Physiological properties of identified neurons. In E. G. Jones & A. Peters (Eds.), *Cerebral cortex* (Vol. 2, pp. 205–236). New York: Plenum Press.

Rajkowska, G., & Goldman-Rakic, P. (1995). Cytoarchitectonic definition of pre-frontal areas in the normal human cortex II. Variability in locations of areas 9 and 46, and relationship to the Talairach coordinate system. *Cerebral Cortex, 5,* 323–337.

Rakic, P. (1982). Early developmental events: Cell-lineages, acquisition of neuronal positions and a real and laminar development. *Neuroscience Research Program Bulletin, 20*(4), 439–451.

Ramon y Cajal, S. (1995). *Histology of the nervous system* (Trans. N. Swanson & L. W. Swanson). New York: Oxford University Press.

Rauch, U., Gao, P., Janetzko, A., Flaccus, A., Hilgenberg, L., Tekotte, H., Margolis, R. K., & Margolis, R. U. (1991). Isolation and characterization of developmentally regulated chondroitin sulfate and chondroitin/keratan sulfate proteoglycans of brain identified with monoclonal antibodies. *Journal of Biological Chemistry, 266,* 14785–14801.

Rauch, U., Karthikeyan, L., Maurel, P., Margolis, R., & Margolis, R. K. (1992). Cloning and primary structure of neurocan, a developmentally regulated, aggregating chondroitin sulfate proteoglycan of brain. *Journal of Biological Chemistry, 267,* 19536–19547.

Reed, G. B., Claireaux, A. E., & Bain, A. D. (Eds.). (1989). *Diseases of the fetus and newborn.* St. Louis: Mosby.

Sanides, F. (1969). Comparative architectonics of the neocortex of mammals and their evolutionary interpretation. *Annals of the New York Academy of Science, 167,* 404–423.

Sanides, F. (1972). Representation in the cerebral cortex and its gene lamination pattern. In G. F. Bourne (Ed.), *Structure and function of nervous tissue* (Vol. 5, pp. 329–455). New York: Academic Press.

Selemon, L. D., Rajkowska, G., & Goldman-Rakic, P. S. (1995). Abnormally high neuronal density in the schizophrenic cortex: A morphometric analysis of prefrontal area 9 and occipital area 7. *Archives of General Psychiatry, 52,* 805–818.

Sinha, U. K., Hollen, K. M., & Miller, C. A. (1993). Abnormal neuritic architecture identified by DI-I in Pick's disease. *Journal of Neuropathy and Experimental Neurology, 52,* 411–418.

VanHoesen, G. W. & Damasio, A. R. (1987). Neural correlates of cognitive impairment in Alzheimer's disease. In F. Plum (Ed.), *Higher functions of the nervous system (the handbook of physiology).* Bethesda, MD: American Physiologic Society.

Vickers, J. C., Huntley, G. W., Hof, P. R., Bederson, J., Defelipe, J., & Morrison, J. H. (1995). Immunocytochemical localization of non-NMDA ionotropic excitatory amino acid receptor subunits in human neocortex. *Brain Research, 671*(1), 175–180.

Vissavajjhala, P., Janssen, W. G. M., Hu, Y. L., Gazzaley, A. H., Moran, T., Hof, P. R., & Morrison, J. H. (1996). Synaptic distribution of the AMPA-GLU-R2 subunit and its co-localization with calcium-binding proteins in rat cerebral cortex: An immunohistochemical study using a GLU-R2-specific monoclonal antibody. *Journal of Experimental Neurology, 142*(2), 296–312.

Wallace, M. N., Brown, I. E., Cox, A. T., & Harper, M. S. (1995). Pyramidal neurons in human precentral gyrus contains nitric-oxidase synthase. *Neuroreport, 6,* 2532–2536.

5

Evolution and Phylogenetic History of the Frontal Lobes

CAROL A. BANYAS

There is grandeur in this view of life, with its several powers,
having been originally breathed into a few forms or into one;
and that, whilst this planet has gone cycling on according to
the fixed law of gravity, from so simple a beginning endless
forms most beautiful and most wonderful have been, and are
being evolved.

—DARWIN (1958, p. 450)

Where do we come from? Where are we going? Of all animals, humans have a deep desire to understand their origins and continue to question the beginnings of life and the reasons for our existence. Man has been concerned with his origin throughout history, particularly the evolution of his underlying thinking process, mechanism of behavior, and social functioning of the brain. Most individuals with scientific training believe that man descended from animal ancestors and that the unique cerebral development is fundamental to human behavior, thinking, and self-understanding. The ultimate concern now is for our continued survival and the future of man.

How did man achieve his unique position among the higher animals? Before the present century no real basis of discussion existed for this question, and today a definite answer cannot be determined. However, a partial answer can be offered to the question of man's origin in which the essentials of man's phylogeny can be supported by an immense wealth of material and literature. Observations have been based on factual data drawn from the fields of paleontology, comparative anatomy, neurology, neuroscience and cultural history.

EVOLUTIONARY THEORISTS

For many years, there seemed to be little doubt of the Biblical account of creation. It was believed that the human species and the universe was formed by a grand design. It was not until the 19th century that other interpretations were made based on the observations of nature. Human beings were no longer considered a creation but, rather, part of a history of evolvement through natural selection.

In 1735, Carolus Linnaeus, in his *Systema Naturae,* proposed a daring new idea to classify humans close to a few great apes. He also proposed a system of nomenclature for classifying living beings which he felt accounted for the plan of divine creation.

In 1809, Jean Baptiste Chevalier de Lamarck, in his *Philosophie Zoologique* wrote that all organisms living today came gradually from primitive forms such as apes. He also believed that new forms were being spontaneously created, then carried up the chain. He also postulated another mechanism, which carries his name, Lamarckism: the inheritance of acquired characteristics (Ruse, 1996). Unfortunately, his ideas were not widely accepted during that time.

The fundamental idea that humans might be descended from apes did not take shape until Charles Darwin published his theory of evolution in *Origin of Species.* He saw the living world as changing in that new species emerge while others fall into extinction and demonstrated that existing plants and animals cannot have been separately created in their present forms but must have evolved from earlier forms by slow transformation and that more are born than can survive. He also believed that all animals share a common descent. He even speculated that all life, including both plants and animals, might have come from a common ancestor. Finally, he believed that change occurred through natural selection, whereby those with improved characteristics leave behind the most offspring which favors some animals over others.

NERVOUS SYSTEM DEVELOPMENT

Invertebrate

Animals such as jellyfish had the first developed nervous systems, which were simple nerve nets. This represented a great advance because their behavior demonstrated the ability to swim for nutrients. These multicellular organisms move through muscle contraction and communicate through an electrochemical transmission process at the cell membrane via neurons. This primitive mechanism became fixed in evolution.

Many invertebrates, such as the earthworm, have simple nervous systems, consisting of only a few thousand neurons. This system is a collection of neurons called ganglia concerned with segments of the animal body. Within each ganglion there are sensory input fibers and output motor fibers. These actions are coordinated by nerve pathways that interconnect them. The ganglion at the head of the worm is larger than the others and performs the coordinating role. The head ganglion was found to be the beginning of a brain. Over the course of evolution, the head ganglion became larger and took more command over the other ganglia.

So far, it is known that neurons in animals, from jellyfish to humans, use the same electrochemical mechanisms for conducting information. To progress to more sophisticated and adaptive behaviors, more neurons needed to be organized in more complex ways.

Vertebrate

The vertebrates fall into five classes. Fish are the lowest, then amphibians, and reptiles. From the latter arose the two remaining classes, the birds and mammals. The two most important features of the phylogenetic development of the vertebrates were bilateral symmetry and cephalization or progressive development of the anterior end of the animal (Johnston, 1906). This involved the development of organs of special senses, enlargement of the brain, formation of a cranium to protect the brain, the disappearance of some myotomes and a change in position of others, a shift in position of cranial nerve nuclei, and, finally, extensive growth of the forebrain.

A vertebrate nervous system of the simplest type began with development of the neural tube formed by infolding dorsal ectoderm surrounding a central lumen. Intersegmental connections between sensory and motor elements allowed for a behavioral repertoire of simple reflexive acts. For complex behaviors to occur, intersegmental connections developed at the rostral part of the neural tube that became the brain. This process of encephalization has occurred to different degrees in the brains of the five vertebrae classes. The brain operated as a control center for the input of information from distance receptors, and visual, auditory, and olfactory inputs converged directly upon the brain, giving rise to stimulus behavior. The output of the system developed connections from the brain to the segments of the neural tube and then to muscles.

BRAIN DEVELOPMENT

When neurons performing a common function move closer together, as the phylogenetic scale is ascended, synaptic relations among the cells within these groups becomes more complex. The general trend of evolution toward greater differentiation and complexity increases the capacity for interpretation of sensory data and behavioral responses.

Phylogeny refers to the individual species of vertebrates to all other species, living or extinct, with respect to their place in evolution (Sarnot & Netsky, 1981). The arbitrary place that each class of vertebrates and each species occupies on the phylogenetic scale is based on many anatomical features of the body and brain.

The vertebrate brain represents the continuation of a trend from the primitive invertebrate nervous system. A vast increase in the number of neurons developed in the vertebrate brain which is the reason for the generation of more complex aspects of behavior and experience. The most outstanding feature of vertebrates is a segmented backbone (spinal cord). Their muscular systems are well developed, and their nervous systems are highly coordinated. They have a three-part brain and well-developed senses, as well as respiratory and circulatory systems.

The brain of primitive vertebrates, such as fish or even amphibia, is essentially brainstem. The forebrain is no more than an olfactory center which receives impulses almost exclusively. The structure of the reticular system stems from the very beginning of the evolutionary process. The functions originally controlled by lower systems were taken over by the cerebrum. This shift of dominance to the higher centers, encephalization, has been a major principle in the evolution of the brain.

The basic plan of the vertebrate brain can be seen most clearly in the stages of embryological development, because the growth and development of the individual animal from the fertilized ovum to the newborn tend to reflect evolutionary history. In the first stage, the most rostral part of the neural tube develops three swellings that will later become the hindbrain, midbrain, and forebrain. At the second stage, the forebrain divides into the telencephalon and diencephalon (thalamus and hypothalamus); the olfactory bulbs become differentiated. In the hindbrain, the cerebellum, pons, and medulla then form. The dorsal part of the midbrain develops the superior and inferior colliculi. Stage three occurs in the mammal, where there is considerable development of the telencephalon, ultimately to form the cerebral hemispheres. The telencephalon bulges outward and folds back over the brainstem to accommodate itself within the confines within the skull. The older parts of the telencephalon become unfolded between the outermost cortical layer and the thalamus and form the archicortex and the striatum or basal ganglia. The most recently developed part of the telencehpalon is the neopallium or the neocortex. This folded neural tissue reaches its greatest level of development in man.

The three divisions of the telencephalon are the paleocortex, which is a phylogenetically old structure seen as pyriform lobes; the archicortex, which is represented by the hippocampus and the amygdala; and the neocortex, which appears first in reptiles and develops in mammals (Oakley & Plotkin, 1979).

The cerebrum of the lowest vertebrates is only a small smooth (lissencephalic) pair of lobes at the forepart of the brain. Bulbs which project from them receive sensations of smell and other senses are received by the cerebrum itself. Other functions are responded to lower parts of the brain. Reptiles have a more advanced cerebrum with a small patch on its surface (neopallium) which assumes more sensory and motor functions. It specifically exists in an area in which associations can be stored from reflex action and simple conditioning where patterns are formed. In a primitive mammal (insectivorous shrew), most of the cortex is related to smell; the paleopallium is large with a prominent bulb in front, where the olfactory nerve leads from the nose. The neopallium is still small. In a monkey (macaque), the neopallium is expanded and olfactory areas are recessed under the forebrain. The neopallium in mammals extends over other parts of the brain and expands its own surface area so greatly that it folds in on itself to form cortices convoluted with gyri and sulci (gyrencephalic brains). The addition of sulci and gyri can be seen in the progressively more convoluted brains of monkeys, apes, and man. In higher primates and man, the brain is so greatly enlarged that there is a vast capacity in which associations can be stored.

The last step in phylogenetic development is the cerebral cortex, which brings to order all systemic functions of the brain. To understand the functional organization of the cortex, the overall significance of the cortex as a relay station for different systems must be described.

The evolution of the cortex leads to tremendous changes in practically all parts of the brain. The dorsal part of the thalamus becomes dependent on the cortex in that it receives fibers carrying sensory messages, filters them, and sends them on to the cortex. The midbrain divides into dorsal and ventral regions and then develops superior and inferior colliculi. In fish and amphibians, the superior colliculus, or optic tectum, becomes the most important visual center.

The basal ganglia originates in the walls of the telencephalon and moves centrally within the cerebral hemispheres. The reptilian forebrain has a somewhat developed striatum and the neocortex emerges dorsally.

In the mammalian forebrain, the basal ganglia occupy a central position within the hemispheres and direct striatal–neocortical connections are established. Also in mammalian telencephalon is the formation of interhemispheric connections via the corpus callosum, where information is exchanged between the hemispheres. Other commissures are represented in all vertebrate classes: The anterior commissure interconnects archicortical structures and also the neocortical temporal lobe in primates. Commissures of the superior and inferior colliculi are also found in all species.

During evolution, the neocortex increases in size faster than the archicortex and paleocortex. The limbic system is formed when the archicortex (hippocampus and amygdala) becomes medially displaced and the paleocortex (pyriform lobes) is displaced laterobasally and both become confined to a belt around the stalk of the forebrain (Creutzfeldt, 1995). These structures are interconnected with the thalamus and hypothalamus and begin to develop pathways to the cortex.

All vertebrates have developed segmental motor connections from the brain, which control specific motor areas. In fish, amphibians, and reptiles, the mesencephalon and diencephalon form these connections; in mammals, telencephalic regions become dominant as motor areas but the phylogenetically older connections continue. The most primitive motor system found in all vertebrates is a multisynaptic pathway through the reticular formation—the reticulospinal tract.

The medial longitutidinal fasciculus is the oldest descending tract in the central nervous system (CNS) carrying information from the vestibular nuclei and the cerebellum to the spinal cord. In lower vertebrate brains, the main center of coordination is the optic tectum which has direct motor control via the tectospinal tract. In more encephalized vertebrates, the lateral vestibular tract is an important spinal input of vestibular information. The reticulospinal tract is still to be found, but it has developed a direct connection, bypassing the old multisynaptic pathway.

The development of the forebrain allows a shifting of motor control into higher regions. The extrapyramidal motor system becomes developed in recently evolved vertebrates and is centered around the basal ganglia. In mammals, the basal ganglia has many reciprocal connections with many areas of the neocortex, including motor and sensory cortex.

Mammals also have developed another direct system of motor control, known as the pyramidal motor system. This pyramidal tract descends through the brainstem and decussates in the medulla, then goes to the spinal cord, and is most important in primates and man. Lesions of this system produce only transient deficits in other mammals, whereas in primates, long-lasting or permanent deficits in fine, skilled movements may be seen (Oakley & Plotkin, 1979).

EVOLUTION OF EARLY HUMANS

To provide a clear understanding of the phylogeny of the frontal lobe, it is necessary to further describe the evolution of man and the intricacies of the brain as it evolved in the beginning. This includes the origin of early humans and its most accurate time lines, the environment, climate, fossil records, and their periods of extinction.

Primate Classification

There are two groups in the classification of the order of Primates: the archaic primates (plesiadapiformes), which became extinct, and the modern primates (euprimates). Primate classification consists of two major groups: the suborder of Prosimii (prosimians), which includes lemurs, lorises, galagos and tarsiers, and the suborder of Anthropedia, which includes simians or higher primates (e.g., monkeys, apes, and humans).

To illustrate a continuing process of evolutionary change, biologists developed evolutionary trees allocating species to groups based on their body structures and giving them individually distinctive names (nomenclature) and later studying the patterns of relationships. Phylogenetic relationships are inferred on patterns of similarities shared between species; however, because of the rates of evolution, geological age, and embryonic development, certain conditions can obscure findings.

One of the most important features that distinguishes primates from other mammals is their ability to adapt to living in trees. Another important difference between primates and mammals is that the former rely on vision rather than olfaction; consequently, the optic nerve gets much bigger and contains more fibers than in other forms.

The mammalian progression to man may have started with Plesiadapis, a fossil prosimian resembling a rodent, which lived about 70 million years ago and disappeared in an unknown time. This gap was closed by the finding of *Ramapithecus,* dating back 12 million years, who was considered part of the hominidae family because he could walk erect and oppose fingers and thumb. The successor of *Ramapithecus* formed two species of *Australopithecus,* who had greater mobility of the thumb and a hand grasp. This was a milestone in evolution (Sarnot & Netsky, 1981).

Australopithecines

In 1924, a fossil with the skull of a baboon was discovered near the South African town of Taung. It became one of the most important fossil finds in the history of anthropology. Professor Raymond Dart (1967), an Australian born anatomist working in Johannesburg, named this find *Australopithecus africanus,* the southern ape, which, in his view, was the missing link between apes and humans. This Taung skull had a brain case not much bigger than an ape, and the skull showed a configuration that represented an ape-brained animal that stood upright (Stanley, 1996).

Several distinct groups of Australopithecines were found. One was composed of small "gracile" forms: *Australopithicus afarensis* and *Australopithecus africanus.* These were the most ape-like dating back 4.4 million years ago. The other group consisted of three "robust forms," namely, *Australopithecus robustus.* This genus persisted for approximately 1.5 million years without much evolutionary change.

The bodily skeleton of *Australopithecus* appeared more human than ape-like, but this was not true for the skull. A skull's cranial capacity appears to be a good measure of the weight of the brain housed in it. The estimated volumes of the skulls ranged from about 438–485 cubic centimeters. It has been estimated that these cranial capacities are similar in size to chimps and orangutans. Human cranial capacity is between 1,280 and 1,560 cubic centimeters.

The physique of the species *Australopithecus afrensis* can be attributed to a discovery of Donald Johanson in 1974 of the skeleton he named "Lucy" (Johanson & Shreer, 1989). Her bones were those of a bipedal animal. In 1978, Mary Leakey and Paul Abell came upon a set of footprints in North Tanzania which provided evidence that *Australopithecus* spent some time walking upright (Leakey, 1994). However, in the early 1980s, further study revealed that *Australopithecus* had features that made them much more adept at tree climbing.

Australopithecus had a brain that was only slightly larger than the brain of a chimpanzee. They produced no stone tools or other artifacts, which suggests that their mental capacity was more ape-like than human. Similar to chimps, they passed information from generation to generation by example and imitation of behaviors rather than by language and symbols.

Darwin believed the development of upright posture and tool making would lead to the evolution of a more human-like brain. However, the emergence of bipedal from quadrupedal posture did not lead to the development of a larger brain in the *Australopi-*

thecus and they did not make tools, yet this species survived 100,000 generations or more.

Dr. Steven M. Stanley (1996), professor of paleobiology at Johns Hopkins University, proposes a compelling and provocative theory that addresses the evolutionary stability of *Australopithecus* and the sudden origin of *Homo* (the origin of the human genus) and its emergence of a larger brain. What led to the transition from *Australopithecus* to *Homo,* and what prevented *Australopithecus* from evolving a much larger brain?

Stanley argues that before the transition of development of a larger brain, our ancestors had to abandon the habit of regularly climbing trees. He believed that abandoning the trees was an evolutionary requisite for large brains, because the animals that evolved into *Homo* needed to have their hand free to carry and tend to their helpless infants. No mother could have climbed trees every day with an infant under one arm.

Highly immature infants are unique to humans, among all primates. Human offspring remain helpless and uncoordinated for many months after birth; young chimpanzees and orangutans are mature enough to crawl and cling to their active mothers almost immediately. Humans, during the first year of life, have a brain that is twice as large as that of an adult chimpanzee. Yet it is this delayed development for humans, in which infants are weak and helpless, that is responsible for the cerebral expansion that occurs during the first year.

Stanley argues that this human pattern of brain growth resulted in an "evolutionary compromise"—the restriction of the mother. This was the price that early *Homo* paid for its large brain. This helplessness after birth could never have evolved in a group of animals that climbed trees.

By the mid-1980s the current literature on human evolution began to show arguments that *Australopithecus* spent a great deal of time in trees, thus substantiating Stanley's theory. It would appear that *Australopithecus* probably was both terrestrial and a tree climber. Evidence showed that they did not match apes in their pattern of climbing. *Australopithecus* perhaps used their forelimbs primarily for ascending trees and for grasping branches as they walked horizontally along supportive limbs. However, the question still to be answered was, how did a large brain then abruptly evolve?

Stanley also gives the argument that about 2.5 million years ago an environmental change, called the "Modern Ice Age," forced the transition from *Australopithecus* to *Homo.* During this period, the rain forests of Africa shrunk, which was the beginning of the demise of *Australopithecus.* The woodland habitat narrowed, and they were unable to rely on trees for refuge. There was also increased predation that may have brought about the demise of *Australopithecus.*

Emergence of *Homo*

What was it that transformed prehuman creatures into modern man? The unfolding drama of human origins still eludes us, but the many discoveries during the past several decades have brought us closer to be able to say what made us human. We have been around for about 100,000 years or so. One of our forebears of the *Hominidae* class, *Homo erectus* seemed to have lasted for 1.5 million years and before that, *Homo habilis* occupied Africa for about 1 million years. Monkeys evolved about 40 million years ago followed by apes 10 million years ago, and last of all, the hominids came between 14 and 4 million years ago. Of the primates, the gorilla and the orangutan are distant relatives to man, whereas the chimpanzee is the closest. Unfortunately, the fossil record for hominids is incomplete and for apes almost blank, to know how modern man and the ancestral hominids have evolved from a common ancestor. There is a major gap between 8 and 4 million years ago. When considering the incomplete record of human evolution, the thinking is that new human ancestors suddenly appear, as do intermediate forms (Leakey, 1981).

Is it conceivable that evolution has progressed in stages and led to the emergence of man or did man evolve through the same process as the rest of evolution (random mutation, gene arrangement and conditions of selection)? Or is our existence assumed by some other forces not yet identified (Rensch, 1972)?

What traits separate modern humans from lower animals? With the emergence of *Homo*, traits that require large frontal lobes began to appear, particularly the ability to create. This ability involved the capacity to construct tools and weapons. This ability also brought with it the capacity to construct a language. The expanding frontal lobes of *Homo* allowed them to develop and plan strategies and plan for the future. Social communication and cooperation also evolved.

Homo habilis

In 1961, Mary Leakey and her son Richard discovered in Olduvai Gorge a skull of a new human species, *Homo habilis*. They lived in Africa 2 to 1.8 million years ago. They differed from *Australopithecus* in their larger size, a flattened face with no ridge above the eyes, smaller molars and premolars, and a much bigger brain, with a capacity up to 800 cubic centimeters or approximately 50 cubic inches. However, the habilines were in many ways more similar to Austalopithecines than humans. In 1964, Louis Leakey named this new type of hominid *Homo habilis*—"skillful person," because the study of its fingers revealed an ability to grip that was sufficient for making stone tools (Thomas, 1995).

Thus, the habilines appeared to be a borderline hominid species, a transition type for *Australopithecus* to *Homo erectus*. Their tools were very primitive and there did not appear to be a great cognitive difference from the *Australopithecines* (Donald, 1993).

Homo erectus

The situation changed drastically with the advent of the next species of hominid, *Homo erectus*. The key innovation in erectus was the emergence of the most basic level of human representation, the ability to mimic, or reenact events (Donald, 1993). *Homo erectus* were different from *Australopithecus* and habilines in that they were more human in appearance, brain size, stature, and culture. With this species, a major advance in human evolution emerged.

There was a migration out of Africa by *Homo erectus* approximately 1 million years ago. *Homo erectus*—also called pithecanthropes, a name used for the *Java Homo erectus*—gradually spread throughout the temperate regions of the Old World. *Homo erectus* eventually inhabited North Africa, Asia (Peking), and probably Europe. The oldest *Homo erectus* populations were descendants of *Homo habilis* and showed features of a more evolved species. They appeared approximately 1.7 million years ago in the Lake Turkana region of Kenya. The stature of *Homo erectus* was similar to man with some reaching a height of 5½ feet. Their cranial capacity varied between 775 and 1,250 cubic centimeters or 80% of modern human capacity and approximately 47–76 cubic inches. They occupied the Old World for approximately 1.5 million years. Overall, they looked human but had a prominent brow ridge over the eyes and a forehead sloped back.

Endocasts showed landmarks of the Rolandic and Sylvian fissures, large temporal and frontal lobes, an expanded parietal lobe, and an enlarged cerebellum. With the expansion of the brain was an enlargement and sophistication of tool manufacture. The main tools were hand axes, choppers, scrapers, and points. They were of higher quality than previous habilines in that a certain amount of planning and organization was required to produce them.

There is also evidence of a cultural advance for *Homo erectus* in the use of fire, which occurred around 450,000 years ago. Some anthropologists believe that the first humans had to overcome their fear of fire, which is shared with all animals. This control of fire involved a change in behavior and the capacity to create (Thomas, 1995). This use of fire also brought people together, the beginnings of social and family cohesion.

Many historians are also convinced that *Homo erectus* communicated by speech. The extent of their activities seemed to have called for a highly developed means of communication, though others disagree and this remains controversial in the literature in that others believe that language was a more recent phenomenon.

Neanderthals

In 1856 a unique set of skull and bones were uncovered in the Neander Valley near Duesseldorf, Germany. There was a flattened cranium and a heavy ridge above large eye sockets. Similar fossils were also found in Africa, and other specimens were found throughout Europe. There is little question that the *Neanderthal* lineage was established in Europe, slightly before 300,000 years ago. Some workers refer to them as "archiac *Homo sapiens*"; however, they have come into view as a distinct species, for which the name *Homo neanderthalis* takes precedence.

The greatest mystery about *Neanderthals* is their brain size, which has been estimated to be approximately 13% greater than humans. The average *Neanderthal* brain measured 1,500 milliliters in volume, whereas humans are 1,400 milliliters. However, their crania were not shaped as humans. They exhibited a large brow ridge, a long sloping forehead formed at the front of a flat-topped brain case. It appears that less of the *Neanderthal* brain than ours was concentrated in the frontal lobes, yet the large brain size allowed for large cerebral hemispheres.

The need to have a large volume of brain tissue dependent on motor activities was evident in the physical robustness of *Neanderthals*. An average male stood about 5½ feet but was very sturdy, most likely outweighing humans. He was long-waisted with short legs and much brawnier than humans. They also lacked a predominant chin.

Neanderthals possessed advanced skills using fire for cooking and heating. They may have crafted leather and fur garments and had a relatively advanced tool- and weapon-making culture. They produced up to 60 identifiable items, including knives, scrapers, and projectile points, each of which was prepared by a flaking technique in which well-chosen stones were hit by a hammer stone to dislodge fine flakes of stone and then trimmed for a specific purpose (Leakey, 1981). These tools were more precise and finer than in previous cultures. This provided evidence of their ability to plan, think, and scheme. Fossil remains also indicate that *Neanderthals* may have possessed advanced language skills as their larynx was capable of making the same sounds as humans.

Neanderthals also showed evidence of abstract thought. It appears that the oldest musical instrument in the world, the flute, seems to have been made by *Neanderthals*.

Neanderthal culture possessed a sense of community spirit by performing ritual burials and caring for the old and sick. Remains of physically impaired individuals have been uncovered, some displaying healed injuries. Archeologists have also uncovered skeletons of individuals buried together with soil containing pollen of flowers which upon closer examination may have had some therapeutic properties.

Neanderthals showed signs of being a social race in their concern over the concept of life, death, and humanity, which suggested the acquisition of abstract thought and reasoning. Yet, unlike humans, there is no evidence of couples or family-oriented activities. In fact, *Neanderthals* were cruel warriors and fighters and may also have practiced cannibalism (Thomas, 1995).

Homo sapiens

Exactly when *Homo sapiens* came into existence has not been determined, but fossils, artifacts, and data point to the origin of the species in Africa more than 100,000 years ago, long before *Neanderthals* had disappeared from Europe. It appears that our species, *Homo sapiens,* was present long before *Neanderthals* died out. The fossils found are dated between 100,000 and 120,000 years old.

Was it selection pressure that propelled the species toward *Homo sapiens*? In each part of the world that there had been *Homo erectus,* there would eventually arise an early grade of *Homo sapiens.* As the selection pressure continued through the demands of culture, each population of early *Homo sapiens* ultimately emerged as *Homo sapiens sapiens,* modern man (Leakey, 1981).

The evolution of *Homo sapiens,* about 200,000 years ago involved a considerable expansion of the brain which was clearly manifested in their way of life. The cerebrum once again expanded to its present size, the vocal apparatus changed, and cultural innovation became more rapid.

The skulls exhibited our high-vaulted forehead, sunken cheeks, and sharp chin. There were reductions in the buttressing of the skull and the projection of the face in front of the braincase, a more prominent face and nose, and changes in the base of the skull that may relate to the presence of a larynx of modern type. This population also had a larger brain (1,100–1,300 ml) than *Homo erectus* and an expanded parietal region.

Researchers working in caves in Israel have found the remains of both *Neanderthals* and modern humans. The *Neanderthal* remains dated back some 60,000 years; and modern human remains (*Homo sapiens sapiens*) dated back 92,000 years. Thus, it would appear that modern humans existed before *Neanderthals* appeared and may have coexisted for some time until the *Neanderthals* became extinct. Within 3,000 or 4,000 years after the arrival of *Homo sapiens sapiens,* the *Neanderthals* vanished. Did our species intentionally kill off *Neanderthals* or is it that *Homo sapiens* displaced *Neanderthals* in competition for food and shelter?

There was a distinct leap in manipulative and organizational abilities following the appearance of *Homo sapiens sapiens.* This was accompanied by a rich emergence of art: cave painting, carving, and engraving, which became an integral part of human life. Their tools were sophisticated, finely chipped, and thinly flaked, and blades for carving were developed.

Cro-Magnons were the direct ancestors of the first modern humans, *Homo sapiens sapiens.* They appeared in Europe 35,000 years ago and bore a close resemblance to modern humans. They were larger and averaged about 6 feet in height. Their culture quickly advanced far above the *Neanderthals.* They were sophisticated game hunters.

One of the most prominent aspect of the Cro-Magnon age was the development of esthetic feelings, which may have been linked to religion and magic (Thomas, 1995). During the Upper Paleothic period, they produced radiant cave paintings of the animals in their environment and were discovered in the cave of Lascaux, France, which has become one of the centerpieces of prehistoric art. They also appeared to have developed a social structure, burying a few of their dead in elaborate costumes and painted symbolic figures. Small animal carvings were also among their artifacts—particularly Venus figurines, presumed to be fertility totems.

What set early *Homo sapiens* apart from the other species that had preceded them was that they engineered a constantly changing relationship to their environment: They created an evolving culture (Stanley, 1996). Furthermore, technical innovations, spiritual concerns, and rituals began to appear. In other words, cultural evolution predominated. Was an increase in brain size alone responsible for the changes that occurred with the emergence of *Homo*; moreover, did brain function play a role in this evolutionary development?

See Figure 5.1 for a summary of the characteristics of hominid evolution.

	Brain size	Skull form	Domain	Existence (years ago)	Capacity
Australopithecus 	438–435 cc	Massive face, projecting jaws	Eastern and Southern Africa	4.4 million	Tools: none
Homo Habilis 	800 cc	Larger cranial capacity, flattened face, no ridge above eyes	East Africa	2–1.8 million	Ability to grasp, primitive tools
Homo Erectus 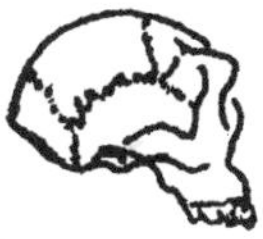	775–1,250 cc	Enlarged temporal, parietal, frontal and occipital lobes; brow ridge over eyes; forehead sloped back	Africa, Asia, Indonesia, Europe	1.5 million	Tools: axes, choppers, scrapers, and points
Neanderthal 	1,500 ml	Flattened cranium, heavy brow ridge, large eye sockets, long sloping forehead; parietal lobe larger than frontal	Europe, Western Asia, Africa	300,000	Advanced tools, spiritual life, music, hunting methods
Homo Sapiens 	1,100–1,300 ml	Expansion of cerebrum greater in parietal region; reduction of brow ridge; more prominent face, nose, chin; skull base reflects larynx	Africa, Western Asia	200,000–3,500	Art carvings, sophisticated tools, cave paintings

FIGURE 5.1. Characteristic findings of hominid evolution.

FOSSIL FORMS

Because a brain does not fossilize, its signature is left on the inner surface of the fossilized cranium. The general anthropoid pattern consisted of a strongly marked middle frontal sulcus which began near the rostrum and made its course directly backward to terminate on the precental sulcus (Broom, Robinson, & Scheper, 1950). In the chimpanzee, Bailey, Von Bonin, and McCulloch (1950) found that the middle frontal sulcus was inconsistent and occasionally fused with the frontomarginal sulcus. The brain of the original Pithecanthropus was found to have three depressions which appeared as frontal sulci with numerous branches as described by Ariens Kappers (1929).

The brain of the *Neanderthal* revealed a strong development of the middle frontal sulcus and a lesser development of the inferior frontal convolution (Ariens Kapers, 1929).

Are we able to determine how the brain grows in phylogenesis? The parietal area becomes larger; however, the main addition is right in the center between the somesthetic, the acoustic, and the visual fields; in other words, not a peripheral addition but a growth by interclation (Von Bonin, 1963). In ape brains, it was found that the parietal and temporal lobes are much smaller than the human brain.

Ralph Holloway, an anthropologist at Columbia University, concluded that the basic shape of the human brain is clearly evident in the hominids of at least 2 million years ago. If *Homo* emerged some 4 million years ago, does this mean that the human brain may have developed late on the evolutionary scale? With the emergence of the *Homo*, the size of the brain steadily increased with the forebrain being his most distinguishing feature. The shape also differs from that of a chimpanzee with the temporal and parietal lobes becoming dominant (Leakey, 1981).

It appears that the frontal lobe of the fossil forms differs but little in size from that of modern man. The frontal lobe of the fossil forms is relatively large as that of modern man and larger than that of the macaque (monkey). However, the occipital and parietal lobes are rather different from those of modern man and even smaller than those of the macaque. The great expansion of the parietal lobe which occurs during anthropogenesis is impressive. The associative centers in the frontal and temporal lobes are much more developed in *Homo sapiens* than in the anthropoid apes. See Figure 5.2.

In the *Neanderthals*, the picture changes considerably. The occipital lobe remains about the same relative size, but the parietal lobe appears to increase at the cost of the frontal lobe. Whether this change is a real one or merely due to a difference in the estimate of the site of the central sulcus is debatable. However, most of what has been said and written on the sulci of the brain as seen on endocasts is worth very little. Many detailed accounts on the frontal sulci have been written about, but it is unclear and doubtful if these identifications can be upheld. There was little besides the Sylvian fissure, the superior and middle temporal sulci, and the orbital sulci that could be identified in the casts.

In the upper Paleolithics (old stone age or agricultural era), the same conditions are seen as in modern man, except that the brains are larger on the whole than those of modern man, especially by the area of the frontal lobe.

It is often maintained that it is the third frontal convolution that has been added in man; however, upon evaluation of the cytoarchitectural picture, it is seen that the areas of the third frontal convolution are present both in monkey and man. It is the part above the third convolution, an "associational area" that is enlarged in man.

In the collection of endocasts, some factors complicate the analysis. The cortical forwarding of larger brains becomes tighter and the dura more thickened and less pliable;

(a)

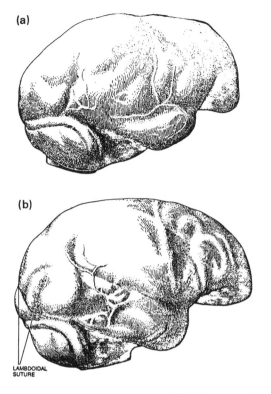

(b)

LAMBDOIDAL
SUTURE

FIGURE 5.2. Endocranial casts of (a) chimpanzee, *Pan troglodytes,* and (b) a gracile *Australopithecus africanus.* In both casts details of the gyral and sulcal markings of the cerebral cortex are minimal. A differing neurological organization, however, can be seen. The hominid brain is higher, particularly in the parietal region. The orbital surface of the frontal lobe is displaced downward in contrast to the chimpanzee's forward-thrusting olfactory rostrum. From Holloway (1974). Copyright 1974 by *Scientific American.* Reprinted by permission of the estate of Tom Prentiss.

therefore, details are more difficult to see than on smaller primate brains. For instance, the position of the lunate sulcus in Australopithecine brains, is significant because it appears to mark the area between the primary and secondary visual areas. The position of the lunate sulcus could possibly show that the functional divisions of the brain changed towards a more human pattern. The accuracy in identifying the exact position are debated in the literature.

The hominid bipedal locomotion was also an important contributor to brain morphology. The adoption of a more upright posture made the orientation of the brainstem more vertical than that of apes. It lowered the position of the cerebellum with respect to the occipital lobes (which filled in the vacated space) and moved some of the visual cortex on the lateral surface into the posterior midline. These changes would produce a more posterior position of the lunate sulcus in *Australopithecus* and later hominids.

The presence or absence of a central sulcus distinguishes brains of monkeys from prosimians. Because the central sulcus divides somatic from motor cortex in monkeys, its first appearance in the fossil record may represent some restructuring of these functional divisions. The Sylvian fissure is the most visible of all surface landmarks. It delineates the upper boundary of the temporal lobe and is lower and longer on the left side than on the right in most modern human brains. This is also seen in some endocasts of the genus *Homo.* This is also correlated with the larger size of Wernicke's language area in the left in modern man.

The sulcal markings associated with Broca's language area have been seen in *Homo habilis* and *Homo erectus* endocasts but do not appear on the endocasts of Australopithacine brains. Whether these hominids may have used Broca's area for language has not been proven by endocasts alone. We can define in morphological terms only that

Broca's area first appeared in the brains of early *Homo*. However, the evolution of language functions cannot be proven by endocasts alone. See Figure 5.3.

Finally, the increase in brain size between Australopithecines and early *Homo* increased in the number of folds in all parts of the cerebral cortex. The new folds may be an effect of this overall size rather than a specific change. The value of the endocasts provides a source of information about brain evolution but is limited by our minimal understanding of how surface morphology correlates with brain function (Deacon, 1990).

THE GROWTH OF THE BRAIN

The increase in brain size between *Australopithecus* and early *Homo* increased in the number of folds in all parts of the cerebral cortex, especially the neocortex. In general, primate brains have large expanded volumes of neocortex. Also, the association cortex, the area not involved with motor or sensory function but, rather, the area devoted to thinking, becomes especially large.

Terrance Deacon (1990) argues for a model of brain expansion that applies to the evolution of *Homo*. As the brain grew in size, it outstripped body size, and the excess brain tissue—the portion not required to operate the body—was available for higher functions. The "principle of proper mass" a term coined by Jerison (1973) states that "The mass of neural tissue devoted to a particular function is appropriate to the amount of information processing that the function entails" (pp. 8–9).

Terrance Deacon's hypothesis builds onto the principle of proper mass. He states that the body automatically sends a particular number of fibers to the brain that are proportional to its own size. Thus, as the brain enlarges, it outstrips the body and the body cannot recruit excess neuronal connections that develop within the brain. Moreover,

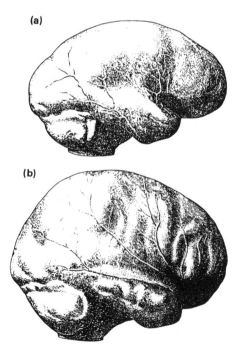

(a)

(b)

FIGURE 5.3. (a) Brain cast of *Homo erectus*. This shows evidence similar to Figure 5.1b of human organization. As it is true in most human casts, the position of the lunate sulcus cannot be determined, but the expansion of the temporal lobe and the human shape of the frontal lobe are evident. This is a cast of Java specimen VIII; it reflects the flat-topped skull conformation typical of the fossil forms of *Homo erectus* found in Indonesia. (b) Brain cast of *Homo sapiens* made from a cranium in the collection at Columbia University. The height of the cerebral cortex, measured from its summit to the tip of the temporal lobe, and the fully rounded, expanded frontal lobe, showing a strong development of Broca's area, typify the characteristic *Homo sapiens* pattern of neurological organization. From Holloway (1974). Copyright 1974 by *Scientific American*. Reprinted by permission of the estate of Tom Prentiss.

when the brain suddenly expands without a corresponding expansion of the body, the sensory, motor, auditory, and visual regions are at a disadvantage in competition for connections with new brain cells. Thus, neurons in areas such as the prefrontal cortex are connected only to neurons within other parts of the brain itself, not to neurons of the rest of the body. Thus, when the brain expanded, the prefrontal cortex enlarged dramatically, which is devoted to conceptual functions and plays a major role in thinking. Those areas associated with bodily functions underwent little change.

Brain Asymmetry

The human brain is asymmetrical not only in its functioning but also in its physical form. The front part of the right cerebral hemisphere projects farther forward, whereas the back of the left hemisphere projects farther backward. Also, the Sylvian fissure is usually larger in the left hemisphere, and the left planum temporal, which connects Wernicke's area, is also larger, suggesting that these asymmetries are related to language function.

Many researchers believed that the development of advanced communication was the most important aspect of our ancestors' cerebral ascendance above the animal world. However, recent research has uncovered cerebral asymmetries in lower mammals that in many ways resemble those of humans. The brains of apes are asymmetrical in the same way as ours, and this feature even extends to simpler animals such as monkeys. See Figure 5.4.

Debates have arisen over the link between brain asymmetry and handedness. It is known that the left part of our brain controls our right hand as well as governing speech. These two skills, manual and linguistic, are used in sign language. There have been suggestions that it was not the origins of spoken language that led to the lateral partitioning of the human brain but the earlier advent of sign language—communication in which the right hand took the lead and the left hemisphere, which controlled this hand, took on the role of organizing its sequential gestures (Stanley, 1996).

Did right-hand gesturing arise in our primate ancestors? MacNeilage, Studdert-Kennedy, and Lindblom (1987) argue that scientists have found that monkeys and other primates tend to use the left hand for reaching and grasping, leaving the right hand available for food handling and gesturing.

Many scientists have suggested theories for cerebral asymmetry claiming that evolution has saved brain tissue by positioning certain functions mainly on one side instead of duplicating them on the other. However, Stanley proposes a different explanation. He begins with a proposal of a symmetrical brain and then considers what will happen when the capacity for some new function evolves within it. Thus, the new function must displace a preexisting function. Moreover, if this change takes place in only one hemisphere, the original function can be totally conserved in the other hemisphere.

In other words, if the brain grows larger while a new function adds to an original function on only one side, then the original function does not suffer. Thus, when the brain expanded in *Homo*, asymmetric positioning made it possible for brain expansion not to amplify existing functions but to make room for new ones.

Language

The intellectual or integrative functions of the brain were not clearly recognized until 1870. However, in 1792, Franz Josef Gall, an anatomist, hypothesized that intellectual

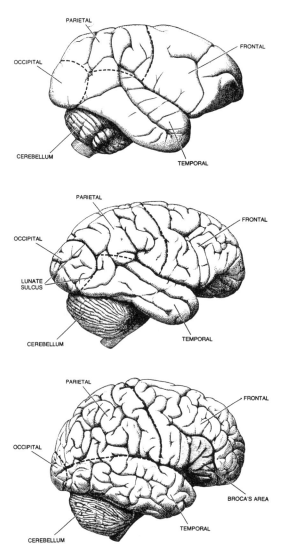

FIGURE 5.4. Gross differences in the neurological organization of three primate brains are apparent in the size of the cerebral components of a ceboid monkey (top), a chimpanzee (middle), and modern man (bottom). The small occipital lobe and the large parietal and temporal lobes in man compared with the other primates, typify the hominid pattern. Lunate sulcus, or furrow, on the chimpanzee's brain bounds its large occipital lobe. From Holloway (1974). Copyright 1974 by *Scientific American*. Reprinted by permission of the estate of Tom Prentiss.

and moral powers were located in certain areas of the brain, particularly the ability to speak, in the front half of the brain. He and other scientists laid the foundations for anatomical and functional markings of cortical areas (Creutzfeldt, 1995).

For almost a century, it has been suggested that animals, particularly primates, can be taught to speak. In the last few years, experiments have been conducted with chimpanzees and orangutans. It was questionable whether the animals could combine the vocabulary syntactically and develop grammatical constructions. It has been concluded that they only utilize symbols as tools to satisfy their immediate needs. It should be noted that no subhominid species have developed grammar to communicate with each other.

No area corresponding to the anterior speech area of Broca has been recognized in apes. However, the usually large inferior temporal area, Wernicke's area, is just detectable in the orangutan brain and doubtfully present as a small area of the chimpanzee brain.

Fleschsig (1920) found that of all areas of the human cortex, areas 39 and 40 are the last to myelinate. Myelination is delayed until after birth and is completed in late childhood. These findings indicate that areas 39 and 40 are phylogenetically developed as a new region of the cortex. (Geschwind, 1965; Tobias, 1983). Comparison of human with ape brains indicates that this late development of areas 39 and 40 has displaced the visual areas backward by a powerful evolutionary force (Eccles, 1989).

On examining endocasts, Tobias (1983, 1987) found little development in the Australopithacine brain relative to the modern ape brain, just a small "fullness" over the "future" site of Broca's area in the inferior frontal lobe. However, in the brains of *Homo habilis*, there was also a "fullness" evident over the inferior parietal lobe, indicating that phylogenetic development of areas 39 and 40 had already occurred (Holloway, 1983; Tobias, 1983, 1987). *Homo erectus* displayed a progression in these developments of the anterior and posterior speech areas, and with *Neanderthals*, the large brain presumably had full development to the *Homo sapiens sapiens* level. Tobias (1983, 1987) regards *Homo habilis* as the initiator of spoken language because of evidence from endocasts for the existence of anterior and posterior speech areas.

The ability to speak depends not only on the development of the brain but also on the development of the peripheral apparatus—the position of the larynx, size and shape of the pharynx, and the form of the mouth cavity. It was found that the mandible of the *Neanderthal* allowed about the same amount of room for the tongue as that of modern man; therefore, there is reason to believe that the ability to speak was ascribed to that race, and there is justification in ascribing the faculty of articulate speech to the *Neanderthals*.

The lateral precentral cortex in nonhuman primates may be the counterpart of Broca's area, which regulates mouth and facial gestures used in communication. Such gestures in conjunction with the evolution of the supralaryngeal airway may have promoted the evolution of Broca's area in humans.

Comparative anatomy of hominid fossils and living primates suggests that the evolution of the human supralaryngeal vocal tract probably started in the early *Homo erectus* and was not completed until the appearance of modern man. The later *Neanderthals* were the last to retain the ancient nonhuman supralaryngeal vocal tract. The existence of a supralaryngeal airway in a fossil hominid suggests there were matching neural motor circuits and mechanisms.

The literature on the primate brain is voluminous; however, comprehensive analyses of even portions of the nervous system are very complex. Functional and structural analyses of the brain of man and of the macaques dominate the literature. The problem of evaluating the phylogenetic implications of neural structures in both morphological and physiological terms is compounded by the fact that the functional significance of many structures cannot be stated in finite terms. For example, structures such as the basal ganglia are integrated with other structures (cerebral cortex and thalamus) into complex feedback systems.

Thus far, a historical background has been given of the early beginnings of man to provide an understanding in the development of the brain from an evolutionary perspective. The purpose of this chapter is not to go into detail about the evolution and workings of all brain structures but, rather, to focus on specific areas pertinent to the development of the cerebral cortex and the frontal lobes.

ORGANIZATION OF THE CORTICAL AREAS

During phylogeny, as the frontal lobes increased in size, all the sensory areas were displaced backward. The parietal association cortex increased in size between the visual, auditory, and somatosensory areas and pushed those regions apart. As the temporal association cortex enlarged, the auditory cortex, which was located visibly on the lateral cortex in mammals, was pushed into the Sylvian fissure and covered by Heschl's transverse convolutions in man.

The frontal lobes are the most recent in the phylogenetic development of the brain. They are hardly visible in lower animals but are larger in primates, they occupy up to one-fourth of the total mass of the cerebral hemispheres in man, and they are presumed to be involved in creative thinking, planning, and achieving goal-directed acts. On the ongenetic scale, the frontal lobes do not mature until a child is between 4 and 7 years of age (Luria, 1973).

The three major areas of the frontal cortex in primates are the precentral (pre- and supplementary motor), the anterior (prefrontal, orbitofrontal, and far frontal), and the cingulate (limbic). The major divisions can be defined on their thalamic input: precentral cortex receives input from the ventrolateral group of nuclei, anterior frontal from the nucleus medialis dorsalis, and cingulate from the anterior group (Pribram, 1958a, 1958b).

The subdivisions of the cingulate cortex (limbic) follow the subdivisions of the anterior thalamic nuclei: *nucleus anterior medialis* projects to the anterior congulate cortex, *n. anterior lateralis* to the posterior, and *n. lateralis dorsalis* to the retospinal portion of the congulate gyrus (Pribram & Fulton, 1954).

Phylogenetically, the prefrontal region is one of the last areas to mature due to tardy myelination. It should not be assumed that the development of cortical functions in the parietal, temporal, and association area only begin to function in later life. In fact, these areas, with their functional importance, are more likely to be at work from the beginning of life. In the course of evolution, the prefrontal cortex undergoes more expansion than does the rest of the cortex. Studies indicate that the dorsal and lateral areas undergo development and further differentiation much later than do the medial and ventral areas.

Precentral Motor Cortex and Efferents

Cytoarchitectonically, Brodmann's areas 4,6, and 8 are characterized by an agranular structure in that layer IV has a lower neuronal density than in the primary sensory areas. Area 4 is characterized by the occurrence of giant pyramidal cells in layer V, called Betz cells. These increase in number from the primates to man, and send axons into the corticospinal or pyramidal tract.

Only a small portion of the efferents of the motor cortex reach the spinal pyramidal tract, even though the functional significance of these direct corticospinal connections increases in the phylogenetic scale. In the primate, only a minority terminate in the anterior horn directly on motor neurons; the majority of the fibers regulate motor activity via the spinal interneural system. Also in the primate, the number of pyramidal fibers terminating on the anterior horn, derived mainly from area 4, is much greater than in lower mammals. Thus, in primates and man there is greater control directly over neuronal activity from the motor cortex (Philips & Poster, 1977). Direct corticomotor neuronal connections have been shown to exist in the primate, rat, and raccoon and are primarily directed to the cervical motor neurons that innervate distal muscles of the forearm and regulate fine finger movements.

The change from quadrupedality to bipedality demonstrates that there was a transformation of the neural machinery of the brain. Unfortunately, little is known about the detail of neural control of human bipedal walking.

There are two major descending pathways, the cortico and reticular spinal tract and the pyramidal tract, which arises mainly from the motor cortex of the frontal lobes. The former descends to the brainstem where it forms two descending tracts on both sides of the spinal cord and activates motor neurons innervating axial and proximal limb muscles. The latter crosses in the medulla to descend as the pyramidal tract to innervate the distal muscles of the contralateral limbs. These tracts play a role in bipedal walking.

The movements of walking are dependent on the rhythmic discharges from the motor cortex under the influence of activities from other regions of the cerebral cortex, basal ganglia, and cerebellum. All of this neural circuitry had to be reorganized in the evolution of locomotion from quadrupedal to the bipedal mode of *Australopithecus*. It appears that the prehominids may have had a very efficient and complex motor control system, as exhibited by primates today, which have a more versatile and well-controlled motor apparatus than that of other mammals.

The motor responses in hominids showed an additional evolutionary development of the motor system. There was an enormous expansion of the motor cortical representation for the thumb and fingers. This relates to the development of fine motor skills of the hand necessary for the development of stone tools. With the evolution of *Homo habilis* to *Homo erectus* to *Homo sapiens sapiens*, there was a change in the variety and elegance of the tools. This change is attributable to the progressively enhanced creative imagination and motor skill that would derive from the evolutionary development of the cerebellar hemispheres and especially the premotor and motor cortices with all of their ancillary activities (Eccles, 1989).

The voluntary initiation of movements is associated with the supplementary motor area (SMA) located in the frontal lobe. Experiments on monkeys show increases in regional cerebral blood flow (rCBF) during motor-sequence testing over the SMA. In hominid evolution there appears to have been no change in the manner by which "voluntary" movements are initiated. However, in hominid evolution, the development of area 6 was much greater compared to area 4. SMA projects to the primary motor area (M1) largely via premotor area 6, where there is refinement in the instructions to the motor cortex. Further refinements with influences from motor learning are given to the instructions to the motor cortex via the thalamus. It is known that a motor skill involves a complicated cerebral set of functions, but hominids would have already developed this ability. It would have been much further developed in hominid evolution (Eccles, 1989).

Frontal Association Cortex

The frontal association cortex includes the granular cortex of fields 9–12 as well as 45 and 46, according to Brodmann. This region is also known as the prefrontal cortex. The remaining agranular frontal cortex are fields 6 and 8 (premotor) and motor speech area 49. During phylogenesis, the size of the prefrontal cortex (granular) increases in size much more significantly than that of other neocortical fields, and there is a dominance of dorsolateral over ventralmedial surface (Fuster, 1980).

The prefrontal cortex is where associations of different kinds of information are processed to make decisions. In the evolution of the human skulls from *Australopithecus* to *Homo*, one of the most striking changes was the transformation of a frontal region that was low and sloping, like that of an ape into man's nearly vertical forehead. This change reflected an expansion of the prefrontal cortex, which gave rise to the increase in the thinking power seen in hominids.

Prefrontal Association Cortex

Thalamic afferents also transmit activity from the limbic system and most of the efferents project to the basal ganglia, mesencephalic structures, and pontine nuclei. Through the efferent connections, the prefrontal influences the motor systems.

The afferents from the limbic give the frontal cortex the role of a distinct link between limbic functions and neocortical behavior (Nauta, 1971). From the afferent connections, limbic system, diencephalon structures, hippocampus, and amygdala, short- and long-term memory reach the prefrontal cortex and are integrated into behavioral control.

It has been considered that the limbic system, via the temporal lobe, is also under the influence of neocortical action, and that neocortical activity also reaches the prefrontal cortex directly via association fibers. Thus, it can be concluded that the prefrontal cortex represents internal states of forebrain, particularly emotion and motivation in a social and cognitive context, and through efferent connections adapts the neocortical sensorimotor control of behavior to the emotional and social cortex (Creutzfeldt, 1995).

The increase in the prefrontal cortex of mammals, and especially in man, correlates with the increasing control of behavior by the neocortex. With the increasing corticalization during evolution, a corresponding neocortical representation of inner conditions and of social expression becomes necessary to integrate the cortically controlled behavior with emotional and social conditions (Creutzfeld, 1995). Lower mammals have less corticalization of sensorimotor functions. Cortical representation of sensorimotor functions is less necessary because the corresponding subcortical structures control behavior through instinct by efferent connections.

Limbic System

The limbic system is involved in monitoring, mediation, and expression of emotional, motivational, sexual, and social behavior. It mediates such responses as fight or flight, attraction or avoidance, arousal or calming, hunger, thirst, satiation, fear, sadness, affection, happiness, and the control of aggression. Important limbic structures are the amygdala and hippocampus. The limbic system is considered to be the seat of emotion and emotional control.

Archicortex: Hippocampus and Amygdala

The hippocampus is associated with learning and memory. It comprises the dorsomedial part of the inverted, unspecialized forebrain of amphibians. In reptiles, the hippocampus differentiates into a loosely laminated structure but does not closely resemble its mammalian counterpart in cytoarchitecture.

During the course of evolution, the hypothalamus initially controlled and expressed raw and reflexive emotion in response to monitoring of internal homeostasis and basic needs. The development of the amygdala enabled the organism to monitor and test the emotional features of the environment and to act on them (Joseph, 1992). In phylogenesis, the amygdala hierarchically takes over control of emotion from the hypothalamus. The amygdala is interconnected with various neocortical and subcortical regions and monitors and abstracts information from the environment. It assigns emotional or motivational meaning to experiences. It allows an individual to distinguish and express subtle emotional nuances such as friendliness, fear, distrust, and anger. This structure is also involved in attention, learning, and memory as well as emotional functioning.

The amygdala are structures with only rudimentary lamination in some parts. Several nuclei differentiate within the amygdala, some early, others late in phylogeny. The amygdala gather olfactory impulses and other visceral information essential to the function of the limbic system.

The central amygdala nucleus is found in all vertebrates. It is a continuation of the lateral olfactory nucleus (stria terminalis). The medial amygdaloid nucleus is primordial in lower vertebrates and well developed in reptiles, birds, and mammals. A cortical portion is found only in mammals. The basolateral amygdala nuclei are developed only in mammals and are the best differentiated part of the amygdala in man, which is continuous with the overlying hippocampus.

Among primates, the small-cell part of the corticobasolateral amygdaloid group is the most progressive in development. The large basal amygdaloid nuclei also undergo constant phylogenetic development. The centromedial group remain unchanged. These changes suggest increased amygdaloid involvement in the limbic system and decreased importance of olfactory input (Stephan & Andy, 1977).

The hippocampus is also associated with learning and memory and complements the amygdala in regard to attention and emotion. As the amygdala and hippocampus develop, individuals can tend to the external environment based on hypothalamically monitored needs. Moreover, individuals can differentiate what occurs externally, determine what is satisfying, and remember this information. This eventually leads to the development of further associations, memories, and more specific complex emotional responses to the environment. These emotional responses determine behavior and play a role in organization of external experiences and the development of consciousness.

THE BEGINNING OF SELF-CONSCIOUSNESS

The frontal lobes of the brain are considered our emotional center and home to our personality. They are believed to be involved in the highest levels of goal-directed activities such as complex sequencing and the creation of long- and short-term plans. They have also come to be associated with behaviors linked to consciousness such as self-awareness, self-regulation, intentionality, and altruism. Luria (1973) stated that the frontal lobes play a fundamental role in constructing and maintaining human conscious activity.

This recognition, that the frontal lobes are the seat of consciousness, is consistent with the fact that the frontal lobes are the last to develop phylogenetically in the brain. The development and functions of the frontal lobes are what differentiate human beings from other animals. Even as far back as 1928, the American neurologist Tilney suggested that the entire period of human evolutionary existence could be viewed as the age of the frontal lobe. (Stuss & Benson, 1986).

For the greater part of the hominid evolution, there is increasing evidence of frontal lobe evolvement, provided by evidence of a stone culture and tool-making abilities. This evolvement resulted in the development of conceptual tasks such as planning and sequencing. Initial tool-making abilities of *Homo habilis* were primitive and crude, then came an advance with *Homo erectus* and finally up to the Paleolithic era of art revealing a sophistication in design and the use of a cognitive system and abstraction.

What is it that makes us uniquely human? Self-awareness and the emergence of consciousness and altruism imply the highest mental experience. The first traces of this behavior were seen with food sharing at communal living sites (Isaac, 1978). Evidence of consciousness was also evidenced by *Neanderthals* by their respect for the dead with burial customs. There was also evidence that they cared for those individuals of the tribe who were injured. Dobzhansky (1967) articulates well the emergence of human self-consciousness or self-awareness:

> Self-awareness is, then, one of the fundamental, possibly the most fundamental, characteristic of the human species. This characteristic is an evolutionary novelty; the biological species from which mankind has descended had only rudiments of self-awareness, or perhaps lacked it altogether. Self-awareness has, however, brought in its train somber companions—fear, anxiety and death awareness. Man is burdened by death awareness. A being who knows that he will die arose from ancestors who did not know. (p. 68)

CONCLUDING REMARKS

Charles Darwin, in *Origin of Species,* had a profound influence on man's thoughts in regard to the origin of our existence. Yet, questions still arise as to how the past affects the present and, more important, the future of mankind.

In the past, as man settled in tribal and village life, defense mechanisms appeared regarding property, adaptability to authority began, and crimes and other kinds of behavior evolved, thus increasing man's potential for good and evil and moral ramifications. Throughout history, despite wars and threatening powers of annihilation, we continue to evolve to the present age of information. It is with this past that man's increased awareness becomes concerned with the future.

Environmentalists today are strong advocates for the protection of species and their habitat. Could it be that mass extinctions of the past threaten us as individuals and that one day our species will be no more? Or do we believe that our evolution has been completed? Charles Darwin suggested that early man was not as highly evolved as modern man, and as animal brains have evolved, so has the nature of consciousness and mind. Geneticists state that humanity will not become superhuman. We will always build on our present weaknesses rather than make a new evolutionary start. Humanists believe that the nature of man is to continue to advance and the need to grow is imperative if humanity is to survive. That growth is to be directed to a transformation of human nature that would give the truest meaning to the existence on earth.

Modern man has not solved the problem of his relationship to society. Good and evil are shifting quantities, changing from time to time in meaning and value. A change of consciousness is the next major evolutionary transformation. The spiritual aspiration in man is innate; for man, unlike the animal, is aware of his limitations and weaknesses and feels the need to attain beyond what he now is. The human mental status will always be there, striving toward the supermental and spiritual development. As individuals advance spiritually, they become more united with the whole.

REFERENCES

Ariens Kappers, C. U. (1929). The fissures of the frontal lobes of Pithecanthropus erectus Dubois compared with those of Neanderthal man, homorecens, and chimpanzee. *Proceedings of the Koninklijke Akademie van Wetenschoppen, 32,* 182–195.

Bailey, P., von Bonin, G., & McCulloch, W. S. (1950). *The neocortex of the chimpanzee.* Urbana: University of Illinois Press.

Broom, R., Robinson, J. T., & Scheper, G. W. H. (Eds.). (1950). *The Sterdonkin ape-man Plesianthropus.* Pretoria: Transvaal Museum Mem. 4.

Creutzfeldt, O. D. (1995). *Cortex cerebri: Performance, structural, and functional organization of the cortex.* New York: Oxford University Press.

Dart, R. (1967). *Adventures with the missing link.* Philadelphia: Institutes Press.

Darwin, C. (1958). *Origin of species.* New York: American Library of World Literature.

Deacon, T. W. (1990). Rethinking mammalian brain evolution. *American Zoologist, 30,* 629–705.

Dobzhansky, T. (1967). *The biology of ultimate concern.* New York: New American Library.

Donald, M. (1993). *Origin of the modern mind: Three stages in the evolution of culture and cognition.* Cambridge: First Harvard University Press.

Eccles, J. C. (1989). *Evolution of the brain: Creation of the self.* New York: Routledge.

Fleschsig, P. (1920). *Anatomie des menschlichen Gehirns unds Rückemnarks auf myelogenetischer Grundlage.* Leipzig: Thieme.

Fuster, J. M. (1980). *The prefrontal cortex: Anatomy, physiology and neuropsychology.* New York: Raven Press.

Gall, F. J. (1792). *Anatomie et physiologie du système nerveux en général, et du cerveau en particulier.* Paris: Shoell.

Geschwind, N. (1965). Disconnection syndromes in animal and man: 1. *Brain, 88,* 237–294.

Holloway, R. L. (1974). The casts of fossil hominid brains. *Scientific American, 231*(1), 106–115.

Holloway, R. L. (1983). Human paleontological evidence relevant to language behavior. *Human Neurobiology, 2,* 105–114.

Isaac, C. (1978). Food-sharing behavior of protohuman hominids. *Scientific American, 288*(4), 90–180.

Jerison, H. J. (1973). *Evolution of the brain and intelligence.* New York: Academic Press.

Johanson, D., & Shreer, J. (1989). *Lucy's child: The discovery of a human ancestor.* New York: William Morrow.

Johnston, J. B. (1906). *The nervous system of vertebrates.* Philadelphia: P. Blakiston's Son.

Joseph, R. (1992). The limbic system: Emotion, laterality, and unconscious mind. *Psychoanalytic Review, 3,* 406–456.

Leakey, R. (1981). *The making of mankind.* New York: Elsevier-Dutton.

Leakey, R. (1994). *The origin of humankind.* New York: Basic Books.

Luria, A. R. (1973). *The working brain.* New York: Basic Books.

MacNeilage, P. F., Studdert-Kennedy, M. G., & Lindblom, B. (1987). Primate handedness reconsidered. *Behavioral and Brain Sciences, 10*(2), 247–303.

Nauta, J. H. (1971). The problem of the frontal lobe: A reinterpretation. *Journal of Psychiatric Research, 8,* 167–187.

Oakley, D., & Plotkin, H. C. (Eds.). (1979). *Brain, behavior and evolution.* Cambridge, UK: Cambridge University Press.

Philips, C. G., & Poster, R. (1977). *Corticospinal neurons: Their role in movement.* London: Academic Press.

Pribram, K. H. (1958a). Comparative neurology and the evolution of behavior. In A. Roe & G. G. Simpson (Eds.). *Behavior and evolution* (pp. 140–164). New Haven, CT: Yale University Press.

Pribram, K. H. (1958b). Neocortical functions in behavior. In H. F. Harlow & C. N. Woolsey (Eds.), *Biological and biochemical bases of behavior* (pp. 151–172). Madison: University of Wisconsin Press.

Pribram, K. H., & Fulton, J. F. (1954). An experimental critique of the effects of anterior cingulate ablations in monkey. *Brain, 77,* 34–44.

Rensch, B. (1972). *Homosapiens: From man to demigod.* New York: Columbia University Press.

Ruse, M. (1996). *Monad to man: The concept of progress in evolutionary biology.* Cambridge, MA: Harvard University Press.

Sarnot, H. B., & Netsky, M. G. (1981). *Evolution of the nervous system* (9th ed.). New York: Oxford University Press.

Stanley, S. M. (1996). *Children of the ice age: How a global catastrophe allowed humans to evolve.* New York: Harmony Books.

Stephan, H., & Andy, O. J. (1977). Quantitative comparison of the amygdala in insectivores and primates. *Acta Anatomy, 98,* 130–153.

Stuss, D. T., & Benson, D. F. (1986). *The frontal lobes.* New York: Raven Press.

Thomas, H. (1995). *Human origins: The search for our beginnings.* New York: Harry N. Abrams.

Tilney, F. (1928). *The brain: From ape to man.* New York: Hoeber.

Tobias, P. V. (1983). Recent advances in the evolution of the hominids with special reference to brain and speech. In C. Chagas (Ed.), *Recent advances in the evolution of primates* (pp. 50–140). Vatican City: Pontificiae Academiae Scientarium Scripta Varia.

Tobias, P. V. (1987). The brain of homo habilis: A new level of organization in cerebral evolution. *Journal of Human Evolution, 16,* 741–761.

Von Bonin, G. (1963). *The evolution of the human brain.* Chicago: University of Chicago Press.

6

Neuroimaging and the Frontal Lobes

Insights from the Study
of Neurodegenerative Diseases

WILLIAM JAGUST

The application of brain imaging techniques to the study of the frontal lobes is a potentially vast topic. Although modern neuroimaging modalities, such as computed tomography (CT), magnetic resonance imaging (MRI), positron emission tomography (PET), and single photon emission computed tomography (SPECT) have been used for a relatively short period, a large literature encompassing technical, radiological, clinical, and neurobiological disciplines has developed. Thus, any review of the subject cannot possibly encompass the field and must be concerned with only a few key topics. This review first notes some of the features and differences in these techniques to provide a review of the strengths and weaknesses of various imaging modalities and to define what each modality can explain about either brain structure or function. Subsequently, by reviewing a limited number of degenerative neurological diseases, relationships between frontal lobe structure and function and behavior, as revealed with these techniques, are explored. An important theme of the review is that both direct and remote effects of brain disease exert influences on frontal lobe function, and that these different effects may be separately explored through the use of appropriate techniques and models.

NEUROIMAGING TECHNIQUES

The primary structural brain imaging techniques used by clinicians and scientists are CT and MRI. Although the two modalities use fundamentally different physical properties and have correspondingly different strengths and limitations, the information they provide is similar. In general, these techniques provide measures of the sizes of brain structures and can detect abnormalities of tissue as well.

CT scanning measures tissue interactions with X-rays transmitted through the patient's brain from an external source and thus make measurements which primarily reflect tissue density. Contrast material with high density may be employed to penetrate a disrupted blood–brain barrier and localize regional pathology which disrupts the blood–brain barrier. CT is widely available and relatively inexpensive and thus is a commonly used technique for measuring brain structure. However, although the resolution is excellent, contrast sensitivity is not great. This results in poor discrimination between gray matter and white matter, and between some types of tissue abnormalities and normal brain. In addition, beam-hardening artifacts, produced by differential attenuation of X-rays by bone, limit visualization of brain structures close to bone, such as the posterior fossa and some areas of cerebral cortex. These limitations have been largely overcome with MRI.

MRI utilizes entirely different principles to image the brain, taking advantage of the fact that nuclei with a magnetic moment, such as ^{1}H, ^{13}C, ^{23}Na, and ^{31}P, emit energy when placed in a magnetic field and excited with a radiofrequency pulse. Although many such nuclei are found in biological samples, protons are the most abundant and consequently the simplest to image with high signal to noise characteristics. The principles of MRI have been reviewed in detail elsewhere (Budinger & Lauterbur, 1984). A great advantage of MRI is that differences in the application of the radiofrequency pulse enable an investigator to tailor the images so that they reflect either a T1 or T2 relaxation parameter. These parameters, which reflect changes in the alignment of protons in the magnetic field, differ in different tissue types such that the MR image can show high-contrast sensitivity, allowing good differentiation of gray matter, white matter, and cerebrospinal fluid (CSF). Thus, MR images display relatively distinct margins between these different tissue types so that, for example, the boundaries of gray matter can be relatively well delimited from surrounding CSF and white matter. In addition, the capacity for true three-dimensional data acquisition with MR permits reformatting of images in multiple planes of view and full characterization of brain morphology.

CT and MRI clearly provide measures of brain structure. However, diseases affecting frontal lobe function may produce their primary effects not by direct involvement of frontal structures but by involvement of other brain regions with projections to frontal cortex. Such diseases may have profound functional consequences, with no measurable structural changes in the frontal lobes. Within the past 15 years, the application of functional imaging techniques has clearly demonstrated relationships between frontal lobe functioning and behavior that have not been obvious when brain structure was studied.

Both PET and SPECT are emission tomographic techniques which use similar principles permitting the three-dimensional mapping of the distribution of an injected radiotracer. The signal, detected by a tomograph, is provided by a radionuclide attached to the molecule of interest. Most studies of brain function have utilized tracers which measure regional cerebral metabolic rates for glucose (rCMRglc) such as the PET tracer [^{18}F]fluorodeoxyglucose (FDG) or regional cerebral blood flow (rCBF) such as the PET tracer [^{15}O]water or the SPECT tracers [^{99m}Tc]hexamethyl propyleneamine oxime (HMPAO), and [^{99m}Tc]cysteinate dimer (ECD). For the most part, studies of blood flow and glucose metabolism show similar results, because flow and metabolism are normally coupled in the majority of diseases. Other tracers, such as fluorodopa, measure neurochemical characteristics of the tissue by providing a substrate or receptor ligand which traces a particular feature of a neurochemical system of interest.

PET and SPECT differ according to the type of radioactivity utilized to generate the image. PET utilizes radionuclides such as ^{11}C, ^{15}O, and ^{18}F, which decay by positron emission and produce two photons which travel in directions 180 degrees opposite to each other. Because these annihilation photons can be detected by the simultaneous excitation of a pair of opposing crystal detectors, the tomograph can localize the positron emission to a line. Reconstruction of an image is accomplished by the back projection of multiple such lines through each pair of detectors. SPECT imaging detects radionuclides such as ^{99m}Tc and ^{123}I, which decay by emitting single photons in random directions. Because collimation is required to determine the location of the emitted activity, the sensitivity of SPECT, in terms of the number of counts detected per unit time, is lower than PET. Furthermore, resolution can be increased with PET with little trade-off of sensitivity, whereas with SPECT, increased resolution comes at the price of reduced sensitivity. PET is capable of higher resolution and more accurate quantitation and also, because PET radionuclides have short half-lives, repeated studies of the sort necessary for activation experiments are far simpler. Nevertheless, the two techniques are comparable in terms of detecting functional brain changes in basic physiological processes.

STRUCTURE–FUNCTION RELATIONSHIPS IN THE FRONTAL LOBE: DEMENTIA

Studies of patients with dementing diseases provide good examples of how changes in the structure and function of the frontal lobes may differ, and how these changes are related to behavior. Undoubtedly, the dementia that has been subject to the most study in this regard is the most common dementia in adults, Alzheimer's disease (AD). It is well-known that structural brain changes in AD are widespread. Patients with AD have greater cerebral atrophy than do nondemented subjects throughout the cerebral hemispheres (Gado et al., 1982; Jacoby, Levy, & Dawson, 1980; Sandor et al., 1992). However, this atrophy is also commonly seen in normal older subjects (DeCarli, Kaye, Horwitz, & Rapoport, 1990; Jernigan, Press, & Hesselink, 1990).

Regional changes in brain atrophy have not been specifically found in the frontal lobes in AD patients. Indeed, pathological and clinical studies have suggested that the temporal lobes in particular show the predominant effects of AD (Brun & Englund, 1981; Hyman, Van Hoesen, Damasio, & Barnes, 1984). Congruent with such effects, several CT studies have suggested that measures of temporal lobe structures, such as the size of the temporal horns and sylvian fissures, are most effective in differentiating AD patients from controls (Kido et al., 1989; Sandor, Albert, Stafford, & Harpley, 1988). Perhaps most specifically, structural imaging studies have evaluated changes in the hippocampus in AD patients. Both CT and MR studies have found that evaluation of hippocampal size was effective in differentiating clinically diagnosed AD patients from patients with other dementias and also was highly related to postmortem diagnoses (de Leon, George, Stylopoulos, Smith, & Miller, 1989; Jack, Petersen, O'Brien, & Tangalos, 1992; Jobst et al., 1992; Kesslak, Nalcioglu, & Cotman, 1991; Seab et al., 1988). Thus, from a diagnostic imaging perspective, it is not the frontal lobes but rather temporal lobes in AD which appear to be most useful. Nevertheless, AD patients provide an interesting model for the evaluation of a number of brain–behavior relationships precisely because the frontal lobes are not uniformly severely involved pathologically, structurally, or functionally. By evaluating groups of patients with a continuum of frontal lobe damage revealed with imaging modalities, and relating such changes to behavior, insights into brain–behavior relationships can be elucidated.

In fact, relatively few structural imaging studies have evaluated relationships between regional brain structure and cognitive function in nontemporal brain regions of AD patients, although some relationships between the degree of frontal atrophy and cognitive functions have emerged. Frontal lobe size is clearly diminished in AD as are all cortical regions whether studied with MRI (Jernigan, Salmon, Butters, & Hesselink, 1991) or CT (Pfefferbaum et al., 1990). Using CT, one study (Pfefferbaum et al., 1990) suggested that frontal reductions were greater in younger AD patients and in patients with greater language disturbances. Stout, Jernigan, Archibald, and Salmon (1996) used MR to differentiate gray matter from white matter and abnormal white matter and found that nonlimbic gray matter volumes were related to dementia severity but not independently from limbic gray matter volumes. That is, global gray matter volume was a significant determinant of dementia severity. Rusinek et al. (1991) found significant reductions in frontal lobe gray matter volume in AD patients relative to controls, but these reductions were not as great as those seen in temporal lobes. A recent report by Lehtovirta et al. (1995) evaluated MRI measures of atrophy in a group of AD subjects stratified according to whether they carried the Apolipoprotein E (ApoE) ε4 risk factor for AD. These investigators found that the subjects with 3/3 or 3/4 genotypes showed smaller frontal lobes than controls, whereas the group with 4/4 genotypes showed smaller hippocampi than did controls. This is an interesting, though as yet unconfirmed, report of a genetic basis for differential brain atrophy in AD. Thus, taken together, frontal lobe atrophy may be more common in younger subjects, those with language disorders, and those without the ApoE risk for AD. Clearly, such associations appear reasonable in terms of concepts of language localization, although genetic effects on brain structure are much more poorly understood.

Thus, in AD there is generalized atrophy, and when regional effects are evaluated, atrophy is seen in most brain regions examined. In addition, few studies have specifically evaluated frontal lobe atrophy; in those that have, some relationships between atrophy and cognitive function have emerged. A major concern with such studies is the potential confounding of brain atrophy, cognitive function, and dementia severity. This concept can best be understood by appreciating that a diagnosis of dementia usually necessitates dysfunction of neocortex—the isolated disturbance of amnesia, in all diagnostic schema, does not satisfy criteria for dementia. Thus, once amnesia has progressed to frank dementia, a variety of neocortical brain regions may become dysfunctional, any one of which may be highly correlated to dementia severity and, through this correlation, to a host of other cognitive functions. These issues are well appreciated when studies of functional brain changes in AD are reviewed.

In parallel with structural brain imaging, most studies of AD patients using functional imaging modalities have found reductions in glucose metabolism and blood flow in the temporal cortex, with abnormal function seen in parietal cortex as well (Duara et al., 1986; Foster et al., 1984; Frackowiak et al., 1981; Friedland et al., 1983). Both cross-sectional and longitudinal studies have shown that more severely demented subjects develop frontal lobe hypometabolism and hypoperfusion as the dementia progresses (Eberling, Jagust, Reed, & Baker, 1992; Jagust, Friedland, Budinger, Koss, & Ober, 1988). This finding is illustrated in Figure 6.1. Based on such studies, frontal lobe function should be linked to global dementia severity.

The impairment in frontal lobe metabolism has been specifically evaluated in AD in a number of respects. Haxby et al. (1988) found reductions in premotor cortex in a group

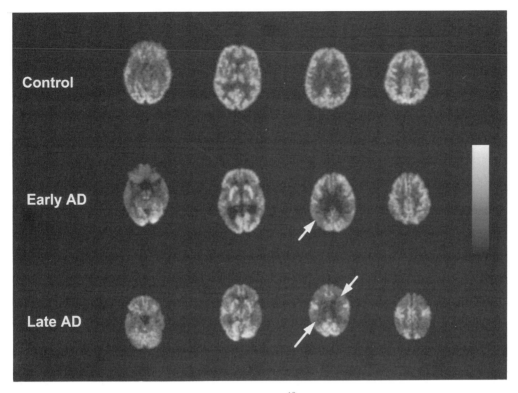

FIGURE 6.1. PET images obtained using the tracer [^{18}F]fluorodeoxyglucose of a control patient and two patients with Alzheimer's disease (AD) in early and late stages. Note that in early AD, the metabolic lesion is relatively confined to the parietal and temporal cortex (arrow), whereas in late AD frontal and parietal lobe lesions are evident (arrows).

of AD patients which appeared relatively early in the disease. These frontal lobe metabolic rates correlated with dementia severity more robustly than did metabolic rates in parietal lobes. Frontal hypometabolism was also related to impairment of verbal fluency and attention. Another study using SPECT found that frontal lobe hypoperfusion was better correlated with dementia severity than temporal lobe hypoperfusion (Eberling et al., 1992). Both of these studies suggest that frontal lobe function is a more sensitive measure of severity than is temporal or parietal function because of floor effects in temporal and parietal function. However, they also raise concerns about spurious correlations with specific cognitive functions that are really dependent on correlations with dementia severity. Because frontal lobe perfusion and metabolism are related to dementia severity, it is likely that numerous specific cognitive functions will decline in proportion to frontal lobe physiology.

Eberling, Reed, Baker, and Jagust (1993) performed a detailed analysis of relationships between regional perfusion as measured with SPECT and neuropsychological testing, using a series of cluster scores derived from grouping neuropsychological tests into measures of frontal lobe function, perseveration, visuospatial ability, language ability, and memory. When these neuropsychological test scores were correlated with regional brain perfusion, a host of significant relationships emerged. However, when global dementia severity was accounted for by using performance on the Mini-Mental Status Examination (MMSE; Folstein, Folstein, & McHugh, 1975) as a forced variable in a stepwise multivariate procedure, many of these correlations disappeared. Nevertheless, relationships between frontal lobe perfusion and performance on tests of frontal lobe ability and perseveration scores remained significant.

The degree of involvement of the frontal lobes in AD patients also appears related to a number of non–cognitive-behavioral features seen in AD. Some AD patients, for example, experience distress and show considerable awareness of their cognitive deficits, whereas other patients are unaware and others experience considerable anosognosia. These differences do not appear to be simply related to psychological factors such as the presence of depression, but they may be related to fundamental differences in frontal lobe function. Two studies have found that right dorsolateral hypoperfusion in AD patients is linked to the presence of anosognosia (Reed, Jagust, & Coulter, 1993; Starkstein et al., 1995). Apathy has also been related to the degree of frontal lobe and anterior temporal lobe perfusion in AD (Craig et al., 1996).

Thus, a number of clinical differences in the presentations of AD patients are related to variability in frontal lobe function. However, as noted, this frontal lobe involvement, while interesting from the perspective of understanding the basis of behavioral and cognitive disturbance, is not a diagnostic feature of AD. In this respect, another group of dementias characterized specifically by frontal lobe involvement has received considerable recent attention because of dramatic changes in the frontal lobes apparent with a number of different imaging modalities which are also related to behavioral changes. This disorder, frontotemporal dementia, is characterized by behavioral disturbances reflecting varying degrees and location of frontal and anterior temporal lobe damage, along with imaging characteristics that parallel these clinical findings. A recent monograph (Pasquier, Lebert, & Scheltens, 1996) summarizes many features of the syndrome, and clinical diagnostic and pathologic criteria have been proposed the Lund and Manchester Groups (1994), two of the leading entities studying this disorder. Genetic linkages of some cases with frontotemporal types of dementias have been reported on chromosome 17 (Heutink et al., 1997; Lynch et al., 1994).

As noted, the overwhelming feature of the disorder is pathological, imaging, and clinical involvement of the frontal lobes. A number of functional imaging studies have demonstrated reductions in frontal lobe cerebral blood flow in patients clinically diagnosed with the condition (Jagust, Reed, Seab, Kramer, & Budinger, 1989; Miller et al., 1991; Neary, Snowden, Northen, & Goulding, 1988). Similar findings using PET and FDG have been observed in autopsy-confirmed Pick's disease, a condition with clinical and pathological overlap with frontotemporal dementias (Friedland et al., 1993; Kamo et al., 1987). Figure 6.2 provides an example of a PET image of glucose metabolism in a patient with clinically diagnosed frontal lobe dementia. These metabolic and flow reductions are usually quite different from the reductions seen in AD patients, as they are more limited to the frontal lobes (and the anterior temporal lobes) and they are more severe in degree. As noted in multiple studies, they are related to behavior, as most of these patients present with varying combinations of disinhibition and apathy, and demonstrate profound disturbances in frontal and executive function on neuropsychological testing. It is this very combination of impaired frontal lobe abilities and imaging features that has been proposed as a diagnostic criterion.

Patients with vascular dementia may, at times, also demonstrate alterations in either perfusion or metabolism in the frontal lobes. A number of investigators have drawn attention to the fact that vascular dementia patients show clinical signs of frontal lobe damage and demonstrate dementia syndromes which are often described as "subcortical–

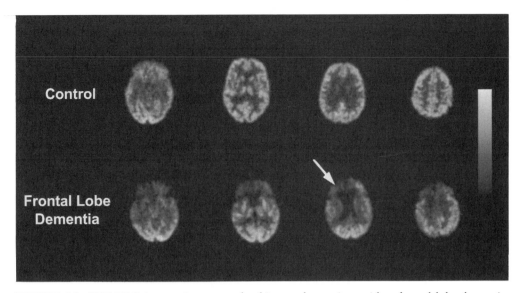

FIGURE 6.2. PET–FDG images in a control subject and a patient with a frontal lobe dementia. In this case, clear metabolic reductions which predominate in frontal lobes are seen (arrow).

frontal." This may be especially true in cases of subcortical infarction which can functionally disconnect the frontal lobes (Ishii, Nishihara, & Imamura, 1986). Although these patients are not clinically confused with patients with frontotemporal dementia because of the presence of focal signs and structural brain lesions, their behavioral characteristics may overlap. Not surprisingly, some reports have noted reduced frontal perfusion or metabolism in cases of vascular dementia (Cohen et al., 1986). Such vascular dementia patients are interesting to compare with frontotemporal dementia patients. Although the two contrast in terms of mechanism, with frontotemporal dementia patients exhibiting direct pathological involvement of the frontal lobes and vascular dementia patients exhibiting frontal disconnection via subcortical infarction of white matter tracts, the two conditions may show similar functional imaging characteristics at times. Figure 6.3 shows an example of PET and MRI findings in a patient with subcortical infarction which resulted in frontal lobe hypometabolism. Behavioral disturbances in these vascular dementia patients may also overlap considerably with the behavioral symptoms shown by patients with frontal lobe degenerations.

It is important to recognize that because of the locus of pathology in cases of AD and frontotemporal dementia, the functional imaging presumably parallels anatomic changes which may be present at the microscopic or gross level. Although the fundamental basis of changes in metabolism and perfusion are not well understood, they are felt primarily to reflect reductions in metabolic demand rather than tissue ischemia because of the normal oxygen extraction ratio (Frackowiak et al., 1981). Most workers have attributed these changes to loss of synapses or neurons, as both are key determinants of tissue metabolism (Schwartz et al., 1979), both are lost in AD (Terry et al., 1991), and metabolic rates parallel histological indices of neuronal loss and gliosis (McGeer, McGeer, Harrop, Akiyama, & Kamo, 1990). In addition, in frontotemporal dementia, frontal lobe atrophy has been reported in a number of structural brain imaging studies (Cummings & Duchen, 1981; Knopman et al., 1989; Mendez, Selwood, Mastri, & Frey, 1993; Miller

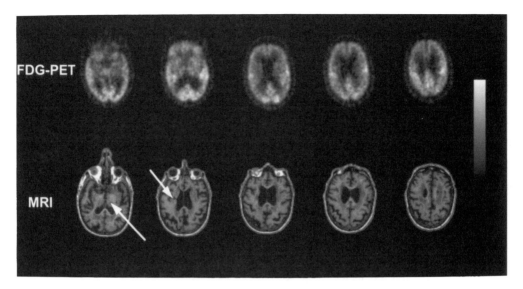

FIGURE 6.3. PET–FDG scan and MRI of a patient with multiple subcortical lacunar infarcts in basal ganglia, thalamus, and white matter. MRI lesions are denoted with arrows, whereas the PET image demonstrates metabolic reductions which predominate in frontal cortex.

et al., 1991). Figure 6.4 shows an example of severe frontal lobe atrophy revealed with structural imaging. As noted, such changes contrast with the changes that occur remotely in cases of vascular dementia. The pathophysiological process related to remote effects of lesions on the frontal lobes is also repeated in a number of subcortical neurodegenerative diseases, although in these conditions the pathological process which exerts these distant effects is neurochemical rather than structural.

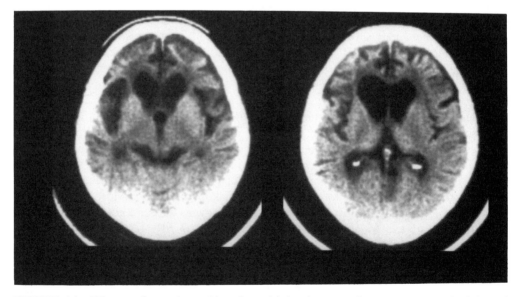

FIGURE 6.4. CT scan of a patient with a frontal lobe dementia demonstrating marked frontal atrophy.

FRONTAL LOBE IMAGING FINDINGS IN SUBCORTICAL NEURODEGENERATIVE DISEASES

Insights into frontal lobe functioning have also been obtained from brain imaging studies of patients with idiopathic Parkinson's disease (PD). Structural imaging studies have demonstrated that generalized atrophy accompanies PD (Drayer, 1988; Steiner, Gomori, & Melamed, 1985), in a manner indistinguishable from that seen in normal aging. MRI has also demonstrated signal changes in subcortical and brainstem nuclei in PD patients (Hauser & Olanow, 1994). However, specific structural changes in the frontal lobes are not a characteristic feature of the disease.

Initial functional imaging studies in PD measured both changes in rCBF and rCMRglc in this disease. Early rCBF studies, performed with the ^{133}Xe inhalation technique, generally revealed blood flow reductions that were widespread in cerebral cortex (Lavy, Melamed, Cooper, Bentin, & Rinot, 1979) and appeared to predominate in the frontal lobes (Bes et al., 1983). However, this technique suffers from limitations of resolution and technical difficulties in measuring changes in subcortical structures, such as the striatum, which are of considerable interest. Initial PET studies of rCMRglc also showed reductions in cortical glucose utilization, which were especially severe and predominated in posterior brain regions in a demented parkinsonian patient (Kuhl, Metter, & Riege, 1984). Thus, initial findings suggested that PD patients who were not demented showed reductions in global rCMRglc with some predominance in frontal cortex, whereas demented PD patients showed more severe temporal and parietal hypometabolism akin to that seen in AD. This is particularly interesting when one considers that AD and PD pathology frequently coexist (Boller, Mizutani, Roessmann, & Gambetti, 1980; McKeith et al., 1996).

Changes in subcortical glucose metabolism have been more controversial, with some studies reporting increased metabolic rates in the basal ganglia contralateral to more affected limbs (Martin et al., 1984) and other studies reporting no changes or lower metabolic rates in subcortical structures (Eidelberg et al., 1990; Karbe et al., 1992; Kuhl et al., 1984; Otsuka et al., 1991). Similar inconsistent results have been obtained with PET measures of oxygen metabolism and blood flow, with increases, decreases, and no changes reported (Otsuka et al., 1991; Wolfson, Leenders, Brown, & Jones, 1985). Although these findings often appear confusing and contradictory, differences between studies appear to be related to a few key issues. First, differences are frequently noted between unilaterally and bilaterally affected PD patients, with the former often demonstrating increased flow and metabolism contralateral to the affected extremity, and the latter demonstrating reductions bilaterally. This may well reflect the duration of the disease, because nigral lesions in animals acutely increase striatal metabolism with smaller effects over time. In addition, other clinical characteristics of patients, such as the relative degree of tremor and the relationship between timing of the scan and levodopa dosage, may be related to the PET findings. Finally, technical issues related to inaccurate recovery of radioactivity values from low-resolution tomographs may obscure hypermetabolism in some cases (Eidelberg et al., 1994).

The general trends in cortical function reported in the inital work have been well replicated, with considerable data supporting the finding of cortical glucose metabolic reductions in cognitively well-characterized patients who are not demented and more severe disturbances in demented patients. Furthermore, patterns of glucose metabolism in PD appear to bear strong relationships to clinical features of the subjects, such as the presence or absence of dementia, depression, and specific cognitive incapacities.

Peppard et al. (1992) found that rCMRglc was globally reduced in PD patients, with more extensive reductions in posterior brain regions in more demented subjects. Pizzolato et al. (1988) reported similar findings when rCBF was studied with SPECT. Eberling, Richardson, Reed, Wolfe, and Jagust (1994) studied a group of nondemented subjects and reported global reductions which were accentuated in posterior brain regions as well. On the surface, these findings might suggest a lack of frontal lobe functional abnormalites in PD. However, when patients are grouped according to clinical symptomatology, clear findings emerge.

Mayberg et al. (1990) characterized a group of nondemented PD patients as depressed or nondepressed and found that metabolic rates in caudate and orbitofrontal cortex were lower in the depressed patients than in nondepressed patients and controls. In addition, scores on depression scales correlated significantly with the degree of orbitofrontal rCMRglc. Ring et al. (1994) used PET and found that depressed PD patients, in comparison to nondepressed PD patients and controls, showed reduced rCBF which centered on medial prefrontal and cingulate cortex bilaterally. In addition, there were no differences in rCBF in these regions when PD patients were compared to patients without PD who suffered from primary depression. These authors have also noted that the PET findings seen in depressed PD patients parallel those reported for patients with primary depression (Baxter et al., 1989). These findings have been explained through conceptualizations of the importance of frontal–subcortical circuits in determining both behavioral and cognitive features of a variety of disease states.

In addition to relationships between PD, depression, and frontal lobe functional imaging findings, a number of studies have reported that PD patients perform poorly on a variety of tests of frontal lobe functions (Lees & Smith, 1983; Starkstein et al., 1989; Taylor, Saint-Cyr, & Lang, 1986). Although the basis for cognitive deterioration in PD is clearly complex, some data exist to support relationships between frontal lobe blood flow and metabolism and cognitive function. Jagust, Reed, Martin, Eberling and Nelson-Abbott (1992) found that in a group of nondemented PD patients, relative dorsolateral frontal lobe rCBF seen with SPECT correlated significantly with performance on cognitive tests of both frontal/executive ability and measures of perseveration. In addition, scores on a depression test were related to frontal lobe function. Playford et al. (1992) found that PD patients failed to activate both putamen and a group of frontal cortical regions (cingulate, supplementary motor area, and dorsolateral prefrontal cortex) in response to an internally cued motor task. Although the task used was motor, these data are important in linking the internal cued aspect of the task to frontal functions. Furthermore, in a separate study, increased supplementary motor area activation was seen when PD patients' akinesia responded to apomorphine infusions (Jenkins et al., 1992). Thus, considerable evidence links performance on frontal-related tasks with frontal brain regions affected by the dopaminergic system.

Frontal lobe changes in metabolic and flow images are even more profound in other extrapyramidal disorders, especially in progressive supranuclear palsy (Steele–Richardson–Olszewski syndrome). Resting PET studies using both flow and metabolic tracers have demonstrated significant reductions in function throughout frontal cortex in these patients (D'Antona et al., 1985; Foster et al., 1988; Leenders, Frackowiak, & Lees, 1988). Perhaps related to these striking frontal lobe abnormalities, in comparison to idiopathic PD, atypical parkinsonism appears to metabolically affect the striatum more severely (Otsuka et al., 1991). Although these findings have not specifically correlated with cognitive function (in general most of these studies had small sample sizes), they do reflect the frontal–subcortical type of dementia frequently exhibited by such patients (Albert,

Feldman, & Willis, 1974). The application of neurochemically specific PET tracers, such as [^{18}F]6-fluorodopa (FDOPA) (Garnett, Firnau, & Nahmias, 1983), has demonstrated clear reductions of dopaminergic function in the striatum of PD patients and patients with atypical parkinsonian syndromes. Interestingly, in PD, the neurochemical lesion as revealed with PET and FDOPA predominates in caudal putamen, with relative sparing of rostral putamen and caudate, whereas in these other syndromes, FDOPA uptake is abnormal throughout the striatum (Brooks et al., 1990; Otsuka et al., 1991). Actual measurement of FDOPA uptake in frontal cortex has proven difficult because of the low signal to noise in this brain region (Otsuka et al., 1995), and it is consequently difficult to implicate direct involvement of nigral–frontal pathways in the genesis of frontal lobe disorders. However, the use of dopamine transporter ligands such as [^{11}C]S-nomifensine (Marie et al., 1995) suggests the possibility that loss of frontal lobe dopaminergic terminals can be measured *in vivo* in parkinsonian syndromes.

These findings taken together clearly support the involvement of frontal–subcortical systems in Parkinson's disease and related parkinsonian degenerations. The anatomy and functional relationships of these systems is more thoroughly discussed in Chapter 1, this volume. However, findings obtained in functional imaging studies of these disorders provides evidence of their importance in neurological disease. Considerable evidence links the functions of the frontal lobes to circuitry involving basal ganglia and thalamus (Alexander, DeLongh, & Strick, 1986; Selemon & Goldman-Rakic, 1985). In addition, well-recognized dopaminergic projections from the medial substantia nigra (ventral tegmental area, A10 cell group) to frontal and limbic cortex exist (Glowinski, Tassin, & Thierry, 1984; Lindvall & Bjrklund, 1974). Thus, the features of parkinsonian degenerations which are so clearly delineated as involving the frontal lobes with functional imaging may be related to direct involvement of either nigral projections or subcortical frontal loops.

SUMMARY AND CONCLUSIONS

Studies of neurodegenerative diseases that utilize brain imaging modalities have thus demonstrated several key findings in relationship to frontal lobe functions. First, performance on frontal lobe tests is related to these imaging measures of frontal lobe atrophy or hypofunction when such measurements show wide enough variation and differentiation from global effects of dementia severity. Furthermore, behavioral features of degenerative diseases, such as apathy, awareness of deficits, and depression, are related to frontal lobe function. Similar functional and behavioral deficits may be produced by either degenerative lesions which directly affect the frontal lobes or by lesions which interrupt frontal subcortical connections. Finally, neurochemical lesions of the dopaminergic system produce deficits in both behavioral tasks mediated by the frontal lobes and frontal lobe perfusion and metabolism. Whether such changes are related to disturbances in dopaminergic projections to the frontal lobes or via striatal circuitry is unknown. In addition, it is unclear whether direct frontal lobe lesions differ substantially from deafferenting frontal lobe lesions in terms of the nature and severity of the behavioral deficits produced.

These results are important in providing, along with the results of lesion studies, converging evidence concerning the role of the frontal lobes in behavior. Future research which may refine this understanding is likely to derive from other developments in functional imaging as well. The use of activation studies (reviewed Chapter 12, this volume) offers the potential of defining the component processes of cognitive functions subserved by frontal cortex, with precise localization of each specific process. The evolution of techniques for neuropharmacological measurement of a host of different neurotransmitter systems also offers the promise of identifying specific neurochemical factors which may be related to specific cognitive functions mediated by the frontal lobes.

REFERENCES

Albert, M. L., Feldman, R. G., & Willis, A. L. (1974). The "subcortical dementia" of progressive supranuclear palsy. *Journal of Neurology, Neurosurgery, and Psychiatry, 37,* 121–130.

Alexander, G. E., DeLongh, R. M., & Strick, P. L. (1986). Parallel organization of functionally segregated circuits linking basal ganglia and cortex. *Annual Review of Neuroscience, 9,* 357–381.

Baxter, L. R., Schwartz, J. M., Phelps, M. E., Mazziotta, J. C., Guze, B. H., Selin, C. E., Gerner, R. H., & Sumida, R. M. (1989). Reduction of prefrontal cortex glucose metabolism common to three types of depression. *Archives of General Psychiatry, 46,* 243–250.

Bes, A., Guell, A., Fabre, N., Dupui, P., Victor, G., & Geraud, G. (1983). Cerebral blood flow studied by [133]Xenon inhalation technique in parkinsonism: Loss of hyperfrontal pattern. *Journal of Cerebral Blood Flow Metabolism, 3,* 33–37.

Boller, F., Mizutani, T., Roessmann, U., & Gambetti, P. (1980). Parkinson disease, dementia, and Alzheimer disease: Clinicopathological correlations. *Annals of Neurology, 7,* 329–335.

Brooks, D. J., Ibanez, V., Sawle, G. V., Quinn, N., Lees, A. J., Mathias, C. J., Bannister, R., Marsden, C. D., & Frackowiak, R. S. J. (1990). Differing patterns of striatal ^{18}F-Dopa uptake in Parkinson's disease, multiple system atrophy, and progressive supranuclear palsy. *Annals of Neurology, 28,* 547–555.

Brun, A., & Englund, E. (1981). Regional pattern of degeneration in Alzheimer's disease: Neuronal loss and histopathological grading. *Histopathology, 5,* 549–564.

Budinger, T. F., & Lauterbur, P. C. (1984). Nuclear magnetic resonance technology for medical studies. *Science, 226,* 288–298.

Cohen, M. B., Graham, L. S., Lake, R., Metter, E. J., Fitten, J., Kulkarni, M. K., Sevrin, R., Yamada, L., Chang, C. C., Woodruff, N., & Kling, A. S. (1986). Diagnosis of Alzheimer's disease and multiple infarct dementia by tomographic imaging of iodine-123 IMP. *Journal of Nuclear Medicine, 27,* 769–774.

Craig, A. H., Cummings, J. L., Fairbanks, L., Itti, L., Miller, B. L., Li, J., & Mena, I. (1996). Cerebral blood flow correlates of apathy in Alzheimer disease. *Archives of Neurology, 53,* 1116–1120.

Cummings, J. L., & Duchen, L. W. (1981). Kluver–Bucy syndrome in Pick disease: Clinical and pathological correlations. *Neurology, 31,* 1415–1422.

D'Antona, R., Baron, J. C., Samson, Y., Serdaru, M., Viader, F., Agid, Y., & Cambier, J. (1985). Subcortical dementia: Frontal cortex hypometabolism detected by positron emission tomography in patients with progressive supranuclear palsy. *Brain, 108,* 785–799.

DeCarli, C., Kaye, J. A., Horwitz, B., & Rapoport, S. I. (1990). Critical analysis of the use of computer-assisted transverse axial tomography to study human brain in aging and dementia of the Alzheimer type. *Neurology, 40,* 872–883.

de Leon, M. J., George, A. E., Stylopoulos, L. A., Smith, G., & Miller, D. C. (1989). Early marker for Alzheimer's disease: The atrophic hippocampus. *Lancet, 2,* 672–673.

Drayer, B. P. (1988). Imaging of the aging brain. Part II. Pathologic conditions. *Radiology, 166,* 797–806.

Duara, R., Grady, C., Haxby, J., Sundaram, M., Cutler, N. R., Heston, L., Moore, A., Schlageter, N., Larson, S., & Rapoport, S. I. (1986). Positron emission tomography in Alzheimer's disease. *Neurology, 36,* 879–887.

Eberling, J. L., Jagust, W. J., Reed, B. R., & Baker, M. G. (1992). Reduced temporal lobe blood flow in Alzheimer's disease. *Neurobiology of Aging, 13,* 483–491.

Eberling, J. L., Reed, B. R., Baker, M. G., & Jagust, W. J. (1993). Cognitive correlates of regional cerebral blood flow in Alzheimer's disease. *Archives of Neurology, 50,* 761–766.

Eberling, J. L., Richardson, B. C., Reed, B. R., Wolfe, N., & Jagust, W. J. (1994). Cortical glucose metabolism in Parkinson's disease without dementia. *Neurobiology of Aging, 15,* 329–335.

Eidelberg, D., Moeller, J. R., Dhawan, V., Sidtis, J. J., Ginos, J. Z., Strother, S. C., Cedarbaum, J., Greene, P., Fahn, S., & Rottenberg, D. A. (1990). The metabolic anatomy of Parkinson's disease: Complementary [18F]Fluorodeoxyglucose and [18F]Fluorodopa positron emission tomographic studies. *Movement Disorders, 5,* 203–213.

Eidelberg, D., Moeller, J. R., Dhawan, V., Spetsieris, P., Takikawa, S., Ishikawa, T., Chaly, T., Robeson, W., Marouleff, D., Przedborski, S., & Fahn, S. (1994). The metabolic topography of parkinsonism. *Journal of Cerebral Blood Flow Metabolism, 14,* 783–801.

Folstein, M. F., Folstein, S. E., & McHugh, P. R. (1975). Mini-Mental State: A practical method for grading the cognitive state of patients for the clinician. *Journal of Psychiatry Research, 12,* 189–198.

Foster, N. L., Chase, T. N., Mansi, L., Brooks, R., Fedio, P., Patronas, N. J., & DiChiro, G. (1984). Cortical abnormalities in Alzheimer's disease. *Annals of Neurology, 16,* 649–654.

Foster, N. L., Gilman, S., Berent, S., Morin, E. M., Brown, M. B., & Koeppe, R. A. (1988). Cerebral hypometabolism in progressive supranuclear palsy studied with positron emission tomography. *Annals of Neurology, 24,* 399–406.

Frackowiak, R. S. J., Pozzili, C., Legg, N. J., Du Boulay, G. H., Marshall, J., Lenzi, L., & Jones, T. (1981). Regional cerebral oxygen supply and utilization in dementia: A clinical and physiological study with oxygen-15 and positron tomography. *Brain, 104,* 753–778.

Friedland, R. P., Budinger, T. F., Ganz, E., Yano, Y., Mathis, C. A., Koss, B., Ober, B. A., Huesman, R. H., & Derenzo, S. E. (1983). Regional cerebral metabolic alterations in dementia of the Alzheimer type: Positron emission tomography with [18F]Fluorodeoxyglucose. *Journal of Computer Assisted Tomography, 7,* 590–598.

Friedland, R. P., Koss, E., Lerner, A., Hedera, P., Ellis, W., Dronkers, N., Ober, B. A., & Jagust, W. J. (1993). Functional imaging, the frontal lobes, and dementia. *Dementia, 4,* 192–203.

Gado, M., Hughes, C. P., Danziger, W., Chi, D., Jost, G., & Berg, L. (1982). Volumetric measurements of the cerebrospinal fluid spaces in demented subjects and controls. *Radiology, 144,* 535–538.

Garnett, E. S., Firnau, G., & Nahmias, C. (1983). Dopamine visualized in the basal ganglia of living man. *Nature, 305,* 137–138.

Glowinski, J., Tassin, F. P., & Thierry, A. M. (1984). The mesocortical-prefrontal dopaminergic neurons. *Trends in Neuroscience,* 418–451.

Hauser, R. A., & Olanow, C. W. (1994). Magnetic resonance imaging of neurodegenerative diseases. *Journal of Neuroimaging, 4,* 146–158.

Haxby, J. V., Grady, C. L., Koss, E., Horwitz, B., Schapiro, M., Friedland, R. P., & Rapoport, S. I. (1988). Heterogeneous anterior–posterior metabolic patterns in dementia of the Alzheimer type. *Neurology, 38,* 1853–1863.

Heutink, P., Stevens, M., Rizzu, P., Bakker, E., Kros, J. M., Tibben, A., Niermeijer, M. F., van Duijn, C. M., Oostra, B. A., & van Swieten, J. C. (1997). Hereditary frontotemporal dementia is linked to chromosome 17q21-q22: A genetic and clinicopathological study of three Dutch families. *Annals of Neurology, 41,* 150–159.

Hyman, B. T., Van Hoesen, G. W., Damasio, A. R., & Barnes, C. L. (1984). Alzheimer's disease: Cell-specific pathology isolates the hippocampal formation. *Science, 225,* 1168–1170.

Ishii, N., Nishihara, Y., & Imamura, T. (1986). Why do frontal lobe symptoms predominate in vascular dementia with lacunes. *Neurology, 36,* 340–345.

Jack, C. R., Petersen, R. C., O'Brien, P. C., & Tangalos, E. G. (1992). MR-based hippocampal volumetry in the diagnosis of Alzheimer's disease. *Neurology, 42,* 183–188.

Jacoby, R. J., Levy, R., & Dawson, J. M. (1980). Computed tomography in the elderly: II. Senile dementia: Diagnosis and functional impairment. *British Journal of Psychiatry, 136,* 256–269.

Jagust, W. J., Friedland, R. P., Budinger, T. F., Koss, E., & Ober, B. (1988). Progression of regional cerebral metabolic abnormalities in Alzheimer's disease. *Neurology, 38,* 909–912.

Jagust, W. J., Reed, B. R., Martin, E. M., Eberling, J. L., & Nelson-Abbott, R. A. (1992). Cognitive function and regional cerebral blood flow in Parkinson's disease. *Brain, 115,* 521–537.

Jagust, W. J., Reed, B. R., Seab, J. P., Kramer, J. H., & Budinger, T. F. (1989). Clinical–physiologic correlates of Alzheimer's disease and frontal lobe dementia. *American Journal of Physiological Imaging, 4,* 89–96.

Jenkins, I. H., Fernandez, W., Playford, E. D., Lees, A. J., Frackowiak, R. S. J., Passingham, R. E., & Brooks, D. J. (1992). Impaired activation of the supplementary motor area in Parkinson's disease is reversed when akinesia is treated with apomorphine. *Annals of Neurology, 32,* 749–757.

Jernigan, T. L., Press, G. A., & Hesselink, J. R. (1990). Methods for measuring brain morphologic features on magnetic resonance images: Validation and normal aging. *Archives of Neurology, 47,* 27–32.

Jernigan, T. L., Salmon, D. P., Butters, N., & Hesselink, J. R. (1991). Cerebral structure on MRI, Part II: Specific changes in Alzheimer's and Huntington's diseases. *Biological Psychiatry, 29,* 68–81.

Jobst, K. A., Smith, A. D., Szatmari, M., Molyneux, A., Esiri, M. E., King, E., Smith, A., Jaskowski, A., McDonald, B., & Wald, N. (1992). Detection in life of confirmed Alzheimer's disease using a simple measurement of medial temporal lobe atrophy by computed tomography. *Lancet, 340,* 1179–1183.

Kamo, H., McGeer, P. L., McGeer, E. G., Calne, D. B., Martin, W. R., & Pate, B. D. (1987). Positron emission tomography and histopathology in Pick's disease. *Neurology, 37,* 439–445.

Karbe, H., Holthoff, V., Huber, M., Herholz, K., Weinhard, K., Wagner, R., & Heiss, W. D. (1992). Positron emission tomography in degenerative disorders of the dopaminergic system. *Journal of Neural Transmission (Parkinson's Disease Section), 4,* 121–130.

Kesslak, J. P., Nalcioglu, O., & Cotman, C. W. (1991). Quantification of magnetic resonance scans for hippocampal and parahippocampal atrophy in Alzheimer's disease. *Neurology, 41,* 51–54.

Kido, D. K., Caine, E. D., LeMay, M., Ekholm, S., Booth, H., & Panzer, R. (1989). Temporal lobe atrophy in patients with Alzheimer's disease: A CT study. *American Journal of Neuroradiology, 10,* 551–555.

Knopman, D. S., Christensen, K. J., Schut, L. J., Harbaugh, R. E., Reeder, T., Ngo, T., & Frey, W. (1989). The spectrum of imgaging and neuropsychological findings in Pick's disease. *Neurology, 39,* 362–368.

Kuhl, D. E., Metter, E. J., & Riege, W. H. (1984). Patterns of local cerebral glucose utilization determined in Parkinson's disease by the [^{18}F]Fluorodeoxyglucose method. *Annals of Neurology, 15,* 419–424.

Lavy, S., Melamed, E., Cooper, G., Bentin, S., & Rinot, Y. (1979). Regional cerebral blood flow in patients with Parkinson's disease. *Archives of Neurology, 36,* 344–348.

Leenders, K. L., Frackowiak, R. S. J., & Lees, A. J. (1988). Steele–Richardson–Olszewski syndrome: Brain energy metabolism, blood flow and fluorodopa uptake measured by positron emission tomography. *Brain, 111,* 615–630.

Lees, A., & Smith, E. (1983). Cognitive deficits in the early stages of Parkinson's disease. *Brain, 106,* 257–270.

Lehtovirta, M., Laakso, M. P., Soininen, H., Helisalmi, S., Mannermaa, A., Helkala, E. L., Partanen, K., Ryynanen, M., Vainio, P., Hartikainen, P., & Riekkinen, P. J. (1995). Volumes of hippocampus, amygdala, and frontal lobe in Alzheimer patients with different apolipoprotein E genotypes. *Neuroscience, 67,* 65–72.

Lindvall, O., & Bjrklund, A. (1974). The organization of the ascending catecholamine neuron systems in the rat brain as revealed by the glyoxylic acid florescence method. *Acta Physiologica Scandinavica, 412,* 1–48.

Lund and Manchester Groups. (1994). Clinical and neuropathological criteria for frontotemporal dementia. *Journal of Neurology Neurosurgery, and Psychiatry, 57,* 416–418.

Lynch, T., Sano, M., Marder, K. S., Bell, K. L., Foster, N. L., Defendini, R. F., Sima, A. A. F., Keohane, C., Nygaard, T. G., Fahn, S., Mayeux, R., Rowland, L. P., & Wilhelmsen, K. C. (1994). Clinical characteristics of a family with chromosome 17-linked disinhibition–dementia–parkinsonism–amyotrophy complex. *Neurology, 44,* 1878–1884.

Marie, R. M., Barre, L., Rioux, P., Allain, P., Lechevalier, B., & Baron, J. C. (1995). PET imaging of neocortical monoaminergic terminals in Parkinson's disease. *Journal of Neural Transmission, 9,* 55–71.

Martin, W. R. W., Beckman, J. H., Calne, D. B., Adam, M. J., Harrop, R., Rogers, J. G., Ruth, T. J., Sayre, C. I., & Pate, B. D. (1984). Cerebral glucose metabolism in Parkinson's disease. *Canadian Journal of Neurological Science, 11,* 169–173.

Mayberg, H. S., Starkstein, S. E., Sadzot, B., Preziosi, T., Andrezejewski, P. L., Dannals, R. F., Wagner, H. N., & Robinson, R. G. (1990). Selective hypometabolism in the inferior frontal lobe in depressed patients with Parkinson's disease. *Annals of Neurology, 28,* 57–64.

McGeer, E. G., McGeer, P. L., Harrop, R., Akiyama, H., & Kamo, H. (1990). Correlations of regional postmortem enzyme activities with premortem local glucose metabolic rates in Alzheimer's disease. *Journal of Neuroscience Research, 27,* 612–619.

McKeith, I. G., Galasko, D., Kosaka, K., Perry, E. K., Dickson, D. W., Hansen, L. W., Salmon, D. P., Lowe, J., Mirra, S. S., Byrne, E. J., Lennox, G., Quinn, N. P., Edwardson, J. A., Ince, P. G., Bergeron, C., Burns, A., Miller, B. L., Lovestone, S., Collerton, D., Jansen, E. N. H., Ballard, C., deVos, R. A. I., Wilcock, G. K., Jellinger, K. A., & Perry, R. H. (1996). Consensus guidelines for the clinical and pathologic diagnosis of dementia with Lewy bodies (DLB). *Neurology, 47,* 1113–1124.

Mendez, M. F., Selwood, A., Mastri, A. R., & Frey, W. H. (1993). Pick's disease versus Alzheimer's disease: A comparison of clinical characteristics. *Neurology, 43,* 289–292.

Miller, B. L., Cummings, J. L., Villaneuva-Meyer, J., Boone, K., Mehringer, C. M., Lesser, I. M., & Mena, I. (1991). Frontal lobe degeneration: Clinical, neuropsychological, and SPECT characteristics. *Neurology, 41,* 1374–1382.

Neary, D., Snowden, J. S., Northen, B., & Goulding, P. (1988). Dementia of frontal lobe type. *Journal of Neurology, Neurosurgery, and Psychiatry, 51,* 353–361.

Otsuka, M., Ichiya, Y., Hosokawa, S., Kuwabara, Y., Tahara, T., Fukumura, T., Kato, M., Masuda, K., & Goto, I. (1991). Striatal blood flow, glucose metabolism and 18F-Dopa uptake: Difference in Parkinson's disease and atypical parkinsonism. *Journal of Neurology, Neurosurgery, and Psychiatry, 54,* 898–904.

Otsuka, M., Ichiya, Y., Kuwabara, Y., Sasaki, M., Yoshida, T., Fukumura, T., & Masuda, K. (1995). Nigrofrontal dopaminergic function as assessed by ^{18}F-dopa PET. *Nuclear Medicine Communications, 16,* 1021–1025.

Pasquier, F., Lebert, F., & Scheltens, P. (1996). *Frontotemporal dementia.* Dordrecht, The Netherlands: ICG.

Peppard, R. F., Martin, W. R. W., Carr, G. D., Grochowski, E., Schulzer, M., Guttman, M., McGeer, P. L., Phillips, A. G., Tsui, J. K. C., & Calne, D. B. (1992). Cerebral glucose metabolism in Parkinson's disease with and without dementia. *Archives of Neurology, 49,* 1262–1268.

Pfefferbaum, A., Sullivan, E. V., Jernigan, T. L., Zipursky, R. B., Rosenbloom, M. J., Yesavage, J. A., & Tinklenberg, J. R. (1990). A quantitative analysis of CT and cognitive measures in normal aging and Alzheimer's disease. *Psychiatry Research: Neuroimaging, 35,* 115–136.

Pizzolato, G., Dam, M., Borsato, N., Saitta, B., Da Col, D., Perlotto, N., Zanco, P., Ferlin, G., & Battistin, L. (1988). 99mTc-HM-PAO SPECT in Parkinson's disease. *Journal of Cerebral Blood Flow Metabolism, 8,* S101–S108.

Playford, E. D., Jenkins, I. H., Passingham, R. E., Nutt, J., Frackowiak, R. S. J., & Brooks, D. J. (1992). Impaired mesial frontal and putamen activation in Parkinson's disease: A positron emission tomography study. *Annals of Neurology, 32,* 151–161.

Reed, B. R., Jagust, W. J., & Coulter, L. (1993). Anosognosia in Alzheimer's disease: Relationships to depression, cognitive function, and cerebral perfusion. *Journal of Clinical and Experimental Neuropsychology, 15,* 231–244.

Ring, H. A., Bench, J., Trimble, M. R., Brooks, D. J., Frackowiak, R. S. J., & Dolan, R. J. (1994). Depression in Parkinson's disease: A positron emission study. *British Journal of Psychiatry, 165,* 333–339.

Rusinek, H., de Leon, M. J., George, A. E., Stylopoulos, L. A., Chandra, R., Smith, G., Rand, T., Mourino, M., & Kowalski, H. (1991). Alzheimer's disease: Measuring loss of cerebral gray matter with MR imaging. *Radiology, 178,* 109–114.

Sandor, T., Albert, M., Stafford, J., & Harpley, S. (1988). Use of computerized CT analysis to discriminate between Alzheimer patients and normal control subjects. *American Journal of Neuroradiology, 9,* 1181–1187.

Sandor, T., Jolesz, F., Tieman, J., Kikinis, R., Jones, K., & Albert, M. (1992). Comparative analysis of computed tomographic and magnetic resonance imaging scans in Alzheimer's patients and controls. *Archives of Neurology, 49,* 381–384.

Schwartz, W. J., Smith, C. B., Davidsen, L., Savaki, H., Sokoloff, L., Mata, M., Fink, D. J., & Gainer, H. (1979). Metabolic mapping of functional activity in the hypothalmo–neurohypophysial system of the rat. *Science, 205,* 723–725.

Seab, J. P., Jagust, W. J., Wong, S. T. S., Roos, M. S., Reed, B. R., & Budinger, T. F. (1988). Quantitative NMR measurements of hippocampal atrophy in Alzheimer's disease. *Magnetic Resonance Medicine, 8,* 200–208.

Selemon, L. D., & Goldman-Rakic, P. S. (1985). Longitudinal topography and interdigitation of corticostriatal projections in the rhesus monkey. *Journal of Neuroscience, 5,* 776–794.

Starkstein, S. E., Preziosi, T. J., Berthier, M. L., Bolduc, P. L., Mayberg, H. S., & Robinson, R. G. (1989). Depression and cognitive impairment in Parkinson's disease. *Brain, 112,* 1141–1153.

Starkstein, S. E., Vazquez, S., Migliorelli, R., Teson, A., Sabe, L., & Leiguarda, R. (1995). A single-photon emission computed tomographic study of anosognosia in Alzheimer's disease. *Archives of Neurology, 52,* 415–420.

Steiner, I., Gomori, J. M., & Melamed, E. (1985). Features of brain atrophy in Parkinson's disease: A CT scan study. *Neuroradiology, 27,* 158–160.

Stout, J. C., Jernigan, T. L., Archibald, S. L., & Salmon, D. P. (1996). Association of dementia severity with cortical gray matter and abnormal white matter volumes in dementia of the Alzheimer type. *Archives of Neurology, 53,* 742–749.

Taylor, A. E., Saint-Cyr, J. A., & Lang, A. E. (1986). Frontal lobe dysfunction in Parkinson's disease. *Brain, 109,* 845–883.

Terry, R. D., Masliah, E., Salmon, D. P., Butters, N., DeTeresa, R., Hill, R., Hansen, L. A., & Katzman, R. (1991). Physical basis of cognitive alterations in Alzheimer's disease: Synapse loss is the major correlate of cognitive impairment. *Annals of Neurology, 30,* 572–580.

Wolfson, L. I., Leenders, K. L., Brown, L. L., & Jones, T. (1985). Alterations of regional cerebral blood flow and oxygen metabolism in Parkinson's disease. *Neurology, 35,* 1399–1405.

Part II

NEUROCHEMISTRY AND NEUROPHYSIOLOGY OF THE FRONTAL LOBES

7

Serotonin and the Frontal Lobes

PHILIPPE H. ROBERT
VALERIE AUBIN-BRUNET
GUY DARCOURT

Serotonin, or 5-hydroxytryptamine (5-HT), initially identified in peripheral tissues, was first detected in the mammalian central nervous system 40 years ago. Very rapidly its heterogeneous distribution suggested that this amine could be a cerebral neurotransmitter. It is now clearly established that neurons that synthesize and release 5-HT participate in the control of many central functions, and that alterations of serotoninergic transmission are associated with various neuropsychiatric conditions such as depression, anxiety, impulsivity, and behavioral disorders in dementias. In addition, interactions between serotonin and the dopaminergic system imply that serotonin is involved in schizophrenic disorders. It should be noted that frontal dysfunctions have been described in most of these disorders. The present chapter is divided into three main sections. The first is devoted to the description of central serotonin receptors. The second describes relationships between alterations of the serotoninergic system and the neuropsychiatric manifestations usually associated with frontal dysfunction. Finally, the third part deals with potential therapeutic uses of 5-HT receptor ligands.

SEROTONIN RECEPTOR SUBTYPES

Organization of Serotoninergic Neurons

5-HT neurons arise from midbrain nuclei. 5-HT cell bodies are systematically organized in the median and dorsal raphe nuclei (Molliver, 1987). Ascending fibers from the dorsal raphe project preferentially to the cortex and striatal regions, whereas the median raphe projects to the limbic regions (Jacobs & Azmitia, 1992). Cowen (1991) reported that each projecting 5-HT neuron sends more than 500,000 terminals to the cerebral cortex. Indeed, the average density of 5-HT innervation in the cortex is greater than that of dopamine or noradrenaline. Most of the different 5-HT receptor subtypes are located on the postsynaptic targets of serotoninergic neurons. Furthermore, some receptors are located on the soma and dendrites (5-HT1A somatodendritic autoreceptors) or on the terminals (5-HT1B/5-HT1D presynaptic autoreceptors) of serotoninergic neurons (Hamon & Gozlan, 1993).

5-HT Receptors

The general definition of a receptor is now relatively consensual. The three most important criteria are the operational aspects (drug-related characteristics; agonists, antagonists, and ligand-binding affinities), the transductional aspects (receptor–effect coupling events) and the structural aspects (gene and receptor structural sequence). Until recently, 5-HT receptors were classified into three main categories. However, more discoveries have extended the number to seven, and others may await identification. The information provided here is based on a provisional consensus which led to publication of the "International Union of Pharmacology Classification of Receptors for 5-Hydroxytryptamine" (Hoyer et al., 1994). Table 7.1 summarizes the operational characteristics and main locations of each receptor subtype. It should be noted that, with the exception of the 5-HT3 subtype, all 5-HT receptors are coupled to G proteins.

5-HT1 Receptors

These were first identified in the course of radioligand-binding studies on brain homogenates with [³H]5-HT (Peroutka & Snyder, 1979), through their high affinity for 5-HT. 5-HT1A receptors were located in limbic structures such as the hippocampus, septum, and amygdala but also in the frontal cortex (Radja et al., 1991; Biegon, Kargman, Snyder, & McEwen, 1986; Dillon, Gross-Isseroff, Israeli, & Biegon, 1991), striatum and raphe nuclei. A recent study of human brain areas obtained from autopsied samples (Marazziti et al., 1994) showed that the highest density of 5-HT1A receptors in the human brain, labeled with the selective ligand [³H]8-OH-DPAT, was found in the hippocampus, followed by the prefrontal cortex and striatum. A parallel study of the distribution of 5-HT1A receptor mRNA was consistent with the binding results, except in the striatum (Pazos, Probst, & Palacios, 1987). Even if the consensus is not perfect, 5-HT1A receptors are generally considered postsynaptic in the hippocampus (Verge et al., 1986), presynaptic in the striatum (Hall et al., 1986), and both post- and presynaptic in the frontal cortex (Hall et al., 1985). Finally, in the anterior raphe nuclei, 5-HT1A receptors are situated at the surface of the somas and the dendrites of serotoninergic neurons.

The strongest concentration of 5-HT1B receptor binding sites was found in the globus pallidus and pars reticula of the substantia nigra. These sites are situated in the presynaptic nerve endings (Hamon et al., 1990). The distribution of their mRNA shows a preference for the striatum.

There are also 5-HT1D receptor binding sites in the substantia nigra, but, like 5-HT1E receptors, they are also present in the frontal cortex, subiculum, and entorhinal cortex (Barone, Jordan, Atger, Kopp, & Fillion, 1994). 5-HT1D and 5-HT1E receptors are distributed homogeneously in the frontal cortex, in layers II to VI. It is thus possible that these receptors are present on nerve endings other than those of serotoninergic fibers, which are most dense in layer IV (Azmitia & Gannon, 1986; Morrison, Foote, Molliver, Bloom, & Lidow, 1982).

TABLE 7.1. Operational Characteristics and Locations of 5-HT Receptor Subtypes

Receptor	Radioligands	Agonists	Antagonists	Localization
5-HT1A	[^{3}H]8-OH-DPAT [^{3}H]Ipsapirone	8-OH-DPAT Flesinoxan Ipsapirone	Cyanopindolol Pindolol Spiperone	Limbic system Raphe Prefrontal cortex
5-HT1B	[^{125}I]Iodocyanopindolol [^{3}H]5-HT S-CM-G[^{125}I]TNH2	RU 24969 Metergoline Methysergide	Cyanopindolol Propanolol Pindolol	Basal ganglia Globus pallidus
5-HT1D	[^{3}H]5-HT	L 694247 Metergoline Methysergide	Methiothepin Mianserin	Frontal cortex Hippocampus Substantia nigra
5-HT1E	[^{3}H]5-HT	5-HT	None	Frontal cortex Hippocampus
5-HT1E	[^{3}H]5-HT	5-HT	None	Dorsal raphe Hippocampus
5-HT2A	[^{3}H]Ketanserine [^{3}H]Spiperone	DOI Methyl-5-HT	Pirenperone Ketanserin	Frontal cortex Claustrum Limbic system
5-HT2B		Methyl-5-HT	Mesulergine	Mainly peripheral
5-HT2C	[^{3}H]Mesulergine	Methyl-5-HT DOI mCPP	Metergoline Mesulergine Methysergide	Basal ganglia Limbic system Choroid plexus
5-HT3	[^{3}H]Zacopride	2 Methyl-5-HT	Tropisetron Zacopride	Limbic system
5-HT4	[^{3}H]GR113808	Cisapride 5-MeOT	SB 204070 GR113808	Substantia nigra Hippocampus
5-HT5				Cortex Hippocampus
5-HT6				Not known; central nervous system
5-HT7	[^{125}I]LSD [^{3}H]5-HT			Forebrain

5-HT2 Receptors

It is now clear that at least three 5-HT2 receptor subtypes exist. 5-HT2A receptors (corresponding to the former 5-HT2 receptors) are present in different regions of the cortex (Cook et al., 1994; Hoyer, Pazos, Probst, & Palacios, 1986; Pazos, Cortes, & Palacios, 1985) and the limbic system. They are situated on postsynaptic targets of serotoninergic neurons. The distribution of their mRNA corresponds to that of the receptors in the frontal cortex (Mengod, Pompeiano, Martinez-Mir, & Palacios, 1990). In an *in vivo* study based on positron emission tomography (PET) with the ligand F18N-methylspiperone, Wang et al. (1995) showed a gradual decay of these receptors with age, which was more marked in the frontal cortex than in the occipital cortex. The receptors initially known as 5-HT1C are now called 5-HT2C (Humphrey, Hartig, & Hoyer, 1993) because of their pharmacological and structural relatedness to 5-HT2A. In humans, they are particularly abundant.

Other 5-HT Receptors

Contrary to the receptors described previously, which are all coupled to G proteins, 5-HT3 is an "ion-channel receptor" whose stimulation opens a sodium/potassium channel (Yakel, Shao, & Jackson, 1990). In the central nervous system it is most abundant in the amygdala, hippocampus, and entorhinal cortex (Laporte, Kidd, Verge, Gozlan, & Hamon, 1992; Palacios, Waeber, Mengod, & Pompeiano, 1991). There are few data on 5-HT4 receptors. They appear to be present in the frontal cortex, where they mediate adenylyl cyclase stimulation (Monferini et al., 1993).

Serotonin–Dopamine Interactions

These relationships are important for several reasons.

1. The dopaminergic (DA) system has held an important place in the study of prefrontal function.
2. As described earlier, there is a high density of serotoninergic receptors in the striatum and frontal cortex.
3. In the midbrain, dopaminergic cell bodies of the substantia nigra are innervated by serotoninergic projections of the medial and dorsal raphe.

In a review of the literature on clinical, physiological, and anatomical data, Kapur and Remington (1996) underlined that one role of the serotoninergic system is to inhibit dopaminergic operation at different levels. In the midbrain, inhibition of the firing of dopaminergic neurons seems to be modulated by 5-HT2 receptors located on the somatodendritic surface of DA neurons (Jacobs & Azmitia, 1992; James & Starr, 1980; Ugedo, Grenhoff, & Svensson, 1989). In the forebrain, serotoninergic neurons projecting via the raphe striatal pathway provoke the inhibition of striatal DA neuronal firing. Lesions of these serotoninergic projections disinhibit the dopaminergic system (Dray, Davies, Oakley, Tongroach, & Velluci, 1978; Dray, Gonye, Oakley, & Tanner, 1976), whereas 5-HT2 antagonists, by blocking the serotoninergic inhibitory effect, increase the level of DA in the striatum.

BEHAVIORAL DISTURBANCES, FRONTAL LOBE, AND SEROTONIN

Many studies have shown a relationship between frontal region dysfunction and clinical behavioral disorders (Mega & Cummings, 1994; Cummings, 1993). At the same time, the role of serotonin was demonstrated in a wide variety of human and animal disorders (see Table 7.2).

Serotonin, Depression, and Anxiety

In 1976, Asberg, Traskman, and Thoren were the first to study links between behavioral and biological disturbances. They demonstrated the existence of two subgroups of depressed subjects, one with low levels of 5-hydroxyindoleacetic acid (5-HIAA) in the cerebrospinal fluid (CSF) and the other with normal levels. This bimodal distribution has been confirmed (Brown & Linnoila, 1990; Van Praag, 1982), but clinical characterization

TABLE 7.2. Behavior Related to Frontal Lobe Disorders and Serotoninergic (5-HT) System Abnormalities

Frontal lobe disorders	5-HT system disturbances
Depressive mood	Depression
Emotional lability	General anxiety
Perseverative behaviors	Panic attack
Compulsion	Obsessive–compulsive disorder
Agitation	Aggressiveness
Anxiety	Impulsivity
Disinhibition	Sleep disorders
Irritability	Eating disorders
Apathy	Pain
Loss of initiative	Retardation

Note. Frontal lobe disorders include disorders occurring in different areas (e.g., dorsolateral, orbitofrontal and anterior cingulum), as well as dysfunction of connections between the frontal–subcortical regions. (Bibliographic references are listed in the text.)

of these low-serotonin depressed patients has remained unconvincing (Goodwin, Post, Dunner, & Gordon, 1973). The strongest correlation was with a history of attempted suicide (Asberg, Schalling, Taskman-Bendz, & Wagner, 1987). Studies on endocrine responses to agents increasing central serotoninergic activity have the potential advantage of examining the physiological operation of the serotoninergic system. Through their hypothalamic connections, central monoaminergic systems act on the endocrine hypo-thalamus–pituitary axis. Intravenous tryptophan and oral fenfluramine (Cowen & Charig, 1987) both increase plasma prolactin levels and have been used to explore the serotoninergic system. Cocaro, Siever, Owen, and Davis (1990) demonstrated a fall in the prolactin response to fenfluramine in 33% of depressed subjects with a history of suicide attempts against only 6% of other depressed subjects. Extending this methodology, Mann et al. (1996b) used PET [^{18}F]fluorodeoxyglucose (18FDG) method to examine the fenfluramine-induced changes in regional glucose metabolism (rCMR glu) as an indicator of changes in regional neuronal activity and therefore in serotonin responsivity. These authors demonstrated in healthy subjects an increase of rCMRglu on the anterior cingulate and the lateral prefrontal cortex. In contrast, using the same fenfluramine challenge test, depressed patients (Mann et al., 1996a) had no areas of increase in frontal rCMRglu. This result provides the first direct *in vivo* evidence of a blunted regional brain response to serotonin release in depressed patients.

All studies on selective serotonin reuptake inhibitors (SSRIs) have shown that these agents have an antidepressive action (Blier, De Montigny, & Chaput, 1994). However, the hypothesis that an isolated rise in serotoninergic neurotransmission is sufficient to explain the antidepressant effect is controversial (Poldinger, Calanchini, & Schwarz, 1991), and it seems important to refine our knowledge of interactions between the serotoninergic system and the other neurotransmitter systems.

The serotoninergic system is also involved in anxiety disorders. In generalized anxiety, clinical trials have demonstrated the efficacy of selective serotoninergic drugs. Serotoninergic treatments are effective on panic disorders, too (Giesecke, 1990). The putative presynaptic origin (Kahn, Van Praag, Weltzer, Asnis, & Barr, 1988) of the deficiency remains to be confirmed, however. Finally, it is in obsessive–compulsive disorders (OCD) that the serotoninergic system plays the clearest role. SSRI have both an antiobsessive and an anticompulsive action (Fontaine & Chouinard, 1989). Serotoninergic modulation is particularly important in the left orbitofrontal region. This region is where the largest increase in regional cerebral blood flow was observed during delayed symptom exacerbation by a single dose of metergoline (a 5-HT antagonist) in fluoxetine-treated OCD patients.

Transnosological Approach

Given the discrepancies between clinical classifications and biological features, a dimensional, transnosographical approach to these disturbances appears to be more relevant than a conventional categorial diagnostic approach. Among the various behavioral manifestations in which serotonin is involved (Benkelfat, 1993) one of the most important is represented by control and compulsion disorders, which are also common in frontal dysfunction.

The role of central serotoninergic function in suicidal behavior was shown many years ago, and it is now agreed that serotonin exerts an inhibitory function on the other neuronal systems (Golden, Gilmore, & Carson, 1991). On the other hand, it is not known if fluctuations in the serotoninergic system are a marker of traits correlating with a threshold of attempted suicide or a marker of a state correlating with an acute stressor triggering the pathway to suicide (Abbar, Amadeo, & Malafosse, 1992). The majority of postmortem studies of suicide victims have shown reductions in 5-HIAA and 5-HT in the cerebral cortex. Conflicting results between the different studies (for review, see Aubin-Brunet, 1996a; Little & Sparks, 1990) can be due to methodological biases, especially those linked to the victim's psychiatric history. Similarly, the results of studies on serotoninergic receptors must also be interpreted with care (for review, see Mann, Arango, & Marzuk, 1989). It is generally agreed that suicide victims show a fall in presynaptic receptors and a rise in postsynaptic 5-HT2 receptors (Sparks & Little, 1990). In regard to suicide attempts, the consensus is that 5-HIAA levels fall in the CSF during unipolar depression and personality disorders. The lowest levels have been found in subjects who make violent suicide attempts (shooting, hanging, falls) relative to those who commit suicide with poisons, drugs, or CO_2 (Coccaro, 1992). Dynamic neuroendocrine studies show similar trends, and suggest the existence of 5-HT2 receptor hypersensitivity in suicides (Mann et al., 1992). Genetic studies have suggested that the tryptophan hydroxylase genotype correlates with the CSF 5-HIAA level and could be associated with behaviors controlled by serotonin (Virkkunen, Rawlings, & Tokola, 1994). Many studies (see Roy, Virkkunen, & Linnoila, 1990, for a review) have also explored CSF 5-HIAA levels in aggressive patients. These studies show a decrease in 5-HIAA in the CSF of impulsively violent criminals, mothers who kill their children and then attempt to commit suicide, impulsive arsonists, compulsive gamblers, and people with antisocial or borderline personality disorders. Serotonin is also involved in inability to delay actions and to tolerate frustration. Most studies point to a fall in serotoninergic neurotransmission in alcoholics (Ballanger, Goodwin, & Major, 1979), bulimic subjects (Fernstrom, 1985), impulsive arsonists, and violent delinquents. It is interesting to note that the frontal lobe plays an important role in controlling both impulsive behaviors (Miller, 1992) and central serotonin turnover (Linnoila, Virkkunen, & Higley, 1993). Finally, it must be underlined that the serotoninergic system is also involved in the pain tolerance threshold (Basbaum & Fields, 1984), sleep (Hartmann & Greewald, 1984) and eating disorders such as carbohydrate "bingeing" and nocturnal bulimia (Brewerton, Brandt, Lessem, Murphy, & Jimerson, 1990).

The serotoninergic system is therefore involved in phenomena as varied as depression and anxiety, behavioral disorders occurring in various conditions, and physiological functions. Aubin, Jouvent, Widlocher, and Darcourt (1993) constructed the Aubin Jouvent Rating Scale (AJRS) based on the identification and measurement of the previously discussed manifestations. The main value of this scale is for the study of potential relationships between these clinical dimensions and serotoninergic dysfunctions. In its final version, AJRS is composed of 10 items scored from 0 to 6. It has been validated in subjects over 6 years of age. The first study (Aubin-Brunet, 1993) assessed 155 subjects with an average age of 73 years (dementia, *n* = 41; major affective disorders, *n* = 71; residual schizophrenia, *n* = 18; healthy subjects, *n* = 25). The results for each of the 10 items showed a mean score of more than 1, with an overall mean of 2.095, providing statistical validation of their clinical relevance. The standard deviation was greater than 1, reflecting a good distribution of the scores. Principal-components analysis after Varimax oblique rotation showed that the 10 items were distributed into factors accounting for 78% of the variance (see Table 7.3). Each item was pure; that is, it was not distributed among several factors but, on the contrary, was saturated in a single factor. This saturation varied from 0.62 to 0.90. Finally, the factorial distribution (factor 1 = loss of control; factor 2 = anxiety, insomnia; factor 3 = depression; factor 4 = physiological disturbances) is in keeping with categories used in clinical practice. These results were confirmed in other populations of elderly subjects (Aubin-Brunet, 1996a; Aubin-Brunet, Beau, Asso, Robert, & Darcourt, 1996b). It is also interesting to observe the relationships between clinical assessments and biological parameters. The clomipramine test is a dynamic neuroendocrine test, and the prolactin response it entails is the most specific for the serotoninergic system (Cowen, 1991; Golden et al., 1991). A preliminary study (Thiery, Aubin-Brunet, Candito, & Darcourt, 1997) demonstrated that the prolactin response of 9 subjects (mean age = 73.13, range = 62 to 89) characterized by a score higher than 20 (mean = 23.2) on the AJRS scale (serotoninergic deficiency) was significantly lower (Δ PRL = 0.67 ± 2.24 vs. 8.64 ± 15.94; *p* < .06) than that of 11 subjects (mean age = 83, range = 70 to 95) with a score lower than 8 (mean = 7). It should also be noted that there was no difference between the two groups in regard to the intensity of stress and adverse effects. These results obtained in very old subjects with diminished biological reactivity are the first to verify the hypothesis whereby a deficiency in the serotoninergic system can be identified by a biological index in subjects with an elevated AJRS score.

TABLE 7.3. Factor Analysis on the 10 AJRS Items:
Four-Factor Solutions after Oblique Rotation

	Factor 1	Factor 2	Factor 3	Factor 4
% of variance	45	14	10	9
Mood swings	0.89			
Aggressiveness	0.88			
Irritability	0.87			
Impatience	0.67			
Sleep disorders		0.90		
Anxiety		0.62		
Suicidal			0.88	
Intolerance of isolation			0.67	
Eating disorders				0.71
Pain				0.74

THERAPEUTIC IMPLICATIONS

Knowledge of the relationships between serotonin and the frontal lobe has already found therapeutic applications. The best known is the treatment of depression and anxiety disorders. Indeed, SSRIs increase the extracellular concentration of 5-HT, leading to the stimulation of the various classes of specific receptors by endogenous neurotransmitters. However, some of these receptors are autoreceptors whose activation inhibits central serotoninergic transmission (i.e., the opposite phenomenon to the aim of treatment). This explains the potential value of 5-HT1A/B/D autoreceptor antagonists. Finally, it should be remembered that 5-HT1A receptors are directly involved in the control of mood and emotions, and that agonists of these receptors (buspirone, ipsapirone) have proven clinical efficacy, notably in anxiety disorders.

Another implication is in the treatment of "negative" symptoms of schizophrenia. An early hypothesis suggested that these symptoms could be mediated by a serotoninergic deficiency and could therefore be improved by treatments that enhanced serotoninergic transmission in the frontal lobes (Breier, 1995), such as 5-HT reuptake inhibitors (Goff, Midha, Saridsegal, Hubbard, & Amico, 1995; Spina et al., 1994). For these agents to be effective, the serotoninergic terminals must be intact. If the clinical manifestations are due to a loss of these nerve endings, another approach would be to use a 5-HT agonist acting directly on the receptors. A second hypothesis is based on the relationships between serotonin and dopamine. Negative symptoms would result from hypodopaminergic activity in the frontal cortex. The 5-HT2 antagonist would allow the dopaminergic system to be disinhibited (Moghaddam & Bunney, 1990), thereby leading to a rise in dopaminergic transmission in the prefrontal cortex. The first clinical data supporting this hypothesis were provided by the demonstration that, in schizophrenic subjects, setoperone (Ceulemans, Gelders, Hoppenbrouwers, Reyntjens, & Janssen, 1985) and ritanserin (Gelders, 1989) improved negative symptoms such as emotional withdrawal. More recently, new antipsychotic agents such as risperidone have been developed to combine the 5-HT2 and D2 actions in as balanced a manner as possible. The paradox is that agents used in these two schemas have opposite effects on the serotoninergic system. There is currently no universally accepted explanation for this phenomenon, but investigations will probably have to take into account both the anatomical location of the serotoninergic target and the precise description of so-called negative symptoms, which are in fact heterogeneous and reflect the involvement of separate neurophysiological entities.

A third therapeutic implication is in the treatment of behavioral disorders in patients with dementias. In dementia of Alzheimer type for example, clinical trials have demonstrated the efficacy of serotoninergic agents (Lebert, Pasquier, & Petit, 1994; Nyth & Gottfries, 1990). In addition, the preservation of postsynaptic 5-HT1A receptors in these patients (Chen, Adler, & Bowen, 1996) suggests that subjects with depressive symptoms could benefit from SSRIs or even 5-HT1A agonists. Similarly, the selective preservation of 5-HT2A receptors in the orbitofrontal and temporal neocortex of anxious Alzheimer's disease patients (Chen et al., 1994) suggests that products acting on 5-HT2A receptors would be of value (Esiri, 1996). Behavioral disorders are a major problem in frontal lobe dementia. Anderson, Scott, and Harborne (1996) reported two cases in which a combination of SSRIs and lithium improved depressive symptoms. In the clinical case reported here, illustrating the course of frontal lobe dementia, the SSRI acted on a larger spectrum of behavioral disorders, some of which correspond to those described previously as being linked to a serotoninergic dysfunction.

Case Study

The following case report demonstrates the utility of serotoninergic agonists in a patient with a dementia syndrome.

Mme A is a right-handed, 60-year-old woman with higher education and no psychiatric history. She presented in late November 1994 accompanied by her daughter. For about 6 months she had been sad, impatient, and sometimes irritable. This was out of character, and her daughter persuaded her to consult when she started having morbid ideas. Mme A continued to play bridge regularly and to visit her grandchildren but seemed to have lost interest. A neuropsychological examination was done in December 1994 (Mini-Mental State, 28/30; Signoret Mnesic Efficiency Battery, 61.5, score normal for age and education; Wisconsin Card Sorting Test, 3/6 categories completed, and increased number of perseverations). Cerebral scintigraphy with the hexamethyl propyleneamine oxime tracer showed discrete orbitofrontal hypoperfusion. During a subsequent visit in January 1995, her daughter reported inappropriate behavior. She had caught her mother stealing a packet of sweets in a shop. On another occasion she left a cafe without paying. Antidepressive treatment with paroxetine (10 mg for 7 days, then 20 mg) considerably improved her emotional disorders and inappropriate behavior: "She seems to be more present when she's with us, is interested in more things and, especially, no longer has morbid ideas and no longer does silly things."

In July 1995, during another visit, Mme A's children reported that she had stopped taking her treatment for 3 weeks. She had started to become withdrawn, lying on her bed and reading, watching TV games, and chatting to the portrait of her husband, who had died 19 years previously. The interview showed that she was again having morbid ideas and pessimistic thoughts, although she broached these subjects without sadness. On the contrary, she was very lively and even socially disinhibited (she lay on a table in the waiting room, and greeted the doctor with a kiss). In addition, her daughter reported the following events:

> "She only shoplifted once, in a department store, but what is new is that she has become very careful with her money. Sometimes she even goes to the kitchen in a restaurant to discuss the price of a meal. . . . She is also more and more interested in games. She wants to go on playing bridge, but I think she's finding it difficult to get someone to play with her. According to what she has told me, she has been to the casino several times. . . . What's more, she tries to pick up men and is quite successful! Finally, she has put on weight, but it's true that she does eat a lot. I am amazed by the size of the meals she eats. Meals seem to have become very important. At home, she can't bear waiting once the meal is on the table!"

Mme A agreed with what her daughter said, then asked when the interview would end because it was "time to be getting home." Renewed treatment with paroxetine led to a disappearance of depressive ideas, a reduction in her appetite, and less interest in games.

In September 1996, a new neuropsychological examination was undertaken (Mini-Mental State, 15/30; altered immediate recall and inability to complete memory tests). Her daughter said Mme A had again stopped taking her treatment during the summer. Her behavior had changed. She would spend long hours lying in bed, was no longer interested in games, and went out for only two reasons: the church and the supermarket. She had recently become very religious and often attended services; she would ask the priest questions on irrelevant subjects during the services. Her eating behavior had also changed. She said she only liked minced steak, bought a great deal of it, and ate two helpings at each meal. Furthermore, she no longer tolerated the cold; her favorite drink was mint cordial with warm water. This time paroxetine only partially improved her apathy and had no effect on the other disorders.

Dementias illustrate the value of serotoninergic agents in the treatment of behavioral disorders observed during the course of various neuropsychiatric conditions. Controlled clinical trials are now required to determine the effect of different serotoninergic agents on behavioral disorders that are clearly defined from a clinical standpoint.

REFERENCES

Abbar, M., Amadeo, S., & Malafosse, A. (1992). An association study between suicidal behavior and tryptophan hydroxylase markers. *Clinical Psychopharmacology, 15*(Suppl. 1), 299.

Anderson, I. M., Scott, K., & Harborne, G. (1996). Serotonin and depression in frontal lobe dementia (letter). *American Journal of Psychiatry, 152,* 645.

Asberg, M., Traskman, L., & Thoren, P. (1976). 5-HIAA in the cerebrospinal fluid: A biochemical suicide predictor? *Archives of General Psychiatry, 33,* 1193–1197.

Asberg, M., Schalling, D., Taskman-Bendz, L., & Wagner, A. (1987). Psychobiology of suicide, impulsivity, and related phenomena. In H. Y. Meltzer (Ed.), *Psychopharmacology: Third generation of progress* (pp. 665–668). New York: Raven Press.

Aubin-Brunet, V. (1996a). *De l'hypothése biologique à la quantification clinique: L'exemple des relations sérotonine vieillissement.* Université Paris 6: Thèse de Sciences de la Vie.

Aubin-Brunet, V., Beau, C. H., Asso, G., Robert, P. H., & Darcourt, G. (1996b). Serotoninergic symptomatology in dementia. In E. Giacobini, R. Becker, & P. H. Robert (Eds), *Alzheimer disease: Therapeutic strategies* (pp. 520–555). Boston: Birkhauser.

Aubin, V., Jouvent, R., Widlocher, D., & Darcourt, G. (1993). Modelisation hypothetique du déficit serotoninergique chez le suject âgé: Construction et validation d'une echelle clinique. *L'Encéphale, 19,* 37–46.

Azmitia, E. C., & Gannon, P. J. (1986). Anatomy of the serotonergic system in the primate and the sub-primate brains. *Advances in Neurology, 43,* 407–468.

Ballanger, J. C., Goodwin, F. K., & Major, L. F. (1979). Alcohol and central serotonin metabolism in man. *Archives of General Psychiatry, 36,* 224–229.

Barone, P., Jordan, D., Atger, F., Kopp, N., & Fillion, G. (1994). Quantitative autoradiography of 5-HT1D and 5-HT1E binding sites labelled by [^{3}H]5-HT, in frontal cortex and the hippocampal region of the human brain. *Brain Research, 638,* 85–94.

Basbaum, A. I., & Fields, H. L. (1984). Endogenous pain controls systems: Brainstem spinal pathways and endorphin circuits. *Annual Review of Neurosciences, 7,* 309–338.

Benkelfat, C. (1993). Serotonergic mechanisms in psychiatric disorders: New research tools, new ideas. *International Clinical Psychopharmacology, 8*(Suppl. 2), 53–62.

Biegon, A., Kargman, S., Snyder, L., & McEwen, B. (1986). Characterization and localization of serotonin receptors in human brain postmortem. *Brain Research, 363,* 91–98.

Blier, P., De Montigny, C., & Chaput, Y. (1994). Current advances and trends in the treatment of depression. *Trends in Pharmacological Sciences, 15,* 220–226.

Breier, A. (1995). Serotonin, schizophrenia and antipsychotic drug action. *Schizophrenia Research, 14, 187–202.*

Brewerton, T. D., Brandt, H. A., Lessem, M. D., Murphy, D. L., & Jimerson, D. C. (1990). Serotonin and eating disorders. In E. F. Coccaro & D. L. Murphy (Eds), *Serotonin in major psychiatric disorders—Progress in psychiatry* (pp. 153–184). Washington, DC: American Psychiatric Press

Brown, G. L., & Linnoila, M. (1990). Serotonin metabolite (5-HIAA) studies in depression, impulsivity, and violence. *Journal of Clinical Psychiatry, 51*(Suppl. 4), 31–41.

Ceulemans, D. L., Gelders, Y. G., Hoppenbrouwers, M. L., Reyntjens, A. J., & Janssen, P. A. (1985). Effect of serotonin antagonism in schizophrenia: A pilot study with setoperone. *Psychopharmacology, 85,* 329–332.

Chen, C. P. L. H., Adler, J. T., & Bowen, D. M. (1996). Presynaptic serotonergic markers in community-acquired cases of Alzheimer's disease: Correlations with depression and medication. *Journal of Neurochemistry, 66,* 1592–1598.

Chen, C. P. L. H., Hope, R. A., Adler, J. T., Keene, J., McDonald, B., Francis, P. T., Esiri, M. M., & Bowen, D. M. (1994). Loss of 5-HT2A receptors in Alzheimer's disease neocortex is associated with disease severity while preservation of 5-HT2A receptors is associated with anxiety [Abstract]. *Annals of Neurology, 36,* 308–309.

Coccaro, E. F. (1992). Impulsive aggression and central serotonergic system function in humans: An example of a dimensional brain–behavior relationship. *International Clinical Psychopharmacology, 7,* 3–12.

Coccaro, E. F., Siever, L. J., Owen, K. R., & Davis, K. L. (1990). Serotonin in mood and personality disorders. In E. F. Coccaro & D. L. Murphy (Eds.), *Serotonin in major psychiatric disorders* (pp. 69–98). Washington, DC: American Psychiatric Press.

Cook, E. H., Fletcher, K. E., Wainwright, M., Marks, N., Yan, S., & Leventhal, B. L. (1994). Primary structure of the human platelet serotonin 5-HT2A receptor: Identity with frontal cortex serotonin 5-HT2A receptor. *Journal of Neurochemistry, 63,* 465–469.

Cowen, P. J. (1991). Serotonin receptor subtypes: Implications for psychopharmacology. *British Journal of Psychiatry, 159*(Suppl. 12), 7–14.

Cowen, P. J., & Charig, E. M. (1987). Neuroendocrine responses to intraveneous tryptophan in major depression. *Archives of General Psychiatry, 44,* 958–966.

Cummings, J. L. (1993). Frontal–subcortical circuits and human behavior. *Archives of Neurology, 50,* 873–880.

Dillon, K. A., Gross-Isseroff, R., Israeli, M., & Biegon, A. (1991). Autoradiographic analysis of serotonin 1A receptor binding in the human brain postmortem: Effects of age and alcohol. *Brain Research, 554,* 56–64.

Dray, A., Gonye, T. J., Oakley, N. R., & Tanner, T. (1976). Evidence for the existence of a raphe projection to the substancia nigra in rat. *Brain Research, 113,* 45–57.

Dray, A., Davies, J., Oakley, N. R., Tongroach, P., & Velluci, S. (1978). The dorsal and media raphe projections to the substancia nigra in the rat: Electrophysiological, biochemical and behavioural observations. *Brain Research, 151,* 431–442.

Esiri, M. M. (1996). The basis for behavioural disturbances in dementia [Editorial]. *Journal of Neurology Neurosurgery and Psychiatry, 61,* 127–130.

Fernstrom, J. D. (1985). Dietary effects on brain serotonin synthesis: Relationship to appetite regulation. *American Journal of Clinical Nutrition, 42,* 1072–1082.

Fontaine, R., & Chouinard, G. (1989). Fluoxetine in the long term maintenance treatment of obsessive compulsive disorder. *Psychiatric Annals, 19,* 88–91.

Gelders, Y. G. (1989). Thymosthenic agents, a novel approach in the treatment of schizophrenia. *British Journal of Psychiatry, 155,* 33–36.

Giesecke, M. E. (1990). Overcoming hypersensivity to fluoxetine in a patient with panic disorder. *American Journal of Psychiatry, 147,* 532–533.

Goff, D. C., Midha, K. K., Saridsegal, O., Hubbard, J. W., & Amico, E. (1995). A placebo-controlled trial of fluoxetine added to neuroleptic in patients with schizophrenia. *Psychopharmacology, 117,* 417–423.

Golden, N. R., Gilmore, J. H., & Carson, S. W. (1991). Serotonin, suicide and aggression: Clinical studies. *Journal of Clinical Psychiatry, 52*(Suppl. 12), 61–69.

Goodwin, F. K., Post, R. M., Dunner, D. L., & Gordon, E. K. (1973). Cerebrospinalfluid amine metabolites in affective illness; the probenecid technique. *American Journal of Psychiatry, 130,* 73–79.

Hall, M. D., El Mestikawy, S., Emerit, M. B., Pichat, L., Hamon, M., & Gozlan, H. (1985). [^{3}H]8 Hydroxy-2(di-*n*-propylamino)tetralin binding to pre- and postsynaptic 5-hydroxytryptamine sites in various region of the rat brain. *Journal of Neurochemistry, 44,* 1685–1696.

Hall, M. D., Gozlan, H., Emerit, M. B., El Mestikawy, S., Pichat, L., & Hamon, M. (1986). Differentiation of pre- and postsynaptic high-affinity serotonin receptor binding sites using physico-chemical parameters and modifying agents. *Neurochemistry Research, 11*, 891–892.

Hamon, M., Collin, E., Chantrel, D., Daval, G., Verge, D., Bourgoin, S., & Cesselin, F. (1990). Serotonin receptors and the modulation of pain. In J. M. Besson (Ed.), *Serotonin and pain* (pp. 53–72). Amsterdam: Elsevier.

Hamon, M., & Gozlan, H. (1993). Les rcepteurs centraux de la srotonine. *Mdecine/Sciences, 9*, 21–30.

Hartmann, E., & Greewald, D. (1984). Tryptophan and human sleep: An analysis of 43 studies. In H. G. Schlossberger, W. Kochen, & B. Linzen (Eds.), *Tryptophan and serotonin research* (pp. 297–304). Berlin: Walter de Gruyter.

Hoyer, D., Clarke, D. E., Fozard, J. R., Hartig, P. R., Martin, G. R., Mylecharane, E. J., Saxena, P. R., & Humphrey, P. P. (1994). International Union of Pharmacology Classification of receptors for 5-hydroxytryptamine. *Pharmacological Reviews, 46*, 157–203.

Hoyer, D., Pazos, A., Probst, A., & Palacios, J. M. (1986). Serotonin receptors in the human brain. II: Characterisation and autoradiographic localisation of 5-HT1C and 5-HT2 recognition sites. *Brain Research, 376*, 97–107.

Humphrey, P. P., Hartig, P. R., & Hoyer, D. (1993). A proposed new nomenclature for 5-HT receptors. *Trends in Pharmacological Sciences, 14*, 233–236.

Jacobs, B. L., & Azmitia, E. C. (1992). Structure and function of the brain serotonin system. *Physiological Review, 72*, 165–229.

James, T. A., & Starr, M. S. (1980). Rotational behaviour elicited by 5-HT in the rat: Evidence for an inhibitory role of 5-HT in the substancia nigra and corpus striatum. *Journal of Pharmaceutical Pharmacology, 32*, 196–200.

Kahn, R. S., Van Praag, H. M., Weltzer, S., Asnis, G., & Barr, G. (1988). Serotonin and anxiety revisited. *Biological Psychiatry, 23*, 189–208.

Kapur, S., & Remington, G. (1996). Serotonin–dopamine interaction and its relevance to schizophrenia. *American Journal of Psychiatry, 153*, 466–476.

Laporte, A. M., Kidd, E., Verge, D., Gozlan, H., & Hamon, M. (1992). Autoradiographic mapping of central 5-HT3 receptors. In A. M. Hamon (Ed.), *Central and peripheral 5-HT3 receptors*. London: Academic Press.

Lebert, F., Pasquier, F., & Petit, H. (1994). Behavioral effects of trazodone in Alzheimer's disease. *Journal of Clinical Psychiatry, 55*, 536–538.

Linnoila, M., Virkkunen, M., & Higley, G. (1993). Impulse control disorders. *International Clinical Psychopharmacology, 8*(Suppl. 1), 53–56.

Little, K. Y., & Sparks, D. L. (1990). Brain markers and suicide: Can a relationship be found? *Journal of Forensic Sciences, 35*, 1393–1403.

Mann, J. J., Arango, V., & Marzuk, P. M. (1989). Evidence for the 5-HT hypothesis of suicide: A review of post-mortem studies. *British Journal of Psychiatry, 155*(Suppl. 8), 7–14.

Mann, J. J., Malone, K. M., Diehl, D. J., Perel, J., Cooper, T. B., & Mintun, M. A. (1996a). Demonstration *in vivo* of reduced serotonin responsivity in the brain of untreated depressed patients. *American Journal of Psychiatry, 153*, 174–182.

Mann, J. J., Malone, K. M., Diehl, D. J., Perel, J., Nichols, T. E., & Mintun, M. A. (1996b). Positron emission tomographic imaging of serotonin activation effects on prefrontal cortex in healthy volunteers. *Journal of Cerebral Blood Flow and Metabolism, 16*, 418–426.

Mann, J. J., McBride, P. A., Brown, R. P., Linnoila, M., Leon, A. C., De Meo, M., Mieczkowsky, T., & Myers, J. (1992). Relationship between central and peripheral serotonin indexes in depressed and suicidal psychiatric inpatients. *Archives of General Psychiatry, 49*, 442–446.

Marazziti, D., Marracci, S., Palego, L., Rotondo, A., Mazzanti, C., Nardi, I., Ladinsky, H., Giraldo, E., Borsini, F., & Cassano, G. B. (1994). Localisation and gene expression of Serotonin 1A receptors in human brain postmortem. *Brain Research, 658*, 55–59.

Mega, M. S., & Cummings, J. L. (1994). Frontal–subcortical circuits and neuropsychiatric disorders. *Journal of Neuropsychiatry and Clinical Neurosciences, 6*, 358–370.

Mengod, G., Pompeiano, M., Martinez-Mir, M. I., & Palacios, J. M. (1990). Localisation of the mRNA for the 5-HT2 receptor by in situ hybridization histochemistry. Correlation with the distribution of receptor sites. *Brain Research, 524,* 139–143.

Miller, L. A. (1992). Impulsivity, risk taking, and the ability to synthesize fragmented information after frontal lobectomy. *Neuropsychologia, 30,* 69–79.

Moghaddam, B., & Bunney, B. S. (1990). Acute effects of typical and atypical antipsychotic drugs on the release of dopamine from prefrontal cortex, nucleus accumbens, and striatum of the rat: *In vivo* microdialysis study. *Journal of Neurochemistry, 54,* 1755–1760.

Molliver, M. (1987). Serotoninergic neuronal systems: What their anatomic organisation tell us about their function. *Clinical Psychopharmacology, 7,* 3–23.

Monferini, E., Gaetani, P., Rodriguez y Baena, R., Giraldo, E., Parenti, M., Zoccheti, A., & Rizzi, C. A. (1993). Pharmacological characterization of the 5-HT receptor coupled to adenylyl cyclase stimulation in human brain. *Life Sciences, 52,* 61–65.

Morrison, J. H., Foote, S. L., Molliver, M. E., Bloom, F. E., & Lidow, G. W. (1982). Noradrenergic and serotonergic fibers innervate complementary layers in monkey visual cortex: An immunohistochemical study. *Proceedings of the National Academy of Sciences, USA, 79,* 2401–2405.

Nyth, A. L., & Gottfries, C. G. (1990). The clinical efficacy of citalopram in treatment of emotional disturbances in dementia disorders. *British Journal of Psychiatry, 157,* 894–901.

Palacios, J. M., Waeber, C., Mengod, G., & Pompeiano, M. (1991). Molecular neuroanatomy of 5-HT receptors. In J. R. Fozard & P. R. Saxena (Eds.), *Serotonin: Molecular biology, receptors and functional effects* (pp. 121–134). Basel: Birkhauser Verlag.

Pazos, A., Cortes, R., & Palacios, J. M. (1985). Quantitative autoradiographic mapping of serotonin receptors in the rat brain. *Brain Research, 346,* 241–249.

Pazos, A., Probst, A., & Palacios, J. M. (1987). Serotonin receptors in the human brain. Autoradiographic mapping of serotonin-1 receptors. *Neuroscience, 21,* 97–122.

Peroutka, S. J., & Snyder, S. H. (1979). Multiple serotonin receptors: Differential binding of [^{3}H]5-hydroxytryptamine, [^{3}H]lysergic acid diethylamide and [^{3}H]spiroperidol. *Molecular Pharmacology, 16,* 687–699.

Poldinger, W., Calanchini, B., & Schwarz, W. (1991). A functional–dimensional approach to depression: Serotonin deficiency as a target syndrome in a comparison of 5-hydroxytryptophan and fluvoxamine. *Psychopathology, 24,* 53–81.

Radja, F., Laporte, A. M., Daval, G., Verge, D., Gozlan, H., & Hamon, M. (1991). Autoradiography of serotonin receptor subtypes in the central nervous system. *Neurochemistry International, 18,* 1–15.

Roy, A., Virkkunen, M., & Linnoila, M. (1990). Serotonin in suicide, violence and alcoholism. In E. F. Coccaro & D. L. Murphy (Eds.), *Serotonin in major psychiatric disorders—Progress in Psychiatry Series* (pp. 185–208). Washington, DC: American Psychiatric Press.

Sparks, D. L., & Little, K. Y. (1990). Altered serotonin binding in some suicides. *Psychiatry Research, 32,* 19–28.

Spina, E., Dedomenico, P., Ruello, C., Longobardo, N., Gitto, C., Ancione, M., Dirosa, A. E., & Caputi, A. P. (1994). Adjunctive fluoxetine in the treatment of negative symptoms in chronic schizophrenic patients. *International Clinical Psychopharmacology, 9,* 281–285.

Thiery, C., Aubin-Brunet, V., Candito, M., & Darcourt, G. (1997). Neuroendocrine responsivity to clomipramine in elderly: Correlation with clinical evaluation. *Biological Psychiatry, 42,* 212.

Ugedo, L., Grenhoff, J., & Svensson, T. H. (1989). Ritanserin, a 5-HT2 receptor antagonist, activate midbrain dopamine neurons by blocking serotonergic inhibition. *Psychopharmacology, 98,* 45–50.

Van Praag, H. M. (1982). Depression, suicide and metabolism of serotonin in the brain. *Journal of Affective Disorders, 4,* 275–290.

Verge, D., Daval, G., Marcinkiewicz, M., Patey, A., El Mestikawy, S., Gozlan, H., & Hamon, M. (1986). Quantitative autoradiography of multiple 5-HT1 receptor subtypes in the brain of control and 5,7-DHT treated rats. *Journal of Neurosciences, 6,* 3474–3482.

Virkkunen, M., Rawlings, R., & Tokola, R. (1994). CSF biochemistries, glucose metabolism and diurnal activity rhythms in alcoholic, violent offenders, fire setters and healthy volunteers. *Archives of General Psychiatry, 51,* 20–27.

Wang, G. J., Volkow, N. D., Logan, J., Fowler, J. S., Schlyer, D., MacGregor, R. R., Hitzemann, R. J., Gur, R. C., & Wolf, A. P. (1995). Evaluation of age related changes in serotonin 5-HT2 and dopamine D2 receptor availability in healthy human subjects. *Pharmacology Letters, 14,* 249–253.

Yakel, J. L., Shao, X. M., & Jackson, M. B. (1990). The selectivity of the channel coupled to the 5-HT3 receptor. *Brain Research, 533,* 46–52.

8

Acetylcholine and Frontal Cortex "Signal-to-Noise Ratio"

MICHAEL E. HASSELMO
CHRISTIANE LINSTER

The processes of normal cognition may depend crucially on levels of acetylcholine in the brain. This may seem surprising to many neuroscientists, for whom the role of acetylcholine in cognition is overshadowed by the vital role of acetylcholine in the peripheral nervous system. In addition, many researchers think of cholinergic modulation as subtly altering the tone of a system that functions quite effectively without cholinergic modulation. But this viewpoint proves invalid in the face of evidence about the effects of muscarinic cholinergic antagonists on cognitive function. For example, the drug scopolamine, which blocks muscarinic acetylcholine receptors in the brain as well as the periphery, causes a state of delirium, characterized by confusion, visual hallucinations, and a profound memory impairment (Beach, Fitzgerald, Holmes, Phibbs, & Stuckendoff, 1969; Crawshaw & Mullen, 1984; Safer & Allen, 1971). These effects suggest that acetylcholine effects at muscarinic receptors do not just subtly alter cortical processes within a narrow dynamic range but actually play an integral role in normal function. Loss of this cholinergic component of cortical function causes such dramatic alterations in glutamatergic and γ-aminobutyric acid (GABA)ergic function that hallucinations can result. The only reason that the role of acetylcholine in behavior appears subtle is that drugs must be given at doses sufficiently low that they only partially block cholinergic receptor function.

Although hallucinations may reflect a role of cholinergic modulation within extrastriate visual cortex, the confusional state suggests a possible role for cholinergic modulation in the frontal cortex. Some recent reports described the use of muscarinic antagonists for inducing a highly suggestive state (Ardila & Moreno, 1991), an effect that has been used for interrogation and for criminal activities (Geis, 1961). Unfortunately, there has not been extensive investigation of the effects of muscarinic blockade on higher cognitive functions of planning and reasoning, but the confusional state associated with muscarinic antagonists suggests that the frontal cortex may be strongly affected by muscarinic blockade.

MODELING THE PHYSIOLOGICAL SUBSTRATES OF BEHAVIOR

To understand the effects of pharmacological agents on cognitive function, we must be able to model cognition in terms of the specific physiological substrates which are influenced by drugs. Thus, a primary focus of psychopharmacology should be the effects of modulatory agents at a cellular level. When scopolamine causes a state of confusion or hallucinations, this effect is due to a change in the dynamics of neural circuits, which results from the blockade of the normal activation of muscarinic acetylcholine receptors. We only converge on a coherent theory of pharmacological influences on cognition when we structure such a theory in terms of the cellular physiology of cortical circuits.

Here we present an overview of research attempting to link these multiple levels. The chapter starts with a review of available physiological data on the effects of acetylcholine within cortical structures, with a particular emphasis on prefrontal cortex. Subsequently, we present an overview of a computational model used to analyze how specific cellular effects of acetylcholine relate to signal-to-noise ratio—a measure of how much neuronal activity depends upon sensory input relative to how much appears to reflect background activity. Finally, we propose some links to behavioral phenomena.

PHYSIOLOGY OF ACETYLCHOLINE IN THE CORTEX

Physiological Data on Cholinergic Modulation in Frontal Cortex

Data have been available for a number of years on the effects of cholinergic modulation in cortical structures. The seminal work of Krnjevic and Phillis (1963), who performed extracellular recording of action potentials from neocortical neurons during the infusion of acetylcholine and various cholinergic pharmacological agents, marked the beginning. They found populations of neurons selectively sensitive to acetylcholine—these neurons greatly increase their firing rate during infusion of acetylcholine into the cortex.

Later work focused on understanding circuit-level effects such as these in the context of specific effects of cholinergic modulation at a cellular level. Much of this research involved intracellular and extracellular recording from brain slice preparations of cortical structures, allowing dose-regulated infusions of acetylcholine and other cholinergic agents. The increases in firing rate induced by acetylcholine in the studies of Krnjevic and others may be due to direct depolarization of neuronal membranes by acetylcholine. For example, in slice preparations of a variety of cortical structures, perfusion of cholinergic agonists causes a depolarization on the order of 3–5 mV in pyramidal cells (Barkai & Hasselmo, 1994; Cole & Nicoll, 1984), and even larger depolarizations in inhibitory interneurons (McQuiston & Madison, 1996; Reece & Schwartzkroin, 1991). Andrade (1991; Hajdahmane & Andrade, 1996) described muscarinic depolarization of pyramidal cells in rat prefrontal cortex.

In addition to the direct depolarization of cortical neurons, activation of acetylcholine receptors decreases the adaptation characteristics of these neurons. Most cortical pyramidal cells respond to depolarization with an initial high frequency of firing which gradually decreases until the neuron stops firing at an appreciable rate. This adaptation appears to be due to influx of calcium during each spike, which activates a calcium-dependent potassium current that slows down firing (Madison, Lancaster, & Nicoll, 1987; Schwindt, Spain, & Crill, 1992). Cholinergic modulation decreases these calcium-dependent potassium currents, resulting in a decrease of pyramidal cell adaptation and, hence, stronger firing in response to input.

In addition to these effects on the intrinsic properties of neurons, acetylcholine also modulates synaptic release of glutamate and GABA, thereby suppressing synaptic potentials. Activation of muscarinic receptors causes suppression of glutamate and GABA release in slice preparations of a variety of structures, including somatosensory cortex (Hasselmo & Cekic, 1996), primary visual cortex (Brocher, Artola, & Singer, 1992); piriform cortex (Hasselmo & Bower, 1992; Williams & Constanti, 1988), and hippocampus (Hasselmo & Schnell, 1994; Hounsgaard, 1978; Valentino & Dingledine, 1981). Muscarinic suppression of synaptic transmission has also been described in slice preparations of prefrontal cortex (Vidal & Changeux, 1993) along with a novel nicotinic enhancement of afferent input to the prefrontal cortex. Note that in this last study (Vidal & Changeux, 1993), the muscarinic suppression of potentials occurred in 100% of cells, whereas the nicotinic enhancement of potentials only occurred in 14% of the cells. Nicotinic enhancement of glutamatergic synaptic transmission has also been demonstrated in the hippocampus (Gray, Rajan, Radcliffe, Yakehiro, & Dani, 1996). Anatomical data also support the existence of muscarinic modulation of excitatory transmission in the prefrontal cortex, because M2 receptors have been observed on the presynaptic terminals of asymmetric (noncholinergic) synapses in prefrontal cortex (Mrzljak, Levey, & Goldman-Rakic, 1993). Effects of acetylcholine on inhibitory synaptic potentials have been shown in the hippocampus (Pitler & Alger, 1992) and in the piriform cortex (Patil & Hasselmo, 1997; Patil, Linster, & Hasselmo, 1997).

In addition to the direct depolarization of pyramidal cells, acetylcholine also appears to cause an activity-dependent enhancement of neuronal response (Andrade, 1991). Thus, in slice preparations, neurons that spike during cholinergic modulation are more prone to spike subsequently, due to an afterdepolarization effect replacing the standard afterhyperpolarization. This response greatly alters the population response of a network of neurons, biasing activity toward neurons that were previously active. A similar type of effect has been described in the piriform cortex (Constanti, Bagetta, & Libri, 1993; Sciancalepore & Constanti 1995). This phenomenon has been used in computational models of cortical short-term memory function (Lisman & Idiart, 1995), and indeed this effect provides an ideal mechanism for maintaining individual memories for short periods within a population of neurons. However, the absence of an effect of cholinergic antagonists such as scopolamine on short-term memory phenomena such as digit span (Broks et al., 1988; Drachman, 1978; Ostfeld & Aruguete, 1962) or the recency component of a serial position curve (Crow & Grove-White, 1973; Frith, Richardson, Samuel, Crow, & McKenna, 1984) suggests that this is not the essential feature for the role of frontal cortex in short-term memory function (Fuster, 1990).

Because of the considerable data on effects of cholinergic drugs on memory function, considerable physiological research has focused on the role of acetylcholine in learning. Cholinergic agonists have been shown to enhance long-term potentiation and other forms of synaptic modification in the dentate gyrus (Burgard & Sarvey, 1990) region CA1 of the hippocampus (Blitzer, Gil, & Landau, 1990; Huerta & Lisman, 1993, 1995), piriform cortex (Hasselmo & Barkai, 1995), and primary visual cortex (Brocher et al., 1992). Some of these effects may involve alterations in synaptic efficacy without the usual high-frequency stimulation necessary to induce long-term potentiation (Auerbach & Segal, 1994; Markram & Segal, 1990). In addition, cholinergic agonists have been shown to alter response properties of cortical neurons in other manners which enhance responsiveness to sensory stimuli. For example, cholinergic modulation of potassium currents has been proposed to mediate classical conditioning in motor cortex (Berner & Woody, 1991; Woody & Gruen, 1987) and cholinergic agonists have been shown to enhance the alteration of auditory tuning curves in response to conditioning (Ashe & Weinberger, 1991; Metherate & Weinberger, 1990) and to cause long-term enhancement of the response to somatosensory stimulation (Metherate, Tremblay, & Dykes, 1987; Rasmussen & Dykes, 1988).

Anatomy of Cholinergic Innervation

Cortical structures receive cholinergic innervation from a series of nuclei in the basal forebrain (Mesulam, Mufson, Warner, & Levey, 1983). Whereas many studies focus on specific synaptic contacts by cholinergic axons, a few studies have suggested that there may be additional nonsynaptic release of acetylcholine which could have its effect through a mechanism referred to as volume transmission: the longer-range diffusion of acetylcholine to sites not at a specific junction (Mrzljak, Pappy, Leranth, & Goldman-Rakic, 1995; Umbriaco, Watkins, Descarries, Cozzari, & Hartman, 1994). This has been determined by staining cholinergic fibers with choline acetyltransferase antibodies and reconstructing axonal varicosities with electron microscopy. Use of these techniques has shown that in the rat somatosensory cortex, only 14% of the axonal varicosities are associated with postsynaptic densities (Umbriaco, Watkins, Descarries, Cozzari, & Hartman, 1994), whereas a study of macaque prefrontal cortex showed that only 44% of the cholinergic boutons were associated with synaptic specializations on postsynaptic neurons (Mrzljak et al., 1995), suggesting that the remainder of varicosities cause effects via volume transmission. In our computational models, we have drawn on this data for volume transmission, modeling effects of acetylcholine as being relatively homogeneous within a cortical region. Ultimately, there is likely to be considerable heterogeneity of cholinergic effects between different cortical regions, but assuming homogeneity in models of local regions allows us to understand how setting the global modulatory tone of a local cortical region can alter its processing dynamics.

COMPUTATIONAL MODELING OF CHOLINERGIC EFFECTS ON SIGNAL-TO-NOISE RATIO

Research on the cellular effects of acetylcholine in cortical structures provides an overwhelming variety of selective effects on different aspects of neuronal function. In fact, the extent of detailed data makes it difficult to synthesize this information into an intuitive notion of modulatory effects. Computational modeling proves a useful tool for understanding these effects. Because computational models allow analysis of dynamics in distributed populations of neurons, they aid the understanding of how a range of different cellular effects, acting across a broad population of neurons, can change the processing characteristics of a specific cortical region.

The modeling work in our own laboratory has focused on understanding the effects of acetylcholine within cortical structures. In particular, we have focused on how acetylcholine changes the relative processing of input from the environment (extrinsic or afferent input) versus the interpretation of this information based on previous learning (intrinsic or feedback activity). This framework can be used for understanding a range of cellular effects in the context of cortical function.

This general framework for understanding the effects of acetylcholine relates to extensive prior research on a measure termed "signal-to-noise ratio." This term refers to modulatory effects on activation dynamics which enhance the response to sensory stimuli (the "signal") relative to background activity (the "noise"). This refers to both a temporal comparison of response during stimulation versus "spontaneous" activity before and after the stimulation and a spatial comparison of the response of neurons within a receptive field versus those not clearly tuned to the sensory stimulus. This general framework provides a useful measure of the level of afferent influence on activity within a cortical region, but we propose that signal to noise should be replaced with the term "extrinsic to intrinsic," because the "spontaneous" activity and background activity most likely reflects neuronal activity driven by interpretation or predictions about the environment rather than random noise.

The term "signal to noise" has primarily been used in describing effects of norepinephrine on cortical activity (Sara 1985; Servan-Schreiber, Printz, & Cohen, 1990; Woodward, Moises, Waterhouse, Hoffer, & Freedman, 1979). Norepinephrine has been shown to reduce background spontaneous activity and enhance the response of cortical neurons to sensory stimuli in a range of modalities, including auditory (Foote, Bloom, & Aston-Jones, 1983) somatosensory (Waterhouse & Woodward, 1980) and visual (Kasamatsu & Heggelund, 1982; Madar & Segal, 1980). Recordings from hippocampal pyramidal cells during iontophoretic application of norepinephrine (Segal & Bloom, 1974) demonstrate reduced neuronal activity during behaviorally irrelevant auditory tones but enhanced excitatory responses to tones indicating food.

The same term can be used to describe the effects of acetylcholine on cortical responsiveness to sensory stimuli. Application of cholinergic agonists enhances the response of neurons to sensory stimuli in the primary visual cortex (Sillito & Kemp, 1983) and in auditory cortex (Ashe & Weinberger, 1991). These similarities are not surprising in that acetylcholine and norepinephrine have similar effects on most cellular parameters. Both substances block neuronal adaptation (Madison & Nicoll, 1986; Madison et al., 1987). Both substances activate inhibitory interneurons (Doze, Cohen, & Madison, 1991; Gellman & Aghajanian, 1993; Pitler & Alger, 1992; Reece & Schwartzkroin, 1991). Both substances appear to suppress excitatory transmission in certain cortical structures (Hasselmo & Cekic, 1996; Hasselmo, Linster, Patil, Ma, & Cekic, 1997; Valentino & Dingledine, 1981; Vanier & Bower, 1993), and both substances reduce inhibitory synaptic potentials (Doze et al., 1991; Pitler & Alger, 1992). The primary differences between the two substances concerns the relative amount of pyramidal cell depolarization.

The analysis of effects of acetylcholine on signal-to-noise ratio gives a notion of how much neural activity within a region depends on environmental influences versus how much depends on the internal spread of activity. This measure is therefore relevant to a range of different behaviors. Behavioral tasks which measure attention naturally require a strong influence of environment on neural activity (strong "signal"). Modulators such as acetylcholine and norepinephrine, which enhance signal-to-noise ratio, therefore appear important for performance in tasks requiring storage of new information or detection of infrequent or indistinct stimuli. Muscarinic antagonists such as scopolamine strongly impair the learning of new information (Crow & Grove-White, 1973; Ghoneim & Mewaldt, 1975) and impair performance in certain attention tasks (Wesnes & Warburton, 1983). In contrast, amphetamines, which enhance norepinephrine release, greatly enhance performance in attention tasks (Koelega, 1993) and learning of new information (Mewaldt & Ghoneim, 1979). A simple understanding of how cellular effects relate to signal to noise could be helpful for understanding the role of modulators in these tasks. To this end, we have developed a mathematical framework for cortical activity based on the Wilson-Cowan equations (Hasselmo et al., 1997; Hasselmo, Schnell, & Barkai, 1995; Hasselmo & Linster, (1998); Van Vreeswijk & Hasselmo, in press; Wilson & Cowan, 1972, 1973). This framework allows us to link these various cellular effects to steady-state signal-to-noise ratio. We have also investigated these effects using integrate and fire models of cortical networks (Hasselmo et al., 1997).

Mathematical Analysis

We have used a mathematical framework as well as computer simulations to relate modulatory effects on specific cellular parameters to signal-to-noise ratio. This framework is based on a simplified representation of cortical pyramidal cells and inhibitory interneurons as threshold linear input–output functions. Thus, when input is below threshold, the neurons do not fire, and when input is above threshold, the output of the neuron is represented by a continuous variable representing firing rate. These simple units are then coupled with variables representing the strength of recurrent excitatory connections between pyramidal cells (W_{pp}), excitatory connections from pyramidal cells to interneurons (W_{pi}), inhibitory connections from interneurons to pyramidal cells (W_{ip}) and inhibitory connections between interneurons (W_{ii}). A simple version of such a network is illustrated in Figure 8.1.

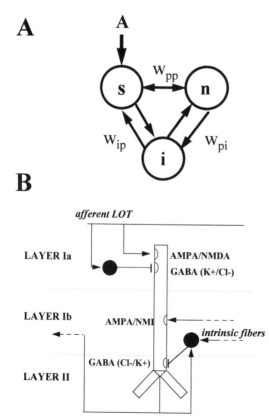

FIGURE 8.1. (A) Simplified network for mathematical analysis. *s* represents the activation of an excitatory neuron receiving afferent input, *n* represents the activation of an excitatory neuron which does not receive direct afferent input, and *i* represents the activation of the inhibitory interneuron. A = direct afferent input (layer Ia), W_{pp} = feedback excitation, W_{pi} = excitatory connections to inhibitory interneuron, W_{ip} = inhibitory connections on excitatory neurons. (B) Architecture of the computer simulation of piriform cortex: 50 pyramidal cells each receive input connections from the lateral olfactory tract (LOT). In addition, 50 feedforward interneurons also receive input from the LOT and inhibit pyramidal cells via GABA-A and GABA-B receptors. In layer Ib, pyramidal cells receive recurrent excitatory input from other pyramidal cells. Pyramidal cells also excite 50 feedback interneurons, which in turn inhibit pyramidal cells. Feedback interneurons inhibit each other via GABA-A receptors.

All the primary modulatory effects of acetylcholine and norepinephrine described previously can be related to signal-to-noise ratio using this framework. Here, we analyze the effects of suppression of excitatory synaptic transmission between pyramidal cells, suppression of excitatory synaptic transmission from pyramidal cells to interneurons, suppression of neuronal adaptation in pyramidal cells, and depolarization of interneurons.

In this example, pyramidal cells receiving afferent input are modeled with the activation variable s, pyramidal cells not receiving afferent input are modeled with the activation variable n, and interneurons are modeled with the activation variable i. If we assume that the number of neurons in the network is large, the connectivity and input A are scaled to the time constants of the neurons, and the input A is present on a time scale much larger than the time constant of the neurons, then we can write the equations for the network as

$$\tau \frac{ds}{dt} = W_{pp}s + W_{pp}n - W_{pi}i - s + A$$

$$\tau \frac{dn}{dt} = W_{pp}s + W_{pp}n - W_{pi}i - n$$

$$\tau \frac{di}{dt} = W_{pi}s + W_{pi}n - i$$

where A is the external afferent input to neurons s, W_{pp} is the average connection strength between pyramidal cells, W_{pi} is the average strength of excitatory connections from pyramidal cells to interneurons, and W_{ip} is the average strength of inbitory connections from interneurons to pyramidal cells. All connection strengths are normalized between 0 and 1. Note that we neglect feedback inhibition among interneurons for this example. Feedforward inhibition adds a constant inhibitory term to the equations and thus does not influence the relationships between parameters in the resulting equation; it results in a linear shift of the obtained results in parameter space.

We can then calculate the steady state (equilibrium) state by setting $ds/dt = dn/dt = di/dt = 0$, and replacing i in the equations for s and n:

$$s = W_{pp}s + W_{pp}n - W_{ip}W_{pi}s - W_{ip}W_{pi}n + A$$
$$n = W_{pp}s + W_{pp}n - W_{ip}W_{pi}s - W_{ip}W_{pi}n$$

In this network, the signal-to-noise ratio can be easily analyzed as the ratio of s to n (the ratio of the activation of neurons receiving afferent input to that of neurons not receiving afferent input). This ratio can be obtained by focusing on the equation for neurons not receiving afferent input (the equation starting with n), and separating the variables for this steady state value. This gives us the following ratio:

$$\frac{s}{n} = \frac{1 - W_{pp} + W_{ip}W_{pi}}{W_{pp} + W_{ip}W_{pi}}$$

Effect of Suppression of Excitatory Synaptic Transmission on Signal-to-Noise Ratio

Here we can see that suppression of recurrent excitation W_{pp} increases the signal to noise ratio, but this effect depends on the relation of W_{pp} to the product of W_{ip} and W_{pi}. As can be seen from this equation, the signal-to-noise ratio *s/n* expressed here tends toward infinity as the value W_{pp} approaches the product of W_{ip} and W_{pi}. Note that for the ratio to be positive, W_{pp} must be greater than the product of W_{ip} and W_{pi}, and less than $W_{ip} \cdot W_{pi} + 1$. Figure 8.2 shows a surface plot of the output of this equation. In this plot, decreases in W_{pp} (going leftward) can cause a progressive increase in *s/n* up to the discontinuity, but the location of this increase depends on the value of W_{pi}. Note that a similar plot would be obtained if W_{pi} were kept fixed and W_{ip} were varied.

Thus, for certain strengths of feedback inhibition, suppression of feedback excitation can enhance the relative response to afferent input. This can be understood on an intuitive level by thinking in terms of the source of background activity ("noise"). This background activity depends on the spread of activity across excitatory synapses within cortical structures and is decreased when these excitatory neurons are suppressed. Whether this activity reflects internal predictions about the environment or a particular interpretation of the input stimuli, this activity can only arise from spread across intrinsic excitatory connections. Thus, suppression of intrinsic excitatory synapses decreases the background activity and correspondingly increases the relative amount of activity due to afferent input ("signal").

Effect of Suppression of Neuronal Adaptation on Signal-to-Noise Ratio

The simplified representation also allows analysis of the effect of neuronal adaptation on the steady-state signal-to-noise ratio. Modulatory agents have been shown to alter neuronal adaptation in piriform cortex pyramidal cells, particularly in deep pyramidal cells (Tseng & Haberly, 1989). In previous articles (Hasselmo et al., 1995), we modeled adaptation with a buildup of intracellular calcium *c* proportional to activation of pyramidal cells according to coefficient *W* and decreasing in proportion to a diffusion coefficient *g*. This influenced activation via an increase in inhibitory current proportional to the coefficient μ times intracellular calcium, as represented in the following equations.

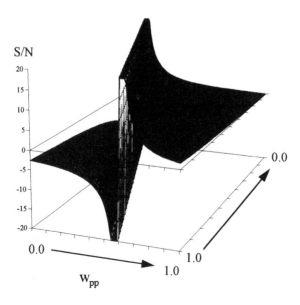

FIGURE 8.2. Surface plot of signal-to-noise ratio changes across a wide range of values as generated by the mathematical analysis. In this representation, decreases in excitatory connections between pyramidal cells (W_{pp}) can enhance signal-to-noise ratio for a range of values of excitatory input to interneurons (W_{pi}), but the magnitude of the effect depends on the relationship of W_{pp} with W_{pi}.

$$\tau \frac{ds}{dt} = W_{pp}s + W_{pp}n - W_{pi}i - s - \mu c_s + A$$

$$\tau \frac{dn}{dt} = W_{pp}s + W_{pp}n - W_{pi}i - n - \mu c_n$$

$$\tau \frac{di}{dt} = W_{pi}s + W_{pi}n - i$$

$$\frac{dc_s}{dt} = \Omega s - \gamma c_s, \quad \frac{dc_n}{dt} = \Omega s - \gamma c_n$$

In the steady state, this adds an inhibitory component to each excitatory population dependent on its own activation but not that of the other population. This additional inhibitory component therefore influences only the numerator of the signal-to-noise equation.

$$\frac{s}{n} = \frac{1 - W_{pp} + W_{ip}W_{pi} + \mu\Omega / \gamma}{W_{pp} - W_{ip}W_{pi}}$$

This yields the somewhat paradoxical result that the reduction in adaptation induced by acetylcholine and norepinephrine should actually reduce the signal-to-noise ratio due to reduced adaptation of the neurons not receiving direct afferent input. However, this effect on signal-to-noise ratio will appear more slowly due to the slower time constant of neuronal adaptation.

Effect of Depolarization of Interneurons

As mentioned previously, experimental evidence demonstrates the depolarization of interneurons in cortical structures by both acetylcholine (Pitler & Alger, 1992) and norepinephrine (Gellman & Aghajanian, 1993). This depolarization of interneurons appears rather paradoxical when combined with the suppression of evoked inhibitory potentials. Why would the same substance simultaneously increase inhibition via direct depolarization while suppressing total feedback inhibition? The analytical framework presented here provides a possible explanation of this paradox (Patil & Hasselmo, 1997). We can analyze the effect of depolarization of inhibitory interneurons by representing it as a direct depolarizing afferent input to interneurons A'. To fully understand this effect, we must incorporate the effect of having firing thresholds in both the excitatory and inhibitory neurons in the network. When we incorporate these thresholds (represented by θ) and solve for the equilibrium state (Q) as done previously (Hasselmo et al., 1995; Patil & Hasselmo, 1997), we obtain the following equation:

$$Q = \frac{I - A'W_{ip} + W_{ip}\theta_i}{1 - W_{pp} + W_{ip}W_{pi}} + \theta$$

In this equation Q represents the equilibrium state of any pyramidal cell in the network receiving afferent input with strength $A = I + \theta$. The threshold of the excitatory pyramidal cell is represented by θ and the inhibitory cell has threshold θ_i. The direct depolarizing input to inhibitory interneurons is represented with A'. As shown in Figure 8.3, increases in this direct depolarization of interneurons A' will shift the equilibrium state of the network by equal amounts for all values of input to the excitatory neurons A. This means

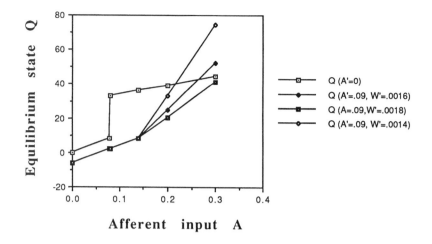

FIGURE 8.3. Effect of modulation on equilibrium state in the network shown in Figure 8.1. Equilibrium state Q is shown for different values of excitatory afferent input A to the excitatory neuron. A combination of increases in A' (depolarization of interneurons) with decreases in W_{pi} (suppression of excitatory input to interneurons) makes the network show less spontaneous activity and less response to weak input (low values of A) but makes the network respond more strongly to strong input (high values of A).

that the excitatory population does not respond until afferent input A reaches higher values. Thus, although there is no change in the threshold value θ, the functional threshold is increased. At the same time, suppression of W_{pi} will alter the slope of the relationship between afferent input A and the equilibrium state Q, resulting in a steeper increase. As shown in Figure 8.3, combination of direct depolarization with suppression of W_{pi} results in a network which responds less to weak inputs but responds more strongly to stronger afferent input. Thus, these two effects could interact to make the spontaneous and background activity of the network weaker while enhancing the response to strong afferent input. This would increase signal-to-noise ratio because the response to afferent input would be enhanced while the spontaneous background activity of the network would decrease.

Computer Simulations

To illustrate the analytical results described in the previous section, we ran computer simulations using a simplified representation of a cortical network (see Hasselmo et al., 1997, for a detailed description). The model consists of 50 pyramidal cells, and 50 of each feedback and feedforward interneurons. Afferent input is given to pyramidal cells and feedforward interneurons. Each pyramidal cell makes recurrent excitatory connections to 20 surrounding pyramidal cells; the strength of these connections decays linearly as a function of the distance between the two cells. These connections are made via synapses using both fast time courses (AMPA) and slow time courses (NMDA). Each feedforward interneuron connects to 10 pyramidal cells. These connections are made via fast (20%) and slow (80%) time courses representing GABA-A and GABA-B receptors. Each pyramidal cell connects to five feedback interneurons and receives input from the same five interneurons (via fast [80%] and slow [20%] synapses). Feedback interneurons make feedback inhibitory connections among each other (via fast synapses).

Suppression of Feedback Excitation

The computer simulations show that in a network with high background activity, suppression of excitatory transmission between pyramidal cells (feedback excitation) enhances the signal-to-noise ratio. Indeed, suppression of feedback excitation decreases background activity and reduces the recruitment of cells that do not receive direct afferent input. Figure 8.4(A) shows membrane potentials and action potentials of 16 pyramidal cells in the network in response to stimulation in the absence (modulation OFF) and in the presence (modulation ON) of a 60% suppression of feedback excitation. Pyramidal cells receiving input are indicated by arrows, stimulus onset and offset are indicated by arrowheads below the traces. With no modulation, feedback excitation results in a large number of pyramidal cells showing increased spiking activities during stimulation. In contrast, when feedback excitation is suppressed by 60%, background activity is lower and increases in spike rates are confined primarily to pyramidal cells receiving direct afferent input. Figure 8.4(B) shows the average spike rates of each pyramidal cell during spontaneous and stimulus-driven activity in the absence (modulation OFF) and in the presence (modulation ON) of suppression of feedback excitation. For each cell, the average output activity (number of spikes) during 120 msec is shown in each panel. Pyramidal cells receiving external input are indicated by arrows.

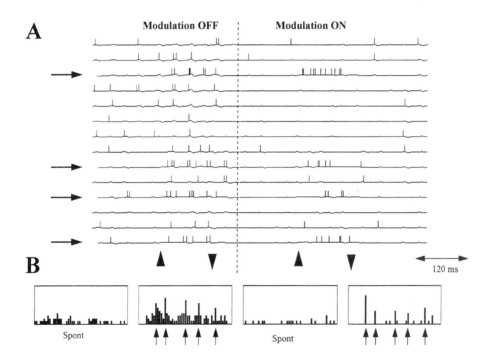

FIGURE 8.4. Effect of suppression of feedback excitation on pyramidal cell response to afferent input. (A) Membrane potentials and action potentials of 16 pyramidal cells are shown. Pyramidal cells receiving afferent input are indicated by horizontal arrows. Stimulus onset and offset are indicated by arrowheads below the traces. Background activity and response to afferent input are shown in the absence (modulation OFF) and in the presence (modulation ON) of 60% suppression of feedback excitation. (B) Average activities of the 50 pyramidal cells in the network during 120-msec background activity (spont) and in response to input. Pyramidal cells receiving input are indicated by arrows.

Suppression of Feedback Inhibition

In addition to the suppression of intrinsic excitatory synaptic transmission by acetyl-choline and norepinephrine, data suggest that these modulators also suppress excitatory input from pyramidal cells to inhibitory interneurons in the hippocampus (Doze et al., 1991; Pitler & Alger, 1992). Our simulations show that suppression of excitatory input to interneurons (feedback inhibition), in addition to suppression of feedback excitation, can further enhance signal-to-noise ratio. Figure 8.5(A) shows membrane potentials and action potentials of 16 pyramidal cells in the network in response to stimulation in the absence (modulation OFF) and in the presence (modulation ON) of a 60% suppression of feedback excitation and 40% suppression of the excitatory input to inhibitory interneurons (feedback inhibition). Pyramidal cells receiving input are indicated by arrows; stimulus onset and offset are indicated by arrowheads below the traces. With no modulation, feedback excitation results in a large number of pyramidal cells showing increased spiking activities during stimulation. In contrast, when both feedback excitation and feedback inhibition are suppressed, background activity is lower and only pyramidal cells receiving external input have increased spike rates. In this case, pyramidal cells receiving afferent input are more active in the presence of modulation than in the absence

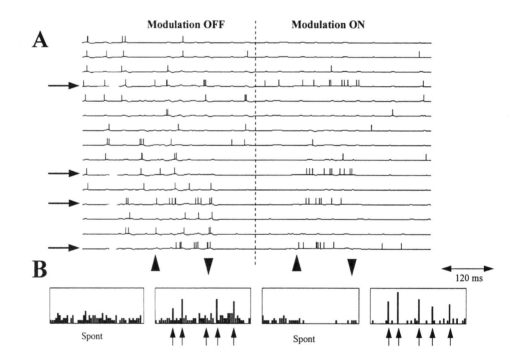

FIGURE 8.5. Effect of suppression of feedback excitation and feedback inhibition on pyramidal cell response to afferent input. (A) Membrane potentials and action potentials of 16 pyramidal cells are shown. Pyramidal cells receiving afferent input are indicated by horizontal arrows. Stimulus onset and offset are indicated by arrowheads below the traces. Background activity and response to afferent input are shown in the absence (modulation OFF) and in the presence (modulation ON) of 60% suppression of feedback excitation and 40% of feedback inhibition. (B) Average activities of the 50 pyramidal cells in the network during 120-msec background activity (spont) and in response to input. Pyramidal cells receiving input are indicated by arrows. Note the greater activity of these neurons compared to those receiving input in Figure 8.4(B).

of stimulation. Figure 8.5(B) shows the average spike rates of each pyramidal cell during spontaneous and stimulus-driven activity in the absence (modulation OFF) and in the presence (modulation ON) of suppression of feedback excitation. For each cell, the average output activity (number of spikes) during 120 msec is shown in each panel. Pyramidal cells receiving external input are indicated by arrows. Note that the neurons receiving direct afferent input show higher response in this histogram compared to the histogram presented in Figure 8.4(B).

Parameter Space

To verify these results, we ran a large number of different simulations with varying amounts of suppression of feedback excitation and feedback inhibition. For each point in parameter space, we constructed a new network with random connectivity, and we presented random input patterns to the network. The signal-to-noise ratio was computed across the full set of different simulations for each parameter value as explained in the section on "Mathematical Analysis." The simulation results show that signal-to-noise ratio is maximal when both feedback excitation and feedback inhibition are suppressed (Figure 8.6[A]). Suppression of feedback excitation of 40% to 60% led to increased signal-to-noise ratios. When suppression of feedback inhibition was also included, the signal-to-noise ratio was considerably improved.

In our simulations, W_{ip} was kept constant, and we varied W_{pp} and W_{pi}. In the simulations, W_{ip} was chosen to be 0.6. For comparison with the analytical results described previously, we computed the value of s/n for both W_{pp} and W_{pi} varying between 0 and 1. Figure 8.6(B) shows the values obtained with the same resolution used in the large-scale spiking network simulations described earlier, illustrating a similar qualitative change in s/n to the change observed in the spiking network model.

Summary

Many assumptions are inherent in this framework, especially concerning the notion that cortical firing represents some kind of steady state. However, in this framework simple relationships between effects on cellular parameters and signal-to-noise ratio can be stated:

1. Suppression of excitatory connections between pyramidal cells within a region (W_{pp}) enhances signal-to-noise ratio.
2. Suppression of feedback inhibition (W_{pi} or W_{ip}) enhances or decreases signal to noise depending on the relative value of W_{pp}.
3. Suppression of adaptation decreases signal-to-noise ratio.
4. Depolarization of inhibitory interneurons enhances signal-to-noise ratio.

The interaction of these terms is complex—much depends on the relative values of these variables and the nature of the afferent input. However, this framework provides a starting point for understanding the complex interaction between a number of cellular effects of modulators. This type of analysis is necessary to understand the often paradoxical interaction of cellular effects (e.g., this suggests why a modulator would simultaneously depolarize inhibitory interneurons while suppressing synaptic connections to and from these interneurons).

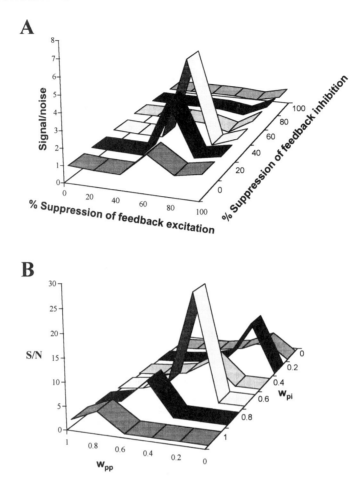

FIGURE 8.6. Signal-to-noise ratio as a function of feedback excitation and inhibition in the spiking network model (A) and in the simplified mathematical analysis (B). (A) For each point in parameter space, 50 networks were constructed and presented with random input patterns. The signal-to-noise ratio is computed as the number of spikes generated by neurons receiving input divided by the total number of spikes during the time of input presentation (120 msec). Suppression of feedback excitation and suppression of feedback inhibition are varied from 0% to 100% in 20% steps. The maximal signal-to-noise ratio occurs when feedback excitation is suppressed by 60% and feedback inhibition by 40%. (B) The equation for single-to-noise ratio presented in the results section was utilized to generate values of s/n for the same parameter values presented for the spiking network model. Note a similar qualitative structure to the change in signal-to-noise ratio. Note that W_{pp} decreases to the right in this plot, whereas in Figure 8.2 W_{pp} decreases to the left.

BEHAVIORAL SIGNIFICANCE OF CHOLINERGIC MODULATION

As described previously, the effect of cholinergic modulation on cortical signal-to-noise ratio could underlie its role in behavioral tasks, including learning of new information (Crow & Grove-White, 1973; Ghoneim & Mewaldt, 1975) and attention (Wesnes & Warburton, 1983). Naturally, it is not enough to simply compute the signal-to-noise ratio to understand this effect. The signal-to-noise framework describes the strength of extrinsic versus intrinsic influences but does not put these influences into a specific functional context. However, the relationship between extrinsic and intrinsic influences proves relevant to the possible role of neuromodulation in two functions that have been the focus of considerable neural network modeling: associative memory function and self-organization. This provides the basis for linking signal-to-noise ratio to the memory function of more complex network models of cortical function.

In associative memory function, associations are formed between patterns of neuronal activity determined by extrinsic input (Anderson, 1983; Hasselmo & Bower, 1993; Hasselmo & Schnell, 1994; Hasselmo, 1995; Kohonen, 1984). The modifiable synapses must not be the predominant influence on postsynaptic activity or the representations will be distorted by previous representations. To ensure accurate learning of new associations in these types of networks, activity is commonly clamped to the input pattern during learning (Anderson, 1983; Kohonen, 1984). This corresponds to an extreme case of the extrinsic-to-intrinsic ratio. Namely, learning in these types of networks requires a high extrinsic-to-intrinsic ratio, whereas retrieval involves a decrease in this ratio (a greater dependence of neuronal activity on previous representations). Thus, a high signal-to-noise ratio might simply be a means of increasing the accuracy of storage of new associations—preventing their contamination by previous expectation.

In contrast, during self-organization, new patterns of neuronal activity are determined by the competition between different afferent input patterns over time (usually using some type of interleaved learning). In these types of neural network models, the modifiable synapses are usually the afferent input synapses, and they are the predominant influence on postsynaptic activity during learning. However, the signal-to-noise ratio must again be very high to ensure effective function. If intrinsic connectivity is strong, the formation of representations will be slowed or prevented by continuous distortion due to intrinsic spread of activity. Most models of self-organization assume very strong afferent (extrinsic) input, neglecting the fact that 80% of excitatory cortical synapses are intrinsic. Again, enhancement of signal-to-noise ratio enhances the formation of new representations. Thus, for both associative memory function and self-organization, increases in extrinsic-to-intrinsic ratio help in the storage of new information, whereas decreases in extrinsic-to-intrinsic ratio might be associated with retrieval of previously stored information.

Bottom-Up and Top-Down Interactions

The previous section describes how modulation of cortical dynamics could be very important for learning of associations and self-organization of new cortical representations. However, this focus on learning dynamics ignores the complexities of activation during retrieval. Once representations are stored, the issue of the ongoing interaction of afferent input and stored representations still remains. What determines that a noisy or degraded input should evoke a particular representation? How are conflicts between competing interpretations of the same ambiguous stimulus resolved?

These issues involve an interaction of what are sometimes referred to as bottom-up and top-down influences. Bottom-up influences refer to the flow of sensory information from the periphery. The greater the extrinsic-to-intrinsic ratio in most networks, the greater the bottom-up influence. Top-down influences refer to the interpretation of sensory input based on previously formed representations or associations. The activity generated by top-down interpretations or predictions about the environment could be what is referred to as "noise" in the phrase "signal-to-noise." In contrast to noise, however, these top-down predictions are generated by highly structured cortical representations which might be continuously generated and matched with sensory input.

The capacity of neuromodulators to influence extrinsic-to-intrinsic ratios could play a very important role in regulating the interaction of top-down and bottom-up influences. For example, high levels of acetylcholine or norepinephrine could enhance the influence of bottom-up sensory input, resulting in greater accuracy in attentional tasks but perhaps impairing the retrieval of information. In contrast, blockade of cholinergic modulation might result in an unusual predominance of top-down influences, and this might underlie the visual hallucinations reported under the influence of scopolamine (Crawshaw & Mullen, 1984; Safer & Allen, 1971). These hallucinations might be the result of cortical interpretations which have not been vetoed by an ongoing matching process with bottom-up sensory input.

Changes in the dynamics of top-down and bottom-up interactions could underlie the effect of muscarinic receptor blockade on various high-order cognitive tasks. In fact, cholinergic blockade would be expected to perturb those functions often attributed to frontal cortex, such as response monitoring. In fact, there is ongoing controversy about whether the effects of damage due to aneurysms in the anterior communicating artery are due to lesions of cortical cholinergic innervation or to lesions of frontal cortex structures (DeLuca, 1993). Patients with this type of damage show an increase in confabulations, which could be attributed to a decrease in the ability to evaluate retrieval of information (top-down activity) in the context of environmental input (bottom-up activity).

During blockade of cholinergic effects, the ability to efficiently process multiple competing forms of afferent input will be affected. This could underlie the observed effect of blockade of muscarinic acetylcholine receptors on performance in the Stroop task (Callaway & Band, 1958), on tasks requiring discrimination between several simultaneous stimuli such as face matching (Flicker, Serby, & Ferris, 1990), and on searches conducted in parallel but not those done in serial (Brandeis, Naylor, Halliday, Callaway, & Yano, 1992). The decreased influence of afferent input can also be seen in the slower response to visual targets that normally capture attention (Callaway, Halliday, Haylor, & Schechter, 1985).

Just as muscarinic influences increase signal-to-noise ratio by suppressing intrinsic transmission, nicotinine effects may enhance signal-to-noise ratio by enhancing transmission at afferent synapses (Gray et al., 1996). This could give nicotinic receptors an important role in the dynamics of retrieval, allowing afferent input to more strongly select a particular response. Blockade of nicotinic receptor has been shown to impair response selection by rats in the delayed match to sample task (Granon, Poucet, Thinusblanc, Changeux, & Vidal, 1995). The more rapid time course of synaptic modulation mediated by nicotinic receptors, or GABA-B receptors, could allow important changes in the dynamics of retrieval over shorter periods than the change in muscarinic modulation. For example, in recent research we have proposed that rapid changes in modulation of signal-to-noise ratio provides a method of retrieval similar to simulated annealing in neural network architectures (Sohal & Hasselmo, 1998).

Analysis of signal-to-noise ratio provides a simple framework for describing the interaction of afferent input and intrinsic retrieval within cortical structures. As shown here, cellular effects of modulators such as acetylcholine can clearly enhance signal-to-noise ratio on a network level. Understanding the role of these changes in network dynamics in terms of specific behavioral tasks requires further elaboration of computational models to address the complexity of behaviors involving frontal cortex function.

REFERENCES

Anderson, J. A. (1983). Cognitive and psychological computation with neural models. *IEEE Transactions Systems Man Cybernetics, SMC-13*, 799–815.

Andrade, R. (1991). Cell excitation enhances muscarinic cholinergic responses in rat association cortex. *Brain Research, 548*, 81–93.

Ardila, A., & Moreno, C. (1991). Scopolamine intoxication as a model of transient global amnesia. *Brain and Cognition, 15*, 236–245.

Ashe, J. H., & Weinberger, N. M. (1991). Acetylcholine modulation of cellular excitability via muscarinic receptors: Functional plasticity in auditory cortex. In R. T. Richardson (Ed.), *Activation to acquisition: Functional aspects of the basal forebrain cholinergic system* (pp. 189–246). Boston: Birkhauser.

Auerbach, J. M., & Segal, M. (1994). A novel cholinergic induction of long-term potentiation in rat hippocampus. *Journal of Neurophysiology, 72*, 2034–2040.

Barkai, E., & Hasselmo, M. E. (1994). Modulation of the input/output function of rat piriform cortex pyramidal cells. *Journal of Neurophysiology, 72*, 644–658.

Beach, G. O., Fitzgerald, R. P., Holmes, R., Phibbs, B., & Stuckendoff, H. (1969). Scopolamine poisoning. *New England Journal of Medicine, 270*, 1354–1355.

Berner, J., & Woody, C. D. (1991). Local adaptation of 2 naturally-occurring neuronal conductances. GK+(A) and GK+(CA) allow for associative contiguity judgments in artificial neural networks. *Biological Cybernetics, 66*, 79–86.

Blitzer, R. D., Gil, O., & Landau, E. M. (1990). Cholinergic stimulation enhances long-term potentiation in the CA1 region of rat hippocampus. *Neuroscience Letters, 119*, 207–210.

Brandeis, D., Naylor, H., Halliday, R., Callaway, E., & Yano, L. (1992). Scopolamine effects on visual information processing, attention and event-related potential map latencies. *Psychophysiology, 29*, 315–336.

Brocher, S., Artola, A., & Singer, W. (1992). Agonists of cholinergic and noradrenergic receptors facilitate synergistically the induction of long-term potentiation in slices of rat visual cortex. *Brain Research, 573*, 27–36.

Broks, P., Preston, G. C., Traub, M., Poppleton, P., Ward, C., & Stahl, S. M. (1988). Modelling dementia: Effects of scopolamine on memory and attention. *Neuropsychologia, 26*, 685–700.

Burgard, E. C., & Sarvey, J. M. (1990). Muscarinic receptor activation facilitates the induction of long-term potentiation (LPT) in the rat dentate gyrus. *Neuroscience Letters, 116*, 34–39.

Callaway, E., & Band, R. I. (1958). Some psychopharmacological effects of atropine. *AMA Archive of Neurology and Psychiatry, 79*, 91–102.

Callaway, E., Halliday, R., Haylor, H., & Schechter, G. (1985). Effects of oral scopolamine on human stimulus evaluation. *Psychopharmacology, 85*, 133–138.

Cole, A. E., & Nicoll, R. A. (1984). Characterization of a slow cholinergic postsynaptic potential recorded in vitro from rat hippocampal pyramidal cells. *Journal of Physiology, 352*, 173–188.

Constanti, A., Bagetta, G., & Libri, V. (1993). Persistent muscarinic excitation in guinea-pig olfactory cortex neurons—involvement of a slow poststimulus after depolarizing current. *Neuroscience, 56*, 887–904.

Crawshaw, J. A., & Mullen, P. E. (1984). A study of benzhexol abuse. *British Journal of Psychiatry, 145*, 300–303.

Crow, T. J., & Grove-White, I. G. (1973). An analysis of the learning deficit following hyoscine administration to man. *British Journal of Pharmacology, 49*, 322–327.

DeLuca, J. (1993). Predicting neurobehavioral patterns following anterior communicating artery aneurysm. *Cortex, 29*, 639–647.

Doze, V. A., Cohen, G. A., & Madison, D. V. (1991). Synaptic localization of adrenergic disinhibition in the rat hippocampus. *Neuron, 6*, 889–900.

Drachman, D. A. (1978). Central cholinergic system and memory. In M. A. Lipton, A. DiMascio, & K. F. Killam (Eds.), *Psychopharmacology: A generation of progress* (pp. 651–662). New York: Raven Press.

Flicker, C., Serby, M., & Ferris, S. H. (1990). Scopolamine effects on memory, language, visuospatial praxis and psychomotor speed. *Psychopharmacology (Berl.), 100*, 243–250.

Foote, S. L., Bloom, F. E., & Aston-Jones, G. (1983). Nucleus locus coeruleus: new evidence of anatomical and physiological specificity. *Physiology Review, 63*, 844–913.

Frith, C. D., Richardson, J. T. E., Samuel, M., Crow, T. J., & McKenna, P. J. (1984). The effects of intravenous diazepam and hyoscine upon human memory. *Quarterly Journal of Experimental Psychology, 36A*, 133–144.

Fuster, J. M. (1990). Behavioral electrophysiology of the prefrontal cortex of the primate. *Progress in Brain Research, 85*, 313–324.

Geis, G. (1961). The status of interrogation drugs in the United States. *Journal of Forensic Medicine, 8*, 29.

Gellman, R. L., & Aghajanian, G. K. (1993). Pyramidal cells in piriform cortex receive a conovergence of inputs from monoamine activated GABAergic interneurons. *Brain Research, 600*, 63–73.

Ghoneim, M. M., & Mewaldt, S. P. (1975). Effects of diazepam and scopolamine on storage, retrieval, and organisational processes in memory. *Psychopharmacology, 44*, 257–262.

Granon, S., Poucet, B., Thinusblanc, C., Changeux, J. P., & Vidal, C. (1985). Nicotinic and muscarinic receptors in the rat prefrontal cortex—differential roles in working-memory, response selection and effortful processing. *Psychopharmacology, 119*, 139–144.

Gray, R., Rajan, A. S., Radcliffe, K. A., Yakehiro, M., & Dani, J. A. (1996). Hippocampal synaptic transmission enhanced by low concentrations of nicotine. *Nature, 383*, 713–716.

Hajdahmane, S., & Andrade, R. (1996). Muscarinic activation of a voltage-dependent cation nonselective current in rat association cortex. *Journal of Neuroscience, 16*, 3848–3861.

Hasselmo, M. E. (1995). Neuromodulation and cortical function: Modeling the physiological basis of behavior. *Behavioral Brain Research, 67*, 1–27.

Hasselmo, M. E., & Barkai, E. (1995). Cholinergic modulation of activity-dependent synaptic plasticity in the piriform cortex: Brain slice physiology and computational modeling. *Journal of Neuroscience, 15*, 6592–6604.

Hasselmo, M. E., & Bower, J. M. (1992). Cholinergic suppression specific to intrinsic not afferent fiber synapses in rat piriform (olfactory) cortex. *Journal of Neurophysiology, 67*(5), 1222–1229.

Hasselmo, M. E., & Bower, J. M. (1993). Acetylcholine and memory. *Trends in Neurosciences, 16*(6), 218–222.

Hasselmo, M. E., & Cekic, M. (1996). Suppression of synaptic transmission allows combination of associative feedback and self-organizing feedforward connections in a model of neocortex. *Behavioral Brain Research, 79*, 153–161.

Hasselmo, M. E., & Linster, C. (1998). Modeling the piriform cortex. In E. G. Jones & P. S. Ulinski (Eds.), *Cortical models: Cerebral cortex* (Vol. 12). New York: Plenum.

Hasselmo, M. E., Linster, C., Patil, M., Ma, D., & Cekic, M. (1997). Noradrenergic suppression of synaptic transmission may influence cortical signal-to-noise ratio. *Journal of Neurophysiology, 77*, 3326–3339.

Hasselmo, M. E., & Schnell, E. (1994). Laminar selectivity of the cholinergic suppression of synaptic transmission in rat hippocampal region CA1: Computational modeling and brain slice physiology. *Journal of Neuroscience, 14*, 3898–3914.

Hasselmo, M. E., Schnell, E., & Barkai, E. (1995). Dynamics of learning and recall at excitatory recurrent synapses and cholinergic modulation in hippocampal region CA3. *Journal of Neuroscience, 15*, 5249–5262.

Hounsgaard, J. (1978). Presynaptic inhibitory action of acetylcholine in area CA1 of the hippocampus. *Experimental Neurology, 62*, 787–797.

Huerta, P. T., & Lisman, J. E. (1993). Heightened synaptic plasticity of hippocampal CA1 neurons during a cholinergically induced rhythmic state. *Nature, 364*, 723–725.

Huerta, P. T., & Lisman, J. E. (1995). Bidirectional synaptic plasticity induced by a single burst during cholinergic theta-oscillation in CA1 in vitro. *Neuron, 15*, 1053–1063.

Kasamatsu, T., & Heggelund, P. (1982). Single cell responses in cat visual cortex to visual stimulation during iontophoresis of noradrenaline. *Experimental Brain Research, 45*, 317–324.

Koelega, H. S. (1993). Stimulant drugs and vigilance performance—A review. *Psychopharmacology, 111*, 1–16.

Kohonen, T. (1984). *Self-organization and associative memory.* Berlin: Springer-Verlag.

Krnjevic, K., & Phillis, J. W. (1963). Acetylcholine-sensitive cells in the cerebral cortex. *Journal of Physiology, 166*, 296–327.

Lisman, J. E., & Idiart, M. A. P. (1995). Storage of 7 ± 2 short-term memories in oscillatory subcycles. *Science, 267*, 1512–1515.

Madar, Y., & Segal, M. (1980). The functional role of the noradrenergic system in the visual cortex: Activation of the noradrenergic pathway. *Experimental Brain Research, 41*, 814.

Madison, D. V., Lancaster, B., & Nicoll, R. A. (1987). Voltage clamp analysis of cholinergic action in the hippocampus. *Journal of Neuroscience, 7*, 733–741.

Madison, D. V., & Nicoll, R. A. (1986). Actions of noradrenaline recorded intracellularly in rat hippocampal CA1 pyramidal cells, *in vitro. Journal of Physiology, 372*, 221–244.

Markram, H., & Segal, M. (1990). Long-lasting facilitation of excitatory postsynaptic potentials in the rat hippocampus by acetylcholine. *Journal of Physiology, 427*, 381–393.

McQuiston, A. R., & Madison, D. V. (1996). Postsynaptic actions of cholinergic receptor activation on multiple types of interneurons in CA1 region of the rat hippocampus. *Society for Neuroscience Abstracts, 22*, 786.

Mesulam, M. M., Mufson, E. J., Wainer, B. H., & Levey, A. I. (1983). Central cholinergic pathways in the rat: An overview based on an alternative nomenclature (Ch1–Ch6). *Neuroscience, 10*, 1185–1201.

Metherate, R., Tremblay, N., & Dykes, R. W. (1987). Acetylcholine permits long-term enhancement of neuronal responsiveness in cat primary somatosensory cortex. *Neuroscience, 22*, 75–81.

Metherate, R., & Weinberger, N. M. (1990). Cholinergic modulation of responses to single tones produces tone-specific receptive-field alterations in cat auditory-cortex. *Synapse, 6*, 133–145.

Mewaldt, S. P., & Ghonheim, M. M. (1979). The effects and interactions of scopolamine, physostigmine and methamphetamine on human memory. *Pharmacology and Biochemical Behavior, 10*, 205–210.

Mrzljak, L., Levey, A. I., & Goldman-Rakic, P. S. (1993). Association of M1 and M2 muscarinic receptor proteins with asymmetric synapses in the primate cerebral cortex—Mophological evidence for cholinergic modulation of excitatory neurotransmission. *Proceedings of National Academy of Science, USA, 90*, 5194–5198.

Mrzljak, L., Pappy, M., Leranth, C., & Goldman-Rakic, P. S. (1995). Cholinergic synaptic circuitry in the macaque prefrontal cortex. *Journal of Comparative Neurology, 357*, 603–617.

Ostfeld, A. M., & Aruguete, A. (1962). Central nervous system effects of hyoscine in man. *Journal of Pharmacology and Experimental Therapy, 137*, 133–139.

Patil, M., & Hasselmo, M. E. (1997). *Modulation of inhibitory synaptic potentials in the piriform cortex.* Manuscript submitted for publication.

Patil, M., Linster, C. E., & Hasselmo, M. E. (1997). Cholinergic modulation of synaptic inhibition and the role of interneurons in the piriform cortex. In J. M. Bower (Ed.), *Computational neuroscience.* New York: Academic Press.

Pitler, T. A., & Alger, B. E. (1992). Cholinergic excitation of GABAergic interneurons in the rat hippocampal slice. *Journal of Physiology, 450*, 127–142.

Rasmusson, D. D., & Dykes, R. W. (1988). Long-term enhancement of evoked potentials in cat somatosensory cortex produced by co-activation of the basal forebrain and cutaneous receptors. *Experimental Brain Research, 70*, 276–286.

Reece, L. J., & Schwartzkroin, P. A. (1991). Effects of cholinergic agonists on 2 nonpyramidal cell-types in rat hippocampal slices. *Brain Research, 566*, 115–126.

Safer, D. J., & Allen, R. P. (1971). The central effect of scopolamine in man. *Biological Psychiatry, 3*, 347–355.

Sara, S. J. (1985). The locus coeruleus and cognitive function: Attempts to relate noradrenergic enhancement of signal/noise in the brain to behavior. *Physiological Psychology, 13,* 151–162.

Schwindt, P. C., Spain, W. J., & Crill, W. E. (1992). Calcium-dependent potassium currents in neurons from cat sensorimotor cortex. *Journal of Neurophysiology, 67,* 216–226.

Sciancalepore, M., & Constanti, A. (1995). Patch-clamp study of neurons in rat olfactory cortex slices—Properties of a slow poststimulus afterdepolarizing current (I-ADP). *Neuroreport, 6,* 2489–2494.

Segal, M., & Bloom, F. E. (1974). The action of norepinephrine in the rat hippocampus. II. Activation of the input pathway. *Brain Research, 72,* 99–114.

Servan-Schreiber, D., Printz, H., & Cohen, J. D. (1990). A network model of catecholamine effects—Gain, signal-to-noise ratio and behavior. *Science, 249,* 892–895.

Sillito, A. M., & Kemp, J. A. (1983). Cholinergic modulation of the functional organization of the cat visual cortex. *Brain Research, 289,* 143–155.

Sohal, V. S., & Hasselmo, M. E. (1998). GABAB modulation improves sequence disambiguation in computational models of hippocampal region CA3. *Hippocampus, 8*(2), 171–193.

Tseng, G. F., & Haberly, L. B. (1989). Deep neurons in piriform cortex. II. Membrane properties that underlie unusual synaptic responses. *Journal of Neurophysiology, 62,* 386–400.

Umbriaco, D., Watkins, K. C., Descarries, L., Cozzari, C., & Hartman, B. K. (1994). Ultrastructural and morphometric features of the acetylcholine innervation in adult rat parietal cortex: An electron microscopic study in serial sections. *Journal of Comparative Neurology, 348,* 351–373.

Valentino, R. J., & Dingledine, R. (1981). Presynaptic inhibitory effect of acetylcholine in the hippocampus. *Journal of Neuroscience, 1,* 784–792.

Vanier, M. C., & Bower, J. M. (1993). Differential effects of norepinephrine on synaptic transmission layers 1A and 1B of rat olfactory cortex. In F. H. Eeckman & J. M. Bower (Eds.), *Computation and neural systems* (pp. 267–272). Boston: Kluwer Academic.

Van Vreeswijk, C. A., & Hasselmo M. E. (in press). Self-sustained memory states in a simple model with excitatory and inhibitory neurons. *Biological Cybernetics.*

Vidal, C., & Changeux, J. P. (1993). Nicotinic and muscarinic modulations of excitatory synaptic transmission in the rat prefrontal cortex in vitor. *Neuroscience, 56,* 23–32.

Waterhouse, B. D., & Woodward, D. J. (1980). Interaction of norepinephrine with cerebrocortical activity evoked by stimulation of somatosensory afferent pathways in the rat. *Experimental Neurology, 67,* 11–34.

Wesnes, K., & Warburton, D. M. (1983). Effects of scopolamine on stimulus sensitivity and response bias in a visual vigilance task. *Neuropsychobiology, 9,* 154–157.

Williams, S. H., & Constanti, A. A. (1988). Quantitative study of the effects of some muscarinic antagonists on the quinea-pig olfactory cortex slice. *British Journal of Pharmacology, 93,* 855–862.

Wilson, H. R., & Cowan J. D. (1972). Excitatory and inhibitory interactions in localized populations of model neurons. *Biophysiology Journal, 12,* 1–24.

Wilson, H. R., & Cowan J. (1973). A mathematical theory of the functional dynamics of cortical and thalamic nervous tissue. *Kybernetik, 13,* 55–80.

Woodward, D. J., Moises, H. C., Waterhouse, B. D., Hoffer, B. J., & Freedman, R. (1979). Modulatory actions of norepinephrine in the central nervous system. *Federation Procedings, 38,* 2109–2116.

Woody, C. D., & Gruen, E. (1987). Acetylcholine reduces net outward currents measured *in vivo* with single electrode voltage clamp techniques in neurons of the motor cortex of cats. *Brain Research, 424,* 193–198.

9

Dopamine Projections and Frontal Systems Function

J. RANDOLPH SWARTZ

Dopamine (DA) is a catecholamine that has both motor and behavioral functions. Decreases in DA lead to parkinsonism, mental slowing, apathy, and possibly depression. Increased DA activity can result in chorea, dyskinesia, tics, psychosis, and mania. Much of DA's influence on motor activity and behavior is mediated through neural pathways in the frontal lobes. I first review the neurochemistry of DA, including metabolism, neural projections, and receptors. Next, the anatomy of frontal systems neural circuitry is summarized. The role that dopamine and the frontal lobes play in various neuropsychiatric disorders is briefly explored. Neuroimaging with positron emission tomography (PET) and single photon emission computed tomography (SPECT) is emphasized as windows into the brain's structure and function in these disorders.

DOPAMINE METABOLISM

Catecholamine synthesis occurs in the nerve terminal (Cooper, Bloom, & Roth, 1991). The amino acid tyrosine is converted to levodopa (L-dopa) by tyrosine hydroxylase in the rate limiting step of catecholamine synthesis. Next, L-dopa is metabolized to DA by aromatic amino acid decarboxylase. If excessive catecholamines build up in the nerve terminal, they inhibit tyrosine hydroxylase, preventing continued synthesis. In some areas of the brain, as well as other parts of the body, DA is converted to norepinephrine by dopamine-β-hydroxylase and to epinephrine by N-methyltransferase.

Synaptically released DA has its activity terminated via two routes: the uptake mechanism or transformation to inactive forms (Baraban & Coyle, 1995). DA can be moved back into the presynaptic nerve terminal via uptake transporters where it is recycled as a neurotransmitter (Amara & Kuhar, 1993), or DA can be metabolized by a series of enzymatic steps to homovanillic acid (HVA). The two main enzymes that metabolize DA are monoamine oxidase (MAO) and catechol-O-methyl transferase (COMT). MAO is located intracellularly, bound to the external side of the mitochondrial membrane, whereas COMT is an extracellular enzyme. There are two types of MAO: MAO_A and MAO_B, although DA is metabolized selectively by MAO_B. MAO_B initiates enzymatic transformations which convert DA to dihydroxyphenylacetic acid (DOPAC). DOPAC is then metabolized via COMT to HVA. Alternatively, DA can be converted by COMT to 3-methoxytyramine, then converted by MAO_B to 3-methoxy-4-hydroxyphenylacetaldehyde, and finally metabolized via a series of enzymatic transformations to HVA.

DOPAMINE PATHWAYS

There are three major dopamine projections: mesocortical, mesolimbic, and nigrostriatal pathways (Cummings & Coffey, 1994). The mesocortical pathway originates in the ventral tegmental area (VTA), located in the midbrain, and projects to the frontal cortex, temporal cortex, and anterior cingulum. The mesolimbic pathway also originates in VTA and projects to a variety of limbic structures, including the nucleus accumbens (located between the caudate head and putamen), the amygdala, the hippocampus, and the septal nuclei. Nigrostriatal pathways originate in the substantia nigra pars compacta, in the midbrain next to the VTA, and project to the striatum (the caudate nucleus and the putamen). Many DA projections arising from the midbrain travel to higher levels of the brain grouped together with ascending and descending pathways of other biogenic amines (e.g., serotonin and norepinephrine). These biogenic amine pathways are collectively referred to as the medial forebrain bundle (MFB) (Moore & Bloom, 1978). In addition, a fourth DA pathway, the tuberoinfundibular pathway, projects from the arcuate nucleus and the periventricular area of the hypothalamus to the infundibulum and the anterior pituitary gland where DA inhibits the release of prolactin.

DOPAMINE RECEPTORS

There are at least five different DA receptors (D1, D2, D3, D4, and D5) (Sibley & Monsma, 1992), all with differing DNA sequences. Most of the known activity of DA receptors has been described in studies of D1 and D2 receptors. Less is known about the D3, D4, and D5 receptors. D1 and D2 receptors are located primarily in areas receiving innervation from dopaminergic neurons. High concentrations are in the postsynaptic neurons of prefrontal cortex, striatum, and the limbic system (especially the nucleus accumbens). The D3 receptor is highly concentrated in the nucleus accumbens whereas the D4 receptor is highly concentrated in the frontal cortex. D2 receptors also are located on the presynaptic dopamine terminal, where they regulate dopamine synthesis and release.

All five DA receptors have been cloned. D2 was the first (Bunzow et al., 1988), while cloning of D3 (Sokoloff, Giros, Martes, Bouthenet, & Schwartz, 1990) and D4 (Van Tol et al., 1991) followed; D3 and D4 have binding characteristics similar to D2. The D1 receptor also has been cloned (Dearry et al., 1990), and a D1-like receptor with distinctive pharmacological traits has been identified as D5 (Sunahara et al., 1991). It is likely that more DA receptors will be identified (Niznik & Van Tol, 1992). DA receptors can be differentiated by selective agonists and antagonists that bind specifically to each: SKF 82526 is a selective D1 agonist; SCH 23390 is a selective D1 antagonist. Sulpiride is a selective D2 antagonist. Both D1 and D2 receptors can exist in high or low affinity states, based on the degree to which agonists or antagonists bind to them. The development of specific pharmacological probes for each receptor should lead to a better understanding of the abnormal gene expression of various DA receptors in studies of different illnesses (Seeman, 1992).

DA receptors have differing effects on protein function via second messengers. D1 and D5 stimulate adenylate cyclase via the receptor-linked stimulatory G-protein, while D2 (and possibly D3 and D4) inhibits adenylate cyclase via the receptor-linked inhibitory G-protein. Adenylate cyclase synthesizes the second messenger cyclic adenosine monophosphate (cAMP), which in turn activates cAMP-dependent protein kinase leading to protein phosphorylation. The addition of a negatively charged phosphate group can change the shape and function of a protein molecule. Thus, DA receptors (along with many other types of receptors) regulate protein function via second messengers and different DA receptors have different effects on protein activity. DA receptor activation may also lead to activation of immediate early genes (e.g., c-fos), which in turn may regulate gene expression. Differences in c-fos activation in various parts of the brain provide clues about neural tract specificity of medications. For example, several lines of evidence suggest that novel antipsychotic medications block DA receptors in the mesolimbic pathway while sparing the DA receptors of the nigrostriatal pathway (Chiodo & Bunney, 1983; Robertson, Matsumura, & Fibuger, 1994; White & Wang, 1983).

FRONTAL SYSTEMS NEURAL CIRCUITRY

Chow and Cummings (Chapter 1, this volume) extensively reviewed this circuitry. Basal ganglia diseases often result in dysfunction of frontal–subcortical circuits and lead to a variety of neuropsychiatric syndromes.

BRAIN REWARD CIRCUITS AND DOPAMINE

The original discovery of the brain's reward circuits (Olds & Milner, 1954) led to a rich legacy of research (Rolls, 1975; Routtenberg, 1978; Yeomans, 1988). Regions involved in this process include neural structures in the brainstem, midbrain, and forebrain which are grouped together into the MFB (Olds & Olds, 1963; Wetzel, 1968). They correspond to the mesotelencephalic dopamine system ascending in the MFB to the forebrain (Crow, 1972). Subsequent studies showed that brain stimulation reward is dependent on intact mesotelencephalic DA neurotransmission (Corbett & Wise, 1980; Fray, Dunnett, Iversen, Bjorklund, & Stenevi, 1983; Mogenson, Takigawa, Robertson, & Wu, 1979; Wise, 1980; Wise & Rompre, 1989; Zarevics & Setler, 1979). DA neurons constitute a "second stage" anatomic convergence within the brain's reward circuitry, upon which "first stage" neurons synapse to form the brain's "in series" reward neural circuit (Wise & Rompre, 1989). Almost every recreationally abused substance (e.g., cocaine, amphetamine, opiates, and cannibis) acts on this second-stage DA covergence to enhance the experience of brain reward, thus providing positive reinforcement for such behavior (Gardner & Lowinson, 1991; Wise 1980; Wise & Rompre, 1989). Loss of DA function in these reward pathways may contribute to apathy (Willner & Scheel-Kruger, 1991).

Alzheimer's Disease

Alzheimer's disease (AD) is the most common degenerative dementia. Brain pathology usually begins in the bilateral parietal or posterior temporal cortex and then spreads anteriorly to the frontal lobes in later stages (Cummings & Benson, 1992). The neuroanatomical progression of AD correlates well with the clinical manifestations of memory loss and visuospatial impairment early in the course followed by personality changes later. The most consistent neurochemical change in AD is a presynaptic cholinergic defect. Many studies of AD show a central nervous system (CNS) cholinergic deficit marked by reduced choline acetyltransferase and reduced acetylcholine (Ach) in the cerebral cortex and the hippocampus (Bowen, Smith, White, & Davison, 1976; Davies & Maloney, 1976; Perry, Perry, Blessed, & Tomlinson, 1977). This may be due to cholinergic neuronal loss in the nucleus basalis of Meynert (Whitehouse et al., 1982).

However, other neurotransmitters including dopamine and serotonin are abnormal in AD (Itoh et al., 1994; Tejani-Butt, Yang, & Pawllyk, 1995). Storga, Vrecko, Birkmayer, and Reibnegger (1996) measured the concentrations of monoamine neurotransmitters, their precursors, and their metabolites in seven brain regions (globus pallidus, putamen, amygdala, caudate nucleus, substantia nigra, cingulum, and raphe nuclei) in eight pathologically verified AD cases and six controls. Concentrations of dopamine, L-dopa, DOPAC, norepinephrine, and serotonin were significantly reduced. These findings show monoaminergic neurotransmitter disturbance in AD and emphasize the significance of dopaminergic deficit in AD.

Pizzolato et al. (1996) used SPECT with a D2 receptor ligand to measure striatal D2 receptors in 15 AD subjects without overt extrapyramidal symptoms. They showed reduced striatal receptor binding in AD subjects compared to controls, supporting the hypothesis that alterations in striatal D2 receptors occur with AD (Pizzolato et al., 1996).

DA dysfunction may play an important role in both the cognitive and the noncognitive symptoms of AD. Itoh et al. (1994) used PET to study striatal DA metabolism and found decreased DA activity in AD. The severity of this DA abnormality correlated with dementia severity (as measured by Mini-Mental Status Examination). Apathy is the most common behavioral disturbance in AD, with a prevalence estimated as high as 90% (Bozzola, Gorelick, & Freels, 1992; Rubin, Morris, & Berg, 1987). Apathy has been associated with anterior cingulate damage (Cummings, 1995; Damasio & Van Hoesen, 1983) and with decreased DA function in the forebrain (Willner & Scheel-Kruger, 1991). In AD, Craig et al. (1996) recently reported a significant association between apathy severity and decreased regional cerebral blood flow (CBF) in the anterior cingulate, orbitofrontal, dorsolateral prefrontal, and anterior temporal brain regions (Craig et al., 1996).

About one-third of AD patients experience psychotic symptoms, such as paranoia or hallucinations. In schizophrenia these symptoms have been attributed to excess DA activity. In AD, cholinergic levels are reduced relative to dopaminergic levels; resulting in a balance toward DA predominance (similar to what is seen in schizophrenia) that may lead to psychosis in AD (Cummings, 1993; White & Cummings, 1996). Psychosis in AD responds to treatment with both cholinergic boosting medications (e.g., physostigmine) and dopamine receptor antagonists (e.g., haloperidol) (Cummings, Gorman, & Shapira, 1993; Flint, 1991; Gorman, Read, & Cummings, 1993). These findings show how DA must be viewed in terms of its balance with other neurotransmitters when considering the etiology of various behavioral symptoms.

Frontotemporal Dementia

Frontotemporal dementia (FTD) is the second most common degenerative dementia. Patients present with personality changes, apathy, disinhibition, hyperphagia, irritability, compulsions, irritability, and depressive symptoms (Brun et al., 1994; Gustafson, 1993; Miller et al., 1991; Miller, Darby, Swartz, Yener, & Mena, 1995; Neary, Snowden, Northen, & Goulding, 1988). There are impaired executive functions marked by perseveration and difficulties with shifting sets (e.g., Wisconsin Card Sorting Test). Memory, visuospatial skills and calculations are often spared in the early stages. FTD can be mistaken for a primary affective disorder (Gustafson, Brun, & Risberg, 1990) and often is misdiagnosed as AD.

Pathology in the frontal–subcortical circuits is closely related to the behavioral phenomenology and cognitive declines observed in FTD. Lesions throughout the anterior cingulate circuit result in apathy. Injury to anterior cingulum can result in akinetic mutism, marked by profound apathy, lack of spontaneous speech, and monosyllabic answers to questions (Cummings & Coffey, 1994). Dysfunction of the orbitofrontal circuit results in personality changes, including increased irritability and social disinhibition, whereas dysfunction of the dorsolateral prefrontal circuit leads to executive function deficits (Cummings, 1995).

Postmortem neurochemical studies of FTD showed profound loss of serotonin receptor binding with spared cholinergic cells (Sparks & Markesbery, 1991). (DA receptor binding was not evaluated in that study.) However, a recent neuroimaging study suggests that low DA function in the frontal lobe may play a role in the pathogenesis of FTD. Frisoni et al. (1994) used SPECT to measure cerebral perfusion and postsynaptic D2 receptors in five FTD subjects, six AD subjects, and six controls. FTD exhibited lower frontal/temporal and frontal/parietal ratios than did AD. Some AD subjects also showed frontal hypoperfusion which was attributed to variation in the severity/staging of the AD subjects. There was significantly reduced ligand uptake of D2 receptors in superior frontal regions in FTD compared to AD, which suggests more severe involvement of the frontal–cortical dopaminergic system in FTD than in AD (Frisoni et al., 1994).

Parkinson's Disease

Parkinson's disease (PD) is a common movement disorder marked by rigidity, bradykinesia, and tremor. About 20–30% of PD patients develop dementia, while 50% suffer from depression. The classical dementia of PD has been described as subcortical, manifesting as impaired memory, slowed information processing speed (bradyphrenia), motoric slowing, dysarthria, abnormal gait and posture, with preservation of language. However, the dementia associated with PD shows diverse brain pathology involving both subcortical and cortical areas. At pathology there is loss of pigmented dopaminergic neurons in the substantia nigra pars compacta and Lewy bodies in various brain regions (substantia nigra, locus ceruleus, nucleus basalis of Meynert, among others). Allard, Rinne, and Marcusson (1994) studied postmortem brains of PD, AD, and controls by measuring [^{3}H]GBR-12935 binding to DA uptake sites in the putamen. Binding was almost completely abolished in the PD group and reduced by 65% in the AD group, suggesting degeneration of DA neurites in the putamen in both PD and AD, but more severe in PD.

In a PET study, Brooks and Frackowiak (1989) showed that cerebral metabolism in PD patients without dementia was globally decreased (especially in the frontal lobes).

Tarczy and Szirmai (1995) measured cerebral perfusion using SPECT and distinguished three patterns of hypoperfusion in PD patients: frontal lobe type, posterior (Alzheimer-like) type, and multiple small vascular defect type. An MAO_B inhibitor which increased DA activity improved Mini-Mental Status Examination scores and verbal fluency in the frontal lobe type. Although the mechanism for this clinical improvement remains unclear, these results suggest that low DA function may be related to the cognitive impairment of these frontal lobe-type PD patients. The overall theme of these studies is that the motor and cognitive impairment of PD is closely related to DA dysfunction in frontal-striatal subcortical circuits.

Huntington's Disease

Huntington's disease (HD) is an autosomal dominant hereditary disorder marked by personality changes, chorea, and dementia. Postmortem pathology reveals atrophy of the caudate head, which is associated with deficiency in γ-amniobutyric acid (GABA), glutamic acid decarboxylase, Ach, choline acetyltransferase, substance P, and enkephalin (Martin & Gusella, 1986). Pearson and Reynolds (1994) measured neurotransmitter markers in postmortem tissue from frontal and temporal cortex of HD patients. Decreased GABA and glutamate concentrations, along with increased concentrations of serotonin and dopamine metabolites, were reported. The dementia of HD classically has been attributed to striatal pathology; many of the early neuroimaging studies of HD pointed to dysfunction of the caudate. Early PET studies showed striatal, but not cortical, hypometabolism (Hayden et al., 1986). More recent neuroimaging evidence points to abnormal frontal–striatal circuits and DA dysfunction as integral to the pathogenesis of HD. Increasing evidence suggests that HD is characterized by decreased DA receptor density in the striatum and also possibly in the frontal cortex.

Ichise, Toyama, Fornazzari, Ballinger, and Kirsh (1993) used SPECT to measure D2 receptor density and cerebral perfusion in 4 symptomatic HD subjects, 20 asymptomatic subjects at risk for HD, and 22 controls. Striatal-to-frontal cortex ratios were measured. All HD subjects had decreased D2 ratios, and three of the four showed decreased perfusion ratios. Five of 20 at-risk subjects showed decreased D2 ratios and 2 showed decreased perfusion ratios. In aggregate, these findings show that decreased D2 receptor density can be detected in both symptomatic HD subjects and, to a lesser degree, asymptomatic subjects at risk for HD. Toyama et al. (1993) used SPECT to measure D2 receptor density in three symptomatic HD patients and also found reduced basal ganglia/frontal cortex ratios. Brucke et al. (1993) used similar imaging techniques and found reduced striatal/frontal cortical ratios of D2 receptor density in 18 HD patients. Saur et al. (1994) used SPECT to measure cerebral perfusion and D2 receptor binding in the frontal cortex and basal ganglia in 26 patients with movement disorders (including 13 with PD and 2 with HD). The HD patients showed lower perfusion and lower D2 receptor binding compared to the other hyperkinetic extrapyramidal disorders. Sedvall et al. (1994) used PET to measure D1 receptor density among five HD patients, one asymptomatic gene carrier, and five control subjects. The total D1 receptor number in the caudate and putamen was reduced by about 75% in the HD patient group. Those with mild to moderate impairment showed a 50% reduction in putamen volume and D1 receptor density compared to controls. The asymptomatic gene carrier had volume and receptor density reductions in the lower range of the control subjects. The HD patients also showed reduced D1 receptor binding in the frontal cortex, supporting the concept that the subcortical dementia of HD is more accurately described as a frontal–striatal dementia with marked DA dysfunction.

Schizophrenia

Schizophrenia is a chronic mental illness marked by deterioration of perceptions, thought content, thought form, and behavior. These symptoms ("positive" symptoms) present as hallucinations, delusions, formal thought disorder (e.g., loose associations), and disorganized behavior. Also, it is marked by social withdrawal, amotivation, apathy, and inappropriate affect ("negative" or "deficit" symptoms) (Crow, 1980). Evidence suggests that dopamine and the frontal lobe play integral roles in the etiology of schizophrenia.

The original dopamine hypothesis of schizophrenia stated that this illness was a manifestation of a hyperdopaminergic state in the brain (Matthysse, 1973). This hypothesis was based on indirect evidence of a correlation between the clinical potency of neuroleptics and their affinity for dopamine receptors (specifically the D2 receptor) (Creese, Burt, & Snyder, 1976; Seeman, Lee, Chau-Wong, & Wong, 1976). Yet, others have challenged the concept that a hyperdopaminergic state explains all the symptoms of schizophrenia (Davis, Kahn, Ko, & Davidson, 1991; Reynolds, 1989). Nevertheless, recent findings suggest that a modified version of the original dopamine hypothesis may improve our understanding of the etiology of schizophrenia (Davis et al., 1991).

Several lines of evidence suggest that schizophrenia is characterized by hypo-dopaminergic function in the mesocortical pathway and hyperdopaminergic function in the mesolimbic pathway (Davis et al., 1991; Csernansky, Murphy, & Faustman, 1991). These conditions may be closely associated in a reciprocal relationship. Many animal studies (Glowinski, Tassin, & Thierry, 1984; Leccesse & Lyness, 1987; Pycock, Kerwin, & Carter, 1980), but not all (Roskin, Deutch, & Roth, 1987), have shown that lesions of the prefrontal cortex DA neurons causes increased levels of DA and its metabolites, as well as increased D2 receptor binding sites, in the striatum and the nucleus accumbens. Conversely, the dopamine agonist apomorphine injected into the prefrontal cortex of rats reduces DA metabolites in the striatum (Scatton, Worms, Lloyd, & Bartholini, 1982). In aggregate, these findings suggest that schizophrenia patients show the simultaneous presentation of both positive symptoms (associated with increased DA activity in the nucleus accumbens and striatum) and negative symptoms (associated with decreased prefrontal dopamine activity) (Davis et al., 1991).

Neuroimaging studies of schizophrenia provide further clues to understanding the etiology of this illness. Structural and functional imaging studies point to three pathological regions in schizophrenia: frontal lobe, temporal lobe, and basal ganglia (Gur & Pearlson, 1993). Of these, the frontal lobes appear most closely related to the negative symptoms of schizophrenia. Some studies (Andreasen et al., 1986; DeMyer et al., 1988), but not all (Rossi et al., 1990), using magnetic resonance imaging (MRI) to image the brains of schizophrenia patients have reported decreased frontal lobe volume. Functional imaging studies of cerebral metabolism or perfusion in schizophrenia have shown a reduced "anterior–posterior gradient" (Mathew, Wilson, Tant, Robinson, & Prakash, 1988), an association between decreased frontal lobe metabolism or perfusion and negative symptoms (Lewis, Ford, Syed, Reveley, & Toome, 1992; Vita et al., 1991), and an association between dorsolateral prefrontal cortex (DLPFC) hypofrontality and cognitive impairment on executive tasks requiring the subjects to change sets (Berman & Weinberger, 1990; Kawasaki et al., 1991; Lewis et al., 1992; Rubin et al., 1991). The hypofrontality of schizophrenia has been reported in neuroleptic-naive schizophrenia patients (Andreasen et al., 1992). In a discordant twin study, Weinberger, Berman, Suddath, and Torrey (1992) found that all twins with schizophrenia showed reduced DLPFC CBF compared to their unaffected co-twins. Satoh, Narita, Someya, Fukuyama and Yonekura (1993) reported a catatonic schizophrenia in whom SPECT and PET showed decreased metabolism and decreased CBF in the dorsal frontal–parietal lobes.

PET studies of DA receptor density in schizophrenia have been inconsistent. Wong et al. (1986) reported increased D2 density, whereas Farde et al. (1990) reported no differences in D2 density between schizophrenia subjects and controls. Recently, Pearlson et al. (1993) found elevated D2 receptor density in young and elderly schizophrenia patients, whereas Sedvall et al. (1995) reported reduced D1 receptor density in the basal ganglia. Seeman and Niznik (1990) found elevated D2 receptor density in the caudate and putamen of schizophrenia patients.

Mood Disorders

Norepinephrine and serotonin play key roles in the etiology of affective disorders. However, dysfunction of the dopaminergic system also contributes to affective disorders, including major depression and mania (Jimerson, 1987). Bromocriptine (Silverstone, 1984) and L-dopa (Butcher & Engel, 1969) have mild antidepressant effects. The antidepressant bupropion acts primarily as a dopamine uptake blocker, thus increasing the amount of DA available in the synapse (Richelson, 1994). Psychotic depression may be related to increased DA activity in some parts of the brain; treatment is more likely to be effective if both antipsychotic and antidepressant medications are used (Chan et al., 1987).

Also, evidence shows that DA dysfunction is associated with mania (Silverstone, 1985). Inhibition of DA hydroxylase (increasing DA availability) has been hypothesized to be related to mania, whereas medications that inhibit DA synthesis may reduce the severity of manic symptoms (Sack & Goodwin, 1974). Manic-like conditions can be induced by stimulants such as amphetamine, which increase DA availability. These conditions can be alleviated by lithium (Van Kammen & Murphy, 1975). Recently, low plasma dopamine-β-hydroxylase was reported in lithium-withdrawn bipolar patients; enzyme activity normalized after lithium was restarted (Sofuoglu et al., 1995).

Neuroimaging studies support the concept that frontal lobe pathology and DA dysfunction are related to affective disorders. Baxter et al. (1985) measured cerebral metabolism with PET in a variety of affective disorders, including unipolar depression and bipolar depression, mixed states, and mania. Bipolar-depressed and bipolar-mixed state patients showed significantly lower whole brain metabolism than the other affective disorder groups and the controls. The whole brain metabolic rates for bipolar-depressed patients increased, going from depression or a mixed state to euthymia or mania. Unipolar depression patients showed lower ratios of caudate nucleus/hemisphere metabolism. SPECT studies have also found abnormal cerebral perfusion in both depression and mania. Lesser et al. (1994) found frontotemporal hypoperfusion, particularly in the right hemisphere, in late-life depression. Rubin et al. (1995) reported hypoperfusion in the anterior cortical areas in both major depression and acute mania.

PET studies of DA receptors have shown abnormal receptor density in some mood disorder patients. An early PET study of D2 receptors in bipolar patients reported no difference between bipolar subjects and controls (Wong et al., 1985), but a more recent study found decreased D1 receptors in frontal cortex of mood disorder patients,independent of their mood state (i.e., mania vs. depression) (Suhara et al., 1992). D'haenen and Bossuyt (1994) measured D2 receptor density in unipolar depression with SPECT and found a significantly higher basal ganglia/cerebellum uptake ratio in depression. Pearlson et al. (1995) used PET to measure D2 receptor density in the caudate and putamen among psychotic and nonpsychotic bipolar patients. Psychotic bipolar patients showed higher D2 receptor density than nonpsychotic bipolar patients or controls. Severity of psychosis among bipolar patients correlated with the D2 receptor density.

Thus, DA dysfunction may play a role in depression and mania, particularly if psychosis is present. Also, evidence points to an association between mood disorders and dysfunction of the frontal–subcortical circuits. However, the results of these studies are not consistently replicated, and the association is at the present best conceptualized as circuit-related rather than circuit-specific behavior (Cummings, 1995).

Tourette's Syndrome

Tourette's syndrome (TS) consists of multiple motor tics and one or more vocal tics that may appear simultaneously or at different times. It is associated with basal ganglia pathology (Peterson et al., 1993) and a response to DA receptor antagonists (Shapiro et al., 1989). Wolf et al. (1996) found that monozygotic twins discordant for TS severity showed differences in D2 receptor binding in the caudate nucleus head but not the putamen, which predicted the differences in tics ($r = .99$). Strong evidence links caudate DA dysfunction to TS.

CONCLUSIONS

Converging lines of evidence suggest that DA and frontal–subcortcial circuits play integral roles in a variety of behavioral symptoms. Low DA in the frontal cortex is associated with cognitive impairment and apathy in dementia, negative symptoms of schizophrenia, and aspects of depression. There is overlap in the clinical presentations of each of these. For example, apathy, indifference, amotivation, and emotional withdrawal can occur in dementia, schizophrenia, and major depression. Also, excessive DA function in subcortical circuits is associated with psychosis in a variety of disorders, including dementia, schizophrenia, and mood disorders. A simple hypothesis of either increased or decreased activity of one chemical in one part of the brain cannot fully explain the etiology of all these symptoms. Yet, it is likely that similar chemical imbalances in the frontal–subcortical neural connections are related to similar symptoms observed in different neuropsychiatric disorders. An improved understanding of these neuroanatomical and neurochemical aberrations will lead to better insight into the pathogenesis of these disorders and improve treatment options.

REFERENCES

Allard, P. O., Rinne, J., & Marcusson, J. O. (1994). Dopamine uptake sites in Parkinson's disease and in dementia of the Alzheimer type. *Brain Research, 637,* 262–266.

Amara, S. G., & Kuhar, M. J. (1993). Neurotransmitter transporters: Recent progress. *Annual Review of Neuroscience, 16,* 73–93.

Andreasen, N. C., Nasrallah, H. A., Dunn, V., Olson, S. C., Grove, W. M., Ehrhardt, J. C., Coffman, J. A., & Crossett, J. H. W. (1986). Structural abnormalities in the frontal system in schizophrenia. *Archives of General Psychiatry, 43,* 136–144.

Andreasen, N. C., Rezai, K., Alliger, R., Swayze, V. W. II, Flaum, M., Kirchner, P., Cohen, G., & O'Leary, D. S. (1992). Hypofrontality in neuroleptic-naive patients and in patients with chronic schizophrenia. *Archives of General Psychiatry, 49,* 943–958.

Baraban, J. M., & Coyle, J. T. (1995). Monoamine neurotransmitters. In H. I. Kaplan & B. J. Sadock (Eds.), *Comprehensive textbook of psychiatry* (6th ed., pp. 25–32). Baltimore: Williams & Wilkins.

Baxter, L. R., Phelps, M. E., Mazziotta, J. C., Schwartz, J. M., Gerner, R. H., Selin, C. E., & Sumida, R. M. (1985). Cerebral metabolic rates for glucose in mood disorders: Studies with positron emission tomography and fluorodeoxyglucose F-18. *Archives of General Psychiatry, 42,* 441–447.

Berman, K. F., & Weinberger, D. R. (1990). Lateralization of cortical function during cognitive tasks: Regional cerebral blood flow studies of normal individuals and patients with schizophrenia. *Journal of Neurological and Neurosurgical Psychiatry, 53,* 150–160.

Bowen, D. M., Smith, C. B., White, P., & Davison, A. N. (1976). Neurotransmitter-related enzymes and indices of hypoxia in senile dementia and other abiotrophies. *Brain, 9,* 459–496.

Bozzola, F. G., Gorelick, P. B., & Freels, S. (1992). Personality changes in Alzheimer's disease. *Archives of Neurology, 49,* 297–300.

Brooks, D. J., & Frackowiak, R. S. (1989, June). PET and movement disorders. *Journal of Neurology, Neurosurgery, and Psychiatry* (Suppl.), 68–77.

Brucke, T., Wenger, S., Asenbaum, S., Fertl, E., Pfafflmeyer, N., Muller, C., Podreka, I., & Angelberger, P. (1993). Dopamine D2 receptor imaging and measurement with SPECT. *Advanced Neurology, 60,* 494–500.

Brun, A., Englund, B., Gustafson, L., Passant, U., Mann, D. M. A., Neary, D., & Snowden, J. S. (1994). Clinical and neuropathological criteria for frontotemporal dementia. *Journal of Neurological and Neurosurgical Psychiatry, 57,* 416–418.

Buchsbaum, M. S., Wu, J. C., DeLisi, L. E., Holcomb, H. H., Kessler, R., Johnson, J., King, A. C., Hazlett, E., Langston, K., & Post, R. M. (1986). Frontal cortex and basal ganglia metabolic rates assessed by positron emission tomography with F-18 2-deoxyglucose in affective illness. *Journal of Affective Disorders, 10,* 137–152.

Bunzow, J. R., Van Tol, H. H. M., Grandy, D. K., Albert, P., Salon, J., Christie, M., Machida, C. A., Neve, K. A., & Civelli, O. (1988). Cloning and expression of a rat D2 dopamine receptor cDNA. *Nature, 336,* 783–787.

Butcher, L. L., & Engel, J. (1969). Behavioral and biochemical effects of L-dopa after peripheral decarboxylase inhibition. *Brain Research, 15,* 233–241.

Carpenter, M. B., & Sutin, J. (1983). *Human neuroanatomy* (8th ed.). Baltimore: Williams, & Wilkins.

Chan, C. H., Janicak, P. G., Davis, J. M., Altman, E., Andriukaitis, S., & Hedeker, D. (1987). Response of psychotic and non-psychotic depressed patients to tricyclic antidepressants. *Journal of Clinical Psychiatry, 48,* 197–200.

Chiodo, L. A., & Bunney, B. S. (1983). Typical and atypical neuroleptics: Differential effects of chronic administration on the activity of A-9 and A-10 midbrain dopaminergic neurons. *Journal of Neuroscience, 3,* 1607–1619.

Cooper, J. R., Bloom, F. E., & Roth, R. H. (1991). *The biological basis of neuropharmacology* (6th ed.). New York: Oxford University Press.

Corbett, D., & Wise, R. A. (1980). Intracranial self-stimulation in relation to the ascending dopaminergic systems of the midbrain: A moveable electrode mapping study. *Brain Research, 185,* 1–15.

Craig, A. H., Cummings, J. L., Fairbanks, L., Itti, L., Miller, B. L., Li, J., & Mena, I. (1996). Cerebral blood flow correlates of apathy in Alzheimer's disease. *Archives of Neurology, 53,* 1116–1120.

Creese, I., Burt, D. R., & Snyder, S. H. (1976). Dopamine receptor binding predicts clinical and pharmacological potencies of antipsychotic drugs. *Science, 192,* 481–483.

Crow, T. J. (1972). A map of the rat mesencephalon for electrical self-stimulation. *Brain Research, 36,* 265–273.

Crow, T. J. (1980). Positive and negative schizophrenic symptoms and the role of dopamine. *British Journal of Psychiatry, 137,* 383–386.

Csernansky, J. G., Murphy, G. M., & Faustman, W. O. Limbic/mesolimbic connections and the pathogenesis of schizophrenia. *Biological Psychiatry, 30,* 383–400.

Cummings, J. L. (1993). Frontal–subcortical circuits and human behavior. *Archives of Neurology, 50,* 873–880.

Cummings, J. L. (1995). Anatomic and behavioral aspects of frontal–subcortical circuits. *Annals of the New York Academy of Science, 769,* 1–13.

Cummings, J. L.,, & Benson, D. F. (1992). *Dementia: A clinical approach* (2nd ed.). Stoneham, MA: Butterworth-Heinemann.

Cummings, J. L., & Coffey, C. E. (1994). Neurobiological basis of behavior. In J. L. Cummings & C. E. Coffey (Eds.), *Textbook of geriatric neuropsychiatry* (1st ed., pp. 71–96). Washington, DC: American Psychiatric Press.

Cummings, J. L., Gorman, D. G., & Shapira, J. (1993). Physostigmine ameliorates the delusions of Alzheimer's disease. *Biological Psychiatry, 33,* 536–541.

Damasio, A. R., & Van Hoesen, G. W. (1983). Emotional disturbances associated with focal lesions of the limbic frontal lobe. In K. M. Heilman & P. Satz (Eds.), *Neuropsychology of human emotion* (pp. 85–110). New York: Guilford Press.

Davies, P., & Maloney, A. J. (1976). Selective loss of central cholinergic neurons in Alzheimer's disease. *Lancet, 2,* 1403.

Davis, K. L., Kahn, R. S., Ko, G., & Davidson, M. (1991). Dopamine in schizophrenia: A review and reconceptualization. *American Journal of Psychiatry, 148,* 1474–1486.

Dearry, A., Gingrich, J. A., Falardeau, P., Fremeau, R. T. Jr., Bates, M. D., & Caron, M. G. (1990). Molecular cloning and expression of the gene for a human D1 dopamine receptor. *Nature, 347,* 72–76.

DeMyer, M. K., Gilmor, R. L., Hendrie, H. C., DeMyer, W. E., Augustyn, G. T., & Jackson, R. K. (1988). Magnetic resonance brain images in schizophrenic and normal subjects: Influence of diagnosis and education. *Schizophrenia Bulletin, 14,* 21–37.

D'haenen, H., & Bossuyt, A. (1994). Dopamine D2 receptors in depression measured with single photon emission computed tomography. *Biological Psychiatry, 35,* 128–132.

Farde, L., Wiesel, F. A., Stone-Elander, S., Halldin, C., Nordstrom, A. L., Hall, H., & Sedvall, G. (1990). D2 dopamine receptors in neuroleptic-naive schizophrenic patients: A positron emission tomography study with ^{11}C raclopride. *Archives of General Psychiatry, 47,* 213–219.

Flint, A. J. (1991). Delusions in dementia: a review. *Journal of Neuropsychiatry and Clinical Neuroscience, 3,* 121–130.

Fray, P. J., Dunnett, S. B., Iversen, S. D., Bjorklund, A., & Stenevi, U. (1983). Nigral transplants reinnervating the dopamine-depleted neostriatum can sustain intracranial self-stimulation. *Science, 219,* 416–420.

Frisoni, G. B., Pizzolato, G., Bianchetti, A., Chierichetti, F., Ferlin, G., Battistin, L., & Trabucchi, M. (1994). Single photon emission computed tomography with [^{99}Tc]-HM-PAO and [^{123}I]-IBZM in Alzheimer's disease and dementia of frontal type: preliminary results. *Acta Neurologica Scandinavica, 89,* 199–203.

Gardner, E. L., & Lowinson, J. H. (1991). Marijuana's interaction with brain reward systems: update 1991. *Pharmacology and Biochemical Behavior, 40,* 571–580.

Glowinski, J., Tassin, J. P., & Thierry, A. M. (1984). The mesocorticoprefrontal dopaminergic neurons. *Trends in Neurosciences, 7,* 415–418.

Gorman, D. G., Read, S. L., & Cummings, J. L. (1993). Cholinergic therapy of behavioral disturbances in Alzheimer's disease. *Neuropsychiatry, Neuropsychology and Behavioral Neurology, 6,* 229–234.

Gur, R. E., & Pearlson, G. D. (1993). Neuroimaging in schizophrenia research. *Schizophrenia Bulletin, 19,* 337–353.

Gustafson, L. (1993). Clinical picture of frontal lobe degeneration of non-Alzheimer type. *Dementia, 4,* 143–148.

Gustafson, L., Brun, A., & Risberg, J. (1990). Frontal lobe dementia of non-Alzheimer type. *Advanced Neurology, 51,* 65–71.

Hayden, M. R., Martin, W. R. W., Stoessl, A. J., Clark, C., Hollenberg, S., Adam, M. J., Ammann, W., Harrop, R., Rogers, J., Ruth, T., Sayre, C., & Pate, B. D. (1986). Positron emission tomography in the early diagnosis of Huntington's disease. *Neurology, 36,* 888–894.

Ichise, M., Toyama, H., Fornazzari, L., Ballinger, J. R., & Kirsh, J. C. (1993). Iodine-123-IBZM dopamine D2 receptor and technetium-99m-HMPAO brain perfusion SPECT in the evaluation of patients with and subjects at risk for Huntington's disease. *Journal of Nuclear Medicine, 34,* 1274–1281.

Itoh, M., Meguro, K., Fujiwara, T., Hatazawa, J., Iwata, R., Ishiwata, K., Takahashi, T., Ido, T., & Sasaki, H. (1994). Assessment of dopamine metabolism in brain of patients with dementia by means of 18F-fluorodopa and PET. *Annals of Nuclear Medicine, 8,* 245–251.

Jimerson, D. C. (1987). Role of dopamine mechanisms in the affective disorders. In H. Meltzer (Ed.), *Psychopharmacology: The third generation of progress* (pp. 505–511). New York: Raven Press.

Kawasaki, Y., Maeda, Y., Suzuki, M., Takeshita, K., Yamguchi, N., Matsuda, H., Miyauchi, T., & Hisada, K. (1991). SPECT analysis of rCBF changes during Wisconsin Card Sorting Test. *Biological Psychiatry, 29,* 333S–701S.

Leccesse, A. P., & Lyness, W. H. (1987). Lesions of dopamine neurons in the medial prefrontal cortex: Effects on self-administration of amphetamine and dopamine synthesis in the brain of the rat. *Neuropharmacology, 26,* 1303–1308.

Lesser, I. M., Mena, I., Boone, K. B., Miller, B. L., Mehringer, C. M., & Wohl, M. (1994). Reduction of cerebral blood flow in older depressed patients. *Archives of General Psychiatry, 51,* 677–686.

Lewis, S. W., Ford, R. A., Syed, G. M., Reveley, A. M., & Toone, B. K. (1992). A controlled study of 99mTc-MPAO single-photon emission imaging in chronic schizophrenia. *Psychological Medicine, 22,* 27–35.

Martin, J. B., & Gusella, J. F. (1986). Huntington's disease: pathogenesis and management. *New England Journal of Medicine, 315,* 1267–1276.

Matthyse, S. (1973). Antipsychotic drug actions: a clue to the neuropathology of schizophrenia? *Federation Proceedings, 32,* 200–205.

Mathew, R. J., Wilson, W. H., Tant, S. R., Robinson, L., & Prakash, R. (1988). Abnormal resting regional cerebral blood flow patterns and their correlates in schizophrenia. *Archives of General Psychiatry, 45,* 542–549.

Miller, B. L., Cummings, J. L., Villanueva-Meyer, J., Boone, K., Mehringer, C. M., Lesser, I. M., & Mena, I. (1991). Frontal lobe degeneration: clinical, neuropsychological and SPECT characteristics. *Neurology, 41,* 1374–1382.

Miller, B. L., Darby, A., Swartz, J. R., Yener, G. G., & Mena, I. (1995). Dietary changes, compulsions and sexual behavior in frontotemporal degeneration. *Dementia, 6,* 195–199.

Mogenson, G. J., Takigawa, M., Robertson, A., & Wu, M. (1979). Self-stimulation of the nucleus accumbens and ventral tegmental area of Tsai attenuated by microinjections of spiroperidol into the nucleus accumbens. *Brain Research, 171,* 247–259.

Moore, R. Y., & Bloom, F. E. (1978). Central catecholamine neuron systems: Anatomy and physiology of the dopamine systems. *Annual Review of Neuroscience, 1,* 129–169.

Nauta, W. J. H., & Feirtag, M. (1986). *Fundamental neuroanatomy.* New York: W. H. Freeman.

Neary, D., Snowden, J. S., & Mann, D. M. A. (1993). The clinical pathological correlates of lobar atrophy. *Dementia, 4,* 154–159.

Neary, D., Snowden, J. S., Northen, B., & Goulding, P. (1988). Dementia of frontal lobe type. *Journal of Neurological and Neurosurgical Psychiatry, 51,* 353–361.

Niznik, H. B., & Van Tol, H. H. (1992). Dopamine receptor genes: New tools for molecular psychiatry. *Journal of Psychiatry Neuroscience, 17,* 158–180.

Olds, J., & Milner, P. (1954). Positive reinforcement produced by electrical stimulation of septal area and other regions of rat brain. *Journal of Comparative Physiology and Psychology, 47,* 419–427.

Olds, M. E., & Olds, J. (1963). Approach-avoidance analysis of rat diencephalon. *Journal of Comparative Neurology, 120, 259–295.*

Pearlson, G. D., Tune, L. E., Wong, D. F., Aylward, E. H., Barta, P. E., Powers, R. E., Tien, A. Y., Chase, G. A., Harris, G. J., & Rabins, P. V. (1993). Quantitative D2 dopamine receptor PET and structural MRI changes in late-onset schizophrenia. *Schizophrenia Bulletin, 19,* 783–795.

Pearlson, G. D., Wong, D. F., Tune, L. E., Ross, C. A., Chase, G. A., Links, J. M., Dannals, R. F., Wilson, A. A., Ravert, H. T., Wagner, H. N. Jr., & DePaulo, J. R. (1995). In vivo D2 dopamine receptor density in psychotic and nonpsychotic patients with bipolar disorder. *Archives of General Psychiatry, 52,* 471–477.

Pearson, S. J., & Reynolds, G. P. (1994). Neocortical neurotransmitter markers in Huntington's disease. *Journal of Neural Transmission (General Section), 98,* 197–207.

Perry, E. K., Perry, R. H., Blessed, G., & Tomlinson, B. E. (1977). Necropsy evidence of central cholinergic defects in senile dementia. *Lancet, 1,* 189.

Peterson, B., Riddle, M., Cohen, D. J., Katz, L., Smith, J., Hardin, M., & Leckman, J. (1993). Reduced basal ganglia volumes in Tourette's syndrome using three-dimensional reconstruction techniques from magnetic resonance images. *Neurology, 43,* 941–949.

Pizzolato, G., Chierichetti, F., Fabbri, M., Cagnin, A., Dam, M., Ferlin, G., & Battistin, L. (1996). Reduced striatal dopamine receptors in Alzheimer's disease: single photon emission tomography study with the D2 tracer [123I]-IBZM. *Neurology, 47,* 1065–1068.

Pycock, C. J., Kerwin, R. W., & Carter, C. J. (1980). Effect of lesion of cortical dopamine terminals on subcortical dopamine in rats. *Nature, 286,* 74–76.

Reynolds, G. P. (1989). Beyond the dopamine hypothesis: The neurochemical pathology of schizophrenia. *British Journal of Psychiatry, 155,* 305–316.

Richelson, E. (1994). The pharmacology of antidepressants at the synapse: Focus on newer compounds. *Journal of Clinical Psychiatry, 55*(9, Suppl. A), 34–39.

Robertson, G. S., Matsumura, H., & Fibiger, H. C. (1994). Induction patterns of c-fos-like immunoreactivity in the forebrain as predictors of atypical antipsychotic activity. *Journal of Pharmacology and Experimental Therapy, 271,* 1058–1066.

Rolls, E. T. (1975). *The brain and reward.* Oxford: Pergamon Press.

Roskin, D. L., Deutch, A. Y., & Roth, R. H. (1987). Alterations in subcortical dopaminergic function following dopamine depletion in the medial prefrontal cortex. *Society for Neuroscience Abstracts, 13,* 560.

Rossi, A., Stratta, P., D'Albenzio, L., Tartaro, A., Schiazza, G., di Michele, V., Bolino, F., & Casacchia, M. (1990). Reduced temporal lobe areas in schizophrenia: Preliminary evidence from a controlled multi-planar magnetic resonance imaging study. *Biological Psychiatry, 27,* 61–68.

Routtenberg, A. (1978). The reward systems of the brain. *Scientific American, 239,* 154–164.

Rubin, E. H., Morris, J. C.,, & Berg L. (1987). The progression of personality changes in patients with mild senile dementia of the Alzheimer type. *Journal of American Geriatric Society, 35,* 721–725.

Rubin, E., Sackeim, H. A., Prohovnik, I., Moeller, J. R., Schnur, D. B., & Mukherjee, S. (1995). Regional cerebral blood flow in mood disorders: IV. Comparison of mania and depression. *Psychiatry Research, 61,* 1–10.

Rubin, P., Holm, S., Friberg, L., Karle, A., Andersen, H. S., Hertel, C., Poulsen, U. J., Madsen, S. M., Lassen, N. A., & Hemmingsen, R. (1991). rCBF (SPECT) and CT measurements during first episode schizophrenia and schizophreniform psychosis. *Biological Psychiatry, 29,* 270.

Sack, R. L., & Goodwin, F. K. (1974). Inhibition of dopamine-hydroxylase in manic patients. *Archives of General Psychiatry, 31,* 649–654.

Satoh, K., Narita, M., Someya, T., Fukuyama, H., & Yonekura, Y. (1993). Functional brain imaging of a catatonic type of schizophrenia: PET and SPECT studies. *Japanese Journal of Psychiatry and Neurology, 47,* 881–885.

Saur, H. B., Bartenstein, P., Schober, O., Oberwittler, C., Lerch, H., & Masur, H. (1994). Comparison of D2 receptor scintigraphy (123I-IBZM) with cerebral perfusion (99m-Tc-HMPAO) in extrapyramidal disorders. *Nuklearmedizin, 33,* 184–188.

Scatton, B., Worms, P., Lloyd, K. G., & Bartholini, G. (1982). Cortical modulation of striatal function. *Brain Research, 232,* 331–343.

Sedvall, G., Karlsson, P., Lundin, A., Anvret, M., Suhara, T., Halldin, C., & Farde, L. (1994). Dopamine D1 receptor number—A sensitive PET marker for early brain degeneration in Huntington's disease. *European Archives of Psychiatry and Clinical Neuroscience, 243,* 249–255.

Sedvall, G., Pauli, S., Karlsson, P., Farde, L., Nordstrom, A. L., Nyberg, S., & Halldin, C. (1995). PET imaging of neuroreceptors in schizophrenia. *European Neuropsychopharmacology, 5*(Suppl.), 25–30.

Seeman, P. (1992). Dopamine receptor sequences: Therapeutic levels of neuroleptics occupy D2 receptors, clozapine occupies D4. *Neuropsychopharmacology, 7,* 261–284.

Seeman, P., Lee, T., Chau-Wong, M., & Wong, K. (1976). Antipsychotic drug doses and neuroleptic/dopamine receptors. *Nature, 261,* 717–719.

Seeman, P., & Niznik, H. B. (1990). Dopamine receptors and transporters in Parkinson's disease and schizophrenia. *FASEB: Federation of American Societies for Experimental Biology Journal, 4,* 2737–2744.

Shapiro, E., Shapiro, A. K., Fulop, G., Hubbard, M., Mandeli, J., Nordlie, J., & Phillips, R. A. (1989). Controlled study of haloperidol, pimozide, and placebo for the treatment of Gilles de la Tourette's syndrome. *Archives of General Psychiatry, 46,* 722–730.

Sibley, D. R., & Monsma, F. J. Jr. (1992). Molecular biology of dopamine receptors. *Trends in Pharmacology Sciences, 13,* 61–69.

Silverstone, T. (1984). Response to bromocriptine distinguishes bipolar from unipolar depression. *Lancet, 1,* 903–904.

Silverstone, T. (1985). Dopamine in manic depressive illness: a pharmacological synthesis. *Journal of Affective Disorders, 8,* 225–231.

Sims, N. R., Bowen, D. M., Allen, S. J., Smith, C. C. T., Neary, D., Thomas, D. J., & Davison, A. N. (1983). Pre-synaptic cholinergic dysfunction in patients with dementia. *Journal of Neurochemistry, 40,* 503–509.

Sofuoglu, S., Dogan, P., Kose, K., Esel, E., Basturk, M., Oguz, H., & Gonul, A. S. (1995). Changes in platelet monoamine oxidase and plasma dopamine-beta-hydroxylase activities in lithium-treated bipolar patients. *Psychiatry Research, 59,* 165–170.

Sokoloff, P., Giros, B., Martes, M. P., Bouthenet, M. W., & Schwartz, J. C. (1990). Molecular cloning and characterization of a novel dopamine D3 receptor as a target for neuroleptics. *Nature, 347,* 146–151.

Sparks, D. L., & Markesbery, W. R. (1991). Altered serotonergic and cholinergic synaptic markers in Pick's disease. *Archives of Neurology, 48,* 796–799.

Storga, D., Vrecko, K., Birkmayer, J. G., & Reibnegger, G. (1996). Monoaminergic neurotransmitters, their precursors and metabolites in brains of Alzheimer patients. *Neuroscience Letter, 203,* 29–32.

Suhara, T., Nakayama, K., Inoue, O., Fukuda, H., Shimizu, M., Mori, A., & Tateno, Y. (1992). D1 dopamine receptor binding in mood disorders measured by positron emission tomography. *Psychopharmacology, 106,* 14–18.

Sunahara, R. K., Guan, H. C., O'Dowd, B. F., Seeman, P., Laurier, L. G., Ng, G., George, S. R., Torchia, J., Van Tol, H. H. M., & Niznik, H. B. (1991). Cloning of the gene for a human dopamine D5 receptor with higher affinity for dopamine than D1. *Nature, 350,* 614–619.

Tarczy, M., & Szirmai, I. (1995). Failure of dopamine metabolism: borderline of parkinsonism and dementia. *Acta Bio-Medica de L'Ateneo Parmense, 66,* 93–97.

Tejani-Butt, S. M., Yang, J., & Pawllyk, A. C. (1995). Altered serotonin transport sites in Alzheimer's disease raphe and hippocampus. *Neuroreport, 6,* 1207–1210.

Toyama, H., Ichise, M., Ballinger, J. R., Fornazzari, L., & Kirsh, J. C. (1993). Dopamine D2 receptor SPECT imaging: Basic in vivo characteristics and clinical applications of 123I-IBZM in humans. *Annals of Nuclear Medicine, 7,* 29–38.

Van Kammen, D. P., & Murphy, D. L. (1975). Attenuation of the euphoriant and activating effects of d-1-amphetamine by lithium carbonate treatment. *Psychopharmacology, 44,* 212–224.

Van Tol, H. H. M., Bunzow, J. R., Guan, H. C., Sunahara, R. K., Seeman, P., Niznik, H. B., & Civelli, O. (1991). Cloning of the gene for a human D4 receptor with high affinity for the antipsychotic clozapine. *Nature, 350,* 610–614.

Vita, A., Giobbo, G. M., Dieci, M., Garbarini, M., Castignoli, G. & Invernizzi, G. (1991). Frontal lobe dysfunction in schizophrenia: evident from neuropsychological testing and brain imaging techniques. *Biological Psychiatry, 29,* 647S.

Weinberger, D. R., Berman, K. F., Suddath, R., & Torrey, E. F. (1992). Evidence of dysfunction of a prefrontal-limbic network in schizophrenia: A magnetic resonance imaging and regional cerebral blood flow study of discordant monozygotic twins. *American Journal of Psychiatry, 149,* 890–897.

Wetzel, M. C. (1968). Self-stimulation's anatomy: Data needs. *Brain Research, 10,* 287–296.

White, F. J., & Wang, R. X. (1983). Differential effects of classical and atypical antipsychotic drugs on A9 and A10 dopamine neurons. *Science, 221,* 1054–1057.

White, K. E., & Cummings, J. L. (1996). Schizophrenia and Alzheimer's disease: Clinical and pathophysiologic analogies. *Comprehensive Psychiatry, 37,* 188–195.

Whitehouse, P. J., Price, D. L., Struble, R. G., Clark, A. W., Coyle, J. T., & DeLong, M. R. (1982). Alzheimer's disease and senile dementia: Loss of neurons in the basal forebrain. *Science, 215,* 1237–1239.

Willner, P., & Scheel-Kruger, J. (Eds.). (1991). *The mesolimbic dopamine system: From motivation to action.* New York: Wiley.

Wise, R. A. (1980). The dopamine synapse and the notion of "pleasure centers" in the brain. *Trends in Neurosciences, 3,* 91–95.

Wise, R. A., & Rompre, P. P. (1989). Brain dopamine and reward. *Annual Review of Psychology, 40,* 191–225.

Wolf, S. S., Jones, D. W., Knable, M. B., Gorey, J. G., Lee, K. S., Hyde, T. M., Coppola, R., & Weinberger, D. R. (1996). Tourette syndrome: prediction of phenotypic variation in monozygotic twins by caudate nucleus D2 receptor binding. *Science, 273,* 1225–1227.

Wong, D. F., Wagner, H. N. Jr., Pearlson, G., Dannals, R. F., Links, J. M., Ravert, H. T., Wilson, A. A., Suneja, S., Bjorvvinssen, E., Kuhar, M. J., & Tune, L. (1985). Dopamine receptor binding of C-11-3-N-methylspiperone in the caudate in schizophrenia and bipolar disorder: a preliminary report. *Psychopharmacology Bulletin, 21,* 595–598.

Wong, D. F., Wagner, H. N., Tune, L. E., Dannals, R. F., Pearlson, G. D., Links, J. M., Tamminga, C. A., Broussolle, E. P., Ravert, H. T., Wilson, A. A., Toung, J. K. T., Malat, J., Williams, F. A., O'Touma, L. A., Snyder, S. H., Kuhar, M. J., & Gjedde, A. (1986). Positron emission tomography reveals elevated D2 receptors in drug-naive schizophrenics. *Science, 239,* 1558–1563.

Yeomans, J. (1988). Mechanisms of brain-stimulation reward. *Progressive Psychobiology, Physiology and Psychology, 13,* 227–266.

Zarevics, P., & Setler, P. E. (1979). Simultaneous rate-independent and rate-dependent assessment of intracranial self-stimulation: Evidence for the direct involvement of dopamine in brain reinforcement mechanisms. *Brain Research, 169,* 499–512.

10

Neurotransmitters and Neuromodulators in Frontal–Subcortical Circuits

DAVID FEIFEL

The neurochemical organization of frontal–subcortical circuits can be conceptualized as being composed of three functional elements. At the heart of frontal–subcortical communication are core circuits which form functional neural loops connecting frontal cortical regions, in turn, to the basal ganglia, the thalamus, and back to the frontal cortex. These core circuits mainly utilize two amino acid neurotransmitters—glutamate and γ-aminobutyric acid (GABA)—and thus may seem, from a neurochemical perspective, austere relative to the complex and manifold functions they subserve. Neurochemical diversity and distinction across subcortical circuits, however, are provided by the contribution of two additional neurochemical elements: one from within, the other originating outside of the core system. Neuropeptides colocalized with core neurotransmitters display a heterogeneous distribution across functionally distinct compartments within the core circuitry and provide intrinsic modulation that is neuroanatomically specific. Ascending bioamine-containing pathways (dopamine, serotonin, noradrenaline, and acetylcholine) originating outside the core frontal–subcortical circuits selectively intersect and modulate the activity of the core circuits and, in many cases, each other.

AMINO ACIDS: THE CORE NEUROTRANSMITTERS

The amino acids glutamate and GABA are the two most ubiquitous brain neurotransmitters. They both mediate fast synaptic communication which has a time course in the order of 1 msec. Glutamate and GABA are, respectively, the major excitatory and inhibitory neurotransmitters in the brain as a whole, and together constitute the basic neurochemical signaling elements of the core frontal–subcortical circuits (see Figure 10.1). This core circuitry consists of excitatory glutamatergic (and to a lesser degree aspartergic) afferents emanating from widespread regions, mostly layer V, of the frontal cortex and projecting topographically onto medium spiny neurons throughout the basal ganglia. Excitatory neurons, which are also likely to be glutamatergic, originating from the dorsomedial thalamus project back to these frontal cortical regions (Streit, 1984). Though several distinct glutamate receptors subtypes are known to exist and have been localized in the striatum, the ion channel-coupled, N-methyl-D-aspartate (NMDA) receptor appears to play the most significant role vis-à-vis core frontal–subcortical systems.

Intervening between these excitatory connections to and from the frontal lobes are neuronal pathways that link the basal ganglia to the thalamus and thus create closed frontal–subcortical neuronal loops. These basal ganglia connections are predominately GABAergic and inhibitory in function (Parent, 1990; Penny & Young, 1981). They are configured in two basic parallel pathways which, depending on the number of inhibitory synapses involved (two or three), can either inhibit or disinhibit excitatory thalamocortical transmission and, in so doing, inhibit or disinhibit overall signal transmission within the frontal–subcortical loop (Alexander, Crutcher, & Delong, 1990). By splitting a simple frontal–subcortical loop into parallel facilitatory or "direct" and inhibitory or "indirect" subcircuits, the basal ganglia affords the frontal–subcortical system with a "gain-control" device which can selectively attenuate or potentiate signals passing through it.

In addition to this simple feed-forward pathway, glutamate and GABA exist in several other pathways within the core frontal–subcortical circuits. For example, gluta-

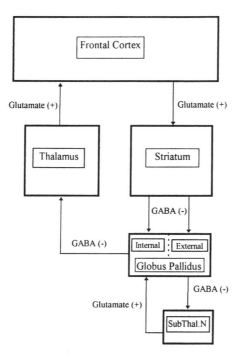

FIGURE 10.1. The core system in frontal–subcortical circuits. Signals projecting from the striatum to the globus pallidus can be transmitted to the thalamus via a "direct" pathway, which is mediated by the internal globus pallidus and involves two inhibitory synapses, or via an "indirect" pathway, which is mediated by the external global pallidus and subthalamic nucleus and involves three inhibitory synapses. The direct pathway produces disinhibition of thalamocortical transmission, whereas the indirect pathway produces inhibition of the thalamacortical pathway.

matergic projections from the frontal cortex directly innervate the substantia nigra pars compact (SNpc) and the subthalamic nucleus. Furthermore, a large number of glutamatergic and GABAergic neurons exist intrinsic to the frontal cortex and act to integrate cortical activity as corticocortical connections.

Despite their central role in frontal–subcortical circuits, there has been, until recently, little understanding of the role of amino acid neurotransmitters in specific clinical syndromes in comparison, for example, to the monoamines. Glutamate deficiency has become increasingly implicated in contributing to the symptomatology of schizophrenia, particularly the negative or deficit features such as paucity of thought, emotional expression, and volitional behavior (Kim, Kornhuber, Schmid-Burgk, & Holzmuller, 1980). Supporting this belief is the fact that noncompetitive antagonists of NMDA receptors such as phencyclidine are psychotogenic and unlike psychostimulants such as amphetamine and cocaine, they may produce the negative as well as the positive symptoms (e.g., hallucinations and delusions) associated with schizophrenia.

Functional antagonists of NMDA receptors also demonstrate an antidepressant-like profile in some preclinical paradigms sensitive to antidepressants (Trullas & Skolnick, 1990), and their chronic administration leads to downregulation of forebrain β-adrenergic receptors (Paul, Trullas, Skolnick, & Nowak, 1992), a neurochemical event associated with the clinically therapeutic effects of antidepressants. This has led to some speculation that NMDA systems may play a role in depression, a condition associated with frontal–subcortical dysregulation, and that NMDA systems may contribute to the therapeutic actions of antidepressants. This notion is indirectly supported by the finding of lower glutamate receptor binding in the frontal cortex of suicide victims (Nowak, Ordway, & Paul 1995). Hyperexcitation of glutamatergic neurons is thought to occur in many brain injury states, such as stroke, which may in turn lead to a neurotoxic cascade that is responsible for extending the area of damage beyond the direct site of injury. As an outcome of this occurrence, glutamate antagonists are being investigated as putative neuroprotective agents. Glutamate, via non-NMDA receptors in memory circuits in the limbic system, is thought to be a critical substrate for long-term potentiation, a neuroplastic event associated with memory. As a result, glutamate agonists which act upon these receptors are generating interest as putative nootropic agents.

Given that more than one-third of brain neurons use GABA as a neurotransmitter, and the critical role GABA plays in frontal–subcortical signaling, it is surprising that GABA has not been more strongly implicated in the etiology of specific neuropsychiatric disorders. However, a growing body of evidence suggests that GABA may be directly or indirectly involved in the pathogenesis of several neuropsychiatric disorders, including Alzheimer's disease, epilepsy, Huntington's chorea, schizophrenia, alcoholism, and mood and anxiety disorders (Sherif & Ahmed, 1995). Benzodiazepines act on the GABA receptor complex and are arguably the most potent of psychotropic agents in regard to their speed of action and efficacy in the treatment of conditions such as epilepsy, anxiety, and insomnia. They are also useful adjuncts to neuroleptic agents for the treatment of psychosis. GABA has also been linked to mood disorders (Petty, 1995). Animal models of depression show regional brain GABA deficits, and GABA agonists show antidepressant activity in such models. In humans, lowered cerebrospinal fluid GABA levels have been found in patients with depression and many effective somatic treatments for depression and mania including valporate and electroconvulsive shock significantly alter GABAergic activity in the brain. Some authors suggest that low GABA function may be an inherited predisposing factor for mood disorders (Petty, 1995).

PEPTIDES: INTRINSIC MODULATION OF CORE CIRCUITS

In the past 25 years, over 100 peptides have been discovered in the brain. Many have been shown to meet the criteria for neurotransmission or neuromodulation, and evidence for others is accumulating. One remarkable property of neuropeptides is that they often coexist in nerve terminals with other neurotransmitters whose action they frequently modulate (Hokfelt et al., 1986). This colocalization is often pathway-selective. Colocalized peptides may thus provide neurochemical heterogeneity across otherwise chemically indistinguishable classical neurotransmitter systems, which seems to be the case in frontal–subcortical circuits.

Differential peptide distribution in the striatum is a major part of the basis for compartmentalizing this structure into striasome patches and the surrounding nonstriosomal matrix. Stiasomes are rich in the neuropeptides substance P and dynorphin, the later being an endogenous opiate, whereas matrix regions are rich in enkephalin, another endogenous opiate neuropeptide (Ragsdale & Graybiel, 1990). These striatal neuropeptides are colocalized in nerve terminals with GABA, the main striatal neurotransmitter, which is equally represented in both compartments. This differential neuropeptide–GABA colocalization corresponds to anatofunctional divisions because the two compartments have distinct afferent and efferent connections. For example, striosomes receive a highly restricted input from specific prefrontal–cortical areas such as the posterior orbitofrontal, insular, medial–frontal and anterior cingulate cortex as well as from limbic areas such as the amygdala and hippocampus (Eblen & Graybiel, 1995). Other regions of the frontal cortex, including the dorsolateral prefrontal and premotor areas, project mainly to matrix regions. Striosomes and matrix may also be differentially innervated by distinct populations of ascending dopamine afferents and may express distinct D1/D2 receptor ratios (Loopuijit, Sebens, & Korf, 1987). Dopamine has been shown to have opposing tonic regulatory effects on the expression of basal ganglia enkephalin and dynorphin (Parent & Lavoie, 1993).

The distribution of striatal neuropeptides may also chemically distinguish frontal–subcortical transmission via the direct (facilitatory) and indirect (inhibitory) pathways. The GABAergic striatopallidal projection to the external globus pallidus, associated with the indirect pathway, is rich in enkephalin and neurotensin. The GABAergic striatopallidal projection to the internal globus pallidus, associated with the direct pathway, is rich in substance P and dynorphin (Graybiel, 1990).

In addition to GABA, neuropeptide colocalization is associated with other neurotransmitters that are involved in frontal–subcortical signaling. The best example of these neurotransmitters is dopamine. Approximately half of all mesolimbic dopamine neurons contain cholecysotokinin (CCK), and a lesser proportion contain neurotensin (Hokfelt et al., 1986). Electrophysiological, neurochemical and behavioral studies suggest that both CCK (Crawley, 1991) and neurotensin (Nemeroff & Bissette, 1992) can significantly modulate mesolimbic dopamine activity. For example, preclinical studies indicate that neurotensin appears to act as an antagonist of dopamine function.

Aside from providing neuroanatomical resolution, neuropeptides may have other functional implications for frontal–subcortical signaling. Optimal neuropeptide release occurs under conditions of high-frequency neural firing (Hokfelt, 1991). Under normal conditions, therefore, release of colocalized neuropeptides from GABAergic and dopaminergic neurons is likely to be minimal because the basal activity of these neurons is characterized by tonic low-frequency activity with phasic activation. Release of neuropeptides from frontal–subcortical neurons is likely to be increased in degenerative states when surviving neurons may be hyperactivated to compensate for the death or dysfunction of neighboring cells. In some instances, therefore, neuropeptides may play a more significant role in abnormal rather than in normal states of frontal–subcortical signaling. Depending on the specific neuropeptide-neurotransmitter interaction, neuropeptides released under these conditions may counter the level of neural activity or facilitate it further. Colocalized neuropeptides may therefore provide a second level, gain-control mechanism embedded within the primary gain control mechanism represented by the core circuits of the basal ganglia. Such a secondary system could provide greater anatomical resolution of frontal–subcortical circuits owing to the anatomic specificity of neuropeptide distribution across these circuits. Colocalized neuropeptides may also provide frontal–subcortical circuits a greater degree of temporal plasticity because the neuropeptide influence on synaptic transmission is much slower than that of classical neurotransmitters, operating in the time order of seconds and minutes (Hokfelt, 1991).

The role of neuropeptides in specific clinical disorders associated with frontal–subcortical circuits remains highly speculative. Based on their neuroanatomical distribution it is possible that neuropsychiatric syndromes strongly associated with orbitofrontal, cingulate cortex, and/or limbic dysfunction such as depression, akinetic mutism, and obsessive–compulsive disorder may preferentially involve striosomal neural circuits and their distinct neuropeptide substrates. On the other hand, clinical syndromes associated with dysfunction of the dorsolateral prefrontal cortex, which has an important role in executive functions, or the frontal motor areas, which have a role in sensorimotor processing, may be mediated more substantially by matrix-associated neuropeptide substrates. Evidence also suggests that diseases involving frontal–subcortical circuits (e.g., Parkinson's disease and Huntington's chorea) are associated with selective changes in expression of dynorphin and enkephalin in the striatum (Parent & Lavoie, 1993). These changes in peptide activity may produce changes in the balance between transmission via direct and indirect circuits and thus may contribute to the clinical features associated with these disorders.

Peptides colocalized with ascending dopamine pathways may play an important role in the normal and abnormal behaviors associated with this neurotransmitter. For example, neurotensin's ability to antagonize mesolimbic dopamine's effects led to speculation that it may act as an endogenous neuroleptic, and alterations of CCK and neurotensin systems have been implicated in the dysregulation of mesolimbic dopamine function thought to underlie schizophrenia. Mesolimbic peptides may also play an important role in the action of neuropharmacological treatments for schizophrenia as chronic treatment with haloperidol or other neuroleptics significantly alters the expression of these peptides (Nemeroff & Bissette, 1992).

BIOAMINES: EXTRINSIC MODULATION OF CORE CIRCUITS

Dopamine

Dopamine circuits intersect the core frontal–subcortical circuitry at several points and modulate them in critical ways. The dopaminergic projections to frontal–subcortical circuits originate from a relatively small region in the ventral mesencephalon but provide relatively distinctive innervation of these circuits via a mesocorticolimbic pathway, which innervates the ventral striatum, paralimbic areas, and the frontal cortex and via the nigrostriatal pathway, which innervates the dorsal striatum (Lindvall & Bjorklund, 1984).

Nigrostriatal Pathway

Cells originating in the SNpc (A9) and retrorubral (A8) areas project to the dorsal striatum, including the head of the caudate and the putamen, where they terminate on medium spiny GABA-containing neurons that also receive glutamatergic projections from the frontal cortex (Di Chiara & Morelli, 1993). Functionally, this pathway has been most strongly associated with regulation of voluntary motor function and initiation of behavioral responses to environmental stimuli. Increased dopamine activity in this system resulting from localized injections of stimulants produces stereotyped behaviors in animals. Dopamine deficiency in this system results in motor deficits such as those observed following chemical lesions of the dopamine system in rats and in humans with Parkinson's disease, which has been strongly linked to loss of nigrostriatal dopamine. It appears, therefore, that the role of nigrostriatal dopamine is to tonically facilitate transmission of frontal–subcortical signals responsible for voluntary motor function as they pass through the basal ganglia. This may be accomplished by differential modulation of the direct and indirect pathways within the basal ganglia. Indeed, dopamine appears to facilitate transmission in GABAergic neurons within the direct pathway via D1 receptors, which produce postsynaptic excitation, whereas dopamine inhibits GABAergic neurons in the indirect pathway via D2 receptors, which produce postsynaptic inhibition (Gerfen, 1992). Such dopaminergic innervation would result in facilitation of the amplifier action and inhibition of the dampening action produced by the direct and indirect pathways, respectively, on frontal–subcortical signaling, and would account for the behavioral effects associated with dopamine excess and deficiency.

Mesocorticolimbic Pathway

Another set of dopamine cells which originate in the ventral tegmentum (A10) project to the ventral striatum (including the nucleus accumbens), the septum, amygdala, and bed nucleus stria terminalis (Fallon, 1988). They also send separate projections to the prefrontal cortex, where they innervate the deepest cortical layers (layers V and VI) most intensely. Both in the striatum and in the cortex, dopamine terminals seem positioned to modulate the responsiveness of target neurons to excitatory glutamatergic input, and there is good experimental support for an reciprocal regulation of frontal–subcortical activity by dopamine and glutamate (Riederer, Lange, Kornuber, & Danielczyk, 1992).

Mesocorticolimbic dopamine, particularly the subcortical component, plays a critical role in a wide variety of appetitive behaviors including food and water intake, reproduction, and exploratory behavior, and it is thought to be an important neural substrate for motivation and reward (Fibinger & Phillips, 1988). Chemical or electrical stimulation of the mesocorticolimbic dopamine system produces heightened locomotor exploration in animals and produces evidence of positive reinforcement in operant paradigms such as electrical intracranial self-stimulation and drug self-administration. In humans, activation of the mesocorticolimbic dopamine system has been implicated in the heightened appetitive drive associated with drug addiction (Wise, 1988). Hypofunction of this system, on the other hand, has been associated with syndromes involving decreased volitional behavior and reinforcement. The cingulate cortex and medial–frontal cortex have strong reciprocal connections with the mesocorticolimbic dopamine system and a frontal–subcortical circuit involving these connections is thought to regulate motivational states in humans (Mega & Cummings, 1994). Lesions of these cortical areas in humans sometimes result in akinetic mutism, a syndrome characterized by profound apathy and lack of volitional behavior.

The role of cortical dopamine and subcortical dopamine appear thematically related. It is possible that prefrontal dopamine provides integration of higher cognitive aspects of the actions regulated by subcortical dopamine. For example, dopamine in the prefrontal cortex seems to be critical for cognitive processes that support the temporal organization of motor behavior (Sawaguchi, Matsumura, & Kubota, 1986). Cortical dopamine is also important for cognition, and cognitive disturbances such as memory loss are produced experimentally by depletion of dopamine in the prefrontal cortex (Goldman-Rakic, Lidow, Smiley, & Williams, 1992). Perturbation in cortical dopamine may also strongly contribute to the cognitive disturbances seen in Parkinson's disease and schizophrenia, which resemble those produced by frontal lobe damage (Robbins, 1991).

Mesocorticolimbic dopamine has been strongly implicated in the pathophysiology of schizophrenia. Interestingly, excessive subcortical dopamine activity appears to be important in the production of positive features of schizophrenia, whereas deficient cortical dopamine activity appears to be important in the production of negative features. Traditional antipsychotic drugs, which are without exception D2 antagonists, are more effective against positive features and have little effect on, and may even exacerbate, negative features. On the other hand, some clinical studies have reported that functional agonists of dopamine transmission such as bromocriptine and selegeline improve the negative features of schizophrenia.

Serotonin

Like dopamine, serotonin (5-hydroxytryptamine; 5-HT) containing neurons originating in a relatively localized region in the mesencephalon intersect with frontal–subcortical circuits at several anatomical points where they can modulate neural transmission. Ascending 5-HT fibers from the dorsal raphe nucleus in the pons and upper brainstem project predominately to the frontal cortex, thalamus, hippocampus, and basal ganglia structures (Azmitia & Segal, 1978). Over 15 distinct 5-HT receptor subtypes have been identified. Most attention, however, has focused on 5-HT1A and 5-HT2 receptors which are the key postsynaptic receptors. 5-HT1A receptors also constitute the main soma-todendendritic autoreceptors located on cell bodies in the raphe. Among the most important actions of serotonin vis-à-vis frontal–subcortical circuits is its ability to modulate dopamine transmission. Serotonergic fibers innnervate the dopamine cell bodies in the substantia nigra and ventral tegmental area. They also innervate dopamine terminal fields in the nucleus accumbens, dorsal striatum, and frontal cortex (Azmitia & Segal, 1978). Electrophysiological and behavioral evidence supports an inhibition of dopamin-ergic transmission by serotonin. This effect appears to be mediated by postsynaptic 5-HT2 receptors on the cell bodies and axon terminals of dopamine neurons resulting in a decrease in the firing rate and neurotransmitter release from dopamine cells (Ennis, Kemp, & Cox, 1981). In addition, 5-HT1A receptors are located on glutamate-containing pyramidal cells in the frontal cortex and have been shown to produce a hyperpolarizing effect on these. Consistent with this idea, administration of 5-HT1A antagonists stimulate glutamate release in the striatum cells (McCormick & Williamson, 1989).

Serotonin has been implicated in the regulation of numerous important behavioral functions, including aggression, mood, memory, appetite, sexual activity, and pain. Serotonin and noradrenaline are the neurotransmitters most strongly implicated in the neurochemistry of depression, which is associated with prefrontal and cingulate cortex hypoactivity. Rapid depletion of brain serotonin produced by dietary modification can cause a rapid transient lowering of mood in patients with a history of depression (Delgado et al., 1994). Most antidepressants alter brain serotonergic function, and the antidepressant efficacy of selective serotonin reuptake inhibitors (SSRIs) such as fluoxetine indicates that direct pharmacological alteration of serotonergic function alone is sufficient to successfully treat a large proportion of depressed patients. The fact that some clinically effective antidepressants have no measurable serotonergic actions suggests that changes in this neurotransmitter are not exclusively responsible for regulation of mood.

Serotonergic dysregulation has also been heavily implicated in obsessive–compulsive disorder, a condition linked anatomically with abnormal function of frontal–subcortical circuits. Functional imaging studies of brains of patients with obsessive–compulsive disorder show hyperactivity in the orbitofrontal cortex and caudate nucleus. SSRIs effectively decrease the symptoms associated with this disease, and successful treatment has been associated with normalization of activity in these structures (Baxter, Schwartz, & Bergman, 1992).

Recent advances in the treatment of schizophrenia provide additional evidence for the importance of serotonin in the regulation of frontal–subcortical circuits. A new generation of "atypical" antipsychotics is providing greater therapeutic efficacy in the treatment of schizophrenia with a more favorable side effect profile than "typical" antipsychotics such as haloperidol. These newer agents, of which clozapine is the protoype, have in common antagonism of 5-HT2 receptors, in addition to the D2 antagonism, although to a lesser degree, produced by "typical" antipsychotics. These "atypical" antipsychotics or dopamine–serotonin antagonists are more effective than "typical" antipsychotics for the treatment of the negative symptoms of schizophrenia, which have been attributed to decreased prefrontal dopamine (Weinberger, Aloia, Goldberg, & Berman, 1994). They also produce fewer of the motor abnormalities associated with the typical antipsychotics that are attributed to postsynaptic blockade of dopamine in the nigrostriatal circuit. The proposed mechanism of these actions is a release of dopamine transmission from 5-HT2-mediated inhibition in the striatum and prefrontal cortex, respectively (Kapur & Remington, 1996).

Perturbations in serotonergic function may underlie many of the behavioral changes seen in syndromes associated with frontal lobe damage. Serotonin plays an important role in the regulation of appetite, and serotonin agonists decrease appetite in animals and humans. Loss of serotonergic tone may cause the hyperphagia seen in many patients with frontal lobe syndromes (Miller, Darby, Swartz, Yener, & Meni, 1995). Destruction of 5-HT neurons leads to behavior suggestive of impulsivity and aggressiveness in laboratory animals and reduced central serotonin has been found in cerebrospinal fluid and postmortem brains of patients with high levels of impulsive, disinhibited, and violent behavior. Similar behaviors are frequently displayed by patients with orbitofrontal damage, and loss of serotonin may contribute to this syndrome. Considerable effort is currently being directed toward developing "serenics," drugs which selectively target 5-HT1A receptors in the hopes that these drugs will be useful in decreasing aggressiveness and impulsivity.

Noradrenaline

The majority of brain noradrenergic neurons are concentrated in the locus coeruleus, a well-delineated cluster of approximately 15,000 cells per hemisphere within the pontine brainstem. Noradrenergic efferent fibers originating in the locus coeruleus project with a remarkable widespread distribution throughout much of the brain. Of particular functional importance is a dense noradrenergic innervation of layer I pyramidal cells in the prefrontal cortex (Morrison, Molliver, Grazanna, & Coyle, 1981). A large body of experimental evidence suggests that this noradrenergic innervation of the prefrontal cortex plays a critical role in the tonic regulation of attention. These neurons are relatively quiescent during sleep and are most active during waking periods, particularly those associated with enhanced alertness, in which novel stimuli are presented to an animal. This neuronal response rapidly habituates with repetitive exposure to the stimulus in a manner commensurate with the animal's disinterest in the stimulus (Aston-Jones, Chiang, & Alexinsky, 1991). Depletion of forebrain noradrenaline has relatively little detrimental effect on learning or memory of simple tasks; however, in the context of more complex tasks involving distracting stimuli, performance is markedly decreased by noradrenergic dysregulation (Berridge, 1993). This set of findings is consistent with the role of the prefrontal cortex in inhibiting the processing of irrelevant stimuli. For example, humans and monkeys with prefrontal damage show marked deficits in regulation of attention and inhibiting responses to distracting stimuli (Woods & Knight, 1986). Overall, increased noradrenergic activity in the prefrontal cortex appears to have the effect of increasing signal (relevant stimuli)-to-noise (irrelevant stimuli) ratio for cognitive processing (Foote, Bloom, & Aston-Jones, 1983).

Noradrenaline can enhance the cognitive function of humans and nonhuman primates, seemingly via the actions of α-2 receptors in the prefrontal cortex (Arnsten, Steere, & Hunt, 1996). α-2 agonists, such as clonidine or guanfacine, improve performance in tasks of executive function—those requiring planning, foresight, mental flexibility and abstraction—in catecholamine-depleted monkeys and in intact aged monkeys (Cai, Ma, & Xu, 1993). Whereas α-2 receptors exist as postsynaptic heteroreceptors and presynaptic autoreceptors, the cognitive enhancing action of α-2 agonist is probably mediated by postsynaptic heteroreceptors in the prefrontal cortex. The α-2 agonist-induced enhancement of executive function is lost when the prefrontal cortex is ablated. The ability of α-2 agonists to enhance cognitive functioning on tasks dependent on prefrontal function has also been demonstrated in aged human and nonhuman primates, as well as in patients with known prefrontal-related attentional deficits such as schizophrenia, attention-deficit disorder, and Korsakoff's syndrome (Coull, 1994).

Acetylcholine

Most acetylcholine-containing neurons in the brain originate in the basal forebrain and the brainstem. The basal forebrain cholinergic neurons are found in nuclear aggregates in the median and ventral regions of each cerebral hemisphere. One such aggregate, the nucleus basalis of Meynert, projects diffusely, in particular to the prefrontal cortex where acetylcholine terminals are abundant in deep layers. Microiontophoretic application of acetylcholine increases, via muscarinic receptors, the spontaneous firing rate of more than half of the cells in the dorsolateral prefrontal cortex. The activity of prefrontal neurons can be potentiated by electrical stimulation of the nucleus of Meynert, an effect blocked by atropine, a cholinergic antagonist (Inoue et al., 1983). Cholinomimetic drugs increase glutamate transmission in corticocortical and corticostriatal pathways (Dijk, Francis, Stratman, & Bowern, 1995). The cholinergic projections to the cortex are thought to play an important role in cortical arousal, memory, and learning. Marked cell loss in the nucleus basalis and significant decrease in acetylcholine content of the cortex are the most consistent neurochemical findings in Alzheimer's disease and are thought to be major contributors to the cognitive decline in this disorder. First-generation therapeutic agents for Alzheimer's disease, such as tacrine hydrochloride, employ a strategy based on countering reductions in central cholinergic content that occur in this disease.

In addition to the basal forebrain, acetylcholine-containing neurons originate in several nuclei within the upper brainstem. Two of these, the peduculopontine nucleus and the laterodorsal nucleus give rise to extensive ascending projections which innervate most of the thalamic nuclei, where they provide inhibitory input to thalamocortical pathways (Sofroniew, Priestley, Consolazione, Eckenstein, & Cuello, 1985). These cells fire tonically during wakefulness and rapid eye movement (REM) sleep but not during non-REM sleep. Lesions of the tegmental cholinergic cells results in a loss of REM sleep, and the characteristic electroencephalographic correlates of that state (Jones, 1993). The substantia nigra also receives numerous cholinergic fibers, which probably arise from this brainstem population (Lavoie & Parent, 1994). Evidence suggests that these cholinergic cells share a reciprocal inhibitory relationship with dopaminergic cells originating in the midbrain.

Acetylcholine also contributes to frontal–subcortical signaling within the striatum via large aspiny type II cells which act as local interneurons and utilize acetylcholine as their neurotransmitter (Parent, Cote, & Lavoie, 1995). These cholinergic neurons receive tonic facilitation via glutamatergic corticostriatal cells, and perhaps dopaminergic (D1) innervation as well. In turn, they send local inhibitory projections to the main medium spiny GABAergic output neurons (Di Chiara & Morelli, 1993) and may oppose the facilitatory D1 influence onto these same medium spiny neurons. Consistent with this possibility is the fact that acetylcholine antagonists such as benzotropine are effective in ameliorating some of the motor symptoms of Parkinson's disease, presumably by releasing nigrostriatal dopamine inputs from cholinergic opposition.

REFERENCES

Alexander, G. E., Crutcher, M. D., & DeLong, M. R. (1990). Basal ganglia-thalamocortical circuits: Parallel substrates for motor, oculomotor, prefrontal and limbic functions. *Progress in Brain Research, 85,* 119–146.

Arnsten, A. F. T., Steere, J. C., & Hunt, R. D. (1996). The contribution of α-2-noradrenergic mechanisms to prefrontal cortical cognitive function. *Archives of General Psychiatry, 53,* 448–455.

Aston-Jones, G., Chiang, C., & Alexinsky, T. (1991). Discharge of noradrenergic locus coeruleus neurons in behaving rats and monkeys suggest a role in vigilance. *Progress in Brain Research, 88,* 501–520.

Azmitia, E. C., & Segal, M. (1978). An autoradiographic analysis of the differential ascending projections of the dorsal and median raphe nuclei in the rat. *Journal of Comparative Neurology, 179,* 641–659.

Baxter, L. R., Schwartz, J. M., & Bergman, K. S. (1992) Caudate glucose metabolic rate changes with both drug and behavior therapy for obsessive–compulsive disorder. *Archives of General Psychiatry, 49,* 681–689.

Berridge, C. W. (1993). Noradrenergic modulation of cognitive function: Clinical implications of anatomical, electrophysiological and behavioural studies in animal models. *Psychological Medicine, 23,* 557–564.

Cai, J. X., Ma, Y., Xu., L., & Hu, X. (1993). Reserpine impairs spatial working memory performance in monkeys: Reversal by the α-2-adrenergic agonist clonidine. *Brain Research, 614,* 191–196.

Coull, J. T. (1994). Pharmacological manipulations of the α-2-noradrenergic system. *Clinical Pharmacology, 5*(2), 116–128.

Crawley, J. N. (1991). Cholecystokinin–dopamine interactions. *Trends in Neurosciences, 165,* 6147–6151.

Delgado, P. L., Price, L. H., Miller, H. L., Salomon, R. M., Aghajanian, G. K., Heninger, R. R., & Charney, D. S. (1994). Serotonin and the neurobiology of depression: Effects of tryptophan depletion in drug-free depressed patients. *Archives of General Psychiatry, 51*(11), 865–874.

Di Chiara, G., & Morelli, M. (1993). Dopamine–acetylcholine–glutamate interactions in the striatum: A working hypothesis. In H. Narabayashi, N. Yanagisawa, T. Nagatsu, & Y. Mizuno (Eds.), *Advances in neurology: Parkinson's disease: From basic research to treatment* (Vol. 60, pp. 25–33). New York: Raven Press.

Dijk, S., Francis, P. T., Stratmann, G. C., & Bowern, D. M. (1995). Cholinomimetics increase glutamate outflow via an action on the corticostriatal pathway: Implications for Alzheimer's disease. *Journal of Neurochemistry, 65,* 2165–2169.

Eblen, F., & Graybiel, A. M. (1995). Highly restricted origin of prefrontal cortical inputs to striosomes in the macaque monkey. *Journal of Neuroscience, 15*(9), 5999–6013.

Ennis, C., Kemp, J. D., & Cox, B. (1981). Characterization of 5-hydroxytryptamine receptors that regulate dopamine release in the striatum. *Journal of Neurochemistry, 36,* 1505–1520.

Fallon, J. H. (1988). Topographic organization of ascending dopaminergic projections. In P. W. Kalivas & C. B. Nemeroff (Eds.), *The mesocorticolimbic dopamine system* (pp. 1–9). New York: New York Academy of Sciences.

Fibiger, H. C., & Phillips, A. G. (1988). Mesocorticolimbic dopamine systems and reward. In P. W. Kalivas & C. B. Nemeroff (Eds.), *The mesocorticolimbic dopamine system* (pp. 206–215). New York: New York Academy of Sciences.

Foote, S. L., Bloom, F. E., & Aston-Jones, G. (1983) Nucleus locus coeruleus: New evidence of anatomical and physiological specificity. *Physiology Review, 63,* 844–914.

Gerfen, C. R. (1992). The neostriatal mosaic: Multiple levels of compartmental organization. *Trends in Neurosciences, 15,* 133–139.

Goldman-Rakic, P. S., Lidow, M. S., Smiley, J. F., & Williams, M. S. (1992). The anatomy of dopamine in monkey and human prefrontal cortex. *Journal of Neural Transmission, 36*(Suppl.), 163–177.

Graybiel, A. M. (1990). Neurotransmitters and neuromodulators in the basal ganglia. *Trends in Neurosciences, 13*(7), 244–254.

Hokfelt, T. (1991) Neuropeptides in perspective: The last ten years. *Neuron, 7,* 867–879.

Hokfelt, T., Fried, G., Hansen, S., Holets, V., Lundberg, J. N., & Skirboll, L. (1986). Neurons with multiple messengers: Distribution and possible functional significance. *Progress in Brain Research, 65,* 115–137.

Inoue, M., Oomura, Y., Aou, S., Sikdar, S. K., Hynes, M., Mizuno, Y., & Katubuchi, T. (1983). Cholinergic role in monkey dorsolateral prefrontal cortex during bar-press feeding behavior. *Brain Research, 278,* 185–194.

Jones, B. (1993). The organization of central cholinergic systems and their functional importance in sleep-waking states. *Progress in Brain Research, 98,* 61–71.

Kapur, S., & Remington, G. (1996). Serotonin–dopamine interaction and its relevance to schizophrenia. *American Journal of Psychiatry, 153*(4), 446–476.

Kim, J. S., Kornhuber, H. H., Schmid-Burgk, W., & Holzmuller, B. (1980). Low cerebrospinal fluid glutamate in schizophrenic patients and a new hypothesis of schizophrenia. *Neuroscience Letter, 20,* 379–382.

Lavoie, B., & Parent, A. (1994). Pedunculopontine nucleus in the squirrel monkey: Cholinergic and glutamatergic projections to the substantia nigra. *Journal of Comparative Neurology, 344,* 232–241.

Lindvall, O., & Bjorklund, A. (1984). *Monoamine innervation of cerebral cortex.* New York: Alan Liss.

Loopuijit, L. D., Sebens, J. B., & Korf, F. (1987). A mosaic-like distribution of dopamine receptors in rat neostriatum and its relationship to striosomes. *Brain Research, 405,* 405–408.

McCormick, D. A., & Williamson, A. (1989). Convergence and divergence of neurotransmitter action in human cerebral cortex. *Proceedings of the National Academy of Sciences, USA, 86,* 8098–8102.

Mega, M. S., & Cummings, J. L. (1994). Frontal–subcortical circuits and neuropsychiatric disorders. *Journal of Neuropsychiatry, 6*(4), 358–370.

Miller, B. L., Darby, A. L., Swartz, J. R., Yener, G. G., & Meni, I. (1995). Dietary changes, compulsions and sexual behavior in frontotemporal degeneration. *Dementia, 6*(4), 195–199.

Morrison, J. G., Molliver, M. D., Grazanna, R., & Coyle, J. T. (1981). The intra-cortical trajectory of the coeruleocortical projection in the rat: A tangentially organized cortical afferent. *Neuroscience, 6,* 139–158.

Nemeroff, C. B., & Bissette, G. (1992). Neuropeptides, dopamine and schizophrenia. *Annals of the New York Academy of Sciences, 668,* 273–291.

Nowak, G., Ordway, G. A., & Paul, I. A. (1995). Alterations in the N-methyl-D-aspartate (NMDA) receptor complex in the frontal cortex of suicide victims. *Brain Resarch, 675,* 157–164.

Parent, A. (1990). Extrinsic connections of the basal ganglia. *Trends in Neuroscience, 13*(7), 254–258.

Parent, A., & Lavoie, B. (1993). The heterogeneity of the mesostriatal dopaminergic system as revealed in normal and Parkinsonian monkeys. In H. Narabayashi, N. Yanagisawa, T. Nagatsu, & Y. Mizuno (Eds.), *Advances in neurology: Parkinson's disease: From basic research to treatment* (Vol. 60, pp. 25–33). New York: Raven Press.

Parent, A., Cote, P., & Lavoie, B. (1995). Chemical anatomy of primate basal ganglia. *Progress in Neurobiology, 46,* 131–197.

Paul, I. A., Trullas, R., Skolnick, P., & Nowak, G. (1992). Downregulation of cortical-adrenoceptors by chronic treatment with functional NMDA antagonists. *Psychopharmacology (Berlin), 106,* 285–287.

Penny, J. B. Jr., & Young, A. B. (1981). GABA as the pallidothalamic neurotransmitter: Implications for basal ganglia function. *Brain Research, 207,* 195–199.

Petty, F. (1995). GABA and mood disorders: A brief review and hyhpothesis. *Journal of Affective Disorders, 34,* 275–281.

Ragsdale, C. W., & Graybiel, A. M. (1990). A simple ordering of neocortical areas established by the compartmental organization of their striatal projections. *Proceedings of the National Academy of Science, 87,* 6196–6199.

Riederer, P., Lange, K. W., Kornhuber, J., & Danielczyk, W. (1992). Glutamatergic–dopaminergic balance in the brain. *Drug Research, 42*(1), 265–268.

Robbins, T. W. (1991). Cognitive deficits in schizophrenia and Parkinson's disease: Neural basis and the role of dopamine. In P. Willner & J. Schell-Kruger (Eds.), *The mesolimbic dopamine system: From motivation to action* (pp. 497–528). West Sussex, England: Wiley.

Sawaguchi, T., Matsumura, M., & Kubota, K. (1986). Dopamine modulates neuronal activities related to motor performance in the monkey prefrontal cortex. *Brain Research, 371,* 404–408.

Sofroniew, M. V., Priestley, J. V., Consolazione, A., Eckenstein, F., & Cuello, A. C. (1985). Cholinergic projections from the mid-brain and pons to the thalamus in the rat, identified by combined retrograde tracing and choline acetyltransferase immunohistochemistry. *Brain Research, 329,* 213–223.

Streit, P. (1984). Glutamate and aspartate as transmitter candidates for systems of the cerebral cortex. In E. G. Jones & A. Peters (Eds.), *Cerebral cortex* (Vol. 2, pp. 119–143). New York: Plenum.

Sherif, F. M., & Ahmed, S. S. (1995). Basic aspects of GABA-transaminase in neuropsychiatric disorders. *Clinical Biochemistry, 28*(2), 145–154.

Trullas, R., & Skolnick, P. (1990). Functional antagonists at the NMDA receptor complex exhibit antidepressant actions. *European Journal of Pharmacology, 185,* 1–10.

Weinberger, D. R., Aloia, M. S., Goldberg, T. E., & Berman, K. F. (1994). The frontal lobes and schizophrenia. *Journal of Neuropsychiatry and Clinical Neurosciences, 6*(4), 419–427.

Wise, R. A. (1988). Psychomotor stimulant properties of addictive drugs. In P. W. Kalivas & C. B. Nemeroff (Eds.), *The mesocorticolimbic dopamine system* (pp. 228–234). New York: New York Academy of Sciences.

Woods, D. L., & Knight, R. T. (1986). Electrophysiological evidence of increased distractibility after dorsolateral prefrontal lesions. *Neurology, 36,* 212–216.

11

Cognitive Functions of the Frontal Lobes

JOAQUIN M. FUSTER

The frontal neocortex is the highest stage of a hierarchy of neural structures dedicated to the representation and execution of the actions of the organism. At the bottom of that hierarchy are the motoneurons and anterior roots of the spinal cord. Above that, in ascending order, are the motor nuclei of the mesencephalon, the cerebellum, and parts of the diencephalon, including certain nuclei of the hypothalamus, the thalamus, and the basal ganglia.

Hierarchical organization prevails within the frontal cortex itself. At the base of the cortical motor hierarchy is the primary motor cortex, in charge of the representation and execution of elementary skeletal movements. Above it is the premotor cortex, serving more complex movements defined by goal and trajectory, including certain premotor areas involved in speech. At the summit is the cortex of association of the frontal lobe, which is commonly designated prefrontal cortex. This cortex represents the broad schemata of action in the skeletal and speech domains, and in addition is critically involved in the enactment of those schemata or plans.

On account of those representational and operant functions, the prefrontal cortex is essential for the temporal organization of behavior and the spoken language. Included in the functional purview of the prefrontal cortex is the organized action in the mental domain of rational thinking. In sum, the prefrontal cortex is motor cortex of the highest order in that it supports the cognitive functions that coordinate the execution of the most elaborate and novel actions of the organism. For this reason it has been named the executive of the brain and the organ of creativity.

This chapter is dedicated to the cognitive functions of the prefrontal cortex and to the consequences of their failure. Before dealing with these subjects, however, I deal briefly with basic facts of development, anatomy, and neurochemistry (see Fuster, 1997, for more extensive review).

The prefrontal cortex is one of last regions of the neocortex to develop, phylogenetically as well as ontogenetically. It reaches maximum relative growth in the human brain, where it constitutes nearly one-third of the totality of the neocortex. In ontogenetic development, the prefrontal cortex is one of the last regions to undergo the myelination of its afferent, efferent, and intrinsic fibers. It is late to reach full maturity also by other criteria, such as the number and volume of cells and the size and number of the dendritic spines of its neurons. In the normal human individual, full prefrontal maturation is not reached until late adolescence. This long developmental process is probably related to the slow maturation of the cognitive functions that the prefrontal cortex supports, taking into account the slow development of the highest and most characteristically human of all cognitive activities, which is the spoken language. These activities are organized mainly by the cortex of the dorsolateral convexity of the frontal lobe, which in both phylogeny and ontogeny grows relatively more than the orbitomedial prefrontal cortex.

The prefrontal region of the cortex is the most highly interconnected of all neocortical regions. It receives afferent fibers from the brainstem, the hypothalamus, the limbic system (amygdala and hippocampus), the thalamus (especially anterior and mediodorsal nuclei), and other areas of the neocortex, notably the association cortex of postrolandic regions. Brainstem, hypothalamic, and limbic inputs probably bring to the prefrontal cortex information about the internal milieu, whereas the inputs from the hippocampus are probably essential for the formation of motor memory. Inputs from posterior cortex are apparently involved in sensory–motor integrations at the highest level. The prefrontal cortex reciprocates the afferent inputs from all those cerebral structures with output efferents to them.

Several neurotransmitter systems converge on the prefrontal cortex and are active within it. Most prominent among them are dopamine systems, a norepinephrine system, the cholinergic system originating in the basal nucleus of Meynert, and the γ-aminobutyric (GABA)ergic system. Certain types of dopamine receptors of the prefrontal cortex have been postulated to malfunction in schizophrenia. The cholinergic system seems deficient in Alzheimer's disease and other dementias.

THE COGNITIVE SUPPORT OF TEMPORAL ORGANIZATION

In recent years, as a result of neuropsychological and neurophysiological studies in the human and the monkey, the prefrontal cortex has emerged as the highest neural structure in charge of the organization of behavior in the time domain. This role of the prefrontal cortex is now believed essential for the sequencing of new and complex behavior, including speech and extending to logical reasoning. To understand this role of the prefrontal cortex in what has been termed executive function, it is important to consider, above all, that the prefrontal cortex has both representational and operant functions. Let us briefly deal with the former before the latter.

The entire prefrontal cortex is a substrate of motor memory. In this region of the neocortex, especially in its dorsolateral aspects (i.e., in the convexity of the frontal lobe), the highest schemes or plans of behavior are formed and represented. These are established in the prefrontal cortex presumably under the influence and control of inputs from the limbic system, notably the amygdala and the hippocampus, and from posterior (postrolandic) cortex, in addition to inputs from the brainstem thought to be responsible for maintaining the drive and motivation of the organism. The schemata or plans themselves are probably constituted by distributed networks of interconnected prefrontal cells formed by temporal coincidence of those inputs. By temporal coincidence, synapses are modulated, too, the effect of facilitating their conductance and thus weaving the network together (Fuster, 1995). The activation of a given network above a certain level of excitation leads to the enactment of the plan and the sequence of behavior directed to the reaching of its goal.

For behavior to become temporally organized in the execution of the action plan, functions of temporal integration need to enter into play. The formation of temporal structures or gestalts of behavior necessitates, above all, the capacity of the organism to mediate cross-temporal contingencies, in other words, its capacity to fulfill the following logical operations: If now this, then later that; and if earlier that, then now this. It should be emphasized that this applies to thinking and speech as well as to skeletal behavior.

The cross-temporal mediation is carried out by means of at least three subfunctions or operational components. They are thought to be the three basic cognitive functions, or information processing functions, of the prefrontal cortex: (1) short-term motor memory or preparatory set for forthcoming action, (2) short-term perceptual memory (working memory) for retention of sensory information on which that action is to be based, and (3) inhibitory control of interference, namely, a function to suppress all internal or external information that could interfere with the action at hand, that is, with the behavioral gestalt under way.

These three functions of the prefrontal cortex are supported by neuropsychology and primate neurophysiology (Fuster, 1997).

Preparatory Set

Short-term motor memory or preparatory set is motor attention. It may be construed as a form of attention directed to the action in preparation. This form of attention is focused in the representation of the plan and, at the same time, in components of established, long-term motor memory, which is activated temporarily for the execution of all the integral pieces of the sequence of behavior in progress, from its initiation to its goal.

It is not yet clear by what mechanisms a scheme of behavior in an activated motor network of frontal cortex becomes the agent of preparation for action. It appears, however, that one electrical correlate of preparatory set is the so-called contingent negative variation, which is a slow surface negative potential that develops over the frontal lobe in the time interval between a sensory stimulus and a motor response contingent on it. Another electrical correlate is the Bereitschaftspotential or readiness potential, another slow surface potential, this one briefer, that develops over the motor cortex just before an intended movement.

Recording from cells with microelectrodes in behaving monkeys, we have found neurons in the dorsolateral prefrontal cortex that might perform that function of preparatory set. While a monkey delays action and prepares for it, in the context of a delay task (e.g., delayed matching to sample, spatial delayed response), we have observed neurons that by their frequency of discharge seem in tune with the impending motor response. Their discharge is greater or smaller in accord with the characteristics of the monkey's intended action. What is more, the cells' discharge accelerates as that action approaches, and the gradient of acceleration varies proportionally to the certainty with which the animal can predict specific response features. A degree of uncertainty is introduced in the test by associating different colors with different probabilities of required response of the arm, either to one side or to the other.

Summing up, the presence of neurons that seem to predict future actions, though only for the short term, indicates that there are mechanisms in the dorsolateral prefrontal cortex not only for evoking that future, the memory of the future (Ingvar, 1985), but for preparing the motor apparatus for it. Those mechanisms may result in the priming of structures at lower stages of the motor hierarchy for the forthcoming action (e.g., the premotor cortex, the basal ganglia, and the pyramidal system). The relationship is apparent between the discharge of those set cells of the monkey and the well-known role of the human prefrontal cortex in the conception and execution of plans (see the next section).

Working Memory

In addition to set cells, memory cells can be found in the dorsolateral prefrontal cortex of the monkey. Neurons of this second type seem to have a temporally opposite function to those of the first. Instead of looking forward in time to the impending motor action, they look back in time, to the sensory information, a few seconds or minutes before, on which that action is partly dependent. These cells react specifically to the sensory cues, and, during the period of delay before the motor response, their discharge decelerates. They are probably the neuronal components of activated networks that make up the physiological foundation for the widely accepted role of the prefrontal cortex in working memory.

Working memory is also a function initially suspected by neuropsychological study of prefrontal syndromes in the human and the monkey; this study gave presumptive evidence that short-term or recent memory deficits are common components of those syndromes. The evidence from animals was especially persuasive. A long tradition of research initiated by Jacobsen (1935) demonstrated that monkeys with ablations of dorsolateral prefrontal cortex have serious difficulties in learning and performing so-called delay tasks (e.g., delayed response and delayed alternation). In these tasks the animal must retain an item of information in memory for subsequent performance, after a delay, of a motor act. A similar deficit can be produced by reversible (cryogenic) inactivation of prefrontal cortex bilaterally (Bauer & Fuster, 1976; Shindy, Posley, & Fuster, 1994). Microelectrode studies in the monkey, with the resultant discovery of memory cells (Fuster & Alexander, 1971; Niki, 1974), established conclusively that, in the dorsolateral prefrontal cortex of the primate, there is a physiological substrate of neurons for the memory function that fails in the monkey and the human after prefrontal damage.

Subsequently, Baddeley (1986) introduced the term "working memory" to describe the temporary, on-line memory that humans utilize in certain tasks and for solving certain problems. With that term, Baddeley also introduced a theory of the cognitive operations involved in that form of active memory, which primate researchers had been variously naming provisional memory, operant memory, or simply short-term memory. One of those operations, Baddeley assumed, the articulatory loop, is a concept difficult to apply to the monkey, but one with clear implications for the construction of language, which is a form of sequential behavior definitely dependent on working memory.

Thus the recent memory function of humans, which is frequently impaired in prefrontal syndromes, and the short-term memory function of monkeys, which fails after prefrontal lesion and has an obvious electrical correlate in the discharge of memory cells, are one and the same function—that is, what has come to be commonly called working memory. Neurophysiologically, it consists in the transient activation of a wide network of neocortical neurons, which is maintained active by prefrontal cortex as the information contained in that network has to be used for prospective action. The role of the prefrontal cortex in working memory is critical, but it needs emphasizing in view of recent work—microelectrode research and neuroimaging (Swartz et al., 1995)—that that role is based essentially on corticocortical interactions, namely, interactions between prefrontal cortex and areas of postrolandic cortex. The localization of working memory in the prefrontal cortex is an unfortunate misconception.

Inhibitory Control

Patients with prefrontal damage are abnormally distractible, perseverate, and have difficulty controlling impulsivity and instinctual behavior. The convergence of human and animal neuropsychology leads to the conclusion that such symptoms are more frequently produced by lesions of orbitofrontal cortex than by lesions of any other sector of the prefrontal cortex. Because the mentioned symptoms commonly occur together, and because the anatomy and connectivity of the orbital prefrontal cortex point to a common pathophysiology, it is increasingly obvious that all the manifestations of orbitofrontal damage derive from disorder of one common function. Such a function can be appropriately defined as the ability to protect goal-directed structures of behavior from interference.

There are many kinds of interference. Interference can come from sensory stimuli that appear in the context of the behavioral structure and that, if not suppressed, can lead the behavior away from its goal. The interference can also be in the form of internal tendencies, whether inborn or the product of learning. For example, it may be interference from instinctual impulses that, under certain conditions, prevail over current behavior and disrupt it. Or else, for example, the interference may come from well-established memories or patterns of behavior that are appropriate in other circumstances but presently are an impediment to current behavior and the achievement of its goal.

At variance with the physiological evidence of set and memory functions in the prefrontal cortex, the role of this cortex in the inhibitory control of interference does not have as yet recognized electrophysiological correlates. In all probability, however, inhibitory control functions are exercised selectively through the intrinsic cortical GABAergic system and the inhibitory corticohypothalamic pathways that originate in the orbital prefrontal cortex.

FRONTAL PATHOLOGY OF COGNITION

From the evidence outlined previously, it is reasonable to infer that those three prefrontal functions, two chiefly based in dorsolateral cortex (set and working memory) and the other in orbital cortex (inhibitory control), cooperate with one another to ensure the integrity and purpose of all the novel and complex sequences of goal-directed behavior. This functional cooperation engages other cerebral structures connected with the prefrontal cortex. It is a functional cooperation that extends to the spoken language and to mental sequences of logical thought.

Based on these functional inferences, it is appropriate to reexamine the symptomatology of prefrontal damage in the human. The following is not intended as a detailed clinical description of prefrontal syndromes but as an outline of reference to understand the consequences of failure in the human of the physiological functions of the prefrontal cortex just considered.

Above all it has to be acknowledged that there is no such thing as *the* frontal lobe syndrome. The anatomical and functional heterogeneity of the frontal cortex precludes this nosological entity. In its stead, however, we are able to identify three major clusters of symptoms or syndromes depending on the topography of the lesion that originates them after disease or trauma of the prefrontal cortex. Each of the syndromes results from damage to one of the three major aspects of the frontal cortex: dorsolateral, medial/cingulate, and orbital. Figure 11.1 illustrates these regions and the cytoarchitectonic areas they include according to Brodmann's map.

Patients with damaged dorsolateral prefrontal cortex can exhibit a considerable variety of symptoms. The resulting syndrome differs depending on the location and extent of the damage within the dorsolateral region. However, it is possible to identify a number of manifestations of dorsolateral pathology that are most commonly observed; they may appear together or separately.

Most frequent are the disorders of drive, attention, and motivation. Even patients with minor dorsolateral prefrontal damage appear disinterested in the world around them and deprived of spontaneity, to judge from their language as well as their behavior. They display less alertness than normal to events and persons in their environment and seem to lack the motivation to do things for themselves or for others. Their ordinary life is driven by routine and a certain tendency to temporal concreteness: This means that their behavior is anchored in the here and now, without perspective either backward or forward in time. Their memory for recent events is faulty, and so is their capacity to plan for the future.

Temporal concreteness seems to derive directly from impairment of the two functions for temporal integration that we have assigned to dorsolateral cortex (i.e., working memory and preparatory set). The disorder of working memory can be readily recognized on observation of the patient in daily life and can be substantiated by formal testing. To some degree the short-term memory deficit is a consequence of the mentioned disorders of drive and attention. The subject does not remember what he or she is not interested in or motivated to remember. To a large degree, however, the deficit is primary, that is, a consequence of the failure of the basic prefrontal mechanisms of working memory.

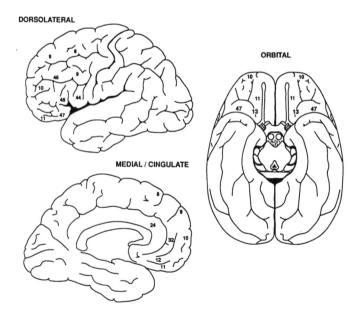

FIGURE 11.1. Three schematic views of the human brain with frontal cytoarchitectonic areas indicated according to Brodmann's map.

Whereas the working memory deficit is a common characteristic of the dorsolateral syndrome, the planning deficit is almost pathognomonic of it. This is the most consistent and typical symptom from dorsolateral prefrontal damage. The patient cannot formulate plans of future action that deviates from ordinary routine. His capacity to create new speech or behavior is severely restricted. Clearly, this deficit is closely related to the deficit in memory of the future mentioned previously and thus a deficit in the ability to represent schemata of action. In addition, however, there is the inability to execute them. In sum, we are dealing again with the lack of drive, the incapacity to make decisions, and the faulty preparation for impending action, in other words, the defect in motor preparation set. These difficulties, in the aggregate, constitute what has been called the dysexecutive syndrome.

The lesions of medial prefrontal cortex induce a disorder of drive and motivation with even more constancy and saliency than lesions of the dorsolateral cortex. Here all disorders of temporal integration are completely attributable to inattention and lack of interest. Thus, apathy is the dominant affective component of the medial/cingulate syndrome. From apathy derives the lack of spontaneity in all aspects of action, including speech. Generally the patient is less mobile than before the damage, hypokinetic in all respects. In extreme cases from large lesions of medial prefrontal cortex, the hypokinesia becomes akinesia. Akinetic mutism is a characteristic disorder from severe damage of medial prefrontal cortex.

The orbital syndrome, resulting from lesion of ventral prefrontal cortex, in many respects differs sharply from the other two. An attention disorder is here again in the foreground, but this one is rather different from the attention disorder of medial and dorsolateral syndromes. The orbital disorder lies not so much in the intensive aspects of attention, that is, in failure to focus and concentrate, but in its exclusionary aspect. The orbital patient is unusually distractible, unable to inhibit interference from external stimuli that are extraneous to present context and not part of the action currently under way. Together with it and probably in part related to it, the patient shows hyperactivity, unable to inhibit spontaneous actions and to react to the extraneous stimuli (hyperreactivity).

The affects of the orbital patient are labile and unpredictable. Euphoria is often the dominant affect, at least more often than in other prefrontal syndromes. Together with it, the patient commonly exhibits inappropriate and childish humor. In addition, he is unable to inhibit instinctual drives and tends to make displays of belligerence, hypersexuality, and hyperphagia. Disinhibition of instincts, in the absence of good moral judgment, often drives the patient to unruly behavior and to break the law. Sociopathy is almost a hallmark of the orbitofrontal syndrome.

To conclude, the patient from damage of the orbital prefrontal cortex exhibits a number of abnormalities of cognition and affect as well as emotional and social behavior. Many of these abnormalities seem to be the result of a deficit in the inhibitory control functions of orbital cortex.

From the previous description it follows that psychological and social disorders of one kind or another are common in patients with any type of frontal lobe pathology. Several of these disorders are easily attributable to the failure of the basic functions of the prefrontal cortex, earlier explained, that define its role in the temporal organization of behavior. In any case, some of the clinical manifestations of frontal pathology are reminiscent of certain psychiatric disorders of unknown etiology. This had led to the presumption that these disorders are the result of frontal dysfunction.

One example of such disorders is attention-deficit disorder (ADD) of childhood. We have no hard evidence demonstrating that the ADD is caused by any disorder of the frontal lobe. However, the similarities between ADD and the orbital–prefrontal syndrome are striking. Both are characterized by an attention disorder, especially distractibility, hyperkinesia, and unruly behavior. Thus it is reasonable to conclude that the ADD has something to do with a disorder of the orbitofrontal cortex (Fuster, 1997). Furthermore, because ADD is often outgrown in late adolescence, it is also reasonable to suppose that the ADD is the clinical manifestation of a lag in the maturation of the orbital–prefrontal cortex.

On the issue of schizophrenia we find another example of extrapolated reasoning for involvement of a diseased frontal lobe in psychiatric illness. This reasoning, however, is more solid than the one pertaining to ADD. The rationale for prefrontal pathology in schizophrenia is based on the following evidence: (1) evidence in the psychotic patient of disordered temporal organization of thinking, speech, and behavior; (2) evidence in that patient of disordered dopamine systems and receptors; (3) evidence of schizophrenics' poor performance of tests of frontal lobe function (e.g., Tower of London for planning, Wisconsin Card Sorting Test [WCST] for working memory and interference control); and (4) evidence, in schizophrenic patients, of frontal metabolic deficit ("hypofrontality") and absence of dorsolateral prefrontal activation, as determined by neuroimaging in performance of frontal tasks (e.g., WCST).

Certainly this evidence can be used to argue for some involvement of the prefrontal cortex in the pathogenesis of schizophrenia. However, it is unreasonable to assume that the illness exclusively, or even principally, affects the prefrontal cortex. This position has to contend with the evidence that no injury to this cortex is known to result in schizophrenia. It is more reasonable to conclude that schizophrenia affects several neurotransmitter systems, notably dopaminergic, that are profusely distributed in the prefrontal cortex. Because such a neurotransmitter disorder affects the connectivity of the prefrontal cortex with limbic structures, the basal ganglia, and the rest of the neocortex, the disorder manifests itself as an impairment of several emotional and cognitive functions that depend on that connectivity. Thus, schizophrenia would be a prefrontal disorder inasmuch as the prefrontal cortex is critical for those functions. It is more appropriate, however, to view this disease, with all its numerous manifestations, as some kind of a disconnection syndrome in which the prefrontal cortex is affected, as are many other cerebral structures connected with it.

REFERENCES

Baddeley, A. (1986). *Working memory.* Oxford: Clarendon Press.

Bauer, R. H., & Fuster, J. M. (1976). Delayed-matching and delayed-response deficit from cooling dorsolateral prefrontal cortex in monkeys. *Journal of Comparative Physiology and Psychology, 90,* 293–302.

Fuster, J. M. (1995). *Memory in the cerebral cortex: An empirical approach to neural networks in the human and nonhuman primate.* Cambridge, MA: MIT Press.

Fuster, J. M. (1997). *The prefrontal cortex: Anatomy, physiology, and neuropsychology of the frontal lobe* (3rd ed.). Philadelphia: Lippincott-Raven.

Fuster, J. M., & Alexander, G. E. (1971). Neuron activity related to short-term memory. *Science, 173,* 652–654.

Ingvar, D. H. (1985). "Memory of the future": An essay on the temporal organization of conscious awareness. *Human Neurobiology, 4,* 127–136.

Jacobsen, C. F. (1935). Functions of the frontal association area in primates. *Archives of Neurological Psychiatry, 33,* 558–569.

Niki, H. (1974). Prefrontal unit activity during delayed alternation in the monkey: I. Relation to direction of response. *Brain Research, 68,* 185–196.

Shindy, W. W., Posley, K. A., & Fustr, J. M. (1994). Reversible deficit in haptic delay tasks from cooling prefrontal cortex. *Cerebral Cortex, 4,* 443–450.

Swartz, B. E., Halgren, E., Fuster, J. M., Simpkins, F., Gee, M., & Mandelkern, M. (1995). Cortical metabolic activation in humans during a visual memory task. *Cerebral Cortex, 3,* 205–214.

12

Neuroimaging and Activation of the Frontal Lobes

CHERYL L. GRADY

The purpose of this chapter is to review the role of the frontal lobes in cognition as illuminated by neuroimaging. Over the past 5 to 10 years, the number of experiments reported in the literature using neuroimaging to study brain and behavior has dramatically increased, and many of these have found activation in some part of the frontal lobes. To keep this review manageable, therefore, I have placed a few limitations on the content. First, the discussion is limited to those processes that are "cognitive" in the sense that they are not purely sensory or motor but require some elaboration of stimuli and a decision to be made about some aspect of the stimuli. Second, I consider only those areas that are part of prefrontal cortex (i.e., Brodmann's areas 8, 9, 10, 11, 45, 46, and 47). Premotor cortex is not included, nor is Brodmann's area 44, which has been excluded, perhaps arbitrarily, on the basis of its traditional role in motor speech output. Third, I consider only those experiments carried out on healthy, young subjects, in an attempt to focus on the "normal" functioning of prefrontal cortex. Finally, I have included only those studies that have utilized positron emission tomography (PET) to measure regional cerebral blood flow (rCBF) and have reported the results in terms of atlas coordinates (Talairach, Szikla, & Tournoux, 1967; Talairach & Tournoux, 1988). These experiments have utilized mathematical procedures that resample the individual brain images and standardize them to match a template brain that conforms to the stereotactic space of the atlas (Friston, Frith, Liddle, & Frackowiak, 1991; Friston et al., 1995). This procedure allows direct comparison across studies by simply comparing the coordinates for each activated region. Functional MRI, although it appears to be more and more the tool of choice for cognitive activation experiments, is not yet at the stage where results are reported routinely in terms of coordinates, making it difficult to compare results from this technique directly to those obtained with PET.

OVERVIEW OF ANATOMY AND FUNCTION OF PREFRONTAL CORTEX

A comprehensive summary of the many studies that have examined the structure and function of prefrontal cortex in humans and monkeys is beyond the scope of this chapter. Thus, a few words that emphasize the specific characteristics of the different parts of prefrontal cortex will suffice. To aid in this task, I focus on two aspects of the frontal lobes that have emerged as important characteristics of frontal function—that is, functional differences based on dorsal versus ventral prefrontal cortex and right–left asymmetries. In this section and those following, I identify the subregions of prefrontal cortex by Brodmann's areas (BAs) wherever possible, based on a recent comparative analysis of prefrontal regions in human and monkey that has resulted in a reformulation of BAs to make them comparable across species (Pandya & Yeterian, 1996; Petrides & Pandya, 1994).

It has long been recognized that lesions of the frontal lobe in humans can lead to personality changes and other behavioral disturbances. One of the earliest demonstrations is the famous 19th-century case of Phineas Gage who survived an accident that drove an iron bar through his head but afterward displayed dramatic changes in personality and judgment (Harlow, 1868). More recently, research found that this type of personality change is more likely to occur after lesions of the ventral or medial aspects of the frontal lobes (e.g., BA 11 and ventromedial portions of BA 10) than after lesions to dorsolateral prefrontal cortex (Stuss & Benson, 1984). In the case of Phineas Gage, a recent reconstruction of his lesion by Damasio, Grabowski, Frank, Galaburda, and Damasio (1994) showed that it primarily involved the ventral and medial aspects of both frontal lobes, confirming the importance of these regions to social behaviors and judgment. Patients with ventromedial prefrontal lesions also have been described as having an "environmental dependency syndrome" (Lhermitte, 1986) in which their behavior is overly controlled by external stimuli, becoming stereotypical and stimulus bound. On the other hand, dorsolateral lesions (e.g., BAs 46, 9, and 8) are associated more with cognitive dysfunction, such as loss of executive function and cognitive flexibility (Cummings, 1993; Eslinger & Grattan, 1993). Prefrontal lesions also have been found to result in impaired episodic memory retrieval, particularly when memory is tested via recall (Mangels, Gershberg, Shimamura, & Knight, 1996; Owen, Sahikian, Semple, Polkey, & Robbins, 1995; Ptito, Crane, Leonard, Amsel, & Caramanos, 1995; Schacter, 1987; Wheeler, Stuss, & Tulving, 1995), although it is sometimes difficult to know if this is the result of dorsolateral or ventral prefrontal damage. Dorsomedial prefrontal lesions (lateral and medial portions of BAs 8 and 9, and the anterior cingulate) impair performance on attentional tasks, such as the Stroop Test and tasks involving target detection (Richer et al., 1993). Thus, human lesion studies have shown a dorsal–ventral dissociation in the types of behavioral problems that occur, but the lesions are generally large and include multiple areas in prefrontal cortex, making it difficult to determine the roles of specific regions within prefrontal cortex.

The issue of laterality in human frontal lobe lesions has not been prominent in this field of research (see Stuss, Eskes, & Foster, 1994, for a review); nevertheless, some differences in the effects of right versus left frontal lesions have been noted. Frontal lobe excisions have been found to be associated with deficits in working memory, with right-sided lesions causing more impairment of nonverbal tasks and left-sided lesions causing greater impairment of verbal working memory (Petrides & Milner, 1982). A similar laterality has been found for the effect of right and left frontal lesions on recency memory for nonverbal and verbal material (Milner, Petrides, & Smith, 1985), as well as a greater effect of right frontal lesions on memory span for visually presented patterns (Pigott & Milner, 1994). The right frontal lobe also has been implicated in attention to extrapersonal space, particularly when exploratory motor movements are required (Daffner, Ahern, Weintraub, & Mesulam, 1990; Spiers et al., 1990), and in olfactory function (Zatorre & Jones-Gotman, 1991). Conversely, the left frontal lobe may be more involved than the right in programming eye movements (De Renzi, Colombo, Faglioni, & Gibertoni, 1982) and in verbal fluency (e.g., Stuss & Benson, 1986; Janowsky, Shimamura, Kritchevsky, & Squire, 1989).

Experiments involving lesions or single-cell recordings in monkeys are able to be more precise than human studies in the specific areas of prefrontal cortex being examined. Many of these experiments have focused on the sulcus principalis and the areas of cortex surrounding this sulcus, which seem to be crucial for the performance of working-memory tasks. Cortex within the sulcus principalis (BA 46) mediates spatial working memory tasks, such as the oculomotor delayed response (Goldman-Rakic, 1990; Funahashi, Bruce, & Goldman-Rakic, 1993), whereas cortex surrounding the sulcus (BAs 46 and 9) is involved in both spatial and nonspatial working memory (Di Pellegrino & Wise, 1991; Mishkin & Manning, 1978; Petrides, 1995). In contrast, ventromedial lesions (e.g., BA 11) in monkeys result in impaired recognition memory but not working memory (Bachevalier & Mishkin, 1986). Some evidence suggests that the dorsal part of BA 8 (8B) is active during working-memory tasks in a manner similar to areas 46 and 9 (Di Pellegrino & Wise, 1991). More caudal parts of lateral prefrontal cortex, including ventral portions of BA 8 (8A), and cortex ventral to the caudal portion of the sulcus principalis, including BA 45, are thought to mediate the associative significance between stimulus cues and behavioral response or reward (i.e., conditional learning) (Quintana & Fuster, 1992; Sakagami & Niki, 1994; Watanabe, 1992). In conditional go/no-go tasks, an additional region of prefrontal cortex on the inferior convexity (BA 47) also shows increased activity (Sasaki, Gemba, Nambu, & Matsuzaki, 1994). Both dorsal and ventral prefrontal lesions in monkeys result in cognitive inflexibility and loss of response inhibition (Ridley, Durnford, Baker, & Baker, 1993). In addition, evidence suggests that dorsal and ventral lesions are responsible for different kinds of inhibitory control (i.e., attentional vs. emotional) (Dias, Robbins, & Roberts, 1996), similar to the dorsal–ventral distinction made in humans. Another dorsal/ventral distinction that has been noted in the frontal lobes of monkeys is related to visual processing in that dorsal areas are more involved in spatial location of objects whereas ventral frontal areas mediate identification of objects (Wilson, Scalaidhe, & Goldman-Rakic, 1993).

In a recent review of the animal literature, Petrides (1994) has suggested that prefrontal cortex in the monkey can be partitioned into three regions with distinct roles in memory. In this formulation, ventromedial prefrontal cortex (BAs 11, 13, and 14) is critical for recognition memory in the monkey, whereas ventrolateral prefrontal cortex (BA 47/12, 45, and ventral 46) is critical for basic working-memory functions. Dorsolateral prefrontal cortex (BA 9 and dorsal 46) is thought to be necessary for tasks that draw heavily on the self-monitoring and planning of behavior. Such tasks in the monkey would primarily be working-memory tasks, although in the human some other memory tasks, such as recall of information, might also involve strategic monitoring. Conspicuously absent from the animal literature is an examination of the role of BA 10, about which almost nothing is known except for its anatomy and connections with other prefrontal regions (Pandya & Yeterian, 1996). In the discussion that follows we shall see how much homology exists between prefrontal functions in the monkey and those in man as defined by neuroimaging, as well as the correspondence between human lesion studies and the neuroimaging data, with particular focus on dorsal–ventral and right–left distinctions.

OVERVIEW OF TASKS AND COGNITIVE FUNCTIONS

Prior to reviewing the data, Table 12.1 presents a brief summary of the cognitive processes that have been studied in relation to frontal function and the experimental tasks used for this purpose. These functions include attention, perception, and various types of memory, and they involve more than one sensory modality as well as multiple modes of response. It should be noted that the list of experiments in Table 12.1 is not a complete list of PET activation experiments in any of the cognitive areas, only those that have reported activation in prefrontal cortex. In addition, Table 12.1 includes a description of the control task for each experiment that served as the comparison task for determining rCBF activation.

Perception

The experiments involving some type of perceptual discrimination that have reported activation in prefrontal cortex are mostly in the visual modality, a predominance that reflects the PET literature as a whole. (See Table 12.1A.) These visual studies include perception of objects (Kosslyn et al., 1993, 1994; Kosslyn, Alpert, & Thompson, 1995; Schacter, Alpert, Savage, Rauch, & Albert, 1995), faces (Grady et al., 1996; Haxby et al., 1994, 1995; Sergent, Ohta, & MacDonald, 1992), including facial emotion (George et al., 1993), and spatial information (George et al., 1993; Parsons et al., 1995). The study by Parsons et al. (1995) is included in the spatial category, even though the task was to view pictures of hands and decide if they were right or left hands, because the hands were depicted in various orientations, thus necessitating a mental rotation. The auditory perception experiments involve a difficult tone discrimination (Holcomb et al., in press) and two studies of pitch discrimination, one using speech stimuli (Zatorre, Evans, Meyer, & Gjedde, 1992) and one using segments of familiar songs (Zatorre, Halpern, Perry, Meyer, & Evans, 1996). In addition, one of the working-memory tasks utilizing faces (see Haxby, Ungerleider, Horowitz, Rapoport, & Grady, 1995) also had a condition in which the memory component was minimal (1-sec delay), so maxima from this task have been classified as perception rather than memory. These perceptual experiments varied in difficulty and complexity of the discrimination required. For example, one study by Kosslyn et al. (1994) required subjects to identify pictures of objects when presented in unusual or noncanonical orientations, whereas another (Grady et al., 1996) varied the difficulty of a face perception task by degrading the stimuli. Two of the experiments also examined rCBF during imagery, either visual or auditory (see Kosslyn, 1993; Zatorre, Halpern, et al., 1996, in Table 12.1).

Attention

Frontal lobe activation has been reported in experiments examining three different types of attentional processing. These experiments include a study of dividing attention among various features of a visual stimulus (Corbetta, Miezin, Dobmeyer, Shulman, & Petersen, 1991), and two studies on sustained attention, one to tactile stimulation (Pardo, Fox, & Raichle, 1991) and one to auditory stimuli (Paus et al., 1997). In addition, two studies

TABLE 12.1. Descriptions of Tasks Used in Reviewed Papers

Reference	Task	Comparison task
Object processing	**A. Perception**	
Kosslyn et al. (1994; 1)	Picture match with name (canonical view)	Neutral response to word–pattern pairs
Kosslyn et al. (1994; 2)	Picture match with name (noncanonical view)	Picture match with name (canonical view)
Kosslyn et al. (1995; 1)	Picture match with object name (e.g., daisy)	Neutral response to word–pattern pairs
Kosslyn et al. (1995; 2)	Picture match with object name (e.g., daisy)	Picture match with object category
Kosslyn et al. (1995; 3)	Picture match with object category (e.g., flower)	Neutral response to word–pattern pairs
Kosslyn et al. (1993; 1)	Does letter cover location in grid? (perception)	Respond to disappearance of x from grid
Kosslyn et al. (1993; 2)	Does letter cover location in grid? (imagery)	Perception task
Schacter et al. (1995)	Object decision: possible or impossible	Passive object viewing
Face processing		
George et al. (1993; 1)	Facial emotion discrimination	Face identity
Grady et al. (1996)	Degraded face matching	Neutral response to visual noise
Haxby et al. (1994)	Face matching	Location matching and visual noise
Haxby et al. (1995; 1)	Face matching (1-sec delay)	Neutral response to visual noise
Sergent et al. (1992)	Famous face identity	Gender decision on unfamiliar faces
Spatial processing		
George et al. (1993; 2)	Location matching	Face matching
Parsons et al. (1995)	View hands, decide if right or left hand	Fixation
Auditory processing		
Holcomb et al. (in press)	Tone discrimination	Neutral response to tones
Zatorre et al. (1992)	Pitch discrimination (speech stimuli)	Neutral response to speech
Zatorre, Halpern, et al. (1996)	Pitch discrimination and imagery using familiar songs (visual cues)	Decision on visual cue words–which has more letters?
	B. Attention	
Bench et al. (1993)	Name incongruent color of word (Stroop)	Name color of colored cross
Corbetta et al. (1991)	Divide attention among 3 visual features	Passive viewing of stimuli
George et al. (1994)	Name incongruent color of word (Stroop)	Name color of colored bar
Pardo et al. (1991)	Attend to left toe stimulation	Rest
Paus et al. (1997)	Listen to tones, respond to rare target	Listen to tones, no targets
Rees et al. (1997)	Attend to feature conjunction	Attend to individual features
	C. Motor learning, classical conditioning	
Blaxton, Zeffiro, et al. (1996)	Eye blink conditioning (paired US and CS)	Pseudoconditioning (unpaired)
Deiber et al. (1991; 1)	Retrieval of learned motor sequence	Fixed motor sequence
Grafton et al. (1994)	Pursuit rotor task	No control task, increase over practice trials
Hazeltine et al. (1997)	Motor sequence learning	No control task, increase over practice trials
Hugdahl et al. (1995)	Extinction of shock-tone conditioning	Preconditioning habituation
Jenkins et al. (1994)	Motor sequence learning	Retrieval of previously learned sequence
Rauch et al. (1995)	Retrieval of learned motor sequence	Performance of random sequence

D. Working memory

Courtney et al. (1996)	DMS for faces	DMS for locations
Deiber et al. (1991; 2)	Subject ordered series of movements	Fixed order
Gold et al. (1996; 1)	Delayed alternation to color cue—unpracticed	Fixed response to color cue
Gold et al. (1996; 2)	Delayed alternation to color cue—practiced	Fixed response to color cue
Haxby et al. (1995; 2)	DMS for faces	Neutral response to visual noise
Jonides et al. (1993)	DMS for location	Feature conjunction
Petrides, Alivastos, Meyer, & Evans (1993; 1)	Say numbers in different order	Count 1–10
Petrides, Alivastos, Meyer, & Evans (1993; 2)	Hear numbers, say missing number	Count 1–10
Petrides, Alivastos, Evans, & Meyer (1993; 1)	Point to different object on each trial	Point to specified target object
Schumacher et al. (1996; 1)	Visual three-back letter match	Visual search for target letters
Schumacher et al. (1996; 2)	Auditory three-back letter match	Auditory search for target letters
Smith et al. (1995)	DMS for location (3,000-msec delay)	DMS for location (250-msec delay)
Zatorre et al. (1994)	Match 1st and 8th tones	Passive listening to tones

E. Episodic memory

Encoding

Haxby et al. (1996; 1)	Face encoding	Face matching
Kapur (1996)	Learn paired associates (visual)	Read word pairs
Owen et al. (1996; 1)	Encode object features	Retrieve object features (recognition)
Shallice et al. (1994; 1)	Learn paired associates (auditory)	Hear same word pair

Retrieval

Andreasen, O'Leary, Arndt, et al. (1995)	Visual word recognition	Word reading
Andreasen, O'Leary, Cizadlo, et al. (1995)	Retrieval of personal experience	Semantic retrieval (verbal fluency)
Andreasen et al. (1996)	Face recognition	Face gender decision
Becker et al. (1994)	Word recall (12-word list)	Word recall (3-word list)
Blaxton, Bookheimer, et al. (1996; 1)	Conceptual cued recall of studied words	Semantic association on nonstudied items
Blaxton, Bookheimer, et al. (1996; 2)	Perceptual cued recall of studied words	Word fragment completion
Buckner, Petersen, et al. (1995)	Word stem recall	Nonstudied word stem completion
Buckner et al. (1996)	Paired associate recall (auditory and visual)	Repeat word
Cabeza et al. (1997; 1)	Paired associate recognition	Word pair reading
Cabeza et al. (1997; 2)	Paired associate recall	Word pair reading
Fiez et al. (1996)	Word free recall	Fixation
Grasby et al. (1993)	Word free recall (15-word list)	Word free recall (5-word list)
Grasby et al. (1994)	Word free recall (increasing list length)	No-control task—linear analysis
Haxby et al. (1996; 2)	Face recognition	Face matching
Kapur et al. (1995)	Visual word recognition	Living–nonliving decision on words
Moscovitch et al. (1995)	Recognition of location	Location matching
Nyberg et al. (1995)	Visual word recognition	Word reading
Nyberg, Cabeza, & Tulving (1996; 1)	Visual word recognition	Recall of word location
Nyberg, Cabeza, & Tulving (1996; 2)	Recall of word location	Word recognition
Owen et al. (1996; 2)	Recognize object features	Encode object features

TABLE 12.1. (*continued*)

Reference	Task	Comparison task
Petrides et al. (1995; 1)	Word free recall	Word repetition
Petrides et al. (1995; 2)	Paired associate recall	Word repetition
Petrides, Alivastos, Evans, & Meyer (1993; 2)	Point to object associated with cue color	Point to specified target object
Roland & Gulyas (1995; 1)	Pattern recall	Rest
Roland & Gulyas (1995; 2)	Pattern recognition	Pattern encoding
Rugg et al. (1996)	Visual word recognition	No control, increase with percentage of "old" words
Schacter et al. (1996)	Word stem recall	Nonstudied word stem completion
Shallice et al. (1994; 2)	Paired associate cued recall	Paired associate generation
Tulving, Kapur, Markowitsch, et al. (1994)	Recognition of studied sentences	Nonstudied sentences
Tulving et al. (1996)	Picture recognition	Nonstudied pictures

F. Semantic memory retrieval

Reference	Task	Comparison task
Andreasen, O'Leary, Cizaldo, et al. (1995)	Semantic retrieval (verbal fluency)	Episodic retrieval (personal experience)
Buckner, Raichle, & Petersen (1995; 1)	Hear noun and generate verb	Repeat word
Buckner, Raiche, & Petersen (1995; 2)	Stem completion	Fixation
Demonet et al. (1994)	Detect target noun–adjective category	Phoneme detection
Frith et al. (1991)	Generate words (fluency)	Repeat words
Jennings et al. (1997)	Living–nonliving decision on word	Decide if word contains letter "a"
Kapur et al. (1994)	Living–nonliving decision on word	Decide if word contains letter "a"
Martin et al. (1995; 1)	Say color associated with object	Name object
Martin et al. (1995; 2)	Say action associated with object	Name object
Martin et al. (1996; 1)	View and silently name pictures of tools	View nonsense objects
Martin et al. (1996; 2)	View and name pictures of animals	View and name pictures of tools
Petersen et al. (1989)	Hear (see) noun and generate verb	Hear (see) and repeat word
Wise et al. (1991)	Hear noun and generate verb	Rest

G. Language

Reference	Task	Comparison task
Bookheimer et al. (1995)	Read word silently	View nonsense figures
Bottini et al. (1994)	Decide if sentence is plausible	Lexical decision (visual presentation)
Klein et al. (1995)	Bilingual production of synonyms, rhymes, and translations	Repetition of words in either language
Petersen et al. (1990)	Read word silently	Fixation
Price et al. (1994; 1)	Lexical decision	Feature decision (false font)
Price et al. (1994; 2)	Read word silently	See false font string
Zatorre, Meyer, et al. (1996)	Phoneme matching	Neutral response to noise bursts

H. Theory of mind

Reference	Task	Comparison task
Fletcher et al. (1995)	Stories requiring judgment of another's actions	Stories requiring factual judgments
Goel et al. (1995)	Inference re Columbus's knowledge	Inference re unfamiliar object

Note. Numbers after the author's name refer to different tasks or statistical comparisons.

of the Stroop effect have been included as examples of selective attention to a particular stimulus feature (Bench et al., 1993; George et al., 1994). (See Table 12.1B.) The Stroop effect (e.g., MacLeod, 1991) refers to the increased response time resulting when subjects are required to name the color of the ink in which a color word is printed (e.g., green) and ignore the word itself. That is, it requires more time to selectively attend to the ink color and suppress the incongruent color word than to name the color of a patch or bar. A recent study by Rees, Frackowiak, and Frith (1997) also examined selective attention by having subjects attend either to single features of a stimulus (color or orientation) or to both features at once (conjunction condition). One additional study (Haxby et al., 1994) examined selective attention to either object identity or object location, but because the activations were the same as during simple perception of these features, this study is discussed as a perceptual task.

Motor Memory Tasks and Classical Conditioning

The learning of specific motor movements is considered a type of procedural or skill learning and is thought to be distinct from other forms of memory (Schacter & Tulving, 1994), such as episodic and semantic memory. This distinction arises, at least in part, because retrieval of such movements can be implicit (i.e., can occur without explicit or conscious knowledge). In this category of procedural memory are four experiments in which subjects either learned or retrieved a sequence of motor movements in conjunction with visual cues (Rauch et al., 1995; Hazeltine, Grafton, & Ivry, 1997), auditory cues (Deiber et al., 1991; Jenkins, Brooks, Nixon, Frackowiak, & Passingham, 1994), or no cues (Grafton, Woods, & Tyszka, 1994). (See Table 12.1C.) In the experiments of Rauch et al. (1995) and Deiber et al. (1991), prefrontal activation was found when subjects were performing the task after it had been learned; in the case of the Jenkins et al. (1994) study, increased prefrontal activation was seen in the unpracticed condition compared to the practiced condition.

In the experiments by Grafton et al. (1994) and Hazeltine et al. (1997), prefrontal activity was measured over sequential trials of motor learning (i.e., as subjects became more practiced). Two experiments of classical conditioning are also included in the category of procedural learning due to the implicit nature of this type of process. One of these conditioning experiments involved the pairing of tones and air puffs to elicit eyeblinks (Blaxton, Zeffiro, et al., 1996), and one paired tones with shocks (Hugdahl et al., 1995). PET scanning was carried out during the conditioning phase in the eyeblink study (when the conditioned stimuli [CS] and unconditioned stimuli [US] were paired), and during the extinction phase in the tone–shock study, which followed conditioning and involved presentation of only the tones (CS).

Working Memory

Working memory is a concept that has evolved over the past few years (Baddeley, 1992). It is usually considered a form of short-term memory in which subjects are required to hold information in short-term stores while continuing to process new information. Thus, working-memory tasks are complex, requiring both stimulus encoding and retrieval. There have been quite a few PET studies using working-memory paradigms over the past few years, and all have found activity in frontal cortex. The studies reviewed here include both visual (Courtney, Ungerleider, Keil, & Haxby, 1996; Gold, Berman, Randolph, Goldberg, & Weinberger, 1996; Haxby et al., 1995; Jonides et al., 1993; Petrides,

Alivisatos, Evans, & Meyer, 1993; Schumacher et al., 1996; Smith et al., 1995) and auditory working-memory experiments (Petrides, Alivisatos, Meyer, & Evans, 1993; Zatorre, Evans, & Meyer, 1994; Schumacher et al., 1996), including one in which tones were used as cues for subject-directed motor sequences (Deiber et al., 1991). (See Table 12.1D.) The majority of these studies used nonverbal stimuli (e.g., faces or locations), although two experiments made use of verbal stimuli, letters, and numbers in both the visual and auditory modalities. Four of the experiments made use of a paradigm known as delayed match to sample (DMS) (Glick, Goldfarb, & Jarvik, 1969), which is commonly used to examine working memory in monkeys (e.g., Mishkin & Manning, 1978). This paradigm involves the presentation of a stimulus or series of stimuli to the subject (the sample stimulus), a delay of some specified time, and the presentation of one or more stimuli (the choice stimuli). The subject's task is to indicate which, if any, of the choice stimuli are the same as the sample stimulus. Another common paradigm used in working-memory experiments is the *n*-back task in which subjects are presented with a series of stimuli, often letters, and required to respond when a stimulus is repeated after a specified number of intervening stimuli.

Episodic Memory

Episodic memory is defined as memory for specific events that have occurred in a person's experience, and thus it is associated with a particular time, place, and context (Tulving, 1983). This distinguishes it from semantic memory, which also involves the retrieval of past knowledge, but the source of that knowledge is not recalled. (See Table 12.1E.) An example of episodic memory would be to remember having dinner at a particular restaurant in Paris on one's 30th birthday, whereas an example of semantic memory would be the knowledge that Paris is the capital of France. In the first case, specific context of the event can be recalled; in the second case, the person cannot recall specifically how this fact was learned, only that this fact is part of his or her general knowledge of the world. The experiments on episodic memory can be subdivided into tasks that measure encoding, or the processing of stimuli that enables them to be stored in memory, and those that measure retrieval of items from memory stores. Retrieval can be further divided into recall, or retrieval in the absence of the learned items, and recognition, or retrieval when the learned items are presented again to the subjects along with new items. Four experiments have examined encoding into episodic memory: two that used verbal material (Kapur et al., 1996; Shallice et al., 1994), one that examined encoding of faces (Haxby et al., 1996), and one that measured brain activity during the encoding of pictures of objects (Owen, Milner, Petrides, & Evans, 1996). Many more have measured brain activity during retrieval, including some that have measured memory using recall (Andreasen, O'Leary, Cizadlo, et al., 1995; Becker et al., 1994; Blaxton, Bookheimer, et al., 1996; Buckner, Raichle, Miezin, & Petersen, 1996; Buckner, Petersen, et al., 1995; Cabeza et al., 1997; Fiez et al., 1996; Grasby et al., 1993, 1994; Nyberg, McIntosh, Cabeza, & Habib et al., 1996; Petrides, Alivastos, Evans, & Meyer, 1993; Petrides, Alivisatos, & Evans, 1995; Roland & Gulyas, 1995; Schacter et al., 1996), and some that have used recognition paradigms (Andreasen, O'Leary, Arndt, et al., 1995; Andreasen et al., 1996; Cabeza et al., 1997; Haxby et al., 1996; Kapur et al., 1995; Moscovitch, Kapur, Kohler, & Houle, 1995; Nyberg et al., 1995; Nyberg, McIntosh, Cabeza, Habib, et al., 1996; Roland & Gulyas, 1995; Rugg, Fletcher, Frith, Frackowiak, & Dolan, 1996; Tulving, Kapur, Markowitsch, et al., 1994; Tulving, Markowitsch, Craik, Habib, & Houle, 1996). These experiments have examined memory for both verbal and nonverbal material, including faces, patterns, and spatial locations, and have utilized both the visual and auditory modalities.

Semantic Memory Retrieval

Consistent with the definition given previously, tests of semantic processing or retrieval from semantic memory involve retrieving knowledge, usually about an object or word, that is not connected with a particular episode in an individual's experience. These tasks include retrieving information about an object, such as its color (Martin, Haxby, Lalonde, Wiggs, & Ungerleider, 1995), viewing objects from different semantic categories (Martin, Wiggs, Ungerleider, & Haxby, 1996), deciding if a word represents a living entity (Jennings, McIntosh, Kapur, Tulving, & Houle, 1997; Kapur et al., 1994), generating words when given a category, initial letter, or associated word (Andreasen, O'Leary, Cizadlo, et al., 1995; Buckner, Raichle, & Petersen, 1995; Frith, Friston, Liddle, & Frackowiak, 1991; Petersen, Fox, Posner, Mintun, & Raichle, 1989; Wise et al., 1991), and detecting when noun–adjective pairs correspond to a specified category (Demonet et al., 1992). (See Table 12.1F.)

Language Tasks

Language tasks consist primarily of the processing of single words (i.e., reading words silently) (Bookheimer, Zeffiro, Blaxton, Gaillard, & Theodore, 1995; Petersen, Fox, Snyder, & Raichle, 1990; Price et al., 1994), or deciding if a letter string is a word or not (lexical decision; Price et al., 1994). One experiment involved bilingual subjects and tested various aspects of word processing (e.g., producing rhymes or synonyms) in both their primary and secondary languages (Klein, Milner, Zatorre, Meyer, & Evans, 1995). The experiment by Zatorre, Meyer, Gjedde, and Evans (1996) is included in this category because the primary purpose of this experiment was to examine how subjects process phonetic information contained in speech and utilized words as stimuli. Only one experiment involved language processing at the level of sentences and consisted of deciding whether sentences were semantically correct (Bottini et al., 1994). Because all these language tasks require retrieval of information from semantic memory, at least to some extent, maxima from these studies have been grouped with those from studies of semantic memory in the tables and figures. (See Table 12.1G.)

Theory of Mind

Finally, two experiments explore the brain areas that are active during so-called "theory of mind" tasks. (See Table 12.1H.) Theory of mind refers to the ability of an individual to infer what another individual might think or how another might act in certain situations. For example, in the study by Goel, Grafman, Sadato, and Hallett (1995), subjects were asked to view unfamiliar objects and decide how their function might be judged by someone alive during the time of Christopher Columbus. The control task asked subjects to decide for themselves what the function of the object might be. In the other experiment (Fletcher et al., 1995), scenarios or stories were presented to the subjects who were then asked to determine how and why individuals in the story acted the way that they did. The only way to answer these questions correctly would be for the subject to infer what the person in the story was thinking (Baron-Cohen, Leslie, & Frith, 1985).

PREFRONTAL ACTIVATIONS REPORTED
IN THE NEUROIMAGING LITERATURE

The activations in frontal cortex reviewed here were derived using the most common method of data analysis in PET experiments: subtracting images obtained during a control condition, usually constructed to control for the sensory and motor aspects of the task, from those obtained during the task of interest. These comparisons result in areas of increased rCBF, or activation, revealing those areas that participate in task performance. To compare results across studies, I have focused here on the reported maxima of activation from the listed papers (i.e., the voxel showing the largest magnitude of rCBF increase within a larger area of activation). This approach necessarily ignores at least two important aspects of brain functioning (see section "Limitations of this Analysis") but allows a preliminary examination of regional similarities and differences of cognitive representations among the various parts of prefrontal cortex. Each reported maximum of activation in prefrontal cortex was first categorized, using the reported coordinates, by Brodmann's area according to the estimated location of each BA in the Talairach and Tournoux (1988) atlas. It is often difficult to assign Brodmann's areas using this atlas, which in some cases is inconsistent depending on which orientation one considers (e.g., coronal or axial). For the purposes of this analysis, the coronal orientation was used in assigning the BA, but if the area was ambiguous on this orientation, the coordinates were checked on the saggital and axial orientations as well. Thus, in some cases Brodmann's area reported here will differ from that reported in the original reference. These individual maxima are listed in Tables 12.2–12.8 for each of Brodmann's areas and are grouped by cognitive function. Figures 12.1–12.7 show the general locations of these maxima, again grouping by function, although in some cases maxima in similar locations and representing the same cognitive process are shown as one locus in the figures. Readers should be aware that these assignments of activation loci to Brodmann's areas are somewhat arbitrary and are to be considered approximations of the actual locations, given that they are based on group data without actual knowledge of where these regions are in individual brains.

BA 11 lies completely on the ventral surface of the frontal lobes, and in the Talairach and Tournoux (1988) atlas includes areas 13 and 14 of Pandya and Yeterian (1996). The cognitive function represented most frequently in this area is episodic retrieval, involving both recognition and recall (Table 12.2). All the maxima from BA 11 are plotted in Figure 12.1, in which it can be seen that episodic retrieval is primarily represented in the right hemisphere. In contrast, retrieval from semantic memory is almost exclusively represented in the left hemisphere, regardless of whether the semantic information retrieved is about words or objects. Activations during working memory, like those from episodic retrieval, are found mainly in the right hemisphere, whereas classical conditioning and perception of faces or objects is bilaterally represented. There were no activations from language, motor memory, verbal working memory, or attention tasks in BA 11.

Dorsal and lateral to BA 11 is the region referred to as BA 47 (or 47/12 in the terminology of Pandya & Yeterian, 1996). Most of the cognitive functions are represented in BA 47 (Table 12.3 and Figure 12.2), with the notable exceptions of verbal working memory and perception. This region of ventral prefrontal cortex has more activations from semantic processing and language tasks than any other region, all but one of which are found in the left hemisphere. In addition, there is one reported area of activation from an episodic encoding task that also is seen in left BA 47. Similar to the pattern seen in BA 11, episodic retrieval, involving both recall and recognition, is represented mainly

TABLE 12.2. rCBF Activations in Brodmann's Area 11

Task	Reference	X	Y	Z
	Episodic memory			
Verbal episodic retrieval	Blaxton, Bookheimer, et al. (1996; 2)	−16	54	−12
Verbal episodic retrieval	Kapur et al. (1995)	−20	40	−8
Verbal episodic retrieval	Andreasen, O'Leary, Cizaldo, et al. (1995; 1)	1	46	−18[a]
Verbal episodic retrieval	Schacter et al. (1996)	5	35	−12[a]
Verbal episodic retrieval	Petrides (1995; 2)	20	48	−8
Verbal episodic retrieval	Kapur et al. (1995)	18	42	−8
Nonverbal episodic retrieval	Andreasen et al. (1996)	13	28	−25
Nonverbal episodic retrieval	Andreasen et al. (1996)	2	35	−14[a]
	Semantic retrieval and language			
Semantic retrieval	Andreasen, O'Leary, Cizaldo, et al. (1995; 2)	−34	45	−13
Semantic retrieval	Martin et al. (1995; 1)	−24	32	−8[b]
Semantic retrieval	Jennings et al. (1997)	−24	28	−8[b]
Semantic retrieval	Andreasen O'Leary, Cizaldo, et al. (1995; 2)	18	18	−21
	Motor memory and classical conditioning			
Eyeblink conditioning	Blaxton, Zeffiro, et al. (1996)	−24	28	−24
Eyeblink conditioning	Blaxton, Zeffiro, et al. (1996)	12	54	−16
Eyeblink conditioning	Blaxton, Zeffiro, et al. (1996)	8	42	−12
	Working memory			
Nonverbal visual WM	Gold et al. (1996; 1)	20	50	−12
Nonverbal visual WM	Gold et al. (1996; 1)	40	46	−8
Nonverbal visual WM	Courtney et al. (1996)	16	38	−8
Nonverbal auditory WM	Zatorre et al. (1994)	38	51	−9
	Perception			
Face processing	Sergent et al. (1992)	−3	25	−17
Object processing	Kosslyn et al. (1994; 2)	−22	40	−8
Face processing	Haxby et al. (1994)	24	34	−12[c]
Face processing	Haxby et al. (1995; 1)	26	33	−8[c]

Note. X, Y, Z, coordinates from the Talairach and Tournoux (1988) atlas. Brief descriptions of tasks involved in each experiment can be found in Table 12.1.
[a] Maxima with the same letters are plotted as one area in Figure 12.1.

in the right hemisphere. Activations during attention tasks and motor or conditioning tasks are found only in the right hemisphere in this region of prefrontal cortex. There are two interesting clusters of activations in BA 47, one in the right hemisphere consisting mainly of episodic retrieval and procedural memory (Figure 12.2, coronal section +20 mm), and one in the left hemisphere comprised of semantic retrieval and episodic encoding (Figure 12.2, coronal section +28 mm).

The areas of activation in BA 45 are shown in Table 12.4 and Figure 12.3. A variety of functions are represented in this area, both verbal and nonverbal, although not verbal working memory. Episodic retrieval and perception are both particularly prominent in BA 45. Like areas 11 and 47, episodic encoding and semantic processing are represented

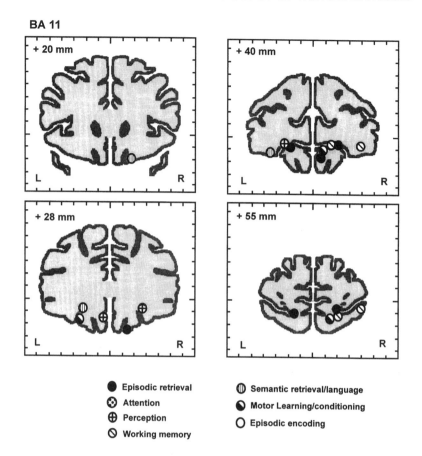

FIGURE 12.1. Maxima of rCBF activations in Brodmann's area 11 shown on coronal sections of the brain from the atlas of Talairach and Tournoux (1988). The following three conventions apply in all figures: (1) The numbers in the top left-hand corner of each section refer to the position, in millimeters, of the section anterior to the anterior commissure (the coronal origin of the atlas). (2) "L" refers to the left hemisphere and "R" to the right hemisphere. (3) The tic marks on the grids are in 10-mm intervals; slightly larger tic marks indicate the origins of the axial and sagittal planes. Coordinates for the plotted activations can be found in Table 12.2.

mainly in the left hemisphere, and episodic retrieval is found mainly in the right hemisphere. Unlike areas 11 and 47, in which activations from recognition and recall were found in roughly equal numbers, the activations from episodic retrieval in BA 45 are mainly from recognition tasks. The most striking thing about cognitive representation in BA 45 is the large number of perceptual activations, more than in any other area of prefrontal cortex. These include both visual and auditory modalities and are seen bilaterally. All but one of the maxima reported from studies of auditory perception and imagery fall in this general area of prefrontal cortex. Clusters of activity in BA 45 are found in the right hemisphere involving episodic retrieval and perception (Figure 12.3, coronal section +20 mm), and in the left hemisphere involving episodic encoding and perception (Figure 12.3, coronal section +35 mm).

Area 46 (Table 12.5 and Figure 12.4) is one of the two prefrontal regions where working memory is most heavily represented in terms of rCBF activations (the other

TABLE 12.3. rCBF Activations in Brodmann's Area 47

Task	Reference	X	Y	Z
	Episodic memory			
Verbal episodic retrieval	Blaxton, Bookheimer, et al. (1996; 1)	−40	28	−4
Episodic encoding	Haxby et al. (1995; 1)	−33	27	−12
Verbal episodic retrieval	Andreasen, O'Leary, Arndt, et al. (1995)	35	19	−5
Verbal episodic retrieval	Shallice et al. (1994; 2)	26	18	0[a]
Verbal episodic retrieval	Cabeza et al. (1997; 1 & 2)	28	22	0[a]
Nonverbal episodic retrieval	Owen et al. (1996)	25	22	−5[a]
	Semantic retrieval and language			
Semantic retrieval	Petersen et al. (1989)	−30	33	−6[b]
Semantic retrieval	Kapur et al. (1994)	−28	34	−4[b]
Semantic retrieval	Buckner, Raichle, & Petersen (1995; 1 & 2)	−49	29	−2
Semantic retrieval	Andreasen, O'Leary, Cizaldo, et al. (1995; 2)	−32	23	−2
Semantic retrieval	Martin et al. (1995; 2)	−32	34	0[c]
Language	Price et al. (1994; 2)	−38	28	−16[d]
Language	Bookheimer et al. (1995)	−40	26	−8[d]
Language	Klein et al. (1995)	−42	39	−6
Language	Zatorre, Meyer, et al. (1996)	−56	20	−5
Language	Bottini et al. (1994)	−38	28	0[c]
Language	Bottini et al. (1994)	34	24	−8
	Motor memory and classical conditioning			
Eyeblink conditioning	Blaxton, Zeffiro, et al. (1996)	32	20	−16
Shock–tone conditioning	Hugdahl et al. (1995)	34	29	−16
Motor sequence learning	Jenkins et al. (1994)	36	20	4
	Working memory			
Nonverbal visual WM	Gold et al. (1996; 1 & 2)	−44	42	−4
Nonverbal visual WM	Gold et al. (1996; 1 & 2)	−50	16	0
Nonverbal visual WM	Jonides et al. (1993)	35	19	−2[e]
Nonverbal visual WM	Smith et al. (1995)	32	18	−1[e]
	Attention			
Sustained attention	Paus et al. (1997)	36	22	−11
Selective attention	Bench et al. (1993)	32	28	−4

Note. X, Y, Z, coordinates from the Talairach and Tournoux (1988) atlas. Brief descriptions of tasks involved in each experiment can be found in Table 12.1.
[a]Maxima with the same letters are plotted as one area in Figure 12.2.

being BA 9). There are numerous activations from both verbal and nonverbal working-memory tasks in both hemispheres, although verbal working memory is somewhat more heavily weighted in the left hemisphere (four out of six maxima) and nonverbal working memory activations occur more frequently in the right hemisphere (four maxima out of five). Thus BA 46 marks the beginning of activations from tasks of verbal working memory (i.e., moving ventrally up through prefrontal cortex). In addition, area 46 is one of two regions to have an activation from spatial processing tasks, which is seen in the right hemisphere. Like the other prefrontal regions examined so far, semantic processing is represented in left hemisphere BA 46, as is episodic encoding, whereas activations

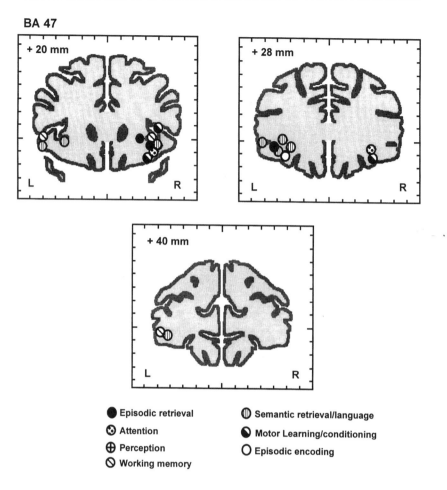

FIGURE 12.2. Maxima of rCBF activations in Brodmann's area 47 shown on coronal sections of the brain from the atlas of Talairach and Tournoux (1988). Coordinates for the plotted activations can be found in Table 12.3.

during episodic retrieval are mainly right hemispheric and attentional maxima are found only in the right hemisphere.

BA 10 is a large region in anterior prefrontal cortex that extends from the ventral surface of the frontal pole to just dorsal of BA 46. The most heavily represented function in BA 10 (Table 12.6 and Figure 12.5) by far is episodic retrieval, particularly retrieval of verbal information and mostly involving recall rather than recognition. A number of activations during classical conditioning, mostly in the right hemisphere, also are found this region, similar to the number seen in BAs 11 and 47. Like the other regions of prefrontal cortex surveyed so far, semantic processing primarily activates the left hemisphere, and rCBF increases during verbal episodic retrieval are seen primarily in the right hemisphere. Activations from tasks of nonverbal retrieval are roughly equivalent in the two hemispheres, although those in the right hemisphere were all from recognition tasks. There are several maxima from working-memory and perception experiments in BA 10 but none from attentional or encoding tasks.

TABLE 12.4. rCBF Activations in Brodmann's Area 45

Task	Reference	X	Y	Z
	Episodic memory			
Verbal episodic retrieval	Petrides et al. (1995; 1)	−23	25	3
Episodic encoding	Kapur et al. (1996)	−48	36	0
Episodic encoding	Shallice et al. (1994; 1)	−31	34	8
Verbal episodic retrieval	Nyberg, Cabeza, Tulving (1996; 1)	34	28	4[a]
Verbal episodic retrieval	Cabeza et al. (1997; 1)	24	24	8
Verbal episodic retrieval	Nyberg et al. (1995)	28	30	8[a]
Verbal episodic retrieval	Kapur et al. (1995)	42	20	20[b]
Verbal episodic retrieval	Blaxton, Bookheimer, et al. (1996; 2)	38	24	24[c]
Nonverbal episodic retrieval	Haxby et al. (1996; 2)	36	22	20[b]
Nonverbal episodic retrieval	Moscovitch et al. (1995)	36	22	24[c]
	Semantic retrieval and language			
Semantic retrieval	Jennings et al. (1997)	−34	28	4
Semantic retrieval	Buckner, Raichle, & Petersen (1995; 1 & 2)	−37	20	11
Semantic retrieval	Martin et al. (1996; 2)	−26	28	16
Semantic retrieval	Petersen et al. (1989)	−42	24	20[d]
Language	Klein et al. (1995)	−44	27	12
Language	Price et al. (1994; 1)	−50	22	20[d]
Semantic retrieval	Martin et al. (1996; 1)	28	28	4
	Motor memory and classical conditioning			
Motor sequence retrieval	Rauch et al. (1995)	−41	28	8
Motor sequence learning	Hazeltine et al. (1997)	40	19	7[e]
Eye blink conditioning	Blaxton, Zeffiro, et al. (1996)	44	20	8[e]
	Working memory			
Nonverbal visual WM	Haxby et al. (1995; 2)	−44	20	8
Nonverbal auditory WM	Zatorre et al. (1994)	−31	22	8
Nonverbal auditory WM	Zatorre et al. (1994)	38	20	5
	Perception			
Face processing	Grady et al. (1996)	−46	32	4
Facial emotion discrimination	George et al. (1993; 1)	−44	20	16
Object processing	Kosslyn et al. (1993; 1)	−31	36	8
Object processing	Schacter et al. (1995)	−40	26	16
Auditory processing/imagery	Zatorre, Halpern, et al. (1996)	−35	24	22
Face processing	Haxby et al. (1995; 1)	42	26	20[f]
Facial emotion discrimination	George et al. (1993; 1)	38	26	20[f]
Object processing	Schacter et al. (1995)	32	22	20[g]
Auditory processing	Holcomb et al. (in press)	28	22	4
Auditory processing	Zatorre et al. (1992)	46	32	9
Auditory proc/imagery	Zatorre, Halpern, et al. (1996)	36	24	18[g]
	Attention			
Sustained attention	Paus et al. (1997)	−34	25	9
Selective attention	George (1994)	−44	32	8
Sustained attention	Paus et al. (1997)	36	27	12

Note. X, Y, Z, coordinates from the Talairach and Tournoux (1988) atlas. Brief descriptions of tasks involved in each experiment can be found in Table 12.1.
[a]Maxima with the same letters are plotted as one area in Figure 12.3.

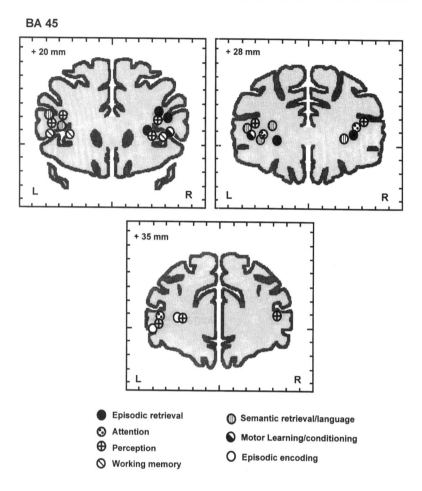

FIGURE 12.3. Maxima of rCBF activations in Brodmann's area 45 shown on coronal sections of the brain from the atlas of Talairach and Tournoux (1988). Coordinates for the plotted activations can be found in Table 12.4.

Activated areas found in BA 9 (Table 12.7 and Figure 12.6) are primarily from tests of episodic retrieval, motor tasks, and working memory. Like BA 10, most of the episodic-retrieval activations came from tests of verbal recall, and most are in the right hemisphere. In the case of the working-memory activations, there are relatively equal numbers in the two hemispheres for both verbal and nonverbal tasks, although there are slightly more nonverbal working-memory areas in the left hemisphere than the right. Semantic processing is again represented in the left hemisphere, although there are fewer maxima for semantic processing in BA 9 than in more ventral areas of prefrontal cortex. Bilateral areas of activation from an experiment on visual imagery are found in BA 9 that are slightly dorsal to those areas participating in auditory imagery (see Table 12.4). Two maxima, both in the left hemisphere, come from studies of spatial processing, making BA 9, along with BA 46, one of two regions of prefrontal cortex with increased activity during perception of spatial information.

The last and most dorsal portion of prefrontal cortex is BA 8. The cognitive processes represented in BA 8 are mainly episodic retrieval (predominantly recall), object process-

TABLE 12.5. rCBF Activations in Brodmann's Area 46

Task	Reference	X	Y	Z
	Episodic memory			
Verbal episodic retrieval	Schacter et al. (1996)	−31	43	8
Nonverbal episodic retrieval	Tulving et al. (1996)	−38	26	24
Episodic encoding	Haxby et al. (1996; 1)	−26	42	16
Episodic encoding	Owen et al. (1996)	−38	46	29
Verbal episodic retrieval	Becker et al. (1994)	40	42	8
Verbal episodic retrieval	Andreasen, O'Leary, Arndt, et al. (1995)	30	44	10[a]
Verbal episodic retrieval	Tulving, Kapur, Markowitsch, et al. (1994)	32	44	12[a]
Verbal episodic retrieval	Blaxton, Bookheimer, et al. (1996; 1)	34	42	20[b]
Verbal episodic retrieval	Rugg et al. (1996)	38	40	20[b]
	Semantic retrieval and language			
Semantic retrieval	Buckner, Raichle, & Petersen (1995; 1)	−39	43	8
Semantic retrieval	Kapur et al. (1994)	−38	38	16
Semantic retrieval	Frith et al. (1991)	−43	29	20[c]
Semantic retrieval	Martin et al. (1995; 1)	−38	30	20[c]
	Motor memory and classical conditioning			
Motor sequence learning	Jenkins et al. (1994)	40	38	16
	Working memory			
Verbal visual WM	Schumacher et al. (1996; 1)	−44	44	18
Verbal auditory WM	Petrides, Alivastos, Meyer, & Evans (1993; 2)	−32	44	18[d]
Verbal auditory WM	Petrides, Alivastos, Meyer, & Evans (1993; 1)	−35	42	22[d]
Verbal auditory WM	Schumacher et al. (1996; 2)	−46	26	25
Nonverbal visual WM	Petrides, Alivastos, Evans, & Meyer (1993; 1)	−35	30	22
Verbal auditory WM	Petrides, Alivastos, Meyer, & Evans (1993; 1)	38	39	26[e]
Verbal auditory WM	Petrides, Alivastos, Meyer, & Evans (1993; 2)	40	34	29[e]
Nonverbal visual WM	Gold et al. (1996; 1)	38	30	20[f]
Nonverbal visual WM	Petrides, Alivastos, Evans, & Meyer (1993; 1)	35	32	21
Nonverbal visual WM	Smith et al. (1995)	40	36	22[e]
Nonverbal visual WM	Courtney et al. (1996)	36	26	24[f]
	Perception			
Face processing	Haxby et al. (1995; 1)	42	41	8
Face processing	Grady et al. (1996)	36	38	24[g]
Spatial processing	Parsons (1995)	36	32	26[g]
	Attention			
Divided attention	Corbetta et al. (1991)	45	37	12
Selective attention	Bench et al. (1993)	26	40	16

Note. X, Y, Z, coordinates from the Talairach and Tournoux (1988) atlas. Brief descriptions of tasks involved in each experiment can be found in Table 12.1.
[a]Maxima with the same letters are plotted as one area in Figure 12.4.

ing, and language (Table 12.8 and Figure 12.7). Semantic processing and language provided the majority of the maxima in the left hemisphere, whereas most of the activated areas in the right hemisphere came from episodic-retrieval tasks, with two maxima each from attention and perception experiments. Most notably, BA 8 was the only area of prefrontal cortex to show activations during the two theory-of-mind experiments, and these maxima were in essentially the same location in the medial portion of BA 8. This

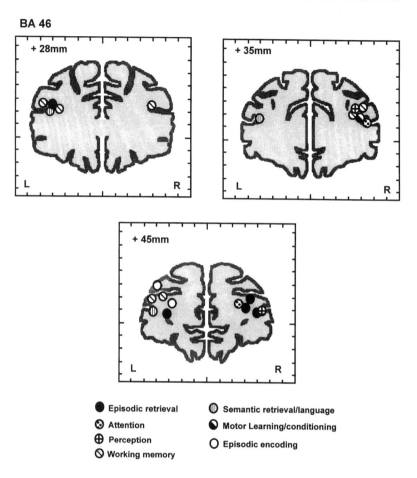

FIGURE 12.4. Maxima of rCBF activations in Brodmann's area 46 shown on coronal sections of the brain from the atlas of Talairach and Tournoux (1988). Coordinates for the plotted activations can be found in Table 12.5.

region of cortex has no activations from tasks of episodic encoding or procedural memory.

SUMMARY OF PREFRONTAL ACTIVATIONS

Table 12.9 provides a summary of the localization and lateralization of each of the cognitive processes in prefrontal cortex. Several interesting conclusions can be drawn from this survey of the neuroimaging literature to date. The first item of interest is that although most of the cognitive functions discussed here are represented widely throughout prefrontal cortex, there are regions where specific functions appear to be concentrated more heavily. For example, all the prefrontal regions have at least several reported maxima from experiments involving episodic retrieval. Nevertheless, activity during episodic retrieval occurs most frequently in BA 10 (25 maxima), followed by areas 9 and 8. Episodic retrieval can be further broken down by whether information was retrieved via recall, represented mostly in BA 10 and dorsal areas 9 and 8, or retrieved via

TABLE 12.6. rCBF Activations in Brodmann's Area 10

Task	Reference	X	Y	Z
	Episodic memory			
Verbal episodic retrieval	Andreasen, O'Leary, Arndt, et al. (1995)	−25	53	−14
Verbal episodic retrieval	Grasby et al. (1994)	−24	48	−8
Verbal episodic retrieval	Becker et al. (1994)	−34	46	−4[a]
Verbal episodic retrieval	Grasby et al. (1993)	−34	46	0[a]
Verbal episodic retrieval	Rugg (1996)	−32	52	0[b]
Verbal episodic retrieval	Blaxton, Bookheimer, et al. (1996; 1)	−30	58	4[b]
Verbal episodic retrieval	Blaxton, Bookheimer, et al. (1996; 2)	−18	56	16[c]
Nonverbal episodic retrieval	Tulving et al. (1996)	−28	52	8[b]
Nonverbal episodic retrieval	Roland & Gulyas (1995; 1)	−18	60	19[c]
Verbal episodic retrieval	Andreasen, O'Leary, Arndt, et al. (1995)	26	48	−15
Verbal episodic retrieval	Buckner et al. (1996)	29	59	−8[d]
Verbal episodic retrieval	Blaxton, Bookheimer, et al. (1996; 1)	8	54	−4
Verbal episodic retrieval	Blaxton, Bookheimer, et al. (1996; 1)	36	44	−4
Verbal episodic retrieval	Becker et al. (1994)	22	54	−4[d]
Verbal episodic retrieval	Grasby et al. (1993)	24	52	0[d]
Verbal episodic retrieval	Blaxton, Bookheimer, et al. (1996; 2)	22	52	0[d]
Verbal episodic retrieval	Tulving, Kapur, Markowitsch, et al. (1994)	30	50	0[e]
Verbal episodic retrieval	Grasby et al. (1994)	30	48	4[f]
Verbal episodic retrieval	Buckner, Petersen, et al. (1995)	32	50	6[e]
Verbal episodic retrieval	Schacter et al. (1996)	30	46	8[f]
Verbal episodic retrieval	Rugg et al. (1996)	40	50	8
Verbal episodic retrieval	Buckner et al. (1996)	27	49	16
Nonverbal episodic retrieval	Andreasen et al. (1996)	24	57	−9
Nonverbal episodic retrieval	Haxby (1996; 2)	34	54	4[e]
Nonverbal episodic retrieval	Roland & Guylas (1995; 2)	3	59	5
	Semantic retrieval and language			
Semantic retrieval	Buckner, Raichle, & Petersen (1995; 1)	−33	49	−6[g]
Semantic retrieval	Martin et al. (1995; 2)	−34	48	16
Language	Bottini et al. (1994)	−2	42	−8
Language	Klein et al. (1995)	−29	48	−3[g]
Language	Petersen et al. (1990)	−26	41	0
Language	Bottini et al. (1994)	−12	54	20
Semantic retrieval	Jennings et al. (1997)	40	48	12
	Motor memory and classical conditioning			
Eyeblink conditioning	Blaxton, Zeffiro, et al. (1996)	−24	58	0
Motor sequence learning	Jenkins et al. (1994)	−30	46	−4
Shock–tone conditioning	Hugdahl et al. (1995)	26	63	−12
Eyeblink conditioning	Blaxton, Zeffiro, et al. (1996)	14	60	−4
Eyeblink conditioning	Blaxton, Zeffiro, et al. (1996)	32	54	0[h]
Motor sequence learning	Jenkins et al. (1994)	28	50	−4[h]
	Working memory			
Nonverbal visual WM	Gold et al. (1996; 1 & 2)	−26	52	−8
Nonverbal visual WM	Haxby et al. (1995; 2)	−31	50	12[i]
Nonverbal visual WM	Gold et al. (1996; 1)	−32	52	8[i]
Verbal auditory WM	Petrides, Alivastos, Meyer, & Evans (1993; 2)	25	58	8
Nonverbal visual WM	Gold et al. (1996; 1)	34	54	4
	Perception			
Auditory processing/imagery	Zatorre, Halpern, et al. (1996)	−29	46	3[j]
Object processing	Kosslyn et al. (1995; 1)	−33	44	4[j]
Object processing	Kosslyn et al. (1994; 1)	24	58	0[k]
Object processing	Kosslyn et al. (1995; 3)	35	57	4[k]

Note. X, Y, Z, coordinates from the Talairach and Tournoux (1988) atlas. Brief descriptions of tasks involved in each experiment can be found in Table 12.1.
[a]Maxima with the same letters are plotted as one area in Figure 12.5.

recognition, seen primarily in BAs 11, 45, and 47. This distribution suggests that recall preferentially activates dorsal and anterior portions of prefrontal cortex, whereas recognition is mediated preferentially by ventromedial and ventrolateral prefrontal cortex. This finding is consistent with the monkey literature, which has indicated a prominent role of ventral prefrontal cortex in recognition memory. The dorsal prefrontal involvement might be due to a greater need for monitoring and strategic search during recall, both of which are functions ascribed to dorsal frontal cortex (Petrides, 1994).

Other types of memory also have differential distributions in prefrontal cortex. Working memory preferentially activates BAs 46 and 9 in mid-dorsolateral prefrontal cortex. This is particularly true of verbal working memory, which, except for one area of activation in BA 10, is represented entirely in these two areas of prefrontal cortex. Similar to the relation between recognition and ventral prefrontal cortex, this indicates a considerable degree of homology with the results from nonhuman primate studies, which have long implicated areas 46 and 9 in working memory. In contrast, retrieval from semantic memory leads to increased activity most frequently in ventrolateral and ventromedial cortex. Thus, the different distributions of activity among prefrontal regions

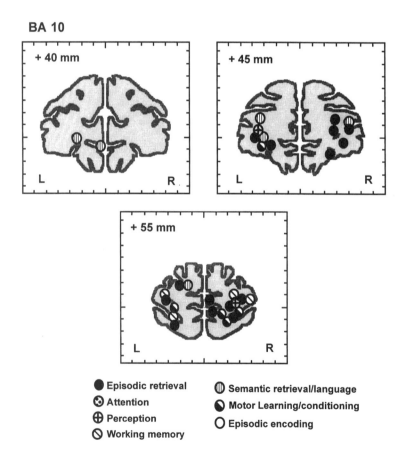

FIGURE 12.5. Maxima of rCBF activations in Brodmann's area 10 shown on coronal sections of the brain from the atlas of Talairach and Tournoux (1988). Coordinates for the plotted activations can be found in Table 12.6.

TABLE 12.7. rCBF Activations in Brodmann's Area 9

Task	Reference	X	Y	Z
Episodic memory				
Verbal episodic retrieval	Petrides (1995; 1)	−40	49	26[a]
Verbal episodic retrieval	Fiez et al. (1996)	−37	45	30[a]
Verbal episodic retrieval	Becker et al. (1994)	−28	16	32
Nonverbal episodic retrieval	Tulving et al. (1996)	−38	24	28
Nonverbal episodic retrieval	Nyberg, Cabeza, & Tulving (1996; 2)	−30	30	40
Episodic encoding	Haxby et al. (1996; 1)	−20	36	32
Verbal episodic retrieval	Blaxton, Bookheimer, et al. (1996a; 1 & 2)	40	22	24[b]
Verbal episodic retrieval	Buckner et al. (1996)	39	23	28[b]
Verbal episodic retrieval	Petrides (1995; 1)	36	51	33
Verbal episodic retrieval	Fiez et al. (1996)	33	33	34
Verbal episodic retrieval	Buckner, Peterson, et al. (1995)	30	29	34
Verbal episodic retrieval	Petrides (1995; 2)	48	30	35
Verbal episodic retrieval	Petrides (1995; 1)	43	32	38
Nonverbal episodic retrieval	Roland & Gulyas (1995; 1)	24	52	33
Semantic retrieval and language				
Semantic retrieval	Martin et al. (1995; 1)	−42	18	28[c]
Language	Klein et al. (1995)	−48	22	26
Language	Klein et al. (1995)	−44	15	30[c]
Semantic retrieval	Jennings et al. (1997)	42	30	28
Motor memory and classical conditioning				
Motor sequence learning	Jenkins et al. (1994)	−40	20	28
Motor sequence retrieval	Grafton et al. (1994)	−14	43	30
Motor sequence learning	Jenkins et al. (1994)	36	32	28[d]
Motor sequence retrieval	Deiber et al. (1991; 1)	38	34	28[d]
Shock–tone conditioning	Hugdahl et al. (1995)	4	52	32
Working memory				
Verbal auditory WM	Petrides, Alivastos, Meyer, & Evans (1993; 1)	−40	32	30[e]
Verbal auditory WM	Petrides Alivastos, Meyer, & Evans (1993; 2)	−35	24	31[f]
Nonverbal visual WM	Gold et al. (1996; 2)	−8	46	24
Nonverbal visual WM	Gold et al. (1996; 1)	−42	20	28[f]
Nonverbal auditory/motor WM	Deiber et al. (1991; 2)	−34	32	28[e]
Nonverbal visual WM	Gold et al. (1996; 1 & 2)	−34	24	28[f]
Nonverbal auditory WM	Zatorre et al. (1994)	−36	29	30
Verbal auditory WM	Petrides, Alivastos, Meyer, & Evans (1993; 2)	27	29	36
Nonverbal visual WM	Gold et al. (1996; 1)	42	24	28
Nonverbal auditory/motor WM	Deiber et al. (1991; 2)	34	36	28[g]
Nonverbal auditory WM	Zatorre et al. (1994)	36	36	31[g]
Perception				
Face processing	Grady et al. (1996)	−48	20	28
Object imagery	Kosslyn et al. (1993; 2)	−40	14	28
Spatial processing	George et al. (1993; 2)	−38	36	28[h]
Spatial processing	Parsons et al. (1995)	−45	36	30[h]
Object processing	Kosslyn et al. (1995; 1)	48	23	32[i]
Object imagery	Kosslyn et al. (1993; 2)	48	20	28[i]
Object processing	Kosslyn et al. (1994; 2)	35	15	28

Note. X, Y, Z, coordinates from the Talairach and Tournoux (1988) atlas. Brief descriptions of tasks involved in each experiment can be found in Table 12.1.
[a]Maxima with the same letters are plotted as one area in Figure 12.6.

seen in the various memory functions lend support to the prevailing notion that these types of memory are indeed distinct from one another (Schacter & Tulving, 1994).

Other processes besides memory also appear to be distributed unevenly throughout prefrontal cortex. Like semantic retrieval, language is represented mainly in ventrolateral prefrontal cortex, although some activity during language tasks also is seen in BA 8. Both object perception and auditory processing are represented primarily in BA 45, which is perhaps not surprising given that ventrolateral prefrontal cortex receives projections from both visual and auditory association cortex in the monkey (see Pandya & Yeterian, 1996, for a review). The heavy representation of both perception and recognition memory in BA 45 indicates a close relation between these two functions and may suggest that this area works in conjunction with perceptual areas in posterior cortex to facilitate the match between incoming stimuli and stored representations. In addition, there is a trend for visuospatial processing to involve more dorsal areas of prefrontal cortex than face perception (see Table 12.9B). This is consistent with monkey experiments showing anatomical and functional connections between ventral object processing regions in occipitotemporal cortex and ventral frontal cortex and between dorsal spatial processing

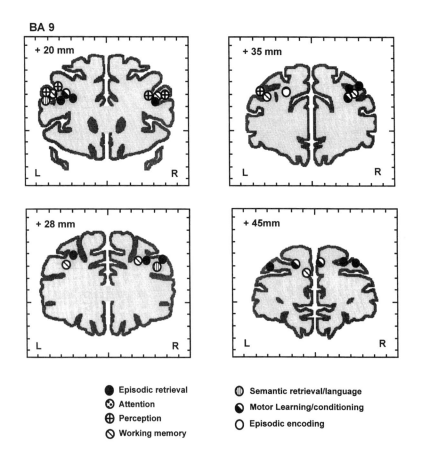

FIGURE 12.6. Maxima of rCBF activations in Brodmann's area 9 shown on coronal sections of the brain from the atlas of Talairach and Tournoux (1988). Coordinates for the plotted activations can be found in Table 12.7.

TABLE 12.8. rCBF Activations in Brodmann's Area 8

Task	Reference	X	Y	Z
	Episodic memory			
Verbal episodic retrieval	Buckner, Petersen, et al. (1995)	−36	19	40[a]
Nonverbal episodic retrieval	Roland & Gulyas (1995; 1)	−39	18	38[a]
Nonverbal episodic retrieval	Petrides, Alivastos, Evans, & Meyer (1993; 2)	−16	24	39
Verbal episodic retrieval	Kapur et al. (1995)	22	22	36
Verbal episodic retrieval	Andreasen, O'Leary, Arndt, et al. (1995)	37	12	39[b]
Verbal episodic retrieval	Buckner, Petersen, et al. (1995)	44	18	39
Verbal episodic retrieval	Blaxton, Bookheimer, et al. (1996; 1)	38	10	40[b]
Verbal episodic retrieval	Buckner, Petersen, et al. (1995)	14	29	43
Verbal episodic retrieval	Blaxton, Bookheimer, et al. (1996; 1)	8	20	48
Nonverbal episodic retrieval	Roland & Gulyas (1995; 1)	38	24	42
Nonverbal episodic retrieval	Roland & Gulyas (1995; 1)	19	35	44
	Semantic retrieval and language			
Semantic retrieval	Wise et al. (1991)	−36	14	40[c]
Semantic retrieval	Demonet et al. (1992)	−20	18	44
Language	Bookheimer et al. (1995)	−32	14	44[c]
Language	Bottini et al. (1994)	−8	30	48
Language	Klein et al. (1995)	−3	22	54[d]
Language	Price et al. (1994; 2)	−6	26	56[d]
Language	Price et al. (1994; 2)	6	40	44
	Working memory			
Nonverbal visual WM	Petrides, Alivastos, Evans, & Meyer (1993; 1)	−38	10	40
	Perception			
Object processing	Kosslyn et al. (1994; 1)	−13	21	40
Object processing	Kosslyn et al. (1995; 1)	−10	33	48
Object processing	Kosslyn et al. (1993; 1)	46	15	40
Object processing	Kosslyn et al. (1995; 2)	4	24	56
	Attention			
Sustained attention	Pardo et al. (1991)	41	7	36
Selective attention	Rees et al. (1997)	42	22	40
	Theory of mind			
Theory of mind	Goel et al. (1995)	−12	38	32[e]
Theory of mind	Fletcher et al. (1995)	−12	36	36[e]

Note. X, Y, Z, coordinates from the Talairach and Tournoux (1988) atlas. Brief descriptions of tasks involved in each experiment can be found in Table 12.1.
[a] Maxima with the same letters are plotted as one area in Figure 12.7.

areas in parietal cortex and more dorsal portions of frontal cortex (Desimone & Ungerleider, 1989; Pandya & Yeterian, 1996; Wilson et al., 1993). The wider representation of non–face object perception is probably due to the more elaborate processing required during these particular object perception tasks, which most likely involved some degree of semantic processing. The other cognitive processes have too few areas of activation to speculate on localization, although it is interesting that the maxima derived from the two independent theory-of-mind experiments were located in essentially the same medial part of BA 8.

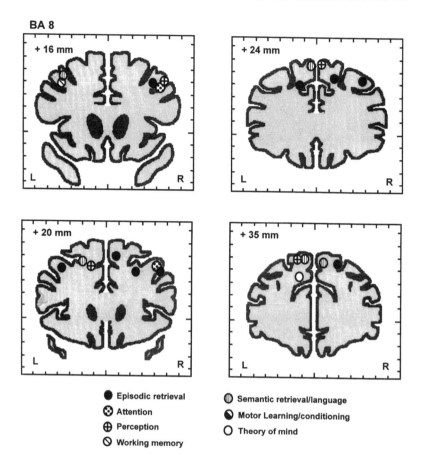

FIGURE 12.7. Maxima of rCBF activations in Brodmann's area 8 shown on coronal sections of the brain from the atlas of Talairach and Tournoux (1988). Coordinates for the plotted activations can be found in Table 12.8.

Another interesting characteristic of prefrontal activation revealed by neuroimaging is that many of the cognitive processes show a striking laterality. Tulving, Kapur, Craik, Moscovitch, and Houle (1994) have previously noted that episodic retrieval is accompanied by activation primarily in the right frontal lobe and semantic retrieval and encoding are associated with left prefrontal activity. They termed this phenomenon "HERA" (hemispheric encoding/retrieval asymmetry), and others have since accumulated more evidence of this asymmetry (Buckner, 1996; Nyberg, Cabeza, & Tulving, 1996). This survey also confirms the HERA concept by showing that semantic retrieval and encoding are strongly lateralized to left prefrontal cortex, whereas episodic retrieval is lateralized to right prefrontal cortex, although the lateralization is not as strong for nonverbal retrieval. Table 12.9B shows that in all areas where semantic retrieval and episodic encoding are represented, activations occur largely, or exclusively, in the left hemisphere. Episodic retrieval for verbal information is represented mainly in right prefrontal cortex throughout all areas, whereas nonverbal retrieval is predominantly right hemispheric in more ventral areas such as BAs 45 and 11 but in dorsolateral prefrontal cortex appears

TABLE 12.9. Localization and Lateralization of Cognitive Processes

A. Localization of cognitive processes[a]

BA	ER	EE	WM	SR	LN	MM	CC	PC	AT	Totals
8	11	0	1	2	5	0	0	4	2	25
9	13	1	11	2	2	4	1	7	0	41
10	25	0	5	3	4	2	4	4	0	47
46	7	2	11	4	0	1	0	3	2	30
45	8	2	3	5	2	2	1	11	3	37
47	5	1	4	5	6	1	2	0	2	26
11	8	0	4	4	0	0	3	4	0	23
Totals	77	6	39	25	19	10	11	33	9	229

B. Lateralization of cognitive processes

BA	VR	NR	EE	VW	NW	SR	LN	ML	MR	CC	FP	SP	OP	AU	AT	TM
8	R	=			L	L	L					=			R	L
9	R	=	L	=	L	=	L	=	=	R	L	L	R			
10	R	=		R	L	=	L	=		R			=	L		
46	R	L	L	L	R	L		R			R	R			R	
45	R	R	L		=	L	L	R	L	R		=		R	=	
47	R	R	L		=	L	L	R		R					R	
11	R	R			R	L				=	=		L			

Note. R, predominant activation in right hemisphere; L, predominant activation in left hemisphere; =, bilateral activation; Underlined letters indicate only one maximum for that process in that brain region; BA, Brodmann's area; ER, episodic retrieval; VR, verbal episodic retrieval; NR, nonverbal episodic retrieval; EE, encoding; WM, working memory; VW, verbal working memory; NW, nonverbal working memory; SR, semantic retrieval; LN, language; MM, motor memory; ML, motor learning; MR, motor retrieval; CC, classical conditioning; PC, perception; FP, face processing; SP, spatial processing; OP, object perception and imagery; AU, auditory processing; AT, attention; TM, theory of mind.
[a] Entries in A are the total number of reported maxima from Tables 12.2–12.8 (theory of mind not included).

to be bilaterally represented. However, there are many more verbal retrieval experiments than nonverbal experiments, so this apparent discrepancy may be a function of too little data from nonverbal tasks. Thus, the HERA model accurately describes the asymmetrical nature of prefrontal involvement in memory function, but, as mentioned previously, we can now move beyond this concept to examine the roles of specific prefrontal regions. It also is interesting to note that although human lesion studies indicated some laterality in frontal lobe function, this right–left dissociation during memory processing was not readily apparent in the lesion literature.

Other processes besides episodic and semantic memory also appear to be lateralized in prefrontal cortex (Table 12.9B). Activation during classical conditioning occurs mainly in the right hemisphere, unlike motor memory activation, which is bilateral. This difference in brain activation suggests that these two types of procedural memory, although similar in some ways, may be distinct in the way they are represented in the brain. Attentional function also appears to be lateralized primarily to right prefrontal cortex, although the number of reported maxima is relatively small. Nevertheless this asymmetry is consistent with other studies showing a predominant role for both right posterior and frontal cortex in attentional function and neglect (Baynes, Holtzman, & Volpe, 1986; Corbetta, Miezin, Shulman, & Petersen, 1993; Daffner et al., 1990; Posner, Walker, Friedrich, & Rafal, 1984; Spiers et al., 1990), and suggests a general right hemisphere bias for attention. On the other hand, perception, including auditory processing, which is not summarized in Table 12.9, and working memory show no clear or consistent lateralization in prefrontal cortex.

LIMITATIONS OF THIS ANALYSIS

This meta-analysis has at least three limitations to keep in mind when considering prefrontal activation. The first of these is the fact that there is considerable variability in neuroanatomical structures from one human brain to another (Paus et al., 1996; Rademacher, Caviness, Steinmetz, & Galaburda, 1993; Rajkowska & Goldman-Rakic, 1995; Steinmetz, Furst, & Freund, 1990). Warping each individual's brain images into the standard atlas coordinate system of Talairach and Tournoux, although it allows us to directly compare across brains, necessarily introduces some degree of error. The localizations presented here, and in the original reports, therefore must be considered approximate. Nevertheless, the summary presented here is based on state-of-the-art methodology and is an adequate beginning for understanding how cognition is represented in prefrontal cortex.

A second limitation of the current review, and one that can be applied to most neuroimaging studies in the literature, is that only rCBF increases are considered. Each task condition may also result in significant rCBF decreases, but these are often ignored. For example, reduced blood flow in auditory cortex has been found in visual perceptual experiments (Courtney et al., 1996; Haxby et al., 1994), and reduced rCBF in visual areas has been noted in an auditory experiment (Paus et al., 1997), which may reflect suppression of activity in unattended modalities, thus serving to focus attention to the attended modality. In addition, the phenomenon of priming, a type of implicit memory for previously presented stimuli, is accompanied by reduced rCBF in the perceptual areas of cortex that process the stimuli (Blaxton, Bookheimer, et al., 1996; Squire et al., 1992). Recently, several investigators have suggested that rCBF decreases may be as important as increases for understanding the brain mechanisms underlying cognition (Blaxton, Bookheimer, et al., 1996; Grady et al., 1996). Thus, it is clear that a complete picture of these brain mechanisms, both within prefrontal cortex and in other cortical areas, will have to include examination of both increases and decreases in brain activity.

Finally, perhaps the most important limitation of this analysis is that it ignores the interactions of prefrontal regions with other parts of the brain, interactions critical for cognitive performance. Recently some investigators in the neuroimaging field have advocated using a systems-level approach that focuses on functional networks of brain regions, under the assumption that these networks will vary depending on the type of cognitive processing required (Friston, Frith, Liddle, & Frackowiak, 1993; Horwitz & Sporns, 1994; McIntosh & Gonzalez-Lima, 1994). Experiments using this analytical approach have shown that the functional interactions among a given set of brain regions do indeed change when task demands change (McIntosh et al., 1994), and that these interactions can explain both the increases and decreases in activity seen in different experimental conditions (Nyberg, McIntosh, Cabeza, Nilsson, et al., 1996). A good example of the complexity of prefrontal participation during cognition can be found in the Nyberg, McIntosh, Cabeza, Nilsson, et al. (1996) study in which a network analysis showed that right prefrontal cortex not only had increased activity during visual episodic retrieval but also, along with other brain areas, inhibited activity in extrastriate cortex. This type of systems-level examination of brain activity is necessary to elucidate fully the role of prefrontal cortex in cognition.

CONCLUSIONS

This review of rCBF activation in prefrontal cortex demonstrates a considerable degree of converging evidence across multiple independent PET experiments for different roles of specific regions of prefrontal cortex in cognition, particularly memory. Indeed, it is remarkable how closely some areas of activation from different studies correspond to one another. Also noteworthy is the degree to which prefrontal representations of cognitive function in the human, as defined through neuroimaging, are homologous to those described in the monkey literature. This homology is evident despite the uncertainty in localizing these functions with current imaging technology and analysis. This finding is encouraging because it confirms the utility of using animal models and extrapolating results from such studies to humans. It also is clear that with these techniques we can overcome the limitations of animal models and begin to define the role of prefrontal cortex in uniquely human behaviors, such as verbal recall. Despite the focus on regional function within the frontal lobes in this review, readers should not conclude that a strict localizationalist approach is being suggested. This review is intended as an initial examination of how different parts of prefrontal cortex participate in cognition, with the understanding that this particpation varies depending on the context of specific cognitive demands and input from other parts of the brain. The task now should be to integrate cognitive activity in prefrontal cortex with activity in the rest of the brain, bringing us one step closer to the ultimate goal of understanding how the brain works.

REFERENCES

Andreasen, N. C., O'Leary, D. S., Arndt, S., Cizadlo, T., Hurtig, R., Rezai, K., Watkins, G. L., Boles Ponto, L. L., & Hichwa, R. D. (1995). Short-term and long-term verbal memory: A positron emission tomography study. *Proceedings of the National Academy of Sciences, USA, 92,* 5111–5115.

Andreasen, N. C., O'Leary, D. S., Arndt, S., Cizadlo, T., Hurtig, R., Rezai, K., Watkins, G. L., Boles Ponto, L. L., & Hichwa, R. D. (1996). Neural substrates of facial recognition. *Journal of Neuropsychiatry and Clinical Neuroscience, 8,* 139–146.

Andreasen, N. C., O'Leary, D. S., Cizadlo, T., Arndt, S., Rezai, K., Watkins, G. L., Boles Ponto, L. L., & Hichwa, R. D. (1995). Remembering the past: Two facets of episodic memory explored with positron emission tomography. *American Journal of Psychiatry, 152,* 1576–1585.

Bachevalier, J., & Mishkin, M. (1986). Visual recognition impairment follows ventromedial but not dorsolateral prefrontal lesions in monkeys. *Behavioral Brain Research, 20,* 249–261.

Baddeley, A. (1992). Working memory. *Science, 255,* 556–559.

Baron-Cohen, S., Leslie, A. M., & Frith, U. (1985). Does the autistic child have a theory of mind? *Cognition, 21,* 37–46.

Baynes, K., Holtzman, J. D., & Volpe, B. T. (1986). Components of visual attention: Alterations in response pattern to visual stimuli following parietal lobe infarction. *Brain, 109,* 99–114.

Becker, J. T., Mintun, M. A., Diehl, D. J., Dobkin, J., Martidis, A., Madoff, D. C., & DeKosky, S. T. (1994). Functional neuroanatomy of verbal free recall: A replication study. *Human Brain Mapping, 1,* 284–292.

Bench, C. J., Frith, C. D., Grasby, P. M., Friston, K. J., Paulesu, E., Frackowiak, R. S. J., & Dolan, R. J. (1993). Investigations of the functional anatomy of attention using the Stroop Test. *Neuropsychologia, 31,* 907–922.

Blaxton, T. A., Bookheimer, S. Y., Zeffiro, T. A., Figlozzi, C. M., Gaillard, W. D., & Theodore, W. H. (1996). Functional mapping of human memory using PET: comparisons of conceptual and perceptual tasks. *Canadian Journal of Experimental Psychology, 50,* 42–56.

Blaxton, T. A., Zeffiro, T. A., Gabrieli, J. D. E., Bookheimer, S. Y., Carrillo, M. C., Theodore, W. H., & Disterhoft, J. F. (1996). Functional mapping of human learning: A PET activation study of eyeblink conditioning. *Journal of Neuroscience, 16,* 4032–4040.

Bookheimer, S. Y., Zeffiro, T. A., Blaxton, T., Gaillard, W., & Theodore, W. (1995). Regional cerebral blood flow during object naming and word reading. *Human Brain Mapping, 3,* 93–106.

Bottini, G., Corcoran, R., Sterzi, R., Paulesu, E., Schenone, P., Scarpa, P., Frackowiak, R. S. J., & Frith, C. D. (1994). The role of the right hemisphere in the interpretation of figurative aspects of language. *Brain, 117,* 1241–1253.

Buckner, R. L. (1996). Beyond HERA: Contributions of specific prefrontal brain areas to long term memory retrieval. *Psychonomic Bulletin Review, 3,* 149–158.

Buckner, R. L., Petersen, S. E., Ojemann, J. G., Miezin, F. M., Squire, L. R., & Raichle, M. E. (1995). Functional anatomical studies of explicit and implicit memory retrieval tasks. *Journal of Neuroscience, 15,* 12–29.

Buckner, R. L., Raichle, M. E., Miezin, F. M., & Petersen, S. E. (1996). Functional anatomic studies of memory retrieval for auditory words and visual pictures. *Journal of Neuroscience, 16,* 6219–6235.

Buckner, R. L., Raichle, M. E., & Petersen, S. E. (1995). Dissociation of human prefrontal cortical areas across different speech production tasks and gender groups. *Journal of Neurophysiology, 74,* 2163–2173.

Cabeza, R., Kapur, S., Craik, F. I. M., McIntosh, A. R., Houle, S., & Tulving, E. (1997). Functional neuroanatomy of recall and recognition: A PET study of episodic memory. *Journal of Cognitive Neuroscience, 9,* 254–265.

Corbetta, M., Miezin, F. M., Dobmeyer, S., Shulman, G. L., & Petersen, S. E. (1991). Selective and divided attention during visual discriminations of shape, color, and speed: Functional anatomy by positron emission tomography. *Journal of Neuroscience, 11,* 2383–2402.

Corbetta, M., Miezin, F. M., Shulman, G. L., & Petersen, S. E. (1993). A PET study of visuospatial attention. *Journal of Neuroscience, 13,* 1202–1226.

Courtney, S. M., Ungerleider, L. G., Keil, K., & Haxby, J. V. (1996). Object and spatial visual working memory activate separate neural systems in human cortex. *Cerebral Cortex, 6,* 39–49.

Cummings, J. L. (1993). Frontal–subcortical circuits and human behavior. *Archives of Neurology, 50,* 873–880.

Daffner, K. R., Ahern, G. L., Weintraub, S., & Mesulam, M. M. (1990). Dissociated neglect behavior following sequential strokes in the right hemisphere. *Annals of Neurology, 28,* 97–101.

Damasio, H., Grabowski, T., Frank, R., Galaburda, A. M., & Damasio, A. R. (1994). The return of Phineas Gage: Clues about the brain from the skull of a famous patient. *Science, 264,* 1102–1105.

Deiber, M. P., Passingham, R. E., Colebatch, J. G., Friston, K. J., Nixon, P. D., & Frackowiak, R. S. J. (1991). Cortical areas and the selection of movement: A study with positron emission tomography. *Experimental Brain Research, 84,* 393–402.

Demonet, J.-F., Celsis, P., Nespoulous, J. L., Viallard, G., Marc-Vergnes, J. P., & Rascol, A. (1992). Cerebral blood flow correlates of word monitoring in sentences: Influence of semantic incoherence. A SPECT study in normals. *Neuropsychologia, 30,* 1–11.

De Renzi, E., Colombo, A., Faglioni, P., & Gibertoni, M. (1982). Conjugate gaze paresis in stroke patients with unilateral damage: An unexpected instance of hemispheric asymmetry. *Archives of Neurology, 32,* 482–486.

Desimone, R., & Ungerleider, L. G. (1989). Neural mechanisms of visual processing in monkeys. In H. Goodglass & A. R. Damasio (Eds.), *Handbook of neuropsychology* (pp. 267–300). Amsterdam: Elsevier.

Dias, R., Robbins, T. W., & Roberts, A. C. (1996). Dissociation in prefrontal cortex of affective and attentional shifts. *Nature, 380,* 69–72.

Di Pellegrino, G., & Wise, S. P. (1991). A neurophysiological comparison of three distinct regions of the primate frontal lobe. *Brain, 114,* 951–978.

Eslinger, P. J., & Grattan, L. M. (1993). Frontal lobe and frontal–striatal substrates for different forms of human cognitive flexibility. *Neuropsychologia, 31,* 17–28.

Fiez, J. A., Raife, E. A., Balota, D. A., Schwarz, J. P., Raichle, M. E., & Petersen, S. E. (1996). A positron emission tomography study of the short-term maintenance of verbal information. *Journal of Neuroscience, 16,* 808–822.

Fletcher, P. C., Happe, F., Frith, U., Baker, S. C., Dolan, R. J., Frackowiak, R. S. J., & Frith, C. D. (1995). Other minds in the brain: A functional imaging study of theory of mind in story comprehension. *Cognition, 57,* 109–128.

Friston, K. F., Ashburner, J., Frith, C. D., Poline, J. B., Heather, J. D., & Frackowiak, R. S. J. (1995). Spatial registration and normalization of images. *Human Brain Mapping, 3,* 165–189.

Friston, K. J., Frith, C. D., Liddle, P. F., & Frackowiak, R. S. J. (1991). Plastic transformation of PET images. *Journal of Computer Assisted Tomography, 15,* 634–639.

Friston, K. J., Frith, C. D., Liddle, P. F., & Frackowiak, R. S. J. (1993). Functional connectivity: The principal-component analysis of large (PET) data sets. *Journal of Cerebral Blood Flow and Metabolism, 13,* 5–14.

Frith, C. D., Friston, K., Liddle, P. F., & Frackowiak, R. S. J. (1991). Willed action and the prefrontal cortex in man: a study with PET. *Proceedings of the Royal Society of London (Biology), 244,* 241–246.

Funahashi, S., Bruce, C. J., & Goldman-Rakic, P. S. (1993). Dorsolateral prefrontal lesions and oculomotor delayed-response performance: Evidence for mnemonic scotomas. *Journal of Neuroscience, 13,* 1479–1497.

George, M. S., Ketter, T. A., Gill, D. S., Haxby, J. V., Ungerleider, L. G., Herscovitch, P., & Post, R. M. (1993). Brain regions involved in recognizing facial emotion or identity: An oxygen-15 PET study. *Journal of Neuropsychiatry and Clinical Neuroscience, 5,* 384–394.

George, M. S., Ketter, T. A., Parekh, P. I., Rosinsky, N., Ring, H., Casey, B. J., Trimble, M. R., Horwitz, B., Herscovitch, P., & Post, R. M. (1994). Regional brain activity when selecting a response despite interference: An H2^{15}O PET study of the Stroop and an emotional Stroop. *Human Brain Mapping, 1,* 194–209.

Glick, S. D., Goldfarb, T. L., & Jarvik, M. E. (1969). Recovery of delayed matching performance following lateral frontal lesions in the monkey. *Communications in Behavioral Biology, 3,* 299–303.

Goel, V., Grafman, J., Sadato, N., & Hallett, M. (1995). Modeling other minds. *Neuroreport, 6,* 1741–1746.

Gold, J. M., Berman, K. F., Randolph, C., Goldberg, T. E., & Weinberger, D. R. (1996). PET validation of a novel prefrontal task: Delayed response alternation. *Neuropsychology, 10,* 3–10.

Goldman-Rakic, P. S. (1990). Cellular and circuit basis of working memory in prefrontal cortex of nonhuman primates. In H. B. M. Uylings, C. G. Van Eden, J. P. C. De Bruin, M. A. Corner, & M. G. P. Feenstra (Eds.), *Progress in brain research* (pp. 325–336). Amsterdam: Elsevier.

Grady, C. L., Horwitz, B., Pietrini, P., Mentis, M. J., Ungerleider, L. G., Rapoport, S. I., & Haxby, J. V. (1996). The effect of task difficulty on cerebral blood flow during perceptual matching of faces. *Human Brain Mapping, 4,* 227–239.

Grafton, S. T., Woods, R. P., & Tyszka, M. (1994). Functional imaging of procedural motor learning: Relating cerebral blood flow with individual subject performance. *Human Brain Mapping, 1,* 221–234.

Grasby, P. M., Frith, C. D., Friston, K. J., Bench, C., Frackowiak, R. S. J., & Dolan, R. J. (1993). Functional mapping of brain areas implicated in auditory–verbal memory function. *Brain, 116,* 1–20.

Grasby, P. M., Frith, C. D., Friston, K. J., Simpson, J., Fletcher, P. C., Frackowiak, R. S. J., & Dolan, R. J. (1994). A graded task approach to the functional mapping of brain areas implicated in auditory–verbal memory. *Brain, 117,* 1271–1282.

Harlow, J. M. (1868). Recovery from the passage of an iron bar through the head. *Publication of the Massachusetts Medical Society, 2,* 327–346.

Haxby, J. V., Horwitz, B., Ungerleider, L. G., Maisog, J. M., Pietrini, P., & Grady, C. L. (1994). The functional organization of human extrastriate cortex: A PET-rCBF study of selective attention to faces and locations. *Journal of Neuroscience, 14,* 6336–6353.

Haxby, J. V., Ungerleider, L. G., Horwitz, B., Maisog, J. M., Rapoport, S. I., & Grady, C. L. (1996). Storage and retrieval of new memories for faces in the intact human brain. *Proceedings of the National Academy of Sciences, USA, 93,* 922–927.

Haxby, J. V., Ungerleider, L. G., Horwitz, B., Rapoport, S. I., & Grady, C. L. (1995). Hemispheric differences in neural systems for face working memory: A PET-rCBF Study. *Human Brain Mapping, 3,* 68–82.

Hazeltine, E., Grafton, S. T., & Ivry, R. (1997). Attention and stimulus characteristics determine the locus of motor-sequence encoding. A PET study. *Brain, 120,* 123–140.

Holcomb, H. H., Caudill, P. J., Medoff, D. R., Zhao, Z., Lahti, A. C., Dannals, R. F., & Tamminga, C. A. (in press). Cerebral blood flow relationships associated with a difficult tone recognition task in trained normal volunteers. *Cerebral Cortex.*

Horwitz, B., & Sporns, O. (1994). Neural modeling and functional neuroimaging. *Human Brain Mapping, 1,* 269–283.

Hugdahl, K., Berardi, A., Thompson, W. L., Kosslyn, S. M., Macy, R., Baker, D. P., Alpert, N. M., & LeDoux, J. E. (1995). Brain mechanisms in human classical conditioning: A PET blood flow study. *Neuroreport, 6,* 1723–1728.

Janowsky, J., Shimamura, A. P., Kritchevsky, M., & Squire, L. R. (1989). Cognitive impairment following frontal lobe damage and its relevance to human amnesia. *Behavioral Neuroscience, 103,* 548–560.

Jenkins, I. H., Brooks, D. J., Nixon, P. D., Frackowiak, R. S. J., & Passingham, R. E. (1994). Motor sequence learning: A study with positron emission tomography. *Journal of Neuroscience, 14,* 3775–3790.

Jennings, J. M., McIntosh, A. R., Kapur, S., Tulving, E., & Houle, S. (1997). Cognitive subtractions may not add up: The interaction between semantic processing and response mode. *Neuroimage, 5,* 229–239.

Jonides, J., Smith, E. E., Koeppe, R. A., Awh, E., Minoshima, S., & Mintun, M. A. (1993). Spatial working memory in humans as revealed by PET. *Nature, 363,* 623–625.

Kapur, S., Craik, F. I. M., Cabeza, R., Jones, C., Houle, S., McIntosh, A. R., & Tulving, E. (1996). Neural correlates of intentional encoding of information into episodic memory: A PET study. *Cognitive Brain Research, 4,* 243–249.

Kapur, S., Craik, F. I. M., Jones, C., Brown, G. M., Houle, S., & Tulving, E. (1995). Functional role of the prefrontal cortex in retrieval of memories: A PET study. *Neuroreport, 6,* 1880–1884.

Kapur, S., Rose, R., Liddle, P. F., Zipursky, R. B., Brown, G. M., Stuss, D., Houle, S., & Tulving, E. (1994). The role of the left prefrontal cortex in verbal processing: semantic processing or willed action? *Neuroreport, 5,* 2193–2196.

Klein, D., Milner, B., Zatorre, R. J., Meyer, E., & Evans, A. C. (1995). The neural substrates underlying word generation: A bilingual functional-imaging study. *Proceedings of the National Academy of Sciences, USA, 92,* 2899–2903.

Kosslyn, S. M., Alpert, N. M., & Thompson, W. L. (1995). Identifying objects at different levels of hierarchy: A positron emission tomography study. *Human Brain Mapping, 3,* 107–132.

Kosslyn, S. M., Alpert, N. M., Thompson, W. L., Chabris, C. F., Rauch, S. L., & Anderson, A. K. (1994). Identifying objects seen from different viewpoints. A PET investigation. *Brain, 117,* 1055–1071.

Kosslyn, S. M., Alpert, N. M., Thompson, W. L., Maljkovic, V., Weise, S. B., Chabris, C. F., Hamilton, S. E., Rauch, S. L., & Buonanno, F. S. (1993). Visual mental imagery activates topographically organized visual cortex: PET investigations. *Journal of Cognitive Neuroscience, 5,* 263–287.

Lhermitte, F. (1986). Human autonomy and the frontal lobes. II. Patient behavior in complex and social situations. The environmental dependency syndrome. *Annals of Neurology, 19,* 335–343.

MacLeod, C. M. (1991). Half a century of research on the Stroop effect: An integrative review. *Psychology Bulletin, 109,* 163–203.

Mangels, J. A., Gershberg, F. B., Shimamura, A. P., & Knight, R. T. (1996). Impaired retrieval from remote memory in patients with frontal lobe damage. *Neuropsychology, 10,* 32–41.

Martin, A., Haxby, J. V., Lalonde, F. M., Wiggs, C. L., & Ungerleider, L. G. (1995). Discrete cortical regions associated with knowledge of color and knowledge of action. *Science, 270,* 102–105.

Martin, A., Wiggs, C. L., Ungerleider, L. G., & Haxby, J. V. (1996). Neural correlates of category-specific knowledge. *Nature, 379,* 649–652.

McIntosh, A. R., & Gonzalez-Lima, F. (1994). Structural equation modeling and its application to network analysis in functional brain imaging. *Human Brain Mapping, 2,* 2–22.

McIntosh, A. R., Grady, C. L., Ungerleider, L. G., Haxby, J. V., Rapoport, S. I., & Horwitz, B. (1994). Network analysis of cortical visual pathways mapped with PET. *Journal of Neuroscience, 14,* 655–666.

Milner, B., Petrides, M., & Smith, M. L. (1985). Frontal lobes and the temporal organization of memory. *Human Neurobiology, 4,* 137–142.

Mishkin, M., & Manning, F. J. (1978). Non-spatial memory after selective prefrontal lesions in monkeys. *Brain Research, 143,* 313–323.

Moscovitch, M., Kapur, S., Kohler, S., & Houle, S. (1995). Distinct neural correlates of visual long-term memory fof spatial location and object identity: A positron emission tomography study in humans. *Proceedings of the National Academy of Sciences, USA, 92,* 3721–3725.

Nyberg, L., Cabeza, R., & Tulving, E. (1996). PET studies of encoding and retrieval: The HERA model. *Psychonomic Bulletin Review, 3,* 135–148.

Nyberg, L., McIntosh, A. R., Cabeza, R., Habib, R., Houle, S., & Tulving, E. (1996). General and specific brain regions involved in encoding and retrieval of events: What, where and when. *Proceedings of the National Academy of Sciences, USA, 93,* 11280–11285.

Nyberg, L., McIntosh, A. R., Cabeza, R., Nilsson, L.-G., Houle, S., Habib, R., & Tulving, E. (1996). Network analysis of positron emission tomography regional cerebral blood flow data: Ensemble inhibition during episodic memory retrieval. *Journal of Neuroscience, 16,* 3753–3759.

Nyberg, L., Tulving, E., Habib, R., Nilsson, L.-G., Kapur, S., Houle, S., Cabeza, R., & McIntosh, A. R. (1995). Functional brain maps of retrieval mode and recovery of episodic information. *Neuroreport, 7,* 249–252.

Owen, A. M., Milner, B., Petrides, M., & Evans, A. C. (1996). Memory for object features versus memory for object location: A positron-emission tomography study of encoding and retrieval processes. *Proceedings of the National Academy of Sciences, USA, 93,* 9212–9217.

Owen, A. M., Sahakian, B. J., Semple, J., Polkey, C. E., & Robbins, T. W. (1995). Visuo-spatial short term recognition memory and learning after temporal lobe excisions, frontal lobe excisions or amygdalo-hippocampectomy in man. *Neuropsychologia, 33,* 1–24.

Pandya, D. N., & Yeterian, E. H. (1996). Morphological correlations of human and monkey frontal lobe. In A. R. Damasio, H. Damasio, & Y. Christen (Eds.), *Neurobiology of decision making* (pp. 13–46). Berlin: Springer-Verlag.

Pardo, J. V., Fox, P. T., & Raichle, M. E. (1991). Localization of a human system for sustained attention by positron emission tomography. *Nature, 349,* 61–64.

Parsons, L. M., Fox, P. T., Downs, J. H., Glass, T., Hirsch, T. B., Martin, C. C., Jerabek, P. A., & Lancaster, J. L. (1995). Use of implicit motor imagery for visual shape discrimination as revealed by PET. *Nature, 375,* 54–58.

Paus, T., Tomaluolo, F., Otaky, N., MacDonald, D., Petrides, M., Atlas, J., Morris, R., & Evans, A. C. (1996). Human cingulate and paracingulate sulci: Pattern, variability, asymmetry, and probabilistic map. *Cerebral Cortex, 6,* 207–214.

Paus, T., Zatorre, R. J., Hofle, N., Caramanos, Z., Gotman, J., Petrides, M., & Evans, A. C. (1997). Time-related changes in neural systems underlying attention and arousal during the performance of an auditory vigilance task. *Journal of Cognitive Neuroscience, 9,* 392–408.

Petersen, S. E., Fox, P. T., Posner, M. I., Mintun, M., & Raichle, M. E. (1989). Positron emission tomographic studies of the processing of single words. *Journal of Cognitive Neuroscience, 1,* 153–170.

Petersen, S. E., Fox, P. T., Snyder, A. Z., & Raichle, M. E. (1990). Activation of extrastriate and frontal cortical areas by visual words and word-like stimuli. *Science, 249,* 1041–1044.

Petrides, M. (1994). Frontal lobes and working memory: Evidence from investigations of the effects of cortical excisions in nonhuman primates. In F. Boller & J. Grafman (Eds.), *Handbook of neuropsychology* (pp. 59–82). Amsterdam: Elsevier.

Petrides, M. (1995). Impairments on nonspatial self-ordered and externally ordered working memory tasks after lesions of the mid-dorsal part of the lateral frontal cortex in the monkey. *Journal of Neuroscience, 15,* 359–375.

Petrides, M., Alivisatos, B., & Evans, A. C. (1995). Functional activation of the human ventrolateral frontal cortex during mnemonic retrieval of verbal information. *Proceedings of the National Academy of Sciences, USA, 92,* 5803–5807.

Petrides, M., Alivisatos, B., Evans, A. C., & Meyer, E. (1993). Dissociation of human mid-dorsolateral from posterior dorsolateral frontal cortex in memory processing. *Proceedings of the National Academy of Sciences, USA, 90,* 873–877.

Petrides, M., Alivisatos, B., Meyer, E., & Evans, A. C. (1993). Functional activation of the human frontal cortex during the performance of verbal working memory tasks. *Proceedings of the National Academy of Sciences, USA, 90,* 878–882.

Petrides, M., & Milner, B. (1982). Deficits on subject-oriented tasks after frontal and temporal lobe lesions in man. *Neuropsychologia, 20,* 249–262.

Petrides, M., & Pandya, D. N. (1994). Comparative architectonic analysis of the human and the macaque frontal cortex. In F. Boller & J. Grafman (Eds.), *Handbook of neuropsychology* (pp. 17–57). Amsterdam: Elsevier.

Pigott, S., & Milner, B. (1994). Capacity of visual short-term memory after unilateral frontal or anterior temporal-lobe resection. *Neuropsychologia, 32,* 969–981.

Posner, M. I., Walker, J. A., Friedrich, F. J., & Rafal, R. D. (1984). Effects of parietal injury on covert orienting of attention. *Journal of Neuroscience, 4,* 1863–1874.

Price, C. J., Wise, R. J. S., Watson, J. D. G., Patterson, K., Howard, D., & Frackowiak, R. S. J. (1994). Brain activity during reading. The effects of exposure duration and task. *Brain, 117,* 1255–1269.

Ptito, A., Crane, J., Leonard, G., Amsel, R., & Caramanos, Z. (1995). Visual-spatial localization by patients with frontal-lobe lesions invading or sparing area 46. *Neuroreport, 6,* 1781–1784.

Quintana, J., & Fuster, J. M. (1992). Mnemonic and predictive functions of cortical neurons in a memory task. *Neuroreport, 3,* 721–724.

Rademacher, J., Caviness, V. S., Steinmetz, H., & Galaburda, A. M. (1993). Topographical variation of the human primary cortices: Implications for neuroimaging, brain mapping, and neurobiology. *Cerebral Cortex, 3,* 313–329.

Rajkowska, G., & Goldman-Rakic, P. S. (1995). Cytoarchitectonic definition of prefrontal areas in the normal human cortex: II. Variability in locations of areas 9 and 46 and relationship to the Talairach coordinate system. *Cerebral Cortex, 5,* 323–337.

Rauch, S. L., Savage, C. R., Brown, H. D., Curran, T., Alpert, N. M., Kendrick, A., Fischman, A. J., & Kosslyn, S. M. (1995). A PET investigation of implicit and explicit sequence learning. *Human Brain Mapping, 3,* 271–286.

Rees, G., Frackowiak, R. S. J., & Frith, C. (1997). Two modulatory effects of attention that mediate object categorization in human cortex. *Science, 275,* 835–838.

Richer, F., Decary, A., Lapierre, M.-F., Rouleau, I., Bouvier, G., & Saint-Hilaire, J.-M. (1993). Target detection deficits in frontal lobectomy. *Brain and Cognition, 21,* 203–211.

Ridley, R. M., Durnford, L. J., Baker, J. A., & Baker, H. F. (1993). Cognitive inflexibility after archicortical and paleocortical prefrontal lesions in marmosets. *Brain Research, 628,* 56–64.

Roland, P. E., & Gulyas, B. (1995). Visual memory, visual imagery, and visual recognition of large field patterns by the human brain: Functional anatomy by positron emission tomography. *Cerebral Cortex, 5*, 79–93.

Rugg, M. D., Fletcher, P. C., Frith, C. D., Frackowiak, R. S. J., & Dolan, R. J. (1996). Differential activation of the prefrontal cortex in successful and unsuccessful memory retrieval. *Brain, 119*, 2073–2084.

Sakagami, M., & Niki, H. (1994). Encoding of behavioral significance of visual stimuli by primate prefrontal neurons: Relation to relevant task conditions. *Experimental Brain Research, 97*, 423–436.

Sasaki, K., Gemba, H., Nambu, A., & Matsuzaki, R. (1994). Activity of the prefrontal cortex on no-go decision and motor suppression. In A.-M. Thierry, J. Glowinski, P. S. Goldman-Rakic, & Y. Christen (Eds.), *Motor and cognitive functions of the prefrontal cortex* (pp. 139–159). Berlin: Springer-Verlag.

Schacter, D. L. (1987). Memory, amnesia and frontal lobe dysfunction. *Psychobiology, 15*, 21–36.

Schacter, D. L., Alpert, N. M., Savage, C. R., Rauch, S. L., & Albert, M. S. (1996). Conscious recollection and the human hippocampal formation: Evidence from positron emission tomography. *Proceedings of the National Academy of Sciences, USA, 93*, 321–325.

Schacter, D. L., Reiman, E., Uecker, A., Polster, M. R., Yun, L. S., & Cooper, L. A. (1995). Brain regions associated with retrieval of structurally coherent visual information. *Nature, 376*, 587–590.

Schacter, D. L., & Tulving, E. (1994). What are the memory systems of 1994? In D. L. Schacter & E. Tulving (Eds.), *Memory systems 1994* (pp. 1–38). Cambridge, MA: MIT Press.

Schumacher, E. H., Lauber, E., Awh, E., Jonides, J., Smith, E. E., & Koeppe, R. A. (1996). PET evidence for an amodal verbal working memory system. *Neuroimage, 3*, 79–88.

Sergent, J., Ohta, S., & MacDonald, B. (1992). Functional neuroanatomy of face and object processing. A positron emission tomography study. *Brain, 115*, 15–36.

Shallice, T., Fletcher, P., Frith, C. D., Grasby, P., Frackowiak, R. S. J., & Dolan, R. J. (1994). Brain regions associated with acquisition and retrieval of verbal episodic memory. *Nature, 368*, 633–635.

Smith, E. E., Jonides, J., Koeppe, R. A., Awh, E., Schumacher, E. H., & Minoshima, S. (1995). Spatial versus object working memory: PET investigations. *Journal of Cognitive Neuroscience, 7*, 337–356.

Spiers, P. A., Schomer, D. L., Blume, H. W., Kleefield, J., O'Reilly, G., Weintraub, S., Osborne-Shaefer, P., & Mesulam, M. -M. (1990). Visual neglect during intracarotid amobarbital testing. *Neurology, 40*, 1600–1606.

Squire, L. R., Ojemann, J. G., Miezin, F. M., Petersen, S. E., Videen, T. O., & Raichle, M. E. (1992). Activation of the hippocampus in normal humans: A functional anatomical study of memory. *Proceedings of the National Academy of Sciences, USA, 89*, 1837–1841.

Steinmetz, H., Furst, G., & Freund, H.-J. (1990). Variation of perisylvian and calcarine anatomic landmarks within stereotaxic proportional coordinates. *American Journal of Neuroradiology, 11*, 1123–1130.

Stuss, D. T., & Benson, D. F. (1984). Neuropsychological studies of the frontal lobes. *Psychology Bulletin, 95*, 3–28.

Stuss, D. T., & Benson, D. F. (1986). *The frontal lobes.* New York: Raven Press.

Stuss, D. T., Eskes, G. A., & Foster, J. K. (1994). Experimental neuropsychological studies of frontal lobe functions. In F. Boller, H. Spinnler, & J. A. Hendler (Eds.), *Handbook of neuropsychology* (pp. 149–186). Amsterdam: Elsevier.

Talairach, J., Szikla, G., & Tournoux, P. (1967). *Atlas d'anatomie stereotaxique du telencephale.* Paris: Masson.

Talairach, J., & Tournoux, P. (1988). *Co-planar stereotaxic atlas of the human brain.* New York: Thieme.

Tulving, E. (1983). *Elements of episodic memory.* New York: Oxford University Press.

Tulving, E., Kapur, S., Craik, F. I. M., Moscovitch, M., & Houle, S. (1994). Hemispheric encoding/retrieval asymmetry in episodic memory: Positron emission tomography findings. *Proceedings of the National Academy of Sciences, USA, 91*, 2016–2020.

Tulving, E., Kapur, S., Markowitsch, H. J., Craik, F. I. M., Habib, R., & Houle, S. (1994). Neuroanatomical correlates of retrieval in episodic memory: Auditory sentence recognition. *Proceedings of the National Academy of Sciences, USA, 91,* 2012–2015.

Tulving, E., Markowitsch, H. J., Craik, F. I. M., Habib, R., & Houle, S. (1996). Novelty and familiarity activations in PET studies of memory encoding and retrieval. *Cerebral Cortex, 6,* 71–79.

Watanabe, M. (1992). Frontal units of the monkey coding the associative significance of visual and auditory stimuli. *Experimental Brain Research, 89,* 233–247.

Wheeler, M. A., Stuss, D. T., & Tulving, E. (1995). Frontal lobe damage produces episodic memory impairment. *Journal of International Neuropsychology Society, 1,* 525–536.

Wilson, F. A. W., Scalaidhe, S. P. O., & Goldman-Rakic, P. S. (1993). Dissociation of object and spatial processing domains in primate prefrontal cortex. *Science, 260,* 1955–1958.

Wise, R. J. S., Chollett, F., Hadar, U., Friston, K. J., Hoffner, E., & Frackowiak, R. S. J. (1991). Distribution of cortical neural networks involved in word comprehension and word retrieval. *Brain, 114,* 1803–1817.

Zatorre, R. J., Evans, A. C., & Meyer, E. (1994). Neural mechanisms underlying melodic perception and memory for pitch. *Journal of Neuroscience, 14,* 1908–1919.

Zatorre, R. J., Evans, A. C., Meyer, E., & Gjedde, A. (1992). Lateralization of phonetic and pitch discrimination in speech processing. *Science, 256,* 846–849.

Zatorre, R. J., Halpern, A. R., Perry, D. W., Meyer, E., & Evans, A. C. (1996). Hearing in the mind's ear: A PET investigation of musical imagery and perception. *Journal of Cognitive Neuroscience, 8,* 29–46.

Zatorre, R. J., & Jones-Gotman, M. K. (1991). Human olfactory discrimination after unilateral frontal or temporal lobectomy. *Brain, 114,* 71–84.

Zatorre, R. J., Meyer, E., Gjedde, A., & Evans, A. C. (1996). PET studies of phonetic processing of speech: Review, replication, and reanalysis. *Cerebral Cortex, 6,* 21–30.

Part III

NEUROPSYCHOLOGICAL FUNCTIONS OF THE FRONTAL LOBES

13

Bedside Frontal Lobe Testing

The "Frontal Lobe Score"

THIERRY ETTLIN
UDO KISCHKA

The clinical diagnosis of prefrontal lobe lesions is difficult even for experienced behavioral neurologists and neuropsychologists. Prefrontal dysfunction is often missed not only in standard neurological examination but also in conventional mental state examinations and neuropsychological testing.

One reason for this difficulty is the complex nature of functions ascribed to the prefrontal lobes. They include high-level mental activities such as motor control and programming (suppression of reflexes and motor impulses, rapid switches in movements, programming and performance of complex series of movements); mental control (flexibility in shifting, resistance to interference, e.g., the ability to reverse automatized series); personality and emotion (initiative, self-monitoring, control of aggressive and sexual impulses); and fluency, creativity, and planning. Deficits in these functions have been categorized as disorders of the executive system (Stuss & Benson, 1986). The impact of executive control on more easily tested brain functions such as attention, memory, language, motor function, and visuospatial abilities has been studied and evidence has been gathered that it is not the numeric test result as such but, rather, the process of how the result was achieved that is indicative of prefrontal lobe dysfunction. Only a few clinical examinations and neuropsychological tests—usually sorting and category tests— were designed to probe prefrontal dysfunctions and have been proposed to be relatively specific for the executive system.

A second reason for the difficulty in diagnosing prefrontal dysfunction is the limited empirical support for the assumptions regarding prefrontal lobe function in man. These assumptions are generally based either on an extensive examination of a single patient with a circumscribed prefrontal lobe lesion, or on studies with larger numbers of patients, but with only one test administered (see, e.g., Boller & Spinnler, 1994; Fuster, 1989;

Luria, 1966; Stuss & Benson, 1986). For the reasons mentioned previously, clinical neurologists still have to rely on their clinical sense, a feeling for prefrontal-type abnormalities based on clinical experience.

Together with D. F. Benson at the Behavioral Neurology Unit at UCLA, we decided to construct a diagnostic instrument for clinical use to assess prefrontal lobe dysfunction confidently and in a reasonable amount of time. To achieve this goal, we assembled a large number of clinical examinations, tests, and rating scales from the literature that had been proposed to indicate prefrontal lobe damage and evaluated them systematically in patients and control subjects. The aim was to select those tests that would prove to yield the highest sensitivity and specificity. Because we were interested in examinations that are fast and easy to perform at bedside, we did not include time-consuming and material-dependent tasks such as the Wisconsin Card Sorting Test (Grant & Berg, 1948) and the Tower of London Test (Shallice, 1982).

The explicit goal of the studies presented here was simply the development of a bedside assessment of prefrontal dysfunction as a tool for the behavioral neurologist. It should not be mistaken for an attempt to propose a comprehensive explanation of the working of the human prefrontal lobes.

Because the vast majority of the literature in this field uses the general term "frontal lobes" when in fact typical prefrontal functions are referred to, we decided to adopt this terminology and will therefore speak of frontal lobe functions.

The following clinical examinations, mental status tests, and rating scales were reported in the literature as indicative of frontal lobe damage.

MOTOR CONTROL AND PROGRAMMING

Maintaining a Voluntary Movement

Motor Impersistence (Ben-Yishay, Diller, Gerstmann, & Haas, 1968). The subject is instructed to hold his/her eyes closed until told otherwise. Failure to hold the eyes closed for 30 seconds is scored.

Conjugate Eye Movement (De Renzi, Colomba, Faglioni, & Gibertoni, 1982; Luria, 1966). The subject has to follow the examiner's fingers with his or her eyes in all directions and then perform these eye movements on command.

Suppression of Reflexes and Motor Impulses

Grasp Reflex (Fulton, 1934). The examiner tests for a tactile grasp reflex by lightly touching with his own hand the first interosseus space of the subject's hands. If positive, it results in a flexion of thumb and fingers.

Conflicting Commands (Christensen, 1979; Luria, 1966). The instruction is: "Tap once, when I tap twice; tap twice, when I tap once."

Go/No-Go (Christensen, 1979; Luria, 1966). The instruction is: "Tap twice, when I tap once, but when I tap twice, don't tap at all." A typical error of patients with frontal dysfunction would be the inability to stop the impulse to tap after the examiner tapped twice.

Programming and Performance of Series of Movements

Rhythm Tapping (Luria, 1966). The subject is asked to repeat two different rhythms tapped by the examiner: (-..-..-..) (—...—...—...-). Patients with frontal lesions are expected to have trouble repeating the second, complex pattern that requires constant switches in rhythm.

Luria's Hand Sequences (Luria, 1966). Two steps: In this easier version, the examiner makes a fist, then extends his fingers, holding his hand horizontally. The subject has to repeat this alternating movement 10 times. Three steps: The third movement is added, the examiner turning his hand by 90° with the extended fingers still pointing forward. Number of trials necessary to learn the sequence, fluency and perseverations are rated. (See Figure 13.1.)

Alternating Pattern (Luria, 1966). The subject is told to copy a drawing (see Figure 13.2) without lifting the hand from the paper. The test requires alternating between peaks and blocks; a typical error ascribed to frontal lobe dysfunction would be to draw two peaks in a row.

Multiple Loops (Bouman & Grunbaum, 1930). The subject has to copy double loops. Failure and perseverations are scored.

MENTAL CONTROL

Resistance to Interference (e.g., Ability to Reverse Automated Series)

Serial 7's (Smith, 1967). The subject is instructed to count backward by 7 starting from 100 (100–93–86 . . . all the way down to 2). According to Luria (1966), typical errors of patients with frontal lobe lesions are stereotypes (e.g., 100–93–83–73 . . .) or the

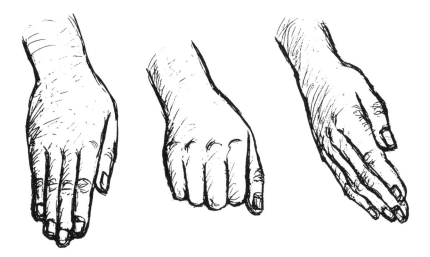

FIGURE 13.1. Luria's hand sequences (Luria, 1966).

FIGURE 13.2. Alternating pattern (Luria, 1966).

switch to multiples of 7 as learned at school (e.g., 79–70–63–56 . . .). Numbers of errors, time to complete the task, stereotypes or perseverations are scored.

Reverse Spelling (Weinberg, Diller, Gerstman, & Schulman, 1972). We use "earth" for the American subjects and "Stich" for the Swiss and German subjects. Both words contain pairs of letters (ea, th, st, ch) that commonly occur in this order. They are expected to elicit a stereotype when trying to spell them backward (e.g., t–h–r–e–a).

Weekdays in Reverse, Months in Reverse (Bender, 1979). Numbers of errors, time, stereotypes, and perseverations are scored.

Flexibility in Shifting

Trail Making Test (Reitan, 1958). We use numbers and months instead of numbers and letters to minimize a recognition effect in eventual subsequent neuropsychological testing. For part A, the 7 weekdays are written in random distribution on a sheet and have to be connected from Monday through Sunday by a line drawn with a pen. For part B, the subject has to alternate between numbers and months (101–January–102–February . . . up to 112–December). Time and numbers of errors are scored and, additionally, the failure to alternate between numbers and months (e.g., 101–January–102–103–104 . . .).

CONCEPT FORMATION

Coin Test (Wang, 1987). The subject has to guess in which hand the examiner is holding a coin. Because the examiner changes the hand regularly (A: once right, once left; B: once right, twice left), the subject has to find out this pattern. The number of trials required to recognize the pattern is rated.

FLUENCY AND CREATIVITY

Word Fluency (Benton & Hamsher, 1976; Milner, 1964). The subject is told to (1) name as many cities as possible in one minute; (2) name as many words as possible in one minute beginning with an "S." Repetitions are not counted.

Five-Point Test (Regard, Strauss, & Knapp, 1982). As a test of nonverbal fluency, the subject is instructed to draw different patterns by connecting the dots in each five-dot matrix using four lines (see Figure 13.3). We allow 2 minutes instead of 5 minutes. Repetitions are not scored.

FIGURE 13.3. The five-point test. The sheet comprises five columns and seven rows of blocks, each of which contains five points. Adapted from Regard, Strauss, and Knapp (1982). Copyright 1982 by *Perceptual and Motor Skills*. Adapted by permission.

Alternate Use Test (Eslinger & Grattan, 1993). More recently, this test has been proposed to be specific for frontal lobe dysfunction. The instruction to come up with unusual uses for common objects (e.g., a pencil) is supposed to be difficult for patients with frontal dysfunction. Unfortunately, we were not able to incorporate this test as it was published after our studies had started.

UNILATERAL INATTENTION

Double Simultaneous Stimulation (Russel, Neuringer, & Goldstein, 1970). This is an examination of unilateral neglect and is performed for the visual and the tactile modalities. The instructions are: "Look at my nose and tell me which hand I am moving, right, left or both"; and "Tell me which of your hands I am touching, right, left or both."

MEMORY

Digit Span (Wechsler, 1955). The patient is asked to repeat a string of digits at a rate of one per second. The average number of digits normal adults can repeat is 6 1 (Spitz, 1972).

Word List Learning (McCarthy, Ferris, Clark, & Crook, 1981; Rey, 1964). The lists were "spinach, table, dog, baseball, Chevrolet, rose, belt, blue" for English-speaking subjects and "Spinat, Tisch, Hund, Fussball, Opel, Rose, Gürtel, blau" for German-speaking subjects. At the beginning of the whole test battery, the examiner reads the word list four times. After each reading, the subject has to repeat as many items as possible. At the end, the subjects are asked to recall as many items as possible without another reading. At this delayed trial, the examiner gives clues for the items that are not recalled: vegetable, furniture, animal, sport, car, flower, garment, color.

PERSONALITY AND EMOTION

Initiative, self-monitoring, control of aggressive and sexual impulses, emotionality, and social behavior are often reported to be affected by frontal lobe dysfunction. For the assessment of these functions, we included items from the Neurobehavioral Rating Scale by Levin et al. (1987). (See Table 13.1.)

To score the Neurobehavioral Rating Scale, examiners take into consideration not only their evaluation of the patient's behavior during the test situation but also observations by the patients themselves, their relatives, nurses, and physicians on the ward.

LANGUAGE

Spontaneous Speech. Based on Luria (1966) and Stuss and Benson (1986), we selected the following criteria regarding spontaneous speech and narrative discourse: reduced production, fixation on details, lack of distance, discursive discourse, missing chronology, and perseveration. The examiner rates the subject's speech by each of these criteria as present or not present.

DEVELOPMENT OF THE "FRONTAL LOBE SCORE"

The construction of a battery of clinical examinations and tests for bedside assessment of frontal dysfunction was performed in two steps: In a first step, we used all the tests listed previously to examine a sample of 118 patients and control subjects. By statistical analysis, we selected those examinations that differentiated best between patients with frontal lobe lesions and control subjects as well as patients with cerebral lesions without involvement of the frontal lobes.

In a second step, we attempted to evaluate the validity of the resulting Frontal Lobe Score (FLS) in a prospective, blinded setup and to compare its sensitivity and specificity with the Wisconsin Card Sorting Test (WCST) and the Stroop Test in a new sample of 108 patients and controls.

Study 1

The first study included four groups: 27 patients with cerebral lesions confined to the frontal lobes (frontal), 25 patients with cerebral lesions without involvement of the frontal lobes (nonfrontal), 18 patients with mixed frontal–nonfrontal lesions (mixed), and 48 normal control subjects (controls). Statistical analysis of the data was performed using stepwise discriminant analysis as well as multiple *t*-tests for the numeric variables and chi-square tests for the dichotomous (present–not present) variables. In this way, we

---

TABLE 13.1. Instructions for Application of the Frontal Lobe Score

- *Serial 7's*: The subject is instructed to count backward by 7 starting from 100 (100–93–86 . . . all the way down to 2). Typical frontal errors are stereotypes (e.g., 100–93–83–73 . . .) or the switch to multiples of 7 as learned at school (e.g., 79–70–63–56 . . .). They are scored additionally.

- *Reverse Spelling*: We use "earth" for English-speaking subjects and "Stich" for German-speaking subjects. Typical frontal errors are stereotypes, in which the subject spells the letter pairs in the habitual order (e.g., t–h–r–e–a).

- *Weekdays in Reverse*: Numbers of errors and time are scored.

- *Months in Reverse*: In addition to errors and time, stereotypes (e.g., . . . July–June–May–June) are scored as frontal error pattern.

- *Grasp Reflex*: The examiner tests for a tactile grasp reflex by lightly touching with his own hand the first interosseus space of the subject's hands. If positive, it results in a flexion of thumb and fingers.

(continued)

TABLE 13.1. (*continued*)

- *Go/No-Go*: The instruction by the examiner is: "Tap twice, when I tap once, but when I tap twice, don't tap at all." The examiner taps once or twice in random order (five times once and five times twice). There are two typical frontal errors: the inability to stop the impulse to tap after the examiner tapped twice and the imitation of the examiner's rhythm.

- *Rhythm Tapping*: The subject is asked to repeat the following two different rhythms tapped by the examiner: (-..-..-..) (—...—...—...-). A typical frontal error would be tapping a simple rhythm instead of the second, complex rhythm.

- *Luria's Hand Sequences*: Two steps: In this easier version, the examiner makes a fist, then extends his fingers, holding his hand horizontally. The subject has to repeat this alternating movement 10 times. Three steps: The third movement is added, the examiner turning his hand by 90° with the extended fingers still pointing forward. Number of trials necessary to learn the sequence and fluency are rated. Perseverations (the repetition of the two steps when the three steps are tested) are scored additionally as a frontal error.

- *Alternating Pattern*: The subject is told to copy a drawing without lifting the hand from the paper. A typical frontal error would be to draw two peaks in a row.

- *Trail Making Test*: For part A, the 7 weekdays are written in random distribution on a sheet and have to be connected from Monday through Sunday by a line drawn with a pen. For part B, the subject has to alternate between numbers and months (101–January–102–February . . . up to 112–December). Time and numbers of errors are scored and, additionally, the failure to alternate between numbers and months (e.g., 101–January–102–103–104 . . .) as a frontal error.

- *Five-Point Test*: The subject is instructed to draw different patterns by connecting the five dots in each matrix using four lines. We allow two minutes instead of five minutes. Word list learning: the lists are "spinach, table, dog, baseball, Chevrolet, rose, belt, blue" for English-speaking subjects and "Spinat, Tisch, Hund, Fussball, Opel, Rose, Gürtel, blau" for German-speaking subjects. At the beginning of the whole FLS battery, the examiner reads the word list four times. After each reading, the subject has to repeat as many items as possible. At the end, the subjects are asked to recall as many items as possible without another reading.

- *Neurobehavioral Rating Scale*
  - Emotional withdrawal (lack of spontaneous interaction, isolation, deficiency in relating to others).
  - Depressive mood (sorrow, sadness, despondency, pessimism).
  - Decreased initiative/motivation (lack of normal initiative in work or leisure, failure to persist in tasks, reluctance to accept new challenges).
  - Motor retardation (slow movements or speech excluding primary weakness).
  - Blunted affect (reduced emotional tone, reduction in normal intensity of feelings, flatness).
  - Lability of mood (sudden change in mood which is disproportionate to the situation).
  - Disinhibition (socially inappropriate comments and/or actions, including sexual/aggressive content, or inappropriate to the situation, outbursts of temper).
  - Hostility/uncooperativeness (animosity, irritability, belligerence, disdain for others, defiance of authority).
  - Excitement (heightened emotional tone, increased reactivity).
  - Inattention (failure to sustain attention, easily distracted, failure to notice aspects of the environment, difficulty in directing attention, decreased alertness).
  - Poor planning (unrealistic goals, failure to take disability into account, poorly formulated plans for the future, e.g., what will you do when you leave the hospital).
  - Inaccurate insight and self-appraisal (poor insight, exaggerated self-opinion, overrating level of ability and underrating personality change in comparison with evaluation by clinicians and family).

For the scoring of the Neurobehavioral Rating Scale, the examiner takes into consideration not only his evaluation of the patient's behavior during the test situation, but also observations by the patient him- or herself, his or her relatives, nurses and physicians on the ward.

Spontaneous speech: The examiner rates the subject's speech by each of the seven criteria as present or not present.

Note. All errors and the times to complete the tasks are scored. In some of the items, typical frontal errors are scored additionally as indicated in the table.

selected those mental status tests, clinical examinations, and rating scales that make up the FLS (Table 13.1). It consists of 12 tests and rating scales with 56 variables.

The following tests did not differentiate well between the frontal and the nonfrontal group and were therefore not included in the FLS: verbal fluency, digit span, motor impersistence, conflicting commands, multiple loops, coin test, conjugate eye movement, and double simultaneous stimulation.

For the practical use of the resulting battery, we defined cutoff criteria as follows: The dichotomous variables (e.g., the grasp reflex) were noted as present or not present. For the numeric variables, normal score ranges were defined as the mean values of the control group 1 standard deviation. The variables were then weighted: values exceeding this range were deliberately assigned a score value of 1. Those variables, however, that had revealed significant differences between the frontal and the nonfrontal group in t-test or chi-square, respectively, were assigned a score value of 2. By simply adding the scores (0, 1, or 2 for each of the 56 variables), the total FLS was obtained.

Analysis of the distribution of the resulting total scores in each group showed that a cutoff score of 12 gave the highest sensitivity for discriminating the frontal group from the nonfrontal and the control group. A total score of 12 or higher was therefore chosen as indicating frontal lobe dysfunction.

The time required for the administration of the final test battery representing the FLS varies between about 20 minutes for most normal control subjects and 40–45 minutes for the patients with severe deficits.

Study 2

The second study evaluated the validity of the FLS in a prospective, blinded setup and compared its sensitivity and specificity to the WCST and the Stroop Test (Stroop, 1935). It comprised 108 subjects, again divided into four groups: 26 patients with cerebral lesions confined to the frontal lobes (frontal), 28 patients with cerebral lesions without involvement of the frontal lobes (nonfrontal), 31 patients with mixed frontal–nonfrontal lesions (mixed), and 23 control patients without cerebral lesions (controls). In contrast to the first study, we chose patients without cerebral lesions as controls instead of healthy subjects. Because the FLS was assembled as a bedside examination, it has to have a high specificity with regard to hospital patients without cerebral lesions: No such patient should erroneously be diagnosed as having a frontal lobe dysfunction.

In addition to the FLS, we performed the following examinations:

1. *WCST.* A perseverative response score of greater than 19 was regarded as indicating frontal lobe dysfunction.
2. *Stroop Test in the version of Baumler (1985).* On table I, the subject has to read 36 words signifying red, green, blue or yellow, printed in black. Table II shows 36 rectangles printed in the four different colors, and table III contains 36 words from table I but printed in colors incompatible with the significations. The difference in time required to read through the tables III and II (expressed as C-values of 4) was chosen as differentiating criterion.

As in the first study, only patients with circumscribed cerebral lesions were included. Exclusion criteria were generalized cerebral disease and psychiatric disease as well as aphasia that impeded understanding of the instructions.

Results

Frontal Lobe Score

In the frontal group, 24 out of 26 subjects had scores of 12 or higher and were correctly classified as frontal, two subjects had scores of 11 or lower and were false negatively classified.

Sensitivity for detection of frontal lobe lesions was therefore 92.3% (= 24/26).

In the nonfrontal group, 21 out of 28 subjects had scores of 11 or lower, seven subjects had scores of 12 or higher and were false positively classified as frontal. In the control group, no subject had a score of 12 or higher; the highest score in this group was 11 in one subject.

Specificity was therefore 75.0% (= 21/28) compared to the patients with nonfrontal lesions and 100% in comparison with control patients.

In both studies, analyses of each subtest of the FLS separately showed that no single subtest alone had sufficient sensitivity and specificity.

Wisconsin Card Sorting Test

Sensitivity for detection of frontal lobe lesions was 65.4% (= 17/26).

Specificity was 53.6 % (= 15/28) compared to the nonfrontal patients and 60.9% (= 14/23) in comparison with control patients.

Stroop Test

Sensitivity for detection of frontal lobe lesions was 30.8% (= 8/26).

Specificity was 92.9% (= 26/28) compared to the patients with nonfrontal lesions and 95.7% (= 22/23) compared to control patients.

DISCUSSION

To devise a clinical method for the assessment of frontal lobe dysfunction at bedside, we selected 12 tests and two behavioral rating scales that best differentiated patients with frontal lobe lesions from healthy control subjects and from patients with cerebral lesions without involvement of the frontal lobes. The resulting FLS covers a wide variety of functions:

1. *Motor control and programming*: suppression of reflexes and motor impulses (grasp reflex, go/no-go), rapid switches in movements (rhythm tapping), programming and performance of complex series of movements (Luria's hand sequences, alternating pattern).
2. *Mental control*: flexibility in shifting (Trail Making Test); resistance to interference, for example, the ability to reverse automated series (reverse spelling, weekdays and months in reverse).
3. *Fluency and creativity*: five-point test.
4. *Memory*: word list learning.
5. *Personality and emotion*: 12 items from the Neurobehavioral Rating Scale including initiative, emotionality, control of aggressive and sexual impulses, and self-monitoring.
6. *Planning*: assessed qualitatively as an item of the Neurobehavioral Rating Scale.

The FLS yielded satisfactory sensitivity and specificity even under blinded conditions, with the examiners uninformed about presence, localization, and nature of cerebral lesions in their patients.

Several tests that are generally regarded as indicating frontal lobe dysfunction did not differentiate well between patients with lesions of the frontal lobes and those with nonfrontal cerebral lesions. Therefore, they were not included in the FLS. Surprisingly, verbal fluency, which is assumed to be a specific indicator of frontal lobe dysfunction, was one of those that did not differentiate well. In fact, mean word production rate of the patients in the group with nonfrontal lesions was even slightly lower than in the group with frontal lesions. Similarly, Pasquier, Lebert, Grymonprez, and Petit (1995) found that patients with dementia of frontal lobe type did not differ from patients with dementia of Alzheimer type with respect to verbal fluency. Of course, we do not want to suggest from these findings that the frontal lobes are not involved in language processing. Rather, they can simply be regarded as an indication that language production processes are disrupted also by nonfrontal cerebral lesions (e.g., parietal and/or temporal lesions).

Our studies emphasize the necessity of a battery of tests, as none of the tests alone had acceptable sensitivity and specificity. Thus, they are of limited use when applied separately. Several tests (e.g., grasp reflex, serial sevens, and Luria's hand sequences), were highly specific but fell short on sensitivity, showing up only in a few patients. This is plausible because of the multitude of frontal functions probably attributable to different areas of the prefrontal cortex.

The FLS detected pure frontal lesions with high sensitivity (92.3%). Two patients with frontal lobe lesions had a frontal lobe score of 11 or lower and were therefore false negatively categorized: a 54-year-old male after surgical removal of an abscess of the right dorsolateral convexity and a 65-year-old male with a glioblastoma of the left dorsolateral cortex and the PMA.

The FLS discriminated patients with frontal lesions from controls with a specificity of 100% (i.e., no control patient was erroneously classified as having a frontal lobe lesion).

Differentiation from patients with nonfrontal lesions was obtained with a specificity of 75%; 7 out of 28 patients with nonfrontal lesions had FLS scores of 12 or higher. These cases were a 66-year-old female with a hemorrhage of the left basal ganglia, a 72-year-old female with an ischemic infarction of the left caudate and internal capsule, a 65-year-old male with a hemorrhage of the right pallidum and internal capsule, a 71-year-old male with a hemorrhage of the left thalamus, a 47-year-old male with a left parietal glioblastoma, a 74-year-old male with a right parietal hemorrhage, and a 69-year-old female with a left parietooccipital glioblastoma.

Four out of these seemingly incorrect classifications were thus basal ganglia and thalamus lesions. These findings can be explained by the concept of parallel neuronal circuits connecting the frontal cortex with the basal ganglia and the thalamus (Alexander, DeLong, & Strick, 1986; Alexander, Crutcher, & DeLong, 1990). This model describes five such circuits and predicts that a lesion of a specific circuit even on a subcortical level (basal ganglia or thalamus) causes functional deficits resembling those deficits after lesions of the corresponding frontal cortical areas (Cummings, 1993).

The selected items from the Neurobehavioral Rating Scale by Levin et al. (1987) had high sensitivity and specificity for the detection of frontal lobe dysfunction. This underscores the importance of personality, emotional, and motivational changes that can occur after frontal lobe damage. One must bear in mind, however, that the inclusion of this rating scale in the FLS increases the extent by which the examiner's subjective judgment influences the score. The same is true for the rating of the patient's spontaneous speech. The FLS therefore requires some clinical experience.

In contrast with the FLS, the concurrently administered WCST was clearly less sensitive and specific for the demonstration of frontal lobe dysfunction. Not only was the sensitivity very low, but it also erroneously classified as frontal a considerable number of patients with nonfrontal lesions and even patients without cerebral pathology. These findings are in agreement with data from other authors who concluded that WCST scores did not differentiate well between patients with frontal versus nonfrontal lesions (Anderson, Damasio, Jones, & Tranel, 1991).

The Stroop Test, on the other hand, had a high specificity compared to normal controls and compared to nonfrontal lesions. It was, however, not sensitive (i.e., it missed roughly 70% of the patients with frontal lesions).

As a screening instrument for frontal lobe dysfunction, the FLS therefore appears to be superior to the WCST and the Stroop Test. A pathological outcome in the Stroop Test makes a confirmation of a frontal lobe dysfunction possible with a high degree of confidence. The superiority of the FLS surprised us. We had, after all, included the well-known WCST and Stroop Test to validate the FLS and would have been satisfied if the FLS as a bedside screening examination would just have held up against them. A possible explanation for the superior sensitivity of the FLS lies in the fact that it covers a wider variety of frontal lobe functions than do the WCST and Stroop Test. The multitude of functions probably attributable to different areas of the prefrontal cortex makes such an explanation plausible.

Empirical support for the assumptions regarding frontal functions stems mainly from studies of patients with frontal lobe lesions. Only recently demonstrations of frontal lobe activation during such tasks have been made possible in healthy subjects by SPECT and PET techniques (Bench et al., 1993; Frith, Friston, Liddle, & Frackowiack, 1991; Pardo, Pardo, Janer, & Raichle, 1990; Rezai et al., 1993; Shallice et al., 1994). Although these studies had shown activation of prefrontal areas during the performance of the WCST (Rezai et al., 1993) and the Stroop Test (Bench et al., 1993; Pardo et al., 1990), lesions of these areas did not cause relevant deficits in performing these tests in some of our patients. Again, we regard these findings as evidence for the hypothesis that these two tests indicate dysfunctions in specific areas of the frontal lobe and miss lesions in the other frontal areas. In particular, the WCST may involve activation of the left dorsolateral prefrontal cortex (Rezai et al., 1993), the Stroop Test activation of the right anterior cingulate (Bench et al., 1993; Pardo et al., 1990). The latter PET finding, however, is contrasted by recent data of impaired Stroop performance in patients with lesions of the right lateral prefrontal cortex, but not in patients with lesioned right anterior cingulate (Vendrell et al., 1995). This discrepancy points to the fundamental difficulty to deduce the localization of specific cerebral functions from deficits after lesions of these areas. It does, however, also remind us that PET, SPECT, and functional MRI techniques all infer local neuronal activation indirectly only and therefore have to be interpreted with the necessary caution.

We see the clinical relevance of the FLS mainly in bedside screening of patients for frontal lobe dysfunction by the consultant neurologist. It can therefore be regarded as an extension of the standard neurological examination and mental status examination. Modern imaging techniques do not by any means make these clinical examinations redundant, as not all lesions show up on CT and on MRI scans. And even if such a structural lesion is demonstrated in CT or MRI, we are not exempt from the necessity to examine the patient for functional deficits as correlates of the lesions, just as an MRI finding of, for example, an occipital lesion does not exempt us from the necessity to examine the visual functions. Deficits in frontal lobe functions such as impaired mental flexibility and decreased initiative can easily be misinterpreted as dementia or depression. They strongly influence the prognosis of recovery and the planning of rehabilitation and should therefore be recognized as early as possible.

ACKNOWLEDGMENTS

The studies described herein were performed in close collaboration with the following colleagues (in alphabetical order): Michael Beckson, MD, Department of Psychiatry and Biobehavioral Sciences, UCLA Neuropsychiatric Institute, Los Angeles, California; D. Frank Benson, MD, Department of Neurology, UCLA, Los Angeles, California; Klaus Fassbender, MD, Mannheim Medical School, University of Heidelberg, Germany; Manuela Gaggiotti, MD, Department of Neurology, University of Basel, Switzerland; Udo Rauchfleisch, PhD, Department of Psychiatry, University of Basel, Switzerland; and Dirk Wildgruber, MD, Department of Neurology, University of Tübingen, Germany.

REFERENCES

Alexander, G. E., Crutcher, M. D., & DeLong, M. R. (1990). Basal ganglia-thalamocortical circuits: Parallel substrates for motor, oculomotor, "prefrontal" and "limbic" functions. *Progress in Brain Research, 85,* 119–146.

Alexander, G. E., DeLong, M. R., & Strick, P. L. (1986). Parallel organization of functionally segregated circuits linking basal ganglia and cortex. *Annual Review of Neuroscience, 9,* 357–381.

Anderson, S. W., Damasio, H., Jones, R. D., & Tranel, D. (1991). Wisconsin Card Sorting Test as a measure of frontal lobe damage. *Journal of Clinical and Experimental Neuropsychology, 13,* 909–922.

Baumler, G. (1985). *Farbe-Wort-Interferenztest.* Gottingen, Germany: Hogrefe.

Bench, C. J., Frith, C. D., Grasby, P. M., Friston, K. J., Paulesu, E., Frackowiack, R. S., & Dolan, R. J. (1993). Investigations of the functional anatomy of attention using the Stroop test. *Neuropsychologia, 31,* 907–922.

Bender, M. B. (1979). Defects in reversal of serial order of symbols. *Neuropsychologia, 17,* 125–138.

Benton, A. L., & Hamsher, K de S. (1976). *Multilingual Aphasia Examination.* Iowa City: University of Iowa.

Ben-Yishay, Y., Diller, L., Gerstmann, L., & Haas, A. (1968). The relationship between impersistence, intellectual function and outcome of rehabilitation in patients with left hemiplegia. *Neurology, 18,* 852–861.

Boller, F., & Spinnler, H. (Eds.). (1994). The frontal lobes. In F. Boller & J. Grafman (Eds.), *Handbook of neuropsychology, section 12.* Amsterdam, The Netherlands: Elsevier.

Bouman, L., & Grunbaum, A. A. (1930). Uber motorische Momente der Agraphie. *Psychiatrie, Neurologie, medizinische Psychologie, 77,* 223–260.

Christensen, A. L. (1979). *Luria's neuropsychological investigation.* Copenhagen, Denmark: Munksgaard.

Cummings, J. L. (1993). Frontal–subcortical circuits and human behavior. *Archives of Neurology, 50,* 873–880.

De Renzi, E., Colomba, A., Faglioni, P., & Gibertoni, M. (1982). Conjugate gaze paresis in stroke patients with unilateral damage: An unexpected instance of hemispheric asymmetry. *Archives of Neurology, 39,* 482–486.

Eslinger P. J., & Grattan, L. M. (1993). Frontal lobe and frontal–striatal substrates for different forms of human cognitive flexibility. *Neuropsychologia, 31,* 17–28.

Frith, C. D., Friston, K. J., Liddle, P. F., & Frackowiack, R. S. (1991). A PET study of word finding. *Neuropsychologia, 29,* 1137–1148.

Fulton, J. F. (1934). Forced grasping and groping in relation to the syndrome of the premotor area. *Archives of Neurology and Psychiatry, 31,* 221–225

Fuster, J. M. (1989). *The prefrontal cortex: Anatomy, physiology and neuropsychology of the frontal lobe* (2nd ed.). New York: Raven Press.

Grant, D. A., & Berg, E. A. (1948). A behavioral analysis of degree of reinforcement and ease of shifting to new responses in a Weigl-type card-sorting problem. *Journal of Experimental Psychology, 38,* 404–411.

Levin, H. S., High, W., Goethe, R., Sisson, R. A., Overall, J. E., Rhoades, H., Eisenberg, H. M., Kalisky, Z., & Gary, H. (1987). The neurobehavioral rating scale: Assessment of the behaviorial sequelae of head injury by the clinician. *Journal of Neurology, Neurosurgery, and Psychiatry, 50,* 183–193.

Luria, A. R. (1966). *Human brain and psychological processes.* New York: Harper & Row.

Luria, A. R. (1973). *The working brain: An introduction to neuropsychology.* New York: Basic Books.

McCarthy, M., Ferris, S. H., Clark, E., & Crook, T. (1981). Acquisition and retention of categorized material in normal aging and senile dementia. *Experimental Aging Research, 7,* 127–135.

Milner, B. (1964). Some effects of frontal lobectomy in man. In J. M. Warren & K. Akert (Eds.), *The frontal granular cortex and behavior* (pp. 313–334). New York: McGraw-Hill.

Pardo, J. V., Pardo, P. J., Janer, K. W., & Raichle, M. E. (1990). The anterior cingulate cortex mediates processing selection in the Stroop attentional conflict paradigm. *Proceedings of the National Academy of Sciences, USA, 87,* 256–259.

Pasquier, F., Lebert, F., Grymonprez, L., & Petit, H. (1995). Verbal fluency in dementia of frontal lobe type and dementia of Alzheimer type. *Journal of Neurology, Neurosurgery and Psychiatry, 58,* 81–84.

Regard, M., Strauss, E., & Knapp, P. (1982). Children's production on verbal and nonverbal fluency tasks. *Perceptual and Motor Skills, 55,* 839–844.

Reitan, R. M. (1958). Validity of the Trail Making Test as an indication of organic brain damage. *Perceptual and Motor Skills, 8,* 271.

Rey, A. (1964). *L'Examen clinique en psychologie.* Paris: Presses Universitaires de France.

Rezai, K., Andreasen, N. C., Alliger, R., Cohen, G., Swayze, V., & O'Leary, D. S. (1993). The neuropsychology of the prefrontal cortex. *Archives of Neurology, 50,* 636–642.

Russel, E. W., Neuringer, C., & Goldstein, G. (1970). *Assessment of brain damage: A neuropsychological key approach.* New York: Wiley.

Shallice, T. (1982). Specific impairments of planning. *Philosophical transactions of the Royal Society of London, 298,* 199–209.

Shallice, T., Fletcher, P., Frith, C. D., Grasby, P., Frackowiack, R. S., & Dolan, R. J. (1994). Brain regions associated with acquisition and retrieval of verbal episodic memory. *Nature, 368,* 633–635.

Smith, A. (1967). The serial sevens subtraction test. *Archives of Neurology, 17,* 78–80.

Spitz, H. H. (1972). Note on immediate memory for digits: Invariance over the years. *Psychological Bulletin, 78,* 183.

Stroop, J. R. (1935). Studies of interferences in serial verbal reactions. *Journal of Experimental Psychology, 18,* 643–662.

Stuss, D. T., & Benson, D. F. (1986). *The frontal lobes.* New York: Raven Press.

Vendrell, P., Junquè, C., Pujol, J., Jurado, M. A., Molet, J., & Grafman, J. (1995). The role of prefrontal regions in the Stroop task. *Neuropsychologia, 33,* 341–352.

Wang, P. L. (1987). Concept formation and frontal lobe function: The search for a clinical frontal lobe test. In E. Perecman (Ed.), *The frontal lobes revisited*. New York: IRBN Press.

Wechsler, D. (1955). *Manual for the Wechsler Adult Intelligence Scale*. New York: Psychological Corporation.

Weinberg, J., Diller, L., Gerstman, L., & Schulman, P. (1972). Digit span in right and left hemiplegics. *Journal of Clinical Psychology, 28*, 361.

14

Neuropsychological Assessment of Executive Functions

Impact of Age, Education, Gender, Intellectual Level, and Vascular Status on Executive Test Scores

KYLE BRAUER BOONE

The term "executive function" refers to cognitive abilities involved in volition, planning, purposive action, and effective performance (Lezak, 1995). The availability of appropriate tools for measurement of executive functions is critical given that these specific skills appear to be most predictive of functional status in terms of employability (Lysaker, Bell, & Beam-Goulet, 1995) and higher-level activities of daily living, such as money management, cooking, safety, medication administration, community utilization, and social functioning (Aronson & Vroonland, 1993; Nadler, Richardson, & Malloy, 1993).

Standardized clinical assessment of executive functions have traditionally involved tests such as the Wisconsin Card Sorting Test (WCST), Stroop Test, and Verbal Fluency (FAS). More recently, there has been interest in assessing executive function through working memory paradigms such as Auditory Consonant Trigrams (ACT; a variant of the Brown–Peterson task).

The WCST is viewed as a measure of "concept formation sensitive to difficulty forming initial concepts, maintaining a concept once it is attained, recognizing category shifts, and trying new hypotheses when faced with negative feedback" (Perrine, 1993, p. 469). It measures "reactive flexibility" in which the primary requirement is the ability to "freely shift cognition and behavior according to the particular demands and context of a situation" (Eslinger & Grattan, 1993, p. 18). In contrast, FAS has been viewed as a measure of "spontaneous flexibility" requiring "generation of a diversity of responses ... by mounting effective search strategies to move among classes and categories of knowledge" (Eslinger & Grattan, 1993, p. 18). The Stroop Color-Interference Test is considered a measure of cognitive inhibition (Boone, Miller, Lesser, Hill, & D'Elia, 1990). It measures the ability to inhibit overlearned responses in favor of an unusual one (Spreen

& Strauss, 1991). ACT (Brown–Peterson paradigm) is a measure involving working memory/divided attention (Fleming, Goldberg, Gold, & Weinberger, 1995; Marie, Rioux, Eustache, & Travere, 1995; Stuss et al., 1985).

The validity of these tests was first established through lesion studies, although, more recently, functional imaging data have been used to corroborate these brain behavior relationships. For example, during the 1960s and 1970s, lesion studies showed that the WCST was sensitive to frontal lobe functioning (Drewe, 1974; Robinson, Heaton, Lehman, & Stilson, 1980; Milner, 1963). During the 1980s and 1990s, PET and SPECT imaging studies have confirmed the pivotal role of the frontal lobe in WCST performance by documenting activation primarily of dorsolateral prefrontal cortex during test completion (Berman et al., 1991; Marenco, Coppola, Daniel, Zigun, & Weinberger, 1993; Nagahama et al., 1996; Rezai et al., 1993; Rubin et al., 1991; Weinberger, Berman, & Zec, 1986), although studies have differed as to whether test performance is more related to right- (Marenco et al., 1993) or left- (Rezai et al., 1993; Rubin et al., 1991) hemisphere functioning. Similarly, decreased FAS word generation was initially found to be associated with structural damage to the left frontal lobe (Miceli, Caltagierone, Gainotti, Masullo, & Silveri, 1981; Miller, 1984; Milner, 1964, 1971; Perret, 1974), and more recently regional cerebral blood flow (rCBF) and functional MRI (fMRI) studies have supported the role of the left dorsolateral prefrontal cortex in verbal fluency (Elfgren, Ryding, & Passant, 1996; Frith et al., 1995; Liddle, Friston, Frith, & Frackowiak, 1992; Pujol et al., 1996). Initial lesion studies reported that poor performance on the interference section of the Stroop Test was associated with left frontal pathology (Perret, 1974), whereas subsequent functional imaging studies found Stroop performance to be associated with perfusion of the right anterior cingulate (Bench et al., 1993; Liddle et al., 1992; Pardo, Pardo, Janer, & Raichle, 1990), right frontal polar cortex and right orbitofrontal cortex (Bench et al., 1993). The Brown–Peterson paradigm has been reported to be significantly associated with frontal lobe function (Leng & Parkin, 1989) and lateral frontal glucose metabolism (Marie et al., 1995).

EFFECT OF DEMOGRAPHIC VARIABLES, IQ, AND VASCULAR ILLNESS ON EXECUTIVE TEST PERFORMANCE

Although these tests have clear utility for assessing frontal-lobe-mediated executive functions, accurate interpretation of test scores requires information regarding the extent to which performance is confounded by demographic factors (age, education, gender), overall intellectual level, and chronic medical illness. However, as discussed below, the available literature regarding these issues has either been sparse or contradictory.

Demographic Factors

Age

Previously, we examined performance on four executive measures for age-related declines in a sample of 61 healthy, older subjects ages 50 to 79 (Boone et al., 1990). We found no age-related changes in performance for FAS and ACT, although there was a trend for lowered performance with advanced age on the Stroop task. Also, we failed to detect an age-related deterioration in overall WCST performance, although we observed declines in subjects ages 70 to 79 for number of categories completed, percent conceptual level responses, and total errors; we noted no declines for perseverative responses, percent perseverative errors, failure to maintain set, or other responses. The relative lack of age effects on the WCST was corroborated in a subsequent study involving 91 healthy, older subjects (Boone, Ghaffarian, Lesser, Hill-Guiterrez, & Berman, 1993).

The remaining literature regarding age effects on the WCST has been contradictory. Some studies, corroborating ours, generally failed to detect a decline with age until very late life (Haaland, Vranes, Goodwin, & Garry, 1987), whereas other investigations found an earlier age-related deterioration (Axelrod & Henry, 1992; Daigneault, Braun, & Whitaker, 1992; Heaton, 1981; Kramer, Humphrey, Larish, Logan, & Strayer, 1994; Libon et al., 1994; Loranger & Misiak, 1960; Parkin & Lawrence, 1994; Spencer & Raz, 1994).

Although some studies found no age effect on the Stroop Test (Graf, Uttl, & Tuokko, 1995), or an age effect that was equaled by the effect of health status (Houx, Jolles, & Vreeling, 1993), others reported significant or nearly significant age-related decrements in Stroop performance (Comalli, Wapner, & Werner, 1962; Daigneault et al., 1992; Houx et al., 1993; Libon et al., 1994; Swerdlow, Filion, Geyer, & Braff, 1995; Whelihan & Lesher, 1985).

Regarding verbal fluency, other studies, like ours, reported no effect of age (Axelrod & Henry, 1992; Bolla, Lindgren, Bonaccorsy, & Bleecker, 1990; Daigneault et al., 1992; Miller, 1984; Mittenberg, Seidenberg, O'Leary, & DiGiulio, 1989; Ruff, Light, & Parker, 1996; Selnes et al., 1991; Tomer & Levin, 1993) or an effect only after age 80 (Benton, Eslinger, & Damasio, 1981), or observed that FAS shows only a mild nonsignificant decline with age (Libon et al., 1994), particularly in well-educated individuals (Lezak, 1995). Significant declines with age have only been reported in those older cohorts with low educational level (Parkin & Lawrence, 1994). Hultsch, Hammer, and Small (1993) showed that after controlling for self-reported health status and activity levels, age no longer accounted for significant variance on word generation.

The meager literature on the effect of age on ACT/Brown–Peterson performance has been mixed. Our data (Boone et al., 1990) and work from others (Puckett & Lawson, 1989; Stuss, Stethem, & Poirier, 1987) failed to show significant age-related decline, although other investigations documented some losses with age (Inman & Parkinson, 1983; Parkin & Walter, 1991; Parkinson, Inman, & Dannenbaum, 1985; Schonfield, Davidson, & Jones, 1983).

Gender

We analyzed the impact of various demographic factors, including gender, on WCST performance in 91 healthy adults ages 45 to 83 (Boone, Ghaffarian, et al., 1993). Gender was significantly related to six WCST scores; women outperformed men on number of errors, categories, perseverative responses, percent perseverative errors, percept conceptual level responses, and trials to first category. No other literature on the effect of gender on WCST performance was located.

The literature on gender differences in verbal fluency performance is equivocal, with some studies indicating that women outperform men (Bolla et al., 1990; Veroff, 1980), at least at high educational levels (Ruff et al., 1996), or that performance of men and women is equivalent (Lezak, 1995). No gender-related differences in performance have been found for the Stroop Test (Houx et al., 1993; Swerdlow et al., 1995) or ACT (Stuss et al., 1987).

Education

Educational level had a significant impact on four WCST scores in our middle-aged to elderly normal sample (Boone, Ghaffarian, et al., 1993). Subjects with more than 16 years of education outscored subjects with only a high school education on number of errors, perseverative responses, percent perseverative errors, and percent conceptual level responses.

Some evidence suggests that more highly educated subjects may perform better on the Stroop Test (Houx et al., 1993). Of interest, although FAS performance has been found in some studies to increase with higher educational levels (Ruff et al., 1996; Selnes et al., 1991), education may not account for any unique test score variance over and above that attributable to verbal intelligence (Bolla et al., 1990). Educational level has not been found to significantly affect ACT performance (Stuss et al., 1987).

Intellectual Level

In a separate publication in which we compared WCST performance across differing full scale IQ (FSIQ) groupings (Boone, Ghaffarian, et al., 1993), we observed no significant differences in WCST performance. No other studies could be located regarding the issue of the impact of IQ on WCST performance.

Some investigations indicate that intellectual level, especially verbal intelligence, significantly correlates with verbal fluency (Bolla et al., 1990; Borkowski, Benton, & Spreen, 1967; Cauthen, 1978; Miller, 1984). We found no literature regarding the effect of IQ on Stroop or ACT/Brown–Peterson performance.

Medical Illness: Cardiovascular Disease/White Matter Hyperintensities

Signs of cardiovascular illness, such as history of vascular events, presence of plaques in the carotid arteries, and presence of peripheral arterial atherosclerotic disease, are associated with significant declines in cognitive ability in the elderly (Breteler, Claus, Grobbee, & Hofman, 1994), and the negative impact may be greatest on executive skills. For example, Dywan, Segalowitz, and Unsal (1992) found that cardiovascular health status predicted performance on the WCST, accounting for 28% of test score variance. In addition, high-functioning patients with mild to moderate cardiovascular disease exhibited lowered scores on speed and executive tasks (Spieth, 1964). Similarly, declines on executive tasks have been reported in hypertensive patients (Waldstein, Manuck, Ryan, & Muldoon, 1991; Goldman, Kleinman, Snow, Bidus, & Korol, 1974). Factors that positively influence the cardiovascular system, such as regular exercise, decreases in cholesterol and triglyceride levels, and antihypertensive medications, seem to improve cognition, especially executive abilities. For example, vigorous exercise is associated with superior reasoning, concept formation, and abstraction (Elsayed, Ismail, & Young, 1980). Similarly, lowering serum cholesterol and triglycerides improves problem-solving ability and concept formation (Reitan & Shipley, 1963).

In addition to direct effects on cognition, cardiovascular disease, and cerebrovascular risk factors are associated with the white matter hyperintensities (WMHI) that are commonly found on brain MRI scans of older individuals (Bots et al., 1993), and these WMHI appear to have further detrimental effects on cognition, especially executive skills. Small, scattered WMHI appear to be relatively benign in their impact on cognitive function. However, once total WMHI volume exceeded 10 cm^2, we observed significant declines in executive skills, such as those tapped by the ACT and WCST (Boone et al., 1992). The magnitude of this decline was substantial, equivalent to that seen in frontotemporal dementia (Boone, Miller, & Lesser, 1993). Other studies found that WMHI significantly affected performance on the Stroop Test (Fukui, Sugita, Sato, Takeuchi, & Tsukagoshi, 1994; Houx et al., 1993; van Swieten, Staal, Kappelle, Derix, & van Gijn, 1996; Ylikoski et al., 1993), and verbal fluency (Breteler, van Amerongen, et al., 1994).

Purpose of the Present Study

Although some data are available regarding the impact of demographic factors, IQ, and vascular health status on executive measures, it is unclear which of these variables best predict test scores and actually accounts for unique test score variance. For the purposes of this chapter, regression analyses were computed to determine the relative impact of age, gender, education, FSIQ, and vascular health on WCST, Stroop Test, FAS, and ACT performance in a middle-aged and older normal population.

Method and Results

Subjects were 155 middle-aged and older individuals recruited as controls through newspaper ads seeking healthy elderly. Participants ranged in age from 45 to 84, with a mean of 63.07 ± 9.29. Fifty-three were male and 102 were female. Mean educational level was 14.57 ± 2.55 and mean FSIQ was 115.41 ± 14.11. Subjects were free of current or past psychotic, major affective, and alcohol and other drug dependence disorders and spoke English fluently. All had physical and neurological examinations, including a complete blood chemistry panel, complete blood cell count, and thyroid function panel. Subjects were excluded if they had a history of physical findings of neurological disease, such as stroke, Parkinson's disease, or seizure disorder. Also excluded were individuals with laboratory findings showing serious metabolic abnormalities (e.g., low sodium level, elevated glucose level, or thyroid or liver function abnormalities). Fifty-one subjects had vascular illness (defined as cardiovascular disease and/or WMHI) based on self-report or evidence on examination of at least one of the following: current or past history of hypertension ($n = 39$), arrhythmia ($n = 8$), large WMHI on MRI (> 10 cm^2; $n = 7$), coronary artery bypass graft ($n = 3$), angina ($n = 2$), and old myocardial infarction ($n = 1$). Twenty-four subjects were on cardiac and/or antihypertensive medications.

Subjects were administered the Satz–Mogel abbreviation of the Wechsler Adult Intelligence Scale—Revised (Adams, Smigielski, & Jenkins, 1990), the WCST (Heaton, 1981), the Comalli version of the Stroop Test (the word reading, color naming, and color-interference sections consist of 100 items each; Comalli et al., 1962), FAS (Lezak, 1995), and ACT consisting of 0-, 3-, 9-, and 18-second delays (Stuss et al., 1985; Boone et al., 1990). Variables used for analysis included FSIQ; number of categories, perseverative responses, errors, trials to first category, and percent conceptual level responses on the WCST; number of seconds to complete the color-interference section of the Stroop; total words generated on FAS; and total score on ACT.

Stepwise regression analyses were computed for each executive test score, using age, gender, educational level, FSIQ, and vascular status as predictor variables. As shown in Table 14.1, the various WCST scores were predicted by differing independent variables, although vascular illness and FSIQ tended to be the primary predictors, with gender and education level registering a more secondary role. Age was not a significant predictor of any WCST score, whereas vascular status was the primary predictor of number of categories completed and number of trials to completion of first category. Also, vascular status was a secondary predictor of number of perseverative responses, percent conceptual level responses, and number of errors, accounting for between 4 and 6% of score variance. FSIQ was the primary predictor of number of errors and percent conceptual level responses, reflecting 8% and 9% of score variance, respectively. FSIQ was the secondary predictor of number of categories completed and number of trials to first category, accounting for 4% of variance. Educational level was the main predictor of number of perseverative responses (accounting for 7% of score variance), and a minor predictor of number of errors and perceptual conceptual level responses (accounting for 3% of score variance). Gender was a secondary predictor of number of categories, number of errors, and percent conceptual level responses (contributing 4–5% of score variance).

Regarding FAS performance, the only significant predictor was FSIQ, accounting for 15% of test score variance. Scores on ACT were also significantly predicted by FSIQ, responsible for 17% of test score variance, but age and vascular status were secondary predictors, accounting for 6% and 3% of test score variance, respectively.

Stroop interference performance was primarily predicted by age and secondarily predicted by FSIQ; these variables accounted for 15% and 13% of test score variance.

To examine whether relationships between some predictor variables and executive scores could have been obscured by associations between predictor variables, correlations, *t*-tests, and chi-square analyses were used to assess the relationships among predictor variables. Correlations were computed on the three noncategorical predictor variables

TABLE 14.1. Stepwise Regression Results for Executive Test Scores

Test	Variable	Coefficent	Standard error coefficient	Increase in R^2	Total R^2
FAS	FSIQ	.3025	.0580	.1545	
Stroop Comalli	Age	1.6604	.2877	.1468	
	FSIQ	−.9563	.1912	.1248	.2715
WCST					
Categories	Vascular status	−.8101	.3003	.0587	
	FSIQ	.0301	.0099	.0406	.0993
	Gender	.8827	.2955	.0519	.1512
Perseverative responses	Education	−2.0099	.6536	.0650	
	Vascular status	10.4948	3.6071	.0516	.1166
% Conceptual level	FSIQ	.3276	.1250	.0867	
responses	Vascular status	−10.4507	3.3983	.0619	.1486
	Gender	10.0388	3.3529	.0421	.1907
	Education	1.5615	.6890	.0279	.2186
Errors	FSIQ	−.3399	.1357	.0801	
	Gender	−10.5133	3.6476	.0443	.1244
	Vascular status	8.8895	3.6844	.0354	.1598
	Education	−1.7784	.7438	.0323	.1921
Trials to 1st category	Vascular status	11.1542	3.5274	.0704	
	FSIQ	−.3128	.1159	.0439	.1143
ACT	FSIQ	.2376	.0418	.1737	
	Age	−.1585	.0673	.0552	.2288
	Vascular status	−3.0208	1.3516	.0257	.2545

(age, education, and FSIQ). No relationship was found between age and education ($r = -.036$) or between age and FSIQ ($r = .060$); only a modest correlation, accounting for 20% of variance, was detected between educational level and FSIQ ($r = .453$). *t*-test and chi-square analyses showed that men and women did not differ in age (male = 63.83 ± 8.9, female = 62.68 ± 9.5; $t = .73$, $df = 1,153$, $p = .465$), educational level (male = 15.02 ± 2.9, female = 14.34 ± 2.3; $t = 1.57$, $df = 1,153$, $p = .118$), FSIQ (male = 117.74 ± 14.9, female = 114.17 ± 13.6; $t = 1.49$, $df = 1,151$, $p = .138$), or vascular status (vascular = 20 male, 31 female; nonvascular = 33 male, 71 female; chi-square = .85, $p > .30$). In addition, the vascular and nonvascular status groups did not differ in education (vascular = 14.35 ± 2.6, nonvascular = 14.73 ± 2.5; $t = .87$, $df = 1,151$, $p = 386$) or FSIQ (vascular = 113.33 ± 14.01, nonvascular = 116.42 ± 14.24; $t = 1.25$, $df = 1,149$, $p = .215$), but did significantly differ in age, with the vascular group averaging 7 years older than the nonvascular group (vascular = 67.45 ± 8.2, nonvascular = 60.88 ± 9.1; $t = -4.30$, $df = 1,151$, $p = .00001$). There was considerable overlap in age ranges for the vascular and nonvascular groups; 34% of the vascular group was less than 65 years of age, and 34% of the nonvascular group was age 65 or greater. In conclusion, the five predictor variables were not strongly associated with each other, except for age and vascular status.

To further analyze the effects of age and vascular status on executive test scores, a two-way analysis of variance (ANOVA) was computed using vascular status and age (< 65 and ≥ 65) as the two main factors for those executive scores in which vascular status, but not age, had been a significant predictor in the regression equations (i.e., WCST scores). As shown in Table 14.2, there was no significant main effect for age for any of the WCST scores, but there were significant main effects for vascular status for all WCST scores. Thus, the impact of vascular status on WCST performance does not appear to be an artifact of age.

DISCUSSION

We found that a modest but significant amount of executive test score variance was accounted for by demographic, IQ, and/or vascular illness factors, but that the precise variables varied according to the specific executive score. Performance on all tests was substantially affected by overall intellectual level, whereas the WCST and ACT were also affected by vascular health status. Age influenced performance on the Stroop Color-

TABLE 14.2. Two-Way ANOVA Results for Wisconsin Card Sorting Test Scores

WCST score	Vascular status, < age 65		Vascular status, ≥ age 65		Age main effects		Main effects	
	Vascular	Healthy	Vascular	Healthy	*F*	*p*	*F*	*p*
Categories	4.58 ± 2.0	4.95 ± 1.6	3.68 ± 2.3	5.10 ± 1.3	7.57	.007	1.32	.253
Perseverative responses	25.11 ± 27.5	17.24 ± 14.8	32.52 ± 32.4	20.70 ± 14.7	6.52	.012	1.99	.161
% Conceptual level responses	58.02 ± 23.4	64.95 ± 18.6	47.4 ± 24.6	62.84 ± 18.6	8.79	.004	2.85	.094
Errors	35.89 ± 24.5	29.51 ± 20.6	45.41 ± 24.8	33.33 ± 21.5	5.10	.025	2.66	.105
Trials to 1st category	19.16 ± 26.8	14.12 ± 6.0	30.46 ± 40.4	13.3 ± 3.5	8.86	.003	1.98	.162

Interference Test and ACT but not scores on FAS or WCST. The impact of educational level and gender was limited to select WCST scores.

Findings from the regression analyses would seem to be at variance with some other studies, including our own (Boone, Ghaffarian, et al., 1993), which found a role for educational level on WCST and FAS performance. The regression analyses suggest that when FSIQ is included along with educational level, the latter does not account for a significant amount of unique test score variance. Similar findings were documented by Bolla et al. (1990) regarding the relative impact of verbal intelligence versus educational level on FAS performance. The putative protective role of educational level for maintaining cognitive ability in advanced age may be overrated; the overriding factor may instead be native intelligence. Alternatively, Bolla et al. (1990) suggest that the lack of an effect of education may be confined to older cohorts, especially women, who did not have the same access to education that younger generations had.

The fact that only a limited role for advancing age on executive performance was documented is in contrast to previous studies which have suggested that executive skill declines are the primary cognitive deficit seen with aging (Albert & Kaplan, 1980; Mittenberg et al., 1989; Veroff, 1980; Whelihan & Lesher, 1985). We did not study patients over 85 years, which limits conclusions related to the very old. Also, it is possible that the high intellectual level of our sample provided a protection against age-related losses in executive performance.

Alternately, previous studies documenting age effects on executive performance may not have adequately controlled for vascular illness. Our subjects, even those with cardiovascular abnormalities and WMHI, viewed themselves as healthy, and the vascular problems we documented were well-controlled and nonacute and did not appear to interfere with activity level. Yet, these vascular conditions, present in one-third of a self-identified "healthy" population, significantly predicted WCST and ACT scores. Thus, the executive abnormalities associated with the vascular conditions are worrisome because they occur in elderly subjects who may not view themselves, nor are they viewed by medical professionals, as at risk for cognitive problems. Therefore, research analyzing the independent impact of age on the WCST and working memory paradigms must exclude, or control for, vascular illness if accurate conclusions are to be drawn. Similarly, this study raises issues regarding the development of executive test score normative data, especially involving the WCST and ACT, for the elderly. If the normative sample includes a sizable percentage of "healthy" older subjects with subacute cardiovascular illness, the mean scores on these measures will be depressed and not reflective of any "pure" effect of age on performance. As a result, the normative data will not be of use in detecting subtle declines in executive function such as those associated with mild cardiovascular disease.

The consistent finding of a significant impact of overall intellectual level on executive performance raises additional concerns regarding existing normative data. Most normative studies used for test score interpretive purposes provide data according to education, age, and gender, although the analyses from the current study suggest that IQ is the most relevant factor. However, from a practical standpoint, use of normative data based on IQ groupings can be problematic because IQ, in contrast to age, education, and gender, can be affected by the same neurological insults that cause declines in executive scores. A patient's executive abilities might drop significantly, but if IQ has also deteriorated, IQ-based normative data will not detect the loss in executive ability. Thus, the use of IQ-based norms is only appropriate if there has been no appreciable decline in IQ or if actual or estimated premorbid IQ scores are available.

Table 14.3 provides preliminary normative data for the various executive test

TABLE 14.3. Normative Data for Executive Test Scores

FAS normative data stratified by IQ

	Average IQ	*High average IQ*	*≥ Superior IQ*
	(*n* = 53)	(*n* = 39)	(*n* = 59)
	36.45 ± 9.26	38.87 ± 9.22	44.31 ± 11.88

Stroop interference normative data stratified by IQ and age

	Average IQ	*High average IQ*	*≥ Superior IQ*
< *Age 65*	(*n* = 33)	(*n* = 23)	(*n* = 35)
	132.64 ± 34.51	128.65 ± 26.87	110.29 ± 22.37
≥ *Age 65*	(n = 20)	(*n* = 16)	(*n* = 24)
	164.65 ± 51.90	153.75 ± 56.99	137.08 ± 33.14

ACT normative data stratified by IQ and age

	Average IQ	*High average IQ*	*≥ Superior IQ*
< *Age 65*	(*n* = 32)	(*n* = 23)	(*n* = 37)
	45.81 ± 6.05	45.91 ± 6.45	50.38 ± 8.01
≥ *Age 65*	(n = 20)	(*n* = 16)	(*n* = 23)
	39.95 ± 9.99	43.31 ± 9.23	49.22 ± 6.02

WCST normative data stratified by IQ and vascular status

	Average IQ	*High average IQ*	*≥ Superior IQ*
Categories			
Healthy	(*n* = 34)	(*n* = 25)	(*n* = 44)
	4.71 ± 1.70	4.88 ± 1.45	5.27 ± 1.45
Vascular	(*n* = 17)	(*n* = 13)	(*n* = 17)
	3.53 ± 2.53	3.77 ± 2.01	4.76 ± 1.89
Perseverative responses			
Healthy	(*n* = 33)	(*n* = 25)	(*n* = 44)
	21.94 ± 16.41	19.00 ± 12.63	15.07 ± 14.19
Vascular	(*n* = 16)	(*n* = 13)	(*n* = 17)
	39.31 ± 42.68	27.46 ± 25.65	21.71 ± 15.00
% Conceptual level responses			
Healthy	(*n* = 33)	(*n* = 25)	(*n* = 44)
	59.87 ± 18.01	61.10 ± 17.17	69.51 ± 18.79
Vascular	(*n* = 17)	(*n* = 13)	(*n* = 17)
	45.32 ± 29.84	47.19 ± 20.79	61.52 ± 18.49
Trials to 1st category			
Healthy	(*n* = 34)	(*n* = 25)	(*n* = 44)
	14.53 ± 5.22	14.16 ± 6.40	13.23 ± 4.94
Vascular	(*n* = 17)	(*n* = 13)	(*n* = 17)
	40.76 ± 50.14	24.15 ± 30.61	12.35 ± 2.55
Errors			
Healthy	(*n* = 33)	(*n* = 25)	(*n* = 44)
	36.21 ± 20.55	33.72 ± 19.27	24.71 ± 20.82
Vascular	(*n* = 16)	(*n* = 13)	(*n* = 17)
	46.81 ± 30.51	46.77 ± 21.02	32.41 ± 19.73

scores. To maximize cell size, stratification of data for each test was confined to the two predictor variables that contributed the most unique test score variance. In a further effort to maintain adequate cell size, only three IQ groupings (average, high average, superior) and two age groupings (< 65, $\bar{x} = 56.09 \pm 5.34$; ≥ 65, $\bar{x} = 71.54 \pm 5.02$) were used. Given that only four subjects had FSIQs less than average (i.e., < 90), IQ groupings were limited to average range and higher. FAS data are only grouped by IQ because no other variable predicted a significant amount of test score variance. Because most of the WCST scores were predicted primarily by IQ and vascular status, all WCST data are grouped according to these variables. Although providing normative data according to health status is rather unorthodox, it serves the purpose of illustrating the extent of the loss in WCST performance associated with vascular illness. Specifically, the presence of vascular illness virtually removes any benefit of IQ on number of categories achieved and number of perseverative responses; subjects with $\geq$ superior IQ and vascular illness performed comparably to subjects with average IQ and no vascular illness.

ACKNOWLEDGMENTS

This work was supported in part by Grant No. MH43960 from the National Institute of Mental Health, Bethesda, Maryland, a grant from the UCLA Alzheimer's Disease Center, and a grant from the Harbor–UCLA Research and Education Institute.

REFERENCES

Adams, R. L., Smigielski, J., & Jenkins, R. L. (1984). Development of a Satz–Mogel short form of the WAIS-R. *Journal of Consulting and Clinical Psychology, 52,* 908.

Albert, M. S., & Kaplan, E. (1980). Organic implications of neuropsychological deficits in the elderly. In *New directions in memory and aging: Proceedings of the George A. Talland Memorial Conference.* Hillsdale, NJ: Erlbaum.

Aronson, J., & Vroonland, J.P. (1993). The residual cognitive competence of elderly females. *Journal of Clinical Psychology, 49,* 724–731.

Axelrod, B. N., & Henry, R. R. (1992). Age-related performance on the Wisconsin Card Sorting, Similarities, and Controlled Oral Word Association Test. *The Clinical Neuropsychologist, 6,* 16–26.

Bench, C. J., Frith, C. D., Grasby, P. M., Friston, K. J., Paulesu, E., Frackowiak, R. S. J., & Dolan, R. J. (1993). Investigations of the functional anatomy of attention using the Stroop Test. *Neuropsychologia, 31,* 907–922.

Benton, A. L., Eslinger, P. J., & Damasio, A. R. (1981). Normative observations on neuropsychological test performances in old age. *Journal of Clinical Neuropsychology, 3,* 33–42.

Berman, K. F., Ostrem, J. L., Randolph, C., Gold, J., Goldberg, T. E., Coppola, R., Carson, R. E., Herscovitch, P., & Weinberger, D. R. (1991). Physiological activation of a cortical network during performance of the Wisconsin Card Sorting Test: A positron emission tomography study. *Neuropsychologia, 33,* 1027–1046.

Bolla, K. I., Lindgren, K. N., Bonaccorsy, C., & Bleecker, M. (1990). Predictors of verbal fluency (FAS) in the healthy elderly. *Journal of Clinical Psychology, 46,* 623–628.

Boone, K. B., Ghaffarian, S., Lesser, I. M., Hill-Gutierrez, E., & Berman, N. G. (1993). Wisconsin Card Sorting Test performance in healthy, older adults: relationship to age, sex, education, and IQ. *Journal of Clinical Psychology, 49,* 54–60.

Boone, K. B., Miller, B. L., & Lesser, I. M. (1993). Frontal lobe cognitive functions in aging: Methodologic considerations. *Dementia, 4,* 232–236.

Boone, K. B., Miller, B. L., Lesser, I. M., Hill, E., & D'Elia, D. (1990). Performance on frontal lobe tests in healthy, older individuals. *Developmental Neuropsychology, 6*, 215–223.

Boone, K. B., Miller, B. L., Lesser, I. M., Mehringer, C. M., Hill-Gutierrez, E., Goldberg, M. A., & Berman, N. G. (1992). Neuropsychological correlates of white-matter lesions in healthy elderly subjects. *Archives of Neurology, 49*, 549–554.

Borkowski, J. G., Benton, J. G., & Spreen, O. (1967). Word fluency and brain damage. *Neuropsychologia, 5*, 135–140.

Bots, M. L., van Swieten, J. C., Breteler, M. M., de Jong, P. T., van Gijn, J., Hofman, A., & Grobbee, D. E. (1993). Cerebral white matter lesions and atherosclerosis in the Rotterdam Study. *Lancet, 341*, 1232–7.

Breteler, M. M., Claus, J. J., Grobbee, D. E., & Hofman, A. (1994). Cardiovascular disease and distribution of cognitive function in elderly people: The Rotterdam Study. *British Medical Journal, 308*, 1604–1608.

Breteler, M. M., van Amerongen, N. M., van Swieten, J. C., Claus, J. J., Grobbe, D. E., van Gijn, J., Hofman, A., & van Harskamp, F. (1994). Cognitive correlates of ventricular enlargement and cerebral white matter lesions on magnetic resonance imaging: The Rotterdam Study. *Stroke, 25*, 1109–1115.

Cauthen, N. R. (1978). Verbal fluency: Normative data. *Journal of Clinical Psychology, 34*, 126–129.

Comalli, P. E. Jr., Wapner, S., & Werner, H. (1962). Interference effects of Stroop color-word test in childhood, adulthood, and aging. *Journal of Genetic Psychology, 100*, 47–53.

Daigneault, S., Braun, C. M. J., & Whitaker, H. A. (1992). Early effects of normal aging on perseverative and non-perseverative prefrontal measures. *Developmental Neuropsychology, 8*, 99–114.

Drewe, E. A. (1974). The effect of type and area of brain lesion on Wisconsin Card Sorting Test performance. *Cortex, 10*, 159–170.

Dywan, J., Sagalowitz, S. J., & Unsal, A. (1992). Speed of information processing, health, and cognitive performance in older adults. *Developmental Neuropsychology, 8*, 473–490.

Elfgren, C. I., Ryding, E., & Passant, U. (1996). Performance on neuropsychological tests related to single photon emission computerised tomography findings in frontotemporal dementia. *British Journal of Psychiatry, 169*, 416–422.

Elsayed, M., Ismail, A. H., & Young, R. J. (1980). Intellectual differences of adult men related to age and physical fitness before and after an exercise program. *Journal of Gerontology, 35*, 383–387.

Eslinger, P. J., & Grattan, L. M. (1993). Frontal lobe and frontostriatal substrates for different forms of human cognitive flexibility. *Neuropsychology, 31*, 17–28.

Fleming, K., Goldberg, T. E., Gold, J. M., & Weinberger, D. R. (1995). Verbal working memory dysfunction in schizophrenia: use of a Brown–Peterson paradigm. *Psychiatry Research, 56*, 155–161.

Frith, C. D., Friston, K. J., Herold, S., Silbersweig, D., Fletcher, P., Cahill, C., Dolan, R. J., Frackowiak, R. S. J., & Liddle, P. F. (1995). Regional brain activity in chronic schizophrenic patients during the performance of a verbal fluency task. *British Journal of Psychiatry, 167*, 343–349.

Fukui, T., Sugita, K., Sato, Y., Takeuchi, T., & Tsukagoshi, H. (1994). Cognitive functions in subjects with incidental cerebral hyperintensities. *European Neurology, 34*, 272–276.

Goldman, H., Kleinman, K. M., Snow, M. Y., Bidus, D. R., & Korol, B. (1974). Correlation of diatolic blood pressure and signs of cognitive dysfunction in essential hypertension. *Diseases of the Nervous System, 35*, 571–572.

Graf, P., Uttl, B., & Tuokko, H. (1995). Color- and picture–word Stroop tests: Performance changes in old age. *Journal of Clinical and Experimental Neuropsychology, 17*, 390–415.

Haaland, K. Y., Vranes, L. P., Goodwin, G. S., & Garry, P. J. (1987). Wisconsin Card Sorting Test Performance in a healthy elderly population. *Journal of Gerontology, 42*, 345–346.

Heaton, R. K. (1981). *Wisconsin Card Sorting Test Manual.* Odessa, FL: Psychological Assessment Resources.

Houx, P. J., Jolles, J., & Vreeling, F. W. (1993). Stroop interference: Aging effects assessed with the Stroop color–word test. *Experimental Aging Research, 19,* 209–224.

Hultsch, D. F., Hammer, M., & Small, B. J. (1993). Age differences in cognitive performance in later life: Relationships to self-reported health and activity life style. *Journal of Gerontology, 48,* 1–11.

Inman, V. Q., & Parkinson, S. R. (1983). Differences in Brown–Peterson recall as a function of age and retention interval. *Journal of Gerontology, 38,* 58–64.

Kramer, A. F., Humphrey, D. G., Larish, F. J., Logan, G. D., & Strayer, D. L. (1994). Aging and inhibition: Beyond a unitary view of inhibitory processing in attention. *Psychology and Aging, 9,* 491–512.

Leng, N. R., & Parkin, A. J. (1989). Aetiological variation in the amnesic syndrome: A comparisons using the Brown–Peterson task. *Cortex, 25,* 251–259.

Lezak, M. D. (1995). *Neuropsychological assessment* (3rd ed.). New York: Oxford University Press.

Libon, D. J., Glosser, G., Malamut, B. L., Kaplan, E., Goldberg, E., Swenson, R., & Sands, L. P. (1994). Age, executive functions, and visuosopatial functioning in healthy older adults. *Neuropsychology, 8,* 38–43.

Liddle, P. F., Friston, K. J., Frith, C. D., & Frackowiak, R. S. J. (1992). Cerebral blood flow and mental processes in schizophrenia. *Journal of the Royal Society of Medicine, 85,* 224–227.

Loranger, A. W., & Misiak, H. (1960). The performance of aged females on five non-language tests of intellectual functions. *Journal of Clinical Psychology, 16,* 189–191.

Lysaker, P., Bell, M., & Beam-Goulet, J. (1995). Wisconsin Card Sorting Test and work performance in schizophrenia. *Psychiatry Research, 56,* 45–51.

Marenco, S., Coppola, R., Daniel, D. G., Zigun, J. R., & Weinberger, D. R. (1993). Regional cerebral blood flow during the Wisconsin Card Sorting Test in normal subjects studied by xenon-133 dynamic SPECT: Comparison of absolute values, percent distribution values, and covariance analysis. *Psychiatry Research: Neuroimaging, 50,* 177–192.

Marie, R. M., Rioux, P., Eustache, F., & Travere, J. M. (1995). Clues about the functional neuroanatomy of verbal working memory: a study of resting brain glucose metabolsim in Parkinson's disease. *European Journal of Neurology, 2,* 83–94.

Miceli, G., Caltagierone, C., Gainotti, G., Masullo, C., & Silveri, M. C. (1981). Neuropsychological correlates of localized cerebral lesions in nonaphasic brain-damaged patients. *Journal of Clinical Neuropsychology, 3,* 53–63.

Miller, E. (1984). Verbal fluency as a function of a measure of verbal intelligence and in relation to different types of cerebral pathology. *British Journal of Clinical Psychology, 25,* 53–57.

Milner, B. (1963). Effect of different brain lesions on card sorting. *Archives of Neurology, 9,* 90–100.

Milner, B., (1964). Some effects of frontal lobectomy in man. In J. M. Warren & K. Akert (Eds.), *The frontal granular cortex and behavior* (pp. 313–334). New York: McGraw-Hill.

Milner, B. (1971). Interhemispheric differences in the localization of psychological processes in man. *British Medical Bulletin, 27,* 272–277.

Mittenberg, W., Seidenberg, M., O'Leary, D. S., & DiGiulio, D. V. (1989). Changes in cerebral functioning associated with normal aging. *Journal of Clinical and Experimental Neuropsychology, 11,* 918–932.

Nadler, J. D., Richardson, E. D., & Malloy, P. F. (1993). The ability of the Dementia Rating Scale to predict everyday functioning. *Archives of Clinical Neuropsychology, 8,* 449–460.

Nagahama, Y., Fukuyama, H., Yamauchi, H., Matsuzaki, S., Konishi, J., Shibasaki, H., & Kimura, J. (1996). Cerebral activation during performance of a card sorting test. *Brain, 119,* 1667–1675.

Pardo, J. V., Pardo, P. J., Janer, K. W., & Raichle, M. E. (1990). The anterior cingulate cortex mediates processing selection in the Stroop attentional conflict paradigm. *Proceedings of the National Academy of Sciences, USA, 87,* 256–259.

Parkin, A. J., & Lawrence A. (1994). A dissociation in the relation between memory tasks and frontal lobe tests in the normal elderly. *Neuropsychologia, 32,* 1523–1532.

Parkin, A. J., & Walter, B. M. (1991). Aging, short-term memory and frontal dysfunction. *Psychobiology, 19,* 175–179.

Parkinson, S. R., Inman, V. W., & Dannenbaum, S. E. (1985). Adult age differences in short-term forgetting. *Acta Psychologica, 60,* 83–101.

Perret, E. (1974). The left frontal lobe of man and the suppression of habitual responses in verbal categorical behavior. *Neuropsychologia, 12,* 323–330.

Perrine, K. (1993). Differential aspects of conceptual processing in the Category Test and the Wisconsin Card Sorting Test. *Journal of Clinical and Experimental Neuropsychology, 15,* 461–473.

Puckett, J. M., & Lawson, W. M. (1989). Absence of adult age differences in forgetting in the Brown–Peterson task. *Acta Psychologica, 72,* 159–175.

Pujol, J., Vendrell, P., Dues, J., Kulisevsky, J., Marti-Valalta, J. L., Garcia, C., Junque, C., & Capdevila, A. (1996). Frontal lobe activation during word generation studied by functional MRI. *Acta Neurologica Scandinavica, 93,* 403–410.

Reitan, R. M., & Shipley, R. E. (1963). The relationship of serum cholesterol changes to psychological abilities. *Journal of Gerontology, 18,* 350–357.

Rezai, K., Andreasen, N. C., Alliger, R., Cohen, G., Swayze, V., & O'Leary, D. (1993). The neuropsychology of the prefrontal cortex. *Archives of Neurology, 50,* 636–642.

Robinson, A. L., Heaton, R. K., Lehman, R. A. W., & Stilson, D. W. (1980). The utiligy of the Wisconsin Card Sorting Test in detecting and localizing frontal lobe lesions. *Journal of Consulting and Clinical Psychology, 48,* 605–614.

Rubin, P., Holm, S., Friberg, L., Videbech, P., Andersen, H. S., Bendsen, B. B., Stromso, N., Larsen, J. K., Lassen, J. A., & Hemmingsen, R. (1991). Altered modulation of prefrontal and subcortical brain activity in newly diagnosed schizophrenia and schizophreniform disorder: A regional cerebral blood flow study. *Archives of General Psychiatry, 48,* 987–995.

Ruff, R. M., Light, R. H., & Parker, S. B. (1996). Benton Controlled Oral Word Association Test: Reliability and updated norms. *Archives of Clinical Neuropsychology, 11,* 329–338.

Schonfield, A. D., Davidson, H., & Jones, H. (1983). An example of age-associated interference in memorizing. *Journal of Gerontology, 38,* 204–210.

Selnes, O. A., Jacobson, L., Machado, A. M., Becker, J. T., Wesch, J., Miller E. N., Visscher, B., & McArthur, J. C. (1991). Normative data for a brief neruopsychological screening battery. *Perceptual and Motor Skills, 73,* 539–550.

Spencer, W. D., & Raz, N. (1994). Memory for facts, source, and context: Can frontal lobe dysfunction explain age-related differences. *Psychology and Aging, 9,* 149–159.

Spieth, W. (1964). Cardiovascular health status, age, and psychological performance. *Journal of Gerontology, 19,* 277–284.

Spreen, O., & Strauss, E. (1991). *A compendium of neuropsychological tests: administration, norms, and commentary.* New York: Oxford University Press.

Stuss, D. T., Ely, P., Hugenholtz, H., Richard, M. T., LaRochelle, S., Poirier, C. A., & Bell, I. (1985). Subtle neuropsychological deficits in patients with good recovery after closed head injury. *Neurosurgery, 17,* 41–47.

Stuss, D. T., Stethem, L. L., & Poirier, C. A. (1987). Comparison of three tests of attention and rapid information processing across six age groups. *The Clinical Neuropsychologist, 1,* 139–152.

Swerdlow, N. R., Filion, D., Geyer, M. A., & Braff, D. L. (1995). "Normal" personality correlates of sensorimotor, cognitive, and visuospatial gating. *Biological Psychiatry, 37,* 286–299.

Tomer, R., & Levin, B. E. (1993). Differential effects of aging on two verbal fluency tasks. *Perceptual and Motor Skills, 76,* 465–466.

van Swieten, J. C., Staal, S., Kappelle, L. J., Derix, M. M., & van Gihn, J. (1996). Are white matter lesions directly associated with cognitive impairment in patients with lacunar infarcts. *Journal of Neurology, 243,* 196–200.

Veroff, A. F. (1980). The neuropsychology of aging: Qualitative analysis of visual reproductions. *Psychological Research, 41,* 249–268.

Waldstein, S. R., Manuck, S. B., Ryan, C. M., & Muldoon, M. F. (1991). Neuropsychological correlates of hypertension: review and methodolgic considerations. *Psychological Bulletin, 110,* 451–468.

Weinberger, D. R., Berman, K. F., & Zec, R. F. (1986). Physiologic dysfunction of dorsolateral prefrontal cortex in schizophrenia. I. Regional cerebral blood flow evidence. *Archives of General Psychiatry, 43,* 114–124.

Whelihan, W. M., & Lesher, E. L. (1985). Neuropsychological changes in frontal functions with aging. *Developmental Neuropsychology, 1,* 371–380.

Ylikoski, R., Ylikoski, A., Erkinjuntti, T., Sulkava, R., Raininko, R., & Tilvis, R. (1993). White matter changes in healthy elderly persons correlate with attention and speed of mental processing. *Archives of Neurology, 50,* 818–824.

15

Language and the Frontal Lobes

ANDREW KERTESZ

The phylogenetic increase in frontal lobe size in humans has attracted the attention of anatomists and anthropologists, such as Gall, Bouillaud and Broca, who assumed that the increased size was associated with the uniquely human capacity for language. There is an apocryphal story of Gall considering the frontal lobes the seat of language because of the bulgy eyes of those classmates who had exceptional verbal abilities. The publication of the case of Phineas Gage (Harlow, 1848, 1868) brought about a considerable change in the notion about frontal lobe function. This case report described the personality changes of a previously conscientious workman who survived a penetrating injury by a tapping iron that entered his maxilla and orbit exiting in the mediodorsal frontal region resulting in little physical damage but a major change in personality (he became irresponsible, inattentive, superficial, and socially disinhibited). Similar case reports appeared subsequently, such as the one by Welt (1888) who described a patient with a tumor in the orbitofrontal region which was associated with inappropriate jocularity, aggressiveness, and maliciousness. Physiologists who stimulated the frontal lobes at the end of the century did not find much in the way of permanent change, but frontal lobe ablations produced impulsive and hyperactive animals that lost affection and social behavior. Bianchi (1895) formulated rather modern concepts of frontal lobe function of serializing and synthesizing groups of representations. Frontal lobe lesions also produced apathy, decreased activity, decreased speech, and inability to plan and carry out a series of actions. In some animals, rage reactions, experimental neurosis, and aggression were controlled by frontal lobotomies, and subsequently Moniz (1936) began to use lobotomy for severe anxiety and psychosis in patients.

The frontal lobe occupies one-third of the surface of each hemisphere including the motor cortex with its distinctive cytoarchitectonics. Some of this distinctiveness diminishes as the surrounding association areas are reached. Undoubtedly, the frontal lobes have an important motor function in addition to the precentral motor strip. There is a large premotor area consisting of Brodmann's areas 6, 8, 44, and 45, including the cortical eye fields and the supplementary motor area on the medial surface of the hemisphere as well as the posterior third of the inferior frontal gyrus. These last two structures are the well-known language areas in the left frontal lobe in most adults, although evidence demonstrates that they are not the only ones concerned with language. It has been postulated from widely converging evidence that the left inferior posterior frontal lobe has an important role in articulation and the medial supplementary motor area on the left in the initiation of speech in a large majority of individuals. In a minority of left-handers and a few right-handers, the right hemisphere is dominant for language, including the frontal structures.

BROCA'S APHASIA AND BROCA'S AREA

The language syndrome most commonly associated with left frontal lobe impairment is Broca's aphasia. The lesion in persistent Broca's aphasia often involves, in addition to the posterior inferior frontal gyrus, the inferior central Rolandic area (Niessl von Maydendorf, 1911; Levine & Sweet, 1983), the inferior parietal regions, and often a substantial part of the insula and subcortical regions (Kertesz, Harlock, & Coates, 1979; Mohr et al., 1978). Traditionally, Broca's area is thought of as the pars opercularis of the third frontal convolution (Bailey & von Bonin, 1951). Others used the posterior third of the third frontal convolution as the extent of the area, including the pars angularis (F_3). Brodmann (1909) labeled this region as area 44, although the histology is not considered all that unique and the border of areas 45 and 44 is far from well defined histologically. This premotor association cortex is adjacent to the motor cortex subserving the lips, tongue, palate, and pharynx and was considered to carry the memory for movements of articulation (articulatory engrams). Broca's area lesions do not necessarily result in Broca's aphasia, although patients with the so-called Broca's aphasia syndrome regularly have frontal involvement, either the frontal opercular cortex or Broca's area, or the subcortical white matter and the capsulostriatal region.

Broca (1861) described articulatory disturbance, limited speech output, and retained comprehension in two patients. Although he called it aphemia, the syndrome of Broca's aphasia became well established, even though its localization to the posterior frontal region was disputed. Broca's aphasia and the associated syndromes are often defined descriptively, and quantitated taxonomy is infrequently applied. The basis of such taxonomy includes defined fluency, comprehension, repetition, and naming scores (Kertesz, 1979; Kertesz & Phipps, 1977). The descriptive definition of Broca's aphasia includes decreased fluency, phonological paraphasias, and articulatory errors, often called verbal apraxia, agrammatism, and relatively preserved comprehension. In addition, poor repetition and naming and equivalent disturbance of writing and reading with relatively preserved reading comprehension are often mentioned in various definitions. A linguistic definition includes recurrent utterances, verbal stereotypies, condensed sentence structure, poor melodic line, decreased length of uninterrupted word phrases, phonemic paraphasia, decreased verbal agility and articulation, and deficient grammatical form (Goodglass, Quadfasel, & Timberlake, 1964). This is in contrast to what is often called cortical motor aphasia or aphemia or pure motor aphasia, which refers to the articulatory and prosodic disturbance of language output without the agrammatic component. These definitions depend a great deal on the stage of the stroke. Often a more complete Broca's aphasia will recover toward a pure motor aphasia or verbal apraxia.

PURE MOTOR APHASIA

Verbal apraxia is occasionally seen in isolation as the initial symptom as a result of an inferior rolandic lesion. Liepmann (1905) used the term "apraxia of speech" and emphasized it as part of the larger syndrome of Broca's aphasia. Recently, speech pathologists in North America have widely adopted and defined the clinical picture, calling it verbal apraxia (Johns & Darley, 1970). Because of its resemblance to dysarthria, the term "cortical dysarthria" has also been used (Nathan, 1947). The syndrome is characterized by articulatory errors, slowing, segmentation, hesitancy, phonemic paraphasias that involve initial consonant and consonant clusters characteristically with omission and substitution, dysprosody, and occasionally hypophonia. This milder articulatory disturbance is also called aphemia by (Bastian, 1897; Schiff, Alexander, Naeser, & Galaburda, 1983), pure motor aphasia (Dejerine, 1906), anarthria (Marie, 1906), and phonetic disintegration (Lecours & Lhermitte, 1976). Although this condition tends to recover rather quickly, at times persisting cases are seen, especially in association with other components of Broca's aphasia.

Dysphonia, dysprosody, and stuttering are peripheral speech deficits that are also associated with a variety of frontal damage, both right and left. Acquired stuttering has been described with frontal lobe lesion, but some distinctive features of idiopathic stuttering are not replicated by the frontal cases (Rosenbek, 1980).

PERSISTING NONFLUENT APHASIA

Severe persisting Broca's aphasia often evolves from initially global aphasics (Kertesz & McCabe, 1977; Kertesz, 1981; Mohr et al., 1978). Persistent nonfluency was associated with lesions extending to the Rolandic cortical region and underlying white matter in previous studies (Knopman et al., 1983; Lecours & Lhermitte, 1976; Levine & Sweet, 1983; Niessl von Mayendorf, 1930). The involvement of the central and frontal white matter was important for the fluency deficit in the head-injured population of Russell and Espir (1961) and Ludlow et al. (1986), and in stroke (Naeser, Palumbo, Helm-Estabrooks, Stiassny-Eder, & Albert, 1989). The frontal portion of the centrum semiovale and periventricular white matter, which is involved in persistent cases of global or Broca's aphasia, often includes the pyramidal tract, thalamocortical somatosensory projections, the body of the caudate nucleus, striatocortical connections, callosal radiations, the subcallosal fasciculus (Muratoff, 1893), thalamocortical projections from the dorsomedial and ventrolateral nuclei (Yakovlev & Locke, 1961), and the occipitofrontal fasciculus (Dejerine & Dejerine-Klumpke, 1895). Converging evidence suggests that the articulatory network for fluency involves the white matter connecting tracts between the cortical components of the network, and that persisting nonfluent aphasia can be produced mainly by white matter lesions.

There are patients who have significant, albeit recoverable, disturbance of articulation and speech output with preserved comprehension and only Broca's area is involved at the premotor cortex of areas 44 and 45. Inferior Rolandic and subcortical regions, however, may compensate, and recovery tends to be rapid if the cortical deficit is restricted in Broca's area (Mohr, 1973). These patients are often left with somewhat decreased word fluency and some verbal apraxia (Kertesz, 1988). Disturbance of syntactic function and agrammatism have also been related to the frontal lobe component of Broca's aphasia and to frontal lesions (Nadeau, 1988).

FRONTAL–SUBCORTICAL APHASIAS

Subcortical lesions can produce a variety of deficits. As a rule, dominant putaminal and capsulostriatal lesions will produce a nonfluent language disorder that at times resembles Broca's aphasia (Kertesz, 1984; Kirk & Kertesz, 1994; Naeser et al., 1982). Some of these were considered atypical or distinct from the cortical syndromes (Damasio, Damasio, Rizzo, Varney, & Gersh, 1982). Hemiparesis, dysarthria, and dysphonia appeared to be more severe in patients with subcortical lesions. Otherwise, neither the severity of aphasia nor degree of impairment of any of the subtests differentiates reliably between the cortical and subcortical syndromes (Kirk & Kertesz, 1994). Aphasia severity does not always correlate with the lesion volume in the subcortical lesions, and the site may be more important in determining the degree of language impairment (Kirk & Kertesz, 1994; Naeser et al., 1982). Patients who only have capsulostriatal lesions may only have mild anomia (Alexander, Naeser, & Palumbo, 1987). Severely impaired patients tend to have basal ganglia, internal capsule, and extracapsular white matter impaired as well (Damasio et al., 1982). Some of the capsulostriatal patients also have an articulatory disturbance with phonemic paraphasias such as seen in verbal apraxia (Alexander et al., 1987; Kertesz, 1984). The more frontal white matter is involved the less fluency is seen in these patients (Alexander et al., 1987). The variable association with dysarthria is attributable to the variable damage to corticobulbar fibers from the precentral cortex toward the pons (Alexander & Naeser, 1988). A few patients may develop global aphasia with relatively a small subcortical lesion that involves white matter anteriorly, superiorly, and posteriorly (Kirk & Kertesz, 1994). Recently, anterior insular involvement in dysfluency has been reemphasized (Donkers, 1996), similiar to Pierre Marie's (1906) concept of the "quadrilateral" area lesion causing "anarthria."

Aphasia due to subcortical damage has been attributed to secondary cortical hypometabolism or hypoperfusion (Metter et al., 1983; Olsen, Bruhn, & Oberg, 1986; Perani, Vallar, Cappa, Mensa, & Fazio, 1987; Weiller et al., 1993; Weinrich, Ricaurte, Kowall, Weinstein, & Lane, 1987). In cases of capsulostriatal infarcts or anterior subcortical infarcts and hemorrhages this is likely related to frontal lobe dysfunction because of the extensive frontostriatal connections that may be disrupted. SPECT studies suggest subcortical lesions with extensive frontal connections produce ipsilateral cortical hypometabolism and functional deactivation of frontal language areas (Perani et al., 1987). Although dysarthria and hypophonia could be related to the motor disruption of the basal ganglia lesions, severe language disturbance is usually associated with white matter involvement. Motor and premotor phonemic assembly mechanisms are elaborated by a cortical–subcortical network. Partial damage to one or two components of the network is followed by good recovery. However, if all cortical and subcortical components of the network are impaired, the deficit is more severe (Bruner, Kornhuber, Seemuller, Suger, & Wallesch, 1982) and recovery is much less likely (Kertesz, 1988).

TRANSCORTICAL MOTOR APHASIA

A distinctive type of language deficit, seen with lesions of the left frontal lobe, was called transcortical motor aphasia (TMA) by Wernicke (1886), although Lichtheim (1885) provided the first description of this aphasic syndrome. His patient had impaired speech and writing but good repetition, writing to dictation, reading aloud and comprehension, and he used the term "inner commissural aphasia" (innere leitungsaphasie) to underline the concept of disconnection. Others questioned the concept of TMA as soon as it appeared. Bastian (1897) thought TMA represented a mild dysfunction of the motor speech area, which required a stronger stimulus such as external speech than in the normal state where internal cognitive stimuli would elicit spontaneous speech. Goldstein (1915) described TMA in recovering Broca's aphasia after trauma, and he called this form of frontal aphasia a "peripheral motor" aphasia. The term "adynamic aphasia" has also been used for decreased spontaneous speech, since the description by Pick (1892) and Kleist (1934). Luria (1966) used the opposite terminology, calling these cases "frontal dynamic aphasia." Luria (1970) distinguished, in addition to the "dynamic" type of TMA, the perseverative type when frontal type perseverations are prominent. Luria postulated a disturbance of the predicative function of inner speech resulting in a failure of transition from initial thought to verbal proposition in a "linear scheme of the phrase" (Luria & Tsvetkova, 1967). Other formulations suggested a selective impairment of verbal planning (Costello & Warrington, 1989).

TMA is characterized by significantly reduced fluency with relatively normal repetition. The extent of this dissociation, particularly the extent of reduced fluency, is determined with variable methods, and a quantitative definition of the syndrome based on test scores is not often used. Therefore, the lesion localization is divergent to some extent as variable patients tend to be included in some series. For instance, there is a variable naming deficit, although naming tends to be preserved in contrast to Broca's aphasia. Writing is impaired to the same extent as spontaneous speech and may show the same transcortical features. Even though the patient is unable to produce a narrative, written description of a picture, writing to dictation may be quite well preserved.

In an acute phase of TMA, speech production may be limited to the extent of mutism. Subsequently, answers are produced only after a long delay. The output is frequently perseverative and grammatical complexity is reduced. On the other hand, articulation and phonology tend to be normal and generally syntax is preserved when more complex phrases are used. Occasionally, patients only mouth words silently or speak in a whisper or muffled monotone (Rubens, 1975). At times compulsive repetition and forced completion are observed (Rubens, 1975; Stengel, 1947). Echolalia is a feature of some cases with extensive deep damage to the frontal lobe and sometimes posterior spread involving comprehension. Many patients may spontaneously correct syntactic violations, although they may repeat semantically normal sentences unaltered (Davis, Foldi, Gardner, & Zurif, 1978).

In mild cases of TMA, spontaneous speech is brief, laconic consisting only of one or two words. At the same time, the patient can produce lengthy sentences on repetition. Naming may be performed with single-word answers, but the patient cannot describe the attributes of objects in full sentences. These patients may respond to questions about history with automatisms, such as "I don't know" or "I can't remember." However, questions about their illness reveal that their memory is accurate and yes–no questions are successful in eliciting replies (Rubens, 1975). Serial speech and sentence completion are normal but the picture description in connected sentences is poor. These patients may continue to perform well on nonverbal tests and seem to comprehend quite well. They even perform the Wisconsin Card Sorting Test better than do patients with more diffuse brain damage or even with larger parietotemporal strokes, even though card sorting is considered a prototypical frontal lobe test. Even when recovery occurs, these patients still manifest a disturbance of "referential function of speech" consisting of the paucity of descriptive features distinguishing objects. Rubens (1975) considered this function characteristic of TMA with left frontal lobe disease.

At times, the differentiation of those cases with preserved repetition and those with classical Broca's aphasia is not clear-cut. My colleagues and I have defined TMA according to test scores of the Western Aphasia Battery (WAB) (Kertesz & Phipps, 1977; Rubens & Kertesz, 1983). When using a conservative definition, the location of the lesions is most consistently in the left mesial frontal lobe—supplementary motor area (SMA), anterior and superior to Broca's area (Botez & Barbeau, 1971). Anterior cerebral artery infarction on the left side often reproduces the syndrome of TMA (Alexander & Schmitt, 1980; Damasio & Kassel, 1978; Kertesz & McCabe, 1977; Kornyei, 1975; Masdeu, Schoene, & Funkenstein, 1978; Rubens, 1975). Associated neurological deficit with anterior cerebral artery occlusion includes urinary incontinence, and contralateral leg and proximal arm weakness. Sensory loss may be restricted to the contralateral lower extremity, and facial weakness may only be present during spontaneous emotional expression. Even in the absence of significant hemiparesis, motor neglect of the right extremities may be seen (Castaigne, Laplane, & Degos, 1972; Damasio & Van Hoesen, 1983). Bilateral ideomotor apraxia, grasping, and alien hand may be present (Goldberg, Mayer, & Toglia, 1981; Watson, Fleet, Gonzalez-Rothi, & Heilman, 1986).

When TMA is seen with destruction of Broca's area, the preservation of repetition is thought to be related to transcortical mechanisms using right-hemisphere inferior frontal regions for output (Rubens, 1976). The right frontal lobe capacity for language was also supported by a left hemispherectomy in a 12-year-old who was able to repeat sentences and had good auditory comprehension but severely restricted spontaneous speech in effect displaying TMA with only the nondominant functioning hemisphere (Gott, 1973).

Some of the lesions producing TMA are subcortical in the white matter and lateral to the left frontal horn (Freedman, Alexander, & Naeser, 1984; Rothman, 1906). It has been postulated that lesions in this location interrupt connections between SMA and Broca's area. TMA has been observed during recovery from peri-Sylvian lesions or Broca's aphasia (Rubens, 1976). Short-lived mutism is common after Broca's area lesions and large peri-Sylvian lesions can produce persisting mutism if the posterior inferior frontal destruction is extensive (Mohr et al., 1978). The prognosis for TMA due to a SMA infarct is quite good. Most cases evolve over weeks toward anomic aphasia and eventually recover fully (Kertesz & McCabe, 1977).

THE SUPPLEMENTARY MOTOR AREA AND LANGUAGE

The medial surface of both frontal lobes, the SMA, has important specialized motor functions particularly in initiating movements of any kind. Penfield and Roberts (1959) among others recognized the importance of the SMA for speech on the left, and renamed it the supplementary speech area. Stimulation of the supplementary motor cortex of either hemisphere in man has produced arrest of speech or repetitive involuntary vocalization (Brickner, 1940; Erickson & Woolsey, 1951; Penfield & Roberts, 1959). Epileptogenic tumors in the left SMA can also induce vocalization and speech arrest during seizures (Arseni & Botez, 1961; Sweet, 1951). Botez and Barbeau (1971) summarized the literature of speech deficit associated with SMA lesions and described this area as the starting mechanism for speech. The ventral lateral nucleus of the thalamus and the periaqueductal grey matter of the mesencephalon appeared to be the subcortical components of this circuit.

Cytoarchitectonically SMA represents a paralimbic extension from adjacent limbic cortex such as the cingulate gyrus and has extensive reciprocal connections with it (Damasio & Van Hoesen, 1983; Sanides, 1970). SMA is also connected to the striatum via the subcallosal fasciculus (Yakovlev & Locke, 1961). Goldberg (1985) postulated a role of SMA in selecting and executing specific movement sequences from internally generated limbic drive for action and its external realization projecting limbic outflow on to motor executive regions and translating intention to action (Goldberg, 1985). The SMA and cingulate cortex play an important role in the initiation of vocalization in primates (Jürgens & von Cramon, 1982; Myers, 1976).

FRONTAL CORTICAL EXCISIONS, LOBOTOMIES, AND LESION STUDIES

Milner (1964) reported reduction of spontaneous speech in patients with left frontal lobectomy for epilepsy. Most of these frontal resections were anteriorly in the premotor and prefrontal cortex. These patients had a great deal of difficulty with traditional test of word fluency. There is a lesser degree of reduction of word fluency with right frontal lobes which was mainly attributed to defective initiation (Ramier & Hecaen, 1970). Patients with lesions in Brodmann's area 9 in the dorsolateral prefrontal cortex were particularly affected. Robb (1966) reviewed cortical excisions of the left frontal lobe in 26 cases. Sixteen had transient postoperative aphasia and 10 had none. Only one case after excision of Broca's area showed persisting deficit, but most of the excisions were anterior to the opercular portion of the third frontal convolution.

Bilateral frontal lobotomies for psychosurgery provide limited information concerning frontal lobe function because of the variable degree of white matter destruction and lack of standardized testing applied on examining these patients. Most of these patients were psychotic before lobotomy, with altered language function to begin with. Many of the studies used only indirect language tests, such as the verbal intelligence scores from the Wechsler Adult Intelligence Scale or tests of verbal reasoning (Stuss et al., 1981).

Several frontal–subcortical circuits and the behavioral syndromes associated with their lesions were distinguished (Alexander, Benson, & Stuss, 1989; Cummings, 1993). The dorsolateral prefrontal syndrome consists of impaired executive function and motor programming, inflexibility, impersistence, poor organizational strategies, and sequencing. Language is affected by perseveration and decreased word fluency, and in severe cases by mutism. The orbitofrontal syndrome consists of personality changes, irritability, disinhibition, environmental dependency, and distractability. Language is mainly socially affected by altered content and pragmatics. Insensitivity, lack of interest, perseveration, and inappropriate content may render communication difficult, and further impairment leads to abulia, TMA, and mutism. Although the theoretical distinctiveness of these syndromes is attractive, lesions or degenerative disease often produce a mixture of symptoms and various combinations in their evolution. Clinicians may emphasize one or another feature to conform to various theroetical predictions.

WORD FLUENCY

Word fluency, in which the subject is asked to recall as many words as possible in a category in a minute, is one of the commonly tested and most sensitive language functions of the frontal lobes. However, word fluency is impaired in many lesions of the brain, especially in the left hemisphere. Deficits in word fluency occur in aphasic syndromes and in dementia. Impairment can be seen from either the left or right, but a more consistent impairment is seen from left-sided frontal lesions (Milner, 1964). Left medial frontal and SMA lesions particularly tend to result in decreased word-list generation (Alexander & Schmitt, 1980). When a dorsolateral resection and an orbitofrontal leukotomy group were compared, word fluency was affected mainly by the dorsolateral resections (Stuss et al., 1981). Frontal lobe lesions impair letter word fluency (words beginning with the same letter) predominantly rather than word association in semantic categories (Milner, 1964). Ramier and Hecaen (1970) suggested a deficit in initiation which may result after lesions of either frontal lobes. The linguistic component of the deficit, as tested by word fluency, however, would be left-hemisphere sensitive. The right-hemisphere corollary of the word-fluency paradigm is design fluency for the production of drawings (Jones-Gotman & Milner, 1977). However, the specificity of design fluency for frontal lobe damage, just like word fluency, has been questioned. Design-fluency deficit can be seen after lesions in several other cortical areas than the right frontal lobe.

Difficulty with verbal abstraction and abstract reasoning in a verbal mode has been studied with the Proverb Interpretation Test, especially with bilateral frontal lobe disturbance (Benton, 1968). Luria (1966) emphasized the uncoupling of the verbal and motor behaviors as one of the fundamental disturbances in frontal deficit, although some of the experimental studies subsequently investigating Luria's theory showed this theory to be only partially valid (Drewe, 1975). Patients with frontal lobe damage may give an appropriate verbal response to a question of judgment, yet in actual behavior they are unable to carry out actions according to the same principle. Some of these patients may verbalize the consequence of actions yet act as if they were not aware of them. Patients with leukotomies do not show any action–verbalization dissociation in tests where the cue stimulus conflicted with verbal instruction (Benson & Stuss, 1982).

FRONTAL LOBE DEMENTIA

Decreased speech output and mutism are often prominent symptoms in descriptions of Pick's disease (PiD) (Caron, 1934; Pick, 1892) and in frontal lobe dementia (FLD) (Gustafson Brun, Holmkvist, & Risberg, 1985; Neary, Snowden, Northen, & Goulding, 1988). PiD disease is clinically defined as a frontotemporal dementia. Patients with progressive language deficit before other cognitive domains are involved were described as primary progressive aphasia (PPA) by Mesulam (1982, 1987), but eventually many of these cases develop the frontal lobe symptomatology of FLD. There is a great deal of overlap between description of language deficit in FLD and in the cases of PPA (Kertesz, Hudson, Mackenzie, & Munoz, 1994). Initially, most cases of PPA only show anomic aphasia, then later transcortical motor or Broca's aphasia. When short phrases are still reasonably well articulated but a great deal of hesitation and word finding difficulty is seen, the term "logopenia" is applied (Mesulam & Weintraub, 1992). The common nonfluent variety of PPA leads to mutism which is undistinguishable from the cases of mutism described in FLD or as it has been more recently called frontotemporal dementia (FTD) (Lund & Manchester Groups, 1994). Although the pathology of FTD varies in a continuum ranging from classical PiD with Pick bodies to dementia lacking specific histology (Knopman, Mastri, Frey, Sung, & Rustan, 1990), the clinical presentation is similar across pathological variations suggesting that FLD, PPA, and corticobasal degeneration all belong to the same biological entity that may be termed "Pick complex" (Kertesz et al., 1994; Kertesz & Munoz, 1998). Neuroimaging often reveals significant frontal lobe involvement before other atrophy can be detected (Miller et al., 1991; Neary et al., 1986). In cases with primary aphasic presentation, left temporal or frontotemporal atrophy predominates (Mesulam & Weintraub, 1992).

FUNCTIONAL ACTIVATION

Functional imaging has produced additional, albeit at times conflicting, evidence of frontal lobe involvement in language processing. Language tasks of various kinds have shown frontal lobe activation with positron emission tomography (PET) scans and functional magnetic resonance imaging (fMRI). Petersen, Fox, Posner, and Raichle (1988) found left inferior frontal and anterior cingulate activation in verb generation in response to nouns. They thought that the left frontal region was involved in semantic processing intrinsically rather than only in output mechanisms because auditory word tasks also produced activation in the identical left frontal region as well as in the anterior cingulate. At times the activation paradigm produces alteration of cerebral blood flow in the opposite direction such as in the study by Howard et al. (1992) in which the presentation of visual words produced increased blood flow in the left posterior, middle temporal gyrus as well as in the dorsal portion of the anterior cingulate gyrus, but at the same time decreased blood flow was produced in the right inferior and middle frontal gyri. The deep frontal white matter between the cingulate gyrus and the lateral prefrontal cortex (Brodmann's areas 8 and 9) also seem to be activated by semantic judgment tasks which also required phonological processing (Demonet et al., 1992). The same areas that are activated by language tasks in the frontal lobe, namely, the inferior dorsolateral prefrontal cortex and the anterior cingulate, are also activated by the Wisconsin Card Sorting Test and a version of the Delayed Alternation Task, which are more typically frontal executive tasks rather than language paradigms (Berman et al., 1991). Language-mediated processing, however, cannot be excluded in these tests. When the novelty of the task was eliminated or habituation occurred, the subject showed some activation in the dorsolateral cortex, but not in the anterior cingulate. In verbal fluency tasks, in addition to the previously mentioned areas, the left posterior middle frontal gyrus, Broca's area, and left middle SMA were also activated (Wise et al., 1991). No significant difference was found between letter fluency and semantic fluency tasks in contrast to the lesion studies (Frith, Friston, Liddle, & Frackowiak, 1991), which showed letter fluency was affected more by frontal lesions. The right anterior cingulate gyrus was also activated in this paradigm. Reciprocal inhibition was noted between the dorsolateral prefrontal cortex and the superior temporal gyrus during this experiment of intrinsic generation of words.

Activation within Broca's area was shown across a variety of PET studies of phonological processing (Demonet, Fiez, Paulesu, Peterson, & Zatorre, 1996). It has been hypothesized variously that this region may be involved in some form of subvocal articulatory representation or high-level articulatory coding (Fiez et al., 1995). An alternative hypothesis was that the execution of phonological tasks requires the selective engagement of verbal working memory (Paulesu, Frith, & Frackowiak, 1993) or what is also called the articulatory loop (Baddeley, 1986). Dorsolateral frontal convexity activation by language tasks may be related to the nonspecific effort involved to access phonological representations to motor representations and semantic processes (Chertkow

& Bub, 1994). Such tasks may include generating verbs in response to nouns (Petersen et al., 1988). Another area often activated by similar language tasks is the anterior cingulate cortex corresponding to SMA. These are regions of the human frontal lobe involved in attention and executive control of many different activities, not only language (Posner & Petersen, 1990).

FMRI is a noninvasive technique of measuring cerebrovascular response with brain activity similar to PET scanning. Therefore, many fMRI studies of language were initially tended to replicate PET studies. Because of the noninvasive nature of the method, multiple repetitions of each activation are possible and individuals can be studied with reference to their own anatomical structure (Binder et al., 1993). A great deal of frontal lobe activation was produced by semantic processing using semantic monitoring—tone monitoring subtraction technique (Binder et al., 1995). This was, in general, agreement with PET studies using similar tasks (Demonet et al., 1992; Petersen et al., 1988). Silent word generation appeared to activate more area and produce less artefact (Rueckert et al., 1994; Yetkin et al., 1995). Internal speech using silent word generation in alphabetical order of initial letters demonstrated activity in Broca's area (Hinke et al., 1993). In another fMRI study, more widespread activation was seen with a word-generation task, including Broca's area, premotor cortex, and dorsolateral prefrontal cortex, as well as the posterior regions (Cuenod et al., 1995). In most of the studies, not only were the frontal lobes activated by these tasks but posterior heteromodal cortex also appeared to participate in semantic processing. Although the posterior components of this network are postulated to be sites of highly structured forms of semantic information (Hart & Gordon, 1990), the left frontal components appear to facilitate access to these representations and influence retrieval and search strategies of various executive functions (Shallice, 1989).

The primary focus of activation during a word-generation task appeared to include the anterior insula, Brodmann's area 47, and area 10 in the inferior frontal cortex on the left side, and also in the homologous regions in the right frontal lobe (McCarthy, Blamire, Rothman, Gruetter, & Shulman, 1993). Right-hemisphere activation in addition to the left side suggested that response factors or more general frontal lobe functions, rather than specific language processing, play a major role in activation of this region. Activity from the anterior cingulate mostly in the dominant hemisphere was achieved by both silent word generation and word generation aloud. It seems that fMRI studies confirm that frontal lobes play an important executive function in language, in addition to a specific role in phonological selection and motor execution. The anterior attentional system through the cingulate and the dorsolateral executive control system allows the selection, integration, and matching of various cortical representations of language.

SUMMARY

The role of the frontal lobes in language can be summarized as follows:

1. The executive functions of initiation, selection, and activation are subserved by the mesial frontal area (SMA).
2. Lesions in the cortical–subcortical circuit activating speech movements (motor engrams) produce linguistic and articulatory disturbances.

3. Phonological and semantic selection utilizes inferior dorsolateral premotor cortex, inferior precentral cortex (Broca's area), and anterior cingulate cortex (SMA) and forms a network with more posterior language areas.

4. Prosody inflection and similar pragmatic functions of language are probably subserved by the right-hemisphere frontal lobe in a closely integrated network with the previously mentioned left frontal language function.

The neuronal systems mediating these functions may be damaged selectively or in various combinations, influencing the language profiles associated with frontal lobe deficits.

REFERENCES

Alexander, M. P., Benson, D. F., & Stuss, D. T. (1989). Frontal lobes and language. *Brain and Language, 37,* 656–691.

Alexander, M. P., & Naeser, M. A. (1988). Cortical-subcortical differences in aphasia. In F. Plum (Ed.), *Language, communication and the brain* (pp. 215–228). New York: Raven Press.

Alexander, M. P., Naeser, M. A., & Palumbo, C. L. (1987). Correlations of subcortical CT lesion sites and aphasia profiles. *Brain, 110,* 961–991.

Alexander, M. P., & Schmitt, M. A. (1980). The aphasia syndrome of stroke in the left anterior cerebral artery territory. *Archives of Neurology, 37,* 97–100.

Arseni, C., & Botez, M. I. (1961). Speech disturbances caused by tumors of the supplementary motor area. *Acta Psychiatrica Scandinavica, 36,* 379–399.

Baddeley, A. D. (1986). *Working memory.* Oxford, UK: Oxford University Press.

Bailey, P., & von Bonin, G. (1951). *The isocortex of man.* Urbana: University of Illinois.

Bastian, H. (1897). Some problems in connexion with aphasia and other speech defects. *Lancet, 1,* 933–942, 1005–1017, 1131–1137, 1187–1194.

Benson, D. F., & Stuss, D. T. (1982). Motor abilities after frontal leukotomy. *Neurology, 32,* 1353–1357.

Benton, A. L. (1968). Differential behavioral effects on frontal lobe disease. *Neuropsychologia, 6,* 53–60.

Berman, K. F., Randolph, C., Gold, J., Holt, D., Jones, D. W., Goldberg, T. E., Carson, R. E., Herscovitch, P., & Weinberger, D. R. (1991). Physiological activation of frontal lobe studies with positron emission tomography and oxygen—15 water during working memory tasks. *Journal of Cerebral Blood Flow and Metabolism, 11,* S851.

Bianchi, L. (1895). The functions of the frontal lobes. *Brain, 18,* 497–522.

Binder, J. R., Rao, S. M., Hammeke, T. A., Bandettini, P. A., Jesmanowicz, A., & Frost, J. A. (1993). Temporal characteristics of functional magnetic resonance signal change in lateral frontal and auditory cortex. *Proceedings for the Society of Magnetic Resonance Medicine, 3,* 5.

Binder, J. R., Rao, S. M., Hammeke, T. A., Frost, J. A., Bandettini, P. A., Jesmanowicz, A., & Hyde, J. S. (1995). Lateralized human brain language systems demonstrated by task subtraction functional magnetic resonance imaging. *Archives of Neurology, 52,* 593–601.

Botez, M. I., & Barbeau, A. (1971). Role of subcortical structures and particularly the thalamus in the mechanism of speech and language: A review. *International Journal of Neurology, 8,* 300–320.

Brickner, R. (1940). A human cortical area producing repetitive phenomena when stimulated. *Journal of Neurophysiology, 3,* 128–130.

Broca, P. (1861). Remarques sur le siège de la faculté du langage articulé suivés d'une observation d'aphésie (perte de la parole). *Bulletin de la Société d'Anthropologie, 2,* 235–257.

Brodmann, K. (1909). *Vergleichende Lokalisationslehre der Grosshirnrinde in ihren Prinzipien dargestellt auf Grund des Zellenbaues.* Leipzig: Barth.

Bruner, R. J., Kornhuber, H. H., Seemuller, E., Suger, G., & Wallesch, C. W. (1982) Basal ganglia participation in language pathology. *Brain and Language, 16,* 281–299.

Caron, M. (1934). *Etude clinique de la maladie Pick.* Paris: Vigot.

Castaigne, P., Laplane, D., & Degos, J. D. (1972). Trois cas de négligence motrice par lésion frontale pré-rolandique. *Revue Neurologique, 126,* 5–115.

Chertkow, H., & Bub, D. (1994). Functional activation and cognition: The ^{15}O PET subtraction method. In A. Kertesz (Ed.), *Localization and neuroimaging in neuropsychology* (pp. 152–184). San Diego: Academic Press.

Costello, A., & Warrington, E. K. (1989). Dynamic aphasia: The selective impairment of verbal planning. *Cortex, 25,* 103–114.

Cuenod, C. A., Bookheimer, S. Y., Hertz-Pannier, L., Zeffiro, T. A., Theodore, W. H., & Le Bihan, D. (1995). Functional MRI during word degeneration, using conventional equipment: A potential tool for language localization in the clinical environment. *Neurology, 45,* 1821–1827.

Cummings, J. L. (1993). Frontal–subcortical circuits and human behavior. *Archives of Neurology, 50,* 873–880.

Damasio, A. R., Damasio, H., Rizzo, M., Varney, N., & Gersh, F. (1982). Aphasia with nonhemorrhagic lesions in the basal ganglia and internal capsule. *Archives of Neurology, 39,* 15–20.

Damasio, A. R., & Kassel, N. F. (1978). Transcortical motor aphasia in relation to lesions of the supplementary motor area [Abstract]. *Neurology, 28,* 396.

Damasio, A. R., & Van Hoesen, G. W. (1983). Emotional disorders associated with focal lesions of the limbic frontal lobe. In K. M. Heilman & P. Satz (Eds.), *Neuropsychology of human emotion* (pp. 85–110). New York: Guilford Press.

Davis, L., Foldi, N. S., Gardner, H., & Zurif, E. B. (1978). Repetition in the transcortical aphasias. *Brain and Language, 6,* 226–238.

Dejerine, J. (1906). L'aphasie motrice: Sa localisation et sa physiologie pathologique. *Presse Medicale, 55,* 453–457.

Dejerine, J., & Dejerine-Klumpke, A. (1895). *Anatomie des centres nerveux.* Paris: Ruef et Cie.

Demonet J. F., Chollet, F., Ramsay, S., Cardebat, D., Nespoulous, J. L., Wise, R., Rascol, A., & Frackowiak, R. (1992). The anatomy of phonological and semantic processing in normal subjects. *Brain, 115,* 1753–1768.

Demonet, J. F., Fiez, J. A., Paulesu, E., Peterson, S. E., & Zatorre, R. J. (1996). PET studies of phonological processing. *Brain and Language, 55,* 352–370.

Donkers, N. F. (1996). A new brain region for coordinating speech articulation. *Nature, 384,* 159–161.

Drewe, E. A. (1975). An experimental investigation of Luria's theory on the effects of frontal lesions in man. *Neuropsychologia, 13,* 421–429.

Erickson, T. C., & Woolsey, C. N. (1951). Observations on the supplementary motor area of man. *Transaction of the American Neurological Association, 76,* 50–56.

Fiez, J. A., Raichle, M. E., Miezin, F. M., Petersen, S. E., Tallal, P., & Katz, W. F. (1995). PET studies of auditory and phonological processing: Effects of stimulus characteristics and task demands. *Journal of Cognitive Neuroscience, 7,* 357–375.

Freedman, M., Alexander, M. P., & Naeser, M. A. (1984). Anatomic basis of transcortical motor aphasia. *Neurology, 34,* 409–417.

Frith, C. D., Friston, K. J., Liddle, P. F., & Frackowiak, R. S. J. (1991). A PET study of word finding. *Neuropsychologia, 29,* 1137–1148.

Goldberg, F. (1985). Supplementary motor area structure and function: Review and hypothesis. *The Behavioral and Brain Sciences, 8,* 567–616.

Goldberg, G., Mayer, N. H., & Toglia, J. U. (1981). Medial frontal cortex infarction and the alien hand sign. *Archives of Neurology, 38,* 683–686.

Goldstein, K. (1915). Die transkortikalen Aphasien. *Ergebnisse Neurologie und Psychiatrie.* Jena: G. Fischer.

Goodglass, H., Quadfasel, F. A., & Timberlake, W. H. (1964). Phrase length and the type and severity of aphasia. *Cortex, 1,* 133–153.

Gott, P. S. (1973). Language after dominant hemispherectomy. *Journal of Neurology, Neurosurgery and Psychiatry, 36,* 1082–1088.

Gustafson, L., Brun, A., Holmkvist, A. F., & Risberg, J. (1985). Regional cerebral blood flow in degenerative frontal lobe dementia of non-Alzheimer type. *Journal of Cerebral Blood Flow and Metabolism 5*(Suppl. 1), 141–142.

Harlow, J. M. (1848). Passage of an iron bar through the head. *Boston Medical and Surgical Journal, 39,* 389–393.

Harlow, J. M. (1868). Recovery from the passage of an iron bar through the head. *Publication of the Massachusetts Medical Society, 2,* 327–347.

Hart, J., & Gordon, B. (1990). Delineation of single-word semantic comprehension deficits in aphasia, with anatomic correlation. *Annals of Neurology, 27,* 226–231.

Hinke, R. M., Hu, X., Stillman, A. E., Kim, S. G., Merkle, H., Salmi, R., & Ugurbil, K. (1993). Functional magnetic resonance imaging of Boca's area during internal speech. *Neuroreport, 4,* 675–678.

Howard, D., Patterson, K., Wise, R., Brown, W. D., Friston, K., Weiller, C., & Frackowiak, R. (1992). The cortical localization of the lexicons. Positron emission tomography evidence. *Brain, 115,* 1769–1782.

Johns, D. F., & Darley, F. L. (1970). Phonetic variability in apraxia of speech. *Journal of Speech and Hearing Disorders, 13,* 556–583.

Jones-Gotman, M., & Milner, B. (1977). Design fluency: The invention of nonsense drawings after focal cortical lesions. *Neuropsychologia, 15,* 643–652.

Jürgens, U., & von Cramon, D. (1982). On the role of the anterior cingulate cortex in phonation: A case report. *Brain and Language, 15,* 234–248.

Kertesz, A. (1979). *Aphasia and associated disorders: Taxonomy, localization and recovery.* New York: Grune & Stratton.

Kertesz, A. (1981). Evolution of aphasia syndromes. *Topical Language Disorders, 1,* 15–27.

Kertesz, A. (1984). Subcortical lesions and verbal apraxia. In J. C. Rosenbek, M. McNeil, & A. E. Aronson (Eds.), *Apraxia of speech* (pp. 73–90). San Diego: College Hill Press.

Kertesz, A. (1988). What do we learn from recovery from aphasia? In S.G. Waxman (Ed.), *Advances in Neurology—Functional recovery in neurological disease* (Vol. 47, pp. 175–196). New York: Raven Press.

Kertesz, A., Harlock, W., & Coates, R. (1979). Computer tomographic localization, lesion size and prognosis in aphasia and nonverbal impairment. *Brain and Language, 8,* 34–50.

Kertesz, A., Hudson, L., Mackenzie, I. R. A., & Munoz, D. G. (1994). The pathology and nosology of primary progressive aphasia. *Neurology, 44,* 2065–2072.

Kertesz, A., & McCabe, P. (1977). Recovery patterns and prognosis in aphasia. *Brain, 100,* 1–18.

Kertesz, A., & Munoz, G. D. (1998). *Pick's disease and Pick complex.* New York: Wiley-Liss.

Kertesz, A., & Phipps, J. (1977). Numerical taxonomy of aphasia. *Brain & Language, 4,* 1–10.

Kirk, A., & Kertesz, A. (1994). Cortical and subcortical aphasias compared. *Aphasiology, 8,* 65–82.

Kleist, K. (1934). *Gehirnpathologie.* Leipzig: Barth.

Knopman, D. S., Mastri, A. R., Frey, W. H. II, Sung, J. H., & Rustan, T. (1990). Dementia lacking distinctive histologic features: a common non-Alzheimer degenerative dementia. *Neurology, 40,* 251–256.

Knopman, D. S., Selnes, O. A., Niccum, N., Rubens, A. B., Yock, D., & Larson, D. (1983). A longitudinal study of speech fluency in aphasia: CT correlates of recovery and persistent nonfluency. *Neurology, 33,* 1170–1178.

Kornyei, E. (1975). Aphasie transcorticale et echolalie: Le probleme de l'initiative de la parole. *Revue Neurologique, 131A,* 347–363.

Lecours, A. R., & Lhermitte, F. (1976). The "pure form" of the phonetic disintegration syndrome (pure anarthria): Anatomo-clinical report of a historical case. *Brain and Language, 3,* 88–113.

Levine, D. N., & Sweet, E. (1983). Localization of lesions in Broca's motor aphasia. In A. Kertesz (Ed.), *Localization in neuropsychology* (pp. 185–208). New York: Academic Press.

Lichtheim, L. (1885). On aphasia. *Brain, 7,* 433–484.

Liepmann, H. (1905). Die linke Hemisphäre und das Handeln. *Medizin Wochenschrift, 2,* 2375–2378.

Ludlow, C. L., Rosenberg, J., Fair, C., Buck, D., Schesselman, S., & Salazar, A. (1986). Brain lesions associated with nonfluent aphasia fifteen years following penetrating head injury. *Brain, 109,* 55–80.

Lund & Manchester Groups (1994). Clinical and neuropathological criteria for frontotemporal dementia. *Journal of Neurology, Neurosurgery and Psychiatry, 57,* 416–418.

Luria, A. R. (1966). *Higher cortical functions in man.* London: Tavistock.

Luria, A. R. (1970). *Traumatic aphasia.* Hague: Mouton.

Luria, A. R., & Tsvetkova, L. S. (1967). The mechanism of "dynamic aphasia." *Foundations of Language, 4,* 296–307.

Marie, P. (1906). Revision de la question de l'aphasie: La troisieme circonvolution frontale gauche ne joue aucun role special dans la fonction du langage. *Semaine Medicale, 21,* 241–247.

Masdeau, J. C., Schoene, W. C., & Funkenstein, H. (1978). Aphasia following infarction of the left supplementary motor area. A clinicopathologic study. *Neurology, 28,* 1220–1223.

McCarthy, G., Blamire, A. M., Rothman, D. L., Gruetter, R., & Shulman, R. G. (1993). Echo-planar magnetic resonance imaging studies of frontal cortex activation during word generation in humans. *Proceedings of the National Academy of Sciences, USA, 90,* 4952–4956.

Mesulam, M. M. (1982). Slowly progressive aphasia without dementia. *Annals of Neurology, 11,* 592–598.

Mesulam, M. M. (1987). Primary progressive aphasia—Differentiation from Alzheimer's disease. *Annals of Neurology, 22,* 533–534.

Mesulam, M. M., & Weintraub, S. (1992). Primary progressive aphasia: Sharpening the focus on a clinical syndrome. In F. Boller, F. Forette, Z. Khachaturian, M. Poncet, & Y. Christen (Eds.), *Heterogeneity of Alzheimer's disease* (pp. 43–66). Berlin: Springer-Verlag.

Metter, E. J., Riege, W. H., Hanson, W. R., Kuhl, D. E., Phelps, M. E., Squire, L. R., Wasterlaw, C. G., & Benson, D. F. (1983). Comparison of metabolic rates, language, and memory in subcortical aphasias. *Brain and Language, 19,* 33–47.

Miller, B. L., Cummings, J. L., Villanueva-Meyer, J., Boone, K., Mehringer, C. M., Lesser, I. M., & Mena, I. (1991). Frontal lobe degeneration: Clinical, neuropsychological, and SPECT characteristics. *Neurology, 41,* 1374–1382.

Milner, B. (1964). Some effects of frontal lobectomy in man. In J. M. Warren & K. Akert (Eds.), *The frontal granular cortex and behavior* (pp. 313–334). New York: McGraw-Hill.

Mohr, J. P. (1973). Rapid amelioration of motor aphasia. *Archives of Neurology, 28,* 77–82.

Mohr, J. P., Pessin, M. S., Finkelstein, S., Funkenstein, H. H., Duncan, G. W., & Davis, K. R. (1978). Broca aphasia: Pathologic and clinical. *Neurology, 28,* 311–324.

Moniz, E. (1936). Premiers essais de psycho-chirurgie. Technique et résultats. *Lisboa Medica, 12,* 152.

Muratoff W. (1893). Secundare degenerationen nach Durchschneidung des Balkens. *Neurologisches Centralblatt, 12,* 714–729.

Myers, R. E. (1976). Comparative neurology of vocalization and speech: proof of a dichotomy. In S. R. Harnad, H. D. Steklis, & J. Lancaster (Eds.), *Origins and evolution of language and speech* (pp. 745–747). New York: New York Academy of Sciences.

Nadeau, S. E. (1988). Impaired grammar with normal fluency and phonology: implications for Broca's aphasia. *Brain, 111,* 1111–1137.

Naeser, M. A., Alexander, M. P., Helm-Estabrooks, N., Levine, H. L., Laughlin, S. A., & Geschwind, N. (1982). Aphasia with predominantly subcortical lesions sites: Description of three capsular/putaminal syndromes. *Archives of Neurology, 39,* 2–14.

Naeser, M. A., Palumbo, C. L., Helm-Estabrooks, N., Stiassny-Eder, D., & Albert, M. L. (1989). Severe nonfluency in aphasia. Role of the medial subcallosal fasciculus and other white matter pathways in recovery of spontaneous speech. *Brain, 112,* 1–38.

Nathan, P. W. (1947). Facial apraxia and apraxic dysarthria. *Brain, 7,* 449–478.

Neary, D., Snowden, J. S., Bowen, D. M., Sims, N. R., Mann, D. M. A., Benton, J. S., Northen, B., Yates, P. O., & Davison, A. A. (1986). Neuropsychological syndromes in presenile dementia due to cerebral atrophy. *Journal of Neurology, Neurosurgery and Psychiatry, 49,* 163–174.

Neary, D., Snowden, J. S., Northen, B., & Goulding, P. (1988). Dementia of frontal lobe type. *Journal of Neurology, Neurosurgery and Psychiatry, 51,* 353–361.

Niessl von Maydendorf, E. (1911). *Die aphasischen Symptome und ihre kortikale Lokalization.* Leipzig: Barth.

Niessl von Mayendorf, E. (1930). *Vom Lokalisationsproblem der artikulierten Sprache.* Leipzig: Barth.

Olsen, T S., Bruhn, P., & Oberg, R. G. E. (1986). Anomia from pulvinar and subcortical parietal stimulation. *Brain, 91,* 99–116.

Paulesu, E., Frith, C. D., & Frackowiak, R. S. J. (1993). The neural correlates of the verbal component of working memory. *Nature, 362,* 342–345.

Penfield, W., & Roberts, L. (1959). *Speech and brain mechanisms.* Princeton, NJ: Princeton University Press.

Perani, D., Vallar, G., Cappa, S., Mensa, C., & Fazio, F. (1987). Aphasia and neglect after subcortical stroke: A clinical/cerebral perfusion correlation study. *Brain, 110,* 1211–1229.

Petersen, S. E., Fox, P. T., Posner, M. I., & Raichle, M. E. (1988). Positron emission tomographic studies of the cortical anatomy of single word processing. *Nature, 331,* 585–589.

Pick, A. (1892). Über die Beziehungen der senilen Hirnatrophie zur Aphasie. *Prag Med Wchnschr 17,* 165–167.

Posner, M. I., & Petersen, S. E. (1990). The attention system of the human brain. *Annual Review of Neuroscience, 13,* 25–42.

Ramier, A. M., & Hecaen, H. (1970). Role respectif des atteintes frontales et de la lateralisation lesionnelle dans les deficits de lat fluence verbale. *Revue Neurologique, 123,* 17–22.

Robb, J. P. (1966). Effect of cortical excision and stimulation on the frontal lobe on speech. *Proceedings of the Association for Research in Nervous and Mental Diseases.* New York: Hafner.

Rosenbek, J. (1980). Apraxia of speech—Relationship to stuttering. *Journal of Fluency Disorders, 5,* 233–253.

Rothman, M. (1906). Lichtheimsche motorische Aphasie. *Zeitschrift für Klinische Medizin, 60,* 87–121.

Rubens, A. B. (1975). Aphasia with infarction in the territory of the anterior cerebral artery. *Cortex, 11,* 239–250.

Rubens, A. B. (1976). Transcortical motor aphasia. In H. Whitaker & H. A. Whitaker (Eds.), *Studies in neurolinguistics* (Vol. 1, pp. 293–306). New York: Academic Press.

Rubens, A., & Kertesz, A. (1983). The localization of lesions in transcortical aphasias. In A. Kertesz (Ed.), *Localization in neuropsychology* (pp. 245–268). New York: Academic Press.

Rueckert, L., Appollonio, I., Grafman, J., Jezzard, P., Johnson, R. Jr., Le Bihan, D., & Turner, R. (1994). MRI functional activation of left frontal cortex during covert word production. *Journal of Neuroimaging, 4,* 67–70.

Russell, W. R., & Espir, M. L. E. (1961). *Traumatic aphasia.* London: Oxford University Press.

Sanides F. (1970). Functional architecture of motor and sensory cortices in primates in the light of a new concept of neocortex evolution. In C. R. Noback & W. Montagna (Eds.), *The primate brain* (pp. 137–208). New York: Appleton.

Schiff, H. B., Alexander, M. P., Naeser, M. A., & Galaburda, A. M. (1983). Aphemia—Clinical-anatomic correlations. *Archives of Neurology, 40,* 720–727.

Shallice, T. (1989). *From neuropsychology to mental structure.* Cambridge, UK: Cambridge University Press.

Stengel, E. (1947). A clinical and psychological study of echo-reactions. *Journal of Mental Science,* *93,* 598–612.

Stuss, D.T., Kaplan, E. F., Benson, D.F., Wier, W. S., Naeser, M. A., & Levine, H. L. (1981). Long-term effects of prefrontal leucotomy—An overview of neuropsychologic residuals. *Journal of Clinical Neuropsychology, 3,* 13–32.

Sweet, W. (1951). Discussion of Erickson and Woolsey. *Transactions of the American Neurological Society, 76,* 55.

Watson, R. T., Fleet, W. S., Gonzalez-Rothi, L., & Heilman, K. M. (1986). Apraxia and the supplementary motor area. *Archives of Neurology, 43,* 787–792.

Weiller, C., Willmes, K., Reiche, W., Thron, A., Isensee, C., Buell, U., & Ringelstein, E. B. (1993). The case of aphasia or neglect after striatocapsular infarction. *Brain, 116,* 1509–1525.

Weinrich, M., Ricaurte, G., Kowall, J., Weinstein, S. L., & Lane, B. (1987). Subcortical aphasia revisited. *Aphasiology, 1,* 119–126.

Welt, L. (1888). Über Charakterveranderungen des Menschen infolge von Läsionen des Stirnhirns. *Deutsche Archiv für Klinische Medizin, 42,* 339–390.

Wernicke, C. (1886). Einige neuere Arbeiten über Aphasie. *Fortschritte der Medizin, 4,* 377–463.

Wise, R., Chollet, F., Hadar, U., Friston, K., Hoffner, E., & Frackowiak, R. (1991). Distribution of cortical neural networks involved in word comprehension and word retrieval. *Brain, 114,* 1803–1817.

Yakovlev, P. I., & Locke, S. (1961). Limbic nuclei of thalamus and connections of limbic cortex. III: Corticocortical connections of the anterior cingulate gyrus, the cingulum, and the subcallosal bundle in monkeys. *Archives of Neurology, 5,* 364–400.

Yetkin, F. Z., Hammeke, T. A., Swanson, S. J., Morris, G. L., Mueller, W. M., McAuliffe, T. L., & Haughton, V. M. (1995). A comparison of functional MR activation patterns during silent and audible language tasks. *American Journal of Neuroradiology, 16,* 1087–1092.

16

Frontal Lobe Dysfunction and Patient Decision Making about Treatment and Participation in Research

L. JAIME FITTEN

Possessing the mental capacity to make decisions about events affecting one's health is an indispensable ingredient of giving informed consent for treatment and participating in medical research. Physicians treating medically ill older patients are increasingly asked to provide expert opinion regarding the mental competence of their patients, while researchers investigating the diseases of advanced age recruit ever-growing numbers of elders into research programs and face the uncertainties of this population's capacity to consent to research. This is probably a result of recent demographic trends in this country, in particular of the rapid growth of the most fragile segment of the U.S. population, the oldest old (Fowles, 1991), as well as of advances in the basic and clinical neurosciences and the development of recent cultural trends which in the past generation have evinced growing concern for the protection of patient autonomy in the context of the traditional doctor–patient relationship.

Because the elderly as a group suffer from the greatest number of medical afflictions in the population at large, they need to make a greater number of decisions regarding their medical treatment than do younger individuals. The burgeoning number of clinical trials for age-related disease increases the pressure on seniors for decisions about participation in research. However, the aged population's capacity to make medically related decisions about their own health may be jeopardized by the considerably higher prevalences of age-associated neuropsychiatric diseases, most notably incipient or even frank dementias, which can impair their decision-making ability (Kloezen, Fitten, & Steinberg, 1988). It is estimated that 80% of all guardianships involve persons over age 60 (Bulcroft, Kielkopf, & Tripp, 1991). However, the fact that all adult patient populations are asked, at some point, to make treatment choices expands the scope of the problem. Practitioners' opinions may strongly influence legal decisions about patient competence and may thus significantly affect patient lives. Therefore, physician knowledge of issues concerning patients decisional capacities and their assessment is necessary in everyday clinical practice (Finucane, Myser, & Ticehurst, 1993). Yet, practical, standardized, and reliable instruments to facilitate the assessment of patients' decisional capacities have been difficult to develop and are still largely unavailable—possibly because of the difficulty in operationalizing many of the complex concepts underlying decisional competence (Finucane et al., 1993; Iris, 1988; Janofsky, McCarthy, & Folstein, 1992; Kaplan, Strang, & Ahmed, 1988; Kapp, 1990; Lo, 1990; Rosse, Ciolino, & Guriel, 1986; Stanley, Stanley, & Guido, 1988).

DEMENTIA AND INFORMED CONSENT FOR TREATMENT

Over the past 5 years more than 40 general articles have appeared on the subject of informed consent by patients with dementia. The large majority of these articles were either review or position articles on a variety of topics concerning the informed consent process and its inherent moral dilemmas. Interestingly, only two articles involving prospective, experimental approaches had the potential to add truly new information to the problem of competency and dementia.

In one, Marson, Ingram, Cody, and Harrell (1995) assessed Alzheimer's disease (AD) treatment decision-making capacity in mildly and moderately demented subjects as well as healthy aged controls using the vignette methodology like the one developed by previous investigators (Fitten & Waite, 1990; Fitten, Hamann, Evans, Kelly, & Smith, 1984; Fitten, Lusky, & Hamann, 1990; Kloezen et al., 1988) for clinical situations in previous prospective treatment decision-making competency studies of healthy and medically ill elderly persons. They found increasingly diminished understanding of consent issues in the mildly demented individuals as the legal standard for understanding was made more demanding. However, no differences between groups were found when the minimal standards were used.

This study showed that the vignette methodology, designed to facilitate clinical assessment of consent capacity, was useful when applied to the cognitively impaired and implied that even mildly demented AD patients may have serious impediments to understanding many consent forms. Interestingly, Marson found no significant impediment in understanding or choosing in healthy elderly controls, a similar finding to our results for the same type of healthy population (Fitten & Waite, 1990; Fitten et al., 1990). Marson, Cody, Ingram, and Harrell (1995), in another paper, described the neuropsychological measures that best predicted vignette performance. Although they used no novel measures, the main predictor in his study was word fluency performance, which suggested that frontal systems might be playing an important role in vignette understanding.

DEMENTIA AND INFORMED CONSENT FOR RESEARCH

Giving informed consent for research involves different circumstances and calculations for the individual than consenting to treatment (e.g., treatment is for the specific benefit of a particular individual, whereas research is not). The literature on informed consent for research and the demented patient is surprisingly modest. Over the past 5 years, when interest in the subject has been at its highest, only a handful of articles have addressed the topic. Most of the few papers written either took an ethically oriented position or were general review articles on important issues of informed consent in cognitively impaired individuals (Becker & Kahana, 1993; DeRenzo, 1994; High, 1992; Marson, Schmitt, Ingram, & Harrell, 1994; Resau, 1995; Sachs, 1994). Only one article specifically focused on the problem of competency assessment (Marson et al., 1994), while in another there was a preliminary effort to assess competency to participate in a noninterventional community study (Geiselmann & Helmchen, 1994).

A polarization occurs around AD in these articles without consideration to other forms of cognitive impairment which by their distinctive neuropathology could affect differently the ability to give informed consent. No articles focus on the neural substrates that subserve the cognitive and emotive functions that support judgment and decision-making ability or on their pathology, which can hamper the kind of thinking needed to deliberate and consent.

COMPETENCY AND CAPACITY AS PART OF INFORMED CONSENT

In the clinical field, some confusion surrounds the terms "competency" and "capacity." Competency is a legal category. All adults are presumed competent and, therefore, responsible for their choices, unless determined otherwise by a court. In adjudications of incompetence, most courts require the filing of a medical report documenting the respondent's disability. Such reports usually state the nature of the disability, the respondent's physical and mental condition, and the degree of impairment and limitations on decision-making ability. Bulcroft et al.'s (1991) retrospective record review, however, found physicians' reports to be generally "sketchy, inconclusive, and frequently outdated." The reports were usually lacking in specific assessments of competence. In court, however, physicians' assessments are crucial to the legal proceedings and influence which patients are ruled incompetent to make a variety of decisions.

In contrast, the term "capacity" is often used to refer to assessments by physicians which indicate whether patients have, or lack, the ability to make informed choices about their health care. There are currently no broadly established legal standards for determining a person's capacity to make medical decisions on his or her own behalf, although California has made strides in this direction by the recent enactment of the Due Process in Competence Determinations Act (S.B. Mello, Ch. 842 Stat. 1995), which stipulates a clearer methodology for competency assessment. Similarly, there is no standard or singular model that physicians follow in their assessments of decisional capacity for treatment choices, and there are even fewer guidelines outside individual institutional review boards to direct procurement of informed consent for research from subjects with cognitive impairment. Clearly, clinical guidelines based on research studies would be most beneficial.

In a broad sense, competence refers to the ability to perform a task or series of tasks. It should be evident, however, that the ability to perform one task does not necessarily confer the ability to successfully carry out another. For example, the ability to drive a car safely does not necessarily imply comparable capacity to drive a motorcycle or a truck. As a consequence of this basic observation, several areas of competence have been described and discussed in the literature, including competence to handle financial affairs, to make a will, to enter into a contract, and to consent to medical research, to name some of the more common examples. However, no clear or specific legal criteria to determine competence to make medical treatment decisions or participate in research have been formally established.

In examining this problem, Kaplan et al. (1988) noted that the literature on competency has more or less ignored the equally rich and extensive literature on judgment and decision making. This oversight may result in a relative lack of attention to the nuances of decision-making processes. The judgment and decision-making literature focuses on how cognitive, emotional, biological, and social factors all influence the decision-making process. It examines how presumably healthy individuals attempt to reduce uncertainty, come to an understanding and how they arrive at decisions and establish a plan of action. Equally problematic is that the judgment and decision-making literature has not fully taken into account the connection it has with issues of competency that often involve mentally impaired, medically ill individuals. Over time, a hiatus has developed between these bodies of work. As a consequence, the need has never been fully satisfied for a clinically useful model to assess medical decisional capacity which can, in turn, be more easily used in the courts to facilitate the determination of patients' competency.

CONSIDERATIONS AND SIGNIFICANCE OF INFORMED CONSENT IN NEUROPSYCHIATRIC DISEASES

In medicine most therapeutic actions or research interventions are based on the supposition that fully conscious patients are sufficiently autonomous to participate in treatment or intervention decisions and that they are responsible for their choices. Consequently, as required by law, when treatment or participatory choices must be made by patients, informed consent is obtained. This is in compliance with the legal doctrine of informed consent, which requires that prior to initiating an intervention on a competent person, his or her informed consent must be obtained. Although derived from the moral principle of respect for self-determination, this law more typically has focused on the establishment of rules and procedures, practically enforceable by institutions, that govern the context of consent and regulate the behavior of consent seekers rather than on the confirmation of the ability of the patient to participate autonomously in the decision process. It is a doctrine that has emphasized primarily, although not exclusively, disclosure of facts and risk and freedom from external control.

Several writers concerned with the ethical underpinnings of informed consent continue to express interest in developing approaches for obtaining informed consent that place greater emphasis on the moral theory of respect for autonomous action behind consent procedures (Faden & Beauchamp, 1986; Katz, 1980). However, the concept of autonomous action per se should also be of some interest to those concerned about decision-making processes themselves. Autonomy is a concept more native to philosophy and the law than to medicine, clinical psychology, or clinical neuroscience. It encompasses the problem of the nature of free agency and its relation to the origins and conditions of responsible behavior. It has been proposed that autonomous actions by an individual are those that are (1) intentional, (2) with understanding, and (3) without controlling influences (Faden & Beauchamp, 1986). These particular characteristics of behavior, long debated in philosophy, have not been easily amenable to experimental manipulation. However, recent increases in our knowledge of the relationship between neuroanatomy, neurophysiology, and disordered behavior encourage us to take greater interest in the understanding of those elements of autonomous actions that could be particularly affected by neurodegenerative, neoplastic, traumatic, or vascular disease processes.

The philosophical and psychological literatures are replete with varying analyses of intentional action. Although it is well beyond the scope of this chapter to examine these in any comprehensive or exhaustive manner, generally, it can be stated that they treat autonomous action as synonymous or coextensive with actions described as instrumental, goal-directed, volitional, free-willed, reasoned, deliberate, or planned. However, common threads weave through this complex tapestry of related concepts. Key among them is that intentional acts require plans (i.e., the integration of thoughts into a blueprint for action). An action plan is a representation of the strategies and tactics proposed for the execution of an action (Goldman, 1970). The relationship between intentional action and action plans is direct (Goldman, 1970). Intentional acts correspond to the actor's conception or plan of them. Thus, an intentional action is one that is willed in accordance with a plan, whether the act is wanted or not (Norman, 1981). Without pursuing this analysis further, some clinical relevance may already be found for this concept of intentional action because it requires the development of a plan, and we have come to learn recently that the complex activity of planning for action appears quite dependent on the functional integrity of frontal systems.

What do we mean when we say we understand a fact or concept or situation? There is no simple consensus answer to this question in law, philosophy, or psychology. "Understanding" has many definitions and can be employed to signify comprehension, knowing, practical competence, and so on. Yet, within the context of informed consent, it may be argued that the analysis of a person's understanding is more equivalent to the analysis of "knowing." The type of understanding at issue here is a special case of propositional understanding, or "understanding that" as well as "understanding what" (Faden & Beauchamp, 1986). It is an individual's understanding that his or her action is one of a certain description with consequences of a certain type in a particular context. Thus, what is needed is an account that identifies the conditions under which a person understands the nature and consequences of his or her actions. In philosophy and law the amount of understanding required for informed consent has been the subject of debate and the establishment of standards for understanding has been elusive. However, this issue is of lesser magnitude for our present purpose because our main concern here is not to decide between degrees of understanding but rather to identify some of the most basic thinking activities and skills that must be operative before even a modicum of understanding can be achieved.

For example, it has been argued that to understand a proposed intervention, a subject must comprehend to some adequate degree that he or she is authorizing a procedure (Cassileth, 1980; Harris, 1982) as well as all the important statements that correctly describe the nature of the intervention and the foreseeable consequences and possible outcomes of undergoing or not that intervention. To achieve this end, several types of cognitive operations are necessary. At a minimum, an individual must possess a normal state of consciousness and alertness, followed by the ability to sustain an attentional focus against ordinary distractors and to participate satisfactorily in some form of linguistic communication as well as to retain in memory what has been learned about a proposed treatment long enough to deliberate about it. However necessary these functions may be, they are not sufficient in and of themselves.

Because understanding involves deliberations that will eventually lead to choices, more complex cognitive operations are also required (Fitten & Waite, 1990). These include the ability to engage in "as if" or probabilistic, nonconcrete thinking; to consider or visualize more than one alternative course of action at a time, switching back and forth to compare and contrast them; to recall relevant past deeds and life stories complete with their emotional valence and compare them to the present situation; and to imagine the sequence of events that would follow the choosing of one option over another (Churchland, 1996). Furthermore, these cognitive operations are not possible without the integrative and executive capacity of the frontal lobes, a capacity which is elaborated from predominantly frontal systems functions such as working memory, control of interference, set formation, temporal sequencing of information and behavior, integration of past and present experience into new information, goal selection, planning, and monitoring through self-awareness, to cite some prominent examples.

Another cornerstone in the pyramid of autonomous action is freedom from control. This subject has stimulated a vast area of philosophical inquiry and debate and I intend no rigorous or detailed review here. However, I do note that a major focus of the informed consent literature on this topic has been on freedom from control by others (DeFelice, 1974) in the form of coercion, manipulation, or persuasion, an area of undeniable importance to philosophy and the law. Not developed to the same extent is the difficult yet more interesting area from the point of view of brain–behavior relationships, of freedom from internal controlling influences—"controlling" in the sense that they would detract by their influence from ideally autonomous actions arising from individual thinking. Among the more obvious examples of this "lack of freedom" would be the case of a person who heard loud voices (hallucination) directing and compelling him or her to commit an illegal, dangerous, or morally objectionable act or the insidiously dementing individual who unexpectedly exhibited inappropriate social behavior at a gathering of family and friends.

The current view would be that both of these individuals are exhibiting behavioral manifestations of brain disease, however incompletely understood each disease may be, and as a consequence it is unlikely they would be viewed as having performed truly voluntary or autonomous acts and would therefore not be held responsible for their socially unacceptable behavior. However, until it was strongly suspected or made clear that these individuals suffered from brain diseases affecting behavior and suppressing free choice, they would probably receive the repudiation reserved for those who transgress either moral or legal codes or other social tenets. This is because in everyday life we assume a person to be responsible for his or her acts unless specific exculpatory conditions exist.

However, until recently, our knowledge of the brain as the organ of experience and behavior was sufficiently rudimentary to lead to a totally different evaluation of the previously described aberrant behaviors, resulting in a very different personal and societal response to those individuals whose acts were the consequence of brain physiology gone wrong. Yet, whereas the examples just cited may have gained wider acceptance today as instances of persons having lost freedom of choice or "voluntariness" due to internally generated events that are outside an individual's control, a clear or categorical demarcation cannot always be made between the strictly voluntary and the clearly involuntary. Illegal actions performed due to the impulsive behavior of youths are usually considered legally binding, even though they may be the result of functional neuronal immaturities resulting from either variation in genetic programming and/or suboptimal timely environmental influences such as appropriate emotional parental interventions (Stuss & Benson 1986), none of which are under the younger individual's control.

As our understanding of brain activity–behavior relationship increases, our understanding of what constitutes uncontrolled internal influence over choice and behavior will probably also be modified. Consider reports by Eslinger and Damasio (1985) and Damasio (1994) on patients with ventromedial frontal cortex lesions. These persons have well-preserved cognitive functions such as language, recall, visual–spatial skills, and mathematical abilities and can interact appropriately in a normal and ordinary manner. Yet, they seem unable to organize and conduct their lives with any reasonable amount of success. This is exemplified by the case of EVR (Eslinger & Damasio, 1985), a successful professional who after sustaining a lesion to his ventromedial cortex (extirpation of a tumor) was able to maintain his high IQ but not the success and integrity of his professional and personal life, both of which progressively unraveled. His deficit appeared to reside in his inability to reason in ordinarily familiar circumstances, rendering his decision-making abilities for everyday matters largely ineffective.

Through the study of this and other similar cases, Damasio (1994) hypothesized a role for this area of the human frontal cortex in planning and decision making. He views human reasoning as the interplay of neuronal mechanisms at several levels of organization, ranging from those that perform basic body regulation to those that control complex strategies based on language, but he adds a clinically derived concept, based on observation, yet disputed in the history of philosophy. This concept is that reasoning depends heavily on the process of feeling, its visceral precursors, and the intimately linked images that relate to the state of the body. Thus, reasoning is not just the application of formal rules but also uses visceral and somatic information, which becomes elaborated into feeling states that guide decision making through a complex maze of possible options and outcomes of relevance to the individual.

The problem for EVR posed by his ventromedial frontal cortex lesion is the breakdown in the integration between cognitive and affective domains in the reasoning and decision-making process. His frontal lobes, needed for complex deliberations and decisions, have no access to information about the valence of a complex situation, concept, or plan. Consequently, EVR is vulnerable to making frequent unwise or foolish decisions. The connection of ventromedial frontal cortex to limbic structures is critical to the elaboration and modulation of feeling states. Although abnormalities in frontal ventromedial function could have a significant impact on an individual's decision-making capabilities, how such dysfunctions could be evaluated, and at what point they could be considered sufficient to impede autonomous choice, can only be left to speculation at this stage of our knowledge. However, such questions could resound persistently in the clinics and the courts as understanding of brain–behavior relationships increases.

EVR has a particular significance for the concept of autonomy in the context of informed consent. For several theorists on autonomy, such as Dworkin (1978) and Macklin (1982), an additional critical element for autonomous action is authenticity. The concept of authenticity has been influential and requires that actions faithfully represent the values, attitudes, and motivations and life plans that the individual personally accepts upon due consideration of the way he or she wishes to live.

The requirement of authenticity for autonomous action has not been universally accepted by all theorists on the grounds that it puts excessive restrictions on autonomous actions and, in a majority of cases, conscious, reflective consideration will not have taken place before an action is taken (Faden & Beauchamp, 1986). This objecting argument seems less valid in the context of patients with distinctive but not obvious impairments in their ability to integrate deliberation with feelings about relevant past experiences to reach adequately reasoned decisions. Such is the case with the patient EVR, and it can be argued that many of his decisions will lack authenticity and will be significantly less than autonomous. Thus, it appears that the authenticity model of autonomous action may have greater applicability in populations with frontal disorders.

Clearly, the near simultaneous operation of many neuronal networks will be necessary to process the relevant information and the role of the individual in it. Supporting these distributed networks are several important anatomical structures: ventromedial and lateral frontal cortex, temporoparietal association cortex, and the hippocampus as well as other limbic structures known to be critical to the elaboration and modulation of feeling states and visceral changes such as the amygdala, cingulate gyrus, hypothalamus, portions of the basal ganglia, and the anterior thalamus (Pandya & Yeterian, 1996). Many of these structures are profoundly affected by AD and frontotemporal dementia (FTD), and can be dramatically affected by cerebrovascular disease, tumor, or trauma yet are relatively well preserved in normal aging. Therefore, it is important not only to increase our knowledge about the particular impairments to understanding of consent issues in research and treatment found in the most common brain diseases, such as those of the aged, and to contrast these impairments with the performance of the well elderly, but also to gain a better understanding of which larger brain structures play a role in the understanding of complex concepts and decision making.

PRELIMINARY STUDIES OF TREATMENT AND RESEARCH DECISION-MAKING CAPACITY

Recently, my group collected data concerning the ability to understand consent to research and consent to medical treatment issues on 55 healthy, independently living, older community volunteers and 25 nondemented, hospitalized, stable, medically ill elders (Fitten & Waite, 1990; Fitten et al., 1990, Fitten, Wieland, & Waite, 1997), as well as 4 subjects with early-stage AD and FTD (1998), using our standard informed consent for research and clinical "vignette" methodology where the subject is asked questions about clinical situations presented to the subject as if he or she were the patient in that situation. Testing involves the use of three increasingly complex clinical scenarios (vignettes) to examine the subject's understanding of issues of the highest relevance to his or her proposed scenario treatment. This approach has permitted the generation of normative values for the performance of healthy, cognitively unimpaired older persons which overall show good basic initial understanding of consent issues at all levels of understanding tested, even in the more complicated scenarios. Clinical vignette scores were consistently higher than scores for understanding of the standard Veterans Administration informed consent form for research. In a recent iteration of the vignette methodology (Fitten et al., 1997), we added scripted prompting of questions when needed, a measure intended to reduce the role of memory for details in the overall understanding score. In this study, we demonstrated improved subject performance after prompting on standard VA informed consent for research and clinical vignettes alike irrespective of subject age or education. Based on these findings, we were able to propose preliminary normative error thresholds for decisional impairment which we are using in currently ongoing work.

Our preliminary work on the assessment of understanding of consent issues in early-stage but otherwise healthy FTD and AD (two FTD, two AD) is beginning to reveal interesting results. The Folstein Mini-Mental Status Examination (MMSE) score for the FTD patients was 30 and 22, whereas the AD patients' scores were 26 and 25. The performance on the questions requiring a higher order of understanding (understanding who is authorizing, understanding risks benefits and alternatives, etc.) was better for the AD than for the FTD patients. This was particularly true for the FTD subject with a MMSE of 30, whose neuroimaging and neuropsychological testing revealed predominantly dominant hemisphere frontal lobe pathology. This individual is a lawyer who specialized in medicolegal cases, yet he failed the informed consent for research and performed poorly on two of the three vignettes. In contrast, the two AD patients with lower Folstein MMSEs performed at a higher level on all three vignettes although both failed the most difficult vignette which is in contrast to the performance of healthy, older subjects. These preliminary findings are suggestive of the importance of frontal lobe function to decision-making operations. SPECT brain images of these patients show different patterns of cortical hypoperfusion, each consistent with the respective diagnosis of FTD (frontal hypoperfusion) and AD (temporoparietal hypoperfusion).

CONCLUSIONS

The changing demographics of an aging society with ever greater numbers of elders needing medical treatment, advances in the basic and clinical neurosciences with a growing requirement for subjects to study, and a gradual shift toward more egalitarian ethics over the past three decades have generated a need to better understand and implement the informed consent process. Several neuropsychiatric conditions, most common in the elderly, may pose serious barriers to informed consent to treatment or research participation through their impact on the neural substrates that support specific cognitive and cognitive–affective processes. Frontal lobe integrity appears critical to the understanding of treatment or research issues and to decision making in the consent process. Even modest damage to any of the frontal lobe's functional subdivisions may seriously reduce an individual's capacity to give authentic, truly informed consent.

REFERENCES

Becker, D., & Kahana, Z. (1993). Informed consent in demented patients: A question of hours. *Medicine and Law, 12*(3–5), 271–276.

Bulcroft, K., Kielkopf, M. R., & Tripp, K. (1991). Elderly wards and their legal guardians: Analysis of country probate records in Ohio and Washington. *Journal of Gerontology, 31,* 156–164.

Cassileth, B. R. (1980). Informed consent: Why are its goals imperfectly realized? *New England Journal of Medicine, 302,* 896–900.

Churchland, P. (1996). Feeling reasons. In A. Damasio, H. Damasio, & Y. Christen (Eds.), *Neurobiology of decision-making.* Berlin, Springer-Verlag.

Damasio, A. (1994). *Descartes error: Emotion, reason and the human brain.* New York: Grosset/Putnam.

DeFelice, S. L. (1974). Analysis of the relationship between human experimentation and drug discovery in the United States. *Drug Metabolism Review, 3,* 175.

DeRenzo, E. (1994). Surrogate decision making for severely cognitively impaired research subjects: The continuing debate. *Cambridge Quarterly of Healthcare Ethics, 3*(4), 539–548.

Dworkin, G. (1978). Moral autonomy. In H. T. Engelhardt, Jr. & D. Callahan (Eds.), *Morals, science, and sociality.* Hastings-on-Hudson, NY: Hastings Center.

Eslinger, P., & Damasio, A. (1985). Severe disturbance of higher cognition after bilateral frontal lobe ablation: Patient EVR. *Neurology, 35,* 1731–1741.

Faden, R., & Beauchamp, T. (1986). *A history and theory of informed consent.* New York: Oxford University Press.

Finucane, P., Myser, C., & Ticehurst, S. (1993). "Is she fit to sign, doctor?"—Practical ethical issues in assessing the competence of elderly patients. *Medical Journal of Austria, 159,* 400–403.

Fitten, L. J., Hamann, C., Evans, G., Kelly, F., & Smith, E. (1984). Relationship of cognitive impairment to decision-making competence in nursing home residents: Development of a competence assessment protocol. *Journal of the American Geriatric Society, 32*(Suppl. 4), 519.

Fitten, L. J., Lusky, R., & Hamann, C. (1990). Assessing treatment decision-making capacity in elderly nursing home residents. *Journal of the American Geriatric Society, 38,* 1097–1104.

Fitten, L. J., & Waite M. (1990). Impact of acute hospitalization on treatment decision-making capacity in medically ill geriatric patients. *Archives of Internal Medicine, 150,* 1717–1721.

Fitten, L. J., Wieland, D., & Waite, M. (1997). *The medical decisional capacity assessment protocol (MDCAP): Assessing the cognitive aspects of treatment decision-making capacity.* Unpublished manuscript.

Fowles, D. G. (1991). *A profile of older Americans.* Washington, DC: American Association of Retired Persons.

Geiselmann, B., & Helmchen, H. (1994). Demented subjects' competence to consent to participate in field studies: The Berlin Aging Study. *Medicine and Law, 13*(1–2), 177–84.

Goldman, A. I. (1970). *A theory of human action.* Englewood Cliffs, NJ: Prentice-Hall.

Harris, L. (1982). *Views of informed consent and decision making: Parallel surveys of physicians and the Public* (Vol. 1, pp. 17–18). President's Commission for the Study of Ethical Problems in Medicine and Biomedical and Behavioral Research, Making Health Care Decisions. Washington, DC: U.S. Government Printing Office.

High, D. M. (1992, September). Research with Alzheimer's disease subjects: informed consent and proxy decision making. *Journal of the American Geriatric Society, 40*(9), 950–957.

Iris, M. A. (1988). Guardianship and the elderly: A multi-perspective view of the decision-making process. *Gerontologist, 28,* 39–45.

Janofsky, J. S., McCarthy, R. J., & Folstein, M. F. (1992). The Hopkins competency assessment test: A brief method for evaluating patients' capacity to give informed consent. *Hospital and Community Psychiatry, 43,* 132–136.

Kaplan, K. H., Strang, J. P., & Ahmed, I. (1988). Dementia, mental retardation and competency to make decisions. *General Hospital Psychiatry, 10,* 385–388.

Kapp, M. B. (1990). Liability issues and assessment of decision-making capability in nursing home patients. *American Journal of Medicine, 89,* 639–642.

Katz, J. (1980). Disclosure and consent. In A. Milunsky & G. Annas (Eds.), *Genetics and the law* (Vol. 2, pp. 122, 128). New York: Plenum Press.

Kloezen, S., Fitten, L. J., & Steinberg, A. (1988). Assessment of treatment decision-making capacity in a medically ill patient. *Journal of the American Geriatric Society, 36,* 1055–1058.

Lo, B. (1990). Assessing decision-making capacity. *Law, Medicine, and Health Care, 18,* 193–201.

Macklin, R. (1982). *Man, mind, and morality: The ethics of behavior control.* Englewood Cliffs, NJ: Prentice-Hall.

Marson, D. C., Cody, H. A., Ingram, K. K., & Harrell, L. E. (1995). Neuropsychologic predictors of competency in Alzheimer's disease using a rational reasons legal standard [Comment]. A prototype instrument. *Archives of Neurology, 52*(10), 995–999.

Marson, D. C., Ingram, K. K., Cody, H. A., & Harrell, L. E. (1995). Assessing the competency of patients with Alzheimer's disease under different legal standards: A prototype instrument. *Archives of Neurology, 52*(10), 949–954.

Marson, D. C., Schmitt, F. A., Ingram, K. K., & Harrell, L. E. (1994). Determining the competency of Alzheimer patients to consent to treatment and research. *Alzheimer Disease and Associated Disorders, 8*(4), 5–18.

Norman, D. A. (1981). Categorization of action slips. *Psychology Review, 88,* 1–15.

Pandya, D., & Yeterian, E. (1996). Morphological correlations of human and monkey frontal lobe. In A. Damasio, H. Damasio, & Y. Christen (Eds.), *Neurobiology of decision-making.* Berlin, Springer-Verlag.

Resau, L. S. (1995). Obtaining informed consent in Alzheimer's research. *Journal of Neuroscientific Nursing, 27*(1), 57–60.

Rosse, R. B, Ciolino, C. P., & Guriel, L. (1986). Utilization of psychiatric consultation with an elderly medically ill inpatient population in a VA hospital. *Military Medicine, 151,* 583–586.

Sachs, G. A. (1994). Advance consent for dementia research. *Alzheimer Disease and Associated Disorders, 8*(4), 19–27.

Stanley, B., Stanley, M., & Guido, J. (1988). The functional competency of elderly at risk. *Gerontologist, 28,* 53–58.

Stuss, D. T., & Benson, D. F. (1986). *The frontal lobes.* New York: Raven Press.

17

Memory and the Frontal Lobes

GORSEV G. YENER
ADAM ZAFFOS

In 1935, Jacobsen was the first to suggest that the frontal cortex was involved in memory when he noticed that frontal lobe-lesioned monkeys performed well in immediate responses but failed when delayed response was required (Moscovitch & Winocur, 1995). Later studies concluded that some subjects with frontal injury performed normally on classical memory tests (Benson et al., 1981; Cochrane & Kljajic, 1979; Pigott & Milner, 1993). Yet, studies using elaborate neuropsychological testing paradigms implied a close relationship between memory and the frontal lobes (Fuster, 1995; Goldman-Rakic, 1995; Ingvar, 1985; Mesulam, 1985; Milner, Petrides, & Smith, 1985; Moscovitch & Winocur, 1995; Stuss & Benson, 1984). Clearly, there are different views about the frontal lobes and memory.

According to one school of thought, the frontal lobes are on top of a hierarchical pyramid which organizes memory (Benson, 1993a, 1993b; Fuster, 1990; Petrides, 1995a). With this model, largely derived from clinical experience, functional divisions of human cortex have been proposed (Benson, 1993a; Mesulam, 1985): (1) primary (isotopic) cortex, (2) unimodal association cortex, (3) heteromodal association cortex, and (4) supramodal association cortex. In this organization, primary cortex receives sensory stimuli, unimodal association receives input from primary cortex; heteromodal association areas collect information from multiple sensory modalities and from memory, while the prefrontal cortex, as supramodal association cortex, directs all the these activities and monitors and selects responses.

Alternatively, some researchers favor distributed neural networks as the organizational structure encompassing memory and the frontal lobes (Goldman-Rakic, 1988; Olton, 1989). Studies using a variety of different paradigms support this network concept. For example, in single-unit studies on monkeys, during delay-related memory tasks, activation simultaneously occurs in prefrontal and parietal regions (Batuev, Shaefer, & Orlov, 1985); sensory and prefrontal circuits are organized in parallel but are not convergent on prefrontal cortex; and both depth electrode studies (Seeck et al., 1995) and positron emission tomography (PET) studies (Fletcher et al., 1995; Jonides et al.,

1993) show simultaneous activation of prefrontal and posterior cortex during memory tests.

Memory processing evolves through several stages: (1) encoding (i.e., receiving new information), (2) working (i.e., keeping information in short-term storage), (3) consolidation (i.e., placing the encoded material into a permanent storage), and (4) retrieval (i.e., recalling of information that has been stored). In PET studies, consolidation has been shown to be closely related to the hippocampus and surrounding medial temporal lobe (Fazio et al., 1992; Squire & Zola-Morgan, 1991; Zola-Morgan & Squire, 1993). However, the frontal cortex appears to be involved in many aspects of mnemonic processing including encoding, retrieval, working memory, spatial memory, nonspatial memory, context memory, temporal sequencing, categorization, attention, conditional associative learning, and planning.

FRONTAL LOBE ANATOMY: ITS RELATION TO MEMORY FUNCTIONING

Between the days E40 and E90, all cortical areas including prefrontal cortex complete development. In contrast to widely held beliefs, the production of neurons targeted for prefrontal cortex, is completed earlier than those targeted for visual cortex and columnar organization of prefrontal cortex occurs earlier than that for visual cortex. But, myelination occurs later in prefrontal cortex than in all other areas (Rakic, 1995). Frontal cortex can be divided into three parts: motor, premotor, and prefrontal regions. The precentral sulcus separates motor cortex from premotor cortex, and the arcuate sulcus separates premotor from prefrontal cortex. Posterior parts of frontal cortex play a major role in the organization of movement, while the anterior parts prefrontal cortex participate in broader behaviors.

Most prefrontal cortex in high primates consists of granular heteromodal isocortex. Many afferents to that part of brain come from primary sensory or heteromodal (especially parietal) association areas and cingulate–orbitofrontal regions. Therefore, prefrontal cortex encompasses a template for the cross-correlation of sensory experiences and their integration into a purposive behavior (Mesulam, 1986).

The extensive connections between prefrontal cortex and other brain regions, including hippocampus and temporal lobe, explain the importance of the frontal lobes in memory functions. As is shown in Chapter 1, this volume (Chow & Cummings), frontal–subcortical structures are connected in parallel circuits, which involve frontal lobes, striatum, globus pallidus, and thalamus (Cummings, 1993, 1995). Among these, lesions of dorsolateral prefrontal cortex and connected loop structures (i.e., caudate lesions) (Schmaltz & Isaacson, 1968; Wikmark, Divac, & Weiss, 1973) result in memory deficit characterized by poor retrieval (poor recall, intact recognition) (Cummings 1993, 1995). However, in medial temporal and thalamic-type memory deficits, declarative memory (i.e., fact learning) is impaired (Pepin & Auray-Pepin, 1993; Squire 1982, 1986; Zola-Morgan & Squire, 1993) due to interference at the stages of consolidation. Memory for the past is encoded in lateral and medial temporal system, the information for current status is processed in the sensory system, future memory is related to frontal–prefrontal cortex systems (Fuster, 1995; Ingvar, 1985) (see Figure 17.1).

There are also close connections between thalamus and frontal cortex (Goldman-Rakic & Porrino, 1985; Nauta, 1971). Thalamic nuclei contribute to parallel circuits important for mnemonic processing (Cummings, 1993; Morecraft, Geula, & Mesulam, 1992; Nauta, 1971). Septal regions, ventromedial midbrain tegmentum, and inferior

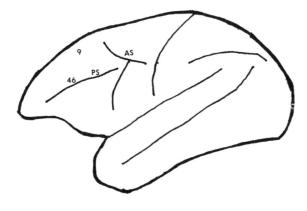

FIGURE 17.1. Schematic diagram of the frontal cortex of the macaque brain. AS, arcuate sulcus; PS, principal sulcus. Areas 46 and 9 consist of the middorsolateral frontal cortex. Adapted from Petrides (1992). Copyright 1992 by Raven Press. Adapted by permission.

temporal regions give rise to pathways to mediodorsal nucleus which projects to orbitofrontal cortex. Orbitofrontal cortex has connections with hippocampus, septum, hypothalamus, and nonspecific thalamic nuclei. Connections between frontal lobe and brainstem include extensions of frontal–limbic and frontal–thalamic pathways. Because the behavioral significance of a stimuli is assessed in the prefrontal cortex (Boussaoud & Wise, 1993; Rosenkilde, Bauer, & Fuster, 1981; Yamatani, Ono, Nyshijo, & Takaku, 1990; Yajeya, Quintana, & Fuster, 1988), prefrontal cortex may direct a role in attention processes which in turn may contribute to regulate the arousal and tone.

In prefrontal cortex, regions surrounding the principal sulcus (Brodmann's area 46), were found to be important sites for spatial memory in many experimental studies (Funahashi, Bruce, & Goldman-Rakic, 1989, 1993). This region of dorsolateral prefrontal cortex has reciprocal connections by parallel tracts with area 7 of parietal cortex (Goldman-Rakic, 1988). Areas 7 and 46 of prefrontal cortex also share common targets such as supplementary motor area (Brodmann's area 6), orbitoprefrontal cortex, opercular area, presubiculum, parahippocampal area, superior temporal sulcus (Brodmann's area 20), anterior and posterior cingulate (Brodmann's area 24, 23), prestriate cortex (Brodmann's area 19), and parahippocampal gyrus (Goldman-Rakic, 1995).

Frontal lobe and thalamic connections, especially from medial pulvinar, ventral anterior, and mediodorsal nucleus, are also organized in parallel tracts (Goldman-Rakic & Porrino, 1985) which carry different information (Schwartz & Goldman-Rakic, 1984). Prefrontal cortex is also connected reciprocally with hippocampus (Leichnetz & Astruc, 1975; Rosene & van Hoesen, 1977), entorhinal cortex, parahippocampal gyrus, presubicular cortex, and anterior and posterior cingulate cortex (Goldman-Rakic, 1987). Because presubicular area relays the hippocampal output to most cortical and subcortical structures (Hyman, van Hoesen, Damasio, & Barnes, 1984), it is reasonable to infer that prefrontal cortex interacts with hippocampal formation. Besides these direct reciprocal connections, prefrontal cortex and hippocampal formation meet indirectly in the multisynaptic connections of anterior and posterior cingulate cortex. This area is also primary target for parietal projections. Through these connections, parietal cortex and prefrontal cortex communicate through limbic targets.

Ventromedial prefrontal cortex is considered part of integrated medial temporal–medial thalamic memory system (Bachevalier & Mishkin, 1986), and in clinical studies, patients with unilateral dorsolateral frontal lobe lesions were found to perform better than those with medial frontal lesions (Wallesch, Kornhuber, Köllner, Haas, & Hufnagl, 1983). When monkeys with orbital and lateral frontal ablations were compared on visual discrimination learning tasks, the orbitofrontal group was unsuccessful in both learning and retention but not the lateral frontal group. This finding was interpreted as resulting from a deficit in response inhibition in the orbitofrontal group (Passingham, 1972). Another reason proposed for the dissociation of memory deficits in dorsolateral and medial frontal areas is the involvement of basal forebrain with its cholinergic projections with hippocampus (Damasio, Graff-Radford, Eslinger, Damasio, & Kassell, 1985). Ventromedial frontal cortex, as a part of the limbic–thalamic system, appears to monitor the output of the system and may have role in initiation and retrieval (Moscovitch & Winocur, 1995).

MEMORY AND ITS RELATION TO THE FRONTAL LOBES

The term "frontal" lobe dysfunction has to be carefully used because the tests for the detection of frontal lobe impairment are complex, and frontal lobe functions may be affected by psychiatric or medical disorders (Boone, Miller, & Lesser, 1993) or aging (Moscovitch & Winocur, 1995). Subjects can fail these tests for many reasons, and relation of the test and a focal brain region may be difficult to demonstrate (Stuss, 1993).

Explicit memory (declarative memory, i.e., fact learning) may be normal (Benson et al., 1981; Hirst & Volpe, 1988; Shimamura, Gershberg, Jurica, Mangels, & Knight, 1992) or mildly affected (Janowsky, Shimamura, Kritchevsky, & Squire, 1989) in patients with frontal lobe damage. Similarly, memory for complex visual scenes can be unimpaired in patients with unilateral partial frontal lobectomy (Pigott & Milner, 1993). Routine memory investigations may not reveal the frontal lobe deficits as they do not tap memory for the anticipated future (Ingvar, 1985). Several psychometric tests are well established for estimating frontal lobe functioning, such as the Wisconsin Card Sorting Test (Milner, 1963), which requires set shifting, or the Stroop Test, which measures interference (Cohn, Dustman, & Bradford, 1984). However, these tasks are not considered memory tasks.

Experimental Tests for Memory Related to the Frontal Lobes

Various neuropsychological tests have been used in either experimental animal studies or, in patient studies with frontal lobe damage. This section summarizes some of these tests and their relation to frontal lobe function.

Spatial Delayed-Response and Delayed Matching-to-Sample Tasks

The spatial delayed-response task (DR) is a well-established marker of frontal lobe function in nonhuman primates. In this task, the subject watches as the experimenter hides a desired object in one of two identical wells. After a brief delay, the subject is allowed to reach for an object that is hidden in the same well (Diamond & Doar, 1989; Kojima & Goldman-Rakic, 1984). Performance on these tasks is impaired after unilateral frontal ablations (Warren, Cornwell, & Warren, 1969) or cooling (Bauer & Fuster, 1976) in monkeys. In infants, frontal lobe myelination is not fully developed until the age of 20 years, and 7- to 9-months-old infants fail DR task (Diamond & Doar, 1989).

In the delayed matching-to-sample task (DMST), nonhuman primates are required to find the same, trial-unique stimulus after a delay period. DMST scores were found to be low in monkeys with prefrontal lesions (Fuster, 1990). On the other hand, the delayed non-matching-to-sample task (DNMST) is used in studies of hippocampus and related structures (Zola-Morgan & Squire, 1993). In the DNMST task, the subject has to find the stimulus different from that which was shown before the delay period (Fuster, 1990). This task tends to be impaired in animals with ventromedial lesions.

Neuronal activity in behaving monkeys during delay tasks is investigated by means of single-unit recordings. The dorsolateral prefrontal cortex (DLPFC) is directly involved in active memory processing (Niki & Watanabe, 1976; Joseph & Barone, 1987; Quintana, Yajeya, & Fuster, 1988; Funahashi et al., 1989, 1993). In the oculomotor DR task, monkeys are trained to fixate on a central spot and a visual target appears on the screen for 0.5 seconds in the periphery; then, after a delay, monkeys are supposed to remember the target direction and make a saccade toward the target. During the delay time, single-unit activities are recorded in the prefrontal cortex, as well as in posterior parietal cortex, visual association cortex, limbic cortex, hippocampus, supplementary motor area, premotor cortex, caudate–putamen, and superior colliculus (Funahashi et al., 1989, 1993). All these structures contribute to the spatial processing and memory, but the activity in the prefrontal cortex is the most significant. Two types of cells are activated during the delay: spatially oriented delay cells, and pure memory cells. Spatially oriented delay cells activate in accordance with the spatial orientation of given stimuli (Joseph & Barone, 1987; Kojima, Kojima, & Goldman-Rakic, 1982), and pure memory cells continue to discharge after the response. Pure memory cells consist of 60% of all prefrontal neurons (Niki & Watanabe, 1976).

The sustained single-unit activity in the prefrontal cortex during the delay imposed between the sensory cue and production of a response (Fuster, 1973; Niki & Watanabe, 1976) is related to "working memory" (Wilson, Scalaidhe, & Goldman-Rakic, 1993) or "mediation of cross-temporal contingencies" (Fuster, 1990). This neuronal delay activity has important characteristics. First, it occurs independently from the stimulus modality (Iversen, 1967), which implies that attentional filtering occurs in the prefrontal area (Mesulam, 1985). Second, duration of activity is related to the duration of delay. Increased delay time results in prolonged activity (Kojima et al., 1982; Batuev et al., 1985). Third, the level of performance is related to the amount of neuronal delay activation (Watanabe, 1986).

According to Wilson et al. (1993), object and spatial processing domains in primate prefrontal cortex are diffentially located. Spatial processing occurs on the principal sulcus (area 46) and anterior banks of arcuate sulcus, and object (item) processing, on the inferior convexity of dorsolateral cortex. Although the principal sulcus (Goldman, Rosvold, Vest, & Galkin, 1971) situated on the DLPFC is mainly related to spatial memory (Stamm, 1970), there are also color memory cells in this region (Fuster, 1990), implying that nonspatial memory processing also may take place in the principal sulcus.

Nonspatial Memory

Monkeys with orbital and lateral frontal ablations perform differently in visual discrimination learning tasks. The orbitofrontal group is unsuccessful in both learning and retention but not the lateral frontal group. This finding was interpreted as revealing a deficit in response inhibition produced by orbitofrontal lesions (Passingham, 1972). In similar clinical study of humans, both frontal lobe groups showed impairment in visual discrimination tasks (Oscar-Berman, 1978). Cooling of prefrontal cortex, but not parietal cortex, causes impairment in performance of a visual DMST (Fuster & Bauer, 1974). Inferior frontal convexity lesions result in impairment of delayed color matching in monkeys (Mishkin & Manning, 1978). Tactile memory deficits in monkeys (Iversen, 1967) or transient odor recognition deficits in rats have been reported after frontal ablation (Koger & Mair, 1994). In humans, odor memory is impaired after right orbitofrontal or temporal lesions (Jones-Gotman & Zatorre, 1993), auditory short-term memory tests are more severe in ptaitnes with frontal lobe damage than in patients with posterior damage (Lewisohn, Zieler, Libet, Eyeberg, & Nielson, 1972). In single-unit recordings, prefrontal activation is observed during visual delayed tasks (Matsunami & Kubota, 1983). These findings demonstrate that the relation of frontal lobe to the is not modality specific.

Temporal Sequencing

Even though frank amnesia is not characteristic of patients with frontal lobe damage, impairments on tests of temporal order or recency discrimination (Milner et al., 1985; Shimamura, Janowsky, & Squire, 1990) are common. When remembering the temporal sequence of items is required, patients with left frontal lobe lesions show impairment in verbal tests only, whereas patients with right frontal dysfunction fail in both verbal and nonverbal tests. Lateralization is also evident in the temporal organization of memory, and right frontal lobe lesions cause more severe deficits than does left-sided pathology (Milner et al., 1985; MacAndrews & Milner, 1991).

Frontal lobes are also important in memory of event frequency (Pigott & Milner, 1993; Smith & Milner, 1988): Frontal lobe excision results in difficulty with estimating the frequency of abstract designs, but patients perform as well as controls in recognition of the designs. Patients with right-sided lesions have worse performance than do patients in the left-sided lesion group (Smith & Milner, 1988).

Attention

Attention deficit may play a role in memory abnormalities observed following frontal lesions (Boussaoud & Wise, 1993; Rosenkilde et al., 1981; Yamatani et al., 1990; Yajeya et al., 1988). In clinical studies, patients with frontal lesion may have deficits in attention despite an IQ within normal ranges (Black, 1976). In divided-attention tasks (i.e., two stimuli are simultaneously given), rats with frontal cortex lesions ignore one stimuli; this contrasts with the performance of animals with hippocampal lesions (Olton, Wenk, Church, & Meck, 1988).

Encoding

Encoding deficits may lead to memory impairment (Freedman & Cermak, 1986; Kojima et al., 1982). In PET studies, encoding and retrieval of verbal material result in prefrontal activation (Grasby et al., 1993). Encoding is more dependent on left than right prefrontal cortex (Fletcher et al., 1995).

Retrieval

In verbal memory tests, retrieval deficits (i.e., poor recall with relatively spared recognition) are common in patients with frontal lobe dysfunction (Stuss et al., 1994). In a study that compared the retrieval in patients with prefrontal, temporal, and diencephalic lesions, those with medial temporal and diencephalic disorders scored the worst and did not improve with cuing. Patients with unilateral lateral temporal and prefrontal pathology performed better, scored worse in free recall than controls, but improved with cueing (Jetter, Poser, Freeman, & Markowitsch, 1986). In these patients, recognition memory was relatively better than free recall (Vogel, Markowitsch, Hempel, & Hackenberg, 1987). In Korsakoff's and Alzheimer's disease patients, frontal lobe dysfunction may contribute impairment or retrieval of retrograde memories (Kopelman, 1991). In PET studies with normal subjects, retrieval has been found to be related to the right prefrontal cortex (Buckner et al., 1995; Fletcher et al., 1995).

Conditional Associative Learning

In conditional associative learning tasks, subjects are required to respond to the different colored stimuli by pointing to specific designs. Patients with frontal lobe lesions of either side are impaired in learning this task, but patients with temporal lobe lesions do not differ from controls. These findings show that particular memory types depend on the integrity of specific brain regions. Self-generated responses depend on midlateral frontal cortex (areas 46 and 9) (Petrides, 1995b), whereas conditional learning depends on posterior frontal regions (areas 6 and 8) (Petrides, 1992; Petrides, Alivisatos, Evans, & Meyer, 1993).

Planning and Strategy Application

Short-term spatial memory is normal after unilateral or bilateral frontal lobe lesions, but patients are not successful in planning effective strategies and using spatial working memory Owen, Downes, Sahakian, Polkey, & Robbins, 1990; Shallice & Burgess, 1991).

Categorization

Patients with frontal lobe lesions obtain normal scores on the Wechsler Memory Scale, but their scores for categorization tasks are lower than those of controls (Hirst & Volpe, 1988). In a study that requires the categorical classification of objects, patients with frontal lobectomies showed impairments whereas those with temporal lobectomy did not. Verbal categorical recall was impaired with lesions of either frontal loss group, being worse on left-sided lesions (della Rocchetta, 1986).

Context Memory

Frontal lobe dysfunction causes impairment in the ability to associate information with its context, as shown by Janowsky, Shimamura, and Squire (1989). Recall and recognition memory were within normal ranges, but source memory for time and place of learning the information was impaired.

Self-Ordered Tasks

Self-ordered tasks, in which subjects are required to indicate the item that has not been shown before on a card that holds all the items, are impaired with frontal lobe damage (Milner et al., 1985; Petrides, 1995b; Wiegersma, van der Scheer, & Hijman, 1990). The same items are placed in different positions on each card. In this experiment the subject must keep a record of their earlier responses and plan the subsequent move. In monkeys, a self-ordered task was impaired within midlateral frontal (areas 46 and 9) lesions; however, animals with area 8 and area 6 lesions (posterior dorsolateral frontal region) performed as well as controls. Based on these findings, Petrides (1992) proposed a functional model of prefrontal cortex that separated dorsolateral prefrontal cortex into two subdivisions: ventrolateral and middorsal lateral. The former relates to the active retrieval of information when planning or decision making is needed; the latter to self-ordered tasks requiring a monitoring system.

Implicit and Explicit Memory

Implicit (procedural) memory refers to skill learning, whereas explicit (declarative) memory refers to fact learning. Explicit memory deteriorates with medial temporal-medial thalamic lesions (Squire & Zola-Morgan, 1991; Zola-Morgan & Squire, 1993), but not with frontal lesions (Shimamura et al., 1992). The patients with frontal lobe lesions performed as well as controls in word recognition, cued recall and word associate learning, but there were deficits on tasks of explicit memory, such as free recall (Janowsky, Shimamura, Kritchevsky, & Squire, 1989). Study of implicit memory in patients with frontal dysfunction, have produced discrepant results, some showing deficits (Martone, Butters, Payne, Becker, & Sax, 1984) and others showing normal results (Shimamura et al., 1992).

Behavioral Significance

The significance of the stimulus is also partially mediated by the frontal lobe (Pandya & Yeterian, 1984). Neuronal activity following attentional or intentional cues indicates that dorsal premotor cortex cells reflect the motor significance of stimuli, whereas the ventrolateral part of the DLPFC plays a relatively small role (Boussaoud & Wise, 1993). Also, a study of visual delay tasks showed that DLPFC discriminates stimuli according to this behavioral significance (Yajeya et al., 1988; Yamatani et al., 1990). Interaction between amygdala and frontal lobe may constitute the anatomic basis of this function of the frontal lobe (Gaffan, Murray, & Fabre-Thorpe, 1993). All these findings support the hypothesis that prefrontal cortex integrates motivational input into behavioral action.

Proactive Interference

Proactive interference (PI) refers to the negative effect of previously learned material on the recall of newly acquired information (Kopelman, 1991). Increasing the intertrial interval results in improvement in performance in delayed alternation tasks in primates (Pribram & Tubbs, 1967), presumably due to reduction of proactive interference effects (Fuster, 1990). Pigott and Milner (1993) showed that spatial memory may be normal in frontal lobe-damaged patients, although there may be impairment in spatial tasks with proactive interference (Milner, 1995). A relationship between failure to release from proactive interference and performance in WCST was found in patients with unilateral left frontal lobectomies (Moscovitch, 1982). Bilateral orbitofrontal lesions do not impair most aspects of memory in standart tests, but the patients are open to PI effects (Stuss et al., 1982). Freedman and Cermak (1986) compared Korsakoff's patients to patients with frontal lobe lesions and found that the latter showed memory impairment and the Korsakoff's group had failure of release from PI. Janowsky, Shimamura, Kritchevsky, and Squire (1989) examined PI in amnesics, patients with frontal lobe lesions, and patients with Korsakoff's syndrome. Only the Korsakoff's group failed the test. This finding implies that frontal lobe impairment or memory deficit alone is not sufficient to cause failure in this paradigm, but presumably the association of both regions is. In schizophrenia, the release from PI is also impaired and these patients fail both frontal and mnemonic tests (Randolph, Gold, Carpenter, Goldberg, & Weinberger, 1992). Perseveration may be due to decreased release from PI (Vilkki, 1989).

Contingent Negative Variation, Event-Related Potentials, and Their Relation to Frontal Lobes

Contingent negative variation (CNV), a slow negative potential, is elicited when an associative motor response must be given after a previously conditioned sensory stimulus. The source of CNV is presumed to be the frontal cortex, as it is recorded at maximal amplitude over frontal regions (Akdal, 1996).

FACTORS AFFECTING THE MEMORY FUNCTION MEDIATED BY THE FRONTAL LOBES

Laterality Effects

It has been suggested that the right frontal lobe is related more than the left to the temporal organization of memory (Milner et al., 1985; MacAndrews & Milner, 1991). Patients with unilateral frontal lesions on the left fail in verbal and nonverbal self-ordered tasks, whereas the right frontal lobe lesions caused impaired performance on nonverbal self-ordered tasks (Petrides & Milner, 1982). Patients with right frontal lobe damage may display poor retention of visually presented letters or geometric designs (Butters, Samuels, Goodglass, & Brody, 1970). Working memory mechanisms have also been lateralized. Oculomotor DRs are processed in contralateral prefrontal cortex (Funahashi et al., 1993).

Age and Sex Effects

Minimal age differences in frontal lobe abilities can be documented in healthy aged individuals (Boone, Miller, Lesser, Hill, & D'Elia, 1990). In rats, no effect of sex difference was observed in delayed spatial response alternation tasks before or after the ablation of medial prefrontal cortex (van Haaren, de Bruin, Heinsbroek, & van de Poll, 1985).

Neurotransmitters

Some neurotransmitters, such as acetylcholine, glutamate, and dopamine, are involved in memory functions. Memory deficit can be observed after the injection of acetylcholine antagonists but not after injection of dopaminergic antagonists into the prelimbic sector of the medial frontal cortex in rats. Thus, in rats, memory function in that region may be related more to the cholinergic system than to the dopaminergic system (Brito, Silva, & Brito, 1989). However, other studies show that dopamine and glutamate can regulate cell firing on the memory-related neurons in prefrontal cortex (Goldman-Rakic, 1995), and the retention of maze performance in rats has been found to be inversely related to the number of N-methyl-D-aspartate receptors in hippocampus and frontal cortex (Wenk, Grey, Ingram, Spangler, & Olton, 1989).

MEMORY DEFICITS SEEN AFTER THE DISEASES
THAT CAUSE FRONTAL LOBE DYSFUNCTION

Frontotemporal Dementias

Frontotemporal dementia is characterized by apathy, disorganized planning for the future, stereotyped behavior and speech, restlessness, utilization behavior (Gustafson, 1993), and changes of oral dietary/behavior (Miller, Darby, Swartz, Yener, & Mena, 1995). The neuropathological attention involves the frontal and anterior temporal lobes (Brun, 1987): SPECT typically shows hypofrontality (Ingvar, 1983b; Miller et al., 1991) and EEG in these patients reveals slowing over the frontal regions (Yener et al., 1996). Declarative memory (explicit memory) is relatively intact at the beginning of the disease (Knopman et al., 1989).

Parkinson's Disease and Multisystem Atrophies

Cognitive aspects of Parkinson's disease (PD) have been extensively studied (Daum et al., 1995; Owen et al., 1990). Memory deficits in PD share features with frontal dysfunction, such as impaired matching-to-sample test (Sahakian et al., 1988) and poor recall with preserved recognition (Daum et al., 1995). In multiple system atrophy, cognitive deficits are also similar to those seen in frontal lobe damage, including deficits in set shifting (Robbins et al.,1992).

Korsakoff's Syndrome

There are similarities between the neuropsychological status of patients with frontal lobe damage and patients with Korsakoff's syndrome, such as decrease in Wisconsin Card Sorting Test scores or increased perseveration, deficits in initiation, or defective retrieval of retrograde memories (Kopelman, 1991). The major difference between the two groups is that the frontal group is not amnesic (Janowsky, Shimamura, Kritchevsky, & Squire, 1989) whereas the patients with Korsakoff's syndrome have the dementia pattern of poor recall and impairment in temporal order.

Schizophrenia

Retrieval may be compromised whereas recognition is spared, and anergia accompanies the memory deficit in schizophrenia (Goldberg, Weinberg, Pliskin, Berman, & Podd, 1989). Release from PI is also impaired as these patients (Randolph et al., 1992).

CONCLUSION

The frontal lobes play a role in adequate memory functioning. The temporal gap between the stimulus and the response (i.e., perception–action cycle) is closed by the frontal lobes. This function is provided by widespread connections of prefrontal cortex with limbic and cortical structures. Context memory, source memory, retrieval, encoding, categorization, temporal sequencing, planning, strategy application, attention, and release from proactive interference contribute to the many aspects of cognitive functioning related to the role of the frontal lobes in memory.

ACKNOWLEDGMENT

We are indebted to Dr. Idil Cavus and her incredible help on this chapter.

REFERENCES

Aggleton, J. P., Neave, N., Nagle, S., & Sahgal, A. (1995). A comparison of the effects of medial prefrontal, cingulate cortex, and cingulum bundle lesions on tests of spatial memory: Evidence of a double dissociation between frontal and cingulum bundle contributions. *Journal of Neuroscience, 15*(11), 7270–7281.

Akdal, G. (1996). *Contingent negative variation and P300 activity in complex partial and generalized epilepsy.* Doctoral dissertation, Dokuz Eylül University, Izmir, Turkey.

Awh, E., Smith, E. E., & Jonides, J.(1995). Human rehearsal processes and the frontal lobes: PET evidence. *Annals of the New York Academy of Sciences, 769,* 97–117.

Bachevalier, J., & Mishkin, M. (1986). Visual recognition impairment follows ventromedial but not dorsolateral prefrontal lesions in monkeys. *Behavioral Brain Research, 20,* 249–261.

Batuev, A. S., Shaefer, V. I., & Orlov, A. A. (1985). Comparative characteristics of unit activity in the prefrontal and parietal areas during delay performance in monkeys. *Behavioral Brain Research, 16,* 57–70.

Bauer, R. H., & Fuster, J. M. (1976). Delayed-matching and delayed-response deficit from cooling dorsolateral prefrontal cortex in monkeys. *Journal of Comparative and Physiological Psychology, 90,* 293–302.

Benson, D. F. (1993a). Prefrontal abilities. *Behavioral Neurology, 6*(2), 75–82.

Benson, D. F. (1993b). Progressive frontal dysfunction. *Dementia, 4,* 149–153.

Benson, D. F., Stuss, D. T., Naeser, M. A., Weir, W. S., Kaplan, E. F., & Kline, H. L. (1981). The long term effects of prefrontal leucotomy. *Archives of Neurology, 38,* 165–169.

Black, W. (1976). Cognitive deficits in patients with unilateral war related frontal lobe lesions. *Journal of Clinical Psychology, 32*(2), 366–372.

Boone, K. B., Miller, B. L., Lesser, I. M., Hill, E., & D'Elia, L. (1990). Performance on frontal lobe tests in healthy, older individuals. *Developmental Neuropsychology, 6*(3), 215–223.

Boone, K. K., Miller, B. L., & Lesser, I. M. (1993). Frontal lobe cognitive functions in aging: Methodologic considerations. *Dementia, 4,* 232–236.

Boussaoud, D., & Wise, S. P. (1993). Primate frontal cortex: neuronal activity following attentional versus intentional cues. *Experimental Brain Research, 95,* 15–27.

Brito, G. N. O., Silva, S. P., & Brito, L. S. O. (1989). The Cholinergic and dopaminergic systems of the prelimbic sector of frontal cortex and memory in the rat. *Brazilian Journal of Medicine and Biological Research, 22,* 1155–1158.

Brun, A. (1987). Frontal lobe degeneration of non-Alzheimer type. I. Neuropathology. *Archives of Gerontology and Geriatry, 6,* 193–208.

Buckner, R. L., Petersen, S. E., Ojemann, J. G., Miezin, F. M., Squire, L. R., & Raichle, M. E. (1995). Functional anatomical studies of explicit and implicit memory retrieval tasks. *Journal of Neuroscience, 15*(1), 12–29.

Butters, N., Samuels, I., Goodglass, H., & Brody, B. (1970). Short term visual and auditory memory disorders after parietal and frontal lobe damage. *Cortex, 6*(4), 440–459.

Cochrane, N., & Kljajic, I. (1979). The effects on intellectual functioning of open refrontal leucotomy. *Medical Journal of Australia, 1,* 258–260.

Cohn, N. B., Dustman, R. E., & Bradford, D. C. (1984). Age related decrements in Stroop color test performance. *Journal of Clinical Psychology, 40,* 1244–1250.

Cummings, J. L. (1993). Frontal–subcortical circuits and human behavior. *Archives of Neurology, 50,* 873–880.

Cummings, J. L. (1995). Anatomic and behavioral aspects of frontal-subcortical circuits. *Annals of the New York Academy of Sciences, 769,* 1–13.

Damasio, A. R., Graff-Radford, N. R., Eslinger, P. J., Damasio, H., & Kassell, N. (1985). Amnesia following basal forebrain lesions. *Archives of Neurology, 42,* 263–271.

Daum, I., Schugens, M. M., Spieker, S., Poser, U., Schönle, P. W., & Birbaumer, N. (1995). Memory and skill acquisition in Parkinson's disease and frontal lobe dysfunction. *Cortex, 31,* 413–432.

della Rocchetta, A. I. (1986). Classification and recall of pictures after unilateral frontal or temporal lobectomy. *Cortex, 22,* 189–211.

Diamond, A., & Doar, B. (1989). The performance of human infants on a measure of frontal cortex function, delayed response task. *Developmental Psychobiology, 22*(3), 271–294.

Fazio, F., Perani, D., Gilardi, M. C., Colombo, F., Cappa, S. F., Vallar, G., Bettinardi, V., Paulesu, E., Alberoni, M., Bressi, S., Franceschi, M., & Lenzi, G. (1992). Metabolic impairment in human amnesia: a PET study of memory networks. *Journal of Cerebral Blood Flow and Metabolism, 12,* 353–358.

Fletcher, P. C., Frith, C. D., Grasby, P. M., Shallice, T., Frackowiak, R. S. J., & Dolan, R. J. (1995). Brain systems for encoding and retrieval of auditory–verbal memory: An *in vivo* study in humans. *Brain, 118,* 401–416.

Freedman, M., & Cermak, L. S. (1986). Semantic encoding deeficits in frontal lobe disease and amnesia. *Brain and Cognition, 5,* 108–114.

Funahashi, S., Bruce, C. J., & Goldman-Rakic, P. S. (1989). Mnemonic coding of visual space in the monkey's dorsolateral prefrontal cortex. *Journal of Neurophysiology, 61*(2), 331–348.

Funahashi, S., Bruce, C. J., & Goldman-Rakic, P. S. (1993). Dorsolateral prefrontal lesions and oculomotor delayed-response performance: Evidence for mnemonic "scotomas." *Journal of Neurosciences, 13*(4), 1479–1497.

Fuster, J. M. (1973). Unit activity in prefrontal cortex during delayed-response performance: Neuronal correlates of transient memory. *Journal of Neurophysiology, 36*(1), 61–78.

Fuster, J. M. (1990). Prefrontal cortex and the bridging of temporal gaps in the perception-action cycle. *Annals of the New York Academy of Sciences, 608,* 318–329.

Fuster, J. M. (1992). Prefrontal neurons and the cognitive foundation of motor action. In P. Chauvel, A. V. Delgado-Escueta, E. Halgren, & J. Bancaud (Eds.), *Frontal lobe seizures and epilepsies* (pp. 351–360). New York: Raven Press.

Fuster, J. M. (1995). Memory and planning. Two temporal perspectives of frontal lobe function. In H. H. Jasper, S. Riggio, & P. S. Goldman-Rakic (Eds.), *Epilepsy and the functional anatomy of the frontal lobe* (pp. 9–20). New York: Raven Press.

Fuster, J. M., & Bauer, R. H. (1974). Visual short term memory deficit from hypothermia of frontal cortex. *Brain Research, 81,* 393–400.

Gaffan, D., Murray, E. A., & Fabre-Thorpe, M. (1993). Interaction of the amygdala with the frontal lobe in reward memory. *European Journal of Neuroscience, 5,* 968–975.

Goldberg, T. E., Weinberger, D. R., Pliskin, N. H., Berman, K. F., & Podd, M. H. (1989). Recall memory deficit in schizophrenia. A possible manifestation of prefrontal dysfunction. *Schizophrenia Research, 2,* 251–257.

Goldman, P. S., Rosvold, H. E., Vest, B., & Galkin, T. W. (1971). Analysis of the delayed alternation deficit produced by dorsolateral prefrontal lesions in the rhesus monkey. *Journal of Comparative and Physiological Psychology, 77*(2), 212–220.

Goldman-Rakic, P. S. (1987). Circuitry of the frontal association cortex and its relevance to dementia. *Archives of Gerontology and Geriatry, 6,* 299–309.

Goldman-Rakic, P. S. (1988). Topography of cognition; parallel distributed networks in primate association cortex. *Annual Reviews in Neurosciences, 11,* 137–156.

Goldman-Rakic, P. S. (1995). Anatomical and functional circuits in prefrontal cortex of nonhuman primates. Relevance to epilepsy. In H. H. Jasper, S. Riggio, & P. S. Goldman-Rakic (Eds.), *Epilepsy and the functional anatomy of the frontal lobe* (pp. 51–65). New York: Raven Press.

Goldman-Rakic, P. S., & Porrino, L. J. (1985). The primate mediodorsal (MD) nucleus and its projection to the frontal lobe. *Journal of Comparative Neurology, 242,* 535–560.

Grasby, P. M., Frith, C. D., Friston, K. J., Bench, C. J., Frackowiak, R. S. J., & Dolan, R. J. (1993). Functional mapping of brain areas implicated in auditory-verbal memory function. *Brain, 116,* 1–20.

Gustafson, L. (1993). Clinical picture of frontal lobe degeneration of non-Alzheimer type. *Dementia, 4,* 143–148.

Hirst, W., & Volpe, B. T. (1988). Memory strategies brain damage. *Brain and Cognition, 8,* 379–408.

Hodges, J. R., & Gurd, J. M. (1994). Remote memory and lexical retrieval in a case of frontal Pick's disease. *Archives of Neurology, 51,* 821–827.

Hyman, B. T., van Hoesen, G. W., Damasio, A. R., & Barnes, C. L. (1984). Alzheimer's disease:cell specific pathology isolates the hippocampal formation. *Science, 225,* 1168–1170.

Ingvar, D. H. (1983). Serial aspects of language and speech related to prefrontal cortical activity: A selective review. *Human Neurobiology, 2(3),* 177–189.

Ingvar, D. H. (1985). Memory of the future: An essay on the temporal organization of consciousness awareness. *Human Neurobiology, 4,* 127–136.

Iversen, S. D. (1967). Tactile learning and memory in baboons after temporal and frontal lesions. *Experimental Neurology, 18,* 228–238.

Janowsky, J. S., Shimamura, A. P., Kritchevsky, M., & Squire, L. R. (1989). Cognitive impairment following frontal lobe damage and its relevance to human amnesia. *Behavioral Neurosciences, 103(3),* 548–560.

Janowsky, J. S., Shimamura, A. P., & Squire, L. R. (1989). Source memory impairment in patients with frontal lobe lesions. *Neuropsychologia, 27(8),* 1043–1056.

Jetter, W., Poser, U., Freeman, R. B., & Markowitsch, H. J. (1986). A verbal long term memory deficit in frontal lobe damaged patients. *Cortex, 22,* 229–242.

Jones-Gotman, M., & Zatorre, R. J. (1993). Odor recognition memory in humans: Role of right temporal and orbitofrontal regions. *Brain and Recognition, 22,* 182–198.

Jonides, J., Smith, E. E., Koeppe, R. A., Awh, E., Minoshima, S., & Mintun, M. A. (1993). Spatial working memory in humans as revealed by PET. *Nature, 363,* 623–625.

Joseph, J. P., & Barone, P. (1987). Prefrontal unit activity during a delayed oculomotor task in the monkey. *Experimental Brain Research, 67,* 460–468.

Knopman, D. S., Christensen, K. J., Schute, L. J., Harbaugh, R. E., Reeder, T., Ngo, T., & Frey, II, W. (1989). The spectrum of imaging and neuropsychological findings in Pick's disease. *Neurology, 39,* 362–368.

Koger, S. M., & Mair, R. G. (1994). Comparison of the effects of frontal cortical and thalamic lesions on measures of olfactory learning and memory in the rat. *Behavioral Neuroscience, 108(6),* 1088–1100.

Kojima, S., & Goldman-Rakic, P. S. (1984). Functional analysis of spatially discriminative neurons in prefrontal cortex of rhesus monkey. *Brain Research, 291,* 229–240.

Kojima, S., Kojima, M., & Goldman-Rakic, P. S. (1982). Operant behavioral analysis of memory loss in monkeys with prefrontal lesions. *Brain Research, 248,* 51–59.

Kopelman, M. D. (1991). Frontal dysfunction and memory deficits in the alcoholic Korsakoff syndrome and Alzheimer type dementia. *Brain, 114,* 117–137.

Leichnetz, G. R., & Astruc, J. (1975). Preliminary evidence for a direct projection of the prefrontal cortex to the hippocampus in the squirrel monkey. *Brain and Behavioral Evolution, 11,* 355–364.

Lewisohn, P. M., Zieler, R. E., Libet, J., Eyeberg, S., & Nielson, G. (1972). Short term memory: A comparison between frontal and non frontal right and left hemisphere brain damaged patients. *Journal of Comparative and Physiological Psychology, 81(2),* 248–255.

MacAndrews, M. P., & Milner, B. (1991). The frontal cortex and memory for temporal order. *Neuropsychologia, 29(9),* 849–859.

Martone, M., Butters, N., Payne, M., Becker, J. T., & Sax, D. S. (1984). Dissociation between skill learning and verbal recognition in amnesia and dementia. *Archives of Neurology, 41,* 965–970.

Matsunami, K., & Kubota, K. (1983). Radioactive deoxyglucose uptake into the prefrontal cortex during a delayed response task of the monkey. *Neuroscience Letters, 36,* 329–333.

Mesulam, M.-M. (1985). Attention, confusional states, and neglect. In M.-M. Mesulam (Ed.), *Principles of behavioral neurology* (pp. 125–168). Philadelphia: F. A. Davis.

Mesulam, M.-M. (1986). Frontal cortex and behavior. *Annals of Neurology, 19*(4), 320–324.

Miller, B. L., Cummings, J. L., Villanueva-Meyer, J., Boone, K., Mehringer, C. M., Lesser, I. M., & Mena I. (1991). Frontal lobe degeneration: Clinical, neuropsychological, and SPECT characteristics. *Neurology, 41,* 1374–1382.

Miller, B. L., Darby, A. L., Swartz, J. R., Yener, G. G., & Mena, I. (1995). Dietary changes, compulsions and sexual behavior in frontotemporal degeneration. *Dementia, 6,* 195–199.

Milner, B. (1963). Effects of different brain lesions on card sorting. *Archives of Neurology, 9,* 90–100.

Milner, B. (1995). Aspects of human frontal lobe function. In H. H. Jasper, S. Riggio, & P. S. Goldman-Rakic (Eds.), *Epilepsy and the functional anatomy of the frontal lobe* (pp. 67–81). New York: Raven Press.

Milner, B., Petrides, M., & Smith, M. L. (1985). Frontal lobes and temporal organization of memory. *Human Neurobiology, 4,* 137–142.

Mishkin, M., & Manning, F. J. (1978). Non spatial memory after selective prefrontal lesions in monkeys. *Brain Research, 143,* 313–323.

Morecraft, R. J., Geula, C., & Mesulam, M.-M. (1992). Cytoarchitecture and neural afferents of orbitofrontal cortex in the brain of the monkey. *Journal of Comparative Neurology, 123,* 341–358.

Moscovitch, M. (1982). Multiple dissociations of function in amnesia. In L. Cermak (Ed.), *Human memory and amnesia* (pp. 337–370). Hillsdale, NJ: Erlbaum.

Moscovitch, M., & Winocur, G. (1995). Frontal lobes, memory, and aging. *Annals of the New York Academy of Sciences, 769,* 119–150.

Nauta, W. J. H. (1971). The problem of the frontal lobe: A reinterpretation. *Journal of Psychological Research, 8,* 167–187.

Niki, H., & Watanabe, M. (1976). Cingulate unit activity and delayed response. *Brain Research, 110,* 381–386.

Olton, D. S. (1989). Frontal cortex, timing and memory. *Neuropsychologia, 27*(1), 121–130.

Olton, D. S., Wenk, G. L., Church, R. M., & Meck, W. H. (1988). Attention and the frontal cortex as examined by simultaneous temporal processing. *Neuropsychologia, 26*(2), 307–318.

Oscar-Berman, M. (1978). The effects of dorsolateral-frontal and ventrolateral-orbitofrontal lesions on nonspatial test performance. *Neuropsychologia, 16,* 259–267.

Owen, A. M., Downes, J. J., Sahakian, B. J., Polkey, C. E., & Robbins, T. W. (1990). Planning and spatial working memory following frontal lobe lesions in man. *Neuropsychologia, 28*(10), 1021–1034.

Pandya, D. N., & Yeterian, E. H. (1984). Proposed neural circuitry for spatial memory in primate brain. *Neuropsychologia, 2,* 109–122.

Passingham, R. E. (1972). Visual discrimination learning after selective prefrontal ablation in monkeys (Macaca mulatta). *Neuropsychologia, 10,* 27–39.

Pepin, E. P., & Auray-Pepin, L. (1993). Selective dorsolateral frontal lobe dysfunction associated with diencephalic amnesia. *Neurology, 43,* 733–741.

Petrides, M. (1992). Functional specialization within dorsolateral frontal cortex. In P. Chauvel, A. V. Delgado-Escueta, E. Halgren, & J. Bancaud (Eds.), *Frontal lobe seizures and epilepsies* (pp. 379–388). New York: Raven Press.

Petrides, M. (1995a). Functional organization of the human frontal cortex for mnemonic processing. Evidence from neuroimaging studies. *Annals of the New York Academy of Sciences, 769,* 85–96.

Petrides, M. (1995b). Impairments on nonspatial self-ordered and externally ordered working memory tasks after lesions of the mid-dorsal part of the lateral frontal cortex in the monkey. *Journal of Neurosciences, 15*(1), 359–375.

Petrides, M., Alivisatos, B., Evans, A. C., & Meyer, E. (1993). Dissociation of human mid-dorsao-lateral from posterior dorsolateral frontal cortex in memory processing. *Proceedings of the National Academy of Sciences, USA, 90,* 873–877.

Petrides, M., & Milner, B. (1982). Deficits on subject-ordered tests after frontal- and temporal-lobe lesions in man. *Neuropsychologia, 20,* 249–262.

Pigott, S., & Milner, B. (1993). Memory for different aspects of complex visual scenes after unilateral temporal- or frontal-lobe resection. *Neuropsychologia, 31*(1), 1–15.

Pribram, K. H., & Tubbs, W. E. (1967). Short term memory, parsing, and the primate frontal cortex. *Science, 156,* 1765–1767.

Quintana, J., Yajeya, J., & Fuster, M. (1988). Prefrontal representations of stimulus attributes during delay tasks. I. Unit activity in cross temporal integration of sensory and sensory information. *Brain Research, 474,* 211–221.

Rakic, P. (1995). The development of the frontal lobe. A view from the rear of the brain. In H. H. Jasper, S. Riggio, & P. S. Goldman-Rakic (Eds.), *Epilepsy and the functional anatomy of the frontal lobe* (pp. 1–8). New York: Raven Press.

Randolph, C., Gold, J. M., Carpenter, C. J., Goldberg, T. E., & Weinberger, D. R. (1992) Release from proactive interference: Determinants of performance and neuropsychological correlates. *Journal of Clinical and Experimental Neuropsychology, 14*(5), 785–800,

Robbins, T. W., James, S., Lange, K. W., Owen, A. M., Quinn, N. P., & Marsden, C. D. (1992). Cognitive performance in multiple system atrophy. *Brain, 115,* 271–291.

Rosene, D. L., & van Hoesen, G. W. (1977). Hippocampal efferents reach widespread areas of cerebral cortex and amygdala in the rhesus monkey. *Science, 198,* 315–317.

Rosenkilde, C. E., Bauer, R. H., & Fuster, J. M. (1981). Single cell activity in ventral prefrontal cortex of behaving monkeys. *Brain Research, 209,* 375–394.

Sahakian, B. J., Morris, R. J., Evenden, J. L., Heald, A., Levy, R., Philpot, M., & Robbins, T. W. (1988). A comparative study of visuospatial memory and learning in Alzheimer-type dementia and Parkinson's disease. *Brain, 111,* 695–718.

Schmaltz, L. W., & Isaacson, R. L. (1968). Effects of caudate and frontal lesions on retention and relearning of a DRL schedule. *Journal of Comparative and Physiological Psychology, 65*(2), 3343–348.

Schwartz, M. W., & Goldman-Rakic, P. S. (1984). Callosal and intrahemispheric connectivity of the prefrontal association cortex in rhesus monkey: Relation between intraparietal and principal sulcal cortex. *Journal of Comparative Neurology, 226,* 403–420.

Seeck, M., Schomer, D., Mainwaring, N., Ives, J., Dubuisson, D., Blume, H., Cosgrove, R., Ransil, B. J., & Mesulam, M.-M. (1995). Selectively distributed processing of visual object recognition in the temporal and frontal lobes of the human brain. *Annals of Neurology, 37,* 538–545.

Shallice, T., & Burgess, P. W. (1991). Deficits in strategy application following frontal lobe damage in man. *Brain, 114,* 727–741.

Shimamura, A. P., Gershberg, F. B., Jurica, P. J., Mangels, J. A., & Knight, R. T. (1992). Intact implicit memory in patients with frontal lobe lesions. *Neuropsychologia, 30*(10), 931–937.

Shimamura, A. P., Janowsky, J. S., & Squire, L. R. (1990). Memory for the temporal order of events in patients with frontal lobe lesions and amnesic patients. *Neuropsychologia, 28*(8), 803–813.

Smith, M. L., & Milner, B. (1988). Estimation of frequency of occurrence of abstract designs after frontal or temporal lobectomy. *Neuropychologia, 26*(2), 297–306.

Squire, L. R. (1982). The neuropsychology of human memory. *Annual Reviews in Neurosciences, 5,* 241–273.

Squire, L. R. (1986). Mechanisms of memory. *Science, 232,* 1612–1619.

Squire, L. R., & Zola-Morgan, S. (1991). The medial temporal lobe system. *Science, 253,* 1380–1385.

Stamm, J. S. (1970). Dorsolateral frontal ablations and response processes in monkeys. *Journal of Comparative and Physiological Psychology, 70*(3), 437–447.

Stuss, D. T. (1993). Assessment of neuropsychological dysfunction in frontal type degeneration. *Dementia, 4,* 220–225.

Stuss, D. T., Alexander, M. P. M., Palumbo, C. L., Buckle, C. L., Buckle, L., Sayer, L., & Pogue, S. J. (1994). Organizational strategies of patients with unilateral or bilateral frontal lobe injury in word list learning. *Neuropsychology, 8,* 355–373.

Stuss, D. T., & Benson, D. F. (1984). Neuropsychological studies of the frontal lobes. *Psychology Bulletin, 95,* 3–28.

Stuss, D. T., Kaplan, E. F., Benson, D. F., Weir, W. S., Chiulli, S., & Sarazin, F. F. (1982). Evidence for the involvement of orbitofrontal cortex in memory functions: An interference effect. *Journal of Comparative and Physiological Psychology, 96*(6), 913–925.

van Haaren, F., de Bruin, J. P. C., Heinsbroek, R. P. W., & van de Poll, N. E. (1985). Delayed spatial response alternation: effects of delay-interval duration and lesions of the medial prefrontal cortex on response accuracy of male and female Wistar rats. *Behavioral Brain Research, 18,* 41–49.

Vilkki, J. (1989). Perseveration in memory for figures after frontal lobe lesion. *Neuropsychologia, 27*(8), 1101–1104.

Vogel, C. C., Markowitsch, H. J., Hempel, U., & Hackenberg, P. (1987). Verbal memory in brain damaged patients under different conditions: a study of retrieval aids in frontal, temporal and diencephalic damaged subjects. *International Journal of Neurosciences, 33*(3–4), 237–256.

Wallesch, C. W., Kornhuber, H. H., Köllner, C., Haas, H. C., & Hufnagl, J. M. (1983). Language and cognitive deficits resulting from medial and dorsolateral frontal lobe lesions. *Archiv für Psychiatrie und Nervenkrankheiten, 233,* 279–296.

Warren, J. M., Cornwell, P. R., & Warren, H. B. (1969). Unilateral frontal lesions and learning by Rhesus monkeys. *Journal of Comparative and Physiological Psychology, 69*(3), 498–505.

Watanabe, M. (1986). Prefrontal unit activity during delayed conditional go/no-go discrimination in monkey. I. Relation to the stimulus. *Brain Research, 382,* 1–14.

Wenk, G. L., Grey, C. M., Ingram, D. K., Spangler, E. L., & Olton D. S. (1989). Retention of maze performance inversely correlates with NMDA receptor number in hippocampus and frontal neocortex in the rat. *Behavioral Neurosciences, 103*(3), 688–690.

Wiegersma, S., van der Scheer, E., & Hijman, R. (1990). Subjective ordering, short term memory, and the frontal lobes. *Neuropsychologia, 28*(1), 95–98.

Wikmark, R. G. E., Divac, I., & Weiss, R. (1973). Retention of spatial delayed alternation in rats with lesions in the frontal lobes. *Brain and Behavioral Evolution, 8,* 329–339.

Wilson, F. A. W., Scalaidhe, S. P. O., & Goldman-Rakic, P. S. (1993). Dissociation of object and spatial processing domains in primate prefrontal cortex. *Science, 260,* 1955–1958.

Winocur, G. (1991). Conditional learning in aged rats: Evidence of hippocampal and prefrontal cortex impairment. *Neurobiology of Aging, 13*(1), 131–135.

Yajeya, J., Quintana, J., & Fuster, J. M. (1988). Prefrontal representation of stimulus attributes during delay tasks. II. The role of behavioral significance. *Brain Research, 474,* 222–230.

Yamatani, K., Ono, T., Nishijo, H., & Takaku, A. (1990). Activity and distribution of learning related neurons in monkey (Macaca fuscata) prefrontal cortex. *Behavioral Neuroscience, 104*(4), 503–531.

Yener, G. G., Leuchter, A. F., Jenden, D. J., Read, S. L., Cummings, J. L., & Miller, B. L. (1996). Quantitative EEG in frontotemporal dementia. *Clinical Electroencephalography, 7*(2), 61–68.

Zola-Morgan, S., & Squire, L. R. (1993). Neuroanatomy of memory. *Annual Reviews in Neurosciences, 16,* 547–563.

18

Neuropsychiatry of the Right Frontal Lobe

TERRI A. EDWARDS-LEE
RONALD E. SAUL

The frontal lobes comprise the portion of the brain responsible for programming, regulating, and verifying all mental activity (Luria, 1980). In humans they encompass as much as 33% of the brain and are believed to control many of the qualities that distinguish humans from lower primates (Absher & Cummings, 1995). Emotion, will, judgment, foresight, creativity, and abstract reasoning are abilities that have been attributed to the frontal lobes (Absher & Cummings, 1995; Mattson & Levin, 1990; Petrides & Milner, 1982; Stuss & Benson, 1986). Despite these known functions, at times it is still referred to as "noneloquent cortex." This term is most often used to refer to the right prefrontal region, which mediates few language functions. This chapter demonstrates why this view of the right frontal cortex is erroneous.

The right hemisphere appears to be dominant for attention and for the interpretation and expression of emotions: the right frontal lobe mediates the expression of emotion and the posterior right hemisphere mediates perception of emotionally relevant stimuli. The right frontal lobe probably functions in choosing the appropriate emotional response to situations and has a role in the expression of mood and the tone of the mood expressed. It functions in communication through prosody and the paralingusitic aspects of language. These plus other yet undefined aspects of right frontal lobe function constitute the right hemisphere's contribution to personality.

The aim of this chapter is to review the role of the right frontal lobe as it pertains to behavior. However, many of the functions of the right frontal lobe are not well characterized, in part due to the difficulty of testing executive functions and in part due to the rarity of lesions confined to the right frontal lobe without lateral or posterior extension. In many cases the right and the left hemispheres are compared, but there are few studies of lesions involving only the right frontal lobe. Thus, although this chapter analyzes the role of the right frontal lobe in behavior, much of the information derives from studies of lesions of the right hemisphere with comments on anterior or posterior location of the lesion.

TABLE 18.1. Right Frontal Lobe Functions

Sensory
    Hue discrimination
    Olfactory discrimination (orbital frontal)*
    Modulation and filtering of sensory input

Motor
    Complex motor functions (Supplementary motor area)*
    Motor impersistence[a]

Executive
    Response preparation and inhibition (supplementary motor area)*
    Cognitive estimation
    Design fluency
    Motor sequence generation (ventral lateral or orbital cortex)*
    Hooper Visual Organization test
    Picture arrangement[c]
    Graphic pattern generation[d]

Attention
    Left-hemisphere neglect/decreased leftward exploration
    Auditory sustained attention (dorsolateral prefrontal cortex)*
    Simple continuous performance task
    Nonverbal continuous performance task[d]

Visuospatial
    Visual organization test
    Visuoconstructional apraxia[b]
    Topographical disorientation[b]
    Visuospatial learning[b]
    Construction and design copying[c]

Memory
    Nonverbal subject-ordered tasks
    Verbal and nonverbal recency judgment tasks

Emotion[e]
    Primary emotions
    Emotional expression
    Facial gestures
    Body gestures
    Speech intonation

Note. Information taken from Stuss, Eskes, and Foster (1994) except where noted by superscript letter. Asterisk (*) indicates probable localization.
[a]Kertesz, Nicholson, Cancelliere, Kassa, and Black (1985).
[b]McDonald (1993).
[c]Stuss and Benson (1984).
[d]Glosser and Goodglass (1990).
[e]See text for references.

The neuropsychological functions of attention and language that have been attributed to the right frontal lobe and their relation to the behavioral functions of the right frontal lobe are discussed (see Table 18.1).

ATTENTION

The right frontal lobe helps maintain attention to the environment. The attention embraces the external surroundings as a whole and allows accurate reading of world

(Borod, 1992). It is believed that whereas the left hemisphere is analytical and attends to details, the right hemisphere maintains a global attention to the environment (Borod, 1992). For example, Luria, Karpov, and Yarbuss (1966) described a patient with a right frontal lobe tumor who when asked to scan a picture and answer questions or describe a scene would base his erroneous conclusions on one detail instead of integrating all the details in the picture to form a more accurate conclusion. Global attention enables a person to react appropriately to a situation. It has been theorized that the right hemisphere monitors the environment and plans the reaction to threatening situations (Borod, 1992). Heilman (1995) hypothesized that the right hemisphere directs attention to extrapersonal space whereas the left hemisphere directs attention to peripersonal space. They based this hypothesis on the fact that cognitive activities controlled by the left hemisphere, such as reading, writing, and praxis, are performed close to the body, whereas activities performed by the right hemisphere, such as facial and emotional recognition and route finding, occur away from the body.

Neuropsychological testing confirms the presence of attentional deficits in patients with right frontal lesions. Following right frontal lobe injury, visual attention is diminished. Subjects have longer delays in locating a target in the left hemispace despite intact visual fields (Teuber, Battersby, & Bender, 1949) and are impaired on tests of visualized movement (Albert & Hecaen, 1971). Heilman, Watson, and Valenstein (1985) attributed this left-hemispace deficit in visual attention to a failure to initiate leftward exploration or a "directional hypokinesia."

The role of the right prefrontal lobe in attention was evaluated in a study of response to tones during dichotic listening (Woods & Knight, 1986). Patients with right frontal damage had no responses to sounds presented in the left ear and reduced attention to ipsilateral tones preceded by a distracting stimulus when compared to patients with comparable left-hemisphere damage and normal controls (Woods & Knight, 1986). Tests of attention requiring sequence identification were impaired in patients with right frontal lobe lesions compared to patients with lesions in other sites and with normal controls.

The attentional abilities of the right frontal lobe contribute to its function in visuospatial cognition. Intact visuospatial cognition requires that a person be able to attend and assimilate many different stimuli simultaneously. The role of the right frontal lobe in executing visuospatial tasks involving learning, memory, and cognition is well established. Right frontal lesions cause impairment of three-dimensional constructional tasks, copying of designs (Benton, 1968; Stuss & Benson, 1984), and design fluency (Jones-Gotman & Milner, 1977). Learning of mazes, both tactile (Corkin, 1965) and visual (Corkin, 1965; Jones-Gotman & Milner, 1977; Milner, 1965), is impaired with right frontal lobe dysfunction.

LANGUAGE AND COGNITION

The right frontal cortex contributes to language and communication. Language is amenable to standardized testing. The right frontal lobe mediates language prosody, organizes and forms a cohesive discourse, interprets abstract communication in spoken and written language, and interprets the inferred relationships involved in communication.

Also, it is responsible for the prosodic elements of language (Ross, 1981; Ross & Mesulam, 1979). Ross (1981) reported that the prosodic aspects of speech were arranged in an analogous way in the right hemisphere to the verbal aspects of language in the left hemisphere. In broad terms this means that the anterior right hemisphere is responsible for prosodic output and the posterior right hemisphere is responsible for prosodic comprehension. He suggests that lesions corresponding to Broca's area in the right hemisphere lead to a motor aprosodia. Following right frontal lobe damage, the prosodic contours that signal a question, that end a declarative statement, or that carry meaning through emphasis may be impaired (Alexander, Benson, & Stuss, 1989; Weintraub, Mesulam, & Kramer, 1981). Patients with motor aprosodia have difficulty placing melodic contours into their verbal output to represent their underlying emotional feelings. Speech is monotonous and lacks the usual melodic qualities despite preserved dialectical accent. When attempting to sing, these patients are also amelodic (Alexander et al., 1989). The changes in tone that reflect sadness, happiness, or surprise are reduced or may even be lost (Alexander et al., 1989; Ross & Mesulam, 1979).

Cancelliere and Kertesz (1990) however, have an opposing view that the aprosodias more commonly follow basal ganglia injury of either hemisphere and challenge the model of a pattern of aprosodias in the right hemisphere analogous to the aphasias of the left hemisphere.

Though not aphasic, subjects with right frontal lobe damage have difficulty producing a concise, cohesive discourse and often have difficulty formulating an idea (Kaczmarek, 1984; Mattson & Levin, 1990). When attempting to tell a story, they complain that their minds are blank and their speech is characterized by long pauses and stereotyped phrases. During conversation there are many free associations (Novoa & Ardila, 1987) and confabulations (Alexander et al., 1989; McDonald, 1993; Novoa & Ardila, 1987). Patients with right hemisphere lesions have speech described as verbose and tangential, with less meaning for the same amount of output when compared to normal subjects (Diggs & Basili, 1987; Joanette, Goulet, Ska, & Nespoulous, 1986; McDonald, 1993; Rivers & Love, 1980; Roman, Brownell, Potter, & Seibold, 1987; Wapner, Hamby, & Gardner, 1981).

Subjects with right-hemisphere and right frontal pathology have difficulty interpreting abstract meaning in communication and exhibit difficulty with comprehension of metaphors (Winner & Gardner, 1977), proverbs (Hier & Kaplan, 1980), and idiomatic phrases (Van Lancker & Kempler, 1987). Also, there is difficulty recognizing and utilizing abstract relationships between words (Brownell, Potter, & Michelow, 1984; Villardita, 1987). They often cannot understand the punch line of jokes (Bihrle, Brownell, & Powelson, 1986; Brownell, Michel, Powelson, & Gardner, 1983; Gardner, Ling, Flamm, & Silverman, 1975; Wapner et al., 1981), and interpretation of complex situations is impaired. They have difficulty elucidating the motive of actors in complex narratives (McDonald, 1993; Wapner et al., 1981) and predicting plausible story outcomes in the absence of explicit clues (McDonald, 1993; Rehak, Kaplan, Weylman, & Kelly, 1992).

Unfortunately, the specific role of the right frontal lobe in these functions is somewhat less well characterized. Disturbances in the following paralinguistic domains have been described following right frontal lobe lesions: proverb interpretation (Benton, 1968), nonliteral verbal humor (Brownell et al., 1983), indirect requests (Brownell, Potter, Bihrle, & Gardner, 1986), sarcasm (Weylman, Brownell, & Gardner, 1988), and affect (Cicone, Wapner, & Gardner, 1980). After reviewing the literature on language abilities in patients with bilateral frontal lobe damage compared to patients with selective right-hemisphere damage, McDonald (1993) argued that more anterior right-hemisphere damage leads to a failure to ignore the concrete attributes of verbal information (i.e., failure to derive verbal inference) and the loss of control of verbal behavior. He based this argument on the few studies that remark on anterior versus posterior location of lesions within the hemisphere. In these studies, the greatest preference for literal responses (Foldi, 1987; Weylman, Brownell, Roman, & Gardner, 1989), embellishment of responses (Wapner et al., 1981), tendency for confabulation with verbal recall (Hough, 1990), and errors in deducing verbal inference (Benowitz, Moya, & Levine, 1990) were found following anterior lesions.

The right hemisphere governs production of abstract verbal formulations. Split brain experiments have shown that the disconnected right hemisphere can produce parts of speech including pause fillers, overlearned phrases, and emotional expletives, contrasted with only limited ability to understand nouns, verbs, adverbs, and simple verbal commands (Gazzaniga & Hillyard, 1971; Sperry & Gazzaniga, 1967; McDonald, 1993; Zaidel, 1977). Similar language output, such as nonliteral speech—expletives, social formulas, stereotyped phrases, and clichés—and serial and memorized speech (Benson, 1979; Jackson, 1915; Van Lancker, 1973, 1988) has been found in aphasics with preserved right-hemisphere function. Though able to make nonliteral utterances, the aphasics are unable to use words from the utterances in propositional context; for example, the patient who says "son of a gun" is unable to use the word "son" to refer to his male offspring (Van Lancker, 1990).

The the importance of the frontal lobes in producing abstract formulations is seen in Alzheimer's disease (AD), which affects the temporal and parietal lobes early and spares the frontal lobes until later in the disease progression. Patients with AD are characteristically able to produce social formulas with ease and fluency until the late stages of the disease, though they may not understand these when spoken by someone else. This argues that the spared frontal lobes function to produce these stereotyped phrases (Van Lancker, 1990). The right hemisphere, perhaps the right frontal lobe specifically, is primarily responsible for the production of abstract verbal formulations.

Alexander et al. (1989) divided the language disturbances following right frontal lesions into five syndromes (see Table 18.2). These disturbances are somewhat analogous to the language disturbance produce by contralateral lesions in the left hemisphere. Lesions in the *right lower motor cortex and posterior operculum* cause "affective motor dysprosody" (Ross & Mesulam, 1979). Patients with this disorder have difficulty placing melodic contours in their voice to indicate the underlying emotional feelings. Speech is flat and lacks musical quality even though inflection and dialectical accent elements are intact. The voice is monotonous. Changes in the voice that reflect sadness, happiness, surprise, and so on are reduced or lost. Facial and body gestures are decreased in an analogous manner (Ross, Harney, de Lacoste-Utamsing, & Purdy, 1981).

Larger lesions involving the *right operculum/lower motor cortex* produce a syndrome similar to the previous one but with disturbance of additional aspects of verbal communication. They have an affective dysprosody and amelodic singing. In addition to an affective dysprosody they have difficulty in comprehension in several paralinguistic domains including nonliteral verbal humor (Brownell et al., 1983), sarcasm (Weylman et al., 1988), and affect (Cicone et al., 1980). They have a visuospatial disturbance with a mild left hemispatial neglect and segmental production of complex constructions. The hemineglect is neither prominent nor lasting. A similar syndrome is seen with subcortical lesions in the anterior limb of the internal capsule, striatum and periventricular white matter lateral to the frontal horn and anterior body of the lateral ventricle.

The syndrome resulting from *right dorsolateral frontal lesions* is less well anatomically defined. These subjects have problems with pragmatics of discourse, such as sarcasm, irony, and inference (Alexander et al., 1989; Brownell et al., 1986; Joanette et al., 1986). Larger right prefrontal lesions cause greater limitations in the pragmatic

TABLE 18.2. Language Syndromes of the Right Hemisphere

Right lower motor cortex and posterior operculum
    Decreased prosodic contours in voice
    Decreased prosodic gestures of face and body

Right anterior operculum/lower motor cortex (can also occur with subcortical lesions
involving the anterior limb of the internal capsule, striatum, and periventricular white matter)
    Decreased prosodic contours in voice
    Decreased prosodic gestures of face and body
    Amelodic singing
    Disturbed comprehension of paralinguistic domains
      Nonliteral verbal humor
      Sarcasm
      Affect
    Temporary hemineglect and impaired constructions

Right dorsolateral frontal
    Impaired language pragmatics
    Poor organization of dialogue
    Impaired use of analogy, irony, and related types of language
    Blunt and impolite discourse
    Discourse may seem confabulatory due to poor social awareness and speech organization

Medial frontal
    Loss of affective prosody, but intact prosodic imitation
    Pervasive reduction in speech output

Right anterior frontal (including basal forebrain, medial orbital surface, frontal pole,
superior medial brain, supplementary motor area, and cingulate gyrus)
    Loss of affective prosody
    Socially inappropriate
    Impulsive responses
    Confabulation
    Poor social awareness

aspects of communication, particularly in organizing a coherent narrative (Delis, Wapner, Gardner, & Moses, 1983; Joanette et al., 1986). Their output has frequent tangential irrelevant comments, and a vague rambling quality characterizes their verbal communication (Weylman et al., 1988). They have a reduced ability to use analogy, irony, and similar types of language. They appear excessively literal and direct. Their discourse tends to be blunt and impolite. In severe cases, inattention to communication context, blunted social awareness, and the piecemeal tangential style produce an apparently confabulated content to the narrative, even in the absence of any memory deficit (Weinsteim & Kahn, 1955).

The disorder produced by *medial frontal lesions* is characterized by a reduction in output. The patients are not mute but have a persistent and pervasive reduction in total speech output. Affective prosody may be reduced in range. There is loss of prosodic variation even with marked emotional feelings, but imitation of affective prosody is intact.

Lesions causing the *right anterior frontal lobe* disorder involve the entire right medial prefrontal area including the basal forebrain, medial orbital surface, frontal pole, superior medial brain including supplementary motor area and anterior cingulate gyrus. This lesion produces a dramatic behavioral syndrome that includes emotional flattening, inappropriate actions, apathy, and confabulation. Patients have even greater deficits in appreciating social content. They respond impulsively with their first association to stimuli. Narrative discourse is disorganized, with perseveration and confabulation (Alexander & Freedman, 1984; Stuss, Alexander, Lieberman, & Levine, 1978).

The contributions of the right frontal lobe to communication include affective prosody, the paralinguistic aspects of speech, and the abstract elements of speech. They aid in the communication of emotion through speech and help provide for the higher level of cognitive abstractions that characterize adult speech. The right frontal lobe aids in the understanding of emotional and abstract communication.

EMOTION

Altered emotional processes and personality following right-hemisphere brain damage have been recognized since Babinski observed that anosognosia most commonly accompanied left hemiparesis. Following right-hemisphere damage, patients are often indifferent or euphoric and minimize the symptoms of their deficit (Sackeim et al., 1982).

The right hemisphere is dominant for both the comprehension and expression of emotion in all modalities (Tucker, Luu, & Pribram, 1995). It has been hypothesized that the role of the right hemisphere in emotion is a spatial one. The right hemisphere appears to mediate perception of the relationships among emotional interactions and determines the appropriate behavior for a given situation (Borod, 1992). The right hemisphere is believed to integrate perceptions from different sensory modalities and allow a complete and thorough assessment of the emotional and physical environment and, therefore, an appropriate response (Borod, 1992).

The right hemisphere is responsible for the aural and visual comprehension of emotion. Visually, the right hemisphere interprets affective gestures and facial expressions (Borod, 1992; Borod, Koff, Lorch, & Nicholas, 1985; DeKosky, Heilman, Bowers, & Valenstein, 1980; Etcoff, 1984). Tachistoscopic studies show a left visual field advantage for interpretation of emotion in facial expressions (Strauss & Moscovitch, 1981). Studies in brain-damaged patients showed more deficits in interpretation of facial expression following right-hemisphere damage than left (Borod et al., 1985; DeKosky et al., 1980; Etcoff, 1984), which is independent of deficits in processing nonemotional faces (Bowers, Bauer, Coslett, & Heilman, 1985; Cicone et al., 1980).

The auditory comprehension of emotion has been investigated in a number of ways. Dichotic listening experiments have demonstrated a left ear (right-hemisphere) advantage for processing the emotional tone of natural speech, nonverbal vocalization, and musical passages (Borod, 1992; Bryden & MacRae, 1988; Ley & Bryden, 1982; Safer & Leventhal, 1977). The identification (Heilman, Scholes, & Watson, 1975; Tucker, Watson, & Heilman, 1977), discrimination (Tucker et al., 1977), and comprehension (Ross, 1981) of emotional prosody is impaired in subjects with right-hemisphere damage.

The interpretation of emotional material presented linguistically is governed by the right hemisphere. Processing words with emotional meaning was studied tachistoscopically. Male subjects were shown emotional and nonemotional words. They processed emotional words more accurately when they were presented in the left visual field. Others found that subjects with right brain damage were more impaired on discrimination and identification tasks involving emotional than nonemotional words. Subjects with left brain damage (or intact right hemispheres) read visually presented emotional words and wrote aurally presented emotional words better than nonemotional words (Landis, Graves, & Goodglass, 1982).

Verbal expression of emotion is also impaired following right-hemisphere damage. A diminished ability to express emotion and mood verbally was found in comissuroto-mized patients who had reduced access to right-hemisphere processing during verbal expression (TenHouten, Hoppe, Bogen, & Walter, 1985, 1986). Subjects with right brain damage were found to use less appropriate words (Borod et al., 1985) and words of lower emotional intensity (Bloom, Borod, Obler, & Koff, 1990) when describing emotional situations.

The right hemisphere is involved in the retrieval of emotional memory. Subjects with right-sided brain damage have poorer recall of emotionally charged material than do subjects with left-sided brain damage (Borod, 1992; Wechsler, 1973). Ross, Homan, and Buck (1994) hypothesized that the right hemisphere is responsible for the retrieval of memory of primary emotions. Patients undergoing Wada testing of the right hemisphere were asked to relate an emotionally charged life event before and during the testing. The majority of the patients changed the related emotion surrounding the event from a primary to a social emotion during the Wada testing. This lead Ross et al. (1994) to hypothesize that the right hemisphere is dominant for the expression of primary emotions and the left hemisphere is dominant for the expression of social emotions.

The right frontal lobe is responsible for the expression of emotion through speech intonation (Ross, 1981; Ross & Mesulam, 1979) and body gesturing (Ross, 1981). It is implicated in these functions by the finding that normal subjects show a greater expressivity for spontaneous and posed expression on the left hemiface (Borod, 1992; Tucker et al., 1995). In subjects with right anterior hemispheric lesions, spontaneous and posed facial expressions are less accurate, although anterior left-hemisphere lesions also impair facial expression compared to normal controls (Borod, 1992; Weddell, Miller, & Trevarthen, 1990). Subjects with right-hemisphere damage (Borod et al., 1985; Borod, Welkowitz, Alpert, & Brozgold, 1990; Ross, 1981; Ross & Mesulam, 1979; Shapiro & Danly, 1985; Tucker et al., 1977), and specifically right frontal damage (Ross, 1981), show deficits in producing emotional intonation in their speech relative to subjects with left brain damage or normal controls.

The right hemisphere is dominant for the expression and comprehension of emotion. Its role in emotion has been confirmed with many studies of multiple modalities of emotional interpretation and expression. The right frontal lobe mediates emotional expression, and more posterior regions (Ross, 1981) are involved in emotional perception. Patients with right frontal dysfunction exhibit disorders of behavior, due in part to their inability to interact appropriately in their social context.

MOOD

The prefrontal cortex is involved in maintaining one's apparent emotional tone or mood. Mood is the internal experience of a feeling state (Stuss, Gow, & Hetherington, 1992). Alterations in patients' mood following damage to bilateral or unilateral frontal lobes have been widely reported. Depression is reported with lesions of either frontal lobe, and mania is reported with lesions to the right frontal lobe. In general, patients are more euphoric and unconcerned following right frontal lobe lesions, but there have been a number of exceptions.

Left hemisphere and specifically left frontal damage has been associated most commonly with a depressed mood. Robinson, Kubos, Starr, Rao, and Price (1984) reported that depression is more severe after left anterior lesions than with left-posterior or right-hemisphere lesions. It was found that the severity of depression in this series correlated with the proximity of the lesion's anterior border to the left frontal pole. Other investigators have found similar evidence with subjects showing a dysphoric reaction manifest by feelings of despair, hopelessness, and anger. In these studies the patients had heightened tendencies toward self-blame, self-deprecation, and fits of crying (Gainotti, 1972; Hall, Hall, & Lavoie, 1968).

Right-sided lesions have been associated with an indifferent–euphoric reaction, characterized by minimization of symptoms, emotional placidity, joking, elation, or social disinhibition (Sackeim et al., 1982). Inappropriate cheerfulness has been seen in patients with right frontal lesions (Robinson et al., 1984). Mania or hypomania is a rare postlesion event that has been found most commonly following right-hemisphere pathology (Bakchine, Lacombley, Benoit, & Parisot, 1989; Starkstein, Boston, & Robinson, 1988; Stuss et al., 1992). Responsible lesions have involved the orbitofrontal cortex or limbic or paralimbic areas with strong connections to the orbitofrontal cortex (Bakchine et al., 1989; Starkstein et al., 1988; Stuss et al., 1992). Robinson and Starkstein (1990) found that right posteroinferior medial frontal lobe lesions that also involved the thalamic and perithalamic areas produced mania. In a study of 14 patients following right hemispherectomy, 12 of the patients were described as euphoric. In this particular study, there were too few patients with left hemispherectomy to make any conclusions regarding distinguishing lateralized features (Sackeim et al., 1982). This same study reviewed the literature of gelastic (laughing) and dacrystic (crying) ictal phenomena. Their review revealed that laughter was more likely to occur with left-hemisphere foci and crying was more likely with right-hemisphere foci. This suggested that exaggerated functioning of these areas produced the affective manifestation.

Depressive syndromes following right frontal lesions are more controversial. Robinson et al. (1984) observed depression with posterior right-hemisphere strokes. The severity of the depression correlated with the proximity of the lesion to occipital pole (Robinson et al., 1984). Other investigators found depression related to lesions in the right frontal area as well (Ross & Rush, 1981; Stuss et al., 1992). Patients with depression following right-hemisphere damage were found to have more psychological symptoms including irritability, loss of interest, and difficulty in concentration. In a series of patients with frontotemporal dementia, those with right frontal or frontotemporal degeneration were found to have symptoms of atypical depression. They showed increased irritability and motor activity and some showed increased appetite and weight gain (Miller, Chang, Mena, Boone, & Lesser, 1993). Ross and Rush (1981) reported pathological crying following right operculum lesions in patients with a premorbid major depressive disorder. In agreement with the report of increased psychological symptoms following right-hemisphere damage, Grafman, Vance, Weingartner, Salazar, and Amin (1986) and others (Hillbrand, Sokol, Waite, & Foster, 1993) found that patients with right orbitofrontal lesions reported increased edginess, anxiety, and depression compared with patients with nonfrontal lesions and a group of matched control subjects. Left dorsolateral frontal injury, in contrast, produced more anger and hostility. These observations support a role for the right hemisphere in depression though the symptoms may be atypical.

The reported changes in mood, positive or negative, produced by right frontal lesions are inconsistent. The variability in findings may reflect varying definitions of mood (Stuss et al., 1992) as well as varying lesion location and size within the right frontal lobe. Though the patients show increased activity and speech, this may not be accompanied by a positive mood. Independence of mood and affect has been reported in a series of patients with frontal lesions who were objectively rated for emotional expression and then asked to complete a survey to state their subjective emotion (Weddell, Trevarthen, & Miller, 1988). Right frontal lobe lesions can cause increased activity and denial of illness, but this hyperactivity and positive affect may not correlate with happiness or a feeling of well-being.

PERSONALITY

The role of the frontal lobes in personality was first documented in 1835 in the description of a 16-year-old male of morose, shut-in character who shot himself in the lower midforehead. The medial–orbital parts of his frontal lobe were extensively damaged and he lost his sight entirely. After the injury he was unconcerned over his blindness and assumed a gay, vivacious, and jocular disposition (Blumer & Benson, 1975; Stuss & Benson, 1984). The best known early case of personality change following frontal lobe injury was that of Phineas Gage, a previously reserved, hard-working man who became obstinate and socially unrestrained after a tamping rod caused severe damage to his frontal lobes (Harlow, 1868; Stuss & Benson, 1984).

Though the range of personality changes seen with frontal lobe pathology have been well described, the effects of unilateral frontal lobe pathology are not well characterized. The right and left hemispheres as a whole are somewhat better classified for personality, mood, and emotion. It has recently been suggested that the right hemisphere is dominant for the nuances of social conduct and interaction (Miller et al., 1993). Luria (1973a) stated that there was a disturbance of social judgment following right-hemisphere lesions. Many divergent lines of evidence support this theory. Descriptions of social inappropriateness in predominantly right-hemisphere disease and the absence of social deficiencies in predominantly left-hemisphere disease provide support for this theory. The right hemisphere's dominance in emotional expression and comprehension is also consistent with this interpretation.

The right frontal lobe may have a role in the adherence to social rules and performance of appropriate social behavior. Luria (1973b) reported that the disinhibited behavior of the frontal lobe personality syndrome was more likely to follow right frontal lobe lesions. Increased rule breaking was found by Milner as discussed in Regard and Landis (1994) in patients with right frontal lobe pathology. This may be an empirical correlate to a disregard for socially governed expectations.

Miller et al. (1993) have studied a population of patients with frontotemporal dementia (FTD) with predominantly unilateral degeneration. They found that those with right predominant degeneration were more socially inappropriate and more likely to present with psychiatric syndromes. Emotional alienation from their family was a prominent part of their clinical course. They were irritable and severely disinhibited and had excess motor activity. During the interview, many of the patients with right frontal syndromes manifested impatience and irritability. In their daily activities, they were impatient, demanding, and aggressive. Two displayed grossly disinhibited and socially unacceptable behavior (e.g., masturbating in public view and changing clothes in a public parking lot).

Those with left predominant degeneration were more socially appropriate than those with right predominant degeneration. Patients with left predominant degeneration were generally pleasant with hyperacute insight into their disorder and admitted to a dysphoric mood. These patients were hypercritical of themselves, typically being aware of their impairments long before others were. Many remained functional in their jobs despite severe language impairment. This is in contrast to the patients with right degeneration who had no personal insight and denied their problems despite glaring changes in functioning. Those with left degeneration were pleasant, some with enhanced interpersonal relations. One woman described her affected spouse as being more caring and showing greater humility. Those with right predominant degeneration had frequent arguments and generally had difficulty with interpersonal relations. Findings in FTD patients are congruent with observations in right- and left-hemisphere damage (Mesulam, 1982; Sackeim et al., 1982). These clinical presentations argue that intact functioning of the right frontotemporal area is important in maintaining socially appropriate behavior.

The role of the right-hemisphere in social interaction and the social aspects of personality is supported by the evidence of social dysfunction in patients with known right hemisphere damage and the proven role of the right hemisphere in emotion (discussed previously). The contribution of the right frontal lobe is more difficult to define. Social appropriateness is probably affected most severely after right prefrontal damage but currently there is insufficient data to be certain (Alexander et al., 1989). Miller et al.'s (1993) study of patients with frontal or frontotemporal degeneration supports the role of the frontal lobe in social monitoring and planning.

NEUROBIOLOGICAL BASIS OF BEHAVIOR CHANGES FOLLOWING RIGHT FRONTAL LOBE DYSFUNCTION

The right hemisphere, particularly the right frontal lobe, is functionally and anatomically structured for multimodal processing. The right hemisphere is involved in processes, such as attention, visuospatial skills, and emotional interpretation and expression, that require integration of diverse sensory and cognitive input. Heilman (1975) speculated that the right hemisphere is more integrated with the subcortical systems that are important for arousal and attention. This connectivity would explain the unilateral spatial neglect that occurs with right-hemisphere pathology. Semmes (1968) found sensory and motor functions to be more diffusely represented in the right hemisphere than the left. She hypothesized that diffuse representation of these elementary functions in the right hemisphere could enhance integration of dissimilar units and hence specialization for behaviors requiring multimodal coordination.

Gur et al. (1980) found the right hemisphere to have an increased ratio of white to gray matter compared to the left hemisphere. They determined the amount of gray matter based on the clearance of inhaled xenon-133. They concluded that verbal analytical processes of the left hemisphere are subserved by an organization that emphasizes processing or transfer within a region, whereas the spatial–gestalt functions of the right hemisphere are subserved by an organization that optimizes transfer across regions.

Tucker, Roth, and Bair (1986) found increased right coherence by EEG in a study of 14 volunteers. EEG coherence is an index of the synchrony of EEG signal at two sites which reflects the degree of shared electrical activity between two brain regions. Tucker and his colleagues recorded weekly EEG data from 14 volunteers over many months. Using spectral analysis, they determined the coherence between frontal, temporal, parietal, and occipital regions bilaterally. They found increased intrahemispheric coherence over the right hemisphere and increased interhemispheric coherence in the right frontal lobe. They concluded that the finding of increased EEG coherence in the right hemisphere and an increased ratio of white to gray matter (Gur et al., 1980) is consistent with the right hemisphere's function in global perception and conceptualization.

COMMENTS

Two syndromes that may be related to right-hemisphere dysfunction are attention-deficit/hyperactivity disorder (ADHD) and Asperger's syndrome. Disturbances of the right-hemisphere attentional functions may contribute to the syndrome of ADHD. Voeller (1996; Denckla, 1996) studied children with a characteristic neuropsychological profile and neurological findings consistent with right-hemisphere damage or dysfunction and found that the majority had ADHD. The children with left-hemisphere damage were much less likely to have ADHD. This supports the proposal that right-hemisphere dysfunction is responsible for some cases of ADHD.

Asperger syndrome is theorized to be a selective learning disability of the right hemisphere (Ellis, Ellis, Fraser, & Deb, 1994; McKelvey, Lambert, Mottron, & Shevell, 1995). It is characterized by naively inadequate social interaction, inability to make friends, impaired emotional intonation and gesturing, pedantic monologues, restricted repertoire of interests such as rail or air time tables, and the appearance of a lack of empathy with others (Wing, 1981). Patients with this syndrome have feelings for others and care about social relationships but lack the skills needed for social interaction (Denckla, 1996). Though language skills are intact, the patients do poorly on visuospatial tasks and tasks related to right-hemisphere functioning. This syndrome of social ineptitudes and intact left-hemisphere functioning suggest a role for the right hemisphere in this disorder.

CONCLUSION

The right frontal lobe maintains global attention to the environment and is dominant for the expression of emotion through mood and all forms of communication. Its contribution to personality lies in its role in emotional expression and in selecting behaviors that comply with social standards. Though the right hemisphere appears dominant for emotion, both frontal lobes function together to produce one's personality. The mechanism of this interplay is not known. Unilateral pathology provides a view of the individual functions of each frontal lobe. After a left frontal lobe lesion, patients usually are acutely aware of their deficits and become dysphoric and hopeless with self-blame and self-deprecation, but with preserved social emotions and interactions with others. Following a right frontal lobe lesion, a patient is more likely to become disinhibited with increased verbal output and activity and an absence of self-reflection as manifested by a denial of their deficit. These changes in behavior following unilateral lesions support the right hemisphere's, and more specifically the right frontal lobe's, role as the modulator for socially appropriate behavior.

REFERENCES

Absher, J. R. & Cummings, J. L. (1995). Neurobehavioral examination of frontal lobe functions [Special issue for A. R. Luria]. *Aphasiology, 9*(2), 181–192.

Albert, M. L., & Hecaen, H. (1971). Relative movement perception following unilateral cerebral damage. *Transactions of the American Neurological Association, 96,* 200–202.

Alexander, M. P., Benson, D. F., & Stuss, D. T. (1989). Frontal lobes and language. *Brain and Language, 37*(4), 656–691.

Alexander, M. P., & Freedman, M. (1984). Amnesia after anterior communicating artery aneurysm rupture. *Neurology, 34*(6), 752–757.

Bakchine, S., Lacomblez, L., Benoit, N., & Parisot, D. (1989). Manic-like state after bilateral orbitofrontal and right temporoparietal injury: Efficacy of clonidine. *Neurology, 39*(6), 777–781.

Benowitz, L. I., Moya, K. L., & Levine, D. N. (1990). Impaired verbal reasoning and constructional apraxia in subjects with right hemisphere damage. *Neuropsychologia, 28*(3), 231–241.

Benson, F. (1979). *Aphasia, alexia, and agraphia.* New York: Churchill Livingston.

Benton, A. L. (1968). Differential behavioral effects in frontal lobe disease. *Neuropsychologia, 6*(1), 53–60.

Bihrle, A. M., Brownell, H. H., & Powelson, J. A. (1986). Comprehension of humorous and nonhumorous materials by left and right brain-damaged patients. *Brain and Cognition, 5*(4), 399–411.

Bloom, R. L., Borod, J. C., Obler, L. K., & Koff, E. (1990). A preliminary characterization of lexical emotional expression in right and left brain-damaged patients. *International Journal of Neuroscience, 55*(2–4), 71–80.

Blumer, D., & Benson, D. F. (1975). Personality changes with frontal and temporal lobe lesions. In D. Blumer & D. F. Benson (Eds.), *Psychiatric aspects of neurologic disease* (pp. 151–170). New York: Grune & Stratton.

Borod, J. C. (1992). Interhemispheric and intrahemispheric control of emotion: A focus on unilateral brain damage [Special section: The emotional concomitants of brain damage]. *Journal of Consulting and Clinical Psychology, 60*(3), 339–348.

Borod, J. C., Koff, E., Lorch, M. P., & Nicholas, M. (1985). Channels of emotional expression in patients with unilateral brain damage. *Archives of Neurology, 42*(4), 345–348.

Borod, J. C., Welkowitz, J., Alpert, M., Brozgold, A. Z. (1990). Parameters of emotional processing in neuropsychiatric disorders: Conceptual issues and a battery of tests [Special issue: Faces, voices, and feelings. Experimental techniques and clinical implications]. *Journal of Communication Disorders, 23*(4-5), 247–271.

Bowers, D., Bauer, R. M., Coslett, H. B., & Heilman, K. M. (1985). Processing of faces by patients with unilateral hemisphere lesions: I. Dissociation between judgments of facial affect and facial identity. *Brain and Cognition, 4*(3), 258–272.

Brownell, H. H., Michel, D., Powelson, J., & Gardner, H. (1983). Surprise but not coherence: Sensitivity to verbal humor in right-hemisphere patients. *Brain and Language, 18*(1), 20–27.

Brownell, H. H., Potter, H. H., Bihrle, A. M., & Gardner, H. (1986). Inference deficits in right brain-damaged patients. *Brain and Language, 27*(2), 310–321.

Brownell, H. H., Potter, H. H., & Michelow, D. (1984). Sensitivity to lexical denotation and connotation in brain-damaged patients: A double dissociation? *Brain and Language, 22*(2), 253–265.

Bryden, M. P., & MacRae, L. (1988). Dichotic laterality effects obtained with emotional words. *Neuropsychiatry, Neuropsychology, and Behavioral Neurology, 1*(3), 171–176.

Cancelliere, A. E. B., & Kertesz, A. (1990). Lesion localization in acquired deficits of emotional expression and comprehension. *Brain and Cognition, 13*, 133–147.

Cicone, M., Wapner, W., & Gardner, H. (1980). Sensitivity to emotional expressions and situations in organic patients. *Cortex, 16*(1), 145–158.

Corkin, S. (1965). Tactually-guided maze learning in man: Effects of unilateral corical excisions and bilateral hippocampal lesions. *Neuropsychologia, 3*, 339–351.

Cummings, J. L. (1985). *Clinical neuropsychiatry.* New York: Grune & Stratton.

Cummings, J. L. (1993). Frontal–subcortical circuits and human behavior. *Archives of Neurology, 50*, 873–880.

DeKosky, S. T., Heilman, K. M., Bowers, D., & Valenstein, E. (1980). Recognition and discrimination of emotional faces and pictures. *Brain and Language, 9*(2), 206–214.

Delis, D. C., Wapner, W., Gardner, H., & Moses, J. A. (1983). The contribution of the right hemisphere to the organization of paragraphs. *Cortex, 19*(1), 43–50.

Denckla, M. B. (1996, March 23–30). *Clinical disorders providing impetus for the study of social–emotional development.* Paper presented at the 48th annual meeting of the American Academy of Neurology, San Francisco.

Diggs, C. C., & Basili, A. G. (1987). Verbal expression of right cerebrovascular accident patients: Convergent and divergent language. *Brain and Language, 30*(1), 130–146.

Ellis, H. D., Ellis, D. M., Fraser, W., & Deb, S. (1994). A preliminary study of right hemisphere cognitive deficits and impaired social judgments among young people with Asperger syndrome. *European Child and Adolescent Psychiatry, 3*(4), 255–266.

Etcoff, N. L. (1984). Selective attention to facial identity and facial emotion. *Neuropsychologia, 22*(3), 281–295.

Foldi, N. S. (1987). Appreciation of pragmatic interpretations of indirect commands: Comparison of right and left hemisphere brain-damaged patients. *Brain and Language, 31*(1), 88–108.

Gainotti, G. (1972). Emotional behavior and hemispheric side of the lesion. *Cortex, 8*(1), 41–55.

Gardner, H., Ling, P. K., Flamm, L., & Silverman, J. (1975). Comprehension and appreciation of humorous material following brain damage. *Brain, 98*(3), 399–412.

Gazzaniga, M. S., & Hillyard, S. A. (1971). Language and speech capacity of the right hemisphere. *Neuropsychologia, 9*(3), 273–280.

Glosser, G., & Goodglass, H. (1990). Disorders in executive control functions among aphasic and other brain-damaged patients. *Journal of Clinical and Experimental Neuropsychology, 12*(4), 485–501.

Grafman, J., Vance, S. C., Weingartner, H., Salazar, A. M., & Amin, D. (1986). The effects of lateralized frontal lesions on mood regulation. *Brain, 109*(pt. 6), 1127–1148.

Gur, R. C., Packer, I. K., Hungerbuhler, J. P., Reivich, M., Obrist, W. D., Amarnek, W. S., & Sackeim, H. A. (1980). Differences in the distribution of gray and white matter in human cerebral hemispheres. *Science, 207*(4436), 1226–1228.

Hall, M. M., Hall, G. C., & Lavoie, P. (1968). Ideation in patients with unilateral or bilateral midline brain lesions. *Journal of Abnormal Psychology, 73*(6), 526–531.

Harlow, J. M. (1868). Recovery from the passage of an iron bar through the head. *Publication of the Massachusetts Medical Society, 2,* 327–347.

Heilman, K. M. (1995). Attentional asymmetries. In R. J. Davidson, & K. Hugdahl (Eds.), *Brain asymmetry* (pp. 228–230). Cambridge, MA: MIT Press.

Heilman, K. M., Scholes, R., & Watson, R. T. (1975). Auditory affective agnosia: Disturbed comprehension of affective speech. *Journal of Neurology, Neurosurgery and Psychiatry, 38*(1), 69–72.

Heilman, K. M., Watson, R. T., & Valenstein, E. (1985). Neglect and related disorders. In K. M. Heilman & E. Valenstein (Eds.), *Clinical neuropsychology* (2nd ed., pp. 243–293). New York: Oxford University Press.

Hier, D. B., & Kaplan, J. (1980). Verbal comprehension deficits after right hemisphere damage. *Applied Psycholinguistics, 1*(3), 279–294.

Hillbrand, M., Sokol, S. J., Waite, B. M., & Foster, H. G. (1993). Abnormal lateralization in finger tapping and overt aggressive behavior. *Progress in Neuro-Psychopharmacology and Biological Psychiatry, 17*(3), 393–406.

Hough, M. S. (1990). Narrative comprehension in adults with right and left hemisphere brain damage: Theme organization. *Brain and Language, 38*(2), 253–277.

Jackson, J. H. (1915). Affections of speech from disease of the brain. *Brain, 38,* 106–174.

Joanette, Y., Goulet, P., Ska, B., & Nespoulous, J. L. (1986). Informative content of narrative discourse in right-brain-damaged right-handers. *Brain and Language, 29*(1), 81–105.

Jones-Gotman, M., & Milner, B. (1977). Design fluency: The invention of nonsense drawings after focal cortical lesions. *Neuropsychologia, 15*(4–5), 653–674.

Kaczmarek, B. L. (1984). Neurolinguistic analysis of verbal utterances in patients with focal lesions of frontal lobes. *Brain and Language, 21*(1), 52–58.

Kertesz, A., Nicholson, I., Cancelliere, A., Kassa, K., & Black, S. E. (1985). Motor impersistence: A right-hemisphere syndrome. *Neurology, 35*(5), 662–666.

Landis, T., Graves, R., & Goodglass, H. (1982). Aphasic reading and writing: Possible evidence for right hemisphere participation. *Cortex, 18*(1), 105–112.

Ley, R. G., & Bryden, M. P. (1982). A dissociation of right and left hemispheric effects for recognizing emotional tone and verbal content. *Brain and Cognition, 1*(1), 3–9.

Luria, A. R. (1973a). The frontal lobes and the regulation of behavior. In K. H. Pribram & A. R. Luria (Eds.), *Psychophysiology of the frontal lobes* (pp. 3–26). New York: Academic Press.

Luria, A. R. (1973b). *The working brain; an introduction to neuropsychology.* New York: Basic Books.

Luria, A. R. (1980). *Higher cortical functions in man.* London: Tavistock.

Luria, A. R., Karpov, B. A., & Yarbuss, A. L. (1966). Disturbances of active visual perception with lesions of the frontal lobes. *Cortex, 2*(2), 202–212.

Mattson, A. J., & Levin, H. S. (1990). Frontal lobe dysfunction following closed head injury: A review of the literature. *Journal of Nervous and Mental Disease, 178*(5), 282–291.

McDonald, S. (1993). Viewing the brain sideways? Frontal versus right hemisphere explanations of non-aphasic language disorders. *Aphasiology, 7*(6), 535–549.

McKelvey, J. R., Lambert, R., Mottron, L., & Shevell, M. I. (1995). Right-hemisphere dysfunction in Asperger's syndrome. *Journal of Child Neurology, 10*(4), 310–314.

Mesulam, M. M. (1982). Slowly progressive aphasia without generalized dementia. *Annals of Neurology, 11*(6), 592–598.

Miller, B. L., Chang, L., Mena, I., Boone, K., & Lesser, I. M. (1993). Progressive right frontotemporal degeneration: clinical, neuropsychological and SPECT characteristics. *Dementia, 4*(3–4), 204–213.

Milner, B. (1965). Visually-guided maze-learning in man: Effects of bilateral hippocampal, bilateral frontal, and unilateral cerebral lesions. *Neuropsychologia, 3*, 339–351.

Novoa, O. P., & Ardila, A. (1987). Linguistic abilities in patients with prefrontal damage. *Brain and Language, 30*(2), 206–225.

Petrides, M., & Milner, B. (1982). Deficits on subject-ordered tasks after frontal- and temporal-lobe lesions in man. *Neuropsychologia, 20*(3), 249–262.

Regard, M., & Landis, T. (1994). The "Smiley": A graphical expression of mood in right anterior cerebral lesions. *Neuropsychiatry, Neuropsychology, and Behavioral Neurology, 7*(4), 303–307.

Rehak, A., Kaplan, J. A., Weylman, S. T., & Kelly, B. (1992). Story processing in right-hemisphere brain-damaged patients. *Brain and Language, 42*(3), 320–336.

Rivers, D. L., & Love, R. J. (1980). Language performance on visual processing tasks in right hemisphere lesion cases. *Brain and Language, 10*(2), 348–366.

Robinson, R. G., Kubos, K. L., Starr, L. B., Rao, K., & Price, T. R. (1984). Mood disorders in stroke patients. Importance of location of lesion. *Brain, 107*(pt. 1), 81–93.

Robinson, R. G., & Starkstein, S. E. (1990). Current research in affective disorders following stroke. *Journal of Neuropsychiatry and Clinical Neurosciences, 2*(1), 1–14.

Roman, M., Brownell, H. H., Potter, H. H., & Seibold, M. S. (1987). Script knowledge in right hemisphere-damaged and in normal elderly adults. *Brain and Language, 31*(1), 151–170.

Ross, E. D. (1981). The aprosodias: Functional–anatomic organization of the affective components of language in the right hemisphere. *Archives of Neurology, 38*(9), 561–569.

Ross, E. D., Harney, J. H., de Lacoste-Utamsing, C., & Purdy, P. D. (1981). How the brain integrates affective and propositional language into a unified behavioral function: Hypothesis based on clinicoanatomic evidence. *Archives of Neurology, 38*, 745–748.

Ross, E. D., Homan, R. W., & Buck, R. (1994). Differential hemispheric lateralization of primary and social emotions: Implications for developing a comprehensive neurology for emotions, repression, and the subconscious. *Neuropsychiatry, Neuropsychology, and Behavioral Neurology, 7*(1), 1–19.

Ross, E. D., & Mesulam, M. M. (1979). Dominant language functions of the right hemisphere? Prosody and emotional gesturing. *Archives of Neurology, 36*(3), 144–148.

Ross, E. D., & Rush, A. J. (1981). Diagnosis and neuroanatomical correlates of depression in brain-damaged patients: Implications for neurology of depression. *Archives of General Psychiatry, 38*(12), 1344–1354.

Sackeim, H. A., Greenberg, M. S., Weiman, A. L., Gur, R. C., Hungerbuhler, J. P., & Geschwind, N. (1982). Hemispheric asymmetry in the expression of positive and negative emotions. Neurologic evidence. *Archives of Neurology, 39*(4), 210–218.

Safer, M. A., & Leventhal, H. (1977). Ear differences in evaluating emotional tones of voice and verbal content. *Journal of Experimental Psychology: Human Perception and Performance, 3*(1), 75–82.

Semmes, J. (1968). Hemispheric specialization: A possible clue to mechanism. *Neuropsychologia, 6*(1), 11–26.

Shapiro, B. E., & Danly, M. (1985). The role of the right hemisphere in the control of speech prosody in propositional and affective contexts. *Brain and Language, 25*(1), 19–36.

Sperry, R., & Gazzaniga, M. S. (1967). Language following surgical disconnection of the hemisphere. In C. Millikan & F. Dailey (Eds.), *Brain mechanisms underlying speech and language* (pp. 108–114). New York: Grune & Stratton.

Starkstein, S. E., Boston, J. D., & Robinson, R. G. (1988). Mechanisms of mania after brain injury: 12 case reports and review of the literature. *Journal of Nervous and Mental Disease, 176*(2), 87–100.

Strauss, E., & Moscovitch, M. (1981). Perception of facial expressions. *Brain and Language, 13*(2), 308–332.

Stuss, D. T., Alexander, M. P., Lieberman, A., & Levine, H. (1978). An extraordinary form of confabulation. *Neurology, 28*(1), 1166–1172.

Stuss, D. T., & Benson, D. F. (1984). Neuropsychological studies of the frontal lobes. *Psychological Bulletin, 95*(1), 3–28.

Stuss, D. T., & Benson, D. F. (1986). *The frontal lobes.* New York: Raven Press.

Stuss, D. T., Eskes, G. A., & Foster, J. K. (1994). Experimental neuropsychological studies of frontal lobe functions. In F. Boller & J. Grafman (Eds.), *Handbook of neuropsychology* (Vol. 9, pp. 149–185). Amsterdam. Elsevier.

Stuss, D. T., Gow, C. A., & Hetherington, C. R. (1992). "No longer gage": Frontal lobe dysfunction and emotional changes [Special section: The emotional concomitants of brain damage]. *Journal of Consulting and Clinical Psychology, 60*(3), 349–359.

TenHouten, W. D., Hoppe, K. D., Bogen, J. E., & Walter, D. O. (1985). Alexithymia and the split brain: I. Lexical-level content analysis. *Psychotherapy and Psychosomatics, 43*(4), 202–208.

TenHouten, W. D., Hoppe, K. D., Bogen, J. E., & Walter, D. O. (1986). Alexithymia: An experimental study of cerebral commissurotomy patients and normal control subjects. *American Journal of Psychiatry, 143*(3), 312–316.

Teuber, H. L., Battersby, W. S., & Bender, M. B. (1949). Changes in visual searching performance following cerebral lesions [Abstract]. *American Journal of Physiology, 159,* 592.

Tucker, D. M., Luu, P., & Pribram, K. H. (1995). Social and emotional self-regulation, *Annals of the New York Academy of Sciences, 769,* 213–239.

Tucker, D. M., Roth, D. L., & Bair, T. B. (1986). Functional connections among cortical regions: Topography of EEG coherence. *Electroencephalography and Clinical Neurophysiology, 63*(3), 242–250.

Tucker, D. M., Watson, R. T., & Heilman, K. M. (1977). Discrimination and evocation of affectively intoned speech in patients with right parietal disease. *Neurology, 27*(10), 947–958.

Van Lancker, D. (1973). Language lateralization and grammers. In J. P. Kimball (Ed.), *Studies in syntax and semantics.* New York: Seminar Press.

Van Lancker, D. (1988). Nonpropositional speech: Neurolinguistic studies. In A. E. Ellis (Ed.), *Progress in the psychology of language.* Hillsdale, NJ: Erlbaum.

Van Lancker, D. (1990). The neurology of proverbs. *Behavioural Neurology, 3*(3), 169–187.

Van Lancker, D. R., & Kempler, D. (1987). Comprehension of familiar phrases by left- but not by right-hemisphere damaged patients. *Brain and Language, 32*(2), 265–277.

Villardita, C. (1987). Verbal memory and semantic clustering in right brain-damaged patients. *Neuropsychologia, 25*(1-B), 277–280.

Voeller, K. K. (1986). Right-hemisphere deficit syndrome in children. *American Journal of Psychiatry, 143*(8), 1004–1009.

Wapner, W., Hamby, S., & Gardner, H. (1981). The role of the right hemisphere in the apprehension of complex linguistic materials. *Brain and Language, 14*(1), 15–33.

Wechsler, A. F. (1973). The effect of organic brain disease on recall of emotionally charged versus neutral narrative texts. *Neurology, 23*(2), 130–135.

Weddell, R. A., Miller, J. D., & Trevarthen, C. (1990). Voluntary emotional facial expressions in patients with focal cerebral lesions. *Neuropsychologia, 28*(1), 49–60.

Weddell, R. A., Trevarthen, C., & Miller, J. D. (1988). Reactions of patients with focal cerebral lesions to success or failure. *Neuropsychologia, 26*(3), 373–385.

Weinsteim, E. A., & Kahn, R. C. (1955). *Denial of illness: Symbolic and physiologic aspects.* Springfield, IL: Thomas.

Weintraub, S., Mesulam, M. M., & Kramer, L. (1981). Disturbances in prosody. A right-hemisphere contribution to language. *Archives of Neurology, 38*(12), 742–744.

Weylman, S. T., Brownell, H. H., & Gardner, H. (1988). "It's what you mean, not what you say": Pragmatic language use in brain-damaged patients. In F. Plum (Ed.), *Language, communication and the brain* (pp. 229–244). New York: Raven Press.

Weylman, S. T., Brownell, H. H., Roman, M., & Gardner, H. (1989). Appreciation of indirect requests by left- and right-brain-damaged patients: The effects of verbal context and conventionality of wording. *Brain and Language, 36*(4), 580–591.

Wing, L. (1981). Asperger's syndrome: A clinical account. *Psychological Medicine, 11*(1), 115–129.

Winner, E., & Gardner, H. (1977). The comprehension of metaphor in brain-damaged patients. *Brain, 100*(4), 717–729.

Woods, D. L., & Knight, R. T. (1986). Electrophysiologic evidence of increased distractibility after dorsolateral prefrontal lesions. *Neurology, 36*(2), 212–216.

Zaidel, E. (1977). Unilateral auditory language comprehension on the token test following cerebral commissurotomy and hemispherectomy. *Neuropsychologia, 15*(1), 1–17.

19

Experimental Assessment of Adult Frontal Lobe Function

JORDAN GRAFMAN

Investigators have proposed a number of different models of the functions of the prefrontal cortex (Grafman, 1994b). Many of these models share certain common traits (e.g., "keeping information/knowledge stored in posterior cortex active for a limited period of time"). On the other hand, discussing their distinctive qualities (e.g., models that incorporate temporal or serial order processing vs. those that do not) can also help researchers devise experiments designed to test model-based alternative hypotheses that characterize this effort (Goldman-Rakic, 1987, 1992; Fuster, 1991, 1997; Stuss & Benson, 1986; Luria & Tsvetkova, 1990; Anderson, Damasio, Jones, & Tranel, 1991; Bechara, Damasio, Damasio, & Anderson, 1994; Bechara, Damasio, Tranel, & Damasio, 1997; Damasio, 1994; Damasio, Grabowski, Frank, Galaburda, & Damasio, 1994; Damasio, Tranel, & Damasio, 1990, 1991; Damasio & Tranel, 1993; Schwartz, Reed, Montgomery, Palmer, & Mayer, 1991; Schwartz, 1995; Grafman 1989, 1994a, 1994b, 1995). Each investigator has approached the functions of the prefrontal cortex from a somewhat unique perspective. I briefly outline their ideas here before indicating which experimental tasks might prove useful in evaluating the validity of each of these frameworks. Certain experimental tasks may also be useful, despite having no relationship to established cognitive models, because they so mimic real-life situations that they can be used to make inferences about functional behaviors impaired by frontal lesions (Tiihonen et al., 1994).

Several methodological questions should be kept in mind when determining the link between an experimental task and the theoretical model being tested. Does the researcher conceive of a level of knowledge representation within the prefrontal cortex? If so, what are the characteristics of that knowledge, what are the implications of activation of that knowledge for ongoing cognitive processing? Is there an explicit attempt to map these cognitive structures and processes to brain? If so, at what level? Does the model provide testable hypotheses? What is the replicability and reliability of the experimental test results that led to the development of the model? Last, but not least for the purposes of this chapter, what experimental tests and methods can be used to test that model?

NORMAN AND SHALLICE'S FRAMEWORK

Norman and Shallice (1986; Shallice, 1988) proposed two basic "control" mechanisms that determine how we monitor our activities. One mechanism, the contention scheduler, operates via automatic and direct priming of stored knowledge either by stimuli in the environment or conceptual thought.

The second mechanism, the supervisory attention system (SAS), reflects conscious awareness (operating within working memory limitations) of internal knowledge states which could set the priorities for action despite contrary or absent environmental stimuli. Because this stored knowledge reached consciousness, it could override the automatic contention scheduling mechanism.

Dividing the attention system between automatic contention scheduling and controlled supervisory mechanisms seemed to make sense and accounted for a great deal of data regarding attention and action failures in patients with prefrontal lobe lesions. That is, such patients have a general tendency to be overresponsive to the automatic demands of the environment, which can be seen in their impulsivity and rule-breaking behaviors (Shallice, Burgess, Schon, & Baxter, 1989).

The homeostasis between the two attentional control systems is critical to maintaining conventional behavioral interactions with the environment. The SAS, more than the contention scheduler, is subserved by anterior brain systems that included large-scale knowledge units. Recently, Shallice utilized the memory operation packet (MOP) conception favored by Schank to describe such large-scale knowledge units (Schank, 1982). When damage occurs to this knowledge base, the SAS cannot operate effectively to, at times, override the contention scheduler (which is subserved by subcortical structures composing the basal ganglia). Norman and Shallice's framework has had a significant impact on other models of memory and cognition. For example, Baddeley included a version of the SAS as the primary mechanism operating within the central executive component of his working-memory model (Baddeley & Wilson, 1988).

GOLDMAN-RAKIC AND PRIMATE WORKING MEMORY

Goldman-Rakic adapted a framework for examining prefrontal cortex functions based primarily on her electrophysiological studies of monkeys (Goldman-Rakic, 1987, 1992). Within this framework, the prefrontal cortex serves as a "working memory" which temporarily keeps active a representation of a stimulus (including its precise spatial coordinates) until a response is required (e.g., a choice discrimination) (Awh, Smith, & Tonides, 1995). She has demonstrated that selected prefrontal cortical neurons fire only during the delay between the presentation of a stimulus set to memorize and the presentation of a probe for response (Guigon, Dorizzi, Burnod, & Schultz, 1995). These prefrontal cortical cells are also specifically linked to where in space the stimulus was seen and not just to a simple memory of the stimulus itself (Funahashi, Chafee, & Goldman-Rakic, 1993; Wilson, Scalaidhe, & Goldman-Rakic, 1993).

Diamond (1991) demonstrated that certain delayed-response tasks are only performed well after a certain stage of prefrontal lobe development in human infants and children (see also Roberts, Hager, & Heron, 1994). Furthermore, there is some evidence of prefrontal lobe involvement in memory processes in adult humans—in particular, during human working-memory activity and retrieval (Cohen et al., 1997; McCarthy et al., 1994). Patients with prefrontal lobe lesions also have diminished contingent negative variation slow waves, which has been thought to reflect interstimulus interval preparatory and rehearsal behavior—a key component of working memory (e.g., Ruchkin, Johnson, Grafman, Canoune, & Ritter, 1997; Ruchkin et al., 1994).

FUSTER'S TEMPORAL PROCESSING MODEL

Fuster has proposed that the prefrontal cortex, although it has multiple functions, is principally involved with representing the "temporal structure of behavior." Temporal structure refers to the coding of place within a sequence of actions or perceptual observations. These action sequences tend to be goal related (i.e., conceptually driven). Fuster has also argued that the prefrontal cortex, to completely encode the temporal aspects of behaviors, must be involved in the formation of "cross-temporal contingencies." Cross-temporal contingencies can be interpreted as the ties between events that are not simply adjacent in time but related to each other because they are part of a set of actions that have a common goal. These temporal operations are unique to prefrontal cortex according to Fuster (1991, 1997).

STUSS AND BENSON'S BEHAVIORAL/ANATOMICAL THEORY

Stuss and Benson (1986) presented exhaustive neurobehavioral reviews of the frontal lobe literature in their monograph on the frontal lobes. They divided the functions of the frontal lobes into two groups. One group is concerned with sequencing behaviors, forming mental sets, and integrating various behaviors (Levine, Stuss, & Milberg, 1995). The other group is concerned with more primitive processes such as drive, motivation, and will. The former group is associated with dorsolateral prefrontal cortex activation whereas the latter group is associated with ventromedial prefrontal cortex activation. These behaviors are at the top of a hierarchy of behaviors that control a person's interactions with the world. Stuss and colleagues (Stuss, Shallice, Alexander, & Picton, 1995; Foster, Eskes, & Stuss, 1994) have has now gone beyond this simple characterization of the role of the prefrontal cortex and have distinguished among a large set of top-down attentional processes that may be subserved by prefrontal cortex. He and his colleagues are currently testing whether these independent attentional processes can be selectively impaired by prefrontal cortical lesions.

LURIA'S VIEW OF PROBLEM SOLVING AND THE FRONTAL LOBE

Luria was particularly interested in failures of problem solving. His approach was qualitative and relied on the analysis of verbal protocols of patients trying to solve multistep arithmetic problems (Luria & Tsvetkova, 1990). In Luria's view, impaired programming and regulation of behavior were the principal deficits exhibited by patients with prefrontal lobe lesions on problem-solving tasks. The patients responses were frequently impulsive and they had difficulty switching from one type of problem-solving strategy to another (Miller, 1992). Patients who developed characteristic stuck-in-set responses often relied on these stereotypical behaviors even when they were obviously inappropriate. Patients could access fragmentary operations but could not combine them into an overall schema to solve a problem. Luria believed that focal lesions of the prefrontal cortex could dissociate types of problem-solving failures.

DAMASIO'S SOMATIC MARKER THEORY

Damasio and his colleagues (Anderson et al., 1991; Bechara et al., 1994, 1997; Damasio, 1994; Damasio et al., 1994) have investigated the failure of patients with prefrontal lesions to correctly select appropriate social behaviors and make social decisions. They claim that such patients fail to behave appropriately due to a "defect in the activation of somatic markers." This somatic signal binds to social behaviors and helps ensure their appropriateness or relevance by providing a modulating or biasing signal to the person when he or she has to make a social decision (Saver & Damasio, 1991). This tag may be mediated by the autonomic nervous system and physiologically measured by recording the galvanic skin response (GSR) during various tasks (Tranel & Damasio, 1994). Failures in somatic activation (e.g., a diminished GSR response) have been identified when patients with ventromedial lesions have to passively watch evocative stimuli rather than actively respond. In addition, GSR responses are seen in normal subjects preceding an appropriate cognitive decision to conserve winnings in a gambling task, whereas patients with ventromedial frontal lesions demonstrate poor decision making and little GSR responsivity in this same task (resulting in inappropriate risk taking) (Bechara et al., 1997). Ventromedial frontal cortex has been implicated as a crucial member of a larger neural network devoted to the normal integration of somatic tags with stored knowledge during decision making (Damasio, 1994).

SCHWARTZ'S ACTION FRAMEWORK

Schwartz and her colleagues (Schwartz, 1995; Schwartz et al., 1991) developed a coding scheme to break down components of simple action sequences into their constituent parts that allows for a componential error analyses. Such an action coding scheme was developed for two different but typical actions: pouring a cup of coffee and brushing teeth. Errors were coded over different temporal epochs and for uniquely defined components of behavior. Furthermore, different error types were defined, including object substitutions, anticipatory errors, omissions, and execution failures. Using this approach, the disorganization of simple actions was described in a consistent, systematic fashion. Frontal apraxia, as seen in their patients, was described as a failure of top-down mechanisms concerned with activation of sequentially stored behaviors (Schwartz, 1995). This detailed approach to coding ongoing behavior offers a real opportunity to more precisely define and describe the breakdown in executing typical actions so often seen in patients with apraxia (Gonzalez-Rothi & Heilman, 1997; Tyrrell, 1994).

GRAFMAN'S STRUCTURAL EVENT COMPLEX/ MANAGERIAL KNOWLEDGE UNIT FRAMEWORK

Grafman has argued that the most parsimonious approach to building a model of the cognitive architecture of knowledge stored in the prefrontal cortex would be to adapt an architecture similar to that used in other representational domains (Barsalou, 1989; Barsalou & Sewell, 1985; Neisser, 1987; Smith & Sloman, 1994). Thus, items stored in such an architecture would be interrelated on the basis of similarity, frequency of exposure or expression, category membership, association values, and other psychometric variables. The more related an item was to another item using any one of the metrics, the more likely that such items would be neighbors in a psychological space. The boundaries encompassing such a domain-specific psychological space would probably be fuzzy to accommodate cognitive plasticity during learning or following brain-damage.

Within these cognitive architectures, a unit of knowledge represents a single assembly of information such as an edge, word, meaning, form, location in space, or syntactic frame. Grafman argues that single units of memory could also be capable of storing a structured event complex (SEC) that varies in the number of individuated events it encapsulates. This structured event complex contains macrostructure level information relevant to the consequences of past and current behavior by virtue of its storing events that occurred in the past and will occur in the future. Each SEC representation would store both the theme and boundaries of events assigned to it and not simply rerepresent the other features of events such as words, sentences, visual features, and so on that might be stored in other specific cognitive architectures (both spatially and functionally independent from the SEC cognitive architecture) but that might be temporally bound together with the SEC in any given situation. It is this kind of unitized macrostructure knowledge (i.e., the SEC) that Grafman argues is stored in the prefrontal cortex. Grafman calls the particular kind of SEC that governs our cognitive behavior the managerial knowledge unit (Grafman, 1989, 1995; Grafman & Hendler, 1991; Grafman, Sirigu, Spector, & Hendler, 1993).

THE MANAGERIAL KNOWLEDGE UNIT

Cognitive science has long been concerned with trying to understand how people represent in memory event series that occur in our lives (e.g., Buonomano, & Merzenich, 1995; Miller, Galanter, & Pribram, 1960). A variety of cognitive structures have been hypothesized to account for this kind of macroknowledge. These structures include action procedures, schemas, scripts, frames, cases, and story grammars (Abelson, 1981; Allen, Hendler, & Tate, 1990; Avrahami & Kareev, 1994; Baron-Cohen et al., 1994; Barrett & Weld, 1993, 1994; Casson, 1983; Corson, 1990; Davidson, 1994; Demorest & Alexander, 1992; Eldridge, Barnard, & Bekerian, 1994; Halford, 1993; Hammond, 1989; Johnson & Seifert, 1992; Medin, Goldstone, & Gentner, 1993; Minsky, 1986; Pea & Hawkins, 1987; Schank, 1982; Tipper, Weaver, & Houghton, 1994; Weld, 1994; Wyer & Srull, 1989; Zajonc, 1984). All these knowledge structures are composed of a set of events, actions, or ideas that when linked together form a knowledge unit (e.g., a schema) containing macrostructure information such as the theme of a story (i.e., the SEC). The managerial knowledge unit (MKU; Grafman, 1989) is the SEC specifically involved with cognitive planning, social behavior, and the management of knowledge. The MKU is composed of a series of events. There should be a typical order to the occurrence of these events. The rigidity of event order within an MKU obeys multiple constraints. Some constraints are physical. An individual cannot sip coffee from a cup unless it is first poured into the cup. Some constraints are cultural. In the United States, people generally shower on a daily basis in the morning before eating breakfast. Some constraints are purely individual. Some people brush their teeth twice in the morning—once before and once after eating breakfast. The rigidity of the event order also depends on the frequency of its activation. That is, a rigid event order carried out daily should have a "stronger" representation than one carried out monthly. Each MKU has a typical duration of activation, and each event that is a member of an MKU has a typical event duration.

In general, for the typical MKU, there is a beginning event that specifies a setting, a following set of events that specify goals and activities to achieve those goals, and an event that signifies the setting that deactivates the MKU. Events within an MKU may have different "strength" values. That is, certain events may be more central or critical to the activation, execution, retrieval, or meaning of an MKU.

Parallel Activation

A limited number of MKUs can be activated in "parallel." That is, both categorically and hierarchically distinct MKUs may be simultaneously activated (Grafman, 1995). This parallel activity would, in effect, represent a cascade of activation because different MKUs have different temporal durations (e.g., eating dinner vs. going out on a date) (Nichelli, Clark, Hollnagel, & Grafman, 1995). Therefore, certain MKUs could be activated and deactivated within the duration of other activated MKUs.

Category Specificity

Given that MKUs represent a form of knowledge, like other kinds of knowledge (e.g., lexical), it is probable that there are categorical distinctions within the MKU cognitive architecture. Two potential categories of MKU knowledge that have already been mentioned in this chapter are social behavior (Cohen & Servan-Schreiber, 1992; Damasio et al., 1991; Grafman et al., 1996; Grafman, Vance, Weingartner, Salazar, & Amin, 1986; Partiot, Grafman, Sadato, Wachs, & Hallett, 1995; Rolls, Hornak, Wade, & McGrath, 1994) and abstract-symbolic reasoning (Anderson et al., 1991; Dehaene & Changuex, 1991; Duncan, Burgess, & Emslie, 1995; Grafman, Jonas, & Salazar, 1990; Petrides, 1991). A broadening of the number of categorical distinctions in MKU knowledge would not be surprising.

MKU Metric Relations

What might the metric relations in a cognitive architecture made up of MKUs be? There is no a priori reason why certain metric relations between units of memory would not be similar across knowledge domains. Therefore, such matrices as frequency of exposure or use, similarity, and associative strength, which are relevant to the semantic storage of words, are also candidate matrices in the case of the MKU cognitive architecture (Smith & Sloman, 1994). MKUs that are more frequently activated should also have the lowest thresholds for activation (Neisser, 1987).

Associative relations between MKUs would also determine the spread of activation. MKUs that were most similar within—and across—categories of MKUs would be more strongly related. Therefore, when one MKU among these associatively related MKUs would be activated, those MKUs within this immediate associative network (i.e., the MKU neighbors) would be more likely to be activated than less related MKUs (which might even be inhibited).

MKU Development

Primitive SECs made up of just a few events, such as simple rules or, of more relevance, conditional associates, may develop early in childhood and only later expand into a large multievent MKU based on the frequency with which adjacent events occur together (and in a preferred order) in time (Case, 1992; Eslinger, Gratton, Damasio, & Damasio, 1992; Halford, 1993; Pascual-Leone & Johnson, 1991; Rattermann, Spector, Grafman, Levin, & Howard, 1998). Based on repeated exposure to an SEC, the boundaries of that event series would become more firmly established, leading to a well-formed MKU. Another possibility is that fully formed MKUs could be stored quite early in life but only in sparse numbers, and that growth in the MKU population would depend primarily on expanding life experiences (which are highly controlled when we are children and are still dependent on our cognitive capabilities in other domains (e.g., language understanding). Both possibilities are consistent with a biologically based explanation that argues that because the prefrontal cortex does not fully mature until adolescence and early adulthood, it is impossible that a rich MKU cognitive architecture could be developed until adolescence or adulthood regardless of the richness of experience in childhood. Also note that this hypothesis suggests that the individual and paired events that make up an SEC are first processed as independent or paired events, thereby creating a partial redundancy of representation where the events, event pairs, and MKUs retain their topographical and psychological independence within the prefrontal cortex.

SPECIFIC FORMS OF KNOWLEDGE STORED IN PREFRONTAL CORTEX

Support for permitting information to be encoded and stored across events must be obtained from the neural architecture of the human prefrontal cortex. A number of knowledge and grammar domains might be stored in prefrontal cortex as SECs or MKUs. For example, within this framework, event and SEC boundaries and sequences must be coded and stored. An example of such coding can be seen in the story grammar models proposed in the literature. These grammatical operating constraints would support the storage of coarse and discrete macroknowledge structures concerned with cross-event semantics. For example, to understand the moral of a story, an individual must accumulate and integrate meaning across the numerous propositions contained in the story (Kintsch, 1994). Given the time durations that this knowledge encompasses (from minutes to hours), this form of knowledge, when activated in memory, should gain prioritized control over other behavior that occurs at the resolution of seconds or minutes (e.g., Tipper et al., 1994). By virtue of being bound together with other forms of knowledge (e.g., object, motor action, and spatial coordinate stores), when activated, it would supervise the activation of these other forms of knowledge (Minsky, 1986). Therefore, some types of so-called top-down attentional processes can be considered the by-product of activation of this form of knowledge (Grafman & Weingartner, 1996).

Within any representational domain (including the MKU cognitive architecture), there is great predictability in how a particular memory unit is activated and expressed. However, in the process of binding together an MKU with other units of knowledge, there should be a fair amount of unpredictability in terms of which exact configuration of memory units across the brain will be active at any one time (Grafman & Weingartner, 1996). For example, imagine the changing dynamics of your office in terms of which people and objects are transient and somewhat randomly appearing in time versus those that are constant in time and try pairing all those "units of memory" with the particular set of MKUs that might be active at any time. Arguably these "routinely" novel encoded episodes appear in unpredictable ways, are dynamic, and require people to reactively plan on a regular basis.

SYNTHESIS OF THE FRAMEWORKS

All of the previous frameworks suggest that the human prefrontal cortex is especially involved in tasks that require processing over relatively long periods; require subjects to determine the temporal sequence of events; require subjects to maintain control over their actions in the environment by dividing their resources; induce time sharing and switching between tasks; require subjects to integrate information across events and across time; require subjects to produce actions in real or imagined time; require subjects to focus their attention and to ignore distractors; require subjects to plan, reason, and problem solve; and require subjects to retrieve appropriate social rules for behavior. Thus, by highlighting the main points of the frameworks described previously, it is possible to suggest a modest number of experimental paradigms for the examination of the functions of the human prefrontal cortex that complement the more traditional clinical neurobehavioral approach and qualitative observations.

EXPERIMENTAL NEUROPSYCHOLOGICAL TESTING
IN THE CONTEXT OF THEORETICAL FRAMEWORKS

The tasks suggested in this section can readily be appreciated for their connection to the hypothesized prefrontal cortex functions and theoretical frameworks briefly described earlier in this chapter. However, several limitations must be mentioned. There are no norms for most of the tasks described. Small numbers of controls are available from independent studies, but those controls often cannot be pooled because of differences in age, education, and other etiological variables across control groups or changes in administrative procedures in a test paradigm used across studies. The experimental tasks, while relevant to testing a specific theoretical hypothesis, may not always be directly relevant to the real-life concerns of the patient or his or her family (Lezak, 1982). The psychometric properties of the experimental tasks are often underspecified so that comparisons across tasks within a cognitive domain are limited by differences in between-task difficulty (e.g., Miller, Chapman, Chapman, & Collins, 1995; Miller, Fujioka, Chapman, & Chapman, 1995). Finally, some familiarity with the theoretical frameworks that gave birth to these tasks is required for proper interpretation of the results. With these caveats in mind, there are experimental tasks that can be used to probe the cognitive and social functions of the patient with a frontal lobe lesion. Almost all these tasks are unavailable in commercial form and must be acquired by abstracting the experimental procedure from the published work or by directly communicating with the authors of a particular paper to obtain a copy of the task. Neither of these strategies are particularly onerous, and the interested investigator should be able to assemble a supplemental experimental battery of tests to examine patients with frontal lobe lesions quite easily. To be warned, experimental tasks may occasionally achieve "classic status" but are always subject to modification to examine the fine points of a theory or to accommodate changes in the theory itself. This dynamic status of experimental tests require that they be used with "a grain of salt" and always in the context of a (usually changing) theoretical framework. For the sake of clarity, I divided the following sections into familiar testing domains based on function rather than a specific model noted by a bracketed name where a particular theory/framework is relevant.

Attention

Patients with frontal lobe lesions have been described as having difficulty in their supervisory attention capability [Norman & Shallice (Norman & Shallice, 1986)]. In addition, they have been reported as being especially sensitive to distracting elements in the environment and have difficulty sustaining attention (Rueckert & Grafman, 1996). A number of attentional tasks can be called on to examine these processes [Stuss & Benson].

Sustained attention can be examined using a version of the traditional continuous performance test. An example of such a task can be seen in the recent paper by Rueckert and Grafman (1996). In this version, the procedure is controlled for the number of stimuli presented, the kind of distractors presented, the interval between targets, and the duration of the task. Their results indicated that patients with prefrontal lobe lesions had particular difficulty in the second half of the task when there was a greater interval between targets. Several of the models described earlier predict that patients with frontal lobe lesions should perform more poorly as task performance is extended in time. The observation that patients become less able to identify targets over time suggests that they may have more difficulty focusing their attention over time and may become more distractable. A classic experimental task used to measure distractability and selective attention is the flanker task developed by Eriksen (1995). This task controls for kind of distractor (related or unrelated) and the spatial position of distractors (close vs. far). Although a recent study of patients with frontal lobe lesions and another group of patients with Parkinson's disease found no specific decrement in performance on this task (Lee & Grafman, in press), it is nevertheless useful to document the ability of patients to selectively attend to novel stimuli. Another way to examine effortful selective attention in patients with frontal lobe lesions is to administer a serial search task. A classic paradigm developed by Treisman and her colleagues may be useful for this purpose (Treisman, 1996). In the pop-out condition, subjects should see the target instantly because it has no featural conjunctions with the distractors. In the serial-search condition, the target has significant featural overlap with the distractors requiring more careful, and serial, search. The more distractors, the longer the serial search takes until a target is identified. This task may be used to examine the search strategies of patients with frontal lobe lesions and is a useful contrast between automatic recognition and effortful-search processes.

Supervisory attention requires that the subject overcome a prepotent mode of behavior to respond effectively to a current task demand (Cockburn, 1995; Karnath & Wallesch, 1992). The classic task to examine this ability is the go/no-go task where the subject is first trained to respond in one way to a specific cue and a different way to a second cue. The order is then reversed in the second half of the task, and an increase in subject false-positive errors and slowed response times can indicate a failure to inhibit the prepotent response. Various versions of the Stroop task can also be used for this purpose (Vendrell et al., 1995).

How a subject allocates resources during performance on a dual task is also a measure of supervisory attention. Resource allocation can be measured by the experimental task of divided attention using a dichotic listening task or a divided visual field task (e.g., Godefroy & Rousseaux, 1996). In this case, subjects have to monitor two or more inputs and are required to respond to each input individually or to a combination of input. Resource allocation can also be examined in the context of a task-switching experiment (e.g., Allport, Styles, & Hsieh, 1994), or it may observed in a dual-task scenario where a secondary task drains some of the resources required to perform the primary task (D'Esposito et al., 1995). In the case of task switching, subjects are asked to consistently or randomly switch between two tasks. The signal to switch can either be exogenous (a signal in the task environment) or endogenous (the subject determines when to switch on the basis of instructions). Instituting supervisory attention means controlling the allocation of resources in these special task conditions allowing for an optimal performance to emerge.

A more functional approach to supervisory attention has been advocated by Shallice and Burgess (1991a, 1991b) who have developed tasks that require the subject to perform multiple errands within a certain time frame. Subjects have to determine how to allocate their attention and prioritize their time to successfully accomplish the targeted tasks.

By utilizing a combination of these attentional tasks or conditions, investigators can more precisely identify the nature of what appears to be an "attentional failure" in patients with frontal lobe lesions.

Memory

Although recognition memory is often intact in patients with frontal lobe lesions, and recall, although mildly impaired, does not seem to be a major problem for patients with frontal lobe lesions, certain aspects of memory appear strikingly impaired in these patients [Goldman-Rakic, Fuster, Grafman, Stuss & Benson]. These aspects include memory for the sequence of a stimulus, integrating complex information over time such as remembering or interpreting the theme of a story (Nichelli, Grafman, et al., 1995), new associative memory for previously unassociated material, remembering where and when a fact was learned, and autobiographical memory (Baddeley & Wilson, 1988; Eldridge et al., 1994; Eslinger & Grattan, 1994; Shallice, 1988; Kesner, Hopkins, & Fineman, 1994; Stuss & Benson, 1986).

Sequence order of information can be tested by using sorting, verification, and simple retrieval tasks (Kesner et al., 1994). The material can be composed of words, objects, events, stories, or scripts. I would suggest that both sequence production and verification tasks be considered as there is some clinical evidence that there can be a dissociation between performance on production versus verification tasks (Grafman et al., 1993; Pascual-Leone et al., 1993; Pascual-Leone, Grafman, & Hallett, 1994, 1995). Several methods for scoring the adequacy of a reproduced sequence are available (e.g., see Puff, 1982).

Integrating information over time is usually associated with story processing and requires anaphoric linkage, inference, binding of story propositions and elements together, and synthesizing individual events within a story to obtain its moral or overall thematic content (Kintsch, 1994). Some evidence exists that patients with frontal lobe lesions have difficulty in performing this analysis on-line and may have trouble encoding and retaining this kind of information in memory. When attempting to recall integrated information, subjects may confabulate or embellish story information (Fischer, Alexander, D'Esposito, & Otto, 1995). There is a large story grammar and content psychological literature to borrow from, but the basic task should include stories that have been well studied in the literature along with an established discourse processing scoring methodology (Kintsch, 1994). The latter detailed methodological approach distinguishes this kind of evaluation from the standard story analysis used in the Wechsler Memory Scale (Wechsler, 1987) and other commercially available memory batteries (Lezak, 1995).

Associative memory deficits have been observed in patients with frontal lobe lesions even when they can remember the individual items making up the test (Petrides, 1991, 1994, 1995). Associative memory can be tested in a number of ways, including verifying whether two presented items were paired together earlier or using one member of the pair to cue memory for the second item. In either of these cases, recognition or recall of individual items should be contrasted to recognition or cued recall of the item pairs. The more unusual the item pairing (e.g., using unrelated items such as corn–neuron), the more sensitive this task should be.

Partly because of their difficulty in remembering the sequence of presented information and in integrating it over time, patients with frontal lobe lesions may have difficulty identifying the source of their knowledge (Conway & Dewhurst, 1995; Hoffman, 1997; Schacter, Koutstaal, & Norman, 1996; Schacter, Osowiecki, Kaszniak, Kihlstrom, & Valdiserri, 1994; Spencer & Raz, 1994). In that event, they may have difficulty distinguishing between events to which they were recently exposed versus events to which they were exposed in their past as well as events that are of historical or personal significance versus events that have no historical significance. A number of source memory paradigms available in the literature can be used to test patients with frontal lobe lesions (Conway & Dewhurst, 1995; Hoffman, 1997; Schacter et al., 1994, 1996). Almost all of them expose subjects to a large set of faces, facts, or events—some of the studies used materials that are famous or of historical value. Later on, subjects are shown a large number of new and old items and asked to say whether they represent old or famous events, faces, facts, and so on. The key finding is that patients with frontal lobe lesions make a large number of errors falsely verifying the nonfamous events to which they were exposed earlier as famous events, although they are unable to say when or where they were exposed to these items or events. Thus, we get the term "source amnesia."

Finally, autobiographical memory has been reported to be impaired in patients with frontal lobe lesions (Eldridge et al., 1994; Fink et al., 1996; Greene, Hodges, & Baddeley, 1995; Kapur, 1997; Kopelman, 1994, 1995; Kopelman, Greene, Guinan, Lewis, & Stanhope, 1994). There are a number of reasons that they may be impaired in this memory domain, including having difficulty in being able to sequence life events properly, distinguishing between events that they experienced versus events they observed, dating life events, and knowing the relevance or centrality of certain events they experienced in their life to the building of their character and personality. There is a wide range of autobiographical procedures available to the investigator (Eldridge et al., 1994; Fink et al., 1996; Greene et al., 1995; Kapur, 1997; Kopelman, 1994, 1995; Kopelman et al., 1994). All of them require family members to corroborate the reported autobiographical history. The task should require the subject to remember at least 5 to 10 events per period and to describe the importance of the event, to date it, to say where it took place, and to indicate the names of other important people who participated in that event. Subjects may also be asked to verify whether they participated in a particular event (that relatives attest happened). Autobiographical memory can be compared to memory for famous events that occurred roughly in the same period as the personal memories patients are asked to retrieve or verify.

Patients with frontal lobe lesions may have difficulty in one or more of the memory processes described. These deficits do not imply that patients with frontal lobe lesions are amnesic but that they have difficulty in retrieving certain forms of knowledge that we ordinarily use to make an episodic memory complete (e.g., context or the order of events). It is useful to keep in mind that if a patient has a frontal lobe lesion that extends to the basal forebrain region (including the septum, nucleus of Mynert, diagonal band of broca, etc.) of the frontal lobes, they may have a much more serious memory deficit than does the average patient with frontal lobe lesions (Damasio, Graff-Radford, Eslinger, Damasio, & Kassell, 1985; Salazar et al., 1986). A basal forebrain lesion-induced memory deficit resembles a moderately severe amnesia because of damage to the cholinergic-rich neurons in that area that project to many cortical regions (Damasio et al., 1985; Salazar et al., 1986).

Planning

Planning impairment has frequently been reported in patients with frontal lobe dsyfunction [Luria, Schwartz, Grafman]. However, planning is a complicated activity that demands a number of subcomponents of cognition be managed in parallel (Shallice & Burgess, 1991a; Grafman & Hendler, 1991; Minton, Drummond, Bresina, & Phillips, 1992). Planning, moreover, can be divided into both motoric and cognitive components (Pascual-Leone et al., 1994). Finally, planning can be divided into development and execution phases (Rattermann et al., 1998). Although many experimental tests are used to determine how well a subject plans, few were designed specifically for that purpose.

People may be asked to plan common activities, and they may be asked to plan unusual activities. In the realm of the unusual falls most of the visuomotor and cognitive tasks we administer in psychological experiments. A number of visuomotor learning tasks require planning behavior (Flitman, O'Grady, Cooper, & Grafman, 1997; Pascual-Leone et al., 1993; Pascual-Leone, Wassermann, Grafman, & Hallett, 1996). For example, the hand posture sequence devised by Luria is a task that requires the subject to shift from one hand posture to another in rapid succession (Luria & Tsvetkova, 1990). To do this, patients must store in memory the postures and their sequence before executing the action series. Many subjects report imaging the movements either before or in concert with their actions (this imaging procedure is a type of cognitive planning). The motor actions themselves could represent executing a plan. Most tests of ideational apraxia (see Gonzalez-Rothi & Heilman, 1997) demand that a succession of postures and movements be achieved to demonstrate an action or achieve a goal (e.g., putting on an article of clothing). In this case, planning which piece of clothing to wear ahead of time is followed by the act of putting on the clothing.

More abstract planning tasks also exist (e.g., see Allen et al., 1990). Tests like the Tower of Hanoi, Tower of Toronto, and Tower of London all purport to measure planning behavior (Goel & Grafman, 1995; Grafman et al., 1992). In all these Tower tasks, the subject sees a set of pegs (usually three) on which sit anywhere from three to five disks (although not all disks are always on the same peg). The pattern of disks on pegs in this initial state can be varied from trial to trial. The subject also sees a goal state which represents the final position of the disks on the pegs and is instructed to move the disks to the appropriate pegs to achieve the goal state. The subject usually has to obey some rules for moving the disks (only move one disk at a time, a larger disk cannot be put on top of a smaller disk, etc.). Subjects err by making illegal moves, not attaining the final state because they make too many irrelevant moves (e.g., backtracking), or because they run out of some allotted time to achieve the goal state (Goel & Grafman, 1995; Grafman et al., 1992). Two aspects of performance on these tests tend to be of particular interest to neuropsychologists: (1) the duration of time that expires from when the initial disk state is shown to when the subject's first move is made, and (2) rule violations that subjects make during plan execution. Increased or diminished planning time and an increase in rule violations in patients compared to controls have been associated with lesions to the prefrontal cortex and appear to be independent from problems in motor control, imagery, or memory. Work by Goel and Grafman (1995) suggests that at least for the Tower of Hanoi task, subjects with frontal lobe lesions are particularly susceptible for missing a counterintuitive move (i.e., inhibiting a prepotent response) that facilitates attaining the goal state. Because the Tower of Hanoi allows for reversible moves compared to the Tower of London, it may not be as useful for assessing actual preexecution planning as the Tower of London. Because of its stimulus simplicity and ease of performance, the Tower task has become an experimental staple for the evaluation of planning and plan execution in abnormal populations.

Another way to assess planning ability is to take real-life scenarios and goals and to ask the subject to achieve goals by structuring and/or executing a series of events (Nichelli et al., 1994). There are very large psychological and artificial intelligence experimental literatures on script event processing, real-world planning, and reactive planning that allow for the construction of myriad experimental tasks with which to assess real-life planning (Eldridge et al., 1994; Grafman, 1989; Shallice & Burgess, 1991a). For example, it is possible to choose high-exposure (planning a vacation) and low-exposure (planning to repel an invasion of wild penguins) activities for which subjects can be asked to generate plans. The experimenter can then examine the generated event sequence for sequence order errors, for the importance (to achieving the plan goal) of each generated event, for the intrusion of irrelevant events, and so on. Besides being administered generation tasks, subjects can also be asked to verify whether or not two events from the same plan are in the correct order. The tasks may be verbal using written statements for events, they may be pictorial with images depicting the events, or subjects may even be asked to carry out the activity in real time (Partiot, Grafman, Sadato, Flitman, & Wild, 1996). A wide range of such designs are available to the experimenter. In sum, most studies have demonstrated that patients with frontal lobe lesions are particularly susceptible to making sequence errors, to generating irrelevant actions, and even to distorting the estimated duration of the generated events compared to patients with nonfrontal lesions (Sirigu, Zalla, Pillon, Grafman, Agid, & Dubois, 1995; Sirigu, Pillon, Grafman, Dubois, & Agid, 1995; Sirigu et al., 1996). This particular form of planning experiment has the added advantage that it uses materials that may have some immediate relationship to real-life activities (Grafman et al,, 1993; Grafman, Thompsen-Putnam, Sunderland, & Weingartner, 1991).

Reasoning

Reasoning is a complex cognitive skill. While relying on other cognitive processes such as working memory, language comprehension, and categorization, its essential operations involve analogical mapping, inference, coherence, and deduction/induction (Gentner & Holyoak, 1997; Spellman & Holyoak, 1996). An ability to benefit from feedback and to adapt to circumstances is a part of everyday reasoning (Holyoak & Thagard, 1997). Many scholars believe that this is the highest of all cognitive abilities and an essential part of what makes us human. Many neuropsychologists have clinically observed that patients with frontal lobe lesions have a difficult time reasoning [Damasio, Grafman]

(Brazelli, Colombo, Della Salla, & Spinnler, 1994; Damasio, 1994). Although there are a number of competing theories of reasoning, there is little in the way of neuropsychological tools available for the interested cognitive neuroscientist (Holyoak & Kroger, 1995).

A number of tests of concept formation and shifting appear to require reasoning operations. A recently introduced experimental task, the California Card Sorting Test (Delis, Squire, Bihrle, & Massman, 1992), appears to offer several advantages over the well-worn Wisconsin Card Sorting Test in evaluating the reasons why a subject with frontal lobe lesions might fail on a concept formation task (Arnett et al., 1994; Grafman, Jonas, & Salazar, 1990, 1992; Heaton, Chelune, Talley, Kay, & Curtiss, 1993). Besides the usual free-sorting condition, there are also conditions where the examiner sorts and the subjects explain the reason for the sort, or the subject's own sort is cued by the examiner. No feedback is given and the scoring parameters include number of sorts, appropriate sorts, perseverative responses, and a host of other variables. There is no evidence for the specificity of the California Card-Sorting Test, but several studies indicate it is sensitive to frontal lobe dysfunction (e.g., see Dimitrov, Grafman, Soares, & Clark, in press).

A number of other reasoning paradigms could be easily adapted to neuropsychological testing. For example, in a recent study, Wharton et al. (in press) used an analogical mapping technique in conjunction with positron emission tomography to study the brain–blood flow activity of normal subjects performing this task. They used configurations of geometric stimuli for this particular study and asked subjects either to make a match to sample decision (basically a working memory task) or to decide on whether the source stimulus configuration conceptually mapped onto the target stimulus. The main finding was that the left prefrontal cortex was highly activated during the analogical mapping condition compared to the working memory condition. The stimuli and paradigm used in this study would be easily adaptable for patient studies, as are many other similar paradigms recently reviewed by Robin and Holyoak (1995). Almost all these experiments utilize a comparison between a memory condition and one requiring some form of analogical mapping. Both nonverbal and a variety of verbal stimuli (from words to stories) can be used to explore the ability of patients to see analogies between two kinds of stimuli. Cronin-Golumb (1990) reviewed the few experimental studies that have been conducted looking at the reasoning capabilities of older normal subjects and patients with degenerative neurological disorders. In essence, the key task for patients with frontal lobe lesions is whether they can hold two sets of information in mind while finding the conceptual correspondence between the two sets when their surface features may be different. This mapping of conceptual correspondence is the process to evaluate.

Social Cognition and Decision Making

A relatively large literature contains qualitative observations of patients with ventromedial prefrontal cortex lesions whose behavior was seen as abnormal [Damasio, Stuss & Benson, Grafman]. Practically all the studies from the first two-thirds of the 20th century only obtained family or "significant other" ratings or remembrances of the patient's abnormal behavior (Barker, 1995; Brickner, 1934). Of course, at least for the 110 years after Harlow's first description of the rather dramatic changes in patient Gage's behavior, there was no experimental social cognition literature that could be drawn on to better control the circumstances in which the abnormal social behavior was elicited (Damasio et al., 1994; Harlow, 1848, 1868). However, over the last 40 years, a sophisticated social cognition literature has emerged which has, for the most part, been ignored by the greater neuropsychological community (Wyer & Srull, 1989, 1994). A number of recent reviews offer a sophisticated range of tasks, only some which are easily adaptable to patient populations. Part of the difficulty in adapting social cognition tasks to neuropsychology stems from the fact that large numbers of usually college-age students have to be tested to obtain a subtle but desired significant effect in these paradigms. However, not all paradigms need be so difficult to borrow (Dimitrov, Grafman, & Hollnagel, 1996; Goel, Grafman, Sadato, & Hallett, 1995). They include tasks measuring social attitudes, priming social attribute ratings of characters in a story, and recognition of social cues (Wyer & Srull, 1994). In addition, other tasks that are not directly examining social behavior, such as the gambling task (discussed earlier [Bechara et al., 1997]), nevertheless assay such cognitive processes as judgment and decision making that are an important part of social and risk-evaluation behavior (Damasio, 1994).

Structured Event Processing Variables

Most of the experimental tasks described in the previous sections either directly or indirectly test a number of processing variables. These variables include the ability of patients to recognize a sequential order of events, to hold information over time, to appreciate certain semantic characteristics of the information that is being held, and to express knowledge and behavior via a set of connected actions or events. However, if the experimental study is theoretically driven (as are most of the experimental tests described previously), then a number of other structural variables need to be considered as they would be in almost any other cognitive study examining features of a cognitive architecture, including frequency of exposure to the item/event knowledge being tested, the category specificity of the item/event, the centrality of a set of items/events to the routinized behavior of the subject, and the kinds of inhibitory behavior that may be evoked as a secondary effect of activating the targeted knowledge, as well as many other variables that are relevant for characterizing the stimuli and tasks used.

The SEC/MKU framework allows for a number of these variables to be manipulated when constructing a test [Schwartz, Grafman]. There can be tests of the MKU structure itself. For example, a strong prediction would be that events within an MKU or SEC are rigidly ordered. This notion can be tested by categorizing pairs of events varying in their physical, social, and individual constraints. Response times obtained during event-pair order verification tasks and production frequencies of event pairs during script generation tasks should be fastest for item pairs with physical constraints and slowest for item pairs based on individual constraints. The MKU event structure could be tested by similar verification and production measures designed to evaluate the frequency with which an MKU event is activated, its associative strength to related events, and the category specificity of a particular event (e.g., which can serve to select the most promising of the models [and tasks] for further investigation).

To examine the validity of the SEC model, one could ask a subject to generate all the activities they might do on a Saturday (getting dressed, eating breakfast, working in the garden, etc.). Error analyses can be used to determine whether patterns of MKU or event activation failure correspond to proposed or obtained centrality, frequency, and MKU boundary metrics. Patients may only have difficulty in generating, verifying, or acting out low-frequency MKUs. There may be dissociations in performance between the verbal generation, visual verification, or real-time acting out of MKUs. Category-specific deficits could be expected in certain patients with frontal lobe damage such as a selective deficit in appropriately activating MKUs concerned with social behavior. Finally, a variety of "deactivation failures" of MKU events may occur in some patients who may have difficulty in the initial activation, fluctuations in activation, or premature deactivation of MKU events. Such activation failures may result from a problem in maintaining appropriate suprathreshold activation of the MKU knowledge domain (otherwise described as an attention deficit).

Summary of Experimental Test Section

I have described a set of tasks and variables that are considered experimental but can be used to supplement the standard clinical evaluation when the functions of the frontal lobes need to be examined in greater detail. These experimental tests are generally theoretically driven (and the interpretation of any test's results are both constrained and burdened by the theoretical framework that led to its development), and the investigators using such tests need to be familiar with the particular theory that inspired the development of the particular test they are using. Perhaps there is no other region of the brain that inspires such spirited theoretical debate as the human prefrontal cortex. The determination of clinical researchers to learn more about their patient's behavior and to describe it in sufficient detail will no doubt lead to a more sophisticated view of the human prefrontal cortex in the years ahead.

SIMILARITIES AND DISTINCTIONS AMONG THE MODELS

Given the inextricable link of experimental tests to the models that gave birth to them, it is perhaps useful to list what is common and distinct among the various models I have described earlier in this chapter. Although the models and experimental neuropsychological tasks would each like to stand on their own merits, there are similarities across them. They all operate over extended time domains (seconds +). They all argue for what have been called controlled attentional processes. That is, many of the models suggest a process, subserved by prefrontal cortex, that is monitored within consciousness and responsible for shifting the conceptual set of the subject. Many of the models presume that the processes they describe depend on or are biased toward examining the internal mental state of the subject as opposed to analyzing the surface features of environmental stimuli. All the models consider the prefrontal cortex a member of a distributed set of neural regions concerned with almost all functional behaviors that require the activation of a mental model of the world (especially when aspects of that model are no longer present in the environment).

There are some distinctions between these models as well. Some focus more on general attentional mechanisms [Norman & Shallice/Stuss et al.], whereas others focus on a specific domain of cognition [Damasio's somatic marker theory]. Some frameworks focus on working memory processes [Goldman-Rakic] whereas others focus more on action set representation [Schwartz]. Finally, some are interested in the notion of executive function deficits that cut across the territory of the prefrontal cortex [Baddeley] whereas others are concerned with specifying the role of specific regions of the prefrontal cortex [Fuster].

These similarities and differences can be a guide to our own test development. Any test of the cognitive and social functions of the frontal lobe must require the subject to mentally manipulate the stimuli they are shown, process the sequence of stimulus order, and attend to the conceptual aspects of the task. Additional task "dressing" truly depends on the particular model you adapt.

CONCLUSIONS

It remains difficult for neurobehaviorists (and other health professionals) to reveal through their tests why the patient with frontal lobe damage who is intellectually sound, and may even have average item memory, still persistently displays abnormal planning, reasoning, and social conduct. The framework(s) and tasks presented in this chapter, when used appropriately, can aid in providing a more coherent explanation for knowledge deficits and behavioral abnormalities that may appear in the context of human frontal lobe lesions.

ACKNOWLEDGMENT

This chapter is dedicated to the memory of Charles G. Matthews and D. F. "Frank" Benson.

REFERENCES

Abelson, R. P. (1981). Psychological status of the script concept. *American Psychologist, 36*(7), 715–729.

Allen, J., Hendler, J., & Tate, A. (Eds.). (1990). *Readings in planning*. San Mateo, CA: Morgan Kaufmann.

Allport, A., Styles, E. A., & Hsieh, S. (1994). Shifting attentional set: Exploring the dynamic control of tasks. In C. Umilta & M. Moscovitch (Eds.), *Attention and performance* (pp. 421–452). Cambridge, MA: MIT Press.

Anderson, S. W., Damasio, H., Jones, R. D., & Tranel, D. (1991). Wisconsin Card Sorting Test performance as a measure of frontal lobe damage. *Journal of Clinical and Experimental Neuropsychology, 13*(6), 909–922.

Arnett, P. A., Rao, S. M., Bernardin, L., Grafman, J., Yetkin, F. Z., & Lobeck, L. (1994). Relationship between frontal lobe lesions and Wisconsin Card Sorting Test performance in patients with multiple sclerosis. *Neurology, 44*(3 Pt. 1), 420–425.

Avrahami, J., & Kareev, Y. (1994). The emergence of events. *Cognition, 53,* 239–261.

Awh, E., Smith, E. E., & Jonides, J. (1995). Human rehearsal processes and the frontal lobes: PET evidence. *Annals of New York Academy of Science, 769,* 97–117.

Baddeley, A., & Wilson, B. (1988). Frontal amnesia and the Dysexecutive syndrome. *Brain and Cognition, 7,* 212–230.

Barker, F. G. (1995). Phineas among the phrenologists: The American crowbar case and nineteenth-century theories of cerebral localization. *Journal of Neurosurgery, 82*(4), 672–682.

Baron-Cohen, S., Ring, H., Moriarty, J., Schmitz, B., Costa, D., & Ell, P. (1994). Recognition of mental state terms. *British Journal of Psychiatry, 165,* 640–649.

Barrett, A., & Weld, D. S. (1993). Characterizing subgoal interactions for planning. In *Proceedings of the Thirteenth International Joint Conference on Artificial Intelligence*. Chambery, France: Morgan Kaufmann.

Barrett, A., & Weld, D. S. (1994). Partial-order planning: Evaluating possible efficiency gains. *Artificial Intelligence, 67,* 71–112.

Barsalou, L. W., & Sewell, D. R. (1985). Contrasting the representation of scripts and categories. *Journal of Memory and Language, 24,* 646–665.

Barsalou, L. W. (1989). Intraconcept similarity and its implications for interconcept similarity. In S. Vosniadou & A. Ortony (Eds.), *Similarity and analogical reasoning* (pp. 76–121). New York: Cambridge University Press.

Bastian, H. C. (1892). On the neural processes underlying attention and volition. *Brain, 15*(Pt. 1), 1–34.

Bechara, A., Damasio, A. R., Damasio, H., & Anderson, S. W. (1994). Insensitivity to future consequences following damage to human prefrontal cortex. *Cognition, 50*(1), 7–15.

Bechara, A., Damasio, H., Tranel, D., & Damasio, A. R. (1997). Deciding advantageously before knowing the advantageous strategy. *Science, 275(5304)*, 1293–1295.

Brazzelli, M., Colombo, N., Della Salla, S., & Spinnler, H. (1994). Spared and impaired cognitive abilities after bilateral frontal lobe damage. *Cortex, 30*(1), 27–51.

Brickner, R. M. (1934). An interpretation of frontal lobe function based upon the study of a case of partial bilateral frontal lobectomy. In *Research publications: Association for research in nervous and mental disease* (pp. 259–351). New York: Association for Research in Nervous and Mental Disease.

Buonomano, D. V., & Merzenich, M. M. (1995). Temporal information transformed into a spatial code by a neural network with realistic properties. *Science, 267*, 1028–1030.

Case, R. (1992). The role of the frontal lobes in the regulation of cognitive development. *Brain and Cognition, 20*(1), 51–73.

Casson, R. W. (1983). Schemata in cognitive anthropology. *Annual Review of Anthropology, 12*, 429–462.

Cockburn, J. (1995). Task interruption in prospective memory: A frontal lobe function. *Cortex, 31*, 87–97.

Cohen, J. D., Perlstein, W. M., Braver, T. S., Nystrom, L. E., Noll, D. C., Jonides, J., & Smith, E. E. (1997). Temporal dynamics of brain activation during a working memory task. *Nature, 386*(6625), 604–608.

Cohen, J. D., & Servan-Schreiber, S. D. (1992). Context, cortex, and dopamine: A connectionist approach to behavior and biology in schizophrenia. *Psychological Review, 99*(1), 45–77.

Conway, M. A., & Dewhurst, S. A. (1995). Remembering, familiarity, and source monitoring. *Journal of Experimental Psychology, 48*(1), 125–140.

Corson, Y. (1990). The structure of scripts and their constituent elements. *European Bulletin of Cognitive Psychology, 10*(2), 157–183.

Cronin-Golumb, A. (1990). Abstract thought in aging and age-related neurological disease. In F. Boller & J. Grafman (Eds.), *Handbook of neuropsychology* (Vol. 4, pp. 279–310). Amsterdam: Elsevier Science.

Damasio, A. R. (1994). Descartes' error: Emotion, reason, and the human brain. New York: Grosset/Putnam.

Damasio, H., Grabowski, T., Frank, R., Galaburda, A. M., & Damasio, A. R. (1994). The return of Phineas Gage: Clues about the brain from the skull of a famous patient. *Science, 264*, 1102–1105.

Damasio, A. R., Graff-Radford, N. R., Eslinger, P. J., Damasio, H., & Kassell, N. (1985). Amnesia following basal forebrain lesions. *Archives of Neurology, 42*, 263–271.

Damasio, A. R., & Tranel, D. (1993). Nouns and verbs are retrieved with differently distributed neural systems. *Proceedings of the National Academy of Sciences, USA, 90*(6), 4957–4960.

Damasio, A. R., Tranel, D., & Damasio, H. (1990). Individuals with sociopathic behavior caused by frontal damage fail to respond autonomically to social stimuli. *Behavioral Brain Research, 41*, 81–94.

Damasio, A. R., Tranel, D., & Damasio, H. C. (1991). Somatic markers and the guidance of behavior: Theory and preliminary testing. In H. S. Levin, H. M. Eisenberg, & A. L. Benton (Eds.), *Frontal lobe function and dysfunction* (pp. 217–229). New York: Oxford University Press.

Davidson, D. (1994). Recognition and recall of irrelevant and interruptive atypical actions in script-based stories. *Journal of Memory and Language, 33*, 757–775.

Dehaene, S., & Changeux, J. P. (1991). The Wisconsin Card Sorting Test: Theoretical analysis and modeling in a neuronal network. *Cerebral Cortex, 1*(1), 62–79.

Delis, D. C., Squire, L. R., Bihrle, A., & Massman, P. (1992). Componential analysis of problem-solving ability: Performance of patients with frontal lobe damage and amnesic patients on a new sorting test. *Neuropsychologia, 30,* 683–697.

Demorest, A. P., & Alexander, I. E. (1992). Affective scripts as organizers of personal experience. *Journal of Personality, 60*(3), 645–663.

D'Esposito, M., Detre, J. A., Alsop, D. C., Shin, R. K., Atlas, S., & Grossman, M. (1995). The neural basis of the central executive system of working memory. *Nature, 378*(6554), 279–81.

Diamond, A. (1991). Guidelines for the study of brain-behavior relationships during development. In H. S. Levin, H. M. Eisenberg, & A. L. Benton (Eds.), *Frontal lobe function and dysfunction* (pp. 339–380). New York: Oxford University Press.

Dimitrov, M., Grafman, J., & Hollnagel, C. (1996). The effects of frontal lobe damage on everyday problem solving. *Cortex, 32*(2), 357–366.

Dimitrov, M., Grafman, J., Soares, A. H. R., & Clark, K. (in press). Concept formation and shifting in frontal lesion and Parkinson's disease patients. *Neuropsychology.*

Divac, I. (1988). A note on the history of the term "prefrontal." *IBRO News, 16*(2), 5.

Duncan, J., Burgess, P., & Emslie, H. (1995). Fluid intelligence after frontal lobe lesions. *Neuropsychologia, 33*(3), 261–268.

Ebdon, M. (1993). Is the cerebral neocortex a uniform cognitive architecture? *Mind and Language, 8*(3), 368–403.

Eldridge, M. A., Barnard, P. J., & Bekerian, D. A. (1994). Autobiographical memory and daily schemas at work. *Memory, 2*(1), 51–74.

Eriksen, C. W. (1995). The flankers task and response competition: A useful tool for investigating a variety of cognitive problems. *Visual Cognition, 2*(2–3), 101–118.

Eslinger, P. J., & Grattan, L. M. (1994). Altered serial position learning after frontal lobe lesion. *Neuropsychologia, 32*(6), 729–739.

Eslinger, P. J., Grattan, L. M., Damasio, H., & Damasio, A. R.(1992). Developmental consequences of childhood frontal lobe damage. *Archives of Neurology, 49*(7), 764–769.

Eslinger, P. J., & Damasio, A. R. (1985). Severe disturbance of higher cognition after bilateral frontal lobe ablation: Patient EVR. *Neurology, 35,* 1731–1741.

Fink, G. R., Markowitsch, H. J., Reinkemeier, M., Bruckbauer, T., Kessler, J., & Heiss, W. D. (1996). Cerebral representation of one's own past: Neural networks involved in autobiographical memory. *Journal of Neuroscience, 16*(13), 4275–4282.

Fischer, R. S., Alexander, M. P., D'Esposito, M., & Otto, R. (1995). Neuropsychological and neuroanatomical correlates of confabulation. *Journal of Clinical and Experimental Neuropsychology, 17*(1), 20–28.

Flitman, S., O'Grady, J., Cooper, V., & Grafman, J. (1997). PET imaging of maze processing. *Neuropsychologia, 35*(4), 409–420.

Fodor, J. A. (1983). *The modularity of mind.* Cambridge, MA: MIT Press.

Foster, J. K., Eskes, G. A., & Stuss, D. T. (1994). The cognitive neuropsychology of attention: A frontal lobe perspective [Special issue]: The cognitive neuropsychology of attention. *Cognitive Neuropsychology, 11*(2), 133–147.

Funahashi, S., Chafee, M. V., & Goldman-Rakic, P. S. (1993). Prefrontal neuronal activity in Rhesus monkeys performing a delayed anti-saccade task. *Nature, 365,* 753–756.

Fuster, J. (1997). *The prefrontal cortex.* New York: Raven Press.

Fuster, J. M. (1991). The prefrontal cortex and its relation to behavior. *Progress in Brain Research, 87*(201), 201–211.

Gentner, D., & Holyoak, K. J. (1997). Reasoning and learning by analogy. *American Psychologist, 52*(1), 32–34.

Godefroy, O., & Rousseaux, M. (1996). Divided and focused attention in patients with lesion of the prefrontal cortex. *Brain Cognition, 30*(2), 155–174.

Goel, V., & Grafman, J. (1995). Are the frontal lobes implicated in "planning" functions?: Interpreting data from the Tower of Hanoi. *Neuropsychologia, 33*(5), 623–642.

Goel, V., Grafman, J., Sadato, N., & Hallett, M. (1995). Modeling other minds. *Neuroreport, 6*(13), 1741–1746.

Goldman-Rakic, P. S. (1987). Circuitry of primate prefrontal cortex and regulation of behavior by representational memory. In F. Plum & V. Mountcastle (Eds.), *Handbook of physiology—The nervous system* (Vol. 5, pp. 373–417). Washington, DC: American Physiological Society.

Goldman-Rakic, P. (1992). Working memory and the mind. *Scientific American, 267*(3), 110–117.

Gonzalez-Rothi, L. J., & Heilman, K. M. (Eds.). (1997). *Apraxia: The neuropsychology of action.* East Sussex, UK: Psychology Press.

Grafman, J. (1989). Plans, actions, and mental sets: Managerial knowledge units in the frontal lobes. In E. Perecman (Ed.), *Integrating theory and practice in clinical neuropsychology* (pp. 93–138). Hillsdale, NJ; Erlbaum.

Grafman, J. (1994a). Alternative frameworks for the conceptualization of prefrontal lobe functions. In F. Boller & J. Grafman (Eds.), *Handbook of neuropsychology* (pp. 187–202). Amsterdam: Elsevier Science.

Grafman, J. (1994b). Neuropsychology of higher cognitive processes. In D. Zaidel (Ed.), *Handbook of perception and cognition* (pp. 159–181). San Diego: Academic Press.

Grafman, J. (1995). Similarities and distinctions among current models of prefrontal cortical functions. *Annals of New York Academy of Science, 769,* 337–368.

Grafman, J., & Hendler, J. (1991). Planning and the brain. *Behavioral and Brain Sciences, 14*(4), 563–564.

Grafman, J., Jonas, B., & Salazar, A. (1990). Wisconsin Card Sorting Test performance based on location and size of neuroanatomical lesion in Vietnam veterans with penetrating head injury. *Perceptual and Motor Skills, 71*(3 Pt. 2), 1120–1122.

Grafman, J., Jonas, B., & Salazar, A. (1992). Epilepsy following penetrating head injury to the frontal lobes: Effects on cognition. *Advances in Neurology, 57,* 369–378.

Grafman, J., Litvan, I., Gomez, C., & Chase, T. (1990). Frontal lobe function in progressive supranuclear palsy. *Archives of Neurology, 47*(5), 553–558.

Grafman, J., Litvan, I., Massaquoi, S., Stewart, M., Sirigu, A., & Hallett, M. (1992). Cognitive planning deficit in patients with cerebellar atrophy. *Neurology, 42*(8), 1493–1496.

Grafman, J., Schwab, K., Warden, D., Pridgen, A., Brown, H. R., & Salazar, A. M. (1996). Frontal lobe injuries, violence, and aggression: A report of the Vietnam Head Injury Study. *Neurology, 46*(5), 1231–1238.

Grafman, J., Sirigu, A., Spector, L., & Hendler, J.(1993). Damage to the prefrontal cortex leads to decomposition of structured event complexes. *Journal of Head Trauma Rehabilitation, 8*(1), 73–87.

Grafman, J., Thompsen-Putnam, K., Sunderland, T., & Weingartner, H. (1991). Script generation as an indicator of knowledge representation in patients with Alzheimer's disease. *Brain and Language, 40*(3), 344–358.

Grafman, J., Vance, S. C., Weingartner, H., Salazar, A. M., & Amin, D. (1986). The effects of lateralized frontal lesions on mood regulation. *Brain, 109*(Pt. 6), 1127–1148.

Grafman, J., & Weingartner, H. (1996). A Combinatorial Binding and Strength (CBS) model of memory: Is it a better framework for amnesia?. In D. Herrmann, M. Johnson, C. McEvoy, C. Hertzog, & P. Hertel (Eds.), *Basic and applied memory research: Theory in context* (pp. 259–276). Hillsdale, NJ: Erlbaum.

Greene, J. D., Hodges, J. R., & Baddeley, A. D. (1995). Autobiographical memory and executive function in early dementia of Alzheimer type. *Neuropsychologia, 33*(12), 1647–1670.

Guigon, E., Dorizzi, B., Burnod, Y., & Schultz, W. (1995). Neural correlates of learning in the prefrontal cortex of the monkey: A predictive model. *Cerebral Cortex, 5*(2), 135–147.

Halford, G. S. (1993). *Children's understanding: The development of mental models.* Hillsdale, NJ: Erlbaum.

Hammond, K. J. (1989). *Case-based planning: Viewing planning as a memory task.* Boston: Academic Press.

Harlow, J. M. (1868). Recovery From the passage of an iron bar through the head. *Publication of the Massachusetts Medical Society, 2*, 327–347.

Heaton, R. K., Chelune, G. J., Talley, J. L., Kay, G. G., & Curtiss, G. (1993). Wisconsin Card Sorting Test Manual. Odessa, Florida: Psychological Assessment Resources.

Hoffman, H. G. (1997). Role of memory strength in reality monitoring decisions: Evidence from source attribution biases. *Journal of Experimental Psychology, Learning, Memory, and Cognition, 23*(2), 371–383.

Hokkanen, L., Salonen, O., & Launes, J. (1996). Amnesia in acute herpetic and nonherpetic encephalitis. *Archives of Neurology, 53*(10), 972–978.

Holyoak, K. J., & Kroger, J. K. (1995). Forms of reasoning: Insight into prefrontal functions? *Annals of the New York Academy of Science, 769*, 253–263.

Holyoak, K. J., & Thagard, P. (1997). The analogical mind. *American Psychologist, 52*(1), 35–44.

Johnson, H. M., & Seifert, C. M. (1992). The role of predictive features in retrieving analogical cases. *Journal of Memory and Language, 31*, 648–667.

Kapur, N. (1997). How can be best explain retrograde amnesia in human memory disorder? *Memory, 5*(1–2), 115–129.

Karnath, H. O., & Wallesch, C. W. (1992). Inflexibility of mental planning: A characteristic disorder with prefrontal lesions. *Neuropsychologia, 30*(11), 1011–1016.

Kesner, R., Hopkins, R. P., & Fineman, B. (1994). Item and order dissociation in humans with prefrontal cortex damage. *Neuropsychologia, 32*(8), 881–891.

Kien, J., & Kemp, A. (1994). Is speech temporally segmented?: Comparison with temporal segmentation in behavior. *Brain and Language, 46*, 662–682.

Kintsch, W. (1994). The psychology of discourse processing. In M. A. Gernsbacher (Ed.), *Handbook of psycholinguistics* (pp. 721–736). San Diego, CA: Academic Press.

Kopelman, M. D. (1994). The Autobiographical Memory Interview (AMI) in organic and psychogenic amnesia. *Memory, 2*(2), 211–235.

Kopelman, M. D. (1995). The Korsakoff syndrome. *British Journal of Psychiatry, 166*(2), 154–173.

Kopelman, M. D., Green, R. E., Guinan, E. M., Lewis, P. D., & Stanhope, N. (1994). The case of the amnesic intelligence officer. *Psychology of Medicine, 24*(4), 1037–1045.

Lee, S. S., Wild, K., Hollnagel, C., & Grafman, J. (in press). Selective visual attention in patients with frontal lobe lesions or Parkinson's disease. *Neuropsychologica.*

Levine, B., Stuss, D. T., & Milberg, W. P. (1995). Concept generation: Validation of a test of executive functioning in a normal aging population. *Journal of Clinical and Experimental Neuropsychology, 17*(5), 740–758.

Lezak, M. (1982). The problem of assessing executive functions. *International Journal of Psychology, 17*, 281–297.

Lezak, M. (1995). *Neuropsychological assessment.* New York: Oxford University Press.

Luria, A. R., & Tsvetkova, L. S. (1990). *The neuropsychological analysis of problem solving.* Orlando, FL: Paul M. Deutsch Press.

Markowitsch, H. J. (1995). Which brain regions are critically involved in the retrieval of old episodic memory? *Brain Research Review, 21*(2), 117–127.

McCarthy, G., Blamire, A. M., Puce, A., Nobre, A. C., Bloch, G., Hyder, F., Goldman-Rakic, P., & Shulman, R. G. (1994). Functional magnetic resonance imaging of human prefrontal cortex activation during a spatial working memory task. *Proceedings of the National Academy of Sciences, USA, 91*, 8690–8694.

Medin, D., Goldstone, R. L., & Gentner, D. (1993). Respects for similarity. *Psychological Review, 100*(2), 254–278.

Miller, E. N., Fujioka, T. A., Chapman, L. J., & Chapman, J. P. (1995). Psychometrically matched tasks for assessment of hemispheric asymmetries of function. *Brain Cognition, 28*(1), 1–13.

Miller, G. A., Galanter, E., & Pribram, K. H. (1960). *Plans and the structure of behavior.* New York: Holt, Rinehart & Winston.

Miller, L. A. (1992). Impulsivity, risk-taking, and the ability to synthesize fragmented information after frontal lobectomy. *Neuropsychologia, 30*(1), 69–79.

Miller, M. B., Chapman, J. P., Chapman, L. J., & Collins, J. (1995). Task difficulty and cognitive deficits in schizophrenia. *Journal of Abnormal Psychology, 104*(2), 251–258.

Minsky, M. (1986). *Society of mind.* New York: Simon & Schuster.

Minton, S., Drummond, M., Bresina, J., & Phillips, A. (1992). Total order versus partial order planning: Factors influencing performance. In *Principles of knowledge representation and reasoning: Proceedings of the Third International Conference (KR-92).* Chambery, France: Morgan Kaufmann Publishers.

Neisser, U. (Ed.). (1987). *Concepts and conceptual development: Ecological and intellectual factors in categorization.* Cambridge, UK: Cambridge University Press.

Nichelli, P., Clark, K., Hollnagel, C., & Grafman, J. (1995). Duration processing after frontal lobe lesions. *Annals of the New York Academy of Sciences, 769,* 183–190.

Nichelli, P., Grafman, J., Pietrini, P., Alway, D., Carton, J. C., & Miletich, R. (1994). Brain activity in chess playing [letter]. *Nature, 369*(6477), 191.

Nichelli, P., Grafman, J., Pietrini, P., Clark, K., Lee, K. Y., & Miletich, R. (1995). Where the brain appreciates the moral of a story. *Neuroreport, 6*(17), 2309–2313.

Norman, D. A., & Shallice, T. (1986). Attention to action: Willed and automatic control of behavior. In R. J. Davidson, G. E. Schwartz, & D. Shapiro (Eds.), *Consciousness and self-regulation: Advances in research and theory* (pp. 1–18). New York: Plenum.

Partiot, A., Grafman, J., Sadato, N., Flitman, S., & Wild, K. (1996). Brain activation during script event processing. *Neuroreport, 7*(3), 761–766.

Partiot, A., Grafman, J., Sadato, N., Wachs, J., & Hallett, M. (1995). Brain activation during the generation of non-emotional and emotional plans. *Neuroreport, 6*(10), 1397–1400.

Pascual-Leone, A., Wassermann, E. M., Grafman, J., & Hallett, M. (1996). The role of the dorsolateral prefrontal cortex in implicit procedural learning. *Experimental Brain Research, 107*(3), 479–485.

Pascual-Leone, A., Grafman, J., & Hallett, M. (1995). Procedural learning and prefrontal cortex. *Annals of New York Academy of Science, 769,* 61–70.

Pascual-Leone, A., Grafman, J., & Hallett, M. (1994). Modulation of cortical motor output maps during development of implicit and explicit knowledge. *Science, 263*(5151), 1287–1289.

Pascual-Leone, A., Grafman, J., Clark, K., Stewart, M., Massaquoi, S., Lou, J.-L., & Hallett, M.(1993). Procedural learning in Parkinson's disease and cerebellar degeneration. *Annals of Neurology, 34*(4), 594–602.

Pascual-Leone, J., & Johnson, J. (1991). The psychological unit and its role in task analysis: A reinterpretation of object permanence. In M. Chandler & M. Chapman (Eds.), *Criteria for competence: Controversies in the conceptualization and assessment of children's abilities* (pp. 153–187). Hillsdale, NJ: Erlbaum.

Pea, R. D., & Hawkins, J. (1987). Planning in a chore-scheduling task. In S. L. Friedman, E. K. Scholnick, & R. R. Cocking (Eds.), *Blueprints for thinking* (pp. 273–302). Cambridge, UK: Cambridge University Press.

Petrides, M. (1991). Functional specialization within the dorsolateral frontal cortex for serial order memory. *Proceedings of the Royal Society of London B, 246,* 299–306.

Petrides, M. (1994). Frontal lobes and behaviour. *Current Opinions in Neurobiology, 4*(2), 207–211.

Petrides, M. (1995). Functional organization of the human frontal cortex for mnemonic processing. Evidence from neuroimaging studies. *Annals of New York Academy of Science, 769,* 85–96.

Puff, C. R. (Ed.). (1982). *Handbook of research methods in human memory and cognition.* New York: Academic Press.

Rattermann, M. J., Spector, L., Grafman, J., Levin, H., & Howard, H. (1998). *Partial and total-order planning: Evidence from normal and prefrontally damaged populations.* Manuscript submitted for publication.

Roberts, R. J., Hager, L. D., & Heron, C. (1994). Prefrontal cognitive processes: Working memory and inhibition in the anti-Saccade Task. *Journal of Experimental Psychology: General, 125*(4), 374–393.

Robin, N., & Holyoak, K. J. (1995). Relational complexity and the functions of prefrontal cortex. In M. S. Gazzaniga (Ed.), *The cognitive neurosciences* (pp. 987–998). Cambridge, MA: MIT Press.

Roland, P. (1993). *Brain activation*. New York: Wiley-Liss.

Rolls, E. T., Hornak, J., Wade, D., & McGrath, J. (1994). Emotion-related learning in patients with social and emotional changes associated with frontal lobe damage. *Journal of Neurology, Neurosurgery, and Psychiatry, 57,* 1518–1524.

Ruchkin, D. S., Grafman, J., Krauss, G. L., Johnson, R., Jr., Canoune, H., & Ritter, W. (1994). Event-related brain potential evidence for a verbal working memory deficit in multiple sclerosis. *Brain, 117*(Pt. 2), 289–305.

Ruchkin, D. S., Johnson, R., Jr., Grafman, J., Canoune, H., & Ritter, W. (1997). Multiple visuospatial working memory buffers: evidence from spatiotemporal patterns of brain activity. *Neuropsychologia, 35*(2), 195–209.

Rueckert, L., & Grafman, J. (1996). Sustained attention deficits in patients with right frontal lesions. *Neuropsychologia, 34*(10), 953–63.

Rueckert, L., Appollonio, I., Grafman, J., Jezzard, P., Johnson, R., Jr., Le Bihan, D., & Turner, R. (1994). Magnetic resonance imaging functional activation of left frontal cortex during covert word production. *Journal of Neuroimaging, 4*(2), 67–70.

Salazar, A. M., Grafman, J., Schlesselman, S., Vance, S. C., Carpenter, M., Pevsner, P., Ludlow, C., Weingartner, H., & Mohr, J. P. (1986). Penetrating war injuries to basal forebrain: Neurologic and cognitive correlates. *Neurology, 36*(4), 459–465.

Saver, J. L., & Damasio, A. R. (1991). Preserved access and processing of social knowledge in a patient with acquired sociopathy due to ventromedial frontal damage. *Neuropsychologia, 29*(12), 1241–1249.

Schacter, D. L., Koutstaal, W., & Norman, K. A. (1996). Can cognitive neuroscience illuminate the nature of traumatic childhood memories? *Current Opinion Neurobiology, 6*(2), 207–214.

Schacter, D. L., Osowiecki, D., Kaszniak, A. W., Kihlstrom, J. F., & Valdiserri, M. (1994). Source memory: Extending the boundaries of age-related deficits. *Psychology of Aging, 9*(1), 81–89.

Schank, R. (1982). *Dynamic memory: A theory of reminding and learning in computers and people.* Cambridge, MA: Cambridge University Press.

Schwartz, M. F. (1995). Re-examining the role of executive functions in routine action production. *Annals of New York Academy of Science, 769,* 321–335.

Schwartz, M. F., Reed, E. S., Montgomery, M. W., Palmer, C., & Mayer, N. H. (1991). The quantitative description of action disorganization after brain damage: A case study. *Cognitive Neuropsychology, 8*(5), 381–414.

Shallice, T. (1988). *From neuropsychology to mental structure.* New York: Cambridge University Press.

Shallice, T., & Burgess, P. W. (1991a). Deficits in strategy application following frontal lobe damage in man. *Brain, 114,* 727–741.

Shallice, T., & Burgess, P. (1991b). Higher-order cognitive impairments and frontal lobe lesions. In H. S. Levin, H. M. Eisenberg, & A. R. Benton (Eds.), *Frontal lobe function and dysfunction* (pp. 125–138). New York: Oxford University Press.

Shallice, T., Burgess, P. W., Schon, F., & Baxter, D. M. (1989). The origins of utilization behaviour. *Brain, 112,* 1587–1598.

Sirigu, A., Zalla, T., Pillon, B., Grafman, J., Agid, Y., & Dubois, B. (1995). Selective impairments in managerial knowledge following pre-frontal cortex damage. *Cortex, 31*(2), 301–316.

Sirigu, A., Zalla, T., Pillon, B., Grafman, J., Agid, Y., & Dubois, B. (1996). Encoding of sequence and boundaries of scripts following prefrontal lesions. *Cortex, 32*(2), 297–310.

Sirigu, A., Zalla, T., Pillon, B., Grafman, J., Dubois, B., & Agid, Y. (1995). Planning and script analysis following prefrontal lobe lesions. *Annals of the New York Academy Sciences, 769,* 277–288.

Smith, E. E., & Sloman, S. A. (1994). Similarity- versus rule-based categorization. *Memory and Cognition, 22*(4), 377–386.

Spellman, B. A., & Holyoak, K. J. (1996). Pragmatics in analogical mapping. *Cognitive Psychology, 31*(3), 307–346.

Spencer, W. D., & Raz, N. (1994). Memory for facts, source, and context: Can frontal lobe dysfunction explain age-related differences? *Psychology of Aging, 9*(1), 149–159.

Stuss, D. T., & Benson, D. F. (1986). *The frontal lobes* (2nd ed.). New York: Raven Press.

Stuss, D. T., Shallice, T., Alexander, M. P., & Picton, T. W. (1995). A multidisciplinary approach to anterior attentional functions. *Annals of the New York Academy Sciences, 769,* 191–211.

Tiihonen, J., Kuikka, J., Kupila, J., Partanen, K., Vainio, P., Airaksinen, J., Eronen, M., Hallikainen, T., Paanila, J., & Kinnunen, I. (1994). Increase in cerebral blood flow of right prefrontal cortex in man during orgasm. *Neuroscience Letters, 170,* 241–243.

Tipper, S. P., Weaver, B., & Houghton, G. (1994). Behavioural goals determine inhibitory mechanisms of selective attention. *Quarterly Journal of Experimental Psychology, 47a*(4), 809–840.

Tranel, D., & Damasio, H. (1994). Neuroanatomical correlates of electrodermal skin conductance responses. *Psychophysiology, 31,* 427–438.

Treisman, A. (1996). The binding problem. *Current Opinions in Neurobiology, 6*(2), 171–178.

Tyrrell, P. J. (1994). Apraxia of gait or higher level gait disorders: Review and description of two cases of progressive gait disturbance due to frontal lobe degeneration. *Journal of the Royal Society of Medicine, 87,* 56–58.

Vendrell, P., Junque, C., Pujol, J., Jurado, M. A., Molet, J., & Grafman, J. (1995). The role of prefrontal regions in the Stroop task. *Neuropsychologia, 33*(3), 341–352.

Wechsler, D. (1987). Wechsler Memory Scale—Revised Manual. San Antonio, TX: Psychological Corporation.

Weld, D. S. (1994). An Introduction to Least Commitment Planning. *AI Magazine, 15*(4), 27–61.

Wharton, C. M., Grafman, J., Flitman, S. K., Hansen, E. K., Brauner, J., Marks, A., & Honda, M. (in press). Analogical mapping is mediated by left dorsolateral prefrontal cortex. *Cognitive Psychology.*

Wheeler, M. A., Stuss, D. T., & Tulving, E. (1997). Toward a theory of episodic memory: The frontal lobes and autonoetic consciousness. *Psychology Bulletin, 121*(3), 331–354.

Wilson, F. A. W., Scalaidhe, S. P. O., & Goldman-Rakic, P. (1993). Dissociation of object and spatial processing domains in primate prefrontal cortex. *Science, 260,* 1955–1958.

Wyer, R. S., Jr., & Srull, T. K. (1989). *Memory and cognition in its social context.* Hillsdale, NJ: Erlbaum.

Wyer R. S., Jr., & Srull, T. K. (Eds.). (1994). *Handbook of social cognition: Vol. 1. Basic processes* (2nd ed.). Hillsdale, NJ: Erlbaum.

Zajonc, R. B. (1984). On the primacy of affect. *American Psychologist, 39*(2), 117–123.

Part IV

DISEASES
OF THE
FRONTAL LOBES

Section A

NEUROLOGY

20

Clinical and Pathological Aspects of Frontotemporal Dementia

ARNE BRUN
LARS GUSTAFSON

Considering certain properties of the frontal lobes, and especially those that can be related to developmental features can help to understand the degenerative group of frontotemporal dementias (FTD) (Brun et al., 1994). From a phylogenetic point of view, the frontal lobes have expanded from a small percentage of the neocortex in cats to about 30% in man; at the same time the cortex has increased in width and achieved increasing organizational complexity in terms of lamination, synaptic, and dendritic density and appearance of granular neurons. One late structural addition, and a new feature in man, is the fetal subpial granular layer of the telencephalon (Brun, 1965). It consists largely of neuroblasts which may be presumed to offer a new set of cortical neurons capable of creating new connections through inward migration primarily to the superficial associative cortical laminae. It is the last morphogenetic feature in the formation of the neocortex, not present in lower mammals and not or just barely noticeable in monkeys but well developed in man. It may be regarded as the feature that places man first among species in regard to brain development. Ontogenetically it is the last to mature and regionally speaking latest in the phylogenetically young frontal lobe. Also other maturational features such as myelinization, synaptogenesis, and dendritic outgrowth follow the same time schedule, meaning a late and protracted maturation of the frontal lobe. All this carries with it a selective vulnerability to certain diseases and thus relates to the theme of this chapter.

In contrast, the sensorimotor cortex expands and matures in previously mentioned respects much earlier than the frontal lobes and, at 26 fetal weeks, stands out as a landmark raised above the frontal and parietal lobes. Hence, and also from a functional point of view, it can be regarded as a distinct part of the brain, deserving a name of its own, namely, the central lobe. Because the central lobes are phylogenetically older and mature earlier than the frontal lobes, they show a selective vulnerability, different from that of the frontal lobes, and are selectively relatively spared by certain degenerative disorders such as FTD and Alzheimer's disease (AD). This makes it a convenient posterior demarcation structure of the frontal lobes and a dividing structure between the frontal and parietal lobes It thus defines the frontal lobes in relation to adjoining areas from an anatomical, phylogenetic, and ontogenetic point of view and functionally as a pure "associative" lobe contrasting with the sensorimotor central lobe from a functional point of view and also with respect to vulnerability and participation in disease patterns.

Within the neocortex, the ontogeny indicates a difference between the cortical layers. The neurons of the deeper layers are the earliest to take up their final position and to mature; thus they seem older than the superficial layers where in addition the granularity marks the further developmental progress and sophistication. This might correlate with a difference in vulnerability between the cortical laminae as it is expressed in some of the FTD disorders.

The cingulate gyrus, divided in an anterior (area 24) and a posterior (area 23) part on the basis of a difference in terms of cytoarchitectonics, also differ with respect to main cortical connections (Divac, 1972; Nauta, 1973). The anterior part connects mainly with the frontal lobes and the posterior part with the parietal lobes which also finds its correlate in the degenerative topographic patter in disorders such as FTD and Alzheimer's disease, respectively. The striatum and medial nuclei of the thalamus also have special connections with the frontal lobes, and are consequently of interest in the context of frontal lobe disease.

In relation to this frame of frontal properties and features, the newly defined group of primary degenerative frontotemporal dementias is discussed with a reference to some other dementing disorders which often show a clinically relevant tendency to involve the frontal lobes.

PATHOLOGICAL ASPECTS

FTD comprise a group of disorders with a common basic, degenerative pattern seen in frontal lobe degeneration of non-Alzheimer type (FLD), progressive aphasia (PA) and motor neuron disease with dementia (MNDD), thus a homogenous group from the point of view of pathology. Also included is Pick's disease, which has much of the basic changes of the disorders mentioned earlier but which departs from the picture through additional changes of a partly different type and distribution. The main reason for including Pick's disease in the group is its frontal cortical involvement and thereby frontal clinical character, making it *in vivo* more or less indistinguishable from FLD. However, it constitutes only a minor part of the FTD case material which is dominated by FLD, the model for the description that follows.

FLD was so named at the time of its first clinicopathological presentation (Brun, 1987; Gustafson, 1987) to mark its dissimilarity to Alzheimer's disease, the then and often still dominating disorder overshadowing the existence of the other important dementing disorders.

Among the more than 30 pathoanatomically studied cases, only a minority show a grossly obvious frontal atrophy whereas the majority are largely unremarkable on inspection in keeping with the normal for age brain weight. Sectioning of the brain reveals a slight widening of the anterior portion of the ventricular system but not of the temporal or occipital horns. Other structures as the striatum, the amygdalar nucleus, hippocampus, and basal ganglia show mild or no gross changes, but the substantia nigra in some cases reveals a mild depigmentation (see Table 20.1).

TABLE 20.1. Pathological Changes in FLD

Grossly mild frontal atrophy
Microscopic changes in frontal or frontotemporal cortex
    Includes anterior cingulate gyrus
    Rare parietal involvement (advanced stages)
    Cortical laminae 1–3 show:
        Microvaculation
        Neuronal loss or atrophy
        Gliosis
        Synapse loss
    Sometimes also in amygdala and striatum
Superficial white matter gliosis
Moderate nigral neuronal loss
No inclusions or prions, plaques, tangles, or amyloid

Under the microscope, a degenerative process is noted in the frontal convexity cortex and the anterior cingulate gyrus (area 24), and sometimes also in the insular cortex and in about a third of the cases of the anterior temporal cortex. Changes are restricted to the supragranular cortical layers 1, 2, and 3, the dominating change being a microvacuolation and increase in astrocytes. The latter is most easily noted in lamina 1 where cell counting reveals an increase by 70%, whereas other regions, including the parietal lobe, show no such increase (Brun, Liu, & Erikson, 1995). This is accompanied by an increase in immunostaining for glial fibrillary acidic protein marking the site of reactive astrocytes. Neurons show atrophy and some loss in lamina 2 and 3, though with little consequence for the cytoarchitecture. The infragranular deeper laminae 4, 5, and 6 are largely spared. These changes can also be seen in the most advanced cases in the parietal postcentral areas but then only of a mild type. The sensory and motor gyri, the occipital lobes, and posterior cingulate gyrus (area 23) are spared.

These cortical changes never produce a severe or knife blade atrophy but may vary in severity to some extent between left and right hemisphere, creating a slight asymmetry, though never consistently in favor of one side or the other.

Besides these changes seen on routine microscopy, immunostaining and computerized density calculations reveal a striking loss of synapses, frontally amounting to 40–50% in supragranular layers but not, or only insignificantly, in the deeper laminae. The parietal, posterior temporal, or posterior cingulate gyral cortex shows no such loss when compared with age-matched controls (Liu & Brun, 1996).

The subcortical, superficial white matter of the frontal lobes is the site of a mild gliosis and a mild loss of myelin, invisible on gross inspection (Englund & Brun, 1987).

The same changes as in the cortex though milder are, in some cases, found also in the amygdalar nucleus and, in a few cases, in the striatum. Other structures such as the basal ganglia and the hippocampus, are spared. The grossly visible pigment loss in the substantia nigra corresponds microscopically to a mild or moderate loss of pigmented neurons which is not of the severity seen in Parkinson's disease and which is devoid of Lewy bodies. There may also be a slight loss of neurons from the anterior spinal horns but the pyramidal tracts are unremarkable (Brun, 1993).

The histopathological picture is homogeneous, varying only to some extent in terms of distribution and severity within the outlined cortical areas, both in sporadic cases and in families, even in those represented by several cases. Alzheimer changes such as plaques, tangles, amyloid angiopathy, and diffuse amyloid deposits are not seen except in the oldest cases and then to a degree compatible with what is expected for age. Lewy bodies, inflated neurons, and Pick bodies are not encountered. The cortical microvacuolation is not of the coarse type seen in Creutzfeldt–Jakob disease and prions and protease-resistant prion protein cannot be demonstrated (Collinge, Hardy, Brown, & Brun, 1994).

PA, a further member of the FTD group, shows the same changes with microvacuolation in supragranular layers together with astrocytic gliosis in the subpial region, and there are no Pick type cell changes. According to Snowden, Neary, and Mann (1996), the changes predominate on the left side, although the right is also involved, and there is furthermore a loss of neurons not only from the supragranular layers but also from lamina 5, constituting a slight difference from the picture in FLD.

One might speculate that this is basically the same disorder as FLD, though initially predominating in frontal cortical language areas, and might later progress to a more globalized dementia or, at least, dementia of the frontal type (Clark et al., 1986), something also hinted at by Green, Morris, Sandson, McKeel, and Miller (1990) on the basis of a study of progressive aphasia.

MNDD has been described mostly in Japan (Mitsuyama, 1993) but also in other countries (e.g., Ferrer, Roig, Espino, Peiro, & Matias Guiu, 1991; Neary, Snowden, & Mann, 1990; Wikström, Pateau, Palo, Sulkava, & Haltia, 1982). The cortical pathology found has been that described for FLD, in some materials also with involvement of the substantia nigra and globus pallidus, and in other cases also the basolateral amygdala (Mitsuyama, 1993; Morita, Kaiya, Ikeda, & Namba, 1987). Other features diverging from FLD pertain to the concomitant MND component, namely, spinal and bulbar motor neuron degeneration and the various types of inclusions described in this disorder. Indications of frontal dysfunction in classical MND (Lopez, Becker, & De Kosky, 1994; Ludolph et al., 1993) in addition to the combination of the two disorders mentioned earlier, from a morphological point of view, are food for thought along the line of a system disorder where the two diseases are the expressions at the extremes of this system but in other cases they combine to produce MNDD.

Pick's disease is defined here neuropathologically as a disorder with severe frontotemporal cortical atrophy leading to a true lobar atrophy with knife-blade appearance of the gyri within a circumscribed area where all cortical laminae are involved not only with microvacuolation, gliosis, loss of synapses, and neuronal loss of both infra and supragranular layers but also with Pick bodies and ballooned nerve cells. Subcortically, it is also marked by severe white matter degeneration and involvement of the striatum, amygdalar nucleus, and hippocampus with argentophilic inclusions. Due to its partly different and wider distribution and additional microscopical features, it would seem to fall somewhat out of the frame set previously for the FTD group. A link may exist, however, in the shape of the Pick type of FLD (Snowden et al., 1996). Also, the cases of primary PA described by Kertesz, Hudson, and Mackenzie (1994), where Pick cells and inflated neurons were reminiscent of Pick's disease, may point to a link with the FTD group. The position of Pick's disease might become clearer with the advancement of genetics in this field.

Alzheimer's disease is the most common differential diagnostic alternative to dementias involving the frontal lobes (see Table 20.2). Even if AD probably starts in the limbic, and especially the hippocampal structures and in the average case it later has its neocortical main point in the postcentral parietotemporal areas, sparing, relatively speaking, the sensory motor cortex, it involves in the late stages also the frontal cortex (Brun & Englund, 1981). In some 5–7% of cases, however, the frontal lobes become prominently involved at an earlier stage in the presenile form and even more so in the

TABLE 20.2. Organic Dementias with Frontal Features of Differential Diagnostic Interest

ALS with dementia	Creutzfeldt–Jakob disease with frontal emphasis
Progressive aphasic disorders	Alzheimer's disease with frontal emphasis
Pick's disease	Binswanger's disease
Dementia lacking distinctive histology	Selective incomplete white matter infarction
Rare familial forms (Kim)	Strategic infarct dementia
Chromosome 17 linked disorders	Huntington's disease
Corticobasal degeneration	Progressive supranuclear paralysis
Progressive subcortical gliosis	

senile variety, even if hippocampal and parietal areas are more severely deranged. In the cingulate gyrus, the posterior (area 23) is involved in contrast to its anterior portion (area 24) being involved in FLD. Thus, as an exception to the rule, Alzheimer's disease may clinically appear at least superficially as a frontal dementing disorder particularly in the more global senile form (Brun & Gustafson, 1991).

Vascular dementia (VaD) is, in general, a less systematized and more haphazardly localized disorder. Some small vessel dementias do, however, show a clear-cut preference for the frontal lobes and in particular its white matter. The two disorders that are prevalent in this brain region are Binswangers disease or progressive subcortical vascular encephalopathy (PSVE) and selective incomplete white matter infarction (SIWI).

PSVE is often related to hypertension and its consequences on small intracerebral vessels and is therefore marked by small, lacunar infarcts not only in the basal ganglia and brain stem structures but also, and often preferentially, in the white matter of the frontal lobes (Ishii, Nishihara, & Imamura, 1986). This was the situation in 11 "pure" cases, namely, PSVE with only subcortical white matter and basal ganglia lacunes but without the large infarcts of the large vessel multiinfarct dementia type and without the stigmata of other dementing disorders (Brun, Fredriksson, & Gustafson, 1992). The reason for this frontal preference is unknown but may be related to the length of the penetrating arteries supplying the deep frontal structures, maybe again a consequence of phylogeny with expansion of the frontal lobes in excess of the supply capacity at critical levels. The lacunar infarcts are, however, surrounded by incomplete infarcts several times larger than the lacunes and which tend to coalesce to produce large areas of partial loss of axons and myelin sheaths undermining the frontal cortex. The incomplete infarct is a kind of penumbra zone created by the paucity of supplying vessels which, in addition, have the character of end arteries with few or no anastomoses, whereas the more densely vascularized cortex escapes damage.

SIWI also predominates in the frontal white matter although it can be seen also in the parietal lobes. The pathological substrate is here a purely incomplete infarction of the white matter, similar to what is seen in PSVE but without the complete, lacunar infarcts and without involvement of the basal ganglia or the brain stem. The pathogenetic mechanism here is believed to be a fibrohyaline narrowing and stiffening but not occlusion of the penetrator arteries of the white matter in combination with a blood pressure fluctuating between normal and hypotensive levels. This repeatedly creates temporary episodes of hypoperfusion of the white matter on the basis of the narrowing and stiffening preventing autoregulatory adaptation to the flow situation (Brun & Englund, 1986). Both disorders seem to have a stepwise progress of the structural changes but with steps small enough to impress clinically as a slowly progressive disorder. They also both produce dementia, mainly through a partial undermining of the frontal cortex, which is largely normal in both disorders.

There are few systematic neurochemical studies of FTD. Choline acetyltranferase activities, within a normal range, have been reported in Pick's disease and FLD (Francis et al., 1993; Hansen, Deteresa, Tobias, Alford, & Terry, 1988; Knopman, Mastri, Frey, Sung, & Rustan, 1990) and in MNDD (Clark et al., 1986), and nigrostriatal dopamine decrease was found in Pick's disease (Kanazawa et al., 1988) and FLD (Gilbert et al., 1988). Cerebrospinal fluid (CSF) analyses have shown reduced somatostatin levels both in FTD and AD (Edvinsson, Minthon, Ekman, & Gustafson, 1993; Minthon, Edvinsson, Ekman, & Gustafson, 1990). Moreover, the delta sleep-inducing peptide (DSIP) was significantly reduced in AD but not in FTD whereas the corticotrophin-releasing factor (CRF) was significantly reduced in FTD but not in AD. These differences in peptide expression might be related to localization of the disease processes or the sequence in which different neurons are affected. Increased levels of tau and paired helical filament (PHF)-tau in the CSF in AD and low levels in FTD have been reported. Blennow et al. (1996) and Vermersch et al. (1995) found pathological tau proteins in the frontal lobe and the temporal poles in FTD despite the absence of neurofibrillary lesions.

There is evidence of genetic factors with a history of a similar disorder in a first degree relative in about 50% of patients with FLD and Pick's disease (Gustafson, 1987; Knopman et al., 1990; Neary, Snowden, Northen, & Goulding, 1988; Sjögren, Sjögren, & Lindgren, 1952; Van Mansvelt, 1954). Passant, Gustafson, and Brun (1993) described a Swedish pedigree with FTD in 10 out of 21 family members in three generations and typical FLD confirmed postmortem in three cases.

The chromosome 17 linked dementia group has recently become defined on genetic grounds and is composed of disorders with a basic frontotemporal degenerative common denominator of the type seen in the FTD group but with additional structural features of a greater variety than those reported in the FTD group (Sima et al., 1996).

Foster et al. (1997) suggested the name "Frontotemporal dementia with parkinsonism linked to chromosome 17" and the designation "chromosome 17 linked dementias" was given to these disorders by Wilhemsen, Lynch, Pavlou, Higgins, and Nygaard (1994). These writings expand the spectrum of dementing frontotemporal disorders and the spectrum of histological features in spite of a common etiology, namely, chromosome 17 q21–22 linked mutations. Three multigeneration kindreds with FTD linked to chromosome 17 have been described in the Netherlands (Heutink et al., 1977). With one disorder within this group of diseases presented by Basun et al. (1997) being identical to FLD, a connection between the FTD and chromosome 17 linked dementias can be suspected. A common ground may thus be a mutation or mutations on this gene, a candidate gene for the frontal dementing disorders under consideration. Another possibility offered by Brown et al. (1995) indicates a link to chromosome 3 p11–q11 based on a study of a Danish family with a nonspecific dementia with features in common with the FTD group.

Conflicting results concerning an abnormal ApoE allele pattern have been found (Farrer et al., 1995; Frisoni et al., 1994; Gustafson, Abrahamsson, Grubb, Nilsson, & Fex, 1997) and denied (Pickering-Brown et al., 1995).

In conclusion, the developmental background of the frontal lobes, pointed out in the introduction, might be an important reason for its vulnerability in certain situations. The phylogenetically young age of the frontal lobes, with its additional and partly new features, may hold a key to its vulnerability as may also its ontogenetic character with a late and protracted development and maturation. Both features carry with them a tendency to a selective vulnerability that may be expressed particularly in conjunction with certain mutations such as the chromosome 17 q21–22 linked mutation. This contrasts with the robust nature of the phylo- and ontogenetically different and older central sensory and motor gyri. Also, the magnificent growth and expansion of the frontal lobes have placed increasing demands on its vascular supply, especially to distant areas as the deep white matter, a "recent" long-distance irrigation arrangement displaying another form of vulnerability that is expressed in certain vascular disorders. Finally, the changing and growing frontal lobes may require a rearrangement or reinforcement of its connections with phylogenetically older central gray structures, which might further add to its vulnerability.

CLINICAL ASPECTS

Our clinical experience of degenerative FTD derives from a prospective dementia study started 30 years ago whose goal was to develop criteria for early recognition and differential diagnosis of dementia. We soon recognized a group of patients with a predominant frontal lobe clinic and frontotemporal decrease of the regional cerebral blood flow (rCBF) (Gustafson, Brun, & Ingvar, 1977). The clinical diagnosis was usually Pick's disease, in consequence with the current nosological classification. Postmortem examination in the majority of these cases revealed, however, a cortical degeneration that was neither AD nor typical Pick's disease (Brun & Gustafson, 1978) and for which the designation of FLD was introduced. The clinicopathological entity of FLD developed, and after expanded clinicopathological experience, the concept of FTD was introduced.

Some explanations for the large number of FTD patients in our dementia study are the focus on early-onset dementia, the consequent use of functional brain imaging, the postmortem follow-up, and the influence of geographic and genetic factors. In a recent survey, no less than 9% of the neuropathological diagnoses were FTD, FLD in 8%, and Pick's disease in 1% (Gustafson, 1993). Similar and even higher proportions of FTD have been presented by other research groups. Neary et al. (1988) in Manchester described "dementia of frontal lobe type," Knopman et al. (1990) introduced the term "dementia lacking distinctive histological features," and Clark et al. (1986) reported on cases with frontal and/or temporal cortical atrophy without Alzheimer pathology. The clinical similarity between all these materials is striking. Important information on clinical, neuropsychological, brain imaging, and genetic findings in FTD have been added through other studies in the United States, Germany, France, Italy, and the Netherlands (Frisoni et al., 1996; Förstl et al., 1994; Miller, Chang, Mena, Boone, & Lesser, 1993; Pasquier, Lebert, Grymonprez, & Petit, 1995; Van Swieten, Stevens, de Knijff, & Van Duijn, 1996).

The following description of the clinical picture in FTD is mainly referring to FLD (Gustafson, 1987, 1993). Pick's disease has not yet been possible to distinguish with certainty from FLD on pure clinical grounds. The clinical onset is insidious, with a slow gradual progression. Therefore, the patients age at onset and, consequently, also the duration of the disease are difficult to decide. The mean age at onset in our first 30 postmortem-verified FLD cases was 56 ± 7.6 years (range 45–70 years) and the estimated duration of the illness was 3–17 years (mean 8.1 ± 3.4 years). The duration in 8 cases with pure Pick's disease was somewhat longer, 11.0 ± 4.1 years (range 4–17 years), and in a control sample with presenile AD 10.6 ± 3 years (range 5–16 years).

The initial stage of FTD is characterized by changes of personality and behavior, affective symptoms, and a progressive speech disorder. An abbreviated version of the clinical criteria in the Lund–Manchester consensus on FTD is presented in the appendix at the end of this chapter. Most patients also show memory impairment, lack of concentration, and a general mental rigidity and stereotypy. These cognitive changes are, however, often overshadowed by other more obvious and dramatic manifestations of the brain disease. The changes of habitual personality traits are described as emotional leveling and unconcern, lack of empathy, and impaired judgment. The patient becomes self-centered, emotionally cold, and less concerned about his family, friends, work and own appearance. A main problem is that the patient does not understand that his or her present condition and conflicts are due to a pathological change of his or her mental state.

Signs of disinhibition often appear early as restlessness, impulsivity, irritability, aggressiveness, and excessive sentimentality. Craving for affection and sexual contacts may become frequent and easily provoked, but usually such expressions of sexual disinhibition are rather harmless and possible to divert. Unrestrained stereotypical behavior such as impulse buying, hoarding, and shoplifting may, however, cause serious social and economical problems.

The differential diagnosis between FTD and nonorganic affective disorder may sometimes be difficult. The patient may appear unconcerned, at times even euphoric. When accompanied by impulsivity, increased talkativeness, and confabulation, these emotional symptoms may be difficult to differentiate from a hypomanic or manic state. Increased tearfulness and inadequate smiling may also blunt the clinical picture. A diagnosis of major depression may also be suggested in FTD patients with episodes of dysphoria or low mood with suicidal ideation. Suicide was suspected in one postmortem-verified FLD case and in one additional case lacking autopsy. Mimical movements become sparse often at an early stage, which, in combination with the patient's aspontaneity, social withdrawal, and reduced speech, may be misinterpreted as nonorganic depression. The majority of our FLD and Pick cases had received antidepressant medication at an early stage of the disease. In spite of impaired insight, several patients asked for medical examinations and treatment referring to various somatic complaints such as pain and hyperesthesia often combined with bizarre hypochondriacal ideas.

Most FTD cases are judged to have a fairly normal premorbid personality, although restlessness and anxiety are sometimes reported (Gustafson, 1987). The emotional symptoms do not, however, seem related to premorbid personality traits but rather to the distribution of cerebral dysfunction on brain imaging (Lebert, Pasquier, & Petit, 1995; Luaute, Favel, Remy, Sanabria, & Bidault, 1994; Miller et al., 1993).

The personality changes in FTD with social and personal neglect, impaired judgment, and unpredictable behavior may easily lead to conflicts within family and with the society, especially as long as there is no reasonable explanation for the patient's bizarre "pseudopsychopathic" behavior. The heavy strain on the family may cause economic and legal problems and even divorce and suicide. Such complications are less common in families with an Alzheimer patient. A consequence of the relatively preserved practical and spatial abilities is that FTD patients may continue to drive in spite of impaired judgment and a number of near-accidents. This urgent problem may be handled with a firm consequent attitude from the doctor and the family. By contrast, most AD patients are self-critical and anxiously aware of increasing practical difficulties and impaired sense of locality and are therefore ready to give up driving.

Psychotic features are prevalent in FTD as well as in AD (Burns, Jacoby, & Levy, 1990; Gustafson & Risberg, 1992; Lopez et al., 1996; Van Mansvelt, 1954). In our longitudinal study, hallucinations and delusions were reported in 20% of FTD and early-onset AD cases and in 50% of the late-onset AD group. The psychotic symptoms in FTD are often bizarre and badly controlled and the combination, with signs of disinhibition, loss of insight, stereotyped behavior, and language dysfunction of frontal type, may give the impression of functional psychosis, most often schizophrenia. This association between psychosis and frontal lobe syndrome has also been described in AD with marked frontal lobe involvement and in patients with ischemic white matter lesion in the frontal lobes (Brun & Gustafson, 1991; Miller et al., 1991). The psychotic symptoms in early-onset AD, however, seem more strongly related to cognitive failure and the degeneration of the temporoparietal association cortex. Thus, the differences in psychotic symptoms between AD and FTD seem related to differences in the degenerative patterns (Gustafson & Risberg, 1992; Lopez et al., 1996).

Various elements of the human Klüver–Bucy syndrome (Klüver & Bucy, 1938) (e.g., blunted affects, hyperorality, and hypersexuality) are found in FLD, Pick's disease, and other types of FTD. The hyperorality manifests in changes of oral/dietary behavior, gluttony, excessive smoking, and alcohol overconsumption. FTD may therefore be misdiagnosed as alcohol-related dementia (Groen & Endtz, 1982; Gustafson, 1987). Certain types of food, especially sweets, are preferred and the patient may also try uneatable objects. This may, at a later stage of the disease, lead to aspiration and other complications. Utilization behavior (Lhermitte, Pillon, & Serdaru, 1986), which is similar to the hypermetamorphosis of the Klüver–Bucy syndrome in animals, is common in FTD, sometimes as an early sign. This feature has been related to frontal and frontothalamic lesions (Eslinger, Warner, Grattan, & Easton, 1991; Hashimoto, Yoshida, & Tanaka, 1995; Schallice, Burgess, Schon, & Baxter, 1989).

The progressive dynamic aphasia in FTD has been described as *Sprachverödung* (Schneider, 1927) and *dissolution du language* (Delay, Neveu, & Desclaux, 1944; Escourolle, 1958). Speech becomes adynamic with word-finding difficulties and frequent use of stereotyped comments and set phrases. During the early stage, there may be a period of increased unrestrained talking and, at times, also confabulation. Imitating behavior, especially echolalia, was observed in about 50% of FLD and Pick cases (Gustafson, 1993; Van Mansvelt, 1954). Finally, the patients become mute, which, in combination with the amimia, makes communication extremely difficult. The ability to understand information and instructions may, however, remain comparatively late, as does also the ability to write. The handwriting may, however, change in various ways such as magnitude, type of letters, spelling, and speed of writing. These disturbances are unlike the temporoparietal type of dysgraphia and global dysphasia observed in AD. The speech disorder in FTD seems strongly related to the involvement of the speech-dominant hemisphere. The symptom constellation of palilalia, echolalia, mutism, and amimia, the so-called PEMA syndrome of Guiraud (1956), is typical of FTD and rare in AD and may therefore strongly contribute to the differential diagnosis. The speech disorder in FTD has been described in a similar way by various research groups (Knopman et al., 1990; Neary et al., 1988; Snowden & Neary, 1993)

There are important similarities between FTD at an early stage and the clinical spectrum of PA (Mesulam, 1982; Neary, Snowden, & Mann, 1993; Snowden, Neary, Mann, Goudling, & Testa, 1992). PA is dominated by language disturbances and relative preservation of memory and practical abilities. Ultimately, however, many of these cases seem to develop global dementia (Green et al., 1990; Snowden et al., 1992). PA in FTD may be caused by the same degenerative process, although with a somewhat different topographic distribution. The behavioral changes in semantic dementia are less severe than in FTD with brain pathology, mainly restricted to the middle and inferior temporal gyri (Snowden et al., 1996). Progressive supranuclear palsy may also present a speech disorder similar to that in FTD (Esmonde, Giles, Xuereb, & Hodges, 1996).

Several studies (Mitsuyama, 1993; Morita et al., 1987; Neary et al., 1990) showed an association with MND and dementia of frontal lobe type. The clinical onset is usually in the sixth decade and the mean duration of MNDD is about 30 months. The clinical picture is similar to that of FTD, with early changes of personality and behavior, impaired insight, and signs of disinhibition such as restlessness, irritability, unrestrained sexuality, and hyperorality. The speech becomes stereotyped and preservative, developing into echolalia and mutism. Receptive speech function, orientation, and practical abilities may remain relatively untouched by the degenerative process. The diagnosis is based on a rapidly progressive course in combination with signs of anterior horn involvement. Brain imaging shows predominant, precentral pathology, and EEG may remain normal as in FLD and Pick's disease.

NEUROPSYCHOLOGICAL ASSESSMENT

Neuropsychological studies of FTD show cognitive deficits, implicating disordered function of the anterior cortex (Elfgren et al., 1994; Frisoni et al., 1995; Johanson & Hagberg, 1989; Knopman et al., 1989; Neary et al., 1988). The cognitive functions are, however, difficult to evaluate because of the patient's emotional changes and speech dysfunction. The early test profile is characterized by slow verbal production and relatively intact reasoning and memory, while intellectual and motor speed are reduced (Johanson & Hagberg, 1989). By contrast, the early AD patients show a relatively intact verbal ability and a simultaneous impairment of reasoning ability, verbal and spatial memory dysfunction, dysphasia, and visuospatial dysfunction (Johanson & Hagberg, 1989). Memory disturbances are found at an early stage of FTD but within normal range in some patients, namely, those with the best preserved hippocampal structures at autopsy. Remote memory is also affected, although to a lesser extent than in AD and with a relative sparing of memory for daily events (Frisoni et al., 1994; Gustafson, 1987). Memory impairment and confabulation may be more prominent in Pick's disease, probably due to the more severe hippocampal involvement. Dyscalculia is often mentioned as an early dysfunction in FTD.

In our experience, neuropsychological testing can be used for early recognition of FTD and differential diagnosis against AD and other dementias, normal aging, and nonorganic mental disease. The cognitive impairments in FTD and AD correlate significantly with localization and severity of the cortical dysfunction as revealed by rCBF measurements (Elfgren et al., 1991). Elfgren et al. (1994) suggested that a discrimination between AD and FTD could be based on a short test battery when used in the context of a neuropsychological examination, thus underlining the need of qualitative as well as quantitative assessment of test performances (Johanson, Gustafson, & Risberg, 1986). Systematic evaluation of the patient's behavior, such as cooperation, self-criticism, distractibility, flight reactions, and strategy in the test situation, strongly contributes to the differentiation from AD (Johanson & Hagberg, 1989; Pachana, Brauer-Boone, Miller, Cummings, & Berman, 1996). The tests selected by Elfgren et al. (1994) were verbal ability, visuospatial ability, and verbal memory with 89% correctly identified in a retrospective postmortem varied sample, and 84% in a prospective study. Gregory, Orrell, Sahakian, and Hodges (1997), using a screening instrument for FTD based on frontal release signs, awareness of social/ethical dilemma in a short story, and the number of perseveration errors in an oral word association test, correctly classified 92% of AD and 83% of FTD validated against clinical diagnosis. The Mini-Mental State Examination (MMSE; Folstein, Folstein, & McHugh, 1975), which is a useful tool for screening of different types of organic brain dysfunction, does not seem useful for the diagnosis of

FTD. Patients with a typical clinic of FTD may achieve a normal score on MMSE (Gregory & Hodges, 1996; Miller et al., 1991). The score on MMSE does not truly reflect the FTD patient's competence, due to motivational and behavioral factors (Jagust, Reed, Seab, Kramer, & Budinger, 1989; Pasquier, 1996). "Rotations" of test items in 45–180 deviation from the presented pattern were significantly more common in AD than in FLD (Johanson & Hagberg, 1989), and Neary showed better preserved spatial and practical abilities in FTD in spite of the patient's lack of strategy and self-criticism. Elfgren, Passant, and Risberg (1993), in a factor-analytic approach, described three different levels of cognitive impairment in FTD accompanied by corresponding levels of reduced cerebral blood flow in frontotemporal areas. The lack of correlation between the cognitive impairment level and illness duration indicates a considerable individual variation in the clinical course and the difficulty in recognizing clinical onset in FTD (Elfgren et al., 1993).

Elfgren, in a recent study (Elfgren, Ryding, & Passant, 1996), also showed highly significant correlations between a global impairment score and relative blood flow in lateral and medial frontal and left orbital frontal areas, measured with single photon emission computerized tomography (SPECT). Moreover, verbal fluency scores correlated highly significantly with left lateral frontal, medial frontal, and left anterior inferior temporal blood flow. The reduced verbal fluency in FTD seems related to a lack of strategies to generate words (Pasquier et al., 1995). They did not, however, find significant differences between FTD and AD in verbal letter fluency and verbal category tests while Frisoni et al. (1995) reported poorer verbal fluency in FTD compared to AD.

SOMATIC FINDINGS

There are few pathological somatic findings in FLD and Pick's disease, whereas in MNDD, symptoms of frontal lobe dysfunction may appear early and even precede neurological features such as fasciculations, muscular wasting, dysarthria, and dysphagia. The presence of grasp, pout, and other primitive reflexes may contribute to the clinical diagnosis while extrapyramidal signs appear at a late stage. EEG may remain normal even when dementia is evident (Johannesson, Brun, Gustafson, & Ingvar, 1977; Rosén, Gustafson, & Risberg, 1993) and epileptic seizures, especially myoclonus are rare. Quantitative EEG mapping and repeated EEG recordings may strongly improve the differential diagnosis between FTD and AD (Rosén, 1997; Yener et al., 1995). Normal EEG is also prevalent in MNDD (Neary et al., 1990; Talbot et al., 1995). Low blood pressure and orthostatic blood pressure drops were found in more than 50% of unmedicated FTD cases with a similar prevalence also reported in AD and vascular dementia patients of similar age (Passant, Warkentin, & Gustafson, 1997). In that study, hypertension and heart disease were found only in AD and vascular dementia. Urinary incontinence that appears late in uncomplicated AD was reported early in about 50% of our FTD cases. This is probably due to the frontal lobe involvement because incontinence is also a common feature in vascular dementia and AD with lesions in the frontobasal cortex and the anterior cingulate gyrus (Andrew & Nathan, 1964; Wilson & Chang, 1974). Endocrine functions in FTD are mainly normal, although thyroid hormone abnormalities are rather common in FTD (38%) compared to AD (9%) (Fäldt, Passant, Nilsson, Wattmo, & Gustafson, 1996). There are no simple explanations for these somatic findings, although the prefrontal and anterior cingulate cortex seem to have important effects on autonomic and endocrine functions (Devinsky, Morell, & Vogt, 1995).

BRAIN IMAGING

Cortical atrophy, with more or less focal accentuation, was shown with computer tomography (CT) and magnetic resonance imaging (MRI) in Pick's disease and FLD, but the findings are often nonconclusive with important overlap with findings in normals. The anterior–posterior gradient of atrophic changes may however contribute to the differentiation from AD (Förstl et al., 1994, 1996; Gustafson et al., 1989; Knopman et al., 1989). The recognition of vascular lesions in frontal gray and white matter and subcortical strategical infarcts are important because such lesions may cause dementia of a frontal lobe type (Frisoni et al., 1996; Brun & Gustafson, 1991; Miller et al., 1991). Brain imaging may also contribute to differential diagnosis between FTD and Huntington's disease (Kuhl et al., 1982; Mazziotta, 1989).

The rapid development of functional imaging of brain metabolism and blood flow has radically improved recognition and differential diagnosis of dementing diseases. The frontotemporal abnormalities in FLD and Pick's disease were shown with rCBF measurements with the Xenon-clearance technique (Gustafson et al., 1977; Risberg, 1987; Risberg & Gustafson, 1997) and with SPECT (Jagust et al., 1989; Kitamura, Araki, Sakamotot, Ilio, & Terashi, 1990; Miller et al., 1995; Pasquier et al., 1997; Talbot, Snowden, Lloyd, Neary, & Testa, 1995). This was also shown with positron emission tomography (PET) in Pick's disease (Friedland et al., 1993; Kamo et al., 1987; Salmon & Franck, 1989), in progressive supranuclear palsy (D'Antona et al., 1985), and in MMND (Ludolph et al., 1993). SPECT studies of PA often show predominant left-hemisphere frontal pathology (Neary et al., 1993). The flow pathology in FTD is, however, not disease specific but also found in vascular brain damage, Creutzfeldt–Jakob disease, and AD with frontal accent (Brun & Gustafson, 1991). Activation with frontal lobe sensitive tests during the rCBF measurement may improve the detection of frontotemporal lobe dysfunction (Warkentin & Passant, 1997).

DIFFERENTIAL DIAGNOSIS

Differential diagnosis of FTD on one hand and AD and other dementias on the other hand is often possible using well-defined clinical criteria, neuropsychological testing, and brain imaging techniques. The differences between FTD and AD are most clear at an early stage of the disease. The initial stage of FTD is dominated by emotional and personality changes and progressive reduction of speech, but memory failure, severe dyspraxia, and spatial disorientation develop comparatively late in consequence with a relative sparing of the temporoparietal occipital cortical areas. By contrast, early-onset AD is characterized by memory failure, dyspraxia, and impaired visuospatial ability, whereas habitual personality traits, social competence, and insight are better preserved in agreement with the predominant temporoparietal and temporal limbic cortical involvement and sparing of frontal areas.

Vascular brain damage may also mimic FTD. Patients with frontal SIWI often display psychiatric features of frontal lobe type (Brun & Gustafson, 1991; Englund, Brun, & Gustafson, 1989) and, as in PSVE, the dementia may develop gradually or stepwise with emotional lability, periods of euphoria and low mood, apathy, psychomotor retardation, and various psychotic features (Fredriksson, Brun, & Gustafson, 1992). Differential diagnosis of FTD against Huntington's disease and Creutzfeldt–Jakob disease may be critical when personality changes and psychotic features prevail and the neurological characteristics are less obvious. Patients with progressive supranuclear palsy may also show a frontal lobe metabolic and symptom pattern (D'Antona et al., 1985) as well as progressive subcortical gliosis (Neumann & Cohn, 1967). This rare disease has become increasingly important because linkage studies suggest a relation to chromosome 17 (Petersen et al., 1995).

The Lund–Manchester consensus (1994) is recommended as a guideline for clinical recognition of FTD (see appendix). In our clinical work we use a combination of three diagnostic assessment scales for recognition of AD, FTD (Brun & Gustafson, 1993; Gustafson & Nilsson, 1982), and vascular dementia (Hachinski, Ischemic Score, Hachinski et al., 1975). Diagnoses based on the scoring profile in these diagnostic rating scales have been validated against rCBF findings, neuropathological diagnoses, EEG, and CSF findings (Brun & Gustafson, 1988; Risberg & Gustafson, 1988; Rosén et al., 1993; Edvinsson et al., 1993).

Most guidelines for diagnosis of dementia, such as the NINCDS–ADRDA criteria for diagnosis of AD (McKhann et al., 1984), may easily also include FLD and Pick's disease. The revised third edition of the *Diagnostic and Statistical Manual of Mental Disorders* (DSM-III-R; American Psychiatric Association, 1987) presents Pick's disease without further diagnostic guidelines, whereas DSM-IV (American Psychiatric Association, 1994) introduces Pick's disease as "one of the pathologically distinct etiologies associated with frontotemporal brain atrophy." The 10th edition of *The International Classification of Diseases* (World Health Organization, 1992) describes "dementia in Pick's disease" as a slowly progressive dementia, commencing in middle life, with predominance of frontal lobe features and selective atrophy of the frontal and temporal lobes and without the pathological changes of AD.

FTD is a group of dementias with a common pattern of cortical and clinical pathology and increasing evidence of underlying genetic factors. From the clinical point of view, FTD stands out as a diagnostic and therapeutic challenge. The early diagnosis is a prerequisite for adequate treatment and care. The long duration of the disease has a strong impact on the family, which needs professional support through the many difficult years. The clinical picture in FTD shows a wide spectrum of mental and behavioral disorders: schizophrenia, mood disorder, mania, hypochondriasis, obsessive–compulsive disorder, and sociopathical behavior, probably strongly related to the involvement of prefrontal, anterior temporal, and anterior cingulate cortex. Many clinical and experimental studies (Devinsky et al., 1995) show the central role of the anterior cingulate gyrus in the executive system involved in emotions and cognition, social interaction, vocalization, mimical movements, and responses to pain, and our observations strongly support such ideas. The clinical dissimilarity between FTD and AD is in accordance with the almost contrary topographic degenerative patterns in these two major degenerative dementias. This is also valid for the cingulate gyrus, its anterior part (area 24) being involved in FTD and its posterior part (area 23) in AD. This difference was also shown *in vivo* with PET (Minoshima, Norman, & Kuhl, 1994; Kumar, Schapiro, Haxby, Grady, & Friedland, 1990). The importance of the frontal association cortex and its connections to anterior limbic structures in "functional" mental diseases such as schizophrenia (Ingvar & Franzen, 1974; Sabri et al., 1997) has to be considered in the search for etiology and therapeutic strategies in FTD.

APPENDIX: Clinical Diagnostic Features of Frontotemporal Dementia (Abbreviated). Consensus Statement by the Research Groups in Lund and Manchester

Core Diagnostic Features

Behavioral Disorder

Insidious onset and slow progression
Early loss of personal and social awareness
Early loss of insight
Early signs of disinhibition (such as unrestrained sexuality, violent behavior, inappropriate jocularity, restless pacing)
Mental rigidity and inflexibility
Stereotyped and perseverative behavior (wandering, clapping, singing, as well as hoarding of objects and rituals involving hygiene and dressing)
Hyperorality (oral/dietary changes, overeating, food fads, excessive smoking and alcohol consumption, oral exploration of objects)
Distractibility, impulsivity, and impersistence
Utilization behavior (unrestrained exploration/use of objects in the environment)

Affective Symptoms

Depression, anxiety, excessive sentimentality, suicidal ideation, delusion (early and evanescent)
Hypochondriasis, bizarre somatic preoccupation (early and evanescent)
Emotional unconcern and remoteness, lack of empathy
Amimia (inertia, aspontaneity)

Speech Disorder

Progressive reduction and stereotypy of speech
Echolalia and perseveration
Late mutism

Preserved Spatial Skills and Praxis

(Intact abilities to negotiate the environment)

Physical Signs

Early primitive reflexes
Early incontinence
Late akinesia, rigidity, and tremor
Low and labile blood pressure

Investigations

Normal EEG despite clinically evident dementia
Brain imaging (structural and/or functional): predominant frontal and/or anterior temporal abnormality

Neuropsychology: profound failure on "frontal lobe" tests in the absence of severe amnesia, aphasia, or perceptual spatial disorder

Supportive Diagnostic Features

Onset before 65
Positive family history or similar disorder in a first-degree relative
Bulbar palsy, muscular weakness and wasting, fasciculations (motor neuron disease)

REFERENCES

American Psychiatric Association. (1987). *Diagnostic and statistical manual of mental disorders* (3rd ed., rev.). Washington, DC: Author.

American Psychiatric Association. (1994). *Diagnostic and statistical manual of mental disorders* (4th ed.). Washington, DC: Author.

Andrew, J., & Nathan, P. W. (1964). Lesions of the anterior frontal lobes and disturbances of micturition and defeacation. *Brain, 87,* 232–262.

Basun, H., Almqvist, O., Axelman, K., Brun, A., Campbell, T. A., Collinge, J., Forsell, C., Froelich, S., Wahlund, L. O., Wetterberg, L., & Lannfelt, L. (1997). Clinical characteristics of a family with chromosome 17-linked rapid by progressive frontotemporal dementia. *Archives of Neurology, 54,* 539–544.

Blennow, K., Wallin, A., Agren, H., Spenger, C., Sigfrid, J., & Vanmechelen, E. (1996). Tau protein in cerebrospinal fluid: A biochemical marker for axonal degeneration in Alzheimer's disease? *Molecular Chemical Neuropathology, 26,* 231–245.

Brown, V., Asworth, A., Gydesen, S., Soranden, A., Rossor, M., Hardy, D., & Colinge, J. (1995). Familial nonspecific dementia maps to chromsome 3. *Human Molecular Genetics, 4*(9), 1625–1628.

Brun, A. (1965). The subpial granular layer of the fetal cerebral cortex in man: its ontogeny and significance in congenital malformations. *Acta Pathologica Microbiologica Scandinavica*(Suppl. 179), 1–98.

Brun, A. (1987). Frontal lobe degeneration of non-Alzheimer type: I. Neuropathology. *Archives of Gerontology and Geriatrics, 6,* 193–208.

Brun, A. (1993). Frontal lobe degeneration of non-Alzheimer type revisited. *Dementia, 4,* 126–131.

Brun, A., & Englund, E. (1981). Regional pattern of degeneration in Alzheimer's disease: Neuronal loss and histopathological grading. *Histopathology, 5,* 549–564.

Brun, A., & Englund, E. (1986). A white matter disorder in dementia of the Alzheimer type: A pathoanatomical study. *Annals of Neurology, 19,* 253–262.

Brun, A., Englund, B., Gustafson, L., Passant, U., Mann, D. M. A., Neary, D., & Snowden, J. S. (1994). Clinical and neuropathological criteria for frontotemporal dementia. *Journal of Neurology, Neurosurgery and Psychiatry, 57,* 416–418.

Brun, A., Fredriksson, K., & Gustafson, L. (1992). Pure subcortical arteriosclerotic encephalopathy (Binswanger's disease). A clinicopathologic study. Part II: Pathological features. *Cerebrovascular Diseases, 2,* 87–92.

Brun, A., & Gustafson, L. (1978). Limbic lobe involvement in presenile dementia. *Archiv für Psychiatrie und Nervenkrankheiten, 226,* 79–93.

Brun, A., & Gustafson, L. (1988). Zerebrovaskuläre erkrankungen. In K. P. Kisker, H. Lauter, J. E. Meyer, C. Muller, & E. Stromgren (Eds.), *Psychiatrie der Gegenwart, band 6, Organishe Psychosen* (pp. 253–295). Heidelberg: Springer-Verlag.

Brun, A., & Gustafson, L. (1991). Psychopathology and frontal lobe involvement in organic dementia. In K. Iqbal, D. R. C. McLachlan, B. Winbald, & H. M. Wisniewski (Eds.), *Alzheimer's disease: Basic mechanisms, diagnosis, and therapeutic strategies* (pp. 27–33). London: Wiley.

Brun, A., & Gustafson, L. (1993). I. The Lund longitudinal dementia study: A 25-year perspective on neuropathology, differential diagnosis and treatment. In B. Corain, M. Nicolini, B. Winblad, H. Wisniewski, & P. Zatta (Eds.), *Alzheimer's disease: Advances in clinical and basic research* (pp. 4–18). New York: Wiley.

Brun, A., Liu, X., & Erikson, S. (1995). Synapse loss and gliosis in the molecular layer of cerebral cortex in Alzheimer's disease and frontal lobe degeneration. *Neurodegeneration, 4,* 171–177.

Burns, A., Jacoby, R., & Levy, R. (1990). Psychiatric phenomena in Alzheimer's disease. I: Disorders of thought content. *British Journal of Psychiatry, 157,* 72–76.

Clark, A. W., White, C. L. III, Manz, J. H., Parhad, I. I., Curry, B., Whitehouse, P. J., Lehman, L., & Cole, J. T. (1986). Primary degenerative dementia without Alzheimer pathology. *Canadian Journal of Neurological Science, 13,* 462–470.

Collinge, J., Hardy, J., Brown, J., & Brun, A. (1994). Familial Pick's disease and dementia in frontal lobe degeneration of non-Alzheimer type are not variants of prion disease. *Journal of Neurology, Neurosurgery and Psychiatry, 57,* 762.

D'Antona, R., Baron, J. C., Samson, Y., Serdaru, M., Viader, F., Agid, Y., & Cambier, J. (1985). Subcortical dementia. *Brain, 108,* 785–799.

Delay, J., Neveu, P., & Desclaux, P. (1944). Les dissolutions du langage dans la maladie de Pick. *Revue Neurologique, 76,* 37–38.

Devinsky, O., Morrell, M. J., & Vogt, B. A. (1995). Contributions of anterior cingulate cortex to behaviour. *Brain, 118,* 279–306.

Divac, I. (1972). Neostriatum and functions of prefrontal cortex. *Acta Neurobiologie Experimentalis (Warsz.), 32,* 461–477.

Edvinsson, L., Minthon, L., Ekman, R., & Gustafson, L. (1993). Neuropeptides in cerebrospinal fluid of patients with Alzheimer's disease and dementia with frontotemporal lobe degeneration. *Dementia, 4,* 167–171.

Elfgren, C., Brun, A., Gustafson, L., Johanson, A., Minthon, L., Passant, U., & Risberg, J. (1994). Neuropsychological tests as discriminators between dementia of Alzheimer type and frontotemporal dementia. *International Journal of Geriatric Psychiatry, 9,* 635–642.

Elfgren, C., Gustafson, L., Johanson, A., Minthon, L., Passant, U., Risberg, J. (1991). Cognitive function in dementia of Alzheimer type and in frontal lobe dementia related to regional cerebral blood flow. *Journal of Cerebral Blood Flow and Metabolism, 11*(2), 176.

Elfgren, C., Passant, U., & Risberg, J. (1993). Neuropsychological findings in frontal lobe dementia. *Dementia, 4,* 214–219.

Elfgren, C., Ryding, E., & Passant, U. (1996). Performance on neuropsychological tests related to Single Photon Emission Computerised Tomography findings in frontotemporal dementia. *British Journal of Psychiatry, 169,* 416–422.

Englund, E., & Brun, A. (1987). Frontal lobe degeneration of non-Alzheimer type II: White matter changes. *Archives of Gerontology Geriatrics, 6,* 235–243.

Englund, E., Brun, A., & Gustafson, L. (1989). A white-matter disease in dementia of Alzheimer's type—clinical and neuropathological correlates. *International Journal of Geriatric Psychiatry, 4,* 87–102.

Escourolle, R. (1958). *La maladie de Pick: Etude critique d'ensamle et synthèse anatomoclinique.* Paris: Foulon.

Eslinger, P. J., Warner, G. C., Grattan, L. M., & Easton, J. D. (1991). "Frontal lobe" utilization behavior associated with paramedian thalamic infarction. *Neurology, 41,* 450–452.

Esmonde, T., Giles, E., Xuereb, J., & Hodges, J. (1996). Progressive supranuclear palsy presenting with dynamic aphasia. *Journal of Neurology, Neurosurgery, and Psychiatry, 60,* 403–410.

Fäldt, R., Passant, U., Nilsson, K., Wattmo, C., & Gustafson, L. (1996). Prevalence of thyroid hormone abnormalities in elderly patients with symptoms of organic brain disease. *Aging— Clinical and Experimental Research, 8,* 347–353.

Farrer, L. A., Abraham C. R., Volicer, L., Foley, E. J., Kowall, N. W., McKee, A. C., & Wells, J. M. (1995). Allele ε4 of apolipoprotein E shows a dose effect on age at onset of Pick disease. *Experimental Neurology, 136,* 162–170.

Ferrer, I., Roig, C., Espino, A., Peiro, G., & Matias Guiu, X. (1991). Dementia of frontal lobe type and motor neuron disease: A Golgi study of the frontal cortex. *Journal of Neurology and Psychiatry, 54,* 932–934.

Folstein, M. F., Folstein, S. E., & McHugh, P. R. (1975). "Mini-Mental State": A practical method for grading the cognitive state of patients for the clinician. *Journal of Psychiatric Research, 12,* 189–198.

Förstl, H., Besthorn, C., Hentschel, F., Geiger-Kabisch, C., Sattel, H., & Schreiter-Gasser, U. (1996). Frontal lobe degeneration and Alzheimer's disease: Clinical findings, volumetric brain changes and quantitative electroencephalography data. *Dementia, 7,* 27–34.

Förstl, H., Hentschel, F., Besthorn, C., Geiger-Kabisch, C., Sattel, H., Schreiter-Gasser, U., Bayerl, J. R., Schmitz, F., & Schmitt, H. P. (1994). Frontal und temporal beginnende Hirnatrophie. *Nervenarzt, 65,* 611–618.

Foster, N. L., Wilhelmsen, K., Sima, A. A. F., Jones, M. Z., D'Amato, C., & Gildman, S. (in press). Frontotemporal dementia and parkinsonism linked to chromosome 17: A consensus. *Annals of Neurology, 41,* 706–715.

Francis, P. T., Holmes, C., Webster, M. T., Stratmann, G. C., Procter, A. W., & Bowen, D. M. (1993). Preliminary neurochemical findings in non-Alzheimer dementia due to lobar atrophy. *Dementia, 4,* 172–177.

Fredriksson, K., Brun, A., & Gustafson, L. (1992). Pure subcortical arterioslecortic encephalopathy (Binswanger's disease): A clinicpathologic study. Part 1: Clinical features. *Cerebrovascular Disease, 2,* 82–86.

Friedland, R. P., Koss, E., Lerner, A., Hedera, P., Ellis, W., Dronkers, N., Ober, B. A., & Jagust, W. J. (1993). Functional imaging, the frontal lobes, and dementia. *Dementia, 4,* 188–191.

Frisoni, G. B., Beltramello, A., Geroldi, C., Weiss, C., Bianchetti, A., & Trabucchi, M. (1996). Brain atrophy in frontotemporal dementia. *Journal of Neurology, Neurosurgery, and Psychiatry, 61,* 157–165.

Frisoni, G. B., Calabresi, L., Geroldi, C., Bianchetti, A., D'Acquarica, A. L., Govoni, S., Sirtori, C. R., Trabucchi, M., & Franceschini, G. (1994). Apolipoprotein E ε4 allele in Alzheimer's disease and vascular dementia. *Dementia, 5,* 240–242.

Frisoni, G. B., Pizzolato, G., Geroldi, C., Rossato, A., Bianchetti, A., & Trabucchi, M. (1995). Dementia of the frontal type: neuropsychological and (^{99}Tc)-HM-PAO SPET features. *Journal of Geriatric Psychiatry and Neurology, 8,* 42–48.

Gilbert, J. J., Kish, S. J., Chan, L.-J., Morito, C., Shammak, K., & Hornykiewicz, O. (1988). Dementia, parkinsonism and motor neuron disease: Neurochemical and neuropathological correlates. *Neurology, 24,* 688–691.

Green, J., Morris, J. C., Sandson, J., McKeel, D. W., & Miller, J. W. (1990). Progressive aphasia: A precursor of global dementia? *Neurology, 40,* 423–429.

Gregory, C. A., & Hodges J. R. (1996). Frontotemporal dementia: Use of consensus criteria and prevalence of psychiatric features. *Neuropsychiatry, Neuropscychology, and Behavioral Neurology, 9,* 145–153.

Gregory, C. A., Orrell, M., Sahakian, B., & Hodges J. R. (1997). Can frontotemporal demenita and Alzheimer's disease be differentiated using a brief battery of tests? *International Journal of Geriatric Psychiatry, 12,* 375–383.

Groen, J. J., & Endtz, L. J. (1982). Hereditary Pick's disease: Second re-examination of a large family and discussion of other hereditary cases, with particular references to electroencephalography and computerized tomography. *Brain, 105,* 443–459.

Guiraud, P. (1956). *Psychiatrie clinique.* Paris, 553–550.

Gustafson, L. (1987). Frontal lobe degeneration of non-Alzheimer type. II. Clinical picture and differential diagnosis. *Archives of Gerontology and Geriatrics, 6,* 209–233.

Gustafson, L. (1993). Clinical picture of frontal lobe degeneration of non-Alzheimer type. *Dementia, 4,* 143–148.

Gustafson, L., Abrahamsson, M., Grubb, A., Nilsson, K., & Fex, G. (1997). Apolipoprotein E genotyping in Alzheimer's disease and frontotemporal dementia. *Dementia and Geriatric Cognitive Disorders, 8,* 240–243.

Gustafson, L., Brun, A., Cronqvist, S., Dalfelt, G., Risberg, J., Riesenfeld, V., & Rosén, I. (1989). Regional cerebral blood flow, MRI, and BEAM in Alzheimer's disease. *Journal of Cerebral Blood Flow and Metabolism, 9*(Suppl. 7), 513.

Gustafson, L., Brun, A., & Ingvar, D. H. (1977). Clinical neurocirculatory findings in presenile dementia, related to neuropathological changes. *Activitas Nervosa Superior, 19*, 351–353.

Gustafson, L., & Nilsson, L. (1982). Differential diagnosis of presenile dementia on clinical grounds. *Acta Psychiatrica Scandinavica, 65*, 194–209.

Gustafson, L., & Risberg, J. (1992). Deceptions and delusions in Alzheimer's disease and frontal lobe dementia. In C. Katona & R. Levy (Eds.), *Delusions and hallucinations in old age* (pp. 218–229). London: Gaskell.

Hachinski, V. C., Iliff, L. D., Zilhka, E., du Boulay, G. H., McAllister, V. L., Marhsall, J., Ross Russel, R. W., & Symon L. (1975). Cerebral blood flow in dementia. *Archives of Neurology, 32*, 632–637.

Hashimoto, R., Yoshida, M., & Tanaka, Y. (1995). Utilization behaviour after right thalamic infarction. *European Neurology, 35*, 58–62.

Hansen, L. A., Deteresa, R., Tobias, H., Alford, M., & Terry, R.D. (1988). Neocortical morphometry and cholinergic neurochemistry in Pick's disease. *American Journal of Pathology, 131*, 507–528.

Heutink, P., Stevens, M., Rizzu, P., Bakker, E., Kros, J. M., Tibben, A., Niermeijer, M. F., van Duijn, C. M., Oostra, B. A., & van Swieten, J. C. (1997). Hereditary frontotemporal dementia is linked to chromosome 17q21–q22: A genetic and clinicopathological study of three Dutch families. *Annals of Neurology, 41*, 150–159.

Ingvar, D. H., & Franzén, G. (1974). Abnormalities of cerebral blood flow distribution in patients with chronic schizophrenia. *Acta Psychiatrica Scandinavica, 50*, 425–462.

Ishii, N., Nishihara, Y., & Imamura, T. (1986). Why do frontal lobe symptoms predominate in vascular dementia with lacunes? *Neurology, 36*, 340–345.

Jagust, W. J., Reed, B. R., Seab, J. P., Kramer, J. H., & Budinger, T. F. (1989). Clinical-physiologic correlations of Alzheimer's disease and frontal lobe dementia. *American Journal of Physiological Imaging, 4*, 89–96.

Johannesson, G., Brun, A., Gustafson, L., & Ingvar, D. H. (1977). EEG in presenile dementia related to cerebral blood flow and autopsy findings. *Acta Neurologica Scandinavica, 56*, 89–103.

Johanson, A., Gustafson, L., & Risberg, J. (1986). Behavioral observations during performance of the WAIS block design test related to abnormalities of regional cerebral blood flow in organic dementia. *Journal of Clinical and Experimental Neuropsychology, 8*, 201–209.

Johanson, A., & Hagberg, B. (1989) Psychometric characteristics in patients with frontal lobe degeneration of non-Alzheimer type. *Archives of Gerontology and Geriatrics, 8*, 129–137.

Kamo, H., McGeer, P. L., Harrop, R., McGeer, E. G., Calne, D. B., Martin, W. R., & Pate, B. D. (1987). Positron emission tomography and histopathology in Pick's disease. *Neurology, 37*, 439–445.

Kanazawa, I., Kwak, S., Sasaki, H., Muramoto, O., Mizutani, T., Hori, A., & Nukina, N. (1988). Studies on neurotransmitter markers of the basal ganglia in Pick's disease, with special reference to dopamine reduction. *Journal of Neurological Science, 83*, 63–74.

Kertesz, A., Hudson, L., Mackenzie, I. R. A., & Munoz, D. (1994). The pathology and nosology of primary progressive aphasia. *Neurology, 44*, 2066–2072.

Kitamura, S., Araki, T., Sakamotot, S., Ilio, M., & Terashi, A. (1990). Cerebral blood flow and cerebral oxygen metabolism in patients with dementia of frontal lobe type. *Rinsho Shinkeigaku, 30*, 1171–1175.

Klüver, H., & Bucy, P. C. (1938). An analysis of certain effects of bilateral temporal lobectomy in the rhesus monkey, with special reference to "psychic blindness." *Journal of Psychology, 5*, 33–54.

Knopman, D. S., Christensen, K. J., Schut, L. J., Harbaugh, R. E., Reeder, T., Ngo, T., & Frey, W. (1989). The spectrum of imaging and neuropsychological findings in Pick's disease. *Neurology, 39*, 362–368.

Knopman, D. S., Mastri, A. R., Frey, W. H., Sung, J. H., & Rustan, T. (1990). Dementia lacking distinctive histologic features: A common non-Alzheimer degenerative dementia. *Neurology, 40,* 251–256.

Kuhl, D. E., Phelbs, M. E., Markham, C. H., Metter, E. J., Riege, W. H., & Winter, J. (1982). Cerebral metabolism and atrophy in Huntington's disease determined by [18]FDG and computed tomographic scan. *Annals of Neurology, 12,* 425–434.

Kumar, A., Schapiro, M. B., Haxby, J. V., Grady, C. L., & Friedland, R. P. (1990). Cerebral metabolic and cognitive studies in dementia with frontal lobe behavioral features. *Journal of Psychiatric Research, 24*(2), 97–109.

Lebert, F., Pasquier, F., & Petit, H. (1995). Personality traits and frontal lobe dementia. *International Journal of Geriatric Psychiatry, 10,* 10476–1049.

Lhermitte, F., Pillon, B., & Serdaru, M. (1986). Human autonomy and the frontal lobes. Part I: Imitation and utilization behavior: A neuropsychological study of 75 patients. *Annals of Neurology, 19,* 326–334.

Liu, X., & Brun, A. (1996). Regional and laminar synaptic pathology in frontal lobe degeneration of non-Alzheimer type. *International Journal of Geriatric Psychiatry, 2,* 47–55.

Lopez, O. L., Becker, J. T., & De Kosky, S. T. (1994). Dementia accompanying motor neuron disease. *Dementia, 5,* 42–47.

Lopez, O. L., Gonzales, M. P., Becker, J. T., Reynolds, C. F., Sudilovsky, A., & DeKosky, S. T. (1996). Symptoms of depression of psychosis in Alzheimer's disease and frontotemporal dementia. *Neuropsychiatry, Neuropsychology, and Behavioral Neurology, 9,* 154–161.

Luauté, J. P., Favel, P., Remy, C., Sanabria, E., & Bidault, E. (1994). Troubles de l'humeur et démence de type frontal: Hypothèse d'un rapport pathologénique. *L'Encéphale, 20,* 27–36.

Ludolph, A. C., Langen, K. J., Regard, M., Herzog, H., Kemper, B., Kuwert, T., Böttger, I. G., & Feinendegen, L. (1993). Frontal lobe function in amyotrophic lateral sclerosis: A neuropsychologic and positron emission tomography study. *Acta Neurologica Scandinavica, 85,* 81–89.

Mazziotta, J. C. (1989). Huntington's disease: Studies with structural imaging techniques and positron emission tomography. *Seminars in Neurology, 9,* 360–369.

McKhann, G., Drachman, D., Folstein, M., Katzman, R., Price, D., & Stadlan, E. M. (1984). Clinical diagnosis of Alzheimer's disease: Report of the NINCDS–ADRDA Work Group under the auspices of the Department of Health and Human Services Task Force on Alzheimer's Disease. *Neurology, 34,* 939–944.

Mesulam, M. M. (1982). Slowly progressive aphasia without generalized dementia. *Annals of Neurology, 11,* 592–598.

Miller, B. L., Chang, L., Mena, I., Boone, K., & Lesser, I. M. (1993). Progressive right frontotemporal degeneration: Clinical, neuropsychological and SPECT characteristics. *Dementia, 4,* 204–213.

Miller, B. L., Cummings, J. L., Villanueva-Meyer, J., Boone, K., Mehringer, C. M., Lesser, I. M., & Mena, I. (1991). Frontal lobe degeneration: Clinical, neuropsychological and SPECT characteristics. *Neurology, 42,* 1374–1382.

Miller, B. L., Itti, L., Li, J., Darby, A. I., Booth, R., Chang, L., & Mena, I. (1995). Atrophy-corrected cerebral blood flow in frontotemporal dementia. *Facts and Research in Gerontology,* 93–103.

Minoshima, S., Norman, L. F., & Kuhl, D. (1994). Posterior cingulate cortex in Alzheimer's disease. *Lancet, 344,* 895.

Minthon, L., Edvinsson, L., Ekman, R., & Gustafson, L. (1990). Neuropeptide levels in Alzheimer's disease and dementia with frontotemporal degeneration. *Journal of Neurological Transmission, 30,* 57–67.

Mitsuyama, Y. (1993). Presenile dementia with motoneuron disease. *Dementia, 4,* 137–142.

Morita, K., Kaiya, H., Ikeda, T., & Namba, M. (1987). Presenile dementia combined with amyotrophy. A review of 34 Japanese cases. *Archives of Gerontology and Geriatrics, 6,* 263–277.

Nauta, W. J. H. (1973). Connections of the frontal lobe with the limbic system. In L. V. Laitinen & K. E. Livingston (Eds.), *Surgical approaches in psychiatry* (pp. 303–314). Lancaster: Medical and Technical Publishing.

Neary, D., Snowden, J. S., & Mann, D. M. A. (1990). Frontal lobe dementia and motoneuron disease. *Journal of Neurology, Neurosurgery, and Psychiatry, 53,* 23–32.

Neary, D., Snowden, J. S., & Mann, D. M. A. (1993). The clinic pathological correlates of lobar atrophy. *Dementia, 4,* 154–159.

Neary, D., Snowden, J. S., Northen, B., & Goulding, P. J. (1988). Dementia of frontal lobe type. *Journal of Neurology, Neurosurgery, and Psychiatry, 51,* 353–361.

Neumann, M. A., & Cohn, R. (1967). Progressive subcortical gliosis: A rare form of presenile dementia. *Brain, 90,* 405–418.

Pachana, N. A., Brauer-Boone, K., Miller, B. L., Cummings, J. L. & Berman, N. (1996). Comparison of neuropsychological functioning in Alzheimer's disease and frontotemporal dementia. *Journal of the International Neuropsychological Society, 2,* 505–510.

Pasquier, F. (1996). Neuropsychological features and cognitive assessment in frontotemporal dementia. In D. Paquier, F. Lebert, & P. Scheltens (Eds.), *Frontotemporal denebtua* (pp. 46–69). Netherlands: ICG Publ.

Pasquier, F., Lebert, F., Grymonprez, L., & Petit, H. (1995). Verbal fluency in dementia of frontal lobe type and dementia of Alzheimer type. *Journal of Neurology, Neurosurgery, and Psychiatry, 58,* 81–84.

Pasquier, F., Lebert, F., Lavenu, I., Jacob, B., Steinling, M., & Petit, H. (1997). The use of SPECT in a multidisciplinary memory clinic. *Dementia and Geriatric Cognitive Disorders, 8,* 85–91.

Passant, U., Gustafson, L., & Brun, A. (1993). Spectrum of frontal lobe dementia in a Swedish family. *Dementia, 4,* 160–162.

Passant, U., Warkentin, S., & Gustafson, L. (1997). Orthostatic hypotension and low blood pressure in organic dementia: A study of prevalence and related clinical characteristics. *International Journal of Geriatric Psychiatry, 12,* 395–403.

Petersen, R. B., Tabaton, M., Chen, S. G., Monari, L., Richardson, S. L., Lynch, T., Menetto, V., Lanska, D., & Markesbery, W. R. (1995). Familial progressive subcortical gliosis. Presence of prions and linkage to chromosome 17. *Neurology, 45,* 1062–1067.

Pickering-Brown, S. M., Siddons, M., Mann, D. M. A., Owen, E., Neary, D., & Snowden, J. S. (1995). Apolipoprotein E allelic frequencies in patients with lobar atrophy. *Neuroscience Letters, 188,* 205–207.

Risberg, J. (1987). Frontal lobe degeneration of non-Alzheimer type. III. Regional cerebral blood flow. *Archives of Gerontology and Geriatrics, 6,* 225–233.

Risberg, J., & Gustafson, L. (1988). Regional cerebral blood flow in psychiatric disorders. In S. Knezevic, V. A. Maximilian, Z. Mubrin, I. Prohovnik, & J. Wade (Eds.), *Handbook of regional cerebral blood flow* (pp. 219–240). Hillsdale, NJ: Erlbaum.

Risberg, J., & Gustafson, L. (1997). Regional cerebral blood flow measurements in the clinical evaluation of demented patients. *Dementia and Geriatric Cognitive Disorders, 8,* 92–97.

Rosén, I. (1997). Electroencephalography as a diagnostic tool in dementia. *Dementia and Geriatric Cognitive Disorders, 2,* 110–116.

Rosén, I., Gustafson, L., & Risberg, J. (1993). Multichannel EEG frequency analysis and somatosensory-evoked potentials in patients with different types of organic dementia. *Dementia, 4,* 43–49.

Sabri, O., Erkwoh, R., Schreckenberger, M., Owega, A., Sass, H., & Buell, U. (1997). Correlation of positive symptoms exclusively to hyperperfusion or hypoperfusion of cerebral cortex in never-treated schizophrenics. *Lancet, 349,* 1735–1739.

Salmon, E., & Franck, G. (1989). Positron emission tomographic study in Alzheimer's disease and Pick's disease. *Archives of Gerontology and Geriatrics, 1,* 241–247.

Schallice, T., Burgess, P. W., Schon, F., & Baxter, D. M. (1989). The origins of utilization behaviour. *Brain, 112,* 1587–1598.

Schneider, C. (1927). Über Picksche Krankheit. *Monatsschrift Psychiatrie und Neurologie, 65,* 230–275.

Sima, A. A. F., Defendini, R. D., Koehande, D., D'Amato, C., Foster, N. L. Parchi, P., Gambetti, P., Lynch, T., & Wilhelmsen, K. C. (1996). The neuropathology of chromosome 17-linked dementia. *Annals of Neurology, 39,* 734–744.

Sjören, T., Sjören, H., & Lindgren, A. G. H. (1952). Morbus Alzheimer and morbus Pick: A genetic clinical and patho-anatomical study. *Acta Psychiatrica et Neurologica Scandinavica, 82,* 1–152.

Snowden, J. S., & Neary, D. (1993). Progressive language dysfunction and lobar atrophy. *Dementia, 4,* 226–231.

Snowden, J. S., Neary, D., & Mann, D. M. A. (1996). *Frontotemporal lobar degeneration: Frontotemporal dementia, progressive aphasia, semantic dementia.* Edinburgh, New York: Churchill Livingstone.

Snowden, J. S., Neary, D., Mann, D. M. A., Goulding, P. J., & Testa, H. J. (1992). Progressive language disorder due to lobar atrophy. *Annals of Neurology, 31,* 174–183.

Talbot, P. R., Goulding, P. J., Lloyd, J. J., Snowden, J. S., Neary, D., & Testa, H. J. (1995). The inter-relationship between "classical" motor neurone disease and frontotemporal dementia: A neuropsychological and single photon emission tomographic study. *Journal of Neurology, Neurosurgery, and Psychiatry, 58,* 541–547.

Talbot, P. R., Snowden, J. S., Lloyd, J. J., Neary, D., & Testa, H. J. (1995). The contribution of single photon emission tomography to the clinical differentiation of degenerative cortical brain disorders. *Journal of Neurology, 242*(9), 579–586.

van Mansvelt, J. (1954). *Pick's disease. A syndrome of lobar, cerebral atrophy; its clinico-anatomical and histopathological types.* Master's thesis. Enschede, Utrecht.

van Swieten, J. C., Stevens, M., de Knijff, P., van Duijn, C. M. (1996). A genetic-epidemiological study of frontal lobe dementia in the Netherlands. *Neurobiology of Aging, 17,* 556.

Vermersch, P., Bodet, R., Ledoze, F., Ruchoux, M.-M., Chapon, F., Thomas, P., Destee, A., Lechevallier, B., & Delacourte, A. (1995). Mise en évidence d'un profil particulier de protéines Tau pathologiques dans les cas de démences fronto-temporales. *Neuroscience, 318,* 439–445.

Warkentin, S., & Passant, U. (1997). Functional imaging of the frontal lobes in organic dementia. Regional cerebral blood flow findings in normals, in patients with frontotemporal dementia and in patients with Alzheimer's disease, performing a word fluency test. *Dementia and Geriatric Cognitive Disorders, 8,* 105–109.

Wikström, J., Paetau, A., Palo, J., Sulkava, R., & Haltia, M. (1982). Classic amyotrophic lateral sclerosis with dementia. *Archives of Neurology, 39,* 681–683.

Wilhelmsen, K., Lynch, T., Pavlou, G., Higgins, M., & Nygaard, T. (1994). Localization of disinhibition-dementia-parkinsonism-amyotrophy complex to chromosome 17 q21–22. *American Journal of Human Genetics, 55,* 1159–1165.

Wilson, D. H., & Chang, A. E. (1974). Bilateral anterior cingulectomy for the relief of intractable pain (report of 28 patients). *Contina Neurologica, 36,* 61–68.

World Health Organization. (1992). *The ICD-10 classification of mental and behavioural disorders. Clinical descriptions and diagnostic guidelines.* Geneva: Author.

Yener, G. G., Leuchter, A. F., Jenden, D., Read, S. L., Cummings, J. L., & Miller, B. L. (1996). Quantitative EEG in frontotemporal dementia. *Clinical Electroencephalography, 27*(2), 61–68.

21

Vascular Diseases of the Frontal Lobes

HELENA CHUI
LEE WILLIS

CONTENT AND ORGANIZATION

The anatomical and functional boundaries of the frontal lobes are not coextensive. Topographically, the frontal lobes are defined as the cerebral cortex and underlying white matter located anterior to the central sulcus. Functionally, the frontal lobes are interconnected with multimodal association and limbic cortices, as well as the basal ganglia and thalamus, which technically lie outside of the frontal lobes. It can be argued that it is more meaningful to consider the frontal lobes as an integral part of several larger functional networks. A lesion in any part of the network may give rise to similar clinical and behavioral syndromes. For example, akinetic mutism, although classically associated with bilateral infarction of the anterior cingulate gyri, may also emerge following lacunar infarction of the head of the caudate (Mendez, Adams, & Lewandoski, 1989) or the thalamus (Park-Matsumoto et al., 1995). Hence, in this chapter, rather than limit ourselves to cortical anatomical demarcations, we consider the larger functional systems.

Because the frontal cortices constitute approximately half of the cerebral mantle, vascular lesions commonly affect the frontal lobes. The frontal lobes are largely supplied by two of the three major pairs of intracerebral arteries. The medial and medial–orbital sides of the frontal lobes are nourished by the anterior cerebral artery (ACA) (see Figure 21.1), while the dorsolateral and lateral–orbital portions are fed by the middle cerebral artery (MCA) (see Figure 21.2). However, deep midline structures, which are intimately connected with the frontal cortex, receive their blood supply from other sources, including penetrating arteries that emanate from the Circle of Willis, as well as the posterior cerebral artery (PCA) and basilar arteries (see Figure 21.3).

The frontal cortices are the keystones of numerous distributed networks, including those related to movement, motivation, emotion, and higher intellectual function. Also, the subcortical basal forebrain is an integral component of the medial temporal–

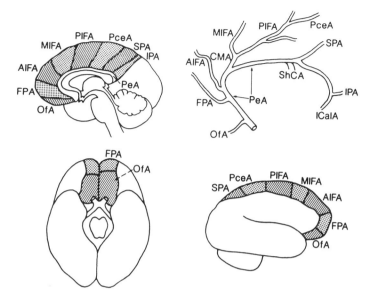

FIGURE 21.1. Distribution of the distal anterior cerebral artery. From Weir (1987, p. 324). Copyright 1987 by Bruce Weir. Reprinted by permission.

diencephalic memory circuit. The anatomical connections of frontal lobe networks are outlined in detail in earlier sections of this book. In this chapter, we focus on the details of the vascular systems that supply some of these frontal lobe networks, the pathophysiological changes that may disrupt blood flow, and the clinical disturbances that consequently ensue.

FUNCTIONAL NEUROANATOMY AND CORRESPONDING VASCULAR SUPPLY

From a heuristic, oversimplified point of view, the frontal cortex may be divided into four major anatomical-functional components. Lying immediately anterior to the central sulcus, the motor and premotor cortices play a pivotal role in motor control. Further anteriorly, the prefrontal cortex can be divided into three sectors: The medial prefrontal cortex relates to motivation and initiation, the orbital frontal cortex mediates social and emotional behavior, and the dorsolateral prefrontal cortex subserves higher-order analysis, planning, and execution. Disturbances associated with damage to prefrontal cortex are frequently referred to as "frontal lobe" syndromes.

An extraordinarily complex network of interconnections underlie frontal lobe function. The motor cortex gives origin to a long-descending efferent pathway (i.e., the pyramidal or corticospinal tract) that initiates and directs movement. This pathway begins in the motor cortex, funnels via the corona radiata into the posterior limb of the internal capsule, passes through the midbrain cerebral peduncles and the basis pontis, crosses to the opposite side in the medullary pyramids, and descends in the lateral corticospinal tracts to synapse on motor neurons in the anterior horn of the spinal cord. A vast array of intrahemispheric, interhemispheric, and cortical–subcortical networks interconnect the

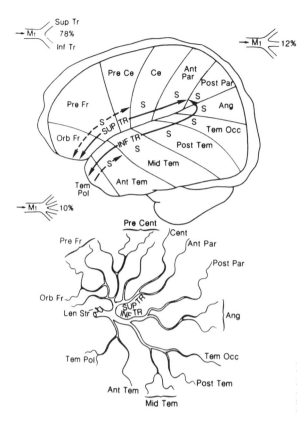

FIGURE 21.2. Distribution of the distal middle cerebral artery. From Weir (1987, p. 328). Copyright 1987 by Bruce Weir. Reprinted by permission.

frontal lobes with paralimbic and posterior multimodal association areas, as well as basal ganglia and thalamus to provide the substrate for balanced motor, emotional and intellectual response. A distinctly organized circuit, which subserves declarative or secondary memory, connects the hippocampus and amygdala in the medial temporal lobes with diencephalic nuclei but also involves the basal forebrain, anterior cingulate, and orbital cortices of the frontal lobes.

The vascular supply for these distributed networks is complex, with tributaries sometimes originating from widely separated arterial trunks and branches (Figure 21.3). In the discussion that follows, a certain degree of interpolation has been involved in identifying the corresponding vascular supply (see Figure 21.4). Detailed information about anatomical connectivity is derived largely from work in nonhuman primates (G. E. Alexander, DeLong, & Strick, 1986), whereas information about the blood supply comes from studies of humans (Pullicino, 1993; Schlesinger, 1976; Stephens & Stilwell, 1969).

Corticobasal Ganglia–Thalamocortical Loops

Segregated, but parallel, corticobasal ganglia–thalamocortical pathways have been tentatively identified in nonhuman primates for each of the major functional divisions (i.e., motor, motivational, emotional, and cognitive) of frontal cortex (G. E. Alexander & Crutcher, 1990; G. E. Alexander et al., 1986). A somatotopical organization is maintained throughout each functional circuit. Each circuit contains multiple, partially overlapping

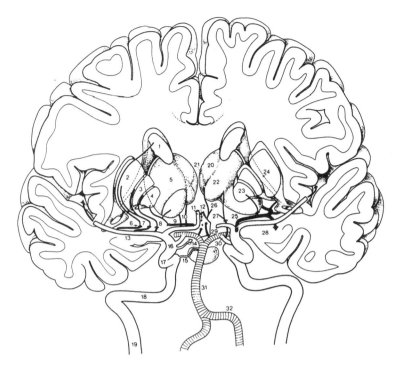

FIGURE 21.3. Frontal view of the central arteries from the carotid and vertebral–basilar system. 1, caudate nucleus; 2, putamen; 3, external globus pallidus (Gpe); 4, internal globus pallidus (Gpi); 5, thalamus; 6, anterior perforated substance; 7, lateral lenticulostriate arteries; 8, medial lenticulostriate arteries; 9, recurrent artery of Heubner; 10, perforating arteries of the anterior cerebral artery; 11, anterior cerebral artery (ACA); 12, posterior perforated substance; 13, sphenoid portion of the middle cerebral artery (M1 portion of the MCA); 14, superior hypophyseal artery; 15, inferior hypophyseal artery; 16, intracranial portion of the internal carotid artery; 17, cavernous portion of the internal carotid artery; 18, petrous portion of the internal carotid artery; 19, cervical portion of the internal carotid artery; 20, dorsomedial thalamic nucleus; 21, medial thalamic nucleus; 22, anterior thalamic nucleus; 23, internal globus pallidus (Gpi); 24, tail of the caudate nucleus; 25, anterior choroidal artery (AChA); 26, paramedian thalamic artery; 27, tuberothalamic artery; 28, amygdala; 29, posterior cerebral artery (PCA); 30, posterior communicating artery; 31, basilar artery; 32, vertebral artery. From Nieuwenhuys, Voogd, and van Huijzen (1983, p. 41). Copyright 1983 by Springer-Verlag. Reprinted by permission.

corticostriate inputs to striatum, which become progressively integrated as they pass through the pallidum or substantia nigra pars reticulata (SNr) to restricted areas of the thalamus and then back to a single cortical area. The cortical areas which project to striatum within a given functional loop are functionally related and usually interconnected. Thus, the circuits integrate and converge or "funnel" information from multiple-related cortical areas back to a single primary cortical area. In this way, the primary cortical area becomes part of a closed feedback loop, whereas the secondary cortical areas contribute to part of an open loop.

Motor Circuit

Multiple somatotypically organized circuits reciprocally connect motor, premotor, and supplementary motor cortical areas with striatum, substantia nigra, and thalamic nuclei

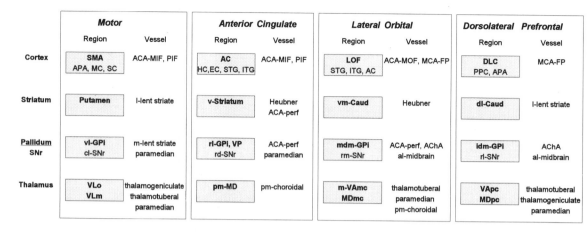

FIGURE 21.4. Blood supply of the cortical basal ganglia thalamo-cortical circuits. AC, anterior cingulate; ACA, anterior cerebral artery; ACA-MIF, anterior cerebral artery middle internal frontal; ACA-MOF, anterior cerebral artery medial orbital frontal; ACA-PIF, anterior cerebral artery posterior internal frontal; AChA, anterior choroidal artery; APA, arcuate premotor area; Caud, caudate; cl, caudolateral; dl, dorsolateral; DLC, dorsolateral prefrontal cortex; EC, entorhinal cortex; GPi, globus pallidus internus; HC, hippocampal cortex; ITG, inferior temporal gyrus; ldm, lateral dorsomedial; LOF, lateral orbitofrontal cortex; m, medial; MC, motor cortex; MCA-FP, middle cerebral artery frontopolar artery; MDmc, medialis dorsalis magnocellularis; MDpc, medialis dorsalis pars cellularis; mdm, medial dorsomedial; l, lateral, lent, lenticulostrate; perf, perforator; pm, posteromedial; PPC, posterior parietal cortex; rd, rostrolateral; rl, rostrolateral; rm, rostromedial; SC, somatosensory cortex; SMA, supplementary motor area; SNr, substantia nigra pars reticulata; STG, superior temporal gyrus; VAmc, ventralis anterior pars magnocellularis; VApc, ventralis anterior pars cellularis; VLm, ventralis lateralis pars medialis; VLo, ventralis lateralis pars oralis; vm, ventromedial. Based partly on G. E. Alexander, DeLong, and Strick (1986, p. 364).

(G. E. Alexander & Crutcher, 1990). Lesions at any of these sites may disrupt complex motor behaviors. Even the most elementary motor function (e.g., force generation) appears to result from the action of distributed cortical–subcortical circuitry (Kunesch, Binkofski, Steinmetz, & Freund, 1995). Reciprocal connections between parietal association areas, prefrontal, and anterior cingulate cortices (Goldman-Rakic, 1988) provide the basis for a distributed network underlying motor performance when guided by intrinsic or extrinsic sensory input.

The motor basal ganglia-thalamocortical circuit is involved in the control of movement speed and amplitude, and possibly in the programming and initiation of internally generated movement. In the motor circuit, corticostriate projections originate from the supplementary motor area, lateral arcuate premotor area, primary motor and somatosensory cortices (Brodmann's areas 6, 4, and 3,1,2). Cortical areas located on the mesial side of the cerebral hemisphere are supplied by branches from the ACA (posterior internal frontal branch), while those situated on the dorsolateral side are perfused by branches of the MCA (precentral and central branches) (Figure 21.4). Axons from these cortical areas terminate primarily in the putamen (which is supplied by the lateral lenticulostriate arteries emanating from the middle cerebral artery) (Figures 21.3, 21.4, and 21.5). Neurons in the putamen project to the ventrolateral two-thirds of both the internal and external segments of the globus pallidus (which are fed by medial lenticulostriate arteries) and to the caudolateral portions of the SNr (which are fed by anterolateral branches coming off the basilar artery). Output from the pallidum and SNr project to the oral part of the ventrolateral nucleus of the thalmus (VL-o) (which is supplied by the thalamotuberal and thalamogeniculate arteries). Finally, VL-o projects back to the supplementary motor area. Thus, disturbances of blood flow in the proximal or distal branches of the ACA and MCA, and also branches of the Circle of Willis and proximal branches of the PCA, may impact various components of the motor circuit.

Anterior Cingulate Limbic Circuit

A "limbic" circuit has been identified that is connected in a closed loop with the anterior cingulate gyrus (area 24). Other corticostriate contributions to this circuit originate in the hippocampus, amygdala, and other limbic and paralimbic areas (entorhinal, perirhinal, temporal pole, superior, and inferior temporal gyri and posterior medial orbitofrontal area [Brodmann's areas 24, 28, 38, 22, 20, 11]) These iso- and allocortical areas send projections to the ventral striatum (i.e., nucleus accumbens) (supplied anteriorly by the recurrent artery of Heubner and posteriorly by other perforating branches from the ACA).

The anterior cingulate gyrus plays an important role in attending and responding to the motivational content of internal and external stimuli (Devinsky, Morrell, & Vogt, 1995). In nonhuman primates, experimental ablations of both anterior cinguli are associated with hypokinesia and social indifference (Smith, 1944). Ablation of unilateral anterior cingulate gyrus results in contralateral motor neglect (Watson, Heilman, Cauthen, & King, 1973). In humans, infarction of bilateral anterior cingulate gyri (which is supplied by the middle internal and posterior internal frontal branches of the ACA) is associated with diminished emotional response and drive (Nielsen & Jacobs, 1951). Few data are available in the primate literature about the behavioral consequences of lesions in the ventral striatum. However, Mesulam and Geschwind (1978) have proposed that the nucleus accumbens may be part of a limbic-inferior parietal cicuit concerned with attention.

The ventral striatum projects to the rostrolateral internal globus pallidus and the ventral pallidum (also supplied by perforating branches of the ACA), as well as the rostrodorsal SNr. In turn, these nuclei project on the posterior medial portion of the medial dorsal (MD) nucleus of the thalamus (fed by the posterior medial choroidal artery coming off the proximal PCA). Finally, the MD projects back on the anterior cingulate area. Thus, the limbic corticobasal ganglia–thalamocortical loop may be affected by altered blood flow in proximal and distal branches of the ACA, or proximal branches of the PCA. It is notable that the branches of the MCA do not contribute a significant blood supply to the principal components of the limbic circuit.

Orbital Limbic Circuit

A lateral orbital limbic circuit in nonhuman primate comprises corticostriate projections from the lateral orbitofrontal cortex (Brodmann's area 10) (supplied by the orbital frontal branches from the ACA and MCA), as well as auditory and visual association cortices in the temporal lobes (areas 22 and 37). The functional nature of this circuit is not well-characterized. In animals, bilateral lesions restricted to the lateral orbitofrontal cortex result in perseverative responses (Mishkin & Manning, 1978), impairments in visual recognition (Bachevalier & Mishkin, 1986), and visual discrimination learning (Voytko, 1985). In humans with bilateral lesions in orbital and orbital–mesial frontal regions, Damasio, Tranel, and Damasio (1991) demonstrated impaired autonomic responses to emotionally charged visual stimuli. They postulate that underactivation of somatic markers may contribute to psychopathic behavior, while overactivation may lead to obsessive–compulsive behavior.

Corticobasal ganglia projections from lateral orbitofrontal cortex terminate in the ventromedial sector of the head of the caudate (supplied by the recurrent artery of Heubner coming from the proximal ACA). The ventromedial caudate projects to the medial dorsomedial internal pallidum (supplied by the anterior choroidal artery and by perforators from the ACA), as well as rostromedial SNr. Projections continue to the medial portions of the ventral anterior (VA) nucleus of the thalamus (fed by the thalamotuberal artery) and the magnocellular portion of the medial dorsal (MD-mc) nucleus of the thalamus (supplied jointly by the thalamotuberal, paramedian thalamic, and posterior medial choroidal arteries). Finally, the thalamic nuclei project back to the lateral orbital frontal cortex. The lateral orbital circuit is thus vulnerable to impaired perfusion in perforating arteries coming from proximal ACA and PCA, as well as the carotid, posterior communicating, and basilar arteries. In addition, the lateral orbital frontal cortex itself might be selectively damaged by a strategic occlusion of the orbital frontal branches of the ACA or MCA.

Dorsolateral Prefrontal Circuit

In primates, the dorsolateral prefrontal circuit originates from and converges back upon the cortex around the principal sulcus (Brodmann's areas 9 and 10) (supplied by precentral branches of the MCA). Secondary contributions arise from multimodal association areas in the posterior parietal cortex and arcuate premotor areas, which are involved in the analysis of motion and space. Monkeys with lesions in dorsolateral prefrontal cortex are impaired in delayed-spatial alternation tasks (Goldman-Rakic, 1988; Goldman-Rakic & Friedman, 1991), which require the ability to retain in working memory the location of a target over time. Humans with prefrontal lesions are impaired in free recall, temporal sequencing, and manipulating memories (Shimamura, Janowsky, & Squire, 1991). Shallice and Burgess (1991) identify the dorsolateral prefrontal cortex as an essential component of a supervisory attentional system, which regulates selection among contentious choices. They postulate that this supervisory or executive system is normally required for planning and decision making, error correction or troubleshooting, in novel, dangerous, or technically difficult situations or in overcoming strong habitual or tempting responses. It would appear that the dorsolateral frontal network creates a work area for assembling, analyzing, and manipulating multiple actual as well as imagined contingencies over time and space.

Corticostriate fibers in the dorsolateral prefrontal circuit terminate in the dorsolateral head of the caudate (supplied by the lateral lenticulostriates coming from the proximal MCA). The circuit continues its topographic projection onto the lateral dorsomedial portion of the internal segment of the globus pallidus (supplied by the anterior choroidal artery), as well as the rostrolateral SNr, and then on to two thalamic nuclei: the ventral anterior pars parvocellularis (VA-pc) and the medial dorsal pars parvocellularis (MD-pc) thalamic nuclei (which are jointly supplied by the thalamotuberal, thalamogeniculate, and paramedian thalamic arteries). To complete the loop, these thalamic nuclei project back on the dorsolateral prefrontal cortex. Like the motor circuit, the dorsolateral circuit depends on the MCA for its blood supply, as well as on deep penetrating arteries. For the dorsolateral circuit, these include the anterior choroidal artery and arteries near the posterior Circle of Willis.

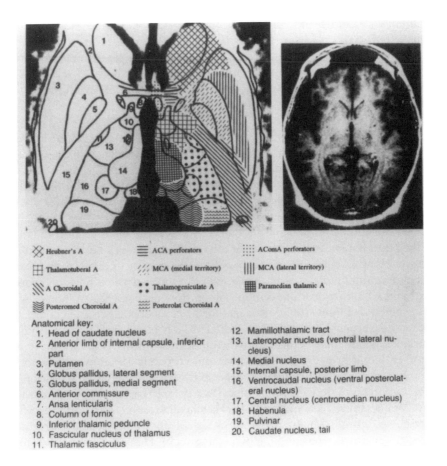

Anatomical key:

1. Head of caudate nucleus
2. Anterior limb of internal capsule, inferior part
3. Putamen
4. Globus pallidus, lateral segment
5. Globus pallidus, medial segment
6. Anterior commissure
7. Ansa lenticularis
8. Column of fornix
9. Inferior thalamic peduncle
10. Fascicular nucleus of thalamus
11. Thalamic fasciculus
12. Mamillothalamic tract
13. Lateropolar nucleus (ventral lateral nucleus)
14. Medial nucleus
15. Internal capsule, posterior limb
16. Ventrocaudal nucleus (ventral posterolateral nucleus)
17. Central nucleus (centromedian nucleus)
18. Habenula
19. Pulvinar
20. Caudate nucleus, tail

FIGURE 21.5. Axial schematic through the midthalamus showing the vascular supply of the basal ganglia and thalamus. From Pullicino (1993, p. 47). Copyright 1993 by Raven Press. Reprinted by permission.

Medial Temporal Limbic–Diencephalic Memory System

The basal forebrain represents a relatively small but strategic component of the medial temporal limbic–diencephalic memory system. These nuclei include the septal nuclei, nucleus of the diagonal band (Broca), and nucleus basalis of Meynert (fed by perforating arteries from the ACA and anterior communicating artery). They are interconnected with the hippocampus and amygdala (supplied by the anterior choroidal artery), critical areas for declarative memory and learning. The hippocampus is connected via the fornix to the septal nuclei, mammillary bodies, and the anterior nucleus of the thalamus (supplied by the tuberothalamic artery). The anterior thalamic nucleus projects in turn to the anterior cingulate gyrus (Papez, 1937). The basolateral amygdala is connected via the ventral amygdalofugal projection to the basal forebrain and then to the lateral preoptic and hypothalamic areas (Carpenter & Sutin, 1983). Other fibers enter the inferior thalamic peduncle and project to the magnocellular part of the medial dorsal nucleus of the thalamus (MD-mc) (which is jointly supplied by the thalamotuberal, thalamogeniculate, and paramedian thalamic arteries). This thalamic nucleus projects in turn to orbital frontal cortex. Thus, the declarative memory system is interlinked with other frontal–

subcortical circuits and depends in part on blood supply from arteries originating from or near the anterior and posterior Circle of Willis.

PATHOPHYSIOLOGY OF VASCULAR DISEASE

Risk Factors for Stroke

Cerebrovascular disease causes brain injury by two basic, non-mutually exclusive, pathophysiological mechanisms, namely, ischemia and hemorrhage. In addition, several anatomical patterns of brain injury are recognized: large or small arterial border zone, and venous. Risk factors, prevention, and treatment differ, depending on the pathophysiological mechanisms involved. Due to lack of space, neither disorders of the venous system nor treatment issues are covered in this chapter.

Ischemia refers to conditions where blood flow is insufficient to meet the metabolic needs of the brain tissue. Autoregulatory mechanisms maintain a fairly constant cerebral blood flow, as long as mean perfusion pressure falls between certain limits (i.e., 50 to 120 mm Hg in normal individuals) (Lassen, 1959). Once perfusion pressure drops below the lower limits of autoregulation, cerebral blood flow declines. When blood flow drops to approximately 17 ml/min/100 g, neuronal membranes depolarize and clinical dysfunction appears (Sharbrough, Messick, & Sundt, 1973). If blood flow is promptly restored, normal brain function may return, and the clinical diagnosis is a "transient ischemic attack." When blood flow diminishes below approximately 10 ml/min/100 g for greater than 30 minutes, neuronal membranes degenerate irreversibly causing neuronal death and cerebral infarction (Heiss, 1983). Clinically, a completed "stroke" or cerebrovascular accident (CVA) is said to have occurred. Focal ischemia results from occlusion of a single blood vessel. A more global pattern of ischemia follows systemic disturbances in circulation (e.g., cardiac arrest and hypovolemic shock). Here, the most vulnerable brain areas are the border zones located at the far reaches of the major cerebral arteries and the periventricular deep white matter where the long-penetrating arterioles end (Bogousslavsky & Regli, 1986; Mounier-Vehier et al., 1994; Mull, Schwarz, & Thron, 1997; Torvik, 1984). In the United States and Europe, roughly 80% of strokes are due to brain ischemia.

Hemorrhage refers to the rupture of blood vessels walls and the extravasation of blood into the brain parenchyma (intracerebral hemorrhage, or ICH), subarachnoid space (subarachnoid hemorrhage, or SAH), or into the subdural, extradural, or ventricular spaces. Saccular aneurysms, arteriovenous malformations, and amyloid angiopathy generally weaken the walls of the larger cerebral arteries, whereas chronic hypertension weakens the walls of smaller penetrating arteries. Hemorrhage in the subarachnoid space may produce secondary ischemia by increasing extravascular tissue pressure or by causing vasospasm; both result in decreased perfusion pressure. In the United States and Europe, approximately 20% of strokes are due to hemorrhage. Intracerebral hemorrhage is twice as common as subarachnoid hemorrhage. In Japan, the percentage of strokes due to hemorrhage is higher, because of an increased incidence of ICH.

Stroke or brain injury due to cerebrovascular disease is the third leading cause of death in most industrialized countries. According to the American Heart Association (1994), there are 3 million survivors of stroke in the United States and nearly 500,000 new strokes each year. The incidence of stroke increases exponentially with age, particularly in elderly persons. In Rochester, Minnesota, the incidence rate increased 10% per year of age after age 60. Between 1980–1984, the age- and sex-adjusted average annual incidence of stroke was 102 per 100,000, overall, and 572/100,000 in persons 60–74 years of age (Broderick, Phillips, Whisnant, O'Fallon, & Begstrahl, 1989). In North Manhattan, the incidence rate is significantly higher among Asians and African Americans, compared to Caucasians or Hispanics (Sacco, Hauser, & Mohr, 1991).

The major risk factors for stroke are similar, regardless of which lobe of the brain is involved. Age is the strongest risk factor for stroke. Some other risk factors are modifiable: atrial fibrillation, hypertension, cardiac disease, diabetes mellitus, smoking, alcoholism, and hyperlipidemia (Prospective Studies Collaboration, 1995; Sacco, 1994; Schoenberg & Schulte, 1988; Tell, Crouse, & Fuberg, 1988; Wolf, D'Agostino, Belanger, & Kannel, 1991). The effect size of each risk factor often differs for large versus small arteries. Hyperlipidemia and smoking primarily accelerate atherosclerosis of the larger arteries, and hypertension also increases arteriolar sclerosis in small vessels. Diabetes mellitus enhances atherogenesis in both large and small arteries (Caplan, 1996). Cardiac emboli associated with atrial fibrillation tend to lodge in the early branches of the larger arteries (Feinberg et al., 1990; Wolf, Dawber, Thomas, & Kannel, 1978). Meningitis (e.g., due to neurosyphilis, neurocysterercosis, tuberculosis, and bacteria) is most commonly associated with small vessel arteritis (Levy, Lillehei, Rubinstein, & Stears, 1995; Muller, Merkelbach, Huss, & Schimrigk, 1995). Coagulopathies may predispose to either thrombosis (protein S deficiency, activated protein C resistance) or bleeding (Factor VIII, X deficiencies). During the past two decades, the death rate due to stroke has declined by 60%, probably due in part to the early detection of risk factors and the institution of appropriate preventive measures (Higgins, 1993).

Stroke and the Frontal Lobes

By virtue of its relative mass and proportionate blood flow, the frontal lobe is frequently the site of infarcts. The distribution of infarcts, by location and subtype, varies depending on the demographic characteristics of the sample and the sophistication of the workup. Approximately 20–30% of hemispheric infarcts are small lacunes in the territory of deep-penetrating arteries, 60% fall into the distribution of either the MCA or ACA, and 15% fall in the distribution of the PCA (Lindgren, Norrving, Rudling, & Johannson, 1994). Lacunar infarcts usually result from occlusion of small penetrating arteries. In roughly 20–30% of cases, the infarct is attributed to a cardiogenic source. Emboli from the heart tend to lodge in the anterior circulation: about 60% in the MCA, 20% in the ACA, and 20% in the PCA territory (Wijdicks & Jack, 1996). Roughly 15% of large vessel strokes are attributed to thromboembolism from atherosclerotic extracranial or intracranial arteries (Lindgren et al., 1994; Sacco, 1994). In approximately one-third of cases, the cause of the infarct cannot be determined with confidence. When one considers that (1) occlusion of the ACA virtually always affects the frontal lobe, (2) occlusion of the MCA affects the frontal lobes in the majority of instances, and (3) occlusion of a small penetrating artery usually involves a frontal–subcortical circuit, the frontal lobe or its networks are damaged in well over half of all ischemic strokes.

Intraparenchymal hemorrhage frequently affects frontal lobe structures. Approximately 50% are located in the basal ganglia or thalamus, 40% lobar, 10% cerebellar, and 5% brainstem. The most common risk factor for ICH is hypertension, which is found in approximately 75% of patients, regardless of race or gender (Broderick, 1994). Chronic hypertension accelerates arteriolar sclerosis, a progressive degeneration of smooth muscle cells in the media of small arteries. Arteriolar sclerosis not only narrows the blood vessel lumen (thereby increasing the likelihood of lacunar infarction) but also weakens the wall and leads to the formation of small (0.2 to > 1 mm) miliary aneurysms (thereby increasing the risk of hemorrhage) (Charcot & Bouchard, 1868). Although hypertension is typically associated with hemorrhages in deep brain structures, it also increases the risk for lobar hemorrhages. Cerebral amyloid angiopathy (CAA) is the second most common cause of ICH in the elderly. In CAA, the characteristic site of hemorrhage is lobar, often with extension into the subarachnoid space. In a review of the literature, Vinters (1987) noted that 35% of 107 hemorrhages due to nonfamilial CAA were located in the frontal lobes.

Finally, subarachnoid hemorrhage from ruptured scaccular aneurysms also have a predlilection for the frontal lobes (Fox, 1983). Stehbens (1972) analyzed the location of intracranial saccular aneurysms in 5267 cases, reported in seven clinical series between 1952 and 1967. Most aneurysms (85% to 95%) were located at major branch sites from the anterior Circle of Willis: internal carotid in 38%, ACA in 31%, and MCA in 20%. The most common sites were at the bifurcation of the intracranial carotid, the carotid origin of the posterior communicating artery (PComA) or the anterior choroidal artery, the first 3 cm of the MCA, and the region of the anterior communicating artery (ACoA). Thus, the frontal lobe is at disproportionate risk following rupture of saccular aneurysms from either dissection of blood into the brain parenchyma itself or ischemia associated with vasospasm of nearby arteries.

CLINICAL LITERATURE

For several reasons, It is not possible to make one-to-one correlations between cerebrovascular disease, structural anatomy, and clinical behavior. First, anatomically contiguous areas may belong to distinct functional systems; thus, disruption of blood flow at different points along an arterial tree may be associated with a variety of behavioral disturbances. Various combinations of behavioral, intellectual, motor, or sensory disturbance are seen with lesions of either the anterior or middle cerebral artery, depending on the site of blood flow disturbance. Clinical lesions are not limited to single anatomical units but often encroach on neighboring structures. Second, functional systems are often widely distributed in space; thus, similar behavioral symptoms may arise when blood supply is disrupted in completely different arterial systems. For example, weakness may result when either the anterior or middle cerebral artery and either a large cortical or deep penetrating branch is affected. Third, anatomical units, particularly those located in the deeper portions of the brain, may receive their supply from multiple arteries (e.g., the head of the caudate is supplied by perforating arteries from both the ACA and MCA; the dorsomedial nucleus of the thalamus is supplied by the thalamotuberal, paramedian, and posterior choridal arteries). Identification of the vessel involved may be difficult, particularly when a small artery is involved. Fourth, there are individual variations in the anatomical development of the arterial tree. For example, in some individuals, the right and left ACA or the right and left paramedian artery may arise from a common root. A review of these complex interrelations could be approached from a vascular, brain, or behavioral perspective.

In this chapter, we would have preferred to maintain a vascular approach. However, where deeper brain structures and smaller arteries are concerned, this becomes difficult. In such situations, the clinical literature approaches the subject primarily from an anatomical rather than a vascular point of view. With these limitations in mind, we review the behavioral disturbances associated with vascular disease affecting the large and small arteries of the anterior circulation (i.e., ACA and MCA), as well as some of the small arteries of the posterior circulation. For larger arteries, we use a vascular approach; for smaller arteries, we switch to an anatomical approach.

LARGE ARTERIES AND CORTICAL STROKES

Anterior Cerebral Artery

Vascular Anatomy

The ACA supply the anterior four-fifths of the corpus callosum as well as the anterior and medial portions of the basal forebrain, basal ganglia, and cerebral hemispheres. The proximal A1 segment (average diameter = 2.6 mm, average length = 13 mm) originates from the intracranial carotid artery and gives rise to several small perforating arteries, including the recurrent artery of Heubner (Weir, 1987). These small arteries supply the tuberculum olfactorium, septal nuclei, medial portion of the globus pallidus internus, ventromedial head of the caudate, anterior third of the putamen, and anterior limb of the internal capsule (Critchley, 1930; Pullicino, 1993). A single short ACoA joins the right and left ACA in 74% of cases, with variations including rare absence in the remaining cases (Krayenbühl & Yasargil, 1968). The ACA distal to the ACoA arches around the genu and over the body of the corpus callosum. From its concave side, the ACA gives origin to numerous short twigs which supply the genu and body of the corpus callosum, septum pellucidum, medial anterior commissure, and anterior pillars of the fornix. From its convex side, the ACA gives rise to approximately eight major branches (e.g., orbitofrontal, frontopolar, anterior internal frontal, middle internal frontal, posterior internal frontal, paracentral, superior internal parietal, and inferior internal parietal branches) which supply the medial surface and 2.5 cm deep into the adjacent white matter of the frontal and parietal lobes. Thus, all but the most distal two of the eight centrifugal branches of the ACA supply key structures of the frontal lobe or components of frontal–subcortical circuits.

Vascular Disease

Major branch points around the Circle of Willis represent sites of predilection for the development of saccular or Berry aneurysms; approximately 25% of saccular aneurysms are found at the ACoA (Weir, 1987). Infarction in the distribution of the ACA results most commonly from vasospasm following rupture of an aneursym taking origin from the ACoA (Greene et al., 1995). ACA strokes may occur as a consequence of local narrowing or hypoplastic changes (Kazui, Sawada, Naritomi, Kuriyama, & Yamaguchi, 1993), and less frequently from cardiac emboli.

Clinical Syndromes

Distinct clinical syndromes are noted when the ACA is occluded unilaterally at successive points along its course (Critchley, 1930). Proximal occlusion of the ACA, including Heubner's artery and the ACoA, results in hemiplegia involving both the arm and the leg, sensory loss of the distal leg, ipsilateral deviation of the eyes, ideomotor apraxia of the left side of the body, some degree of cognitive impairment, and aphasia (if the lesion is in the dominant hemisphere). When occlusion is limited to Heubner's artery, weakness predominantly affects the arm, face, and bulbar musculature (with irritability, forgetfulness, and some emotional incontinence). On the other hand, when occlusion occurs distal to Heubner's artery and the ACoA, weakness and sensory loss predominantly affect the leg. Regardless of the side of the lesion, the left arm may become apraxic due to callosal disconnection. The arm contralateral to the lesion, while maintaining good power, may exhibit forced grasping and groping (so-called alien hand). Forced grasping is not seen, when occlusion of the main trunk occurs distal to the origin of the posterior internal frontal artery.

Crural Predominant Weakness

Occlusion of ACA distal to the ACoA leads to greater weakness in the leg compared to the arm (i.e., crural predominant weakness). In a series of 12 cases, when the lesion involved the medial precentral gyrus, medial premotor cortex, and supplementary motor area (SMA), the pattern of weakness in the leg was greater distally than proximally, and recovery of function was poor (Schneider & Gautier, 1994). When the precentral gyrus was spared, the leg weakness appeared to be greater proximally than distally and recovery was better. Crural paresis due to infarction in the ACA may also be associated with homolateral ataxia (Moulin et al., 1995).

Akinetic Mutism

Bilateral occlusion of the ACA supplying the medial frontal cortex, particularly the anterior cingulate gyri and supplementary motor area, is associated with decreased spontaneous speech and body movement. In the extreme form of akinetic mutism, the patient is alert and able to follow stimuli with his or her eyes but otherwise shows little or no speech or body movements (Barris & Schuman, 1953; Cummings, 1993; Nielsen & Jacobs, 1951). Akinetic mutism is observed when both ACA are occluded (Freemon, 1971) or in the rare (4%) anomalous condition where a single A1 segment, which feeds both hemispheres, is occluded (Borggreve, de Deyn, Marien, Cras, & Dierckx, 1994).

Milder forms of diminished emotional and motor responsiveness may follow unilateral damage to the anterior cingulate and supplementary area (Damasio & Van Hoesen, 1983) or to various combinations of cortical and subcortical components in the "limbic" frontal–basal ganglia–thalamic circuit. Mochizuki and Saito (1990) described motor neglect of the left extremities with lesions in the right superior mesial prefrontal, supplementary, and motor cortices. Meador, Watson, Bowers, and Heilman (1986) described a patient with decreased and slowed motion (hypokinesia and bradykinesia) as well as reduced range of motion (hypometria) in the contralateral limbs following right mesial frontal lobe hemorrhage. Degos, da Fonseca, Gray, and Cesaro (1993) reported a woman who became docile and emotionally unconcerned following ischemic lesions in left anterior cingulate and right head of caudate. Akinesia and mutism may also follow damage to basal ganglia and thalamus (see below).

Alien Hand

In the alien hand syndrome, the patient perceives loss of control over or alienation from one or both upper extremities. The "alien" limb will not do the patient's bidding and may even undo the desired actions of the other limb. Feinberg, Schindler, Flanagan, and Haber (1992) defined two alien hand syndromes: One due to frontal release of spontaneous exploratory movements of the dominant hand coupled with nondominant hemisphere inhibition; the other resulting from callosal disconnection and intermanual conflict. In the frontal release variety, Feinberg proposed that damage to frontal components (cingulate gyrus, Brodmann's area 8, and supplementary motor cortex) release exploratory grasping and groping behaviors generated in the parietal lobes. Alternatively, disconnection of frontal cortex from parietal association cortex may produce motor behaviors that are isolated from the feedforward and feedback circuits necessary for accurately guided movements. In the callosal variety, Gasquoine (1993) proposed that disruption of the coordination between the right and left supplementary motor areas, during the generation of action plans, leaves a "free running" hand. There is debate over the site and extent of damage necessary to produce the alien hand syndrome. The disorder has been reported following lesions in the SMA, anterior corpus callosum (fed by the pericallosal and callosal marginal arteries), but also with lesions in the posterior two-thirds of the corpus callosum (Geschwind et al., 1995; Levin et al., 1987) and the right internal capsule–thalamus–midbrain (Ventura, Goldman, & Hildebrand, 1995).

Callosal Apraxia

Apraxia, specifically of the left hand, also follows anterior callosal disconnection. Liepmann and Maas (1907) proposed that motor centers in the right hemisphere (necessary for controlling movements of the left hand) are disconnected from space–time representations (necessary for skilled movements) located in the left hemisphere. Geschwind and Kaplan (1962) described a patient who developed left-hand apraxia following infarction of the anterior four-fifths of the corpus callosum Similar reports have followed (Graff-Radford, Welsh, & Godersky, 1987; Watson & Heilman, 1983).

Aphasia

Disruption of spoken language may result from interruption of the blood supply to mesial left hemisphere structures, including the SMA and proximal regions of cingulate cortex. These structures are supplied by the posterior internal frontal and paracentral arteries—distal branches of the callosal marginal artery. SMA aphasia is characterized initially by mutism, which later improves although there is usually persistent impairment of speech initiation (Goodglass, 1993). Some patients with small left frontal infarcts in the distribution of the ACA present with transcortical motor aphasia, namely, limited spontaneous speech, intact repetition, normal articulation, and good auditory comprehension (Freedman, Alexander, & Naeser, 1984). Freedman et al. (1984) view the SMA as the most anterior portion of an integrated brain mechanism responsible for the initiation of speech. They postulate that destruction of fibers from the SMA to frontal premotor cortex may disconnect the limbic "starter mechanism" from cortical regions that control speech.

Amnesia

Impaired memory may be seen following rupture of Berry aneurysms, regardless of their location around the Circle of Willis (Richardson, 1989), but may be particularly dramatic when the aneursym originates from the ACoA (M. P. Alexander & Freedman, 1984; Damasio, Graff-Radford, Eslinger, Damasio, & Kassell, 1985; Lindqvist & Norlen, 1966; Talland, Sweet, & Ballantine, 1967; Volpe & Hirst, 1983; Walton, 1953). Here, several stages of behavior typically evolve, beginning with confusion and agitation, followed by confabulation with denial of illness, and evolving to amnesia with personality change. On closer analysis, confabulations can often be related to fragments from the patient's past, strung together in the wrong context and sequence. Over several weeks, confabulation may wane, leaving impaired anterograde memory with other changes in personality (e.g., lack of concern, apathy, irritability, fatuousness, and socially inappropriate behavior). Both the quality of the amnesia and the accompanying personality disturbances are consistent with prefrontal and paralimbic dysfunction.

The ACoA gives rise to several small perforating branches that supply the anterior hypothalamus, septal nuclei, lamina terminalis, columns of the fornix, medial–ventral corpus callosum, and anterior cingulate (Dunker & Harris, 1976). Several of these structures (i.e., septal nuclei, columns of the fornix, and anterior cingulate) are integral components of the limbic–diencephalic memory system, and injury may contribute to temporary or permanent amnesia. Vasospasm may constrict other parts of the ACA, both proximal and distal to the ACoA, leading to more widespread infarction, neurological deficits, and behavioral disturbances. Anatomical localization by computed tomography and neuropsychological studies in patients with ACoA rupture suggest that a combination of basal forebrain with either neostriatal or frontal lesions is necessary for the development of amnesia (Irle, Wowra, Kunert, Hampl, & Kunze, 1992).

Regulation of Mood

Branches from the anterior cerebral artery (ACA) supply a number of cortical and subcortical structures which are implicated in the regulation of mood. Secondary depression has been associated consistently with left prefrontal strokes, particularly when there is proximity to the frontal pole (Eastwood, Rifat, Nobbs, & Ruderman, 1989; Sinyor, Kaloupek, Becker, Goldenberg, & Coopersmith, 1986; Starkstein, Robinson, & Price, 1987; Talland et al., 1967). The area is supplied by the orbital frontal and frontal polar arteries from the ACA and the orbital frontal and prefrontal arteries from the MCA. Stroke lesions involving the left head of caudate, supplied by lenticulostriate artery branching, are also associated with secondary depression (Starkstein, Robinson, Berthier, Parikh, & Price, 1988).

Mania, irritable mood, and disinhibited behaviors have also been reported following stroke to orbitofrontal, basolateral polar temporal areas as well as head of caudate and thalamus. In these cases, a predilection is observed for the lesion to be in the right hemisphere (Bogousslavsky & Regli, 1990b; Cummings & Mendez, 1984; Starkstein, Pearlson, Boston, & Robinson, 1987; Starkstein, Boston, & Robinson, 1988). Orbitofrontal, frontal polar, and lenticulostriate branches of the ACA supply respectively these frontal, temporal, and subcortical regions. When anterior cingulate and orbital lesions co-occur, devastating social agnosia results (Devinsky et al., 1995).

Middle Cerebral Artery

Vascular Anatomy

The MCA, the largest and most complex of the three major cerebral arteries, supplies the lateral basal ganglia, insula, and lateral convexity of the frontal and temporal lobes (Figure 21.2). The MCA has been divided into four segments: M1, lying posterior to the sphenoid ridge; M2, lying on the insula; M3, coursing over the frontoparietal and temporal opercula; and M4, spreading over the cortical surface. The M1 segment (average diameter = 3 mm, average length = 15 mm) takes its origin from the intracranial internal carotid artery. The M1 and proximal M2 segments give rise to approximately 10 lenticulostriate arteries (medial and lateral groups) which supply the lateral substantia innominata, lateral anterior commissure, dorsolateral head of the caudate, dorsolateral globus pallidi, and the middle and posterior putamen (Figures 21.3 and 21.5). These structures are intimately interconnected with the frontal cortex. The MCA subsequently reaches the insula, divides into two or three trunks, which give rise to roughly 8 stems, which divide into numerous cortical branches supplying the following 12 territories of the lateral frontotemporal lobe: orbitofrontal, prefrontal, precentral, central, anterior parietal, posterior parietal, angular, temporo-occipital, and temporopolar (Figure 21.2). Altered perfusion in the proximal M1 segment or upper division of the MCA is most likely to affect frontal lobe circuits and functions.

Vascular Disease

Among the three major cerebral arteries, the MCA is the most common site of symptomatic vascular disease. In a review of 3,110 cases of single saccular aneurysms, Fox (1983) noted that 13% were located at MCA bi- or trifurcation. Approximately 45% of cardiac emboli find their destination within the MCA territory (Yamaguchi, Minematsu, Choki, & Ikeda, 1984). Approximately 60% of hypertensive hemorrhages originate from weakened lenticulostriate arteries.

Clinical Syndromes

Occlusion of the stem of the MCA stem will affect the temporal and parietal as well as the frontal lobes. When occlusion is limited to the upper division of the MCA, on the other hand, the brunt of injury is borne by the frontal lobes. Such a lesion causes ischemia in the territories of the frontal–polar, prefrontal, precentral, central, and posterior parietal branches. Infarction involves the lateral prefrontal, lateral premotor, primary sensorimotor cortices, and underlying white matter. Contralateral weakness and sensory loss appear with more severe deficits in the face and arm than in the leg. Visual fields are generally preserved. The behavioral syndromes associated with MCA strokes are largely determined by the side, as well as the site, of occlusion. Strokes in the left (usually language-dominant) hemisphere are associated with greater disturbances in language, whereas strokes in the right hemisphere are associated with greater disturbances in attention. In complete occlusions of the MCA, which destroy frontal, parietal, and temporal lobes, the resulting global aphasia or severe neglect may overshadow other behavioral changes, making it difficult to sort out the nature of accompanying memory or cognitive impairments. Nonetheless, when occlusions are confined to the lenticulostriate arteries or the upper division of the MCA, circumscribed frontal lobe syndromes of the MCA may be recognized.

Nonfluent Aphasias

The principal cortical area supporting speech output extends posteriorly from classical Broca's area (in the left frontal operculum) along the lower frontal lobe to the Rolandic fissure. This area is supplied by the prefrontal and orbitofrontal branches of the upper MCA trunk. Broca's aphasia is characterized by suppression of speech output, agrammatism, limited vocabulary access, and relatively spared comprehension (Benson, 1993;

Goodglass, 1993). Although persistent Broca's aphasia has been associated with damage to basal ganglia, it is now believed that complete loss of voluntary speech implies damage to deep white matter pathways supplied by the lenticulostriate branches of the left middle cerebral artery. These pathways include the subcallosal fasciculus, the middle portion of periventricular white matter adjacent to the lateral ventricle, and the genu of the internal capsule (Goodglass, 1993; Naeser, Palumbo, Helm-Estabrooks, Stiassny-Eden, & Albert, 1989). Lesions in the speech outflow path of speech (i.e., the genu of the internal capsule) are characterized by severe dysarthria and dysprosody but have no linguistic component and are referred to as aphemia or subcortical motor aphasia (Goodglass, 1993).

Transcortical Motor Aphasia

Transcortical motor aphasia is most often caused by insufficient blood supply to the vascular border zone between left middle and anterior cerebral artery territories, anterior or superior to Broca's area (Goodglass, 1993; Stuss & Benson, 1986). Transcortical motor aphasia shares features with SMA aphasia without the accompanying right-sided leg weakness. Freedman et al. (1984) proposed that transcortical motor aphasia results from the disconnection of Broca's area from the supplementary motor cortex.

Inattention or Neglect

While the left hemisphere is specialized for language, the right hemisphere plays a predominant role in directing attention toward extrapersonal space. In concert with the reticular activating system and the inferior parietal lobule, two areas (3 and 4 below) of the frontal lobe participate in a distributed cortical network for attention (Mesulam, 1981): (1) the reticular activating system sets the level of arousal and vigilance, (2) the inferior parietal lobe provides an internal sensory map, (3) the cingulate gyrus signals the motivational priority, and (4) the dorsolateral frontal cortex (including the frontal eye fields) directs motor exploration. Although profound unilateral neglect classically follows damage to the right inferior parietal lobule, neglect also emerges subsequent to vascular injury to the medial or dorsolateral frontal lobes (Damasio, Damasio, & Chui, 1980; Heilman & Valenstein, 1972; Mesulam, 1981).

Intentional Motor Disorders

"Motor impersistence" is a term introduced by M. Fisher (1956) to describe the inability to sustain simple acts such as conjugate gaze, eye closure, or tongue protrusion. Motor impersistence can be seen with bilateral or unilateral infarcts, particularly if the latter are located in the central or frontal regions of the right hemisphere (Kertesz, Nicholson, Cancelliere, Kassa, & Black, 1985). Heilman and Watson (1991) postulated that as part of a cortical–subcortical circuit, the dorsolateral frontal cortices play a key role in intentional motor activity.

SMALL ARTERIES AND SUBCORTICAL STROKES

The frontal lobe, together with its intimate connections with the basal ganglia and thalamus, integrates motor, attentional, emotional, and executive response. The basal ganglia and thalamus are perfused by small penetrating arteries that arise from or near the Circle of Willis. In the basal ganglia, the "limbic" and lateral orbital circuits, which subserve attention and emotion, are positioned in the ventromedial caudate and receive their blood supply primarily from perforating branches of the ACA. The motor and dorsolateral frontal–subcortical circuits, which make major contributions to movement and executive function, are positioned more laterally and are fed predominantly from the lenticulostriate arteries, taking origin from the M1 segment of the MCA. The vascular supply of these circuits as they pass through the thalamus is overlapping and complex. Chronic hypertension and diabetes mellitus are the main risk factors for the development of arteriolar sclerosis in these small penetrating arteries. Occlusion leads to small lacunar infarcts (C. M. Fisher, 1965, 1979). Rupture leads to deep intracerebral hemorrhages. A wide variety of motor, cognitive, and behavioral deficits become manifest, many having a "frontal lobe" quality.

Basal Ganglia

Head of Caudate

The head of the caudate is supplied by penetrating arteries from both the ACA and the MCA. The ventromedial portion is fed by Heubner's artery and other small penetrating arteries from the proximal ACA, whereas the dorsolateral portion is supplied by medial–striate branches from the proximal MCA (Pullicino, 1993) (Figures 21.3–21.5). Based on anatomical connectivity, three distinct behavioral syndromes are predicted: (1) lesions in the ventromedial head of the caudate, by virtue of its connections with the orbital frontal cortex, will be associated with irritability and disinhibition; (2) lesions in the dorsolateral head of the caudate, as part of the feedback circuit to the principal sulcus, will be associated with dysexecutive function; and (3) lesions in the nucleus accumbens or ventral striatum, which is closely connected with the anterior cingulate, will be associated with apathy and hypokinesia. One must bear in mind that accuracy of lesion localization varies, and that lesions are often not confined to the head of the caudate but encroach on the anterior striatum and the anterior limb or genu of the internal capsule (Pedrazzi, Bogousslavsky, & Regli, 1990).

Bilateral damage to the head of the caudate is characterized by prominent disturbances in the regulation of emotion, behavior, and cognition. Richfield, Twyman, and Berent (1987) reported a woman with bilateral infarction of the head of the caudate. Personality changes included impulsive behaviors, indifference, hypersexuality, minor criminal acts, low tolerance for frustration, and angry outbursts. Neuropsychological testing revealed deficits in delayed recall, complex problem solving, and decline in intellect. Croisile, Tourniaire, Confavreux, Trillet, and Aimard (1989) reported a patient who initially presented with apathy, word-finding difficulty, and incoherent writing in association with an infarct in the left head of the caudate. Two months later, she suffered a second infarct in the right head of the caudate and showed decreased initiative and emotional reactivity, reduced spontaneous speech, hyposexuality, and obsessive and compulsive behaviors. Habib and Poncet (1988) described two cases with multiple lacunar lesions in bilateral striatum and caudate. Both showed marked personality changes, including a loss of interest and drive, loss of curiosity, and flattened affect. Thus, the behaviors associated with bilateral infarction of the head of the caudate are reminiscent of all three prefrontal syndromes.

Side of lesion correlates with clinical syndrome. Caplan et al. (1990) reviewed 10 left- and 8 right-sided lesions involving the head of the caudate in the distribution of

Heubner's artery. In four cases, the lesions were confined to the caudate; in the others, involvement extended into the anterior putamen and internal capsule. With the more extensive lesions, neurological signs included temporary motor weakness, decreased spontaneous and associative movements, and dysarthria. Behavioral abnormalities included abulia, restlessness, and hyperactivity. Contralateral neglect was noted with right-sided lesions, whereas speech and memory deficits were noted with left-sided ones. These differences correspond with lateralization of these functions following cortical lesions.

Attempts have also been made to localize the site of a lesion within the head of the caudate. Mendez et al. (1989) reviewed 12 cases with caudate lesions, 11 unilateral, and 1 bilateral. In 7 cases, where neuropsychological testing was available, impairments were noted in planning and sequencing, attention, and recent and remote memory. When the lesions were predominantly ventromedial, the patients tended to be disinhibited, inappropriate, and impulsive. When lesions were more extensive and involved most of the head of the caudate, affective disturbances such as anxiety and depression were prominent. When the dorsolateral was more affected than the ventromedial head of the caudate, the patients tended to be apathetic and abulic. In this study, behavioral patterns appeared to correlate with the size and location but not with the side of the lesion. These clinical brain–behavior correlations correspond in a general way to predictions suggested by anatomical connectivity in nonhuman primates.

Putamen

The putamen is the major striatal component of the motor system and is largely supplied by the lateral bank of lenticulostriate arteries. A variable degree of contralateral weakness is commonly noted, probably due to concomitant involvement of the internal capsule (Fries, Danek, Scheidtmann, & Hamburger, 1993). Behavioral disturbances, such as neglect or aphasia, are also reported. Damasio, Damasio, and Chui (1980) described two cases of neglect following infarcts in the basal ganglia. Weiller et al. (1993) reviewed 57 cases with striatocapsular infarcts and hemiparesis, 12 with neglect, and 15 with aphasia. All the patients with neglect had right-sided lesions; all but one of the patients with aphasia had left-sided lesions. Patients with neglect or aphasia had larger lesions, but no apparent specific pattern of involvement of the putamen, pallidum, head of caudate, or white matter. Ferro, Kertesz, and Black (1987) found extinction and hemispatial neglect in 86% of 15 subjects with right subcortical lesions. The most severe neglect syndromes were caused either by a large caudate–putaminal–capsular infarct (in the distribution of the lateral lenticulostriate branches) or by smaller infarcts of the capsule and pallidum (in the distribution of the anterior choroidal artery). Lesser degrees of neglect or extinction was noted with capsular–pallidal lesions in the distribution of the mesial lenticulostriate arteries.

Relatively minor degrees of dysexecutive function are reported with lenticular lesions. Godefroy et al. (1992) searched specifically for evidence of executive dysfunction in patients with unilateral lenticulostriate infarcts. The six patients with unilateral subcortical lesions were impaired in crossed tapping (a motor task) but not in other tasks sensitive to executive dysfunction (e.g., trail making or card sorting). Significant executive defects were only noted in four patients who had additional cortical lesions.

In summary, language or attentional disturbances are commonly reported with striatocapsular lesions. On the other hand, personality changes and dysexecutive problems are less frequently reported than with lesions of the head of the caudate. This is in keeping with the pattern of anatomical connectivity: putamen with the motor system and head of the caudate with lateral–orbital and dorsolateral prefrontal cortices.

Globus Pallidus

The globus pallidus externus is nourished by the medial lenticulostriate arteries, whereas the globus pallidus internus is fed by the anterior choroidal artery and ACA perforators. At this point, there is little physical separation between the parallel cortical–basal ganglia–thalamocortical loops. LaPlane, Baulac, Widlocher, and Dubois (1984) describe three patients with absent spontaneous movements reminiscent of akinetic mutism, following bilateral lesions in basal ganglia, mainly affecting the globus pallidi. Strub (1989) described a 60-year-old man, who experienced major changes in personality following bilateral hemorrhages in the globus pallidi. He exhibited poor initiative and apathy, mild extrapyramidal signs, decreased memory, poor visual sequencing and organization, and marked impairment in set shifting. Elements of his behavior were suggestive of both mediofrontal and dorsofrontal syndromes.

Thalamus

The thalamus represents a key way station in the parallel, but segregated, organization of the frontal–subcortical circuits. The three prefrontal behavioral circuits converge on the anterior thalamic or dorsomedial nucleus. (In turn, the anterior thalamic nucleus projects to the anterior cingulate gyrus, whereas the dorsomedial thalamic nucleus projects to dorsolateral and orbitofrontal cortices.) The motor circuit projects to the ventral anterior/ventral lateral nucleus of the thalamus, and subsequently back upon the supplementary motor area.

Ventral Anterior and Anterior Thalamus

The ventral anterior thalamic nucleus participates in two of the three prefrontal circuits (G. E. Alexander et al., 1986): (1) the pars parvocellularis projects to the dorsolateral prefrontal cortex, and (2) the pars magnocellularis to the lateral–orbital prefrontal cortex. The anterior nucleus of the thalamus is an integral component of the limbic–diencephalic memory system. The anterior thalamic nucleus (together with portions of the ventrolateral nucleus) is supplied by the tuberothalamic artery, which arises from the posterior communicating artery (Bogousslavsky, Regli, & Uske, 1988). Severe neuropsychological deficits have been observed following infarction of the anterolateral thalamus (Graff-Radford, Damasio, Yamada, Eslinger, & Damasio, 1985). Left-sided lesions are associated with impairments in language, visuoperception, construction, temporal orientation, memory, and intellect. Right-sided lesions produce deficits particularly in nonverbal abilities (e.g., nonverbal intellect, visual memory, and construction). Daum and Akerman (1994) described frontal-type memory problems (including impaired spatial working memory, increased forgetting rates, poor prospective memory, inadequate elaborative encoding), as well as prefrontal-type personality change (e.g., irritability, lability, disinhibition, inappropriateness, and distractability) following right anterior thalamic infarction. Mania and left hemiballism have been reported following infarction of the right ventral lateral and ventromedial nuclei (Kulisevsky, Berthier, & Pujol, 1993). Variable degrees of hemiparesis are associated with infarction of the anterolateral thalamus, presumably due to involvement of the ventrolateral nucleus (Graff-Radford et al., 1985).

Dorsomedial Thalamus

The dorsomedial nucleus of the thalamus is interwoven with all three prefrontal–subcortical circuits (G. E. Alexander et al., 1986): (1) the pars parvocellularis has reciprocal connections with the dorsolateral prefrontal cortex, (2) the pars magnocellularis has reciprocal connections with orbital–frontal cortex, and (3) the posteromedial dorsomedial nucleus is interconnected with the anterior cingulate (Sandson, Daffner, Carvalho, & Mesulam, 1991). The dorsomedial nucleus is also integrated within the limbic–diencephalic memory system. The principal vascular supply to the dorsomedial thalamic nuclei are branches of the paramedian artery arising from the basilar communicating artery and, to a lesser degree, branches of the tuberothalamic artery, which arises from the posterior communicating artery (Bogousslavsky, Regli, & Uske, 1988).

Not surprisingly, a wide range of cognitive and behavioral deficits have been described in association with infarction of the dorsomedial thalamus. Visual and verbal memory deficits, cognitive deficits, and confusion or dementia often unfold with hemispheric differences (Bogousslavsky, Ferrazzini, et al., 1988; Bogousslavsky, Delaloye, Asal, & Uske, 1991; Graff-Radford et al., 1985; Guberman & Stuss, 1983; Malamut, Graff-Radford, Chawluk, Grossman, & Gur, 1992; Stuss, Guberman, Nelson, & Larochelle, 1988). Right-sided lesions tend to be associated with hemineglect, deficits in visuospatial processing, and impairments in memory. Left-sided lesions are accompanied by deficits in verbal processing and memory (Bassetti, Mathis, Gugger, Löublad, & Hess, 1996; Baumgartner & Regard, 1993; Bogousslavsky, Regli, & Uske, 1988; Graff-Radford et al., 1985; Sandson et al., 1991; Watson, Valenstein, & Heilman, 1981). Behavioral changes include decreased response initiation and inhibition, perseverative behaviors, poor judgment and insight (Baumgartner & Regard, 1993; Sandson et al., 1991) or manic delirium (Bogousslavsky, Ferrazzini, et al., 1988). Akinetic mutism may also follow infarction of the anteriomedial portions of the thalamus (Segarra, 1970). In summary, the behavioral sequelae of dorsomedial thalamic lesions run the gamut and recapitulate all of the principal features of the three prefrontal syndromes.

Internal Capsule

Small deep infarcts or lacunes confined to the internal capsule typically cause unilateral isolated weakness (50%), although other syndromes such as motor–sensory loss (30%) or ataxic hemiparesis (20%) are also seen (Tei, Uchiyama, & Maruyama, 1993). The blood supply to the fan-shaped internal capsule is complex (Figures 21.5, 21.6, and 21.7). Most of the upper internal capsule is fed by the lenticulostriate branches of the MCA (although the most posterior part is supplied by the anterior choroidal artery). Perfusion of the lower portions of the internal capsule (i.e., below the head and body of the caudate nucleus) is multiplex: (1) the anterior limb of the lower internal capsule is fed by Heubner's artery, (2) the lower genu is fed by perforators arising from the apex of the internal carotid artery of ACA (Figure 21.4), and (3) the posterior limb of the lower capsule is supplied by the anterior choroidal artery. In a series of 72 single capsular infarcts (Tei et al., 1993), 71% were in the MCA distribution, 21% were in anterior choroidal, and 8% were in the ACA distribution.

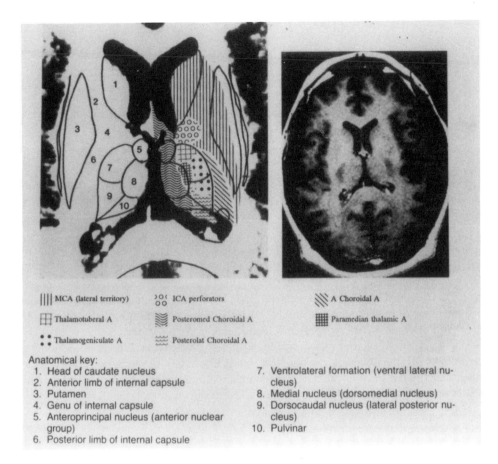

FIGURE 21.6. Axial schematic through the genu of the internal capsule showing the vascular supply of the basal ganglia and thalamus. From Pullicino (1993, p. 48). Copyright 1993 by Raven Press. Reprinted by permission.

Anterior Limb

The anterior limb of the internal capsule conveys axons from the supplementary motor area (Fries et al., 1993), as well as frontopontine and frontobulbar fibers. The anterior limb is usually fed by Heubner's artery, which also supplies the medial head of the caudate. Thus, ischemic lesions are rarely confined to the anterior limb and usually extend into the medial portions of the head of the caudate, globus pallidus, or putamen (Kashihara & Matsumoto, 1985; Weiller et al., 1993). Infarction of the anterior limb is initially associated with hemiparesis predominantly affecting the arm, face, and bulbar musculature (see ACA), slow gait, urinary incontinence, and a variety of behavioral disturbances (see head of caudate). Motor recovery is usually good (Fries et al., 1993).

Genu

The genu carries fibers that originated from the supplementary area and coursed initially through the anterior limb of the internal capsule (Fries et al., 1993). Infarction of the

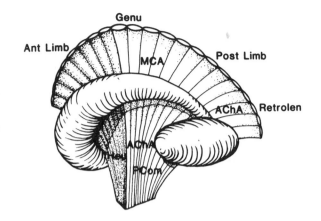

FIGURE 21.7. Schematic diagram depicting the blood supply of the internal capsule. From Weir (1987, p. 337). Copyright 1987 by Bruce Weir. Reprinted by permission.

genu of the internal capsule is associated with contralateral facial or lingual weakness and dysarthria (Bogousslavsky & Regli, 1990). Tatemichi, Desmond, Prohovnik, et al. (1992) and Tatemichi, Desmond, and Prohovnik (1995) reviewed six patients who developed confusion, memory loss, or dementia associated with lacunar infarction of the inferior genu of the internal capsule (fed by IC or ACA perforators). These authors posited that these lesions strategically disrupted the inferior and medial thalamic peduncles carrying thalamocortical fibers related to cognition and memory.

Posterior Limb

The posterior limb of the internal capsule contains fibers from dorsolateral premotor cortex (anteriorly, near the genu) and from primary motor cortex (in the middle and posterior portions) (Fries et al., 1993). The predominant consequence of infarction in the posterior limb of the internal capsule is contralateral hemiparesis, with no or mild sensory loss. As it passes from the upper to lower posterior limb, the cortical spinal tract shifts progressively more posteriorly within the posterior limb of the internal capsule (Fries et al., 1993; Ross, 1980). The superior portion of the posterior limb is supplied by lenticulostriate arteries, whereas the inferior–posterior portion of the posterior limb is supplied by the anterior choroidal artery. Kashihara and Matsumoto (1985) described more favorable recovery of motor function with lesions located more laterally and superiorly compared to those located more posteriorly. Fries et al. (1993) noted excellent motor recovery when lesions were confined to the white matter of the posterior limb (e.g., distribution of anterior choroidal artery) and less favorable recovery if the lesion also affected the thalamus. Differences in recovery might reflect the extent of damage to the descending motor pathways, as well as the degree of concomitant sensory loss.

Mild ataxia, without hemiparesis or proprioceptive loss, has been infrequently reported following small ischemic lesions in the posterior limb of the internal capsule (Luijckx, Boiten, Lodder, Heuts-van Raak, & Wilmink, 1994) that may extend into the neighboring thalamus. Such lesions are purported to interrupt corticocerebellar pathways—either the ascending dentatorubrothalamocortical or the descending corticopontocerebellar fibers.

MULTI-INFARCT DEMENTIA

Dementia is a common finding after stroke. In a study of 251 patients examined after the onset of acute ischemic stroke, Tatemichi, Desmond, and Mayeux (1992; Tatemichi et al., 1993) found evidence of dementia in 26%. The presence of dementia was associated with certain demographic factors, including age, education, and race, as well as certain atherogenic factors such as diabetes mellitus. Dementia was also associated with certain stroke-related characteristics: either small lacunar infarction (odds ratio [OR] = 2.7; 95% confidence interval = 1.3–5.9) or large cortical infarction (OR = 3.9 [1.3–11.3]), and was more common with a left compared to right hemispheric location [not explained by aphasia] (OR = 4.7 [1.7–12.9]). Within the left hemisphere, dementia was associated with strokes in the distribution of the left posterior or anterior cerebral arteries. It is unclear whether the latter findings are related to small strategic lacunar infarctions in the thalamus or basal ganglia, or to large cortical infarcts in these two arterial distributions.

The pattern of cognitive deficits associated with vascular brain injury is highly heterogeneous, depending on the vascular territories involved. In a neuropsychological study of 227 patients, 3 months after admission for ischemic stroke, impairment in memory, orientation, language, and attention were commonly observed (Tatemichi et al., 1994). Certain patterns may be noted in subgroups of patients with vascular dementia. For example, patients with small vessel infarcts demonstrate more severe frontal lobe dysfunction, assessed by cerebral blood flow or neuropsychological testing, compared to patients with Alzheimer's disease (Starkstein et al., 1996; Wolfe, Linn, Babikian, Knoefel, & Albert, 1990). This pattern is consistent with the distribution of small infarcts in the basal ganglia, thalamus, and frontal white matter, where they are prone to interrupt frontal–subcortical circuitry.

Lacunar State

The syndrome of dementia associated with multiple lacunar infarcts or lacunar state was first described by Marie (1901) and Ferrand (1902) in 50 residents of a chronic-care facility. Clinical features included sudden hemiparesis, dementia, dysarthria, pseudobulbar affect, small-stepped gait, and urinary incontinence. Aphasia and heminopsia were notably absent. Similar clinical features were confirmed by C. M. Fisher (1965). Ishii, Nishihara, and Imamura (1986) noted the predominance of frontal lobe symptoms, including lack of volition and akinetic mutism, as well as the corresponding predilection for lacunes and diffuse white matter softenings to occur in the subcortical gray and white matter of the frontal lobes.

Strategic-Infarct Dementia

At times, a dementia syndrome may result from a single strategically placed lesion. In some individuals, a single paramedian branch supplies both anteromedial thalamic regions. Occlusion of the paramedian artery in these cases leads to bilateral infarction of the dorsomedial nucleus and the mammillothalamic tracts (Bogousslavsky, Ferrazzini, et al., 1988). The resulting thalamic dementia is characterized by marked apathy, impaired attention and mental control, and anterograde and retrograde amnesia (Katz, Alexander, & Mandell, 1987; Stuss et al., 1988). As discussed previously, an infarct in the inferior genu of the internal capsule may also strategically disrupt the inferior and medial thalamic peduncles carrying thalamocortical fibers related to cognition and memory (Tatemichi, Desmond, Prohovnik, et al., 1992; Tatemichi et al., 1995).

Subcortical Arteriolar Sclerotic Encephalopathy (Binswanger's Syndrome)

The periventricular and deep white matter in the centrum semiovale are fed by long-penetrating end arterioles. These areas are particularly susceptible to global ischemia due to diffuse arteriolar sclerosis or global hypoperfusion (De Reuck, Crevits, de Coster, Sieben, & van der Eecken, 1980). Binswanger (1894) described eight patients with slowly progressive mental deterioration and pronounced white matter changes, with secondary dilatation of the ventricles. Alzheimer (1902) described the corresponding microscopic features, including hyalination, intimal fibrosis, and onion skinning of the long medullary arteries, together with severe gliosis of the white matter. More recently, loss of myelin, oligodendrocytes, and axons was described (Englund, Brun, & Alling, 1988; Yamanouchi, Sugiura, & Tomonaga, 1989; Yamanouchi, 1991).

Investigators have reviewed the clinical features of subcortical arteriolar sclerotic encephalopathy or Binswanger's syndrome (Babikian & Ropper, 1987; Caplan & Schoene, 1978; Olszewski, 1962; Román, 1987). Usually, there is a history of persistent hypertension or vascular disease (e.g., atheriosclerosis or amyloid angiopathy) and the presence of focal neurological signs (including asymmetric weakness, pyramidal signs, pseudobulbar palsy, and gait disturbance). In a genetic disorder known as cerebral autosomal dominant arteriopathy with subcortical infarcts and leukoencephalopathy (CADASIL), the media of small arterioles become thickened and accumulate eosinophilic, electron-dense granular material (Baudrimont, Dubas, Joutel, Tournier-Lasserve, & Bousser, 1993; Davous & Fallet-Bianco, 1991; Gray et al., 1994). The gene responsible for CADASIL has been linked to chromosome 19p12 (Tournier-Lasserve et al., 1993) Unlike other forms of vascular dementia, the clinical course in subcortical arteriolar sclerotic encephalopathy may be insidious, with long plateaus and periods of slowly progressive dementia. Apathy, lack of drive, mild depression, and alterations of mood (Libon, Scanlon, Swenson, & Coslett, 1990; Loizou, Kendall, & Marshall, 1981) give a characteristic prefrontal flavor.

CONCLUSION

Our understanding of the vascular diseases of the frontal lobes reflects a dynamic interplay between clinical observation, experimental studies, and cognitive neuroscience. Early observations in patients with large vessel strokes outlined the principle features of the major motor, cognitive, and behavioral syndromes. Essentially identical observations are recapitulated in connection with much smaller infarcts located deep in the brain. These similarities make sense once frontal lobe functions are conceptualized as a distributed network—even more so, when segregated, but parallel, frontal–subcortical circuits are mapped in nonhuman primates. Sensitive and noninvasive neuroimaging tools are now available for brain–behavioral correlations. These developments promise a new level of investigation and insight regarding vascular diseases of the frontal lobe.

ACKNOWLEDGMENTS

This work was supported by grants from the National Institute on Aging (Nos. 1P01 AG12435 and 1P50 AG05142) and the State of California Department of Health Services.

REFERENCES

Alexander, G. E., & Crutcher, M. D. (1990). Functional architecture of basal ganglia circuits: neural substrates of parallel processing. *Trends in Neuroscience, 13,* 266–271.

Alexander, G. E., DeLong, M. R., & Strick, P. L. (1986). Parallel organization of functionally segregated circuits linking basal ganglia and cortex. *Annual Review of Neuroscience, 9,* 357–381.

Alexander, M. P., & Freedman, M. (1984). Amnesia after anterior communicating artery aneurysm rupture. *Neurology, 34,* 752–757.

Alexander, M. P. & Naeser, M. A. (1988). Cortical–subcortical differences in aphasia. In F. Plum (Ed.), *Language and communication.* New York: Raven Press.

Alzheimer, A. (1902). Die Seelenstorungen auf arterisclroticsher Grundlage. *Allgemeine Zeitschrift für Psychiatrie und Psychisch-Gerichtlich Medicin, 59,* 695–711.

American Heart Association. (1994). *Heart and stroke facts: Statistical supplement.* Dallas, TX: American Heart Association.

Babikian, V., & Ropper, A. H. (1987). Binswanger's disease: A review. *Stroke, 18,* 2–12.

Bachevalier, J. B., & Mishkin, M. (1986). Visual recognition impairment follows ventromedial but no dorsolateral prefrontal lesions in monkeys. *Behavioral Brain Research, 20,* 249–261.

Barris, R. W., & Schuman, H. R. (1953). Bilateral anterior cingulate gyrus lesions. Syndrome of the anterior cingulate gyri. *Neurology, 3,* 44–52.

Bassetti, C., Mathis, J., Guger, M., Löublad, K. O., & Hess, C. W. (1996). Hypersomnia following paramedian thalamic stroke: A report of 12 patients. *Annals of Neurology, 39,* 471–481.

Baudrimont, M., Dubas, F., Joutel, A., Tournier-Lasserve, E., & Bousser, M. G. (1993). Autosomal dominant leukoencephalopathy and subcortical ischemic stroke. *Stroke, 24,* 122–125.

Baumgartner, R. W., & Regard, M. (1993). Bilateral neuropsychological deficits in unilateral paramedian thalamic infarction. *European Neurology, 33,* 195–198.

Benson, D. F. (1993). Aphasia. In K. M. Heilman & E. Valenstein (Eds.), *Clinical neuropsychology* (pp. 17–36). New York: Oxford University Press.

Binswanger, O. (1894). Die Abgrenzung der allgemeinen progressiven Paralyse. *Berliner Klinische Wochenschrift, 31,* 1102–1105, 1137–1139.

Bogousslavsky, J., Delaloye, B., Asal, G., & Uske, A. (1991). Loss of psychic self-activation with bithalamic infarction. Neurobehavioral, CT, MRI, and SPECT correlates. *Acta Neurologica Scandinavica, 83,* 309–316.

Bogousslavsky, J., Ferrazzini, M., Regli, F., Asal, G., Tanabe, H., & Delyloye-Bischof, A. (1988). Manic delirium and frontal-like syndrome with paramedian infarction of the right thalamus. *Journal of Neurology, Neurosurgery, and Psychiatry, 51,* 116–119.

Bogousslavsky, J., & Regli, F. (1986). Borderzone infarction distal to internal carotid occlusion: Prognostic implications. *Archives of Neurology, 20,* 346–350.

Bogousslavsky, J., & Regli, F. (1990a). Anterior cerebral artery territory infarction in the Lausanne Stroke Registry. *Archives of Neurology, 47,* 144–150.

Bogousslavsky, J., & Regli, F. (1990b). Capsular genu syndrome. *Neurology, 40,* 1499–1502.

Bogousslavsky, J., Regli, F., & Uske, A. (1988). Thalamic infarcts: Clinical syndrome, etiology, and prognosis. *Neurology, 38,* 837–848.

Borggreve, F., de Deyn, P. P., Marien, P., Cras, P., & Dierckx R. A. (1994). Bilateral infarction in the anterior cerebral artery vascular territory due to an anomaly of the Circle of Willis. *Stroke, 25,* 1279–1281.

Broderick, J. P. (1994). Intracerebral hemorrhage. In P. B. Gorelick & M. Alter (Eds.), *Handbook of neuroepidemiology* (pp. 141–164). New York: Marcel Decker.

Broderick, J. P., Phillips, S. J., Whisnant, J. P., O'Fallon, W. M., & Begstrahl, E. J. (1989). Incidence rates of stroke in the eighties: the end of the decline in stroke? *Stroke, 20,* 577–582.

Caplan, L. R. (1996). Diabetes and brain ischemia. *Diabetes, 45*(Suppl. 3), S95–S97.

Caplan, L. R., Schmahmann, J. D., Kase, C. S., Feldmann, E., Baquis, G., Greenberg, J. P., Gorelick, P. B., Helgason, C., & Hier, D. (1990). Caudate infarcts. *Archives of Neurology, 47,* 133–143.

Caplan, L. R., & Schoene, W. C. (1978). Clinical features of subcortical arteriosclerotic encephalopathy (Binswanger disease). *Neurology, 28,* 1206–1215.

Carpenter, M. B., & Sutin, J. (1983). *Human neuroanatomy.* Baltimore: Williams & Wilkins.

Charcot, J. M., & Bouchard, C. H. (1868). Nouvelles recherches sur la pathogénie de l'hemorrhagie cerebrale. *Archives of Physiology, 1,* 110–127, 643–665, 725–734.

Critchley, M. (1930). The anterior cerebral artery and its syndromes. *Brain, 53,* 120–165.

Croisile, B., Tourniaire, D., Confavreux, C., Trillet, M., & Aimard, G. (1989). Bilateral damage to the head of the caudate nuclei. *Annals of Neurology, 25,* 313–314.

Cummings, J. L. (1993). Frontal–subcortical circuits and human behavior. *Archives of Neurology, 50,* 873–880.

Cummings, J. L., & Mendez, M. F. (1984). Secondary mania with focal cerebrovascular lesions. *American Journal of Psychiatry, 141,* 1084–1087.

Damasio, A. R., Damasio, H., & Chui, H. C. (1980). Neglect following damage to frontal lobe or basal ganglia. *Neuropsychologia, 18,* 123–132.

Damasio, A. R., Graff-Radford, N. R., Eslinger, P. J. Damasio, H., & Kassell, N. (1985). Amnesia following basal forebrain lesions. *Archives of Neurology, 42,* 263–271.

Damasio, A. R., Tranel, D., & Damasio, H. C. (1991). Somatic markers and the guidance of behavior: Theory and preliminary testing. In H. S. Levin, H. M. Eisenberg, & A. L. Benton (Eds.), *Frontal lobe function and dysfunction* (pp. 217–229). Oxford: Oxford University Press.

Damasio, A. R., & Van Hoesen, G. W. (1983). Focal lesions of the limbic frontal lobe. In K. M. Heilman & P. Satz (Eds.), *Neuropsychology of human emotion* (pp. 85–110). New York: Guilford Press.

Daum, I., & Akerman, H. (1994). Frontal-type memory impairment associated with thalamic damage. *International Journal of Neuroscience, 75,* 153–165.

Davous, P., & Fallet-Bianco, C. (1991). Démence sous-corticale familiale avec leucoencéphalopathie artériopathique: Observation clinico-pathologique. *Revue Neurologique (Paris), 147,* 376–384.

Degos, J. D., da Fonseca, N., Gray, F., & Cesaro, P. (1993). Severe frontal syndrome associated with infarcts of the left anterior cingulater gyrus and the head of the right caudate nucleus: A clinico-pathological case. *Brain, 116,* 1541–1548.

De Reuck, J., Crevits, L., de Coster, W., Sieben, G., & van der Eecken, H. (1980). Pathogenesis of Binswanger chronic progressive subcortical encephalopathy. *Neurology, 30,* 920–928.

Devinsky, O., Morrell, M. J., & Vogt, B. A. (1995). Contributions of the anterior cingulate cortex to behavior. *Brain, 118,* 279–306.

Dunker, R. O., & Harris, A. B. (1976). Surgical anatomy of the proximal anterior cerebral artery. *Journal of Neurosurgery, 44,* 359–367.

Eastwood, M. R., Rifat, S. L., Nobbs, H., & Ruderman, J. (1989). Mood disorder following cerebrovascular accident. *British Journal of Psychiatry, 154,* 195–200.

Englund, E., Brun, A., & Alling, C. (1988). White matter changes in dementia of Alzheimer's type. *Brain, 111,* 1425–1439.

Ferrand, J. (1902). *Essai sur l'hémiplégie des vieillards: Les lacunes de désintegration cérébrale.* Paris: These.

Feinberg, T. E., Schindler, R. J., Flanagan, N. G., & Haber, L. D. (1992). Two alien hand syndromes. *Neurology, 42,* 19–24.

Feinberg, W. M., Seeger, J. F., Carmody, R. F., Anderson, D. C., Hart, R. G., & Pearce, L. A. (1990). Epidemiologic features of asymptomatic cerebral infarction in patients with nonvalvular atrial fibrillation. *Archives of Internal Medicine, 150,* 2340–2344.

Ferro, J. M., Kertesz, A., & Black, S. E. (1987). Subcortical neglect: Quantitation, anatomy, recovery. *Neurology, 37,* 1487–1492.

Fisher, C. M. (1965). Lacunes: Small deep cerebral infarcts. *Neurology, 15,* 774–784.

Fisher, C. M. (1979). Capsular infarcts, the underlying vascular lesions. *Archives of Neurology, 36,* 65–73.

Fisher, M. (1956). Left hemiplegia and motor impersistence. *Journal of Nervous and Mental Diseases, 123,* 201–218.

Fox, J. L. (1983). *Intracranial aneurysms.* New York: Springer-Verlag.

Freedman, R. B., Alexander, M. P., & Naeser, M. A. (1984). The anatomical basis of transcortical motor aphasia. *Neurology, 34,* 409–417.

Freemon, F. R. (1971). Akinetic mutism and bilateral anterior cerebral artery occlusion. *Journal of Neurology, Neurosurgery, and Psychiatry, 34,* 693–698.

Fries, W., Danek, A., Scheidtmann, K., & Hamburger, C. (1993). Motor recovery following capsular stroke. *Brain, 116,* 369–382.

Gasquoine, P. G. (1993). Alien hand sign. *Journal of Clinical Experiments in Neuropsychiatry, 15,* 653–667.

Geschwind, D. H., Iacoboni, M., Mega, M. S., Zaidel, D. W., Cloughesy, T., & Zaidel, E. (1995). Alien hands syndrome. *Neurology, 45,* 802–808.

Geschwind, N., & Kaplan, E. (1962). A human cerebral disconnection syndrome. *Neurology, 12,* 675–685.

Godefroy, O., Rousseaux, M., Leys, D., Destée, A., Scheltens, P., & Pruvo, J. P. (1992). Frontal lobe dysfunction in unilateral lenticulostriate infarcts: Prominent role of cortical lesions. *Archives of Neurology, 49,* 1285–1289.

Goldman-Rakic, P. S. (1988). Topography of cognition: Parallel distributed networks in primate association cortex. *Annual Review of Neuroscience, 11,* 137–156.

Goldman-Rakic, P. S., & Friedman, H. R. (1991). The circuitry of working memory revealed by anatomy and metabolic imaging. In H. S. Levin, H. M. Eisenberg, & A. L. Benton (Eds.), *Frontal lobe function and dysfunction* (pp. 72–91). Oxford: Oxford University Press.

Goodglass, H. (1993). *Understanding aphasia.* New York: Academic Press.

Graff-Radford, N. R., Damasio, H., Yamada, T., Eslinger, P. J., & Damasio, A. R. (1985). Non-haemorrhagic thalamic infarction: Clinical, neuropsychological, and electrophysiological findings in four anatomical groups defined by computerized tomography. *Brain, 108,* 485–516.

Graff-Radford, N. R., Welsh, K., & Godersky, J. (1987). Callosal apraxia. *Neurology, 37,* 100–105.

Gray, F., Robert, F., Labrecques, R., Chrétien, F., Baudrimont, M., Fallet-Bianco, C., Mikol, J., & Vinters, H. V. (1994). Autosomal dominant arteriopathic leuko-encephalopathy and Alzheimer's disease. *Neuropathology and Applied Neurobiology, 20,* 22–30.

Greene, K. A., Marciano, F. F., Dickman, C. A., Coons, S. W., Johnson, P. C., Bailes, J. E., & Spetzler, R. F. (1995). Anterior communicating artery aneurysm paraparesis syndrome: Clinical manifestations and pathologic correlates. *Neurology, 45,* 45–50.

Guberman, A., & Stuss, D. (1983). The syndrome of bilateral paramedian thalamic infarction. *Neurology, 33,* 540–546.

Habib, M., & Poncet, M. (1988). Perte de l'élan vital, de l'intérêt et de l'affectivité (syndrome athymhormique) au cours de lésions lacunaires des corps striés. *Review of Neurology, 144,* 571–577.

Heilman, K. M., & Valenstein E. (1972). Frontal neglect in man. *Neurology, 22,* 660–664.

Heilman, K. M., & Watson, R. T. (1991). Intentional motor disorders. In H. S. Levin, H. M. Eisenberg, & A. L. Benton (Eds.), *Frontal lobe function and dysfunction* (pp. 200–213). Oxford: Oxford University Press.

Heiss, W. D. (1983). Flow thresholds of functional and morphological damage of brain tissue. *Stroke, 14,* 329–331.

Higgins, M. (Ed). (1993). Proceedings of the National Heart, Lung and Blood Institute conference on the decline in stroke mortality. *Annals of Epidemiology, 3,* 453–575.

Irle, E., Wowra, B., Kunert, H. J., Hampl, J., & Kunze, S. (1992). Memory disturbances following anterior communicating artery rupture. *Annals of Neurology, 31,* 473–480.

Ishii, N., Nishihara, Y., & Imamura, T. (1986). Why do frontal lobe symptoms predominante in vascular dementia with lacunes? *Neurology, 36,* 340–345.

Kashihara, M., & Matsumoto, K. (1985). Acute capsular infarction, location of lesions and the clinical features. *Neuroradiology, 27,* 248–253.

Katz, D. I., Alexander, M. P., & Mandell, A. M. (1987). Dementia following strokes in the mesencephalon and diencephalon. *Archives of Neurology, 44,* 1127–1133.

Kazui, S., Sawada, T., Naritomi, H., Kuriyama, Y., & Yamaguchi, T. (1993). Angiographic evaluation of brain infarction limited to the cerebral artery territory. *Stroke, 24,* 549–553.

Kertesz, A., Nicholson, I., Cancelliere, A., Kassa, K., & Black. (1985). Motor impersistence: A right-hemisphere syndrome. *Neurology, 35,* 662–666.

Krayenbühl, H., & Yasargil, M. G. (1968). Radiological anatomy and topography of the cerebral vessels. In H. A. Krayenbuhl & M. G. Yasargie (Eds.), *Cerebral angiography* (2nd ed.). Philadelphia: J. B. Lippincott.

Kulisevsky, J., Berthier, M. L., & Pujol, J. (1993). Hemiballismus and secondary mania following a right thalamic infarction. *Neurology, 43,* 1422–1424.

Kunesch, E., Binkofski, F., Steinmetz, H., & Freund, H.-J. (1995). The pattern of motor deficits in relation to the site of stroke lesions. *European Neurology, 35,* 20–26.

LaPlane, D., Baulac, M., Widlocher, D., & Dubois, B. (1984). Pure psychic akinesia with bilateral lesions of basal ganglia. *Journal of Neurology, Neurosurgery, and Psychiatry, 47,* 377–385.

Lassen, N. A. (1959). Cerebral blood flow and oxygen consumption in man. *Physiological Review, 39,* 183–238.

Levin, H. S., Goldstein, F. C., Ghostine, S. Y., Wiener, R. L., Crofford, M. J., & Eisenberg, H. M. (1987). Hemispheric disconnection syndrome persisting after anterior cerebral artery aneurysm rupture. *Neurosurgery, 21,* 831–838.

Levy, A. S. M., Lillehei, K. O., Rubinstein, D., & Stears, J. C. (1995). Subarachnoid neurocystercercosis with occlusion of the major intracranial arteries: Case report. *Neurosurgery, 36,* 183–188.

Libon, D. J., Scanlon, M., Swenson, R., & Coslett, M. B. (1990). Binswanger's disease: Some neuropsychological considerations. *Journal of Geriatric Psychiatry and Neurology, 3,* 23–32.

Liepmann, H., & Maas, O. (1907). Fall von linksseitiger Agraphie und Apraxie bei rechtseitiger Lähmung. *Zeitung für Psychologie und Neurologie, 10,* 214–227.

Lindgren, A., Norrving, B., Rudling, O., & Johannson, B. B. (1994). Comparison of clinical and neuroradiological findings in first-ever stroke. *Stroke, 25,* 1371–1377.

Lindqvist, G., & Norlen, G. (1966). Korsakoff's syndrome after operation on ruptured aneurysm of the anterior communicating artery. *Acta Psychiatrica Scandinavica, 42,* 24–34.

Loizou, L. A., Kendall, B. E., & Marshall, J. (1981). Subcortical arteriosclerotic encephalopathy: A clinical and radiological investigation. *Journal of Neurology, Neurosurgery, and Psychiatry, 44,* 294–304.

Luijckx, G. J., Boiten, J., Lodder, J., Heuts-van Raak, L., & Wilmink, J. (1994). Isolated hemiataxia after supratentorial brain infarction. *Journal of Neurology, Neurosurgery, and Psychiatry, 57,* 742–744.

Malamut, B. L., Graff-Radford, N., Chawluk, J., Grossman, R. I., & Gur, R. C. (1992). Memory in a case of bilateral thalamic infarction. *Neurology, 42,* 163–169.

Marie, P. (1901). Des foyers lacunaires de désintegration et de différents autres étâts cavitaires du cerveau. *Revue Médicale, 21,* 281–298.

Meador, K. L., Watson, R. T., Bowers, D., & Heilman, K. M. (1986). Hypometria with hemispatal and limb motor neglect. *Brain, 109,* 293–305.

Mendez, M. F., Adams, N. L., & Lewandowski, K. S. (1989). Neurobehavioral changes associated with caudate lesions. *Neurology, 39,* 349–354.

Mesulam, M. M. (1981). A cortical network for directed attention and unilateral neglect. *Annals of Neurology, 10,* 309–325.

Mesulam, M. M., & Geschwind, N. (1978). On the possible role of neocortex and its limbic connections in the process of attention and schizophrenia: Clinical cases of inattention in man and experimental anatomy in monkey. *Journal of Pyschiatric Research, 14,* 249–260.

Mishkin, M., & Manning, F. J. (1978). Nonspatial memory after selective prefrontal lesions in monkeys. *Brain Research, 143,* 313–323.

Mochizuki, H., & Saito, H. (1990). Mesial frontal lobe syndromes: Correlations between neurological deficits and radiological localizations. *Tohoku Journal of Experimental Medicine, 161,* 231–239.

Moulin, T., Bogousslavsky, J., Chopard, J. L., Ghika, J., Crepin-Leblond, T., Martin, V., & Maeder, P. (1995). Vascular ataxic hemiparesis: A re-evaluation. *Journal of Neurology, Neurosurgery, and Psychiatry, 58,* 422–427.

Mounier-Vehier, F., Leys, D., Godefroy, O., Rodepierre, P., Marchau, M., & Pruvo, J. P. (1994). Borderzone infarct subtypes: Preliminary study of the presumed mechanism. *European Neurology, 34,* 11–15.

Mull, M., Schwarz, M., & Thron, A. (1997). Cerebral hemispheric low-flow infarct in arterial occlusive disease: Lesion patterns and angiomorphological conditions. *Stroke, 28,* 118–123.

Muller, M., Merkelbach, S., Huss, G. P., & Schimrigk, K. (1995). Clinical relevance and frequency of transient stenoses of the middle and anterior cerebral arteries in bacterial meningitis. *Stroke, 26,* 1399–1403.

Naeser, M. A., Palumbo, C. L., Helm-Estabrooks, N., Stiassny-Eden, D., & Albert, M. L. (1989). Severe nonfluency in aphasia: Role of the medial subcallosal fasciculus and other white matter pathways in recovery of spontaneous speech. *Brain, 112,* 1–38.

Nielsen, J. M., & Jacobs L. L. (1951). Bilateral lesions of the anterior cingulate gyri. *Bulletin of the Los Angeles Neurological Society, 16,* 230.

Nieuwenhuys, R., Voogd, J., & van Huijzen, C. (1983). *The human central nervous system.* New York: Springer-Verlag.

Olszewski, J. (1962). Subcortical arteriosclerotic encephalopathy: Review of the literature on the so-called Binswanger's disease and presentation of two cases. *World Neurology, 3,* 359–374.

Papez, J. W. (1937). A proposed mechanism of emotion. *Archives of Neurology and Psychiatry, 38,* 725–743.

Park-Matsumoto, Y. C., Ogawa, K., Tazawa, T., Ishiai, S., Tei, H., & Yuasa, T. (1995). Mutism developing after bilateral thalamo-capsular lesions by neuro-Behcet disease. *Acta Neurologica Scandinavica, 91,* 297–301.

Pedrazzi, P., Bogousslavsky, J., & Regli, F. (1990). Hématomes limités à la tête du noyau caudé. *Revue Neurologique, 146,* 726–738.

Prospective Studies Collaboration. (1995). Cholesterol, diastolic blood pressure, and stroke: 13,000 strokes in 450,000 people in 45 prospective cohorts. *Lancet, 346,* 1647–1683.

Pullicino, P. M. (1993). Diagrams of perforating artery territories in axial, coronal, and sagittal planes. In P. M. Pullicino, L. R. Caplan, & M. Hommel (Eds.), *Advances in neurology* (Vol. 62, pp. 41–72). New York: Raven Press.

Richardson, J. T. E. (1989). Performance in free recall following rupture and repair of intracranial aneurysm. *Brain Cognition, 9,* 210–226.

Richfield, E. K., Twyman, R., & Berent, S. (1987). Neurological syndrome following bilateral damage to the head of the caudate. *Annals of Neurology, 22,* 768–771.

Román, G. C. (1987). Senile dementia of the Binswanger type. *Journal of the American Medical Association, 258,* 1782–1788.

Ross, E. D. (1980). Localization of the pyramidal tract in the internal capsule by whole brain dissection. *Neurology, 30,* 59–64.

Sacco, R. (1994). Ischemic stroke. In P. B. Gorelick & M. Alter (Eds.), *Handbook of neuroepidemiology* (pp. 77–119). New York: Marcel Decker.

Sacco, R. L., Hauser, W. A., & Mohr, J. P. (1991). Hospitalized stroke incidence in blacks and Hispanics in northern Manhattan. *Stroke, 22,* 1491–1496.

Sandson, T. A., Daffner, K. R., Carvalho, P. A., & Mesulam, M. -M. (1991). Frontal lobe dysfunction following infarction of the left-sided and medial thalamus. *Archives of Neurology, 48,* 1300–1302.

Schlesinger, B. (1976). *The upper brainstem in the human.* Berlin: Springer-Verlag.

Schoenberg, B. S., & Schulte, B. P. M. (1988). Cerebrovascular disease: Epidemiology and geopathology. In P. J. Vinken, G. W. Bruyn, & H. L. Klawans (Eds.), *Handbook of clinical neurology, vascular diseases, Part I* (Vol. 53, pp. 1–26). Amsterdam: Elsevier.

Schneider, R., & Gautier, J. C. (1994). Leg weakness due to stroke: Site of lesions, weakness patterns, and causes. *Brain, 117,* 347–354.

Segarra, J. M. (1970). Cerebral vascular disease and behavior. I. The syndrome of the mesencephalic artery (basilar artery bifurcation) *Archives of Neurology, 22,* 408–418.

Shallice, T., & Burgess, P. (1991). Higher-order cognitive impairments and frontal lobe lesions in man. In H. S. Levin, H. M. Eisenberg, & A. L. Benton (Eds.), *Frontal lobe function and dysfunction* (pp. 125–138). Oxford: Oxford University Press.

Sharbrough, F. W., Messick, J. M., & Sundt, T. M. (1973). Correlation of continuous electroen-cephalograms with cerebral blood flow measurements during carotid endarterectomy. *Stroke, 4,* 674–683.

Shimamura, A. P., Janowsky, J. S., & Squire, L. R. (1991). What is the role of frontal lobe damage in memory disorders? In H. S. Levin, H. M. Eisenberg, & A. L. Benton (Eds.), *Frontal lobe function and dysfunction* (pp. 173–195). Oxford: Oxford University Press.

Sinyor, D., Kaloupek, J. P., Becker, D. G., Goldenberg, M., & Coopersmith, H. M. (1986). Post-stroke depression and lesion location: An attempted replication. *Brain, 109,* 537–546.

Smith, W. K. (1944) The results of ablation of the cingular region of the cerebral cortex. *Federation Proceedings, 3,* 42.

Starkstein, S. E., Boston, J. D., & Robinson, R. G. (1988). Mechanisms of mania after brain injury: 12 case reports and review of the literature. *Journal of Nervous Mental Diseases, 176,* 87–100.

Starkstein, S. E., Pearlson, G. D., Boston, J., & Robinson, R. G. (1987). Mania after brain injury: A controlled study of causative factors. *Archives of Neurology, 44,* 1069–1073.

Starkstein, S. E., Robinson, R. G., Berthier, M. L., Parikh, R. M., & Price, T. R. (1988). Differential mood changes following basal ganglia vs. thalamic lesions. *Archives of Neurology, 45,* 725–730.

Starkstein, S. E., Robinson, R. G., & Price, T. R. (1987). Comparison of cortical and subcortical lesions in the production of post-stroke mood disorders. *Brain, 110,* 1045–1059.

Starkstein, S. E., Sabe, L., Vazquez, S., Teson, A., Petracca, G., Chemerinski, E., Di Lorenzo, G., & Leiguarda, R. (1996). Neuropsychological, psychiatric, and cerebral blood flow findings in vascular dementia and Alzheimer's disease. *Stroke, 27,* 408–414.

Stehbens, W. E. (1972). Intracranial arterial aneuryms. In W. E. Stehbens (Ed.), *Pathology of the cerebral blood vessels* (pp. 351–470). St. Louis: C. V. Mosby.

Stephens, R. B., & Stilwell, D. L. (1969). *Arteries and veins of the human brain.* Springfield: Charles C Thomas.

Strub, R. L. (1989). Frontal lobe syndrome in a patient with bilateral globus pallidus lesions. *Archives of Neurology, 46,* 1024–1027.

Stuss, D. T., & Benson, D. F. (1986). *The frontal lobes.* New York: Raven Press.

Stuss, D. T., Guberman, A., Nelson R., & Larochelle, S. (1988). The neuropsychology of paramedian thalamic infarction. *Brain Cognition, 8,* 348–378.

Talland, G. A., Sweet, W. H., & Ballantine, H. T. (1967). Amnesic syndrome with anterior communicating artery aneurysm. *Journal of Nervous and Mental Diseases, 145,* 179–192.

Tatemichi, T. K., Desmond, D. W., & Mayeux, R. (1992). Dementia after stroke: Baseline frequency, risks, clinical features in a hospitalized cohort. *Neurology, 42,* 1185–1193.

Tatemichi, T. K., Desmond, D. W., Paik, M., Figueroa, M., Gropen, T. I., Stern, Y., Sano, M., Remien, R., Williams, J. B. W., Mohr, J. P., & Mayeux, R. (1993). Clinical determinants of dementia related to stroke. *Annals of Neurology, 33,* 568–575.

Tatemichi, T., Desmond, D. W., Prohovnik, I. (1995). Strategic infarcts in vascular dementia: A clinical and brain imaging experience. *Drug Research, 45,* 371–385.

Tatemichi, T., Desmond, D. W., Prohovnik, I., Cross, D. T., Gropen, T. I., Mohr, J. P., & Stern, Y. (1992). Confusion and memory loss from capsular genu infarction: A thalamocortical disconnection syndrome? *Neurology, 42,* 1966–1979.

Tatemichi, T. K., Desmond, D. W., Stern, Y., Paik, M., Sano, M., & Bagiella, E. (1994). Cognitive impairment after stroke: Frequency, patterns, and relationship to functional abilities. *Journal of Neurology, Neurosurgery, and Psychiatry, 57,* 202–207.

Tei, H., Uchiyama, S., & Maruyama, S. (1993). Capsular infarcts: Location, size, and etiology of pure motor hemiparesis, sensorimotor stroke, and ataxic hemiparesis. *Acta Neurologica Scandanavica, 88,* 264–268.

Tell, G., Crouse, J., & Furberg, C. (1988). Relation between blood lipids, lipoproteins, and cerebrovascular atherosclerosis: A review. *Stroke, 19,* 423–430.

Torvik, A. (1984). The pathogenesis of watershed infarcions in the brain. *Stroke, 15,* 221–223.

Tournier-Lasserve, E., Joutel, A., Melki, J., Weissenbach, J., Lathrop, M., Chabriat, H., Mas, J. L., Cabanis, E. A., Baudrimont, M., Maciazek, J., Bach, M. A., & Bousser, M. G. (1993). Cerebral autosomal dominant arteriopathy with infarcts and leukoencephalopathy maps to chromosome 19q12. *Nature Genetics, 3,* 256–259.

Ventura, M. G., Goldman, S., & Hildebrand, J. (1995) Alien hand syndrome without a corpus callosum lesion. *Journal of Neurology, Neurosurgery, and Psychiatry, 58,* 735–737.

Vinters, H. V. (1987). Cerebral amyloid angiopathy: A critical review. *Stroke, 18,* 311–324.

Volpe, B. T., & Hirst, W. (1983). Amnesia following the rupture and repair of an anterior communicating artery aneurysm. *Journal of Neurology, Neurosurgery, and Psychiatry, 46,* 704–709.

Voytko, M. L. (1985). Cooling orbital frontal cortex disrupts matching-to-sample and visual discrimination learning in monkeys. *Physiological Psychology, 13,* 219–229.

Walton, J. N. (1953). The Korsakov syndrome in spontaneous subarachnoid hemorrhage. *Journal of Mental Science, 99,* 521–530.

Watson, R. T., & Heilman, K. M. (1983). Callosal apraxia. *Brain, 106,* 391–403.

Watson, R. T., Heilman, K. M., Cauthen, J. C., & King, F. A. (1973). Neglect after cingulectomy. *Neurology, 23,* 1003–1007.

Watson, R. T., Valenstein, E., & Heilman, K. M. (1981). Thalamic neglect: Possible role of the medial thalamus and nucleus reticularis in behavior. *Archives of Neurology, 38,* 501–506.

Weiller, C., Willmes, K., Reiche, W., Thron, C. I., Buell, U., & Rigelstein, E. B. (1993). The case of aphasia or neglect after striatocapsular infarction. *Brain, 16,* 1509–1525.

Weir, B. (1987). *Aneurysms affecting the nervous system.* Baltimore: Williams & Wilkins.

Wijdicks, E. F., & Jack, C. R. (1996). Coronary artery bypass grafting-associated ischemic stroke. A clinical and neuroradiological study. *Journal of Neuroimaging, 6,* 20–22.

Wolf, P. A., D'Agostino, R. B., Belanger, A. J., & Kannel, W. B. (1991). Probability of stroke: A risk profile from the Framingham Study. *Stroke, 22,* 312–318.

Wolf, P. A., Dawber, T. R., Thomas, H. E., & Kannel, W. B. (1978). Epidemiological assessment of chronic atrial fibrillation and risk of stroke: The Framingham Study. *Neurology, 28,* 973–977.

Wolfe, N., Linn, R., Babikian, V. L., Knoefel, J. E., & Albert, M. L. (1990). Frontal systems impairment following multiple lacunar infarcts. *Archives of Neurology, 47,* 129–132.

Yamaguchi, T., Minematsu, K., Choki, J., & Ikeda, M. (1984). Clinical and neuroradiological analysis of thrombotic and embolic cerebral infarction. *Japan Circulation Journal, 48,* 50–58.

Yamanouchi, H. (1991). Loss of white matter oligodendrocytes and astrocytes in progressive subcortical vascular encephalopathy of Binswanger type. *Acta Neurologica Scandinavica, 83,* 301–305.

Yamanouchi, H., Sugiura, S., & Tomonaga, M. (1989). Decrease in nerve fibres in cerebral white matter in progressive subcortical vascular encephalopathy of Binswanger type. An electron microscopic study. *Journal of Neurology, 236,* 382–387.

22

Extrapyramidal Disorders and Frontal Lobe Function

IRENE LITVAN

The extrapyramidal disorders are a heterogeneous group of clinical syndromes with a common anatomic lesion in the basal ganglia. There is a vast literature on the characterization of the motor aspects of extrapyramidal disorders, but less is known about the pathophysiology of the neuropsychiatric and cognitive aspects of these disorders. Few studies have attempted to correlate neuropathological lesions with behavioral or cognitive abnormalities. As discussed in Chapter 1 (this volume), five frontosubcortical circuits unite regions of the frontal lobe with the striatum, globus pallidus, and thalamus in functional systems that mediate motor activities, eye movements, cognition and behavior (Alexander & Crutcher, 1990; Alexander, DeLong, & Strick, 1986; Cummings, 1995). The five circuits originate in the supplementary motor area, frontal eye fields, dorsolateral prefrontal cortex, orbitofrontal cortex, and anterior cingulate cortex and mediate volitional motor activity, saccadic eye movements, executive functions, motivation and social behavior, respectively. Thus, it is not surprising that functional and behavioral abnormalities reflecting interruption of these circuits are present in extrapyramidal disorders such as Parkinson's disease (PD), progressive supranuclear palsy (PSP, also called Steele–Richardson–Olszewski syndrome), multiple system atrophy (MSA), or Huntington's disease (Agid et al., 1987; Cummings, 1995; Cummings & Benson, 1984, 1988; Forno, 1992; Gibb, 1992; Pillon, Dubois, Ploska, & Agid, 1991). Understanding the behavioral and cognitive abnormalities of extrapyramidal disorders extends our knowledge of basal ganglia functions. In addition, because neurobehavioral abnormalities can be powerful predictors of institutionalization, their recognition and management may delay this course of action for patients (Goetz & Stebbins, 1993, 1995; Morriss, Rovner, Folstein, & German, 1990; Steele, Rovner, Chase, & Folstein, 1990).

This review examines the differential frontosubcortical pattern of anatomic lesions of four major extrapyramidal disorders, and the consequent motor, eye movement, executive, motivation, and social behavioral dysfunction observed.

ANATOMIC FRONTOSUBCORTICAL INVOLVEMENT

The frontal lobe projects to the caudate, putamen, and nucleus accumbens. It is hypothesized that normal basal ganglia function is a result of a balance between the direct and indirect striatal output pathways (see Figures 22.1A, 22.1B). Overall, the direct pathway facilitates the flow of information while the indirect pathway inhibits it. The globus pallidus interna and subtantia nigra pars reticulata connect to the thalamus. Normal function results from a balance between thalamic disinhibition by the direct pathway and subthalamic inhibition by the indirect pathway. The thalamus, in turn, completes the circuit by projecting back to the frontal lobes. The involvement of the five circuits in these disorders is discussed; the motor is the best known.

Motor Circuit

The variety of clinical manifestations of the extrapyramidal disorders are associated with changes in the function of striatal projection neurons (Albin, Young, & Penney, 1995; Alexander & Crutcher, 1990; DeLong, 1990). The differential involvement of the two major parallel striatal output pathways accounts for the hypokinesia or hyperkinesia observed in the extrapyramidal disorders (Figure 22.1). For example, in PD (Figure 22.1A), the chief problem is a decreased dopaminergic nigrostriatal stimulation resulting in both an excess outflow of the indirect striatal pathway and an inhibition of the direct striatal pathway. Both networks increase the thalamic inhibition and decrease the thalamocortical stimulation of motor cortical areas. The decreased motor cortical activity explains the hypokinesia. In PSP and MSA, in addition to involvement of the dopaminergic nigrostriatal pathways, several output nuclei (putamen, pallidum, and subthalamic nuclei) and afferent areas (motor cortex, less consistently premotor) are involved. However, cortical lesions are probably secondary to subcortical degeneration (Hof, Delacourte, & Bouras, 1992).

In contrast to parkinsonian disorders, in the early stages in Huntington's disease, there is a selective loss of γ-aminobutyric acid (GABA)ergic enkephalinergic intrinsic striatal neurons projecting to the lateral globus pallidus and substantia nigra pars reticulata. The decreased inhibitory stimulation to the thalamus increases the activity of the excitatory glutamatergic thalamocortical pathway, which in turn increases neuronal activity in the premotor–motor–supplementary motor cortex and overfacilitates motor program execution, resulting in chorea (Figure 22.1B). In Huntington's disease, frontal and prefrontal cortical involvement has also been reported in pathological studies.

Oculomotor Circuit

There is a different degree of involvement of the oculomotor circuitry in these extrapyramidal disorders, with PSP being the most affected (see Figure 22.2). Striatal dopaminergic deafferentation may explain the minimal oculomotor involvement in PD. Degeneration of the caudate, dorsolateral cortex, and the output pathways in PSP, MSA, and Huntington's disease may contribute to the oculomotor abnormalities observed in all these disorders. However, lesions in Huntington's disease initially affect GABAergic enkephalinergic striatal interneurons, whereas in PSP, striatal cholinergic interneurons are involved. Thus, the output pathways are differently affected in PSP and in Huntington's disease (Figure 22.2A, 22.2B). In addition, in PSP, the frontal and parietal eye field and several brainstem nuclei (Verny, Duyckaerts, Agid, & Hauw, 1996) are all involved. Damage to brainstem nuclei

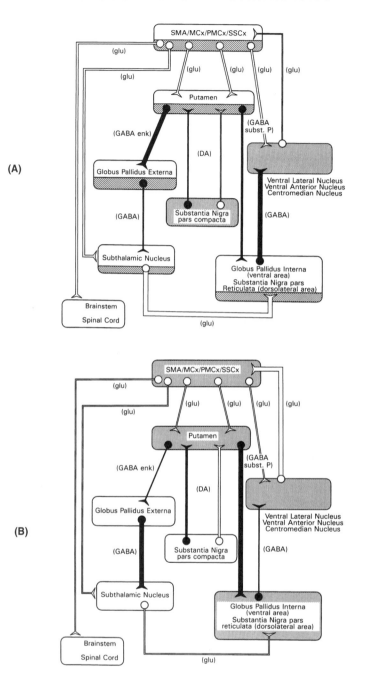

FIGURE 22.1. (A) Schematic diagram of the motor circuit in hypokinetic disorders (PD, PSP, MSA). Stippled areas represent affected nuclei in PD, PSP, and MSA; hatched areas represent affected nuclei in PSP and MSA. Inhibitory neurons are shown as filled symbols, excitatory neurons as open symbols. Overall effects are postulated in PD. (B) Schematic diagram of the motor circuit in Huntington's disease. Stippled areas represent affected nuclei in Huntington's disease. Inhibitory neurons are shown as filled symbols, excitatory neurons as open symbols. DA, dopamine; GABA, γ-aminobutyric acid; enk, enkephalin; subst P, substance P; glu, glutamate; SMA, supplementary motor area; MCx, primary motor cortex; PMCx, premotor cortex; SSCx, somatosensory cortex.

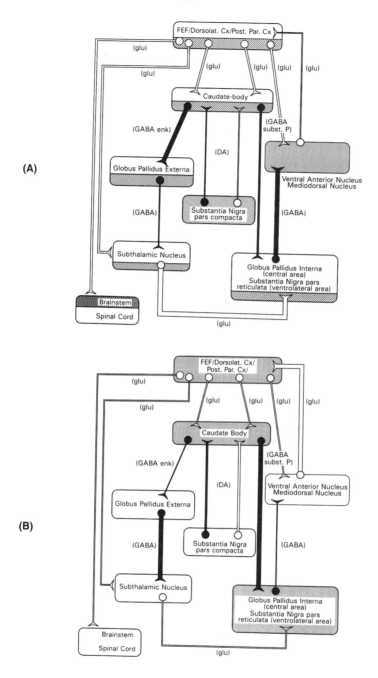

FIGURE 22.2. (A) Schematic diagram of the oculomotor circuit in PD, PSP, MSA. Stippled areas represent lesions in PD, PSP, MSA; hatched areas represent lesions in PSP and MSA; double-hatched areas represent affected nuclei in PSP. Inhibitory neurons are shown as filled symbols, excitatory neurons as open symbols. Overall effects are postulated in PD. (B) Schematic diagram of the oculomotor circuit in Huntington's disease. Stippled areas represent affected nuclei in Huntington's disease. Inhibitory neurons are shown as filled symbols, excitatory neurons as open symbols. DA, dopamine; GABA, γ-aminobutyric acid; enk, enkephalin; subst P, substance P; glu, glutamate; FEF, frontal eye field; Cx, cortex; dorsolat, dorsolateral; post, posterior; par, parietal.

such as the rostral interstitial nucleus of the medial longitudinal fasciculus, interstitial nucleus of Cajal, superior colliculus, and the adjacent reticular formation is thought to account for the vertical gaze palsy (Juncos et al., 1991), while alteration of horizontal saccades is better correlated with pontine neuronal loss (paramedian pontine reticular formation) (Malessa et al., 1991, 1994). Careful morphometric investigations (Revesz, Sangha, & Daniel, 1996) suggest that severe involvement of the GABAergic nucleus raphe interpositus and/or perhaps of the cholinergic pedunculopontine nuclei (Verny et al., 1996) may explain the supranuclear palsy observed in PSP patients.

Dorsolateral Prefrontal Circuit

The dorsolateral prefrontal circuit is particularly affected in PSP but less so in the other disorders (see Figure 22.3). In PD, there is no degeneration but deafferentation of the caudate, which is much less compromised than the putamen. Lesions in the frontal cortex, including the dorsolateral frontal and premotor cortices, are more consistently found in PSP than in MSA or Huntington's disease (Arai, Papp, & Lantos, 1994; Vermersch et al., 1994; Verny et al., 1996). Degeneration of the dorsolateral caudate is seen in PSP and MSA (Gibb, 1992; Graham & Lantos, 1997) but in MSA is relatively preserved (Brooks et al., 1990). The dorsal caudate is severely affected in Huntington's disease (Graham & Lantos, 1997). Again, because lesions in Huntington's disease affect the GABAergic enkephalinergic interneurons of the caudate but in PSP affect the cholinergic interneurons, the output pathways are differently involved at early stages (Figure 22.3A, 22.3B). In addition, in PSP, there is severe neuronal loss in the mediodorsal thalamic nuclei affecting the matrix (75%), which projects to the dorsal frontal cortex (Brandel et al., 1991). Thus, a severe executive dysfunction is predicted in PSP, whereas motor, rather than executive dysfunction, is expected in PD and MSA (see following section). In addition, we would expect a different type of errors in PSP, PD, and MSA than in Huntington's disease.

Orbitofrontal Circuit

In PD, orbitofrontal circuit involvement is less conspicuous; the anterior cingulate cortex is affected with Lewy bodies and the caudate is deafferented (Forno, 1996). Mesocortical dopaminergic, noradrenergic and serotonergic pathways are consistently affected in PD (but relatively spared in PSP) (Agid et al., 1987; Ruberg et al., 1985). Depressed PD patients have more severe neuronal loss in the dorsal raphe than do nondepressed patients (Paulus & Jellinger, 1991). In addition, serotonin binding sites are severely decreased in the frontal cortex and basal ganglia in PD (Chinaglia, Landwehrmeyer, Probst, & Palacios, 1993). Thus, in PD, impaired ascending serotonergic, noradrenergic, and dopaminergic mesocortical pathways contribute to the medial frontosubcortical circuit dysfunction and may explain the increased frequency of associated depression (see following section).

In PSP, the anterior cingulate cortex, superior and inferior temporal gyri, ventral striatum, subthalamic, and mediodorsal thalamic nuclei have neurofibrillary tangles (Graham & Lantos, 1997; Jellinger & Bancher, 1992) (see Figure 22.4A). In fact, the patch, which is the mediodorsal thalamic area thought to project to the orbitofrontal cortex, degenerates in PSP (Brandel et al., 1991).

In MSA, the anterior cingulate cortex, ventral striatum, and subthalamic nuclei are involved (Graham & Lantos, 1997). Thus, the orbitofrontal circuit is more severely and

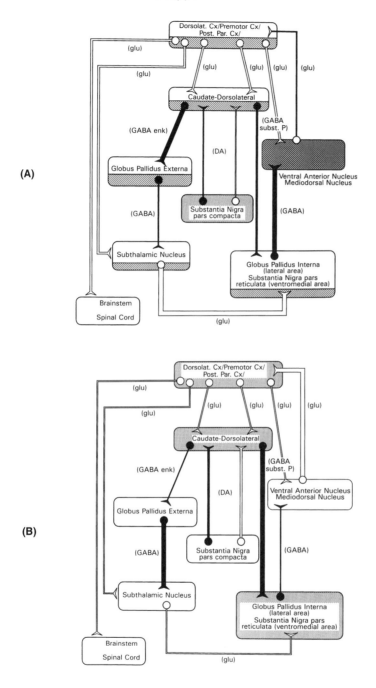

FIGURE 22.3. (A) Schematic diagram of the dorsolateral circuit in PD, PSP, MSA. Stippled areas represent lesions in PD, PSP, MSA; hatched areas represent lesions in PSP and MSA; double-hatched areas represent affected nuclei in PSP. Inhibitory neurons are shown as filled symbols, excitatory neurons as open symbols. Overall effects are postulated in PD. (B) Schematic diagram of dorsolateral circuit in Huntington's disease. Stippled areas represent affected nuclei in Huntington's disease. Inhibitory neurons are shown as filled symbols, excitatory neurons as open symbols. DA, dopamine; GABA, γ-aminobutyric acid; enk, enkephalin; subst P, substance P; glu, glutamate; Cx, cortex; dorsolat, dorsolateral; par, parietal; post, posterior.

differently involved in PSP and PD than in MSA, and scientists expect the effects on the patients' moods to be different in these three disorders. In Huntington's disease, the orbitofrontal and anterior cingulate cortices, ventromedial caudate, and subthalamic nuclei are affected, and to differing degrees, depending on the stage of the disease (postulated early stage, see Figure 22.4B). Therefore, it is hypothesized that in this disorder effects on mood vary at different disease stages (see following section).

Medial Frontal Circuit

In PD, involvement is more restricted to the anterior cingulate, ventral tegmental area, and nucleus accumbens; the entorhinal cortex and hippocampus are inconsistently affected. In PSP, the medial frontal circuit is partially or totally disconnected because several relay nuclei are considerably damaged. There is an increased number of neurofibrillary tangles found in the anterior cingulate cortex, entorhinal cortex, hippocampus, ventral striatum, and mediodorsal thalamic nucleus (Braak, Jellinger, Braak, & Bohl, 1992; Brandel et al., 1991; Hof et al., 1992; Jellinger & Bancher, 1992) (Figure 22.5A). In MSA, medial frontal circuit involvement is minor; there may be inconsistent lesions in the anterior cingulate cortex and hippocampus (Arai et al., 1994; Graham & Lantos, 1997), but it is unclear whether the entorhinal cortex is affected.

In Huntington's disease, the anterior cingulate cortex, entorhinal cortex, and hippocampus are usually affected, but the ventral striatum is less consistently affected (Jellinger, 1995) (Figure 22.5B). The medial frontal circuit is variously involved, in the examined extrapyramidal disorders, that is, more severely affected in PSP, less so in MSA, and qualitatively differently compromised in Huntington's disease (see Figure 22.5A, 22.5B). Thus, effects on motivation are expected to be more severe in PSP than in any of the other disorders.

ASSOCIATED LESIONS MODULATING FRONTOSUBCORTICAL CIRCUITS

In PSP, the cholinergic pedunculopontine nuclei are severely degenerated and, to a lesser degree, so is the cholinergic nucleus basalis of Meynert. However, the reverse is true in PD (Hirsch, Graybiel, Duyckaerts, & Javoy-Agid, 1987; Jellinger & Bancher, 1992; Rogers, Brogan, & Mirra, 1985). Decreased innominatocortical cholinergic activity in PSP probably contributes to the cognitive deficit observed in this disorder (Hirsch et al., 1987). Data on MSA are somewhat limited, but glial cytoplasmic inclusions have been found in these areas (Papp, Kahn, & Lantos, 1989). Neither the pedunculopontine nuclei nor the nucleus basalis of Meynert is involved in Huntington's disease.

CLINICAL FRONTOSUBCORTICAL INVOLVEMENT

Motor abnormalities are associated with dysfunction of the subcortical projections to the premotor–motor and supplementary motor subcortical circuit; supranuclear gaze palsy is related to disturbances of the frontal eyefield subcortical circuit; executive dysfunction is a result of an affected dorsolateral prefrontal subcortical circuitry; disinhibition is the behavioral correlate of orbitofrontal subcortical involvement; and apathy correlates with dysfunction of the medial frontal subcortical circuit. The resulting major clinical dysfunction, secondary to the abnormalities in each of these circuits, is discussed. Of note, the

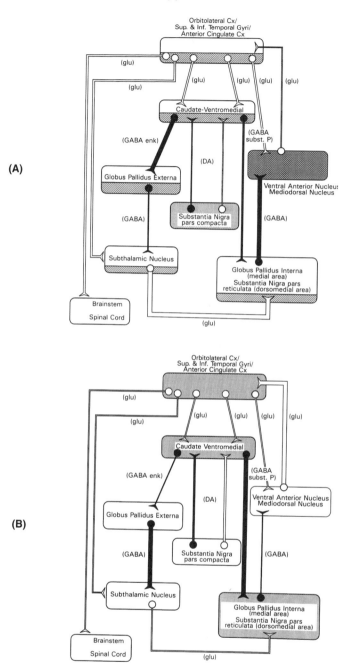

FIGURE 22.4. (A) Schematic diagram of the orbitofrontal circuit in PD, PSP, MSA. Stippled areas represent lesions in PD, PSP, MSA; hatched areas represent lesions in PSP and MSA; double-hatched areas represent affected nuclei in PSP. Inhibitory neurons are shown as filled symbols, excitatory neurons as open symbols. Overall effects are postulated in PD. (B) Schematic diagram of the orbitofrontal circuit in Huntington's disease. Stippled areas represent affected nuclei in Huntington's disease. Inhibitory neurons are shown as filled symbols, excitatory neurons as open symbols. DA, dopamine; GABA, γ-aminobutyric acid; enk, enkephalin; subst P, substance P; glu, glutamate; Cx, cortex; sup, superior; inf, inferior.

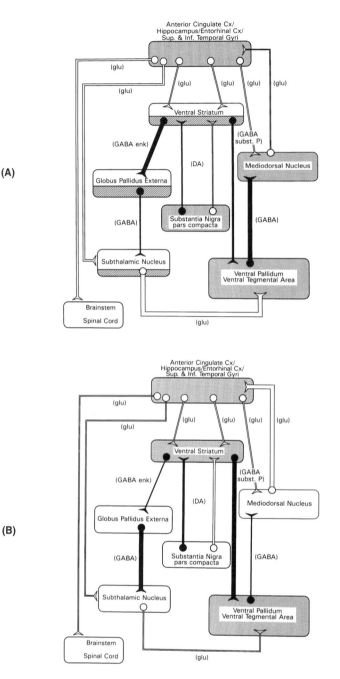

FIGURE 22.5. (A) Schematic diagram of the medial frontal circuit in PD, PSP, MSA. Stippled areas represent lesions in PD, PSP, MSA; hatched areas represent lesions in PSP and MSA. Inhibitory neurons are shown as filled symbols, excitatory neurons as open symbols. Overall effects are postulated in PD. (B) Schematic diagram of the medial frontal circuit in Huntington's disease. Stippled areas represent affected nuclei in Huntington's disease. Inhibitory neurons are shown as filled symbols, excitatory neurons as open symbols. DA, dopamine; GABA, γ-aminobutyric acid; enk, enkephalin; subst P, substance P; glu, glutamate; Cx, cortex; sup, superior; inf, inferior.

relatively distinct anatomic involvement observed during the early stages in the extrapyramidal disorders becomes less evident at the end stage of the disease. This is particularly true in Huntington's disease. Thus, it is not surprising to find, particularly at later stages, considerable symptomatological overlap.

Motor Dysfunction

In PD, the asymmetric onset of bradykinesia, rigidity, and resting tremor benefiting from levodopa therapy are associated with the asymmetrical striatal deafferentation secondary to nigral damage as shown in PET studies. [^{18}F]2-Deoxyglucose PET studies in patients with early unilateral PD show mildly increased metabolism in the lentiform nucleus, whereas PET studies with [^{18}F]Dopa show reduced radioactivity in the putamen contralateral to the affected limbs but with normal caudate activity. In more advanced stages of PD, there is normal striatal metabolism, a symmetrical decrease accumulation of fluorodopa in the caudate, and a marked decrease in the putamen (Martin & Hayden, 1987; Brooks, 1994). Additional degeneration of the putamen, pallidum, and subthalamic nuclei may account for the poor levodopa response observed in PSP and MSA. In PSP, symptoms are generally symmetrical. [^{18}F]Dopa PET studies show that the uptake is significantly reduced in both putamen and caudate in PSP and MSA (Brooks, 1994).

On the other hand, in adult-onset Huntington's disease, the chorea, evident at early stages, is related to a decreased flow in the indirect pathway, but widespread involvement of the output pathways accounts for the rigidity and dystonia observed at later stages. [^{18}F]2-Deoxyglucose PET studies in patients with early Huntington's disease show caudate hypometabolism prior to development of caudate atrophy (Martin & Hayden, 1987). At more advanced stages in Huntington's disease, PET hypometabolism is also evident in the putamen (Young et al., 1986). The fact that in early stages of the disease there is hypometabolism in the caudate but not in the putamen reinforces the pathological information that the disorder begins in the caudate and then progresses to the putamen. In these studies, motor functions (chorea, fine motor functions) correlate highly with indices of putamen metabolism.

Motor learning also relies on the frontal motor circuit, procedural learning is severely affected in patients with extrapyramidal disorders. Patients with PD, PSP, MSA, and Huntington's disease have significant difficulty in acquiring motor skills, whereas controls or patients with cortical lesions, such as those with Alzheimer's disease, significantly improve their learning performance. These findings provide evidence that the basal ganglia are critically involved not only in the performance of elemental motor tasks but also in the acquisition of motor skills (Daum et al., 1995; Grafman, Weingartner, et al., 1990; Heindel, Butters, & Salmon, 1988; Heindel, Salmon, Shults, Walicke, & Butters, 1989; Martone, Butters, Payne, Becker, & Sax, 1984). This finding also implies that episodic, semantic, and procedural memory depend on different neuronal networks. On the other hand, another type of motor learning, classical eyeblink conditioning, seems to be independent of basal ganglia functions because PD patients compared to controls, show intact unconditioned eyeblink responses and similar acquired learning ability (Daum, Schugens, Breitenstein, Topka, & Spieker, 1996).

Oculomotor Dysfunction

The frontal eye field is principally involved in controlling intentional saccades to visible or predicted targets, the supplementary eye field contributes to trigger saccades concerned with motor complex programming, and the prefrontal cortex controls the inhibition of unwanted reflexive saccades (Pierrot-Deseilligny, Rivaud, Gaymard, Muri, & Vermersch, 1995). There is little or no saccade impairment in patients with PD and striatonigral-type MSA (Kennard & Lueck, 1989; Vidailhet et al., 1994; White, Saint-Cyr, Tomlinson, & Sharpe, 1988). However, PSP patients experience all these difficulties and have severe saccade and smooth pursuit paresis, secondary, in part, to bilateral lesions affecting both the frontal and parietal eye fields. Vertical saccade abnormalities in PSP occur earlier than horizontal ones and are secondary to involvement of the previously described mesencephalic nuclei. With careful oculomotor testing, early PSP patients show a decreased horizontal saccade amplitude but not latency (Vidailhet et al., 1994). The antisaccade task (looking in the direction opposite to a visual stimulus), which correlates well with frontal lobe dysfunction, is bilaterally impaired in patients with PSP (Vidailhet et al., 1994) but not in those with PD or striatonigral-type MSA. In Huntington's disease, the major involvement appears to be generating voluntary saccades and suppressing reflex saccades (Kennard & Lueck, 1989).

Eyeblink has been proposed as a putative marker of central dopaminergic activity, as blink rate is significantly decreased in PSP and PD patients but normal in patients with Huntington's disease (Karson, Burns, LeWitt, Foster, & Newman, 1984).

Executive Dysfunction

When patients with extrapyramidal disorders are examined neuropsychologically, they are frequently found to have cognitive disturbances. Approximately 60–70% of the PSP patients examined in two series at relatively early stages had impaired cognition (Maher, Smith, & Lees, 1985; Pillon et al., 1991). The impairments found in PSP patients are similar to those seen in patients with frontal lobe lesions and helped develop the concept of "subcortical dementia" (Albert, Feldman, & Willis, 1974). These deficits include executive dysfunction, slowness of thought, forgetfulness, and changes in personality without aphasia, apraxia, or agnosia. Almost all PSP patients examined neuropsychologically demonstrate an early and prominent executive dysfunction, which includes difficulty with planning, problem solving, concept formation, and social cognition (when evaluated with a series of neuropsychological tests that included the Wisconsin Card Sorting Test [WCST], Trail Making Tests, Tower of Hanoi, fluency test, the Similarity and Picture Arrangement subtests of the Wechsler Adult Intelligence Scale—Revised, motor series of Luria, or imitation behavior). These deficits are also observed in other extrapyramidal disorders such as PD, MSA, and Huntington's disease (Beatty & Monson, 1990; Butters, Wolfe, Martone, Granholm, & Cermak, 1985; Cambier, Masson, Viader, Limodin, & Strube, 1985; Grafman, Litvan, Gomez, & Chase, 1990; Lawrence et al., 1996; Maher et al., 1985; Pillon, Dubois, Lhermitte, & Agid, 1986; Pillon et al., 1991, 1995; Robbins et al., 1994; Rosser & Hodges, 1994; Saint-Cyr, Taylor, & Lang, 1988; Salmon, Kwo-on-Yuen, Heindel, Butters, & Thal, 1989; Taylor, Saint-Cyr, & Lang, 1986). However, the executive functions of PSP patients, such as concreteness of thought, decreased verbal fluency, and difficulty with placing events in the correct sequence, are more severely affected than in most patients with PD, striatonigral-type MSA, and Huntington's disease (Pillon et al., 1991, 1995; Rosser & Hodges, 1994). The mechanism of frontal lobe dysfunction found in various extrapyramidal disorders may have minor differences (Robbins et al., 1994). For example, in the Tower of London planning task, PSP and PD patients are slower in the initial thinking time, MSA patients in a measure of thinking time subsequent to the first move (Robbins et al., 1994), and Huntington's disease patients at both initial and subsequent times (Lawrence et al., 1996).

Measures of glucose consumption (hypometabolism in the frontal cortex) and visualization of the nigrostriatal dopaminergic system (decreased striatal dopamine D2 receptor uptake ratios) show convergent evidence that the dorsolateral frontosubcortical circuit is affected premortem, disconnected by prominent subcortical pathology in PSP, but this is not a consistent feature in PD and MSA (Blin et al., 1990; Blin, Ruberg, & Baron, 1992; Brooks, 1994; Brooks et al., 1990, 1992; D'Antona et al., 1985; De Volder et al., 1989). Conversely, frontocortical cerebral blood flood is not reduced in Huntington's disease patients even while they manifest overt prefrontal-type cognitive deficits (Weinberger, Berman, Iadarola, Driesen, & Zec, 1988). Although striatal structures are primarily affected in Huntington's disease, neuropathological studies also report changes in frontocortical structures. PET studies show that in contrast to the decreased glucose utilization in the caudate and putamen, frontal metabolism is normal in Huntington's disease patients with less than 6 years following symptom onset and mildly decreased thereafter (Kuhl et al., 1982). Moreover, patients with Huntington's disease were reported to have normal regional cerebral blood flow (rCBF) while engaged in a reasoning task (WCST), even when manifesting overt cognitive impairment (Weinberger et al., 1988). Although the Huntington's disease patients did not tend to activate the prefrontal cortex during the WCST as the normals did in the single photon emission tomography study (SPECT), the differences were not significant. These results suggest that in Huntington's disease, the prefrontal cortex is overstimulated at baseline levels by an hyperactive thalamus. Additional evidence is provided by the fact that the more widespread the caudate atrophy, the more cortical rCBF was found during the WCST, and the more it increased over baseline. Similarly, the poorer the performance on the WCST, the greater the cortical activation (Weinberger et al., 1988). These results are in contrast to those found in patients with PSP in whom frontal metabolism is reduced both at rest and during mental activation (Litvan, Weinberger, Berman, & Chase, 1980), suggesting that the mechanism in PSP is mostly secondary to frontal hypoactivation as well as to direct damage of cortical neurons. Similar changes, although not as evident, were also found in PD (Weinberger et al., 1988). PET and SPECT studies also show that in patients with Huntington's disease, prefrontal perfusion or caudate metabolism correlate with cognitive measures (Gomez-Tortosa et al., 1996; Sax et al., 1996; Young et al., 1986). Frontal dysfunction in early Huntington's disease is largely independent of the underlying motor disability (Cooper, Sagar, Jordan, Harvey, & Sullivan, 1991; Lawrence et al., 1996). Thus, it appears that degeneration of the dorsolateral and motor circuits are independent of each other. Moreover, in early stages of Huntington's disease, tasks related to dorsolateral prefrontal functions (set shifting) are disrupted before those that are associated with the orbitofrontal region (visual discrimination reversal) (Lawrence et al., 1996), following the dorsal-to-ventral progression of striatal pathology in this disease.

Patients with frontal lobe lesions, in contrast to those with extrapyramidal disorders, inaccurately solve problems but are not slow. Cognitive slowness can be evaluated with complex reaction time tasks or with cognitive evoked potentials. PSP patients have slowed movement and information processing, but cognitive slowness may be task-dependent in PD, MSA, and Huntington's disease (Cooper, Sagar, Tidswell, & Jordan, 1994; Dubois, Pillon, Legault, Agid, & Lhermitte, 1988; Johnson, Litvan, & Grafman, 1991; Lawrence et al., 1996; Pierrot-Deseilligny et al., 1989). Event-related brain potentials recorded while PSP patients perform an Oddball task show a normal N1 component but dramatically increased latencies and decreased amplitudes of the P2 and P300 components (almost twice that of PD patients) (Johnson et al., 1991). The remarkably delayed latencies found in PSP have not been reported in any other type of extrapyramidal disorder (Johnson, 1992).

The memory disturbances observed in patients with extrapyramidal disorders are thought to be related to an impaired ability to organize their retrieval strategies likely due to their frontal lobe deafferentation. Retrieval is more impaired than learning in PD, PSP, MSA, and Huntington's disease (Beatty, Salmon, Butters, Heindel, & Granholm, 1998; Beatty & Butters, 1986; Hodges, Salmon, & Butters, 1990; Litvan, 1994; Litvan, Grafman, Gomez, & Chase, 1989; Massman, Delis, Butters, Levin, & Salmon, 1990; Orsini et al., 1987; Pillon et al., 1986, 1991, 1994, 1995). Recently Pillon et al. (1994) tested the hypothesis that the memory dysfunction present in extrapyramidal disorders is the result of an inefficient retrieval process of stored information. They found that PSP patients had impaired immediate memory span, disturbed learning, and consistency of recall; however, these abnormalities were considerably alleviated by controlled encoding associated with cued recall. The memory profile observed in PSP patients is similar to that of PD and Huntington's disease patients, suggesting that the memory disturbance in all these disorders is secondary to striatofrontal system damage (Granholm & Butters, 1988). Because the memory profile observed in patients with extrapyramidal disorders differs from that of patients with Alzheimer's disease, which is characterized by more rapid forgetting and less improvement in the controlled situation (Hodges et al., 1990; Pillon et al., 1994), it appears that the hippocampal lesions found in PSP are insufficiently severe to interfere with memory.

Some researchers have stated that the deficits in spatial memory and visual pattern recognition memory observed in early Huntington's disease patients but not in patients with other extrapyramidal disorders are related to disturbances throughout a network that encompasses the dorsolateral prefrontal cortex and posterior parietal area (Lawrence et al., 1996). These features, again, point to a slightly distinct frontosubcortical pathway involvement in these disorders. However, in view of the divergent involvement of the striatofrontal circuit in Huntington and parkinsonian disorders (PD, PSP, and MSA), a more striking between-group difference in performance is expected. On the other hand, only a few studies have investigated these two groups of disorders during their early stages, and a detailed analysis of errors has not been reported.

Orbitofrontal Syndrome

In PD, depression (mean = 40%; range = 4–90%) and anxiety (66%) are very common(Cummings, 1992; Cummings, Diaz, Levy, Binetti, & Litvan, 1996; Starkstein, Mayberg, Leiguarda, Preziosi, & Robinson, 1992; Starkstein, Preziosi, Bolduc, & Robinson, 1990; Tandberg, Larsen, Aarsland, & Cummings, 1996) and may antedate the motor symptomatology (Santamaria, Tolosa, & Valles, 1986). However, depression seems to be less prevalent in PD patients in the general population (Tandberg et al., 1996). Regional cerebral glucose metabolism, visualized with [^{18}F]2-Deoxyglucose PET scans, suggests that depression in PD is associated with dysfunction in the caudate and orbital–inferior area of the frontal lobe (Mayberg et al., 1990). There is not only a significant hypometabolism in these regions in depressed PD patients as compared to both nondepressed PD patients and controls but also a significant inverse correlation between the depression scores and the reported decreased metabolic activity (Mayberg et al., 1990).

Neuropsychiatric disturbances were recently studied in detail in PSP patients (Litvan, Mega, Cummings, & Fairbanks, 1996). PSP patients may exhibit depression (18%), but apathy is much more frequent. In practice, PSP patients' apathy is often mistaken for a depressive disorder and they are frequently, but unsuccessfully, treated with antidepressants. Differentiation of apathy and depression may help focus therapeutic interventions in PSP. The Neuropsychiatric Inventory can help differentiate the common behavioral features of apathy and depression. Disinhibition and impulsive behavior occur in one-third of PSP patients (Litvan et al., 1996). Disinhibition is manifested by acting impulsively without considering the consequences (e.g., crossing the road without considering traffic; getting up without assistance in spite of being aware of their instability). Less frequently, PSP patients may be tactless. Disinhibition is less evident in patients with other extrapyramidal disorders and is only seen in 12% of patients with PD (Cummings et al., 1996). MSA patients were reported to exhibit depression similar to PD patients (Pilo, Ring, Quinn, & Trimble, 1996), but no data are available on other neuropsychiatric symptoms.

Depression is also present in Huntington's disease (40%). [^{18}F]2-Deoxyglucose PET studies in Huntington's disease patients with depression, compared to those without, showed orbitofrontal and thalamic hypometabolism (Mayberg et al., 1992). Although the patients that Mayberg et al. (1992) described had a short symptom duration, these authors estimated disease duration excluding psychiatric symptoms. Interestingly, mania and intermittent explosive disorder (30%) are also features of Huntington's disease. Patients with Huntington's disease may also exhibit obsessive–compulsive disorder (Cummings & Cunningham, 1992). However, because this behavior is rarely, if ever, observed in PD or PSP patients, it is possible that this is secondary to an increased excitatory subcortical output flow to the orbitofrontal cortex. Convergent evidence supporting this possibility is provided by a PET study showing increased orbitofrontal metabolism in patients with idiopathic obsessive–compulsive disorder (Baxter, Phelps, Mazziotta, Guze, & Schwartz, 1987). We could hypothesize that at early stages in Huntington's disease there is orbitofrontal cortex overexcitation resulting in mania or obsessive–compulsive disorder. Mania or obsessive–compulsive disorder is also seen in other hyperkinetic disorders such as neuroacantocytosis, Wilson's disease, and Gilles de la Tourette's syndrome (Cummings, 1993). Conversely, at later stages, depression would occur as a result of reduced orbitofrontal stimulation, secondary to more widespread frontal or caudate degeneration, although it has been also suggested that the paralimbic abnormality, seen in depressed Huntington's disease patients, may be secondary to a state effect (Mayberg et al., 1992). Thus, depression is present in all the examined extrapyramidal disorders. It is not known at what stage of these disorders these abnormalities occur. To better understand the pathophysiology of the extrapyramidal disorders, scientists need to evaluate the behavioral disturbances of all these types of disorders using the same instrument.

In addition to mood disturbances, the orbitofrontal syndrome is associated with automatic imitation of gestures or actions of others and enforced utilization of objects in the environment. In PSP, patients' imitation and utilization behaviors are frequently observed (Pillon et al., 1991, 1994). In my experience, these behaviors occur during the relatively late stages of the disease and are rarely observed in any other extrapyramidal disorder.

Anterior Cingulate Syndrome

Apathy in PD patients (41%) is less common than depression (91%) (Cummings et al., 1996). Conversely, apathy (91%) is the dominant behavioral change found in PSP and is only occasionally accompanied by depression (18%). The apathy of PSP patients is characterized by decreased spontaneous activity (91%), initiation of conversation (86%), and interest (64%) and is likely to be related to decreased medial frontal cortex stimulation. Disinhibition and apathy in PSP are not associated with disease duration, suggesting that the dysfunction of different subcortical circuits does not proceed in parallel. It is now known whether MSA patients exhibit apathy.

In Huntington's disease, the mood disorder may precede the motor or cognitive disturbances, but apathy seems to be more frequent in advanced stages of the disease. Recent studies indicate that patients with Huntington's disease do not discriminate anger from fear and from other emotions except happiness (Sprengelmeyer et al., 1996), secondary perhaps to lesions observed in the amygdala (Mann, Oliver, & Snowden, 1993). These studies have not been performed in other extrapyramidal disorders.

CONCLUSION

The five frontosubcortical circuits are somewhat differentially involved in the four extrapyramidal disorders examined (PD, PSP, MSA, and Huntington's disease). Moreover, involvement of the different circuits in these disorders apparently does not proceed in parallel. PSP severely affects all five frontosubcortical circuits, while there is less involvement in the other extrapyramidal disorders. In the parkinsonian disorders, the behavioral and cognitive disturbances are secondary to inactivation of the frontal cortex, whereas in Huntington's disease, it seems that some behaviors, such as obsessive–compulsive disorder, may be related to a hyperactivated frontal cortex. Careful neuropsychological and behavioral testing may help elucidate the function of the less described frontosubcortical circuits. In addition, neuropsychological and behavioral testing may delineate the extent and progression of the disability found in patients with extrapyramidal disorders and, potentially, can be used to plan a rehabilitation program for such individuals.

REFERENCES

Agid, Y., Javoy-Agid, F., Ruberg, M., Pillon, B., Dubois, B., Duyckaerts, C., Hauw, J. J., Baron, J. C., & Scatton, B. (1987). Progressive supranuclear palsy: Anatomoclinical and biochemical considerations. *Advances in Neurology, 45,* 191–206.

Albert, M. L., Feldman, R. G., & Willis, A. L. (1974). The "subcortical dementia" of progressive supranuclear palsy. *Journal of Neurology, Neurosurgery, and Psychiatry, 37*(2), 121–130.

Albin, R. L., Young, A. B., & Penney, J. B. (1995). The functional anatomy of disorders of the basal ganglia. *Trends in Neurosciences, 18,* 63–64.

Alexander, G. E., & Crutcher, M. D. (1990). Functional architecture of basal ganglia circuits: Neural substrates of parallel processing. *Trends in Neuroscience, 13*(7), 266–271.

Alexander, G. E., DeLong, M. R., & Strick, P. L. (1986). Parallel organization of functionally segregated circuits linking basal ganglia and cortex. *Annual Review of Neuroscience, 9,* 357–381.

Arai, N., Papp, M. I., & Lantos, P. L. (1994). New observation on ubiquitinated neurons in the cerebral cortex of multiple system atrophy (MSA). *Neuroscience Letter, 182,* 197–200.

Baxter, L. R., Phelps, M. E., Mazziotta, J. C., Guze, B. H., & Schwartz, J. M. (1987). Local cerebral glucose metabolic rates in obsessive–compulsive disorder. *Archives of General Psychiatry, 44,* 211–218.

Beatty, W. W., & Butters, N. (1986). Further analysis of encoding in patients with Huntington's disease. *Brain and Cognition, 5*(4), 387–398.

Beatty, W. W., & Monson, N. (1990). Picture and motor sequencing in Parkinson's disease. *Journal of Geriatry, Psychiatry and Neurology, 3*(4), 192–197.

Beatty, W. W., Salmon, D. R., Butters, N., Heindel, W. C., & Granholm, E. L. (1998). Retrograde amnesia in patients with Alzheimer's disease or Huntington's disease. *Neurobiology of Aging, 9,* 181–186.

Blin, J., Baron, J. C., Dubois, B., Pillon, B., Cambon, H., Cambier, J., & Agid, Y. (1990). Positron emission tomography study in progressive supranuclear palsy: Brain hypometabolic pattern and clinico metabolic correlations. *Archives of Neurology, 47*(7), 747–752.

Blin, J., Ruberg, M., & Baron, J. C. (1992). Positron emission tomography studies. In I. Litvan & Y. Agid (Eds.), *Progressive supranuclear palsy: Clinical and research approaches* (pp. 155–168). New York: Oxford University Press.

Braak, H., Jellinger, K., Braak, E., & Bohl, J. (1992). Allocortical neurofibrillary changes in progressive supranuclear palsy. *Acta Neuropathologica (Berlin), 84*(5), 478–483.

Brandel, J. P., Hirsch, E. C., Malessa, S., Duyckaerts, C., Cervera, P., & Agid, Y. (1991). Differential vulnerability of cholinergic projections to the mediodorsal nucleus of the thalamus in senile dementia of Alzheimer type and progressive supranuclear palsy. *Neuroscience, 41*(1), 25–31.

Brooks, D. J. (1994). PET studies in progressive supranuclear palsy. *Journal of Neural Transmission, 42*(Suppl.), 119–134.

Brooks, D. J., Ibanez, V., Sawle, G. V., Playford, E. D., Quinn, N., Mathias, C. J., Lees, A. J., Marsden, C. D., Bannister, R., & Frackowiak, R. S. (1992). Striatal D2 receptor status in patients with Parkinson's disease, striatonigral degeneration, and progressive supranuclear palsy, measured with ^{11}C-raclopride and positron emission tomography. *Annals of Neurology, 31*(2), 184–192.

Brooks, D. J., Ibanez, V., Sawle, G. V., Quinn, N., Lees, A. J., Mathias, C. J., Bannister, R. U., Marsden, C. D., & Frackowiak, R. S. (1990). Differing patterns of striatal ^{18}F-dopa uptake in Parkinson's disease, multiple system atrophy, and progressive supranuclear palsy. *Annals of Neurology, 28*(4), 547–555.

Butters, N., Wolfe, J., Martone, M., Granholm, E., & Cermak, L. S. (1985). Memory disorders associated with Huntington's disease: Verbal recall, verbal recognition and procedural memory. *Neuropsychologia, 23*(6), 729–743.

Cambier, J., Masson, M., Viader, F., Limodin, J., & Strube, A. (1985). Frontal syndrome of progressive supranuclear palsy. *Revue Neurologie (Paris), 141*(8–9), 528–536.

Chinaglia, G., Landwehrmeyer, B., Probst, A., & Palacios, J. M. (1993). Serotoninergic terminal transporters are differentially affected in Parkinson's disease and progressive supranuclear palsy: An autoradiographic study with [^{3}H] citalopram. *Neuroscience, 54*(3), 691–699.

Cooper, J. A., Sagar, H. J., Jordan, N., Harvey, N. S., & Sullivan, E. V. (1991). Cognitive impairment in early, untreated Parkinson's disease and its relationship to motor disability. *Brain, 114*(5), 2095–2122.

Cooper, J. A., Sagar, H. J., Tidswell, P., & Jordan, N. (1994). Slowed central processing in simple and go/no-go reaction time tasks in Parkinson's disease. *Brain, 117*(3), 517–529.

Cummings, J. L. (1992). Depression and Parkinson's disease: A review. *American Journal of Psychiatry, 149,* 443–454.

Cummings, J. L. (1993). Frontal–subcortical circuits and human behavior. *Archives of Neurology, 50,* 873–880.

Cummings, J. L. (1995). Anatomic and behavioral aspects of frontal-subcortical circuits. *Annals of the New York Academy of Sciences, 769,* 1–13.

Cummings, J. L., & Benson, D. F. (1984). Subcortical dementia. Review of an emerging concept. *Archives of Neurology, 41*(8), 874–879.

Cummings, J. L., & Benson, D. F. (1988). Psychological dysfunction accompanying subcortical dementias. *Annual Review of Medicine, 39,* 53–61.

Cummings, J. L., & Cunningham, K. (1992). Obsessive–compulsive disorder in Huntington's disease. *Biological Psychiatry, 31*(3), 263–270.

Cummings, J. L., Diaz, C., Levy, M., Binetti, G., & Litvan, I. (1996). Behavioral syndromes in neurodegenerative diseases: frequency and significance. *Seminars in Neuropsychiatry, 1*(4), 241–247.

D'Antona, R., Baron, J. C., Samson, Y., Serdaru, M., Viader, F., Agid, Y., & Cambier, J. (1985). Subcortical dementia. Frontal cortex hypometabolism detected by positron tomography in patients with progressive supranuclear palsy. *Brain, 108*(Pt. 3), 785–799.

Daum, I., Schugens, M., Breitenstein, C., Topka, H., & Spieker, S. (1996). Classical eyeblink conditioning in Parkinson's disease. *Movement Disorders, 11,* 639–646.

Daum, I., Schugens, M. M., Spieker, S., Poser, U., Schonle, P. W., & Birbaumer, N. (1995). Memory and skill acquisition in Parkinson's disease and frontal lobe dysfunction. *Cortex, 31*(3), 413–432.

DeLong, M. R. (1990). Primate models of movement disorders of basal ganglia origin. *Trends in Neurosciences, 13*(7), 281–285.

De Volder, A. G., Francart, J., Laterre, C., Dooms, G., Bol, A., Michel, C., Goffinet, A. M. (1989). Decreased glucose utilization in the striatum and frontal lobe in probable striatonigral degeneration. *Annals of Neurology, 26,* 239–247

Dubois, B., Pillon, B., Legault, F., Agid, Y., & Lhermitte, F. (1988). Slowing of cognitive processing in progressive supranuclear palsy: A comparison with Parkinson's disease. *Archives of Neurology, 45*(11), 1194–1199.

Forno, L. S. (1992). Neuropathologic features of Parkinson's, Huntington's and Alzheimer's diseases. *Annals of the New York Academy of Science, 648,* 6–16.

Forno, L. S. (1996). Neuropathology of Parkinson's disease. *Journal of Neuropathology and Experimental Neurology, 55,* 259–272.

Gibb, W. R. (1992). Neuropathology of Parkinson's disease and related syndromes. *Neurology Clinics, 10*(2), 361–376.

Goetz, G. C., & Stebbins, G. T. (1993). Risk factors for nursing home placement in advanced Parkinson's disease. *Neurology, 43,* 2227–2229.

Goetz, G. C., & Stebbins, G. T. (1995). Mortality and hallucinations in nursing home patients with advanced Parkinson's disease. *Neurology, 45,* 660–671.

Gomez-Tortosa, E., Arias Navalon, J. A., del Barrio Alba, A., Barroso Fernandez, T., Pardo, C., Sanchez Martin, J. A., & Garcia Yebenes, J. (1996). Relation between frontal lobe blood flow and cognitive performance in Huntington's disease. *Neurologia, 11*(7), 251–256.

Grafman, J., Litvan, I., Gomez, C., & Chase, T. N. (1990). Frontal lobe function in progressive supranuclear palsy. *Archives of Neurology, 47*(5), 553–558.

Grafman, J., Weingartner, H., Newhouse, P. A., Thompson, K., Lalonde, F., Litvan, I., Molchan, S., & Sunderland, T. (1990). Implicit learning in patients with Alzheimer's disease. *Pharmacopsychiatry, 23*(2), 94–101.

Graham, D. I., & Lantos, P. L. (1997). *Greenfield's neuropathology* (6th ed.). London: Arnold.

Granholm, E., & Butters, N. (1988). Associative encoding and retrieval in Alzheimer's and Huntington's disease. *Brain and Cognition, 7*(3), 335–347.

Heindel, W. C., Butters, N., & Salmon, D. P. (1988). Impaired learning of a motor skill in patients with Huntington's disease. *Behavioral Neuroscience, 102*(1), 141–147.

Heindel, W. C., Salmon, D. P., Shults, C. W., Walicke, P. A., & Butters, N. (1989). Neuropsychological evidence for multiple implicit memory systems: A comparison of Alzheimer's, Huntington's, and Parkinson's disease patients. *Journal of Neuroscience, 9*(2), 582–587.

Hirsch, E. C., Graybiel, A. M., Duyckaerts, C., & Javoy-Agid, F. (1987). Neuronal loss in the pedunculopontine tegmental nucleus in Parkinson disease and in progressive supranuclear palsy. *Proceeding of the National Academy of Sciences, U.S.A., 84*(16), 5976–5980.

Hodges, J. R., Salmon, D. P., & Butters, N. (1990). Differential impairment of semantic and episodic memory in Alzheimer's and Huntington's diseases: A controlled prospective study. *Journal of Neurology, Neurosurgery, and Psychiatry, 53*(12), 1089–1095.

Hof, P. R., Delacourte, A., & Bouras, C. (1992). Distribution of cortical neurofibrillary tangles in progressive supranuclear palsy: A quantitative analysis of six cases. *Acta Neuropathologica (Berlin), 84*(1), 45–51.

Jellinger, K. A. (1995). Neurodegenerative disorders with extrapyramidal features. *Journal of Neural Transmission, 46*(Suppl.), 33–57.

Jellinger, K. A., & Bancher, C. (1992). Neuropathology. In I. Litvan & Y. Agid (Eds.), *Progressive supranuclear palsy: Clinical and research approaches* (pp. 44–88). New York: Oxford University Press.

Johnson, R. J. (1992). Event-related brain potentials. In I. Litvan & Y. Agid (Eds.), *Progressive supranuclear palsy: Clinical and research approaches* (pp. 122–154). New York: Oxford University Press.

Johnson, R. J., Litvan, I., & Grafman, J. (1991). Progressive supranuclear palsy: Altered sensory processing leads to degraded cognition. *Neurology, 41*(8), 1257–1262.

Juncos, J. L., Hirsch, E. C., Malessa, S., Duyckaerts, C., Hersh, L. B., & Agid, Y. (1991). Mesencephalic cholinergic nuclei in progressive supranuclear palsy. *Neurology, 41*(1), 25–30.

Karson, C. N., Burns, R. S., LeWitt, P. A., Foster, N. L., & Newman, R. P. (1984). Blink rates and disorders of movement. *Neurology, 34*(5), 677–678.

Kennard, C., & Lueck, C. J. (1989). Oculomotor abnormalities in diseases of the basal ganglia. *Revue de Neurologie (Paris), 145*(8–9), 587–95.

Kuhl, D. E., Phelps, M. E., Markham, C. H., Metter, E. J., Riege, W. H., & Winter, J. (1982). Cerebral metabolism and atrophy in Huntington's disease determined by ^{18}FDG and computed tomographic scan. *Annals of Neurology, 12,* 425–434.

Lawrence, A. D., Sahakian, B. J., Hodges, J. R., Rosser, A. E., Lange, K. W., & Robbins, T. W. (1996). Executive and mnemonic functions in early Huntington's disease. *Brain, 119,* 1633–1645.

Litvan, I. (1994). Cognitive disturbances in progressive supranuclear palsy. *Journal of Neural Transmission, 42*(Suppl.), 69–78.

Litvan, I., Grafman, J., Gomez, C., & Chase, T. (1989). Memory impairment in patients with progressive supranuclear palsy. *Archives of Neurology, 46*(7), 765–767.

Litvan, I., Mega, M. S., Cummings, J. L., & Fairbanks, L. (1996). Neuropsychiatrical aspects of progressive supranuclear palsy. *Neurology, 47,* 1184–1189.

Litvan, I., Weinberger, D., Berman, K., & Chase, T. N. (1988). Cerebral blood flow changes with physostigmine in progressive supranuclear palsy [Abstract]. *Neurology, 38*(3), 308.

Maher, E. R., Smith, E. M., & Lees, A. J. (1985). Cognitive deficits in the Steele–Richardson–Olszewski syndrome (progressive supranuclear palsy). *Journal of Neurology, Neurosurgery, and Psychiatry, 48*(12), 1234–1239.

Malessa, S., Gaymard, B., Rivaud, S., Cervera, P., Hirsch, E., Verny, M., Duyckaerts, C., Agid, Y., & Pierrot-Deseilligny, C. (1994). Role of pontine nuclei damage in smooth pursuit impairment of progressive supranuclear palsy: A clinical–pathological study. *Neurology, 44*(4), 716–721.

Malessa, S., Hirsch, E. C., Cervera, P., Javoy-Agid, F., Duyckaerts, C., Hauw, J. J., & Agid, Y. (1991). Progressive supranuclear palsy: Loss of choline acetyltransferase-like immunoreactive neurons in the pontine reticular formation. *Neurology, 41*(10), 1593–1597.

Mann, D. M., Oliver, R., & Snowden, J. S. (1993). The topographic distribution of brain atrophy in Huntington's disease and progressive supranuclear palsy. *Acta Neuropathologica (Berlin), 85*(5), 553–559.

Martin, W. W. R., & Hayden, M. R. (1987). Cerebral glucose and dopa metabolism in movement disorders. *Canadian Journal of Neurological Sciences, 14,* 448–451.

Martone, M., Butters, N., Payne, M., Becker, J. T., & Sax, D. S. (1984). Dissociations between skill learning and verbal recognition in amnesia and dementia. *Archives of Neurology, 41*(9), 965–970.

Massman, P. J., Delis, D. C., Butters, N., Levin, B. E., & Salmon, D. P. (1990). Are all subcortical dementias alike? Verbal learning and memory in Parkinson's and Huntington's disease patients. *Journal of Clinical and Experimental Neuropsychology, 12*(5), 729–744.

Mayberg, H. S., Starkstein, S. E., Peyser, C. E., Brandt, J., Dannals, R. F., Folstein, S. E. (1992). Paralimbic frontal lobe hypometabolism in depression associated with Huntington's disease. *Neurology, 42,* 1791–1797.

Mayberg, H. S., Starkstein, S. E., Sadzot, B., Preziosi, T., Andrezejewski, P. L., Dannals, R. F., Wagner, H. N., Jr., & Robinson, R. G. (1990). Selective hypometabolism in the inferior frontal lobe in depressed patients with Parkinson's disease. *Annals of Neurology, 28*(1), 57–64.

Morriss, R. K., Rovner, B. W., Folstein, M. F., & German, P. S. (1990). Delusions in newly admitted residents of nursing homes. *American Journal of Psychiatry, 147*(3), 299–302.

Orsini, A., Fragassi, N. A., Chiacchio, L., Falanga, A. M., Cocchiaro, C., & Grossi, D. (1987). Verbal and spatial memory span in patients with extrapyramidal diseases. *Perceptual Motor Skills, 65*(2), 555–558.

Papp, M. I., Kahn, J. E., & Lantos, P. L. (1989). Glial cytoplasmic inclusions in the CNS of patients with multiple system atrophy (striatonigral degeneration, olivopontocerebellar atrophy and Shy-Drager syndrome). *Journal of Neurological Science, 94,* 79–100.

Paulus, W., & Jellinger, K. (1991). The neuropathologic basis of different clinical subgroups of Parkinson's disease. *Journal of Neuropathology and Experimental Neurology, 50*(6), 743–755.

Pierrot-Deseilligny, C., Rivaud, S., Gaymard, B., R., Muri, R., & Vermersch, A. (1995). Cortical control of saccades. *Annals of Neurology, 37,* 557–567.

Pierrot-Deseilligny, C., Turell, E., Penet, C., Lebrigand, D., Pillon, B., Chain, F., & Agid, Y. (1989). Increased wave P 300 latency in progressive supranuclear palsy. *Journal of Neurology, Neurosurgery, and Psychiatry, 52*(5), 656–658.

Pillon, B., Deweer, B., Michon, A., Malapani, C., Agid, Y., & Dubois, B. (1994). Are explicit memory disorders of progressive supranuclear palsy related to damage to striatofrontal circuits? Comparison with Alzheimer's, Parkinson's, and Huntington's diseases. *Neurology, 44*(7), 1264–1270.

Pillon, B., Dubois, B., Lhermitte, F., & Agid, Y. (1986). Heterogeneity of cognitive impairment in progressive supranuclear palsy, Parkinson's disease, and Alzheimer's disease. *Neurology, 36*(9), 1179–1185.

Pillon, B., Dubois, B., Ploska, A., & Agid, Y. (1991). Severity and specificity of cognitive impairment in Alzheimer's, Huntington's, and Parkinson's diseases and progressive supranuclear palsy. *Neurology, 41*(5), 634–643.

Pillon, B., Gouider-Khouja, N., Deweer, B., Vidailhet, M., Malapani, C., Dubois, B., & Agid, Y. (1995). Neuropsychological pattern of striatonigral degeneration: comparison with Parkinson's disease and progressive supranuclear palsy. *Journal of Neurology, Neurosurgery, and Psychiatry, 58*(2), 174–179.

Pilo, L., Ring, H., Quinn, N., & Trimble, M. (1996). Depression in multiple system atrophy and in idiopathic Parkinson's disease: A pilot comparative study. *Biological Psychiatry, 39,* 803–807.

Revesz, T., Sangha, H., & Daniel, S. E. (1996). The nucleus raphe interpositus in the Steele–Richardson–Olszewski syndrome (progressive supranuclear palsy). *Brain, 119,* 1137–1143.

Robbins, T. W., James, M., Owen, A. M., Lange, K. W., Lees, A. J., Leigh, P. N., Marsden, C. D., Quinn, N. P., & Summers, B. A. (1994). Cognitive deficits in progressive supranuclear palsy, Parkinson's disease, and multiple system atrophy in tests sensitive to frontal lobe dysfunction. *Journal of Neurology, Neurosurgery, and Psychiatry, 57*(1), 79–88.

Rogers, J. D., Brogan, D., & Mirra, S. S. (1985). The nucleus basalis of Meynert in neurological disease: A quantitative morphological study. *Annals of Neurology, 17*(2), 163–170.

Rosser, A. E., & Hodges, J. R. (1994). The Dementia Rating Scale in Alzheimer's disease, Huntington's disease and progressive supranuclear palsy. *Journal of Neurology, 241*(9), 531–536.

Ruberg, M., Javoy-Agid, F., Hirsch, E., Scatton, B., L'Heureux, R., Hauw, J. J., Duyckaerts, C., Gray, F., Morel-Maroger, A., Rascol, A., Serdaru, M., & Agid, Y. (1985). Dopaminergic and cholinergic lesions in progressive supranuclear palsy. *Annals of Neurology, 18*(5), 523–529.

Saint-Cyr, J. A., Taylor, A. E., & Lang, A. E. (1988). Procedural learning and neostriatal dysfunction in man. *Brain, 111,* 941–959.

Salmon, D. P., Kwo-on-Yuen, P. F., Heindel, W. C., Butters, N., & Thal, L. J. (1989). Differentiation of Alzheimer's disease and Huntington's disease with the Dementia Rating Scale. *Archives of Neurology, 46*(11), 1204–1208.

Santamaria, J., Tolosa, E., & Valles, A. (1986). Parkinson's disease with depression: A possible subgroup of idiopathic parkinsonism. *Neurology, 36,* 1130–1133.

Sax, D. S., Powsner, R., Kim, A., Tilak, S., Bhatia, R., Cupples, L. A., & Myers, R. H. (1996). Evidence of cortical metabolic dysfunction in early Huntington's disease by single-photon-emission computed tomography. *Movement Disorders, 11*(6), 671–677.

Sprengelmeyer, R., Young, A. W., Calder, A. J., Karnat, A., Lange, H., Homberg, V., Perett, D. I., & Rowland, D. (1996). Loss of disgust. Perception of faces and emotions in Huntington's disease. *Brain, 119,* 1647–1665.

Starkstein, S. E., Mayberg, H. S., Leiguarda, R., Preziosi, T. J., & Robinson, R. G. (1992). A prospective longitudinal study of depression, cognitive decline, and physical impairments in patients with Parkinson's disease. *Journal of Neurology, Neurosurgery, and Psychiatry, 55,* 377–382.

Starkstein, S. E., Preziosi, T. J., Bolduc, P. L., & Robinson, R. G. (1990). Depression in Parkinson's disease. *Journal of Nervous and Mental Disorders, 178,* 27–31.

Steele, C., Rovner, B., Chase, G. A., & Folstein, M. (1990). Psychiatric symptoms and nursing home placement of patients with Alzheimer's disease. *American Journal of Psychiatry, 147*(8), 1049–1051.

Tandberg, E., Larsen, J. P., Aarsland, D., & Cummings, J. L. (1996). The occurrence of depression in Parkinson's disease: A community-based study. *Archives of Neurology, 53*(2), 175–179.

Taylor, A. E., Saint-Cyr, J. A., & Lang, A. E. (1986). Frontal lobe dysfunction in Parkinson's disease: The cortical focus of neostriatal outflow. *Brain, 109,* 845–883.

Vermersch, P., Robitaille, Y., Bernier, L., Wattez, A., Gauvreau, D., & Delacourte, A. (1994). Biochemical mapping of neurofibrillary degeneration in a case of progressive supranuclear palsy: Evidence for general cortical involvement. *Acta Neuropathologica (Berlin), 87*(6), 572–577.

Verny, M., Duyckaerts, C., Agid, Y., & Hauw, J. J. (1996). The significance of cortical pathology in progressive supranuclear palsy—Clinicopathological data in 10 cases. *Brain, 119,* 1123–1136.

Vidailhet, M., Rivaud, S., Gouider-Khouja, N., Pillon, B., Bonnet, A. M., Gaymard, B., Agid, Y., & Pierrot-Deseilligny, C. (1994). Eye movements in Parkinsonian syndromes. *Annals of Neurology, 35,* 420–426.

Weinberger, D. R., Berman, K. F., Iadarola, M., Driesen, N., & Zec, R. F. (1988). Prefrontal cortical blood flow and cognitive function in Huntington's disease. *Journal of Neurology, Neurosurgery, and Psychiatry, 51*(1), 94–104.

White, O. B., Saint-Cyr, J. A., Tomlinson, R. D., & Sharpe, J. A. (1988). Ocular motor deficits in Parkinson's disease: III. Coordination of eye and head movements. *Brain, 111,* 115–129.

Young, B. A., Penney, J. B., Starosta-Rubinstein, S., Markel, D. S., Berent, S., Giordani, B., Ehrenkaufer, R., Jewett, D., & Hichwa, R. (1986). PET scan investigations of Huntington's disease: Cerebral metabolic correlates of neurological features and functional decline. *Annals of Neurology, 20,* 296–303.

23

Lewy Body Disorders

IAN G. McKEITH

Scientists have recognized Lewy bodies (LB) as an important histological characteristic of idiopathic Parkinson's disease (PD) in which their characteristic distribution is associated with neuronal loss in the nuclei of the brainstem and diencephalon. More recently, LB have also been identified in other locations within the central nervous system, in association with a variety of overlapping clinical syndromes. Lowe, Mayer, and Landon (1996) proposed that a family of primary LB disorders may exist and is only now being recognized in the wake of advances in immunocytochemical staining techniques. The key common pathological feature of these LB disorders is neuronal loss associated with LB and Lewy neurite formation in the absence of other essential neuropathological lesions. Pure clinical syndromes occur when Lewy pathology is restricted to one site, with a mixed clinical picture being seen when several sites are involved. Table 23.1 shows a proposed classification of the primary LB disorders that have been described to date.

Frontal lobe dysfunction in idiopathic (LB) PD is considered in detail in Chapter 22, this volume; this chapter therefore focuses upon specific aspects of the relatively recently described disorder of dementia with LB (DLB). In DLB, frontal lobe function may be compromised in at least two ways. There is diffuse cortical (including frontal lobe) LB pathology, in addition to which there is frontostriatal dysfunction related to subcortical disease, similar to that seen in PD. These deficits are reflected in the clinical presentation of the disorder and may be usefully exploited to help differentiate DLB from Alzheiemer's Disease (AD) and other causes of dementia.

THE PATHOLOGICAL DIAGNOSIS OF DEMENTIA WITH LEWY BODIES

Lewy Bodies and Lewy Neurites

Consensus criteria for the pathological assessment and diagnosis of DLB recently have been developed (McKeith et al., 1996) and researchers hope that these will help reduce the bewildering array of diagnostic labels that have previously been given to these cases by independent groups of investigators. Both subcortical and cortical LB need to be present for a diagnosis to be made, and to visualize LB, it is necessary to perform

TABLE 23.1. Primary Lewy Body Disorders

Region affected	Clinical syndrome	Name
Nigrostriatal system	Extrapyramidal movement disorder	Parkinson's disease
Cerebral cortex	Cognitive decline	Dementia with Lewy bodies
Sympathetic neurones in spinal cord	Autonomic failure	Primary autonomic failure
Dorsal vagal nuclei	Dysphagia	Lewy body dysphagia

Note. From Lowe, Mayer, and Landon (1996). Copyright 1996 by Cambridge University Press. Reprinted by permission.

appropriate brain sampling and sectioning routines. These adhere in most aspects to the Consortium to Establish a Registry for Alzheimer's Disease (CERAD) protocol, particularly for the substantia nigra (SN), locus coeruleus (LC), and dorsal nucleus of vagus (DNV), in which classic "core and halo" LB are usually readily recognizable using hematoxylin and eosin (H&E) staining. Although the distribution of subcortical LB in DLB cases cannot be distinguished from that seen in idiopathic motor PD, associated neuronal loss is typically less. The SN, for example, shows up to a 60% reduction in numbers of neurones in DLB (Perry, Irving, Blessed, Fairbairn, & Perry, 1990), a decrement significantly less than the neuronal loss of 70% or more needed to produce clinically apparent motor deficits, typically seen in PD. The profile of SN loss in DLB is consistent with the clinical observation that most DLB patients have either no or mild spontaneous extrapyramidal features, but that they are unduly sensitive to the effects of medications that acutely block nigrostriatal dopaminergic neurotransmission (McKeith, Fairbairn, Perry, Thompson, & Perry, 1992). (See Table 23.2.)

Cortical LB are, by contrast, usually rather poorly defined spherical inclusions lacking the characteristic core and halo appearance which facilitates recognition of their brainstem counterparts. Although cortical LB may be seen by an experienced eye using conventional H&E staining, they are more readily visualized by antiubiquitin immunocytochemistry (using tau immunostaining to distinguish them from small tangles). Cortical LB are scattered throughout the cerebral cortex but are preferentially found in the frontal, anterior cingulate, insular, and temporal cortices where they are usually present in small nerve cells in cortical layers five and six (Kosaka, Yoshimura, Ikeda, & Budka, 1984). LB are also often seen in the amygdala, especially in the medial parts of the accessory basal and basal nuclei and in the corticoamygdaloid transition area (Kosaka & Iseki, 1996). These nuclei are associated with the hippocampus and parahippocampus and their involvement may contribute to memory disturbance in DLB. Hippocampal LB are rare, although tau-negative–ubiquitin-positive Lewy neurites are found in hippocampal areas CA 2–3 (Dickson et al., 1991) and the extent of this neuritic degeneration

TABLE 23.2. Pathological Features Associated with DLB

Essential for diagnosis of DLB
    Lewy bodies
Associated but not essential
    Lewy-related neurites
    Plaques (all morphologic types)
    Neurofibrillary tangles
    Regional neuronal loss—especially brainstem (SN and locus coeruleus) and nucleus basalis of Meynert
    Microvacuolation (spongiform change) and synapse loss
    Neurochemical abnormalities and neurotransmitter deficits

Note. From McKeith et al. (1996). Copyright 1996 by the American Academy of Neurology. Reprinted by permission.

appears to be correlated with the density of cortical LB (Pollanen, Dickson, & Bergeron, 1993). Lewy neurites have also been described in other brain regions including the amygdala (Braak et al., 1994), basal forebrain, SN, pedunculopontine nuclei, raphe nuclei, and DNV (Dickson, Crystal, Davies, & Hardy, 1996).

Areas recommended for sampling the neocortex include frontal (Brodmann's areas [BA] 8 and 9), temporal (BA 21), and parietal regions (BA 40). Anterior cingulate (BA 24) and transentorhinal cortex (BA 28) should also be routinely examined in view of the LB predilection for limbic and paralimbic regions. Based on these sampling routines and using a semiquantitative scoring system based on a combination of LB density and distribution, cases can be divided into three main pathological subtypes: (1) brainstem-predominant LB disease, (2) limbic (transitional) LB disease, and (3) neocortical LB disease. The precise clinicopathological correlates of these three regionally defined categories remain to be determined, but the majority of cases reported so far in the literature in the various guises of Lewy body dementia (LBD) (Gibb, Esiri, & Lees, 1987), diffuse LB disease (DLBD) (Kosaka et al., 1984; Lennox, Lowe, Morrell, Landon, & Mayer, 1989), senile dementia of LB type (SDLT; Perry, Irving, et al., 1990) or LB variant of AD (LBV) (Hansen et al., 1990) or, can all be recognized as limbic or neocortical LB disease using the new consensus criteria.

Lewy Bodies and Dementia

It is uncertain to what extent the cortical LB contributes to cognitive impairment. Samuel, Galasko, Masliah, and Hansen (1996) found LB concentrations in cingulate and superior temporal cortex to correlate with the severity of dementia assessed using the Mini Mental Status Examination (MMSE). They did not find significant clinicopathological correlations in midfrontal or inferior parietal regions. Neocortical plaque and tangle counts were not associated with mental status. Lennox et al. (1989) previously reported similar findings. Perry, Marshall et al. (1990) were unable to find a relationship between LB density in the limbic cortex and severity of dementia or between cortical LB densities and other key clinical variables such as the presence or absence of hallucinations. This lack of consistent correlation between LB density and clinical parameters may reflect the methodological problems inherent in comparing lifetime clinical measures with pathological data which reflect an "end stage" of disease months or even years later. Perry et al. (1996) also suggested that the presence of LB in the cortex may represent a "tip of the iceberg" phenomenon—the remainder of the iceberg consisting of unidentified cell loss in a select, but critical, population of cortical neurones. Quantitative assessments of neuronal populations and synaptic connectivity in key cortical areas are needed to address this issue.

Alzheimer Pathology in Dementia with Lewy Bodies

Most cases of DLB have some Alzheimer pathology. Kosaka (1990) suggested that cases with few or no "senile" changes should be regarded as "pure" LB disease, the "common" form being associated with numerous cortical plaques and, to a lesser extent, parahippocampal and hippocampal neurofibrillary tangles (NFT). Most investigators now agree that plaques are present in 75% or more of all DLB cases but neocortical NFT are absent or sparse in almost all individuals (Hansen, Masliah, Galasko, & Terry, 1994). NFT density is, on average, only slightly, and not significantly, above age-matched normal control values and over tenfold lower than the average in AD (Perry et al., 1996). The precise interpretation of these observations remains contentious. Some authorities regard them as evidence of coexistent AD, the clinical manifestations of which have been brought forward by the additional burden of LB formation and associated neuronal loss to produce the "LB variant of AD" (Hansen et al., 1990). Others find the Alzheimer pathology merely to constitute "pathological aging" in the majority of LBD cases—the senile plaques being diffuse deposits of amyloid protein (A) with few or no neuritic components (Dickson et al., 198, 1992). Hansen has eloquently pointed out that this debate about the interpretation of Alzheimer pathology spins more on long-standing, unresolved issues concerning the precise pathological definition of AD, in particular the relative significance of plaques versus tangles, than it does on the classification of the newcomer DLB.

THE MOLECULAR GENETICS OF DEMENTIA WITH LEWY BODIES

It becomes apparent that the relationships between AD, DLB, and PD are likely to be complex and multifaceted, and in the glimmer of present knowledge it is probably both premature and unhelpful to try to draw strict boundaries between them. The results of molecular genetic investigations bear this statement out. For example, the apolipoprotein E (Apo E) ε4 allele is overrepresented to a similar extent (51.9%) in pathologically confirmed DLB cases as in AD (58%) compared with aged controls (22.4%)—frequencies quoted are totals of ε3/ε4 and ε4/ε4 genotypes from pooled data (reviewed by Saitoh & Katzman, 1996). Relatively fewer DLB cases (6.6%) than AD (13.7%) are ε4 homozygotes, suggesting that the ε4/ε4 state predisposes so strongly to Alzheimer pathology, that the expression of LB is muted. ε4 allele frequency is not increased in PD without dementia (22.2%). The Apo E ε4 allele appears then to be associated with an increased risk of Alzheimer's but not LB disease, and this may be taken as circumstantial evidence that DLB lies within the spectrum of AD.

There are, however, genetic data from the same group of patients which seem to link DLB with PD rather than with AD, suggesting that DLB belongs within the spectrum of primary LB disorders. This is based on the observation that the B allelic variant of the CYP2D6 gene is increased both in DLB (43%) and in nondemented PD cases (41%), but neither in AD (26%) nor age-matched normal controls (25%) (Saitoh & Katzman, 1996). The San Diego group has tried to resolve this issue by suggesting, on the basis of the neuropathological data, that DLB is a neurodegenerative hybrid, separate and distinct from AD and PD, but with features of each. The group uses the analogy of DLB as a mule. Just as a mule is neither horse nor donkey, despite being composed of nothing other than horse or donkey, so too, in their view (Samuel et al., 1996), DLB is a "different animal" than AD or PD, despite sharing features with both. Whether or not PD and AD can be regarded as separate entities in the same way that horses and donkeys can is, however, open to question.

THE NEUROCHEMISTRY OF DEMENTIA WITH LEWY BODIES

Activity of the cholinergic enzyme, choline acetyltransferase (ChAT), is reduced in both neo- and limbic cortex in DLB, the neocortical decrement (particularly in temporal and parietal lobes) comprising a reduction of over 80% compared with age-matched normal controls and significantly greater than the 50% reductions in ChAT, which are typically seen in AD (Langlais, Thal, & Hansen, 1993; Perry et al., 1994). The clinical symptom most highly correlated with this cholinergic deficit is visual hallucinosis, particularly in patients with evidence of relatively hypermonoaminergic function as measured by an increased index of 5-HT (5-hydroxytryptamine) turnover and preserved, or even increased, 5-HT2 receptor binding (Perry, Smith, Court, & Perry, 1990). Attentional deficits, delirium, and visual hallucinations, are all well recognized consequences of anticholinergic drug toxicity and bear a striking resemblance to some of the central symptoms of DLB, suggesting that the neocortical cholinergic deficit plays an important role in symptom formation.

Subcortical pathology is likely to influence these important cortical cholinergic–monoaminergic interactions. For example, acetylcholine release in the hippocampus is known to be inhibited by septal dopamine, scopolamine-induced deficits in spatial working memory in rats being reversed by D1 receptor blockade (Levin, McGurk, Roso, & Butcher, 1990). In DLB, degeneration of the mesolimbic dopaminergic system may thus offset hypocholinergic activity in the hippocampus as a consequence of diminished inhibitory inputs. This hypothesis is supported by measures of ChAT in hippocampus and entorhinal cortex, which are reduced substantially less in DLB than in AD, and is also consistent with the relative preservation of recent memory function in DLB patients.

The neuromodulatory role of mesocortical dopaminergic systems appears to be considerably less important than those systems projecting to the limbic system. The neocortical association areas most likely to be involved in the formation of complex hallucinations (e.g., in the temporal lobe) do not receive a major input from the septum. Mesocortical dopamine and homovanillic acid (HVA) do not appear to be reduced in DLB or PD (Perry et al., 1993), suggesting that the cholinergic deficits due to cortical (including frontal) pathology are unopposed. A further source of frontal lobe dysfunction in DLB results from the degeneration of nigrostriatal dopaminergic fibers with secondary effects on frontostriatal function. The anatomical and functional aspects of this fronto-subcortical circuitry have been considered in detail in Chapters 1, 8, and 9, this volume.

DEMOGRAPHIC AND EPIDEMIOLOGICAL ASPECTS OF DEMENTIA WITH LEWY BODIES

Several hospital–specialist clinic-based autopsy series indicate DLB to be the second most common pathological cause of degenerative dementia in elderly subjects besides AD. Estimates range from 12% (Burns, Luthert, Levy, Jacoby, & Lantos, 1990) to 36% (Hansen et al., 1990) of all demented cases, the modal frequency being 15–20% (Jellinger, 1996; Lennox et al., 1989; Perry, Smith et al., 1990). In a review of 98 autopsy confirmed cases published between 1961 and 1992 (McKeith, 1993), the mean age of onset of common DLB (that is with Alzheimer-type pathology, and accounting for 85% or more of all cases) was 73.8 years (95% confidence intervals 71.5–76.1), with death following, on average, 6.2 (5.2–7.2) years later. The male:female ratio was 1.4:1 suggesting either that men are more susceptible to DLB (as they are to PD) or, because this is autopsy-based data, that men with DLB have a worse prognosis than women. Pure cases (lacking Alzheimer pathology) had a significantly younger age of onset of 57.4 (45.9–67.9) years ($p < .0001$), a tendency to increased duration of illness, 8.5 (4.5–12.5) years, and a greatly increased tendency to male predominance with a ratio of 3.3:1. Approximately 25% of demented patients attending specialist assessment facilities in the United Kingdom were found to have a clinical presentation suggestive of DLB (Ballard, Mohan, Patel, & Bannister, 1993; Shergill, Mullen, D'Ath, & Katona, 1994), but, as yet, no estimates of the prevalence of DLB in community populations have been reported.

THE CLINICAL DIAGNOSIS OF DEMENTIA WITH LEWY BODIES

Table 23.3 proposes clinical diagnostic criteria that predict with high likelihood that dementia is associated with limbic (transitional) or neocortical LB disease (McKeith et al., 1996). They are also applicable to patients with a preexisting diagnosis of PD, in whom the onset of the characteristic neuropsychiatric symptoms, 12 months or more after first onset of the extrapyramidal motor symptoms, justifies a diagnosis of PD plus DLB.

The central feature of DLB is cognitive impairment which progresses, sometimes rapidly, to an end stage of severe dementia. Attentional impairments and disproportionate problem-solving and visuospatial difficulties are often early and prominent. Fluctuation in cognitive function, persistent well-formed visual hallucinations, and spontaneous motor features of parkinsonism are core features of diagnostic significance. Other features commonly seen in DLB include repeated falls, syncope, and transient losses of consciousness, which may represent the extension of LB pathology to involve the brainstem and autonomic nervous system. Abnormal sensitivity to neuroleptic medication is associated with a threefold increase in mortality and appears to be mediated via D2 receptor antagonism imposed upon nigrostriatal transmission which is already critically compromised by neurodegeneration and lacks the capacity of compensatory autoregulation (McKeith, Fairbairn, et al, 1992). Auditory, olfactory, and tactile hallucinations may also occur in DLB, and if these precede significant cognitive impairment, an initial diagnosis

---

TABLE 23.3. Consensus Criteria for the Clinical Diagnosis of Probable and Possible DLB

1. The central feature required for a diagnosis of DLB is progressive cognitive decline of sufficient magnitude to interfere with normal social or occupational function. Prominent or persistent memory impairment may not necessarily occur in the early stages ,but it is usually evident with progression. Deficits on tests of attention and of frontal–subcortical skills and visuospatial ability may be especially prominent.

2. Two of the following core features are essential for a diagnosis of probable DLB, and one is essential for possible DLB:
   a. Fluctuating cognition with pronounced variations in attention and alertness
   b. Recurrent visual hallucinations that are typically well formed and detailed
   c. Spontaneous motor features of parkinsonism

3. Features supportive of the diagnosis are:
   a. Repeated falls
   b. Syncope
   c. Transient loss of consciousness
   d. Neuroleptic sensitivity
   e. Systematized delusions
   f. Hallucinations in other modalities

4. A diagnosis of DLB is less likely in the presence of:
   a. Stroke disease, evident as focal neurological signs or on brain imaging
   b. Evidence on physical examination and investigation of any physical illness or other brain disorder sufficient to account for the clinical picture

Note. From McKeith et al. (1996). Copyright 1996 by the American Academy of Neurology. Reprinted by permission.

of temporal lobe epilepsy may be made, frequently supported by focal transient EEG slow wave activity in one or both temporal lobes.

The differential diagnosis of DLB, particularly in those presenting with intermittent delirium, includes exclusion of infective, metabolic, inflammatory, pharmacological, or other etiological factors sufficient to produce the clinical picture. Vascular dementia may be suspected because of the apparently sudden onset, fluctuating performance, frequent falls, and syncope and needs to be excluded using clinically and radiologically based criteria (e.g., Roman et al., 1993). Frontal lobe dementia may be suspected because of attentional deficits, relative preservation of recent memory, apathy, and mental slowing. Behavioral disturbances, such as agitation or aggressiveness, may occur early in DLB, and when they do, they are invariably a response to troublesome psychotic symptoms, usually in the form of vivid and persistent visual hallucinations. Behavioral disturbance in FLD is, in contrast, usually based on social disinhibition and impaired judgment, persistent hallucinosis being uncommon in this group.

The most frequent clinical misdiagnosis of DLB is probably as AD (McKeith, Fairbairn, Bothwell, et al., 1994), an almost inevitable consequence of the clinical diagnostic systems for AD having been developed over the last three decades unaware of the existence of DLB patients. Although up to 85% of DLB patients can be identified antemortem (McKeith, Fairbairn, Perry, et al., 1994) using operationalized clinical criteria similar to those in Table 23.3, a significant minority of DLB cases may prove impossible to distinguish from AD on clinical grounds alone. Scientists have not yet established the role of investigations in aiding differential diagnosis. Förstl, Burns, Luthert, Cairns, and Levy (1993) reported a frontal accentuation of generalized cortical atrophy on CT scan of five out of eight autopsy-confirmed LBV cases. The Newcastle upon Tyne group has not found differences between frontal lobe volumes of clinically diagnosed AD and DLB cases, but the AD cases do have greater temporal lobe atrophy.

MEMORY DYSFUNCTION IN DEMENTIA WITH LEWY BODIES

Progressive, disabling mental impairment is a mandatory requirement for the diagnosis of DLB. Symptoms of prominent or persistent memory impairment are not always present early in the course of DLB but are likely to develop in most patients as the disease progresses. For example, at the time of first presentation with symptoms of dementia, only 30% of 21 autopsy-confirmed DLB patients scored 0 points (out of a maximum of 5) on a test of short-term recall, whereas 93% of AD cases did so ($p = .001$). Only 3% of the AD patients scored 3 or more points on this test, whereas 33% of DLB patients did so ($p = .0013$) (McKeith, Perry, Fairbairn, Jabeen, & Perry, 1992). Although Hansen et al. (1990) did not find differences in episodic memory performance between LBV and AD patients, a subgroup of five autopsy-confirmed pure DLB cases (without Alzheimer-type pathology) were found to lack the poor retention over delay intervals, increased propensity to produce intrusion errors in the cued recall condition, and poor recognition discrimanibility typical of AD patients (Salmon & Galasko, 1996). These DLB patients were characterized as having a predominantly subcortical type retrieval deficit, similar to that seen in PD. This relative sparing of memory function in DLB compared to AD may be understood not only in terms of the reduced burden of pathology in the hippocampus and related structures (entorhinal cortex and parahippocampal gyrus) that are thought to underlie memory storage (consolidation) (Salmon & Galasko, 1996) but also in the proposed neuromodulatory effects of the septal dopaminergic deficit on cholinergic neurotransmission in the archicortex. In summary, DLB patients experience particular difficulty on tests of memory retrieval, in contrast to AD patients who experience difficulty in memory acquisition and consolidation.

VISUOSPATIAL DYSFUNCTION IN DEMENTIA WITH LEWY BODIES

Salmon et al. (in press) conducted a study that showed striking differences between the pure DLB and AD patients using tests of visuospatial and visuoconstructional ability. Despite only borderline to mild impairment on the MMSE (range 22–26), four of the five DLB patients performed at floor levels on the Wechsler Intelligence Scale for Children—Revised block design test, and the fifth was severely impaired. DLB patients showed more severe impairment than did AD patients relating to the copy condition of the clock drawing test, producing errors related to the spatial layout of the clock. Disproportionate visuospatial impairment as demonstrated by tests such as block design, clock drawing, or figure copying may therefore be a useful diagnostic indicator of DLB. Byrne (1995) previously drew attention to the function of the clock drawing test as a useful clinical indicator of disease progression in DLB.

EXECUTIVE DYSFUNCTION IN DEMENTIA WITH LEWY BODIES

The term "executive functions" refers to the mental processes involved in the realization of goal-directed behavior, whether expressed through a mental or a motor act (Dubois, Boller, Pillon, & Agid, 1991). These processes include concept formation, planning and sequencing, set shifting, mental flexibility, self-generation of strategies in the absence of external cues, and regulation of behavior according to environmental cues. Executive functions are often impaired following damage to the frontal lobes or to other related parts of the brain, particularly the nigrostriatal–frontal circuits. Nigrostriatal degeneration is thought to be a major determinant of executive dysfunction in PD patients who demonstrate a decreased ability to form concepts, difficulty in maintaining and changing sets, and deficits in planning and execution.

Commonly used clinical tests of executive function include the Wisconsin Card Sorting Test (WCST), the Trail Making test, and the Stroop Test, whereas, to a lesser extent, the verbal fluency test investigates the ability to maintain a mental set and generate a search strategy. Planning and programming capacities are best studied by more complex procedures such as the Tower of London task. Although there have not yet been extensive studies on the subject, one would predict that DLB patients, with their combination of cortical and nigrostriatal pathology, should be substantially impaired on such tests of executive function. Salmon and Galasko (1996) found pure DLB patients to be severely impaired on parts A and B of the Trail Making tests and significantly slower than AD patients in both conditions. These results were not, however, regarded as strong evidence of impaired executive function because the patients were only mildly impaired on other tests of executive functions such as the Wechsler Adult Intelligence Scale—Revised (WAIS-R) similarities subtest and the Conceptualization subtest from the Dementia Rating Scale. Patients who were clinically diagnosed as AD with extrapyramidal features (EPF) have been more extensively investigated and may be considered paradigmatic of DLB (Salmon & Galasko, 1996). Indeed, at autopsy, many such patients will have proven to have DLB rather than pure AD. Merello et al. (1994) found that AD patients with severe EPF performed significantly worse than AD patients without EPF on the WCST, the Trail Making test, a verbal fluency task, Raven's progressive Matrices test, a backward digit span test, and the Block Design test. AD patients with fewer and milder EPF performed worse than those without EPF on the WCST, the Trail Making test, Raven's Progressive Matrices test, the Block Design test, and Benton's Visual Retention test. There were no differences between the three groups on tests of long-term memory, verbal comprehension, or confrontation naming. The pattern of cognitive impairments exhibited by the AD patients with EPF, is indicative of frontostriatal dysfunction superimposed on the typical cortical deficits of AD and is reminiscent of the performance of patients with autopsy-confirmed DLB.

ATTENTIONAL DYSFUNCTION IN DEMENTIA WITH LEWY BODIES

Attentional deficits in DLB may be clinically manifested in different ways. Caregivers frequently report somnolence, reduced awareness of surroundings, and confusion in DLB patients. Episodes of going blank or "switching off" suggest a diagnosis of DLB, especially if other systemic and pharmacological causes of disturbed consciousness have been excluded (McKeith, Perry et al., 1992). Variations in attention and alertness may also contribute to the characteristic fluctuation in cognitive function which occurs in at least 80% of DLB patients. It has been postulated that the deficits in attention and consciousness seen in DLB are related to substantial cholinergic deficits in the brainstem and cortex (Perry et al., 1993), and that perturbations in cholinergic function may account for the fluctuating clinical picture. Hansen et al. (1990) found that nine autopsy-confirmed LBV patients performed significantly worse than did AD patients on a test of attention (the Digit Span subtest from the WAIS-R) despite equivalent levels of global dementia.

Ayre, Sahgal, Wesnes, and McKeith (1996) started to use the computer-based Cognitive Drug Research Computerized Assessment Battery—Dementia (COGDRAS-D) (Simpson, Surmon, Wesnes, & Wilcock, 1991) to investigate DLB attentional deficits in greater depth. On a test of attentional vigilance, subjects were required to respond each time a rapidly changing target digit on a video display unit (VDU) coincided with a constantly displayed single digit. DLB patients responded correctly to only 50% of matching stimuli, significantly worse than AD patients matched for global severity of dementia (87% correct, $p = .001$). AD patients did not score significantly worse than controls (96% correct, $p = .34$). This test included a working-memory component which was tested by asking the subjects to remember three digits to which responses were to be made (rather than providing a constant display of a single digit as in the pure attentional task). This addition required subjects to interpret and manipulate information being held on-line, thereby increasing the frontal demands of the task. Again, controls and AD patients performed similarly, but DLB patients were significantly more impaired ($p = .001$). In contrast, the DLB patients were less impaired than AD patients on a verbal recognition memory task; both groups, however, performed significantly worse than controls.

THE NEUROANATOMICAL BASIS OF COGNITIVE DEFICITS IN DEMENTIA WITH LEWY BODIES

The neuropathological, neurochemical, and clinical evidence presented so far supports the view that patients with DLB have neuropsychological deficits related not only to diffuse cortical disease and neuronal loss but also to dopaminergic frontostriatal dysfunction. To test this proposition further, Sahgal and colleagues carried out a series of investigations using the relatively recently developed computer-based test system CANTAB (Cambridge Neuropsychological Test Automated Battery). CANTAB includes tests of recognition memory sensitive to temporal lobe (cortical, hippocampal) damage. Other tests require intact frontal or frontostriatal structures and circuitry necessary to efficiently execute attentional, strategic planning and certain memory functions. DLB and AD patients matched for age, estimated premorbid verbal IQ, and global severity of dementia were compared with each other and with elderly normal subjects. Nondemented PD patients and age-matched controls were also tested. (Galloway et al., 1992; Sahgal et al., 1991; Sahgal, Galloway, McKeith, Edwardson, & Lloyd, 1992; Sahgal, Galloway, McKeith, Lloyd, et al., 1992; Sahgal, Lloyd, et al., 1992; Sahgal, McKeith, Galloway, Tasker, & Steckler, 1995).

The demented groups were similarly impaired on a simple test of recognition memory, but DLB patients required more trials in a conditional pattern–location paired-associate learning task in which they were required to identify the location of a target stimulus that had previously been presented in one of six possible locations in a spatial array. This test is sensitive to right-sided hippocampal damage and the conditional element also has the potential to detect evidence of frontal lobe dysfunction.

Both demented groups performed worse than controls under conditions of simultaneous matching to sample (no delay) and did not differ from one another. DLB patients performed significantly worse than AD patients in a delayed matching to sample task as well as with all delay intervals. The investigators speculated that the exceptionally marked impairment demonstrated by DLB patients, who were unable to tolerate even short delays, reflects relatively severe posterior temporal cortical degeneration at an early stage of the disease. DLB patients were also significantly impaired on a visual search task testing focal attentional ability and requiring intact frontostriatal circuits for efficient performance, whereas AD patients performed the same as, or similar to, control levels. Interestingly, PD patients were not impaired on this task when compared to their controls. On a more complex visual attentional discrimination (set-shifting) problem, indirectly related to the WCST, and designed to be sensitive to frontal lobe damage, both DLB and AD patients performed worse than controls. None of the DLB patients solved an intradimensional shift stage within the test and, at this level, their performance was significantly worse than the AD group. This is the level of the task at which efficient attentional capacity, mediated by frontal lobe structures, is particularly necessary (Downes et al., 1989).

Finally, DLB patients made more errors than AD patients on a spatial working-memory task which assessed spatial working memory and the ability to use an efficient search strategy. PD patients also performed poorly on this test, which represents a development of the radial maze techniques used to assess memory in rodents, and which is known to be affected by temporal, and especially frontal, lobe damage. Taken together, the CANTAB and COGDRAS-D studies suggest that the neuroanatomical foci of DLB and AD show differences with relatively greater temporal lobe and hippocampal involvement in AD, and evidence of greater damage to frontostriatal structures in DLB similar to, but less severe than, that seen in PD. The preliminary data from the COGDRAS study (Ayre et al., 1996) suggest that these anatomical differences may be exploited, producing a double discrimination on test performance to assist in the diagnostic differentiation between DLB (recall memory > attentional performance) and AD (attentional performance > recall memory).

SUMMARY

DLB appears to be a relatively common form of degenerative dementia, most prevalent in elderly men and identifiable in the majority of patients by a combination of fluctuating cognitive impairment, visual hallucinations, and mild parkinsonism. In clinical practice, the important distinctions are from AD, vascular dementia, and delirium of systemic or pharmacological origin.

There are at least two pathological mechanisms with the potential to compromise frontal lobe function in DLB. One is cortical and the other principally subcortical in origin. Diffuse cortical LB formation and neuronal loss in frontal cortex are mirrored by reductions in measures of frontal–cortical cholinergic activity. These localized pathological changes do not appear to be highly correlated with severity of cognitive impairment, added to which, DLB patients do not present with the behavioral changes or other symptoms typically seen in the frontal lobe atrophies. There is, therefore, little compelling evidence in the data currently available to support a view that frontal lobe degeneration plays a primary role in DLB symptom formation, which does not exclude the possibility that it may contribute to it. The major functional correlate of cortical pathology in DLB appears to be with the genesis of persistent visual hallucinations; the temporal association cortex being the region most strongly implicated.

The second, and apparently more significant factor contributing to frontal dysfunction in DLB, is a consequence of nigrostriatal degeneration which is similar to, but not as severe as, that seen in PD. Experimental evidence cited in this chapter demonstrated attentional and executive impairments in DLB, which are indicative of frontostriatal dysfunction. Similar deficits are seen in PD patients. In contrast, DLB patients show less impairment on tests of recognition memory than do AD patients, reflecting the relative sparing of the hippocampus and related structures in DLB.

REFERENCES

Ayre, G. A., Sahgal, A., Wesnes, K., & McKeith, I. G. (1996). Psychological function in dementia with Lewy bodies and senile dementia of Alzheimer's type. *Neurobiology of Aging, 17*(45), 205.

Ballard, C. G., Mohan, R. N. C., Patel, A., & Bannister, C. (1993). Idiopathic clouding of consciousness—Do the patients have cortical Lewy body disease? *International Journal of Geriatric Psychiatry, 8,* 571–576.

Braak, H., Braak, E., Yilmazer, D., de Vos, R. A., Jansen, E. N., Bohl, J., & Jellinger, K. (1994). Amygdala pathology in Parkinson's disease. *Acta Neuropathologica, 88,* 493–500.

Burns, A., Luthert, P., Levy, R., Jacoby, R., & Lantos, P. (1990). Accuracy of clinical diagnosis of Alzheimer's disease. *British Medical Journal, 301,* 1026.

Byrne, E. J. (1995). Cortical Lewy body disease: An alternative view. In R. Levy & R. Howard (Eds.), *Developments in dementia and functional disorders in the elderly* (pp. 21–30). Petersfield, UK: Wrightson.

Dickson, D. W., Crystal, H. A., Davies, P., & Hardy, J. (1996). Cytoskeletal and Alzheimer-type pathology in Lewy body disease. In R. H. Perry, I. G. McKeith, & E. K. Perry (Eds.), *Dementia with Lewy bodies* (pp. 224–237). New York: Cambridge University Press.

Dickson, D. W., Crystal, H. A., Mattiace, L. A., Kress, Y., Schwagerl, A., Ksiezak-Reding, H., Davies, P., & Yen, S. H. (1989). Diffuse Lewy body disease: Light and electron microscopic immunocytochemistry of senile plaques. *Acta Neuropathologica, 78,* 572–584.

Dickson, D. W., Ruan, D., Crystal, J., Mark, M., Davies, P., Kress, Y., & Yen, S. H. (1991). Hippocampal degeneration differentiates diffuse Lewy body disease (DLBD) from Alzheimer's disease: Light and electron microscopic immunohistochemistry of CA-3 neurites specific to DLBD. *Neurology, 41*, 1402–1409.

Dickson, D. W., Wu, E., Crystal, H. A., Mattiace, L. A., Yen, S. H., & Davies, P. (1992). Alzheimer and age-related pathology in diffuse Lewy body disease. In F. Boller, F. Forcette, Z. Khachaturian, M. Poncet, & Y. Christen (Eds.), *Heterogeneity of Alzheimer's disease* (pp. 168–186). Berlin: Springer-Verlag.

Downes, J. J., Roberts, A. C., Sahakian, B. J., Evenden, J. L., Morris, R. G., & Robbins, T. W. (1989). Impaired extradimensional shift performance in medicated and unmedicated Parkinson's disease: Evidence for a specific attentional dysfunction. *Neuropsychologia, 27*, 1329–1343.

Dubois, B., Boller, F., Pillon, B., & Agid, Y. (1991). Cognitive deficits in Parkinson's disease. In F. Boller & J. Grafman (Eds.), *Handbook of neuropsychology* (pp. 195–240). New York: Elsevier.

Förstl, H., Burns, A., Luthert, P., Cairns, N., & Levy, R. (1993). The Lewy body variant of Alzheimer's disease: Clinical and pathological findings. *British Journal of Psychiatry, 162*, 385–392.

Galloway, P. H., Sahgal, A., McKeith, I. G., Lloyd, S., Cook, J. H., Ferrier, I. N., & Edwardson, J. A. (1992). Visual pattern recognition memory and learning deficits in senile dementias of Alzheimer and Lewy body types. *Dementia, 3*, 101–107.

Gibb, W. R., Esiri, M. M., & Lees, A. J. (1987). Clinical and pathological features of diffuse cortical Lewy body disease (Lewy body dementia). *Brain, 110*, 1131–1153.

Hansen, L. A., Masliah, E., Galasko, D., & Terry, R. D. (1994). Plaque-only Alzheimer disease is usually Lewy body variant, and vice versa. *Journal of Neuropathology and Experimental Neurology, 52*, 648–654.

Hansen, L., Salmon, D. P., Galasko, D., Masliah, E., Katzman, R., De Teresa, R., Thal, L., Pay, M. M., Hofstetter, R., Klauber, M., Rice, V., Butters, N., & Alford, M. (1990). The Lewy body variant of Alzheimer's disease: A clinical and pathological entity. *Neurology, 40*, 1–8.

Jellinger, K. A. (1996). Structural basis of dementia in neurodegenerative disorders. *Journal of Neural Transmission, 47*, 1–29.

Kosaka, K. (1990). Diffuse Lewy body disease in Japan. *Journal of Neurology, 237*, 197–204.

Kosaka, K., & Iseki, E. (1996). Diffuse Lewy body disease within the spectrum of Lewy body disease. In R. H. Perry, I. G. McKeith, & E. K. Perry (Eds.), *Dementia with Lewy bodies* (pp. 238–247). New York: Cambridge University Press.

Kosaka, K., Yoshimura, M., Ikeda, K., & Budka, H. (1984). Diffuse type of Lewy body disease: Progressive dementia with abundant cortical Lewy bodies and senile changes of varying degree—A new disease? *Clinical Neuropathology, 3*, 185–192.

Langlais, P. J., Thal, L., & Hansen, L. (1993). Neurotransmitters in basal ganglia and cortex of Alzheimer's disease with and without Lewy bodies. *Neurology, 43*, 1927–1934.

Lennox, G., Lowe, J., Morrell, K., Landon, M., & Mayer, R. (1989). Antiubiquitin immunocytochemistry is more sensitive than conventional techniques in the detection of diffuse Lewy body disease. *Journal of Neurology, Neurosurgery, and Psychiatry, 52*, 67–71.

Levin, E. D., McGurk, S. R., Roso, J. E., & Butcher, L. L. (1990). Cholinergic–dopaminergic interactions in cognitive performance. *Behavioral and Neural Biology, 54*, 271–299.

Lowe, J. S., Mayer, R. J., & Lanon, M. (1996). Pathological significance of Lewy bodies in dementia. In R. M. Perry, I. G. McKeith, & E. K. Perry (Eds.), *Dementia with Lewy bodies* (pp. 195–202). New York: Cambridge University Press.

McKeith, I. G. (1993). *The clinical diagnosis of Lewy body dementia.* M.D. thesis, University of Newcastle upon Tyne.

McKeith, I. G., Fairbairn, A. F., Bothwell, R. A., Moore, P. B., Ferrier, I. N., Thompson, P., & Perry, R. H. (1994). An evaluation of the predictive validity and inter-rater reliability of clinical diagnostic criteria for senile dementia of Lewy body type. *Neurology, 44*, 872–877.

McKeith, I. G., Fairbairn, A. F., Perry, R. H., & Thompson, P. (1994). The clinical diagnosis and misdiagnosis of senile dementia of Lewy body type (SDLT). *British Journal of Psychiatry, 165*, 324–332.

McKeith, I. G., Fairbairn, A. F., Perry, R. H., Thompson, P., & Perry, E. K. (1992). Neuroleptic sensitivity in patients with senile dementia of Lewy body type. *British Medical Journal, 305,* 673–678.

McKeith, I. G., Galasko, D., Kosaka, K., Perry, E. K., Dickson, D. W., Hansen, L. A., Salmon, D. P., Lowe, J., Mirra., S. S., Byrne, E. J., Lennox, G., Quinn, N. P., Edwardson, J. A., Ince, P. G., Bergeron, C., Burns, A., Miller, B. L., Lovestone, S., Collerton, D., Jansen, E. N. H., Ballard, C., de Vos, R. A. I., Wilcock, G. K., Jellinger, K. A., & Perry, R. H. (1996). Consensus guidelines for the clinical and pathologic diagnosis of dementia with Lewy bodies (DLB): Report of the consortium on DLB international workshop. *Neurology 47(5),* 1113–1124.

McKeith, I. G., Perry, R. H., Fairbairn, A. F., Jabeen, S., & Perry, E. K. (1992). Operational criteria for senile dementia of Lewy body type. *Pathological Medicine, 22,* 911–922.

Merello, M., Sabe, L., Teson, A., Migliorelli, R., Petracchi, M., Leiguarda, R., & Starkstein, S. (1994). Extrapyramidalism in Alzheimer's disease: Prevalence, psychiatric, and neuropsychological correlates. *Journal of Neurology, Neurosurgery, and Psychiatry, 57,* 1503–1509.

Perry, E. K., Haroutunian, V., Davis, K. L., Levy, R., Lantos, P., Eagger, S., Honavar, M., Dean, A., Griffiths, M., McKeith, I. G., & Perry, R. H. (1994). Neocortical cholinergic activities differentiate Lewy body dementia from classical Alzheimer's disease. *Neuroreport, 5,* 747–749.

Perry, E. K., Irving, D., Kerwin, J. M., McKeith, I. G., Thompson, P., Collerton, D., Fairbairn, A. F., Ince, P. G., Morris, C. M., Cheng, A. V., & Perry, R. H. (1993). Cholinergic transmitter and neurotrophic activities in Lewy body dementia: similarity to Parkinson's and distinction from Alzheimer's disease. *Alzheimer's Disease and Associated Disorders, 7(2),* 69–79.

Perry, E. K., Marshall, E., Kerwin, J. M., Smith, C. J., Jabeen, S., Cheng, A. V., & Perry, R. H. (1990). Evidence of a monoaminergic: Cholinergic imbalance related to visual hallucinations in Lewy body dementia. *Journal of Neurochemistry, 55(4),* 1454–1456.

Perry, E. K., Smith, C. J., Court, J. A., & Perry, R. H. (1990). Cholinergic nicotinic and muscarinic receptors in dementia of Alzheimer, Parkinson and Lewy body types. *Journal of Neural Transmission, 2,* 149–158.

Perry, R. H., Irving, D., Blessed, G., Fairbairn, A., & Perry, E. K. (1990). Senile dementia of Lewy body type: A clinically and neuropathologically distinct type of Lewy body dementia in the elderly. *Journal of Neurological Sciences, 95,* 119–135.

Perry, R. H., Jaros, E. B., Irving, D., Scoones, D. J., Brown, A., McMeekin, W. M., Perry, E. K., Morris, C. M., Kelly, P. J., & Ince, P. G. (1996). What is the neuropathological basis of dementia associated with Lewy bodies? In R. H. Perry, I. G. McKeith, & E. K. Perry (Eds.), *Dementia with Lewy bodies* (pp. 212–223). New York: Cambridge University Press.

Pollanen, M. S., Dickson, D. W., & Bergeron, C. (1993). Pathology and biology of the Lewy body. *Journal of Neuropathology and Experimental Neurology, 52,* 183–191.

Roman, G. C., Tatemich, I. T. K., Erinjuntti, T., Cummings, J. L., Masdeu, J. C., & Garcia, J. H. (1993). Vascular dementia: Diagnostic criteria for research studies. Report of the NINDS-AIREN international workshop. *Neurology, 43,* 240–260.

Sahgal, A., Sahakian, B. J., Robbins, T. W., Wray, C. J., Lloyd, S., Cook, J. H., McKeith, I. G., Disley, J. C. A., Eagger, S., Boddington, S., & Edwardson, J. A. (1991). Detection of visual memory and learning deficits in Alzheimer's disease using the Cambridge Neuropsychological Test Automated Battery. *Dementia, 2,* 150–158.

Sahgal, A., Galloway, P. H., McKeith, I. G., Edwardson, J. A., & Lloyd, S. (1992). A comparative study of attentional deficits in senile dementias of Alzheimer and Lewy body types. *Dementia, 3,* 350–354.

Sahgal, A., Galloway, P. H., McKeith, I. G., Lloyd, S., Cook, J. H., Ferrier, I. N., & Edwardson, J. A. (1992b). Matching-to-sample deficits in senile dementias of Alzheimer and Lewy body types. *Archives of Neurology, 49,* 1043–1046.

Sahgal, A., Lloyd, S., Wray, C. J., Galloway, P. H., Robbins, T. W., Sahakian, B. J., McKeith, I. G., Cook, J. H., Disley, J. C. A., & Edwardson, J. A. (1992). Does visuospatial memory in senile dementia of the Alzheimer type depend on the severity of the disorder? *International Journal of Geriatric Psychiatry, 7,* 427–436.

Sahgal, A., McKeith, I. G., Galloway, P. H., Tasker, N., & Steckler, T. (1995). Do differences in visuospatial ability between senile dementias of the Alzheimer and Lewy body types reflect differences solely in mnemonic function? *Journal of Clinical and Experimental Neuropsychology, 17,* 35–43.

Saitoh, T., & Katzman, R. (1996). Genetic correlations in Lewy body disease. In R. H. Perry, I. G. McKeith, & E. K. Perry (Eds.), *Dementia with Lewy bodies* (pp. 336–349). New York: Cambridge University Press.

Salmon, D. P., & Galasko, D. (1996). Neuropsychological aspects of Lewy body dementia. In R. H. Perry, I. G. McKeith, & E. K. Perry (Eds.), *Dementia with Lewy bodies* (pp. 99–113). New York: Cambridge University Press.

Samuel, W., Galasko, D., Masliah, E., & Hansen, L. A. (1996). Neocortical Lewy body counts correlate with dementia in the Lewy body variant of Alzheimer's disease. *Journal of Neuropathology and Experimental Neurology, 55*(1), 44–52.

Shergill, S., Mullen, E., D'Ath, P., & Katona, C. (1994). What is the clinical prevalence of Lewy body dementia? *International Journal of Geriatric Psychiatry, 9,* 907–912.

Simpson, P. M., Surmon, D. J., Wesnes, K. A., & Wilcock, G. K. (1991). The cognitive drug research computerised assessment system for demented patients: A validation study. *International Journal of Geriatric Psychiatry, 6,* 95–102.

24

Frontal Lobe Tumors

TOMOKO Y. NAKAWATASE

Tumors commonly occur in the frontal lobes, and the diverse clinical manifestations of the patients who suffer from them make the clinical diagnosis a challenge. The symptoms exhibited in these patients are easily confused with "psychiatric" rather than "neurological" disorders. Patients with slow-growing frontal lobe lesions often exhibit vague symptoms and may not get medical attention until the tumor has grown large enough to produce increased intracranial pressure.

Botez (1974) presented a comprehensive chapter describing the pathology, neurophysiology, neuropsychiatry, and clinical methods for investigation of frontal lobe tumors. He emphasized the difficulty in describing with accuracy the exact location of a tumor in relation to the major anatomical and physiological subdivisions of the frontal lobes, and partly attributed this difficulty to differences in anatomical descriptions used by anatomists and neurosurgeons. According to his review, frontal lobe tumors are the most common of all cerebral tumors, comprising 16% of all supratentorial tumors, and occur in approximately equal frequency in the left and the right frontal lobes. Botez further stated that mental disorders are the most important symptom in the semiology of frontal lobe tumors and noted that the frequency of mental disorders in this group has been variably reported from 38% to 100%. This chapter reviews the historical literature describing frontal lobe functions based on tumor patients and illustrates the individual symptoms associated with specific regions within the frontal lobes. It also provides an overview of the neuropsychiatric and the neurobehavioral syndromes found in tumor patients and discusses the differential diagnosis and treatment of frontal lobe tumors.

HISTORICAL PERSPECTIVES

Investigators studied extensively the functions of the frontal lobe using tumor patients. Brickner (1936) described patient A before and after the resection of his frontal lobe tumor. Over a period of 12 years, patient A complained of progressive occipital headaches and memory problems. His family described him as being "absent-minded" and "slow." Patient A fell into a coma and immediately underwent a craniotomy with resection of a bifrontal tumor.

Using A as a model, Brickner established the following two major categories of frontal behavior: symptoms in the intellectual sphere, with an emotional coloring, and symptoms in the intellectual sphere, without emotional coloring. The first category consisted of impairment of restraint in controlling or concealing emotion, which included boasting, reminiscing, free expression of mild hostility, free expression of angry, aggressive, negativistic puerile impulses, impairment of "social sense," character and personality change, and impairment of "moral sense." The second category consisted of limitation of the capacity to associate or synthesize mental engrams to a complex degree, which included difficulty in maintaining attention as indicated by distractability and incapacity to select and segregate units of intellectual activity, and impairment in retention and learning capacity. Additional categories of impairments manifested in patient A included the impairment of judgment, abstraction, sense of humor, temporal and spatial orientation, and initiative and abnormalities in the capacity to bluff. Brickner demonstrated other abnormalities in frontal lobe function, including inability to determine the gravity of a given situation, euphoria, use of jargon, compulsiveness, and incontinence. He also added the "special symptoms" of aphasia, perseveration, and condensation. Through his detailed analysis of A's behavior, Brickner offered elaborate descriptions of frontal lobe functions.

Hebb and Penfield (1940) followed a 27-year-old male who sought treatment for posttraumatic epilepsy. Presurgically, the patient had weekly seizures, and in between his attacks, he exhibited significant behavioral problems including irresponsibility, restlessness, childish behavior, and amnesia. The patient underwent a bilateral frontal lobectomy which reduced his seizure frequency to only two during the 15-month follow-up and significantly improved his personality and memory.

Hebb and Penfield's patient showed few of the behavioral and mental defects demonstrated by Brickner's patient. Hebb and Penfield provided two possible explanations for the difference between the two patients. The first explanation was that Brickner's patient suffered a greater amount of tissue destruction than was apparent at operation because the anterior cerebral arteries may have been ligated during the two-stage removal of the encapsulated bilateral frontal tumor. The second explanation entailed possible interference of cerebral function in Brickner's case from the pathological tissue that was left behind during surgery. Hebb and Penfield emphasized the possibility of vascular change and necrosis extending beyond the immediate field of operation during any invasive surgical procedure on the brain. However, they stated that this complication was more likely to occur during tumor resections as a consequence of preoperative displacement and pressure exerted by the mass, compared to surgical procedures involving removal of atrophic tissue. They concluded that human behavior and mental activity are more likely to be impaired by the positive action of an abnormal brain region than by the negative effect of disabling a specific brain region by brain resection.

In 1938, Cushing and Eisenhardt published an excellent detailed report of the clinical aspects of meningiomas (Cushing & Eisenhardt, 1938/1962). Out of 2,203 personally observed and verified tumors listed in the Brain Tumor Registry, 13.4% (295) were intracranial meningiomas. Out of the 295 tumors, 65 were described as parasagittal meningiomas, and within this group, 13 were located in the frontal parasagittal region. All 13 patients presented with a long history of headaches. Vision failure was the most common complaint for which patients sought medical care. Only four of the patients had frequent seizures, but a majority displayed mental status changes including impairment in memory, personality changes, euphoria, jocularity, and untidiness. Cushing indicated that the prodromal symptoms of this group of patients were those indicating increased intracranial pressure, and that patients did not present until the tumors reached a large size as tumors often remained "wholly silent."

Twenty-nine cases of olfactory groove meningiomas were described. Only 14 of these patients complained of defective olfaction, 7 had the Foster–Kennedy syndrome (Kennedy, 1911), and 6 showed "personality changes."

The "frontal lobe syndrome," consisting of changes in personality, such as apathy, impulsiveness, facetiousness, euphoria, lack of initiative and spontaneity, and the inability to plan and follow through on a course of action, has been most often attributed to injury of the frontal lobes bilaterally. To alter the then generally accepted view that lesions of the left and the right hemispheres produced similar deficits, Benton (1968) published a paper reporting the results of neuropsychological tests he felt were more specific either to the left or the right hemisphere in patients with frontal lobe injuries. He evaluated 25 patients of whom 8 had lesions in the right frontal lobe, 10 had lesions in the left frontal lobe, and 7 had bilateral frontal lobe lesions. Fifty percent and 43% of the unilateral and bilateral cases, respectively, had intrinsic tumors, and 25% and 20% of the right frontal and left frontal cases, respectively, had extrinsic tumors. All patients were subjected to a series of neuropsychological tests to determine whether there were differences in scores between those patients with left versus right frontal injury.

Benton found that on the test of verbal associative fluency, in which the patient is asked to say as many words as he or she can think of that begin with the letters "F," "A," and "S," the patients with left frontal lobe disease and the ones with bilateral lesions did worse than patients with right frontal lobe lesions. On the test of paired-associate verbal learning, the left-hemisphere group did better than the bilateral or the right-sided group. On a test of three-dimensional block construction and copying designs, the results of the patients with bilateral dysfunction were inferior to the results of the patients with left-sided lesions, and there was no difference in performance between the right-sided and the bilateral groups. On the tests of temporal orientation and proverbs, the result of the patients with bilateral injuries were inferior to the results of both unilateral groups. Benton concluded that some of the interhemispheric differences in performance that have been shown in patients with unilateral post-Rolandic lesions may also be demonstrated in patients with unilateral frontal lobe lesions, and that certain task performances are more susceptible to the effects of bilateral frontal lobe injury.

LOCALIZING SYNDROMES

Neurological signs play an important role in the localization of symptoms, and the astute clinician can often localize specific symptoms to certain parts of the frontal lobes. Much of the literature on brain–behavior relationship of the frontal lobe has been based on patients with tumors, massive head trauma, aneurysm rupture, or surgical procedures to treat intractable seizures or psychiatric disease (Mesulam, 1986). However, conclusions made about brain–behavior relationships based on such structural lesion cases are often difficult to interpret because the lesions may extend beyond the frontal lobes, or there may be differential effects of other factors, such as the amount of edema, which may alter the brain and thus the clinical manifestation of the patient.

Anderson, Damasio, and Tranel (1990) compared the neuropsychological profile of patients with either a tumor or a stroke in the same location and found major differences in the neuropsychological findings between the two groups. Their series included three patients with left frontal gliomas, four patients with right frontal gliomas, and one patient

TABLE 24.1. Localization of Eye Movements

Location of tumor	Function	Eye findings
Frontal eye field	Clearinghouse for all cortically mediated saccades	Eyes deviated toward the lesion
Supplementary eye field	Spatial planning center	—
Dorsolateral prefrontal cortex	Saccade-suppressing center	Saccadic eye movements

with a right frontal meningioma. The cognitive impairments of tumor patients were found to be mild compared to those of stroke patients, supporting the hypothesis that tumors infiltrate or displace neural tissue without impairing neuronal function.

With frontal lobe tumors, clinicians may miss the diagnosis until the tumor becomes large enough to cause compression of the motor strip leading to a noticeable hemiparesis. Tumors in the premotor areas cause subtle neurological signs of eye deviation, spasticity, contralateral ataxia, and frontal release signs. Table 24.1 demonstrates localization of the mass lesion based on eye findings. Seizures may also be the presenting sign of frontal lobe tumors (see Table 24.2), and the type of seizure may indicate the localization. For example, focal motor seizures may occur in patients with lesions abutting the primary motor cortex, and partial complex seizures with complex motor automatisms, such as bicycling motion, may occur in patients with parasagittal or prefrontal tumors (Kraemer & Bullard, 1994).

If the tumor is located posteriorly in the motor strip of the frontal lobe, the patient often presents with a hemiparesis, whereas if the tumor occurs in the supplementary motor area (SMA), a different syndrome occurs. To better understand the functional significance of this area, Rostomily, Berger, Ojermann, and Lettich (1991) retrospectively analyzed the postoperative deficits and functional recovery patterns of six patients who had undergone removal of the dominant hemisphere SMA during tumor resection. All patients presented with a seizure, and two patients had speech arrest associated with the seizures. Three patients were neurologically intact, and the other three had a mild right hemiparesis. Pathological confirmation revealed a low-grade astrocytoma in four cases, anaplastic astrocytoma in one, and, in the last case, metastatic breast adenocarcinoma. All five patients with a glioma became mute within 24 hours of resection, without disturbance of sensorium or comprehension. Partial speech function returned within 3 to 5 days postoperatively, and fluent spontaneous speech returned within 4 to 12 days. However, all patients showed hesitation and speech initiation difficulties. The patient with the metastatic lesion showed no speech or cognitive deficits.

A characteristic syndrome of reversible contralateral weakness and/or neglect and mutism without cognitive impairment was termed the "SMA syndrome" by this group which advocated appropriate counseling to these patients of the potential severity, yet reversibility, of this neurological impairment. Although this study contributed to our understanding of the SMA, inclusion of right-sided cases and detailed neurobehavioral and neuropsychological evaluations would further enhance this type of study.

TABLE 24.2. Localization of Incontinenece and Seizures

Location of tumor	Incontinence	Seizures
Orbitofrontal	—	Confusional state
Parasagittal	Spastic bladder	Bicycling or other complex motor automatisms
Dorsolateral	Incontinence of apathy	Focal motor seizures

NEUROPSYCHIATRIC MANIFESTATIONS

The investigation of patients with frontal lobe tumors has provided much information about the neuropsychiatric syndromes associated with frontal lobe dysfunction. Frontal lobe tumors often present as a mood disorder. In a prospective series by Irle, Peper, Wowra, and Kunze (1994), neuropsychological information on patients was collected pre- and postresection of their tumor. In this series, they had 18 patients with tumors in the ventral frontal area, 16 patients with tumors in the lateral frontal area, and 26 patients with tumors in the frontal lobe. In the ventral frontal group, 7 patients had meningiomas, 5 had grade I–II gliomas, 3 had grade III–IV gliomas, 2 patients had metastases, and 1 had a cavernoma. In the lateral frontal group, 5 had gliomas, 3 had metastases, and 1 had a cavernoma. In the frontal group, 10 patients had meningiomas, 5 had grade I–II gliomas, 9 had grade III–IV gliomas, and 2 had metastases.

The series investigated by Irle and colleagues is one of the best documented studies in recent years, in which mood state was correlated to lesion type, size, location, and laterality. One hundred and one patients completed the mood questionnaire, and the results of neuropsychological testing were included in the analysis. Mood aspects which were assessed included vigor, fatigue, extraversion, irritability/anger, and anxiety/depression. The lesion size, edema, and degree of compression of the sylvian fissure, cortical sulci, lateral ventricles, and cisterns and displacement of the midline were positively correlated with negative mood states. However, laterality and grade of the tumor had no significant effect on the severity of emotional changes. Patients with lesions of the heteromodal cortical areas (ventral frontal cortex or the temporoparietal cortex) showed significant worsening of mood postoperatively compared to patients with lesions in other areas. These investigators proposed that heteromodal cortices are concerned with emotionally relevant operations and that the loss of function in these areas, such as occurs with destruction from brain tumors, deprives limbic structures of one of their main sources of input and, therefore, leads to changes in emotions.

Hunter, Blackwood, and Bull (1968) reported three patients with frontal meningiomas presenting psychiatrically: a 62-year-old woman who presented after 3 years of a dementing process, a 65-year-old woman who presented after 25 years of seizures and personality change, and a 75-year-old woman who presented after 43 years of delusions and hallucinations. Lesions in the middle and superior frontal regions were associated with "negative" symptoms of apathy, unconcern, dementia, and incontinence, whereas lesions affecting the base of the frontal lobes or orbital cortex caused "positive" symptoms of excitement, disinhibition, euphoria, and hallucinosis. I have had my own experience with a 56-year-old female who presented with personality change, new-onset urinary incontinence, and ataxia, who was found to have a large frontal parasagittal meningioma (see Figure 24.1).

Delusions imply a disturbance of reality testing such that affected individuals cannot evaluate the accuracy of their perceptions or thoughts. Bilateral frontal lobe damage may lead to delusional syndromes such as reduplicative paramnesia, Capgras syndrome, and bizarre confabulations. Patients with Capgras syndrome believe that known persons or objects have been replaced by impostors or "doubles." The syndrome has been reported in patients with bilateral frontal lobe lesions (Alexander, Stuss, & Benson, 1979).

Psychiatric symptoms, including hallucinations, delusions, catatonia, mania, schizophreniform psychosis, and depression, have been reported with frontal tumors. Tumors and other focal lesions should be suspected especially in elderly patients who present with

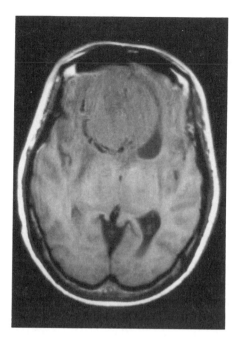

FIGURE 24.1. A 56-year-old female with personality change of disinhibition and inappropriate behavior, and new-onset urinary incontinence and ataxia.

late-life psychosis or depression. In the elderly, meningiomas, gliomas, and pituitary tumors predominate in cases associated with prominent mental symptoms, and the most common sites are the frontal and temporal lobes and the diencephalon (Galasko, Kwo-On-Yuen, & Thal, 1988).

NEUROBEHAVIORAL AND NEUROPSYCHOLOGICAL MANIFESTATIONS

Various neurobehavioral syndromes may be seen in patients with frontal lobe tumors. Table 24.3 summarizes the clinical findings by tumor location. Patients with orbitofrontal tumors tend to exhibit disinhibited behavior, manifesting as social inappropriateness, irritability, profanity, and jocularity. Patients with dorsal midline tumors are more likely to show abulia and poor initiation of thought and movement. Anterior aphasia symptoms of decreased verbal output, decreased fluency, and circumlocutory speech with frequent word-finding pauses may be present in frontal lobe tumor patients with lesions of the left hemisphere. Patients with dorsolateral convexity tumors demonstrate apathy, reduced drive, depressed mentation, and poor planning. A 33-year-old male with a left frontal dorsolateral tumor was found lying in his own feces and urine, apathetic, and refusing medical evaluation (see Figure 24.2).

Meningiomas occur commonly in the falx and may lead to deficits in complex attentional tasks. A 50-year-old woman who underwent psychiatric treatment for 3 years was found to have a large meningioma of the falx, involving the medial aspects of the bilateral frontal lobes. Neuropsychological testing revealed deficits in complex attentional tasks, including the go/no-go test. The go/no-go deficit completely resolved after surgical resection of the tumor, implicating that the medial frontal lobe may be responsible for the ability to do the go/no-go task (Leimkuhler & Mesulam, 1985). Reduplicative

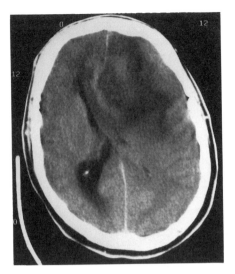

FIGURE 24.2. A 33-year-old male found lying in his own feces and urine, apathetic, uncooperative, with inappropriate laughter.

paramnesia is identified when a patient claims that a particular place is located somewhere else, usually close to the patient's home. The full syndrome includes some impairment of memory function, decreased drive and foresight, disturbed topographical orientation and disturbed awareness, and self-criticism (Benson & Stuss, 1990). All reported cases of reduplicative paramnesia showed evidence of brain damage, particularly of both frontal lobes. Confabulation occurred in variable degrees from the patient making mild elaborations to making wild outright bizarre fabrications. Frontal dysfunction is thought to be predisposed to confabulation (Kapur & Coughlan,1980).

TYPES OF FRONTAL LOBE TUMORS

Neoplasms of the frontal lobes are the most common of all cerebral tumors compromising 16–20% of all supratentorial tumors (Botez, 1974). Table 24.4 illustrates the differential diagnosis of frontal lobe tumor type. Gliomas and meningiomas are the most common, and in a review of the literature, out of 1,690 frontal lobe tumors, 1,217 were gliomas and 473 were meningiomas (Botez, 1974). The glioma series include astrocytomas, oligodendrogliomas, and glioblastoma multiformae. Frontal glioblastomas often grow quickly, causing symptoms of headache, behavioral disturbance, and seizures at a fairly early stage. The slower-growing gliomatous tumors often produce vague behavioral symptoms for many years and may not be diagnosed until the patient develops elementary

TABLE 24.3. Summary of Clinical Findings by Tumor Location

Location of tumor	Motor	Behavioral symptoms	Psychiatrical symptoms
Olfactory groove (orbitofrontal)	Spared unless huge	Often spared	Disinhibition
Parasagittal (dorsal–midline)	Leg weakness greater than arm	Go/no-go	Abulia
Intraparenchymal (dorsolateral)	Contralateral hemiparesis	Poor executive function	Apathy

TABLE 24.4. Types of Frontal Lobe Tumors

Extraparenchymal tumors	Intraparenchymal tumors
Meningioma	Astrocytoma
Optic nerve glioma	Glioblastoma multiforme
Olfactory groove glioma	Oligodendroglioma
Orbital lymphoma	Hemangioma
Pituitary tumor	Hemangioblastoma
Craniopharyngioma	Ependymoma
Chordoma	Tuberculoma
Cavernoma	Lymphoma
Metastases	Metastases

neurological signs or has a seizure (Benson & Stuss, 1986). A parasagittal meningioma is classically known to cause symptoms of spastic paraparesis and bowel and bladder dyscontrol, whereas an olfactory groove meningioma may cause symptoms of dementia and anosmia (Morantz & Walsh, 1994).

Although gliomas and meningiomas are the most common frontal lobe tumors, pathological confirmation may reveal other types of mass lesions. A 51-year-old woman who presented 1 day after a generalized seizure was found to have a stage 1E non-Hodgkins lymphoma involving the dura around the frontal lobe (Miranda et al., 1996). A 60-year-old male with left leg jerks and gait disturbance was found, on CT, to have a highly enhanced flat lesion within the interhemispheric region of the frontal and parietal lobes. The patient underwent a right craniotomy and histological examination of the biopsied thickened falx revealed a caseous necrotic tissue surrounded by epitheloid cells and Langhans giant cells—a tuberculoma (Okada, Yoshida, Asai, & Shintani, 1993).

In the pediatric population, brain tumors are the second most common neoplasm, and seizures are a common manifestation of brain tumors in children (Kim, Wang, & Cho, 1995). In Kim et al.'s (1995) retrospective study of 10 pediatric brain tumor patients with intractable seizures who underwent lesionectomy, 4 had tumors in the frontal region. Three out of the four had a pathological diagnosis of oligodendroglioma, and the fourth case was identified as a ganglioglioma. A rare tumor in infants, a cystic cavernous hemangioma of the frontal lobe was reported in a 4-month-old infant who presented with a generalized seizure (Okada et al., 1989). This type of tumor has been found in every age group but is most commonly found in patients 20–50 years of age (Giombini & Morell, 1978)

A frontal lobe tumor causes effects not only by direct infiltration but through distant alterations secondary to asymmetrically increased intracranial pressure. Pressure from the tumor can cause compression of the cerebral blood vessels and acute ischemic neurological symptoms at a site distant from the tumor (Benson & Stuss, 1986).

DIAGNOSIS

The techniques used in the diagnosis of frontal lobe tumors have evolved and have improved over time. In the past, plain X-rays of the skull were widely used to diagnose brain tumors. Special contrast techniques, including air encephalography and angiography, often helped localize tumors by outlining the mass while pneumoencephalography and ventriculography sharply outlined the ventricular system and an abnormality of the normal ventricular pattern indicated the presence of a mass lesion or tissue loss. Radioisotope scans were useful for demonstrating highly vascular tumors, but their poor resolution and limited anatomical specificity have made this type of scan unpopular for use as a diagnostic tool (Benson & Stuss, 1986).

The recently developed computed tomography and magnetic resonance imaging scans readily facilitate the diagnosis of frontal lobe tumors. However, the patient may not get an imaging scan until the tumor grows large enough to cause seizures, hemiparesis, or symptoms of increased intracranial pressure. The tumor may be diagnosed earlier if the clinician is knowledgeable about frontal lobe functions and is able to observe signs of frontal lobe dysfunction. After the diagnosis has been made, a collaborative team approach with the neurologist, the neurosurgeon, and the oncologist will best serve the patient with a frontal lobe tumor.

REFERENCES

Alexander, M. P., Stuss, D. T., & Benson, D. F. (1979). Capgras syndrome: A reduplicative phenomenon. *Neurology, 29,* 334–339.

Anderson, S. W., Damasio, H., & Tranel, D. (1990). Neuropsychological impairments associated with lesions caused by tumor or stroke. *Archives of Neurology, 47,* 397–405.

Benson, D. F., & Stuss, D. T. (1986). *The frontal lobes.* New York: Raven Press.

Benson, D. F., & Stuss, D. T. (1990). Frontal lobe influences on delusions: A clinical perspective. *Schizophrenia Bulletin 16,* 403–411.

Benton, A. L. (1968). Differential behavior effects in frontal lobe disease. *Neuropsychologia, 6,* 53–60.

Botez, M. I. (1974). *Handbook of clinical neurology.* (Vol. 17, pp. 234–280). New York: Elsevier.

Brickner, R. M. (1936). *The intellectual functions of the frontal lobes* (pp. 4–7, 40–43). New York: Macmillan.

Cushing, H., & Eisenhardt, L. (1962). *Meningiomas: Their classification, regional behavior, life history, and surgical end results.* New York: Hafner. Original work published 1938

Galasko, D., Kwo-On-Yuen, P. F., & Thal, L. (1988). Intracranial mass lesions associated with late-onset psychosis and depression. *Psychiatric Clinics of America, 1,* 151–166.

Giombini, S., & Morell, G. (1978). Cavernous angiomas of the brain. Account of fourteen personal cases and review of the literature. *Acta Neurochirurgica (Wein), 40,* 61–82.

Hebb, D. O., & Penfield, W. (1940). Human behavior after extensive bilateral removal from the frontal lobes. *Archives of Neurology and Psychiatry, 44,* 421–438.

Hunter, R., Blackwood, W., & Bull, J. (1968). Three cases of frontal meningiomas presenting psychiatrically. *British Medical Journal, 3,* 9–16.

Irle, E., Peper, M., Wowra, B., & Kunze, S. (1994). Mood changes after surgery for tumors of the cerebral cortex. *Archives of Neurology, 51,* 164–174.

Kapur, N., & Coughlan, A. K. (1980). Confabulation and frontal lobe dysfunction. *Journal of Neurology, Neurosurgery, and Psychiatry, 43,* 461–463.

Kennedy, F. (1911). Retrobulbar neuritis as an exact diagnostic sign of certain tumors and abscessed in the frontal lobes. *American Journal of Medical Science, 142,* 355–368.

Kim, S. K., Wang, K. C., & Cho, B. K. (1995). Intractable seizures associated with brain tumor in childhood: Lesionectomy and seizure outcome. *Child's Nervous System, 11,* 634–638.

Kraemer, D. L., & Bullard, D. E. (1994). Clinical presentation of the brain tumor. In R. A. Morantz & J. W. Walsh (Eds.), *Brain tumors: A comprehensive text* (pp. 183–193). New York: Marcel Dekker.

Leimkuhler, M. E., & Mesulam, M. M. (1985). Reversible go-no go deficits in a case of frontal lobe tumor. *Annals of Neurology, 18,* 617–619.

Mesulam, M. M. (1986). Editorial—frontal cortex and behavior. *Annals of Neurology, 19,* 320–325.

Miranda, R. N., Glantz, L. K., Myint, M. A., Levy, N., Jackson, C. L., Rhodes, H., Glantz, M., & Medeiros J. (1996). Stage IE non-Hodgkin's lymphoma involving the dura: A clinicopathologic study of five cases. *Archives of Pathological Laboratory Medicine, 120,* 254–260.

Morantz, R. A., & Walsh J. W. (1994). *Brain tumors: A comprehensive text.* New York: Marcel Dekker.

Okada, T., Yoshida, T., Asai, T., & Shintani, A. (1993). Unusual meningeal tuberculoma—Case report. *Neurologia Medico-Chirugica, 33,* 710–712.

Okada, Y., Shima, T., Matsumura, S., Nishida, M., Yamada, T., & Hatayama, T. (1989). Cystic cavernous hemangioma in the frontal lobe in an infant—Case report. *Neurologia Medico-Chirugica, 29,* 40–43.

Rostomily, R. C., Berger, M. S., Ojemann G. A., & Lettich, E. (1991). Postoperative deficits and functional recovery following removal of tumors involving the dominant hemisphere supplementary motor area. *Journal of Neurosurgery, 75*(1), 62–68.

25

Psychosurgery

SETH M. WEINGARTEN

This chapter reviews the history of psychosurgery. The review of these procedures provides information regarding the anatomical and functional relationships of the frontal lobe and the limbic system in neuropsychiatric disorders.

At the turn of the 20th century, reports were published suggesting an organic basis for mental disease. Kraeplin and Alzheimer each had found subtle neuropathology in the brains of schizophrenic patients at postmortem examination. Burckhardt, in Switzerland, and Puusepp, in Russia, performed surgeries involving the frontal lobe on patients with psychotic disorders. Some of the patients were "calmer" after surgery, but the morbidity of the surgery was excessive (Diering & Bell, 1991).

Trauma and tumors of the frontal lobe of the brain are associated with personality changes. In 1841, Phineas Gage, a construction foreman, suffered a frontal lobe injury when a steel tamping iron was driven into his frontal lobes by blasting powder; he lived for 15 years after this accident but changed from a smart and energetic worker and a well-balanced man to a fitful, irreverent man who was unemployable and indulged in gross profanity publicly. Soldiers in World War I who suffered frontal lobe injuries also underwent significant personality changes. These personality changes were also present in patients with tumors of the frontal lobe (Jasper, 1995).

Patients who presented with personality changes after frontal lobe trauma or brain tumors had extensive lesions. Kraeplin and Alzheimer noted that patients with schizophrenia, however, had subtle neuropathological changes. The psychoanalytic concepts of Freud seemed a better explanation than organic cerebral pathology as the cause of mental illness (Swayze, 1995).

Surgeons initially made large lesions in the frontal lobe to alter behavior, but as they gained more experience, they found that more focal lesions could be effective in altering abnormal emotional activity. This review of psychosurgery, therefore, permits an assessment of the effects of discrete frontal lobe and limbic system lesions on behavior.

THE DEVELOPMENT OF PSYCHOSURGERY IN THE 20TH CENTURY

The Second World Congress of Neurology held in London in 1935 brought together the ideas of people doing basic behavioral research and clinical neurologists; this created the environment for the development of psychosurgery in the 20th century (Diering & Bell, 1991; Jasper, 1995; Swayze, 1995).

Jacobsen presented the experimental work being done in Fulton's laboratory at Yale, which demonstrated changes in the emotional reactions of monkeys after ablation of their frontal lobes. Monkeys trained to do a task and receive a food reward became frustrated when they failed to perform and did not receive a reward. After bilateral resection of the prefrontal lobes, the monkeys accepted the failure to perform a learned task and the loss of a food reward with a calm attitude. Moniz, a prominent neurologist from Portugal who was respected for his pioneering efforts in cerebral angiography, felt that Fulton's work should be adapted to patients with psychotic agitation. Fulton cautioned against using this surgery on human beings; he noted that not only were the monkeys' frustration and anxiety ameliorated but the monkeys also lost the intellectual ability to perform the task they had mastered before surgery.

One has to understand the treatment available for agitated psychotic patients at that time to appreciate Moniz's enthusiasm to use Fulton's technique to calm agitated patients. Psychiatric hospitals were overcrowded with psychotic patients; convulsive therapy gave only temporary relief of their symptoms. Freudian analytical techniques did not help this group of patients. Before the introduction of chlorpromazine in 1954, the possibility of quieting psychotic patients with psychosurgery to discharge them from institutions seemed worthy of clinical trial (Diering & Bell, 1991; Jasper, 1995; Swayze, 1995).

Moniz returned to Portugal and with the help of Lima, a neurosurgical colleague, operated on 20 patients with agitated psychotic behavior. The initial procedure involved the injection of absolute alcohol into each frontal lobe through bifrontal burr holes to disrupt frontothalamic fiber connections. A leucotome was later used instead of the injection of alcohol in an attempt to control the extent of the frontal lesion. They succeeded, using this procedure in their first 20 patients. Success was defined as the patient being quieter; this calming effect of the procedure permitted psychiatric patients to leave the hospital. Moniz published the results of these surgeries in journals in six different countries. His efforts represented a great advance in the treatment of agitated psychotic patients. Although psychosurgery did not cure the patients of their psychiatric disease, it supported Osler's belief that "doctors should intend to cure sometimes, to give relief often, and to give comfort always"(p. 514). Moniz was awarded the Nobel prize for the treatment of agitated psychotic behavior with his frontal lobotomy technique (Dagi, 1975).

FIRST GENERATION OF PSYCHOSURGERY

Freeman, a neurologist from George Washington University, was also at the Second World Congress of Neurology to present his work on ventriculography. He, too, felt that Fulton's work could be effective in treating agitated psychotic patients. After Moniz reported the success of his first group of patients, Freeman joined with his neurosurgical colleague, Watts, and performed the Moniz frontal lobotomy procedure. In 1942, they reported on the results of frontal lobotomy in their personal series of 80 patients (Freeman & Watts, 1942).

Initially, Freeman and Watts copied Moniz's method in approaching the frontal lobe through burr holes placed at the top of the skull, but they later changed to their "precision method" of frontal lobotomy. This surgery approached the frontal lobe through a laterally placed burr hole in the frontotemporal area. They then severed the frontothalamic fibers bilaterally by sweeping an instrument through the upper and then the lower half of each frontal lobe; the lobotomy, therefore, resulted from four separate incisions. The procedure was performed with the patients awake. Successful procedures were associated with the development of a confusional state in the patient as the last quadrant was cut. The patient had to remain in the hospital for 1 month after surgery because of disorientation, inability to dress, and the loss of bowel and bladder control. The results of the precision method were better for patients with anxiety and depression than for patients who suffered from schizophrenia. Relief of emotional tension was noted in 35% of schizophrenic patients and 60% of patients with depression and anxiety; this calming effect was often associated with apathy and loss of social inhibition.

Autopsy studies (Freeman & Watts, 1948; Meyer, Beck, & McLardy, 1947; Meyer, Bonn, & Beck, 1945) indicated great variability in the area of the brain destroyed with the precision method of lobotomy; there was asymmetry of the lesions placed in each frontal lobe in most patients. Lesions which included the medial ventral frontal lobe or the cingulum, however, were associated with the best clinical results. In addition, the lesions in the frontal lobe were associated with secondary degeneration in the mediodorsal and anterior nuclei of the thalamus.

Good results of the precision method of frontal lobotomy were explained in Freudian terms as follows: The severance of the frontothalamic connections isolated the "superego" of the frontal lobe from the "id" of the thalamus. The extreme variability of the lesions found at the autopsy of these patients made this thesis untenable (Meyer et al., 1947).

Yakovlev found that secondary degeneration after frontal lobotomy could be traced to the midbrain and pontine nuclei as well as to the thalamic nuclei; he theorized that the degeneration of the thalamic and brainstem nuclei was an important aspect of the clinical effects of frontal lobotomy (Yakovlev, Hamlin, & Sweet, 1950).

Many patients who underwent frontal lobotomies had a loss of intelligence and a change in their preoperative personality. An organic brain defect had been substituted for a psychotic state. If psychosurgery was to be judged in terms of returning a patient to the premorbid state, all procedures had to be judged a failure (Diering & Bell, 1991; Koskoff, Dennis, Lazovik & Wheeler, 1948; Rylander, 1948).

SECOND GENERATION OF PSYCHOSURGERY

In the second generation of psychosurgery, an attempt was made to minimize the unwanted side effects of frontal lobotomy by making the lesions within the brain less destructive. The targets for the smaller lesions were made partially on the basis of the empirical knowledge gained from the study of the effects of psychosurgery on patients and the study of autopsy material in this group of surgically treated mental patients.

In addition to empirical knowledge, however, there was a growing body of neuroanatomical knowledge which helped select targets for psychosurgery. In 1878, Broca described the "grand lobe limbique" (Nauta & Domesick, 1981). Papez further defined this system in the 20th century, noting that a reverberating cerebral circuit existed within the brain, which connected the frontal lobe of the brain with the "seat of emotional experience," the hypothalamus. The circuit consisted of the hypothalamus, the anterior nucleus of the thalmus, the cingulate gyrus, and the hippocampus; the circuit had reciprocal connections with the cortex of the brain. Papez theorized that the rhinencephalon, which was a major part of this system, was primarily concerned with emotion and not olfaction; this was a major innovative concept in neuroanatomy (Papez, 1937).

Yakovlev also recognized the importance of the limbic lobe of Broca in emotional activity. He conceptualized the brain in the following three interconnecting rings: the innermost—the entopallium (the pyriform lobe, the hippocampus, and the hypothalamus); the intermediate ring—the mesopallium (the limbic lobe of Broca and the insula); and the third ring—the ectopallium (the neocortex). He felt that the expansion of the limbic system (mesopallium), which was interconnected with the hypothalamus (entopallium), was related to the development of the expression of internal feelings in humans. He also noted the importance of the interconnection of these systems for the expression of emotions (Yakovlev, 1948).

MacLean expanded on Papez and Yakovlev's observations by adding the amygdala to the circuit of the "visceral brain" or the "limbic system." The orbitomedial frontal lobe, the anterior insula, the temporal pole, and the amygdala were all part of Yakovlev's mesopallium and were related to autonomical activity and emotional behavior. The output from the amygdala was connected to the hypothalamus, and from there to the anterior thalamus which was part of Papez's circuit (MacLean, 1949, 1952).

With the anatomical knowledge gained empirically from frontal lobotomy procedures and the basic neuroanatomy learned from scientists such as Papez, Yakovlev, and MacLean, surgeons developed procedures with smaller areas of cerebral destruction within the frontal and temporal lobes with the hope of achieving the calming effects of frontal lobotomy without the unwanted loss of intellect and social inhibition.

Fulton noted that the improvement of 50% of the 20,000 patients who were operated on by Freeman's technique was at the sacrifice of their intellect and social behavior. He felt that the autopsy studies of patients who had undergone frontal lobotomy suggested that lesions restricted to the medial ventral quadrant of the frontal lobes and the cingulum might achieve the same reduction in anxiety as after more extensive lobotomy with less unwanted side effects of loss of intellect and inappropriate social behavior. Although Fulton remained concerned with the negative side effects of the Moniz technique and recommended a less destructive surgical approach, he dedicated his review of psychosurgery to the courage and insight of Moniz (Fulton, 1951).

Frontal Cortical Resections

Penfield attempted to achieve the calming effects of frontal lobotomy in a group of psychotic patients with resection of areas of the dorsolateral frontal cortex. He found that this surgery brought about a decrease in the patient's anxiety but also a loss of intellectual capacity (Penfield, 1948). Pool and Heath did similar frontal cortical resections in psychotic patients and noted diminished patient anxiety without loss of intelligence, abstraction, or learning ability after resection of the dorsolateral frontal cortex. The resected cortex was normal to microscopic exam (Mettler, 1949).

Other surgeons found that surgery for the relief of anxiety was more effective if the cortical resection involved the medial and ventral areas of the frontal lobes rather than the dorsolateral convexity (Saubidet, Lyonnet, & Brichetti, 1975).

Transorbital Frontal Lobotomy

Freeman and Watts revised their precision method of lobotomy and made a restricted lesion in the frontal lobe through a transorbital approach in which an "ice-pick"-like instrument was inserted through the thin area of the orbital roof and moved through the white matter of the frontal lobe to sever the thalamofrontal connections in the medioventral quadrant of the frontal lobes (Freeman & Watts, 1950). The results of 400 cases treated with transorbital lobotomy were similar to the results obtained after the precision method of lobotomy but were described as "spectacular" because of the quick recovery of the patients from surgery: The patients were up and ready for a meal 1 hour after surgery, and could be discharged to their home in a calmer state a few days later. The procedure was effective for 50% of patients with anxiety and depression; it helped calm 30% of patients with schizophrenia. Other surgeons also found the results of the limited excision of transorbital lobotomy to equal the results of the precision method of frontal lobotomy (Wilson, Pittman, Bennett, & Garber, 1951).

Medial Ventral Frontal Lobotomy

Based on the results of autopsy studies that demonstrated the importance of the medial ventral quadrant of the frontal lobes in successful lobotomy procedures (Freeman & Watts, 1948; Meyer et al., 1945; Meyer et al., 1947; Yakovlev et al., 1950), Poppen approached this area through bifrontal burr holes and used a suction technique to remove the medial orbitofrontal area of the brain; he visualized the area of surgery in order to control intraoperative bleeding. Poppen operated on a series of 500 patients, 116 of whom were available for follow-up. Autopsy studies were done on 15 of these patients; the area of tissue destruction was greater and more variable than anticipated in all autopsy cases. He achieved success in more than one-half of his patients; success was defined as a lessening of anxiety in schizophrenic patients (Greenblatt & Solomon, 1953; Poppen, 1948).

Pool then reviewed a series of patients treated with either frontal–cortical resection, or a lobotomy restricted to the medial ventrofrontal lobe; in a series of 500 patients, he found that medial lobotomy was easier, safer, and as effective as cortical resection. The patients were not cured of core psychotic symptoms but were relieved of anxiety and suffering. Pool did not notice loss of intellect after either procedure (Slocum, Bennet, & Pool, 1959).

Tractotomy

Scoville approached the ventral medial quadrant of the frontal lobes through a low anterior frontal burr hole and performed an orbital undercutting using a suction technique which severed the white matter that connected the medial ventrofrontal cortex to the thalamus and the temporal lobe (Scoville, 1949). Scoville reviewed the long-term effects of frontal orbital undercutting and found that 70–80% of patients with anxiety and depression were relieved of tensions; the procedure was less effective for schizophrenic patients. Many patients could return to their premorbid activities after surgery. The effectiveness of surgery to reduce the patient's level of anxiety could take as long as a year after surgery to develop (Scoville, Bettis, & Scanlon, 1975; Scoville, 1960).

Autopsy study of patients who underwent the Scoville procedure of orbital undercutting demonstrated degeneration outside the immediate area of surgery which involved the mediodorsal nucleus of the thalamus, the uncinate fasiculus running from the orbitofrontal cortex to the temporal lobe, and the fornix and mammilary bodies (Beck, 1960).

In England, Knight (1964) adopted the Scoville approach and refined it. He noted that the lateral extension of the incision was associated with intellectual deficits postoperatively; he narrowed the width of the incision to include only the medial ventral aspect of the frontal lobe. In addition, he noted that cases that failed to improve after surgery were improved with reoperation which extended the incision posteriorly to the area which underlay the head of the caudate nucleus. He called this area "the area innominata" and felt that this area contained fiber tracts connecting the frontal and temporal lobes with each other as well as with the hypothalamus and thalamus.

Using anatomical studies, Nauta demonstrated that multiple limbic connection funneled through the subcaudate area where Scoville and Knight found lesions effective for the relief of anxiety and depression (Nauta, 1962). The ventral outflow from the amygdala (the ventral amygdalofugal tract) went beneath the globus pallidus in this area (the substantia innominata) to connect with the hypothalamus and the nucleus basalis of Meynert. The ventral amygdalofugal fibers also joined the inferior thalamic peduncle in this area and connected to the dorsomedial nucleus of the thalamus, which then connected to the orbitofrontal–cortical system. This compact area beneath the caudate nucleus, therefore, contained fibers connecting the frontal and temporal lobes with the thalamus and hypothalamus.

Knight (1964) performed 200 operations with this approach to the medial ventral quadrant of the frontal lobes. Psychological testing postoperatively demonstrated that the successful cases had less anxiety and depression without the blunting of personality associated with more extensive frontal lobotomy. The relief of anxiety and depression could either be immediate, or could take as long as 3 years to develop after surgery.

Anterior Cingulotomy

Ward (1948) demonstrated that bilateral resection of the anterior cingulate area in monkeys produced a behavioral change in the monkeys: They became tame, docile, and no longer fearful of man or other animals. This "taming" result was similar to the result achieved in Fulton's laboratory animals after frontal lobectomy. Surgery of the anterior cingulate area caused degeneration in the anteromedial aspect of the thalamus; this was also noted after frontal lobectomy. Ward felt that this more limited resection of the anterior cingulate area would be helpful to relieve anxiety in psychiatric patients, without the unwanted loss of intellect and emotional inhibition seen after the more extensive destruction of the frontal lobotomy procedure.

Le Beau (1954) adopted Ward's technique and performed a resection of the anterior cingulate area through a craniotomy approach. He operated on 50 patients and reported good results in more than 60% of them, with a decrease in anxiety, agitation, and violence without a decrease in intelligence. Other surgeons found that surgery on the anterior cingulum helped decrease anxiety in obsessional neurosis but was ineffective for relief of anxiety in psychosis (Lewin, 1960).

Temporal Lobectomy

Scoville evaluated temporal lobectomy for the relief of anxiety in a group of psychotic patients. The results of this surgery were not as good as frontal surgical resections.

Obrador, in Spain, similarly found temporal lobectomy to be less effective than frontal lobe surgery (Scoville, Dunsmore, Liberson, Henry, & Pepe, 1953). In addition, Scoville reported a patient (H.M.) who developed an amnesia for recent events and was unable to encode new information after bilateral temporal lobe resection (Scoville & Milner, 1957).

STEREOTACTIC PSYCHOSURGERY

Descartes noted in the 17th century that any point in space could be defined by relating it to three intersecting right triangles. The Horsely–Clarke frame made use of this principle to reach intracerebral targets in animals; the external skull, which was used to define the coordinates of the intracerebral target, was too irregular to provide the accuracy needed in humans. Spiegel, who had worked with Horsely in Vienna, revised Horsely's system. He used a stereotactic frame based on Horsely's system but did a ventriculogram and used internal ventricular landmarks rather than the contour of the skull to define the coordinates of the intracerebral target and guide the probe to its target (Spiegel, Wycis, Freed, & Orchinik, 1953).

Thalamotomy

Spiegel was aware that the good results of frontal lobotomy were associated with secondary degeneration in the dorsomedial nucleus of the thalamus. Spiegel, a neurologist, and Wycis, a neurosurgeon, theorized that by placing a stereotactic lesion into the dorsomedial nucleus of the thalamus, they might achieve the same result as from frontal lobotomy. They felt that the loss of intellect and change in personality noted in patients after frontal lobotomy was related to the excessive tissue destruction of the procedure; they hoped that the relatively small lesion in the dorsomedial nucleus of the thalamus would achieve the benefits of frontal lobotomy without its unwanted side effects (Spiegel, Wycis, Freed, & Orchinik, 1951, 1953, 1956). They operated on both schizophrenic and nonschizophrenic patients and achieved good results with about 50% of them. A good result was specifically defined as diminished anxiety and depression in the patient without the loss of the core psychiatric symptomatology. Good results were obtained more often in nonschizophrenic patients. Spiegel and Wycis placed pantopaque within the lesions that they made, and confirmed postoperatively, with X-ray, that they could place their probes accurately in the intended target sites. They found, however, that even with these restricted dorsomedial nuclear lesions, they often got diminution of memory, intellect, and drive after surgery. In patients with a relapse, they often resorted to a second or third operation, placing additional lesions in the cingulum or the hypothalamus, or to a lobotomy.

Tractotomy

Knight (1969) developed a method of destroying the posterior 2-cm target which he had found important for good results with open frontal tractotomy by stereotactic techniques. This technique permitted him to spare the frontal lobe tissue anterior to the target; by doing this, he hoped to reduce the 10% incidence of seizures associated with the more destructive open surgery. This lesion was most helpful in patients with anxiety and depression but not as helpful with schizophrenic patients. Symptoms were relieved either immediately or 2 years later. His method was rather primitive in terms of stereotactic technique. He manually placed Yttrium seeds into the posterior medial orbitofrontal lobe using bone landmarks at the base of the skull as reference points. Knight felt that the effectiveness of this lesion was to sever the thalamocortical fibers traversing this area. Several studies of patients who were operated on by Knight indicated that 65% of affective disorders and 50% of schizophrenic patients were improved after this procedure (Cosyns & Gybels, 1978; Lewin, 1960).

Knight, who reviewed 660 patients followed over a 12-year period, noted that this lesion cured 50% of patients with resistant depression. These patients became "free" of medical care after the operation. The results were not as good with anxiety. The benefit of surgery could either be apparent immediately or take several months to develop. Knight (1973) did not note changes in personality as seen with lobotomy patients.

A study of 1,300 subcaudate tractotomies done by Knight revealed that 40–60% of patients returned to near normal lives (Bridges et al., 1994). Depression and anxiety were improved in more than 75% of cases. A prior good response to antidepressant medication predicted a good response to surgery. Contraindications to surgical intervention included schizophrenia, Alzheimer's disease, stroke, and cerebral atrophy. After surgery, the patients had a period of confusion, which lasted for about 1 month. Seizures occurred in 1.6% of patients. There was only one operative hemmorhage. The suicide rate was reduced in patients with depression.

Patients with obsessive–compulsive disorder (OCD) experienced a decrease in their anxiety after the tractotomy; their compulsive thoughts and rituals persisted. The results of this type of surgery on these patients have been studied with positron emission tomography (PET). Patients with OCD have increased metabolism in the orbitofrontal lobe and caudate nucleus with PET brain scans. After surgical tractotomy, these patients show a decrease in the hypermetabolism of the orbitofrontal area (Biver et al., 1995; Insel, 1992). The hypermetabolism of the orbitofrontal cortex and the head of the right caudate nucleus in patients with OCD is also reduced with successful medical treatment with clomiprimine (Baxter et al., 1992). This suggests that sub-caudate stereotactic lesion surgery and clomiprimine seem to be affecting similar anatomical systems: the orbitofrontal–basal ganglia circuits involved in OCD (Baxter et al., 1992; Biver et al., 1995).

Cingulotomy

Ballantine adopted the open surgical results of cingulotomy of Ward and LeBeau (Le Beau, 1954; Lewin, 1960; Ward, 1948) and performed stereotactic anterior cingulotomies on 465 patients over a 25-year span beginning in 1962. Patient selection was made by an investigational review board which consisted of a neurosurgeon, a psychiatrist, and a neurologist. A ventriculogram provided the stereotactic coordinates to place probes into the anterior cingulate area where bilateral radiofrequency lesions were made. Ballantine reported on 198 patients whom he had followed for at least 8 years (Ballantine, Bouckoms, Thomas, & Giriunas, 1987). He noted that the symptoms of 60% of patients with depression or anxiety were improved after cingulotomy; the procedure was significantly less effective in patients with schizophrenia. The rate of suicide over the 8 years of follow-up was reduced. There were no operative deaths, although there were two hemiplegias associated with ventricular hemmorhage. There was a 1% incidence of seizures which were controlled with dilantin. There was improvement in postoperative IQ testing.

Limbic Leucotomy

Richardson (1973) noted that anatomical studies indicated two parallel circuits in the limbic system. The medial circuit involved the following: the medial frontal lobe, cingulum, hippocampus, fornix, mammillary body, anterior thalamic, and medial frontal lobe. The lateral circuit involved the following: orbitofrontal cortex, temporal pole, amygdala, dorsomedial thalamus, and orbitofrontal lobe. Richardson (1973) recommended placing stereotactic lesions into both of these systems to achieve good results.

Kelly also noted the importance of the fact that the median forebrain bundle connected the brainstem centers with the medial and lateral limbic circuits. He made cryogenic lesions in the cingulum and the orbitofrontal lobes to involve both circuits in his lesions (Kelly, Richardson, & Mitchell-Heggs, 1973). In his earlier work, he found that patients with intractable depression and anxiety were best relieved with lesions of the orbitofrontal lobe, whereas patients with obsession and anxiety were more effectively treated with cingulotomy. He noted later, however, that the combination of these lesions was more effective for both groups of patients and resulted in 50% of patients who were symptom free and another 30% who were improved (Kelly, 1973; Kelly & Nita, 1973). Psychosurgery reduced the suffering and lowered the incidence of suicide in these patients. The main indications for surgery were anxiety, depression, and obsessions. Anxiety was relieved either immediately after surgery or months later.

The patients suffered from transitory confusion after surgery. IQ testing demonstrated that intelligence improved above the preoperative level after the initial postoperative confusion had cleared. All patients were placed on prophylactic Dilantin for 6 months after surgery and none of them experienced seizures on this regimen.

Yakovlev observed degeneration of brainstem nuclei after frontal lobotomy; he considered this degeneration an important aspect of the effect of frontal lobotomy on behavior (Yakovlev et al., 1950). Nauta demonstrated the connections of the frontal lobe to these nuclei through the median forebrain bundle. These brainstem nuclei included the nucleus basalis of Meynert, the locus ceruleus, the raphe nuclei, and the ventral tegmentum, which regulate the production within the brain, respectively, of acetylcholine, norepinephrine, serotonin, and dopamine. The median forebrain bundle connected these brainstem centers not only with the frontal lobe but also with the temporal lobe, amygdala, thalamus, and hypothalamus (Nauta & Domesick, 1981). The delayed effects of psychosurgical procedures, therefore, could have been related to the secondary degeneration of these brainstem centers which brought about changes in the chemical environment of the brain; these are the same brainstem centers that are the targets of current psychopharmacological interventions.

Capsulotomy

Leksell placed lesions in the anterior aspect of the interior capsule to interrupt the frontothalamic projections; this procedure is known as "capsulotomy" (Herner, 1961). A ventriculogram was done, and lesions were placed lateral to and 6–7 mm behind the anterior tips of the frontal horns. This procedure relieved anxiety symptoms in 65% of schizophrenic patients and 80% of OCD patients without curing the core symptoms of their illness. There was a tendency for the recurrence of the anxiety within 3 years after surgery (Bingley, Leksell, & Meyerson, 1975). The best results were obtained in patients with in obsessional neurosis and depression. Capsulotomy was slightly more effective than cingulotomy for patients with OCD and generalized anxiety, but the capsulotomy procedure was associated with more postoperative loss of social inhibition than was the cingulotomy procedure (Fodstad, Strandman, Karlsson, & West, 1982; Kullberg, 1975).

Leksell hoped that he could limit the unwanted side effect of capsulotomy, the loss of social inhibition, by diminishing the amount of tissue destruction associated with creating the lesion. He used a "gamma knife" to focus radiation beams within the brain and created stereotactic radiotherapy lesions in the anterior part of the internal capsule. This did away with the tissue destruction associated with passing a probe through the cortex and into the internal capsule in the depth of the frontal lobe (Leksell & Backlund, 1978). The gamma knife created a lesion by collimating 179 beams of radiation from Co-60 radiation sources and produced an 8 × 10 mm lesion. Leksell initially determined the target by identifying the ventricles with pneumoencephalography and then calculating the position of the anterior aspect of the internal capsule. He later was able to identify the internal capsule directly using computerized axial tomography (Meyerson, Bergstrom, & Greitz, 1978). The lesions developed by gamma radiation took several weeks to develop. The results of anterior capsulotomy lesions after radiofrequency lesions and after gamma radiation lesions were equally good after either technique. There was less operative morbidity in terms of postoperative confusion after the gamma knife procedure. There was no loss of intellect in either group of patients (Rylander, 1978). More formal psychometric testing was also done on patients with anxiety disorders after capsulotomy. Anxiety was definitely reduced by the procedure. Perseverative errors were noted in approximately 50% of the patients after surgery. The psychometric studies were similar in capsulotomy patients whether the lesions were made with radiofrequency or gamma knife techniques (Mindus, 1995).

The lesion in the anterior internal capsule is best seen with postoperative magnetic resonance imaging (MRI). This imaging is more sensitive to white matter edema and degeneration than CAT (Mindus et al., 1987). The perilesional edema seen on MRI is associated with demyelination and subsides within 2 years (Kihlstrom, Guo, Lindquist, & Mindus, 1995).

A multicenter study of capsulotomy for relief of anxiety confirmed the effectiveness of this procedure with other surgical centers: A 65% success rate was achieved in a group of 350 patients with anxiety disorders. Psychometric studies demonstrated lowered impulsiveness and less autonomic disturbance in the group of patients improved by surgery. The improvement in patients with OCD was associated with improvement in the metabolism in the orbitofrontal and caudate areas noted on PET scans after capsulotomy (Mindus & Nyman, 1991).

Amygdalotomy

Patients with intractable temporal lobe epilepsy have been studied with cortical and depth electrodes in an attempt to analyze the source of their intractable seizures. Stimulation studies of the temporal lobe cortex and depth structures, such as the amygdala and hippocampus, have been associated with varied psychological responses including anxiety, anger, autonomic responses, déjà vu experiences, delusions, and hallucinations (Weingarten, 1975).

Patients with intractable temporal lobe epilepsy have also been noted to have aggressive behavioral disturbances, and multiple surgical centers have noted that these disturbances can be reduced in 50–80% of patients after bilateral stereotactic amygdalotomies (Balasubramaniam & Ramamurthi, 1970; Kelly, 1973; Kiloh, Gye, Rushworth, Bell, & White, 1974; Narabayashi, Nagao, Saito, Yoshida, & Naghata, 1963).

Andy studied patients with temporal lobe epilepsy and aggressive behavior with depth electrodes placed bilaterally in the amygdala. He noted that patients with seizures and aggressive behavior had more interictal spiking activity in the amygdala. He hypothesized that the lesions in the amygdala had a calming effect by interrupting the discharge from the amygdala into the hypothalamus (Andy & Jurko, 1975).

DISCUSSION

The initial psychosurgical procedures produced massive frontal lobe destruction; the patients were quieted by the procedure but suffered a loss of intellect and a change in personality (Diering & Bell, 1991; Koskoff et al., 1948; Rylander, 1948).

Empirical knowledge gained from the correlation of autopsy findings with the patient's clinical changes after surgery (Beck, 1960; Freeman & Watts, 1948; Fulton, 1951; Meyer et al., 1945; Meyer et al., 1947; Yakovlev et al., 1950) suggested that more focal lesions could be made within the brain to achieve a decrease in anxiety and depression without these unwanted side effects. In addition, anatomical studies identified, and further defined, the limbic system which contained the targets of successful psychosurgical procedures (MacLean, 1949, 1952; Nauta, 1962; Nauta & Domesick, 1981; Papez, 1937; Richardson, 1973; Yakovlev, 1948).

The loss of intellect and the change in personality noted after frontal lobotomy were minimized, with the more discrete lesions made with stereotactic techniques. Lesions made in the frontal lobe in the cingulum, the anterior aspect of the internal capsule, and the area innominata were effective for treating intractable anxiety and depression.

Laitinen and Kelly independently found that specific frontal lobe lesions were more effective to relieve specific neuropsychiatric syndromes (Kelly et al., 1973; Laitinen, 1979). Valenstein, on the other hand, did a review of psychosurgery in the 1970s and found, in a poll of neurosurgeons, that the specificity of intracerebral targets for specific psychiatric diagnostic categories was quite variable and was usually based on the operating surgeon's "pseudo-physiological" reasoning. On the other hand, most operating psychosurgeons agreed that depression and anxiety were the diagnostic categories that mostly benefited from surgical intervention and chose a target within the frontal limbic system. Stereotactic surgery lowered the incidence of operative mortality to less than 1%; seizures to less than 1%; and impulsive behavior to 5%. Although many follow-up studies described results only in general terms of improvement, when formal testing was done, subtle deficits were often found in abstract thinking, learning, memory, and language even after the more discrete focal stereotactic lesions (Valenstein, 1977).

Lesions made within the temporal lobe have not been as effective as frontal lobe psychosurgical lesions in spite of the fact that patients with temporal lobe epilepsy have been noted to have delusions, hallucinations, and other psychopathology (Weingarten, 1975). Lesions of the amygdala have been effective, however, in calming agitated patients with temporal lobe epilepsy (Andy & Jurko, 1975; Balasubramaniam & Ramamurthi, 1970; Kelly, 1973; Kiloh et al., 1974; Narabayashi et al., 1963).

Some findings suggested that the effects of the more focal lesions within the frontal lobe were similar to the effects of psychotropic medications. Although some patients responded immediately to frontal lobe psychosurgical lesions, it took others a month to lessen their anxiety or depression. This time lag in improvement may reflect the time necessary for the retrograde degeneration of brainstem nuclei, which occurs after frontal limbic lesions (Nauta & Domesick, 1981; Yakovlev et al., 1950). These nuclei influence the cholinergic, noradrenergic, and serotonergic balance within the brain and are the target of current psychopharmacology agents (Azmitia & Whitaker-Azmitia, 1995; Holmes & Crawley, 1995; Mesulam, 1995).

The improvement, after psychosurgery, of patients with OCD has been associated with changes in physiological brain imaging studies, which are similar to the changes noted after treatment with clomiprimine (Baxter et al., 1992; Biver et al., 1995; Insel, 1992; Mindus & Nyman, 1991).

Currently, gamma knife technology permits radiation to stereotactically create intracerebral lesions in patients with intractable anxiety and depression (Leksell & Backlund, 1978). The effectiveness of these lesions, which are associated with minimal morbidity, should be compared to the effectiveness and the morbidity of modern psychopharmacology. In the future perhaps a neuropsychiatric team will use a combination of stereotactic surgery and medication to treat anxiety and depression.

REFERENCES

Andy, O., & Jurko, M. (1975). The human amygdala: Excitability state and aggression. In W. Sweet, S. Obrador, & J. Martin-Rodriguez (Eds.), *Neurosurgical treatment in psychiatry, pain and epilepsy* (pp. 417–427). Baltimore: University Park Press.

Azmitia, E., & Whitaker-Azmitia, P. (1995). Anatomy, cell biology, and plasticity of the serotonergic system. In F. Bloom & D. Kupfer (Eds.), *Psychopharmacology, a fourth generation of progress* (pp. 443–450). New York: Raven Press.

Balasubramaniam, V., & Ramamurthi, B. (1970). Stereotaxic amygdalotomy in behavior disorders. *Confinia Neurology, 32,* 367–373.

Ballantine, H. T., Bouckoms, A. J., Thomas, E. K., & Giriunas, I. E. (1987). Treatment of psychiatric illness by stereotactic cingulotomy. *Biological Psychiatry, 22,* 807–819.

Baxter, L. R., Schwartz, J. M., Bergman, K. S., Szuba, M. P., Guze, B. H., Mazziota, J. C., Alazraki, A., Selin, C. E., Ferng, H. K., Munford, P., & Phelps, M. E. (1992). Caudate glucose metabolic rate changes with both drug and behavior therapy for OCD. *Archives of General Psychiatry, 49,* 681–688.

Beck, E. (1960). Pathological and anatomical aspects of orbital undercutting. *Proceedings of the Royal Society of Medicine, 53,* 737–740.

Bingley, T., Leksell, L., & Meyerson, B. (1975). Long-term results of anterior capsulotomy in chronic obsessive compulsive neurosis. In W. Sweet, S. Obrador, & J. Martin-Rodriguez (Eds.), *Neurosurgical treatment in psychiatry, pain and epilepsy.* Baltimore: University Park Press.

Biver, F., Goldman, S., François, A., De La Porte, C., Liuxen, A., Gribomont, B., & Lotstra, F. (1995). Changes in metabolism of cerebral glucose after stereotactic leukotomy for refractory OCD. *Journal of Neurology, Neurosurgery, and Psychiatry, 58,* 502–505.

Bridges, P., Bartlett, J., Hale, A., Poynton, A., Malizia, A. L., & Hodgkiss, A. D. (1994). Psychosurgery: Stereotactic subcaudate tractotomy. *British Journal of Psychiatry, 165,* 599–611.

Cosyns, P., & Gybels, J. (1978). Psychiatric process analysis of obsessive compulsive behavior modification by psychiatric surgery. In E. Hitchcock, H. Ballantine, & B. Meyerson (Eds.), *Modern concepts in psychiatric surgery* (pp. 225–233). New York: Elsevier.

Dagi, T. (1975). Psychiatric surgery and the thics of uncertainty. In W. Sweet, S. Obrador, & J. Martin-Rodriguez (Eds.), *Neurosurgical treatment in psychiatry, pain and epilepsy* (pp. 513–523). Baltimore: University Park Press.

Diering, S. L., & Bell, W. O. (1991). Functional neurosurgery for psychiatric disorders: A historical perspective. *Stereotactic and Functional Neurosurgery, 57,* 175–194.

Fodstad, H., Strandman, E., Karlsson, B., & West, K. A. (1982). Treatment of chronic obsessive compulsive states with stereotactic capsulotomy or cingulotomy. *Acta Neurochirurgica, 62,* 1–23.

Freeman, W., & Watts, J. W. (1942). *Psychosurgery; Intelligence, emotion, and social behavior following prefrontal lobotomy for mental disorders.* Springfield, IL: Charles C Thomas.

Freeman, W., & Watts, J. W. (1948). The thalamic projection to the frontal lobe. *Research Publications Association for Research in Nervous and Mental Disease, 27,* 200–209.

Freeman, W., & Watts, J. W. (1950). *Psychosurgery.* Springfield, IL: Charles C Thomas.

Fulton, J. F. (1951). *Frontal lobotomy and affective behavior.* New York: Norton.

Greenblatt, M., & Solomon, H. C. (1953). *Frontal lobes and schizophrenia.* New York: Springer.

Herner, T. (1961). Treatment of mental disorders with frontal stereotaxic thermo-lesions. *Acta Psychiatrica et Neurologica Scandinavica, 36*(Suppl. 158), 7–134.

Holmes, P., & Crawley, J. (1995). Coexisting neurotransmittors in central noradrenergic neurons. In F. E. Bloom & D. J. Kupfer (Eds.), *Psychopharmacology, a fourth generation of progress* (pp. 346–355). New York: Raven Press.

Insel, T. R. (1992). Toward a neuroanatomy of OCD. *Archives of General Psychiatry, 49,* 739–744.

Jasper, H. H. (1995). A historical perspective: the rise and fall of prefrontal lobotomy. In J. H. Jasper, S. Riggio, & P. S. Goldman-Rakic (Eds.), *Epilepsy and the functional anatomy of the frontal lobe* (pp. 97–114). New York: Raven Press.

Kelly, D. (1973). Psychosurgery and the limbic system. *Postgraduate Medical Journal, 49,* 825–833.

Kelly, D., & Nita, M.-H. (1973). Stereotactic limbic leucotomy—a follow-up study of 30 patients. *Postgraduate Medical Journal, 49,* 865–882.

Kelly, D., Richardson, A., & Mitchell-Heggs, N. (1973). Stereotactic leucotomy: Neurophysiologic aspects and operative technique. *American Journal of Psychiatry, 123,* 133–140.

Kihlstrom, L., Guo, W.-Y., Lindquist, C., & Mindus, P. (1995). Radiobiology of radiosurgery for refractory anxiety disorders. *Neurosurgery, 36,* 294–302.

Kiloh, L., Gye, R., Rushworth, R., Bell, D. S., & White, R. T. (1974). Stereotactic amygdalotomy for aggressive behavior. *Journal of Neurology, Neurosurgery, and Psychiatry, 37,* 437–444.

Knight, G. (1964). The orbital cortex as an objective in the surgical treatment of mental illness. *British Journal of Surgery, 51*(2), 114–124.

Knight, G. C. (1969). Bifrontal stereotactic tractotomy: An atraumatic operation of value in the treatment of intractable psychoneurosis. *British Journal of Psychiatry, 115,* 257–266.

Knight, G. C. (1973). Further observations from an experience of 660 cases of stereotactic tractotomy. *Postgraduate Medical Journal, 49,* 845–854.

Koskoff, D., Dennis, W., Lazovik, D., & Wheeler, E. T. (1948). Psychological effects of frontal lobotomy performed for the alleviation of pain. *Research Publications Association for Research in Nervous and Mental Disease, 27,* 723–752.

Kullberg, G. (1975). Differences in effect of capsulotomy and cingulotomy. In W. Sweet, S. Obrador, & J. Martin-Rodriguez (Eds.), *Neurosurgical treatment in psychiatry, pain and epilepsy* (pp. 301–307). Baltimore: University Park Press.

Laitinen, L. (1979). Emotional responses to subcortical electrical stimulation in psychiatric patients. *Clinical Neurology and Neurosurgery, 81,* 148–157.

Le Beau, J. (1954). Anterior cingulectomy in man. *Journal of Neurosurgery, 11,* 268–276.

Leksell, L., & Backlund, E. O. (1978). Stereotactic gammacapsulotomy. In E. Hitchcock, H. Ballantine, & B. Meyerson (Eds.), *Modern concepts in psychiatric surgery* (pp. 213–216). New York: Elsevier.

Lewin, W. (1960). Selective leucotomy. *Proceedings of the Royal Academy of Medicine, 53,* 732–734.

MacLean, P. D. (1949). Psychosomatic disease and the "Visceral Brain." *Psychosomatic Medicine, 11*(6), 338–353.

MacLean, P. D. (1952). Some psychiatric implications of physiologic studies on frontotemporal portion of limbic system (visceral brain). *Electroencephalography and Clinical Neurophysiology, 4,* 407–418.

Mesulam, M. (1995). Structure and function of cholinergic pathways in the cerebral cortex, limbic system, basal ganglia, and thalamus of the human brain. In F. Bloom & D. Kupfer (Eds.),

Psychopharmacology, the fourth generation of progress (pp. 135–146). New York: Raven Press.

Mettler, F. A. (1949). *Selective partial ablation of the frontal cortex; A correlative study of its effects on human psychotic subjects.* New York: Paul B. Hoeber (Harper & Bros.).

Meyer, A., Beck, E., & McLardy, T. (1947). Prefrontal leucotomy: A neuroanatomical report. *Brain, 70,* 18–49.

Meyer, A., Bonn, M. D., & Beck, E. (1945). Neuropathological problems arising from prefrontal leucotomy. *Journal of Mental Science, 91,* 411–421.

Meyerson, B., Bergstrom, M., & Greitz, T. (1978). Target localization in stereotactic capsulotomy with the aid of computed tomography. In E. Hitchcock, H. Ballantine, & B. Meyerson (Eds.), *Modern concepts in psychiatric surgery* (pp. 217–224). New York: Elsevier.

Mindus, N. H. (1995). Neuropsychological correlates of intractable anxiety disorder before and after capsulotomy. *Acta Psychiatrica Scandinavica, 91,* 23–31.

Mindus, P., Bergstrom, K., Levander, S., Noren, G., Hind, T., & Thuomas, K. A. (1987). Magnetic resonance images related to clinical outcome after psychosurgical intervention in severe anxiety disorder. *Journal of Neurology, Neurosurgery, and Psychiatry, 50,* 1288–1293.

Mindus, P., & Nyman, H. (1991). Normalization of personality characteristics in patients with incapacitating anxiety disorders after capsulotomy. *Acta Psychiatrica Scandinavica, 83,* 283–291.

Narabayashi, H., Nagao, T., Saito, Y., Yoshida, M., & Naghata, M. (1963). Stereotactic amygdalotomy for behavior disorders. *Archives of Neurology, 9,* 11–16.

Nauta, W. J. (1962). The neural associations of the amygdala complex in the monkey. *Brain, 85,* 505–520.

Nauta, W. J., & Domesick, V. B. (1981). Ramifications of the limbic system. In S. Matthysse (Ed.), *Psychiatry and the biology of the human brain* (pp. 165–188). New York: Elsevier.

Papez, J. (1937). A proposed mechanism of emotion. *Archives of Neurological Psychiatry, 38,* 725–743.

Penfield, W. (1948). Symposium on gyrectomy. *Research Publications Association for Research in Nervous and Mental Disease, 27,* 519–563.

Poppen, J. L. (1948). Technic of prefrontal lobotomy. *Journal of Neurosurgery, 5,* 514–520.

Richardson, A. (1973). Stereotactic limbic leucotomy. *Postgraduate Medical Journal, 49,* 860–864.

Rylander, G. (1948). Personality analysis before and after frontal lobotomy. *Research Publications Association for Research for Nervous and Mental Disease, 27,* 691–704.

Rylander, G. (1978). Stereotactic radiosurgery in anxiety and obsessive compulsive states. In E. Hitchcock, H. Ballantine, & B. Meyerson (Eds.), *Modern concepts in psychiatric surgery* (pp. 235–240). New York: Elsevier.

Saubidet, R., Lyonnet, J., & Brichetti, D. (1975). Undercutting of frontal lobes for treatment in the chronic paranoid psychosis, paraphrenia. In W. Sweet, S. Obrador, & J. Martin-Rodriguez (Eds.), *Neurosurgical treatment in psychiatry, pain and epilepsy* (pp. 225–228). Baltimore: University Park Press.

Scoville, W. B. (1949). Selective orbital undercutting as a means of modifying and studying frontal lobe function in man. *Journal of Neurosurgery, 6,* 65–73.

Scoville, W. B. (1960). Late results of orbital undercutting. *Proceedings of the Royal Society of Medicine, 53,* 721–728.

Scoville, W. B., Bettis, D., & Scanlon, W., (1975). Results of orbital undercutting today. In W. Sweet, S. Obrador, & J. Martin-Rodriguez (Eds.), *Neurosurgical treatment in psychiatry, pain, and epilepsy* (pp. 189–202). Baltimore: University Park Press.

Scoville, W. B., Dunsmore, R., Liberson, W., Henry, C. E., & Pepe, A. (1953). Observations on medial temporal lobotomy and uncotomy in the treatment of psychotic states. *Journal of Neurosurgery, 31,* 347–369.

Scoville, W. B., & Milner, B. (1957). Loss of recent memory after bilateral hippocampal lesions. *Journal of Neurology, Neurosurgery, and Psychiatry, 20,* 11–20.

Slocum, J., Bennet, C., & Pool, J. L. (1959). The role of prefrontal lobe surgery as a means of eradicating intractable anxiety. *American Journal of Psychiatry, 116*, 222–230.

Spiegel, E., Wycis, H., Freed, H., & Orchinik, C. W. (1951). The central mechanism of the emotions. *American Journal of Psychiatry, 108*, 426–432.

Spiegel, E., Wycis, H., Freed, H., & Orchinik, C. W. (1953). Thalamotomy and hypothalamotomy for the treatment of psychoses. *Journal of Neurosurgery, 31*, 379–391.

Spiegel, E., Wycis, H., Freed, H., & Orchinik, C. W. (1956). Follow-up study of patients treated by thalamotomy and by combined frontal and thalamic lesions. *Journal of Nervous and Mental Disease, 124*, 399–404.

Swayze, V. W. (1995). Frontal leukotomy and related psychosurgical procedures in the era before antipsychotics (1935–1954). *American Journal of Psychiatry, 152*(4), 505–515.

Valenstein, E. (1977). The practice of psychosurgery: a suvey of the literature (1971–1976). In K. Ryan, J. V. Brady, D. Height, et al. (Eds.), *Psychosurgery* (pp. 1–183). Washington, DC: U. S. Government Printing Office.

Ward, A. A. (1948). The anterior cingulate gyrus and personality. *Research Publications Association for Nervous and Mental Disease, 27*, 438–445.

Weingarten, S. (1975). The relationship of hallucinations to depth structures of the temporal lobe. In W. Sweet, S. Obrador, & J. Martin-Rodriguez (Eds.), *Neurosurgical treatment in psychiatry, pain and epilepsy* (pp. 559–569). Baltimore: University Park Press.

Wilson, W., Pittman, A., Bennett, R., & Garber, A. (1951). Transorbital lobotomy in chronically disturbed patients. *American Journal of Psychiatry, 108*, 444–449.

Yakovlev, P. I. (1948). Motility, behavior and the brain. *Journal of Nervous and Mental Disease, 107*(4), 313–335.

Yakovlev, P. L., Hamlin, H., & Sweet, W. H. (1950). Anatomical Study of Lobotomy. In M. Greenblatt, R. Arnot, & H. C. Solomon (Eds.), *Studies in lobotomy* (pp. 309–329). New York: Grune & Stratton.

26

Infectious, Inflammatory, and Demyelinating Disorders of the Frontal Lobes

DOUGLAS W. SCHARRE

Acquired diseases of the brain commonly affect the frontal lobes. They may have a direct impact on the frontal lobes as part of a more widespread region of dysfunction or the frontal lobes may be the sole area of involvement. Conditions primarily affecting the frontal–cortical regions give rise to different signs and symptoms depending on their location in the orbital, dorsal lateral, posterior, or mesial regions. Other disorders affect primarily the frontal–subcortical white matter tracts. Disconnection syndromes can occur which disrupt the frontal–subcortical circuits or the frontal–cortical to temporal, parietal, or occipital cortical circuits. Due to the multiple neural networks that connect with the frontal lobes, many destructive conditions can also affect frontal lobe functioning at a distance. The great variety of neuropsychiatric manifestations due to frontal lobe dysfunction caused by these disorders is immensely fascinating but also very characteristic so as to direct the clinician to suspect frontal lobe dysfunction. In this chapter, I discuss the major infectious, inflammatory, and demyelinating disorders of the brain and how they affect the frontal lobes.

INFECTIOUS DISORDERS OF THE FRONTAL LOBES

Infectious conditions that affect the frontal lobes are common at all ages. Although some infections appear to involve the brain nonspecifically, many infections have a predilection for a particular brain region or regions. The frontal lobes are a favorite site of involvement for many of the disorders discussed here. Table 26.1 lists central nervous system infections that may involve the frontal lobes. The most common ones are discussed in detail later.

TABLE 26.1. Causes of Central Nervous System Infections Affecting the Frontal Lobes

Prions

Creutzfeldt–Jakob disease (CJD)
Gerstmann–Straussler–Scheinker syndrome (GSS)
Fatal familial insomnia (familial thalamic dementia)
Kuru

Virus

Acute
    Herpes simplex encephalitis
    Other meningoencephalities
Slow
    Human immunodeficiency virus–type 1 (HIV-1)
    Progressive multifocal leukoencephalopathy (PML)

Bacteria

Acute bacterial meningitis
Tuberculosis meningitis
Brain abscess
Subdural empyema
Whipple's disease

Fungus

Chronic meningitis

Spirochetes

Neurosyphilis
Lyme disease

Parasites

Toxoplasma
Cysticercosis
Amoeba

Prion Infections

Prions are made of protein and have no functional nucleic acid. They can cause transmissible diseases, can be inherited in 10%–15% on chromosome 20, or may occur sporadically (DeArmond & Prusiner, 1995; Prusiner, 1995). The normal prion protein is hypothesized to be converted posttranslationally from an alpha-helix to an abnormal beta-sheet conformation which is insoluble to detergents, tends to aggregate, and can induce normal prion proteins to change their conformation to the abnormal form, causing accumulation of prions to sufficient levels to cause a progressive neurodegenerative disease state (Prusiner & Hsiao, 1994).

Creutzfeldt–Jakob Disease

Creutzfeldt–Jakob disease (CJD) has a worldwide incidence of approximately 1 per 1 million. About 90% of the cases arise sporadically, 5% to 15% are familial, with an autosomal dominant inheritance, and only rarely transmitted cases have occurred (Rappaport, 1987; Will et al., 1996). The clinical course is typically very rapid: Death usually comes within several months to 1 year. Occasionally, individuals have survived for several years.

Initially, the patient has complaints of generalized fatigue, neurovegetative symptoms, and forgetfulness. After a few weeks, a progressive dementia ensues with aphasia, amnesia, apraxia, and agnosia. Myoclonus, chorea, tremor, ataxia, cerebellar signs, pyramidal signs, spasticity, rigidity, and seizures typically occur after the dementia has started (Brown, Cathala, Castaigne, & Gajdusek, 1986; Cummings & Benson, 1992). The frontal lobes are involved as part of the widespread cortical and subcortical multifocal process and contribute to the cognitive deficits, aphasia, and motor abnormalities.

Pathology shows a spongiform state in the cortical and subcortical gray matter with loss of neurons and gliosis. Frontal, temporal, and occipital lobes may be more affected than parietal lobes. MRI scans may reveal areas of increased signal on T_2 images (Milton, Atlas, Lavi, & Mollman, 1991). Positron emission tomography (PET) and single photon emission computed tomography (SPECT) shows multiple diffuse areas of hypometabolism in both cortical and subcortical regions (Goldman et al., 1993; Watanabe et al., 1996). Cerebrospinal fluid (CSF) showing a positive immunoassay for the 14-3-3 brain protein is strongly supportive of CJD (Hsich, Kenney, Gibbs, Lee, & Harrington, 1996) (see Table 26.2). The EEG shows background slowing and a very characteristic periodic polyspike discharge (Chiofalo, Fuentes, & Galvez, 1980). Diagnosis can be made by the clinical features, EEG, and CSF and is confirmed by brain biopsy if the features are atypical. Treatment is not available except for supportive care.

Gerstmann–Straussler–Scheinker Disease

Gerstmann–Straussler–Scheinker (GSS) disease is a rare autosomal dominant disorder with onset between 40 to 60 years of age. There are seven known point mutations in the prion protein gene that can result in the GSS syndrome (Prusiner, 1996). GSS is characterized by a mild dementia with pyramidal, extrapyramidal, and cerebellar signs (Farlow et al., 1989). Marked frontal atrophy on MRI and neuronal loss with severe gliosis in the frontal lobes have been described in the codon 105 mutation form (Kitamoto et al., 1993; Kubo, Nishimura, Shikata, Kokubun, & Takasu, 1995).

Fatal Familial Insomnia

Fatal Familial Insomnia (FFI), sometimes referred to as familial thalamic dementia, is inherited and does not appear to be transmissible (Medori et al., 1992; Petersen et al., 1992). FFI has a course and presentation similar to CJD with the addition of progressive insomnia and dysautonomia. Although the neuropathology in FFI seems mostly restricted to the anterior and dorsal medial thalamic nuclei, these nuclei have tremendous connections with specific frontal lobes regions, and neuropsychological evaluation of these patients reveals "frontal" dysfunction with difficulties in working memory, sequencing, and planning abilities (Gallassi, Morreale, Montagna, Gambetti, & Lugaresi, 1992).

Viral Infections

Viral infections can be classified as either acute, with a rapid onset of symptoms, or slow, with a chronic course over months to years (Table 26.1). The clinical features of the infection relate to the selective vulnerability of certain cell types to the particular virus (Johnson, 1982). Some infections appear to have a predilection for the frontal lobes.

TABLE 26.2. Cerebrospinal Fluid Profiles of Various Conditions

Infection	White cells (cells/mm^3)	Protein (mg/dl)	Glucose (mg/dl)	Miscellaneous
Creutzfeldt–Jakob disease	0–15 lymphocytes	nl, 50–120	nl	occ IgG inc, 14-3-3 brain protein
Herpes simplex encephalitis	50–1,000 lymphocytosis	50–400	nl	culture, PCR
Aseptic meningoencephalitis	5–1,000 lymphocytosis	45–80	20–40, nl	culture
HIV-1 dementia complex	0–8 lymphocytosis	< 80	occ dec	IgG inc, culture
PML	0–8 lymphocytosis	< 80	nl	PCR for JC virus DNA
Acute bacterial meningitis	100–60,000 PMN	100–1,000	5–40	culture, antigen detection
Brain abscess	0–500 PMN, lymphocytes	40–100	occ dec	
Fungal meningitis	5–800 lymphocytosis	45–500	10–40, nl	culture, crypto ag
Neurosyphilis	5–1,000 lymphocytosis	50–100	< 40, nl	VDRL, IgG inc
Neuroborreliosis (Lyme)	0–150 lymphocytosis	40–100	nl	IgG inc, PCR, intrathecal antibodies
Isolated angiitis of the CNS	0–800 lymphocytosis	40–600	occ dec	occ IgG inc
Lymphomatoid granulomatosis	0–225 atypical lymphocytes	40–780	nl	occ OCB
Behcet's syndrome	0–500 lymphocytosis	nl–160	nl	occ IgG inc, BBB
SLE	0–50 lymphocytosis	nl–100	nl	OCB, IgG inc, BBB, antineuronal antibodies
Sjogren's syndrome	Mild lymphocytosis	nl–100	nl	OCB, IgG inc
MS	0–20 lymphocytosis	nl–100	nl	OCB, IgG inc
Acute disseminated encephalomyelitis	10–4,000 PMN, lymphocytes	nl–344	nl	inc pressure, occ OCB

Notes. Compiled from multiple sources: Alexander (1993); Ashwal (1995); Bale (1991); Brink and Miller (1996); Bushunow et al. (1996); Fishman (1992); Geerts et al. (1991); Halperin et al. (1991); Hsich et al. (1996); Kirschbaum (1968); Kleinschmidt-DeMasters et al. (1992); Levy, Bredesen, and Rosenblum (1985); Marshall et al. (1988); McLean et al. (1995); Navia, Jordan et al. (1986); Pachner (1995); Schmidt (1989); West et al. (1995); Whitley and Lakeman (1995); and Younger et al. (1988).
BBB, blood–brain barrier breakdown; crypto ag, cryptococcal antigen; dec, decrease; IgG, immunoglobulin G; inc, increased; nl, normal; occ, occasional; OCB, oligoclonal bands; PCR, polymerase chain reaction; PMN, polymorphonuclear cells.

Herpes Simplex Encephalitis

This acute infection is a common cause of encephalitis affecting the frontal lobes, and it is often treatable but mortality is high.

Initial clinical features include headache, fever, stiff neck, and photophobia. These symptoms progress over a few days to produce lethargy, mental status changes, memory impairment, aphasia, focal neurological deficits, seizures, and eventually coma (Whitley, 1991). Recovery may be complete or partial. Frontal and temporal lobe involvement are very common (Kapur et al., 1994). Frontal lobe injury often causes grasp reflexes, frontal release signs, motor impersistence, disinhibition, impulsivity, psychomotor hyperactivity, hyperoral behavior, apathy, echolalia, mutism, anomia, inattention, and utilization behaviors (Brazzelli, Colombo, Della Sala, & Spinnler, 1994). Temporal lobe damage often results in amnesia and, if bilateral, the Klüver–Bucy syndrome. Aphasia or dementia may also be permanent (Cummings & Benson, 1992).

Hemorrhagic necrosis and petechial hemorrhages are seen in the brain at autopsy. In the frontal lobes, the mesial, prefrontal, and basal forebrain regions are more effected than dorsolateral regions (Kapur et al., 1994). Periodic lateralized epileptiform discharges (PLEDs) are the usual focal EEG abnormality, seen in 80% of patients (Bale, 1991). MRI scan often shows focal areas of increased T_2 signal in the temporal/insular or frontal regions. Lumbar puncture usually suggests a viral infection and application of polymerase chain reaction (PCR) has allowed for a specific diagnosis of herpes simplex virus infections in the brain (Whitley & Lakeman, 1995) (Table 26.2). Brain biopsy is also diagnostic. Therapy with acyclovir is started empirically and immediately as the toxic effects are minimal and mortality is reduced from 70% to 19% (Whitley, 1991).

Human Immunodeficiency Virus–Type 1

Human Immunodeficiency Virus–Type 1 (HIV-1) is a retrovirus that preferentially infects T-helper cells (Pantaleo, Graziosi, & Fauci, 1993). As the number of T-helper cells decline, acquired immunodeficiency syndrome (AIDS) occurs making the individual susceptible to numerous opportunistic infections (Centers for Disease Control, 1992). The most common signs and symptoms of HIV-1 infection include lymphadenopathy, diarrhea, fever, night sweats, weight loss, and lethargy (Bale, 1991). Neurological symptoms occur early and opportunistic infections account for many additional clinical syndromes.

Direct HIV-1 infection can cause aseptic meningitis, minor cognitive/motor disorder, dementia, myelopathy, variety of peripheral neuropathies, and myopathy. The brain can also be affected by opportunistic infections, central nervous system (CNS) lymphoma, metastatic neoplasms, cerebrovascular events, metabolic disturbances, and medication effects. Frontal lobe involvement is common and can occur in any of the conditions affecting the brain.

At the time of seroconversion, some individuals develop a primary HIV-1 meningitis consisting of fever, headache, meningismus, and CSF pleocytosis (Cooper et al., 1985). Once systemic findings appear (lymphadenopathy syndrome or AIDS-related complex), 50% have neurological signs or symptoms and 50% have abnormalities on neuropsychological testing (Janssen et al., 1988). Mental and motoric slowness (Kieburtz & Schiffer, 1989) suggesting disruption of frontal–subcortical circuits is referred to as the HIV-1 associated minor cognitive/motor disorder and is the most common abnormality (American Academy of Neurology AIDS Task Force, 1991).

HIV-1 associated dementia (HIVD) has been called by many names, including subacute encephalopathy, HIV encephalopathy, or AIDS dementia complex. HIVD affects 15% to 20% of AIDS patients (Power & Johnson, 1995). It is characterized by progression over weeks to months of a subcortical dementia syndrome with mental slowness, impaired concentration, forgetfulness, cognitive abnormalities, apathy, social withdrawal, slowed motor skills, ataxia, and weakness, potentially resulting in severe global cognitive dysfunction, paraplegia, mutism, and incontinence (American Academy of Neurology AIDS Task Force, 1991; Price, Sidtis, Navia, Pumarola-Sune, & Ornitz,

1988). Neuropsychological testing reveals deficits particularly in nonverbal tasks and frontal lobe tasks including Trails B and verbal fluency (Hestad et al., 1993; Power & Johnson, 1995), which suggests frequent frontal lobe involvement. CT and MRI show generalized cerebral atrophy and periventricular white matter abnormalities (Ekholm & Simon, 1988; Navia, Jordan, & Price, 1986). CSF is abnormal but nonspecific (Marshall et al., 1988; Navia, Jordan et al., 1986) (Table 26.2). The pathology of the HIV-1 associated dementia complex consists of reactive gliosis and microglial nodules, especially in the subcortical white and gray matter (Masliah, Achim, et al., 1992; Navia, Cho, Petito, & Price, 1986). Loss of cortical neurons occurs in the orbitofrontal, temporal, and parietal cortical regions but do not correlate well with the severity of dementia (Ketzler, Weis, Huag, & Budka, 1990; Masliah, Ge, Achim, Hansen, & Wiley, 1992). Since the advent of azidothymidine, it appears that HIVD occurs less frequently and its progression is slowed (Atkinson & Grant, 1994; Schmitt et al., 1988). Using combinations of newer antiviral agents, treatment of the neurological complications of AIDS has dramatically improved (Henry, 1995).

The common opportunistic diseases that frequently involve the frontal lobes include cryptococcal meningitis, CMV encephalitis, cerebral toxoplasmosis, primary CNS lymphoma, and progressive multifocal leukoencephalopathy (PML) (Price, 1996). Cryptococcal meningitis and PML are discussed later below. CMV encephalitis in its severe forms causes diffuse, bilateral cerebral dysfunction with impaired alertness. Neuroimaging can occasionally show subependymal enhancement (Price, 1996). Cerebral toxoplasmosis and primary CNS lymphoma can be diagnosed by clinical presentation, neuroimaging, and a treatment trial or occasionally a brain biopsy (Bale, 1991). Cerebral toxoplasmosis evolves in only a few days, with focal neurological findings and ring-enhancing lesions with mass effect and edema on MRI. Primary CNS lymphoma also causes focal neurological deficits but progresses more slowly, and MRI lesions are more diffuse in the deep white matter. Treatment with azidothymidine lowers the frequency and mortality of opportunistic infections (Schmitt et al., 1988). Specific treatments are also available for many of the opportunistic infections and neoplasms (Bale, 1991).

Progressive Multifocal Leukoencephalopathy

Progressive multifocal leukoencephalopathy (PML), caused by the papovavirus, JC virus, typically occurs in patients with deficits in cell-mediated immunity (Holman, Janssen, Buehler, Zelasky, & Hooper, 1991). Onset is usually between ages 30 and 70 and typically progresses over several weeks or months to death in less than 1 year.

The frontal lobes are commonly affected as part of the multifocal brain involvement. Typical neurological manifestations include deficits in attention, visuospatial skills, memory, language, calculation, motor speed, strength, sensation, vision, and coordination (Berger, Kaszovitz, Post, & Dickinson, 1987; Cummings & Benson, 1992). Fever or other systemic signs are not present.

Pathologically, multifocal demyelination is found in the subcortical white matter particularly in the frontal or parieto-occipital regions (Whiteman et al., 1993). MRI shows areas of demyelination without mass effect or contrast enhancement (Brink & Miller, 1996; Berger et al., 1987). CSF may confirm PML by detection of the CSF JC virus DNA (Brink & Miller, 1996) (see Table 26.2). Diagnosis is also made by brain biopsy and treatment is supportive.

Bacterial Infections

Acute Bacterial Meningitis

The incidence of bacterial meningitis is 5 per 100,000 per year. The frontal lobes are frequently involved as a result of direct intracranial extension of paranasal sinusitis, orbital cellulitis, otitis media, dental abscesses, facial and skull fractures, head trauma, endonasal sinus surgery, and neurosurgical procedures (Dolan & Chowdhury, 1995; Weber et al., 1996). Common organisms causing acute bacterial meningitis in the newborn are gram-negative bacilli, Group B streptococci, and *Listeria monocytogenes*; in children they are *Hemophilus influenzae* type B, *Neisseria meningitidis, Streptococcus pneumoniae*; and in adults they are *S. pneumoniae, N. meningitidis*, and *H. influenzae* type B (Ashwal, 1995; Durand et al., 1993).

Initial symptoms of a bacterial meningitis include fever, headache, stiff neck, photophobia, nausea, and vomiting. Agitation, lethargy, and acute confusional states follow. Focal neurological deficits and seizures are usually due to cerebrovascular complications or acute obstructive hydrocephalus (Durand et al., 1993). When the frontal lobes are involved, long-term sequela include dementia, aphasia, hemiparesis, anger control problems, disinhibition, and other personality changes.

CT or MRI may show evidence of hydrocephalus, edema, or infarct (see Figure 26.1). CSF is diagnostic revealing increased intracranial pressure, polymorphonuclear pleocytosis,

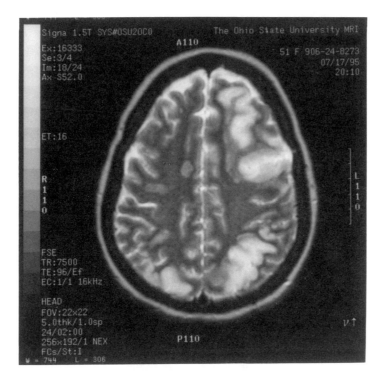

FIGURE 26.1. MRI of a 51-year-old women with *Streptococcus pneumoniae* meningitis showing multiple areas of cortical edema and underlying white matter changes. The frontal lobes are prominently involved. CSF revealed 10,000 cells/mm³ (99% polymorphonuclear cells), protein 1,000 mg/dl, low glucose, and detection of pneumococcal antigen.

elevated protein, hypoglycorrhachia, positive cultures, and bacterial antigen detection (Ashwal, 1995) (Table 26.2). Antibiotics are required for treatment. Adjunctive steroid use is now being considered more frequently for bacterial meningitis at any age (Ashwal, 1995). Vaccination for some of the more common pathogens protects against disease.

Brain Abscess

The incidence of brain abscess is 4 per 1 million per year. The frontal lobes are a common site of abscesses caused by direct intracranial extension of paranasal sinusitis, orbital cellulitis, otitis media, dental abscesses, neoplasms eroding through facial bones, chronic intranasal abuse of cocaine, facial and skull fractures, cranial trauma from penetrating wounds, and neurosurgical procedures (Dolan & Chowdhury, 1995; Richter, 1993; Wispelwey & Scheld, 1992). *Staphylococcus aureus,* anaerobic bacteria, and gram-negative organism infections are frequent causes of brain abscesses after an extension from a frontal sinusitis or middle ear infection (Luby, 1992). Other organisms include streptococci, bacteroides, fusobacteria, and clostridium species. In immunocompromised individuals, various fungal species, cysticercosis, and toxoplasmosis are prevalent (Wispelwey & Scheld, 1992).

Headache, fever, mental status changes, and focal neurological signs are common initial symptoms (Wispelwey & Scheld, 1992). Seizures, increased intracranial pressure, and persistent focal neurological deficits affecting the frontal lobes may occur. Enhanced MRI is very helpful in diagnosing brain abscesses (Sze & Zimmerman, 1988), and EEG usually shows focal delta activity. Lumbar puncture may precipitate a herniation syndrome and is contraindicated in brain abscesses (see Table 26.2). Treatments for brain abscesses include broad coverage antibiotics and occasionally surgical drainage (Wispelwey & Scheld, 1992).

Fungal Infections

Half of all chronic fungal meningitis infections occur in individuals with depressed immune systems or chronic debilitation (Cummings & Benson, 1992). Cryptococcal meningitis is the most common of these infections (Jones & Nathwani, 1995). Other causative organisms include coccidioidomycosis, histoplasmosis, candida species, blastomycosis, and aspergillus.

The disease begins insidiously and progresses slowly over weeks to months. Headache, fever, and stiff neck are common but may not always be present whereas mental status changes occur frequently and often suggest frontal lobe dysfunction. Focal neurological deficits, cranial nerve dysfunction, gait imbalance, dementia, or hydrocephalus may also occur (Cummings & Benson, 1992). Cryptococcal antigen in the CSF is specific for cryptococcal meningitis (Fishman, 1992) (see Table 26.2). Cultures or titers are necessary for diagnosis of other infections. Fluconazole and other new azole antifungal agents are safe and effective as first-line therapies without the severe toxicity seen with amphotericin B (Slavoski & Tunkel, 1995).

Spirochete Infections

Neurosyphilis

Syphilis, caused by the spirochete *Treponema pallidum,* is spread by intimate contact, and CNS invasion occurs in many patients although most are asymptomatic (Scheck &

Hook, 1994). Syphilis recently is increasing in frequency especially in HIV-1 patients. Tertiary neurosyphilis occurs 1 to 50 years after the primary infection and in various forms, including meningovascular, paretic, and tabetic. The frontal lobes are classically involved in general paresis and may be affected by a stroke in meningovascular neurosyphilis.

General paresis results from syphilitic invasion into the brain parenchyma. Prior to penicillin treatment, general paresis accounted for up to 20% of all admissions to mental hospitals (Hook & Marra, 1992), but now it is extremely uncommon. Many of the clinical features suggest frontal lobe involvement and include inattention, dementia, tremulous speech, impaired judgment, irritability, pseudobulbar palsy, paralysis, tremor, ataxia, incontinence, optic atrophy, and Argyll–Robertson pupils. Mania is seen in 20% to 40% and psychosis with grandiose delusions, paranoia, and hallucinations in 3% to 6% (Cummings & Benson, 1992). MRI shows bilateral frontal and/or temporal lobe atrophy and subcortical abnormalities (Zifko et al., 1996). The most abundant numbers of *Treponema pallidum* organisms are found in the frontal lobes. Neuronal loss, gliosis, inflammatory infiltrates, and rarely gumma formation are also seen (Cummings & Benson, 1992).

Screening for neurosyphilis should be done with the fluorescent treponemal antibody–absorption (FTA-ABS) test as other screening tests may be nonreactive in tertiary syphilis (Simon, 1985). If the FTA-ABS is positive, a lumbar puncture is indicated. CSF in neurosyphilis shows lymphocytic pleocytosis, elevated protein, and positive Venereal Disease Research Laboratory (VDRL) test (see Table 26.2). Penicillin is the treatment of choice for all forms of syphilis, with the intravenous route and longer duration of treatments required for patients with neurosyphilis and syphilis associated with HIV-1 (Hook & Marra, 1992).

Lyme Disease

Lyme disease is caused by the tick-borne spirochete *Borrelia burgdorferi*. After the tick bite, an acute localized erythema chronicum migrans (ECM) rash and a viral-like syndrome occur. Dissemination occurs within a few weeks to months, with symptoms including a multifocal ECM rash, acute arthritis, cardiac conduction block, myocarditis, myositis, hepatitis, meningitis, or radiculoneuritis. Some individuals develop a chronic course leading to chronic arthritis, radiculoneuritis, seventh nerve palsies, encephalomyelitis, or encephalopathy, where frontal lobe dysfunction is observed.

The encephalopathy typically results in mild dementia, depression, sleep disturbances, fatigue, and irritability. Deficits in executive function, attention, working memory, organization, initiation, abstract concept formation, and verbal fluency are typical and suggest frontal lobe dysfunction (Fallon & Nields, 1994; Waniek, Prohovnik, Kaufman, & Dwork, 1995). Neuropathological findings include vasculitis, focal demyelination, and, in the late stages, neuronal loss, gliosis, and signs of brain parenchyma infection. MRI may reveal multifocal regions of increased signal in the white matter consistent with demyelination (Halperin, Volkman, & Wu, 1991). Diagnosis is made with a positive serology in the setting of appropriate clinical findings. Demonstration of intrathecal antibody production and CSF PCR for the spirochete may help with diagnosis (Pachner, 1995) (see Table 26.2). Intravenous antibiotics can prevent or halt the neurological complications and may lead to significant improvement.

INFLAMMATORY DISORDERS OF THE FRONTAL LOBES

The inflammatory disorders affecting the frontal lobes of the brain include the vasculitides, the collagen vascular diseases, and paraneoplastic conditions. Most have systemic manifestations and they have a direct impact on the frontal lobes as part of a more widespread process of brain dysfunction. In some cases, the brain is the primary site of involvement and the frontal lobes can be a significantly affected. Table 26.3 lists causes of inflammatory disorders involving the frontal lobes of the brain. Of the collagen vascular diseases, scleroderma, rheumatoid arthritis, and Cogan's syndrome only rarely affect the CNS. Neoplastic-related disorders are discussed in Chapter 24, this volume.

Vasculitides

Isolated Angiitis of the Central Nervous System

This rare vasculitis of unknown etiology is confined to the CNS; the frontal lobes are routinely involved. Lymphoma, sarcoidosis, and herpes zoster conditions are occasionally associated with this vasculitis. Fever and weight loss are noted in 25% of cases. In most cases, there is an initial subacute presentation with severe headache and encephalopathy gradually followed by focal deficits including strokes and progressing to a vascular dementia syndrome affecting medium and small vessels (Vollmer, Guarnaccia, Harrington, Pacia, & Petroff, 1993). Both cortical and subcortical frontal regions may be involved, causing seizures, aphasia, hemiparesis, psychosis, and behavioral changes.

TABLE 26.3. **Causes of Inflammatory Disorders Involving the Frontal Lobes of the Brain**

Vasculitides

Isolated angiitis of the central nervous system
Polyarteritis nodosa
Churg–Strauss angiitis
Wegener's granulomatosis
Lymphomatoid granulomatosis
Giant cell (temporal) arteritis
Takayasu's arteritis
Behcet's syndrome

Collagen vascular diseases

Systemic lupus erythematosus (SLE)
Antiphospholipid antibody syndrome
Sneddon's syndrome
Sjogren's syndrome
Scleroderma
Rheumatoid arthritis
Cogan's syndrome
Mixed connective tissue disease

Other

Acute disseminated encephalomyelitis
Neoplastic-related disorders
Infectious-related disorders
Drug/toxin-induced
Sarcoid

Supranuclear cranial nerve palsies, cerebellar signs, and myelopathy have also been reported. Increased intracranial pressure may occur, leading to papilledema and coma.

A segmental vasculitis with necrosis and giant cells is typically found. The sedimentation rate is increased in 60% of the patients but only to a mean of about 35 mm/h. CT or MRI may be normal or reveal focal, occasionally enhancing, lesions, hemorrhage, or edema, which are found most commonly in the temporal and frontal cortical regions. SPECT tends to show patchy frontal hypoperfusion (Vollmer et al., 1993). Angiography may show vasculopathy but usually does not. CSF findings are nonspecific (see Table 26.2). Diagnosis is made clinically and confirmed by brain biopsy as early as possible. Treatment with prednisone and cyclophosphamide is often ineffective, and there is an 87% mortality rate with deaths occurring a mean of 6 months after onset of symptoms (Younger, Hays, Brust, & Rowland, 1988).

Polyarteritis Nodosa

Polyarteritis nodosa (PAN) characterizes a group of acute systemic necrotizing vasculitides, which includes Churg–Strauss angiitis. Immune complex deposition in PAN causes a relapsing and remitting vasculitis, which eventually leads to infarction or hemorrhage in multiple organs. Common systemic findings include fever, weight loss, headache, anorexia, asthma, dyspnea, proteinuria, hypertension, arthralgias, skin rash, congestive heart failure, and gastrointestinal pain.

Neurological manifestations occur in up to 80% of cases, mostly resulting from peripheral nervous system involvement giving rise to mononeuritis multiplex, polyneuropathy, cranial neuropathy, or myopathy. CNS involvement, including frontal lobe dysfunction, is seen in about 40% of cases and typically occurs later in the course with dementia, encephalopathy, psychosis, seizures, or strokes (Moore & Calabrese, 1994).

Pathology shows a necrotizing vasculitis of the small and medium muscular arteries. Diagnosis is made clinically and confirmed by tissue biopsy (muscle, skin, nerve, or kidney) and angiography. Corticosteroids and immunosuppressive agents are the treatments of choice and often lead to remissions or recovery (Nadeau & Watson, 1990).

Wegener's Granulomatosis

Wegener's granulomatosis is a granulomatosis systemic necrotizing vasculitis that always affects the respiratory tract and often the kidneys. Typical systemic clinical manifestations include fever, weight loss, sinusitis, otitis media, saddle-nose deformity, cough, hemoptysis, pleuritis, glomerulonephritis, visual symptoms, ulcerative or papular skin lesions, arthralgias, myalgias, and pericarditis (Duna, Galperin, & Hoffman, 1995).

Neurological involvement consists mostly of cranial and peripheral neuropathies, including mononeuritis multiplex. The brain can be affected by infarction, hemorrhage, diffuse periventricular white matter lesions, meningeal inflammation, or granulomatous mass lesions causing seizures, focal deficits, and encephalopathy that can involve the frontal lobes (Duna et al., 1995). Contiguous extension of granulomatous inflammation from the paranasal sinuses to the brain and often the frontal lobes is typical (Geiger, Garrison, & Losh, 1992).

Vasculitis, necrosis, and granulomas are seen pathologically on biopsy. Diagnosis is made by cytoplasmic antineutrophil cytoplasmic antibodies (c-ANCA) with a sensitivity and specificity of about 90% (Duna et al., 1995). Angiography is not very helpful, neuroimaging is useful but nonspecific, and CSF can rule out infection. Corticosteroids and cytotoxic agents are needed for successful treatment.

Lymphomatoid Granulomatosis

This rare condition typically affecting the lungs, skin, and nervous system is characterized by a perivascular mature T-cell lymphocytic infiltrate suggestive of a lymphomatous condition. In 60% of cases, a malignant lymphoma does develop (Bushunow, Casas, & Duggan, 1996). Common manifestations include fever, weight loss, cough, chest pain, skin ulcers and papules, and peripheral neuropathies.

CNS dysfunction occurs in 20% to 40% of cases and includes a broad spectrum of deficits such as monocular blindness, internuclear ophthalmoplegia, dysphagia, dysarthria, spasticity, paraparesis, hemiparesis, ataxia, aphasia, encephalopathy, dementia, and frontal lobe signs (e.g., personality change, irritability, disinhibition, impulsivity, distractibility, mood disturbance, and memory loss) (Bushunow et al., 1996; Kleinschmidt-DeMasters, Filley, & Bitter, 1992).

CSF shows pleocytosis with atypical cells (Bushunow et al., 1996) (see Table 26.2). Angiography may show a vasculitic pattern and neuroimaging may show mass lesions, enhancement, or white matter changes. Treatment with prednisone and cyclophosphamide is usually necessary to maintain prolonged remissions. Adjunctive radiotherapy or chemotherapy can also be effective.

Giant Cell (Temporal) Arteritis

This is a systemic vasculitis; women are affected twice as often as men. Nearly all patients are over age 50. Systemic symptoms are rarely absent and include fever, weight loss, anorexia, and malaise. The classic features of the polymyalgia rheumatica syndrome are seen in 50% of those with temporal arteritis. Headache, jaw claudication, scalp tenderness, and tenderness and nodularity of the superior temporal artery are common.

Except for visual disturbances, CNS involvement is infrequent. Blurred vision, amaurosis fugax, and diplopia are reported with blindness occurring, usually without warning, in 8% to 23% of cases (Caselli & Hunder, 1993). Multiple infarcts, more common in the posterior circulation territories, have been reported, but dementia syndromes involving frontal lobe function that is unexplained by strokes are also seen (Caselli, 1990).

Pathology frequently involves the branches of the external carotid, ophthalmic, and vertebral arteries. Anemia is common and an elevated Westergren sedimentation rate (over 50 and often over 100 mm/h), is almost always found. A superior temporal artery biopsy is positive in about 70% of cases (Nadeau & Watson, 1990). Prednisone, typically in doses of 40 to 60 mg per day, is an effective treatment.

Behcet's Syndrome

Behcet's syndrome is an inflammatory disorder of uncertain etiology characterized by recurrent oral and genital ulcers, uveitis, thrombophlebitis, and arthritis (Moore & Calabrese, 1994). Fever and gastrointestinal complaints are also common.

Up to 40% have neurological symptoms—the most common neurological manifestation is a relapsing focal meningoencephalitis affecting the brainstem with headache, cranial neuropathies, dysarthria, long tract signs, and bulbar and pseudobulbar palsies.

Seizures, and increased intracranial pressure have also been reported (Serdaroglu et al., 1989). Frontal lobe dysfunction suggested by reports of dementia, personality change, disinhibition, apathy, emotional disturbance, and akinetic mutism is frequently described (Yamamori et al., 1994).

A chronic small vessel vasculitis is seen pathologically, often involving the frontal white matter (Totsuka, Hattori, Yazaki, Nagao, & Mizushima, 1985; Yamamori et al., 1994). MRI sometimes reveals venous thrombosis and frequently shows subcortical abnormalities (Al Kawi, Bohlega, & Banna, 1991). SPECT may show cortical hypoperfusion, including frontal lobe involvement (Arai et al., 1994; Watanabe et al., 1995). Angiography is usually normal whereas CSF is abnormal but nonspecific (McLean, Miller, & Thompson, 1995) (see Table 26.2). Diagnosis is based on clinical features. Treatment for CNS disease includes high-dose steroids and immunosuppressive agents.

Collagen Vascular Diseases

Systemic Lupus Erythematosus

Systemic lupus erythematosus (SLE) is an immunological disorder of uncertain etiology. Systemic manifestations may include fever, anorexia, rash, lymphadenopathy, arthralgias, pericarditis, valvular disease, pleuritis, Raynaud's phenomenon, alopecia, renal insufficiency, nephrotic syndrome, and hypertension (Nadeau & Watson, 1990).

SLE has the highest incidence of neuropsychiatric and focal CNS manifestations of any of the collagen vascular disorders. Frontal lobe involvement is common. CNS dysfunction may occur from primary involvement of the brain or secondarily from complications of the disease including infection, embolism from endocarditis, steroid treatment toxicity, and severe hypertension.

Neuropsychiatric CNS disease is seen in 40% to 75% of cases and often occurs early in the disease course. Disturbances of frontal and frontal–subcortical circuits contribute to neuropsychiatric manifestations, which typically include acute confusional states/delirium, dementia, psychosis, depression, mania, phobias, and anxiousness (West, 1994). Relative to the frontal lobes, neuropsychological testing shows deficits in information processing, cognitive flexibility, working memory, attention, and verbal fluency (Denburg, Denburg, Carbotte, Fisk, & Hanly, 1993). Focal CNS involvement, including seizures, strokes, supranuclear cranial nerve deficits, chorea, ataxia, parkinsonism, transverse myelitis, and focal paresis, is present in 10% to 35% of cases (West, 1994).

Occasionally associated with SLE is the antiphospholipid antibody syndrome consisting of the presence of antiphospholipid (APL) antibodies (particularly the lupus anticoagulant and anticardiolipin antibodies), venous or arterial thrombotic strokes or ischemia, recurrent abortions, and thrombocytopenia (Brey, Gharavi, & Lockshin, 1993). APL antibodies are present in up to 50% of SLE patients. The frontal lobes can be affected by multiple infarctions, which result in a dementia syndrome. Sneddon's syndrome, recurrent strokes often causing dementia in patients with livedo reticularis, is also associated with APL antibodies.

Diagnosis of SLE is based on clinical features, a positive antinuclear antibody (ANA) test, and other specific antibody tests (Tan et al., 1982). The main pathological feature of SLE is a small vessel vasculopathy that angiography usually is unable to identify. An autoimmune process with antineuronal antibodies may be an important cause of neuropsychiatric CNS involvement and serum antiribosomal-P antibodies are often seen in patients with psychosis and depression (Teh & Isenberg, 1994). MRI is useful in localizing strokes but is often normal in neuropsychiatric lupus (West, Emlen, Wener, & Kotzin, 1995). SPECT scanning is very sensitive, with focal cortical hypoperfusion found most often in the frontal regions followed by the parietal and temporal regions (Colamussi et al., 1995). Nearly all individuals with neuropsychiatric CNS involvement have abnormal CSF IgG index, oligoclonal bands, CSF antineuronal antibodies, and/or serum antiribosomal-P antibodies, which may improve with response to therapy (West et al., 1995) (see Table 26.2). Treatments include nonsteroidal anti-inflammatory agents, steroids, and immunosuppressive agents. Oral anticoagulants are advisable to prevent the recurrent thrombotic events seen with antiphospholipid antibodies (Khamashta et al., 1995). Neuroleptics are used for psychosis and anticonvulsants for seizures.

Sjogren's Syndrome

Sjogren's syndrome, seen mostly in women, is a systemic autoimmune disorder characterized by symptoms of dry eyes and dry mouth and may involve the lung, liver, kidney, heart, blood vessels, skin, muscles, joints, peripheral nerves, spinal cord, and brain. CNS manifestations, reported in up to 25% in some centers (Alexander, 1993) and rarely observed in others (Moutsopoulos, Sarmas, & Talal, 1993), includes migraine, focal neurological deficits, intracerebral hemorrhage, subarachnoid hemorrhage, seizures, myelitis, aseptic meningitis, dementia, and psychiatric symptoms (Alexander, 1993).

The frontal lobes are affected mostly by subcortical pathology, and their dysfunction contributes to the subcortical dementia syndrome and deficits in attention, concentration, mood disturbances (including depression), and obsessive–compulsive traits (Alexander, 1993; Moutsopoulos et al., 1993).

Lymphocytic infiltration of the exocrine glands causes dry eyes and dry mouth. In the CNS, Sjogren's causes a vasculopathy of the small vessels and so angiography only shows a vasculitis in 20% of cases (Alexander, 1993). Laboratory evaluations are frequently positive for antinuclear antibodies and occasionally for anti-SS-A (Ro) (seen with more serious CNS disease) and anti-SS-B (La) antibodies. Biopsy of a minor salivary gland is diagnostic. MRI shows subcortical and periventricular white matter lesions in 80%. SPECT, however, can show cortical hypoperfusion in patients with neuropsychiatric dysfunction without cortical MRI lesions (Alexander, 1993). Corticosteroids and rarely other immunosuppressive agents are used for treatment.

DEMYELINATING DISORDERS OF THE FRONTAL LOBES

Most demyelinating conditions can involve the frontal–subcortical white matter. Table 26.4 presents a comprehensive list of white matter disorders involving the frontal lobes. Primary demyelination involves the loss of the myelin sheath, leaving the axon intact but denuded. Many of the hereditary–metabolic etiologies are actually dysmyelinating conditions that show an impairment in the formation or development of the myelin sheath. Although I do not specifically discuss dysmyelinating disorders, they share many clinical features with the demyelinating conditions. Vascular and neoplastic causes of demyelinating disorders are discussed in Chapters 21 and 24, this volume and many of the autoimmune and infectious causes were discussed earlier in this chapter.

TABLE 26.4. Causes of Demyelinating Disorders
Involving the Frontal Lobes of the Brain

Autoimmune

Multiple sclerosis (MS)
Behcet's syndrome
Systemic lupus erythematosus (SLE)
Sjogren's syndrome
Acute disseminated encephalomyelitis

Vascular

Binswanger's disease

Toxic–metabolic

Marchiafava–Bignami disease
Vitamin B_{12} deficiency
Folate deficiency
Thiamine deficiency (vitamin B_1)
Vitamin B_6 deficiency
Vitamin E deficiency
Anoxic/hypoxic leukoencephalopathy
Radiation leukoencephalopathy
Chemotherapy-related leukoencephalopathy

Hereditary–Metabolic

Metachromatic leukodystrophy (MLD)
Adrenoleukodystrophy (ALD)
Cerebrotendinous xanthomatosis
Membranous lipodystrophy
Hereditary adult onset leukodystrophy
Globoid cell leukodystrophy, late onset

Infectious

HIV-1 associated cognitive/motor complex
Progressive multifocal leukoencephalopathy (PML)
Lyme disease

Neoplastic

Lymphoma of the central nervous system
Paraneoplastic syndromes

Autoimmune Disorders

Multiple Sclerosis

Multiple sclerosis (MS) is the most common demyelinating disorder of the CNS. It is rare in the tropics, but its frequency increases in more northern latitudes and women are affected more than men by a 2-to-1 ratio. The clinical course has several forms which all show dissemination in time and space: exacerbating–remitting, acute progressive, and chronic progressive.

Brainstem and spinal cord regions are frequently affected and may cause internuclear ophthalmoplegia, trigeminal neuralgia, myelopathy, acute transverse myelitis, bladder dysfunction, sensory disturbances, gait imbalance, and pain syndromes. Brain demyelination often results in weakness, sensory dysfunction, gait disturbance, ataxia, movement disorders, and neuropsychiatric syndromes. Treatment with steroids or other medications can complicate and contribute to the cognitive and psychiatric disturbances.

When the frontal lobes are involved, cognitive dysfunction, neuropsychiatric symptoms, and impaired motor control may occur. Cognitive dysfunction occurs in 30% to 50% of MS patients (Fennell & Smith, 1990; Rao, Leo, Bernardin, & Unverzagt, 1991), with typical symptoms including slowed information processing, retrieval memory deficits, visuospatial difficulties, and frontal–executive dysfunctioning—a pattern suggestive of a subcortical dementia syndrome (Rao, 1986). Corpus callosal atrophy on MRI and increased plaque volume correlate with the severity of cognitive impairment (Huber et al., 1992b; Swirsky-Sacchetti et al., 1992). Frontal lobe dysfunctioning on neuropsychological testing is found in 33% of MS patients (McIntosh-Michaelis et al., 1991; Mendozzi, Pugnetti, Saccani, & Motta, 1993) and may include deficits in verbal fluency, conceptual reasoning, the Wisconsin Card Sorting Test (WCST), planning abilities, organizational skills, sustained attention, and set shifting (Fennell & Smith, 1990; Mendozzi et al., 1993). Individuals with demyelination of frontal–subcortical circuits in MS on MRI performed worse on tasks of conceptual reasoning abilities (WCST) and had more perseverative errors than others without significant frontal involvement but with similar overall white matter burden (Arnett et al., 1994). Frontal white matter lesions are also correlated with apathy, diminished spontaneity of speech, executive dysfunction, and slowed information processing speed (Comi et al., 1995; Huber et al., 1992a).

Behavioral and psychiatric symptoms in MS are common and include emotional lability, depression, euphoria, mania, psychosis, personality changes, fatigue, and sexual dysfunction. Frontal cognitive impairment has been shown to be significantly related to depression symptoms, suggesting involvement of shared anatomical circuits (Filippi et al., 1994). Euphoria, seen in about 25% of MS patients, is a cheerful affect inappropriate to the situation (Rabins, 1990). Euphoria has been associated with bilateral subfrontal demyelination (Minden & Schiffer, 1990) and with a higher rate of neurological and cognitive deficits (Rabins, 1990). Apathy, lack of concern over their disabilities, lack of initiation, impaired insight, irritability, and poor judgment are personality changes observed in as many as 40% of MS patients (Mahler, 1992) and may be related to frontal lobe dysfunctioning (Mendez, 1995).

Impaired motor function caused by frontal lobe dysfunction in MS has also been described and includes weakness, loss of motor control, a frontal gait apraxia, and frontal release signs (Franklin, Nelson, Filley, & Heaton, 1989; Mendez, 1995).

MS is believed to be caused by an immune-mediated response triggered by exposure to an unknown environmental agent in the genetically predisposed individual. This results in multifocal discrete demyelinated areas scattered throughout the white matter, which can often be seen as plaques on MRI (see Figure 26.2). Gadolinium contrast can distinguish active from inactive plaques (Bastianello et al., 1990). Cortical brain atrophy most often seen in the frontal lobes on MRI occurs in 33% (Bekiesinska-Figatowska, Walecki, & Stelmasiak, 1996). Cortical hypoperfusion in the frontal lobes on SPECT (Pozzilli et al., 1991), especially in the chronic progressive form (Lycke, Wikkelso, Bergh, Jacobsson, & Andersen, 1993), may represent frontal disconnection from other subcortical and cortical regions. Diagnosis is aided by finding increased immunoglobulin production and oligoclonal bands in the CSF (see Table 26.2).

Prednisone, methylprednisolone, and ACTH appear to speed the recovery of an acute exacerbation. Immunotherapies including intravenous immune globulin (Achiron et al., 1996) and new therapies for relapsing-remitting MS, including copolymer 1 (Johnson et

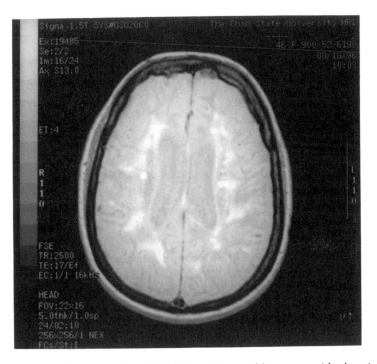

FIGURE 26.2. Proton density weighted MRI of a 46-year-old women with chronic progressive multiple sclerosis affecting the frontal lobes showing bilateral, multiple regions of increased signal in the periventricular and deep white matter of the corona radiata.

al., 1995) and interferon beta-1a (Jacobs et al., 1996) and -1b (IFNB Multiple Sclerosis Study Group & University of British Columbia MS/MRI Analysis Group, 1995; Lublin et al., 1996) may decrease the rate of disease progression.

Treatments for the neuropsychiatric manifestations are also available. Cognitive impairment may be helped with cholinesterase inhibitors (Leo & Rao, 1988) or the use of memory aids, lists, routinization of daily activities, and other cognitive retraining strategies (LaRocca, 1990). Depression and mood disturbances are treated with antidepressants, antimanic agents, support groups, and psychotherapy.

Acute Disseminated Encephalomyelitis

Acute necrotizing hemorrhagic, postinfectious, postvaccinal, multiphasic, and recurrent are all forms of disseminated encephalomyelitis, an immune-mediated condition resulting in CNS demyelination. It is typically, but not exclusively, a monophasic, acute illness presenting with fever, headache, and altered consciousness and typically preceded days or weeks earlier by either viral or other illness or vaccination (Geerts, Dehaene, & Lammens, 1991). Hemiparesis, sensory deficits, seizures, dysarthria, or dysphasia may be present initially (Geerts et al., 1991). Frontal lobe dysfunction contributes to a subcortical dementia syndrome similar to that seen in MS. Inflammation, demyelination, and variable hemorrhage occurs in the white matter. Neuroimaging studies show multifocal abnormalities and large lesions that often involve the cortex with very little periventricular or callosal involvement (Kesselring et al., 1990) (see Figure 26.3). CSF cultures are negative (see Table 26.2). A brain biopsy may be required to rule out infection or tumor. Treatment is supportive and may require reduction of increased intracranial pressure. Immunosuppression has been used with some success (Seales & Greer, 1991).

Toxic–Metabolic Disorders

Marchiafava–Bignami Disease

Marchiafava–Bignami disease is characterized by demyelination of the corpus callosum and adjacent white matter. It is rare and occurs mostly in male, chronic alcoholics in middle to late adult life. Many individuals exhibit a chronic dementia syndrome which progresses over months to years. Remissions are possible. Severe cases present in stupor or coma and die rapidly.

The CNS manifestations include frontal lobe dysfunction, dementia, dysarthria, incontinence, aphasia, hemiparesis, seizures, and signs of corpus callosum interhemispheric disconnection such as left-sided limb apraxia, left-hand anomia, and agraphia (Lechevalier, Andersson, & Morin, 1977; Victor, 1993). Bilateral frontal lobe syndromes with apathy, slow information processing, frontal release signs (grasp and suck), paratonia, and frontal-related apraxic gait with incontinence occur frequently (Victor, 1993). Personality changes, violence, and sexual deviations have also been reported.

Demyelination of the anterior commissure and corpus callosum with relative sparing of the splenium and absence of inflammatory changes is the characteristic pathology. Many cases also have frontal–cortical (layer 3) neuronal loss and gliosis which some have

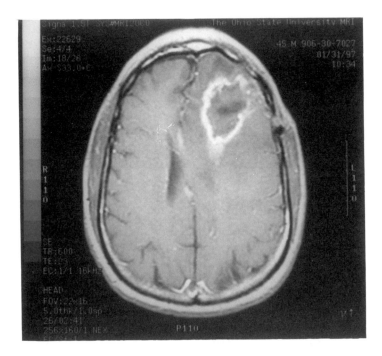

FIGURE 26.3. Gadolinium-enhanced T1 weighted MRI showing a large, irregular, heterogeneous, ring-enhancing lesion in the left frontal lobe causing some midline shift. This 45-year-old man with postinfectious, acute disseminated encephalomyelitis had three other foci of abnormal signal in the white matter, negative CSF cultures, and two brain biopsies unrevealing for tumor or infection.

thought to be due to interruption of callosal fibers (Lechevalier et al., 1977; Victor, 1993). Therefore, frontal lobe dysfunction may be the result of direct frontal pathology or may be the result of a frontal disconnection syndrome. Although MRI scans show demyelination essentially limited to the callosum (Chang et al., 1992), PET studies have shown hypometabolism in frontal and posterior association cortices (Pappata, Chabriat, Levasseur, Legault-Demare, & Baron, 1994), perhaps reflecting this cortical gliosis. Alcoholic abstinence and proper nutrition is recommended.

Vitamin B$_{12}$ Deficiency

Vitamin B$_{12}$ deficiency may be secondary to pernicious anemia, malabsorption syndromes, AIDS, stomach or small bowel resections, stomach acid-reducing agents, or rarely from a dietary B$_{12}$ deficiency (Swain, 1995). Both folate and vitamin B$_{12}$ deficiency can produce megaloblastic anemias and demyelination in the spinal cord and brain, causing peripheral neuropathy, myelopathy, gait disturbance, incontinence, visual impairment, and neuropsychiatric syndromes.

Symptoms suggestive of frontal lobe involvement include slow reaction time, dementia, apathy, confusion, perseveration, aggressiveness, depression, psychosis, and personality changes (Clementz & Schade, 1990; Cummings & Benson, 1992; Lindenbaum et al., 1988).

The dorsal and lateral columns of the spinal cord and the white matter in the brain show areas of spongiform degenerative demyelination. A low serum B$_{12}$ level is usually diagnostic. Serum methylmalonic acid and homocysteine are good confirmatory tests, and malabsorption is demonstrated by performing a Schilling's test. Administration of vitamin B$_{12}$ may reverse or stop the progression of the neurological symptoms and dementia.

REFERENCES

Achiron, A., Barak, Y., Goren, M., Gabbay, U., Miron, S., Rotstein, Z., Noy, S., & Sarova-Pinhas, I. (1996). Intravenous immune globulin in multiple sclerosis: Clinical and neuroradiological results and implications for possible mechanisms of action. *Clinical and Experimental Immunology, 104*(Suppl. 1), 67–70.

Alexander, E. L. (1993). Neurologic disease in Sjogren's syndrome: Mononuclear inflammatory vasculopathy affecting central/peripheral nervous system and muscles, a clinical review and update of immunopathogenesis. *Rheumatic Disease Clinics of North America, 19*, 869–908.

Al Kawi, M. Z., Bohlega, S., & Banna, M. (1991). MRI findings in neuro-Behcet's disease. *Neurology, 41*, 405–408.

American Academy of Neurology AIDS Task Force. (1991). Nomenclature and research case definitions for neurologic manifestations of human immunodeficiency virus-type 1 (HIV-1) infection. *Neurology, 41*, 778–785.

Arai, T., Mizukami, K., Sasaki, M., Tanaka, Y., Shiraishi, H., Horiguchi, H., & Ogata, T. (1994). Clinicopathological study on a case of neuro-Behcet's disease: In special reference to MRI, SPECT and neuropathological findings. *Japanese Journal of Psychiatry and Neurology, 48*, 77–84.

Arnett, P. A., Rao, S. M., Bernardin, L, Grafman, J., Yetkin, F. Z., & Lobeck, L. (1994). Relationship between frontal lobe lesions and Wisconsin Card Sorting Test performance in patients with multiple sclerosis. *Neurology, 44*(3, Part 1), 420–425.

Ashwal, S. (1995). Neurologic evaluation of the patient with acute bacterial meningitis. *Neurologic Clinics, 13*(3), 549–577.

Atkinson, J. H., & Grant, I. (1994). Natural history of neuropsychiatric manifestations of HIV disease. *Psychiatric Clinics of North America, 17*(1), 17–33.

Bale, J. F. Jr. (1991). Encephalitis and other virus-induced neurologic disorders. In A. B. Baker & R. J. Joynt (Eds.), *Clinical neurology* (Chapter 26). New York: Harper & Row.

Bastianello, S., Pozzilli, C., Bernardi, S., Bozzao, L., Fantozzi, L. M., Buttinelli, C., & Fieschi, C. (1990). Serial study of gadolinium–DPTA MRI enhancement in multiple sclerosis. *Neurology, 40,* 591–595.

Bekiesinska-Figatowska, M., Walecki, J., & Stelmasiak, K. (1996). The value of magnetic resonance imaging in diagnosis and monitoring of treatment in multiple sclerosis. *Acta Neurobiologiae Experimentalis, 56,* 171–176.

Berger, J. R., Kaszovitz, B., Post, J. D., & Dickinson, G. (1987). Progressive multifocal leukoencephalopathy associated with human immunodeficiency virus infection. *Annals of Internal Medicine, 107,* 78–87.

Brazzelli, M., Colombo, N., Della Sala, S., & Spinnler, H. (1994). Spared and impaired cognitive abilities after bilateral frontal damage. *Cortex, 30,* 27–51.

Brey, R. L., Gharavi, A. E., & Lockshin, M. D. (1993). Neurologic complications of antiphospholipid antibodies. *Rheumatic Disease Clinics of North America, 19*(4), 833–850.

Brink, N. S., & Miller, R. F. (1996). Clinical presentation, diagnosis and therapy of progressive multifocal leukoencephalopathy. *Journal of Infection, 32,* 97–102.

Brown, P., Cathala, F., Castaigne, P., & Gajdusek, D. C. (1986). Creutzfeldt–Jakob disease: Clinical analysis of a consecutive series of 230 neuropathologically verified cases. *Annals of Neurology, 20,* 597–602.

Bushunow, P. W., Casas, V., & Duggan, D. B. (1996). Lymphomatoid granulomatosis causing central diabetes insipidus: Case report and review of the literature. *Cancer Investigation, 14,* 112–119.

Caselli, R. J. (1990). Giant cell (temporal) arteritis: A treatable cause of multi-infarct dementia. *Neurology, 40,* 753–755.

Caselli, R. J., & Hunder, G. G. (1993). Neurologic aspects of giant cell (temporal) arteritis. *Rheumatic Disease Clinics of North America, 19*(4), 941–953.

Centers for Disease Control. (1992). 1993 revised classification system for HIV infection and expanded surveillance case definition for AIDS among adolescents and adults. *Morbidity and Mortality Weekly Report, 41*(RR-17), 1–19.

Chang, K. H., Cha, S. H., Han, M. H., Park, S. H., Nah, D. L., & Hong, J. H. (1992). Marchiafava–Bignami disease: Serial changes in corpus callosum on MRI. *Neuroradiology, 34,* 480–482.

Chiofalo, N., Fuentes, A., & Galvez, S. (1980). Serial EEG findings in 27 cases of Creutzfeldt–Jakob disease. *Archives of Neurology, 37,* 143–145.

Clementz, G. L., & Schade, S. G. (1990). The spectrum of vitamin B_{12} deficiency. *American Family Physician, 41,* 150–162.

Colamussi, P., Giganti, M., Cittanti, C., Dovigo, L., Trotta, F., Tola, M. R., Tamarozzi, R., Lucignani, G., & Piffanelli, A. (1995). Brain single-photon emission tomography with 99mTc-HMPAO in neuropsychiatric systemic lupus erythematosus: Relations with EEG and MRI findings and clinical manifestations. *European Journal of Nuclear Medicine, 22,* 17–24.

Comi, G., Filippi, M., Martinelli, V., Campi, A., Rodegher, M., Alberoni, M., Sirabian, G., & Canal, N. (1995). Brain MRI correlates of cognitive impairment in primary and secondary progressive multiple sclerosis. *Journal of the Neurological Sciences, 132,* 222–227.

Cooper, D. A., Gold, J., MacLean, P., Donovan, B., Finlayson, R., Barnes, T. G., Michelmore, H. M., Brooke, P., & Penny, R. (1985). Acute AIDS retrovirus infection. *Lancet, 1,* 537–540.

Cummings, J. L., & Benson, D. F. (1992). *Dementia: A clinical approach* (2nd ed.). Stoneham, MA: Butterworth.

DeArmond, S. J., & Prusiner S. B. (1995). Etiology and pathogenesis of prion diseases. *American Journal of Pathology, 146*(4), 785–811.

Denburg, S. D., Denburg, J. A., Carbotte, R. M., Fisk, J. D., & Hanly, J. G. (1993). Cognitive deficits in systemic lupus erythematosus. *Rheumatic Disease Clinics of North America, 19*(4), 815–831.

Dolan, R. W., & Chowdhury, K. (1995). Diagnosis and treatment of intracranial complications of paranasal sinus infections. *Journal of Oral and Maxillofacial Surgery, 53*, 1080–1087.

Duna, G. F., Galperin, C., & Hoffman, G. S. (1995). Wegener's granulomatosis. *Rheumatic Disease Clinics of North America, 21*(4), 949–986.

Durand, M. L., Calderwood, S. B., Weber, D. J., Miller, S. I., Southwick, F. S., Caviness, V. S. Jr., & Swartz, M. N. (1993). Acute bacterial meningitis in adults: A review of 493 episodes. *New England Journal of Medicine, 328*, 21–28.

Ekholm, S., & Simon, J. H. (1988). Magnetic resonance imaging and the acquired immunodeficiency syndrome dementia complex. *Acta Radiology, 29*, 227–230.

Fallon, B. A., & Nields, J. A. (1994). Lyme disease: A neuropsychiatric illness. *American Journal of Psychiatry, 151*, 1571–1583.

Farlow, M. R., Yee, R. D., Dlouhy, S. R., Conneally, P. M., Azzarelli, B., & Ghetti, B. (1989). Gerstmann–Straussler–Scheinker disease. I. Extending the clinical spectrum. *Neurology, 39*, 1446–1452.

Fennell, E. B., & Smith, M. C. (1990). Neuropsychological assessment. In S. M. Rao (Ed.), *Neurobehavioral aspects of multiple sclerosis* (pp. 63–81). New York: Oxford University Press.

Filippi, M., Alberoni, M., Martinelli, V., Sirabian, G., Bressi, S., Canal, N., & Comi, G. (1994). Influence of clinical variables on neuropsychological performance in multiple sclerosis. *European Neurology, 34*, 324–328.

Fishman, R. A. (1992). *Cerebrospinal fluid in diseases of the nervous system* (2nd ed.). Philadelphia: Saunders.

Franklin, G. M., Nelson, L. M., Filley, C. M., & Heaton, R. K. (1989). Cognitive loss in multiple sclerosis: Case reports and review of the literature. *Archives of Neurology, 46*, 162–167.

Gallassi, R., Morreale, A., Montagna, P., Gambetti, P., & Lugaresi, E. (1992). "Fatal familial insomnia": Neuropsychological study of a disease with thalamic degeneration. *Cortex, 28*, 175–187.

Geiger, W. J., Garrison, K. L., & Losh, D. P. (1992). Wegener's granulomatosis. *American Family Physician, 45*, 191–196.

Geerts, Y., Dehaene, I., & Lammens, M. (1991). Acute hemorrhagic leucoencephalitis. *Acta Neurologica Belgica, 91*, 201–211.

Goldman, S., Liard, A., Flament-Durand, J., Luxen, A., Bidaut, L. M., Stanus, E., Hildebrand, J., & Przedborski, S. (1993). Positron emission tomography and histopathology in Creutzfeldt–Jakob disease. *Neurology, 43*, 1828–1830.

Halperin, J. J., Volkman, D. J., & Wu, P. (1991). Central nervous system abnormalities in Lyme neuroborreliosis. *Neurology, 41*, 1571–1582.

Henry, K. (1995). Management of HIV infection: A 1995–96 overview for the clinician. *Minnesota Medicine, 78*, 17–24.

Hestad, K., McArthur, J. H., Dal Pan, G. J., Selnes, O. A., Nance-Sproson, T. E., Aylward, E., Mathews, V. P., & McArthur, J. C. (1993). Regional brain atrophy in HIV-1 infection: Association with specific neuropsychological test performance. *Acta Neurologica Scandinavica, 88*, 112–118.

Holman, R. C., Janssen, R. S., Buehler, J. W., Zelasky, M. T., & Hooper, W. C. (1991). Epidemiology of progressive multifocal leukoencephalopathy in the United States: Analysis of national mortality and AIDS surveillance data. *Neurology, 41*, 1733–1736.

Hook, E. W. III., & Marra, C. M. (1992). Acquired syphilis in adults. *New England Journal of Medicine, 326*, 1060–1069.

Hsich, G., Kenney, K., Gibbs, C. J., Lee, K. H., & Harrington, M. G. (1996). The 14-3-3 brain protein in cerebrospinal fluid as a marker for transmissible spongiform encephalopathies. *New England Journal of Medicine, 335*, 924–930.

Huber, S. J., Bornstein, R. A., Rammohan, K. W., Christy, J. A., Chakeres, D. W., & McGhee, R. B. Jr. (1992a). Magnetic resonance imaging correlates of executive function impairments in multiple sclerosis. *Neuropsychiatry, Neuropsychology, and Behavioral Neurology, 5*, 33–36.

Huber, S. J., Bornstein, R. A., Rammohan, K. W., Christy, J. A., Chakeres, D. W., & McGhee, R. B. (1992b). Magnetic resonance imaging correlates of neuropsychological impairment in multiple sclerosis. *Journal of Neuropsychiatry and Clinical Neuroscience, 4*, 152–158.

IFNB Multiple Sclerosis Study Group and University of British Columbia MS/MRI Analysis Group. (1995). Interferon beta-1b in the treatment of multiple sclerosis: Final outcome of the randomized controlled trial. *Neurology, 45*, 1277–1285.

Jacobs, L. D., Cookfair, D. L., Rudick, R. A., Herndon, R. M., Richert, J. R., Salazar, A. M., Fischer, J. S., Goodkin, D. E., Granger C. V., Simon, J. H., Alam, J. J., Bartoszak, D. M., Bourdette, D. N., Braiman, J., Brownscheidle, C. M., Coats, M. E., Cohan, S. L., Dougherty, D. S., Kinkel, R. P., Mass, M. K., Munschauer, F. E. III, Priore R. L., Pullicino, P. M., Scherokman, B. J., Weinstock-Guttman, B., Whitham, R. H., & Multiple Sclerosis Collaborative Research Group. (1996). Intramuscular interferon beta-1a for disease progression in relapsing multiple sclerosis. *Annals of Neurology, 39*, 285–294.

Janssen, R. S., Saykin, A. J., Kaplan, J. E., Spira, T. J., Pinsky, P. F., Sprehn, G. C., Hoffman, J. C., Mayer, W. B. Jr. & Schonberger, L. B. (1988). Neurological complication of human immunodeficiency virus infection in patients with lymphadenopathy syndrome. *Annals of Neurology, 23*, 49–55.

Johnson, K. P., Brooks, B. R., Cohen, J. A., Ford, C. C., Goldstein, J., Lisak, R. P., Myers, L. W., Panitch, H. S., Rose, J. W., Schiffer, R. B., Vollmer, T., Weiner, L. P., Wolinsky, J. S., & Copolymer 1 Multiple Sclerosis Study Group. (1995). Copolymer 1 reduces relapse rate and improves disability in relapsing-remitting multiple sclerosis: Results of a phase III multicenter, double-blind, placebo-controlled trial. *Neurology, 45*, 1268–1276.

Johnson, R. T. (1982). Viruses and chronic neurologic diseases. *Johns Hopkins Medical Journal, 150*, 132–140.

Jones, G. A., & Nathwani, D. (1995). Cryptococcal meningitis. *British Journal of Hospital Medicine, 54*, 439–445.

Kapur, N., Barker S., Burrows, E. H., Ellison, D., Brice, J., Illis, L. S., Scholey, K., Colbourn, C., Wilson, B., & Loates, M. (1994). Herpes simplex encephalitis: Long term magnetic resonance imaging and neuropsychological profile. *Journal of Neurology, Neurosurgery and Psychiatry, 57*, 1334–1342.

Kesselring, J., Miller, D. H., Robb, S. A., Kendall, B. E., Moseley, I. F., Kingsley, D., du Boulay, E. P., & McDonald, W. I. (1990). Acute disseminated encephalomyelitis. MRI findings and the distinction from multiple sclerosis. *Brain, 113*, 291–302.

Ketzler, S., Weis, S., Huag, H., & Budka, H. (1990). Loss of neurons in the frontal cortex in AIDS brains. *Acta Neuropathology, 80*, 92–94.

Khamashta, M. A., Cuadrado, M. J., Mujic, F., Taub, N. A., Hunt, B. J., & Hughes, G. R. V. (1995). The management of thrombosis in the antiphospholipid-antibody syndrome. *New England Journal of Medicine, 332*, 993–997.

Kieburtz, K., & Schiffer, R. B. (1989). Neurologic manifestations of human immunodeficiency virus infections. *Neurologic Clinics, 7*, 447–468.

Kirschbaum, W. R. (1968). *Jakob–Creutzfeldt Disease*. New York: American Elsevier.

Kitamoto, T., Amano, N., Terao, Y., Nakazato, Y., Isshiki, T., Mizutani, T., & Tateishi, J. (1993). A new inherited prion disease (PrP–P105L mutation) showing spastic paraparesis. *Annals of Neurology, 34*, 808–813.

Kleinschmidt-DeMasters, B. K., Filley, C. M., & Bitter, M. A. (1992). Central nervous system angiocentric, angiodestructive T-cell lymphoma (lymphomatoid granulomatosis). *Surgical Neurology, 37*, 130–137.

Kubo, M., Nishimura, T., Shikata, E., Kokubun, Y., & Takasu, T. (1995). [A case of variant Gerstmann–Straussler–Scheinker disease with the mutation of codon P105L]. *Rinsho Shinkeigaku—Clinical Neurology, 35*, 873–877.

LaRocca, N. G. (1990). A rehabilitation perspective. In S. M. Rao (Ed.), *Neurobehavioral aspects of multiple sclerosis* (pp. 215–229). New York: Oxford University Press.

Lechevalier, B., Andersson, J. C., & Morin, P. (1977). Hemispheric disconnection syndrome with a "crossed avoiding" reaction in a case of Marchiafava–Bignami disease. *Journal of Neurology, Neurosurgery, and Psychiatry, 40*, 483–497.

Leo, G. J., & Rao, S. M. (1988). Effects of intravenous physostigmine and lecithin on memory loss in multiple sclerosis: Report of a pilot study. *Journal of Neurological Rehabilitation, 2*, 123–129.

Levy, R. M., Bredesen, D. E., & Rosenblum, M. L. (1985). Neurological manifestations of the acquired immunodeficiency syndrome (AIDS): Experience at UCSF and review of the literature. *Journal of Neurosurgery, 62*, 475–495.

Lindenbaum, J., Healton, E. B., Savage, D. G., Brust, J. C. M., Garrett, T. J., Podell, E. R., Marcell, P. D., Stabler, S. P., & Allen, R. H. (1988). Neuropsychiatric disorders caused by cobalamin deficiency in the absence of anemia or macrocytosis. *New England Journal of Medicine, 318*, 1720–1728.

Lublin, F. D., Whitaker, J. N., Eidelman, B. H., Miller, A. E., Arnason, B. G. W., & Burks, J. S. (1996). Management of patients receiving interferon beta-1b for multiple sclerosis: Report of a consensus conference. *Neurology, 46*, 12–18.

Luby, J. P. (1992). Southwestern internal medicine conference: Infections of the central nervous system. *American Journal of the Medical Sciences, 304*, 379–391.

Lycke, J., Wikkelso, C., Bergh, A. C., Jacobsson, L., & Andersen, O. (1993). Regional cerebral blood flow in multiple sclerosis measured by single photon emission tomography with technetium-99m hexamethylpropyleneamine oxime. *European Neurology, 33*, 163–167.

Mahler, M. E. (1992). Behavioral manifestations associated with multiple sclerosis. *Psychiatric Clinics of North America, 15*, 427–438.

Marshall, D. W., Brey, R. L., Cahill, W. T., Houk, R. W., Zajac, R. A., & Boswell, R. N. (1988). Spectrum of cerebrospinal fluid findings in various stages of human immunodeficiency virus infection. *Archives of Neurology, 45*, 954–958.

Masliah, E., Achim, C. L., Ge, N., DeTeresa, R., Terry, R. D., & Wiley, C. A. (1992). Spectrum of human immunodeficiency virus-associated neocortical damage. *Annals of Neurology, 32*, 321–329.

Masliah, E., Ge, N., Achim, C. L., Hansen, L. A., & Wiley, C. A. (1992). Selective neuronal vulnerability in HIV encephalitis. *Journal of Neuropathology, and Experimental Neurology, 51*, 585–593.

McIntosh-Michaelis, S. A., Roberts, M. H., Wilkinson, S. M., Diamond, I. D., McLellan, D. L., Martin, J. P., & Spackman, A. J. (1991). The prevalence of cognitive impairment in a community survey of multiple sclerosis. *British Journal of Clinical Psychology, 30*(Part 4), 333–348.

McLean, B. N., Miller, D., & Thompson, E. J. (1995). Oligoclonal banding of IgG in CSF, blood–brain barrier function, and MRI findings in patients with sarcoidosis, systemic lupus erythematosus, and Behcet's disease involving the nervous system. *Journal of Neurology, Neurosurgery, and Psychiatry, 58*, 548–554.

Medori, R., Tritschler, H.-J., LeBlanc, A., Villare, F., Manetto, V., Chen, H. Y., Xue, R., Leal, S., Montagna, P., Cortelli, P., Tinuper, P., Avoni, P., Mochi, M., Baruzzi, A., Hauw, J. J., Ott, J., Lugaresi, E., Autilio-Gambetti, L., & Gambetti, P. (1992). Fatal familial insomnia, a prion disease with a mutation at codon 178 of the prion protein gene. *New England Journal of Medicine, 326*, 444–449.

Mendez, M. F. (1995). The neuropsychiatry of multiple sclerosis. *International Journal of Psychiatry in Medicine, 25*, 123–130.

Mendozzi, L., Pugnetti, L., Saccani, M., & Motta, A. (1993). Frontal lobe dysfunction in multiple sclerosis as assessed by means of Lurian tasks: Effect of age at onset. *Journal of the Neurological Sciences, 115*(Suppl.), S42–S50.

Milton, W. J., Atlas, S. W., Lavi, E., & Mollman, J. E. (1991). Magnetic resonance imaging of Creutzfeldt–Jakob disease. *Annals of Neurology, 29*, 438–440.

Minden, S. L., & Schiffer, R. B. (1990). Affective disorders in multiple sclerosis. Review and recommendations for clinical research. *Archives of Neurology, 47*, 98–104.

Moore, P. M., & Calabrese, L. H. (1994). Neurologic manifestations of systemic vasculitides. *Seminars in Neurology, 14*, 300–306.

Moutsopoulos, H. M., Sarmas, J. H., & Talal, N. (1993). Is central nervous system involvement a systemic manifestation of primary Sjogren's syndrome? *Rheumatic Disease Clinics of North America, 19*(4), 909–912.

Nadeau, S. E., & Watson, R. T. (1990). Neurologic manifestations of vasculitis and collagen vascular syndromes. In A. B. Baker & R. J. Joynt (Eds.), *Clinical neurology* (Chapter 59). New York: Harper & Row.

Navia, B. A., Cho, E-S., Petito, C. K., & Price, R. W. (1986). The AIDS Dementia Complex: II. Neuropathology. *Annals of Neurology, 19*, 525–535.

Navia, B. A., Jordan, B. D., & Price, R. W. (1986). The AIDS Dementia Complex: I. Clinical Features. *Annals of Neurology, 19*, 517–524.

Pachner, A. R., (1995). Early disseminated Lyme disease: Lyme meningitis. *American Journal of Medicine, 98*(Suppl. 4A), 30S–37S.

Pantaleo, G., Graziosi, C., & Fauci, A. S. (1993). The immunopathogenesis of human immunodeficiency virus infection. *New England Journal of Medicine, 328*, 327–335.

Pappata, S., Chabriat, H., Levasseur, M., Legault-Demare, F., & Baron, J. C. (1994). Marchiafava–Bignami disease with dementia: Severe cerebral metabolic depression revealed by PET. *Journal of Neural Transmission—Parkinson's and Dementia Section, 8*, 131–137.

Petersen, R. B., Tabaton, M., Berg, L., Schrank, B., Torack, R. M., Leal, S., Julien, J., Vital, C., Deleplanque, B., Pendlebury, W. W., Drachman, D., Smith, T. W., Martin, J. J., Oda, M., Montagna, P., Ott, J., Autilio-Gambetti, L., Lugaresi, E., & Gambetti, P. (1992). Analysis of the prion protein gene in thalamic dementia. *Neurology, 42*, 1859–1863.

Power, C., & Johnson, R. T. (1995). HIV-1 associated dementia: clinical features and pathogenesis. *Canadian Journal of Neurological Sciences, 22*, 92–100.

Pozzilli, C., Passafiume, D., Bernardi, S., Pantano, P., Incoccia, C., Bastianello, S., Buzzao, L., Lenzi, G. L., & Fieschi, C. (1991). SPECT, MRI and cognitive functions in multiple sclerosis. *Journal of Neurology, Neurosurgery, and Psychiatry, 54*, 110–115.

Price, R. W. (1996). Neurological complications of HIV infection. *Lancet, 348*, 445–452.

Price, R. W., Sidtis, J. J., Navia, B. A., Pumarola-Sune, T., & Ornitz, D. B. (1988). The AIDS dementia complex. In M. L. Rosenblum, R. M. Levy, & D. E. Bredesen (Eds.), *AIDS and the nervous system* (pp. 203–219). New York: Raven Press.

Prusiner, S. B. (1995). The prion diseases. *Scientific American, 272*(1), 48–51, 54–57.

Prusiner, S. B. (1996). Human prion diseases and neurodegeneration. *Current Topics in Microbiology and Immunology, 207*, 1–17.

Prusiner, S. B., & Hsiao, K. K. (1994). Human prion diseases. *Annals of Neurology, 35*, 385–395.

Rabins, P. V. (1990). Euphoria in multiple sclerosis. In S. M. Rao (Ed.), *Neurobehavioral aspects of multiple sclerosis* (pp. 180–185). New York: Oxford University Press.

Rao, S. M. (1986). Neuropsychology of multiple sclerosis: A critical review. *Journal of Clinical and Experimental Neuropsychology, 8*, 503–542.

Rao, S. M., Leo, G. J., Bernardin, L., & Unverzagt, F. (1991). Cognitive dysfunction in multiple sclerosis. I: Frequency, patterns, and prediction. *Neurology, 41*, 685–691.

Rappaport, E. B. (1987). Iatrogenic Creutzfeldt–Jakob disease. *Neurology, 37*, 1520–1522.

Richter, R. W. (1993). Infections other than AIDS. *Neurologic Clinics, 11*(3), 591–603.

Scheck, D. N., & Hook, E. W. III. (1994). Neurosyphilis. *Infectious Disease Clinics of North America, 8*(4), 769–795.

Schmidt, R. P. (1989). Neurosyphilis. In A. B. Baker & R. J. Joynt (Eds.), *Clinical neurology* (Chapter 28). New York: Harper & Row.

Schmitt, F. A., Bigley, J. W., McKinnis, R., Logue, P. E., Evans, R. W., Drucker, J. L., & AZT Collaborative Working Group. (1988). Neuropsychological outcome of zidovudine (AZT) treatment of patients with AIDS and AIDS-related complex. *New England Journal of Medicine, 319,* 1573–1578.

Seales, D., & Greer, M. (1991). Acute hemorrhagic leukoencephalitis: A successful recovery. *Archives of Neurology, 48,* 1086–1088.

Serdaroglu, P., Yazici, H., Ozdemir, C., Yurdakul, S., Bahar, S., & Atkin, E. (1989). Neurologic involvement in Behcet's syndrome: A prospective study. *Archives of Neurology, 46,* 265–269.

Simon, R. P. (1985). Neurosyphilis. *Archives of Neurology, 42,* 606–613.

Slavoski, L. A., & Tunkel, A. R. (1995). Therapy of fungal meningitis. *Clinical Neuropharmacology, 18,* 95–112.

Swain, R. (1995). An update of vitamin B_{12} metabolism and deficiency states. *Journal of Family Practice, 41,* 595–600.

Swirsky-Sacchetti, T., Mitchell, D. R., Seward, J., Gonzales, C., Lublin, F., Knobler, R., & Field, H. L. (1992). Neuropsychological and structural brain lesions in multiple sclerosis: A regional analysis. *Neurology, 42,* 1291–1295.

Sze, G., & Zimmerman, R. D. (1988). The magnetic resonance imaging of infections and inflammatory diseases. *Radiology Clinics of North America, 26,* 839–859.

Tan, E. M., Cohen, A. S., Fries, J. F., Masi, A. T., McShane, D. J., Rothfield, N. F., Schaller, J. G., Talal, N., & Winchester, R. J. (1982). The 1982 revised criteria for the classification of systemic lupus erythematosus. *Arthritis and Rheumatism, 25,* 1271–1277.

Teh, L-S., & Isenberg, D. A. (1994). Antiribosomal P protein antibodies in systemic lupus erythematosus. A reappraisal. *Arthritis and Rheumatism, 37,* 307–315.

Totsuka, S., Hattori, T., Yazaki, M., Nagao, K., & Mizushima, S. (1985). Clinicopathologic studies on neuro-Behcet's disease. *Folia Psychiatrica et Neurologica Japonica, 39,* 155–166.

Victor, M. (1993). Persistent altered mentation due to ethanol. *Neurologic Clinics, 11,* 639–661.

Vollmer, T. L., Guarnaccia, J., Harrington, W., Pacia, S. V., & Petroff, O. A. C. (1993). Idiopathic granulomatous angiitis of the central nervous system. *Archives of Neurology, 50,* 925–930.

Waniek, C., Prohovnik, I., Kaufman, M. A., & Dwork, A. J. (1995). Rapidly progressive frontal-type dementia associated with Lyme disease. *Journal of Neuropsychiatry and Clinical Neurosciences, 7,* 345–347.

Watanabe, N., Seto, H., Sato, S., Simizu, M., Wu, Y. W., Kageyama, M., Nomura, K., & Kakishita, M. (1995). Brain SPECT with neuro-Behcet disease. *Clinical Nuclear Medicine, 20,* 61–64.

Watanabe, N., Seto, H., Shimizu, M., Tanii, Y., Kim, Y-D., Shibata, R, Kawaguchi, M., Tsuji, S., Morijiri, M., Kageyama, M., Wu, Y-W., Kakishita, M., & Kurachi, M. (1996). Brain SPECT of Creutzfeldt–Jakob disease. *Clinical Nuclear Medicine, 21*(3), 236–241.

Weber, R., Keerl, R., Draf, W., Schick, B., Mosler, P., & Saha, A. (1996). Management of dural lesions occurring during endonasal sinus surgery. *Archives of Otolaryngology, 122,* 732–736.

West, S. G. (1994). Neuropsychiatric lupus. *Rheumatic Disease Clinics of North America, 20*(1), 129–158.

West, S. G., Emlen, W., Wener, M. H., & Kotzin, B. L. (1995). Neuropsychiatric lupus erythematosus: A 10-year prospective study on the value of diagnostic tests. *American Journal of Medicine, 99,* 153–163.

Whiteman, M. L. H., Post, M. J. D., Berger, J. R., Tate, L. G., Bell, M. D., & Limonte, L. P. (1993). Progressive multifocal leukoencephalopathy in 47 HIV-seropositive patients: Neuroimaging with clinical and pathologic correlation. *Radiology, 187,* 233–240.

Whitley, R. J. (1991). Herpes simplex virus infections of the central nervous system. Encephalitis and neonatal herpes. *Drugs, 42,* 406–427.

Whitley, R. J., & Lakeman, F. (1995). Herpes simplex virus infections of the central nervous system: Therapeutic and diagnostic considerations. *Clinical Infectious Diseases, 20,* 414–420.

Will, R. G., Ironside, J. W., Zeidler, M., Cousens, S. N., Estibeiro, K., Alperovitch, A., Poser, S., Pocchiari, M., Hofman, A., & Smith, P. G. (1996). A new variant of Creutzfeldt–Jakob disease in the UK. *Lancet, 347*(9006), 921–925.

Wispelwey, B., & Scheld, W. M. (1992). Brain abscess. *Seminars in Neurology, 12,* 273–278.

Yamamori, C., Ishino, H., Inagaki, T., Seno, H., Iijima, M., Torii, I., Harada, T., & Morikawa, S. (1994). Neuro-Behcet disease with demyelination and gliosis of the frontal white matter. *Clinical Neuropathology, 13,* 208–215.

Younger, D. S., Hays, A. P., Brust, J. C. M., & Rowland, L. P. (1988). Granulomatous angiitis of the brain: An inflammatory reaction of diverse etiology. *Archives of Neurology, 45,* 514–518.

Zifko, U., Wimberger, D., Lindner, K., Zier, G., Grisold, W., & Schindler, E. (1996). MRI in patients with general paresis. *Neuroradiology, 38,* 120–123.

27

Traumatic Brain Injury

ARMIN SCHNIDER
KLEMENS GUTBROD

Quite clearly, head trauma may lead to damage of any part of the brain, including the frontal lobes. So, why would a whole chapter of a book on the frontal lobes be devoted to traumatic brain injury (TBI)? The reason is that TBI frequently involves the frontal lobes, in particular the orbital and polar aspects. Penetrating head injuries may involve any part of the brain, but closed head injury (CHI) has some specificity for the orbitofrontal areas. This chapter is limited to a discussion of CHI; penetrating head injury is not considered.

The orbitofrontal predilection of damage following CHI results from external constraints rather than the internal structure of the orbitofrontal areas. The movements of the brain on impact of the head are restricted by the bony skull, the falx, and the tentorium. The mesencephalic tegmentum and the splenium of the corpus callosum are candidate regions for damage following CHI as they may be squeezed against the falx and the tentorium (Adams, 1975). Among the cortical regions, those adjacent to rough bony surfaces are primarily damaged: Autopsy studies revealed that severe CHI preferentially involves the orbitofrontal areas, including the frontal poles, and the anterior temporal convexity (see Figure 27.1) (Adams, 1975; Courville, 1945). Neuroimaging studies (CT and MRI) have confirmed these lesion sites in less severely affected TBI subjects (Levin et al., 1987).

Studying the effects of TBI offers an opportunity to look at the effects of orbitofrontal and frontopolar damage. However, some caveats must be considered:

1. Damage after CHI is never circumscribed. Although many lesions can readily be visualized by modern imaging techniques (Levin et al., 1987), the extent of microscopic damage due to diffuse axonal injury, edema, herniation, infarction, or systemic conditions (e.g., hypoxia) (Adams, 1975) cannot be fully documented. In addition, lesions may evolve; both early and late scans may miss areas of hemorrhage indicating axonal damage. Likewise, a scan may overestimate the true lesion area by demonstrating perifocal edema.

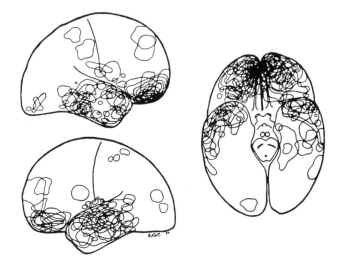

FIGURE 27.1. Areas most commonly damaged in patients with closed head injury. From Courville (1945).

2. Frontal dysfunction does not necessarily indicate frontal damage. For example, disconnection of the prefrontal lobes by a lesion of the dorsomedial thalamic nucleus or its anterior connections may imitate the effects of a frontal lesion (Sandson, Daffner, Carvalho, & Mesulam, 1991; Schnider, Gutbrod, Hess, & Schroth, 1996). More relevant to TBI is the observation that a lesion of the ascending reticular activating system (ARAS; Brodal, 1981) may be associated with frontal dysfunction in the absence of frontal damage (Goldberg, Bilder, Hughes, Antin, & Mattis, 1989).

Due to these uncertainties inherent in the analysis of TBI lesions, conclusions from TBI regarding brain–behavior relationships have to be considered carefully and should normally be based on the analysis of patient groups rather than single cases.

Despite these caveats, a fairly distinct syndrome following CHI can be recognized. Early recovery from severe CHI is characterized by restitution of basic attentional processes (i.e., gross wakefulness) then purposeful wakefulness and return of speech (Alexander, 1982). Although the behavior observed in this early phase can be attributed to failed hemispheric activation due to an impaired ARAS, it primarily reflects frontal, in particular anterior cingulate, malfunction, as apathy, lack of drive, and akinetic mutism may ensue from focal damage involving the anterior cingulate and the supplementary motor area (Bogousslavsky & Regli, 1990; Cummings, 1993). Attention gradually improves and many patients eventually have normal focused attention; deficits in divided attention and mental slowness with decreased information-processing speed, however, often linger (Gronwall & Wrightson, 1974; Stuss et al., 1985; van Zomeren & Saan, 1990). CHI patients typically have memory disturbances. Patients recovering from CHI often go through a stage of confusion and disorientation. In this stage, they fail to retrieve new, and often remote, information from memory; confabulation is common. This period is called posttraumatic amnesia (PTA). It has been defined as the interval between injury and regaining continuous day-to-day memory with intact orientation (Brooks, 1972). In recent studies, we found that both disorientation and confabulations, the key features of PTA, reflect temporal confusion of information within memory, a deficit based on orbitofrontal damage or disconnection (Schnider, von Däniken, & Gutbrod, 1996a, 1996b). Anterograde amnesia may outlast the period of PTA. PTA patients are mostly unaware of their false memories. Lack of concern and overestimation of one's own cognitive capacities (Prigatano, 1991) are typical aspects of the personality and emotional disorders following frontal, especially orbitofrontal and frontopolar, damage. The personality changes may feature hypersexuality, irritability, restlessness, childishness, talkativeness, and blunting of affect with inappropriate emotional responses (Brooks, Aughton, Bond, Jones, & Rizvi, 1980; Levin & Grossman, 1978; Miller, Cummings, McIntyre, Ebers, & Grode, 1986). Personality and behavioral changes are the best predictors of the burden experienced by relatives of TBI patients (Brooks, Campsie, Symington, Beattie, & McKinlay, 1986). Severe personality changes following frontal damage need not be accompanied by measurable neuropsychological deficits (Eslinger & Damasio, 1985).

In the following paragraphs, attentional deficits, posttraumatic amnesia, and personality changes—the characteristic behavioral consequences of frontal lobe damage following CHI—are discussed in more detail.

ATTENTIONAL DEFICITS

Investigators frequently observe deficits of attention in patients with frontal lobe damage (Fuster, 1989; Luria, 1980; Mesulam, 1990; Posner, 1995; Stuss & Benson, 1986). TBI patients often complain that concentrating on mental activities is unusually tiring for them or that they have difficulty in performing two tasks simultaneously (Ponsford & Kinsella, 1991; van Zomeren & Brouwer, 1994). Gronwall (1987) reviewed the incidence of posttraumatic attentional complaints. He concluded that although self-report of attentional problems usually decreases within 3 months after head injury, a significant proportion of head-injured patients, particularly those with more severe injuries, still report attentional deficits 2 years after injury.

It is generally accepted that attention is not a unitary cognitive process but, rather, comprises a variety of different components (Cohen, 1993; Davies, Jones, & Taylor, 1984; Posner & Rafal, 1987; van Zomeren & Brouwer, 1994): Sustained attention, also termed "vigilance" or "tonic alertness," involves the ability to maintain attention over a prolonged period of time. Phasic alertness, also termed "arousal," "activation," or "orienting reaction," describes the increased attentiveness that immediately follows a signal warning a subject that a quick response will soon be required. Selective attention involves both focused attention (the ability to focus attention on one source of information while inhibiting responses to others) and divided attention (the simultaneous processing of various sources of information or the simultaneous performance of various mental operations). Control and monitoring processes allow voluntary control of behavior (Baddeley, 1986; Shallice, 1982; Shiffrin & Schneider, 1977).

Sustained Attention

A critical structure for sustained attention is the ARAS (Mesulam, 1985; Stuss & Benson, 1986). Damage or dysfunction of the brainstem ARAS may cause coma (Plum & Posner, 1980). Less severe pathology presents with clouding of consciousness and drifting of attention; patients can attend to stimuli only for brief periods, then their attention drifts off (Benson & Geschwind, 1975). Several neuropsychological, psychophysiological, blood flow, and metabolic studies also suggest that the frontal lobes, particularly the right midfrontal regions, are involved in sustained attention (Cohen, Semple, Gross, & Holcomb, 1988; Deutsch, Papanicolaou, Borbon, & Eisenberg, 1988; Pardo, Pardo, Janer, & Raichle, 1990; Posner, 1995; Salmoso & Denes, 1982; Wilkins, Shallice, & McCarthy, 1987).

Sustained attention has two aspects of performance (van Zomeren & Brouwer, 1994; Sohlberg & Mateer, 1989): the time over which a given level of performance can be maintained (time-on-task effects) and the consistency of performance over that period (intraindividual variability or lapses of attention). Chronic head-injured patients can maintain their level of performance (i.e., sustained attention is intact), although they work more slowly and less accurately than do control subjects (Brouwer & van Wolffelaar, 1985; Parasuraman, Mutter, & Molloy, 1991; Ponsford & Kinsella, 1992; van Zomeren, Brouwer, Rothengatter, & Snoek, 1988). In contrast to the acute stage, chronic head-injured subjects also do not appear to have markedly increased lapses of attention or intraindividual variability of performance (Jennett & Bond, 1975; Newcombe, 1982; van Zomeren, & Saan, 1990)

Phasic Alertness

Patients with disorders of phasic alertness are easily distracted by external stimuli, although sustained attention may be intact (Benson & Geschwind, 1975). Stuss and Benson (1986) suggested that the diffuse thalamic projection system of the ARAS mediates phasic changes in alertness. Descending fibers from the orbital and medial frontal cortex in turn influence the activity of ascending fibers of the ARAS in the thalamus and the brainstem reticular formation (Luria, 1973; Mesulam, 1985). Thus, the prefrontal cortex regulates the level of alertness in a subtler way than sustained attention alone would allow (van Zomeren & Brouwer, 1994). In chronic TBI patients, phasic alertness—studied with the effect of a warning signal on reaction times—appears to be intact (Ponsford & Kinsella, 1992).

A presumed electrophysiological correlate of phasic alertness is the "contingent negative variation" (CNV), also termed "Bereitschaftspotential" (i.e., the slow negative shift in EEG between a warning signal and the imperative stimulus). In head-injured patients a significant decrease of the CNV amplitude has been repeatedly reported (Curry, 1981; Rizzo et al., 1978; Rugg et al., 1989; Segalowitz, Unsal, & Dywan, 1992). It is controversial, however, whether CNV really reflects the mental capacity of phasic alertness (Rugg et al., 1989).

Selective Attention

Selective attention comprises both focused and divided attention. Determining aspects of focused attention are the inhibition of irrelevant stimuli and the suppression of interference by automatic responses (Schneider & Shiffrin, 1977; Shiffrin & Schneider, 1977). Head-injured patients often report that they are disturbed by noise and they complain about their increased distractibility. In contrast to patients' reports and clinical impression (e.g., Lezak, 1995), several studies found no deficit of the ability to inhibit irrelevant stimuli after CHI (Gronwall & Sampson, 1974; Kewman, Yanus, & Kirsch, 1988; Miller & Cruzat, 1980; Stablum, Leonardi, Mazzoldi, Umilt, & Morra, 1994; Stuss et al., 1989; van Zomeren & Brouwer, 1987). In contrast to the acute stage (van Zomeren & Brouwer, 1994), no increased interference by habitual responses (e.g., in the Stroop Color Word

Test) was found in the chronic stage after CHI (Elting, van Zomeren, & Brouwer, 1989; McLean, Temkin, Dikmen, & Wyler, 1983; Stuss et al., 1985).

Determining aspects of divided attention are the speed of information processing (the amount of information being processed in a given time) and the ability to shift the focus of attention (the time necessary to switch attention between subtasks that cannot be executed simultaneously) (Cohen, 1993; Sohlberg & Mateer, 1989; van Zomeren & Brouwer, 1994). Patients with TBI often complain about mental slowness and failure to concentrate on several tasks simultaneously. Evidence suggests that even patients with mild head injury have deficits in both aspects of divided attention (Gronwall & Sampson, 1974; Hicks & Birren, 1970; Norman & Svahn, 1961; O'Shaugnessy, Fowler, & Reid, 1984; Stablum et al., 1994; van Zomeren, 1981; van Zomeren & Deelman, 1978). A typical clinical manifestation of these deficits is a lack of flexibility with perseveration (Stablum et al., 1994; Stuss & Benson, 1986; Zimmermann, North, & Fimm, 1993).

The anatomical basis of these attentional components is vague. Stuss and Benson (1986) postulated a frontal–thalamic gating system involved in selective attention. Subcortical structures are also involved: through participation in frontal–subcortical loops originating from and ending in specific parts of the frontal lobes (dorsolateral prefrontal, lateral orbital, and anterior cingulate cortex), the striatum, pallidum, substantia nigra, and specific thalamic nuclei influence attention (Alexander, Crutcher, & DeLong, 1990; Cummings, 1995; Foster, Eskes, & Stuss, 1994; Luria, 1973). Damage of these subcortical structures may provoke behavioral disturbances similar to damage of the respective frontal cortex itself, for example, difficulties in set shifting (dorsolateral prefrontal, lateral orbital loop), impaired response inhibition (dorsolateral prefrontal loop), or lack of motivation and apathy (anterior cingulate loop) (Cummings, 1995; Fuster, 1989).

The anatomical basis of the specific aspects of selective attention has hardly been examined. Right dorsolateral frontal areas appear to be crucial for focused attention in that they mediate inhibition of irrelevant stimuli (Alivisatos & Milner, 1989; Knight, Hillyard, Woods, & Neville, 1981; Ruff, Niemann, Allen, Farrow, & Wylie, 1992; Woods & Knight, 1986), whereas the left frontal lobe appears to be critical for the ability to suppress interference by automatic behavior (Drewe, 1975; Holst & Villki, 1988; Luria, 1980; Perret, 1974; Stuss et al., 1982). The repeated finding of intact focused attention after TBI is in accord with the relative preservation of dorsolateral prefrontal areas in CHI. Failures of divided attention have been attributed to frontal lobe damage; no precise focus of damage could be determined, however (Stablum et al., 1994; Stuss & Benson, 1986; Zimmermann et al., 1993). The fact that disturbances of divided attention have repeatedly been found after CHI could indicate that the orbitofrontal areas, which are most consistently damaged in CHI, may be critical for this component of attention.

Supervisory Attentional System

In addition to strategies guiding the sustaining, focusing, and dividing of attention, another component was postulated: a supervisory attentional system (SAS; Shallice, 1982), which is thought to supervise the execution of specialized cognitive routines. The SAS controls what stimuli will receive selective attention. The SAS, considered an executive function with the prefrontal lobes playing a crucial role, may be considered a determinant of divided attention. Shallice (1982) demonstrated a deficit of the SAS in patients with focal left frontal lesions using the Tower of London test. Failures of the SAS have not been sufficiently studied in TBI patients. In the Tower of London test, TBI patients made the same numbers of errors as a control group but they needed more time (Ponsford & Kinsella, 1992; van Wolffelaar, Brouwer, & van Zomeren, 1990).

In summary, in the acute stage after TBI, deficits of all components of attention may be present. In the chronic stage, sustained attention is mostly intact, except when there is extensive damage or dysfunction of the brainstem or midfrontal regions. Phasic alertness appears to be mostly intact after TBI, although CNV data have indicated a weakened alertness response. Focused attention, too, is normally intact in patients with chronic TBI both regarding the effects of distraction and susceptibility to interference. There is little evidence for an impairment of the SAS in patients with CHI. However, a deficit of divided attention has repeatedly been reported in TBI patients; both the amount of information being processed and the ability to shift the focus of attention are reduced. We contend that frontal lobe damage contributes to select deficits of attention observed in patients with TBI. In particular, the observation that CHI most consistently impairs divided attention indicates an important role of orbitofrontal areas for this component of attention.

POSTTRAUMATIC AMNESIA

TBI may produce various types of memory failure. Both anterograde and retrograde amnesia have been described (van Zomeren & Saan, 1990), whereas implicit memory functions (e.g., procedural memory) appear to be typically preserved (Ewert, Levin, Watson, & Kalisky, 1989). Although the anatomical basis of these disturbances is difficult to determine given the often widespread damage caused by TBI, it appears most likely that temporal lobe damage plays a crucial role, particularly in cases of severe, persistent retrograde amnesia (Kapur, Ellison, Smith, McLellan, & Burrows, 1992; Markowitsch et al., 1993). This section discusses PTA, whose distinguishing features—disorientation and confabulation—appear to share a common mechanism and to be dependent on orbitofrontal damage or disconnection.

PTA describes the early condition of patients recovering from coma after severe head injury: They are usually confused and disoriented, often confabulate, and fail to learn and to recall information from memory (van Zomeren & Saan, 1990). Retrograde amnesia is variable and tends to shrink; even if it initially covers several months, it may eventually shrink to only a few minutes before the injury (Russel, 1971; Benson & Geschwind, 1967; Levin et al., 1985). PTA has been defined as the interval between injury and regaining continuous day-to-day memory with intact orientation (Brooks, 1972). Disorientation is considered a sine qua non for the diagnosis; the return of normal orientation has been used to define the termination of PTA (Brooks, 1972; Levin, Lilly, Papanicolaou, & Eisenberg, 1992; Russel, 1971). Patients who recover from PTA either do not recall this period or perceive details from it as if it was a dream. Thus, it seems that some patients do store some information during PTA. The duration of PTA correlates with the severity and the outcome of TBI (Russel, 1971; Levin et al., 1992; van Zomeren & Saan, 1990; Ellenberg, Levin, & Saydjary, 1996).

Despite a wealth of studies establishing the characteristics, course, and prognostic value of PTA, astonishingly little is known about its mechanism. Disorientation has commonly been attributed to anterograde and retrograde amnesia; disoriented patients have been thought to have insufficient new and old information available in memory to maintain orientation (Benton, Van Allen, & Fogel, 1964; High, Levin, & Gary, 1990). The observation that temporal orientation, the only aspect of orientation depending on constantly changing information, is more vulnerable to and recovers later after brain injury than orientation to place or situation might support such an interpretation. However, orientation may vary from one interview to another; a patient's answers may be correct at one time and wrong at other times (Daniel, Crovitz, & Weiner, 1987). In addition, PTA may subside despite persistence of amnesia (Levin et al., 1992). It thus appears that neither anterograde nor retrograde amnesia can account for PTA. Confabulations, another typical, albeit not universal, feature of PTA, have received many interpretations: They have been attributed to the combined occurrence of amnesia and a frontal dysexecutive syndrome or to impaired "self-monitoring" (DeLuca & Cicerone, 1991; Dalla Barba, 1993; Fischer, Alexander, D'Esposito, & Otto, 1995; Shapiro, Alexander, Gardner, & Mercer, 1981; Stuss, Alexander, Lieberman, & Levine, 1978). Another common interpretation attributes confabulations to a desire to "fill gaps in memory" (American Psychiatric Association, 1994). Albeit intuitively plausible terms, neither the notion of the "dysexecutive syndrome" (a broad class of cognitive failures following frontal damage) nor "impaired self-monitoring" (a convenient label for many types of behavioral disturbances with unknown mechanism) is precise enough to explain the basic mechanisms of confabulations. The possibility that confabulations may result from insufficient temporal labeling of information in memory has been advanced (Van der Horst, 1932) with no evidence, however, to support it.

Comparably little is known about the anatomical basis of PTA. An amnesia similar to PTA can occur after rupture of an aneurysm of the anterior communicating artery (Alexander & Freedman, 1984; Damasio, Graff Radford, Eslinger, Damasio, & Kassel, 1985; DeLuca & Diamond, 1995), in the acute stage of Wernicke–Korsakoff syndrome (Victor, Adams, & Collins, 1989), after bilateral paramedian thalamic infarction (Guberman & Stuss, 1983), or after infarction of the thalamo-frontal connections in the capsular genu (Schnider, Gutbrod, et al., 1996; Tatemichi et al., 1992). In contrast to PTA, patients with severe amnesia following medial temporal lesions are concerned about the failure of their memory, do not confabulate, and soon reestablished orientation (Volpe & Hirst, 1983; Schnider, Regard, & Landis, 1994; Schnider, Gutbrod, Ozdoba, & Bassetti, 1995). This comparison indicates that the core features of PTA emanate from damage or disconnection of the basal forebrain and orbitofrontal cortex rather than from medial temporal damage. To our knowledge, only one study has indicated that disorientation after TBI concurs with relatively more severe frontal lobe damage (High et al., 1990).

Mechanisms of Confabulations

We recently studied the mechanisms of confabulations and disorientation in amnestic patients. The observation of a patient with a right capsular genu infarct who was severely amnestic and disoriented and produced abundant confabulations (Schnider, Gutbrod, et al., 1996) indicated that confabulations may not depend on an inability to store new information but may, rather, be associated with an increased tendency to confuse the temporal order of newly acquired information within memory. This patient performed normally in two continuous recognition tasks with novel information (nonwords and nonsense designs), demonstrating that she was able to learn new information. However, she failed to recall the temporal sequence of pairs of words from two lists she had learned 1 hour apart from each other. In a study of a group of amnestic subjects, we further explored the mechanisms of confabulations (Schnider et al., 1996b). Confabulations were classified according to strict criteria: Patients were classified as "spontaneous confabulators" if they ever acted according to their spontaneous confabulations; no assumptions regarding the content of the confabulations were made. Provoked confabulations were measured as the total number of intrusions in all runs of the California Verbal Learning Test (CVLT; Delis, Kramer, Kaplan, & Ober, 1987). We endeavored to answer the following questions:

1. Are provoked and spontaneous confabulations different disorders or different degrees of the same disorder?
2. Are confabulations dependent on an inability to store new information?
3. Are confabulations due to an increased tendency to confuse the temporal order of information within memory?

Because we intended to study the mechanisms of confabulations rather than to describe various degrees of severity of a particular type of amnesia, patients with diverse etiologies of amnesia were included (hemorrhage from an anterior communicating artery aneurysm, hypoxia, Wernicke–Korsakoff syndrome, etc.); 5 of 16 patients had suffered a head injury, among them 3 of the 5 spontaneous confabulators. All patients had severe amnesia as reflected by a severely deficient free late recall in the CVLT (Delis et al., 1987). Only patients who had been in our rehabilitation unit for at least 2 weeks and who were still hospitalized at the time of the study were included in order to make sure that their behavior (in particular, the occurrence of spontaneous confabulations) could be directly observed. The ability to simply store newly presented information was assessed with a continuous recognition test with meaningful designs, in which eight target stimuli were interspersed six times among 72 distracter items. The subjects were asked to indicate each recurrence of a design (maximum correct responses: 40 "yes" and 80 "no" responses). A continuous recognition test is conceptually simple and is probably the purest way to assess simple information storage. The tendency to confuse the temporal order of information acquisition within memory was tested in a similar fashion: One hour after the first run of the recognition test, a second run with precisely the same design was made, except that eight distracters from the first run now served as the targets, whereas the eight targets from the first run were now among the distracters. Subjects were again asked to answer the question: "Have you seen precisely this picture in this run, yet?" for each picture. The idea behind the experiment was that false familiarity with a distracter item in the second run (i.e., a false-positive response) was based on a confusion of the item's previous occurrence in the first rather than the second run. Thus, temporal context confusion was measured as the relative increase of false-positive responses in the second over the first run (see more extensive discussion of the experiment in Schnider et al. (1996b).

We found the following:

1. Provoked and spontaneous confabulations doubly dissociate; that is, they are distinct disorders rather than different degrees of the same disorder.

2. Neither provoked nor spontaneous confabulations are accounted for by a failure to store new information; several patients even performed in the normal range, a finding demonstrating that a failure to learn new information is not even necessary for confabulations to occur.

3. Provoked, but not spontaneous, confabulations correlate with relatively better performance in memory tests and verbal fluency tasks, indicating that provoked confabulations may reflect a normal strategy to compensate for an impaired memory. In

agreement with this interpretation, we observed several patients who started to produce provoked confabulations (i.e., intrusions in memory tests and confabulations on questioning) only after several months. This type of evolution suggests that provoked confabulations are not a component of PTA.

4. Spontaneous, but not provoked, confabulations were invariably associated with an increased tendency to confuse the temporal order of information acquisition, whereas all other amnestic patients (i.e., amnestics who did not spontaneously confabulate) performed in the controls' range. Thus, spontaneous confabulations apparently reflect the erroneous recollection of elements of memory that do not belong together.

No measure of executive functions (verbal and nonverbal fluency, color–word interference) distinguished between spontaneous confabulators and other amnestics. All spontaneous confabulators were also disoriented and none of them had any insight into the failure of his memory. Thus, spontaneous confabulations—the type accounted for by increased temporal context confusion in memory—rather than provoked confabulations are typical for PTA.

Mechanisms of Disorientation

The observation that spontaneously confabulating patients were also disoriented led us to examine the mechanisms of disorientation (Schnider et al., 1996a). We hypothesized that disorientation, similar to spontaneous confabulations, might ensue from an increased tendency to confuse the temporal context of information acquisition rather than a failure to learn new information. The same experiment as described previously (two runs of the continuous recognition task) was used to test these components of memory. Inclusion criteria were similar to the first study (Schnider et al., 1996b). In particular, the fact that only hospitalized patients were included ensured that all patients had been living in a similar setting with equal amounts of information to help orientation. Eight of 21 patients had suffered TBI. Orientation was assessed with a 20-item questionnaire containing five questions probing orientation to person, time, place, and situation (Von Cramon & Sring, 1982). All patients were normally oriented to person, the domain of orientation most resistant to organic brain damage (Daniel et al., 1987; High et al., 1990). We found that orientation was only weakly associated with a failure to store new information ($r = 0.54$, $p < .05$); the correlation was only significant due to three patients with extremely severe amnesia with no significant recognition ability (performance on chance level in the first run of the continuous recognition test). Orientation apparently can be maintained despite a reduced amount of stored information. In contrast, all aspects of orientation (i.e., orientation to time, place, and situation) were very closely associated with the level of temporal context confusion (total orientation score, $r = -.90$, $p < .0001$). Orientation apparently cannot be maintained if recently stored information fails to be recognized as recent, making it impossible to realize what piece of stored information pertains to the present situation. These findings indicate that disorientation more often reflects a confusion of memory traces from different events rather than an inability to store new information. Wrong answers to questions of orientation may reflect a problem in selecting the currently correct response rather than a lack of this knowledge. This interpretation is in accord with the observations that disoriented patients may occasionally give correct responses to questions of orientation (Daniel et al., 1987), that PTA may subside despite continuing anterograde amnesia (Levin et al., 1992), and that some patients later partially recall events that occurred during their PTA (van Zomeren & Saan, 1990).

Anatomical Basis of Disorientation and Spontaneous Confabulations

To determine the anatomical basis of increased temporal context confusion (i.e., the anatomical basis of disorientation and spontaneous confabulations), lesions reconstructed from CT or MRI scans of patients were superimposed on a brain template (see Figure 27.2) (Schnider et al., 1996a). Patients were separated according to their recognition performance in the first run of the experiment ("Item recognition" in Figure 27.2, reflecting pure information storage) and their temporal context confusion (relative increase of false positives in the second run over the first run). We found that increased temporal context confusion was associated with lesions involving the orbitofrontal cortex or the basal forebrain. An impairment of simple information storage (impaired item recognition) had less anatomical specificity; it could be based on cortical, medial temporal, or basal forebrain damage. Confabulations and disorientation thus appear to ensue from damage or disconnection of the orbitofrontal cortex. Based on these results and previous reports of a similar type of amnesia in Wernicke–Korsakoff syndrome, acute paramedian thalamic infarction and capsular genu infarction (Schnider, Gutbrod, et al., 1996), we suggested that spontaneous confabulations and disorientation result from interruption of the loop connecting the orbitofrontal cortex directly (via ventral amygdalofugal pathways) and indirectly (via the dorsomedial thalamic nucleus) with the amygdala (see Figure 27.3). An impairment of simple information storage may be based on an interruption of the loop connecting the

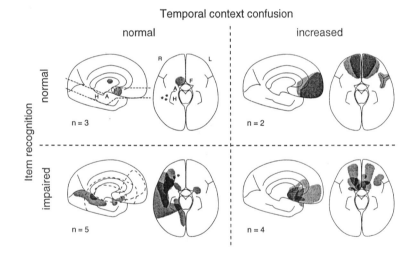

FIGURE 27.2. Anatomy of increased temporal context confusion in memory. All patients with increased temporal context confusion (right column) were disoriented and confabulated spontaneously. The lesion reconstruction shows the projection of lesions to the midsagittal plane and a combined axial plane encompassing the hippocampus (H), the amygdala (A), and the orbitofrontal area (including basal forebrain, F) as indicated in the upper-left design. Patients are separated according to whether their item recognition and temporal context confusion were within ("normal") or outside the controls' range ("impaired" item recognition, "increased" temporal context confusion). In the sagittal plane, shaded areas indicate lesions close to the midline, empty polygons with dashed lines indicate lateral hemispheric lesions. *n*, number of patients in the respective group. From Schnider, von Däniken, and Gutbrod (1996a). Copyright 1996 by Oxford University Press. Reprinted by permission.

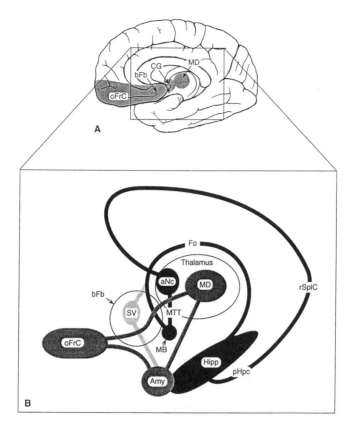

FIGURE 27.3. Disorientation and confabulations in amnesia. (A) Lesions that have been reported in patients with disorientation and spontaneous confabulations. (B) Main connections in this area. The black loop designates the classic Papez circuit (hippocampal loop). The mid-gray loop represents the lateral limbic loop connecting the orbitofrontal cortex with the amygdala. The bright gray connection indicates pathways of both loops with the septum verum. Amy, amygdala; aNc, anterior nucleus of the thalamus; bFb, basal forebrain; CG, capsular genu; MB, mamillary bodies; Fo, fornix; Hipp, hippocampus; MD, dorsomedial nucleus of the thalamus; MTT, mamillo-thalamic tract; oFrC, orbitofrontal cortex; pHpc, parahippocampal gyrus; rSplC, retrosplenial cortex; SV, Septum verum (medial and lateral parts). Adapted from Schnider (1997). Copyright 1997 by Thieme. Adapted by permission.

hippocampus with the anterior thalamic nucleus (i.e., damage of the hippocampus, the fornix, possibly the mamillary bodies, the anterior thalamic nucleus, the cingulate bundle, and the retrosplenial cortex) or direct damage of the neocortex storing the information. Lesions of the basal forebrain and the thalamus may lead to either type of memory failure because both loops have multiple, spatially close connections in these areas (Schnider et al., 1996a; Schnider, Gutbrod, et al., 1996).

Assuming that the characteristics of an amnesia depend on the precise localization rather than the type of brain damage, our results are directly relevant to PTA. Although we tested patients only when they had good sustained attention (which was necessary to conduct the experiments), that is, in a relatively late phase of PTA, it appears reasonable to assume that the mechanisms of the specific characteristics of PTA remain constant throughout the whole period of PTA. We posit that the core features of PTA—disorientation, occasional spontaneous confabulations, and possibly also lack of concern—are based on increased temporal context confusion in memory rather than an inability to store new information, and that the occurrence of PTA depends on damage or disconnection of the orbitofrontal cortex.

PERSONALITY AND EMOTIONAL CHANGES

Fifty to 76% of TBI patients show persistent changes of personality and emotion up to 15 years after the injury (Brooks & McKinlay, 1983; Thomsen, 1984). Personality and emotional changes represent a heavier burden for family members of head-injured patients than do physical disability and residual cognitive deficits (Brooks, Campsie, Symington, Beattie, & McKinlay, 1987; Panting & Merry, 1972; Thomsen, 1984). Alterations of personality and emotion adversely affect the patient's functioning in the workplace (Humphrey & Oddy, 1981; van Zomeren & Saan, 1990). The mechanisms of emotional changes after TBI are manifold: They may be a direct result of structural brain damage or they may be emotional reactions to the injury. The high frequency of frontal lobe damage after CHI (in particular, damage of the orbitofrontal area) has been suggested as the main reason for the high incidence of personality and emotional changes after TBI (Bond, 1984; Teasdale & Mendelow, 1984).

The components of emotion have been defined in many different ways. In this section, we use Benson's (1984) definitions: "mood" designates a subject's inner feeling; "affect" denotes the external manifestation of emotions (e.g., prosody and facial expression); it often reflects an underlying mood; "drive" is the force or need that energizes human activities; and "cognitive control" designates the ability to govern action by thought. Emotion is considered the result of mood, affect, drive, and cognitive control. "Personality" denotes a stable behavioral state of a subject, based on both learned and inherent qualities, against which various mental alterations react.

Personality disorders following brain damage often reflect the failure of specific cognitive or mental abilities. For example reduced drive, poor planning, or confabulation, disorders reflecting specific frontal failures, markedly influence a subject's personality. Rarely, however, personality alterations after brain damage emerge in isolation with no measurable accompanying cognitive or mental defect (Eslinger & Damasio, 1985).

Personality changes following frontal damage have been crudely divided into two broad classes (Blumer & Benson, 1975; Fuster, 1989; Kleist, 1934): The pseudodepressed or apathetic syndrome is characterized by low awareness, lack of initiative, hypokinesia, blunting of affect, reduced sexual interests, and an inability to plan for the future. The IQ is mostly normal. It has been suggested that this syndrome is based on damage of the convexity and the medial aspects of the frontal lobes. The pseudopsychopathic or euphoric syndrome is characterized by facetiousness, irritability, distractability, puerilism, hyperactivity, impulsivity, sexual disinhibition, inappropriate social and personal behavior, and little concern for others. The pseudopsychopathic syndrome has been attributed to damage of the orbitofrontal regions. The side of damage also appears to be important: Left frontal damage more often leads to the pseudodepressed syndrome, right frontal damage to the pseudopsychopathic syndrome (Kolb & Whishaw, 1990). TBI patients often manifest traits of both personality types, resulting in the apparently paradoxical combination of apathy, irritability, and euphoria (Geschwind, 1965).

The right and left frontal lobes appear to play different roles in mood regulation. Left-hemisphere lesions more often produce depression, whereas right-hemisphere lesions more often produce indifference and euphoria (Gainotti, 1972; Starkstein & Robinson,

1991). Major depression is far more common with left anterior frontal lesions than with left posterior lesions, with the severity of depression significantly correlating with the proximity of the lesion to the left frontal pole (Robinson & Szetela, 1981). A similar correlation—based on CT data—was also found in patients with TBI (Robinson & Szetela, 1981).

Hemispheric differences have also been postulated with respect to affect (i.e., the external manifestation of emotion). Patients with right-hemisphere lesions—particularly lesions of the right frontal operculum—were found to have deficits in emotional intonation: The patients' voices became monotonous and lacked emotional inflection (Ross, 1997). Emotional facial expression, too, was found to be less modulated after right brain damage, especially with anterior lesions (Borod, 1992). Although these hemispheric differences may also be important for affective changes after TBI, they have not been substantiated in this group of patients yet.

Disturbances of drive and cognitive control have also been attributed to frontal lobe damage (Benson, 1984; Stuss & Benson, 1986). Patients with supplementary motor area or anterior cingulate lesions may have a reduced drive for both motor and cognitive activities (Damasio & Van Hoesen, 1983; Luria, 1966). The most striking clinical manifestation is akinetic mutism. A possibly related disturbance is the inability to act on the basis of knowledge. The reported patients precisely knew and correctly recited instructions or plans but failed to incorporate them into their actions; action appeared to be dissociated from knowledge (Benson, 1984; Eslinger & Damasio, 1985; Luria, 1966). The patients had bilateral frontal lesions involving the convexities or the orbitofrontal area, in particular the frontal poles.

Personality disorders after TBI cannot always be deduced to basic mental failures. In particular, frontopolar lesions may produce socially incapacitating personality disturbances despite normal measurable cognition (Eslinger & Damasio, 1985). Figure 27.4 displays the lesion of such a patient. This 51-year-old patient suffered a CHI in a bicycle accident. In the first weeks after the injury, he had severe amnesia, was severely disoriented, confabulated spontaneously, and showed no insight into his failures; he had typical PTA. Within 6 weeks he recovered virtually completely except that people caring for him conceived discussions with him as tedious and uncomfortable; no specific

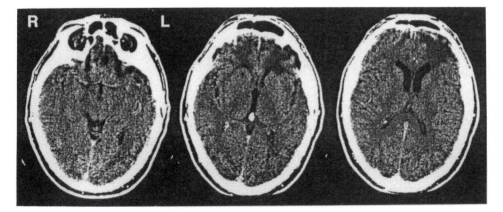

FIGURE 27.4. CT scan of a patient with severe personality changes 18 months after CHI. Extensive neuropsychological evaluations were entirely normal. From Schnider (1997). Copyright 1997 by Thieme. Reprinted by permission.

complaints could be formulated, however. In the following months, marital problems escalated and problems in the workplace arose: Whereas he had been considered creative and highly efficient before his accident, he was now described as awkward, unproductive, overly meticulous and subservient, a person needing an unambiguous structure for any working step. He appeared to have lost his natural feeling for social hierarchies. He eventually realized and severely suffered from his personal isolation but could not explain it. A CT scan performed 18 months after the injury demonstrated a predominantly rostral orbitofrontal lesion (frontal pole) with extension toward the dorsolateral convexity on the left side (see Figure 27.4). The basal forebrain was intact. Despite the severe changes of personality, extensive neuropsychological evaluations yielded entirely normal results. Refined instruments to classify and quantify behavioral disorders will have to be developed to elucidate the mechanisms of such isolated, hitherto "unmeasurable," personality disorders that may follow frontopolar and orbitofrontal damage.

ACKNOWLEDGMENT

This work was supported in part by the Swiss National Science Foundation (Grant Nos. 32-50882.97 and 4038-044052).

REFERENCES

Adams, J. H. (1975). The neuropathology of head injury. In P. J. Vinken & G. W. Bruyn (Eds.), *Handbook of clinical neurology: Head injury* (Vol. 23, pp. 35–65). Amsterdam: Elsevier Science.

Alexander, G. E., Crutcher, M. D., & DeLong, M. R. (1990). Basal ganglia–thalamocortical circuits: Parallel substrates for motor, oculomotor, "prefrontal" and "limbic" functions. *Progress in Brain Research, 85,* 119–146.

Alexander, M. P. (1982). Traumatic brain injury. In D. F. Benson & D. Blumer (Eds.), *Psychiatric aspects of neurologic disease* (pp. 219–249). Orlando, FL: Grune & Stratton.

Alexander, M. P., & Freedman, M. (1984). Amnesia after anterior communicating artery aneurysm rupture. *Neurology, 34,* 452–757.

Alivisatos, B., & Milner, B. (1989). Effects of frontal and temporal lobectomy on the use of advance information in a choice reaction time task. *Neuropsychologia, 27,* 495–503.

American Psychiatric Association. (1994). *Diagnostic and statistical manual of mental disorders* (4th ed.). Washington, DC: Author.

Baddeley, A. D. (1986). *Working memory.* Oxford: Oxford University Press.

Benson, D. F. (1984). The neurology of human emotion. *Bulletin of Clinical Neurosciences, 49,* 23–42.

Benson, D. F., & Geschwind, N. (1967). Shrinking retrograde amnesia. *Journal of Neurology, Neurosurgery, and Psychiatry, 30,* 539–544.

Benson, D. F., & Geschwind, N. (1975). Psychiatric conditions associated with focal lesions of the central nervous system. In S. Arieti & M. Reiser (Eds.), *American handbook of psychiatry* (pp. 208–243). New York: Basic Books.

Benton, A. L., Van Allen, M. W., & Fogel, M. L. (1964). Temporal orientation in cerebral disease. *Journal of Nervous and Mental Disease, 139,* 110–119.

Blumer, D., & Benson, D. F. (1975). Personality changes with frontal and temporal lobe lesions. In D. F. Benson & D. Blumer (Eds.), *Psychiatric aspects of neurologic disease* (pp. 151–170). New York: Grune & Stratton.

Bogousslavsky, J., & Regli, F. (1990). Anterior cerebral artery territory infarction in the Lausanne stroke registry. Clinical and etiologic patterns. *Archives of Neurology, 47,* 144–150.

Bond, M. (1984). The psychiatry of closed head injury. In N. Brooks (Ed.), *Closed head injury. Psychological, social, and family consequences* (pp. 148–178). Oxford: Oxford University Press.

Borod, J. C. (1992). Interhemispheric and intrahemispheric control of emotion: A focus on unilateral brain damage. *Journal of Consulting and Clinical Psychology, 60,* 339–348.

Brodal, A. (1981). *Neurological anatomy* (3rd ed.). New York: Oxford University Press.

Brooks, D. N. (1972). Memory and head injury. *Journal of Nervous and Mental Diseases, 155,* 350–355.

Brooks, D. N., Aughton, M. E., Bond, M. R., Jones, P., & Rizvi, S. (1980). Cognitive sequelae in relationship to early indices of severity of brain damage after severe blunt head injury. *Journal of Neurology, Neurosurgery, and Psychiatry, 43,* 529–534.

Brooks, D. N., Campsie, L., Symington, C., Beattie, A., & McKinlay, W. (1986). The five year outcome of severe blunt head injury: A relative's view. *Journal of Neurology, Neurosurgery, and Psychiatry, 49,* 764–770.

Brooks, D. N., Campsie, L., Symington, C., Beattie, A., & McKinlay, W. (1987). The effects of severe head injury on patient and relatives within seven years of injury. *Journal of Head Trauma Rehabilitation, 2,* 1–13.

Brooks, D. N., & McKinlay, W. (1983). Personality and behavioral change after severe blunt head injury—A relative's view. *Journal of Neurology, Neurosurgery, and Psychiatry, 46,* 336–344.

Brouwer, W. H., & van Wolffelaar, P. C. (1985). Sustained attention and sustained effort after closed head injury. *Cortex, 21,* 111–119.

Cohen, R. A. (1993). *The neuropsychology of attention.* New York: Plenum.

Cohen, R. M., Semple, W. E., Gross, M., & Holcomb, H. H. (1988). Functional localization of sustained attention: Comparison to sensory stimulation in the absence of instruction. *Neuropsychiatry, Neuropsychology, and Behavioral Neurology, 1,* 3–20.

Courville, C. B. (1945). *Pathology of the nervous system* (2nd ed.). Mountain View, CA: Pacific Press.

Cummings, J. L. (1993). Frontal–subcortical circuits and human behavior. *Archives of Neurology, 50,* 873–880.

Cummings, J. L. (1995). Anatomic and behavioral aspects of frontal–subcortical circuits. In J. Grafman, K. J. Holyoak, & F. Boller (Eds.), *Structure and functions of the human prefrontal cortex* (pp. 1–13). New York: New York Academy of Sciences.

Curry, S. (1981). Event-related potentials as indicants of structural and functional damage in closed head injury. *Progress in Brain Research, 54,* 507–515.

Dalla Barba, G. (1993). Different patterns of confabulation. *Cortex, 29,* 567–581.

Damasio, A. R., Graff Radford, N. R., Eslinger, P. J., Damasio, H., & Kassel, N. (1985). Amnesia following basal forebrain lesions. *Archives of Neurology, 42,* 263–271.

Damasio, A. R., & Van Hoesen, G. W. (1983). Emotional distrubances associated with focal lesions of the limbic frontal lobe. In K. M. Heilman & P. Satz (Eds.), *Neuropsychology of human emotion* (pp. 85–110). New York: Guilford Press.

Daniel, W. F., Crovitz, H. F., & Weiner, R. D. (1987). Neuropsychological aspects of disorientation. *Cortex, 23,* 169–187.

Davies, R. D., Jones, D. M., & Taylor, A. (1984). Selective and sustained-attention tasks: Individual and group differences. In R. Parasuraman & D. R. Davies (Eds.), *Varieties of attention* (pp. 395–447). Orlando, FL: Academic Press.

Delis, D. C., Kramer, J. H., Kaplan, E., & Ober, B. A. (1987). *The California Verbal Learning Test.* New York: Psychological Corporation.

DeLuca, J., & Cicerone, K. D. (1991). Confabulation following aneurysm of the anterior communicating artery. *Cortex, 27,* 417–423.

DeLuca, J., & Diamond, B. J. (1995). Aneurysm of the anterior communicating artery: A review of neuroanatomical and neuropsychological sequelae. *Journal of Clinical and Experimental Neuropsychology, 17,* 100–121.

Deutsch, G., Papanicolaou, A. C., Borbon, T., & Eisenberg, H. M. (1988). Cerebral blood flow evidence of right cerebral activation in attention demanding tasks. *International Journal of Neuroscience, 36,* 23–28.

Drewe, E. A. (1975). An experimental investigation of Luria's theory on the effect of frontal lobe lesions in man. *Neuropsychologia, 13,* 421–429.

Ellenberg, J. H., Levin, H. S., & Saydjary, C. (1996). Posttraumatic amnesia as a predictor of outcome after severe closed head injury. *Archives of Neurology, 53,* 782–791.

Elting, R., van Zomeren, A. H., & Brouwer, W. H. (1989). Flexibility of attention after severe head injury. *Journal of Clinical and Experimental Neuropsychology, 11,* 370.

Eslinger, P. J., & Damasio, A. R. (1985). Severe disturbances of higher cognition after bilateral frontal lobe ablation: Patient EVR. *Neurology, 35,* 1731–1741.

Ewert, J., Levin, H. S., Watson, M. G., & Kalisky, Z. (1989). Procedural learning during posttraumatic amnesia in survivors of severe closed head injury: Implications for rehabilitation. *Archives of Neurology, 46,* 911–916.

Fischer, R. S., Alexander, M. P., D'Esposito, M., & Otto, R. (1995). Neuropsychological and neuroanatomical correlates of confabulation. *Journal of Clinical and Experimental Neuropsychology, 17,* 20–28.

Foster, J. K., Eskes, G. A., & Stuss, D. T. (1994). The cognitive neuropsychology of attention: A frontal lobe perspective. *Cognitive Neuropsychology, 11,* 133–147.

Fuster, J. M. (1989). *The prefrontal cortex: Anatomy, physiology, and neuropsychology of the frontal lobes* (2nd ed.). New York: Academic Press.

Gainotti, G. (1972). Emotional behavior and hemispheric side of the lesion. *Cortex, 8,* 41–55.

Geschwind, N. (1965). Disconnection syndromes in animals and man. *Brain, 88,* 237–294.

Goldberg, E., Bilder, R. M., Hughes, J. E. O., Antin, S. P., & Mattis, S. (1989). A reticulo-frontal disconnection syndrome. *Cortex, 25,* 687–695.

Gronwall, D. (1987). Advances in the assessment of attention and information processing after head injury. In H. S. Levin, J. Grafman, & H. M. Eisenberg (Eds.), *Neurobehavioral recovery from head injury* (pp. 355–371). New York: Oxford University Press.

Gronwall, D., & Sampson, H. (1974). *The psychological effects of concussion.* Auckland: Auckland University Press.

Gronwall, D., & Wrightson, P. (1974). Delayed recovery of intellectual function after minor head injury. *Lancet, II,* 605–609.

Guberman, A., & Stuss, D. (1983). The syndrome of bilateral paramedian thalamic infarction. *Neurology, 33,* 540–546.

Hicks, L., & Birren, J. E. (1970). Aging, brain damage, and psychomotor slowing. *Psychological Bulletin, 74,* 377–396.

High, W. M., Levin, H. S., & Gary, H. E. (1990). Recovery of orientation following closed head injury. *Journal of Clinical and Experimental Neuropsychology, 12,* 703–714.

Holst, P., & Villki, J. (1988). Effect of frontomedial lesions on performance on the Stroop test and word fluency tasks. *Journal of Clinical and Experimental Neuropsychology, 10,* 79–80.

Humphrey, M., & Oddy, M. (1981). Return to work after head injury: A review of post-war studies. *Injury, 12,* 107–114.

Jennett, B., & Bond, M. (1975). Assessment of outcome after severe brain damage. *Lancet, i,* 480–487.

Kapur, N., Ellison, D., Smith, M. P., McLellan, D. L., & Burrows, E. H. (1992). Focal retrograde amnesia following bilateral temporal lobe pathology. *Brain, 115,* 73–85.

Kewman, D. G., Yanus, B., & Kirsch, N. (1988). Assessment of distractibility in auditory comprehension after traumatic brain injury. *Brain Injury, 2,* 131–137.

Kleist, K. (1934). *Kriegsverletzungen des Gehirns in ihrer Bedeutung für Hirnlokalisation und Hirnpathologie.* Leipzig: Barth.

Knight, R. T., Hillyard, S. A., Woods, D. L., & Neville, H. J. (1981). The effects of frontal cortex lesions on event-related potentials during auditory selective attention. *Electroencephalography and Clinical Neurophysiology, 52,* 571–582.

Kolb, B., & Whishaw, I. Q. (1990). *Fundamentals of human neuropsychology* (3rd ed.). New York: Freeman.

Levin, H. S., Amparo, E., Eisenberg, H. M., Williams, D. H., High, W. M. Jr., McArdle, C. B., & Weiner, R. L. (1987). Magnetic resonance imaging and computerized tomography in relation to the neurobehavioral sequelae of mild and moderate head injuries. *Journal of Neurosurgery, 66,* 706–713.

Levin, H. S., & Grossman, R. G. (1978). Behavioral sequelae of closed head injury. *Archives of Neurology, 35,* 720–727.

Levin, H. S., High, W. M., Meyers, C. C., Von Laufen, A., Hayden, M. E., & Eisenberg, H. M. (1985). Impairment of remote memory after closed head injury. *Journal of Neurology, Neurosurgery, and Psychiatry, 48,* 556–563.

Levin, H. S., Lilly, M. A., Papanicolaou, A., & Eisenberg, H. M. (1992). Posttraumatic and retrograde amnesia after closed head injury. In L. R. Squire & N. Butters (Eds.), *Neuropsychology of memory* (2nd ed., pp. 290–308). New York: Guilford Press.

Lezak, M. D. (1995). *Neuropsychological assessment* (3rd ed.). New York: Oxford University Press.

Luria, A. R. (1966). *Human brain and psychological processes.* New York: Harper & Row.

Luria, A. R. (1973). *The working brain.* London: Penguin Books.

Luria, A. R. (1980). *Higher cortical functions in man* (2nd ed.). New York: Basic Books.

Markowitsch, H. J., Calabrese, P., Liess, J., Haupts, M., Durwen, H. F., & Gehlen, W. (1993). Retrograde amnesia after traumatic injury of the temporo-frontal cortex. *Journal of Neurology, Neurosurgery, and Psychiatry, 56,* 988–992.

McLean, A., Temkin, N. R., Dikmen, S., & Wyler, A. R. (1983). The behavioral sequelae of head injury. *Journal of Clinical Neuropsychology, 5,* 361–367.

Mesulam, M. M. (1985). Attention, confusional states, and neglect. In M. M. Mesulam (Ed.), *Principles of behavioral neurology.* Philadelphia: F. A. Davis.

Mesulam, M. M. (1990). Large scale neurocognitive networks and distributed processing for attention, language and memory. *Annals of Neurology, 28,* 587–613.

Miller, B. L., Cummings, J. L., McIntyre, H., Ebers, G., & Grode, M. (1986). Hypersexuality or altered sexual preference following brain injury. *Journal of Neurology, Neurosurgery, and Psychiatry, 49,* 867–873.

Miller, E., & Cruzat, A. (1980). A note on the effects of irrelevant information on task performance after mild and severe head injury. *British Journal of Social and Clinical Neuropsychology, 20,* 69–70.

Newcombe, F. (1982). The psychosocial consequences of closed head injury: Assessment and rehabilitation. *Injury, 14,* 111–136.

Norman, B., & Svahn, K. (1961). A follow-up study of severe brain injuries. *Acta Psychiatrica Scandinavica, 37,* 236–264.

O'Shaugnessy, E. J., Fowler, R. S., & Reid, V. (1984). Sequelae of mild closed head injuries. *Journal of Family Practice, 18,* 391–394.

Panting, A., & Merry, P. (1972). The long-term rehabilitation of severe head injuries with particular reference to the need for social and medical support for the patient's family. *Rehabilitation, 38,* 33–37.

Parasuraman, R., Mutter, S. A., & Molloy, R. (1991). Sustained attention following mild closed head injury. *Journal of Clinical and Experimental Neuropsychology, 13,* 789–811.

Pardo, J. V., Pardo, P., Janer, K., & Raichle, M. E. (1990). The anterior cingulate cortex mediates processing selection in the Stroop attention conflict paradigma. *Proceedings of the National Academy of Sciences of the United States of America, 87,* 256–259.

Perret, E. (1974). The left frontal lobe in man and the suppression of habitual responses in verbal categorial behavior. *Neuropsychologia, 12,* 323–330.

Plum, F., & Posner, J. B. (1980). *The diagnoses of stupor and coma.* Philadelphia: F. A. Davis.

Ponsford, J., & Kinsella, G. (1991). The use of a rating scale of attentional behavior. *Neuropsychological Rehabilitation, 1,* 241–257.

Ponsford, J., & Kinsella, G. (1992). Attentional deficits following closed head injury. *Journal of Experimental and Clinical Neuropsychology, 14,* 822–838.

Posner, M. I. (1995). Attention in cognitive neuroscience: An overview. In M. S. Gazzaniga (Ed.), *The cognitive neurosciences* (pp. 615–624). Cambridge: MIT Press.

Posner, M. I., & Rafal, R. D. (1987). Cognitive theories of attention and the rehabilitation of attentional deficits. In R. J. Meier, A. C. Benton, & L. Diller (Eds.), *Neuropsychological rehabilitation* (pp. 182–201). Edinburgh: Churchill Livingstone.

Prigatano, G. P. (1991). Disturbances of self-awareness of deficit after traumatic brain injury. In G. P. Prigantano & D. L. Schacter (Eds.), *Awareness of deficit after brain injury: Clinical and theoretical issues* (pp. 111–126). New York: Oxford University Press.

Rizzo, P. A., Amabile, G., Caporali, M., Spadaro, M., Zanasi, M., & Morocutti, C. (1978). A CNV study in a group of patients with traumatic head injuries. *Electroencephalography and Clinical Neurophysiology, 45,* 281–285.

Robinson, R. G., & Szetela, B. (1981). Mood change following left hemispheric brain injury. *Annals of Neurology, 9,* 447–453.

Ross, E. D. (1997). The aprosodias. In T. E. Feinberg & M. J. Farah (Eds.), *Behavioral neurology and neuropsychology* (pp. 699–711). New York: McGraw-Hill.

Ruff, R. M., Niemann, H., Allen, C. C., Farrow, C. E., & Wylie, T. (1992). The Ruff 2 and 7 selective attention test: A neuropsychological application. *Perceptual and Motor Skills, 75,* 1311–1319.

Rugg, M. D., Cowan, C. P., Nagy, M. E., Milner, A. D., Jacobson, I., & Brooks, D. N. (1989). CNV abnormalities following closed head injury. *Brain, 112,* 489–506.

Russel, W. R. (1971). *The traumatic amnesias.* New York: Oxford University Press.

Salmoso, D., & Denes, G. (1982). Role of the frontal lobes on an attention task: A signal detection analysis. *Perceptual and Motor Skills, 54,* 1147–1150.

Sandson, T. A., Daffner, K. R., Carvalho, P. A., & Mesulam, M. M. (1991). Frontal lobe dysfunction following infarction of the left-sided medial thalamus. *Archives of Neurology, 48,* 1300–1303.

Schneider, W., & Shiffrin, R. M. (1977). Controlled and automatic human information processing. I: Detection, search and attention. *Psychological Review, 84,* 1–66.

Schnider, A. (1997). *Verhaltensneurologie. Die neurologische siete der Neuropsychologie.* Stuttgart: Thieme.

Schnider, A., Gutbrod, K., Hess, C. W., & Schroth, G. (1996). Memory without context. Amnesia with confabulations following right capsular genu infarction. *Journal of Neurology, Neurosurgery, and Psychiatry, 61,* 186–193.

Schnider, A., Gutbrod, K., Ozdoba, C., & Bassetti, C. (1995). Very severe amnesia with acute onset after isolated hippocampal damage due to systemic lupus erythematosus. *Journal of Neurology, Neurosurgery, and Psychiatry, 59,* 644–646.

Schnider, A., Regard, M., & Landis, T. (1994). Anterograde and retrograde amnesia following bitemporal infarction. *Behavioural Neurology, 7,* 87–92.

Schnider, A., von Däniken, C., & Gutbrod, K. (1996a). Disorientation in amnesia: A confusion of memory traces. *Brain, 119,* 1627–1632.

Schnider, A., von Däniken, C., & Gutbrod, K. (1996b). The mechanisms of spontaneous and provoked confabulations. *Brain, 119,* 1365–1375.

Segalowitz, S. J., Unsal, A., & Dywan, J. (1992). CNV evidence for the distinctiveness of frontal and posterior neural process in a traumatic brain-injured population. *Journal of Clinical and Experimental Neuropsychology, 14,* 545–565.

Shallice, T. (1982). Specific impairments of planning. In D. E. Broadbent & L. Weiskrantz (Eds.), *The neuropsychology of cognitive functions* (pp. 199–209). London: The Royal Society.

Shapiro, B. E., Alexander, M. P., Gardner, H., & Mercer, B. (1981). Mechanisms of confabulation. *Neurology, 31,* 1070–1076.

Shiffrin, R. M., & Schneider, W. (1977). Controlled and automatic human information processing: II: Perceptual learning, automatic attending and a general theory. *Psychological Review, 84,* 127–190.

Sohlberg, M. M., & Mateer, C. A. (1989). *Introduction to cognitive rehabilitation.* New York: Guilford Press.

Stablum, F., Leonardi, G., Mazzoldi, M., Umilt, C., & Morra, S. (1994). Attention and control deficits following closed head injury. *Cortex, 30,* 603–618.

Starkstein, S. E., & Robinson, R. G. (1991). The role of the frontal lobes in affective disorder following stroke. In H. S. Levin, H. M. Eisenberg, & A. L. Benton (Eds.), *Frontal lobe function and dysfunction* (pp. 288–303). New York: Oxford University Press.

Stuss, D. T., Alexander, M. P., Lieberman, A., & Levine, H. (1978). An extraordinary form of confabulation. *Neurology, 28,* 1166–1172.

Stuss, D. T., & Benson, D. F. (1986). *The frontal lobes.* New York: Raven Press.

Stuss, D. T., Ely, P., Hugenholtz, H., Richard, M. T., La Rochelle, S., Poirier, C. A., & Bell, I. (1985). Subtle neuropsychological deficits in patients with good recovery after closed head injury. *Neurosurgery, 17,* 41–47.

Stuss, D. T., Kaplan, E. F., Benson, D. F., Weir, W. S., Chiulli, S., & Sarazin, F. F. (1982). Evidence for the involvement of orbitofrontal cortex in memory functions: An interference effect. *Journal of Comparative Physiology and Psychology, 96,* 913–925.

Stuss, D. T., Stethem, L. L., Hugenholtz, H., Picton, T., Pivik, J., & Richard, M. D. (1989). Reaction time after head injury: Fatigue, divided and focused attention, and consistency of performance. *Journal of Neurology, Neurosurgery, and Psychiatry, 52,* 742–748.

Tatemichi, T. K., Desmond, D. W., Prohovnik, I., Cross, D. T., Gropen, T. I., Mohr, J. P., & Stern, Y. (1992). Confusion and memory loss from capsular genu infarction. *Neurology, 42,* 1966–1979.

Teasdale, G., & Mendelow, D. (1984). Pathophysiology of head injuries. In N. Brooks (Ed.), *Closed head injury. Psychological, social, and family consequences* (pp. 4–37). Oxford: Oxford University Press.

Thomsen, I. V. (1984). Late outcome of very severe blunt head trauma: A 10–15 year second follow-up. *Journal of Neurology, Neurosurgery, and Psychiatry, 47,* 260–268.

Van der Horst, L. (1932). Über die psychologie des Korsakowsyndroms. *Monatschrift für Psychiatrie und Neurologie, 83,* 65–84.

Van Wolffelaar, P. C., Brouwer, W. H., & van Zomeren, A. H. (1990). Driving ability 5 to 10 years after severe head injury. In T. Benjamin (Ed.), *Driving behavior in a social context* (pp. 564–574). Caen: Paradigme.

van Zomeren, A. H. (1981). *Reaction time and attention after closed head injury.* Lisse: Swets.

van Zomeren, A. H., & Brouwer, W. H. (1987). Head injury and concepts of attention. In H. Levin & J. Grafman (Eds.), *Neurobehavioral recovery from head injury* (pp. 398–415). New York: Oxford University Press.

van Zomeren, A. H., & Brouwer, W. H. (1994). *Clinical neuropsychology of attention.* New York: Oxford University Press.

van Zomeren, A. H., Brouwer, W. H., Rothengatter, J. A., & Snoek, J. W. (1988). Fitness to drive a car after recovery from severe head injury. *Archives of Physical Medicine and Rehabilitation, 60,* 90–96.

van Zomeren, A. H., & Deelman, B. G. (1978). Long term recovery of visual reaction time after closed head injury. *Journal of Neurology, Neurosurgery, and Psychiatry, 41,* 452–457.

van Zomeren, A. H., & Saan, R. J. (1990). Psychological and social sequelae of severe head injury. In R. Braakman (Ed.), *Handbook of clinical neurology: Head injury* (Vol. 57, pp. 397–420). Amsterdam: Elsevier Science.

Victor, M., Adams, R. D., & Collins, G. H. (1989). *The Wernicke–Korsakoff syndrome* (2nd ed.). Philadelphia: F. A. Davis.

Volpe, B. T., & Hirst, W. (1983). The characterization of the amnesic syndrome following hypoxic ischemic injury. *Archives of Neurology, 40,* 436–440.

Von Cramon, D., & Säring, W. (1982). Störung der Orientierung beim hirnorganischen Psychosyndrom. In D. Bente, H. Coper, & S. Kanowski (Eds.), *Hirnorganische Psychosyndrome im Alter* (pp. 38–49). Berlin: Springer.

Wilkins, A. J., Shallice, T., & McCarthy, R. (1987). Frontal lesions and sustained attention. *Neuropsychologia, 25,* 359–365.

Woods, D. L., & Knight, R. T. (1986). Electrophysiologic evidence of increased distractibility after dorsolateral prefrontal lesions. *Neurology, 36,* 212–216.

Zimmermann, P., North, P., & Fimm, B. (1993). Diagnosis of attentional deficits: Theoretical considerations and presentation of a test battery. In F. J. Stachowiak (Ed.), *Developments in the assessment and rehabilitation of brain-damaged patients* (pp. 3–17). Tübingen: Günter Narr Verlag.

Section B

PSYCHIATRY

28

Schizophrenia and Frontal Lobe Functioning

Evidence from Neuropsychology, Cognitive Neuroscience, and Psychophysiology

WILLIAM PERRY
NEAL R. SWERDLOW
JENNIFER E. McDOWELL
DAVID L. BRAFF

Schizophrenia is a complex brain disorder in which diverse pathophysiological processes produce a "common final pathway" of characteristic clinical manifestations. Recent years have seen major advances in the identification of structural and functional central nervous system abnormalities in schizophrenic patients. For example, morphological studies have led to the observation of ventricular enlargement (Johnstone, Crow, Frith, Husband, & Kreel, 1976; Suddath et al., 1989), diffuse neocortical atrophy (Lawrie et al., 1997), and structural abnormalities of mesial temporal and subcortical nuclei (Andreasen et al., 1994; Bogerts, Mertz, Schonfeldt, & Bausch, 1985; Jernigan et al., 1991; Suddath et al., 1990). Despite the overwhelming evidence of neuroanatomical abnormalities among schizophrenic patients, there is little support for a single underlying pathology of cortex, white matter, or subcortical structures among all schizophrenic patients. Thus, to date neuropathological studies have been neither specific nor sensitive, and a unified theory of schizophrenia as a single disease entity with a single neuropathophysiology appears unlikely. In contrast, theories that focus on complex dysfunctions within multiple brain regions and emphasize circuitry abnormalities have led to an improved understanding of the mechanisms that underlie specific signs and symptoms associated with schizophrenia. Approaches that combine the methods of investigation from the fields of neuropsychology, cognitive neuroscience, and psychophysiology have allowed us to begin to understand the apparent heterogeneity of schizophrenia by parsing schizophrenic patients into groups with shared deficits. Still, it remains difficult to infer structural damage from complex behavioral dysfunctions. This chapter briefly reviews some of the most critical and compelling data, using novel research strategies from neuropsychology, cognitive neuroscience, and psychophysiology with humans and infrahumans that define a frontal lobe neural basis of schizophrenia.

NEUROPSYCHOLOGY

A growing literature suggests that schizophrenic patients have deficits in neuropsychological tests of planning, organizing, and manipulating complex, abstract, and often novel information. These tests are thought to assess executive functioning and have been considered sensitive to integrity of the prefrontal cortical area. Among the many tests used to assess executive functioning, the Wisconsin Card Sorting Test (WCST), which is thought to be regulated primarily by the dorsolateral prefrontal cortex, has received the greatest attention in the literature (Milner, 1963).

The WCST consists of 128 cards, each of which contains geometric figures that may vary along three dimensions (color, form, number). The test subject is instructed to place each card from a deck below one of four key cards. Subjects are not informed of the correct sorting principle to use but are given feedback as to whether their card sort is correct or incorrect. The initial principle is to match the cards by color. Once a subject attains a criterion of 10 correctly sorted cards, the principle is changed without the subject being informed. The test is completed when the subject has completed 6 categories of 10 consecutive correctly sorted cards or has sorted all 128 cards. Several scoring methods and a variety of scores can be obtained from the WCST. The most widely used scoring method is that of Heaton (1981), and the most sensitive score with respect to frontal lobe dysfunction is the perseverative response (Milner, 1963; Braff et al., 1991).

A relatively large number of studies have reported that schizophrenic patients' performance on the WCST is impaired (Fey, 1951; Kolb & Whishaw, 1983; Van der Does & Van der Bosch, 1992). Often these studies have compared the performance of schizophrenic patients to that of brain-damaged patients (Pantelis & Nelson, 1994). However, many of these studies are conducted on schizophrenic patients who are grossly impaired and who are either unmedicated and therefore highly symptomatic or chronically institutionalized and have been taking high doses of neuroleptic medication for many years (e.g., Berman, Zec, & Weinberger, 1986). Braff et al. (1991) studied chronic schizophrenic outpatients and found that they displayed deficits on a range of tests including complex reasoning and cognition. In contrast, performance on the WCST was relatively intact, and when the schizophrenic outpatients were compared to normal controls, the WCST ranked 17th out of 26 measures in terms of sensitivity for group identification. Braff et al. (1991) did find, however, that "there seems to be a significant subgroup of these schizophrenic outpatients with abnormal WCST functioning" (p. 897). Their findings raise questions about the ubiquity of frontal lobe deficits among all schizophrenic patients and speaks to the multidemensional nature of schizophrenia, which is laden with subgroup differences.

An alternative approach to understanding the relationship between the WCST and frontal lobe functioning is to study patients with maximal WCST deficits. In a series of widely cited studies from the National Institute of Mental Health (NIMH), Weinberger and associates (Berman et al., 1986; Weinberger, Berman, & Zec, 1986) used a radioactive isotope inhalation technique to monitor regional cerebral blood flow (rCBF) in normal subjects and schizophrenic patients during their performance on an automated, computer-delivered adaptation of the WCST. The NIMH sample included schizophrenic patients who had "chronic unremitting illness, a population chosen because of the probability that they would perform poorly on the Card Sort" (Goldberg, Weinberger, Berman, Pliskin, & Podd, 1987, p. 1009). They found that while normal subjects showed an increase in rCBF in the dorsolateral prefrontal cortex (DLPFC) region during the WCST, the schizophrenic patients exhibited reduced rCBF in the same region, the degree of which was correlated with the number of perseverative errors committed on the test. This finding and subsequent studies (Weinberger, Berman, & Illowsky, 1988) provide support for the hypothesis that the deficits of schizophrenic patients reflect dysfunction in prefrontal cortex. However, some question remains whether the poor WCST performance of schizophrenic patients is due to a fundamental impairment of the DLPFC or a "behavioral epiphenomena" (Goldberg et al., 1987, p. 1009) due to inattention, poor cooperation, or lack of motivation. Numerous studies have been conducted to address this specific question. Goldberg et al. (1987) studied 44 chronic schizophrenic subjects on the WCST. In one condition, they informed the subjects of the sorting principles underlying the WCST (e.g., color, form, and number) and found that despite being provided with the sorting principles, the patients continued to commit a high number of perseverative responses. In a second condition, the patients were provided card-by-card instruction, which led to an improvement in their performance. However, when the instruction was removed, the patients returned to their baseline level of performance. Goldberg et al. (1987) concluded that the inability to learn the WCST was due to a "trait phenomenon consistent with a failure of cognitive processes traditionally attributed to the prefrontal cortex" (p. 1013). Several authors (Bellack, Mueser, Morrison, Tierney, & Podell, 1990; Green, Ganzell, Satz, & Vaclav, 1990), challenged the conclusions of this study, arguing that the failure to probe the subject's comprehension of their card sorts made the subject an inactive participant, and thus the behavioral contingencies for learning were not optimal to maintain improved performance. To correct for this, Bellack et al. (1990) employed a number of different strategies, including one in which explicit instructions and reinforcement were provided. They found that the schizophrenic patients improved their performance on the WCST when they were provided with the underlying principle of the WCST and were monetarily reinforced for their correct response. They concluded that among schizophrenic patients, subgroups may have different etiologies and structural and functional impairments. Green et al. (1990) conducted a similar study and arrived at similar results. They, too, concluded that the findings of improved performance on the WCST under certain conditions might "reflect separate etiological subtypes and might identify those patients who would benefit from retraining" (p. 92). The findings from these studies stress the critical concept of "density," the "extent to which impaired performance on a measure of a neuropsychological function is more or less modifiable" (Goldman, 1994, p. 99). It follows that if an impairment is dense, providing cues or other performance strategies would not help to modify that performance. In contrast, if providing compensatory strategies does lead to improved performance, that improvement may indicate residual neurobehavioral plasticity and provide great insight into the role of executive functioning and the prefrontal cortex in schizophrenia (Goldman, 1994).

Goldberg and Weinberger (1994) reviewed the work of Green et al. (1990) and Bellack et al. (1990) and pointed out that despite the improved performance of patients using various coaching strategies, the schizophrenic patients were still unable to attain normal perseveration scores. They further stressed that giving patients detailed instructions at the outset disrupted the integrity of the test, which thus no longer could be used to assess the executive functions of planning, hypothesis testing, sequencing, and concept formation. Consequently, the coaching strategies employed did not lead to insights regarding the density of executive functioning. To support their premise, they referred to the research of Bird and Luszcz (1991), which used encoding strategies to improve memory performance in patients with dementia of the Alzheimer's type. In this study, as well as others using patients with known structural neuropathology, performance was improved but not normalized (Gianutsos, 1981).

In a recent study, Potterat, Perry, and Braff (1997) addressed the criticisms of Goldberg and Weinberger (1994) and added that to truly assess the density of executive functioning impairment, a strategy must be used that requires the individual to actively employ the executive functions of attention, working memory, and complex concept formation. If one role of executive functioning is to hold information in "working memory," from which one then develops hypotheses leading to the planning and execution of complex strategies, then executive functioning will be most sensitively assessed under conditions that require the use of working memory from response planning and execution. To this end, they employed the simple intervention of asking the schizophrenic patient to verbally report their sorting strategy after each sort. Half of the subjects were first exposed to the WCST without this intervention while the other half of the patients were asked after each sort, "Why did you put that card there?" Following the administration of the first deck of 64 cards the conditions were switched. The first group of patients were given the modified instruction while the later group was just given the standard feedback, whether the sort was correct or incorrect. They found that simply asking the schizophrenic patient to verbalize the rationale for their sort resulted in significantly fewer perseverations, and this effect continued through the second 64 cards even in the absence of the modified instructions asking why they placed the card where they did. The subjects who were administered the standard version first also showed a significant reduction in their perseverative responses during the second deck of cards when asked to verbalize their strategy. The authors concluded that forcing the patients to verbalize their response may activate the various operations of executive functions such as working memory. They further hypothesized that perseverative responses among schizophrenic patients may be due to a fractured supervisory attentional system (SAS; Norman & Shallice, 1986), which is thought to be mediated by the prefrontal cortical areas. The SAS has been a useful model to explain how one of many different possible actions are selected and carried through to completion (Frith, 1992). According to the SAS model, lower-level competing actions are triggered by the environment. Through a process of mutual inhibition, the highest level of activation is carried through while the competing actions are suppressed. The SAS modulates this process, inhibiting inappropriate routine actions and facilitating actions in the absence of environmental stimulation. In conditions in which the SAS is impaired (e.g., in patients with frontal lobe lesions), the individual is bound to inappropriate stimulus-elicited behavior and subject to perseverations. Therefore, the simple requirement of verbalization of strategy initiates the higher-order functions of self-monitoring, conscious deliberation, planning, and inhibition and allows for processing of novel situations, all essential to successful completion of the WCST task.

Several studies have reported that schizophrenic patients with high levels of negative symptoms, such as alogia, avolition, apathy, and inattention, are more prone to perform poorly on frontally mediated neuropsychological tests (Kolb & Wishaw, 1983; Liddle & Morris, 1991; Palmer et al., 1997). Negative symptoms of schizophrenia have also been compared to the behavioral deficits observed in patients with frontal lesions (Buchanan et al., 1993). Thus, the negative symptoms of schizophrenia provide further support for a role of frontal lobe dysfunction in schizophrenia. In the Potterat et al. (1997) study, perseverative responses on the WCST were positively correlated with intensity of negative symptoms, independent of whether or not subjects were asked to verbalize their WCST strategy. If negative symptoms in schizophrenia truly reflect frontal lobe dysfunction, these findings offer further indirect support for the role frontal lobe dysfunction in mediating WCST perseverative errors.

The previously mentioned studies argue for a central role of frontal lobe impairment in schizophrenia, based on performance on a complex task, which requires numerous cognitive operations for successful completion. It is important to note that there have been descriptions of patients with clear frontal lobe pathology who perform normally on neuropsychological tests of "frontal" function (Eslinger & Damasio, 1986). Such descriptions reinforce the notion that many avenues lead to good or poor test performance on these measures. An alternative strategy for studying the function of the frontal cortex, which has gained popularity in neuropsychology and cognitive neuroscience, is to employ measures that isolate one critical aspect of frontal executive functioning. Lezak (1995) reported that the frontal lobes are responsible for several higher cognitive processes, but among the most critical functions are those of working memory and attention. Consequently, over the past decade, the study of working memory in schizophrenia has become increasingly popular.

Baddeley and Hitch (1974) introduced the concept of working memory to describe a limited capacity "working space" for information processing. In their original conceptualization, working memory consisted of a supraordinate "central executive" system and two slave systems for the transient storage of visuospatial and verbal information. Baddeley (1986) explained that the working memory system has limited storage capacity, is dynamic, and is subject to rapid decay unless rehearsal processes are initiated. The function of this memory system is to provide "temporary storage and manipulation of the information necessary for such complex cognitive tasks as language comprehension, learning, and reasoning" (Baddeley, 1992, p. 556). These higher-level operations are associated with the functional substrate of the prefrontal cortex (Baddeley & Wilson, 1988).

By focusing on one critical element of working memory, Goldman-Rakic and colleagues have provided great insights into the role of working memory dysfunction in schizophrenia. Specifically, their work (Funuhashi, Bruce, & Goldman-Rakic, 1989, 1993; Goldman-Rakic, 1987, 1991; Wilson, Scalaidhe, & Goldman-Rakic, 1993) has provided strong evidence that in nonhuman primates, the prefrontal cortex is the primary site of transient visuospatial information storage. They employed a delayed-response paradigm to study the ability of nonhuman primates to guide behavior by symbolic representation in the absence of external cues. The delayed-response task depends on remembering the previous response and thus indexes the ability to guide behavior by representational memory (Fuster, 1989). Goldman-Rakic (1991) suggested that "at the most elementary level, our basic conceptual ability to appreciate that an object exists when out of view depends on the capacity to keep events in mind beyond the direct experience of those events" (p. 3), and this capacity entails some form of storage or rehearsal.

Using tasks from Goldman-Rakic's studies with primates, several authors have shown that schizophrenic patients and their relatives have impaired performance on visuospatial working memory tasks, and these findings have added strong support for the involvement of the prefrontal cortex in the neuropathology of schizophrenia-spectrum patients (Park & Holzman, 1992; Park, Holzman, & Goldman-Rakic, 1995). For example, Park and Holzman (1992; Park et al., 1995) applied a similar delayed-response task used by Goldman-Rakic to assess working memory deficits in schizophrenic patients. They found that schizophrenic patients exhibited impaired visuospatial working memory but not impaired auditory working memory, as assessed by digit span. Goldberg et al. (1993) found schizophrenic proband twins performed similarly to their nonaffected twin on digit span forward but exhibited poorer performance on digit span backward. They concluded that digit span backward, where numbers are held in working memory and recalled in reverse order, placed a greater cognitive load on the central executive than a pure "hold and repeat" forward span task. Most recently, Gold, Carpenter, Randolph, Goldberg, and Weinberger (1997) introduced a letter–number span task to increase the cognitive demand characteristics of simple digit span tasks. Similar to the digit span backward test, the letter–number span test requires the subject to hold information in a temporary storage but also requires the subject to sort out the numbers from the letters and to separately recall the numbers and letters in successive order. They correctly explained that digit span forward or the simple recall of a series of digits did not require the "cognitive manipulation of stored information and therefore, demanded little of the working memory system" (p. 161). When employing the letter–number span task, Gold et al. (1997) demonstrated that schizophrenic patients do exhibit auditory working memory deficits.

Goldberg, Bigelow, Weinberger, David, and Kleinman (1991) have also demonstrated that working memory performance in schizophrenic patients can be affected by the introduction of a dopamine agonist, such as dextroamphetamine. Similarly, this group demonstrated that when administering amphetamine to schizophrenic patients during the WCST, there was a task-dependent activation of the DLPFC and a significant correlation between working memory performance and neuronal activation (Goldberg et al., 1991). Fleming, Goldberg, and Gold (1994) concluded that these studies lend support to the theory that central dopaminergic activation is responsible for the frontal/working memory impairments observed in schizophrenic patients. Although a considerable number of neuropsychological findings implicate impaired frontal lobe functioning in schizophrenia, the data are not conclusive. For example, Raine et al. (1992) examined schizophrenic patients using magnetic resonance imaging (MRI) and compared their MRI results to neuropsychological tasks including a spatial delayed-response task. They found that although schizophrenic patients had smaller prefrontal areas compared to normal comparison subjects and had impaired performance on tasks of "prefrontal functioning," there was no association between task performance and structural deficits.

COGNITIVE NEUROSCIENCE

Due to the difficulties in interpreting neuroanatomical specificity in relationship to impaired performance on complex neuropsychological tasks, investigators have turned to cognitive neuroscience, linking methodologies from neuropsychology and psychophysiology. One such approach has been to study ocular motor abnormalities in schizophrenic patients. Diefendorf and Dodge (1908) first reported eye movement abnormalities in schizophrenic patients. Since that time, the study of ocular motor or eye movements has provided the opportunity for precise and yet unobtrusive measures of "a complete sub-system of action" (Henderson, Crawford & Kennard, 1996, p. 259). The predominate focus of ocular motor research has been on smooth pursuit and saccadic eye movements. The primary function of smooth pursuit eye movements is to maintain a relatively stable image of a target on the retina. Several authors have reported that approximately 50% of the first-degree relatives of schizophrenic patients have dysfunction of the smooth pursuit system and that these abnormalities correlate with other markers of schizophrenia and their symptoms (Levy, Holzman, Matthysse, & Mendell, 1993; Iacono & Clementz, 1993). Although findings of smooth pursuit abnormalities in schizophrenia have been useful in supporting a theory of frontal-mediated attentional abnormalities in schizophrenia, smooth pursuit deficits are not sensitive or specific. As summarized by Leigh and Zee (1991): "The pursuit system shows considerable intersubject variability. Pursuit is influenced by alertness and by a variety of drugs. Smooth pursuit performance declines in old age. Impaired pursuit is a nonspecific finding of many diffuse neurological disorders" (p. 166).

Recent studies suggest that saccadic measures may be more useful for understanding the neuropathology of schizophrenia. Saccades are fast eye movements and are used to redirect gaze to locations of interest. One particularly interesting task is the antisaccade paradigm. During this task, subjects begin by fixating on a central target. The central fixation light is offset simultaneously with the onset of a peripheral cue. Subjects are instructed to look at the mirror image of the cue (opposite direction, same amplitude). An initial glance in the direction of the cue constitutes an error.

DLPFC pathology is associated with a failure to inhibit reflexive glances to the cue during the antisaccade tasks. Patients with lesions of the DLPFC, but not of other cortical areas, including frontal eye fields, supplementary motor areas, and posterior parietal cortex, made significantly more antisaccade errors than did comparison subjects (Pierrot-Deseilligny, Gaymard, Müri, & Rivand, 1997). Schizophrenic patients, like frontal cortex-lesioned patients, generate a decreased proportion of correct antisaccade responses (Fukushima et al., 1990; Fukushima, Fukushima, Miyasaka, & Yamashita, 1994; McDowell & Clementz, 1997; Thacker, Nguyen, & Tamminga, 1989). The first-degree relatives of schizophrenic patients also generate an increased proportion of antisaccade errors (Clementz, McDowell, & Zisook, 1994; McDowell & Clementz, 1997), suggesting that this result is not an artifact of the numerous special circumstances accompanying a debilitating illness (e.g., medication and hospitalization). Unlike the smooth pursuit findings, proportion of correct responses on the antisaccade task appears to be relatively stable for schizophrenic patients. For example, McDowell and Clementz (1997) varied the stimulus parameters of the antisaccade task to optimize performance. To address concerns that the schizophrenic patients may not be attending to the task, they manipulated the stimulus characteristics to ensure that the schizophrenic patients understood and were engaged in the antisaccade task. As a group, schizophrenic patients and first-degree family members of the schizophrenic patients continued to remain unaffected by the manipulation of the stimulus characteristics. In contrast, other psychiatric patients and nonpatients improved their performance. Most striking was that the schizophrenic patients who did perform normally did not have a single poor-performing relative. The authors concluded that increased antisaccade error rates may index liability for schizophrenia within a subset of families. Although these findings require further investigation, antisaccade tasks are a promising means of identifying schizophrenic patients who may predominately have DLPFC pathology, and combined with linkage studies these tasks may serve as a behavioral marker for a subset of patients.

PSYCHOPHYSIOLOGY

The field of psychophysiology has led to a wealth of important findings in the field of schizophrenia research. Among the most important observations that have developed from psychophysiological studies is that schizophrenia patients are characterized by significant deficits in attention and information processing. Swerdlow and Koob (1987) suggested that the attention and information processing deficits observed in schizophrenia may result from dysfunction at any one of several levels of cortico-striato-pallido-thalamic (CSPT) circuitry. The basic theory is that because of the interconnectedness of specific neuronal pathways, disruptions at different points in the circuit can produce similar functional deficits (Cummings, & Benson, 1992). This circuitry approach has helped to consolidate the recent MRI work that has implicated structural abnormalities in schizophrenic patients in the hippocampus (Suddath et al., 1989, 1990), basal ganglia (Bogerts et al., 1985; Buchsbaum et al., 1992), and thalamic structures (Andreasen et al., 1994).

Using psychophysiological paradigms in which the anatomic substrate of the psychophysiological function is known, and linking those findings with the clinically observed symptoms of schizophrenia, has led to a paradigmatic shift from a search for a single locus to more elaborate schemas of integrated circuits distributed throughout the central nervous system (Swerdlow & Koob, 1987). McGhie and Chapman (1961) noted that schizophrenic patients were unable to "gate" or screen out irrelevant sensory stimuli. Several authors suggested that this gating deficit subjected the schizophrenic patient to sensory inundation which leads to sensory overload, cognitive fragmentation, and thought disorder (Perry & Braff, 1994; Venables, 1964). These clinical observations and theories have helped to stimulate a series of research studies examining defective sensorimotor gating in schizophrenic patients. One approach to assessing critical gating processes which has been particularly fruitful utilizes prepulse inhibition (PPI) of the human startle response as an operational measure of sensorimotor gating. Normally, a strong external stimulus, such as a sudden loud tone, bright light, or air puff elicits a series of flexion and extension responses referred to as a startle response (SR). When the startling stimulus is preceded by 30 to 500 msec by a weak prestimulus in the same or different modality, the SR is inhibited resulting in "prepulse inhibition." It has been hypothesized that when a prepulse is detected and processed, sensorimotor gating is initiated that momentarily decreases or buffers responsivity to other sensory stimulation until the processing of the prepulse has been completed (McDowd, Filion, Harris, & Braff, 1993). In humans, the blink reflex component of the SR is measured using electromyography. The SR is controlled by a simple four-neuron circuit linking the auditory nerve to the spinal motor neuron. However, it is the forebrain-mediated plasticity (e.g., gating) of the SR that makes it a particularly useful behavior for these studies, because a variety of pharmacological, neuroanatomic, and psychopathological factors can modify the gating of the SR. Braff et al. (1978) first reported that schizophrenic patients exhibit a deficit in PPI, experimentally confirming the hypothesized deficit in sensorimotor gating that was clinically observed. This initial finding has been replicated many times and has been extended to hypothetically phenotypically related groups, such as patients with schizotypal personality disorder (Cadenhead, Geyer, & Braff, 1993).

A diminution of PPI, similar to that observed in schizophrenic patients, occurs in laboratory animals in which the functional status of the CSPT circuitry has been altered experimentally in areas that have direct relevance for understanding the neurobiology of schizophrenia, such as the frontal lobes, hippocampus, and nucleus accumbens (Swerdlow, Caine, Braff, & Geyer, 1992). For example, in rats, Geyer, Swerdlow, and their colleagues (Geyer, Swerdlow, Mansbach, & Braff, 1990; Swerdlow, Braff, Geyer, & Koob,

1986; Swerdlow et al., 1992) have demonstrated that activation of D2 dopamine (DA) function in the limbic forebrain produces deficits in PPI that may model those in schizophrenia spectrum patients. Similar PPI deficits follow specific manipulations of medial prefrontal cortex, ventral hippocampus, ventral pallidum, and pontine tegmentum (see Swerdlow & Geyer, in press). Manipulations of CSPT circuitry in animals have been a useful means of understanding the neurobiological substrates of information processing dysfunction in the group of schizophrenic disorders.

Using the PPI paradigm, a number of important correlations between gating deficits and clinical variables pertaining to frontal lobe functioning have been found. For example, it was confirmed that schizophrenic patients with the least PPI show maximal perseverative responses on the WCST (Butler, Jenkins, Geyer, & Braff, 1992). Weinberger (1993) proposed that in schizophrenia, loss of frontally mediated regulation of mesolimbic dopaminergic cells establishes conditions leading to upregulation of mesolimbic dopamine receptors, and consequent overstimulation of these receptors results in mesolimbic hyperdopaminergia. The animal work in PPI supports this hypothesis because mesolimbic hyperdopaminergia disrupts PPI in animals (Braff & Geyer, 1990; Swerdlow et al., 1986; Swerdlow et al., 1992) and patients most deficient in PPI demonstrate maximal perseverative responses on the WCST (Butler et al., 1992). Similarly, Karper et al. (1996) reported that distractibility and impaired vigilance, hypothesized to be frontally mediated cognitive processes, are correlated with reduced sensorimotor gating in schizophrenia. Perry and Braff (1994) demonstrated that schizophrenic patients with the most deficient PPI show the highest rates of thought disturbance when presented with complex, cognitive challenge paradigms. In a follow-up experiment, they demonstrated that this correlation is extremely robust, particularly when measured in a simultaneous paradigm in which the patient is exposed to complex visual stimuli during the assessment of PPI. They found extremely high correlations ($r = .76$) between thought disturbance and PPI. Their findings suggest that there may be a direct relationship between sensorimotor gating failures and thought disturbance, the hallmark characteristic of schizophrenia spectrum disease. These findings are among a growing literature that relates deficits in sensorimotor gating to cognitive deficits in schizophrenia such as perseveration and thought disturbance and clinical features such as age of onset of illness that have been associated with frontal and temporal lobe dysfunction.

CONCLUSION

The aim of this chapter was to briefly review the role of impaired frontal lobe functioning in schizophrenia. Findings from neuropsychology, cognitive neuroscience and psychophysiology have provided a substantive contribution toward understanding the neuropathology of schizophrenia. Many unanswered questions regarding the extent or density of frontal impairment in schizophrenia remain and will be the focus of advances in brain imaging and cognitive neurosciences.

ACKNOWLEDGMENT

This work was supported in part by Grant No. NIMH 42228 from the National Institute of Mental Health and by the Hess Foundation. We thank Joyce Sprock for her assistance in the preparation of the chapter.

REFERENCES

Andreasen, N. C., Arndt, S., Swayze, V., Cizadlo, T., Flaum, M., O'Leary, D., Earhardt, J. C., & Yuh, W. T. C. (1994). Thalamic abnormalities in schizophrenia visualized through magnetic reasonance imaging averaging. *Science, 266,* 294–298.

Baddeley, A. (1986). *Working memory.* Oxford, England: Claredon Press.

Baddeley, A. (1992). Working memory. *Science, 225,* 556–559.

Baddeley, A., & Hitch, G. (1974). Working memory. In G. A. Bower (Ed.), *Psychology of learning and motivation* (Vol. 8, pp. 47–89). New York: Academic Press.

Baddeley, A., & Wilson, B. A. (1988). Frontal amnesia and the dysexecutive syndrome. *Brain and Cognition, 7,* 212–224.

Bellack, A. S., Mueser, K. T., Morrison, R. L., Tierney, A., & Podell, K. (1990). Remediation of cognitive deficits in schizophrenia. *American Journal of Psychiatry, 147,* 1650–1655.

Berman, K. F., Zec, R. F., & Weinberger, D. R. (1986). Physiologic dysfunction of dorsolateral prefrontal cortex in schizophrenia: Role of neuroleptic treatment, attention and mental effort. *Archives of General Psychiatry, 45,* 814–821.

Bird, M., & Luszcz, M. (1991). Encoding specificity, depth of processing, and cued recall in Alzheimer's disease. *Journal of Clinical and Experimental Neuropsychology, 13,* 508–520.

Bogerts, B., Mertz, E., Schonfeldt, M., & Bausch, R. (1985). Basal ganglia and limbic system pathology in schizophrenia: A morphometric study of brain volume and shrinkage. *Archives of General Psychiatry, 42,* 784–791.

Braff, D. L., & Geyer, M. A. (1990). Sensorimotor gating and schizophrenia: Human and animal model studies. *Archives of General Psychiatry, 47,* 181–188.

Braff, D. L., Heaton, R., Kuck, J., Cullum, M., Moranville, J., Grant, I., & Zisook, S. (1991). The generalized pattern of neuropsychological deficits in outpatients with chronic schizophrenia with heterogeneous Wisconsin Card Sorting Test results. *Archives of General Psychiatry, 48,* 891–898.

Braff, D. L., Stone, C., Callaway, E., Geyer, M. A., Glick, I. D., & Bali, L. (1978). Prestimulus effects on human startle reflex in normals and schizophrenics. *Psychophysiology, 14,* 339–343.

Buchanan, R. W., Breier, A., Kirkpatrick B., Elkashef, A., Munson, R. C., Gellad, F., & Carpenter, W. T., (1993). Structural abnormalities in deficit and nondeficit schizophrenia. *American Journal of Psychiatry, 150,* 59–65.

Buchsbaum, M. S., Haier, R. J., Potkin, S. G., Nuechterlein, K., Bracha, H. S., Katz, M., Lohr, J., Wu, J., Lottenberg, S., Jerabeck, P. A., Trenary, M., Tafalla, R., Reynolds, C., & Bunney, W. E. (1992). Frontostriatal disorder of cerebral metabolism in never-medicated schizophrenics. *Archives of General Psychiatry, 49,* 935–942.

Butler, R. W., Jenkins, M. A., Geyer, M. A., & Braff, D. L. (1991). Wisconsin Card Sorting deficits and diminished sensorimotor gating in a discrete subgroup of schizophrenic patients. In C. A. Taminga & S. C. Schultz (Eds.), *Advances in neuropsychiatry and psychopharmacology: Vol. 1. Schizophrenia* (pp. 163–168). New York: Raven Press.

Cadenhead, K. S., Geyer, M. A., & Braff, D. L. (1993). Impaired startle prepulse inhibition and habituation in schizotypal personality disordered patients. *American Journal of Psychiatry, 150,* 1862–1867.

Clementz, B. A., McDowell, J. E., & Zisook, S. (1994). Saccadic system functioning among schizophrenia patients and their first-degree biological relatives. *Journal of Abnormal Psychology, 103,* 277–287.

Cummings, J. L., & Benson, F. D. (1992). *Dementia: A clinical approach* (2nd ed.). Boston: Butterworth-Heinmann.

Diefendorf, A. R., & Dodge, R. (1908). An experimental study of the ocular reactions of the insane from photographic records. *Brain, 31,* 343–489.

Eslinger, P. J., & Damasio, A. R. (1986). Preserved motor learning in Alzheimer's disease: Implications from anatomy and behavior. *Journal of Neuroscience, 6,* 3006–3009.

Fey, E. T. (1951). The performance of young schizophrenics and young normals on the Wisconsin Card Sorting Test. *Consulting Psychology, 15,* 311–319.

Fleming, K., Goldberg, T. E., & Gold, J. M. (1994). Applying working memory constructs to schizophrenic cognitive impairment. In A. S. David & J. C. Cutting (Eds.), *The neuropsychology of schizophrenia* (pp. 197–213). Hillsdale, NJ: Erlbaum.

Frith, C. D. (1992). *The cognitive neuropsychology of schizophrenia.* Hillsdale, NJ: Erlbaum.

Fukushima, J., Fukushima, K., Miyasaka, K., & Yamashita, I. (1994). Voluntary control of saccadic eye movement in patients with frontal cortical lesions and parkinsonian patients in comparison with that in schizophrenics. *Biological Psychiatry, 36,* 21–30.

Fukushima, J., Morita, N., Fukushima K., Chiba, T., Tanaka, S., & Yamashita, I. (1990). Voluntary control of saccadic eye movement in patients with schizophrenia and affective disorders. *Journal of Psychiatric Research, 24,* 9–24.

Funuhashi, S., Bruce, C. J., & Goldman-Rakic, P. S. (1989). Mnemonic coding of visual cortex in monkey's dorsolateral prefrontal cortex. *Journal of Neurophysiology, 61,* 331–348.

Funuhashi, S., Bruce, C. J., & Goldman-Rakic, P. S. (1993). Dorsolateral prefrontal lesions and oculomotor delayed response performance: Evidence for mnemonic "scotomas." *Journal of Neuroscience, 13,* 1479–1497.

Fuster, J. M. (1989). *The prefrontal cortex.* New York: Raven Press.

Geyer, M. A., Swerdlow, N. R., Mansbach, R. S., & Braff, D. L. (1990). Startle response models of sensorimotor gating and habituation deficits in schizophrenia. *Brain Research Bulletin, 25,* 485–498.

Gianutsos, R. (1981). Training the short and long-term verbal recall of a postencephalalitic amnesic. *Journal of Clinical Neuropsychology, 3,* 143–153.

Gold, J. M., Carpenter, C., Randolph, C., Goldberg, T. E., & Weinberger, D. R. (1997). Auditory working memory and Wisconsin Card Sorting Test performance in schizophrenia. *Archives of General Psychiatry, 54,* 159–165.

Goldberg, T. E., Bigelow, L. B., Weinberger, D. R., Daniel, D. G., & Kleinman, J. E. (1991). Cognitive and behavioral effects of coadministration of dextroamphetamine and haloperidol in schizophrenia. *American Journal of Psychiatry, 148,* 78–84.

Goldberg, T. E., Torrey, E. F., Gold, J. M., Ragland, J. D., Bigelow, L. B., & Weinberger, D. R. (1993). Learning and memory in monozygotic twins discordant for schizophrenia. *Psychological Medicine, 23,* 71–85.

Goldberg, T. E., & Weinberger, D. R. (1994). Schizophrenia training paradigms, and the Wisconsin Card Sorting Test redux. *Schizophrenia Research, 11,* 291–296.

Goldberg, T. E., Weinberger, D. R., Berman, K. F., Pliskin, N. H., & Podd, M. H. (1987). Further evidence for dementia of the prefrontal type in schizophrenia. *Archives of General Psychiatry, 44,* 1008–1014.

Goldman, R. S. (1994). Approaches to cognitive training in schizophrenia. *Advances in Medical Psychotherapy, 7,* 95–108.

Goldman-Rakic, P. S. (1987). Circuitry of primate prefrontal cortex and regulation of behavior by representational knowledge. In F. Plum & V. Mountcastle (Eds.), *Handbook of physiology: The nervous system* (Vol. 5, pp. 373–417). Bethesda, MD: American Physiological Society.

Goldman-Rakic, P. S. (1991). Prefrontal cortical dysfunction in schizophrenia: The relevance of working memory. In B. Carroll & J. E. Barrett (Eds.), *Psychopathology and the brain* (pp. 1–23). New York: Raven Press.

Green, M. F., Ganzell, S., Satz, P., & Vaclav, J. (1990). Teaching the Wisconsin Card Sorting Test to schizophrenic patients [letter to the editor]. *Archives of General Psychiatry, 47,* 91–92.

Heaton, R. K. (1981). *A manual for the Wisconsin Card Sort Test.* Odessa, FL: Psychological Assessment Resources.

Henderson, L., Crawford, T. J., & Kenard, C. (1996). The neuropsychology of eye movement abnormalities in schizophrenia. In C. Pantelis, H. E. Nelson, & T. R. E. Barnes (Eds.), *Schizophrenia, a neuropsychological perspective* (pp. 259–277). West Sussex, UK: Wiley.

Iacono, W. G., & Clementz, B. A. (1993). A strategy for elucidating genetic influences on complex psychopathological syndromes. In L. J. Chapman, J. P. Chapman, & D.C. Fowles (Eds.), *Progress in experimental personality and psychopathology research* (pp. 9–24). New York: Springer.

Jernigan, T. L., Zisook, S., Heaton, R. K., Moranville, J. T., Hesselink, J. R., & Braff, D. L. (1991). Magnetic reasonance imaging abnormalities in lenticular nuclei and cerebral cortex in schizophrenia. *Archives of General Psychiatry, 48,* 881–890.

Johnstone, E. C., Crow, T. J., Frith, C. D., Husband, J., & Kreel, L. (1976). Cerebral ventricular size and cognitive impairment in chronic schizophrenia. *Lancet, II,* 924–926.

Karper, L. P., Freeman, G. K., Grillon, C., Morgan, C. A., Charney, D. S., & Krystal, J. H. (1996). Preliminary evidence of an association between sensorimotor gating and distractability in psychosis. *Journal of Neuropsychiatry and Clinical Neurosciences, 8,* 60–66.

Kolb, B., & Whishaw, I. Q. (1983). Performance of schizophrenic patients on tests sensitive to left or right frontal, temporal, or parietal function in neurological patients. *Journal of Nervous and Mental Disease, 171,* 435–443.

Lawrie, S. M., Abukmeil, S. S., Chiswick, A., Egan, V., Santosh, C. G., & Best, J. J. K. (1997). Qualitative cerebral morphology in schizophrenia: A magnetic resonance imaging study and systematic literature review. *Schizophrenia Research, 25,* 155–166.

Leigh, R. J., & Zee, D. S. (1991). *The neurology of eye movements* (2nd ed.) Philadelphia: F.A. Davis.

Levy, D. L., Holzman, P. S., Matthysse, S., & Mendell, N. R. (1993). Eye tracking dysfunction in schizophrenia: A critical perspective. *Schizophrenia Bulletin, 19,* 461–536.

Lezak, M. (1995). *Neuropsychological assessment* (3rd ed.). New York: Oxford University Press.

Liddle, P. F., & Morris, D. L. (1991). Schizophrenic syndromes and frontal lobe performance. *British Journal of Psychiatry, 158,* 340–345.

McDowd, J. M., Filion, D. L., Harris, J., & Braff, D. L. (1993). Sensory gating and inhibitory function in late life schizophrenia. *Schizophrenia Bulletin, 19,* 733–746.

McDowell, J. E., & Clementz, B. A. (1997). The effect of fixation condition manipulations on antisaccade performance in schizophrenia: Studies of diagnostic specificity. *Experimental Brain Research, 115,* 333–344.

McGhie, A., & Chapman, J. (1961). Disorders of attention and perception in early schizophrenia. *British Journal of Medical Psychology, 34,* 103–116.

Milner, B. (1963). Effect of different brain lesions in card sorting: The role of the frontal lobes. *Archives of Neurology, 9,* 100–110.

Norman, D. A., & Shallice, T. (1986). Attention to action: Willed and automatic control of behavior. In R. J. Davidson, G. E. Schwarts, & D. Shapiro (Eds.), *Consciousness and self-regulation: Advances in research and theory* (pp. 1–18). New York: Plenum.

Palmer, B. W., Heaton, R. K., Paulsen, J. S., Kuck, J. K., Braff, D. L., Harris, J. M., Zisook, S., & Jeste, D. V. (1997). Is it possible to be schizophrenic yet neuropsychologically normal? *Neuropsychology, 11*(3), 437–446.

Pantelis, C., & Nelson, H. E. (1994). Cognitive functioning and symptomatology in schizophrenia: The role of frontal–subcortical systems. In A. David & J. C. Cutting (Eds.), *The neuropsychology of schizophrenia* (pp. 215–229). Hove, UK: LEA Press.

Park, S., & Holzman, P. S. (1992). Schizophrenics show spatial working memory deficits. *Archives of General Psychiatry, 49,* 975–982.

Park, S., Holzman, P. S., & Goldman-Rakic, P. S. (1995). Spatial working memory deficits in the relatives of schizophrenic patients. *Archives of General Psychiatry, 52,* 821–828.

Perry, W., & Braff, D. L. (1994). Information-processing deficits and thought disorder in schizophrenia. *American Journal of Psychiatry, 151,* 363–367.

Pierrot-Deseilligny, C., Gaymard, B., Muri, R., & Rivaud, S. (1997). Cerebral ocular motor signs. *Journal of Neurology, 244,* 65–70.

Potterat, E., Perry, W., & Braff, D. L. (1997). Measuring the density of executive functioning impairment in schizophrenia patients. *Biological Psychiatry, 41,* 86S.

Raine, A., Lencz, T., Reynolds, G. P., Harrison, G., Sheard, C., Medley, I., Reynolds, L. M., & Cooper, J. E. (1992). An evaluation of structural and functional prefrontal deficits in schizophrenia: MRI and neuropsychological measures. *Psychiatry Research, 45,* 123–137.

Suddath, R. L., Casanova, M. F., Goldberg, T. E., Daniel, G., Kelsoe, J. R., & Weinberger, D. R. (1989). Temporal lobe pathology in schizophrenia: A quantitative magnetic resonance imaging study. *American Journal of Psychiatry, 146,* 464–472.

Suddath, R. L., Christison, G. W., Torrey, E. F., Casanova, M. F., & Weinberger, D. R. (1990). Anatomical abnormalities in the brains of monozygotic twins discordant for schizophrenia. *New England Journal of Medicine, 322,* 789–794.

Swerdlow, N. R., Braff, D. L., Geyer, M. A., & Koob, G. F. (1986). Central dopamine hyperactivity in rats mimics abnormal acoustic startle response in schizophrenics. *Biological Psychiatry, 21,* 23–33.

Swerdlow, N. R., Caine, S. B., Braff, D. L., & Geyer, M. A. (1992). The neural substrates of sensorimotor gating of the startle reflex: A review of recent findings and their implications. *Journal of Psychopharmacology, 6*(2), 176–190.

Swerdlow, N. R., & Geyer, M. A. (in press). Neurophysiology and neuropharmacology of short lead interval startle modification. In M. E. Dawson, A. Schell, & A. Boehmelt (Eds.), *Startle modification: Implications for neuroscience, cognitive science, and clinical science.* Cambridge, MA: Cambridge University Press.

Swerdlow, N. R., & Koob, G. F. (1987). Dopamine, schizophrenia, mania, and depression: Toward a unified hypothesis of cortico-stratio-pallido-thalamic function. *Behavioural and Brain Sciences, 10,* 197–245.

Thacker, G. K., Nguyen, J. A., & Tamminga, C. A. (1989). Increased saccadic distractibility in tardive dyskinesia: Functional evidence for subcortical GABA function. *Biological Psychiatry, 25,* 49–59.

Van der Does, A. W., & Van der Bosch, R. J. (1992). What determines Wisconsin Card Sorting Test performance in schizophrenia? *Clinical Psychology Review, 12,* 567–583.

Venables, P. H. (1964). Input dysfunction in schizophrenia. In B. A. Maher (Ed.), *Progress in experimental personality research* (Vol. 1, pp. 1–47). New York: Academic Press.

Weinberger, D. R. (1993). A connectionist approach to the prefrontal cortex. *Journal of Neuropsychiatry and Clinical Neurosciences, 5,* 241–253.

Weinberger, D. R., Berman, K. F., & Illowsky, B. P. (1988). Physiological dysfunction of dorsolateral prefrontal cortex in schizophrenia: III. A new cohort and evidence for a monoaminergic mechanism. *Archives of General Psychiatry, 45,* 609–615.

Weinberger, D. R., Berman, K. F., & Zec, R. F. (1986). Physiologic dysfunction of dorsolateral prefrontal cortex in schizophrenia: I. Regional cerebral blood flow evidence. *Archives of General Psychiatry, 4,* 114–124.

Wilson, F. A, Scalaidhe, S. P., & Goldman-Rakic, P. S. (1993). Dissociation of object and spatial processing domains in primate prefrontal cortex. *Science, 260,* 1955–1958.

29

Obsessive–Compulsive Disorder and the Frontal Lobes

ROBERT T. RUBIN
GORDON J. HARRIS

Psychiatric disorders are considered "functional" when there is no clearly understood central nervous system (CNS) pathophysiology underlying them. Thus, schizophrenia, the major affective illnesses, and anxiety disorders have been and are still considered functional psychiatric illnesses. This is a dynamic nomenclature, however—as our knowledge about the pathophysiology of the brain in these disorders increases, the adjective "functional" conveys less and less meaning. The brain substrates of the major psychiatric disorders are being examined in several ways. Complex genetic underpinnings are slowly being defined. Structural and functional imaging studies of the brain are providing some anatomical localization, limited by the resolution of the imaging techniques and the particular methodology of each study. Specific classes of drugs are known to be therapeutic for specific disorders, but the homeostatic balance among CNS neurotransmitter systems clouds inferences that can be made from the pharmacological perturbation of a single neurotransmitter system, and no drug is curative of any psychiatric disorder.

Obsessive–compulsive disorder (OCD) is one of the functional psychiatric illnesses that is giving way to an understanding of its CNS pathophysiology. This chapter summarizes what we know and theorize about the role of the frontal lobes in OCD.

CLINICAL CHARACTERISTICS OF OCD

Contemporary psychiatric diagnostics classifies OCD among the anxiety disorders (American Psychiatric Association, 1994). The hallmarks of OCD are recurrent obsessions and/or compulsions severe enough to be time-consuming (more than 1 hour per day) or to interfere with occupational or social functioning. At some point the individual must recognize that these symptoms are excessive or unreasonable (this does not apply to children), and, if another major psychiatric disorder is present, the content of the obsessions or compulsions must be unrelated to it. Finally, the OCD must not be a direct result of a drug or an underlying medical condition (American Psychiatric Association, 1994; Jenike, 1995).

Obsessions are recurrent and persistent thoughts, impulses, or mental images that are experienced as intrusive and inappropriate, that cause marked anxiety and distress, and that are not simply excessive worries about real-life problems. The individual recognizes that the mental intrusions are a product of his or her own mind (which distinguishes them from psychotic symptoms such as thought insertion) and attempts to neutralize them with other thoughts or actions (e.g., compulsive rituals). The content of obsessions is most often violent (e.g., murder of one's child), sexual, contaminative (e.g., touching unclean objects), or doubting (e.g., worrying repeatedly about having performed a particular act).

Compulsions are repetitive behaviors or mental acts engaged in to reduce anxiety or distress. Common compulsive behaviors are hand washing, ordering of objects, and repetitive checking (e.g., a locked door); common mental acts are repetitive counting, praying, and saying words silently. The frequency and severity of the obsessions and compulsions indicated previously as necessary for a diagnosis are a lower bound for these activities; not infrequently, many hours each day are spent in the throes of OCD, and compulsions may be physically damaging (e.g., washing one's hands until the skin is raw). As mentioned, the individual knows these are alien thoughts and behaviors, is distressed by them, but is powerless to moderate them.

Recent studies suggest different OCD symptom profiles across subjects. For example, factor analysis of Yale–Brown Obsessive–Compulsive Scale (Goodman, Price, Rasmussen, Mazure, Delgado, et al., 1989; Goodman, Price, Rasmussen, Mazure, Fleischmann, et al., 1989) item scores in more than 300 OCD patients yielded four orthogonal factors accounting for more than 60% of the total variance: obsessions and checking, symmetry and order, cleaning and washing, and hoarding (Leckman et al., 1997).

The lifetime prevalence of OCD is 2–3% (Karno, Golding, Sorenson, & Burnam, 1988); thus, it is not rare. OCD occurs equally in men and women and usually begins in early adulthood, although childhood OCD is not uncommon. It may co-occur with other psychiatric illnesses such as major depression, other anxiety disorders, and eating disorders. Of note is the high incidence of OCD (30–50%) in patients with Gilles de la Tourette syndrome, which consists of severe tics and involuntary utterances, occasionally vulgar in nature. Tourette syndrome is quite rare, but approximately 5% of OCD patients may have some form of it, and 20–30% of OCD patients have a history of tics (American Psychiatric Association, 1994). There is a higher concordance of OCD in monozygotic than in dizygotic twins, and there is a higher incidence of OCD in first-degree relatives of both OCD and Tourette syndrome patients than in the general population.

BIOLOGICAL CHARACTERISTICS OF OCD

At present, there are no laboratory findings diagnostic of OCD. An interesting pharmacological finding is that OCD responds best to serotonin uptake inhibitors (SUIs; e.g., clomipramine, fluoxetine, paroxetine, sertraline, and fluvoxamine), which block the serotonin transporter and increase synaptic serotonin concentrations. This implies that reduced serotonergic neurotransmission may underlie OCD (Barr, Goodman, Price, McDougle, & Charney, 1992; Benkert, Wetzel, & Szegedi, 1993; Murphy et al., 1989;

Winslow & Insel, 1990; Zohar & Kindler, 1992), but clear evidence, by measurement of serotonin or its metabolites, transport mechanisms, or receptors, has not been forthcoming. Symptom amelioration by SUIs is not complete (about 35% on average), and only about 50% of patients respond, suggesting that more than one neurotransmitter system may be involved (Goodman, McDougle, & Price, 1992). The addition of dopamine receptor-blocking antipsychotic drugs (e.g., haloperidol) can be effective when there is a comorbid tic disorder, but they are of no additional help in uncomplicated OCD. Other drugs shown to be useful in selected cases are lithium and fenfluramine as adjuncts to SUIs (Goodman et al., 1992). Interestingly, dextroamphetamine, a dopamine- and norepinephrine-potentiating drug, can ameliorate OCD symptoms in some patients (Insel, Hamilton, Guttmacher, & Murphy, 1983; Joffe, Swinson, & Levitt, 1991).

The serotonergic agonist mCPP has been shown to acutely worsen OCD symptoms (Hollander et al., 1992), suggesting that there may be hypersensitivity of serotonergic receptors in OCD and that serotonin uptake-inhibiting drugs may in fact work by producing downregulation of these receptors, making them less sensitive to serotonin. At variance with this hypothesis is the aforementioned observation that fenfluramine, also a serotonergic agonist, may potentiate the therapeutic efficacy of SUIs in some patients. One could postulate differential effects of these serotonin-influencing drugs on the several identified subtypes of serotonin receptors, but this would be speculative at present.

Another dimension of OCD that supports a substrate of CNS pathophysiology is the presence of OCD-like disorders in other mammalian species, including subhuman primates, dogs, cats, horses, pigs, cows, sheep, bears, and parrots (Dodman & Olivier, 1996; Dodman, Moon-Fanelli, Mertens, Pflueger, & Stein, 1997). Compulsive behaviors in these species include repetitive grooming to the point of excoriation; hair and feather pulling; tail chasing, pacing, whirling, bouncing, and somersaulting; sucking, bar biting, and lip flapping; compulsive sexual behaviors; aggression; checking; and marking. Some equine and canine compulsive behaviors are familial and breed specific, providing support for genetic factors in these conditions.

It cannot be determined in which of these behaviors animals engage to reduce anxiety or distress versus which are distressing to the animal but the animal is powerless to control, the latter being a necessary criterion for the diagnosis of OCD in humans, as indicated earlier. Some behaviors, such as pacing, whirling, and compulsive sexual activity, may be engaged in because a captive animal is deprived of necessary physical exercise and environmental stimulation, and these behaviors provide some degree of pleasure and relief from boredom. Nevertheless, some compulsive behaviors are pathological, such as acral lick in dogs, resulting in dermatitis, and avian compulsive feather picking. Of interest, several of these animal behaviors have been treated successfully with SUIs, as well as with dopamine-blocking drugs, and, in some instances, opioid antagonists.

The pharmacology of drugs useful in treating OCD points to which brain areas might be involved. Both the frontal cortex, which has prominent serotonergic afferents from the brainstem raphe nuclei, and the basal ganglia, which receive dopaminergic afferents from the substantia nigra, have been implicated in OCD pathophysiology, as discussed next. However, it must be noted that psychological treatments such as behavior therapy also can have a significant therapeutic result, and similar changes in brain glucose metabolism in OCD with behavior therapy as with pharmacotherapy have been demonstrated (Baxter et al., 1992). Whether psychological therapy induces changes in neurotransmitter activity similar to those induced by pharmacotherapy is as yet unknown. In some instances of severe, incapacitating OCD that were unresponsive to all other treatments, stereotaxic cingulotomy has been partially effective.

FRONTAL LOBE THEORIES OF OCD

As discussed in other chapters in this volume and elsewhere (Cummings, 1995), different frontal cortical–subcortical circuits subserve different aspects of cognition and behavior. Most of the information about these specific circuits comes from lesion studies in animals and neuropathological events in humans, the location of which in patients can be correlated with their neuropsychiatric deficits (Grafman, Holyoak, & Boller, 1995). In a general sense, the frontal lobes mediate, inter alia, executive functions (Goldman-Rakic, 1995)—decision making and behavioral actions based on detailed evaluation of environmental demands, coupled with an appreciation of their historical context and a coordinated affective–emotional component.

Neuropsychological tests can tap some of the components of frontal executive function, but it is difficult to extrapolate from impaired performance on a specific test to involvement of a particular area or function of the frontal lobes in OCD. Candidate areas in OCD include the dorsolateral prefrontal cortex, which mediates executive behavior; the orbitofrontal cortex, which mediates social behavior; and the mediofrontal cortex, which mediates motivation. Each of these areas projects to specific subcortical areas, and both the cortical and subcortical components of the circuit receive afferents from a number of other structures. As summarized by Cummings (1995), the dorsolateral prefrontal circuit includes the dorsal caudate, subthalamic nucleus, and ventral anterior and mediodorsal nuclei of the thalamus; the orbitofrontal circuit includes the ventral caudate, medial globus pallidus/substantia nigra, and ventral anterior and mediodorsal nuclei of the thalamus; and the mediofrontal circuit includes the anterior cingulate, nucleus accumbens, ventral globus pallidus/substantia nigra, and mediodorsal nucleus of the thalamus.

Frontal lobe theories of OCD all represent variations on the postulated involvement of the orbitofrontal and dorsolateral prefrontal cortices and their functional connections with the basal ganglia, thalamus, and other structures, including the hippocampus and amygdala. There also are connections from these structures back to the cortex itself. The underlying theme of the theories is that the orbitofrontal cortex is a generator of afferent impulses to the caudate nucleus, and the caudate in turn serves as a filter or gating area, normally passing to other structures only that activity from the orbitofrontal cortex that produces an emotionally and behaviorally coordinated response. In OCD, this circuit is putatively imbalanced. Baxter et al. (1987) and Baxter (1990) considered that the striatum normally suppresses adventitious thoughts, sensations, and actions, with little need for cortical control. These investigators hypothesized a primary defect in striatal function in OCD, which leads to an increased requirement for cortical participation in the suppression and affective neutralization of intrusive neuronal activity. Modell, Mountz, Curtis, and Greden (1989) viewed overactivity of the orbitofrontal–thalamic circuit as the cause of compulsions in OCD, as they represent unmodulated behavioral drive, and decreased basal ganglia–limbic striatum activity as the cause of the loss-of-control component. The functional result is that the caudate nucleus cannot reasonably filter all the afferent impulses from frontal cortical areas; some inappropriate or otherwise innocuous stimuli therefore are passed to other structures, where they acquire excessive emotional meaning that results in inappropriate thoughts and actions.

EEG studies of OCD subjects undergoing cognitive testing also support involvement of the frontal lobes. Compared to controls, OCD patients have a smaller P300 magnitude on visual evoked potential testing during a go/no-go task (Malloy, Rasmussen, Braden, & Haier, 1989) and greater power in several frontal EEG frequency ranges during rejection versus intake tasks (McCarthy, Ray, & Foa, 1995). Prichep et al. (1993) discerned one subtype of OCD patients who had increased relative power in theta in the frontal and frontotemporal areas and another subtype with increased relative power in alpha in the same areas. Eighty percent of the first group responded to drug treatment, whereas only 18% of the second group were treatment responders. Thus, there may be differential frontal lobe involvement among OCD patients.

As detailed later, a number of functional neuroimaging studies suggest increased blood flow and metabolic overactivity of the orbitofrontal cortex in OCD. Imaging studies of the caudate nucleus, on the other hand, are less consistent in their findings. Thus, it is not possible at present to determine from imaging studies where in the cortical/basal ganglia/thalamic/cortical circuit the primary defect resides. Structural lesions (e.g., infarcts and tumors) of both the frontal cortex and the basal ganglia have been associated with obsessions and stereotyped behaviors resembling compulsions (Swoboda & Jenike, 1995). And, as mentioned previously, pharmacological treatments of OCD do not particularly clarify the matter, as alteration of cortical serotonergic systems with SUIs often results in only partial amelioration of symptoms, and dopaminergic drugs, which act inter alia on striatal dopamine systems, have some role in the management of OCD symptoms, especially when there is comorbid tic disorder. Thus, at present, the broad frontal cortex/basal ganglia/thalamus/frontal cortex theories presented previously are "state of the art" in terms of available data to support them.

NEUROPSYCHOLOGICAL STUDIES SUPPORTING FRONTAL LOBE INVOLVEMENT IN OCD

Otto (1992), summarizing the neuropsychological studies of OCD, divided them into two groups: those that support dysfunction in the aforementioned cortical/basal ganglia/thalamic/cortical circuit and those that indicate visuospatial performance and memory deficits but no frontal cortical impairment. Within the first group (Behar et al., 1984; Flor-Henry, Yeudall, Koles, & Howarth, 1979; Head, Bolton, & Hymas, 1989; Insel, Donnelly, Lalakea, Alterman, & Murphy, 1983; Malloy, 1987), the most consistent frontal lobe finding has been a relative inability of OCD subjects to shift task set compared to normal controls. Malloy (1987) also found those patients who were unable to shift task set on the Wisconsin Card Sorting Test to be less intelligent, lower functioning in daily life, and more psychotic than those who did not demonstrate frontal impairment. In the three studies in which memory was tested, no impairment was noted.

In contrast, in the second group of studies (Boone, Ananth, Philpott, Kaur, & Djenderedjian, 1991; Otto, 1992; Zielinski, Taylor, & Juzwin, 1991), adequate frontal lobe abilities, as well as intellectual and attentional abilities, were found, but there was a consistent deficit in visuospatial memory. Similar memory deficits have been reported in several studies of subjects with checking behaviors but not OCD per se (Otto, 1992).

Reconciliation of these neuropsychological studies is difficult. As noted previously, several studies have pointed toward the heterogeneity of OCD, both in symptom clusters and in biological correlates. In future investigations, multidimensional clinical characterization of OCD cohorts by both *Diagnostic and Statistical Manual of Mental Disorders*

(DSM) and OCD rating scale criteria should help resolve some of the neuropsychological test discrepancies. As with all multivariate studies, sample sizes must be large enough to achieve adequate power of statistical testing and stability of the analysis—studies in which no apparent relationship between symptom subtype and neuropsychological test results was noted have been hampered by relatively small samples (Otto, 1992). Greater attention to the presence of comorbid psychiatric disorder (e.g., major depression) also is needed, because attention, concentration, memory, and the like can be affected by such comorbidity and confound the neuropsychological testing.

The available data indicating deficits in ability to shift task set in OCD are consistent with theories of disrupted response feedback, requiring repeated compulsive acts to determine their adequacy (Otto, 1992). An inherent need for high accuracy in a given individual may aggravate the tendency to lose response feedback, setting up the repetitive behavioral pattern. This theoretical neuropsychological framework can be accommodated within the neuropathological framework of a dysfunction of frontal cortex/basal ganglia/thalamus/frontal cortex circuitry, but only in a general way, because none of the neuropsychological tests used to assess frontal lobe function are highly specific to a given frontal cortical region, and disruptions in caudate function can mimic frontal lobe dysfunction (Otto, 1992). Thus, it is not surprising that neuropsychological studies of OCD to date have not yielded fully concordant findings.

Another issue to be considered is which comes first, neuropsychological deficits or changes in frontal cortical/basal ganglia metabolic activity. Altered metabolic activity may result in the behavioral and neuropsychological test results indicated previously, but it also may be true that the anxiety and need for absolute mastery occasioned by the illness itself underlies the increased cerebral metabolic activity noted on EEG and functional neuroimaging studies. Otto (1992) presented a clear conceptual model for the development of OCD from intrusive thoughts, the two main stages being conditioned or evoked anxiety to the intrusive thought and reinforcement of compulsive behavior aimed at affectively neutralizing the thought. From a neuropsychological standpoint, theoretical models such as this are internally coherent and intuitively appealing, but mapping them onto a putatively dysfunctional neuroanatomical circuit is a more difficult task. And, temporally determining the interaction of the two, especially how they began, represents yet another level of intricacy and demand to be achieved, one hopes, in future studies.

NEUROIMAGING STUDIES SUPPORTING FRONTAL LOBE INVOLVEMENT IN OCD

With the advent of neuroimaging techniques, it now is possible to probe the structure and function of the living human brain. Brain structure can be viewed with X-ray computed tomography (CT) and magnetic resonance imaging (MRI). Nuclear medicine techniques such as single photon and positron emission computed tomography (SPECT and PET) allow the visualization and quantitation of regional cerebral blood flow, glucose metabolic rate, and neurotransmitter receptor occupancy, which are indirect probes of regional neuronal function. SPECT and PET use radiolabeled compounds as tracers; as these compounds decay, high-energy photons are emitted which are counted by external detectors. The distribution of the tracer molecules is computed, and cross-sectional images of the brain are created in which image brightness is proportional to the underlying physiological process being measured.

Structural Imaging Studies

Studies of brain structure with CT and MRI in OCD patients have not demonstrated consistent abnormalities (Aylward et al., 1996; Hoehn-Saric & Benkelfat, 1994; Rubin, Villanueva-Meyer, Ananth, Trajmar, & Mena, 1992). Most of these studies, however, focused on the caudate nucleus or lateral ventricles, and less attention has been paid to the frontal lobes. Robinson et al. (1995) quantitated frontal lobe volumes in 26 OCD patients and 26 control subjects; no significant intergroup difference was found. It is possible, however, that in OCD only parts of the frontal lobes are affected, such as orbitofrontal or mediofrontal cortex, and measurement of total frontal lobe volume might be insensitive to more localized changes. Alternatively, frontal lobe abnormalities in OCD may be only functional and not structural.

With reference to structural imaging studies of other areas of the brain, enlarged lateral ventricles were reported in severely affected, childhood-onset OCD patients (Behar et al., 1984), but this finding was not replicated by the same research group in similar patients (Luxenberg et al., 1988). In some studies, investigators have reported normal lateral ventricle size in OCD patients (i.e., within 4% of that in control subjects) (Aylward et al., 1996; Kellner et al., 1991), and in other studies, investigators found lateral ventricles that were 16% (Insel, Donnelly, et al., 1983) to 28% (Robinson et al., 1995) larger in patients than in controls. These differences, however, were not statistically significant. A study by Stein et al. (1993) may help explain the variability in these reports: Significantly enlarged lateral ventricles were found in those OCD patients with high scores for soft neurological signs but not in patients with low soft-sign scores. Thus, structural abnormalities may be more associated with subtle neurological deficits accompanying OCD in some patients than with the disorder itself.

Similarly, structural studies of the caudate nucleus in OCD have yielded inconsistent findings. Kellner et al. (1991), Stein et al. (1993), and Aylward et al. (1996) reported normal caudate areas or volumes in patients compared to controls. On the other hand, Luxenberg et al. (1988) and Robinson et al. (1995) reported smaller caudate size in OCD, which was associated with considerable, although nonsignificant, ventricular enlargements of 19% and 28%, respectively. And, Scarone et al. (1992) observed a unilateral caudate volume increase in OCD patients. Thus, there is considerable variability among studies of structural brain abnormalities in OCD, and little can be concluded from them at present.

Functional Imaging Studies

In contrast to the contradictory data from structural imaging studies, a consistent finding in SPECT and PET functional neuroimaging studies of OCD has been increased frontal blood flow and glucose metabolism. Although the precise cortical location has varied, nearly all studies have reported hyperactivity in mediofrontal (Harris, Hoehn-Saric, Lewis, Pearlson, & Streeter, 1994; Machlin et al., 1991; Rubin et al., 1992; Swedo et al., 1989), right frontal (Benkelfat et al., 1990; Harris et al., 1994; Nordahl et al., 1989; Swedo et al., 1989), anterior cingulate (Perani et al., 1995; Swedo et al., 1989), and/or orbitofrontal (Baxter et al., 1987; 1988; Benkelfat et al., 1990; Nordahl et al., 1989; Rubin et al., 1992) areas. The elevated perfusion observed in both medial and right middle frontal cortex correlated negatively with anxiety scores (Harris et al., 1994; Machlin et al., 1991), suggesting that hyperfrontality is not a reflection of heightened anxiety in OCD patients.

The differences among studies in the location of frontal abnormalities may have resulted from variation in (1) definition of regions of interest (Baxter & Mazziotta, 1993; Harris, Pearlson, & Hoehn-Saric, 1993; Rauch, Savage, & Alpert, 1994; Rubin & Mena, 1993) and (2) patient characteristics. For example, the definition of orbitofrontal has varied considerably, some research groups considering it as an inferolateral frontal region (Baxter et al., 1987; Harris et al., 1994; Machlin et al., 1991) and others defining it more medially and superiorly (Rubin et al., 1992). Others have described several orbitofrontal subregions (Benkelfat et al., 1990; Nordahl et al., 1989). Fortunately, recently developed stereotaxic methods that define abnormalities in three-dimensional, standardized coordinate space have alleviated somewhat the problem of differing region-of-interest definitions (Harris et al., 1994; McGuire et al., 1994; Rauch et al., 1994). Differences in patient characteristics among studies include age at onset of OCD, comorbid diagnoses such as depression, and medication use (treatment status).

A relationship may exist between OCD hyperfrontality and serotonergic dysfunction, which, as mentioned earlier, has been hypothesized to underlie OCD pathophysiology. SUIs have been effective in reducing not only OCD symptoms but also hyperfrontality as shown by SPECT and PET (Benkelfat et al., 1990; Hoehn-Saric, Harris et al., 1991; Hoehn-Saric, Pearlson, Harris, Machlin, & Camargo, 1991; Perani et al., 1995; Rubin, Ananth, Villanueva-Meyer, Trajmar, & Mena, 1995; Swedo et al., 1992).

A tendency toward lateralized right frontal hyperactivity in OCD also has been noted. Harris et al. (1994) observed increased perfusion in the right middle frontal gyrus in OCD patients, Swedo et al. (1989) noted prefrontal hypermetabolism only on the right side, and Nordahl et al. (1989) and Benkelfat et al. (1990) reported orbitofrontal hypermetabolism primarily in the right hemisphere. Right orbitofrontal activity increased in response to symptom provocation in OCD patients (Greenberg et al., 1994; McGuire et al., 1994; Rauch, Jenicke et al., 1994) and decreased in concert with declining clinical measures of OCD and anxiety severity after pharmacotherapy (Swedo et al., 1992).

Right frontal hypermetabolism in OCD is consistent with theories of frontal emotional lateralization. The right frontal cortex is considered to play a greater role in perception of and reaction to negative primary emotions and stimuli, whereas the left frontal cortex may be more active in response to positive stimuli and positive social emotions (Ross, Homan, & Buck, 1994; Wexler, 1980). The inability of OCD patients to suppress negative primary emotions and thoughts occurs concomitantly with right frontal hyperactivity. Suppression of right-hemisphere cerebral activity, either with the Wada test (transient suppression of a hemisphere by amobarbital injection into the ipsilateral carotid artery (Terzian, 1964; Ross et al., 1994) or as a result of lesions (Robinson & Starkstein, 1989; Sackeim et al., 1982; Starkstein, Robinson, & Price, 1987; Starkstein et al., 1989), is associated with decreased apprehension, euphoric mood, and minimization of negative emotions, whereas left-hemisphere suppression produces feelings of depression, guilt, and worries about the future. Right frontal suppression also is associated with pharmacologically induced euphoria (Pearlson et al., 1993). In contrast to the right frontal hypermetabolism found in OCD, left frontal hypometabolism has been noted in several PET studies of patients with major depression (Bench et al., 1992; Dolan et al., 1992; Martinot, Hardy, et al., 1990). In OCD patients with concomitant major depression, significant frontal hypometabolism was found only on the left side (Baxter et al., 1989).

Theories of OCD pathophysiology also include basal ganglia dysfunction, as mentioned earlier. SPECT and PET studies of the basal ganglia in patients at baseline, however, have been inconsistent in their findings (Aylward et al., 1996; Harris et al.,

1993; Harris & Hoehn-Saric, 1995). Aylward et al. (1996) performed a meta-analysis of patient-control baseline differences, using measures of relative perfusion or metabolism to account for any global group differences in whole-brain metabolic rates. Seven of nine functional imaging studies indicated normal caudate function (Baxter et al., 1987, 1988; Harris et al., 1994; Martinot, Allilaire, et al., 1990; Nordahl et al., 1989; Perani et al., 1995; Swedo et al., 1989), whereas one study noted unilaterally increased caudate function (Benkelfat et al., 1990), and another found caudate hypoperfusion with one radiotracer but normal caudate perfusion with a different radioligand (Rubin et al., 1992). In those studies that reported absolute rates of glucose metabolism, absolute measures of caudate function paralleled the absolute global metabolic rates (Baxter et al., 1987, 1988; Benkelfat et al., 1990; Martinot, Allilaire, et al., 1990; Nordahl et al., 1989; Perani et al., 1995; Swedo et al., 1989). Overall, the meta-analysis, which included 105 OCD patients and 143 controls across nine studies, indicated normal caudate function in OCD, with only a 1% patient–control difference.

Researchers have also investigated the caudate nucleus metabolic response to treatment in OCD. Swedo et al. (1992), Perani et al. (1995), and Rubin et al. (1995) observed no functional caudate changes with pharmacotherapy. In contrast, Benkelfat et al. (1989) reported decreased glucose metabolism in the left caudate with drug treatment, and Baxter et al. (1992) observed decreased metabolism in the right caudate in response to treatment with both a SUI and behavioral therapy. These studies did not report the effect on caudate metabolism that similar interventions might have had in normal controls or other comparison groups, so that the specificity of the changes for OCD remains to be determined.

The cerebral activation response to symptom provocation has been studied as well (Breiter et al., 1996; Greenberg et al., 1994; McGuire et al., 1994; Rauch et al., 1994). All four studies indicated increased right orbitofrontal function in response to symptom provocation; Rauch et al. (1994) and Breiter et al. (1996) reported an increase bilaterally. Basal ganglia findings were not as consistent: McGuire et al. (1994) and Rauch et al. (1994) noted right-sided increases, and Greenberg et al. (1994) noted a right-sided decrease. Breiter et al. (1996) found frontal activation to be stronger and more consistent than basal ganglia changes. As with the before-and-after-treatment studies, caution is necessary in interpreting the activation studies, as they were preliminary and, except for Breiter et al. (1996), did not report responses of control subjects to similarly disturbing stimuli.

As with the structural imaging studies reviewed previously, functional neuroimaging studies also do not strongly substantiate the hypothesis of a caudate abnormality in OCD. They do not rule out this possibility but, rather, indicate that whatever abnormality might exist has not been consistently appreciable with current functional neuroimaging technology.

In summary, the most consistent abnormality reported in OCD functional imaging studies is hyperperfusion and hypermetabolism in mediofrontal, right frontal, anterior cingulate, and/or orbitofrontal regions, consistent with theories of a prefrontal abnormality involving serotonergic dysfunction. The additional, more variable observation of predominantly right frontal abnormalities is consistent with cerebral lateralization theories that postulate a greater role for right frontal cortex in the perception of and reaction to negative primary emotions. There may be an imbalance between right and left frontal lobe function, expressed in OCD as right frontal hyperactivity and in major depression as left frontal hypoactivity, both possibly related to abnormal serotonergic function. The complexity of these disorders is only beginning to be revealed by functional neuroimaging techniques.

CONCLUSIONS

As suggested by this review, evidence from several domains supports the concept of involvement of the frontal lobes in the pathophysiology of OCD. A frontal cortex/basal ganglia/thalamus/frontal cortex circuit represents the core, and there are afferents from and efferents to other areas of the cortex, hippocampus, amygdala, and other subcortical structures. As also indicated by this review, this concept holds only in a general way at present, because not all experimental data are concordant, and probes of this circuit, be they neuropsychological or biological, used in OCD studies to date have been imprecise.

Frontal lobe lesions can produce repetitive behaviors reminiscent of compulsions, but no neuropathology of similar degree has been demonstrated in OCD by structural imaging studies. And, functional studies suggest increased, rather than decreased, blood flow and metabolism in the relevant frontal cortical areas (however, increased metabolism does not necessarily imply increased functional activity). Furthermore, as mentioned earlier, OCD subjects not infrequently have comorbid major depression, and in the latter illness blood flow and metabolism have been shown to be decreased in frontal cortical areas. Neuropsychological assessments also have been contradictory, in that some indicate frontal lobe dysfunction but intact memory function, and others indicate the opposite.

The heterogeneity of OCD as a syndrome likely has contributed to these neuropsychological discrepancies. There also appears to be a continuum of symptom severity from normal, time-limited worry, through obsessive–compulsive personality disorder, to self-perpetuating OCD. As mentioned previously, the DSM criteria defining OCD represent a consensus statement based not only on the nature of the symptoms but also on their frequency and interference with social and occupational functioning. OCD thus remains an arbitrarily defined syndrome, no matter how much expertise underlies the definition, so long as there are insufficient empirical data to validate its qualitative difference from obsessive–compulsive personality disorder, as well as from other major anxiety syndromes such as body dysmorphic disorder. (For example, on what basis is "time-consuming" defined as symptoms present for more than 1 hour per day? How can "significantly interfere with" activities of daily living be applied consistently to all individuals? [American Psychiatric Association, 1994].)

Although animal models of OCD provide an interesting theoretical perspective, as noted earlier, this analogy also suffers from a certain nonspecificity. Repetitive behaviors such as pacing, whirling, hitting oneself, toe walking, and rocking, as well as increased anxiety, also are common symptoms of autism, a pervasive developmental disorder that begins in early childhood and persists into adult life. Dietary tryptophan depletion in autistic adults increases these behaviors (McDougle, Naylor, Cohen, Aghajanian, et al., 1996), and treatment with SUIs decreases them (McDougle, Naylor, Cohen, Volkmar, et al., 1996). This suggests a possibly similar involvement of serotonergic neurotransmission in autism as in OCD.

To objectively decide the boundaries of a syndrome, Kendell (1982) indicated the need to demonstrate a "point of rarity" between related syndromes, based on multivariate discrimination from empirical data. To approach this experimentally, Kendell suggested applying multiple diagnostic schemata to each syndrome, against which discriminant functions are empirically derived. This method is being used to refine the definitions of other psychiatric illnesses such as schizophrenia and affective disorder, and it remains to be done for OCD. Finally, it is interesting to speculate on the phenomenological opposite of OCD, that is, excessive neglect in conducting one's activities of daily living. A large segment of society fails to adequately check their surroundings and to protect themselves from even known threats. Preventable accidents are a leading cause of mortality and morbidity, and epidemics of avoidable diseases such as AIDS are only too well-known. We recognize the ubiquity of denial and risk taking, decry their inappropriateness in many contemporary life circumstances, but approach them only from a cognitive, educational standpoint. Perhaps our relative failure to make headway with such an approach suggests we should take a fresh, psychobiological look at this aspect of behavior. For example, how is "compulsive" risk taking psychobiologically similar to or different from compulsive checking and handwashing? Psychologically they could be intuitively conceptualized as opposite ends of a spectrum, the former representing pathological self-neglect and the latter pathological self-protection. Does this concept also imply opposite states of frontal lobe function? Testing these groups empirically with both neuropsychological and psychophysiological probes might help clarify the natural boundaries of OCD. In other words, is there a psychobiology of pathological denial that includes frontal lobe dysfunction, and how might this inform the psychobiology of OCD? These and other issues remain the exciting areas of future research into OCD and its CNS substrates.

REFERENCES

American Psychiatric Association. (1994). *Diagnostic and statistical manual of mental disorders* (4th ed.). Washington, DC: Author.

Aylward, E. H., Harris, G. J., Hoehn-Saric, R., Barta, P. E., Machlin, S. R., & Pearlson, G. D. (1996). Normal caudate nucleus in obsessive-compulsive disorder assessed by quantitative neuroimaging. *Archives of General Psychiatry, 53*(7), 577–584.

Barr, L. C., Goodman, W. K., Price, L. H., McDougle, C. J., & Charney, D. S. (1992). The serotonin hypothesis of obsessive compulsive disorder: implications of pharmacologic challenge studies. *Journal of Clinical Psychiatry, 53*(Suppl.), 17–28.

Baxter, L. R. (1990). Brain imaging as a tool in establishing a theory of brain pathology in obsessive–compulsive disorder. *Journal of Clinical Psychiatry, 51*(Suppl.), 22–25.

Baxter, L. R., & Mazziotta, J. C. (1993). Single photon emission computed tomography in obsessive–compulsive disorder: In reply. *Archives of General Psychiatry, 50*(6), 499–500.

Baxter, L. R., Phelps, M. E., Mazziotta, J. C., Guze, B. H., Schwartz, J. M., & Selin, C. E. (1987). Local cerebral glucose metabolic rates in obsessive–compulsive disorder: A comparison with rates in unipolar depression and in normal controls. *Archives of General Psychiatry, 44*(3), 211–218.

Baxter, L. R., Schwartz, J. M., Bergman, K. S., Szuba, M. P., Guze, B. H., Mazziotta, J. C., Alazraki, A., Selin, C. E., Ferng, H-K., Munford, P., & Phelps, M. E. (1992). Caudate glucose metabolic rate changes with both drug and behavior therapy in obsessive–compulsive disorder. *Archives of General Psychiatry, 49*(9), 681–689.

Baxter, L. R., Schwartz, J. M., Mazziotta, J. C., Phelps, M. E., Pahl, J. J., Guze, B. H., & Fairbanks, L. (1988). Cerebral glucose metabolic rates in non-depressed patients with obsessive–compulsive disorder. *American Journal of Psychiatry, 145*(12), 1560–1563.

Baxter, L. R., Schwartz, J. M., Phelps, M. E., Mazziotta, J. C., Guze, B. H., Selin, C. E., Gerner, R. H., & Sumida, R. M. (1989). Reduction of prefrontal cortex glucose metabolism common to three types of depression. *Archives of General Psychiatry, 46*(3), 243–250.

Behar, D., Rapoport, J. L., Berg, C. L., Denckla, M. B., Mann, L., Cox, C., Fedio, P., Zahn, T., & Wolfman, M. G. (1984). Computerized tomography and neuropsychological test measures in adolescents with obsessive–compulsive disorder. *American Journal of Psychiatry, 141*(3), 363–369.

Bench, C. J., Friston, K. J., Brown, R. G., Scott, L. C., Frackowiak, R. S., & Dolan, R. J. (1992). The anatomy of melancholia—Focal abnormalities of cerebral blood flow in major depression. *Psychological Medicine, 22*(3), 607–615.

Benkelfat, C., Murphy, D. L., Zohar, J., Hill, J. L., Grover, G., & Insel, T. R. (1989). Clomipramine in obsessive–compulsive disorder: Further evidence for a serotonergic mechanism of action. *Archives of General Psychiatry, 46*(1), 23–28.

Benkelfat, C., Nordahl, T. E., Semple, W. E., King, C., Murphy, D. L., & Cohen, R. M. (1990). Local cerebral glucose metabolic rates in obsessive–compulsive disorder. *Archives of General Psychiatry, 47*(9), 840–848.

Benkert, O., Wetzel, H., & Szegedi, A. (1993). Serotonin dysfunction syndromes: A functional common denominator for classification of depression, anxiety, and obsessive–compulsive disorder. *International Clinical Psychopharmacology, 1*(Suppl.), 3–14.

Boone, K. B., Ananth, J., Philpott, L., Kaur, A., & Djenderedjian, A. (1991). Neuropsychological characteristics of nondepressed adults with obsessive–compulsive disorder. *Neuropsychiatry, Neuropsychology, and Behavioral Neurology, 4*(2), 96–109.

Breiter, H. C., Rauch, S. L., Kwong, K. K., Baker, J. R., Weisskoff, R. M., Kennedy, D. N., Kendrick, A. D., Davis, T. L., Jiang, A., Cohen, M. S., Stern, C. E., Belliveau, J. W., Baer, L., O'Sullivan, R. L., Savage, C. R., Jenike, M. A., & Rosen, B. R. (1996). Functional magnetic resonance imaging of symptom provocation in obsessive–compulsive disorder. *Archives of General Psychiatry, 53*(7), 595–606.

Cummings, J. L. (1995). Anatomic and behavioral aspects of frontal–subcortical circuits. *Annals of the New York Academy of Sciences, 769,* 1–13.

Dodman, N. H., Moon-Fanelli, A., Mertens, P. A., Pflueger, S., & Stein, D. J. (1997). Veterinary models of OCD. In E. Hollander & D. J. Stein (Eds.), *Obsessive–compulsive disorder* (pp. 99–144). New York: Marcel Dekker.

Dodman, N. H., & Olivier, B. (1996). In search of animal models for obsessive–compulsive disorder. *CNS Spectrums 1*(2), 10–15.

Dolan, R. J., Bench, C. J., Brown, R. G., Scott, L. C., Friston, K. J., & Frackowiak, R. S. (1992). Regional cerebral blood flow abnormalities in depressed patients with cognitive impairment. *Journal of Neurology, Neurosurgery, and Psychiatry, 55*(9), 768–773.

Flor-Henry, P., Yeudall, L. T., Koles, Z. J., & Howarth, B. G. (1979). Neuropsychological and power spectral EEG investigations of the obsessive–compulsive syndrome. *Biological Psychiatry, 14*(1), 119–130.

Goldman-Rakic, P. S. (1995). Architecture of the prefrontal cortex and the central executive. *Annals of the New York Academy of Sciences, 769,* 71–83.

Goodman, W. K., McDougle, C. J., & Price, L. H. (1992). The role of serotonin and dopamine in the pathophysiology of obsessive compulsive disorder. *International Clinical Psychopharmacology, 7*(Suppl.1), 35–38.

Goodman, W. K., Price, L. H., Rasmussen, S. A., Mazure, C., Delgado, P., Heninger, G. R., & Charney, D. S. (1989). The Yale–Brown Obsessive–Compulsive Scale, II: Validity. *Archives of General Psychiatry, 46*(11), 1012–1016.

Goodman, W. K., Price, L. H., Rasmussen, S. A., Mazure, C., Fleischmann, R. L., Hill, C. L., Heninger, G. R., & Charney, D. S. (1989). The Yale–Brown Obsessive–Compulsive Scale, I: Development, use, and reliability. *Archives of General Psychiatry, 46*(11), 1006–1011.

Grafman, J., Holyoak, K. J., & Boller, F. (Eds.). (1995). Structure and functions of the human prefrontal cortex. *Annals of the New York Academy of Sciences, 769,* [whole issue].

Greenberg, B. D., Hoehn-Saric, R., George, M. S., Rubenstein, C., Keuler, D., Wang, L., Altemus, M., & Murphy, D. L. (1994). *Symptom activation and rCBF in OCD.* Paper presented at annual meeting of the American Psychiatric Association, Philadelphia.

Harris, G. J., & Hoehn-Saric, R. (1995). Functional neuroimaging in biological psychiatry. In J. Panksepp (Ed.), *Advances in biological psychiatry* (Vol. 1, pp. 113–160). Greenwich, CT: JAI Press.

Harris, G. J., Hoehn-Saric, R., Lewis, R. W., Pearlson, G. D., & Streeter, C. (1994). Mapping of SPECT regional cerebral perfusion abnormalities in obsessive–compulsive disorder. *Human Brain Mapping, 1*(4), 237–248.

Harris, G. J., Pearlson, G. D., & Hoehn-Saric, R. (1993). Single photon emission computed tomography in obsessive–compulsive disorder. *Archives of General Psychiatry, 50*(6), 498–499.

Head, D., Bolton, D., & Hymas, N. (1989). Deficit in cognitive shifting ability in patients with obsessive–compulsive disorder. *Biological Psychiatry, 25*(7), 929–937.

Hoehn-Saric, R., & Benkelfat, C. (1994). Structural and functional brain imaging in obsessive–compulsive disorder. In E. Hollander, J. Zohar, D. Marazziti, & B. Olivier (Eds.), *Current insights in obsessive–compulsive disorder* (pp. 183–211). New York:Wiley.

Hoehn-Saric, R., Harris, G. J., Pearlson, G. D., Cox, C. S., Machlin, S. R., & Camargo, E. E. (1991). A fluoxetine-induced frontal lobe syndrome in an obsessive–compulsive patient. *Journal of Clinical Psychiatry, 52*(3), 131–133.

Hoehn-Saric, R., Pearlson, G. D., Harris, G. J., Machlin, S. R., & Camargo, E. E. (1991). Effects of fluoxetine on regional cerebral blood flow in obsessive–compulsive patients. *American Journal of Psychiatry, 148*(9), 1243–1245.

Hollander, E., DeCaria, C. M., Nitescu, A., Gully, R., Suckow, R. F., Cooper, T. B., Gorman, J. M., Klein, D. F., & Liebowitz, M. R. (1992). Serotonergic function in obsessive–compulsive disorder: Behavioral and neuroendocrine responses to oral m-chlorophenylpiperazine and fenfluramine in patients and healthy volunteers. *Archives of General Psychiatry, 49*(1), 21–28.

Insel, T. R., Donnelly, E. F., Lalakea, M. L., Alterman, I. S., & Murphy, D. L. (1983). Neurological and neuropsychological studies of patients with obsessive–compulsive disorder. *Biological Psychiatry, 18*(7), 741–751.

Insel, T. R., Hamilton, J. A., Guttmacher, L. B., & Murphy, D. L. (1983). D-amphetamine in obsessive–compulsive disorder. *Psychopharmacology, 80*(3), 231–235.

Jenike, M. A. (1995). Obsessive–compulsive disorder. In H. I Kaplan & B. J. Sadock (Eds.), *Comprehensive textbook of psychiatry* (6th ed., pp. 1218–1227). Baltimore: Williams & Wilkins.

Joffe, R. T., Swinson, R. P., & Levitt, A. J. (1991). Acute psychostimulant challenge in primary obsessive–compulsive disorder. *Journal of Clinical Psychopharmacology, 11*(4), 237–241.

Karno, M., Golding, J. M., Sorenson, S. B., & Burnam, A. (1988). The epidemiology of obsessive–compulsive disorder in five US communities. *Archives of General Psychiatry, 45*(12), 1094–1099.

Kellner, C. H., Jolley, R. R., Holgate, R. C., Austin, L., Lydiard, R. B., Laraia, M., & Ballenger, J. C. (1991). Brain MRI in obsessive–compulsive disorder. *Psychiatry Research, 36*(1), 45–49.

Kendell, R. E. (1982). The choice of diagnostic criteria for biological research. *Archives of General Psychiatry, 39*(11), 1334–1339.

Leckman, J. F., Grice, D. E., Boardman, J., Zhang, H., Vitale, A., Bondi, C., Alsobrook, J., Peterson, B. S., Cohen, D. J., Rasmussen, S. A., Goodman, W. K., McDougle, C. J., & Pauls, D. L. (1997). Symptoms of obsessive–compulsive disorder. *American Journal of Psychiatry, 154*(7), 911–917.

Luxenberg, J. S., Swedo, S. E., Flament, M. F., Friedland, R. P., Rapoport, J., & Rapoport, S. I. (1988). Neuroanatomical abnormalities in obsessive–compulsive disorder detected with quantitative X-ray computed tomography. *American Journal of Psychiatry, 145*(9), 1089–1093.

Machlin, S. R., Harris, G. J., Pearlson, G. D., Hoehn-Saric, R., Jeffery, P., & Camargo, E. E. (1991). Elevated medial-frontal cerebral blood flow in obsessive–compulsive patients: A SPECT study. *American Journal of Psychiatry, 148*(9), 1240–1242.

Malloy, P. (1987). Frontal lobe dysfunction in obsessive–compulsive disorder. In E. Perecman (Ed.), *The frontal lobes revisited* (pp. 207–223). New York: New York University School of Medicine.

Malloy, P., Rasmussen, S., Braden, W., & Haier, R. J. (1989). Topographic evoked potential mapping in obsessive–compulsive disorder: Evidence of frontal lobe dysfunction. *Psychiatry Research, 28*(1), 63–71.

Martinot, J. L., Allilaire, J. F., Mazoyer, B. M., Hantouche, E., Huret, J. D., Legaut-Demare, F., Deslauriers, A. G., Hardy, P., Pappata, S., Baron, J. C., & Syrota, A. (1990). Obsessive–compulsive disorder: A clinical, neuropsychological, and positron emission tomography study. *Acta Psychiatrica Scandinavica, 82*(3), 233–242.

Martinot, J. L., Hardy, P., Feline, A., Huret, J. D., Mazoyer, B., Attar-Levy, D., Pappata, S., & Syrota, A. (1990b). Left prefrontal glucose hypometabolism in the depressed state: A confirmation. *American Journal of Psychiatry, 147*(10), 1313–1317.

McCarthy, P. R., Ray, W. J., & Foa, E. B. (1995). Cognitive influences on electrocortical and heart rate activity in obsessive–compulsive disorder. *International Journal of Psychophysiology, 19*(3), 215–222.

McDougle, C. J., Naylor, S. T., Cohen, D. J., Aghajanian, G. K., Heninger, G. R., & Price, L. H. (1996a). Effects of tryptophan depletion in drug-free adults with autistic disorder. *Archives of General Psychiatry, 53*(11), 993–1000.

McDougle, C. J., Naylor, S. T., Cohen, D. J., Volkmar, F. R., Heninger, G. R., & Price, L. H. (1996b). A double-blind, placebo-controlled study of fluvoxamine in adults with autistic disorder. *Archives of General Psychiatry, 53*(11), 1001–1008.

McGuire, P. K., Bench, C. J., Frith, C. D., Marks, I. M., Frackowiak, R. S. J., & Dolan, R. J. (1994). Functional anatomy of obsessive–compulsive phenomena. *British Journal of Psychiatry, 164*(4), 459–468.

Modell, J. G., Mountz, J. M., Curtis, G. C., & Greden, J. F. (1989). Neurophysiologic dysfunction in basal ganglia/limbic striatal and thalamocortical circuits as a pathogenetic mechanism of obsessive–compulsive disorder. *Journal of Neuropsychiatry, 1*(1), 27–36.

Murphy, D. L., Zohar, J., Benkelfat, C., Pato, M. T., Pigott, T. A., & Insel, T. R. (1989). Obsessive–compulsive disorder as a 5-HT subsystem-related behavioural disorder. *British Journal of Psychiatry, 8*(Suppl.), 15–24.

Nordahl, T. E., Benkelfat, C., Semple, W. E., Gross, M., King, A. C., & Cohen, R. M. (1989). Cerebral glucose metabolic rates in obsessive compulsive disorder. *Neuropsychopharmacology, 2*(1), 23–28.

Otto, M. W. (1992). Normal and abnormal information processing: A neuropsychological perspective on obsessive–compulsive disorder. *Psychiatric Clinics of North America, 15*(4), 825–848.

Pearlson, G. D., Jeffery, P. J., Harris, G. J., Ross, C. A., Fischman, M. W., & Camargo, E. E. (1993). Correlation of acute cocaine-induced changes in local cerebral blood flow with subjective effects. *American Journal of Psychiatry, 150*(3), 495–497.

Perani, D., Colombo, C., Bressi, S., Bonfanti, A., Grassi, F., Scarone, S., Bellodi, L., Smeraldi, E., & Fazio. F. (1995). [18F]FDG PET study in obsessive–compulsive disorder: A clinical/metabolic correlation study after treatment. *British Journal of Psychiatry, 166*(2), 244–250.

Prichep, L. S., Mas, F., Hollander, E., Liebowitz, M., John, E. R., Almas, M., DeCaria, C. M., & Levine, R. H. (1993). Quantitative electroencephalographic subtyping of obsessive–compulsive disorder. *Psychiatry Research, 50*(1), 25–32.

Rauch, S. L., Jenike, M. A., Alpert, N. M., Baer, L., Breiter, H., Savage, C. R., & Fischman, A. J. (1994). Regional cerebral blood flow measured during symptom provocation in obsessive-compulsive disorder using oxygen 15-labeled carbon dioxide and positron emission tomography. *Archives of General Psychiatry, 51*(1), 62–70.

Rauch, S. L., Savage, C. R., & Alpert, N. M. (1994). Self-induced dysphoria and neural correlates. *American Journal of Psychiatry, 151*(5),784–785.

Robinson, R. G., & Starkstein, S. E. (1989). Mood disorders following stroke: New findings and future directions. *Journal of Geriatric Psychiatry, 22*(1), 1–15.

Robinson, D., Wu, H., Munne, R. A., Ashtari, M., Alvir, J. M., Lerner, G., Koreen, A., Cole, K., & Bogerts, B. (1995). Reduced caudate nucleus volume in obsessive–compulsive disorder. *Archives of General Psychiatry, 52*(5), 393–398.

Ross, E. D., Homan, R. W., & Buck, R. (1994). Differential hemispheric lateralization of primary and social emotions. *Neuropsychiatry, Neuropsychology, and Behavioral Neurology, 7*(1), 1–19.

Rubin, R. T., Ananth, J., Villanueva-Meyer, J., Trajmar, P. G., & Mena, I. (1995). Regional [133]xenon cerebral blood flow and ^{99m}Tc-HMPAO uptake in patients with obsessive–compulsive disorder before and during treatment. *Biological Psychiatry, 38*(7), 429–437.

Rubin, R. T., & Mena, I. (1993). Single photon emission computed tomography in obsessive–compulsive disorder: In reply. *Archives of General Psychiatry, 50*(6), 500–501.

Rubin, R. T., Villanueva-Meyer, J., Ananth, J., Trajmar, P. G., & Mena, I. (1992). Regional xenon 133 cerebral blood flow and cerebral Technetium 99m HMPAO uptake in unmedicated patients with obsessive–compulsive disorder and matched control subjects. *Archives of General Psychiatry, 49*(9), 695–702.

Sackeim, H. A., Greenberg, M. S., Weiman, A. L., Gur, R. C., Hungerbuhler, J. P., & Geschwind, N. (1982). Hemispheric asymmetry in the expression of positive and negative emotions: Neurological evidence. *Archives of Neurology, 39*(4), 210–218.

Scarone, S., Colombo, C., Livian, S., Abbruzzese, M., Ronchi, P., Locatelli, M., Scotti, G., & Smeraldi, E. (1992). Increased right caudate nucleus size in obsessive–compulsive disorder: Detection with magnetic resonance imaging. *Psychiatry Research 45*(2), 115–121.

Starkstein, S. E., Robinson, R. G., Honig, M. A., Parikh, R. M., Joselyn, J., & Price, T. R. (1989). Mood changes after right-hemisphere lesions. *British Journal of Psychiatry, 155*(7), 79–85.

Starkstein, S. E., Robinson, R. G., & Price, T. R. (1987). Comparison of cortical and subcortical lesions in the production of poststroke mood disorders. *Brain, 110*(4), 1045–59.

Stein, D. J., Hollander, E., Chan, S., DeCaria, C. M., Hilal, S., Liebowitz, M. R., & Klein, D. F. (1993). Computed tomography and neurological soft signs in obsessive–compulsive disorder. *Psychiatry Research, 50*(3), 143–50.

Swedo, S. E., Pietrini, P., Leonard, H. L., Schapiro, M. B., Rettew, D. C., Goldberger, E. L., Rapoport, S. I., Rapoport, J. L., & Grady, C. L. (1992). Cerebral glucose metabolism in childhood-onset obsessive–compulsive disorder: Revisualization during pharmacotherapy. *Archives of General Psychiatry, 49*(9), 690–694.

Swedo, S. E., Schapiro, M. B., Grady, C. L., Cheslow, D. L., Leonard, H. L., Kumar, A., Friedland, R., Rapoport, S. I., & Rapoport, J. (1989). Cerebral glucose metabolism in childhood-onset obsessive–compulsive disorder. *Archives of General Psychiatry, 46*(6), 518–523.

Swoboda, K. J., & Jenike, M. A. (1995). Frontal abnormalities in a patient with obsessive–compulsive disorder: The role of structural lesions in obsessive–compulsive behavior. *Neurology, 45*(12), 2130–2134.

Terzian, H. (1964). Behavioral and EEG effects of intracarotid sodium amytal injection. *Acta Neurochirurgica, 12*(2), 230–240.

Wexler, B. E. (1980). Cerebral laterality and psychiatry: A review of the literature. *American Journal of Psychiatry, 137*(3), 279–291.

Winslow, J. T., & Insel, T. R. (1990). Neurobiology of obsessive compulsive disorder: A possible role for serotonin. *Journal of Clinical Psychiatry, 51*(Suppl.), 27–31.

Zielinski, C. M., Taylor, M. A., & Juzwin, K. R. (1991). Neuropsychological deficits in obsessive–compulsive disorder. *Neuropsychiatry, Neuropsychology, and Behavioral Neurology, 4*(2), 110–126.

Zohar, J., & Kindler, S. (1992). Update of the serotonergic hypothesis of obsessive compulsive disorder. *Clinical Neuropharmacology, 15*(Suppl.), 257A–258A.

30

Depression and Frontal Lobe Disorders

SERGIO E. STARKSTEIN
ROBERT G. ROBINSON

Frontal lobe disorders have frequently been associated with depressive symptoms. Although Adolf Meyer (1904) felt that traumatic insanities were probably due to a combination of biopsychosocial factors, he was among the first to suggest that there may be a direct relationship between traumatic injury to the frontal lobes and emotional disturbances. Both Bleuler (1951) and Kraepelin (1913) recognized an association between manic depressive insanity and cerebrovascular disease. It is only during the past 20 years, however, that empirical studies have examined the association between mood disorders and lesions to specific brain areas. In this chapter, we review the association between depression and dysfunction of the frontal lobes, as demonstrated by patients with neurological disorders, such as cerebrovascular infarction, traumatic brain injury, and Parkinson's disease. We also review the evidence that dysfunction of the frontal lobes may play a role in the pathophysiological mechanism of primary (i.e., no known neurological disease) depression. Finally, based on neuroanatomical structures and recent neuroimaging findings, we propose a theoretical framework for the role of the frontal lobes in the mechanism of depression.

DEPRESSION IN PATIENTS WITH FRONTAL STROKE LESIONS

Several studies examined the association between post-stroke depression and lesions to the frontal lobes. Robinson and Szetela (1981) first reported a significant inverse correlation between the severity of depression and the distance of the anterior border of the lesion from the frontal pole ($r = -.76$) (i.e., the more anterior the lesion, the more severe the depression) (see Figure 30.1). Interestingly, this significant correlation was true for left- but not right-hemisphere lesions.

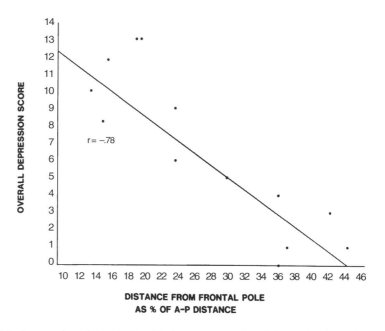

FIGURE 30.1. Scatterplot of the relationship between severity of depression in patients with stroke or traumatic brain injury and distance of the anterior border of the lesion from the frontal pole as measured on CT scan. From Robinson and Szetela (1981). Copyright 1981 by Lippincott Williams & Wilkins. Reprinted by permission.

In a subsequent study, Robinson, Kubos, Starr, Rao, and Price (1984) included only right-handed stroke patients with a negative history of psychiatric disorders and replicated the significant correlation between distance of the lesion from the frontal pole and depression scores ($r = -.92$, $p < .05$). Eastwood, Rifat, Nobbs, and Ruderman (1989) examined a consecutive series of stroke patients admitted to a rehabilitation center and found a significant correlation between distance of the lesion to the frontal pole and depression scores for left ($r = -.74$, $p < .01$) but not right stroke lesions ($r = -.04$, $p = $ NS). Morris, Robinson, and Raphael (1992) also examined a consecutive series of admissions to a rehabilitation unit following stroke. After controlling for personal and family history of depression, they found a significant correlation between distance of left- (but not right-) hemisphere lesions to the frontal pole and severity of depression ($r = -.87$, $p < .0001$). Herrman, Bartels, Schuacher, and Wallesch (1995) examined 20 consecutive aphasic patients, and also found a significant correlation between distance of the lesion to the frontal pole and depression scores (rho $= -.44$, $p < .05$). Sinyor et al. (1986) and House, Dennis, Warlow, Hawton, and Molyneux (1990) could not find a lateralized aspect to the phenomenon but did find significant correlations between proximity of the lesion to the frontal pole and severity of depression for both left- and right-hemisphere lesion patients.

Astrom, Adolfsson, and Asplund (1993) examined neuroradiological correlates of poststroke depression (PSD) in 21 patients with left-hemisphere lesions and 23 patients with right-hemisphere lesions. They found a prevalence of major depression of 86% after left anterior lesions, as compared to 29% after left posterior lesions, and 9% after right-hemisphere lesions. A high prevalence of PSD was also reported after subcortical lesions involving frontal–subcortical circuits (Starkstein, Robinson, & Price, 1987). We found major PSD in 7 of 8 patients with left-sided basal ganglia lesions, and only 1 of 7 patients with right-sided basal ganglia lesions and 0 of 10 with either left or right thalamic lesions ($p < .001$) (Starkstein, Robinson, Berthier, Parikh, & Price, 1988). In a study examining patients with subcortical lesions (without cortical involvement) or cortical lesions (without extension into the basal ganglia or thalamus), we found a significant correlation between distance of the lesion to the frontal pole and depression scores for both cortical ($r = -.52$, $p < .025$), and subcortical lesions patients ($r = -.68$, $p < .05$) (Starkstein et al., 1987). These correlations, however, were not significant for patients with right-hemisphere lesions.

RISK FACTORS FOR POSTSTROKE DEPRESSION

Although a high proportion of patients with left anterior lesions develop depression, not every patient with lesions in this brain area develops depression, raising the issue of whether other factor(s) are necessary for the onset of depression.

We examined this question in a study that included 13 acute stroke patients with major depression and 13 patients without depression but with a stroke lesion of a similar size and location (Starkstein, Robinson, & Price, 1988). Although there were no significant between-group differences in age, gender, socioeconomic, status, education, neurological, deficits, and personal and familial history of psychiatric disorders, depressed patients had significantly more severe subcortical atrophy ($p < .05$) as measured both by the ratio of third ventricle to brain and the ratio of lateral ventricle to brain. This finding suggests that subcortical atrophy may be an important risk factor for the development of major depression after stroke.

In summary, the available evidence strongly suggests an important role for frontal lobe dysfunction in the production of PSD. This conclusion is based primarily on the findings that major PSD was significantly associated with frontal dorsolateral lesions, that anterior lesion location was significantly correlated with depression scores, that left (but not right) frontal lesions were significantly associated with major PSD and finally that anterior subcortical atrophy was a significant risk factor for PSD.

DEPRESSION IN TRAUMATIC BRAIN INJURY

Depression is a frequent finding among patients with traumatic brain injury (TBI), with most studies reporting a prevalence of depression between 25% and 50% (Fedoroff, Jorge, & Robinson, 1993). We found that 17 of 66 (26%) consecutive admissions to a trauma unit showed major depression, whereas another 11 patients (16%) developed major depression at some time during a 1-year follow-up period (Jorge et al., 1993).

Several studies have examined the association between lesion location and depression following TBI. Robinson and Szetela (1981) examined a group of patients with chronic brain injury and found that those with strokes were more severely depressed than patients with TBI. However, when the two groups were matched for lesion location, the severity of depression was similar in both groups. Moreover, the correlation between the distance of the left-hemisphere lesion to the frontal pole and depression scores was true for both stroke and TBI patients, suggesting that depression in both groups may have a similar pathogenesis. In our longitudinal study, 22 of the 66 patients had single focal lesions, and 23 had multiple or bilateral lesions (mostly brain contusions) (Fedoroff, Starkstein,

Forrester, Geisler, & Robinson, 1992). The association between lesion location (as measured from CT scans) and depression was examined using a logistic regression analysis. Lesion location variables were left, right, cortical, subcortical, single, multiple, frontal, orbitofrontal, temporal, temporobasal, left anterior, and parietal–occipital. There was a significant association between the presence of major depression and lesion location (χ^2 = 33.6, df = 12, p < .001) and the presence of a left anterior lesion was the strongest correlate of post-TBI major depression (Wald χ^2 = 12.9, p < .001).

We also examined the long-term correlates of depression after TBI and whether delayed-onset depressions were significantly associated with lesion location (Jorge et al., 1993). We found that at the 3-month follow-up, major depression was no longer significantly associated with lesion location. Moreover, delayed-onset depressions were associated with social factors and previous history of psychiatric disorder, but not with lesion location.

In conclusion, these findings indicate that while major depression after TBI was significantly associated with left anterior lesions, this association between major depression and lesion location was restricted to the acute posttraumatic stage.

DEPRESSION IN PARKINSON'S DISEASE

Depression is a frequent finding in Parkinson's disease (PD), and recent studies have demonstrated a prevalence of major depression of about 20–25% and a similar prevalence for minor (dysthymic) depression (Starkstein & Mayberg, 1993). Whereas depression in PD was usually attributed to social factors, physical disability, or a rigid personality, neuropsychological and neurometabolic studies suggested a significant association between major depression in PD and frontal lobe dysfunction.

We assessed PD patients with either major depression, dysthymia, or no depression using a neuropsychological battery that included the Wisconsin Card Sorting Test (WCST) (which measures the ability to develop new concepts and shift sets and also requires the subject to suppress a previously correct response and produce a new one), the Controlled Word Association Test (which examines visual, conceptual, and visuomotor tracking), the Symbol Digit Test (which examines visuoverbal substitution speed), the Design Fluency Test (a nonverbal counterpart to the Controlled Word Association Test), and the Digit Span (which examines auditory attention) (Starkstein et al., 1989). When major depressed patients were compared with nondepressed PD patients matched for age, education, and Hoehn and Yahr stage of illness, PD patients with major depression showed poorer performance on tasks associated with frontal lobe function such as the WCST (see Figure 30.2), Verbal Fluency, Design Fluency, and section B of the Trail Making Test.

One important question is whether the cognitive impairments associated with major depression in PD were the result of a mood disorder or a specific interaction between the mood disorder and PD. To answer this question, we recently assessed 19 PD patients with and 31 without major depression, 27 patients with primary major depression, and 12 normal controls in a 2 × 2 design (presence or absence of PD; presence or absence of major depression) using a comprehensive neuropsychological battery (Kuzis, Sabe, Tiberti, Leiguarda, & Starkstein, 1997). We found that both groups of major depression patients (with or without PD) had significant deficits in tasks of auditory attention and verbal fluency. This finding suggested that some of the cognitive deficits in PD may be explained by the presence of major depression. However, we also found that PD patients with major depression had significant deficits on frontal lobe tasks (e.g., abstract

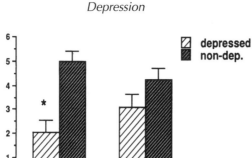

FIGURE 30.2. Patients with PD and major depression showed a significantly worse performance on the WCST compared with patients with PD without depression who were matched for age, duration, and stage of illness. No significant differences were observed between patients with minor and no depression.

reasoning and set shifting) as compared to nondepressed PD patients and normal controls. This suggests a specific association between the neuropathology of PD, major depression, and frontal lobe deficits.

Neuroimaging studies also provided evidence on the role of frontal lobe dysfunction in the mechanism of major depression in PD. We assessed PD patients with or without major depression matched for age and severity of PD using 18 fluorodeoxyglucose (18 FDG) positron emission tomography (PET) (Mayberg et al., 1990). The main finding was the presence of significant bilateral hypometabolism in the caudate and inferior frontal cortex in depressed as compared to nondepressed PD patients. In a recent study, Ring et al. (1994) examined 10 PD patients with major depression and 10 nondepressed patients with PET. They found that depressed patients had bilateral perfusion deficits in anteriomedial regions of the frontal and cingulate cortices, which appeared to be similar to metabolic changes found in patients with primary depression.

Other PET studies in PD have demonstrated significant associations between bradykinesia and reduced perfusion in the mediofrontal cortex (Rascol et al., 1992). One clinical variant of PD is characterized by akinesia and rigidity in the absence of tremor (i.e., the "akinetic–rigid" variant). This syndrome is less frequent than the classical type of PD, which is characterized by tremor, rigidity, and akinesia. If depression in PD is associated with frontal dysfunction, as suggested by PET studies, there should be a higher prevalence of depression in the akinetic rigid as compared to the classic variant of PD. In a recent study we examined the prevalence of major depression and dysthymia in 78 patients with the classical variant of PD and 34 patients with the akinetic–rigid variant (Starkstein et al., 1998). The prevalence of dysthymia was similar in both groups (classic PD, 31%, akinetic–rigid PD, 32%), but patients with akinetic–rigid PD had a significantly higher prevalence of major depression (38% vs. 15%, respectively, $p < .01$). Moreover, a stepwise regression analysis demonstrated that bradykinesia was the extrapyramidal sign with the highest correlation with Hamilton depression scores.

In conclusion, major depression in PD seems to be associated with frontal lobe dysfunction, as these patients showed significant deficits on frontal lobe-related tasks, demonstrated significant metabolic deficits in frontal dorsolateral and frontomedial areas, and showed a higher prevalence of neurological signs associated with frontal lobe dysfunction.

PRIMARY DEPRESSION

Another approach to the study of frontal lobe dysfunction in depression is to examine the presence of metabolic brain deficits among patients with primary depression. Most studies of PET abnormalities in primary depression found significant hypometabolism involving the frontal dorsolateral cortex (primarily on the left hemisphere) and the caudates (Baxter, et al., 1989). A "trait" pattern of cerebral metabolism has been described by Drevets et al. (1992), who reported decreased caudate and increased frontal polar cortex blood flow in patients who were depressed or euthymic at the time of the PET study. They also reported a "state" marker, as an increased flow in bilateral inferior frontal–pars orbitalis was found only in the patients with depression. Other authors also reported an increased caudate metabolism following antidepressant therapy. Finally, Mayberg, Lewis, and Regenold (1994) examined, with SPECT, a group of patients with refractory familial unipolar depression and found significant decreases of blood flow in orbital–inferior frontal, anterior temporal, and cingulate cortex in depressed as compared to normal controls.

Recent PET studies demonstrated that improvement from depression was associated with metabolic decreases in ventral paralimbic areas, such as the anterior insula and the temporal pole (Mayberg, Mahurin, & Brannon, 1995). On the other hand, depressed patients who did not respond to antidepressant treatment had increased metabolism in these ventral areas, suggesting that improvement from depression is not the consequence of the normalization of frontodorsal structures but may result from a complex interaction between ventral and dorsal brain regions.

THE ROLE OF THE FRONTAL LOBES
IN THE PRODUCTION OF DEPRESSION

Although findings in neurological and primary depressed patients suggest an important role for frontal lobe dysfunction in the production of depression, the mechanism of depression still remains highly speculative. However, based on the findings presented previously, it is possible to speculate about a model of depression, and we recently proposed a mechanism for the regulation of inhibition which may apply to mood states as well (Starkstein & Robinson, 1997). For this purpose, we should briefly discuss some relevant evolutionary concepts of brain development.

Development of Frontal Archi- and Paleocortices

Sanides (1969) was the first to propose a dual origin of the cerebral cortex, with the orbitofrontal and basotemporal cortices deriving from the paleocortex and the limbic, prefrontal dorsolateral, and visual, somatosensory, and motor cortices evolving from the archicortex. Petrides and Pandya (1994) discussed important connections within and between paleo- and archicortically derived cortical regions. For instance, there are important connecting pathways between orbitofrontal and frontodorsolateral regions, and a similar pattern of segregated connections may be found in the somatosensory, visual, and auditory domains, as well as within thalamic nuclei. Based on these anatomical findings, Petrides and Pandya (1994) suggested that "the archicortical prefrontal trend serves as the underpinning of the spatial aspects of decision-making, whereas the paleocortical trend provides the temporal backdrop against which decisions in regard to specific objects or events are made and carried out" (p. 52). Goldar (1993) recently proposed that based on contextual information conveying from frontoparietal dorsal areas and object–reward associative memory conveying from temporal and thalamic areas, the ventral paleocortically derived brain areas (primarily the orbitofrontal, anterior insular, and anterior temporal areas) may release or inhibit motor, intellectual, sensory, emotional, and instinctive behaviors programmed in the archicortically derived dorsal cortex.

Mechanism of Depression

Most studies of stroke patients demonstrated a significant association between fronto-dorsolateral lesions and depression, and similar findings were reported among patients with closed head injuries. Neuroimaging studies in depressed patients without neurological disease have also demonstrated dysfunction of the frontodorsolateral cortex (Baxter et al., 1985). Moreover, major depressed patients with PD showed specific cognitive deficits which may be related to frontodorsolateral dysfunction (Starkstein et al., 1989) as well as hypometabolism as demonstrated on PET scan imaging in inferior frontodorsal areas (Mayberg et al., 1990). On the other hand, manic behaviors have been associated with lesions of the orbitofrontal and anterior temporal cortices (Starkstein, Boston, & Robinson, 1988). Based on these findings we suggested that lesions to this "decision making" central system may produce disinhibited behaviors, whereas dysfunction of this area resulting in the overinhibition of the dorsal brain areas may abnormally reduce motor, instinctive, intellectual, and emotional output (Starkstein & Robinson, 1997).

Mayberg (1997) recently discussed relevant findings supporting the model just described. In a recent fluoxetine treatment trial in a group of patients with major depression, she found that a positive clinical response was associated with a significant metabolic increment (as measured with FDG–PET) in the dorsofrontal cortex, and this increase was a normalization of the pretreatment hypometabolic pattern (Mayberg et al., 1995). They also found a significant decrease in ventral brain areas such as the orbitofrontal cortex, and the anterior insula, which, unlike changes seen in dorsal areas, were not a normalization of an abnormal metabolic pattern. On the other hand, depressed patients who did not respond to fluoxetine treatment had increased metabolism in these ventral areas after fluoxetine treatment. Based on these findings, Mayberg (1997) suggested that recovery from depression may require both the inhibition of overactive ventral regions and normalization of frontodorsal hypofunction.

Brain Asymmetries and the Mechanism of Depression

A model for depression should also consider the finding of a significant lateralization of brain lesions associated with depression. We already discussed the significant association between left-hemisphere lesions and depression in patients with acute strokes or closed head injuries, and some PET findings in patients with primary depression reporting significant metabolic deficits in left but not right frontal areas.

We suggested that lateralization of mood disorders after brain lesions may be secondary to asymmetries in biogenic amine systems. Robinson (1979) demonstrated that right (but not left) frontodorsolateral lesions in rodents produced significant locomotor hyperactivity and asymmetric depletions in cortical catecholamine concentrations. A similar lateralized behavior was found after lesions restricted to the dopamine-rich nucleus accumbens (Starkstein, Moran, Bowersox, & Robinson, 1988). Moreover, we also found that locomotor hyperactivity produced by right frontal lesions was significantly correlated with the amount of depletions of norepinephrine in the cortex and locus coeruleus (Robinson, 1979).

Few studies have examined the presence of lateralized biochemical responses to ischemia in humans. We carried out PET studies in patients with or without depression after left- or right-hemisphere lesions using spiperone (which binds to 5-hydroxytrytamine [5-HT]2 [serotonin] receptors) (Mayberg et al., 1988). Patients with right-hemisphere stroke lesions had significantly higher ratios of ipsilateral to controlateral spiperone binding in noninjured temporal and parietal cortices than did patients with left-hemisphere lesions. Moreover, patients with comparable left- (but not right-) hemisphere lesions showed a significant inverse correlation between the amount of spiperone binding in the left temporal cortex and depression scores (i.e., higher depression scores were associated with lower spiperone binding). We suggested that a greater depletion of biogenic amines in patients with right- as compared to left-hemisphere lesions may have produced a compensatory upregulation of receptors that reverted serotonergic dysfunction. On the other hand, the relatively smaller depletions of 5-HT2 receptors following left-hemisphere lesion was insufficient to trigger compensatory upregulation of 5-HT receptors and therefore serotonergic dysfunction occurred. This dysfunction ultimately led to the abnormalities in limbic circuitry, which are manifested as depression.

In conclusion, the lateralization of brain biogenic amine systems, as well as the pattern of connections between dorsal and ventral brain areas, may explain the production of mood disorders after specifically located brain lesions.

CONCLUSIONS

Dysfunction of the frontal lobes may play an important role in the production of depression. We have demonstrated several clinical conditions in which frontal lobe dysfunction was associated with major depression. These conditions include stroke, trauma, Parkinson's disease, and primary depression. Among patients with stroke, left frontal lesions were associated with a high prevalence of depression, and the closer the lesion was to the frontal pole, the more severe the depression. Among patients with Parkinson's disease, major depression was significantly associated with impairments in frontal lobe–related cognitive functions, and PET studies demonstrated significant frontal metabolic deficits in major depressed as compared to nondepressed PD patients. Recent PET findings suggest that depression may not result from frontodorsal dysfunction but from an abnormal interaction between ventral and dorsal brain areas. Finally, the significant association between depression and left-hemisphere lesions may result from asymmetries in the response of the biogenic amine systems to injury. This may lead to lateralized dysfunction of serotonergic and perhaps limbic function and ultimately to depression.

ACKNOWLEDGMENTS

This study was supported in part by grants from the Raúl Carrea Institute of Neurological Research, the Fundación Pèrez Companc, and the CONICET, and by a National Institute of Mental Health Research Scientist Award (No. MH00163) to Robert G. Robinson.

REFERENCES

Astrom, M., Adolfsson, R., & Asplund, K. (1993). Major depression in stroke patients: A 3-year longitudinal study. *Stroke 24*, 976–982.

Baxter, L. R., Phelps, M. E., Mazziotta, J. C., Schwartz, J. M., Gerner, R. H., Selin, C. E., & Sumida, R. M. (1985). Cerebral metabolic rates for glucose in mood disorders: Studies with positron emission tomography and fluorodeoxyglucose F18. *Archives of General Psychiatry, 42*, 441–447.

Baxter, L. R., Schwartz, J. M., Phelps, M. E., Mazziotta, J. C., Guze, B. H., Selin, C. E., Gerner, R. H., & Sumida, R. M. (1989). Reduction of prefrontal cortex glucose metabolism common to three types of depression. *Archives of General Psychiatry, 46*, 243–250.

Bleuler, E. P. (1951). *Textbook of psychiatry*. New York: Macmillan.

Drevets, W. C., Videen, T. O., Price, J. L., Preskorn, S. H., Carmichael, T., & Raichle, M. E. (1992). A functional anatomical study of unipolar depression. *Journal of Neuroscience, 12*, 3628–3641.

Eastwood, M. R., Rifat, S. L., Nobbs, H., & Ruderman, J. (1989). Mood disorder following cerebrovascular accident. *British Journal of Psychiatry, 154*, 195–200.

Fedoroff, J. P., Jorge, R. E., & Robinson, R. G. (1993). Depression in traumatic brain injury. In S. E. Starkstein & R. G. Robinson (Eds.), *Depression in neurologic disease* (pp. 139–151). Baltimore: Johns Hopkins University Press.

Fedoroff, J. P., Starkstein, S. E., Forrester, A. W., Geisler, F., & Robinson, R. G. (1992). Depression in patients with acute traumatic brain injury. *American Journal of Psychiatry, 149*, 918–923.

Goldar, J. C. (1993). *Anatomia de la mente*. Buenos Aires: Salerno.

Herrmann, M., Bartels, C., Schumacher, M., & Wallesch, C. W. (1995). Poststroke depression: Is there a pathoanatomic correlate for depression in the postacute stage of stroke? *Stroke, 26*, 850–856.

House, A., Dennis, M., Warlow, C., Hawton, K., & Molyneux, K. (1990). Mood disorders after stroke and their relation to lesion location. A CT scan study. *Brain, 113*, 1113–1130.

Jorge, R. E., Robinson, R. G., Arndt, S. V., Forrester, A. W., Geisler, F., & Starkstein, S. E. (1993). Comparison between acute and delayed onset depression following traumatic brain injury. *Journal of Neuropsychiatry and Clinical Neurosciences, 5*, 43–49.

Kraepelin, E. (1913). *Ein Lehrbuch für Studierende un Ärzte*. Leipzig: Barth.

Kuzis, G., Sabe, L., Tiberti, C., Leiguarda, R., Starkstein, S. E. (1997). Cognitive functions in major depression and Parkison's disease. *Archives of Neurology, 54*, 982–986.

Mayberg, H. S. (1997). Limbic–cortical dysregulation: A proposed model of depression. *Journal of Neuropsychiatry and Clinical Neurosciences, 9*, 471–481.

Mayberg, H. S., Lewis, P. J., & Regenold, W. (1994). Paralimbic hypoperfusion in unipolar depression. *Journal of Nuclear Medicine, 35*, 929–934.

Mayberg, H. S., Mahurin, R. K., & Brannon, S. K. (1995). Parkinson's depression: Discrimination of mood-sensitive and mood-insensitive cognitive deficits using fluoxetine and FDG PET. *Neurology, 45*, A166.

Mayberg, H. S., Robinson, R. G., Wong, D. F., Parikh, R., Bolduc, P., Starkstein, S. E., Price, T., Dannals, R. F., Links, J. M., Wilson, A. A., Ravert, H. T., & Wagner, H. N. (1988). PET imaging of cortical S2 serotonin receptors after stroke: Lateralized changes and relationship to depression. *American Journal of Psychiatry, 145*, 937–943.

Mayberg, H. S., Starkstein, S. E., Sadzot, B., Preziosi, T., Andrezejewski, P. L., Dannals, R. F., Wagner, H. N., & Robinson, R. G. (1990). Selective hypometabolism in the inferior frontal lobe in depressed patients with Parkinson's disease. *Annals of Neurology, 28*, 57–64.

Meyer, A. (1904). The anatomical facts and clinical varieties of traumatic insanity. *American Journal of Insanity, 60*, 373.

Morris, P. L., Robinson, R. G., & Raphael, B. (1992). Lesion location and depression in hospitalized stroke patients: Evidence supporting a specific relationship in the left hemisphere. *Neuropsychiatry, Neuropsychology, and Behavioral Neurology, 5*, 75–82.

Petrides, M., & Pandya, D. N. (1994). Comparative architectonic analysis of the human and macaque frontal cortex. In J. Grafman & F. Boller (Eds.), *Handbook of neuropsychology* (pp. 17–58). Amsterdam: Elsevier.

Rascol, O., Sabatini, U., Chollet, F., Fabre, N., Senard, J. M., Montastruc, J. L., Celsis, P., Marc-Vergnes, J. P., & Rascol, A. (1992). Supplementary and primary sensory motor area activity in Parkinson's disease. Regional cerebral blood flow changes during finger movements and effects of apomorphine. *Archives of Neurology, 49,* 144–148.

Ring, H. A., Bench, C. J., Trimble, M. R., Brooks, D. J., Frackowiak, S. J., & Dolan, R. J. (1994). Depression in Parkinson's disease: A positron emission study. *British Journal of Psychiatry, 165,* 333–339.

Robinson, R. G. (1979). Differential behavioral and biochemical effects of right and left hemispheric cerebral infarction in the rat. *Science, 205,* 707–710.

Robinson, R. G., Kubos, K. L., Starr, L. B., Rao, K., & Price, T. R. (1984). Mood disorders in stroke patients: Importance of lesion location. *Brain, 107,* 81–93.

Robinson, R. G., & Szetela, B. (1981). Mood changes following left hemisphere brain injury. *Annals of Neurology, 9,* 447–453.

Sanides, F. (1969). Comparative architectonics of the neocortex of mammals and their evolutionary interpretation. *Annals of the New York Academy of Sciences, 167,* 404–423.

Sinyor, D., Jacques, P., Kaloupek, D. G., Becker, R., Goldenberg, M. & Coopersmith, H. M. (1986). Post-stroke depression and lesion location: An attempted replication. *Brain, 109,* 537–546.

Starkstein, S. E., Boston, J. D., & Robinson, R. G. (1988). Mechanisms of mania after brain injury: 12 case reports and review of the literature. *Journal of Nervous and Mental Disease, 176,* 87–100.

Starkstein, S. E., & Mayberg, H. S. (1993). Depression in Parkinson's disease. In S. E. Starkstein & R. G. Robinson (Eds.), *Depression in neurologic disease* (pp. 97–116). Baltimore: Johns Hopkins University Press

Starkstein, S. E., Moran, T. H., Bowersox, J. A., & Robinson, R. G. (1988). Behavioral abnormalities induced by frontal cortical and nucleus accumbens lesions. *Brain Research, 473,* 74–80.

Starkstein, S. E., Petracca, G., Chemerinski, E., TesÛn, A., Sabe, L., Merello, M., & Leiguarda, R. (1998). Depression in classic vs. akinetic-rigid Parkinson's disease. *Movement Disorders, 13,* 29–33.

Starkstein, S. E., Preziosi, T. J., Berthier, M. L., Bolduc, P. L., Mayberg, H. S., & Robinson, R. G. (1989). Depression and cognitive impairment in Parkinson's disease. *Brain, 112,* 1141–1153.

Starkstein, S. E., & Robinson, R. G. (1997). Mechanism of disinhibition after brain lesions. *Journal of Nervous and Mental Disease, 185,* 108–114.

Starkstein, S. E., Robinson, R. G., Berthier, M. L., Parikh, R. M., & Price, T. R. (1988). Differential mood changes following basal ganglia vs. thalamic lesions. *Archives of Neurology, 45,* 725–730.

Starkstein, S. E., Robinson, R. G., & Price, T. R. (1987). Comparison of cortical and subcortical lesions in the production of post-stroke mood disorders. *Brain, 110,* 1045–1059.

Starkstein, S. E., Robinson, R. G., & Price, T. R. (1988). Comparison of patients with and without post-stroke major depression matched for size and location of lesion. *Archives of General Psychiatry, 45,* 247–252.

31

Aggression, Criminality, and the Frontal Lobes

JONATHAN H. PINCUS

Research over the past 20 years has led us to hypothesize that most violence has similar determinants. Violence of street gangs, drug pushers, intrafamily strife, rape, murder and serial murder, arson, assault, and robbery are all associated with a characteristic history and physical findings. All of these instances—the experience of physical abuse in childhood, including sexual abuse, psychiatric disorders with an overly suspicious paranoid attitude, and the presence of brain damage—are important causal factors in the production of violence. Each slightly increases the chance of producing a violent individual, but when all three are combined in one individual, the chances of he or she being violent are very high. These three factors interact: None is ordinarily sufficient, all are unusually necessary. At least two of these have been encountered in all the repeatedly violent individuals whom we have evaluated, and all three have been present in 90% of the more than 100 murders I have personally examined, many on death row.

The portion of the brain most involved has been the frontal lobe. This was surprising because the temporal–limbic system is generally regarded as the center of violent impulses, atavistic reactions, and primitive drives.

I recently evaluated 31 murders. A history of symptoms suggestive of complex partial seizures was elicited in only five of these. Only four demonstrated EEG abnormalities arising from the temporal lobe. Of the 19 who underwent neuroimaging, 3 demonstrated temporal lobe abnormalities with reduced volume of one of the temporal lobes. In all, only 9 of the 31 subjects either had symptoms suggestive of seizures arising from the temporal lobe or had temporal lobe abnormalities on EEG, MRI, or both. Of these nine, one had both symptoms and EEG abnormalities. Of these nine, six also demonstrated frontal signs.

Frontal signs on physical examination were present in 20 of the 31 individuals. Neuropsychological testing indicated frontal abnormalities in many of the remainder. Thirty of the 31 subjects underwent some type of testing other than the neurological examination. Of these 30, no subject was normal in all spheres (i.e., neurological examination, EEG, neuropsychological testing, and neuroimaging). Specific neurological diagnoses could be established in 20 of the 31 subjects. These included fetal alcohol syndrome, mental retardation, cerebral palsy, hypothyroidism, hydrocephalus, and traumatic brain injury. Only two had a history of epilepsy.

Neurological damage is seldom, if ever, the sole cause of violence. It is true that Vietnam veterans who have sustained frontal damage seem more likely to have aggressive displays when they are angry, but this involves only a small number of those who are so damaged (Grafman et al., 1996).

Most psychotic people are not violent, although a few who have command hallucinations ordering them to kill may be dangerous. The vast majority of brain-damaged and psychotic individuals tend to live quiet lives in a back room of the family home, attend special classes, and proceed to a more or less protected work environment with periods in a mental institution, on welfare, or harmlessly remaining on the street with the homeless. None of these are especially desirable outcomes, but criminality and violence are definitely not obligatory or even common results of neurological and/or psychiatric disorder.

There is evidence that most people who have been abused do not become violent criminals (Widom, 1989). Indeed, many abused siblings of violent people do not become violent, yet abuse appears to be a constant feature of the histories of violent individuals.

It may take enormous energy and intact nervous system, one that is unimpaired by neurological or psychiatric disease, to overcome the tendency to violence that is engendered by consistent, long-term abuse delivered by parents or parent substitutes at a tender age. When the impulse to violence that is engendered by abuse is accompanied by brain damage, which makes it difficult for the individual to exercise inhibitory controls over his or her impulses, and the individual also has a psychiatric disorder that has the same effect, making it difficult for him or her to exercise control over impulses, a very dangerous individual may develop.

Thus, abuse, paranoia, and neurological impairment do not act additively. They *interact*. Each quality endows the others with malign significance.

The frontal lobes are enormous, comprising about 40% of the human cortex. The only part of the frontal lobes in which there is a clear, undisputed identity of structure and function are the motor area and Broca's area for speech, which are the most posteriorly located within the frontal lobes. The huge mass of brain that lies in front of the motor area is quite mysterious. Often called "prefrontal," as though it were in front of the brain, it is in fact, *within* the brain and comprises the bulk of the frontal lobes. The region is sometimes considered "silent" because lesions in it often produce no obvious defect in sensation, motor performance, or cognitive function.

It is the region of the brain that makes the human brain recognizably different from the ape, and we should be proud of this measure of our superiority. We have big frontal lobes. It is, therefore, curious, almost embarrassing, that this region of the brain, so highly developed, uniquely, in humans in its size and proportional importance, should seem "silent." The "silence" of frontal lobes lesions, however, is a chimera, the result of inadequate assessment.

When lesions are sustained in the frontal regions anterior to the motor area, behavioral changes may be difficult for a physician to measure, but families, friends, and employers report that the person is no longer the same. Patients may drive through red lights, fail to keep appointments, become slovenly and unkempt, make socially inappropriate remarks, laugh at foolish jokes, urinate on the floor, or leave a child or stove unattended without concern. Some become violent after minor provocation. Some become unable to adapt their behavior to changed circumstances. A prominent feature of the frontal lobe syndrome is poor judgment. The individual may show defects in the ability to foresee, plan, organize, and execute complex behavior (Devinsky, 1992).

One patient of ours, a physician, cured of a falcine bifrontal meningioma but left with large holes instead of frontal lobes, had to stop driving because he had the same accident three times. He drove in a lane that had been closed off. He could see the barrier coming but he did not make the adjustment to change lanes and crashed into the barrier. He could not adapt to a new situation to avoid a disaster. Yet he could drive mechanically, knew where he was going, and knew, intellectually, that two things could not occupy the same space simultaneously. There was something wrong with the processing of this information.

Not everyone with frontal damage has that exact problem in driving or has the same, exact manifestation of poor judgment. Criminal behavior that is not violent can be a manifestation of poor judgment too.

Another patient with frontal lobe dysfunction repeatedly stole cars. On one occasion, in a stolen car, he drove on the interstate highway at excessive speed. When arrested, he explained, "The sign said 95." It was I-95, of course, not the speed limit. On another occasion the stolen auto he drove required repairs, and he drove into a repair shop at 3:00 A.M. That is, he drove through the locked portal of the repair shop for the purpose of repairing the car. It did not occur to him that this was unwise not only because it was illegal but also because he did not know how to repair the car once he entered. The alarm went off, and he remained, hoping the police would help him to repair the car when they came. He was not retarded. His Full Scale IQ was 89; performance IQ, 94; verbal, 87 with little variation among ability areas, but tests of executive (frontal) function were severely abnormal.

The case of Phineas Gage is a famous example of the frontal lobe syndrome. The reason that this case report, written more than a century ago, captured the imagination of physicians, psychologists, and society in general is that it was one of the first intersections between the usually parallel lines of scientific medicine on the one hand and morality, ethics, and the law on the other. Ethics and morality were in the brain. They could be removed without motor, sensory, or cognitive loss. The soul was in the brain. Not in the heart, liver, or gall bladder, or somewhere outside the body in the supracalavarial miasma. No, the soul was actually infracalavarial, supratentorial, and anterior to the motor strip.

The case of Phineas Gage in the 19th century galvanized clergymen and lawyers as it did physicians and neuroscientists, and this galvanization continues to the present. No one who has ever taken an introductory psychology course at college has failed to read or hear about the case of Phineas Gage.

As in most behavioral syndromes, with frontal injury the clinical picture varies from patient to patient. Individual features depend on the nature of the disease, localization, size of the lesion, baseline intellectual endowment of the individual who has been damaged, and, most important, the individual's past experiences and learning.

With frontal injury, individuals become disinhibited. That is, they act instinctually and in accordance with their desires. Their capacity to say to themselves, "Stop! Don't say or do that. It is not wise," is damaged. In people whose instincts are benign, this may not be socially dangerous. It is our contention that in the abused and paranoid, frontal damage is like letting a lion out of his cage.

One subject of ours, a longtime resident on death row, had entered a convenience store at night while his girlfriend waited approvingly and expectantly outside. At knifepoint he took the small amount of cash available in the till and told the young clerk to precede him to the back room.

In reconstructing the crime from the autopsy, it seems that he plunged his knife into the young man's back with a fatal blow. Mortally wounded, the man spun around and offered a weak defense with his arms, and the subject stabbed him repeatedly 54 times in the chest and arms and cut his throat.

Seventy-two hours after the murder, while his girlfriend waited in a nearby room, the subject called a used car dealer and asked him to stay late. The dealer obliged. Our subject, carrying a knife and a tire iron, approached the man, who was alone in his office. A fierce struggle ensued. The victim, though fat and elderly, put up a valiant defense. The office was destroyed, a window frame was broken, furniture and other appointments were scattered. The victim was stabbed 17 times. Many of the wounds were defensive and several were potentially fatal. His throat was deeply slashed. The total amount of money stolen from the two dead men totaled about $100.

Thus, our subject killed two men by multiple stabbing within the space of 72 hours. An investigation led to his arrest, and he confessed. He was accused of premeditated felony murder; the homicides were said to be a means of preventing his being identified. The case against him was strong, as he, himself provided this explanation to the police in his confession.

Stabbing a man 54 times or 17 times is overkill and implies great emotionality and defective impulse control. The commission of two similar murders in less than 3 days for a total of less than $100 suggests terrible judgment, poor planning, and defective prioritizing.

Often, alcohol or drugs contribute to wild, rageful overkilling. Psychotically paranoid individuals, people who, for one reason or another, are out of touch with reality, may, at times, feel inordinately threatened and attack their perceived enemies with a greater intensity than necessary. Brain injury is another condition that commonly underlies extraordinary violence. Brain damage or dysfunction of almost any kind can be associated with impulsiveness, emotional lability, and an intensification of feeling states, especially rage. Therefore, it is not unusual to discover, in cases of overkill, that the perpetrator was under the influence of alcohol or drugs, was psychotically paranoid, had some type of brain damage, or was suffering from some combination of the above.

None of these conditions, intoxication, psychosis, or frontal damage, alone, is sufficient to cause violence. Rather, these individual factors, or combinations of factors, increase an individual's vulnerability to respond to impulses he is unable to check. Brain damage, intoxication, and paranoia impair judgment and the ability to think ahead to the consequences of an act.

In this case, a previous, brief psychiatric evaluation had concluded that the subject simply had "antisocial personality disorder." That he had behaved antisocially there could be no doubt. This kind of essentially useless tautology is the one most commonly used by clinicians who do not wish to take the time to perform a thorough assessment, or who do not like the subject to begin with. The first psychologist who evaluated him concluded that he had demonstrated no evidence of brain damage or neurological impairment. His IQ was normal.

One did not have to be a sophisticated observer to recognize, on first glance, that our subject was brain damaged. It was obvious. He limped. The right side of his face was paralyzed. His right eye was blind and smaller than the left. It had been so from birth.

He carried some impressive facial scars, including a previous tracheostomy. Our subject told us that when he was 16 he had been in a motor vehicle accident and had been in a coma for 2 weeks in intensive care.

Tendon reflexes in his left leg were hyperactive. He showed bilateral Babinski signs. Further evidence of left-sided brain injury was the finding that although he was right-handed, his right hand moved more slowly and was less well coordinated than his left. He demonstrated a snout reflex, saccadic eye movements of the eyes in pursuit, and paratonia, and he was unable to perform reciprocal alternating motor acts with his hands. These are frontal signs (Luria, 1962; Paulson & Gottlieb, 1968; Rodin, 1964).

Just as it should not have required a neurologist to recognize his brain damage, so it should not have taken a psychiatrist to see that there was something very wrong with the subject's behavior. He maintained an "upbeat" attitude that completely belied his physical and legal proximity to the electric chair. Garrulous and high spirited, he seemed utterly oblivious to his status as a condemned prisoner awaiting execution. He rambled; his answers rarely focused on the subject under consideration. His insouciant attitude and inability to feel the seriousness of his situation are characteristic of the thought processes of individuals with frontal lobe injuries. He was also irritable, according to the history, and misinterpreted social situations in a paranoid manner.

On one occasion, before his crime while working in a steel mill, the subject got into a fight with a fellow worker because he mistakenly thought the worker had insulted him rather than a third individual to whom the remarks had actually been addressed. Asked why in either case it was necessary to respond violently, he explained, "I can't think fast enough to respond with words to someone. I'd rather fight than talk. Nothing bothers me except smart mouths."

Despite his irritability and paranoia, it was easy to take advantage of the subject. Anyone who was nice to him could get him to do his work, egg him on to foolhardy feats of daring, and borrow money and not repay it, and still he was amiable. But he had one weak point; if he was teased or belittled, he would instantly turn vicious.

This was a pattern that had begun long before. He never got along well with the other children in his school classes. He was always bigger than they were and his physical size allowed him to protect himself, but he got into many fights which resulted from his being teased. He tended to be "a loner."

The subject said with pride that he had never lost a fight. He seemed to derive a great deal of pride from his capacity to fight and whatever feeling of self-worth he held seemed to derive from his capacity to beat up other people. As he got older he began to carry knives.

When asked why this was necessary, he laughed and said he did not know. But on further questioning, it seemed that he carried the knives for protection, an adaptation to paranoid thinking.

Our prior experience with violent, weapons-carrying delinquents led us to suspect strongly that the subject had been severely physically abused as a child, but no such history could be obtained from him. Like most of the other inmates on death row, he was reluctant to say a critical word about his mother or father. He only hinted at beatings sustained at the hands of his father, minimized them, and alluded in vague terms to ways in which his father "slapped around" his mother. He specifically said that he had never been abused by either of his parents.

In preparation for the second sentencing trial, the judge permitted the completion of the clinical evaluation. At the request of the doctors, the judge ordered neuropsy-chological tests, an MRI scan of the brain, and an EEG, and he permitted the defense to engage the services of an investigator to review the background of the defendant.

Our clinical findings and impression were confirmed and extended by the results of these additional efforts. The neuropsychologist found evidence of damage to both frontal lobes on the Wisconsin Card Sorting Test, Trailmaking A and B, and the Categories Test from the Halstead–Reitan battery. The EEG was abnormal. The MRI scan of the brain showed bilateral frontal white matter lesions, probably of traumatic origin, that effectively represented bifrontal leukotomies. These findings confirmed our prediction of frontal lobe dysfunction.

The social investigator traced a half sibling of the defendant, who was living about 1000 miles away. At the time the investigator was able to contact the half sibling, his children had just been removed from his home by court order. He had been sexually molesting them and caused them to sexually molest each other.

The investigator was able to review the reports of the social workers that had led to the removal of these children from the half sibling's home. These reports recorded some of the activities within the family during our subject's childhood and indicated the kind of home in which he and his sexually abusive half brother had been raised.

From the age of 6 or 7 and continuing for almost a decade, our subject had been used by his mother for her own sexual gratification. The younger children were often locked out of the house when the father was absent so the defendant could perform cunnilingus on his mother. Other sexual games were played as well and the defendant was forced to engage in sexual displays and activities with his younger siblings for her edification and was given license by his mother to beat his younger siblings. His mother rewarded him with something approaching kindness in return for sexually satisfying her and punished him by ridicule and beating.

The (step) father was a brutal man who hated his stepson, probably in part because he was the son of a rival and partly because he was in fact a rival himself, though of tender age. The beatings delivered to our subject were severe and resulted in a report to Child Protective Services even in those days (the 1950s). On one occasion when the subject was about 9 years old, he climbed a tree to escape a beating at the hand of his stepfather. To reach him, the stepfather chopped down the tree with an axe.

As is typical of other individuals who have been horrendously abused as children, our subject had completely repressed these experiences. Even after being confronted with the evidence, he had no recollection of these painful scenes.

Sometimes, when abuse is relentless and intolerable, children totally block it out to survive and experience it as though it were happening to someone else. Later on, they may have absolutely no recollection of the abusive events. This is called dissociation, and it may be confused with epilepsy, especially in brain-damaged individuals.

In view of these new data, we attempted to reconstruct the probable dynamics of the subject's crime. Abuse underlay his violent impulses. His only source of pride was physical strength and its use to intimidate others. The abuse he had experienced as a child diminished any moral compunction that might have prevented his use of physical force. His mother actually encouraged it. He was easily manipulated by anyone who offered him friendship and was much in the power of a woman who directed him to obtain money for her benefit. He planned the robbery and deliberately, exuberantly, and in premeditated fashion intended to murder. He wanted to demonstrate his physical superiority to his girlfriend. The meager reward (less than $100) and the potential cost (his life) were not factors in his planning.

Frontal damage seemed to have interfered with his ability to plan properly. He seemed to be unable to anticipate either dangerous or propitious circumstances, to arrange, invent, postpone, modulate, or discriminate in achieving his goal. Anxiety and fear reactions were dampened by brain damage, but he was left with explosive unmodulated anger that resulted from minimal stimulation. His brain damage created a constant encephalopathy which was very much like that of a man who is constantly drunk. Were it not for brain damage, he might have been able to control his violent impulses because he would have been able to foresee their consequences. Were it not for the abuse, there would have been no violent impulses to control. It was abuse that endowed the frontal brain damage with dire significance and it was frontal damage that opened the door to violence born of abuse.

Curiously, the brain functions that are assayed by standard mental status examination used by psychiatrists and neurologists, and the psychological tests that are encompassed by standard assessment of intelligence, the IQ, are often almost completely unaffected by frontal lobe damage (Damasio, 1985). Memory, speech, mathematical calculation, reading capacity, writing capacity, orientation, and spatial concepts are not affected by frontal lobe damage, but judgment is devastated. A person can be a social imbecile because of frontal damage and still have a normal IQ.

The actual symptoms of frontal lobe damage vary from patient to patient. Judgment is hard to standardize in a test. Yet, there are a large number of other neurological functions that may be abnormal in frontal disorders: reflexes, eye movements, verbal fluency, and complex motor functions can be abnormal (Lezak, 1976; Luria, 1962; Ozeretskii, 1930; Paulson & Gottlieb, 1968; Rodin, 1964; Shahani, Burrows, & Whitty, 1970) These have been standardized for adults (Jenkyn, Walsh, Culver, & Reeves, 1977; Jenkyn et al., 1985). Any or all of these may be abnormal when the frontal lobes are not working properly. Thus, the neurological examination, properly done, can provide independent evidence of frontal damage but does not really deal directly with the assessment of judgment. Every person whose behavior is aberrant, let alone violent, is a possible case of frontal lobe disorder, but it is the rare neurologist or pediatric neurologist who specifically assesses frontal signs, unfortunately.

Psychological tests are available and have also been standardized for frontal damage, but again these have very little to do with judgment. These tests include the Wisconsin Card Sorting Test, Categories, and Trailmaking A and B (Damasio, 1985; Lezak, 1976). Often psychologists omit these tests, seemingly performing tests of lesser sensitivity with relation to frontal lesions such as IQ testing, the Minnesota Multiphasic Personality Inventory battery, and projective tests.

The mind is a major output of the brain. It has many facets, and not all are assayed by any one test any more than are all blood tests encompassed by any single battery.

"What's my blood type, Doc? They did blood tests on me last week," said a patient recently. The answer was, "Yes, but they did not do the test that determines your blood type."

A similar scenario exists with frontal lobe damage and the "ordinary" neurological examination and the "ordinary" psychological tests. These do not assess the functioning of the frontal lobes.

There have been increasing attempts to localize function within the frontal lobe and the circuits subserving it and the subcortical centers that are connected with it. These considerations provide a "new" anatomic meeting place for neurologists and psychiatrists. Cummings (1993) recently provided a useful review of these concepts.

Tests of brain *function* (neurological examination and psychological tests) are often more revealing of frontal dysfunction than are tests of brain *structure*. The standard MRI or CT scan are excellent tests of brain *structure* but give very little insight into the microscopic organization of the brain and little clue to brain *function*. Many serious disorders that may involve frontal lobe functions are not reflected by abnormal MRI scans. Many laymen and even some physicians are surprised to discover that MRI scans may be normal or nonspecifically abnormal in Alzheimer's disease, Huntington's chorea, Parkinson's disease with dementia, learning disorders, schizophrenia, manic–depressive psychosis, mental retardation, and epilepsy.

The electroencephalogram, similarly, is an inconsistent measure of physiological brain abnormality and is characteristically normal in most of the above. Even epileptics can have normal EEGs between seizures. Positron emission (PET), functional magnetic resonance (FMR), and single photon emission computer tomography (SPECT) may provide clinically useful information in the future, but these are not generally available as yet and furnish subjects for investigation as much as they provide tools for the investigation of behavior.

Because of the inadequacies in each kind of testing, *all* may be employed usefully in patients suspected of having frontal lobe disorders, whether or not the subject of the investigation is violent. The most useful have been the neurological examination and neuropsychological tests of frontal functions.

Most of the individuals we have seen on death row have been damaged during their very earliest years, many *in utero* (Blake, Pincus, & Buckner, 1995). Oftentimes mothers of the perpetrators are alcoholics or drug users and abused these drugs during their pregnancies. Many of our subjects have shown the stigmata of fetal alcohol effect. Many of their mothers gave birth in their early teenage years and did not receive prenatal care or counseling regarding diet, vitamin supplements, and the like. Many were exposed to lead during childhood. Most have sustained traumatic brain injuries in childhood and afterward. The stage is clearly set for brain damage.

Most of the violent individuals we have seen had a preceding diagnosis of attention-deficit/hyperactivity disturbance with conduct disorder in childhood. Some had been treated with methylphenidate (Ritalin). The ones not so diagnosed were not necessarily normal. Some who lived in areas remote from a decent standard of medical care did not have access to this diagnosis or any therapy. Proper diagnosis and treatment were often lacking because of the wanderlust of their parents, with frequent moves that made it impossible to provide a sustained relationship with a particular physician, other health care worker, or teacher. Also, some of the parents had odd ideas about the medical care of children and preferred to save money or for other idiosyncratic reasons would not see or consult with medical personnel.

The high frequency with which we encountered the symptoms of attention-deficit/hyperactivity disorder (ADHD) and conduct disorder (CD) in the childhood records of murderers has increased our interest in those conditions. Curiously, there is increasing indication that the frontal lobes of the brain are dysfunctional in ADHD. This is the result of a variety of techniques of study (Castellanos et al., 1996).

What would the behavior of a child in primary school with frontal lobe damage be like? Because the frontal lobes help to focus attention, prioritize, and exclude the extraneous, the child would have a short attention span and would respond to irrelevant stimuli as equally as to relevant ones. Such a child might be hyperactive. He or she would be socially awkward, very likely physically awkward, and yet could have a relatively normal intelligence that he or she was not fully using, "not working to his full potential," in the words of an old schoolmaster. The acquisition of scholastic skills like reading, writing, and arithmetic would be inconsistently achieved because of short attention span. Frustration might lead to irritability and unacceptable temper displays as social inhibitions might not be operative.

Curiously, a primary school child with mania might look quite similar—short attention span, hyperactive, socially inappropriate, unable to focus to exclude stimuli or fully to utilize his or her potential with evidence of easy frustration, irritability, and a "low boiling point." Depressed children also might be similar: withdrawn, preoccupied, unable to concentrate, unable to learn, socially awkward, angry, irritable, and easily provoked to displays of unacceptable emotionality. Both mania and depression have been related to a dysfunctional state of the frontal lobes (Cummings, 1995).

Ritalin, a stimulant, might help frontally damaged children and even those with depression but would not help mania and might make its symptoms worse. Antidepressants would be appropriate for depressed patients. Mood stabilizers like valproic acid (Depakote), lithium, carbamazepine (Tegretol), and gabapentin (Neurontin) might be best for mania but could conceivably help the others, too, if affective instability were prominent.

The very violent individuals we have seen did not simply have ADHD as children. They had ADHD with CD, too—that is, especially destructive behavior with physical harm to people and property, cruelty to animals, and also bedwetting (enuresis) often lasting until the teens. ADHD and CD are not the same. They may coexist, and ADHD is associated with CD in about half the cases. CD with ADHD seemed to characterize all our violent subjects' youth when information was available. We wondered whether we would find the same determinants (abuse, neurological deficit, psychiatric symptoms) in the backgrounds of ADHD children with CD as we found in the background of murderers.

We directed our attention to the question, What factors distinguish children with ADHD from those with ADHD and CD?

Responses to a newspaper advertisement that offered free neurological evaluations to people with "impossible children" were screened and boys with CD and ADHD were matched to boys with ADHD alone, the comparison or control group in this pilot study. The groups were matched for socioeconomic group and age. A standardized interview with examination taking 3 hours was done on each subject, alone and with his parents. Thorough neurological examination was performed. The average age was 9 years and the children were generally from middle-class homes. We found that physical and sexual abuse, familial explosiveness and violence, familial and maternal depression, and suicide distinguished those with CD from those without CD.

Abnormal neurological signs indicating frontal lobe dysfunction were equally prevalent in both groups, which is consistent with the concept that ADHD is probably the result of frontal lobe dysfunction in most cases. Frontal lobe dysfunction, manifested by ADHD, with mental illness and abuse, manifested by CD, would appear to be the childhood matrix from which later serious violence springs. ADHD with CD is a childhood condition with essentially the same determinants as adult violence.

REFERENCES

Blake, P. Y., Pincus, J. H., & Buckner, G. (1995). Neurologic abnormalities in murderers. *Neurology, 45,* 1641–1647.

Castellanos, F. X., Giedd, J. N., Marsh, W. L., Hamburger, S. D., Vaituzis, A. C., & Dickstein, D. P. (1996). Quantitative brain magnetic resonance imaging in attention deficit hyperactivity disorder. *Archives of General Psychiatry, 53,* 607–616.

Cummings, J. L. (1993). Frontal–subcortical circuits and human behavior. *Archives of Neurology, 50,* 873–880.

Cummings, J. L. (1995). Anatomic and behavioral aspects of frontal subcortical circuits. *Annals of New York Academy of Sciences, 769,* 1–13.

Damasio, A. R. (1985). The frontal lobes. In K. M. Heilman & E. Valenstein (Eds.), *Clinical neuropsychology* (2nd ed.). New York: Oxford University Press.

Devinsky, 0. (1992). *Behavioral neuorlogy.* St. Louis: Mosby.

Grafman, J., Schwab, K., Warden, D., Pridgeon, A., Brown, H. R., & Salazar, A. M. (1996). Frontal lobe injuries, violence, and aggression: A report of a Vietnam head injury study. *Neurology, 46,* 1231–1238.

Jenkyn, L. R., Reeves, A. G., Warren, T., Whiting, R. K., Clayton, R. J., & Moore, W. W. (1985). Neurologic signs in senescence. *Archives of Neurology, 42,* 1154–1157.

Jenkyn, L. R., Walsh, D. B., Culver, C. M., & Reeves, A. G. (1977). Clinical signs in diffuse cerebral dysfunction. *Journal of Neurology, Neurosurgery, and Psychiatry, 40,* 956–966.

Lezak, M. D. (1976). *Neuropsychological assessment.* New York: Oxford University Press.

Luria, A. R. (1962). *Higher cortical functions in man* (2nd ed.). New York: Basic Books.

Ozeretskii, N. I. (1930). Techniques of investigating motor function. In M. Gurevich & N. Ozeretskii (Eds.), *Psychomotor functions.* Moscow: Medgiz.

Paulson, G., & Gottlieb, G. (1968). Developmental reflexes: The reappearance of foetal and neonatal reflexes in aged patients. *Brain, 91,* 37–52.

Rodin, E. A. (1964). Impaired ocular pursuit movements. *Archives of Neurology, 10,* 327–331.

Shahani, B., Burrows, P., & Whitty, C. W. M. (1970). The grasp reflex and perseveration. *Brain, 93,* 181–192.

Widom, C. S. (1989). The cycle of violence. *Science, 244,* 160–166.

32

Anterior Temporal Lobes

Social Brain

BRUCE L. MILLER
CRAIG HOU
MICHAEL GOLDBERG
ISMAEL MENA

The frontal lobes have captured the attention and imagination of many scientists (Stuss & Benson, 1986), but the functions of the anterior temporal cortex (AT) have not stimulated such widespread interest. Most temporal lobe research has focused on the posterior temporal structures responsible for encoding vision and language and medial areas, like the hippocampus, involved with memory. However, the AT is functionally related to the basal–frontal regions and both AT and basal–frontal cortex help with the encoding and expression of social signals. Injury to either region causes a dramatic deterioration in many social behaviors.

In 1969, Radinsky speculated that increasing size of prefrontal and polar regions in larger canids such as wolves was associated with more highly developed social behavior, but 25 years later, few studies have explored the social functions of prefrontal cortex or AT, areas for which we use the term "social brain." Unraveling the functions of AT will further understanding of specific neurological and psychiatric conditions including frontotemporal dementia (FTD), autism, and schizophrenia.

Luckily, interest in the AT is beginning to increase, stimulated, in part, by better recognition of the diverse disorders associated with selective dysfunction of this brain region. The establishment of rehabilitation units to cope with head injury has stimulated interest in AT by exposing clinicians to patients with profound social deterioration due to combined anterior temporal and basal–frontal injury. Also, functional imaging and pathological studies of patients with depression (Lesser et al., 1994), psychosis (Chua & McKenna, 1995; Miller, Lesser, Mena, Villanueva-Meyer, & Hill, 1992), and autism

(Baumann & Kemper, 1985) are showing striking abnormalities in AT suggesting an important role for these areas in the regulation of mood and behavior.

Finally, better recognition of FTD (including Pick's disease), which is associated with degeneration of AT structures (Brun, 1987), has helped to catalyze AT research. In about one-quarter of FTD patients, AT injury is selective, and the frontal regions are spared (Edwards-Lee et al., 1997). These temporal lobe–injured but frontal lobe–spared patients offer a fascinating model for understanding the functions of the AT. Of interest, 60 years earlier Spatz suggested that Pick's disease might be the most important brain disorder for helping to understand cortical localization.

This chapter outlines the anatomy and connections of AT, focusing on amygdala and other structures in the anterior temporal lobes. After discussing temporal anatomy, we describe the behavioral alterations observed following AT ablations in animals. The original studies of Klüver and Bucy are contrasted with later work which described the behaviors of monkeys with AT ablations that were released back into their natural environment. In addition, we describe the social deterioration observed in FTD patients with selective dysfunction of the AT. Finally, we hypothesize a central role in social behavior for AT.

ANATOMY AND CONNECTIONS

Excellent reviews of temporal lobe anatomy have been written by Brodal (1981) and Aggleton (1992). Resting in the middle cranial fossa, the temporal lobe is bounded superiorly by the sylvian fissure and posteriorly by a line drawn between the preoccipital notch and the parieto-occipital sulcus. The temporal lobes are bounded by bony structures including parietal bone laterally, temporal and sphenoid bone inferiorly, and the sphenoid bone anteriorly. The AT is particularly vulnerable to trauma because it is easily pushed against the anterior sphenoid bone with shaking of the head. Medial to the temporal lobes lie the brainstem and cerebellum.

The lateral temporal lobe is composed of the superior, middle, and inferior temporal gyri. The superior sulcus separates the superior and middle gyri, while the inferior temporal sulcus divides the middle and inferior temporal gyri. Medially, the basal surface contains the inferior temporal gyrus, collateral sulcus, rhinal sulcus, and the parahippocampal gyrus. Also called the pyriform lobe, the anteriormost portion of the parahippocampal gyrus projects medially to form the uncus. Posterior and lateral to the uncus yet part of the parahippocampal gyrus is the entorhinal area. Signals from the olfactory bulbs travel via the olfactory tracts to the pyriform cortex, which has projections to the entorhinal area. The inferior horns of the lateral ventricles lie within the temporal lobes. At the anterior and dorsomedial end of the inferior horn lies the amygdala, which is continuous with the uncus. The amygdala contains a collection of nuclei, called the amygdaloid nuclear complex. The head of the hippocampus, or *pes hippocampus,* is closely associated with the dorsally located amygdala.

Most temporal lobe is six-layered isocortex, but the hippocampi, dentate gyri, olfactory, and piriform cortex are composed of three-layered allocortex (Brodal, 1981). Allocortex is separated into paleocortex of the olfactory and piriform cortex and archicortex of the dentate gyrus and hippocampus. Posterior medial orbitofrontal and anterior temporal cortex are called transitional cortex, as both have features between isocortex and allocortex. Lateral AT is supplied by the temporal polar artery off the middle cerebral artery. Some of the inferior portions of the AT are supplied by the branches off the posterior cerebral artery (anterior temporal artery).

The orbitofrontal lobes, amygdala, and AT poles are intimately interconnected, and some have suggested that they form a functional unit based on their histological similarities, anatomical interconnectedness, and comparable behavioral responses following stimulation or lesions. Uncinate cortico-cortical fibers serve as a strong connection between orbitofrontal cortex and AT, and both the amygdala and orbital surfaces project fibers to analogous hypothalamic areas.

The amygdala, which sits directly under the uncus, has a corticomedial and basolateral portion. The corticomedial nucleus receives olfactory fibers and projects to the ventromedial hypothalamic nucleus via the stria terminalis. This fiber system is involved with eating behaviors. The basolateral nuclei show evolution between nonhuman primates and humans and are the only, or primary, site of projection for certain areas of cortex including prefrontal and temporal neocortex. The amygdala has two main efferent fiber pathways, the dorsal amygdalofugal pathway passing in stria terminalis and the ventral amygdalofugal pathway. Via amygdalofugal and stria terminalis fibers, the amygdala projects to the forebrain, hypothalamus, thalamus, brainstem, olfactory bulb, hippocampus, and temporal lobe. With forebrain and hypothalamus, the amygdala has extensive reciprocal connections, whereas the connections to dorsomedial thalamus are one way. Likewise, the amygdala receives few afferent fibers from the hippocampus but projects numerous efferents via the entorhinal cortex and perforant pathways. The amygdala has no direct connection to visual cortex but has visual input via the anterior inferior temporal lobe. Other amygdaloid afferents arrive from auditory association areas in the superior temporal gyrus and polysensory association areas in perirhinal cortex, parahippocampal gyrus, and temporal poles.

Entorhinal cortex relays sensory information from primary visual cortex to the amygdala, which in turn projects fibers to higher-order visual cortices in the temporal and occipital lobes. The paraventricular nucleus of the thalamus and entorhinal cortex are also heavily interconnected. Also, the entorhinal cortex receives fibers from the superior temporal, parahipppocampal, perirhinal, and temporal polar cortex. Efferents then project toward the hippocampus.

ANIMAL STUDIES OF AMYGDALA

The amygdala functions in sensory processing, social behavior, memory, and emotion and connects sensory stimuli to emotional and behavioral responses. The amygdala receives input from the olfactory bulb via the lateral olfactory tract and prepyriform cortex, but it is unknown whether the amygdala in humans responds to olfactory stimuli. Similarly, lesions of the amygdala do not directly influence visual, auditory, somatosensory or gustatory sensation in monkeys or humans. However, it is important for organizing social behavior in response to visual stimuli.

Lesions in lizards, rats, cats, and nonhuman primates cause decreased aggression, loss of social rank, and social withdrawal (see review from Kling & Brothers, 1992). Hypersexuality has been observed in cats, dogs, and some species of monkeys. Generally, stimulation leads to behaviors that are opposite to those elicited by lesions. Certain neuronal groups in amygdala respond to complex sensory stimuli with an emotional valence such as faces. Stimulation of amygdala in many animals causes autonomic changes associated with "fight or flight" such as piloerection, hissing, claw displaying, and actual attack or flight. However, in humans, stimulation has produced dreamy sensations memories and hallucinations of fear, *déjà vu*, or epigastric rising.

Experiments from Adolphs, Tranel, Damasio, and Damasio (1995) suggest that the amygdala provide affective and temporal meaning to stimuli. In a patient with Urbach–Wiethe disease, both amygdala were severely injured by calcification, but the hippocampus and surrounding structures were intact. While able to recognize the identity of faces, the patient could not recognize facial expressions. Recognition of fear showed the greatest impairment. Hence, the amygdala has very specific functions in encoding human facial features and emotion. Also, the amygdala plays an important role in encoding fear-associated memory (McGaugh, Cahill, & Roozendaal, 1996).

KLÜVER–BUCY SYNDROME

The Original Caged Animal Experiments

In Klüver and Bucy's experiments, in cage-dwelling macaque monkeys, the anterior one-third of the temporal lobes were ablated. On recovery, the macaques showed a dramatic change in their eating behaviors. This had two main components, a change in dietary preference and a tendency to put objects into their mouths. From fastidious vegetarians, the monkeys became orally indiscriminate, readily ate meat, and placed nonfood items into their mouths. The hyperorality was partially explained by the monkey's inability to recognize objects through vision which led them to explore their environment orally. Although the monkeys could see, they were unable to recognize visually many objects and approached animate and inanimate items without fear, often placing them in their mouths. For this behavior Klüver and Bucy coined the term "psychic blindness." Also, there was excessive attention to new stimuli in the environment: *hypermetamorphosis*. Previously cautious and even aggressive toward strangers, the macaques became placid and allowed humans to touch, pet, or even slap them. Finally, the monkeys frequently masturbated and randomly attempted to copulate with other monkeys. Both heterosexual and homosexual behaviors occurred.

The experiments stimulated decades of research into the functions of the AT and associated structures including the amygdala, hippocampus, and prefrontal cortex. These experiments have shown extraordinary endurance and, even today, investigations are structured to determine what components of AT injury are necessary for the Klüver–Bucy syndrome. Most studies suggest that bilateral injury is required for the emergence of the full-blown syndrome. Also, bilateral amygdalar ablation alone produces oral behavior, placidity, and increased reaction to stimuli, although the visual defects may require lesions of temporal neocortex. Injury to both hippocampi does not produce the behavioral manifestations found with the AT ablations, whereas lesions of anterior temporal neocortex-sparing amygdala produce the syndrome.

As Klüver and Bucy (1939)noted in one of their original papers, "We may consider the outstanding characteristic of the behavioral changes following bilateral temporal lobectomy to be that they affect the relation between animal and environment so deeply." The authors went on to add, "A monkey which approaches every enemy to examine it orally will conceivably not survive longer than a few hours . . . in a region with a plentiful supply of enemies." As will be described, similar disruptions in social behavior also occur in humans with injury to this anatomic region.

Anterior Temporal Ablation Followed by Return to a Natural Environment

One weakness of the original experiments by Klüver and Bucy was that the monkeys were not returned to a natural environment and they made behavioral observations after the animals returned to a cage. In retrospect, this feature of experimental design prevented important observations regarding the role of the AT in complex primate social behavior. Later studies described behavioral changes that occurred in primates after they were returned to an environment which more accurately simulated life in nature (Franzen & Myers, 1973; Kling & Steklis, 1976).

In one set of experiments (Franzen & Myers, 1973), monkeys with ablations of the anterior one-third of the temporal lobes were compared to monkeys with lesions of prefrontal cortex anterior to the frontal eye fields. In both groups, the monkey made indiscriminate approaches toward others, irrespective of rank. Also, the monkeys lost normal facial expressions, body postures, and gestures. The loss of respect for the social rank of others and diminished ability to make appropriate social signals led other monkeys to exclude them from group activities. Monkeys with prefrontal lesions were more passive than the AT group, particularly with regard to both mothering and sexual behavior. The lesioned mothers did not actively look for their babies but would passively feed them when the infants attempted to suckle. Similarly, sexual activity was actively avoided. The AT group were extremely poor parents and the mothers actively prevented their children from nursing. However, they were more likely to engage in sexual behavior than were the prefrontal lesioned monkeys.

In 1976, Kling and Steklis studied behavioral changes in old-world monkeys following lesions to either prefrontal cortex or AT. There was a dramatic change in the social acceptance of the animals following lesions to either region. Most strikingly, there was a dramatic drop in the animals' social rank and decreased socialization with other members of the colony. No longer outgoing or social, the lesioned monkeys became withdrawn and fearful. Animals previously at the top of the social ladder were shunned; some were even aggressively attacked.

These studies eloquently addressed the importance of AT and prefrontal regions in the regulation and control of social behavior. Kling and Steklis (1976) noted that the lesions produced a loss of "socially affiliative behavior," and Myers (1973) suggested that the prefrontal and AT constituted a functional system. Neither Franzen and Myers nor Kling and Steklis noted the bizarre behaviors originally observed by Klüver and Bucy (1939). Rather, they studied ordinary day-to-day social interactions and showed the importance of AT and prefrontal cortex for social bonds. Hence, from a strange syndrome with only remote relevance to most brain disorders, the AT was observed to play a primary role in ordinary social behavior with potential relevance to a variety of brain disorders in humans including FTD, schizophrenia, and autism.

Physiological Studies in Humans

Recent physiological studies have demonstrated changes in the frontal and anterior temporal lobes in association with the elicitation of specific emotional responses. Ekman, Levenson, and Friesen (1983) and others (Wheeler, Davidson, & Tomarken, 1993) showed that emotional responses such as happiness and disgust were associated with unique patterns of physiological activation. Davidson, Ekman, Saron, Senulis, and Friesen (1990) hypothesized that approach-eliciting responses such as happiness activated the left frontotemporal regions, whereas the right frontotemporal areas were activated by withdrawal-eliciting responses such as fear or disgust. The authors showed emotion-inducing scenes from movies while brain electrical activity was simultaneously measured. These studies suggested that the AT and prefrontal cortex had asymmetric functions in humans. Studies of FTD patients support this concept of asymmetric functions for the right and left prefrontal and AT regions.

DISEASES WITH ANTERIOR TEMPORAL LOBE ABNORMALITIES

This book presents a strong focus on the frontal disorders. However, AT involvement is probably an important component of the behavioral deficits seen with a variety of diseases with psychiatric manifestations. Table 32.1 lists some of the disorders associated with AT dysfunction. With these illnesses the main manifestation of AT injury is usually behavioral. Autism and schizophrenia, the two associated with profound abnormalities in social behavior, are briefly discussed.

Frontotemporal Dementia

FTD is a progressive dementing disorder which causes selective degeneration of the prefrontal and AT regions (Brun, 1987; Neary, Snowden, Northen, & Goulding, 1988; Miller et al., 1991). With FTD there is profound disruption of social conduct, and nearly every abnormal behavior found in primates with AT lesions has been described in patients with FTD. FTD is anatomically heterogeneous with variability in the relative involvement of left versus right and prefrontal versus AT areas.

Approximately 25% of the UCLA FTD patients seen by Dr. Miller show selective AT dysfunction with prefrontal cortical sparing. The group with selective AT involvement, which we have called the temporal lobe variant (TLV) of FTD, offers a fascinating model for the clinical manifestations of selective asymmetric but bilateral AT dysfunction (Edwards-Lee et al., 1997). The behaviors found in this group of humans parallel the findings in the AT-lesioned animals described by Franzen and Myers (1973) and Kling and Steklis (1976).

TABLE 32.1. Some Disorders Associated with AT Dysfunction

Tumor	Glioma, sphenoid ridge meningioma, epidermoid
Infection	Bacterial: Abscess (spread from inner ear) Virus: Herpes simplex Parasitic: Toxoplasmosis (HIV)
Trauma	Often bilateral (sometimes associated with hemorrhage
Vascular	Middle cerebral artery emboli or thrombosis (unilateral) Middle cerebral artery aneurysm (unilateral)
Demyelinating	Multiple sclerosis
Development	Autism
Degenerative	Frontotemporal dementia Less commonly Alzheimer's disease
Psychiatric	Schizophrenia? Depression?
Neurological	Epilepsy

Profound social impairment is common in most FTD patients (Miller et al., 1991) and many items in the research criteria established for this condition (Brun et al., 1994) focus on loss of "socially affiliative behaviors." These deficits, which are part of the Lund–Manchester Research Criteria for FTD, include early loss of social awareness, emotional unconcern, disinhibition and amimia. Family members often complain that the FTD patient has become cold, withdrawn, or indifferent and antisocial behaviors occur in nearly 50% (Miller, Darby, Benson, Cummings, & Miller, 1997). This combination of social withdrawal, loss of emotional concern and disinhibition (Miller et al., 1991) can lead to serious disruption of social relationships, and we have seen patients who are divorced by their spouses due to these changes. Hyperorality, stereotyped motor behaviors, and distractibility also contribute to a bizarre presentation. Although the prefrontal dysfunction and/or serotonin deficiency found with FTD account for some of these social changes, AT injury appears to be critical (Edwards-Lee et al., 1997).

Patients with the TLV of FTD show profound social impairment, particularly those with asymmetric right anterior temporal lobe dysfunction, who appear bizarre, remote, and alien. Facial and body expression are diminished, while staring and even grimacing occurs (Miller, Chang, Mena, Boone, & Lesser, 1993). These patients often lose their sense of fear and physically invade the personal space of others. Their social standing invariably drops. This alien and bizarre affect and behavior is sometimes reminiscent of schizophrenia and the first patients that we recognized with right-sided predominant FTD were referred with a diagnosis of late-life onset psychosis (Lesser, Miller, Boone, Hill, & Mena, 1989). In contrast, patients with selective left temporal lesions tend to show sparing of their social demeanor and do not have such dramatic social decline, although depression and social withdrawal and language deficits are common.

Occasionally TLV patients threaten or strike others, but more commonly their affect leads others to incorrectly assume that the FTD patient is a threat to them. Much like the poker-faced monkeys with faulty social signaling who were attacked by their previous friends (Kling & Steklis, 1976), TLV individuals are sometimes harmed by others. Because patients with asymmetric right-sided dysfunction generally show more severe social impairment than do those with asymmetric left-sided involvement, we have suggested that the right temporal and frontal lobes are dominant for social behavior (Miller et al., 1993).

Other behaviors in FTD show parallels with the original syndrome described by Klüver and Bucy. Their distractibility and impulsivity, which is found in the majority of FTD patients (Miller, Ponton, Benson, Cummings, & Mena, 1996), is reminiscent of "hypermetamorphosis." In addition, some patients, particularly those with the TLV, show an intense visual interest in the environment, and we have seen individuals who developed a new and obsessive interest in finding coins, painting, or playing word or computer games (Edwards-Lee et al., 1997). Sometimes this intense visual interest can lead the TLV patient to produce beautiful paintings, astonishing in that creativity is unexpected in the setting of dementia (Miller et al., 1996). Finally, hyperorality is a prominent feature and more than 50% of subjects with FTD show eating changes Miller, Darby, Swartz, Yener, & Mena, 1995). Hence, selective dysfunction of AT in humans leads to profound alterations in social behavior, suggesting that this brain area plays a prominent role in social behavior.

Autism

Autism is found in approximately 2 of 1,000 children and begins before the age of 3 (Wing & Gould, 1979). It is clinically characterized by severe abnormalities in reciprocal social relatedness and communication and restricted and repetitive patterns of behavior and interest (Gillberg & Coleman, 1996). These children are emotionally remote with blunted affect (Kanner, 1943) and repetitive compulsive behaviors such as opening doors or turning on and off of lights. Most autistic individuals are unable to establish normal social contacts. In contrast to the social disorder, many autistic children have normal, or even superior, visuospatial and motor skills. Seizures are common, found in approximately 35–45% of all cases (Olsson, Steffenberg, & Gillberg, 1988). The area localized for the seizures is the temporal lobe in approximately 70% of cases and the high association between autism and temporal lobe seizures suggests that many patients have temporal lobe pathology.

Structural imaging studies of patients with autism have uncovered a variety of brain abnormalities including cerebellar atrophy (Courchesne, Yeung-Courchesne, Press, Hesselink, & Jernigan, 1988), ventricular dilatation (Gaffney & Tsai, 1987) and various abnormalities of cellular migration (Piven et al., 1990). However, most neuroimaging studies suggest that the primary anatomic substrate for autism is AT and medial temporal lobes (Maurer & Damasio, 1982; Bachevalier, 1994). A recent study by Chugani, Da Silve, and Chugani (1996) showed that of 118 patients with infantile spasms, a subgroup of 18 showed bitemporal hypometabolism on positron emission tomography. Fourteen of these individuals were followed and 10 of these 14 developed autism, supporting a strong relationship between abnormal temporal lobe metabolism and autism. Using an entirely different approach, Bolton and Griffiths (1997) evaluated the structural brain abnormalities in 18 patients with tuberous sclerosis; 9 with autism and 9 without. Eight of nine with autism but none of nine without autism had temporal lobe tubers.

Although the number of pathology studies performed are still quite limited, the few performed suggest abnormalities in AT and medial temporal lobes (Bauman & Kemper, 1985). Decreased neuronal cell size and increased cell-packing density has been seen in the hippocampus, entorhinal cortex, and amygdala, suggesting cells fixed at an earlier stage of brain maturation.

Schizophrenia

The early name for schizophrenia was "dementia praecox," which emphasized the presenile onset and progressive deterioration in social and cognitive functions that characterized the course of patients with this illness.

Typically, schizophrenia starts in the teens or early 20s, when abnormalities in behavior and thought emerge. Social withdrawal, blunted and/or bizarre affect, apathy, delusions and hallucinations, abnormal language and thought, and disinhibition are common. Recently, symptom complexes have been divided into the "negative" (apathy, blunted affect, and social withdrawal) and the "positive" (hallucinations, delusions, agitation) types. There is some suggestion that these symptom complexes may have anatomic, prognostic, or therapeutic implications. Swartz (personal communication, May 1997) used similar scales to characterize patients with FTD, and preliminary results suggest that the blunted and bizarre affect seen in FTD is more common with right-sided lesions.

Not surprisingly, studies of patients with early (Katz et al., 1996) and late-life (Miller et al., 1992) schizophrenia show AT perfusion and metabolic defects with functional imaging. Similarly, some autopsy studies suggest AT abnormalities in the medial temporal lobe. Most of the structural (Honer et al., 1995) and functional (Fletcher, Frith, Grasby, Friston, & Dolan, 1996) studies suggest frontal or frontotemporal abnormalities. Similarly, a recent review of the neuropathological findings in schizophrenia (Arnold &

Trojanowski, 1996) suggested that the important abnormalities demonstrated across studies were (1) decreased ventromedial temporal lobe structures and parahippocampal cortical thickness; (2) decreased neuronal density in the limbic, temporal, and frontal regions; and (3) abnormal dendritic spine densities in cortex and various changes in synaptic protein expression in limbic, temporal, and frontal cortices with alterations in glutamatergic, catecholaminergic, and intrinsic innervation in anterior cingulate cortex, sugggesting miswiring or aberrant neurodevelopment.

CONCLUSIONS

The AT structures play an important role in the control of social behavior. Lesions to this region lead to a fundamental change in social demeanor. Generally, the social appeal of individuals with AT injury diminishes, particularly when the lesions are bilateral but worse on the right. Recent work in humans suggests that the right versus the left AT may play different roles in controls of social behavior, with the left AT differentially responsible for aggression and the right AT critical for modifying socially acceptable behavior.

Patients with acquired AT injury are particularly valuable for understanding the function of this area. However, a better understanding of AT function requires meticulous clinical, neuropsychological, and electrophysiological quantitation of the behaviors that emerge following injury to AT structures. The previous neglect of AT has showed an understanding of the anatomic basis of brain behavior.

REFERENCES

Adolphs, B., Tranel, D., Damasio, H., & Damasio, A. R. (1995). Fear and the human amygdala. *Journal of Neuroscience, 15,* 5879–5891.

Aggleton, J. (Ed.). (1992). *Neurobiologic aspects of emotion, memory, and mental dysfunction.* New York: Wiley Liss.

Arnold, S. E., & Trojanowski, J. (1996). Recent advances in defining the neuropathology of schizophrenia. *Acta Neuropathologica, 92*(3), 217–231.

Bachevalier, J. (1994). Medial temporal lobe structures and autism: A review of clinical and experimental findings. *Neuropsychologia, 32*(6), 627–648.

Bauman, M. L., & Kemper, T. L. (1985). Histoanatomic observations of the brain in early infantile autism. *Neurology, 35,* 866–874.

Bolton, P. F., & Griffiths, P. D. (1997). Association of tuberous sclerosis of temporal lobes with autism and atypical autism. *Lancet, 349,* 392–395.

Brodal, A. (Ed.). (1981). *Neurological anatomy in relation to clinical medicine.* New York: Oxford University Press.

Brun, A. (1987). Frontal lobe degeneration of the non-Alzheimer type: I. Neuropathology. *Archives of Gerontology and Geriatrics, 6,* 193–208.

Brun, A., Englund, B., Gustafson, L., Passant, U., Mann, D. M. A., & Neary, D. (1994) Frontal lobe dementia of the non-Alzheimer type revisited. *Dementia, 4,* 126–131.

Chua, S. E., & McKenna, P. J. (1995). Schizophrenia—A brain disease?: A critical review of structural and functional cerebral abnormality in the disorder. *British Journal of Psychiatry, 166*(6), 563–582.

Chugani, H. T., Da Silva, E., & Chugani, D. C. (1996). Infantile spasms: Prognostic implications of bvitemporal hypometabolism on positron emission tomography. *Annals of Neurology, 39*(5), 643–649.

Courchesne, E., Yeung-Courchesne, R., Press, G. A., Hesselink, J. R., & Jernigan, T. L. (1988). Hypoplasia of cerebellar vermal lobules VI and VII. *New England Journal of Medicine, 318,* 1349–1354.

Davidson, R. J., Ekman, P., Saron, C.D., Senulis, J. A., & Friesen, W. V. (1990).. Approach-withdrawal and cerebral asymmetry: Emotional expression and brain physiology. *Journal of Personality and Social Psychology, 58,* 330–341.

Edwards-Lee, T., Miller, B. L., Benson, D. F. Cummings, J. L., Russell G., & Mena I. (1997). The temporal lobe variant of frontotemporal dementia. *Brain, 120,* 1027–1040.

Ekman, P., Levenson, R. W., & Friesen, W. V. (1983). Autonomic nervous system activity distinguishes among emotions. *Science, 221,* 1208-1210.

Fletcher, P. C., Frith, C. D., Grasby, P. M., Friston, K. J., & Dolan, R. J. (1996). Local and distributed effects of apomorphine on fronto-temporal function in acute unmedicated schizophrenia. *Journal of Neuroscience, 16,* 7055–7062.

Franzen, E. A., & Myers, R. E. (1973). Neural control of social behavior: Prefrontal and anterior temporal cortex. *Neuropsychologia, 11,* 141–157.

Gaffney, G. R., & Tsai, L. Y. (1987). Magnetic resonance imaging of high level autism. *Journal of Autism and Developmental Disorders, 17,* 433–438.

Gillberg, C., & Coleman, M. (1996). Autism and medical disorders: A review of the literature. *Developmental Medicine and Child Neurology, 38,* 191–202.

Honer, W. G., Bassett, A. S., Squires-Wheeler, E., Falkai, P., Smith, G. N., Lapointe, J. S., Canero, C., & Lang, D. J. (1995). The temporal lobes, reversed asymmetry and the genetics of schizophrenia. *Neuroreport, 7*(1), 221–224.

Kanner, L. (1943). Autistic disturbances of affective content. *Nervous Child, 2,* 217–250.

Katz, M., Buchsbaum, M. S., Siegel, B. V., Wu, J., Haier, R. J., & Bunney, W. E. (1996). Correlational patterns of cerebral glucose metabolism in never-medicated schizophrenics. *Neuropsychobiology, 33*(1), 1–11.

Kling, A., & Brothers, L. (1992). The amygdala and social behavior. In J. Aggleton (Ed.), *Neurobiologic aspects of emotion, memory, and mental dysfunction* (pp. 353–377). New York: Wiley Liss.

Kling, A., & Steklis, H. D. (1976). A neural substrate for affiliative behavior in nonhuman primates. *Brain Behavior and Evolution, 13,* 216–238.

Klüver, H., & Bucy, P. C. (1939). Preliminary analysis of functions of the temporal lobes in monkeys. *Archives of Neurology and Psychiatry, 42,* 547–554.

Lesser, I. M., Jeste, D. V., Boone, K. B., Harris, M. J., Miller, B. L., Heaton, R. K., & Hill-Gutierrez, E. (1992). Late-onset psychotic disorder, not otherwise specified (NOS): Clinical, neuropsychological and neuroimaging findings. *Biological Psychiatry, 31,* 419–423.

Lesser, I. M., Miller, B. L., Boone, K., Hill, E., & Mena, I. (1989). Psychosis at the first manifestation of degenerative dementia. *Bulletin of Clinical Neuroscience, 4,* 59–64.

Maurer, R. G., & Damasio, A. R. (1982). Childhood autism from the point of view of behavioral neurology. *Journal of Autism and Developmental Disorders, 12,* 195–205.

McGaugh, J. L., Cahill, L., & Roozendaal, B. (1996). Involvement of the amygdala in memory storage: Interaction with other brain systems. *Proceedings of the National Academy of Sciences, 93,* 13508–13514.

Miller, B. L., Cummings, J. L., Villanueva-Meyer, J., Boone, K., Mehringer, C. M., Lesser, I. M., & Mena, I. (1991). Frontal lobe degeneration: Clinical, neuropsychological and SPECT characteristics. *Neurology, 41,* 1374–1382.

Miller, B. L., Chang, L., Mena, I., Boone, K. B., & Lesser, I. (1993). Clinical and imaging features of right focal frontal lobe degenerations. *Dementia, 4,* 204–213.

Miller, B. L., Darby, A., Benson, D. F., Cummings, J. L., & Miller, M. H. (1997). Antisocial behavior in frontotemporal dementia. *British Journal of Psychiatry, 170,* 1–6.

Miller, B. L., Darby, A. L., Swartz, J. R., Yener, G. G., & Mena, I. (1995). Dietary changes, compulsions and sexual behavior in fronto-temporal degeneration. *Dementia, 6,* 195–199.

Miller, B., Lesser, I., Mena, I., Villanueva-Meyer, J., & Hill, E. (1992). Regional cerebral blood flow in late-life-onset psychosis. *Neuropsychiatry Neuropsychology and Behavioral Neurology, 5,* 132–137.

Miller, B. L., Ponton, M., Benson, D. F., Cummings, J. L., & Mena, I. (1996). Enhanced artistic creativity with temporal lobe degeneration. *Lancet, 348,* 1744–1755.

Neary, D., Snowden, J. S., Northen, B., & Goulding, P. J. (1988). Dementia of frontal lobe type. *Journal of Neurology, Neurosurgery, and Psychiatry, 51,* 353–361.

Olsson, I., Steffenburg, S., & Gillberg, C. (1988). Epilepsy in autism and autisticlike conditions: A population-based study. *Archives of Neurology, 45,* 666–668.

Piven, J., Berthier, M. L., Starkstein, S. E., Nehme, E., Pearlson, G., & Folstein, S. (1990). Magnetic resonance imaging evidence for a defect of cerebral cortical development in autism. *American Journal of Psychiatry, 147,* 734–739.

Radinsky, L. B. (1969). Outlines of canid and feline brain evolution. *Annals of the New York Academy of Sciences, 167,* 277–288.

Stuss, D., & Benson, D. F. (1986) *The frontal lobes.* New York, New York: Raven Press.

Wheeler, R. E., Davidson, R. J., & Tomarken, A. J. (1993). Frontal brain asymmetry and emotional reactivity: A biological substrate of affective style. *Psychophysiology, 30,* 82–89.

33

Cholinergic Components of Frontal Lobe Function and Dysfunction

ELAINE K. PERRY
ROBERT H. PERRY

Human frontal lobe functions in initiative, judgment, foresight, monitoring, planning, and motivation, for example, are not widely considered in terms of the neurotransmitter acetylcholine. And yet, the following statements in recent reviews on the cholinergic contribution to neuromodulation in the cerebral cortex indicate the importance of cholinergic nucleus basalis neurons in this context.

> It appears that the ascending cholinergic system alone is capable of keeping the neocortex in its operative mode. Brainstem aminergic afferents may have an important adjuvant effect in neocortical activation but the primary activating system appears to be NB-neocortical projection. (Buzsaki et al., 1988)

> These neurons provide every cytoarchitectonic sector and every cortical layer of the human cerebral cortex with a luxurious innervation of 60–100 cholinergic axons per mm. The high density of cholinergic axons is truly impressive. Its magnitude alone indicates that this pathway is likely to constitute the single most substantial regulatory afferent system of the cerebral cortex. (Mesulam, 1995)

In addition to nucleus basalis projections to the cortex, pedunculopontine cholinergic neurons also project to the frontal cortex while modulating the thalamocortical input. The integrative role of striatal cholinergic interneurons in influencing corticostriatal loop circuitry also impinges on frontal lobe function. Thus, exploration of the frontal lobes would be incomplete without reference to cholinergic modulation.

This chapter reviews aspects of cholinergic anatomy, neurochemistry, and physiology relating to frontal lobe function together with the pathology of frontal–cortical projections in disorders of the human brain and highlights new opportunities for *in vivo* neuroimaging of cholinergic axons that will add to our understanding of the frontal lobes.

568

ANATOMY

Cholinergic innervation of the cerebral, including the frontal, cortex originates from the magnocellular neurons in the basal forebrain, which display their greatest differentiation in human brain. Among the 200,000 neurons (per hemisphere) in this basal forebrain nuclear complex, most belong to the Ch4 group, individual sectors of which innervate different cortical areas (Mesulam, 1995): The Ch4am (anteromedial) provides the major input to medial cortical areas including the cingulate gyrus; Ch4al (anterolateral) to frontoparietal cortex (and also amygdaloid nuclei); Ch4id (intermediate) to laterodorsal frontoparietal (and also to peristriate and midtemporal areas); and Ch4p (posterior) to other temporal areas. These projections, identified in the monkey brain, appear similar to human projections, as judged by pathological conditions such as Alzheimer's disease. Thus, extensive loss of cholinergic fibers in the temporal but not the frontal cortex are associated with cell loss in Ch4p but not Ch4am + Ch4al (Mesulam & Geula, 1988).

Although densities of cholinergic axons (assessed by acetylcholinesterase-rich, choline acetyltransferase positive, or low-affinity nerve growth factor receptor positive fibers) are higher in human limbic and paralimbic cortex compared with primary sensorimotor and sensory association areas (Mesulam & Geula, 1992; Mrzljak & Goldman-Rakic, 1993), all cortical areas are richly innervated (see earlier). Axon densities are higher in more superficial layers of the cerebral cortex, indicating that on entering from underlying gray matter, axons undergo branching as they course toward the pial surface. Cortical cholinergic axons are predominantly unmyelinated and highly varicose and synapse onto the perikarya, dendritic shafts, and spines of pyramidal and nonpyramidal neurons (Frotscher & Leranth, 1985; Wainer, Bolam, Freund, & Henderson, 1984). In primates, the cortex of the frontal lobes, especially prefrontal regions, is proportionally much larger and substantially more differentiated than in nonprimates. Regional choline acetyltransferase activities, measured biochemically in the marmoset brain (Everitt, Sirkia, Roberts, Jones, & Robbins, 1988), range in orbital, dorsolateral, and medial prefrontal cortex and in anterior and posterior dorsolateral frontal, with little variation from 1.5–1.8 (compared with higher values in medial temporal and hippocampus values of 2.2–2.5) moles/g tissue/hour (Everitt et al., 1988). Similarly, in autopsy, human brain enzyme activities are around twofold higher in hippocampus than in frontal neocortical areas (Perry & Perry, 1980). Detailed mapping of choline acetyltransferase immunoreactive axons has been conducted in cynomolgus monkey brain (Lewis, 1991). The greatest density of fibers was apparent in the motor cortex, lower densities in premotor and anterior cingulate cortices, and still lower in the association regions of prefrontal cortex. In agreement with nonprimate laminar studies, immunoreactive axons were concentrated in layers I to upper III, although layer V also contained a distinct band of labeled fibers particularly prominent in a granular (primary motor and premotor) regions of frontal cortex.

The distribution of muscarinic cholinergic receptor binding sites in the macaque brain only partially overlaps with this axonal distribution (Lidow, Gallagher, Rakic, & Goldman-Rakic, 1989). M1 and M2 subtypes are also concentrated in superficial layers of motor cortex, although there are no differences in deeper cortical layers. In prefrontal regions, no laminar difference in M1 receptors is apparent although the M2 subtype parallels cholinergic axon terminals. Different studies have indicated some inconsistency in these receptor distributions, which no doubt reflects the inadequacy of specific ligands as markers of muscarinic receptor subtypes. Immunohistochemical studies of rat cortex have indicated highest M1 densities in the motor cortex, highest densities of M2 in motor and prefrontal cortices, and a coexistence of M2 and nicotinic receptors on both nonpyramidal and pyramidal neurons in cortical layers IV and V (van der Zee, Streetland, Strosberg, Schroder, & Luiten, 1992). Detailed mapping studies of muscarinic and nicotinic receptor subtype distributions in frontal cortex have not yet been conducted. Among a few generalizations are the following: M1, considered to reflect the distribution of cholinoceptive neurons, is the abundant subtype in the cortex as a whole and is as high in frontal as in other areas including the hippocampus; M2 is less abundant in the frontal cortex than the hippocampus and at least partly parallels the density of presynaptic cholinergic density; M3 and M4 are relatively low in the neocortex, including frontal, and M5 is virtually absent; the nicotinic receptor subtype with high affinity for nicotine (predominantly $\alpha 4\beta 2$) is relatively low in ligand binding in the frontal cortex compared to other cortical areas in the temporal lobe such as entorhinal; the nicotinic subtype with high affinity for α-bungarotoxin ($\alpha 7$ subtype) is relatively concentrated in the neocortex as in the hippocampus; the cortical laminar distribution of M1 and M2 tends to be complementary, and the high-affinity nicotine binding site at least partially overlaps with the M2 subtype, being localized in middle layers of the nonmotor frontal cortex (Cortes, Probst, & Palacios, 1987; Court & Perry, 1995; Perry, Court, Johnson, Piggott, & Perry, 1992; Schliebs & Roßner, 1995; Schroder, Zilles, Luiten, & Strosberg, 1990; Schroder, Zilles, Maelicke, & Hajos, 1989).

In contrast to the relatively uniform regional distribution of cholinergic axons in prefrontal regions, both dopaminergic and noradrenergic axons are much more heterogeneous (Lewis, 1991). Dopaminergic axons, for example, primarily innervate the motor cortex in the primate brain, contrasting with the selective innervation of prefrontal and cingulate in rodent. Like cholinergic fibers, dopaminergic axons are densest in superficial cortical layers whereas noradrenergic axons are relatively sparse in these layers and concentrated in lower layers, especially layer V (Lewis, 1991). Interactions between cholinergic (excitatory) and dopaminergic (inhibitory) inputs onto frontal–cortical neurons may then be as relevant in frontal lobe functions as in striatal extrapyramidal motor function.

In addition to the forebrain nucleus basalis system, a second major rostrally projecting nuclear group of cholinergic neurons in the brainstem is also involved in cholinergic modulation in the frontal cortex. Cholinergic neurons of the human pedunculopontine and laterodorsal tegmental nuclei (Ch5 and Ch6) primarily innervate the thalamus (Mesulam, Geula, Bothwell, & Hersh, 1989) and thus via the mediodorsal thalamic nuclear projections to the frontal cortex, cholinergic activity in the reticular formation indirectly influences frontal–cortical activity. In contrast to the cortex, acetylcholine is inhibitory in the thalamus decreasing the responsiveness of inhibitory γ-aminobutyric acid (GABA) neurons (Sillito, 1993). Interestingly, there is dual innervation of the mediodorsal thalamic nucleus (in addition to certain other thalamic nuclei such as the reticular) by both brainstem and forebrain cholinergic cell groups (Heckers, Geula, & Mesulam, 1992). This is evident from the thalamic distribution of low-affinity nerve growth factor receptor p75[NGFR] immunoreactivity, which is selectively localized on nucleus basalis neurons and which occurs as medially situated patches in the mediodorsal nucleus. Thalamocortical input to the frontal cortex is thus jointly governed by forebrain and brainstem cholinergic modulation. The medial prefrontal cortex is also dually innervated by nucleus basalis neurons (see earlier) but also, uniquely, in comparison to other cortical regions, by a regionally selective projection from brainstem Ch6 neurons (Satoh & Fibiger, 1986). Prefrontal cortical neurons thus integrate cholinergic inputs from both major ascending cholinergic nuclear groups, which, by jointly innervating the mediodorsal thalamic nucleus, also indirectly influence frontal lobe function. Thalamic, in contrast to cholinergic, input to the prefrontal cortex terminates primarily in deeper cortical layers (III and IV) (Ginguere & Goldman-Rakic, 1988), providing anatomical segregation of these pathways. The region of the medial prefrontal cortex innervated by the laterodorsal tegmental nucleus is also innervated by dopaminergic terminals from the ventral tegmental area, and it has been suggested that cholinergic–dopaminergic interactions in this area may be important in the control of affect (Satoh & Fibiger, 1986).

Another more circuitous route whereby acetylcholine may exert control of frontal–cortical function involves the basal ganglia. Substantia nigra pars compacta dopaminergic neurons also receive an input from brainstem cholinergic neurons (Bolam, Francis, & Henderson, 1991). Thus dopaminergic input to cortex and also to striatum, which indirectly exerts an important influence on the frontal cortex, is subject to cholinergic modulation. In addition, cholinergic interneurons in the striatum play a major integrative role in governing striatal GABA neurons which project to substantia nigra dopaminergic neurons, providing a further cholinergic–dopaminergic interface.

PHYSIOLOGY

Because all areas of the frontal cortex receive a cholinergic innervation, it can be assumed that acetylcholine is involved to some extent in every aspect of frontal lobe function. Single-unit studies indicate that increased activity in the cholinergic nucleus basalis correlates with behavioral activation and neocortical desynchronization (Buzsaki et al., 1988). This nucleus, rather than the reticular thalamic, is probably the major anatomical substrate of neocortical activation. Evidence based on neuronal discharges in various subcortical nuclei in the awake state and during slow-wave and rapid eye movement sleep indicate that the ascending cholinergic system from the basal forebrain alone is capable of keeping the neocortex in its active, desynchronized state. This essential cortical activating role may be mediated by the dual mechanisms of direct cortical cholinergic excitation from the nucleus basalis and indirect effects of the nucleus basalis projection to thalamic nuclei such as the reticular in dampening oscillatory influences of the thalamus.

In global terms, cortical acetylcholine has been broadly implicated in attention, arousal, memory, and motivation (Blokland, 1996; Buzsaki et al, 1988; Mesulam, 1995), all of which are relevant to the frontal lobe. Frontal–cortical contributions to memory are suggested to involve the monitoring and manipulation of information within working memory (Petrides, 1996). PET and functional MRI studies indicate that the prefrontal cortex in particular is activated during working-memory tasks (Goldman-Rakic, Funahashi, & Bruce, 1990). The following observation by Mesulam (1995) may be particularly relevant to frontal lobe function: "Neurons of the nucleus basalis are sensitive to novel and motivationally relevant sensory events, leading to the expectation that cortical cholinergic innervation should be modulating the impact of sensory events upon cortical circuitry in a manner that reflects their behavioural relevance and novelty."

Increasingly, evidence suggests that cortical acetylcholine acts not so much as initiator but rather as a facilitator of changing membrane potentials. Concepts include enhancing "signal to noise" ratio (Drachman & Sahakian, 1979), increasing the probability of distinguishing postsynaptic potentials from background cortical activity (Warburton, 1981); enhancement of previously less effective synaptic connections (Metherate,

Tremblay, & Dykes, 1987); and, rather more fancifully, the selection of currently relevant information into the conscious stream from parallel information processing occurring at the subconscious level (Perry & Perry, 1995).

Mechanistically, acetylcholine interacts with both muscarinic and nicotinic receptors in the cortex (reviewed in Mesulam, 1995). Muscarinic receptor activation results in a relatively prolonged reduction in potassium conductance so that many types of cholinoceptive neurons are more susceptible to other excitatory inputs. M1 receptors have been identified on assymetric (excitatory amino acid) synapses as well as symmetric (cholinergic) synapses. Muscarinic receptors are linked via G proteins to phospholipase C activation (M1, M3, M5) or adenylylcyclase inhibition (M2 and M4). Nicotinic receptors are cationic channels gating sodium and calcium ions. Less is known of the consequences of nicotinic receptor activation, although release of various transmitters (e.g., acetylcholine and GABA in the cortex and dopamine in the striatum) and alterations in intracellular calcium, which in turn govern gene expression (e.g., c-fos), is documented (Wonnacott, 1997). Evidence that acetylcholine exerts not only short-term electrophysiological effects but also longer-term changes relating to aspects of synaptic plasticity, involving, for example, membrane adhesion, may relate more to nicotinic than muscarinic receptor interactions (Wonnacott, 1997). Nicotinic receptor numbers (specifically of the high-affinity agonist binding subtype) parallel synaptic alterations occurring during development and aging senescence and as a consequence of neurodegenerative disease (Court & Perry, 1994; Court et al., 1997). A further intriguing aspect of such neurotrophic effects of cholinergic activity in the cortex is the presence of intrinsic acetylcholinesterase-rich neurons (Mesulam, 1995). These are not cholinergic but presumed to be cholinoceptive, and they occur in much larger numbers in the neocortex of human compared to other species. They are detected during later development (beyond 10 years of age) and increase in number into adulthood. They decline in old age and in a variety of degenerative diseases such as Alzheimer's.

Anatomically and physiologically there is then sufficient information regarding the cortical cholinergic system to excite interest in the role of this transmitter in human frontal lobe function. Given the complexity of this most highly developed region of the human brain, current knowledge is obviously limited but does provide a useful basis for exploring the contribution of frontal–cortical cholinergic dysfunction in disease.

PATHOLOGY

Differential patterns of cholinergic innervation are apparent during development and aging in different cortical and subcortical regions of the normal human brain. Frontal–cortical regions (e.g., Brodmann's areas 9 and 10) are innervated at an early embryonic stage (around 3 months' gestation), and there is a transient overexpression of choline acetyltransferase activity postnatally (Candy et al., 1985; Court, Piggott, Perry, Barlow, & Perry, 1992). This overexpression likely reflects the stage of synaptic proliferation and elimination typical of early development. Throughout adult life and into old age (up to 100 years) there is, however, no alteration in presynaptic cholinergic activity in this area of frontal cortex to judge by activities of choline acetyltransferane (Figure 33.1). This contrasts with temporal areas (Figure 33.1) and although more detailed regional studies are needed, any alteration in frontal lobe function accompanying senescence cannot as yet be attributed to degeneration or dysfunction of cholinergic projections from either nucleus basalis or brainstem.

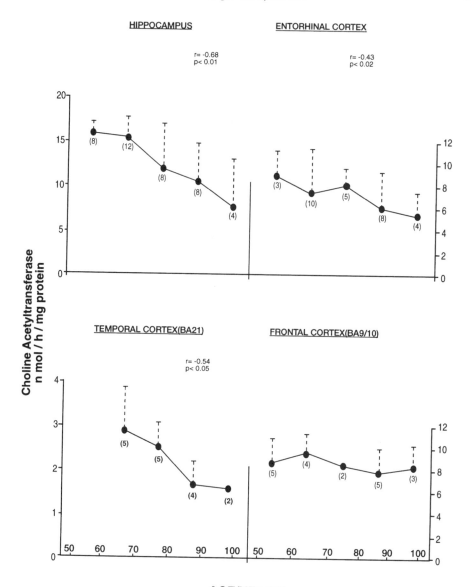

FIGURE 33.1. Cholinergic activity in different regions of the human brain in normal individuals grouped according to age. Mean values with standard deviations (bars) are indicated, with case numbers in parentheses. Correlations were significant in temporal but not frontal areas. BA, Brodmann's area.

In contrast to the stability of prefrontal cholinergic activities in normal aging, some loss of activity is evident in a variety of degenerative diseases associated with cognitive impairment. In Alzheimer's disease, dementia with Lewy bodies (DLB), and Parkinson's disease without dementia, a moderate but not highly significant loss of approximately one-third to one-half the normal choline acetyltransferase activity is apparent (Figure 33.2). The frontal enzyme loss has not yet been correlated with any clinical facet of these diseases, and it is possible that moderate changes are functionally irrelevant or at least associated with only subtle clinical symptoms. The fact that enzyme reductions in prefrontal cortex are similar in three clinically different disorders (Alzheimer's, DLB, and nondemented Parkinsonism) supports this assumption. In a recent study by Geula and Mesulam (1996), of regional variations in the loss of cholinergic fibers in Alzheimer's disease assessed on the basis of acetylcholinesterase histochemistry, various frontal areas—including granular orbitofrontal, dysgranular orbitofrontal, prefrontal association, frontal operculum, prefrontal association, and frontal pole—demonstrated fiber losses ranging from 45% to 75%, whereas in other frontal areas, including primary motor, premotor association, and anterior and posterior cingulate, fiber loss was less than 45%. Greatest fiber loss (> 75%) was apparent in temporal association areas consistent with the many reports on the loss of choline acetyltransferase and memory loss.

In a recent study by Dournaud, Dalaere, Hauw, and Epelbaum (1995), 12 Alzheimer cases showed a significant correlation ($r = .66$, $p < .05$) between choline acetyltransferase in middle frontal gyrus and intellectual status assessed by the Blessed test score. Correlations were nevertheless stronger in parietal and temporal lobe areas ($r = .91$ and .68). In patients presenting with Parkinson's disease and subsequently developing dementia and also in middle-aged cases of Down's syndrome, most of whom are demented, there is a more extensive loss (> 50%) of frontal cholinergic activity (Figure 33.2). These cases are more likely to reflect dysfunction, and although the precise clinical correlate is not established, frontal lobe atrophy has been reported in late-onset Parkinson's disease and DLB (Double et al., 1996). Because anticholinergic drugs, employed to improve extrapyramidal control in Parkinson's disease, exacerbate difficulties in cognitive shifting (monitored using, e.g., the Wisconsin Card Sorting Test [Van Spaendonck, Berger,

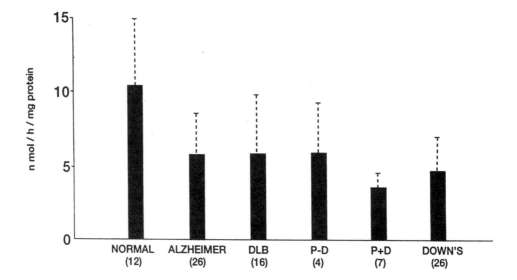

FIGURE 33.2. Activities of choline acetyltransferase in frontal cortex (Brodmann's areas 9 and 10) in Alzheimer's, dementia with Lewy bodies (DLB), Parkinson's disease, without (−) and with (+) dementia (P−D, P+D), and Down's syndrome compared to the normal. Columns represent mean values and bars standard deviations, with case numbers in parentheses. Highly significant differences ($p < .001$) compared with the normal were apparent in demented Parkinson cases and middle-aged cases of Down's syndrome (differences in the other groups were less significant). All groups were matched for age except the Down's group (mean age = 53 years), although the value for normal younger cases matching this age is similar to the normal value shown.

Horstink, Buytenhuijs, & Cools, 1993]), it is likely that the disease-related loss of cholinergic innervation to the frontal cortex is associated with impairment in this type of frontal lobe function. In Alzheimer's disease, patients who are unaware of their cognitive deficits, in addition to being more cognitively impaired, have a specific defect in "frontal/executive" functions (Lopez, Becker, Somsak, Dew, & Dekosky, 1994), which might relate to more extensive cholinergic deficits in this area. In view of the greater neurochemical differences in middle-age Down's than in senile Alzheimer's patients, derangements of frontal lobe function in Down's syndrome as a function of aging might be predicted.

In the anterior cingulate cortex (Figure 33.3), there is a more consistent loss, in some cases extensive, of cholinergic activity in DLB. This area is generally spared in terms of cholinergic activity in Alzheimer's disease (Geula & Mesulam, 1996). The two diseases are differentiated in several clinical respects (McKeith et al., 1996), including increased psychosis (especially visual hallucinations), more marked impairments in cognitive tasks depending on attention or vigilance, and more frequent periods of apparent conscious unawareness or "absences" in DLB. Which, if any, of these symptoms might involve cingulate abnormalities is not established. Hallucinations have been related to cholinergic reductions in the temporal neocortex (Perry, Irving, Blessed, Fairbairn, & Perry, 1990), and in prefrontal cortex hallucinating, individuals are differentiated as a group from nonhallucinating by an imbalance in 5-HT (5-hydroxytryptamine [serotonin], assessed from the metabolic index of turnover, 5-HIAA [5-hydroxyindoleacetic acid] to 5-HT ratio, to be relatively overactive despite an overall reduction in 5-HT levels) and acetylcholine (assessed from the enzyme activity to be hypoactive; Perry et al., 1993). The relatively dense dopaminergic innervation of the cingulate cortex which is also affected in DLB by reductions in dopamine (Marshall & Piggott, 1997) together with evidence that cingulotomy can lead to "absences," suggest that this frontal area should be further investigated in DLB, particularly by neuroimaging (see section on "Neuroimaging").

Attentional deficits, impairments in other functions such as visuospatial memory and immediate recall, and frontal lobe dysfunction are more common in frontotemporal lobe

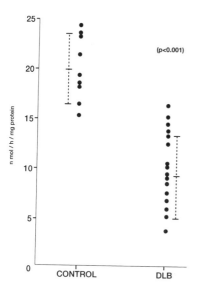

FIGURE 33.3. Choline acetyltransferase in anterior cingulate cortex in individual patients with DLB compared to age-matched controls. Significant difference (Student's *t* test) between the groups is indicated. Means and standard deviations represented by central and upper and lower bars.

dementia (FTD) than in Alzheimer's disease (Pasquier, 1996). In this disorder, and also in Pick's disease, no consistent loss of choline acetyltransferase or overall acetylcholinesterase activities from frontal or temporal cortex has been reported (reviewed by Sjogren, Blennaw, Minthon, Karlsson, & Wallin, 1996). This is interesting in view of the marked loss of neurons in FTD, especially from layers II and III (reviewed by Cooper & Mann, 1996) and claims that in Alzheimer's disease, the cortical cholinergic deficit is secondary to other abnormalities in the cortex. If the latter is correct, it may be inferred that cortical neuron loss does not in itself lead to nucleus basalis dysfunction.

In FTD, most studies of muscarinic receptors have revealed a loss in cortical, including frontal (and also striatal), binding (reviewed by Sjögren et al., 1996), although the particular muscarinic subtype affected has not been identified. This receptor loss, and also the decline in acetylcholinesterase positive cortical neurons in FTD (Mesulam, 1995), probably reflects the disappearance of cholinoceptive cortical neurons. In Alzheimer's disease, there are, with the exception of M2, no consistent reports of muscarinic receptor loss, which may reflect the preservation of cholinoceptive neurons or upregulation of receptors in surviving neurons in response to declining cholinergic input. In contrast, immunocytochemical studies of nicotinic receptor positive neurons have revealed an extensive loss (to < 25% of normal) in Alzheimer's disease and a less extensive loss (50%) in Parkinson's disease (Schroder, Giacobini, Wevers, Birtsch, & Schütz, 1995). Clearly a comprehensive analysis of nicotinic receptor subtypes in different forms of cerebral disorder affecting frontal lobe function is required, especially as it has been suggested that prefrontal cortex may be a major target site for the cognitive actions of nicotine. In rat prefrontal cortex, nicotine selectively enhances the amplitude of excitatory synaptic potentials mediated by glutamate in pyramidal cells (Vidal & Changeux, 1993). In schizophrenia, where frontal, including particularly the cingulate, cortex has been implicated on the basis of psychological and imaging evidence, nicotinic receptors (at least the $\alpha 7$ subtype) have also been implicated (Leonard et al., 1996) although presynaptic cortical including frontal cholinergic deficits are not apparent in the limited postmortem studies so far published (Perry & Perry, 1980).

The cholinergic system has been implicated in schizophrenia because anticholinesterases (e.g., in accidental exposure to organophosphates) can induce auditory hallucinations and problems with referential cognitive thinking, including persecutory and religious delusions (reviewed by Karczmar & Richardson, 1985). Paradoxically, muscarinic receptor blockade also induces hallucinations, although usually of a visual nature and generally without thought disorder. The latter psychopharmacology is more akin to the hallucinatory experiences of patients with DLB (Perry & Perry, 1995). A further reason to consider the cholinergic system and areas of the frontal cortex in schizophrenia is the neuropathological finding of abnormalities (increased number considered to reflect a developmental programming fault) of mesopontine cholinergic neurons (which as discussed include projections to the frontal cortex) in at least some patients with the disease (Garcia-Rill et al., 1995).

Loss of neurons from the nucleus basalis is well documented in Alzheimer's and Parkinson's disease, although the extent of the loss reported in Alzheimer's varies from moderate to severe, and it has been suggested that in this disease, cholinergic dysfunction precedes or exceeds degeneration (Perry et al., 1982. Detailed analysis of subpopulations of cholinergic perikarya in the nucleus basalis have not been reported in most of the disorders discussed previously. An exception is the selective cell loss in Ch4p in Alzheimer's disease (Mesulam & Geula, 1988). In a recent comparison of two sectors of Ch4 (Figure 33.4), the more extensive neuronal loss in Ch4p in Alzheimer's was

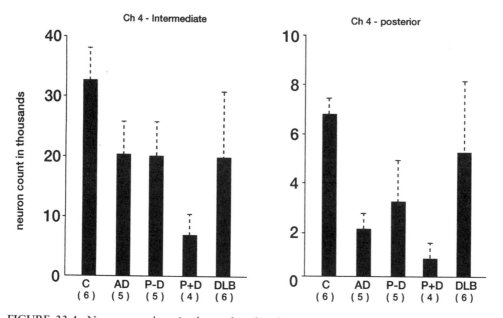

FIGURE 33.4. Neuron numbers in the nucleus basalis sectors Ch4id and Ch4p in controls (C), Alzheimer's disease, Parkinson's disease without and with dementia (P–D, P+D), and DLB. Columns represent mean values and bars standard deviations with case numbers in parentheses. Highly significant differences from controls ($p < .001$) were evident in Alzheimer's and Parkinson's disease in the posterior section projecting to temporal cortex and in Parkinson's disease with dementia in the intermediate sector projecting to frontal cortex.

confirmed (Perry & Irving, 1995). This sector, which projects to temporal areas, is spared in DLB (Figure 33.4), although neuron counts were lower in individuals experiencing hallucinations than in those without this symptom. In the intermediate sector, ch4id, which includes projections to the frontal cortex, neuron loss was modest in both diseases, consistent with the moderate loss of cholinergic enzyme activity. Patients presenting with Parkinson's disease and later developing dementia exhibited the greatest loss of neurons in both sectors; there was also the greatest loss of cholinergic activity in frontal cortex in this subgroup. Thus the function of acetylcholine in human frontal cortex might most appropriately be examined in these patients.

Increasing evidence on the role of acetylcholine in the cortex in attentional rather than specifically mnemonic functions highlights the need to reconsider the original "cholinergic" hypothesis of cognitive impairment in aging and dementia in terms of neuropsychiatric symptoms (Cummings & Kaufer, 1996) and indeed in other diseases with more prominent features of psychosis. More detailed clinical correlative studies based both on autopsy investigations of pre- and postsynaptic cholinergic activities and also on neuroimaging in different areas of the frontal and other lobes are required.

NEUROIMAGING

Diagnostic indices of cortical cholinergic dysfunction applicable *in vivo* have been slow to emerge. Cerebrospinal fluid biochemical parameters such as acetylcholine or acetylcholinesterase are inconsistently reported to reflect abnormalities specific to Alzheimer's disease. Similarly, original reports on hypersensitive pupillary dilatation in response to the cholinergic antagonist tropicamide have not been consistently replicated. Whether such tests will ever be of major diagnostic value is doubtful in view of the complexity of brain cholinergic systems (Figure 33.5) and the inability of such tests to specifically detect cortical cholinergic function let alone the function of particular regions such as frontal lobe. Neuroimaging is far more likely to generate clinically relevant information.

The development of suitable brain imaging markers of the cholinergic system has also been slow, but recently promising advances have been made. Presynaptic markers such as vesamicol, which bind to the vesicular acetylcholine transporter, have not in the past been sufficiently specific to judge from the absence of any reductions in Alzheimer's disease (Kish et al., 1990; Ruberg et al., 1990). Iodobenzovesamicol (Jung et al., 1996; Kuhl et al., 1996), iodobenzyltrozamicol (Efange, Michelson, Khare, & Thomas, 1993), and iodophenylpiperidinocyclohexanol (Shiba, Mori, Matsuda, Ichikawa, & Tonami, 1996) appear to be more promising. *In vivo* (SPECT) mapping of cholinergic terminals using iodobenzovesamicol revealed severe reductions throughout the cerebral cortex in presenile cases of Alzheimer's disease and in demented patients with Parkinson's disease (Kuhl et al., 1996). Other markers of cholinergic transmission studied *in vivo* in animal models which have potential application to human brain chemical (PET or SPECT) imaging (reviewed by Maziere, 1995) are as follows: acetylcholinesterase inhibitors, including [^{11}C]physostigmine and [^{14}N]methylpiperidyl esters of acetylcholine; muscarinic receptor antagonists that cross the blood–brain barrier, such as [^{11}C] or [^{123}I]quinuclidinyl benzilate, [^{11}C]tropanylbenzilate, [^{11}C]methylpiperidylbenzilate, dexetimide labeled with ^{11}C, ^{76}Br, or ^{123}I, [^{11}C]scopolamine and [^{11}C]benzotropine which are not subtype specific,

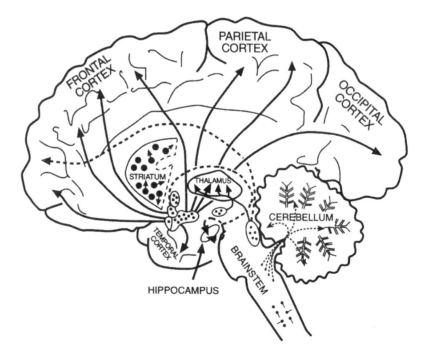

FIGURE 33.5. Human brain cholinergic systems. This diagram depicts projections (arrowheaded lines) from nuclear groups in the basal forebrain and brainstem together with intrinsic neurons in the striatum.

and the antagonist [^{11}C]AF-DX 384 specific for M2 receptors and agonist [^{11}C]butylthio-T2TP specific for M1; [^{11}C]nicotine or [^{123}I]iodonicotine for nicotinic receptors. Where these have been applied to human brain imaging, consistent results indicative of their value in assessing diseases such as Alzheimer's have not been reported. Thus, overall muscarinic receptor binding (assessed using, e.g., QNB) declines only late in the disease as does the M1 subtype, although M2 imaging may be more promising based on one unreplicated study. Acetylcholinesterase imaging is complicated by the presence of the enzyme not only in cholinergic axons but also cholinoceptive neurons. PET imaging with nicotine has generated interesting reductions in Alzheiner's disease, but whether the binding reflects receptor changes or alterations in blood flow is unclear.

THERAPY

With the recent prescription of cholinesterase inhibitors (e.g., tacrine and donepezil) for Alzheimer's disease, the development of cholinergic treatment strategies over the last 20 years has opened a new and exciting area for clinical correlation in a variety of human disorders. Most trials to date have concentrated on cognitive (particularly mnemonic) outcome in Alzheimer's disease, and clinically significant improvement is apparent in a proportion of patients. There is new impetus to assess treatment outcome using other clinical measures (e.g., alleviation of attentional deficits and psychosis, such as hallucinations). In DLB, the more extensive loss of cholinergic activity evident in some cortical areas (Perry et al., 1994), together with the absence or minimal numbers of neocortical tangles compared with Alzheimer's disease, indicates that this group may be more responsive to cholinergic therapy (Perry, Marshall, et al., 1990). In an open trial of tacrine in seven patients presenting with Parkinson's disease and developing dementia, the frequency of hallucinations was greatly reduced after treatment, and in five cases hallucinations were essentially eliminated (Hutchinson & Fazzini, 1996). Although it is not clear to what extent the frontal lobes are implicated in psychotic features such as hallucinations, examination of more specific frontal lobe functions in response to cholinergic therapy, particularly in Parkinson's patients developing dementia, would be interesting.

The prospect that cholinotherapy may be not only symptomatic but also neuroprotective—based on evidence that tacrine postpones institutionalization in Alzheimer patients and that tobacco smoking generally reduces the risk of developing the disease and is associated with a lower density of senile plaques in the cortex of normal elderly individuals (Perry et al., 1996)—provides a further incentive to programs aimed at developing new cholinergic therapies based on inhibiting cholinesterase or stimulating cholinergic (including nicotinic) receptors. Based on current understanding of the neurochemical pathology of frontotemporal dementia, there is no reason to expect cholinergic therapy to be of value. Nevertheless, the presence of nicotinic receptors on intrinsic cortical neurons in this disease suggests that nicotinic neuroprotection therapy might be worth considering.

CONCLUSION

The importance of cholinergic modulation in the frontal cortex, the involvement of frontal cholinergic activities in a variety of degenerative diseases, and new developments in cholinergic imaging and therapy strongly suggest that future human frontal lobe research should take into account the neurotransmitter, which although the first to be discovered is only now entering the neuropsychiatric clinical domain.

ACKNOWLEDGMENTS

Many thanks to Dawn Hinds for manuscript preparation, to Mary Johnson for technical support with the cingulate cortical study, to Andrew Brown for assembling the nucleus basalis data, and to British American Tobacco for partially supporting some of the research mentioned in this chapter.

REFERENCES

Blokland, A. (1996). Acetylcholine: A neurotransmitter for learning and memory? *Brain Research Reviews, 21,* 285–300.

Bolam, J. P., Francis, C. M., & Henderson, Z. (1991). Cholinergic input to dopaminergic neurons in the substantia nigra: A double immunocytochemical study. *Neuroscience, 41,* 483–494.

Buzsaki, G., Bickford, T. G., Ponomareff, G., Thai, L. J., Mandel, R. J., & Gage, F. H. (1988). Nucleus basalis and thalamic control of neocortical activity in the freely moving rat. *Journal of Neuroscience, 26,* 735–744.

Candy, J. M., Perry, E. K., Perry, R. H., Bloxham, C. A., Thompson, J. E., Johnson, M., Oakley, A. E., & Edwardson, J. A. (1985). Evidence for the early prenatal development of cortical cholinergic afferents from the nucleus of Meynert in the human foetus. *Neuroscience Letters, 61,* 91–95.

Cooper, P. N., & Mann, D. M. A. (1996). The neuropathology of frontotemporal dementia. In F. Pasquier, F. Lebert, & P. H. Scheltens (Eds.), *Frontotemporal dementia* (pp. 98–114). The Netherlands: ICG Publications.

Cortes, R., Probst, A., & Palacios, J. M. (1987). Quantitative light microscopic autoradiographic localization of cholinergic muscarinic receptors in the human brain: Forebrain. *Neuroscience, 20,* 65–107.

Court, J. A., Lloyd, S., Johnson, M., Griffiths, M., Birdsall, N. J. M., Piggott, M. A., Oakley, A. E., Ince, P. G., Perry, E. K., & Perry, R. H. (1997). Nicotinic and muscarinic cholinergic receptor binding in the human hippocampal formation during development and aging. *Developmental Brain Research, 101,* 93–105.

Court, J. A., Perry, E. K. (1994). CNS nicotinic receptors: Possible therapeutic targets in neurodegenerative disorders. *CNS Drugs, 2*(3), 216–233.

Court, J. A., & Perry, E. K. (1995). Distribution of nicotinic receptors in the CN. In T. Stone (Ed.), *CNS neurotransmitters and neuromodulators* (pp. 85–104). Boca Raton, FL: CRC Press.

Court, J. A., Piggott, M. A., Perry, E. K., Barlow, R. B., & Perry, R. H. (1992). Age associated decline in high affinity nicotine binding in human brain frontal cortex does correlate with the changes in choline acetyltransferase activity. *Neuroscience Research Communications, 10*(3), 125–133.

Cummings, J. L., & Kaufer, D. (1996). The cholinergic hypothesis revisited. *Neurology, 47,* 876–883.

Double, K. L., Halliday, G. M., McRitchie, D. A., Reid, W. G., Hely, M. A., & Morris, J. G. (1996). Regional brain atrophy in idiopathic Parkinson's disease and diffuse Lewy Body disease. *Dementia, 7*(6), 304–313.

Dournaud, P., Dalaere, P., Hauw, J. J., & Epelbaum, J. (1995). Differential correlation between neurochemical deficits, neuropathology and cognitive status in Alzheimer's disease. *Neurobiology of Aging, 16,* 817–823.

Drachman, D. A., & Sahakian, B. J. (1979). Effects of cholinergic agents on human learning and memory. In A. Barbear, J. H. Growdon, & R. Y. Wurtman (Eds.), *Nutrition and the brain* (pp. 351–366). New York: Raven Press.

Efange, S. M. N., Michelson, R. H., Khare, A. B., & Thomas, Y. R. (1993). Synthesis and tissue distribution of meta-[^{125}I]iodobenzyltrozamiol ([^{125}I]MIBT): Potential radiotracer for mapping central cholinergic innervation. *Journal of Medicinal Chemistry, 36,* 1754–1760.

Everitt, B. J., Sirkia, T. E., Roberts, A. C., Jones, G. H., & Robbins, T. W. (1988). Distribution and some projections of cholinergic neurons in the brain of the common marmoset, Callithrix jacchus. *Journal of Comparative Neurology, 271,* 533–558.

Frotscher, M., & Leranth, C. (1985). Cholinergic innervation of the rat hippocampus as revealed by choline acetyltransferase immunocytochemistry: A combined light and electron microscope study. *Journal of Comparative Neurology, 239,* 237–246.

Garcia-Rill, E., Biedermann, J. A., Chambers, T., Skinner, R. D., Mrak, R. E., Husain, M., & Karson, C. N. (1995). Mesopontine neurons in schizophrenia. *Neuroscience, 68,* 321–335.

Geula, C., & Mesulam, M. M. (1996). Systematic regional variations in the loss of cortical cholinergic fibers in Alzheimer's. *Cerebral Cortex, 6,* 165–177.

Ginguere, M., & Goldman-Rakic, P. S. (1988). Mediodorsal nucleus: A real laminar and tangential distribution of afferents and efferents in the frontal lobe of rhesus monkeys. *Journal of Comparative Neurology, 277,* 195–213.

Goldman-Rakic, P. S., Funahashi, S., & Bruce, C. J. (1990). Neocortical memory circuits. *Journal of Quantitative Biology, 55,* 1025–1038.

Heckers, S., Geula, C., & Mesulam, M. M. (1992). Cholinergic innervation of the human thalamus: Dual origin and differential nuclear distribution. *Journal of Comparative Neurology, 325,* 68–82.

Hutchinson, M., & Fuzzini, E. (1996). Cholinesterase inhibition in Parkinson's disease. *Journal of Neurology, Neurosurgery and Psychiatry, 61,* 324–326.

Jung, Y. W., Frey, K. A., Mulholland, G. K., Del Rosario, R., Sherman, P. S., Raffer, D. M., Van Dort, M. E., Kuhl, D. E., Gildersleeve, D. L., & Wieland, D. M. (1996). Vesamical receptor mapping of brain cholinergic neurons with radioiodine-labelled positional isomers of benzovesamical. *Journal of Medicinal Chemistry, 39,* 3331–3342.

Karczmar, A. G., & Richardson, D. L. (1985). Cholinergic mechanisms, schizophrenia and neuropsychiatric adaptive dysfunction. In M. M. Singh, D. M. Warburton, & H. Lal (Eds.), *Central cholinergic mechanisms and adapted dysfunctions* (pp. 193–221). New York: Plenum Press.

Kish, S. J., Distefano, L. M., Dozic, S., Robitaille, Y., Rajput, A., Deck, J. H. N., & Hornykiewicz, O. (1990). [^{3}H]Vesamicol binding in human brain cholinergic deficiency disorders. *Neuroscience Letters, 117,* 347–352.

Kuhl, D. E., Minoshima, S., Fessler, J. A., Frey, K. A., Foster, N. L., Ficaro, E. P., Wieland, L. D. M., & Koeppe, R. A. (1996). *In vivo* mapping of cholinergic terminals in normal aging, Alzheimer's disease and Parkinson's disease. *Annals of Neurology, 40,* 399–410.

Leonard, S., Adams, C., Breese, C. R., Adler, L. E., Bickford, P., Byerley, W., Coon, H., Griffith, J. M., Miller, C., Myles-Worsley, M., Nagamoto, H. T., Rollins, Y., Stevens, K. E., Waldo, M., & Freedman, R. (1996). Nicotinic receptor function in schizophrenia. *Schizophrenia Bulletin, 22,* 431–445.

Lewis, D. A. (1991). Distribution of choline acetyltransferase—Immunoreactive axons in monkey cortex. *Neuroscience, 40,* 363–374.

Lidow, M. S., Gallagher, D. W., Rakic, P., & Goldman-Rakic, P. S. (1989). Regional differences in the distribution of muscarinic cholinergic receptors in macaque cerebral cortex. *Journal of Comparative Neurology, 289,* 247–259.

Lopez, O. L., Becker, J. T., Somsak, D., Dew, M. A., & Dekosky, S. T. (1994). Awareness of cognitive deficits and anosognosia in probable Alzheimer's disease. *European Neurology, 34,* 277–282.

Marshall, E., & Pigott, M. (1997). *Dopaminergic innervation of the cortex in dementia with Lewy bodies.* Unpublished observations.

Maziere, M. (1995). Cholinergic neurotransmission studied *in vivo* using position emission tomography or single photon emission computerized tomography. *Pharmacology and Therapeutics, 66,* 83–101.

McKeith, I. G., Galasko, D., Kosaka, K., Perry, E. K., Dickson. D. W., Hansen, L. A., Salmon, D. P., & Lowe, J. (1996). Dementia with Lewy bodies: diagnostic criteria and pathological guidelines: report of the Consortium on dementia with Lewy bodies. *Neurology, 47,* 1113–1124.

Mesulam, M. M. (1995). The cholinergic contribution to neuromodulation in the cerebral cortex. *Seminars in the Neurosciences, 7,* 297–307.

Mesulam, M. M., & Geula, C. (1988). Nucleus basalis (Ch4. and cortical cholinergic innervation of the human brain: Observations based on the distribution of acetylcholinesterase and choline acetyltransferase. *Journal of Comparative Neurology, 275,* 216–240.

Mesulam, M. M., & Geula, C. (1992). Overlap between acetylcholinesterase-rich and choline acetyltransferase-positive (cholinergic) axons in human cerebral cortex. *Brain Research, 577,* 112–120.

Mesulam, M. M., Geula, C., Bothwell, M. A., & Hersh, L. B. (1989). Human reticular formation: Cholinergic neurons of the pedunculopontine and laterodorsal tegmental nuclei and some cytochemical comparisons with forebrain cholinergic neurons. *Journal of Comparative Neurology, 281,* 611–633.

Metherate, R., Tremblay, N., & Dykes, R. W. (1987). Acetylcholine permits long term enhancement of neuronal responsiveness in cat primary somatosensory cortex. *Neuroscience, 22,* 75–81.

Mrzljak, L., & Goldman-Rakic, P. S. (1993). Low affinity nerve growth factor receptor (p75^{NGFR}). and choline acetyltransferase (ChAT)—Immunoreactive axons in the cerebral cortex and hippocampus of adult macaque monkeys and humans. *Cerebral Cortex, 3,* 133–147.

Pasquier, F. (1996). Neuropsychologic features and cognitive assessment in frontotemporal dementia. In F. Pasquier, F. Lebert, & P. H. Scheltens (Eds.), *Frontotemporal dementia* (pp. 51–69). The Netherlands: ICG Publications.

Perry, E. K., Court, J. A., Johnson, M., Piggott, M. A., & Perry, R. H. (1992). Autoradiographic distribution of [^{3}H]nicotine binding in human cortex: Relative abundance in subicular complex. *Journal of Chemical Neuroanatomy, 5,* 399–405.

Perry, E. K., Court, J. A., Lloyd, S., Johnson, M., Griffiths, M. H., Spurden, D., Piggott, M. A., Turner, J., & Perry, R. H. (1996). β-Amyloidosis in normal aging and transmitter signalling in human temporal lobe. *Annals of the New York Academy of Sciences, 777,* 389–392.

Perry, E. K., Haroutunian, V., Davis, K. L., Levy, R., Lantos, P., Eagger, S., Honavar, M., Dean, A., Griffiths, M., McKeith, I. G., & Perry, R. H. (1994). Neocortical cholinergic activities differentiate Lewy body dementia from classical Alzheimer's disease. *Neuroreport, 5,* 747–749.

Perry, E. K., Marshall, E., Kerwin, J. M., Smith, C. J., Jabeen, S., Cheng, A. V., & Perry, R. H. (1990). Evidence of a monoaminergic: Cholinergic imbalance related to visual hallucinations in Lewy body dementia. *Journal of Neurochemistry, 55,* 1454–1456.

Perry, E. K., Marshall, E., Thompson, P., McKeith, I. G., Collerton, D., Fairbairn, A. F., Ferrier, I. N., Irving, D., & Perry, R. H. (1993). Monoaminergic activities in Lewy body dementia: Relation to hallucinosis and extrapyramidal features. *Journal of Neural Transmission, 6,* 167–177.

Perry, E. K., & Perry, R. H. (1980). The cholinergic system in Alzheimer's disease. In P. J. Roberts (Ed.), *Biochemistry of dementia* (pp. 135–183). Chichester, UK: Wiley.

Perry, E. K., & Perry, R. H. (1995). Acetycholine and hallucinations: Disease-related compared to drug-induced alterations in human consciousness. *Brain and Cognition, 28,* 240–258.

Perry, R. H., Candy, J. M., Perry, E. K., Irving, D., Blessed, G., Fairbairn, A. F., & Tomlinson, B. E. (1982). Extensive loss of choline acetyltransferase activity is not reflected by neuronal loss in the nucleus of Meynert in Alzheimer's disease. *Neuroscience Letters, 33,* 311–315.

Perry, R. H., & Irving, D. (1995). *Nucleus of meynert in dementia with Lewy bodies.* Unpublished observations.

Perry, R. H., Irving, D., Blessed, G., Fairbairn, A. F., & Perry, E. (1990). A clinically and neuropathologically distinct form of Lewy body dementia in the elderly. *Journal of Neurological Sciences, 95,* 119–139.

Petrides, M. (1996). Lateral frontal cortical contribution to memory. *Neurosciences, 8,* 57–63.

Ruberg, M., Mayo, W., Brile, A., Duyckaerts, C., Kauw, J. J., Simon, H., Lemoal, M., & Agid, Y. (1990). Choline acetyltransferase activity and [³H]vesamicol binding in temporal cortex of patients with Alzheimer's disease, Parkinson's disease and rats with basal forebrain lesions. *Neuroscience, 35,* 327–333.

Satoh, K., & Fibiger, H. C. (1986). Cholinergic neurons of the laterodorsal tegmental nucleus: Efferent and afferent connections. *Journal of Comparative Neurology, 253,* 277–302.

Schliebs, R., & Roβner, S. (1995). Distribution of muscarinic acetylcholine receptors. In T. Stone (Ed.), *CNS neurotransmitters and neuromodulators—acetylcholine* (pp. 67–83). London: CC Press.

Schroder, H., Giacobini, E., Wevers, A., Birtsch, C., & Schütz, U. (1995). Nicotinic receptors in Alzheimer's disease. In E. F. Domino (Ed.), *Brain imaging of nicotine and tobacco smoking* (pp. 73–94). Ann Arbor, MI: NPP Books.

Schroder, H., Zilles, K., Luiten, P. G. M., & Strosberg, A. D. (1990). Immunocytochemical visualization of muscarinic cholinoceptors in the human cerebral cortex. *Brain Research, 514,* 249–258.

Schroder, H., Zilles, K., Maelicke, A., & Hajos, F. (1989). Immunohisto and cytochemical localization of cortical cholinoreceptors in rat and man. *Brain Research, 502,* 287–295.

Shiba, K., Mori, H., Matsuda, H., Ichikawa, A., & Tonami, N. (1996). Radioiodinated (-)-2-[4-(3-iodophenyl) piperidino] cyclohexanol: A potential radioligand for mapping presynaptic cholinergic neurons. *Nuclear Medicine Communications, 17,* 485–492.

Sillito, A. M. (1993). The cholinergic neuromodulatory system: An evaluation of its functional roles. *Progress in Brain Research, 98,* 371–378.

Sjögren, M., Blennaw, K., Minthon, L., Karlsson, I., & Wallin, A. (1996). Neurochemical and treatment studies in frontotemporal dementia. In F. Pasquier, F. Lebert, & P. H. Scheltens (Eds.), *Frontotemporal dementia* (pp. 91–98). The Netherlands: ICG Publications.

van der Zee, E. A., Streetland, C., Strosberg, A. D., Schroder, H., & Luiten, P. G. M. (1992). Visualization of cholinoceptive neurons in the rat neocortex: Colocalization of muscarinic and nicotinic receptors. *Molecular Brain Research, 14,* 326–336.

Van Spaendonck, K. P., Berger, H. J., Horstink, M. W., Buytenhuijs, E. L., & Cools, A. R. (1993). Impaired cognitive shifting in Parkinsonian patients on anticholinergic therapy. *Neuropsychologia, 31,* 407–411.

Vidal, C., & Changeux, J. P. (1993). Nicotinic and muscarinic modulations of excitatory synaptic transmission in the rat prefrontal cortex in vitro. *Neuroscience, 56,* 23–32.

Wainer, B. H., Bolam, J. P., Freund, T. F., & Henderson, Z. (1984). Cholinergic synapses in the rat brain: a correlated light and electron microscopic immunohistochemical study employing a monoclonal antibody against choline acetyltransferase. *Brain Research, 308,* 69–70.

Warburton, D. M. (1981). Neurochemical basis of behaviour. *British Medical Bulletin, 37,* 121–125.

Wonnacott, S. (1997). Presynaptic nicotinic acetylcholine receptors. *Trends in Neuroscience, 20,* 92–98.

34

Frontal Lobe Development in Childhood

CAROLE SAMANGO-SPROUSE

The frontal lobe of the brain has been a fascination to scientists since the turn of the century. Tilney (1928) suggested this period of human evolution should be designated the "age of frontal lobe." Seventy years after Tilney's comment, the function of the frontal lobe and its relationship to cognitive development remains a mystery.

Diversity is the hallmark of frontal lobe function from childhood through adulthood. Frontal lobe is the "governor" of the brain function. The frontal lobe influences initiative, personality, and social consciousness. It possesses a regulatory function which effects the utilization of intellectual resources and integration of multimodality information (Benson & Miller, 1997).

It consists of two hemispheres with the right larger than the left. This asymmetry is functional and influences the development of specific skills. The cortical surface of the frontal lobe evolves prenatally throughout the fourth decade of life (Grattan & Eslinger, 1991). This growth is associated with evolving behavioral stages through the first 16 years of life (Grattan & Eslinger, 1991). Differentiation of frontal lobe is a complex process that is critical and necessary to the development and the integration of higher cortical skills.

ANIMAL STUDIES

Our understanding of the role of the frontal lobe in human behavior has been largely advanced by the research in nonhuman primates within the last decade (Diamond & Goldman-Rakic, 1986; Funahashi, Bruce, & Goldman-Rakic, 1990, 1991, 1993; Goldman-Rakic, 1987). The animal studies primarily investigated the cerebral structures involved in sensorimotor learning. These animal studies have a particular relevance to developmental disorders because they demonstrate the degree to which specific functions are localized within frontal regions.

In a landmark study, Goldman-Rakic (1987) found that Rhesus monkeys with frontal lobe damage were deficient in working-memory skills even though associative memory skills were preserved. Utilization of the general fund of knowledge in a goal-directed organized manner was abnormal. In related studies, Funahashi et al. (1990, 1991, 1993) showed a memory deficit for a specific visual-field location in Rhesus monkeys, although basic sensory and motor deficits were not present. The work of Goldman-Rakic and associates demonstrated that prefrontal cortex was responsible for spatial cognitive behavior through internal representations of the outside world and external stimuli. Goldman-Rakic (1994) postulated that the prefrontal cortex was responsible for multiple working-memory circuits, suggesting specialized functions for specific classes of neurons in the frontal lobe.

Further specialization in the frontal lobe has also been defined by the work in nonhuman primates. In working memory, the dorsolateral prefrontal cortex is responsible for active manipulation and monitoring of working memory. Alternatively, the ventrolateral prefrontal cortex is responsible for retrieval of guided sequential behavior.

EXECUTIVE COGNITIVE FUNCTION

The frontal lobes subserve specific control processes which have been termed "executive functions" (Denckla, 1994a, 1996; Luria, 1973; Shallice, 1982). The complexity of the executive function and its associations and interactions with learning attention and memory has precluded a single well-accepted conceptualization or definition. A recent review of the literature reveals six distinct interpretations (Figure 34.1). In its simplest form, executive function includes four specific target behaviors: (1) planning (motor and time), (2) decision making (across time and space), (3) self-directed goal selection, and (4) monitoring and altering ongoing behavior to achieve a goal (Temple, in press).

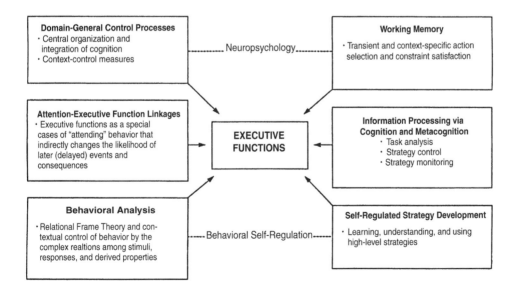

FIGURE 34.1. Summary of theoretical and empirical approaches to executive functions. From Lyon and Krasnegor (1996). Copyright 1996 by Paul H. Brooks. Reprinted by permission.

Readers are referred to *Attention, Memory and Executive Function* (Lyon & Krasnegor, 1996) for an in-depth review of executive cognitive function. Executive function is vital to both human development and to the individual's social and intellectual success. Denckla states that "the difference between child and adult resides in the enfolding of executive function" (Denckla, 1996). Executive function is future oriented, and its primary purpose is to organize the child or adult to the accomplishment of future events.

Denckla (1996) believes that proper assessment of executive function requires the ability to tolerate boredom, to operate independently, and to actively create and execute plans to solve a problem. Denckla's model does not address the social, emotional, or personality aspects of executive function. Denckla believes executive function is central to higher cortical operations and subsequently has a strong overlap with attention and memory.

Pennington defines executive function as "the ability to maintain an appropriate problem-solving set for attainment of a future goal" (Welsh & Pennington, 1988, p. 28). The critical components to Pennington's conceptualization are the concept of working memory and inhibitory control. By definition, working memory is maintaining plans and programs in mind or "on-line" until necessary to complete a specific action or plan. Pennington describes inhibitory control as the ability to override a prepotent or automatic response and shift problem-solving strategies to an alternate solution. Pennington's model further explains the variability of the manifestation of behavioral disorders with diverse neurobiological etiologies yet similar executive function deficits. Pennington emphasizes the need to identify and measure the various aspects of working memory and inhibitory control to further evaluate frontal lobe function and, ultimately, executive function.

Barkley has written extensively on executive function and its relationship to attending behaviors. Barkley (1997) states that the relationship of attention-deficit/hyperactive disorder (ADHD) to executive function as a behavioral inhibition disorder. He identifies five basic constructs of working memory, self-regulation, internalization of speech, reconstitution, and motor control–fluency–syntax. Barkley believes that the development of inhibition is essential to the execution of these higher-order cortical functions. Barkley's hybrid model proposes the incorporation of affect, self-regulation, working memory, and inhibition into one manageable hypothesis.

There are numerous conceptualizations of executive function. The complexity of these higher cortical functions and the breadth of the behaviors presently belies a concise, discrete definition. There is consensus, however, that executive function encompasses a variety of neurocognitive constructs that are governed by the frontal lobe. These constructs influence social, intellectual, and the organizational aspects of a child's life.

PEDIATRIC NEUROPSYCHOLOGY EVALUATION

A unique feature of human cognition and behavior is spoken and written language. Our understanding of the frontal lobe and its relationship to human behavior is lesion based from the adult population (Denckla, 1996). The study of children and the development of the frontal lobe is confounded by the normal learning process of children. In adults, stability is expected and an abrupt change in behavior is usually a reflection of a disease process. In children, the converse is true—stability of cognitive constructs is limited in duration and a change is usually a reflection of brain maturation.

The pediatric neuropsychological assessment identifies the child's array of skills and the deficits within a developmental context. It is bound contextually to narrative data for each age as well as to a comprehensive assessment of the environmental complexity and social dynamics. The purpose of the assessment is the interpretation of the child within the context of developmental expectation for his age and subsequently brain function. The "mental status" examination for any child must assess language, attention, and neuromotor, memory and visual–perceptual development. In addition, self-regulation and mental status should include an examination of the capacity to delay gratification, accept limits, and attend and process to both verbal and nonverbal cues. The assessment of frontal lobe capacity is then a subset of the standard neuropsychological evaluation. The inherent weakness within the assessment of frontal lobe development is the lack of consensus of what the frontal lobe skills are exactly and how they are best assessed.

Assessment of Executive Cognitive Function

There are more than 60 measures of executive cognitive function within frontal lobe development. Two types of skills in the evaluation process must always be considered: (1) determining the degree and control of inhibition and (2) assessing the capabilities of working memory.

Motor sequencing tasks are effective in identifying damage to the frontal lobe. The tasks range from imitating simple hand motions to abstract behavioral sequences. Go/no-go tasks assess the ability to inhibit motoric responses primarily. The premise is that both children and adults with deficient frontal lobe systems are unable to inhibit inappropriate motoric responses. This test is sensitive to level of inhibitory control and has been utilized in the assessment of children with ADHD.

The importance of the frontal lobes for the completion of delayed-response tasks has been documented in nonhuman primates, children, and adult humans. The basic paradigm is the placement of an object in one of two locations. There is a delay of several seconds with the two locations obscured from view. The subject is then allowed to choose where to find the toy. Success on the task is contingent on intact working-memory skills. It assesses the child's internal organization and execution of a memory-driven cognitive construct. Goldman-Rakic (1987) believed that the maturation and intactness of the prefrontal cortex was necessary for completion of delayed-response tasks.

Verbal fluency helps assess frontal function in children (Milner, 1964; Newcombe, 1969; Thurstone, 1958). Children with frontal lobe deficits can demonstrate reduction in word production as well as increased perseverative responses. Hence, the quantity and quality of the verbal responses help in the determination of frontal lobe competence.

The assessment of frontal lobe pathology continues to evolve as our understanding of frontal lobe capacities improves. Frontal lobe dysfunction shows diversity and breadth of impairment, and performance may be impaired in many separate and distinct areas. Responses may be affected by the lack of organizational skills, attentional capacities, and goal-directed behaviors. Therefore, assessment of these diverse behaviors remains a continual challenge in the pediatric population. Neuropsychological assessment of frontal lobe function remains primarily inferential, more so if the child is below school age.

EXECUTIVE COGNITIVE FUNCTION IN THE EARLY CHILDHOOD

Bruner (1973) described evidence of planning and self-monitoring behavior in toddlers. Rakic, Bourgeois, Zecevic, Eckenhoft, and Goldman-Rakic (1986) revealed significant peaks in synaptogenesis in the prefrontal lobe during the first year of life. By 7 to 9 months of age, infants demonstrate cognitive skills attributable to prefrontal cortex in object retrieval tasks. Further development of the frontal lobe region occurs between 12 and 18 months of age (Diamond, 1988).

Early frontal skills emerge in a stage-like fashion similar to the psychological cognitive constructs described by Jean Piaget. There are three critical periods in executive cognitive function— 4–6 years, 9–10 years, and adolescence—with differing developmental trajectories (Welsh, Pennington, & Groissier, 1991). Recognition, memory, and continuous picture recognition reach an adult level by 4 years of age. Visual search and planning on the Tower of Hanoi become indistinguishable from that of an adult by 6 years of age (Welsh et al., 1991). A cognitive spurt seems to occur in development between 5 and 7 years of age (White, 1970). There are rapid advances during this stage in logical thought, verbal mediation, working memory, and selective action (Welsh et al., 1991). By age 10, there is more complexity in organized visual search and greater hypothesis testing and impulse control. Improvement in verbal fluency, motor sequencing, and complex planning are achieved with the advent of adolescence.

Research into early childhood development and executive functions remains limited. There is a need for formal measures of frontal lobe to be incorporated into traditional standardized intelligence testing if the nuances of developmental performance in younger children are to be appreciated. The impact of executive cognitive function on performance and achievement is necessary if educational intervention for children with developmental disorders is to be individualized.

NEUROGENETIC DISORDERS

Behavioral Neurogenetics

"Behavioral neurogenetics" is a novel research approach developed recently to investigate the human brain in specific genetic disorders (Reiss & Denckla, 1996). It studies neuropsychologicaly impaired individuals with a homogeneous genetic etiology which results in common neurobehavioral and neurodevelopmental dysfunction (Reiss & Denckla, 1996).

In behavioral neurogenetics, lesions are defined at the DNA level (Reiss & Denckla, 1996). This research is predicated on two basic assumptions. First, behavioral and/or cognitive dysfunction is a result of a complex pathway. It is easier to understand pathomechanisms when investigating large homogeneous populations of children, and in previous studies, heterogenetiety within populations of children with learning disabilities made it hard to delineate neurobiological markers from environmental or familial influences. By examining known chromosomal disorders, homogeneity of the research sample is significantly increased, therefore, it becomes easier to proceed "from gene to brain to cognitive architecture to manifest learning disabilities" (Denckla, 1994b). The second assumption is that by better understanding cognitive function in children with known genetic disorders, our comprehension of gene–brain–behavior in the normal population will increase. This belief has yet to be realized.

NEUROFIBROMATOSIS—TYPE I

Genetics

Neurofibromatosis—type 1 (NF-1) is the most common autosomal dominant genetic disorder, occurring in approximately 1 of 3,000 live births and currently affecting at least 100,000 individuals in the United States. NF-1 occurs with equal frequency in males and females and has similar incidence in all racial and ethnic populations around the world (Riccardi, 1995; Varnhagen et al., 1988). The diagnosis of NF-1 is determined on the basis of physical findings as defined by the National Institutes of Health Consensus Development Conference (Table 34.1). Clinical manifestations commonly seen are "cafe-au-lait" macules or spots (CLS), neurofibromas, iris (Lisch) nodules, skeletal abnormalities, and central nervous system (CNS) anomalies. CNS lesions include benign and malignant tumors (e.g., astrocytomas, neurofibrosarcomas, and optic pathway gliomas) (Riccardi, 1992). The gene for NF-1 has been mapped to the proximal long arm of chromosome 17 (17q). Its protein product of neurofibromin is usually classified as a tumor suppressor gene (Xu, O'Connell, & Viskochil, 1990).

Neurobehavioral Phenotype

In the last 10 years, research has elicited the effects of this very common genetic disorder on higher cortical functions. The relationship between this gene mutation, neurocognitive disabilities, and neuroimaging findings are of great interest because of the increased prevalence of learning disabilities with NF-1. Estimates of learning disabilities for NF-1 have ranged from 40% to 60% (Eldridge, Denckla, & Bien, 1989; Eliason, 1986; Hofman, Harris, Bryan, & Denckla, 1994; Riccardi, 1995; Varnhegen et al., 1988). The neuropsychological profile of children with NF-1 includes a higher prevalence of nonverbal learning disabilities when compared to both population normals and unaffected siblings (Hofman et al., 1994; North, Joy, & Yuille, 1994, 1995). These problems are often characterized as executive cognitive dysfunction with difficulties in organization, formulation, and execution of written language, poor inhibition, and social dysfunction (Reiss & Denckla, 1996). The school-age child with NF-1 has a depressed intellectual quotient (mean = 89 to 94). A visuospatial deficit on the Judgment of Live Orientation is consistently observed. Also, such a child shows deficits in visual–perceptual organization and fine motor skills. Several recent studies have shown verbal learning deficits in reading and spelling (Hofman et al., 1994; Leguis, Deschumaeker, Spaeper, Casaer, & Fryns, 1994; Mazzocco et al., 1995).

TABLE 34.1. NIH Consensus Criteria for NF-1

The diagnosis of NF-1 is established in anyone having two features in the following list:

1. Six or more cafe-au-lait macules measuring at least 5 mm before puberty or 15 mm after puberty.
2. Two or more neurofibromas or one plexiform neurofibroma.
3. Freckles in the axilla or groin.
4. Lisch nodules on the iris of the eye.
5. Optic glioma.
6. Pseudoarthrosis.
7. NF-1 by above criteria in a parent, sibling, or offspring.

Neurobehavioral Phenotype of Infants

Infants and toddlers with NF-1 have depressed cognitive abilities with abnormal neuro-motor and perceptual motor development compared to their nonhandicapped age-matched peers (Samango-Sprouse et al., 1994). Affect is often described as flattened, with a more passive interactive style. Problem-solving skills observed in play are monochromatic, with one strategy excessively used. Motoric dysfunction includes truncal hypotonia, motor planning deficits, and delayed acquisition of motor skills (Samango-Sprouse et al., 1994).

In the first study, only 1 infant out of 17 had scores within the normal range (i.e., developmental quotient > 85). In the second study, children with familial NF-1 had significantly lower scores in cognition ($p = .04$) and receptive language ($p = .02$) (Table 34.2). Neuromotor evaluation revealed diminished tonus, predominantly in the axial and appendicular regions. This abnormal tone could be an early manifestation of the alterations in brain development caused by the NF-1 gene. The diminished truncal tone may be a precursor to or predictor of the later axial incoordination and gait abnormalities described by others (Eldridge et al., 1989). Because perceptual development and motor behavior are intricately linked, the depressed fine motor development index and gross motor development index scores maybe early indicators of the visual–perceptual dysfunction observed in the school-age population.

Denckla (1996) describes the interdependence of brain regions and ascribes to the importance of motoric integration and execution of refined motor movements as examples of well-organized and highly developed cognitive function. The poorly refined motor movement of these children may signal the early signs of frontal lobe dysfunction. Denckla (1996) also hypothesizes that executive cognitive function may be altered during the course of development in NF-1.

It is possible that early neuromotor dysfunction secondary to the NF-1 lesion may hamper or change the appropriate maturation of specific brain regions. It is appealing to postulate that working memory described in the school-age child could be effected by the actual experience of memory for location in infancy and preschool years. The infant's

TABLE 34.2. NF-1 Developmental Study Results

	SES	Age (mo)	Motor GMDI	Motor FMDI	Cog. MDI	Rec. Lang	Exp. Lang	Tone score	Mom's PPVT	Dad's PPVT
Familial (N = 36)										
Mean	2.94	32.29	82.06	82.96	87.72	84.00	86.97	2.50	73.43	81.00
Standard deviation	1.37	22.33	19.23	20.45	17.22	18.72	22.57	1.22	8.96	27.78
Sporadic (N = 54)										
Mean	2.14	36.17	87.60	91.94	95.26	94.39	92.67	2.44	101.29	104.38
Standard deviation	1.22	21.87	16.58	22.40	16.39	18.17	21.04	1.56	20.65	19.40
Totals for the group (n = 90)										
Mean	2.47	34.62	85.33	88.43	92.24	90.09	90.39	2.47	95.71	98.00
Standard deviation	1.34	22.01	17.81	21.98	17.04	18.98	21.70	1.43	21.93	23.17
Girls (n = 41)										
Mean	2.76	32.55	86.79	89.69	91.29	89.47	88.44	1.78	88.71	83.33
Standard deviation	1.36	21.07	16.94	20.43	16.72	18.76	22.10	1.35	18.75	18.25
Boys (n = 49)										
Mean	2.24	36.35	84.16	87.45	93.04	90.61	92.00	3.10	100.38	115.60
Standard deviation	1.29	22.84	18.59	23.30	17.44	19.38	21.51	1.19	23.06	14.71

Note. From Samango-Sprouse et al. (1994). Copyright 1994 by The American Society of Human Genetics. Reprinted by permission.

ability to develop memory skills and spatial cognition may be affected by the quality of neuromotor experience. However, these theories need empiric substantiation; developmentalists have suggested, for decades, the importance of early neuromotor experience on school-age skills, particularly those in the nonverbal and spatial–perceptual areas of development.

Neuroimaging and NF-1

Children with NF-1 have both gray and white matter MRI abnormalities, with the characteristic findings being foci of the T_2 high-intensity signal often called UBO (unidentified bright object) in the basal ganglia, thalamus, internal capsule, cerebellum, and brainstem (Figure 34.2). The basal ganglia is the most common site for these lesions with brainstem and cerebellar following (Aoki, Berkovich, & Nishimura, 1989; Bognanno et al., 1988; Surik, Barkovich, & Edwards, 1992). There is no mass effect on these lesions, and they are not related to brain tumors, occurring in conjunction less than 5% of the time (Denckla, 1996). These hyperintensities were originally believed to be hamartomas, heterotopias, or dysmyelinated tissue. Limited studies on autopsy reveal these bright foci to be dysplastic glial proliferation related to aberrant myelination (Zimmerman, Yachnis, & Rorke, 1992).

T_2 Hyperintensities and Neurocognitive Outcome

The relationship of these T_2 bright foci with neurocognitive function has been investigated, and it can be hypothesized that these lesions affect brain development and neurocognitive functions. Early studies (Duffner, Cohen, Seidel, & Shucard, 1989; Dunn & Roos, 1989) revealed no cognitive influence attributable to these foci. These studies have two significant limitations—no formal cognitive assessment and no family control subjects.

In more recent studies, a relationship between T_2 bright foci and cognitive impairment was evident (Hofman et al., 1994; Moore, Slopis, Schomet, Jackson, & Levy, in press; North et al., 1994). The presence and the number of locations occupied were associated with lowered IQ in children with NF-1. Denckla (1996) found that the number

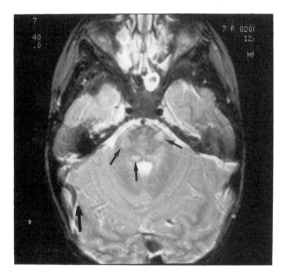

FIGURE 34.2. UBOs of the brain in a child with NF-1.

of locations was critical because it was associated with 40% of the variance in lowered IQ in children with NF-1. Denckla described the importance of the lesions and neuro-cognitive performance with the following story; two males with familial NF-1 and no bright foci had IQs identical to unaffected sibling and affected parent. Conversely, a sporadic case of NF-1 with four brain regions occupied with T_2 bright foci had an average IQ, whereas both parents and a sibling had superior intelligence (Reiss & Denckla, 1996).

Controversy over the association between the T_2 weighted hyperintensities and this relationship to neurocognitive function has continued since several studies demonstrated no effect from these lesions. Moore et al. (in press) evaluated 64 patients and demon-strated a shift to the left in intellectual function (mean Full Scale IQ was 94), but the presence of bright foci was not significantly related to cognitive function. When the site of the lesion was evaluated, thalamic lesions were significantly related to deficits in attention and memory.

Intuitively, it seems likely that T_2 bright foci may have an impact on learning. Perhaps, it may be a cumulative risk related in some way to the number, location, mode of inheritance, and age, or possibly a synergistic effect of multiple factors that result in the observed deficits in frontal lobe function. Both the location and the number of these lesions' effect on neurocognitive function require further study. Riccardi (1995) found improvement in cognitive function in older NF-1 patients. Did regression and/or disap-pearance of lesions influence cognition? A longitudinal study on the relationship of these lesions and the neurocognitive performance would be valuable.

Summary

The neurocognitive phenotype of NF-1 is evolving with characteristic behaviors that suggest executive dysfunction and possible frontal lobe impairment. The atypical profile is evident in early childhood. Cummings (1993) demonstrated that disruption to subcor-tical regions may affect later frontal lobe performance. The presence of T_2 bright lesions in subcortical lesions may alter the learning process during the early years and effect the frontal lobe function observed at school age.

Further study is necessary to evaluate the natural history of this disorder and the interaction of T_2 bright foci on learning and regional brain development. It is reasonable to suspect that early behavioral manifestations of NF-1 are related to later learning. The relationship between these learning curves in children with NF-1 is critical to the develop-ment of appropriate educational and therapeutic interventions. With better understanding of this disorder and its pathogenesis, the care and the education of these children can be more syndrome and symptom specific rather than the generic "one form fits all."

FRAGILE-X

Genetics

Fragile-X is the most common inherited form of mental retardation and was described as a clinically distinct entity in the 1970s. Originally, the fragile site was demonstrated through cytogenetic testing in a culture medium lacking thymidine and folate. In 1991, molecular diagnosis became available with the identification of the fragile-X mental retardation gene (FMR-1). The protein product of FMR-1 is still unknown, but it is believed to play a role in RNA binding (Ashley, Wilkinsen, Reenes, & Warren, 1993; Siomi, Choi, Siomi, Nussbaum, & Dryfuss, 1994). Within FMR-1 locus, there is a repetitive sequence of three DNA nucleotides: cytosine–guanine–guanine (CGG). In the general population, FMR-1 CGG repeats range from approximately 6 to 54 (Fu, Kuhl, Pizzuti, Pierelti, & Sutcliffe, 1994). When 200 or more CGG repeats are present, the clinical presentation of fragile-X is observed (Hansen, Gartler, Scott, Chen, & Laird, 1992).

The FMR-1 gene accounts for a range of effects in females with the full mutation. Unlike other X-linked conditions, females, who are heterozygotes, have atypical and abnormal profiles in behavioral, affective, and cognitive areas (Reiss & Freund, 1990; Freund, Reiss, & Abrams, 1993). Fragile-X and other disorders with expansion of trinucleotide repeat sequence show "genetic anticipation," which is a change for the worse in the effects of a particular genetic disorder as it progresses from one generation to the next (Sutherland & Richards, 1992).

Neurobehavioral Phenotype

Nearly all males and at least 50% of the females with the full mutation have some form of mental retardation ranging from mild to severe. The neurobehavioral phenotype in fragile-X males is a triad of features with atypical behavioral, motoric, and cognitive processes (Reiss & Freund, 1990). The behavioral component of fragile-X phenotype consists of atypical social interactions, unusual responses to sensory stimulation, and hyperactivity (Baumgardner, Green, & Reiss, 1992; Hagerman, 1991; Reiss & Freund, 1990, 1992). Males with fragile-X have difficulty with self-regulation. They show excessive activity, restlessness, and impulsivity. Excessive sensitivity to sound with increased mouthing and/or smelling of objects has been described in school-age boys with fragile-X (Reiss & Freund, 1992).

This lack of neurobehavioral organization is apparent in infants and toddlers with fragile-X. They are very "challenging infants" because of their hyperresponsivity and limited self-regulation, and they have exaggerated responses to many forms of sensory stimulation. They often have difficulty with management of various textures of foods because of the sensory component and motor planning difficulties (Samango-Sprouse et al., 1994). Their lack of behavioral organization, atypical muscle tonus, and developmental delay often results in the initial medical evaluation and eventual diagnosis.

Although many fragile-X boys demonstrate attachment and bonding to their caregivers, some manifest behaviors found within the autistic spectrum disorder (Reiss & Freund, 1992). This includes difficulty with peer social interactions, atypical communication skills, and repetitive motoric behaviors (Reiss & Freund, 1992). In other behavioral studies, fragile-X males were socially avoidant, with increased incidence of gaze aversion and tactile defensiveness. These "autistic-like" behaviors have similar features of patients with frontal lobe dysfunction.

In the motoric domains, the male infant with fragile-X has truncal hypotonia with early motor planning difficulties. These motor planning deficits are evident in gross motor development, feeding, and speech and language development (Samango-Sprouse et al., 1994). These motor deficits have been characterized as a subtype of dyspraxia (Hagerman, 1991). Older males with fragile-X have visual–motor incoordination and visual–perceptual deficits. The neuropsychological profile reveals relative strengths in verbal reasoning with significant deficits in nonverbal areas. Communication skills are atypical in both verbal and nonverbal areas of development (Reiss & Freund, 1992).

Baumgardner, Reiss, Freund, and Abrams (1995) demonstrated difficulties in a triad of behaviors, reflective of deficits in regulation, inhibition, and attention. These early

behaviors of motor incoordination, sensory dysfunction, and communication disturbances may be harbingers of later difficulties in executive function. The degree of
difficulty in these areas is more severe than would be expected based on the level of
cognitive capacity.

Further supporting the concept of frontal lobe dysfunction in fragile-X males is
research illustrating an interaction between cognition and affect in the syndrome. In
periods of increased anxiety, fragile-X children have greater communication dysfunction
manifested by increased word finding and speech difficulties (Sudhalter, Carborough, &
Cohen, 1991). One primary function of the frontal lobe is integration and organization
of behaviors. The increased anxiety may hamper the ability of fragile-X males to organize
and synthesize information with resulting dysfunction in spoken language.

Neuroimaging

Initial neuroimaging suggested that the FMR-1 full mutation had a generalized effect on
brain development (Courchesne, Young-Courchesne, Press, Hesselink, & Jernigan, 1988;
Wesneriwski, Segan, Miezejeski, Sersen, & Rudelli, 1991). Later studies would also
substantiate a selective influence on brain evolution (Reiss, Aylward, Freund, Joshi, &
Bryan, 1991; Reiss et al., 1993).

Early studies revealed that posterior fossa, specifically cerebellar vermis, was decreased with enlarged ventricular volume in fragile-X males. The vermis (lobes VI and
VII) was unusually small in a subgroup of fragile-X males with autism (Reiss, Patel,
Jumar, & Freund, 1988). Further studies by Reiss, Lee, and Freund (1994) revealed
abnormalities in the temporal lobe, particularly the hippocampal areas. Volumetric
analysis with age- and IQ-matched control subjects revealed that the fragile-X individuals
had significantly larger volumes in both right and left hippocampal areas (Reiss et al.,
1994). Evaluation of a larger number of children and young adults with fragile-X (*N* =
51) revealed increased volumes in the caudate nucleus. Fragile-X males have increased
lateral ventriclaar volume when compared to fragile-X females and controls (Reiss et al.,
1994). The caudate nucleus is recognized as a convergence center for information from
the nonmotor regions of the frontal cortex and affects executive function later. Cummings
(1993) and others have postulated that damage to frontal–subcortical areas affects
executive function later. Based on these postulations, many aspects of the neurobehavioral
profile in fragile-X may be related to the disturbances in the development of caudate
nucleus. In addition, both the vermis and the hippocampus are involved in attention and
learning. The vermis is believed to be critical in processing and integrating sensory
information. It modulates attention and movement, whereas the hippocampus supports
learning and memory. The abnormal findings of the brain are supported by the specific
neurobehavioral phenotype observed in fragile-X. However, further research is warranted
to fully understand the cerebral neuroanatomy of children with fragile-X and its
involvement in the neurobehavioral phenotype.

TURNER SYNDROME (MONOSOMY-X)
Genetics

Turner syndrome is characterized by atypical facies with cardiac anomalies, short stature,
abnormal pubertal development, and renal malformations. The various dysmorphic
features frequently enable identification in the newborn period. Fifty-five percent of all

girls with Turner syndrome will be missing an entire X chromosome, whereas the remaining children will only be missing a part of the X chromosome (Lippe, 1990).

Neurobehavioral Phenotype

The developmental prognosis of sex chromosomes aneuploidy (SCA) children was believed to be quite poor in the late 1960s (Robinson, Puck, Pennington, Borelli, & Hudeson, 1979). As a result of prospective studies of SCA and the availability of prenatal diagnosis within the last 20 years, there is growing belief that the neurocognitive problems are related to disturbances in right-hemisphere development, particularly frontal lobe dysfunction.

In the last 30 years, the large preponderance of studies have focused on the school-age or older child with Turner syndrome. As early as 1960s, the deficits in nonverbal areas of development, particularly the visual–spatial deficits, were described (Cohen, 1962; Shaffer, 1962). In 1966, Money and Alexander coined "space-form blindness" to describe the visual spatial difficulties including difficulty in identifying positions in space, rotation of various shapes mentally, and visual–motor incoordination. This constellation of disturbances suggested right-hemisphere dysfunction.

Recognizing the importance of right-hemisphere development in socialization, more recent research studies have focused on both neurocognitive and behavioral manifestations of the school-age child with Turner syndrome. Rovert (1986) demonstrated varying behavioral disturbances in girls according to age. The younger girls (8–12 years) were distractible, hyperactive, and poorly organized, whereas the older females displayed more anxious behaviors and less distractibility. McCauley, Kay, Ito, and Truder (1987) found diminished abilities to interpret facial affect and to read social cues.

Reiss et al. (1993) investigated prepubertal identical female twins who were discordant for Turner syndrome. DNA fingerprinting established zygosity, and no mosaicism was observed chromosomally. Both females had above-average IQ. However, there was an 18-point discrepancy in Performance IQ, in contrast to a 3-point difference in Verbal IQ. Evaluation revealed difficulties in executive function and visual–motor and visual–spatial domains. Behaviorally, the twin with Turner syndrome demonstrated attentional problems, hyperactivity, and anxiety.

Johnson and Ross (1994) investigated 20 Turner syndrome females with matching controls to determine whether there was a critical period for estrogen's effect on brain maturation and cognitive development. In the Oddball paradigm, a simple auditory discrimination task, a maturation effect was shown with older girls (15–20 years) performing less well than the younger girls (9–14 years). In the left-to-right discrimination task, all ages showed task performance deficits. The slowed response in left to right discrimination related to response selection, preparation, and execution. These findings further supported the idea of right-hemisphere dysfunction and frontal lobe involvement.

Neurocognitive and behavioral dysfunction are evident in Turner syndrome. The biological basis for these disturbances is not well understood; however, two primary biological mechanisms have been postulated—the influence of sex hormones and the rate of cell division growth on brain maturation. Insufficient exposure to appropriate levels of estrogen during critical periods of brain development may account for the neurobehavioral dysfunction. Alternatively, atypical rates of cell division may affect the rate of brain growth and subsequently cause cognitive dysfunction. Longitudinal studies that have large cohorts of females with mosaic and nonmosaic Turner syndrome are necessary to address the evolution of the neurobehavioral, neuroimaging, and endocrinological aspect of this neurogenetic disorder.

Neuroimaging and Turner Syndrome

Early studies on the anatomical brain structures of children and adults with Turner syndrome were based on neuropathology. These studies described a variety of heterogeneous findings, including cerebral cortical disorganization, cerebellar hypoplasia, neuronal heterotopias in cerebellar white matter, and posterior fossa abnormalities (Brun & Skold, 1968; Della Giustina, Forabosco, Botticelli, & Pace, 1985; Molland & Purcell, 1974). Autopsy also identified cellular abnormalities in frontal cortex and hippocampus (Nielsen, Nyborg, & Dahl, 1977).

Recent imaging studies have focused on brain architecture and cognitive performance. MRI abnormalities have included Dandy Walker malfunction, agenesis of corpus callosum, and posterior fossa abnormalities. Murphy et al. (1993) studied 18 females with Turner syndrome (9 were mosaic and 9 nonmosaic) and 19 controls. Volumetric analysis revealed decreased volume of cerebral hemisphere and smaller region to whole brain proportions for parietal–occipital, hippocampus, and thalamus. All brain abnormalities were bilateral. Children with mosaic Turner syndrome were between the controls and nonmosaics in measures of brain anatomy as well as neurocognitive performance.

Reiss et al. (1993), evaluating identical female twins who were disconcordant for Turner syndrome, found similar findings neuroanatomically. There was evidence of both specific regional effects and generalized changes in the brain. There was a significant increase in cerebrospinal fluid (25%), with a decrease in gray matter particularly in parietal–occipital, frontal, and left parietal lobes between the affected and nonaffected sibling. The affected twin had significant differences noted in the posterior fossa, with a 10–15% reduction in the size of cerebellar vermis, pons and medulla associated with a 50% relative increase in the volumes of the fourth ventricle and cisterna magna. Neurocognitive findings were consistent with frontal lobe dysfunction.

Reiss, Mazzorio, Greenlaw, Freund, and Ross (1995) completed a study of 30 girls with Turner syndrome and 30 controls individually age matched. Imaging revealed smaller areas of brain tissue (both gray and white matter) in right and left parietal brain regions. There was a suggestion of greater proportion of tissue in the right inferior parietal–occipital region as well.

These consistent studies of females with Turner syndrome support the concept that regional abnormalities of the brain may underlie the described neurocognitive phenotype associated with Turner syndrome. There is abnormally decreased tissue in the parietal–occipital region. These regions of the brain (parietal–occipital) are consistent with the neurocognitive areas of weakness, particularly right-hemisphere and visual–spatial skills.

It is intriguing to consider the importance of posterior fossa abnormalities in behavior and learning in girls with Turner syndrome. At present, no known studies correlate these abnormalities with the unique constellation of learning problems. Additional investigation of the specific nature of the posterior fossa abnormalities and their relationship to cognition is needed to further our understanding of the relationship between neuroanatomy and behavioral performance. The variability in the neurocognitive abilities of the girls with Turner syndrome raises many unanswered questions and possibilities for future research on the relationship between anatomy and genetics. With greater understanding of the behavioral phenotype, therapeutic intervention both medically and educationally can be more specifically tailored for females with this disorder.

ATTENTION-DEFICIT/HYPERACTIVITY DISORDER

Genetics

The genetics of ADHD remain unclear; however, recently some progress has been made. Segregation analysis of ADHD has demonstrated an autosomal transmission with considerable reduction in the penetrance of the hypothesized major gene (Pennington, Grossier, & Welsh, 1993; Pennington, 1997). Linkage studies reveal an association between the genetic marker for thyroid and ADHD (Hauser, Zametkin, & Martinez, 1993). Replication of this study is necessary as the incidence of thyroid deficiency is relatively rare compared to ADHD. More recently, genetic studies showed linkage between the dopamine transporter locus (DATI) and ADHD (Cook et al., 1995). A third possible linkage was recently found between the C4B gene on short arm of chromosome 6 (Warren et al., 1995). Replication of all of these studies is necessary because ADHD appears to be genetically heterogeneous.

Neurobehavioral Phenotype

ADHD is one of the most common childhood developmental disorders. Recent epidemiological studies demonstrate the range of incidence from 1% to 7%. Fifty percent of all children with ADHD qualify for a comorbid diagnosis (Barkley, 1997). The prevalence of multiple diagnoses and the heterogeneity of the population have often precluded a delineation of a specific neurocognitive profile.

The hallmarks of the disorder are deficits in attention, activity, and impulsivity, which are usually identified with standardized questionnaires from parents, teachers, and health care professionals. Peak age for initial symptoms to present are during preschool years—usually 3 to 4 years of age. Sex ratio is disproportionately males to females as high as 7:1 (Pennington, 1997).

The relationship of frontal lobe dysfunction in ADHD has been postulated because of the symptomatology of this disorder—distractibility, hyperactivity, and impulsivity. Douglas (1988) has been a leader in describing the parameters of the new psychological profile and its relationship to frontal lobe function. Recent studies have demonstrated deficits in children with ADHD in tasks that demand inhibition, attention, vigilance, and motor control. Memory tasks, whether verbal or nonverbal, are spared.

Pennington (1997) and Barkley, Grodzinski, and Dupaul (1992) have reviewed most recent studies of executive cognitive function and ADHD. Pennington identified 15 of 18 studies describing executive cognitive function in the children with ADHD. Forty of sixty measures (67%) of the executive function were atypical or abnormal in children with ADHD. Interestingly, the children with ADHD did not score significantly better on any of the measures. There were some specific group differences found across studies in executive function. Children with ADHD were unimpaired in verbal memory, visual–spatial skills, and verbal processes. In contrast, vigilance and perceptual speed were significantly impaired.

Neuroimaging and ADHD

The most conclusive evidence for brain dysfunction in ADHD comes from studies utilizing neuroimaging, regional cerebral blood flow, and electrophysiology measures. A series of research studies (Hynd, Semrud-Clikeman, Lorys, Novey, & Eliopulos, 1990; Hynd et al., 1991) using MRI with children revealed bilaterally smaller anterior cortexes, particularly on the right in children with ADHD. These children did not have the frontal lobe asymmetry typically appreciated in the normal pediatric population (Hynd et al., 1990).

Based on these findings, Hynd hypothesized that the anterior portion of the corpus callosum would be smaller in ADHD population because the frontal lobes, left and right, are connected by the genu of the corpus callosum. Results of the study revealed posterior (splenium) and anterior (genu) significantly smaller in boys and girls with ADHD (Hynd et al., 1991). Hynd, Marshall, and Gonzalez (1993) found that the head of the left caudate nucleus was smaller in children with ADHD than in the control subjects.

Giedd et al. (1994) found that only the anterior portion of the corpus callosum of boys with ADHD was smaller than in control subjects. The Gidd study was larger than the Hynd study (7 vs. 18, respectively) and was matched for several pertinent features, including age, weight, height, Tanner stage, and handedness.

Costellanos et al. (1994) studied 50 males who were matched to a control group of 48 males ranging in age from 6 to 18 years. There was symmetry in caudate nucleus, suggesting a decrease in the volume of right caudate. Lou, Henriksen, Bruhn, Borner, and Nielsen (1989) demonstrated decreased blood flow to frontal lobes in ADHD and increased perfusion to the same region after administration of Ritalin (methylphenidate). In the same study, administration of Ritalin decreased blood flow to both the motor cortex and the primary sensory cortex, with clinical changes of decreased motor restlessness and distractibility.

In a landmark study, Zametkin et al. (1993), using parents with residual ADHD and their affected children, showed reduced cerebral glucose utilization in right frontal lobe with position emission tomography (PET). In another study, Zametkin, Nordahl, Gross, and King (1990) documented a significant reduction in glucose metabolism in 6 of 60 brain regions, including the left anterior frontal lobe.

In summary, studies of brain function and ADHD reveal decreased function in the frontal lobe region of the brain. These findings are consistent with the pathophysiological models of ADHD that have been postulated. With larger sample populations and comorbidity clearly delineated, the link between the frontal lobe, behavior and learning in ADHD will be further elucidated.

CONCLUSION

With the advent of neuroimagery, regional cerebral blood flow, and electroencephalography measures, there has been a resurgence of interest in childhood developmental disorders. Research in neurogenetic disorders such as NF-1, fragile-X, and monosomy-X have enhanced our understanding of the brain, behavior, and learning disabilities. Recent studies reveal a correlation between frontal lobe function, behavior, and neurocognitive outcome. In the next decade, further research is needed into the natural history of the frontal lobe throughout childhood years and its relationship to neurocognitive performance. As the nuances of brain function and behavioral manifestations are further understood, both the medical and educational therapies for children with developmental disorders can be more syndrome specific and individualized.

REFERENCES

Aoki, S., Barkovich, A. J., & Nishimura, J. (1989). Neurofibromatosis Types 1 and 2: Cranial MR findings. *Radiology, 172,* 527–534.

Ashley, C. J., Wilkinsen, K. D., Reenes, D., & Warren, S. T. (1993). FMR 1 protein: Conserved RNP family domains and selective RNA binding. *Science, 262,* 563–566.

Barkley, R. (1997). Behavioral inhibition disorder and attention deficit hyperactivity disorder. *Psychology Bulletin, 121*(1), 65–94.

Barkley, R. A., Grodzinski, G., & DuPaul, G. S. (1992). Frontal lobe functions in attention deficit disorder with and without hyperactivity: A review and research report. *Journal of Abnormal Child Psychology, 20,* 163–188.

Baumgardner, T. L., Green, K. E., & Reiss, A. L. (1992). The psychological effects Associated with fragile X syndrome. *Current Opinion in Pediatrics, 4,* 609–615.

Baumgardner, T. L., Reiss, A. L., Freund, L., & Abrams, M. (1995). Specification of the neurobehavioral phenotype in males with fragile X syndrome. *Pediatrics, 95*(5), 744–752.

Benson, D. F., & Miller, B. L. (1997). Frontal lobes: Clinical and anatomical aspects. In T. E. Feinberg & M. J. Farah (Eds.), *Behavioral neurology and neuropsychology* (pp. 401–408). New York: McGraw-Hill.

Bognanno, J. R., Edwards, M. K., Lee, T. A., Dunn, D. W., Roosk, D., & Klakle, E. C. (1988). Cranial MR imaging in neurofibromatosis. *American Journal of Neuroradiology, 9,* 461–468.

Brun, A., & Skald, G. (1968). CNS malformations in Turner's syndrome. *Neuropathologica Scandinavica, 10,* 159–161.

Bruner, J. (1973). Organization of early skilled action. *Child Development, 44,* 1–11.

Cohen, H. (1962). Psychological test findings in adolescents having ovarian dysgenesis. *Psychosomatic Medicine, 24,* 249–256.

Cook, E. H., Stein, M. A., Krasowski, M. D., Cox, N. J., Olkon, D. M., Kieffer, J. E., & Leventhal, B. L. (1995). Association of attention deficit disorder and the dopamine transporter gene. *American Journal of Human Genetics, 56,* 995–998.

Costellanos, F. X., Giedd, J. N., Eckburg, P., Marsh, W. L., Vaituzis, A. C., Kaysen, D., Hamburger, S. D., & Rapoport, J. L. (1994). Quantitative morphology of the caudate nucleus in attention deficit hyperactivity disorder. *American Journal of Psychiatry, 151,* 1791–1796.

Courchesne, E., Young-Courchesne, R., Press, G. A., Hesselink, J. R., & Jernigan, T. L. (1988). Hypoplasia of cerebellar vermal lobules VI and VII in autism. *New England Journal of Medicine, 318,* 1349–1354.

Cummings, J. L. (1993). Frontal–subcortical circuits and human behavior. *Archives of Neurology, 50,* 873–880.

Della Giustina, E., Forabosco, A., Botticelli, A. R., & Pace, P. (1985). Neuropathology of the Turner syndrome. *Pediatric Media e Chirsurgica, 7,* 49–55.

Denckla, M. B. (1994a). Interpretations of a behavioral neurologist. In S. H. Broman & J. Grafman (Eds.), *Atypical cognitive deficits in developmental disorders: Implications for brain function* (pp. 283–296). New Jersey: Erlbaum.

Denkla, M. B. (1994b). Measurement of executive functioning. In G. R. Lyon (Ed.), *Frames of reference for the assessment of learning disabilities: New views on measurement issues* (pp. 117–142). Baltimore: Brooks.

Denckla, M. B. (1996). A theory and model of executive function: A neuropsychological perspective. In G. R. Lyon & N. A. Krasnegor (Eds.), *Attention, memory and executive function* (pp. 263–278). Baltimore: Brooks.

Diamond, A. (1988). Differences between adult and infant cognition: Is the crucial variable presence or absence of language. In L. Weiskrantz (Ed.), *Thought without language* (pp. 337–370). New York: Oxford University Press.

Diamond, A., & Goldman-Rakic, P. S. (1986). Comparative development in human infants and infant rhesus monkeys of cognitive function that depends on pre-frontal cortex. *Social and Neuroscience Abstracts, 12,* 742.

Douglas, V. I. (1988). Cognitive deficits in children with attention deficit disorder with hyperactivity. In L. M. Bloomindale & J. Sargent (Eds.), *Attention deficit disorder: Criteria, cognition, intervention.* New York: Pergamon Press.

Duffner, P. K., Cohen, M. E., Seidel, G., & Shucard, D. W. (1989). The significance of MRI abnormalities in children with NF-1. *Neurology, 39,* 373–378.

Dunn, D. W., & Roos, K. L. (1989). Magnetic resonance imaging evaluation of learning difficulties and incoordination in neurofibromatosis. *Neurofibromatosis, 2,* 1–5.

Eldridge, R., Denckla, M. B., & Bien, E. (1989). Neurofibromatosis type 1 (Recklinghausen's disease): Neurologic and cognitive assessment with sibling controls. *American Journal of Disease in Children, 143,* 833–837.

Eliason, M. J. (1986). Neurofibromatosis: Implications for learning and behavior. *Journal of Developmental and Behavioral Pediatrics, 7,* 175–179.

Freund, L. S., Reiss, A. L., & Abrams, M. T. (1993). Psychiatric disorders associated with fragile X in the young female. *Pediatrics, 91,* 321–329.

Fu, Y. H., Kuhl, D. P., Pizzuti, A., Pierelti, M., & Sutcliffe, J. S. (1994). Variation of the CGG repeat at the fragile X site results in genetic instability: Resolution of the Sherman paradox. *Cell, 67,* 1047–1058.

Funahashi, S., Bruce, C. J., & Goldman-Rakic, P. S. (1990). Mnemonic coding of visual space in the monkey's dorsolateral prefrontal cortex. *Journal of Neurophysiology, 61,* 331–349.

Funahashi, S., Bruce, C. J., & Goldman-Rakic, P. S. (1991). Neuromal activity related to saccadic eye movements in the monkey's dorsolateral prefrontal cortex. *Journal of Neurophysiology, 65*(6), 1464–1483.

Funahashi, S., Bruce, C. J., & Goldman-Rakic, P. S. (1993). Dorsolateral prefrontal lesions and oculomotor delayed response performance: Evidence for mnemonic scotoma. *Journal of Neuroscience, 13,* 1479–1497.

Giedd, J. N., Costellanos, X., Casey, B. J., Kozuch, P., King, A. C., Hamburger, S. D., & Rapoport, J. L. (1994). Quantitative morphology of the corpus callosum in attentional deficit hyperactivity disorder. *American Journal of Psychiatry, 151,* 665–669.

Goldman-Rakic, P. S. 1987. Development of cortical circuity and cognitive function. *Child Development, 58,* 601–622.

Goldman-Rakic, P. S. (1994). Specification of higher cortical functions. In S. H. Broman & J. Grafman (Eds.), *Atypical cognitive deficits in developmental disorders: Implications for brain function* (pp. 3–22). Hillsdale, NJ: Erlbaum.

Grattan, L. M., & Eslinger, P. J. (1991). Frontal lobe damage in children and adults: A comparative review. *Developmental Neuropsychology, 7*(3), 283–326.

Hagerman, R. T. (1991). Physical and behavioral phenotype. In R. T. Hagerman & A. C. Cronester (Eds.), *Fragile X syndrome* (pp. 3–68). Baltimore: John Hopkins University Press.

Hansen, R. S., Gartler, S. M., Scott, C. R., Chen, S. H., & Laird, C. D. (1992). Methylation analysis of CGG sites in the CPG island of the human FMR-1 gene. *Human Molecular Genetics, 7,* 571–578.

Hauser, P., Zametkin, A. J., & Martinez, P. (1993). Attention deficit hyperactivity disorder in people with generalized resistance to thyroid hormone. *New England Journal of Medicine, 328,* 997–1001.

Hofman, K. J., Harris, E. L., Bryan, R. N., & Denckla, M. B. (1994). Neurofibromatosis type 1: The cognitive phenotype. *Journal of Pediatrics, 124,* 51–58.

Hynd, G. W., Marshall, R., & Gonzalez, J. J. (1993). *Asymmetry of the caudate nucleus in HD: An exploratory study of gender and handedness effects.* Paper presented at the annual meeting of the Society for Research in Child and Adolescent Psychopathology, Santa Fe, NM.

Hynd, G. W., Semrud-Clikeman, M., Lorys, A. R., Novey, E. S., & Eliopulos, D. (1990). Brain morphology in developmental dyslexia and attention deficit disorder/hyperactivity. *Archives of Neurology, 47,* 919–925.

Hynd, G. W., Semrud-Clikeman, M., Lorys, A. R., Novey, E. S., Eliopulos, D., & Lyytinen, H. (1991). Corpus callosum morphology in attention deficit hyperactivity disorder: Morphometric analysis of MRI. *Journal of Learning Disabilities, 24,* 141–146.

Johnson, R. Jr., & Ross, J. L. (1994). Event-related potential indications of altered brain development in Turner syndrome. In S. H. Broman & J. Grafman (Eds.), *Atypical cognitive deficits in developmental disorders: Implications for brain function* (pp. 217–294). Hillsdale, NJ: Erlbaum.

Leguis, E. M., Deschumaeker, M. J., Spaeper, A., Casaer, P., & Fryns, J. P. (1994). Neurofibromatosis type 1 in childhood: A study of the neuropsychological profile in 45 children. *Genetic Counseling, 5,* 51–60.

Lippe, B. (1990). Primary ovarian failure. In S. A. Kaplan (Eds.), *Clinical pediatrics.* Philadelphia: Saunders.

Lou, H. C., Henriksen, L., Bruhn, P., Borner, H., & Nielsen, J. (1989). Strait dysfunction in attention deficit and hyperkinetic disorder. *Archives of Neurology, 46,* 48–52.

Luria, A. R. (1973). The frontal lobes and the regulation of behavior. In K. H. Pribram & Luria (Eds.), *Psychophysiology of the frontal lobes* (pp. 3–26). Orlando, FL: Academic Press.

Lyon, G. R., & Krasnegor, N. A. (1996). *Attention, memory and executive function.* Baltimore: Brooks.

Mazzocco, M. M., Turner, J. E., Denckla, M. B., Hofman, K. J., Scalon, D. C., & Vellutino, F. R. (1995). Language and reading deficits associated with neurofibromatosis type 1: Evidence for a not-go non-verbal learning disability. *Developmental Neuropsychology, 11,* 503–522.

McCauley, E., Kay, T., Ito, J., & Truder, R. (1987). The Turner syndrome: Cognitive deficits, affective discrimination and behavior problems. *Child Development, 58,* 464–473.

Money, J., & Alexander, D. (1966). Turner's syndrome: Further demonstrations of the presence of specific cognitional deficiencies. *Journal of Medical Genetics, 3,* 47–48.

Milner, B. (1964). Some effects of frontal lobectomy in man. In J. M. Warren & K. Akert (Eds.), *The frontal granular cortex and behavior.* New York: McGraw-Hill.

Molland, E. A., & Purcell, M. (1974). Biliary atresea and the Dandy–Walker anomaly in a neonate with 45, X Turner's syndrome. *Journal of Pathology, 115,* 227–230.

Moore, B. D., Slopis, J. M., Schomet, D., Jackson, E. F., & Levy, B. (in press). Neurological significance of areas of high signal intensities on brain MRI of children with neurofibromatosis. *Neurology.*

Murphy, D. G., DeCarli, C., Daly, E., Haxby, J. V., Allen, G., White, R. J., McIntosh, A. R., Powell, C. M., Horwitz, B., Rapport, S. I., & Shapiro, M. B. (1993). X-chromosome effects on female brain: A magnetic resonance imaging study of Turner's syndrome. *Lancet, 13,* 1197–2000.

Newcombe, F. (1969). Missile wounds of the brain: A study of psychological deficits. Oxford, UK: Oxford University Press.

Nielsen, J., Nyborg, H., & Dahl, G. (1977). Turner's syndrome: A psychiatric–psychological study of 45 women with Turner's syndrome compared with their sisters and women with normal karyotypes, growth retardation and primary amenorrhea. *Actu Jutlandica, XLV* (medicine series).

North, K., Joy, P., Yuille, D. (1994). Learning difficulties in neurofibromatosis type 1. The significance of MRI abnormalities. *Neurology, 44,* 878–883.

North, K., Joy, P., & Yuille, D. (1995). Cognitive function and academic performance in children with neurofibromatosis type 1. *Developmental Medicine and Child Neurology, 37,* 427–436.

Pennington, B. F. (1997). Attention deficit hyperactivity disorder. In T. E. Feinberg & M. J. Farah (Eds.), *Behavioral neurology and neuropsychology* (pp. 803–808). New York: McGraw-Hill.

Pennington, B. F., Groisser, D., & Welsh, M. C. (1993). Contrasting cognitive deficits in attention deficit hyperactivity disorder versus reading disability. *Developmental Psychology, 29*(3), 511–523.

Rakic, P., Bourgeois, J. P., Zecevic, N., Eckenhoft, M. F., & Goldman-Rakic, P. S. (1986). Concurrent overproduction of synapses in diverse regions of the primate cerebral cortex. *Science, 232,* 232–235.

Reiss, A. L., Aylward, E., Freund, L. S., Joshi, P. K., & Bryan, R. N. (1991). Neuroanatomy of fragile X syndrome: The posterior fossa. *Annals of Neurology, 29,* 26–32.

Reiss, A. L., & Denckla, M. B. (1996). The contribution of neuroimaging: Fragile X syndrome, Turner syndrome, and neurofibromatosis—1. In G. R. Lyon & J. M. Rumsey (Eds.), *Neuroimaging* (pp. 147–168). Baltimore: Brooks.

Reiss, A., & Freund, L. (1990). Neuropsychiatric aspects of fragile X syndrome. *Brain Dysfunction, 3,* 9–22.

Reiss, A. L., & Freund, L. (1992). Behavioral phenotype of fragile X syndrome: DSM-III-R behavior in male children. *American Journal of Medical Genetics, 43,* 35–46.

Reiss, A. L., Freund, L., Plotnick, L., Baumgardner, T., Green, K., Sozer, A. C., Reader, M., Boehon, C., & Denckla, M. B. (1993). The effects of X monosomy on brain development: Monozygotic twins discordant for Turner's syndrome. *Annals of Neurology, 34,* 95–107.

Reiss, A. L., Lee, J., & Freund, L. (1994). Neuroanatomy of fragile X syndrome: The temporal lobe. *Neurology, 44,* 1317–1324.

Reiss, A. L., Mazzorio, M. M. M., Greenlaw, R., Freund, L. S., & Ross, J. L. (1995). Neurodevelopmental effects of X monosomy: A volumetric imaging study. *Annals of Neurology, 38,* 731–738.

Reiss, A. L., Patel, S., Kumar, A. J., & Freund, L. (1988). Preliminary communication neuroanatomical variations of the posterior fossa in men with the fragile X (Martin–Bell) syndrome. *American Journal of Medical Genetics, 31,* 407–414.

Riccardi, V. M. (1992). Type 1 neurofibromatosis and the pediatric patient. *Current Problems in Pediatrics.*

Riccardi, V. (1995, March). *Consensus conference on learning disabilities and cognitive impairments in children with neurofibromatosis.* Houston, TX.

Robinson, A., Puck, M., Pennington, B., Borelli, J., & Hudeson, M. (1979). Abnormalities of the sex chromosomes: A prospective study on randomly identified newborns. *Birth Defects Original Article Series, 15,* 203–241.

Rovert, J. (1996, May). *Processing deficits in 45, X females.* Paper presented at the annual meeting of the American Association for the Advancement of Science, Philadelphia.

Samango-Sprouse, C., Cohen, M. S., Mott, S. H., Custer, D. A., Vaught, D. R., Stein, H. J., Tifft, C. J., & Rosenbaum, K. N. (1994). The effect of familial vs. sporadic inheritance in the neurodevelopmental profile of young children with neurofibromatoses type 1. *American Journal of Human Genetics, 55*(3), 21.

Shaffer, J. (1962). A specific cognitive deficit observed on gonadol aplasia (Turner syndrome). *Journal of Clinical Psychology, 18,* 403–406.

Shallice, T. (1982). Specific impairments of planning. *Philosophical transactions of the Royal Society of London, Series B: Biological Sciences, 298,* 198–209.

Siomi, H., Choi, M., Siomi, M. C., Nussbaum, R. L., & Dryfuss, G. (1994). Essential role for KH domains in RNA binding: Impaired RNA binding by a mutation in the KH domain in FMR-1 that causes fragile X syndrome. *Cell, 77,* 33–39.

Sudhalter, V., Carborough, H. S., & Cohen, I. L. (1991). Syntactic delay and pragmatic deviance in the language of fragile X males. *American Journal of Medical Genetics, 38,* 493–497.

Surik, R. T., Barkovich, A. J., & Edwards, M. S. B. (1992). Evolution of white matter lesions in neurofibromatosis type-1: MR findings. *American Journal of Radiology, 159,* 171–175.

Sutherland, G. R., & Richards, R. I. (1992). Anticipation legitimized: Unstable DNA to the rescue [editorial]. *American Journal of Human Genetics, 51,* 7–9.

Temple, C. M. (in press), Executive disorders. In C. M. Temple (Ed.), *Development cognitive neuropsychology* (pp. 291–322). East Sussex: Psychology Press.

Thurstone, L. (1958). *Primary mental abilities.* Chicago: University of Chicago Press.

Tilney, F. (1928). *The brain, from ape to man.* New York: Hoeber.

Varnhagen, C. K., Lewin, S., Das, J. F., Bowen, P., Ma, K., & Klimik, M. (1988). Neurofibromatosis and psychological processes. *Journal of Developmental Behavioral Pediatrics, 9,* 257–265.

Warren, R. P., Odell, J. D., Warren, W. L., Burger, R. A., Maciulis, A., Daniels, W. W., & Torres, A. R. (1995). Reading disability, attention deficit hyperactivity disorder and the immune system. *Letter of Science, 268,* 786–787.

Welsh, M. C., & Pennington, B. F. (1988). Assessing frontal lobe functioning in children: Views from developmental psychology. *Developmental Neuropsychology, 4,* 199–230.

Welsh, N. C., Pennington, B. F., & Groisser, D. B. (1991). A normative–developmental study of executive function: A window on prefrontal function in children. *Developmental Neuropsychology, 7*(2), 131–149.

Wesneriwski, E. E., Segan, S. M., Miezejeski, C. M., Sersen, E. A., & Rudelli, R. D. (1991). The fragile X syndrome: Neurological, electrophysiological and neuropathological abnormalities. *American Journal of Medical Genetics, 38,* 480–496.

White, S. H. (1970). Some general outlines of the matrix of developmental changes between five and seven. *Bulletin of the Orton Society, 20,* 41–57.

Xu, G., O'Connell P., & Viskochil, D. (1990). The neurofibromatosis type 1 gene encodes a protein related to GAP. *Cell, 62,* 599–608.

Zametkin, A. J., Liebenauer, L. L., Fitzgerald, G. A., King, A. L., Minkunas, D. V., Herscovitch, P., Yamada, E. M., & Cohen, R. M. (1993). Brain metabolism in children with attention deficit hyperactivity disorder. *American Journal of Psychiatry, 50,* 333–340.

Zametkin, A. T., Nordahl, T. E., Gross, M., & King, A. C. (1990). Cerebral glucose metabolism in adults with hyperactivity of childhood onset. *New England Journal of Medicine, 323,* 1361–1366.

Zimmerman, R. A., Yachnis, A. T., & Rorke, L. B. (1992). Anthology of findings of high signal intensity findings in neurofibromatosis type-1. Abstract from 78th Scientific Assembly and annual meeting of the Radiological Society of North America. *Radiology, 186*(P), 23.

Index